OCEAN YEARBOOK 29

OCEAN
YEARBOOK 29

Sponsored by the
International
Ocean Institute

MARINE &
ENVIRONMENTAL
LAW INSTITUTE

Sponsored by the Marine &
Environmental Law Institute
of the Schulich School of Law

Edited by
Aldo Chircop, Scott Coffen-Smout, and Moira L. McConnell

BRILL
NIJHOFF

LEIDEN | BOSTON

Co-sponsored by the International Ocean Institute and the Marine & Environmental Law Institute, Schulich School of Law, Dalhousie University

Brill Nijhoff Publishers

International Standard Book Number: 978-90-04-29723-4
Library of Congress Catalog Card Number: 79:642855
International Standard Serial Number: 0191-8575
E-International Standard Serial Number: 2211-6001

This publication has been typeset in the multilingual "Brill" typeface. With over 5,100 characters covering Latin, IPA, Greek, and Cyrillic, this typeface is especially suitable for use in the humanities. For more information, please see www.brill.com/brill-typeface.

ISSN 0191-8575
E-ISSN 2211-6001
ISBN 978-90-04-29723-4 (hardback)

Printed by Printforce, the Netherlands

Contents

Issues and Prospects

Law of the Sea and Ocean Governance

Living Resources and Coastal Management

Oil and Gas and Renewable Energy

Maritime Transport

Book Reviews

Appendices

William T. Burke (1926–2014): In Memoriam

One "can only speak of Bill in superlatives... Preeminently successful in both [scholarship and practical affairs]... If you want the best in every way, you have it in Bill." Myres S. McDougal, 1968.

Professor Burke was a colossus of a man. He was short in stature but a giant in every other respect – his legendary intellect, his enormous kind heart, his prodigious energy, his superhuman ability to sustain his focus on a task or a problem, his insatiable interest in and knowledge of an inordinately wide and diverse range of topics... Amongst the international marine law community he was the pre-eminent authority and scholar. As his long-time academic colleague, co-author, and friend, Dr. Edward Miles so eloquently said, "Bill Burke has been the brightest star in the firmament of the international law of the sea since the early 1960s, and even in retirement, no one comes close to his achievement."

For years it was widely believed that William T. Burke was born in Brazil. He was. He was born in Brazil, Indiana in 1926. After completing high school and serving with the US Army, Bill began his illustrious academic career by attending Indiana State University where he completed his bachelor's degree in two and a half short years and at the top of his class. He decided to pursue a law degree at Indiana University School of Law with the hope to effect change and make a contribution. He obtained his JS in 1953. Bill pursued his interest in international law at Yale Law School (LLM 1953–55). Prior to continuing on with his JSD, Bill entered private practice. And as with everything else Bill undertook, he excelled quickly and became world renowned, advising clients including Aristotle Onassis, traveling to Paris, Geneva, and London.

A non-conformist, a self-starter, a man who wanted to control his own schedule and not have to wear a tie if he didn't want to, Bill returned to Yale Law School where he received his JSD in 1959. His thesis "Comprehensive State Authority over Ocean Areas: A Policy Perspective," attests to his abiding interest in ocean space and policy analysis. Bill remained at Yale lecturing and working with Myres S. McDougal as a research associate. Together they authored several articles and published in 1962 their seminal work *Public Order of the Oceans, A Contemporary International Law of the Sea.*

Bill was a formidable scholar. *The Public Order of the Oceans* was a best seller within academic circles, and remains a classic. It was reissued in 1987 with a new introduction summarizing the major legal events that transpired during the 25-year interval, notably the negotiations and acceptance of the 1982 United Nations Convention on the Law of the Sea. His 1994 book *The New*

International Law of Fisheries: UNCLOS 1982 and Beyond, examines the capacity for international law under both treaty and customary law to effectively address high seas fisheries and other emerging problems. This scholarly work was translated into Japanese in 1996. By his retirement he had a vast array of publications – his personal bibliography has pages of monographs, and hundreds of articles in over 300 law journals, as well as contributions to scientific and technical publications.

By 1968, Bill was considered the outstanding American authority on law of the sea, a distinguished international jurist and policy leader on the world scene. He served as an Expert to the US Delegation for the UN Seabed Committee, 1972–1973, as well as the Third Law of the Sea Conference 1974–1976 and attended Conference sessions in Caracas, Geneva and New York from 1972–1976. He lectured throughout the world and substantially shaped the law, policy and many institutions related to ocean law and marine affairs. He was a founding member and served on the Board of Directors of the Law of the Sea Institute from 1965–1978. He was the founding Editor and Editor-in-Chief of the prestigious journal *Ocean Development and International Law* from 1972–79; and was the Associate Editor for many years thereafter. He was on the Board of Directors of the Council on Ocean Law.

Bill was a much loved and revered professor. In 1968, Professor Burke was enticed away from Ohio State University College of Law to join the faculty at the University of Washington School of Law in Seattle. And there he happily remained, retiring in 1996. He continued to work as Professor Emeritus well into his 80s supervising graduate students all over the world, including most recently, the doctoral thesis of Simone Borg, at the IMO International Maritime Law Institute. Like so many before her, Dr. Borg felt herself "particularly lucky to benefit from his inspiring scholarship." As Professor David Attard, Director of IMLI and Judge on International Tribunal for the Law of the Sea, wrote, Professor Burke "influenced generations of professionals." And his sphere of influence was indeed large as well as global.

Bill was a man of great intellectual and personal integrity. Not all his perspectives were shared, yet he commanded the respect of his adversaries. His position that whales and other marine mammals were to be conserved and managed as fisheries, put him at distinct odds with many students, colleagues, governments and environmental NGOs (and soundly in the same camp with many others including the indigenous peoples of the North). Bo Bricklemyer, LLM'77, who went to the University of Washington to "save the whales" and was later hired by Greenpeace in Washington D.C., became a life-long friend of Professor Burke. Bo recently said it was because Bill "was kind, always helpful beyond the classroom, because he had an incredible intellect that I could not resist, and wisdom that reverberates with me to this day... We never fell out. We could always share our points of view – sometimes widely divergent – and end our meetings inevitably laughing."

Bill went way out of his way to help many students. Professor Craig H. Allen Sr., Judson Falknor Professor of Law at the University of Washington noted at Bill's memorial in August, that he was struck how Professor Burke truly exceeded all professional expectations in assisting his students. He was kind and generous to a fault, yet he was always rigorous, demanding and completely honest.

In 1975, Bill became Professor of Law and Marine Affairs having established the interdisciplinary LLM in law and marine affairs at the University of Washington School of Law. This program would deliver and build upon the interdisciplinary policy framework for analysis, comprehensive problem solving and development of international law articulated in the public order of the oceans. It was necessary to have professionals who could rationally and equitably manage the oceans, taking into account the complexity of both the natural and human systems. An understanding of the scientific, technological, economic and social problems associated with marine resource exploitation was essential to formulating a new law of the sea and the cooperative, integrated management of multiple ocean uses.

Towards this end, Bill also created, together with Warren Wooster, Jim Crutchfield, Lee Alverson, amongst others, the interdisciplinary Institute for Marine Studies (now the School for Marine and Environmental Studies). He recruited the brilliant political scientist, Ed Miles, with whom he shared a lifetime of scholarship and friendship.

One would be remiss not to mention Bill's family in any tribute to him. Bill was a devoted father, husband and a doting grandfather. He and his wife Feliciana, whom he met while they were both graduate students at Yale, bought a house in Seattle in 1968 and raised their family there. It remained their home until his death. He loved his family unabashedly. As a graduate student I was well aware of the daily highlights he was quick to share – Liza's swimming accomplishments, Will's activities, and Kate's woes. Kate was ever-present in Bill's world. She was developmentally disabled. Her difficulties often preoccupied him. He was discrete but his concern was patent. A shadow would fall across his face, a phone call, an urgent matter he needed to attend to, to help Kate. Matter solved, he would give his undivided attention to his student or colleague, providing a razor sharp critique, sage advice, a commentary on the issue of the day, a wry laugh about a predicament or engage in respectful debate.

Liza Burke shared how her dad encouraged her to become a lawyer, as a way of finding challenge and meaning in a career. She did. Liza became a criminal defense attorney and wrote that her father "was always interested in my work and quite frequently had a quick and ready analysis of a case that was spot on. He had the ability to slice through the irrelevant and distill the problem down to its essentials. Usually it came from a compassionate understanding of people."

It was my honour and privilege to attend Kate's memorial in May 2010. I went to support Bill. It was me who came away moved to the core having experienced one of life's greatest gifts – the unequivocal validation of the intrinsic value of all human life. And Bill was so amazed and so pleased that unbeknownst to him or the family, his beloved Kate had touched so many people so profoundly.

McDougal wrote in 1968 "Bill wears extraordinarily well as a friend and colleague." How true! Misty (Terrin) Haley LLM'79, who lived in Seattle, saw Bill often. She was struck by how many students remained in touch. "I think he genuinely valued all of us and saw the best in all of us," regardless of our chosen path.

It was my enormous good fortune to have the great Professor Burke as my graduate supervisor, colleague and friend. Like others, we had an enduring friendship and professional relationship. Over the years, we talked periodically, sometimes more often – about family, about the world, about the complex and continually evolving legal framework for responsible, equitable and cooperative ocean use and the ever-growing need for sustainable international fisheries. He attended some meetings where I was presenting the keynote address. Later he was reluctant to travel. He read everything I wrote with great interest, was supportive of my ideas, and was terribly proud. He loved my book and thought it an important contribution to an issue he too considered of critical concern, "the area beyond the 200 mile economic zone." His grandchildren also loved my book – ("Evelyne, the twins love your book too – they love the cover – that's why I keep it on the coffee table," followed by his inimitable laugh).

This is a tribute in memoriam to a wonderful, kind, good human being and a luminary of international fisheries, law of the sea, and marine and environmental affairs. Like the light from a bright star in the night sky that continues to shine long after the star is gone, so too will Bill illuminate our lives for years to come.

Evelyne Meltzer, BA, LLB, LLM*
Halifax, Nova Scotia, Canada
September 2014

* Evelyne.Meltzer@gmail.com.

William A. Tetley (1927–2014): In Memoriam

On the Shoulders of Our Giant: A Reflection on Bill Tetley's Contribution to Maritime Law

Sir Isaac Newton, in a letter to Richard Hooke in 1676, quoting earlier writers, said: "If I have seen further it is by standing on the sholders [sic] of Giants." On Canada Day, 2014, this country and the world bid farewell to a giant in the field of maritime law, in the person of William A. Tetley, C.M., Q.C., better known to his vast cohort of friends and admirers around the globe simply as "Bill."

It is difficult to summarize, in a few pages, the amazing life and outstanding accomplishments of this great man, who, as it were, put Canada on the admiralty law map, in a career spanning some 60 years. Bill in fact had three major careers, in each of which he excelled: first, as a practising lawyer in Montreal with Martineau, Walker, Allison, Beaulieu & Tetley (now Fasken Martineau) from 1952 to 1970; then, as a member of the National Assembly of Quebec from 1968 to 1976 (holding three ministerial portfolios during that period); and finally, as a professor of maritime and admiralty law at McGill University from 1976 to 2012. This piece will focus on the third career, as a member of the academy.

Professor Tetley's books, especially *Marine Cargo Claims*, first published while he was still in practice in 1965, and now in its fourth (two-volume) edition of 2008, came to be regarded almost as a bible, not only by students, but also by lawyers, judges and many categories of business people involved in the shipping industry (shipowners, charterers, brokers, underwriters, marine surveyors, etc.). His other works, in both admiralty law and the conflict of laws, complemented "MCC": *Maritime Liens and Claims*, 1985 and 1998; *International Conflict of Laws: Common, Civil and Maritime,* 1994; and *International Maritime Law,* 2002. The 2002 book was in fact an edited version of his contribution to the *International Encyclopedia of Comparative Law*, published in English by the Max Planck Institute in Hamburg, Germany. It is said that in court, his writings are sometimes quoted by both sides in argument in the same case. Little wonder that his books were translated into Russian, Japanese and Chinese.

In all his books and his plethora of articles published over the decades, Bill strove to study and expound principles and rules of maritime law and private international law in a comparative mode: He examined them in their historical context (over time); he analyzed differences and similarities as between the civil law and the common law traditions reflected in those rules and principles; and he took account of the diverse national legislation of many lands that grew from those legal traditions. Among the most useful aspects of *Marine Cargo Claims*, for example, is its appendix containing national summaries of carriage of goods law of some 45 countries, written by established practitioners or professors from those jurisdictions. This aspect of Tetley's scholarship is particularly noteworthy, in that most legal authors hesitate to write about the laws and legal traditions of other jurisdictions, and this despite the fact that maritime law, by its very nature, is an international activity *par excellence* that calls for such a comparative insight.

Professor Tetley always eagerly sought comments on his writings, and so, when the Internet appeared, hastened to establish a website (now still online at www.mcgill.ca/maritimelaw) and made sure that his articles were posted there for all and sundry to read. He invited, welcomed and responded to comments from anyone. His glossaries of maritime law terms, conflict of laws terms, and his tables of international maritime conventions and national laws, and of the package/kilo limitations of over 40 countries, were and are the object of thousands of "hits" on his website, down to the present day. The site also contains a vast array of other materials, on Canadian and world history, politics and amusing anecdotes from his own long and fascinating life.

Bill Tetley was a tireless worker, with an unbridled passion for maritime law and the conflict of laws, pouring boundless energy (seven days a week), not only into his writings, but into the teaching of students. Christmas Day frequently found him at home, correcting exams! Sundays too were work days for Bill, but only after he had attended the weekly service at St. Peter's Anglican Church, to which he belonged for his entire lifetime. At McGill, he taught at least two, if not three, generations of young people, from all over the world, who eagerly registered for his courses, even when his lectures began at 8:00 a.m.! A few lucky students were also accorded the privilege of working with the great man during their summer holidays, assisting in his research. A very few superprivileged individuals, including the author of these lines, had the opportunity of seconding him in his research and writing, on a full-time basis, for years.

But Tetley's teaching was not restricted to McGill. In his 30 plus years as an educator, he lectured in a "mini-course" every winter (from 1984 to 1998) at Tulane University in New Orleans, which merited him the title of "Distinguished Visiting Professor of Maritime and Commercial Law," and in 1999, Tulane inaugurated the annual "William Tetley Maritime Law Lectures" in his honour. In his three decades as a professor, he lectured in the U.S., the U.K., the U.S.S.R., Belgium, France, Germany, Italy, Sweden, the Netherlands, Spain, Portugal, Greece, Slovenia, Croatia, Malta, South Africa, Australia, Singapore, Hong Kong, China, Puerto Rico, Venezuela, Colombia, Argentina and Brazil – and across Canada. He thus built up a veritable legion of former students, as well as a worldwide network of colleagues on every continent. He was especially proud of being named Visiting Professor at Dalian Maritime University in the People's Republic of China in 1996, and he soon began incorporating references to the Chinese Maritime Code into his books and articles. McGill named three fellowships after him in 2004, for doctoral and master's students.

Some of the main ideas that Bill expounded in maritime law, and defended repeatedly orally and in writing against all critics, are worth recalling here:

- That admiralty law, even in England, as well as in the U.S. and Commonwealth countries, is fundamentally civilian in origin, although the common law has made important contributions to it over the centuries, thus providing us in Canada, in particular, with an especially rich admiralty law tradition – a fact finally recognized by the Supreme Court of Canada only in more recent years;
- That maritime liens are substantive rights in the property of others, rather than only procedural remedies, and therefore should be recognized as such by the courts of other countries, and ranked according to the forum's order of priorities;
- That mandatory rules of other jurisdictions should be afforded greater consideration in the conflict of laws, and that double *renvoi* should be rejected in private international law;
- That shipowners and charterers *jointly* perform the functions of "carrier" and therefore should be held jointly and severally liable, as joint venturers, for their faulty acts and omissions that cause loss or damage to cargo interests (as they are under the Hamburg Rules, for example);
- That the demise clause and the identity of carrier clause, although in general usage in bills of lading and upheld by courts, are of questionable validity, given the public order nature of article 3(8) of the Hague and Hague/Visby Rules, and that they obscure and compromise the true, joint venture character of the carriage of goods by water operation;
- That properly construed, the Hague and Hague/Visby Rules apply to sea waybills, and not merely to bills of lading – a view he maintained, despite the contrary weight of academic opinion, and some judicial pronouncements;
- That legislative reform that makes it easier for carriers to contract out of liability for their negligent conduct is retrograde and should be rejected (one of Tetley's main criticisms of the Rotterdam Rules); and
- That the quest for uniformity in international maritime law requires a greater measure of humility among the actors involved and a willingness to compromise among the States and interests involved, in a sincere quest for justice and harmony.

The above list could go on and on. On all these issues and others, Bill never gave up fighting for the solutions that he believed were just and desirable for the common good, and combating contractual provisions and legislative reform proposals that he deemed ill-advised and counter-productive. Not content with expounding the law as it was, he hastened to state, in no uncertain terms, just what he thought it should be. And he then let the proverbial chips fall where they might. But convinced as he was that his views were correct and progressive, he seemed always able to separate the ideas he opposed from the people who advocated them. He remained courteous and friendly to all, respectful of opinions even when they diverged from his own, and, like the true democrat he was, always open to further reflection and discussion. He completed his 87 years on this earth, leaving few, if any, enemies, and a plethora of warm memories in the minds and hearts of all who had crossed his path, including those who had disagreed with him most strongly on one or another issue.

Professor Tetley held a succession of key positions in maritime-related organizations, both nationally and internationally: President of The Canadian Maritime Law Association (1981–1984); President of the Association of Average Adjusters of Canada (1986–1987); President of the Association of Maritime Arbitrators of Canada (1990–1995); Member of the Executive Council of the Comité Maritime International (CMI) (1986–1990) and its Vice-President (1990–1994); Honorary Life Vice-President of the CMI (1994). In 1986, he chaired a six-person committee in London that settled a dispute between two UN organizations. In 1992, he chaired the task force on the maritime industry in Montreal that issued a unanimous report resolving certain labour problems in the Port of Montreal. He also served as Chair of the International Maritime Arbitration Organization in Paris. In 1999, he was named an arbitrator of the Singapore International Arbitration Centre, and in 2001 as an arbitrator of the China Maritime Arbitration Commission (CMAC). Tetley was also an honorary member of the Maritime Law Association of the United States and of the Maritime Law Associations of Slovenia and Croatia.

He was an editor or contributor to all major maritime law journals and law reports in Europe and North America, including *Lloyd's Maritime and Commercial Law Quarterly*, *Lloyd's Law Reports*, *Droit Maritime Français*, *American Maritime Cases*, *European Transport Law*, the *Journal of Maritime Law & Commerce*, the *Tulane Maritime Law Journal*, the *University of San Francisco Maritime Law Journal*, *La Revue Scapel* and the *Journal of International Maritime Law*.

Bill's awards are no less impressive. They include, in particular, his Queen's Counsel designation in 1968, the Albert Lilar Prize for maritime law, presented only every three years (1981); his admission to the Order of Canada (1995); and the F.R. Scott Award of McGill University (2007), recognizing his significant contribution to law and his exceptional service and leadership to society. The Canadian Bar Association awarded him the Walter S. Owen Book Prize for his third volume of *Marine Cargo Claims* (2009).

As much or more could be said about his awards and career in the Royal Canadian Navy at the end of World War II, and his subsequent achievements in municipal and provincial politics and legal practice, including the writing of his seminal work, *The October Crisis, 1970: An Insider's View*, published in 2006. But the above reflections on his involvement with the maritime world and with the education of tomorrow's leaders in that important domain may suffice to help us all realize how much of a debt we owe him, especially in this country, and how much his counsel and friendship will be missed in the years to come. His total devotion to his wife Rosslyn, their four children and nine grandchildren would require another article.

If we today can see farther into the mists of tomorrow's national and international shipping and the law that may (or should) govern it (hopefully with greater uniformity than at present), it must surely be at least in part because of the sturdy shoulders of Bill Tetley our giant, on which so many have perched and peered out for so very long a time, even as they absorbed something of the giant's spirit and zeal.

May the good professor now at last enjoy "fair winds and following seas" in a better world, and may we who carry on in this one imitate his energy and commitment to promoting the vision, so dear to his big heart, of a more just and harmonious rule of law upon the waves.

Robert C. Wilkins
Secretary-Treasurer
The Canadian Maritime Law Association
Montreal, Quebec
July 14, 2014

The International Ocean Institute

Professor Elisabeth Mann Borgese founded the International Ocean Institute (IOI) in 1972 as a scientific, educational, independent, international, non-profit, non-governmental organisation headquartered in Malta with premises at the University of Malta. The IOI was created to promote education, capacity building, and research as a means to enhance the peaceful and sustainable use and management of ocean and coastal spaces and their resources, as well as the protection and conservation of the marine environment, guided by the principle of the Common Heritage of Mankind.

For more than 40 years the IOI has stood at the forefront of organisations in addressing these issues with the concern of future generations through an inter-disciplinary and comprehensive approach. The IOI has also prepared working papers for the Third United Nations Conference on the Law of the Sea (UNCLOS III: 1973–1982), for the Preparatory Commission for the International Seabed Authority, for the International Tribunal for the Law of the Sea (1982–1994), and for the EU coastal management policy (2006), as well as for various governments. It has provided consultants to UNEP, UNDP, the World Bank, the United Nations Industrial Development Organization (UNIDO), EU, UNESCO/IOC, and the Asian-African Legal Consultative Committee (AALCC). It contributed to the formulation of recommendations of the World Summits in Rio de Janeiro (1992) and Johannesburg (2002), the World Forums on oceans, coasts and islands (2003–2009), as well as to the review of the developments in ocean affairs through the United Nations Open-ended Informal Consultative Process. The IOI was awarded the 2006 South-South Partnership for the special contribution to the tsunami recovery efforts. In 2007, the IOI was granted special consultative status within the Economic and Social Council (ECOSOC) at the United Nations as well as the renewal of formal consultative relations between UNESCO and the IOI from 2011 to 2017.

The goals of the IOI are to:

- contribute to the evolving process of ocean governance through its functions and activities;
- monitor the implementation of international conventions and agreements as they relate to the oceans, participate in and contribute to the evolving

policy dialogue on the ocean in the United Nations System and other international organizations;
· mobilize the political will to elaborate appropriate maritime laws and regulations, to implement national and regional plans and international agreements on the management and sustainable use of the ocean, coasts and
  islands through its organs and bodies;
· raise awareness of the peaceful uses of the ocean, its protection and conservation, as well as the sustainable development of its resources, in accordance with the principle of the common heritage of humankind;
· engage in the dissemination of information and transfer of knowledge and
  experience;
· contribute to the sustainable uses of the ocean as well as to the sustainable
  development of developing countries and countries in transition, through
  institution-building and networking at national and regional levels; and
· respond to the needs of developing countries and countries in transition,
  particularly coastal communities and enhance the role of women by
  increasing their abilities to develop and manage the ocean and coastal
  resources sustainably.

The International Ocean Institute achieves its goals through:

· education and training;
· research and analysis;
· organisation of conferences and meetings;
· institution-building and partnership;
· promotion and communication; and
· fundraising in support of the activities of the Institute and its network.

The IOI's activities include training and capacity building programmes, information dissemination, conferences, research and publications:

· Training of hundreds of decision-makers and professionals, mainly from
  developing countries, through short and long duration interdisciplinary
  courses in ocean and coastal management and the Master of Arts degree in
  Ocean Governance offered at the University of Malta under the aegis of the
  Faculty of Laws;
· Ocean governance advocacy within the United Nations system through
  participation in and contribution to intergovernmental meetings and
  conferences;
· Development work among coastal communities with the objective of
  improving their livelihood while restoring and preserving coastal ecology;

- Information dissemination to international organisations and national institutions through the global IOI Network and the IOI web site;
- Organisation of the *Pacem in Maribus* as an IOI brand to serve as a forum on the ocean, and national and regional leadership seminars and workshops on critical and innovative issues in ocean governance;
- Research on a variety of ocean-related areas such as international and regional agreements and policies on oceans and the coastal zone; on regional and sub-regional co-operation and on scientific and technological approaches to sustainable management of living and non-living marine resources;
- Education and awareness-creation about ocean resources, marine and coastal environments, and the need to care for them;
- Publication of the *Ocean Yearbook* in collaboration with the Marine & Environmental Law Institute, Schulich School of Law, Dalhousie University, Canada;
- Maturing IOI's web site (www.ioinst.org) and publication of an electronic newsletter IOI*nforma* by the IOI HQ. Regional Operational Centres also publish their own newsletters, research papers and reports; and
- Services include advice, consultancy, and information regarding ocean and coastal environments.

The IOI gained worldwide respect and a reputation through its contribution to the codification and implementation of the Law of the Sea Convention, and to the subsequent development of the concept of sustainable development as it applies to the ocean. Furthermore, through the launching of such projects as the coastal and eco-villages projects, dedicated women and youth programmes, training in ocean governance, risk assessment and others, the IOI has contributed positively to the implementation of ocean governance, with a particular focus on developing nations.

The IOI is now developing an international ocean governance and capacity-building education programme that will consist of a network of education, training and research centres with expertise in ocean, coastal and marine affairs and governance. The Centres will be joined together in a partnership so as to provide interdisciplinary and comprehensive coverage of the subject areas. The overall objective will be to enhance the abilities of developing countries to develop and govern their own marine and coastal resources and environment sustainably.

The IOI scope and presence is truly international with 22 Operational Centres and fourteen Focal Points around the globe, with new Focal Points in the development stage. IOI Focal Points are usually selected from alumni and appropriate qualified and experienced persons associated with the IOI. IOI Focal Points are not expected to receive any financial support from IOI, but provide their intellectual contribution to the IOI on a voluntary basis. The IOI network provides a flexible mechanism with a governing and coordinating structure that generates synergism and strategic planning of the network of semiautonomous nodes. This cohesive and comprehensive mechanism is capable of cooperating equally well with other intergovernmental systems and the private sector. The current Operational Centres and their host institutions are:

> IOI–Black Sea, National Research and Development Institute of Marine Geology and Geoecology (GeoEcoMar), Romania; IOI–Canada, Dalhousie University, Canada; IOI–Caspian Sea, Astrakhan State Technical University (ASTU), Astrakhan, Russia; IOI–China, National Marine Data and Information Service, State Oceanic Administration, P.R. China; IOI–Costa Rica, Universidad Nacional, Costa Rica; IOI–Cuba, Centro de Investigaciones Marinas, Ciudad de La Habana, Cuba; IOI–Eastern Africa, Kenya Marine and Fisheries Research Institute, Mombasa, Kenya; IOI–Egypt, National Institute of Oceanography and Fisheries (NIOF), Egypt; IOI–Germany, Centre for Tropical Marine Ecology, Germany; IOI–India, Auroville Centre for Scientific Research, Tamil Nadu, India; IOI–Indonesia, University of Indonesia, Indonesia; IOI–Islamic Republic of Iran, Iranian National Institute for Oceanography and Atmospheric Science (INIOAS), Tehran, Iran; IOI–Japan, INTERCOM, Tokyo, Japan; IOI–Malta, University of Malta, Malta; IOI–Pacific Islands, University of the South Pacific, Suva, Fiji; IOI–Slovenia, Marine Biology Station at the Institute of Biology (MBS), Piran, Slovenia; IOI–South Western Atlantic Ocean, Centre for Marine Studies, Brazil; IOI–Southern Africa, c/o SANBI, Kirstenbosch Gardens, Cape Town, South Africa; IOI–Thailand, Deep Sea Fishery Technology Research and Development Institute, Bangkok, Thailand; IOI–Ukraine, Ecology Initiative NGO, Sevastopol, Ukraine; IOI–United States of America, University of South Florida, St. Petersburg, U.S.A.; and IOI–Western Africa, Nigerian Institute for Oceanography and Marine Research (NIOMR), Lagos, Nigeria.

Each Operational Centre is autonomous, identifying its own priorities for research, capacity building and development within the broad mission of the IOI, while benefiting from the support of the overall IOI Network. Regional approaches to research and capacity building enable the Institute to draw upon the different strengths of the Operational Centres to cater to the needs identified within each region. A director, generally supported by a small staff with a large number of experts and volunteers on call, runs each Centre.

The current Focal Points and their host institutes are:

> IOI–Pakistan, National Centre of Maritime Policy Research (NCMPR), Bahria University, Karachi, Pakistan; IOI–Cyprus, Cyprus University of Technology, Limassol, Cyprus; IOI–China, Shanghai Maritime University, Shanghai, P.R. of China; IOI–Australia, Ocean Technology Group, University of Sydney, Australia; IOI–Lebanon, Lebanese Union of Professional Divers, Sidon, Lebanon; IOI–U.S.A., Collaborative Institute for Oceans, Climate and Security, Venture Development Center, University of Massachusetts, Boston, U.S.A.; IOI–Republic of Korea, Korea Maritime Institute, Seoul, Republic of Korea; IOI–Turkey, Department of Fishing and Processing Technology, Kotekli-Mugla, Turkey; IOI–Singapore, STET Maritime Pte Ltd., Singapore; IOI–Philippines, Office of UN and International Organizations, Department of Foreign Affairs, Pasay City, Republic of the Philippines; IOI–Egypt, Marine Environment Division, National Institute of Oceanography and Fisheries (NIOF), Suez, Egypt; IOI–Malaysia, Borneo Marine Research Institute, Universiti Malaysia Sabah, Sabah, Malaysia; IOI–Finland, Department of Environmental Sciences, University of Helsinki, Finland; IOI–Kazakhstan, Center for Life Sciences, Nazarbayev University, Astana, Republic of Kazakhstan.

The IOI is governed by a Board that makes decisions on policy, programme and budget matters. Five regional representatives were elected from Operational Centre directors in 2009 to replace the IOI Committee of Directors and represent five regions, namely Africa, The Americas, Asia and Oceania, Eurasia, and Europe. These representatives will participate in meetings of the newly constituted Board (Steering Committee), but will not participate in discussions on financial, budgetary and personnel matters. Growing steadily and responding to global changes, the IOI Network is now aimed to multiply its spectrum of activities. It plans to move from direct training to training the trainers and from direct implementation of projects to offering advisory and consultative services.

Marine & Environmental Law Institute
Schulich School of Law

Established in 1883, the Schulich School of Law at Dalhousie University is the oldest common law school in Canada. As a leading law school, it has traditionally played a critical role in the development of national legal education in Canada, in servicing the needs of the Atlantic region and as a focal point for graduate level education globally. The Law School offers the full breadth of undergraduate and graduate level education and is a partner with the International Ocean Institute in supporting, producing and providing a home for the *Ocean Yearbook* in its Marine & Environmental Law Institute (MELAW) (http://www.dal.ca/law/MELAW).

The Schulich School of Law, with its location in the vibrant port city of Halifax, is internationally recognized for excellence in marine and environmental law research and teaching. Since its establishment in 1974 as an area of specialization for the Juris Doctor (J.D., formerly the Bachelor of Laws, LL.B.) students and subsequently for Master of Laws (LL.M.) students and Doctor of Philosophy in Law (Ph.D.) candidates, the Marine & Environmental Law Programme (MELP) has one of the most extensive academic course offerings and supervisory capability in these two fields in the world. With more than 12 full and part-time faculty members currently teaching in the Programme, students have a unique opportunity to learn about public and private law practice in marine (including shipping, fisheries and oil and gas) and environmental law (including land-use planning and energy law) taught from domestic, international and comparative perspectives. At the J.D. level students wishing to specialize in these fields have the option of obtaining a certificate of specialization in either Marine or Environmental Law or both.

The Schulich School of Law also hosts two other research institutes, the Health Law Institute and the Law & Technology Institute, and has additional concentrations in the fields of international law, business law, criminal law and public law. In addition to the required courses in the MELP specialization students are also encouraged to undertake research/courses in those and other fields in the J.D. curriculum. This allows students to engage in the interdisciplinary study of emerging and cross-cutting topics such as biotechnology, environment and health, ethics, indigenous rights, animal rights, international trade law and human rights.

The longstanding research excellence of the Schulich School of Law MELP faculty was formally recognized by the Dalhousie University Board of Governors in 2004 with the creation of the Marine & Environmental Law Institute. In 2014 MELAW celebrates the first ten years as an Institute and the 40th anniversary of the MELP programme, which was originally launched in 1974. The Institute continues to carry out research and consultancy activities and directs the MELP academic specialization. In addition to their scholarly research and publication activities, faculty, staff and others associated with the Institute carry out research projects and provide advisory services to agencies of the United Nations and other inter-governmental organizations, international non-governmental organizations, and regional organizations as well as assisting government departments and non-governmental organizations in Canada and overseas.

The Institute provides law students with the opportunity to gain experience working as research assistants through its research projects, workshops and editing the *Ocean Yearbook*. The Institute supports student collaboration in addressing environmental issues through the Environmental Law Students' Society and the East Coast Environmental Law Association, a non-governmental organization dedicated to environmental law education and advocacy. The Institute encourages interdisciplinary collaborations within the Dalhousie University community including the School for Resource and Environmental Studies, the Marine Affairs Program, the International Development Studies Program, the Institute for Ocean Research Enterprise, the Centre for Foreign Policy Studies, and the Ocean Tracking Network (OTN) led by the Department of Oceanography. The Institute has an extensive network of working partners at the national and international levels.

Acknowledgements

The editors are grateful for the ongoing administrative and substantive support provided by the Marine & Environmental Law Institute and the Sir James Dunn Law Library at the Schulich School of Law, Dalhousie University. The financial support for the editorial office provided by the Schulich School of Law and by the International Ocean Institute's headquarters in Malta is gratefully acknowledged. We wish to extend thanks to Peter L'Esperance for editing assistance, to Susan Rolston for compiling the volume index, and to Lauri MacDougall for administrative support. Warm thanks go to members of the Board of Editors and numerous peer reviewers for their continuing support. Special thanks are extended to staff at Brill for editorial and infrastructural support.

THE EDITORS

Contributors

Anna Antonova

is a graduate student in the Department of Marine Affairs at the University of Rhode Island. She holds a bachelor degree in English and a concentration in maritime studies from Williams College. She also attended Williams-Mystic, an interdisciplinary program in marine affairs. After graduating from Williams in 2012, she became lead author and project leader for the book *Step by Step in Bulgaria*, which was funded by and published for the European Union in 2013. Following her graduation from URI, she plans to pursue a Ph.D. in marine affairs and international relations.

Jay L. Batongbacal

is an assistant professor at the University of the Philippines College of Law and is currently director of the UP Institute for Maritime Affairs and Law of the Sea. He holds a Master of Marine Management and Doctor in the Science of Law from Dalhousie University. He was legal advisor of the technical team that successfully pursued the Philippines' claim to a continental shelf beyond 200 nautical miles in the Benham Rise Region.

Pedro Aníbal Beatón Soler

has a doctorate in science and is a professor at the Multidisciplinary Study Center of Coastal Zones at the Universidad de Oriente, Cuba. He has published on renewable energy, coastal zone management and risk management in different scientific magazines of national and international impact. He is president of the Scientific Committee of the International Conference on Integrated Coastal Zone Management (CARICOSTAS).

Awni Behnam

is honorary president of the International Ocean Institute and a former assistant secretary-general of the United Nations. After serving in the navy (Iraq) and completing his higher education at the University of Wales, Dr. Behnam joined the United Nations Conference on Trade and Development (UNCTAD) in 1977 as economic affairs officer and assistant director in the shipping division. He served as chief of liaison to the Group of 77 and as secretary of the Conference of UNCTAD. In 2000, he was appointed as senior advisor to the secretary-general of UNCTAD.

Meinhard Doelle

is a Professor of Law and Associate Dean, Research, at the Schulich School of Law, Dalhousie University, and is the Director of the Marine & Environmental Law Institute. Professor Doelle specializes in environmental law. He has been involved in the practice of environmental law in Nova Scotia since 1990 and has written on a variety of environmental law topics, including climate change, energy law, invasive species, environmental assessments, and public participation in environmental decision-making.

Godwin Eli Kwadzo Dzah

is a lecturer at the Faculty of Law of the Ghana Institute of Management and Public Administration where he teaches natural resources law and public international law. He graduated with an LL.M. from Harvard Law School, where his research focus was natural resource management and environmental governance. Prior to that, he was a visiting research fellow at the Marine & Environmental Law Institute, Schulich School of Law, Dalhousie University, Canada, and later at the United Nations Secretariat in New York under a United Nations-Nippon Foundation Fellowship. He is admitted to the Ghana Bar.

Daria Gritsenko

is working as a project researcher at Brahea Centre, Centre for Maritime Studies, University of Turku, Finland. She is finalizing her Ph.D. in social research that investigated how public and private actors share the workload of governing quality shipping.

Cheryle Hislop

completed her Ph.D. thesis on the discourse surrounding the concept of high seas marine protected areas in 2010. Her postgraduate studies at the University of Tasmania were complemented with the opportunity to undertake research at the Woods Hole Oceanographic Institution and the University of Delaware as part of a Fulbright Scholarship during 2004–2005. She has a strong and enduring interest in deep ocean geomorphology and the politics of ocean spatial management.

Martin Jes Iversen

is associate professor at the Copenhagen Business School, where he is academic director of the B.Sc. in international shipping and trade, and the tricontinental B.Sc. program GLOBE, which is provided collaboratively by the

Copenhagen Business School, the Chinese University of Hong Kong and the University of North Carolina. He is also co-editor of the international anthology *Global Shipping in Small Nations*, and has published articles in leading international journals such as *Business History Review* and the *International Journal of Maritime History*.

Julia Jabour

is a member of the Ocean & Antarctic Governance Research Program at the Institute for Marine and Antarctic Studies. She has been researching, writing and lecturing on polar governance for 20 years. Julia teaches in a variety of Antarctic law and policy undergraduate and postgraduate units and has had teaching assignments in Iceland, Malaysia, Vietnam and New Zealand. Julia has visited Antarctica six times and been an advisor to the Australian Government at Antarctic Treaty Consultative Meetings on three occasions. She has eclectic research interests relating to the oceans and the polar regions.

Nengye Liu

is a Marie Curie Fellow at the School of Law, University of Dundee, United Kingdom. He has a doctorate of law from the Department of Public International Law, Ghent University, Belgium, a master of law and a bachelor of law from Wuhan University, China. Prior to moving to Dundee, he was a "Future Ocean" research associate at the Walther-Schuecking Institute for International Law, University of Kiel, Germany.

Joseph Loot

is presently an Interdisciplinary Studies Ph.D. student at Dalhousie University, Halifax, Nova Scotia, Canada where he also finished his interdisciplinary Master of Marine Management. Combining the disciplines of law and political science, his areas of study interests are on seafarer rights under the Maritime Labour Convention 2006, child environmental rights, conflict management, and alternative marine resource governance. He was an assistant professor in political science at the University of the Philippines Visayas for 14 years prior to 2012.

Peter Luttmann

is a JD candidate at the Schulich School of Law, Dalhousie University. Mr. Luttmann's interest in maritime and international law stems from: (1) growing up in rural Nova Scotia within easy distance of the Bay of Fundy; (2) pursuing masters studies in Pensacola, Florida, alongside the Gulf of Mexico; and (3) being exposed to international culture and language and a two-month immersion in France following undergraduate studies. Mr. Luttmann hopes to practice law as a member of the Canadian Forces after his call to the bar.

Sarah McDonald

is in the second year of her JD at the Schulich School of Law at Dalhousie University, where she is pursuing a certificate in environmental law. She has a BA in conflict studies and human rights from the University of Ottawa. Sarah currently works as a research assistant for Professor David VanderZwaag, and volunteers as co-chair of the Food Law Action Group and as a copyeditor for the *Dalhousie Journal of Legal Studies*.

Mirka Morales Hierrezuelo

has a master of science in education and as social communication degree. She is an instructor at the Municipal University Center, Guamá, Cuba, and is a graduate of the Program in Integrated Coastal Zone Management by the project Local Integrated Coastal Zone Management in Southeast Cuba (2010–2014). She teaches organizational communication, identity and corporate image, public relations, social marketing, communication and community, art history and the history of Cuban art.

Mary Ann Palma-Robles

is a visiting senior fellow at the Australian National Centre for Ocean Resources and Security, University of Wollongong, Australia. She holds a B.A. in public administration from the University of the Philippines, master of marine management from Dalhousie University, and doctor of philosophy from the University of Wollongong. Her primary research interests are international fisheries law, ocean law and policy and maritime security. Apart from fisheries crime, her most recent research also focuses on trade measures to combat illegal, unreported and unregulated fishing, fishing and naval vessel encounters at sea, and labour conditions in fisheries.

Nuwan Peiris

holds an LL.M. in international trade law (Wales), an LL.B (O.U.S.L.) and is a qualified chartered shipbroker (MICS) (UK). He is an attorney-at-law and state counsel at the Attorney General's Department, Sri Lanka, and a Sri Lankan delegate on fisheries matters. Formerly, he was the independent counsel to the Presidential commission of inquiry investigating human rights violations in Sri Lanka, head of the Human Rights Bureau of the Sri Lanka Legal Aid Commission and a criminal prosecutor. He was a Nippon Fellow of the International Tribunal for the Law of the Sea.

Ofelia Pérez Montero

has sociology and philosophy degrees and is a professor and director at the Multidisciplinary Study Center of Coastal Zones at the Universidad de Oriente, Cuba. She is president of the biennial International Conference on Integrated Coastal Zone Management (CARICOSTAS) in Cuba. She is coordinator of the project Local Integrated Coastal Zone Management in Southeast Cuba (2010–2014) and coordinator of different national and international research projects on integrated coastal zone management, risk, local sustainable development and gender. She has taken part in different international events and published over 50 articles.

José Abelardo Planas Fajardo

has a doctorate in geographic sciences and a geography degree. He is researcher in the Center of Solar Energy Research, Santiago de Cuba, CITMA, Cuba, and is a collaborator at the Multidisciplinary Study Center of Coastal Zones at Universidad de Oriente. He teaches an integrated basin management course at the Universidad de Oriente, and has published on basin management, environmental sustainability indicators and renewable energy.

René Taudal Poulsen

holds a Ph.D. in fisheries history from the University of Southern Denmark, Esbjerg in 2005. He is currently associate professor in shipping economics at the Copenhagen Business School, where he has been employed since 2012. He has published in journals such as *Fish and Fisheries, Scandinavian Economic History Review* and *Business History.*

Isabel Poveda Santana

has a master of sciences in business management and a political economy degree. She is assistant professor at the Universidad de Oriente and a professor and researcher at the Multidisciplinary Study Center of Coastal Zones. She has published in national magazines on themes related to environmental industrial management and local sustainable development and gender.

Karen N. Scott

is a professor of law at the University of Canterbury, New Zealand. She specialises in the areas of international environmental law and the law of the sea and has published extensively on issues relating to oceans management, Antarctica and geoengineering and climate change in journals such as the *Michigan Journal of International Law, International and Comparative Law Quarterly* and the *Melbourne Journal of International Law.* Recent publications include: A.D. Hemmings, D.R. Rothwell and K.N. Scott (eds.), *Antarctic Security in the Twenty-first Century* (Routledge, 2012).

Dikdik Mohamad Sodik

is professor of law at Bandung Islamic University, Bandung, Indonesia, whose research interests primarily focus on the law of the sea. He has published articles, book chapters and books in the area of the law of the sea. Dr. Sodik has bachelor and master of international law degrees from the University of Padjadjaran, Bandung, Indonesia, and a Ph.D. from the Faculty of Law, University of Wollongong, New South Wales, Australia in December 2007.

Henrik Sornn-Friese

is an associate professor at the Copenhagen Business School, where he is academic director of *Copenhagen Business School Maritime* as well as director of the flagship M.Sc. program in economics and business administration. He is author or co-author of several books and book chapters about shipping as well as numerous articles in leading international journals such as *Transportation Journal, Industry and Innovation, Research Policy, International Journal of Maritime History*, and *Business History*. His work on the Danish maritime cluster has impacted directly on recent Danish maritime policy.

Stig Tenold

is a professor of economic history at the Norwegian School of Economics in Bergen. He has published extensively on modern maritime history, and also on Asian economic development and popular music history. Tenold is the co-editor of two recent anthologies: *Global Shipping in Small Nations* and *The World's Key Industry – History and Economics of International Shipping*, both published by Palgrave in 2012.

David L. VanderZwaag

is professor of law and Canada Research Chair (Tier 1) in ocean law and governance at the Schulich School of Law, Dalhousie University. He is a member of the IUCN's World Commission on Environmental Law and co-chairs its Specialist Group on Oceans, Coasts and Coral Reefs. He is an elected member of the International Council of Environmental Law and has authored over 100 papers in marine and environmental law. His educational background includes: Ph.D. (University of Wales, Cardiff), LL.M. (Dalhousie Law School), J.D. (University of Arkansas Law School), M.Div. (Princeton Theological Seminary), and B.A. (Calvin College).

Jenna Viertola

worked as a research assistant at Brahea Centre, Centre for Maritime Studies at University of Turku, Finland. She was responsible for data collection regarding the research which this article is based on.

Johanna Yliskylä-Peuralahti

is working as a project manager at Brahea Centre, Centre for Maritime Studies, University of Turku, Finland. Her recent research has focused on maritime governance and environmental regulation.

Andreas Zink

graduated from the University of Trier, Germany, with a law degree in 2011. Afterwards he joined the Institute for Environmental and Technology Law at the University of Trier where he is currently working on a doctoral thesis about the Ballast Water Management Convention of 2004. His areas of research are mainly the law of the sea, international environmental law and the international regulation of alien invasive species.

Issues and Prospects

∵

The Nexus of Ocean Trade and Climate Change: A Review Essay

Awni Behnam†
Honorary President, International Ocean Institute, Malta
Former Assistant Secretary-General of the United Nations

Introduction

International trade overcomes the restrictions of home markets as it develops an outlet for surplus production above national requirements. There is no doubt that trade is a vital engine of economic growth. By broadening markets, international trade increases the degree of specialization possible and enhances the overall productivity within a country. Exports can be the leading sector in the process because as exports grow they support an increasingly robust sector of intermediate suppliers within the exporting country. This creates growth by stimulating technological change and investment through spillover effects into other sectors. In fact, growth rates of developing countries correlate more with their export performance than with any other single economic indicator.

Trade does not occur in a vacuum. It was the freedom of the seas doctrine that advocated that shipping routes on the high seas are free and open to all nations. The cost of transport impacts on whether goods move at all and/or the size and direction of that movement. The cost and efficiency of the transport mode determines the competiveness of goods shipped and the income of buyers or sellers. Shipping or maritime transport is the backbone of international trade and the use of the ocean and seas for transport of trade is the most valuable of ocean and seas services. According to the United Nations Conference on Trade and Development (UNCTAD) sources, the value of seaborne trade in

† The author acknowledges the support of UNCTAD, the Division on Technology and Logistics and the permission to use presentation material from Jan Hoffman, Frida Youssef, Hassiba Benamara, and Anila Premti of the Trade Logistics Branch. The support of Mary Chehab in preparing this article is acknowledged.

© KONINKLIJKE BRILL NV, LEIDEN, 2015 | DOI 10.1163/9789004297234_002

2012 was estimated at about US$12.9 trillion.[1] Consequently, maritime trade plays a vital role in national and international economies, particularly since seaborne trade accounts for 90 percent of world trade by volume.[2]

However, as important as is maritime transport (shipping), it is the largest contributor to seaborne ocean pollution. Greenhouse gas emissions (GHG) generated by fossil fuel consumption in the shipping sector contributes directly to ocean acidification and to climate change. Hence, the complex and interdependent nexus of ocean trade and climate change.

The two pillars of ocean trade (including cruising vessels) are the ship and the port. Each pillar generates its own carbon footprint and, as such, contributes to the challenge that is climate change. However, climate change impacts the port and the port city more directly than it does the vessels of ocean trade, manifesting itself in the form of extreme weather, such as recurrent cyclones and hurricanes, as well as sea level rise, which may inflict permanent damage on port infrastructure. This article attempts to review this complex relationship focusing specifically on ocean trade.

The Dual Character of Shipping: A Service to Trade and an Industry in Its Own Right

Demand for shipping, as for any other transport service, is always a derived demand, the level of which depends on the type and quantity of goods traded, as well as on the geographic trade structure. The fact that there is no 'original' demand for cargo shipping services underlines the close linkage between trade and shipping. Yet, more important than the fact that demand for shipping services will not materialize unless there is cargo to be moved is the inverse relationship that no trade can take place unless adequate shipping services are at the disposal of the trading community. Consequently, the shipping industry has not only reacted to trading requirements but, in many cases, has created pre-conditions for the expansion of world trade based on an intensified international division of labor.

An example of such development can be seen in the rapid growth of trade in dry bulk commodities over the last three decades, combined with similarly important changes in trade patterns. Reductions in bulk shipping costs based on the exploitation of economies of scale in transport have resulted in a reduction of economic distances. Ocean shipping has experienced and continues to experience an ongoing technological revolution. This is seen in iron

---

1   Estimates obtained directly from H. Benamara, Policy and Legislation Section, DTL, UNCTAD.
2   A. Behnam, "The Ocean Trade in the New Economy," *Ocean Development and International Law* 35 (2004): 115–130. See also *UNCTAD Review of Maritime Transport* and *Annual Reports.*

replacing wood in ship construction, liquid fossil fuels replacing coal in propulsion systems, and dramatic increases in the volume and efficiency of bulk transport, an example being oil tankers of 5,000 dead weight tonnes (dwt) replacing conveying oil in individual barrels. Larger ships have been the hallmarks of the shipping industry. Corresponding decreases in transportation costs have helped open up geographically distant markets, thus reducing the locational distance between raw material suppliers, typically located in developing countries, and the manufacturing centers, typically located in developed countries.

However, it is not the existence of a shipping industry, as such, that preconditions the expansion of world trade but rather the provision of services adequate to serve the differing needs of various trading interests. Such adequacy pertains to all facets of shipping services, e.g., the availability of ships physically suitable for particular transport needs; the frequency of services offered to avoid undue interruptions in commodity flows; and the pricing of such services in line with the ability of the goods traded to bear the cost of transport. Unless these criteria are met, shipping cannot facilitate world trade. Experience has shown that countries, which for one reason or another, have been denied adequate shipping services, or have been deprived of them, face considerable setbacks in their foreign trade, which leads to corresponding interruptions to their development process.

Prior to the acceleration of globalization in the 1980s, it was thought that the most effective way of avoiding such disruptions and ensuring the availability of adequate shipping services was to maintain a certain minimum engagement in shipping. National carriers can reasonably be expected to maintain a closer link with the particular trading interests of their countries than foreign carriers. Furthermore, by controlling substantial tonnage in the national export trades, a country can exercise countervailing power against practices of foreign carriers that are possibly detrimental to its trade interests.

These considerations do not justify limiting the role of shipping to that of a servant to trade. Such a perspective would incur the danger of concealing inefficiencies and consequently misallocating resources. Yet, it is sufficiently clear that decisions to invest in shipping cannot be based solely on criteria of commercial profitability at the level of the firm but must take into account the industry's viability for the country's economy as a whole. From this, it also follows that to compare investment in shipping with investment in other sectors of the economy on the basis of direct returns on that investment is neither feasible nor meaningful. Benefits from allocating resources to other sectors depend on the existence of a functioning transport system, such as shipping and, inversely, the expansion of shipping activities in conjunction with the development of other sectors of the economy.

Apart from providing a service to trade, shipping as an independent industry has a direct bearing on the development process of a country. It helps to improve foreign exchange, creates employment, fosters technology transfer and economic integration, and helps to safeguard national sovereignty, particularly in times of political crises. Apart from these direct effects, shipping investment contributes substantially to the diversification of the economy of the investing country, as it requires a whole range of support industries and services. These include shipbuilding and repairing, supplies, equipment, insurance, banking services, human resources, and telecommunications.

Over the past four decades, world seaborne trade grew at an annual average rate of three percent, rising from 2.6 billion tons in 1970 to 8.4 billion tons in 2010. In 2011, volumes increased at an annual rate of four percent to reach 8.7 billion tons. In 2011, 60 percent of the volume of seaborne world trade originated in developing countries and 57 percent of this trade was delivered in their territories.[3] Figure 1.1 shows the growth of international maritime trade.

As mentioned earlier, the shipping industry has undergone a significant transformation over time through technological innovations involving much larger ships and faster propulsion. This transformation has occasioned dramatic increases in the ability of the shipping industry to navigate vast distances quickly and safely, and absorb the ever-expanding demand for moving trade. The structure and growth of merchant marine vessels is illustrated in Figure 1.2. The magnitude of the shipping industry is illustrated in that the total value of global freight costs of imports (all modes) was estimated at US$1.2 trillion in 2010.[4]

In 2011, the revenue of the global industry exceeded US$400 billion and is expected to reach US$511.8 billion by the end of 2015. Estimates for January 2013 indicate that the total value of the world fleet is worth US$809 billion.[5]

In 2012, world seaborne trade reached a record high of 8.7 billion tons and total maritime activity increased to 45 billion ton-miles. The value of world merchandise exports reached US$18.2 trillion in 2011.[6] In 2012, world seaborne trade accounted for 90 percent of world trade by volume. In the same year, the world merchant fleet serviced 1.5 billion dwt by 104,305 sea-going vessels,[7] of

---

3   UNCTAD, *Review of Maritime Transport, 2011*, UNCTAD/RMT/2011, available online: <http://unctad.org/en/docs/rmt2011_en.pdf>.

4   UNCTAD, *Review of Maritime Transport, 2012*, UNCTAD/RMT/2011, available online: <http://unctad.org/en/PublicationsLibrary/rmt2012_en.pdf>.

5   Figures available from UNCTAD, Trade Logistics Branch, DTL, 2013.

6   UNCTAD, *Review of Maritime Transport, 2012*, n. 4 above, p. 4.

7   Id., p. 36.

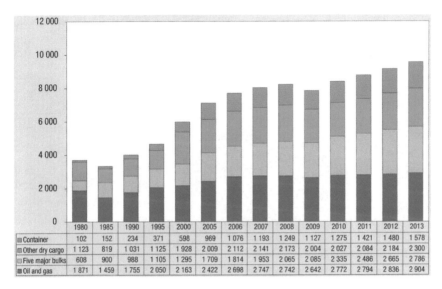

FIGURE 1.1 *International seaborne trade, selected years (millions of tons loaded)*
SOURCE: UNCTAD. REPRINTED WITH PERMISSION.

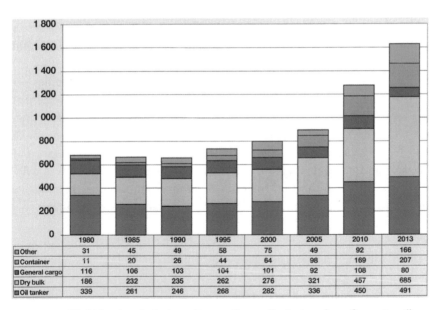

FIGURE 1.2 *World fleet by principal vessel types, 1980–2013 (beginning-of-year figures, in millions*
of dwt)
SOURCE: UNCTAD. REPRINTED WITH PERMISSION.

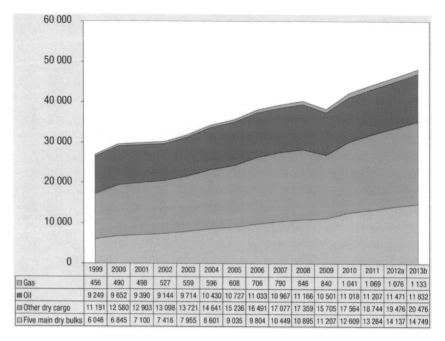

FIGURE 1.3   *World seaborne trade in cargo ton-miles by cargo type, 1999–2013 (billions of ton-miles)*
SOURCE: UNCTAD. REPRINTED WITH PERMISSION.

which 72 percent were oil tankers and bulk carriers. The average age is 12.2 years for tankers and 17.5 years for bulk carriers.[8] Figure 1.3 illustrates world seaborne trade in ton-miles by cargo type.

The productivity of the world fleet is estimated to be 30,000 ton-miles per dwt, the highest level of productivity since 1990. Approximately 71.5 percent of the world fleet is registered under foreign flags and/or in open-registry countries. The sheer size of the global shipping industry, its uninterrupted growth and its preeminent role in the global economy confirm the importance of accounting for ocean trade's contribution to climate change. Additionally, these statistics confirm that solutions must take into account the systemic implications, which will attend reducing ocean trade's carbon footprint.

Climate Change: The Challenge

Perhaps the greatest challenge to the human race in the 21st century is climate change. Simply defined, climate change, or alternatively global warming, is a

---

8   Id., p. 39.

change in global climate patterns apparent from the mid-to-late 20th century onwards, attributed largely to the increased levels of atmospheric carbon dioxide (CO_2) produced by the use of fossil fuels. The long-term consequences of climate change threaten the very survival of the human species. However, in the immediate term, climate change threatens the viability of sustainable development and prosperity. Additionally, it will impact water and food security, coastal infrastructure, human health, ocean health, biodiversity, migration, global trade, as well as security, where flooding, sea level rise, extreme weather, storm surges, hurricanes, melting of the ice and glaciers, and desertification and flooding become more frequent and of greater intensity. Typhoon Haiyan, which devastated the Philippines on 8 November 2013, may be a precursor of what is yet to come. In September 2013, *National Geographic* wrote:

> A profoundly altered planet is what our fossil-fuel-driven civilization is creating, a planet where Sandy-scale flooding will become more common and more destructive for the world's coastal cities. We have irreversibly committed future generations to a hotter world and rising seas. In the last several years we've observed accelerated melting of the ice sheets in Greenland and West Antarctica. The concern is that if the acceleration continues, by the time we get to the end of the 21st century, we could see sea-level rise of as much as six feet globally instead of two to three feet.[9]

The same article states that in 2012, an expert panel convened by the US National Oceanic and Atmospheric Administration adopted a sea level rise of 6.6 feet (two meters) as its highest of four scenarios for 2100. The most recent findings of the Intergovernmental Panel on Climate Change (IPCC) indicate that the reality may be worse than earlier assessed. UNCTAD adds, "One recent study has estimated that assuming a sea level rise of 0.5 meter by 2050, the value of exposed assets in 136 port megacities may be as high as US$28 trillion."[10]

---

9   T. Folger, "Rising Seas," *National Geographic*, September 2013. Available online: <http:// ngm.nationalgeographic.com/2013/09/rising-seas/folger-text>, quoting R. Horton, Earth Institute, Columbia University.

10   UNCTAD, Ad Hoc Expert Meeting on Climate Change and Adaptation: A Challenge for Global Ports, 29–30 September 2011. Information Note by the UNCTAD Secretariat, UNCTAD/DTL/TLB/2011/2, available online: <http://unctad.org/en/Docs/dtltlb2011d2 _en.pdf>, quoting T. Lenton, A. Footitt and A. Dlugolecki. 2009. *Major Tipping Points in the Earth's Climate System and Consequences for the Insurance Sector*. 89 pp.

The *World Ocean Review* warns that:

> ...without doubt sea level will rise slowly at first, speeding up and continu-
> ing beyond the 21st century. Gradually many coastal areas will become
> uninhabitable. People will lose their homes and part of their culture.[11]

According to the same report, rising sea levels threaten over one billion people in
Asia. Such population displacement is a recipe for conflict and a threat to global
security. Militating against climate change is not sufficient and there is an urgent
need to begin the process of adaptation, climate protection and risk minimization for which investment in coastal management must be adequately budgeted.

Globally, an increase in the frequency of natural and human-induced disasters has occurred since the 1950s, coinciding with an increase in urban densifi-
cation. As the climate change process advances, disasters such as landslides,
floods, windstorms and extreme temperatures may occur with greater frequency and intensity.[12] Urban vulnerability to climate change will therefore
depend upon disaster preparedness, defined by the International Strategy for
Disaster Reduction Secretariat as:

> activities and measures taken in advance to ensure effective response to
> the impact of hazards, including the issuance of timely and effective
> early warnings and the temporary evacuation of people and property
> from threatened locations.[13]

The Organisation for Economic Co-operation and Development estimates that
by 2070, 150 million people in the world's largest port cities will be at risk from
coastal flooding, along with $35 trillion worth of property, an amount that will
equal nine percent of the global GDP.[14] The Secretary-General of the United
Nations on 3 October 2011 stated:

> Rising sea levels are [a] major impact of climate change and an urgent
> concern. Sixty million people now live within one meter of sea level

---

11   *World Ocean Review* (WOR.1), 2010, available online: <http://worldoceanreview.com/en>, p. 6.

12   UN-HABITAT, *Impact of Climate Change upon Urban Areas, Cities and Climate Change*, 2011.
      Chapter IV, ISBN 978-1-84971-37-9. See UN-HABITAT, Cities and Climate Change Initiatives,
      Developing local climate change plans, 2012, ISBN 978-92-1-1324006.

13   S. Brinceño, "Today's Education for Tomorrow's Disaster Risk Reduction," in *Risk Wise*
      eds., S. Nicklin, B. Cornwell, J. Dodd, J. Griffiths and S. Townsend (Leicester: Tudor Rose,
      2008), pp. 4–17.

14   *National Geographic*, n. 9 above.

[and] by the end of the century the number will jump to 130 million. Major coastal cites – such as Alexandria, New York, Karachi, Calcutta, Belem, New Orleans, Shanghai, Tokyo, Lagos, Miami, and Amsterdam – could face serious threats from storm surges. The nexus between urbanization and climate change is real and potentially deadly.[15]

Figure 1.4 illustrates predictions of sea level rise until 2100. The 20 major port cities with assets valued at greater than US$20 trillion under sea level rise

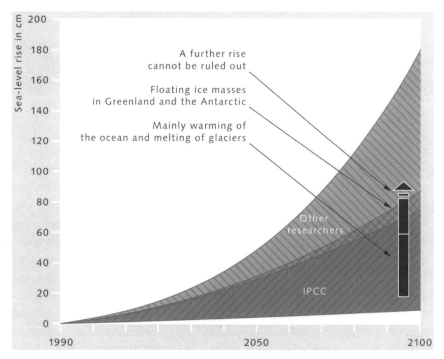

FIGURE 1.4   *Sea level will rise significantly by the end of this century, although the precise extent to which it will rise is unclear. The IPCC forecasts a rise of up to one meter during this century. Other researchers consider that a rise of as much as 180 cm is possible. As there are numerous studies and scenarios to back up both these projections, the findings and figures cover a broad range. There will certainly be feedback effects between the melting of the glaciers and the expansion of water due to global warming. Record rates of sea level rise are predicted in the event of more rapid melting of the Antarctic and Greenland ice sheets.*
SOURCE: *WORLD OCEAN REVIEW 1* (HAMBURG: MARIBUS GGMBH, 2010), P. 59.
REPRINTED WITH PERMISSION.

15   United Nations Secretary-General Ban Ki-moon, United Nations Secretary-General's Message on World Habitat Day, 3 October 2011, available online: <http://www.un.org/sg/statements/index.asp?nid=5582>.

predictions by 2050 are: Guangzhou Guangdong, Miami, Kolkata (Calcutta), Shanghai, New York-Newark, Mumbai (Bombay), Ningbo, Tianjin, Krung Thep (Bangkok), Tokyo, Hong Kong, Osaka-Kobe, New Orleans, Rotterdam, Amsterdam, Dhaka, Qingdao, Thành-Pho-Ho-Chi, Virginia Beach, and Nagoya.[16]

These are examples of the enormity of the challenge coastal port cities face.[17]

The IPCC Fifth Assessment Report (October 2013) provided another wakeup call in a summary released for policy makers:

> Warming of the climate system is unequivocal, and since the 1950s, many of the observed changes are unprecedented over decades to millennia. The atmosphere and ocean have warmed, the amounts of snow and ice have diminished, sea level has risen, and the concentrations of greenhouse gases have increased.[18]

Over the last two decades, the Greenland and Antarctic ice sheets have been losing mass, glaciers have continued to shrink almost worldwide, and Arctic sea ice and Northern Hemisphere spring snow cover have continued to decrease in extent. The rate of sea level rise since the mid-19th century currently exceeds the mean rate during the previous two millennia. Over the period 1901–2010, global mean sea level rose between 0.17 and 0.21 meters.

Human influence on the climate system is clear. Increased scientific understanding of the Earth's climate system confirms that various observed phenomena are symptoms of anthropogenic climate change, such as rising concentrations of atmospheric greenhouse gases (GHG), positive radiative forcing, and observed warming trends. Human influence has been detected in atmospheric and oceanic warming, changes in the global hydrological cycle, reductions in snow and ice cover, accelerations in mean sea level rise, and changes in climatic extremes. Evidence confirming human influence on the Earth's climate has grown since the fourth review of the IPCC. It is extremely likely that human influence has been the dominant cause of the observed warming since the mid-20th century.

The global ocean will continue to warm during the 21st century. Heat will penetrate from the surface to the deep ocean and affect ocean circulation. Cumulative emissions of CO_2 will largely determine global mean surface

---

16   H. Benamara, UNCTAD (TLB – DTL), 2013.

17   See also UN-HABITAT, *Impact of Climate Change upon Urban Areas, Cities and Climate Change*, 2011. Chapter IV, ISBN 978-1-84971-37-9; UN-HABITAT, Cities and Climate Change Initiatives, *Developing Local Climate Change Plans*, 2012, ISBN 978-92-1-1324006.

18   Intergovernmental Panel on Climate Change, *Climate Change 2013: The Physical Science Basis, Fifth Assessment Report 2013*, available online: <http://www.ipcc.ch/report/ar5/>.

warming by the late 21st century and beyond. Most aspects of climate change will persist for many centuries to come, even if emissions of CO_2 are stopped today. This represents a substantial multi-century climate change commitment created by past, present, and future emissions of CO_2.

Maritime Transport as a Contributor to Climate Change

Over recent years, UNCTAD has been carrying out substantial work to help improve the understanding of issues at the interface of maritime transport and climate change. This work focuses particularly on the impacts of climate change on critical transportation infrastructure, considering the implications of sea level rise, extreme weather events, and rising temperatures, as well as the associated adaptation requirements. These issues are of particular importance to coastal developing countries, in particular, for small island developing States (SIDS) that may be vulnerable to climate change impacts but may lack the capacity to take the appropriate adaptation measures.

UNCTAD 13, the Doha Mandate, highlighted the sustainability and facilitation of trade. Maritime trade constitutes 90 percent of world trade. Current freight transportation systems, particularly those in the maritime setting, contribute significantly to global GHG emissions and consequently to ocean acidification. Over 95 percent of fuels in the freight transport supply chain are petroleum-based and the sector consumes 50 percent of all global liquid fossil fuels, a percentage share which is projected to grow over 45 percent from 2008 to 2035. Approximately 25 percent of CO_2 emissions are transport related and are expected to increase by 57 percent by 2030.[19] The evidence indicates that shipping is a highly productive service when compared with other transport industries. However, the most recent studies show that GHG and CO_2 emissions from shipping are major contributors to climate change, amounting to as much as twice the total emissions of airlines, with emissions anticipated to increase by 100 percent by 2050 as seaborne trade continues to expand. Shipping was estimated to have accounted for 3.4 percent of the global GHG emissions during 2007 and was estimated to be responsible for 2.7 percent of CO_2 emissions. The recorded annual emissions from shipping range between 870 and 1,120 million tons of CO_2,[20] with the maritime transport

---

19   UNCTAD, *Review of Maritime Transport, 2012*, n. 4 above, p. 128.

20   UNCTAD, *Maritime Transport and the Climate Change Challenge, Summary of Proceedings*, Geneva, 16–18 February 2009, UNCTAD/DTL/TLB/2009/1, 1 December 2009, p. 7, Table 1, available online: <http://unctad.org/en/docs/dtltlb20091_en.pdf>.

sector accounting for ten percent of all transportation emissions globally, a figure which is greater than the emissions of all African countries combined. It is estimated that the world merchant fleet consumed approximately 350 million metric tons of fuel in 2007 and its consumption is expected to increase by 100 percent by 2050.[21]

GHG emissions from international shipping are of public concern. Those emissions are not covered under the UNFCCC, the United Nations Framework Convention on Climate Change, the international regulatory framework dealing with climate change. Currently, the Kyoto Protocol does not cover maritime emissions, and there is no effective international emission strategy for shipping in place.

Eyring et al. state:

> Although shipping contributes only about 16% to the total fuel consumption of all traffic related sources, ...the ocean-going fleet produces 9.2 (0.8) times more NO_x emissions than aviation...80 (2.7) times more SO_x emissions...[and] approximately 1,200 times more particulate matter than aviation.[22]

This clearly indicates the need for the shipping industry to incorporate environmental considerations into their designated development.

The European Union has committed to taking action to reduce GHG emissions from shipping. Additionally, the International Maritime Organization (IMO) has taken certain initiatives to address emissions in maritime transport, including improving vessel efficiency.[23] However, there is no international accord governing the allocation of emissions from shipping and whether to allocate emissions to countries of registry or otherwise. For example, under the Kyoto Protocol, CO_2 emissions from international shipping cannot be attributed to any particular economy. Consequently, the IMO has had to address this issue from the perspective of GHG emission limitations and reductions. In July 2011, the IMO adopted technical measures for new ships and operational measures for all ships. These measures supplement MARPOL Annex VI by adding a

---

21   Id.

22   V. Eyring, H.W. Köhler, J. van Aardenne and A. Lauer, "Emissions from International Shipping: 1. The last 50 Years," *Journal of Geophysical Research: Atmospheres* 110 (September 2005), 12 pp.

23   A. Premti, "Key Trends in International Transport and Implication for Development," Presentation at UNCTAD Trade and Development Commission, 17–21 June 2013, Geneva.

new Chapter 4 entitled Regulations on Energy Efficiency for Ships.[24] However, the technical and operational measures to improve efficiency may not be sufficient to satisfactorily reduce the amount of GHG emissions from international shipping in view of the growth projections of human population and world trade.

Figures 1.5 and 1.6 illustrate the percentage share of global carbon emissions according to sector, including transport, as well as a comparison to the emissions of maritime shipping.

Two main issues confront the international community in addressing the challenge posed by shipping's contribution to climate change. The first relates to implementing technical solutions to reduce emissions from ships, particularly NO_x, SO_x, and CO_2 emissions. The second relates to regulating shipping more broadly, as it is a competitive international industry operating

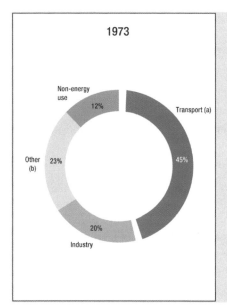
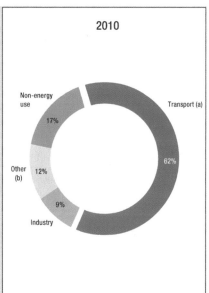

FIGURE 1.5   *World oil consumption, 1973 and 2010*
SOURCE: UNCTAD. REPRINTED WITH PERMISSION.

---

24   International Convention for the Prevention of Pollution from Ships, 1973 (MARPOL). Adoption: 1973 (Convention), 1978 (1978 Protocol), 1997 (Protocol – Annex VI); Entry into force: 2 October 1983 (Annexes I and II); *Main Events in IMO's Work on Limitation and Reduction of Greenhouse Gas Emissions from International Shipping*, Summary Document prepared by the IMO Secretariat, October 2011. See also UNCTAD, *Review of Maritime Transport, 2012*, n. 4 above, p. 130.

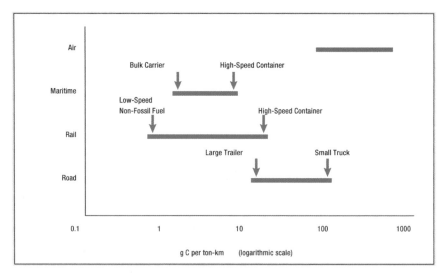

FIGURE 1.6   *Comparison of CO$_2$ emissions in freight transport by mode of transport (grams carbon per ton freight carried per kilometer)*
SOURCE: UNCTAD. REPRINTED WITH PERMISSION.

under the regime of flags of convenience, which undermine governance, jurisdiction, control, and compliance enforcement in shipping and maritime trade.

With regards to the first challenge, potential solutions involve reducing total fuel consumption, employing cleaner fuels, and replacing residual fuel with marine diesel, as well as developing exhaust gas treatment technology and alternative energy systems. Shipping must not be allowed to hide behind the slogan 'little pollution for a lot of movement'. The EU can lead by example by incorporating maritime transport emission reductions as part of its integrated and comprehensive maritime policy. To the credit of the EU, it has adopted a roadmap of 40 concrete initiatives with an overall objective of achieving a total 60 percent reduction in CO$_2$ emissions and comparable reduction in oil dependency by 2050.[25]

The shipping industry is conservative. Correspondingly, changes in behavior do not come easily and there is a culture of procrastination when it comes to reducing pollution from ships. These realities contribute to a widely held

---

25   European Commission White Paper on Transport, adopted in March 2011; Freda Yousef, UNCTAD Trade Logistics Branch, DTL, June 2013.

consensus concerning the difficulty of imposing responsibility for emissions in the shipping industry.

The second issue stems from the existence of flags of convenience and the international character of shipping. Although ultimately it is the flag State that should bear responsibility for monitoring compliance with any agreed measures or solutions, for one half of the global shipping fleet, flag State enforcement is absent; this places the other half in an unfair competitive position. Furthermore, international organizations such as the IMO cannot enforce compliance with potential emission reductions conventions and guidelines. It is up to the flag State to ensure compliance through enforcement opportunities such as port State control measures.

There are two additional obstacles that impede flag States from assuming responsibility for emission reduction strategies. The first is the absence of a mandatory genuine link between flag State and vessel, which renders flag States incapable of exercising jurisdiction and control. The second are the difficulties faced by international agencies such as the IMO in implementing principles such as those issued by the UNFCCC for common but differentiated responsibilities for developed and developing countries, as called for by the most vulnerable of developing countries.[26]

Despite these challenges, policy-makers are actively developing solutions. The EU integrated maritime policy paper has clearly recognized the nexus of oceans and climate change; it recognizes that CO_2-induced acidification of the marine environment is inevitable. The solutions it proposes do not consist in capping emissions. Rather, they consist of developing environment-friendly freight corridors and achieving cuts in shipping emissions through fuel efficiency.

Shipping, and international trade more broadly, has undergone enormous technological change over the past four decades due to the evolution of multimodal transport systems and containerization. The concept of door-to-door transport has forever revolutionized maritime transport by integrating the land transport sector into the shipping sector. Thus it is no longer feasible to address maritime transport of international trade in terms of climate change without taking into account the connectivity paradigm. Therefore it is the concept of sustainable freight transport that has to be addressed, that is, mitigation and adaptation measures to minimize GHG emissions in the integrated transport supply chain.

UNCTAD lists a number of possible mitigation and adaptation measures that may be taken to reduce freight transport emissions at both the national or

---

26   UNCTAD, *Maritime Transport and the Climate Change Challenge*, n. 13 above, p. 10.

international levels. Such measures include technology and energy use improvements (alternative fuel and energy sources), operational measures (cost-cutting strategies, re-routing, vessel speed reduction, improvement of infrastructure and green logistics systems, alternative routing for shorter distances and combinations thereof, enhanced port operations and infrastructures), as well as market-based programs (capping, trade and emissions credits, and fuel tax). For these measures to be successful, two preconditions must be met. First, there must be sufficiently strong political will. Second, there must be abundant financial resources. Unfortunately, neither of these preconditions is currently in place.

Implications of Climate Change to Coastal City Ports

The location of ports at the interface between the land and the sea presents both challenges and opportunities. The adage given to ports as the 'gateway of nations' is indicative of their importance. Ports are the living heart of a country's economy, and they play a strategic role in the international trading system. Concurrently, ports face the challenges associated with climate change (as discussed above) more directly than any other valued infrastructure, due to their exposure and corresponding vulnerability to climate change-driven ocean perturbations.

In September 2011, UNCTAD convened a meeting of International Experts on Climate Change and Impact on Global Ports.[27] The background report identified several factors that ports face in relation to climate change, such as sea level rise, extreme weather conditions, hurricanes, storms, flooding and inundation, erosion of coastal areas, change in wave directions, and temperature change. The economic and social costs of these impacts on ports are immeasurable. One expert from the International Chamber of Shipping warned that "without ports and shipping half the world would starve and the other half would freeze."[28]

In a 2011 article in *The New York Times*, Nathanial Gronewold remarked that there has been little comprehensive investigation into how ports will be affected by climate change and that globally, port authorities lack concrete

---

27   UNCTAD, *Ad Hoc Expert Meeting on Climate Change and Adaptation: A Challenge for Global Ports, 29–30 September 2011. Main Outcomes and Summary of Discussions*, UNCTAD/DTL/TLB/2011/3, available online: <http://unctad.org/en/Docs/dtltlb2011d3_en.pdf>.

28   S. Bennett, International Chamber of Shipping, Presentation at UNCTAD Ad Hoc Expert Meeting, Climate Change and Adaptation, n. 27 above.

data relating to projected adaptation and mitigation costs when considering future scenarios that may require massive investment to prepare for.[29] Further, he emphasized that

> ...with hundreds of ports tied to one another in often intricate and complex trade links, even a temporary disruption to one far-flung port facility can have wide ranging implications on global trade.

It is generally accepted that a sea level rise of one meter will take place during this century. Other experts, such as the IPCC, forecast a rise of 1.80 meters. UNCTAD further warns that when assessing the port vulnerability to climate change, it is important to consider coastal transport networks and port hinterland connections, the integrity of which is vital to port operations.

Based on this reasoning, the 2011 UNCTAD meeting called for devising port adaptation strategies.[30] What is of concern, however, is the apparent lack of global awareness regarding the impacts of climate change and the need for intensive data acquisition, information generation and analytical research.[31]

A Concluding Reflection

We, as vulnerable humans, should not allow for this doomsday prediction to occur. I have said before that human capacity for destructiveness is only matched by human ingenuity for survival. There is no denying that once again the challenge of preparation, adaptation, and mitigation trumps all others. The international community has no alternative but to realize and to build upon a holistic, over-arching governance framework to manage the ocean sustainably and maintain its ecological, economic, and social services upon which humankind depends. Such an approach is encapsulated in the Blue Economy model.

The Blue Economy, defined as "living with the ocean and from the ocean in a sustainable relationship,"[32] is the transition toward a human-ocean centered

---

29   N. Gronewald, "Little Preparation under Way for Climate Change at World's Seaports," *The New York Times*, 28 September 2011. Available online: <http://www.nytimes.com/cwire/2011/09/28/28climatewire-little-preparation-under-way-for-climate-cha-99300.html?pagewanted=all>; M. Savonis, ICF International, US Ports. Addressing the Adaptation Challenge, Presentation at UNCTAD Expert Group, n. 27 above.

30   Report of the Ad Hoc Expert Meeting, UNCTAD/DTL/TLB/2011/3, n. 27 above.

31   Id.

32   A. Behnam, *Tracing the Blue Economy*, Lumen Monograph Series Volume 1 (Malta: Foundation de Malte, 2013), ISBN: 978-1-291-61589-0.

relationship where humankind coexists with the ocean and from the ocean in a sustainable manner. It is also understood that the concept of Blue Economy integrates two dimensions, that of the provision of goods and services and the protection and security of property and life in a manner that is sustainable and guarantees the rights of future generations.

On the one hand, the ocean offers apparently limitless services essential for the survival and prosperity of humans in fields ranging from recreation to research, from travel to trade, from food to medicine, from waste disposal to carbon sequestration, from energy to minerals, from climate control to border control and much more. At the same time the ocean follows the laws of nature in ways that escape human control and can be devastating to humankind. From this, humankind has always sought deliverance or protection through resilience, avoidance, mitigation, and adaptation. Recent tsunamis, hurricanes, cyclones, storm surges, extreme coastal weather events, and other marine hazards are in the majority not triggered by human activities. Of course, anthropogenic sources of climate change (triggered or accelerated by human activity) could be said to exacerbate some of these phenomena, hence the need for humans, individuals, and communities to protect themselves and become more resilient to climatic changes and hazards. If ocean acidification continues unabated, the oceans will die and the human need for the services it produces will be humanity's Achilles heel.

The future of nations and the global economy is dependent on how successfully we will manage the sustainable growth of ocean trade in the face of the challenges posed by climate change. Successfully navigating these challenges will depend in large part on managing the evolving multimodal and logistical aspects of ocean trade, in such a way that reduces its footprint through innovation and technology. Admittedly, a great deal of progress has been made in improving fuel and engine efficiency. The benefits of this, however, are currently negated by the increasing demand for trade.

Policy-makers must avoid sectoral myopia and adopt a broad and forward-looking perspective in crafting solutions. There is a need to realize that when addressing the nexus of climate change and seaborne trade we have in one instance the culprit and the victim; maritime transport is a polluter of the highest degree and hence a primary contributor to climate change. Yet, in order for the shipping sector to confront that problem through adaptation and mitigation measures, significant financial resources will be required that may be overwhelming, particularly for developing countries. Is it not time that maritime shipping, international freight transport, and merchandise pay a levy for the freedom of the seas they enjoy? This is the Blue Economy proposal and a solution embracing the principle that the polluter pays. Such a levy may be administered by an international organization comparable to the International Seabed Authority, which would be responsible for directing resources to developing countries to expand capacity building efforts and enhance climatic resilience.

In this relationship of living with and from the ocean sustainably, humans need to learn and discover innovative means of responding with preparation, adaptation and mitigation measures, which reflect a true accounting of the ecological, economic and social costs and benefits.

Law of the Sea and Ocean Governance

∴

Extended Continental Shelf Claims in the South China Sea: Implications for Future Maritime Boundary Delimitations

Jay L. Batongbacal
Director, University of the Philippines Institute for Maritime Affairs and Law of the Sea, Quezon City, Philippines

Introduction

The Vietnamese and Malaysian submissions for extended continental shelf areas in the South China Sea represent a potential approach to the regional application of the 1982 United Nations Convention on the Law of the Sea (UNCLOS)[1] and the possibility of future overlapping extended continental shelf claims by the littoral States of the South China Sea. This article will analyse the configuration of possible extended continental shelf claims and identify potential maritime boundary delimitation issues under this approach.

A major turning point in relations between the littoral States of the South China Sea (SCS) was reached in 2009 when Malaysia and Vietnam made submissions to the Commission on the Limits of the Continental Shelf (CLCS) for the continental shelf beyond 200 nautical miles (NM), colloquially known as the extended continental shelf (ECS). Pursuant to the terms of UNCLOS Article 76, Vietnam and Malaysia made a joint submission on the continental shelf beyond 200 NM in an area in the southern portion of the SCS between their coasts,[2] and Vietnam made an additional submission for the seabed area

---

1   United Nations Convention on the Law of the Sea, 10 December 1982, 21 *International Legal Materials* 1261 (1982), available online: <http://www.un.org/depts/los/convention _agreements/convention_overview_convention.htm>.

2   See *Continental Shelf – Joint submission to the Commission by Malaysia and Viet Nam*, available online: <http://www.un.org/depts/los/clcs_new/submissions_files/submission _mysvnm_33_2009.htm> [Malaysia/Vietnam Joint Submission].

Ocean Yearbook 29: 21–43

southeast of the Paracel Islands.[3] These implied that Vietnam and Malaysia had foregone their more extensive previous claims to seabed areas in the SCS,[4] and signaled a conservative application of the UNCLOS framework of maritime zones.

The most important feature of these submissions is that they completely disregard all islands and rocks in the Spratly and Paracel Islands in the delineation of the exclusive economic zone and continental shelf (EEZ/CS) areas in the SCS. This is a very significant development in the evolution of maritime disputes since by virtue of plain geography there can be no continental shelf beyond 200 NM in the SCS unless *none* of those small features generate their own EEZ/CS. If even only one island were to be granted an EEZ/CS in either the Paracels or Spratly Islands, such an EEZ/CS could essentially negate the existence of ECS zones.

As of this writing, the Philippines has not made a submission to an ECS in the SCS, preferring instead to secure its claim to the Benham Rise Region on its Pacific seaboard.[5] Technically and legally, there is nothing that prevents the Philippines from making a new submission,[6] but the rise in tensions in the SCS since 2009 appears to have overshadowed action on this key decision point. On

---

3 See *Continental Shelf – Submission to the Commission by Viet Nam*, available online: <http://www.un.org/depts/los/clcs_new/submissions_files/submission_vnm_37_2009 .htm> [Vietnam Sole Submission].

4 Representations of Vietnam's original expansive seabed claim vary, but see V.L. Forbes, *Conflict and Cooperation in Managing Maritime Space in Semi-enclosed Seas* (Singapore: Singapore University Press, 2001), 136; also D. Rosenberg, "Governing the South China Sea: From Freedom of the Seas to Ocean Enclosure Movements," *Harvard Asia Quarterly* 12, no. 3 & 4 (2010): 4–12, p. 5. Malaysia's original seabed claim, on the other hand, was first published in a Malaysian official chart published on 21 December 1979. See J.A. Roach, "Malaysia and Brunei: An Analysis of their Claims in the South China Sea," (CNA Occasional Paper, Arlington: CNA Corporation, 2014), particularly p. 34.

5 See *Continental Shelf – Submission to the Commission by the Philippines*, available online: <http://www.un.org/depts/los/clcs_new/submissions_files/submission_phl_22_2009.htm>.

6 Commission on the Limits of the Continental Shelf (CLCS), *Rules of Procedure of the Commission on the Limits of the Continental Shelf. CLCS /40/Rev. 1*, Annex I, para. 3. The rules permit a coastal State to make a submission for a portion of its continental shelf without prejudice to maritime boundary delimitations in any other portions, for which submissions may be made later. The Philippines invoked this provision in making a reservation for future submission to 'other areas' in its submission. Republic of the Philippines, *A Partial Submission of Data and Information on the Outer Limits of the Continental Shelf of the Republic of the Philippines Pursuant to Article 76(8) of the United Nations Convention on the Law of the Sea, Part I: Executive Summary* [Philippine Submission], p. 12. Executive Summary available online: <http://www.un.org/depts/los/clcs_new/submissions_files/phl22_09/phl_esummary.pdf>.

22 January 2013, the Philippines launched an arbitration case against China[7] seeking to vindicate its entitlement to a full 200-NM EEZ/CS in response to increased Chinese assertiveness that saw China interfere with Philippine petroleum exploration and development in Reed Bank,[8] officially protest the auction of concession areas between Reed Bank and the island of Palawan,[9] as well as take control of Scarborough Shoal.[10] In its Notification and Statement

---

7   See *The Republic of the Philippines v. The People's Republic of China*, available online: <http://www.pca-cpa.org/showpage.asp?pag_id=1529>.

8   In 2011, Chinese patrol ships interfered with the conduct of seismic surveys by the MV *Veritas Voyager*, a ship contracted by a Philippine petroleum concessionaire in the area of Reed Bank. For a detailed description, see I. Storey, "China and the Philippines: Implications of the Reed Bank Incident," China Brief, Vol. XI, no. 8, 6 May 2011 (Washington, D.C.: Jamestown Foundation, 2011), pp. 6–9. Also available online: <http://www .jamestown.org/uploads/media/cb_11_8_03.pdf>.

9   "More companies to bid for oil, gas projects," *Philippine Daily Inquirer*, 1 March 2012, available online: <http://business.inquirer.net/46973/more-companies-to-bid-for-oil-gas -prospects>. When the Philippines announced the opening of the fourth Philippine Energy Contracting Round, which offered certain submerged areas along the Palawan Trough located between Reed Bank and the island of Palawan, China protested the move to have "seriously infringed on China's sovereignty and sovereign rights" and demanded that the Philippines "immediately withdraw the bidding offer...refrain from any action that infringes on China's sovereignty and sovereign rights." Ministry of Foreign Affairs of the People's Republic of China, *Note Verbale No. (11) PG-202*, 6 July 2011. China had also warned ominously that petroleum exploration without its consent would not be successful, and that China would "take all possible measures" against the Philippines' actions when necessary. P. Dutton, "Testimony before the US-China Economic and Security Review Committee Hearing on China's Maritime Disputes in the East and South China Sea," p. 3. Available online: <http://www.uscc.gov/sites/default/files/Dutton%20 Testimony,%20April%204%202013.pdf>.

10   "China has de facto control over Panatag Shoal, says former DFA senior official," *GMA News Online*, 6 October 2012, available online: <http://www.gmanetwork.com/news/ story/277126/news/nation/china-has-de-facto-control-over-panatag-shoal-says-former -dfa-senior-official>; "A year after Panatag stand-off, shoal firmly controlled by China," *GMA News Online*, 23 April 2013, available online: <http://www.gmanetwork.com/news/ story/305062/news/world/a-year-after-panatag-stand-off-shoal-firmly-controlled-by -china#>. For a full account, see J. Batongbacal, "The 2012 Scarborough Shoal Stand-off: A Philippine Perspective," *Chinese Studies Journal* 10 (2013): 60–131; R. de Castro, "The 2012 Scarborough Shoal Stand-off: From stalemate to escalation of the South China Sea dispute?," in *The South China Sea Maritime Dispute: Political, Legal and Regional Perspectives*, eds. L. Buszynski and C. Roberts, (Routledge Security in the Asia Pacific Series. New York: Routledge, 2014), pp. 111–129; C. La Mière, *Maritime Diplomacy in the 21st Century: Drivers and Challenges* (New York: Routledge, 2014), pp. 126–138.

of Claim,[11] the Philippines also impliedly disregards the Spratly Islands in generating EEZ/CS zones.[12] Its claims that certain submerged features are 'unlawfully occupied' by China[13] can only be based on the assumption that none of the Spratly Islands (regardless of which country has sovereignty) can generate any EEZ/CS zones, and instead the area is dominated by an EEZ/CS extending from the Philippine island of Palawan. In this respect, the Philippine position appears to be consistent with those of Vietnam and Malaysia, that none of the contested island groups generate the full EEZ/CS in the SCS.

Incidentally, Brunei has indicated an intention to lay claim to an ECS notwithstanding the fact that its 200-NM EEZ/CS zone may tend to be enclosed by the Malaysian EEZ/CS from Sarawak and Sabah.[14] It asserts that it has delimited its territorial sea and EEZ/CS maritime boundaries with Malaysia, although details of their actual agreement have not been publicly released.[15] Brunei also declares that it is entitled to an ECS area beyond the 200-NM EEZ/CS delimited with Malaysia.[16]

China's continued ambiguity with respect to the precise nature of its nine-dashed line map, formally communicated through a Note Verbale dated 7 May 2009 to the CLCS and the United Nations,[17] remains a source of friction among

---

11   Republic of the Philippines, *Notification and Statement of Claim*, 22 January 2013, available online: <http://www.dfa.gov.ph/index.php/component/docman/doc_download/56-notification-and-statement-of-claim-on-west-philippine-sea?Itemid=546>.

12   This includes the Kalayaan Island Group as described in its domestic legislation, Presidential Decree No. 1596 dated 11 June 1978. The third to seventh claims under para. 41 of the Notification and Statement of Claim ask the arbitral tribunal to declare Mischief and McKennan Reefs to be occupied by China in violation of the sovereign rights of the Philippines under the continental shelf regime; Gaven and Subi Reefs to be submerged features unlawfully occupied by China; and Johnson, Cuarteron, and Fiery Cross Reefs to be entitled to no more than 12-NM territorial seas. However, para. 40 asserts that its claims do not require sea boundary delimitations whether under UNCLOS Article 74 (continental shelf) and/or Article 84 (EEZ). Taken together, these claims may be plausible only if none of the islands in the Spratly Islands region generate EEZ/CS zones. Otherwise, the existence of an EEZ/CS from even one island will require maritime delimitations as a prerequisite to the determination of the status and legality of the rocks and reefs occupied by China.

13   Notification and Statement of Claim, n. 11 above, pp. 13–14, 17–19.

14   *Brunei Darussalam's Preliminary Submission concerning the Outer Limits of its Continental Shelf*, 12 May 2009 [Brunei Preliminary Information]. Available online: <http://www.un.org/depts/los/clcs_new/submissions_files/preliminary/brn2009preliminaryinformation.pdf>.

15   Id., p. 3.

16   Id., p. 4.

17   People's Republic of China, *Note Verbale CML/17/2009*, 7 May 2009, available online: <http://www.un.org/depts/los/clcs_new/submissions_files/mysvnm33_09/chn_2009re_mys_vnm_e.pdf>.

littoral States of the SCS. Despite possible expansive interpretations, an arguably official and legally binding description of the claim may be found in the Note Verbale, and a subsequent one dated 14 April 2011.[18] The first Note asserts that

> China has indisputable sovereignty over the islands in the South China Sea and the adjacent waters, and enjoys sovereign rights and jurisdiction over the relevant waters as well as the seabed and subsoil thereof.[19]

It might be argued that the reference to 'sovereignty' over 'the adjacent waters', combined with the nine-dashed line map, connotes a territorial claim to the entire SCS. However, the reference to 'sovereign rights and jurisdiction over the relevant waters' clearly recognizes the concept of coastal State rights and jurisdictions over the EEZ/CS, so the term 'adjacent waters' can refer only to the 12-NM territorial sea over which a coastal State does have sovereignty.[20] Any other interpretation would contravene the delicate balance of maritime jurisdictions negotiated by all coastal States, including China, which ratified UNCLOS in 1996. China itself professes adherence to an UNCLOS-based delineation of maritime zones, rather than an indiscriminate and unitary claim, in the second Note, which explains:

> Since 1930s, the Chinese Government has given publicity several times [to] the geographical scope of China's Nansha Islands and the names of its components. China's Nansha Islands is therefore clearly defined. In addition, under the relevant provisions of the *1982 United Nations Convention on the Law of the Sea*, as well as the *Law of the People's Republic of China on the Territorial Sea and the Contiguous Zone (1992)* and the *Law on the Exclusive Economic Zone and the Continental Shelf of the People's Republic of China (1998)*, China's Nansha Islands is fully entitled to Territorial Sea, Exclusive Economic Zone (EEZ) and Continental Shelf.[21]

---

18   People's Republic of China, *Note Verbale CML/8/2011*, 14 April 2011, available online: <http://www.un.org/depts/los/clcs_new/submissions_files/mysvnm33_09/chn_2011_re _phl_e.pdf>.

19   Id., p. 1.

20   The subtle nuances in China's declaration are explained more in N.-T.A. Hu, "South China Sea: Troubled Waters or a Sea of Opportunity?," *Ocean Development & International Law* 41, no. 3 (2010): 203–213, pp. 205–206.

21   Note Verbale, 14 April 2011, n. 18 above, p. 2.

Unfortunately, China's assertiveness and actions with respect to the SCS claims have evinced claims to jurisdiction and sovereignty beyond those described even under UNCLOS. These are most evident in assertions of sovereignty over submerged features well within the EEZ/CS zones projected from the mainland of the coastal State. For example, since 2013, the Philippines and China have engaged in tense diplomatic and maritime tussles over Second Thomas Shoal (called 'Ayungin' by the Philippines and 'Ren'ai' by China), a submerged reef approximately 100 NM from Palawan.[22] The Philippines complained of provocative Chinese patrols surrounding and coming close to the *BRP Sierra Madre*, a landing ship aground on the shoal since 1999 and acting as a lonely Philippine outpost to monitor and prevent further Chinese incursions into its EEZ/CS.[23] Chinese ships blocked a Philippine ship attempting to resupply soldiers stationed on the decrepit landing ship, accusing the Philippines of attempting to bring construction materials to the shoal.[24] A month later, a Philippine ship succeeded in running the informal blockade to provide food, supplies, and relief for the soldiers.[25] Having followed Chinese interference and protests against petroleum exploration in Reed Bank and adjacent areas, it is understandable why the Philippines views the actions of China as being tantamount to claiming absolute sovereignty over the entire area of the nine-dashed line.

A recent attempt to explain the nine-dashed line describes it as a line with three purposes: it indicates title to the island groups within them, it preserves Chinese historic rights to fishing, navigation, and other marine activities such as oil and gas development in the waters and continental shelf enclosed by the line, and allows for 'residual functionality' to serve as maritime delimitation lines.[26] While the first purpose of asserting title to islands within the lines may

---

22   "China to PH: Remove ship from Ayungin," Rappler.com, 13 March 2014, available online: <http://www.rappler.com/nation/52918-china-philippines-remove-ship-ayungin>.

23   "China sends ships to another Phl shoal," *Philippine Star*, 22 May 2013, available online: <http://www.philstar.com/headlines/2013/05/22/944871/china-sends-ships-another -phl-shoal>.

24   Ministry of Foreign Affairs of the People's Republic of China. *Foreign Ministry Spokesperson Qin Gang's Remarks on Comments by the US State Department on China's Expulsion of Philippine Ships that Transported Construction Materials to the Ren'ai Reef*, 13 March 2014. Available online: <http://ke.china-embassy.org/eng/fyrth/t1137065.htm>.

25   "Chinese vessels harass, but fail to stop, resupply mission for PH Navy ship at Ayungin Shoal," InterAksyon/Agence France-Presse, 29 March 2014, Available online: <http:// www.interaksyon.com/article/83734/chinese-vessel-harasses-but-fails-to-stop-resupply -mission-for-brp-sierra-madre-at-ayungin>.

26   Z. Gao and B.B. Jia, "The Nine-Dash Line in the South China Sea: History, Status, and Implications," *American Journal of International Law* 107, no. 1 (2013): 98–124.

be understandable given the original title of the map containing the lines issued in 1947,[27] the latter two purposes that attempt to justify recent official actions of China ignite debate and push the envelope of acceptable conduct at sea. It is doubtful whether China's reference to 'historic rights' could be considered in the same sense as historic rights or historic title in international law.[28] As for its residual function as maritime delimitation lines, it should be considered that delimitations cannot be undertaken unilaterally by only one coastal State, and therefore cannot be the basis for asserting and actually enforcing exclusive rights or sovereignty up to the very limit of such lines and completely disregarding the interests of the other coastal State.

Nonetheless, given China's apparent continued acceptance of UNCLOS, it is clear that at minimum it may still claim extensive maritime spaces based on the various islands and features in the SCS. The extent of its legitimate claims depends upon the application of UNCLOS Article 121 and the proper characterization of all features either as fully formed 'islands' capable of human habitation and independent economic life justifying the establishment of a 200-NM EEZ/CS, or as bare 'rocks' entitled only to a 12-NM territorial sea.[29] But while there has been a general trend in maritime delimitation jurisprudence pointing to the diminution of the effect of small islands and rocks on the delimitation of maritime zones vis-à-vis more extensive coastlines,[30] the rules for

---

27   The 1947 map enclosing much of the South China Sea in 11 broken lines was originally entitled "The Location Map of the South Sea Islands (*Nanhai zhudao weizhi tu*)." See L. Jinming and L. Dexia, "The Dotted Line on the Chinese Map of the South China Sea: A Note," *Ocean Development & International Law* 34 (2003): 287–295, p. 290.

28   For an analysis of the nature of 'historic rights' asserted by China in relation to the nine-dashed line map, see F. Dupuy and P.-M. Dupuy, "A Legal Analysis of China's Historic Rights Claim in the South China Sea," *American Journal of International Law* 107, no. 1 (2013): 124–141, p. 124. See also C. Symmons, *Historic Waters in the Law of the Sea: A Modern Reappraisal* (Leiden: Brill, 2008).

29   For discussion of the application of UNCLOS Article 121 to the South China Sea, see C. Symmons, "Maritime Zones from Islands and Rocks," in *The South China Sea Disputes and Law of the Sea*, eds. S. Jayakumar, T. Koh, and R. Beckman (Cheltenham UK/ Northampton MA: Edward Elgar, 2014), pp. 5–11.

30   See *Maritime Delimitation in the Black Sea (Romania v. Ukraine), Judgment, 3 February 2009*, available online: <http://www.icj-cij.org/docket/files/132/14987.pdf>; *Dispute concerning delimitation of the maritime boundary between Bangladesh and Myanmar in the Bay of Bengal (Bangladesh v. Myanmar), Judgement, 14 March 2012*, available online: <http://www.itlos.org/fileadmin/itlos/documents/cases/case_no_16/C16 _Judgment_14_03_2012_rev.pdf>; *Territorial and Maritime Dispute between Nicaragua and Honduras in the Caribbean Sea (Nicaragua v. Honduras), Judgment, 8 October 2007*, available online: <http://www.icj-cij.org/docket/files/120/14075.pdf>; *Territorial and Maritime*

determination of the actual weight and extent of their zones have not been consistent and uniform. What can be said of existing jurisprudence is only that the breadth of the maritime zones of islands and rocks are greatly influenced by their immediate geographical context as appreciated by international tribunals in each special case. Thus, unless there is general agreement among the littoral States concerned on how the islands and rocks of the SCS shall be treated for purposes of maritime boundary delimitation, there is no assurance either way that none or some of such islands may impact on the configuration of EEZ/CS zones.

Possible Extended Continental Shelf Entitlements

It is apparent that a jurisdictional division of the SCS based on UNCLOS is the principal approach considered by the smaller Southeast Asian States for the resolution of maritime disputes. The Vietnamese and Malaysian ECS submissions, as well as the Philippine arbitration claim, all assume the application and interpretation of UNCLOS in the SCS in a manner that leaves a high seas corridor in the middle of the SCS. Presumably, such an application of UNCLOS represents what these States see to be an equitable distribution of jurisdiction over marine resources and the most acceptable compromise between their competing interests. It represents a convergence in the evolution of the respective claims of these smaller States.[31] By their actions, these States clearly do not regard China's nine-dashed line map as representative of any legitimate rights, historical or otherwise, beyond those recognized by UNCLOS.

It is important to examine all of the potential maritime boundaries that could be generated by such an approach, even on a purely hypothetical basis, for several reasons. First, it indicates a common ground among at least three of the four main Southeast Asian claimants as to what may be an acceptable basis for resolution of the competing maritime claims. Second, it clearly reduces the

---

Dispute (Nicaragua v. Colombia), Judgment, 19 November 2012, available online: <http://www.icj-cij.org/docket/files/124/17164.pdf>. See also H.D. Jang, "Diminishing Role of Islands in Maritime Boundary Delimitation: Case Studies of Dokdo/Takeshima Island and the Senkaku/Diaoyu Islands," *Hawaii Law Review* 35 (2013): 139–196, p. 139; V. Prescott and G. Triggs, "Islands and Rocks and Their Role in Maritime Delimitation," in *International Maritime Boundaries*, Vol. 5, eds. D. Colson and R. Smith (Leiden: Martinus Nijhoff, 2005), pp. 3245–3280; H. Jayewardene, *The Regime of Islands in International Law* (Leiden: Martinus Nijhoff, 1990).

31   See R. Beckman, "The UN Convention on the Law of the Sea and the Maritime Disputes in the South China Sea," *American Journal of International Law* 107, no. 1 (2013): 142–163.

extent of the more intractable territorial disputes in the SCS to only the pockets of 12-NM territorial sea surrounding each island and rock above water at high tide, providing a means to authoritatively determine rights and responsibilities of the littoral States when it comes to disputed activities in the marine areas beyond those enclaves. Third, it could provide some insights on specific maritime boundary delimitation issues that the competing States would still have to face, bilaterally or otherwise, in attempting even an UNCLOS-based resolution of their respective claims. And finally, it allows the visualization and consideration of at least one concrete option for an equitable geographic division of the SCS on the basis of international law. Even a purely academic and hypothetical application of UNCLOS under these premises could shed light on possible future evolution, if not resolution, of the SCS disputes. Given that the SCS disputes are seen as being the most complex of all territorial and maritime disputes, an examination of all possible options and outcomes, no matter how unlikely at present, would certainly contribute to the future discussions.

The possible configuration of the 12-NM territorial sea and 200-NM EEZ/CS areas in the absence of the many islands and rocks in the SCS have been demonstrated elsewhere,[32] and the only maritime zone that remains to be drawn are the hypothetical ECS zones that may be subject of submissions by littoral States other than Vietnam and Malaysia. In addition to the latter two States that have already been defined in their respective submissions to the CLCS, it is possible to anticipate additional potential ECS claims through a desktop study undertaken in accordance with the Scientific and Technical Guidelines of the CLCS.[33] This involves the use of publicly available bathymetric data viewed through appropriate geographic information system software, and the generation of two-dimensional bathymetric profiles extending from the various coastlines.[34] By analysing the Vietnamese and Malaysian claims vis-à-vis

---

32   See C. Schofield and A. Arsana, "Map of the South China Sea," *American Journal of International Law* 107, no. 1 (2013): p. 96.

33   CLCS, *Scientific and Technical Guidelines of the Commission on the Limits of the Continental Shelf*, CLCS/11, 13 May 1999 [CLCS Scientific and Technical Guidelines].

34   The desktop study was initially conducted using Google Earth v. 16 and its built-in SRTM30_PLUS digital elevation data with 30 arc-second resolution, then later redone using GlobalMapper v. 15 with GEBCO digital elevation data also with 30 arc-second resolution. For information on the dataset, including its limitations, see Intergovernmental Oceanographic Commission and International Hydrographic Organization, *General Bathymetric Chart of the Oceans*, Gridded Bathymetric Chart, available online: <http://www.gebco.net/data_and_products/gridded_bathymetry_data/>. As a combination of radar altimetry, soundings, and interpolated satellite-derived marine gravity data, these datasets are not adequate for purposes of making submissions to the CLCS. However, they

available bathymetric data and using them as a basis for identifying comparable potential regions of the base of the continental slope, possible Philippine and Chinese ECS claims on the basis of natural prolongation and in accordance with UNCLOS Article 76 may be reasonably anticipated.[35] Although such a desktop study would not be able to produce precise foot of slope points and outer limits, it is sufficient for application of the CLCS' Test of Appurtenance[36] and provides just enough basis for academic discussion of prospective ECS claim areas in general. The point of the study is not to predict the exact outer limits of future submissions, but rather to anticipate maritime zone overlaps for which policy options may be generated and prepared. It also establishes 'minimum case' scenarios for littoral States considering future maritime delimitation strategies and options.[37] Thus, the desktop study results in an interesting and indicative configuration of overlapping and converging ECS claims (Figure 2.1) that illustrate the various kinds of bilateral and multilateral maritime boundary delimitation challenges faced by the littoral States of the SCS.

------

are useful enough for initiating desktop studies that can guide the preparation and conduct of full-blown submissions subject to the acquisition of actual soundings of any given shelf area. The conduct of desktop studies is recommended by the CLCS in its training program. For information on the conduct of desktop studies as part of the CLCS recommended procedures, see CLCS, *The Law of the Sea: Training Module for delineation of the outer limits of the continental shelf beyond 200 nautical miles and for preparation of submission to the Commission on the Limits of the Continental Shelf* (New York: United Nations, 2006), particularly Modules III, IV, and VII. For practical information on the conduct of two-dimensional studies using publicly available data, see D. Monahan, *Claiming a Juridical Continental Shelf under Article 76 of the United Nations Convention on Law of the Sea (UNCLOS)*, Technical Report No. 217 (Fredericton, NB: Geodesy and Geomatics Engineering, University of New Brunswick, 2002). Available online: <http://www2.unb.ca/gge/Pubs/TR217.pdf>.

35   In the absence of actual multi-beam bathymetry survey data and marine geological data from the Philippines and China, it is impossible to determine with absolute certainty the potential foot of slope points from which to determine the ECS outer limits. However, total accuracy is not necessary for this exercise, as the potential Philippine and Chinese ECS claims are drawn only as general approximations to be used for problem identification for future maritime delimitations in this complex region.

36   CLCS Scientific and Technical Guidelines, n. 33 above, p. 12.

37   For a more detailed discussion of the opposite possible extreme of the islands in the Paracels and Spratlys generating 200-NM EEZ/CS and ECS beyond them, see A. Oude Elferink, "Do the coastal states on the South China Sea have a continental shelf beyond 200 nautical miles?," in Jayakumar et al., n. 29 above, pp. 164–191.

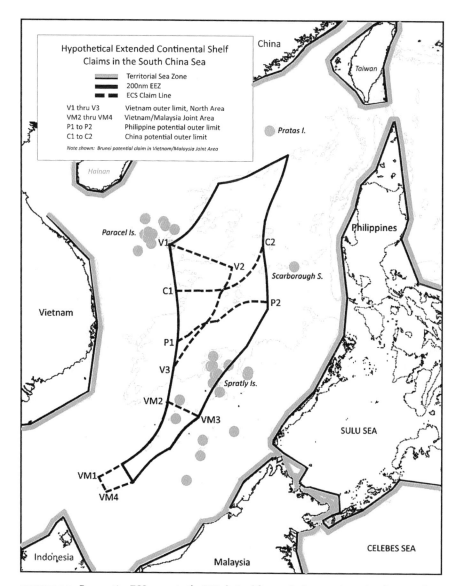

FIGURE 2.1 *Prospective ECS areas in the SCS derived from a desktop study, in the absence of any of the smaller islands generating 200-NM EEZ/CS zones. The 200-NM limit from mainland coasts of the littoral States is indicated, and various circles signify territorial sea enclaves around islands and rocks per Article 121 of UNCLOS.*

Analysis of the Vietnamese and Malaysian Submissions

Vietnam and Malaysia, by virtue of their respective unilateral and joint submissions to the CLCS leave no doubt as to their intention to claim their ECS entitlements. The two countries may actually have very little choice in the matter: by the sheer accident of geography, their coasts do not lie adjacent to any other seas that could accommodate an ECS, and their only available coastal frontages facing high seas beyond 200 NM are in the SCS.

Reference to publicly available bathymetric data indicates plausible evidence of geo-morphological continuity from Vietnam's eastern coast up to the outer limits of the unilateral Vietnamese claim to the North Area. The Vietnamese ECS in this region is based mostly on the foot of slope plus 60-NM formula line in Article 76(4)(i), and the boundary appears to be generated from three dominant foot of slope points.[38] In the northernmost portion of this ECS area, Vietnam has restrained itself from continuing the outer limit northward apparently in deference to future maritime delimitations with the expected location of mainland China's prospective ECS claim. The northern endpoint of the ECS outer limit is described as a "fixed point at intersection of formula line and equidistance line,"[39] the latter presumably referring to an equidistant point from unidentified basepoints or baselines on the eastern coast of Vietnam and the southeastern coast of Hainan Island.[40] This point is also approximately 350 NM from both presumptive basepoints.

It should be noted at the outset that the Vietnamese ECS in the North Area disregards the Paracel Islands completely, and discounts their ability to generate EEZ/CS zones, which impliedly prevents it from generating ECS areas as well. This is an important consideration since recognizing full status to even one of the Paracels could completely eliminate ECS claims in this region and place it entirely within a 200-NM continental shelf zone.

On the other hand, in the area claimed by both Vietnam and Malaysia in their joint submission, questions may be raised as to whether the Joint Area may indeed be considered as a natural prolongation that is joined on both

---

38   Vietnam Sole Submission, n. 3 above, pp. 6–8.

39   Id., p. 6.

40   It is most likely that the basepoints are located within the baselines established by Vietnam in 1977 and those declared by China in 1996. Socialist Republic of Vietnam, "Statement on the Territorial Sea, the Contiguous Zone, the Exclusive Economic Zone, and the Continental Shelf of 12 May 1977," available online: <http://www.un.org/Depts/los/LEGISLATIONANDTREATIES/PDFFILES/VNM_1977_Statement.pdf>.; People's Republic of China, "Declaration of the Government of the People's Republic of China on the Baselines of the Territorial Sea, 15 May 1996," available online: <http://www.un.org/Depts/los/LEGISLATIONANDTREATIES/PDFFILES/CHN_1996_Declaration.pdf>.

western and eastern sides by the coasts of Vietnam and Malaysia respectively. Bathymetric profiles extending from their respective coastlines to the Joint Area reveal the presence of intervening deep troughs; on the Vietnamese side it is roughly 2,100 m deep and approximately 80–140 NM from the coast, while on the Malaysian side it is around 2,800 m deep and 75–140 NM from the coast of North Borneo. These could arguably be considered as discontinuities militating against natural prolongation from the two land territories. This is likely the reason why the joint submission made it a point to locate the continental margin of the Joint Area well to the north, adjacent to the Philippines,[41] in order to show that regardless of the presence of the troughs, the area between Vietnam and Malaysia is still entirely within the southern continental margin in the SCS basin, and not part of the deep ocean floor. The deep ocean floor in that northern region is more than 4,200 m deep, making the aforementioned troughs appear to be mere undulations in the wider continental margin.

Analysis of Potential Natural Prolongations of the Philippines and China

The Philippines and China have a common advantage over Vietnam and Malaysia in one respect. Both countries have coastal areas outside of the SCS: the Pacific Ocean in the case of the former, and the East China Sea in the case of the latter. The Philippines' submission for the Benham Rise Region expressly reserved the right to file submissions for "other areas,"[42] which certainly would include the SCS, while China filed a preliminary information paper with the CLCS on 11 May 2009,[43] followed by a more specific formal submission on 14 December 2012.[44] While the Philippine submission was unopposed and successfully validated by the CLCS in April 2012,[45] China's submission has been

---

41   Malaysia/Vietnam Joint Submission, n. 2 above, Figure 2 and Table 2.

42   Philippine Submission, n. 6 above, p. 12.

43   People's Republic of China, "Preliminary Information Indicative of the Outer Limits of the Continental Shelf Beyond 200 Nautical Miles of the People's Republic of China," available online: <http://www.un.org/depts/los/clcs_new/submissions_files/preliminary/chn2009preliminaryinformation_english.pdf>.

44   People's Republic of China, "Submission by the People's Republic of China Concerning the Outer Limits of the Continental Shelf beyond 200 Nautical Miles in Part of the East China Sea," available online: <http://www.un.org/depts/los/clcs_new/submissions_files/chn63_12/executive%20summary_EN.pdf>.

45   CLCS, "Recommendations of the Commission on the Limits of the Continental Shelf in regard to the Submission made by the Philippines in respect of the Benham Rise Region on 8 April 2009," available online: <http://www.un.org/depts/los/clcs_new/submissions_files/phl22_09/phl_rec.pdf>.

protested by Japan on the ground that the ECS claim is being made in an area where the distance between opposite coasts is less than 400 NM and therefore cannot be the subject of ECS claims.[46] Within the SCS, however, both countries have yet to make any submissions.

Analysis of bathymetric profiles west of the Philippines indicate that there indeed exists a plausible natural prolongation extending west/southwest of the Philippine island of Palawan. The base of the slope region wherein the maximum change in gradient may be found cuts across the 200-NM line in the vicinity of Reed Bank, and continues on a southwesterly course that is unbroken until it reaches the Vietnamese 200-NM limit. At its southern most point, the prospective base of the slope region is well within 60 NM of the outer limits of the Vietnamese ECS area in the north. This implies that the natural prolongation also exists to the south of the base of the slope region, and therefore joins the area of the continental margin identified in the Malaysia/Vietnam Joint Submission. In fact, the natural prolongation from the Philippines is more pronounced and less ambiguous than on the Malaysian side, because the continuity is not seriously interrupted by a prominent trough.

To the northwest, bathymetric profiles demonstrate a plausible natural prolongation extending from the southeastern coast of Hainan Island and the southern mainland of China. Macclesfield Bank could arguably be considered a natural component of the continental margin in this area under Article 76(6), which would place the base of slope region on the southeastern edge of the bank where the possible point of maximum change in gradient is very prominent prior to the relatively flat deep ocean floor. The southern coast of the mainland would contribute additional ECS areas, and a Chinese ECS area here would encompass a considerable portion of the seabed beyond 200 NM. It appears that even the Philippines may find it difficult to establish an ECS area of its own in this region, because from the Philippine island of Luzon, the continuity of the land territory falls far short of 200 NM and stays very close to the coastline (approximately 65 NM offshore). Continuity beyond this area appears to be interrupted by the Manila Trench that runs all the way from just south of the southern tip of Taiwan and along the western side of Luzon down to Mindoro Island, representing a physical break in the natural prolongation.

It would not be amiss to note the situation of Taiwan, which is not formally distinguished by any of the littoral States from mainland China, but has been acting separately from the mainland insofar as UNCLOS is concerned by

---

46   Permanent Mission of Japan to the United Nations, *Note Verbale SC/12/372*, 28 December
      2012, available online: <http://www.un.org/depts/los/clcs_new/submissions_files/chn63
      _12/jpn_re_chn_28_12_2012.pdf>.

enacting its own baselines and maritime zone legislation. Inspection of bathy-metric profiles projecting from Taiwan's coast and into the SCS do not bode well for an ECS area solely in its favor, as the seabed deepens quite rapidly close to the mainland (approximately 60 NM from shore) and is interrupted by a rise that is clearly connected to the continental margin of the southern coast of mainland China. Also, the island of Taiwan is located at the corner of a sharp concave region formed by the southern coast of mainland China and the west-ern and northern coast of the Philippines. The only way by which an ECS in the SCS might appertain to Taiwan is if Pratas Island were to be accorded full sta-tus as an island entitled to a 200-NM EEZ/CS. However, perusal of the bathy-metric profile emanating from Pratas Island casts doubt as to whether this will be of benefit; the continental slope connected to the island drops off approxi-mately 100 NM from shore, marking the deep ocean floor by the time it reaches the 200-NM limit.

Notes on Brunei and Indonesia

Brunei and Indonesia represent cases of coastal States disadvantaged by neigh-boring coastlines, though for different reasons. Both countries may be deemed to be entitled to claim a natural prolongation from their respective land terri-tories extending deep into the SCS. In Brunei's case, the fact that it is a small country with a short coastline flanked on both sides by the much larger Malaysia causes the adjacent boundaries to technically converge upon each other well short of the 200-NM limit and effectively cuts it off from access to areas beyond national jurisdiction due to the rejoining Malaysian maritime zones. Brunei's publicized claim to a zone between two parallel lines extending from its territorial sea boundaries to beyond 200 NM can be understood as a position against this situation, which may be arguable considering that inter-national law recognizes that a coastal State should not be cut off from access to its 200-NM limit and the high seas beyond.[47] This principle appears to have

---

47   *Delimitation of the Maritime Boundary in the Gulf of Maine Area (Canada/United States of America), Judgment,* ICJ Reports 1984 [*Gulf of Maine*], at para. 157. The main opinion iden-tifies as among the equitable criteria for maritime boundary delimitation, "the criterion of preventing, as far as possible, any cut-off of the seaward projection of the coast or of part of the coast of either of the States concerned." The same principle played a promi-nent role in the case of *Barbados v. Trinidad and Tobago* (Award, 11 April 2006, XXVII RIAA 147–251 [2006]) where the tribunal drew a delimitation line extending throughout the 200-NM limit and reaching into the prospective ECS boundary of the parties. The tribunal explained that it was mindful that "as far as possible, there should be no cut-off effects arising from the delimitation line and that the line as drawn by the Tribunal avoids the encroachment that would result from an unadjusted equidistance line." Id., para. 375.

been invoked consistently to result in recognition of an ECS entitlement despite an enclosure resulting from the application of strict equidistance to a concave coastline.[48] It is therefore reasonable to expect Brunei to insist on claiming an ECS, especially since Brunei submitted preliminary information to the CLCS on 12 May 2009 expressing its intention to do so in the future. It asserts that Malaysia and Brunei delimited the Brunei EEZ/CS via an exchange of letters dated 16 March 2009,[49] but thus far no details, particularly precise maritime boundaries, have been released.[50] It is apparent, however, that a Brunei ECS claim will necessarily impinge upon the Joint Area claimed by Vietnam and Malaysia.[51]

Indonesia presents a unique problem, on account of the fact that it had delimited its continental shelf boundaries with its neighbors in separate agreements (with Malaysia on 27 October 1969 and with Vietnam on 26 June 2003). The resulting Indonesian continental shelf falls short of the 200-NM limit measured from the outermost points on the Natuna Islands, and therefore cuts it off from the area beyond 200 NM. The gap between the Indonesian continental shelf under its agreements with Vietnam and Malaysia and the 200-NM limit have thus been claimed by the latter two as part of their Joint Area. Indonesia might argue that its previous continental shelf agreement with Malaysia, which is the one that cuts it off from the 200-NM limit, was negotiated and agreed upon under a different legal regime, that of the 1958 Convention on the Continental Shelf,[52] and did not yet contemplate the possibility of either the 200-NM continental shelf, much less the ECS. At present, the Indonesian continental shelf north of the Natuna Islands ends at roughly the 200 m isobath, proving its basis in the 1958 Convention rather than UNCLOS. Indonesia may still claim the full

---

48   The no cut-off principle was applied in the case of *Bangladesh v. Myanmar* (Judgment, 14 March 2012, available online: <http://www.itlos.org/fileadmin/itlos/documents/cases/case_no_16/C16_Judgment_14_03_2012_rev.pdf>), where the tribunal drew the maritime boundary between the parties so that it could enable Bangladesh access to the seabed beyond 200 NM. Subsequently, in the *Bay of Bengal Maritime Boundary Arbitration* (*Bangladesh v. India*, Award, 7 July 2014), available online: <http://www.pca-cpa.org/showfile.asp?fil_id=2705>), the tribunal similarly deflected the technical equidistance line so that the boundary could intersect with the Bangladesh/Myanmar boundary outside the 200-NM limit. Without the adjustments arising from these two cases, the EEZ/CS area of Bangladesh would not even reach 200 NM as it would be enclosed by converging technical equidistance lines produced by the coasts of India and Myanmar.

49   Brunei Preliminary Information, n. 14 above, p. 3.

50   See also G.B. Poling, *The South China Sea in Focus: Clarifying the Limits of the Maritime Dispute* (Washington, D.C.: Center for Strategic and International Studies, 2013), pp. 7–9.

51   Id., p. 9.

52   1958 Convention on the Continental Shelf, 499 *United Nations Treaty Series* 311.

200-NM EEZ and establish a maritime boundary separate from its delimited continental shelf, and take its jurisdiction over the superjacent waters beyond the existing continental shelf limits north of the Natuna Islands. But nothing prevents Indonesia from understandably seeking to re-negotiate the boundaries, although there may be some legal impediments to changing its position.[53] The *ipso facto* and *ab initio* nature of continental shelf entitlements, combined with the application of the various principles explained above, may have an impact on the consideration of the issues. Perhaps in the future, Indonesia may consider moving toward claiming ECS entitlements as well.

Prospective Continental Shelf Delimitation Challenges

With their respective ECS entitlements foreseen, the desktop exercise may be taken to the logical step of determining where the future ECS delimitation contests under purely UNCLOS-based rules will likely arise, whether at the negotiating table or before an international tribunal. The hypothetical scenario of a full suite of maritime zones in the absence of islands and rocks as demonstrated by the desktop exercise provides a minimum 'base case' that acts as one end of a spectrum of possible divisions of jurisdiction in the SCS. On the assumption that no small islands or rocks in the SCS (Hainan being an exception) will have maritime zone entitlements beyond 12-NM territorial seas, it is possible to establish starting points for discussions of initial delimitation scenarios that consider progressively more complicated ones by appreciating the specific impacts of introducing particular islands and rocks into the process.

China/Taiwan and the Philippines in the North

In the absence of any effect on the part of Pratas Island, the bathymetry in the northern sector of the SCS demonstrates a classic continental shelf, slope, and rise emanating from mainland China's southern coast off the east of Hong

---

53   Notably, Article 59 of the *Vienna Convention on the Law of Treaties* permits States to consider a prior treaty as terminated by a later treaty if "it appears from the later treaty or is otherwise established that the parties intended that the matter should be governed by that treaty; or the provisions of the later treaty are so far incompatible with those of the earlier one that the two treaties are not capable of being applied at the same time." Since the criteria for the definition of the continental shelf in the 1958 Geneva Convention on the Continental Shelf (i.e., 200-m isobath or depth of exploitability) has been entirely superseded and replaced by Article 76 of UNCLOS, it may be argued that there is clear incompatibility between the two treaties in this respect, while at the same time, the parties have clearly demonstrated observance and implementation of UNCLOS.

Kong, with the rise ending just before reaching the Philippine 200-NM limit from Luzon. This slope appears to be a natural prolongation of mainland China's land territory, and interrupts any lines of continuity that could be drawn from Taiwan proceeding through this corner of the SCS. An appreciable natural prolongation into this area is doubtful since the deep ocean floor appears to begin approximately 60 NM from the shore of mainland Taiwan. As stated previously, this can only be avoided if Pratas Island, presently held by Taiwan, were to generate its own EEZ/CS. In such a case, the potential ECS area measured from mainland China would be connected to a 200-NM EEZ/CS from Pratas Island. The Philippines is apparently placed at a disadvantage here due to the presence of the Manila Trench, which interrupts geomorphological continuity from Luzon into this region. Unless it is able to present through other means a reasonable degree of natural prolongation despite the trench, the seabed just outside its western 200-NM EEZ/CS limits may be subject to the ECS claims of China and/or Taiwan in this particular area of the SCS.

Vietnam and China off the Paracels

The ECS areas measured from the Vietnamese and Chinese mainland converge in the area adjacent to the Paracels, with the potential Chinese 350-NM constraint line running a short distance beyond the Vietnamese-defined outer limit. The possibly overlapping ECS areas of Vietnam and China would be described by the envelope created by their respective 350-NM constraint lines, with the potential maritime boundary to be drawn presumably from the point of intersection of the two constraint lines to the endpoint of the agreed maritime boundary in the Gulf of Tonkin. A single maritime boundary would have to traverse the area of the Paracels, which China has cordoned off with straight baselines of dubious legality under UNCLOS. How the boundary would cut across the Paracels would have to consider directly the principles of 'no cut-off' and non-encroachment,[54] as well as non-advantage in favor of either Vietnam or China.[55]

---

54   The principle of non-encroachment is a corollary to the equitable principles/relevant circumstances rule for delimitation of the continental shelf, expressed by the International Court of Justice (ICJ) in the *North Sea Continental Shelf Case*. The ICJ stated the principal rule is that the division of the continental shelf between two parties should be undertaken to ensure that each retains as much as possible of its natural prolongation of land territory into and under the sea, but such division should be "without encroachment on the natural prolongation of the land territory of the other." *North Sea Continental Shelf (Federal Republic of Germany/Denmark; Federal Republic of Germany/Netherlands), Judgment, ICJ Reports* (1969) [*North Sea*], para. 101.

55   The principle of non-advantage is derived from the judgment of the Court in *Tunisia v. Libya*, which emphasized that while coastal States enjoy sovereign rights over the

Macclesfield Bank could be a bone of contention in this sector, as the bathymetry indicates a possible geomorphological continuity extending from both the Vietnamese eastern coast and the Chinese southern mainland coast. The deep ocean floor arguably begins only on the southeastern side of the Bank itself because the areas between the two coasts and the Bank are generally shallower by approximately 2,000 m. It is uncertain why the Vietnamese-drawn outer limits stop just before clearly encompassing Macclesfield Bank, other than possibly an attempt to avoid strenuous objection from China (which if so, unfortunately did not work at all), or to keep the matter open to future negotiations. The prospective single maritime boundary claims in the area of Macclesfield Bank may greatly reflect the situation in *Gulf of Maine*, where both the United States and Canada attempted to place Georges Bank within their respectively proposed boundaries, but ended up with the Bank being divided by the International Court of Justice.

Vietnam and the Philippines

The potential ECS area of the Philippines extending from the island of Palawan could possibly overlap with the southern portion of the Vietnamese area under its unilateral submission. The natural prolongation and geomorphological continuity from the Philippines extends consistently up to the Vietnamese 200-NM limit; thus the outer limits of the Philippine ECS will likely intersect with the outer limits of the Vietnamese ECS. The sliver of overlapping ECS areas would be in a classic position of opposition, and in the absence of intervening islands in the Spratly area should be relatively easy to delimit bilaterally.

However, the location of the islands in light of the surrounding ECS areas raises the issue of whether the principles of no cut-off and non-encroachment would then warrant the creation of maritime corridors to give such islands access to either the Vietnamese or Philippine side, whichever they may end up being adjudged in favor of, or to the seabed beyond national jurisdiction. The minute sizes of the land mass of the contested islands relative to the

---

continental shelf to the full extent authorized by international law in the relevant circumstances, such enjoyment is at the same time subject to the principle that "although all States are equal before the law and are entitled to equal treatment, 'equity does not necessarily imply equality', nor does it seek to make equal what nature has made unequal" and "there can be no question of distributive justice." *Continental Shelf (Tunisia/Libyan Arab Jamarihiya), Judgment, ICJ Reports* (1982), at para. 46. This means that no coastal State should be placed in a position and granted an entitlement markedly superior to the other coastal State in the delimitation of shared continental shelf areas.

mainlands of both coastal States seem to militate against the grant of a large corridor such as that in *Nicaragua v. Colombia*, but even a pinhead-shaped projection like that of *St. Pierre and Miquelon* seems a rather perplexing possibility.[56]

Vietnam, Malaysia, and the Philippines

It appears that the Vietnamese-Malaysian Joint Area presents the most challenges to delimitation. Rather than being a straightforward division between Vietnam and Malaysia, no less than three other States (Philippines, Indonesia, and Brunei) could possibly have legal interests that may be affected by the joint area and may warrant more complex negotiations or arbitration. While Vietnam and Malaysia could theoretically agree simply on an equidistance line to bisect the Joint Area and allocate equivalent areas between them, the fact that the Joint Area also lies in the southern portion of a potential Philippine ECS area measured from Palawan renders the northern portion of the Joint Area subject to a possible Philippine claim for delimitation. Bathymetric profiles indicate that a natural prolongation can be discerned from the island of Palawan, winding along complex banks, saddles, and ridges westward, extending all the way up to the Vietnamese 200-NM limit in this region.

Vietnam, Malaysia, and Brunei

Roughly the center of the Joint Area is subject to a possible Brunei ECS claim, if the latter pushes through with its intention as declared in its

---

56   In *Nicaragua v. Colombia*, the Court rejected the idea of enclaving islands completely within the EEZ/CS, noting that "Nicaragua's proposed solution of enclaving the Colombian islands itself infringes that [no cut-off] principle, since it denies those islands their natural projection to the east up to and, indeed, beyond, the line 200 nautical miles from the Nicaraguan coast." *Judgment, ICJ Reports* (2012), at para. 213. The maintenance of access to the area beyond 200 NM resulted in a huge corridor connecting the islands and area between directly eastward toward Colombia. It is reminiscent, though on a larger scale, of what the Court attempted to do in granting the tiny islands of St. Pierre and Miquelon a 'frontal projection' toward the high seas inside Canada's 200-NM EEZ. *Delimitation of Maritime Areas between Canada and France (Canada v. France)*, XXI RIAA 265–341 (1992), at para. 74 [St. Pierre and Miquelon]. It is quite interesting to note that the issue of delimitation of the ECS projected from St. Pierre and Miquelon was also raised, which would have been logical considering its position that the islands were entitled to the full 200-NM EEZ/CS; however, the tribunal deemed the matter to be beyond its competence and jurisdiction, especially since claims to ECS were expressly placed within the review competence of the CLCS. Id., at para. 75–82.

preliminary information for the CLCS. This may proceed only upon the assumption that Brunei's EEZ/CS have indeed been agreed upon with Malaysia and enables Brunei to directly access an area beyond 200 NM and establish a natural prolongation up to that extent. Brunei could have strong arguments in its favor, emanating from the no cut-off and non-encroachment principles enunciated originally in the *North Sea Continental Shelf Cases* and reinforced in subsequent cases. However, the same trough that could raise a question of interruption of the natural prolongation in the case of Malaysia also raises the same issue for Brunei, so resolution of this matter will have to be consistent with the determination of Malaysia's claim to the Joint Area. It has been noted that it would not be equitable for Malaysia's Sarawak and Sabah coast to be deemed entitled to an ECS but not Brunei, which lies in between.[57]

Vietnam, Malaysia, and Indonesia

And finally, the southern portion of the Joint Area could be subjected to an Indonesian claim, if the latter decides and successfully abrogates its prior continental shelf agreement with Malaysia in order to extend its continental shelf zone beyond 200 NM. The bathymetric profiles from the Natuna Islands also present the classic configuration of a continental shelf, uninterrupted by either seafloor highs or lows and gently sloping consistently into the southern end of the Joint Area. A hypothetical Indonesian ECS will necessarily extend into the Joint Area since the base of slope region is well inside the latter's boundaries. It could legally be pursued on the basis of the no cut-off and non-encroachment principles, as well as the principle of ensuring access to the high seas/seabed area beyond national jurisdiction. In this respect, the two delimitation cases in the Bay of Bengal (*Bangladesh v. Myanmar* and *Bangladesh v. India*) would appear to be the best authorities.

Note on a Possible International Seabed Area

It would not be amiss to note that should all the littoral States claim ECS areas under the conservative presumptions used in this discussion, and under strict application of Article 76 and the Scientific and Technical Guidelines, there could indeed be a small portion of the SCS that would remain an international seabed area, directly adjacent to the Philippine 200-NM limit and located at more or less the center of the deep ocean floor in the SCS.

---

57   Poling, n. 50 above, pp. 8–9.

Conclusion

With or without islands creating distortions on the prospective EEZ/CS boundaries measured from the littoral mainland coasts, the SCS remains a geographically challenging arena for maritime boundary delimitation. The challenges
arise from the application of agreed treaty norms and evolving jurisprudence to
the unyielding geography. Littoral States are situated in adjacent or opposite
positions, sometimes both, in relation to each other. The irregular shape of the
surrounding coastlines bear both convex (e.g., the southern coast of China
and the eastern coast of Vietnam) and concave (e.g., the coasts of Brunei and
Malaysia, the coasts of Vietnam, Malaysia, and Indonesian archipelago) features,
as well as enclosed corners (e.g., the area adjacent to the Gulf of Tonkin).
Examination of the seabed shows that it is likewise quite complex, with broad
shallow areas to the south, sharply defined banks and ridges, and very deep
ocean floor. The bathymetry of the SCS basin produces possibly contentious submarine banks and ridges that could be subject to competing claims. Macclesfield
Bank primarily appears to be a good candidate for this kind of coastal State competition; other smaller banks and ridges may be similarly situated. In any case,
there seems little doubt that the littoral States of the SCS may all claim entitlements to ECS areas as a general rule; the practice of the smaller States to date all
evince the intention to do so, with two already having expressly acted thereon.
While China remains steadfast in its assertion (albeit ambiguously) of the nine-
dashed line, its public adherence to UNCLOS and its system of maritime zones
allows the consideration of a similar practice as a possible option.

It goes without stating that the delimitation issues enumerated and
described would not be relevant if the questions of sovereignty over the various islands in the Paracels and Spratlys are finally resolved with the largest
islands generating the full suite of maritime zones. But even if they do not do
so, the location of the islands within the prospective EEZ/CS or ECS zones still
call for the application of the various delimitation principles applied in jurisprudence that still pose challenges to the littoral States. The desktop study thus
demonstrates that even if the littoral States based their claims on an ideal and
strictly UNCLOS-based division of the SCS that gives no effect to the islands,
there will still be much cause for continued competition for seabed resources
pending final and complete maritime boundary delineations and delimitations. There could still be protracted maritime boundary disputes even without claims not based on UNCLOS like China's nine-dashed line and the original
Malaysian and Bruneian continental shelves.

It is fair to conclude that with or without maritime zones drawn in accordance with UNCLOS, the maritime disputes in the SCS are likely to continue in

the foreseeable future in the absence of conscious and deliberate efforts by the littoral States to actually and finally settle all of the boundary and resource use issues. Resort to UNCLOS may still not provide all the needed answers, although it may clarify the nature of a maritime dispute and more specifically delimit the range of possible rights and obligations legitimately applicable in identified locations. It cannot be assumed that a uniform application of UNCLOS will be enough to establish a well-ordered peace for the region's maritime disputes. The bigger challenge that is therefore posed, to which all littoral States must rise, is whether they should indeed pursue maritime delimitations (and impliedly, a division of the SCS) as their immediate and primary objective, or should think 'outside of the box' to find other cooperative solutions.

Arctic Sunrise from ITLOS: The Arctic Surprise and in Search of a Balanced Order

Nuwan Peiris
Attorney-at-law and State Counsel, Attorney General's Department, Sri Lanka

Introduction

The recent provisional measures case of the *Arctic Sunrise* from the International Tribunal for the Law of the Sea (ITLOS) has undermined the reliability, consistency, and impartiality of the Tribunal's jurisprudence. In this case, ITLOS ordered all Greenpeace personnel on board the Dutch vessel *Arctic Sunrise* arrested by Russia to be released on a financial bond, and not on the undertaking to return to face criminal proceedings for a protest against a Russian oil rig on the continental shelf in the Arctic Ocean. The Tribunal also ordered *Arctic Sunrise* to be released on posting a bond with Russia. Russia protested the Tribunal's jurisdiction and did not appear before ITLOS.

This article provides a brief account of the *Arctic Sunrise* case. It then proceeds to analyse the majority, separate, and dissenting opinions to determine whether the central issues involved were approached correctly. The Tribunal did not give adequate attention to two central issues. First, all of the judges, including the dissent, overlooked a simple point: does the flag State (or the ship) have exclusive jurisdiction over an offence committed by a person *outside* the ship since two individuals were trying to scale the platform? Second, this case also highlights the lack of comity towards the Annex VII tribunal and its growing inability to develop jurisprudence under the United Nations Convention on the Law of the Sea (UNCLOS) in a consistent and structured manner.[1]

Factual Matrix

The ship *Arctic Sunrise* was detained in the Pechora Sea by the Russian Coast Guard on 19 September 2013 for an attempt by Greenpeace to stage a protest against oil extraction on the offshore, ice-resistant, fixed platform Prirazlomnaya, owned by Gazprom Neft Shelf LLC, in the Barents Sea. The *Arctic Sunrise* is an

---

1 United Nations Convention on the Law of the Sea, opened for signature 10 December 1982, 1833 *United Nations Treaty. Series* 396 (entered into force 16 November 1994) [UNCLOS].

icebreaker, built in 1975, and owned by the Stichting Pheonix, Amsterdam and chartered to Stichting Greenpeace Council, Amsterdam under a ferryboat charter.[2] It was registered in, and flew the flag of, the Netherlands. At the time of the protest, Greenpeace had been using the vessel for its environmental campaigns since 1995.[3] Greenpeace is an international organization that has campaigned for environmental protection the world over for the last 40 years.[4] Greenpeace, as the Netherlands' annexure to the pleadings suggests, started a campaign in 2010 called 'Save the Arctic' to ban offshore oil drilling in the Arctic Ocean given its environmentally sensitive character. Two considerations motivated Greenpeace's campaign. First, harsh climatic conditions render cleaning an oil spill difficult if not impossible. Second, because global warming disproportionately impacts the Arctic, Greenpeace sought to prevent the exploitation of additional fossil fuel reserves, which would exacerbate challenges faced by the region.[5]

The Prirazlomnaya platform was located in the Pechora Sea on Russia's continental shelf and within its EEZ.[6] Russian authorities declared a safety zone of three nautical miles (NM) around the platform as opposed to the UNCLOS Article 60 requirement of 500 meters.[7] Operations on the platform began a few months earlier, after they had been called off due to international protests, including by Greenpeace.[8]

On 18 September 2013, *Arctic Sunrise* launched five rigid-hull inflatable boats outside the Prirazlomnaya platform's three NM safety zone.[9] Ten minutes later, the first of five boats approached the oil rig and two of the activists attempted to climb the outside structure of the platform with the objective of unfurling a banner below the main deck.[10] Simultaneously, a group of three boats further back towed a 'safety pod', a foam tube, towards the platform with the intention of hanging it from the side of the platform. The Russian Coast Guard approached the boat and arrested two individuals, Finnish and Swiss nationals, for attempting to climb the rig, and prevented the boats from

---

2   Request for provisional measures submitted by the Netherlands, October 21, 2013, para. 10, available online: <https://www.itlos.org/fileadmin/itlos/documents/cases/case_no.22/Request_provisional_measures_en_withtrnslations.pdf>.

3   Id., para. 2, Annex 2.

4   Id., para. 3, Annex 2.

5   Id., para. 9, Annex 2.

6   Id., para. 7, Annex 2.

7   Id., para. 7, Annex 2.

8   Id., para. 7, Annex 2.

9   Id., para. 11, Annex 2.

10 Id., para. 13, Annex 2.

engaging in any further activities. The boats escaped the Coast Guard and boarded *Arctic Sunrise* despite the Coast Guard's protest.[11]

Thereafter, the Coast Guard fired warning shots at *Arctic Sunrise* and attempted to board the vessel at locations more than three NM away from the platform.[12] The Coast Guard, thereafter, directed the ship to move out to 20 NM for a potential transfer of prisoners and a discussion. It is observed that it is unclear whether ordering the vessel 20 NM away was a safety measure adopted to protect the oil rig by the Russians. Since nothing happened after the direction, *Arctic Sunrise* returned to a position five NM from the oil rig.

According to the version of events offered by Greenpeace,[13] since incorporated by the Netherlands in its request for provisional measures with regard to the arrested Finnish national, the Russian authorities informed the Finnish Consulate that two climbers were rescued from the water after falling off the oil rig and were being treated as guests. On 19 September 2013, in the Russian EEZ, armed agents of the Russian Federal Security Service descended from a Russian helicopter and boarded *Arctic Sunrise*. The Russians took control of and detained the vessel and its crew. The Russian Coast Guard subsequently towed the vessel to Murmansk, and Russia commenced action against the crew in Murmansk.

On 20 September 2013, the Netherlands requested that Russia provide details of the arrest and release the crew and vessel.[14] Russia did not respond. The Netherlands repeated the same request on 23 September 2013. Thereafter, Russia informed the Netherlands of the ongoing criminal proceedings and requested information from the Dutch and invited a Dutch consulate representative to be present during the investigations. The Netherlands refused the request and reiterated their protests. Later, on 3 October 2013, the Netherlands informed Russia that they would resort to an Annex VII tribunal under UNCLOS given the urgency and disparate views of both parties.

Submission of the Parties

In view of the above, the Netherlands applied for provisional measures under ITLOS until the Annex VII tribunal is constituted. The Netherlands submitted to the Annex VII tribunal that Russia's actions in arresting and detaining *Arctic Sunrise* without the Netherlands' prior consent, infringed upon the exercise of

---

11   Id., para. 21, Annex 2.

12   Id., para. 23, Annex 2.

13   Id., para. 29, Annex 2.

14   Id., Annex 3.

its right to protect a vessel flying its flag from the freedom of navigation as provided by Articles 58(1), 87(1)(a) and Part VII of UNCLOS.[15] With respect to the detained crew members, the Netherlands requested the release of the crew on the basis of their right to liberty and security as provided by Articles 9 and 12(2) of the International Covenant on Civil and Political Rights. Further, the Netherlands requested, *inter alia*, that Russia should cease and guarantee the non-repetition of all the above wrongful acts and provide reparation in full. Until the Annex VII tribunal is constituted, the Netherlands requested,[16] *inter alia*, the release of the ship and the crew from the maritime areas under the jurisdiction of the Russian Federation and the recognition of *Arctic Sunrise's* freedom of navigation.

In response to the proceedings instituted by the Netherlands, Russia stated that the Annex VII tribunal has no jurisdiction in view of the Russian declaration filed under Article 298 that excludes Article 287 adjudicatory procedures in Section 2 for matters concerning "…law-enforcement activities in regard to the exercise of sovereign rights or jurisdiction."[17] In view of the fact that the Annex VII tribunal lacked jurisdiction, Russia refused to participate in the provisional measures case before ITLOS.

The Netherlands contended that such a declaration has the effect of modifying the legal provisions of the UNCLOS,[18] rendering Articles 309 and 310, of no legal effect. The reason is that optional exception in Article 298(1)(b), on law enforcement activities and its derogation to Article 287 only applies with respect to "disputes…excluded from the jurisdiction under Article 297, paragraph 2 or 3." Such disputes concern marine scientific research and fisheries, respectively, neither of which is at issue in the present case.

The Order of the Tribunal

The Reasoning of the Order
On the jurisdictional issue of the Russian declaration, the Tribunal held that the law enforcement activities under Article 298(1)(b) *prima facie* applies only

---

15   See Notification and the Statement of Claim, 4 October 2013.

16   Request for provisional measures submitted by the Netherlands, see n. 2 above, para. 47.

17   Request for provisional measures submitted by the Netherlands, 27 October 2013, para. 10, available online: <https://www.itlos.org/fileadmin/itlos/documents/cases/case_no.22/Note_verbale_Russian_Federation_eng.pdf>.

18   See the *Arctic Sunrise* Case, Order dated 22 November 2013, para. 44, available online: <https://www.itlos.org/fileadmin/itlos/documents/cases/case_no.22/Order/C22_Ord_22_11_2013_orig_Eng.pdf>.

to disputes excluded from the jurisdiction under Article 297, paragraph 2 or 3. Hence, the Tribunal found only a *prima facie* finding of jurisdiction through Articles 298(1)(b) and 297(2) or (3).[19] The Tribunal also noted that the absence of a party did not preclude the Tribunal from prescribing provisional measures provided the parties had been given a chance to present their case.[20] Further, the non-appearing party is nevertheless a party with "ensuing rights and obligations,"[21] along with its procedural rights.[22]

The Tribunal noted that a difference of opinion has arisen among the parties on Part V and Part VII, notably Articles 56(2), 58, 87(1)(a), 110(1),[23] and Article 60,[24] indicating the existence of a dispute between parties.[25] The Tribunal ordered Russia to immediately release *Arctic Sunrise* and all persons who have been detained on the posting of a bond or other financial security by the Netherlands in the amount of €3,600,000. Two judges, Russian Judge Golitsyn and Judge Kulyk, dissented.

Did the Order Maintain Comity towards the Arbitral Tribunal as per Article 290(5)?

The interim character of this Tribunal under Article 290(5) was much discussed in the *ARA Libertad* case by Judges Wolfrum and Cot where the issue of comity was spearheaded and discussed until the Annex VII tribunal is constituted to grant provisional measures.[26] In their statements regarding the distinction between Articles 290(5) and 290(1), the Judges opined:

> In this context it seems appropriate to refer to an important consideration concerning provisional measures under article 290 of the Convention. One has to distinguish between provisional measures taken under article 290, paragraph 1, of the Convention and those under article 290, paragraph 5, of the Convention. Whereas under article 290, paragraph 1, of the Convention, the Tribunal is called upon to decide *prima facie* on its own jurisdiction, under article 290, paragraph 5, of the

---

19   Id., para. 45.

20   Id., para. 48.

21   Id., para. 51.

22   Id., para. 53.

23   Id., para. 67.

24   Id., para. 68.

25   Id., para. 71.

26   See the *ARA Libertad* Case, Joint Separate Opinion of Judge Wolfrum and Judge Cot, available online: <http://www.itlos.org/fileadmin/itlos/documents/cases/case_no.20/C20_Ord _15.12.2012_SepOp_Wolfrum-Cot_orig-no_gutter.pdf>.

Convention, it must decide on the *prima facie* jurisdiction of another court or tribunal. Out of respect for the other court or tribunal the Tribunal has to exercise some restraint in questioning *prima facie* jurisdiction of such other court or tribunal. This has to be taken into account in the context of this case. The Tribunal still has to develop a jurisprudence to specify the applicable threshold more clearly. What counts, among other possible considerations, is the urgency and which rights or interests are at stake. It is equally unsatisfactory if the arbitral tribunal under Annex VII denies its jurisdiction which the Tribunal has established *prima facie* as it is for the settlement of the said dispute if the Tribunal denies *prima facie* jurisdiction in a situation where the arbitral tribunal would have voted otherwise.[27]

With respect to the *Arctic Sunrise* case, the Tribunal did not adopt this fine jurisprudential approach, dragging its entire jurisprudence back to its genesis, for the reason that no comity was shown to the Annex VII tribunal. The Tribunal should have been mindful that provisional measures can also be ordered by the Annex VII tribunal, and the Netherlands has seen no urgency to request provisional measures from the Annex VII tribunal as the written pleadings attached show. More importantly, the Tribunal should have kept in mind that their role is to provide for provisional measures until provisional measures are ordered by the Annex VII tribunal and not to pre-empt their role.

The *substantive ground* for provisional measures, like in domestic courts, is to maintain the status quo of the subject matter so that the final relief will not be rendered nugatory. Coupled with that, there also exists an urgency to intervene to maintain that status quo. Apart from the above substantive grounds, there are *procedural grounds* like making a *prima facie* case, balance of convenience, equitable conduct on the part of the plaintiff, etc. It is questionable how the order intends to achieve the status quo of the subject matter when the relief granted is more akin to a final arbitration that adjudicates on merits. Instead of a clear finding on the issue of status quo, the Tribunal saw the mere "difference of opinions exists as to the applicability of 56, 58, 60, 87 and 110" as a sufficient ground to grant provisional relief.

Although the Annex VII tribunal can grant relief that is just and equitable, which encompasses the release of the vessel and the crew on a financial bond, or a provisional measures' forum to maintain the status quo, it is questionable whether financial security can be given for the vessel and crew when the act complained thereof is one of a criminal nature and not commercial in

---

27   Id., para 5.

character. In criminal proceedings a vessel is an instrument of punitive wrong doing and it is needed in a criminal trial as evidence. The crew, who represent the accused, can only be released if bail is posted, on the condition that they will attend court. While in a commercial/civil action the release of the vessel and the crew on a financial bond is possible, in a criminal case the release of the accused with the criminal productions – since the vessel and its equipment will be marked in evidence – should not be done on financial security before the conclusion of the trial by an international court.

It cannot be ignored that not so long ago this Tribunal, in the provisional measures case of M/V *Louisa*,[28] allowed Spain to continue criminal proceedings for the alleged artifacts collected by MV *Louisa* (flagged by St. Vincent and the Grenadines) in its territorial seas, where provisional measures were refused since there was no urgency. MV *Louisa* was arrested while in a Spanish port. The offence complained of was committed in Spain's territorial sea, but in this case it was in the safety zone of the EEZ. The Tribunal, in this case, never thought of allowing criminal proceeding to continue for those personnel arrested within the safety zone. Instead it found an urgency to release them upon posting a bond, irrespective of the location of the alleged conduct. The approach taken in the *Arctic Sunrise* and MV *Louisa* cases are difficult to reconcile.

Status quo of the subject matter would have been preserved had the Tribunal ordered the ship to be maintained in operational condition by Russia rather than releasing the ship on a bond, until the future Annex VII tribunal changes or confirms its stance through its provisional measures or final judgment. Therefore, it would have been preferable had the Tribunal ordered the expedited criminal proceedings and the developments pending the constitution of the Annex VII tribunal to be reported to ITLOS continuously, especially for those who were caught within the vicinity of the oil rig.

The Tribunal seems to have reached a premature conclusion that the arrest and detention of the vessel and the crew to be almost an illegality, though it was not expressly stated in the order to be illegal. In this regard, the Tribunal's order to expedite proceedings may have been adequate, leaving the legality of arrest, detention, and the final outcome of the Russian case to be judged by the Annex VII tribunal.

Further, a more balanced order could have resulted if direction had been given to the flag State (the Netherlands) to share information with Russian authorities for expedited action given the Netherland's own submissions, its collaboration with Greenpeace, and possession of detailed evidence on the

---

28   See Order of 8 October 2003, ITLOS Reports 2003.

organization's conduct.[29] The order therefore should have been reciprocal, which is entirely acceptable even in an *ex parte* case despite Russia's absence.

The Netherlands requested the release of the crew in question as an urgent measure. It is questionable how it would help to maintain the status quo since the release is a substantive relief for the merits tribunal. Further, the applicant nowhere states that any criminal action on the part of the crew will be undertaken by them, nor do they build a case on the line of extradition of the crew to the flag state for prosecution for the alleged wrong doing on the Prirazlomnaya platform.

Despite, the *ex parte* proceedings against Russia, the Tribunal has a duty to act and rule according to law. Needless to say, the absence of a State party does not give the Tribunal the freedom to adjudicate the way it pleases, for example, to introduce a new legal basis not provided in the pleadings or ignore critical pieces of evidence, nor does it pave the way to ignore the jurisprudence the Tribunal had developed during its short period.

Encouragingly, unlike previous provisional measure cases, the Netherlands annexed the pleadings of the Annex VII tribunal. It is observed that to grant provisional measures, ITLOS, as a necessary fact, should know the legal basis upon which the Annex VII tribunal is constituted. ITLOS should have taken this opportunity to judicially emphasize the legal necessity to include the legal submissions upon which the Annex VII tribunal is constituted in future applications. Interestingly, no provisional measures were requested from the Annex VII tribunal. It is observed that ITLOS should have clarified whether it exercises the jurisdiction to grant provisional relief until the conclusion of the Annex VII tribunal proceedings, or, whether the effect of such measures ceases once the Annex VII tribunal is constituted.

Is There an Importance in Relying on Article 60?

It seems that the main issue was how best to reconcile the application of rights in Articles 56(2), 58, 87(1)(a), and 110(1) against the rights in Article 60 (safety zone). The pivot upon which the case may have proceeded was on Article 60 *for the reason* that the protest and arrest had taken place *within* the 500-metre safety zone of the rig and the vessel was arrested outside the said safety zone. It seems that Russia has abused rights vested in them by Article 60, and that abuse of Article 60 should have been raised by the Netherlands as the legal basis. As noted by Judge Golitsyn, Article 60(2) gives the EEZ State the exclusive jurisdiction on safety matters.[30] Interestingly, the Netherlands did not

---

29   The Netherland had already refused to cooperate in the investigations with the Russian authorities stating that the arrest was illegal (*vide* annex 5 and 6 of the written pleadings of the Netherlands). However, the Netherlands could have participated under 'protest'.

30   See Opinion of Judge Golitsyn, n. 39 below, para. 22.

raise Article 60 as a specific basis, despite averring Part VII of the UNCLOS as a basis in the request filed. Rather, the main order later introduced Article 60 and stated (along with the other articles cited) that a dispute exists to grant provisional measures.

Can this protest be ruled as imperiling the safety in a provisional measure case? It seems difficult to limit the exercise of exclusive jurisdiction on safety in Article 60(2) to matters listed in Article 110(1). Had Russia participated in the proceedings this issue could have been raised. Perhaps this shows the importance of participating in the proceedings, where one may have greater control over the outcome despite jurisdictional protests.

Other Declarations and Opinions

In general, there are three distinct and clearly contradictory separate opinions that run against the reasoning of the majority and from each other. From a judicial policy perspective, given the increasing number of separate opinions that have been filed by the Tribunal judges over the years, it is observed that some of these filed opinions go entirely contradictory to the majority decisions, but remain supportive of the outcome of majority decisions for the sake of unanimity. This leaves a question as to whether these separate opinions should be left at their rudimentary stage, or whether they should be developed into full decisions through their application to the contentious facts with definitive conclusions. This in effect is provided with either a concurring decision or a dissenting decision. On the other hand, both dissents by Judges Golitsyn and Kulyk should have preferably addressed all issues raised in the case, and should have stated whether their respective dissents deviate only on the issues they have commented on, or whether they agree on the rest of the issues discussed in the main order. It is important at this juncture to analyse the rest of the opinion and dissents for the reason that it shows how far it deviates from the main order on almost all aspects, including the above discussed issue of comity and exhaustion of local remedies.

Declaration of Judge Ad Hoc Anderson
Judge Anderson,[31] while agreeing with the main order, regretted the non-appearance of Russia and stated that the non-appearance does not help the

---

31   See the *Arctic Sunrise* Case, Declaration of Judge Ad Hoc Anderson, available online: <https://www.itlos.org/fileadmin/itlos/documents/cases/case_no.22/Order/C22_Ord _22.11.2013_decl.Anderson_orig_Eng.pdf>.

efficient application of Part XV of the Convention. Secondly, the learned judge proceeded to observe Article 283, which deals with the obligation to exchange views, does not contemplate exhausting negotiations but to exchange views to find the most appropriate means of peaceful settlement by negotiation or other means. The objective of this being that the other side will not be taken by complete surprise. The learned judge observed that from the Dutch *Note Verbale* dated 3 October 2013 to Russia that the Netherlands had indicated its intention to submit the dispute to arbitration under UNCLOS as soon as feasible, thereby complying with Article 283 *prima facie*. The question of admissibility of the claim will be determined finally by the Annex VII tribunal.

Separate Opinion of Judges Wolfrum and Kelly

First, this opinion deals with the effect of the non-appearance of Russia since the main order failed to clarify this issue in detail. The opinion reasoned that Article 28 of the ITLOS statute on default proceedings applies for proceedings on provisional measures once the Tribunal finds jurisdiction *prima facie*. Secondly, the opinion also explained as to why parties must appear.

As far as the declaration is concerned, the opinion notes that an exclusion of jurisdiction from the declaration made under Article 298 cannot justify the non-appearance by a party since courts have the sole right to interpret the scope of the declaration based on the doctrine of *Kompetenz-Kompetenz*.[32] The opinion nevertheless agreed with the majority decision on the ruling of the scope of declaration, but said it is missing convincing reasoning. The explanation being that to determine the urgency, *prima facie* plausibility of the claim or even the exchange of views under Article 283, the applicability of the declaration must be discussed in detail. The opinion in this regard should have exercised caution in making sweeping statements of this nature since the exchange of views appears in Section 1 of Part XV, and hence are excluded from the application of the limits and exceptions in Section 3.

Next, the opinion noted that the majority decision does not touch upon the issue that *Arctic Sunrise* was arrested within the EEZ of Russia and only a few individuals entered the safety zone. This factor should have been featured in the majority decision given the limited enforcement jurisdiction in the EEZ as reflected in Articles 73, 110, 111, 220, 221, and 226. The context is different in respect of artificial installations where the coastal State enjoys exclusive

---

32   See the *Arctic Sunrise* Case, Separate Opinion of Judges Wolfrum and Kelly, para. 7, available online: <https://www.itlos.org/fileadmin/itlos/documents/cases/case_no.22/Order/C22_Ord_22.11.2013_sep.op.Wolfrum-Kelly_orig_Eng.pdf>.

jurisdiction, including legislative jurisdiction according to Article 60(2).[33] It is equally important to note that

> ...enforcement actions in the exclusive zone in general are concerned the enforcement jurisdiction of the coastal State is limited if it is not legitimized by one of the exceptions mentioned above. It is for the flag State to take the enforcement actions not entrusted to the coastal State by the Convention.

This is feasible and effective since in the past Dutch courts had issued restraining orders to Greenpeace on similar incidents.[34]

This statement of the opinion needs revisiting. It is implicit in this statement that residual jurisdiction is vested with the flag State. However, closer scrutiny of UNCLOS provisions on flag State jurisdiction in Part VII on the high seas reveals that the Convention does not privilege flag State rights over coastal State rights in the EEZ, limiting the application of Article 60. Interestingly, this statement also gives much credence to Dutch domestic cases and practices, perhaps with the intention of hinting that Russia should have followed the same suit. However, the opinion never gave centrality to the pending domestic criminal cases in Russia in the instant case, even in relation to the persons arrested while scaling the platform. More interestingly, the Netherlands did not attempt to support its claim by employing Dutch cases, which are factual matters before ITLOS.

The opinion concluded that the majority decision should have accounted for the division of enforcement functions between the coastal and flag States in granting provisional relief. This opinion observed the necessity to delineate the enforcement functions between the coastal State and the flag State in a provisional measure's case in the safety zone and outside the safety zone that falls in the EEZ of Russia. The opinion correctly observed the majority decision's failure to address this balance given the interim character of the Tribunal under Article 290(5).

Although Wolfrum's and Kelly's opinion summed up the approach in the final paragraph – the necessity to delineate the enforcement functions between the coastal State and the flag State in a provisional measure's case – it ought to be taken as a critical failure on the part of the learned judges to apply this approach to the facts in question. Rather than remaining undecided, they

---

33   Id., para. 11.
34   Id., para. 12.

should have decided whether the Netherlands' claim of release could be granted or not.

Separate Opinion of Judge Jesus

Judge Jesus' opinion agreed with the majority, but expressed a different opinion with regard to jurisdiction, the posting of a bond, and the release of personnel. On the issue of jurisdiction, the opinion expressed its dissatisfaction with the reasoning of the main order,[35] and dealt with the Russian declaration to the effect that Article 297(2) and (3) relates to marine scientific research and fisheries and had nothing to do with the instant arrest.

On the issue of the financial bond, the opinion disagreed for posting a bond which is tantamount to a "...back-door prompt release procedure,"[36] though Judge Jesus had no objection to the release of the vessel.[37] If this argument is taken to its logical conclusion, even a vessel release, as a provisional measure, could be deemed to be prompt release, since vessel release is mentioned only in such a procedure. Article 290 is silent on the type of provisional measures, yet gives jurisdiction to grant any measure "...appropriate under the circumstances to preserve respective rights of the parties..." (Article 290(1)).

To argue to justify the release of the vessel on one hand, but to take out the posting of a bond on the other hand is inconsistent. It is also observed that the UNCLOS, quite rightly, does not deal with the ultimate nature of an award or provisional measure that can be delivered, rather it leaves it to be determined by the law applicable (Article 293). Further into the reasoning the learned judge compares the pending criminal proceedings with prompt release procedure. It is submitted that this reasoning may be of relevance to the Article 292 prompt release procedure, but it does not mean that this is confined only to Article 292.

Separate Opinion of Judge Paik

Judge Paik filed a separate opinion that only focused on the non-appearance of Russia. He took the view that the main order relied on the practice associated in default appearances of the International Court of Justice (ICJ) Statute in

---

35   See the *Arctic Sunrise* Case, Separate Opinion of Judge Jesus, para. 5, available online, <https://www.itlos.org/fileadmin/itlos/documents/cases/case_no.22/Order/C22_Ord _22.11.2013_sep.op.Wolfrum-Kelly_orig_Eng.pdf>.

36   Id., para. 7.

37   Id., para. 6.

interpreting Article 28 of the Tribunal Statute.[38] The opinion took the position that Article 28 represents an improvement of Article 53 of the ICJ Statute based on legal experience. Also, the opinion observed, *inter alia*, that the onus to substantiate its claim to fall within the jurisdiction is not different when the other party fails to appear, and non-appearance alone does not give the Tribunal the right to enter a default judgment against the absent party. Further, Article 28 can also be applied to provisional measures.

Dissenting Opinion of Judge Golitsyn

Judge Golitsyn, the Russian judge, dissented on grounds of lack of *prima facie* jurisdiction and inadmissibility of the Dutch claim. Irrespective of this jurisdictional objection, the learned judge next dissented on grounds relating to the inappropriateness to grant provisional measures, inconsistency of the provisional measures granted with Article 290(1) and (5), and finally on the unsuitability of posting a bond for release.

On the lack of *prima facie* jurisdiction and inadmissibility, the dissent observed that before dealing with *prima facie* jurisdiction and "...law-enforcement activities in regard to the exercise of sovereign rights or jurisdiction," the main order should have ruled the Dutch claim to be inadmissible since the obligation to exchange views under Article 283 has not been complied with.[39]

It is submitted that an obligation to exchange views cannot be considered as a complete jurisdictional bar for provisional measures for the reason that preservation of rights may be rendered nugatory if delayed pending the exchange of views. Furthermore, it would be improper to place an interpretation of Article 283 read with Article 286 for such a negotiation to be a mandatory pre-jurisdictional basis to request interim relief.

Secondly, as far as the inappropriateness to grant provisional measures is concerned, the dissent noted that the objective is the urgent need to preserve the rights of the parties without transgressing on the merits.[40] Therefore, the primary reasons for the Dutch claim leads to a ruling on merits,[41] hence the

---

38　　See the *Arctic Sunrise* Case, Separate Opinion of Judge Paik, paras. 5 and 2, available online, <https://www.itlos.org/fileadmin/itlos/documents/cases/case_no.22/Order/C22 _Ord_22.11.2013_sep.op.Paik_orig_Eng.pdf>; see also Article 53 of the ICJ Statute.

39　　See the *Arctic Sunrise* Case, Dissenting Opinion of Judge Golitsyn, paras. 5 and 7, available online, <https://www.itlos.org/fileadmin/itlos/documents/cases/case_no.22/Order/C22 _Ord_22.11.2013_diss.op.Golitsyn_orig_Eng.pdf>.

40　　Id., para. 18.

41　　Id., para. 19.

Tribunal by granting the same supported the Dutch claim on merits,[42] and resultantly the dissent took the view of analysing the merits.[43]

The dissent observed Article 60(2) gives coastal States exclusive jurisdiction over customs, fiscal, health, safety, and immigration matters in their EEZ.[44] Enforcement measures in Article 60(4) provides for the coastal State to take appropriate measures for safety both of navigation and of the artificial islands.[45] In this regard, Russia has passed laws to enforce safety.[46] Having analysed the facts,[47] the dissent held that the breach of such Russian law is intentional.[48] Further, the dissent noted that it is no defence to violate the regulations of a safety zone by staying outside that zone. Article 111 provides that the right of hot pursuit is available to a mother ship for the activities of its craft when they work as a team.[49] In accordance with Article 111(2), Russia was in hot pursuit of the ship for violations committed within the safety zone and on the continental shelf platform.[50]

With regard to preservation of property pending criminal proceedings, the dissent noted the undertaking given by Russia in this regard,[51] and observed that in *M/V "Louisa" (Saint Vincent and the Grenadines v. Kingdom of Spain, Request for Provisional Measures)* the Tribunal decided that the assurances given by Spain on the conditions of the ship should be adequate and the same approach be taken in this case. However, it is submitted that the Spanish undertaking was a *judicial* undertaking and, in this case, the Russian undertaking was a *private* undertaking to the Netherlands. The difference is significant.

The dissent manifestly fails to make any comment on the non-appearance of Russia when the non-appearance became a central point of discussion in the main order and in other separate opinions. Secondly, the dissent also conspicuously fails to shed any light on the Russian declaration filed under Article 298.

---

42   Id., para. 20.
43   Id., para. 21.
44   Id., para. 22.
45   Id., para. 25.
46   Id., para. 26.
47   Id., paras. 29 and 30.
48   Id., para. 31.
49   Id., para. 35.
50   Id., para. 36.
51   Id., para. 41.

Dissenting Opinion of Judge Kulyk

This dissent mainly deals with the prescription of provisional measures and reservations on the use of a bond as provisional measures. The dissent, unlike the main order and separate opinions, appears to more appropriately focus on the requirements of provisional measures articulated in Article 290(1) and (5). The dissent discusses the necessity to preserve the respective rights of the parties,[52] urgency,[53] and irreversible damage, etc.,[54] drawing from the previous Tribunal jurisprudence.

The dissent criticized the main order in not emphasizing the requirements of 'irreparability' or 'irreversibility' and instead of emphasizing the requirement of urgency.[55] Further, the dissent also highlighted that these standards should be applied in a discretionary manner with the appropriateness to the circumstances at hand.

It is noted that the vessel merely being laid up in a Russian port will not cause any irreversible damage before the Annex VII tribunal is established.[56] As a provisional measure, the dissent advocated the granting of access for the operator to maintain the vessel during its detention rather than outright release.[57] This approach seems to be more meaningful, and balanced, given the pending criminal proceedings. However, the dissent did not take a measured and balanced approach when it characterized releasing the ship's personnel as an urgent provisional measure using the International Covenant on Civil and Political Rights (ICCPR) as a basis.[58] The dissent should have elaborated on employing the ICCPR as basis through Article 293 (applicable law), especially against the backdrop of enforcement powers in Articles 60 and 111.

Finally, on the issue of posting a bond, the dissent questioned this process and stated that a release by posting a bond in favor of Russia will not preserve the rights, if Russia becomes successful in the Annex VII tribunal, because the Netherlands "...assumes [the] obligation to deliver the appropriate persons under the jurisdiction of the court inasmuch as the Annex VII tribunal decides in favor of the Russian Federation."[59]

---

52   See the *Arctic Sunrise* Case, Dissenting Opinion of Judge Kulyk, para. 1, available online, <https://www.itlos.org/fileadmin/itlos/documents/cases/case_no.22/Order/C22_Ord _22.11.2013_diss.op.Kulyk_orig_Eng.pdf>.

53   Id., para. 2.

54   Id., para. 3.

55   Id., para. 7.

56   Id., para. 9.

57   Id., para. 11.

58   Id., para. 12.

59   Id., para. 15.

An Overall Comment on the Order and the Other Opinions

All judges, including the dissenting judges, overlooked a very critical point, although a simple point. Does the flag State (or the ship) have the exclusive jurisdiction over an offence committed by a person *outside* the ship? This is critical because some did not commit the offence *on board* the vessel – two individuals were trying to scale the platform! All the learned judges seem to tussle between the safety zone jurisdiction *simpliciter* and flag State jurisdiction *simpliciter*. The preferred approach should have been, first, to weigh the safety zone jurisdiction and the *extended* flag State jurisdiction to persons caught outside the vessel; second, to weigh the vessel's right to interfere with the safety zone jurisdiction; and third, to determine if the *extended* safety zone jurisdiction and its rights/duties were weighed in relation to pursuing the vessel. No flag State can vindicate itself a superior or an exclusive prerogative for those outside the ship attempting to commit mischief in another's safety zone.

By logical extension, if such persons outside the ship are aided and abetted by the vessel it is even impossible to give primacy to the flag State when it comes to the jurisdiction over the vessel, especially noting the fact that the vessel remained in EEZ waters, where right of navigation needs to be balanced with the enjoyment of EEZ rights of the other. Given all of this, it is almost *impossible* to hold that there is a rule prohibiting Russia from prosecuting the two personnel arrested for scaling the oil rig, and it is even more irreconcilable to prescribe provisional measures in favor of the flag State.

This aspect is critical since the Tribunal did not apply Article 60(2), which grants exclusive jurisdiction (legislative and enforcement) as in internal waters, *over* the offshore structure, encompassing jurisdiction over the protestors illicitly climbing the structure. Nor were the criminal proceedings allowed to continue when a buffer safety zone is created to 'ensure safety' of the structure through Article 60(2). Compliance is mandated for 'all ships' through Article 60(6). Boats directed by a ship outside this buffer zone are equally responsible for the breach of "...international standards regarding navigation" (Article 60(6)). Despite all this, the Tribunal impeded the criminal proceedings brought by Russia against the protesters as an urgent measure. Some opinions were even bold enough to consider ICCPR for the release of all persons, including the two climbing the structure, as an urgent measure, while the pending criminal action was never seen as a justification under Articles 60(2) and 60(6) *even* till the Annex VII tribunal is established.

Conclusion

Like the still waters that run deep, the jurisprudential controversy of this order may create problems. But it seems that the Tribunal's urgency to release the personnel arrested inside the safety zone of the oil rig as an urgent measure disregarding pending criminal proceedings reflects the sweeping nature of the Tribunal's order, an over-simplified approach, and a lack of appreciation of the complexity of the facts involved. In the future, what happens if a crew member of a vessel gets out of the vessel and enters or attempts to enter an artificial island in a coastal State's EEZ to commit mischief? Would the ITLOS order provisional measures in favor of the flag State to release the person who is arrested on the artificial island? Discouragingly, given the previous case of provisional measures, *M/V Louisa* – where criminal proceedings were left to continue – the Tribunal's approach in *Arctic Sunrise* seems to be subjective and fragmented when the personnel arrested inside the safety zone were released on a bond. Given the contradictory approach in these two cases, it remains to be seen how ITLOS would approach a similar case in the future. But what is more worrying is the way all the learned judges gave primacy to flag State juris-diction *simpliciter* without fully appreciating the safety zone jurisdiction and its implications in prescribing provisional measures.

Engineering the 'Mis-Anthropocene': International Law, Ethics and Geoengineering

Karen N. Scott†

Professor of Law, University of Canterbury, Christchurch, New Zealand

Introduction

In May 2013, it was announced that atmospheric concentrations of carbon dioxide (CO_2) had reached 400 parts per million (ppm).[1] Rising from approximately 280 ppm at the onset of the Industrial Revolution,[2] the atmospheric concentration of CO_2 is now substantially higher than at any point in the last 800,000 years.[3] In its Fifth Assessment Report on Climate Change released in late 2013, the Intergovernmental Panel on Climate Change (IPCC) concluded that "[w]arming of the climate system is unequivocal, and since the 1950s, many of the observed changes are unprecedented over decades to millennia. The atmosphere and ocean have warmed, the amounts of snow and ice have diminished, sea level has risen, and the concentrations of greenhouse gases have increased."[4] Anthropogenic climate change extends, as the conclusions of the IPCC demonstrate, beyond the atmosphere and impacts the biosphere, cryosphere and

---

† This article was originally presented as the *5th Annual Douglas M. Johnston Ocean Governance Lecture* at the Schulich School of Law, Dalhousie University, Halifax, Canada, 30 October 2013 under the title of "International Law and the 'Mis-anthropocene': Responding to the Geoengineering Challenge." The author would like to acknowledge the Marine & Environmental Law Institute, Dalhousie University in supporting her visit. Parts of the article also draw on ideas presented at a *Workshop of Multidisciplinary Perspectives on Climate Ethics* held at the Villa del Grumello, Lake Como, Italy, 26–27 September 2013.

1 "400 PPM: Carbon Dioxide in the Atmosphere Reaches Prehistoric Levels," *Scientific American*, 9 May 2013, available online: <http://blogs.scientificamerican.com/observations /2013/05/09/400-ppm-carbon-dioxide-in-the-atmosphere-reaches-prehistoric-levels/>.

2 M.R. Raupach, G. Marland, P. Ciais et al., "Global and Regional Drivers of Accelerating CO_2 Emissions," *Proceedings of the National Academy of Sciences*, Suppl. Ser. 104 (2007): 10288–10293 at 10288.

3 IPCC 2013, "Summary for Policy Makers," in *Climate Change 2013: The Physical Science Basis. Contribution of Working Group I to the Fifth Assessment Report of the Intergovernmental Panel on Climate Change*, eds. T.F. Stocker, D. Qin, G.K. Plattner et al. (Cambridge: Cambridge University Press, 2013), p. 11.

4 Id., p. 4.

Ocean Yearbook 29: 61–84

© KONINKLIJKE BRILL NV, LEIDEN, 2015 | DOI 10.1163/9789004297234_005

hydrosphere. While climate change may have dominated global environmental agendas over the last two decades, the conscious and unconscious transformation of our Earth's environmental systems by humankind has a history extending over millennia and includes, *inter alia,* the alternation of biochemical cycles including nitrogen, phosphorus, and sulphur,[5] the modification of terrestrial ecosystems through agriculture, the transformation of the freshwater cycle through changes in river flow,[6] the alteration of ocean chemistry through an increase in the levels of CO_2 and nitrogen,[7] as well as driving what has been described as the Sixth Extinction.[8] In order to describe these impacts, which are arguably different in *kind* as opposed to merely *extent*, a new term was created in 2000: the Anthropocene. Adopted by Paul Crutzen and Eugene Stooemer,[9] the Anthropocene describes a new geological era, one within which "humankind has become a global geological force in its own right."[10]

In the Anthropocene, global greenhouse gas emissions are more than 40 percent higher today than they were in 1990,[11] despite the adoption of binding emission reduction targets under the 1997 Kyoto Protocol.[12] Twenty years on from the adoption of the 1992 United Nations Framework Convention on Climate Change (UNFCCC)[13] it is difficult to characterize the climate change regime as anything other than a failure. Whether the current climate change regime and the traditional tools of international environmental law are fit for purpose in the age of the Anthropocene is a question worthy of debate.

---

5   W. Steffen, J. Grineveld, P. Crutzen and J. Macneill, "The Anthropocene: Conceptual and Historical Perspectives," *Philosophical Transactions of the Royal Society A* 369 (2011): 842–867 at 843.

6   Id.

7   T. Tyrrell, "Anthropogenic Modification of the Oceans," *Philosophical Transactions of the Royal Society A* 369 (2011): 887–908.

8   Steffen et al., n. 5 above, p. 843. See R. Leakey and R. Lewin, *The Sixth Extinction. Biodiversity and Its Survival* (London: Weidenfield & Nicolson, 1996).

9   P. Crutzen and E.F. Stoemer, "The 'Anthropocene,'" *Global Change Newsletter* 41 (2000): 17–18. See also P.J. Crutzen and W. Steffen, "How Long Have We Been in the Anthropocene Era?" *Climatic Change* 61 (2003): 251–257.

10   Steffen et al., n. 5 above, p. 843. See also W. Steffen, P.J. Crutzen and J.R. McNeill, "The Anthropocene: Are Humans Now Overwhelming the Great Forces of Nature?" *Ambio* 36, no. 8 (2007): 614–621.

11   IPCC 2013, n. 3 above, p. 11.

12   1997 Protocol to the Framework Convention on Climate Change (Kyoto), 37 *International Legal Materials* (1998) 22 (in force 18 June 2001).

13   1992 UN Framework Convention on Climate Change, 31 *International Legal Materials* (1992) 851 (in force 21 March 1994) [UNFCCC].

Increasingly, however, individuals and even States are disengaging from this debate and beginning to explore other strategies to mitigate the impacts of climate change, including geoengineering.

Defined as "the intentional large-scale manipulation of the planetary environment" for climate change mitigation purposes,[14] geoengineering seeks either to reduce atmospheric concentration of greenhouse gases or to lower the surface temperature of the Earth without the need for expensive emissions reductions. What sets geoengineering apart from other strategies for the mitigation of or adaptation to climate change is the *deliberate* large-scale and potentially irreversible interference with natural planetary systems. Although climate change itself results from large scale and potentially irreversible (at least on a human time scale) interference with the atmosphere, that interference has been inadvertent or at least an unintentional by-product of human industrial and other activity. With geoengineering we are not just playing God but we *know* we are playing God. And that knowledge raises significant ethical issues over and above the risks posed to the environment by geoengineering and its economic viability as a climate change mitigation measure.

The question for this article is whether international law provides an appropriate framework within which these important ethical questions can be addressed. Part 2 of this article introduces geoengineering as a climate change mitigation strategy and briefly sets out some of the environmental and economic risks associated with proposed strategies before going on, in Part 3, to summarize the principal components of the international legal framework which currently applies to geoengineering. In Part 4 of this article five ethical questions associated with geoengineering are explored and the extent to which those questions can be addressed within the current legal framework is briefly assessed. This article concludes that the ethical, environmental and economic risks associated with geoengineering can only be effectively addressed within a binding legal framework, and Part 5 of the article identifies three possible options for the development of a future regulatory framework for geoengineering.

Geoengineering as a Climate Change Mitigation Measure

The transition of geoengineering from the fringes to the mainstream of scientific and, increasingly, policy debate arguably began with the publication of an

---

14   D.W. Keith, "Geoengineering the Climate: History and Prospect," *Annual Review of Environment and Resources* 25 (2000): 245–284 at 247.

article by Nobel laureate Paul J. Crutzen in 2006, advocating the injection of sulphur into the stratosphere with the intention of reflecting sunlight and cooling the planet.[15] However, the desire of scientists, governments and even lawyers to manipulate weather and climate for their own ends has a much longer history.[16] First coined as a term to apply to the manipulation of planetary systems for climate change purposes in 1977,[17] geoengineering has gained increasing support over the last five years as a possible technical solution to climate change, and has recently been explored in a series of high profile reports published by the Royal Society[18] and the governments of the United Kingdom[19] and the United States,[20] as well as in a plethora of articles in scientific and technical journals.

Divided into two categories, geoengineering technologies are designed either to remove CO_2 from the atmosphere or to manage solar radiation. Techniques aimed at the removal of CO_2 from the atmosphere primarily focus on enhancing or expanding mechanisms that naturally perform this function. Examples include afforestation or reforestation,[21] soil-carbon

---

15   P.J. Crutzen, "Albedo Enhancement by Stratospheric Sulfur Injections: A Contribution to Resolve a Policy Dilemma?" *Climatic Change* 77 (2006): 211–219.

16   See J.R. Fleming, *Fixing the Sky. The Checkered History of Weather and Climate Control* (New York: Columbia University Press, 2010); Keith, n. 14 above.

17   C. Marchetti, "On geoengineering and the CO_2 Problem," *Climate Change* 1 (1977): 59–68.

18   The Royal Society (UK), *Geoengineering the Climate. Science, Governance and Uncertainty* (Royal Society Policy Document 10/09/2009) [*2009 Royal Society Report on Geoengineering*].

19   See the Fourth Report of Session 2008–2009 of the House of Commons, Innovation, Universities, Science and Skills Committee, *Engineering: Turning Ideas into Reality, Volume 1* (HC 50–1); *Government Response to the Committee's Fourth Report* (House of Commons Innovation, Universities, Science and Skills Committee), *Engineering: Turning Ideas into Reality: Government Response to the Committee's Fourth Report* (Fifth Special Report of Session 2008–09, HC 759); House of Commons Science and Technology Committee, *The Regulation of Geoengineering* (Fifth Report of Session 2009–10) (HC 221); *Government Response to the House of Commons Science and Technology Committee 5th Report of Session 2009–10: The Regulation of Geoengineering*, Cm 7936.

20   K. Bracmort, R.K. Lattanzio and E. Barbour, *Geoengineering: Governance and Technology Policy* (Congressional Research Service Report for Congress, R41371, 2010); Chairman Bart Gordon, Committee on Science and Technology, US House of Representatives, *Engineering the Climate: Research Needs and Strategies for International Coordination Report* (111 Congress, Second Session, October 2010) [*Engineering the Climate Report*].

21   See J.G. Canadell and M.R. Raupach, "Managing Forests for Climate Change Mitigation," *Science* 320 (2008): 1456–1457; L. Ornstein, I. Aleinov and D. Rind, "Irrigated Afforestation of the Sahara and Australian Outback to End Global Warming," *Climatic Change* 97 (2009):

sequestration,[22] the use of CO_2 absorbing algae on building surfaces,[23] and even the capture and storage of atmospheric CO_2 by artificial 'trees'.[24] In terms of capacity, the oceans constitute by far the largest reservoir of CO_2,[25] and it is perhaps unsurprising that significant scientific effort to date has been put into developing ways of enhancing that reservoir. In particular, scientists are exploring ways to improve the efficiency of the biological pump, through which phytoplankton transports CO_2 from the atmosphere to the ocean's depths, in regions where plankton biomass is low, such as the Southern Ocean and the Equatorial Pacific.[26] Thirteen experiments have been carried out to date involving the stimulation of plankton biomass or algal blooms through the addition of missing nutrients such as iron.[27] Although the growth of phytoplankton has increased in each case so far,[28] the effectiveness of this technique as a climate change mitigation measure is as yet unproven.[29] An alternative or

---

409–437; K.R. Richards and C. Stokes, "A Review of Forest Carbon Sequestration Cost Strategies: A Dozen Years of Research," *Climatic Change* 63 (2004): 1–48; B. Sohngen, "Forestry Carbon Sequestration," in *Smart Solutions to Climate Change. Comparing Costs and Benefits*, ed. B. Lomborg (Cambridge: Cambridge University Press, 2010), pp. 114–132; M. Tavoni, B. Sohngen and V. Bosetti, "Forestry and the Carbon Market Response to Stabilize Climate," *Energy Policy* 35 (2007): 5346–5353.

22   See R.K. Shrestha and R. Lal, "Ecosystem Carbon Budgeting and Soil Carbon Sequestration in Reclaimed Mine Soil," *Environment International* 32 (2006): 781–796.

23   E. Jacob-Lobes, C.H.G. Scoparo and T.T. Franco, "Rates of CO_2 Removal by *Aphanothece microscopic Nägeli* in Tubular Photobioreactors," *Chemical Engineering and Processing* 47 (2008): 1365–1373.

24   K.S. Lackner, "Capture of Carbon Dioxide from Ambient Air," *The European Physical Journal: Special Topics* 176 (2009): 93–106.

25   Secretariat of the Convention on Biological Diversity, *Scientific Synthesis of the Impacts of Ocean Fertilization on marine Biodiversity, Biodiversity* (Technical Series No. 46) (Montreal: Secretariat of the Convention on Biological Diversity, 2009), p. 9.

26   H.J.W. de Baar and P.W. Boyd, "The Role of Iron in Plankton Ecology and Carbon Dioxide Transfer of the Global Oceans," in *The Changing Ocean Carbon Cycle: A Midterm Synthesis of the Joint Global Ocean Flux Study*, eds. R.B. Hansen, H.W. Ducklow and J.G. Field (Cambridge: Cambridge University Press, 2000), p. 61 at 107; R.A. Duce and N.W. Tindale, "Atmospheric Transport of Iron and Its Deposition in the Ocean," *Limnology & Oceanography* 36 (1991): 1715.

27   D. Wallace, C. Law, P. Boyd et al., *Ocean Fertilization. A Scientific Summary for Policy Makers* (Paris: IOC/UNCESO, 2010) (OOC/BRO/2011/2), p. 3.

28   R.S. Lampitt, E.P. Achterberg, T.R. Anderson et al., "Ocean Fertilization: A Potential Means of Geoengineering?" *Philosophical Transactions of The Royal Society A* 366 (2008): 3919–3945 at 3928.

29   For a discussion of the results of the key experiments to date see K.O. Buesseler, J.E. Andrews, S.M. Pike et al., "The Effects of Iron Fertilization on Carbon Sequestration in

perhaps additional ocean-based technique is designed to stimulate the ocean solubility pump, which also transports CO_2 from the surface to the depths of the ocean, by means of increasing the alkalinity of the oceans, through the addition of limestone powder or soda ash.[30] Known as 'weathering', this technique is designed to increase the ocean's capacity to store atmospheric CO_2 while also reducing the effects of ocean acidification.[31] By contrast, solar radiation management techniques are not designed to reduce atmospheric concentration of CO_2. Rather, they attempt to offset the temperature increases associated with climate change through reflecting sunlight back into space or deflecting it from the Earth altogether. Techniques range from the benign but likely ineffective urban albedo enhancement[32] to the rather more radical whitening of marine clouds[33] or the stratosphere in order to reflect solar radiation back into space.[34] The most extraordinary solutions seek to deflect rather than

the Southern Ocean," *Science* 304 (2004): 414–417; P. Boyd, "A Mesoscale Phytoplankton Bloom in the Polar Southern Ocean Stimulated by Iron Fertilization," *Nature* 407 (2000): 695–702; R.E. Zeebe and D. Archer, "Feasibility of Ocean Fertilization and its Impact on Future Atmospheric CO_2 Levels," *Geophysical Research Letters* 32 (2005): L09703; S. Blain, B. Quéguiner, L. Armand et al., "Effect of Natural Iron Fertilization on Carbon Sequestration in the Southern Ocean," *Nature* 446 (2007): 1070–1074; R.T. Pollard, I. Salter, R.J. Sanders et al., "Southern Ocean Deep-water Carbon Export Enhanced by Natural Iron Fertilization," *Nature* 457 (2009): 577–580.

30   L.D.D. Harvey, "Mitigating the Atmospheric CO_2 Increase and Ocean Acidification by Adding Limestone Powder to Upwelling Regions," *Journal of Geophysical Research* 113 (2008): C04028 doi: 10.1029/2007JC004373; H.S. Kheshgi, "Sequestering Atmospheric Carbon Dioxide by Increasing Ocean Alkalinity," *Energy* 20 (1995): 915–922.

31   J.C. Stephens and D.W. Keith, "Assessing Geochemical Carbon Management," *Climatic Change* 90 (2008): 217–242 at 228.

32   H. Akbari, S. Menon and A. Rosenfeld, "Global Cooling: Increasing World-wide Urban Albedos to Offset CO_2," *Climatic Change* 94 (2009): 275–298 at 277; R.M. Hamwey, "Active Amplification of the Terrestrial Albedo to Mitigate Climate Change: An Exploratory Study," *Mitigation and Adaptation Strategies for Global Change* 12 (2007): 419–439.

33   J. Latham, P. Rasch, C.C. Chen et al., "Global Temperature Stabilization via Controlled Albedo Enhancement of Low-level Maritime Clouds," *Philosophical Transactions of the Royal Society A* 366 (2008): 3969–3987; S. Salter, G. Sortino and J. Latham, "Sea-going Hardware for the Cloud Albedo Method of Reversing Global Warming," *Philosophical Transactions of the Royal Society A* 366 (2008): 3989–4006.

34   See n. 9 above; R.E. Dickinson, "Climate Engineering: A Review of Aerosol Approaches to Changing the Global Energy Balance," *Climatic Change* 33 (1996): 279–290; Y.A. Izrael, "Field Experiment on Studying Solar Radiation Passing through Aerosol Layers," *Russian Meteorology and Hydrology* 34 (2009): 265–278; P.J. Rasch, S. Tilmes, R.P. Turco et al., "An Overview of Geoengineering of Climate Using Stratospheric Sulphate Aerosols," *Philosophical Transactions of the Royal Society A* 366 (2008): 4007–4037; A. Robock,

reflect solar radiation through the placement of strategic mirrors or sunshades between the Earth and the sun or in orbit around the Earth.[35]

Most of these geoengineering proposals embody a level of risk to the global environment.[36] Stratospheric whitening, for example, risks potential damage to the ozone layer[37] and the disruption of rainfall patterns across Asia and Africa.[38] Ocean fertilization, on the other hand, may lead to toxic algal blooms,[39] eutrophication and anoxia,[40] and even the release of other greenhouse gases such as nitrous oxide.[41] Techniques such as reforestation[42] and

L. Oman and G.L. Stenchikov, "Regional Climate Responses to Geoengineering with Tropical and Arctic SO_2 Injections," *Journal of Geophysical Research* 113 (2008): D16101 doi:10.1029/2008JD010050; A.F. Tuck, D.J. Donaldson, M.H. Hitchman et al., "On Geoengineering with Sulphate Aerosols in the Tropical Upper Troposphere and Lower Stratosphere," *Climatic Change* 90 (2008): 315–331.

35   See R. Angel, "Feasibility of Cooling the Earth with a Cloud of Small Spacecraft Near the Inner Legrange Point (L1)," *Proceedings of the National Academy of the Sciences of the United States of America* 103, no. 46 (2006): 17184–17189; J.T. Early, "Space-based Solar Shield to Offset Greenhouse Effect," *Journal of the British Planetary Society* 42 (1989): 567–569; T. Kosugi, "Role of Sunshades in Space as a Climate Control Option," *Acta Astronautica* 67 (2010): 241–253; D.J. Lunt, A. Ridgwell, P.J. Valdes et al., "'Sunshade World': A Fully Coupled CGM Evaluation of the Climatic Impacts of Geoengineering," *Geophysical Research Letters* 35 (2008): L12710 doi:10.1029/2008GL033674; C.R. McInnes, "Space-based Geoengineering: Challenges and Requirements," *Proceedings of the Institute of Mechanical Engineers, Part C: Journal of Mechanical Engineering Science* 224, no. 3 (2010): 571–580; J. Pearson, J. Oldson and E. Levin, "Earth Rings for Planetary Environment Control," *Acta Astronautica* 58 (2006): 44–57.

36   For a comparison of these risks see P.W. Boyd, "Ranking Geo-engineering Schemes," *Geoscience* 1 (2008): 722–724; T.A. Fox and L. Chapman, "Review: Engineering Geo-engineering," *Meteorological Applications* 18 (2011): 1–8.

37   S. Tilmes, R. Müller and R. Salawitch, "The Sensitivity of Polar Ozone Depletion to Proposed Geoengineering Schemes," *Science* 320 (2008): 1201–1204 at 1204.

38   Robock et al., n. 34 above.

39   C.G. Trick, B.D. Bill, W.P. Cochlan et al., "Iron Enrichment Stimulates Toxic Diatom Production in High-nitrate, Low-chlorophyll Areas," *Proceedings of the National Academy of Sciences* 107 (2010): 5887–5892 at 5587.

40   Lampitt et al., n. 28 above, p. 3930.

41   C.S. Law, "Predicting and Monitoring the Effects of Large-scale Ocean Iron Fertilization on Marine Trace Gas Emissions," *Marine Ecology Progress Series* 364 (2008): 283–288. See also M.G. Lawrence, "Side Effects of Oceanic Iron Fertilization," *Science* 297 (2002): 1993; J.A. Furhrman and D.G. Capone, "Possible Biogeochemical Consequences of Ocean Fertilization," *Limnology and Oceanography* 36, no. 8 (1991): 1951–1959.

42   Reforestation and afforestation may nevertheless create a risk to biodiversity where, for example, old growth forest is replaced with few or even a single species such as pine.

urban albedo enhancement are relatively low risk, but are equally unlikely to make a sufficient contribution to reducing the impacts of climate change to make them worthwhile.[43] More generally, none of these techniques have been proven in terms of their effectiveness to mitigate climate change[44] and most are based on technologies or mechanisms that will require a huge investment of resources and are simply not economic.[45] For example, to draw down a meaningful level of CO_2 from the atmosphere scientists have estimated that an area larger than the Southern Ocean would have to be fertilized with iron.[46] The delivery of sulphate aerosols designed to whiten the stratosphere would apparently require millions of flights of four-hour duration every year.[47] The potential costs associated with space-related geoengineering are even more formidable with commentators and the US government recently concluding that the economics of such technologies are simply not viable.[48] Moreover, all of these strategies, with the exception of ocean weathering, are focused on either removing CO_2 from the atmosphere or reducing the surface temperature of the Earth. They do not seek to address the 'other' climate change problem: ocean acidification.[49] In fact, to the extent that they involve increasing the ocean reservoir of CO_2, deliberately through fertilization or 'naturally' through

---

43   2009 Royal Society Report on Geoengineering, n. 18 above, p. 34.

44   Most research to date has focused on ocean fertilization. For a discussion of the results of the key experiments to date, see Buesseler et al., n. 29 above; Boyd, n. 29 above; Zeebe and Archer, n. 29 above; Blain, Quéguiner and Armand et al., n. 29 above; Pollard et al., n. 29 above.

45   For a discussion of the relative economics of geoengineering, see *2009 Royal Society Geoengineering Report,* n. 18 above; S. Barrett, "The Incredible Economics of Geo-engineering," *Environmental Resource Economics* 39 (2008): 45–54; Boyd, n. 36 above; Fox and Chapman, n. 36 above; T.M. Lenton and N.E. Vaughan, "The Radiative Forcing Potential of Different Climate Geoengineering Options," *Atmospheric Chemistry and Physics* 9 (2009): 5539–5561; J.E. Bickel and L. Lane, "Climate Engineering," in *Smart Solutions to Climate Change. Comparing Costs and Benefits,* ed. B. Borg (Cambridge: Cambridge University Press, 2010), pp. 9–51; R.A. Pielke, Jr, "Climate Engineering: Alternative Perspective," in *Smart Solutions to Climate Change. Comparing Costs and Benefits,* ed. B. Borg (Cambridge: Cambridge University Press, 2010), pp. 52–61.

46   See Buesseler et al., n. 29 above; K.O. Buesseler and P.W. Boyd, "Will Ocean Fertilization Work?" *Science* 300 (2003), p. 67.

47   Rasch et al., n. 34 above, pp. 4030–4031.

48   Kosugi, n. 35 above, p. 253; *Engineering the Climate Report,* n. 20 above, p. 42.

49   Ocean acidity has increased by 30 percent since 1750 and it is estimated that it could increase by 150 percent by 2050. See Secretariat of the Convention on Biological Diversity, *Scientific Synthesis of the Impacts of Ocean Acidification on Marine Biodiversity* (Technical Series No. 46) (Montreal: Secretariat of the Convention on Biological Diversity, 2009), p. 9.

a focus on solar radiation management rather than emissions control, geoengineering is likely to make ocean acidification much worse.[50]

In 'normal' times an assessment of the environmental risks, economic costs and potential benefits of geoengineering would counsel against manipulating planetary systems for any purpose. But these are not normal times. Atmospheric concentration of CO_2 has increased by 40 percent since pre-industrial times.[51] Arctic sea-ice shrank to its lowest recorded level in September 2012.[52] The first decade of the 21st century was characterized by extreme weather events and was the warmest since records began in 1850.[53] The costs of climate change inaction are just beginning to be calculated with one report suggesting that damage could amount to more than 20 percent of annual global GDP.[54] Globally, States have failed to put in place mechanisms to reduce emissions of greenhouse gases, and the rise of newly industrial States such as China, India, and Brazil is now a major contributing factor to emission increases.[55] Notably, none of the major emitters of greenhouse gases has signed up to the Doha Amendments to the 1997 Kyoto Protocol agreed to in 2012.[56] The ethical and legal evaluation of the risks and benefits of geoengineering must therefore be undertaken within the broader ethical context of climate change itself. To an increasing minority, geoengineering provides a potential solution, essentially a 'get out of jail free' option to solve climate change.

Geoengineering and the Current Regulatory Framework

Geoengineering, with two narrow exceptions, is not subject to explicit regulation. However, these activities do not take place within a legal vacuum.[57] To

---

50   Increased levels of ocean acidification have implications for coral, calcifying marine organisms, and coastal defences. See S.C. Doney, W.M. Balch, V.J. Fabry et al., "Ocean Acidification: A Critical Emerging Problem for the Oceans," *Oceanography* 22 (2009): 16–25.

51   IPCC 2013, see n. 3 above, p. 11.

52   J. Blunden, D.S. Arndt, eds., "State of the Climate in 2012: Special Supplement to the *Bulletin of the American Meteorology Society*," *Bulletin of the American Meteorology Society* 94, no. 8 (August 2013), p. 111, available online: <http://dx.doi.org/10.1175/2013BAMSStateo ftheClimate.1>.

53   World Meteorological Organization, *The Global Climate 2001–2010. A Decade of Climate Extremes* (Geneva: World Meteorology Organization, 2013).

54   N. Stern, *The Economics of Climate Change: The Stern Review* (London: HM Treasury, 2007).

55   Available online: <http://www.epa.gov/climatechange/ghgemissions/global.html#four>.

56   The amendments are not yet in force. Available online: <http://unfccc.int/kyoto_protocol/ doha_amendment/items/7362.php>.

57   The legal literature on geoengineering is growing steadily. In particular, see D. Bodansky, "May we Engineer the Climate?," *Climatic Change* 33 (1996): 309–321; W.C.G. Burns,

date, three regimes have sought to address the environmental consequences of geoengineering, using, thus far, primarily soft-law mechanisms in respect of particular geoengineering techniques. More generally, a number of fundamental principles of international environmental law apply to any activity, including geoengineering, that pose a significant risk to the environment and operate to constrain such activities.

The first regime of direct application to geoengineering is the 1997 Kyoto Protocol, which promotes the enhancement of forest sinks and permits States to count reforestation and afforestation activities against their overall targets to reduce greenhouse gases as set out in Article 3 of the Protocol. Initiatives adopted in 2010 and 2011 have, in fact, created new incentives to reduce emissions from deforestation[58] and a wider range of land-use change activities are currently being considered for potential eligibility under the Clean Development Mechanism.[59] Proponents of reforestation and land-use change activities tend not to describe these techniques as geoengineering on account of the negative connotations associated with the term, but these techniques do fall within the classic definition of geoengineering. The climate change regime does not address geoengineering more generally, although its objective, to stabilize "greenhouse gas concentrations in the atmosphere at a level that would prevent dangerous anthropogenic interference with the climate system,"[60] would appear to preclude an endorsement of solar radiation management techniques that seek to reduce surface temperature without addressing the level of atmospheric CO_2.

Second, the 1992 Biodiversity Convention has provided a forum for a discussion of the implications of geoengineering for biodiversity on three occasions. The conference of the parties adopted a decision in 2008, calling on parties to refrain from ocean fertilization until it can be justified by science and

---

"Climate Geoengineering: Solar Radiation Management and its Implications for Intergenerational Equity," *Stanford Journal of Law, Science and Policy* 4 (2011): 38–55; K.N. Scott, "International Law in the Anthropocene: Responding to the Geoengineering Challenge," *Michigan Journal of International Law* 34 (2013): 309–358; D.G. Victor, "On the Regulation of Geoengineering," *Oxford Review of Economic Policy* 24, no. 2 (2008): 322–336; J. Virgo, "International Governance of a Possible Geoengineering Intervention to Combat Climate Change," *Climatic Change* 95 (2009): 103–119.

58   Decision 1/CP.16 *The Cancun Agreements: Outcome of the work of the Ad Hoc Working Group on Long-term Cooperative Action under the Convention* adopted by the Conference of the Parties, eighteenth session, 29 November–10 December 2010, Cancun, Mexico.

59   Decision 2/CMP.7 *Land Use, Land-use Change and Forestry* adopted by the Conference of the Parties, seventeenth session, 28 November–9 December 2011, Durban, South Africa.

60   UNFCCC, n. 13 above, Article 2.

subjected to an effective regulatory mechanism[61] and further decisions were adopted in 2010 and 2012, which more generally cautioned parties against the deployment of climate-related geoengineering in the absence of a science-based, global, transparent, and effective control mechanism.[62] All three decisions, while undoubtedly persuasive, are nevertheless non-binding.

Third, the 1972 London Convention[63] and 1996 London Protocol[64] have collectively provided the principal forum for addressing, and developing a regime in respect of, ocean fertilization.[65] The general applicability of the dumping regime to ocean fertilization activities has been much debated in light of whether the iron or other ocean fertilizer is 'disposed of' for the purpose of the

---

61   CBD Decision IX/16 *Biodiversity and Climate Change* adopted by the Conference of the Parties, ninth meeting, 19–30 May 2008, Bonn, Germany, at para. C.4.

62   CBD Decision X/33 *Biodiversity and Climate Change* adopted by the Conference of the Parties, tenth meeting, 18–29 October 2010, Nagoya, Japan, at para. 8(w); CBD Decision XI/20 (2012) *Climate-related Geoengineering* adopted by the Conference of the Parties, twelfth meeting, 8–19 October 2012, Hyderabad, India.

63   1972 Convention on the Prevention of Marine Pollution by Dumping of Wastes and other Matter, 11 *International Legal Materials* (1972) 1294 (in force 30 August 1975) [London Convention].

64   1996 Protocol to the London Dumping Convention, 36 *International Legal Materials* (1997) 7 (in force 24 March 2006) [1996 Protocol].

65   See C. Bertram, "Ocean Iron Fertilization in the Context of the Kyoto Protocol and the Post-Kyoto Process," *Energy Policy* 38 (2010): 1130–1139; D. Freestone and R. Rayfuse, "Ocean Iron Fertilization and International Law," *Marine Ecology Progress Series* 364 (2008): 227–233; K. Güssow, A. Proelss, A. Oschlies et al., "Ocean Iron Fertilization: Why Further Research is Needed," *Marine Policy* 34 (2010): 911–918; R. Rayfuse, "Drowning Our Sorrows to Create a Carbon Free Future? Some International Legal Considerations Relating to Sequestering Carbon by Fertilizing the Oceans," *University of New South Wales Law Journal* 14 (2008): 919–930; R. Rayfuse, M.G. Lawrence and K.M. Gjerde, "Ocean Fertilisation and Climate Change: The Need to Regulate Emerging High Seas Uses," *International Journal of Marine and Coastal Law* 23 (2008): 297–326; K.N. Scott, "Exploiting the Oceans for Climate Change Mitigation: Case Study on Iron Fertilization," in *Proceedings of the 2011 Law of the Sea Institute Conference: The Limits of Maritime Jurisdiction*, eds. C. Schofield and S. Lee (Leiden: Martinus Nijhoff, 2014), pp. 653–677; P. Verlaan, "Geo-engineering, the Law of the Sea, and Climate Change," *The Carbon and Climate Law Review* 4 (2009): 446–458; P. Verlaan, "Current Legal Developments: London Convention and London Protocol," *International Journal of Marine and Coastal Law* 26 (2011): 185–194; R. Warner, "Preserving a Balanced Ocean: Regulating Climate Change Mitigation Activities in Marine Areas beyond National Jurisdiction," *Australian International Law Journal* 14 (2007): 99–120; R. Warner, "Marine Snow Storms: Assessing the Environmental Risks of Ocean Fertilization," *The Carbon and Climate Law Review* 4 (2009): 426–436.

Convention/Protocol[66] or whether it can be characterized as constituting 'placement' which is not contrary to the aims of either instrument.[67] A detailed analysis of the applicability of the dumping regime to ocean fertilization has been undertaken by the author elsewhere,[68] but as it currently stands, the tighter regulation as developed by the 1996 Protocol would potentially preclude ocean fertilization for climate-related purposes[69] in contrast to the more flexible approach embodied in the 1972 Convention.[70] The Protocol however, binds only 44 States to date,[71] and it is the more permissive standards as set out in the 1972 Convention that are designated the international standards relating to dumping, and which are globally applicable by virtue of Article 210(6) of the 1982 United Nations Convention on the Law of the Sea (UNCLOS).[72] In order to bridge the gap between the two instruments, and to promote a unified approach between the Convention and Protocol, the parties to the dumping regime adopted, in 2008, a resolution which declared ocean fertilization activities, other than legitimate scientific research, to be contrary to the aims of both instruments.[73] While undoubtedly persuasive, this resolution, like those issued by the conference of the parties to the Biodiversity Convention, is formally non-binding. The focus of the parties to the London Protocol since 2008 has been developing principles to govern ocean fertilization for scientific research purposes. Relying on the placement for a purpose other than disposal exception under the Protocol, ocean fertilization for scientific research purposes has

---

66   London Convention, n. 63 above, Article III(1)(a); 1996 Protocol, n. 64 above, Article 1.4.1.

67   London Convention, n. 63 above, Article III(1)(b); 1996 Protocol, n. 64 above, Article 1.4.2.

68   In particular, see K.N. Scott, "Regulating Ocean Fertilization under International Law: The Risks," *The Carbon and Climate Law Review* (2013): 108–116.

69   The 1996 Protocol, n. 64 above, adopts a reverse listing procedure whereby only substances listed in Annex I of the Protocol may be dumped subject to conditions set out under the Protocol. It is unlikely that Annex I of the Protocol can be interpreted to include the substances likely to be used for ocean fertilization such as iron.

70   The 1972 Convention, n. 63 above, lists substances that may not be dumped in Annex I and substances that may be dumped subject to a special permit in Annex II. Substances not listed in either annex may be dumped subject to a general permit. It is unlikely that the ocean fertilizers under consideration are listed in either annex I or II and therefore it might be presumed that they can be dumped subject to the other conditions of the Convention.

71   By contrast, the 1972 Convention has 87 parties.

72   UNCLOS does not specify the origin of the international standards that are binding on all 166 parties but Articles 210 and 216 have been interpreted to refer to the 1972 Convention. See R.R. Churchill and A.V. Lowe, *The Law of the Sea*, 3rd ed. (Manchester: Manchester University Press, 1999), p. 369.

73   Resolution LC-LP.1 (2008) *on the Regulation of Ocean Fertilization* (31 October 2008).

been deemed compatible with the Protocol provided it is carried out in accordance with the risk assessment framework adopted in 2010.[74] This position was formalized in October 2013 when the parties to the Protocol adopted amendments, inserting a new Article 6*bis* and two new annexes into the Protocol. Article 6*bis* prohibits "the placement of matter into the sea from vessels, aircraft, platforms or other man-made structures at sea for marine geo-engineering activities listed in annex 4, unless the listing provides that the activity or sub-category of an activity may be authorised under a permit."[75] Article 6*bis* goes on to stipulate that parties must adopt administrative measures relating to the issue of permits for geoengineering purposes where the activity has undergone an assessment "which has determined that pollution of the marine environment from the proposed activity is, as far as practicable, prevented or reduced to a minimum."[76] While the definition of geoengineering for the purposes of the Protocol is not confined to activities that involve the abandonment, disposal, or placement of matter in the ocean,[77] the regulatory reach of the Protocol is currently confined to ocean fertilization activities.[78] Moreover, these amendments are not yet in force.

The final instrument that is worth highlighting is the 1976 UN Convention on the Prohibition of Military or any Other Hostile Use of Environmental Modification Techniques (the ENMOD Convention).[79] The Convention seeks to regulate 'environmental modification' under Article II of the Convention but the definition of environmental modification undoubtedly encompasses

---

74   Resolution LC.LP.2 (2010) *on the Assessment Framework for Scientific Research Involving Ocean Fertilization.*

75   Article 6*bis*(1) of the amended Protocol (not yet in force).

76   Article 6*bis*(2) of the amended Protocol (not yet in force).

77   For the purposes of the Protocol, geoengineering is defined under Article 1(5)*bis* of the Protocol (not yet in force) as "a deliberate intervention in the marine environment to manipulate natural processes, including to counteract anthropogenic climate change and/ or its impacts, and that has the potential to result in deleterious effects, especially where those effects may be widespread, long lasting or severe."

78   For a more detailed analysis of these amendments and the application of the law of the sea more generally to geoengineering, see K.N. Scott, "Geoengineering and the Law of the Sea," *Research Handbook on International Marine Environmental Law*, ed. R. Rayfuse (*forthcoming*, Edward Elgar, 2015).

79   1976 UN Convention on the Prohibition of Military or any Other Hostile Use of Environmental Modification Techniques, 16 *International Legal Materials* (1977) 88 (in force 5 October 1978) [ENMOD Convention]; J. Goldblat, "The Environmental Modification Convention of 1977: An Analysis," in *Environmental Warfare, A Technical, Legal and Policy Appraisal*, ed. A.H. Westing, (London and Philadelphia: Taylor & Francis, 1984), pp. 53–64.

geoengineering.[80] However, the focus of ENMOD is on limiting environmental modification for military or hostile purposes,[81] and Article III(1) of the Convention expressly stipulates that "[t]he provisions of this Convention shall not hinder the use of environmental modification techniques for peaceful purposes and shall be without prejudice to the generally recognized principles and applicable rules of international law concerning such use."[82] Therefore, while the ENMOD Convention does create a number of obligations relating to cooperation and notification in relation to environmental modification applicable to the 76 States party to the Convention, its value as a broader framework instrument for geoengineering is limited.

More generally, however, geoengineering undoubtedly creates a significant risk of serious harm to the global environment and, as such, is consequently subject to customary and other obligations of international environmental law that are designed to minimize or manage those risks. Such principles arguably include the prevention of harm; the prevention of pollution; the obligation to protect vulnerable ecosystems and species; the precautionary principle; principles of cooperation, information exchange, and environmental impact assessment; the principle of due regard for other users; and the principle of State responsibility.[83] Moreover, to the extent that these principles are customary in nature they are also *erga onmes* in the sense of being owed to the international community as a whole.[84] However, their customary origin, external to any individual treaty regime, also leads to a level of uncertainty with respect to their content and the interpretation of that content by individual States.

---

80   Article II of ENMOD, n. 79 above, defines 'environmental modification techniques' as "any technique for changing – through the deliberate manipulation of natural processes – the dynamics, composition or structure of the Earth, including its biota, lithosphere, hydrosphere and atmosphere, or of outer space."

81   Id., Article I.

82   Interestingly, earlier drafts of ENMOD had a broader application and sought to outlaw environmental modification, including climate modification, for military and other purposes incompatible with the "maintenance of international security, human well-being and health." See L. Juda, "Negotiating a Treaty on Environmental Modification Warfare: The Convention on Environmental Warfare and its Impact on Arms Control Negotiations," *International Organization* 32 (1978): 975–991 at 978. This earlier draft was developed by the then Soviet Union but narrowed at the behest of the United States. See id., p. 979.

83   See further Scott, n. 57 above, pp. 333–350.

84   On the nature of *erga omnes* obligations in international law, see M. Ragazzi, *The Concept of International Obligations* Erga Omnes (Oxford: Clarendon Press, 1997); C.J. Tams, *Enforcing Obligations* Erga Omnes *in International Law* (Cambridge: Cambridge University Press, 2005).

Consequently, while these principles may serve to constrain the most radical of geoengineering activities, designed to have a major impact on the atmosphere, biosphere or hydrosphere, their restraining influence may be more limited with respect to less ambitious proposals or geoengineering-related research. Moreover, the decentralized nature of international law currently places individual States as interpreters and arbiters of these general obligations. International environmental law as it currently stands therefore represents the start but not the end of the regulatory framework for geoengineering.

Regulatory and Ethical Issues Associated with Geoengineering

Today, climate change is as much an ethical problem as an environmental one.[85] No State seriously contests that climate change represents a serious if not the most serious environmental challenge in human history or that humanity bears the overwhelming responsibility for its cause. The climate change regime is arguably the most complex and indeed controversial of any environmental regime. It is also one of the least successful. As individuals, corporations, and governments we know what we *should* do to respond to climate change: reduce emissions, change patterns of consumption, and develop means of sustainable growth. But as individuals, corporations, and governments, we have thus far proven largely unwilling to make those changes, refusing to face the prospect that unsustainable patterns of consumption could be considered morally or ethically wrongful.[86] One commentator has gone so far as to suggest that the typical individual's attitude towards fossil fuels in the 21st century can be compared to the attitude of slave-owners' towards slaves in the 18th and 19th centuries.[87]

Geoengineering, as a solution to climate change, can be similarly characterized as much an ethical issue as an environmental one. In addition to

---

85   See P. Harris, *World Ethics and Climate Change: From International to Global Justice* (Edinburgh: Edinburgh University Press, 2010); T. Hayward, "Human Rights versus Emissions Rights: Climate Justice and the Equitable Distribution of Ecological Space," *Ethics & International Affairs* 21, no. 4 (2007): 431–450; E.A. Posner and D. Weisbach, *Climate Change Justice* (Princeton: Princeton University Press, 2010).

86   See generally C. Hamilton, *Requiem for a Species. Why We Resist the Truth about Climate Change* (London: Earthscan, 2010).

87   J.F. Mouhot, "Past Connections and Present Similarities in Slave Ownership and Fossil Fuel Usage," *Climatic Change* 105 (2011): 329–355. For a response to this thesis see: J.P. Howe, "History and Climate: A Road Map to Humanistic Scholarship on Climate Change," *Climatic Change* 105 (2011): 357–363.

managing the risks posed by geoengineering to the global environment, and responding to the formidable technical and economic challenges it presents, scientists, policy-makers, and individuals also need to engage with the ethics of geoengineering.[88] The central question for this article is whether the ethics of geoengineering can be meaningfully engaged within the framework of international law. The brief description of the regulatory framework of application to geoengineering provided above demonstrates that there are limitations on geoengineering activity where that activity is likely to result in serious environmental harm. However, those limitations are fragmented between multiple regimes and customary obligations, and rely overwhelmingly on interpretation, implementation, and enforcement by States themselves. The opportunity for debating the ethical, as opposed to environmental, risks associated with geoengineering within the international legal framework is currently largely non-existent. Yet these ethical risks are equally important to the decision as to whether we engineer the planet to combat climate change.

In the penultimate section of this article, five ethical concerns associated with geoengineering are identified and examined in order to explore the extent to which those concerns can be addressed within the current framework of international law. These ethical issues comprise: the ethics or morals of large-scale manipulation of planetary systems for climate change mitigation; the relationship between geoengineering and other means of climate change mitigation, particularly emissions reduction; the regulation of geoengineering at the research stage; the extent of public participation in decision-making relating to geoengineering; and the control of private enterprise in geoengineering activities. The need to address these ethical issues – alongside managing environmental concerns associated with geoengineering – will provide the foundation for the development of a proposal for the management of geoengineering in the final part of this article.

The Ethics or Morals of Geoengineering

With its modern secular Anglo-European foundations, international law is traditionally non-hierarchical and has generally refrained from prioritizing one set of values over another. This, however, is beginning to change. The advent of the human rights movement in the 1940s and the recognition of environmental values in the 1970s have begun the process of identifying a core set of international values from which States are creating fundamental concepts and

---

88   For an excellent introduction to the ethics of geoengineering, see C. Hamilton, *Earth Masters. Playing God with the Climate* (New South Wales, Australia: Allen and Unwin, 2013).

principles and even a nascent hierarchy of obligations – through the concept of *jus cogens* – within international law. States have made moral or ethical judgments on issues such as the use of chemical weapons and the prohibition of genocide. Even within the context of climate change itself, States have decided that its affects are the common concern of humankind and have acknowledged the historical responsibility of developed States in terms of both the problem and the solution.[89]

To date, however, there has been little inter-governmental debate over the ethics or morals of geoengineering as a response to climate change.[90] Rather, as a consequence of the absence of an appropriate international forum, the international response to geoengineering so far has been fragmented and limited. Ocean fertilization has received the most regulatory attention to date, under the auspices of the dumping regime, and the efforts of the parties to develop a binding comprehensive and sophisticated risk assessment framework are commendable. However, at no stage have the parties engaged in any real debate as to the ethics of ocean fertilization as a climate change mitigation measure. Furthermore, it might even be suggested that it is not appropriate for the parties to engage with broader ethical issues associated with geoengineering: it is debatable whether the Protocol provides a suitable mandate to address marine geoengineering – not involving the placement of matter in the sea – more generally, and it is quite clear that the dumping regime is not the appropriate forum to address terrestrial, atmospheric, or space-based geoengineering. However, the current pragmatic but fragmented approach to geoengineering regulation risks the inadvertent endorsement of geoengineering, by implication, as a climate change mitigation measure. The adoption of recent amendments to the London Protocol have, for example, effectively endorsed and authorized climate-related ocean fertilization research activities provided those activities meet certain environmental criteria under the Risk Assessment Framework and operate under permits issued by State parties. Other regimes may follow suit. While individual regimes may have the appropriate expertise to regulate individual geoengineering activities and to set down conditions in order to protect the environmental sphere they have responsibility for – whether that is the ocean, biosphere or atmosphere – they do not, and arguably cannot, address the broader ethical question: should we geoengineer our planet in order to mitigate the negative effects of climate change? We need to

---

89   UNFCCC, n. 13 above, Preamble.
90   This is in noted contrast to ethical debates within academic literature and through civil society groups.

identify or create an international forum within which this fundamental debate can take place.

Geoengineering and Emissions Reductions

The question as to whether we *should* mitigate climate change through geoengineering is closely related to the second ethical issue: the relationship between geoengineering and other climate change mitigation strategies, including emissions reductions. Arguably the greatest ethical risk associated with geoengineering is the so-called moral hazard: that geoengineering will divert attention and resources from emissions reductions, and will effectively be regarded as a 'get out of jail free' option for governments reluctant to commit to reductions.[91] Given the urgency of the need to take action, any delay, while States explore alternative technological options, could render measures such as emissions reductions redundant and make the much more drastic option offered by geoengineering inevitable. Geoengineering has to be considered alongside, rather than in isolation of, other climate change mitigation options and its relationship to those options needs to be actively explored.

Regulating the Scientists

The third ethical issue is by no means confined to the context of geoengineering but is perhaps most clearly demonstrated by it: the regulation and control of scientific research. All geoengineering is currently at the research stage and most is at the very early pre-field trial stage of research. To what extent should research and scientists be subject to international regulatory control and should some forms of research be prohibited?

The freedom to engage in scientific research is valued by most if not all societies. While there is no legal right to conduct scientific research,[92] "pursuit of scientific knowledge is an area in which absolute freedom of the individual to act has been a marked philosophical concept."[93] In part, this view is justified on the basis that research and indeed technology are inherently neutral in terms of values, and regulation consequently only becomes relevant at the

---

91   See A.C. Lin, "Does Geoengineering Present a Moral Hazard?" *Ecology Law Quarterly* 40 (2013): 673–712.

92   The closest we have to such a right is Article 27 of the 1948 United Nations Declaration on Human Rights, which asserts that "everyone has the right freely to participate in the cultural life of the community, to enjoy the arts and to share in scientific advancement and its benefits" and "everyone has the right to the protection of the moral and material interests resulting from any scientific, literary or artistic production of which he is the author."

93   A. McKnight, "International Regulation of Science and Technology," *International Journal* 25 (1969–1970): 745–753 at 745.

point of application.[94] However, the division between research and application is increasingly permeable and, in some cases, non-existent.[95] Scientific and technological research carried out by Nazi scientists and engineers during the Second World War perhaps provide the most graphic illustrations of the creation of value-laden technology.[96] But scientists and engineers need not harbor nefarious purposes in order for their research to fundamentally challenge or even transform international society irrespective of application. Moreover, as demonstrated by the history of nuclear research and regulation, controlling a technology once it has been developed can be challenging if not effectively impossible.[97] On a more mundane level, scientists, engineers, and institutions become invested in research, and the longer it is left before that research is subject to regulation the more difficult it is to root out ethically misguided projects.[98]

Research into geoengineering is arguably value-laden. The purpose of that research is to develop a quick-fix for climate change. The distinction between research and application is consequently particularly permeable if not non-existent in the context of geoengineering research. More subtly, the very fact that research is taking place into geoengineering will affect (arguably, is already affecting) how political and policy debates on climate change are framed. Confining regulation to the application as opposed to the research stage of geoengineering constitutes the equivalent of closing the stable door after the proverbial horse has bolted. But how should scientific research into geoengineering be controlled and who should set the scientific agenda?

Traditionally, scientists favor decentralized ethical frameworks either at the individual or institutional level,[99] or within an area or industry, often referred

---

94   H.E. Douglas, *Science, Policy, and the Value-Free Ideal* (Pittsburgh: University of Pittsburgh Press, 2009).

95   See L. Winner, *The Whale and the Reactor. A Search for Limits in an Age of High Technology* (Chicago: The University of Chicago Press, 1986).

96   E. Katz, "The Nazi Engineers: Reflections on Technological Ethics in Hell," *Science and Engineering Ethics* 17 (2011): 571–582; E. Katz, "On the Neutrality of Technology: The Holocaust Death Camps as a Counter Example," *Journal of Genocide Research* 7 (2005): 409–421.

97   See R.E. Goodin, "No Moral Nukes," *Ethics* 90 (1980): 417–449; J. Granoff, "Nuclear Weapons, Ethics, Morals, and Law," *Brigham Young University Law Review* (2000): 1413–1442.

98   R. Roache, "Ethics, Speculation, and Values," *Nanoethics* 2 (2008): 317–327 at 323.

99   See P.A.E. Brey, "Anticipatory Ethics for Emerging Technologies," *Nanoethics* 6, no. 1 (2012): 1–13; European Group on Ethics in Science and New Technologies to the European Commission and S.O. Hansson, "Do we Need a Special Ethics for Research?" *Science and*

to as self-governance.[100] An example of an attempt at self-governance has already occurred with respect to geoengineering. In 2010, a group of geoengineering scientists adopted a set of voluntary guidelines designed to reduce the risks associated with geoengineering at the Asilomar International Conference on Climate Intervention Technologies, modelled on the high-profile 1975 Asilomar Principles on Recombinant DNA Technology.[101] But this highly decentralized approach to the governance of scientific research does not really assist in providing a forum or a framework within which to address those broad ethical questions identified above: *should* we morally engage in geoengineering and how does it relate to other climate change mitigation strategies such as emissions reductions? One potential option is to provide scientists with guidelines or even binding terms and conditions to guide their research. This is the approach which has been adopted within the dumping regime in respect of ocean fertilization. The Risk Assessment Framework developed under the auspices of the 1996 London Protocol, which is not yet binding, sets out detailed conditions and processes that scientists based in States party to the regime should comply with before engaging in ocean fertilization experimentation. The question is: How far should regulation interfere with the freedom of scientific research and who should decide the level of control, or even whether certain areas of research should be prohibited altogether?

Democratizing Geoengineering

The question 'who decides?', raised above in the context of the regulation of scientific research, is fundamental to the fourth ethical issue associated with geoengineering. Just as climate change is likely to affect all States regardless of their respective contributions to greenhouse gas emissions, environmental changes wrought by geoengineers are likely to be equally globally applicable. The question – who decides – is therefore of great significance. Geoengineering technologies are such that a decision to engineer a planetary solution to climate change could potentially be made by a group of States, or a single State or even a corporation acting unilaterally. But all States have an interest in that

---

Engineering Ethics 17 (2011), p. 21; A. Nordmann, "If and Then: A Critique of Speculative NanoEthics," *Nanoethics* 1 (2007), p. 31; Roache, id., p. 317.

100   P.L. Taylor, "Scientific Self-Regulation. So Good, How Can it Fail? Commentary on the Problems with Forbidding Science," *Science Engineering Ethics* 15 (2009), p. 395.

101   M. Leinen, "The Asilomar International Conference on Climate Intervention Technologies: Background and Overview," *Stanford Journal of Law Science and Policy* 4 (2011), p. 1. On the 1975 Asilomar Principles on Recombinant DNA Technology, see S. Wright, "Molecular Biology or Molecular Politics? The Production of Scientific Consensus on the Hazards of Recombinant DNA Technology," *Social Studies of Science* 16 (1986), p. 593.

decision as indeed do groups and interests that transcend typical State boundaries. But does the current international legal framework permit 'democratic'
decision-making (in so far as the notion of democracy can be applied at the
international level) in respect of geoengineering? Certainly the fragmented
regime focusing on the management of environmental risks outlined above is
anything but conducive to maximizing the democratic participation in the
ethical geoengineering debate.

The Geoengineering Philanthropist and Entrepreneur

The final ethical issue, foreshadowed in the previous section, relates to the role
of private actors and geoengineering. Compared to the costs associated with
emissions reductions it has been argued that geoengineering offers a comparatively cheap quick fix.[102] Although the economics of geoengineering are highly
disputed,[103] there exists a very real possibility that technologies could be taken
up by entrepreneurs seeking to make money or generate carbon credits or
even by philanthropists seeking to mitigate climate change for the benefit of
humanity. For example, in July 2012 the Haida Salmon Restoration Corporation
made international headlines when it deliberately dumped 100 metric tonnes
of iron sulphate into the ocean off the coast of western Canada.[104] The scheme,
which dumped five times more iron into the ocean than any of the previous 13
iron fertilization experiments carried out to date,[105] was ostensibly designed to
both increase local salmon populations and, more significantly to sequester
CO_2.[106] Ocean fertilization has in fact generated significant private commercial interest. The most high profile corporation involved in ocean fertilization
is the US-based Climos,[107] however, the Ocean Nourishment Corporation has

---

102   See Barrett, n. 45 above.

103   See the references discussed in n. 45 above.

104   J. Tollefson, "Ocean-fertilization Project Off Canada Sparks Furore," *Nature* 490 (25
       October 2012), p. 458.

105   Id. For an overview of the 13 experiments carried out to date, see D. Wallace, C. Law,
       P. Boyd et al., *Ocean Fertilization. A Scientific Summary for Policy Makers* (Paris: IOC/
       UNESCO, 2010), p. 3.

106   See n. 104 above, p. 458.

107   In 2009, Climos announced plans to fertilize 40,000 square km of the Southern Ocean
       with iron for the sale of carbon offset credits. See A. Strong, "Ocean Fertilization: Time to
       Move On," *Nature* 461 (2009): 347–348. These plans are on hold for the time being. For an
       entertaining description of the activities of Climos, see E. Kintisch, *Hack the Planet.
       Science's Best Hope – or Worst Nightmare – for Averting Climate Catastrophe* (New Jersey:
       John Wiley & Sons, 2010), Chap. 7. See also, M. Leinen, "Building Relationships between
       Scientists and Business in Ocean Iron Fertilization," *Marine Ecology Progress Series* 364

recently conducted urea fertilization experiments in the Sulu Sea[108] and Atmocean, also a US venture, has undertaken experiments with the use of wave-driven pumps to transfer nutrient-rich deep water to the surface.[109] More generally, Bill Gates has been reported to be providing US$1.5 million per year to assist researchers to study geoengineering options.[110] In light of the potential for wide-scale and potentially damaging environmental change to be brought about by private actors, for profit or otherwise, an effective regulatory regime needs to be in place to govern *all* geoengineering activities.

Geoengineering and the Future Regulatory Framework

The response of the international legal community so far to geoengineering has focused on the need to address, manage and minimize its potential negative environmental consequences. The current international legal toolbox is reasonably well-suited to this task. Full-scale and potentially research-related geoengineering activities can be constrained by environmental principles such as no harm and precaution as well as the more specific rules relating to pollution prevention and control and biodiversity conservation established by individual treaty regimes.[111] However, the fragmented, ad hoc approach to geoengineering regulation is much less able to respond to the broader, fundamental ethical questions identified above: is geoengineering a morally appropriate response to climate change and how does it relate to other mitigation measures; what controls should be placed on research activities; and, more generally, who gets to decide – States, scientists or private corporations? Functionally, these questions can only be addressed within a dedicated geoengineering forum and within a legally-binding regulatory framework.[112] There are three potential options for a geoengineering forum.

(2008): 251–256; A.L. Strong, J.J. Cullen and S.W. Chisholm, "Ocean Fertilization. Science, Policy and Commerce," *Oceanography* 22, no. 3 (2009): 236–261.

108   J. Mayo-Ramsay, "Environmental, Legal and Social Implications of Ocean Urea Fertilization; Sulu Sea Example," *Marine Policy* 34 (2010), p. 831. Further trials by the Ocean Nourishment Corporation have also been put on hold.

109   Warner, "Preserving a Balanced Ocean," n. 65 above.

110   See Kintisch, n. 107 above, pp. 8–9.

111   See further Scott, n. 83 above.

112   The preference for a legally binding rather than soft law framework reflects the serious environmental risks associated with geoengineering technologies, which are unlikely to be appropriately managed by non-binding measures.

The first comprises the creation of a designated instrument on geoengineering together with associated institutional bodies such as a conference or meeting of the parties to make decisions and technical bodies to provide advice and supervision. This model follows that typically established by multilateral environmental agreements (MEAs) and provides an effective means of establishing a basic framework agreement within which detailed obligations can follow at a later stage. There are, however, two principal disadvantages to this option. First, as a stand-alone instrument the opportunities for integrating geoengineering options with other climate change mitigation strategies, including emissions reductions, may be limited. Second, more prosaically but just as importantly, States may be unwilling to meet the costs of establishing yet another treaty regime. Treaty congestion is a common lament within the field of international environmental law, with States increasingly preferring to promote cooperation and coordination among existing treaties rather than establishing new ones.[113]

The second option seeks to avoid the full extent of the costs of establishing a new regime by utilizing an existing institution such as the United Nations Environment Programme or the United Nations Educational, Scientific and Cultural Organization (UNESCO). Both organizations provide fora for hosting conferences and the negotiation of treaties and other legal instruments. UNESCO, in particular, has potential in the context of geoengineering given its focus on scientific and research activities. However, many States, including the United States, are traditionally skeptical of the efficacy and efficiency of UN organizations and may be unwilling to support the UN being used as the forum within which geoengineering is ultimately addressed. Like the option of a designated treaty regime, UN bodies may also be seen as operating in isolation to the climate change regime more generally, and geoengineering may be effectively segregated from other climate change mitigation strategies such as emissions reductions.

The final and preferred option utilizes the climate change regime itself as the forum within which a regulatory framework for geoengineering is developed. The 1992 UNFCCC benefits from near universal support and the regime comprises a decision-making body (the conference of the parties) as well as several technical and implementation-related institutions. The framework model developed by the UNFCCC is easily adaptable to addressing new climate-related issues such as geoengineering through the adoption of protocols.

---

113   See K.N. Scott, "International Environmental Governance: Managing Fragmentation through Institutional Connection," *Melbourne Journal of International Law* 12 (2011): 177–216.

The greatest advantage of this option is that geoengineering is properly integrated into the climate change debate and its ethics, environmental risks, and economic costs are evaluated within the broader context of mitigation and adaptation. The biggest risk lies with seeking to address yet another issue within an already stretched and increasingly polarized regime. However, if we want to move beyond our focus on the environmental risks of geoengineering and actually begin to consider its ethics within the framework of international law, the climate change regime represents the best and perhaps the only option.

Concluding Remarks

The failure of the climate change regime to facilitate meaningful State action in reducing emissions demonstrates the dangers of developing a legal response to an environmental problem without sufficient engagement early on with fundamental issues of ethics – in the case of climate change, ethical issues associated with climate justice and the right to (sustainably) develop. But an ethical response to environmental crisis is itself insufficient in the context of actually changing State behavior and providing the institutional infrastructure to enforce and embed that behavioral change. The importance of a combined ethical-legal response is nowhere more clearly demonstrated than in relation to geoengineering. While the ethics of engineering a solution to climate change are increasingly debated in academic literature across multiple disciplines and within civil society arenas, the legal response has thus far been cautiously confined to attempts to manage the negative environmental impacts of particular geoengineering activities within individual regimes. Although this is important, particularly in the short-term, ultimately we need to develop a forum and indeed the tools to address the broader ethical questions posed by geoengineering and, most importantly, whether geoengineering is an efficacious and just response to anthropogenic climate change. We may have unconsciously and inadvertently created the Anthropocene in our relentless quest for progress and civilization but, in the 21st century, we have a conscious responsibility to ensure that we do not create or engineer a 'mis-Anthropocene'.

Ice-Covered Areas under the Law of the Sea Convention: How Extensive are Canada's Coastal State Powers in the Arctic?*

Peter Luttmann[†]
JD Candidate 2015, Schulich School of Law, Dalhousie University
Halifax, Canada

I.   Introduction

In 1970, Canada passed the *Arctic Waters Pollution Prevention Act,*[1] landmark legislation designed to protect its ice-covered waters. Over the ensuing years, Canada added various regulations and measures to complement the Act and carry its purpose into effect. The Act and accompanying measures received a mixed reaction globally, with the United States in particular challenging their validity under international law. Thus, in the wake of and while establishing this controversial Arctic waters regime, Canada endeavored at successive Law of the Sea Conferences to give it international legitimacy.[2] The culmination of these efforts was the inclusion of "Section 8 – Ice-Covered Areas" in Part XII of the 1982 United Nations Convention on the Law of the Sea (LOS Convention). That section contains only one article, Article 234.

The question posed in this article is, did Canada achieve its aim? In other words, does Canada's regulatory scheme for protecting Arctic waters operate

---

*   Editors' Note. – This article was the winning entry in the 2014 *Ocean Yearbook* Student Paper Competition.

†   I wish to thank Professor Aldo Chircop for making this subject area both engaging and challenging, and for his personal encouragement. In particular, he deserves credit for the insight expressed in this article that the wording of Article 234 of the Law of the Sea Convention represents only a snapshot of conditions as they existed in Arctic waters at the time of the Article's drafting, and that the Arctic is an area of dynamic change (See "The Textual Parameters of Article 234: Geographic, Climatic and Temporal Limits" and the concluding paragraph).

1   *Arctic Waters Pollution Prevention Act,* RSC 1985, c A-12 [AWPPA].

2   D. Pharand, "The Arctic Waters and the Northwest Passage: A Final Revisit," *Ocean Development and International Law* 38 (2007): 3–69 at 46; D. McRae, "Rethinking the Arctic: A New Agenda for Canada and the United States," Carleton University Canada-US Project, policy paper 14, 2008, p. 2.

© KONINKLIJKE BRILL NV, LEIDEN, 2015 | DOI 10.1163/9789004297234_006

within the parameters of Article 234 of the LOS Convention? To answer this question, this article first analyses the scope of Article 234, in light of its text and context. Second, it summarizes Canada's Arctic waters regime, noting any inconsistencies with Article 234. Finally, suggestions regarding how Canada might best protect its Arctic waters in the future, via Article 234 or otherwise are offered.

II.   Article 234

A.   *The Contextual Parameters of Article 234*

1.   Historical Context

Prior to the Third United Nations Conference on the Law of the Sea, efforts had failed to draft a comprehensive treaty that would form a 'constitution' for the world's oceans. The primary obstacle to agreement was the tension between, on the one hand, traditional maritime powers such as the United States and the United Kingdom who desired to preserve navigational freedoms, and on the other hand, coastal States who were keen to assert greater influence over the waters off their shores, both to enhance security and to safeguard resources and the marine environment.[3]

Within this setting, there was a push by coastal States to expand their territorial seas beyond the formerly accepted limit of three nautical miles (NM).[4] By the time Canada had declared a 12 NM territorial sea in 1970, there was evidence of customary State practice justifying the extension.[5] By contrast, maritime powers were fighting to maintain freedom of navigation and overflight in and above important navigation routes such as straits.[6] It was in this environment that States negotiated and drafted the LOS Convention, ultimately reaching a compromise entailing a careful balance "between coastal state authority and global freedom of navigation."[7]

So, for example, while under the Convention coastal States enjoy significant powers within the 12 NM limit of their territorial sea, the rights do not

---

3   J. Kraska, "The Law of the Sea Convention and the Northwest Passage," *International Journal of Marine and Coastal Law* 22 (2007): 269–270.

4   J.A. Roach and R.W. Smith, *Excessive Maritime Claims*, 3rd ed. (The Netherlands: Koninklijke Brill NV, 2012), p. 136 (Note trend in table at time when UNCLOS III being drafted (1973–1982)).

5   Pharand, n. 2 above, p. 42.

6   For example, the North Corfu Channel; Pharand, n. 2 above, pp. 30–42.

7   Kraska, n. 3 above, p. 269.

amount to full sovereignty, as in internal waters. Ships of all States retain a right of "innocent passage" through territorial seas,[8] meaning that they may proceed through them "continuously and expeditiously," in a manner that "is not prejudicial to the peace, good order or security of the coastal State."[9] While a coastal State may pass laws and regulations on safe navigation and the prevention, reduction, and control of pollution within its coastal environment,[10] such laws and regulations must not hamper the right of innocent passage and cannot "apply to the design, construction, manning or equipment of foreign ships (CDEM), unless they are giving effect to generally accepted international rules or standards."[11] Throughout the LOS Convention coastal State authority and navigation rights are generally counterpoised in this manner.

In addition to emerging in the atmosphere of competing coastal and maritime State interests prefacing the Convention, Canada's Arctic waters regime arose in the context of United States' assertions of navigational freedom in the Arctic. First, in 1970, following two 1969 transits of the Northwest Passage (NWP) by the S/T Manhattan,[12] Canada extended its territorial sea from three NM to 12 NM and enacted the Arctic Waters Pollution Prevention Act (AWPPA).[13] Second, in 1985, following the westerly crossing of the NWP by the US Coast Guard icebreaker Polar Sea and a dispute over the status of the "Passage" waters, Canada enclosed by Order-in-Council the entire Arctic archipelago with straight baselines,[14] establishing a second ground for claiming these waters as internal.[15] Thus, it was in a context of competing rights, conflict, and compromise that Article 234 was drafted into the LOS Convention.

2.   Statutory Context

The LOS Convention is an extensive multilateral treaty that functions as a kind of 'charter of rights' for States' use of the world's oceans. The Convention

---

8   United Nations Convention on the Law of the Sea, 10 December 1982, *United Nations Treaty Series* 1833, Art. 17 [LOS Convention].

9   Id., Art. 19.

10   Id., Art. 21(1)(a),(f).

11   Id., Art. 24(1), Art. 21(2).

12   A US tanker converted into an ice-breaking vessel that successfully completed the voyage west and return east through the NWP; Pharand, n. 2 above, p. 38.

13   Id. Initially, the AWPPA applied only out to 100 NM (Pharand, n. 2 above, p. 11, 48).

14   Id., pp. 4–5, 11, 13.

15   Id. p. 4, 5, 9 (in additional to an 'historic title' claim).

balances various interests like freedom of navigation and overflight, coastal State sovereignty and security, and marine environmental protection. By the time one reaches Article 234, the Convention has already laid out an extensive framework of rights and responsibilities including defined maritime zones ("territorial sea and contiguous zone," "exclusive economic zone," "continental shelf" and "high seas"),[16] specific navigational rights ("innocent passage," "transit passage," and "freedom of the high seas"),[17] and distinct geographic regimes (e.g., for "archipelagic states," "islands," and "straits used for international navigation").[18]

Article 234 is found in Part XII of the LOS Convention titled, "Protection and Preservation of the Marine Environment." This part contains eleven sections and begins by placing a duty on all States to protect and preserve the marine environment.[19] States are then enjoined individually and collectively to "take...all measures *consistent with this Convention* that are necessary to prevent, reduce and control pollution of the marine environment from any source" [emphasis added].[20] This seeming broad conferral of power is circumscribed not only by the phrase 'consistent with this Convention', but also by paragraph 4 of Article 194 which requires that States "...refrain from unjustifiable interference with activities carried out by other States in the exercise of their rights and in pursuance of their duties in conformity with this Convention." The subsequent provisions of Part XII further refine the meaning of 'unjustifiable interference', reigning in States' pollution prevention powers.

Section 5, in particular, limits this scope by imposing minimum requirements on States' pollution prevention rules. While States are free to adopt laws and regulations to prevent, reduce, and control marine pollution from land-based sources, they must take account of "internationally agreed rules, standards, and recommended practices and procedures."[21] States may pass pollution prevention measures to protect seabed areas under their jurisdiction, but these measures cannot be less effective than international rules and standards.[22] Similarly, national rules governing the activity of a State's vessels

---

16   LOS Convention, n. 8 above, Parts II, V, VI and VII.

17   Id., Part II, Section 3; Part III, Section 3; Art. 52; Id., Part III, Section 2; Id., Art. 87.

18   Id., Part IV; Id., Part VIII; Id., Part III.

19   Id., Art. 192.

20   Id., Art. 194.

21   Id., Art. 207(1).

22   Id., Art. 208.

or dumping in its territorial sea, exclusive economic zone (EEZ), or onto its continental shelf must at least meet global standards.[23]

Up to this point in Part XII, States are permitted to go beyond, but must not dip below international marine pollution prevention standards.[24] This changes in Article 211 where the Convention specifically addresses vessel-source pollution. In Article 211, flag State authority remains unaltered as does States' authority over internal waters; a State may, for example, adopt specific pollution prevention requirements as a condition for entering internal waters or ports.[25] However, coastal State pollution prevention powers are constrained to varying degrees in both territorial waters and the EEZ. First, the laws or regulations that a State adopts to prevent, reduce, or control marine pollution cannot hamper the innocent passage of foreign vessels through its territorial sea.[26] Second, coastal States may only adopt pollution prevention laws for their EEZ that conform and give effect to existing international standards to carry out the enforcement activities permitted in Section 6.[27]

However, what if international standards are not strict enough to adequately protect the unique marine environment of a region's EEZ from vessel-source pollution? Paragraph 6 of Article 211 specifically addresses this scenario. In short, where coastal States on reasonable grounds believe that "a particular, clearly defined area of *their* respective exclusive economic zones" [emphasis added] needs special mandatory measures for adequate protection from vessel-source pollution, they can, after consulting with other concerned States through the International Maritime Organization (IMO), make a submission to the IMO to establish such measures. The submission must include supporting scientific evidence. The IMO makes a determination on the submission within 12 months and, if approved, implements the needed standards for the area which become applicable to foreign vessels 15 months after the initial submission. As will be seen, this process is in sharp contrast to the broad powers outlined in Article 234, which (1) permit a coastal State to act alone rather than collectively; (2) do not require consultation with other States or an IMO submission; and (3) do not impose delayed implementation for the measures adopted.

---

23 Id., Art. 209(2), 210 and 211(2) (pertaining to vessels flying a State's flag or registered in the State or operating under its authority).

24 With exception of pollution from land-based sources, LOS Convention, n. 8 above, Art. 207.

25 Id., Art. 211(3).

26 Id., Art. 211(4).

27 Id., Art. 211(5).

The theme of limited coastal State powers continues in Part XII's enforcement provisions.[28] Vessels detained for unseaworthiness must be allowed to
proceed "immediately" once the causes of a violation are rectified,[29] and
enforcement measures taken when there are clear grounds for believing a foreign vessel has violated pollution prevention laws in a State's territorial waters
must be carried out without prejudice to the right of innocent passage.[30]
A coastal State must be even more cautious when seeking to engage a vessel it
believes has violated pollution laws in its EEZ. In the case of a clear violation, the coastal State may only demand specified information.[31] If the violation
results in "a substantial discharge causing or threatening significant pollution
of the marine environment," the coastal State may inspect the vessel, but only
if certain conditions exist.[32] Only when a violation rises to the level of a discharge causing major damage or a threat of such damage to the coast or
resources of a State's territorial sea or EEZ can that State institute proceedings,
including detention of the foreign vessel.[33] If there is an agreement, international or otherwise, that assures financial security to the coastal State, it must
let the vessel proceed without detention.[34] Significantly, all of the limitations
with respect to enforcement of pollution violations occurring in the EEZ also
apply to areas where "special mandatory measures" have been adopted pursuant to Article 211(6).[35]

Further reinforcing the importance the Convention accords to navigational
freedoms is "Section 7 – Safeguards." Under Article 226, a coastal State investigating a vessel pursuant to Article 220 must not delay it longer than is essential.
Under Article 232 States are made subject to potential liability for imposing
enforcement measures that are either unlawful or exceed what is reasonably
required. The most important article in this section affecting the scope of
Article 234 is the one that immediately precedes it, Article 233.

Article 233 specifies that "nothing in sections 5, 6 and 7 affects the legal
regime of straits used for international navigation" – in other words, the regime

---

28   Id., Part XII, Section 6.

29   Id., Art. 219.

30   Id., Art. 220(2).

31   Id., Art. 220(3).

32   Id., Art. 220(5), (The conditions are (1) the ship refuses to give required info, (2) the info
      supplied by the ship obviously does not match the facts, and/or (3) the circumstances
      justify it.).

33   Id., Art. 220(6), (Additionally, there must be 'clear objective evidence' of such a
      violation).

34   Id., Art. 220(7).

35   Id., Art. 220(8).

that provides States with a right of transit passage. The right of transit passage permits a vessel or aircraft to "proceed without delay" through an international strait using its normal mode of operation (i.e., submarines may travel submerged).[36] States bordering international straits have limited power to regulate in relation to such passage. In the area of navigation safety and marine traffic, bordering States may set up sea lanes and traffic separation schemes provided that they are necessary to promote safe passage;[37] they are first referred to the IMO;[38] the bordering States agree on the measures;[39] and they conform to generally accepted international standards.[40] With respect to vessel-source pollution control in international straits, bordering States are limited to giving effect to applicable international regulations on the discharge of oil, oily wastes, or other noxious substances.[41] Finally, whatever laws are adopted cannot have the effect of denying, hampering, or impairing transit passage.[42] All of this is significant, because while sections 5, 6 and 7 of Part XII are specifically prevented from infringing on this regime, Section 8, the home of Article 234, is not. Given the juxtaposition of Articles 233 and 234, this exclusion cannot be arbitrary, but what does it mean?

From the perspective of many flag States, the Convention places no duty on their vessels transiting international straits with respect to marine pollution laws other than to "comply with generally accepted international regulations, procedures and practices for the prevention, reduction and control of pollution from ships."[43] From Canada's viewpoint as a coastal State bordering an alleged 'strait used for international navigation', coastal States acting pursuant to Article 234 may require foreign vessels transiting an international strait situated in ice-covered waters to comply with national standards that exceed international norms.[44] Since Article 234 is excluded from Article 233's prohibition against affecting the legal regime of international straits, Canada's argument has merit. However, any impact of coastal State measures on a navigational guarantee as important as transit passage could not have been intended to be unlimited. The scope of these powers must be defined by reference to the context of both the Convention and Article 234 itself.

---

36   Id., Art. 39(1).
37   Id., Arts. 41, 42(1)(a); Id., Art. 41(1).
38   Id., Arts. 41(4).
39   Id.
40   Id., Arts. 41(3).
41   Id., Art. 42(1)(b).
42   Id., Art. 42(2).
43   Id., Art. 39(2)(b).
44   Pharand, n. 2 above, pp. 46–47; McRae, n. 2 above, p. 2.

Before considering the text of Article 234, one other detail of this provision's statutory context warrants mention. Article 236 of Part XII excludes government vessels from the application of the Convention's provisions on preservation and protection of the marine environment.[45] Since Article 234 is in Part XII, "Protection and Preservation of the Marine Environment," it must be included in the scope of Article 236's exclusion, and the extensive powers it grants to coastal States thus may not be applied to government vessels.

3.   Contextual Limits

What limits, if any, do Article 234's historical and statutory context place on a correct understanding of its scope? Given the lengthy negotiations that went into completing the LOS Convention, how likely is it that Article 234 can trump important navigation rights? On the other hand, if Canada could simply have used the formula for special mandatory measures outlined in Article 211(6) to protect Arctic waters (and legitimize its Arctic waters regime), why would it have worked so hard for the inclusion of a specific provision like Article 234? Whatever interpretational limits the context may impose, they must harmonize with the text of Article 234 which itself establishes a number of limitations.

B.   *The Textual Parameters of Article 234*

Article 234 reads as follows:

> Coastal States have the right to adopt and enforce *non-discriminatory* laws and regulations for the prevention, reduction and control of marine pollution from vessels in ice-covered areas *within the limits of the exclusive economic zone*, where *particularly severe climatic conditions* and the *presence of ice covering such areas for most of the year* create *obstructions or exceptional hazards to navigation*, and pollution of the marine environment could cause *major harm to or irreversible disturbance of the ecological balance*. Such laws and regulations shall have due regard to *navigation* and the protection and preservation of the marine environment based on *the best available scientific evidence*. [emphasis added][46]

---

45   Government vessels comprise those owned or operated by a State and used for government non-commercial service.

46   LOS Convention, n. 8 above.

The text of Article 234 reveals a number of important limitations on coastal States' pollution prevention powers. These constraints may be grouped as "Geographical, Climatic and Temporal," "Operational" and "Other" limitations. Each will be addressed in turn.

1.   Geographic, Climatic, and Temporal Limits

Article 234, as its section title suggests, applies broadly speaking to 'ice-covered areas'. What is meant by this phrase is further defined throughout the text. First, it is not restricted to regions where ice is always present, but rather applies to areas where ice is present 'for most of the year'. Second, the text identifies ice-covered areas as ones having a harsh climate – one that is 'particularly severe'. Third, the text indicates that in ice-covered areas the combination of the ice and climate conditions must create difficulties for navigation – 'obstructions or exceptional hazards'. Finally, the ice-covered area must be one that is particularly susceptible to the impact of marine pollution. Do these geographic and meteorological characteristics describe Canadian Arctic waters?

Though sea ice extent and thickness is declining in the Arctic, ice still covers the waters in the winter, and remains present to varying extents in the summer.[47] The Arctic winter is particularly harsh with a potent combination of storms, darkness, and extreme cold.[48] While calmer weather and warmer temperatures arrive in the summer, the presence of ice in many areas continues to make navigation hazardous.[49] In fact, some studies show that warming conditions in the Arctic will actually lead to increased migration of old ice from the Arctic Ocean into the Northwest Passage, creating chokepoints and dangerous shipping conditions.[50] Finally, there is consensus that the Arctic is a region that is particularly sensitive to pollutants and for which an oil spill would be catastrophic.[51]

Still, because the Arctic is an area in transition questions remain. What percentage of ice needs to be present to qualify a sea area as 'ice-covered'? Does

---

47   Arctic Council, Protection of the Arctic Marine Environment Working Group (PAME), *Arctic Marine Shipping Assessment 2009 Report* (April 2009), pp. 4, 25, 27, 28, 30, and 35 [AMSA Report].

48   Id., pp. 4, 19–20, 24–25.

49   Id., pp. 22, 25, 26, 32, and 35.

50   K.J. Wilson, J. Falkingham, H. Melling and R. de Abreu, "*Shipping in the Canadian Arctic: Other Possible Climate Change Scenarios*," Research Paper by researchers from the Canadian Ice Service/Meteorological Service of Canada and Fisheries and Oceans Canada (Institute of Ocean Sciences, Victoria, Canada, 2006), p. 4.

51   AMSA Report, n. 47 above, pp. 134–145, 148–149 (Canadian Arctic), 152–153, 168, 186–187.

the thickness or type of ice (e.g., multi-year ice, second-year ice, first-year ice, etc.) matter?[52] Article 234 is silent on these details. Qualifiers like 'obstructions or exceptional hazards to navigation' and 'particularly severe climatic conditions' can however help provide answers. For example, while a sea area completely covered with light nilas ice ("A thin elastic crust of ice, easily bending on waves"[53]) might pose very little 'hazard' to shipping (in the absence of inclement weather), an 'open water'[54] area where bergy bits or growlers ("smaller pieces of icebergs [that] are especially dangerous to ships because they are extremely difficult to detect"[55]) are present could pose 'an exceptional hazard' to shipping. Additionally, as noted before, the 'ice-covering' need not be present all year to engage Article 234 powers.

The most difficult challenge of Article 234's text with respect to climate and ice conditions is that the provision is worded to reflect the Arctic conditions prevailing when the Convention was drafted. While such conditions still largely prevail, and may do so for many years to come, Arctic waters may continue to warrant exceptional environmental protection even when conditions in the region no longer strictly match the Article 234 description. In such an event, on a narrow interpretation, coastal States would cease to enjoy the pollution protection powers granted by the provision. For now though, given Article 234's over-arching pollution prevention purpose, its wording is sufficiently adaptable to encompass the range of ice and climate conditions currently seen in Canadian Arctic waters.

Article 234 presents another interpretively challenging geographic parameter. The power of coastal States to adopt and enforce laws for the prevention, reduction, and control of vessel-source pollution is confined to 'within the limits of the exclusive economic zone'.[56] Some advocate a strict interpretation of this phrase. Under such an approach, the powers granted under Article 234 apply only to the 'area beyond and adjacent to the territorial sea' out to 200 NM, i.e., in the area between the seaward limit of the territorial sea and the limit of the EEZ.[57] Those in this camp further contend that since it would be implausible for a coastal State's pollution prevention powers to be greater in the EEZ (farther from its territory) than in the territorial sea, Article 234

---

52   Arctic Ice Regime Shipping System (AIRSS) Standards 1998, TP12259, at para. 3 [AIRSS
      Standards].
53   Id.
54   Id., para. 3.2.
55   AMSA Report, n. 47 above, p. 22.
56   LOS Convention, n. 8 above.
57   Id., Art. 55, 57; Pharand, n. 2 above, p. 47.

powers must be no greater than those conferred on coastal States for their territorial seas.[58]

By contrast, leading Canadian scholars like Donat Pharand argue that Article 234 warrants a broad interpretation.[59] They contend that since the EEZ is measured from the same baselines as the territorial sea, Article 234 must be meant to include a coastal State's territorial sea in its area of application.[60] Pharand supports this position by citing a Canadian and a US delegate who "participated in the negotiation leading to the adoption of Article 234" and interpreted the provision's geographic parameters in this way.[61] Advocates of a broad interpretation see Article 234 as granting to coastal States (from baselines to the limits of the EEZ) exceptional pollution prevention powers within this wide area, powers that go beyond those granted under the Convention to coastal States in territorial seas.[62]

A further 'hybrid' view accepts the geographic parameters of the broad interpretation, while agreeing with the proponents of a narrow view that pollution prevention powers under Article 234 are no greater than those granted under the Convention to coastal States in the territorial sea.[63] The United States ostensibly holds this position.[64]

Which view of Article 234's geographic scope the international community endorses is vital from a Canadian perspective. Since coastal States' pollution prevention measures for their territorial seas can neither hamper the right of innocent passage nor regulate foreign vessel CDEM, a narrow or hybrid interpretation of the geographic scope of Article 234 powers would significantly restrict the measures Canada could legitimately adopt for non-internal Arctic waters. Conversely, a broad interpretation of Article 234's scope would support the legitimacy of Canada assuming broader regulatory powers as a coastal State over its non-internal Arctic waters.

---

58 Pharand, Id.

59 Professor of Law Emeritus of the University of Ottawa, Professor Pharand has written extensively on the law of the Sea, particularly the Arctic region. He was a founding member and served as president of the Canadian Council on International Law. See "Donat Pharand: 1989 Read Medal Recipient," available online: <http://www.ccil-ccdi.ca/ccil-john-e-read-medal/2011/1/29/donat-pharand.html>.

60 Pharand, n. 2 above at 47.

61 Id.

62 Id., pp. 46–48.

63 Id., p. 47.

64 Roach and Smith, n. 4 above, p. 491.

2.   Operational Limits

The operational limits of Article 234 are threefold. Coastal States (1) may exercise both prescriptive and enforcement jurisdiction ("adopt and enforce"); (2) must restrict their laws and regulations to the "prevention, reduction and control of marine pollution"; and (3), must target only vessel-source pollution (foreign application). Although these requirements are less ambiguous than Article 234's geographic, climatic, and temporal parameters, they still raise the following question: Can a coastal State incidentally impact subject-matter areas like maritime safety or CDEM standards, so long as the overall goal of its legislation is the prevention, reduction, and control of marine pollution from vessels in ice-covered areas? Canada appears to take the position that such impacts are both permitted and necessary.[65]

3.   Other Limits

Several other constraints apply to coastal State powers under Article 234. First, the laws and regulations adopted and enforced must be non-discriminatory. A coastal State's pollution prevention regime for ice-covered waters may not directly or indirectly impose a greater burden on the vessels of a particular State. Second, coastal States are enjoined to "have due regard" to two mandatory considerations: (i) "navigation" and (ii) "the best available scientific evidence."

What does 'have due regard to navigation' mean in this context? As noted before, Article 233 does not explicitly preclude Section 8, Ice-Covered Areas, from affecting transit passage. Further, Article 234 mentions neither innocent passage, transit passage, nor freedom of the high seas. Nevertheless, the term 'navigation' arguably encompasses each of these rights. What Article 234 seems to provide for is a middle ground between, on the one hand, forbidding coastal States to impede navigation, and on the other hand, allowing them free reign to impact navigation, as in internal waters. 'Have due regard' suggests that a coastal State in adopting and enforcing pollution prevention measures for an ice-covered area may affect navigation (possibly hamper, impair, or even deny it), but only insofar as is necessary to carry out Article 234's purpose.

---

65   See, for example, under "Purpose" in the Equivalent Standards for the Construction of Arctic Class Ships 1995 [Equivalent Standards], TP 12260, at viii, which state, "The purpose of the regulations is to minimise the risk of pollution in the waters of the Canadian Arctic. The *Arctic Waters Pollution Prevention Act* is only interested in aspects of pollution. The *Canada Shipping Act* is the applicable act when considerations of the safety of the persons on board and of the vessel itself are to be considered. This standard, although incorporating measures which will lead to the improved safety of those on board of the vessel itself, was not designed with that intent."

The above interpretation is opposed by the United States, which rejects the legitimacy of Canada's straight baselines enclosing the Arctic archipelago's waters as internal[66] and views the Northwest Passage as a strait used for international navigation subject to transit passage.[67] American scholars consider transit passage 'non-suspendable' and thus as surviving any impact coastal States may exert on navigation under Article 234.[68]

The mandatory consideration of best available scientific evidence is particularly challenging in the Arctic, a region difficult to access and about which much is still unknown.[69] However, there is a growing body of scientific evidence available to guide and support Canadian Arctic pollution prevention laws. Though recent science agrees that sea ice coverage and thickness will continue to decline in the Arctic throughout this century, no studies project disappearance of winter sea ice over the same period.[70] While researchers admit that global climate models are too crude to predict "the state of sea ice in the Northwest Passage region,"[71] climate models nonetheless indicate that "...the last regions of the Arctic Ocean with sea ice coverage in summer would be in the northern waterways of the Canadian Archipelago and along the northern coast of Greenland."[72] These projections correspond with the findings of Wilson et al.[73] Their report suggests that, due to drifting of multi-year ice from the Arctic Ocean into areas of the Northwest Passage, warming temperatures in the region may in some years lead to more, rather than less difficult navigation conditions.[74]

For Canada, the challenge is not so much showing that science calls for pollution prevention measures in its Article 234 waters, but rather demonstrating that the measures it has chosen correspond with current scientific data. A recent discussion paper produced for Transport Canada concludes that neither of Canada's current systems for regulating vessel traffic in Arctic waters "has a

---

66   Roach and Smith, n. 4 above, pp. 95–97, 111; Kraska, n. 3 above, p. 272.

67   Roach and Smith, id., pp. 268, 318; Kraska, id., p. 275.

68   Roach and Smith, id., pp. 268–269, 270; Kraska, id., pp. 264, 275 and 279.

69   AMSA Report, n. 47 above, pp. 35, 186–187.

70   Id., p. 35, findings 1 and 2 (AMSA Report employed the Arctic Climate Impact Assessment 2004 (ACIA), the Intergovernmental Panel on Climate Change Fourth Assessment Report 2007, and the Global Climate Models (GCM) used in each).

71   Id., p. 27.

72   Id., p. 32.

73   Wilson et al., n. 50 above.

74   Id., p. 4.

strong scientific basis."[75] Though Canada's Arctic regime is usually challenged by critics on other grounds, and 'have due regard to' is a lower requirement than 'must', Canada should strive to ensure that its laws and regulations for pollution control in Arctic waters conform to the 'best available scientific evidence'.

C.   Conclusion on the Scope of Article 234

Given Article 234's historical and statutory context and the constraints written into its text, the provision should be understood as giving coastal States exceptional pollution prevention powers within the following scope:

(1) *Operational:* Coastal States may both enact and enforce laws and regulations to prevent, reduce, and control vessel-source marine pollution.

  · This should be understood to permit incidental affects outside the strict parameters of pollution control, impacting areas like maritime safety and CDEM standards.
  · Given the characteristics of the Arctic region and the potential impact of any environmental incident there, such subject-matter areas have a direct bearing on pollution prevention and are legitimately and necessarily affected by Article 234 pollution prevention measures.

(2) *Geographic, Climatic, and Temporal:* Coastal States' laws and regulations apply and may be enforced in 'ice-covered areas' of their EEZs.

  · The EEZ should be understood as the area measured from the baselines of a coastal State's territorial sea and reaching out to the 200-NM limit of its EEZ.
  · A broad scope should be accorded to the climatic and temporal criteria of Article 234:

      i. 'For most of the year' should not be interpreted only in light of the percentage of ice in an area, but also in light of the fragility of the Arctic environment and the obstructions and hazards posed to shipping.

---

75   G.W. Timco and I. Kubat, "Regulatory Update for Shipping in Canada's Arctic Waters: Options for an Ice Regime System," Discussion Paper TP 14732 (Canadian National Research Council, March 2007), pp. 1, 8, 12, and 22.

   ii. The presence of multi-year ice in the summer in certain waters should qualify as meeting Article 234's 'ice-presence' criterion. This ice can create chokepoints or, due to its mobility and extreme hardness, imperil even the highest polar class vessels, especially when present in small, hard to detect pieces.

(3)   *With Respect to Navigation*: Coastal States may impact navigation in ice-covered areas, but only to the extent necessary to prevent, reduce, and control marine pollution; and as long as their regime applies equally to all foreign vessels and excludes government vessels.

· The regime of international straits and transit passage does not trump Article 234 powers based on the exclusion of Section 8 from Article 233's limitation.

· Respect for this important navigation right remains very important.

(4)   *With Respect to Scientific Evidence*: Coastal States must consult the 'best available scientific evidence' when adopting pollution prevention measures for ice-covered areas.

· While their measures need not perfectly mirror the scientific data, there should be correspondence with the scientific evidence such that a coastal State's laws and regulations can be said to have a 'sound scientific basis'.

III.   The Canadian Regulatory Regime for Arctic Waters

A.   *Legislation*

Canada's Arctic waters regime began in earnest with passage of the AWPPA in 1970. This legislation was followed by several important implementing regulations. In this section, the AWPPA and key Canadian Arctic waters regulations are summarized and analyzed for Article 234 compliance.

1.   Arctic Waters Pollution Prevention Act

a.   *Summary of the AWPPA*

The AWPPA is specific legislation designed to prevent waste deposits in Canada's Arctic waters, whether the waste originates on land or water and whether it is from a person, undertaking or ship.[76] Since Article 234 is

---

76   AWPPA, n. 1 above, ss. 4–6.

concerned only with vessel-source pollution, only the parts of the AWPPA that impact or address this area are considered here.[77] Section 2 of the AWPPA broadly defines 'arctic waters' as follows:

> ...the internal waters of Canada and the waters of the territorial sea of Canada and the exclusive economic zone of Canada, within the area enclosed by the 60th parallel of north latitude, the 141st meridian of west longitude and the outer limit of the exclusive economic zone; however, where the international boundary between Canada and Greenland is less than 200 nautical miles from the baselines of the territorial sea of Canada, the international boundary shall be substituted for that outer limit.[78]

Since 'arctic waters' confines the scope of the Act's application,[79] the definition is controversial vis-à-vis the United States. The United States does not accept the 141st meridian as the legal boundary for the waters of the Beaufort Sea off Alaska and the Canadian North.[80]

The AWPPA establishes the absolute liability (civil) offence of depositing waste in Arctic waters.[81] The Act defines 'waste' as "any substance that, if added to any water, would degrade or alter or form part of a process of degradation or alteration of the quality of that water to an extent that is detrimental to their use by man or by any animal, fish or plant that is useful to man."[82] It also includes any water containing a substance that would produce the same deleterious effect.[83] Although the Act permits the Governor in Council (GIC) to make regulations providing conditions under which waste may be deposited,[84] this power has been used sparingly. For example, to allow limited deposits of non-vessel-source domestic and industrial waste[85] or to permit scientific research on the effects of depositing specific kinds of waste in Arctic waters and to test the effectiveness of clean-up and recovery techniques there.[86] The

---

77   Note: Since land-sourced pollution emanates from Canadian territory, Article 234 is not required to justify the regulations controlling it.

78   AWPPA, n. 1 above.

79   Id., s. 3(1).

80   Roach and Smith, n. 4 above, p. 470.

81   See n. 1, ss. 7(1), 4(1), 5(2), 6(1)(c) (sections with respect to the ship/ship owner).

82   Id., s. 2.

83   Id.

84   Id., s. 4(3).

85   *Arctic Waters Pollution Prevention Regulations*, CRC, c 354, ss. 4, 5 and 6.

86   *Arctic Waters Experimental Pollution Regulations*, 1978, SOR/78-417; *Arctic Waters Experimental Pollution Regulations*, 1979, SOR/80-9; Arctic Waters Experimental Pollution

bottom line under the Act is that for ships, Canadian Arctic waters are essentially a 'zero discharge' area.[87]

The master of a ship which deposits waste or, due to distress, is in danger of depositing waste into Canadian Arctic waters, has a duty under the Act to report this to a 'pollution prevention officer' (PPO).[88] The ship and cargo owners of the depositing ship are made jointly and severally liable for any "costs, expenses and loss or damage" resulting from the discharge.[89]

Among the AWPPA's provisions, some of the widest-reaching are those found in Sections 11 and 12 which provide for the establishment of Shipping Safety Control Zones (SSCZ). Under these provisions, the GIC may make regulations that *prohibit* ships of a prescribed class from navigating in SSCZs unless (1) the ship complies with specified CDEM and other standards; (2) the ship operates with the help of a pilot or ice navigator with prescribed qualifications or with prescribed-class icebreaker assistance; and (3) the ship operates during a specified time period or under specified ice conditions.[90]

Section 13 of the Act gives the GIC the power to destroy or remove and sell a ship or any of its contents where he "believes on reasonable grounds that waste is being deposited or is likely to be deposited in the arctic waters by a ship that is in distress, stranded, wrecked, sunk or abandoned...."[91] The destruction may only be done "if necessary."[92]

Enforcement under the AWPPA is primarily placed in the hands of pollution prevention officers.[93] These officers are granted extensive authority with respect to ships, as is demonstrated by the following powers: power to board and inspect ships within a SSCZ;[94] when certain circumstances are present, power to order a ship in or near a SSCZ to proceed outside the zone, remain outside it or anchor in a particular place;[95] and where the officer learns that "a

---

Regulations, 1982, SOR/82-276; and *Arctic Waters Experimental Pollution Regulations*, 1982 (Dome Petroleum), SOR/82-832.

87   *Arctic Shipping Pollution Prevention Regulations*, CRC, c. 353, ss. 28 and 29 (create exceptions for sewage generated on board or oil or an oily deposit from a vessel under certain circumstances) [ASPPR].

88   AWPPA, see n. 1 above, s. 5(2) describing 'pollution prevention officer'.

89   Id., s 6(1)(c) (but note s. 7(4): cargo owner not liable if deposit of cargo in Arctic waters would not contravene s. 4(1)).

90   Id., s. 12(1).

91   Id., s. 13.

92   Id.

93   Id., s. 14.

94   Id., s. 15(4)(a).

95   Id., s. 15(4)(b).

substantial quantity of waste has been deposited in the Arctic waters" or "on reasonable grounds" believes there is "a grave and imminent danger" of such a deposit being made, power to order ships in a specified area to report their positions and to "order any ship to take part in the clean-up...or in any action to control or contain the waste."[96] These powers are supplemented by a requirement for masters and those on board to assist pollution prevention officers, and a prohibition against obstructing them in their duties or providing them with false or misleading statements.[97] In addition to the powers listed above, Section 23(1) provides that an officer who suspects on reasonable grounds that a ship has contravened the Act "may, with the consent of the Governor in Council, seize the ship and its cargo anywhere in the Arctic waters or elsewhere in the territorial sea or internal or inland waters of Canada."[98]

Finally, the AWPPA establishes several summary conviction offences which provide a further deterrent for would-be polluters of Arctic waters. A ship that contravenes the Section 4(1) prohibition on discharging waste into Arctic waters, in addition to incurring civil liability, may face a fine of up to C$100,000.[99] Ships that navigate in a SSCZ without meeting prescribed standards or whose master or crew obstruct or make false statements to a pollution prevention officer could be fined up to C$25,000.[100] In obtaining a conviction against a ship under the Act, prosecutors are assisted by Section 20(2) which excuses them from identifying the exact person aboard the ship who committed the act or neglect charged.[101] As long as a prosecutor can prove someone on board did it, she has met the burden.[102]

b.   *Compliance of the AWPPA with Article 234*

Compliance issues for the AWPPA arise in three key areas: (1) the impact of the Act's provisions on navigation freedoms; (2) the imposition of CDEM standards for foreign vessels; and (3) the application of the Act to disputed waters.

First, the waters to which the Act applies extend in the west along the 141st meridian and out to the 200 NM limit of Canada's EEZ. Article 234 allows coastal States to adopt and enforce laws "within the limits of the exclusive

---

96   Id., s. 15(4)(c).

97   Id., s. 17.

98   Id., s. 23(1).

99   Id., s. 18(1).

100   Id., s. 19(2).

101   AWPPA, n. 1 above.

102   The person responsible, however, must be someone other than a PPO or mandatory pilot.

economic zone." However, because the United States rejects the 141st meridian as the legal boundary in the Beaufort Sea, Canada faces a potential enforcement problem within that body of water.

Second, the Act authorizes regulations which address ship construction, design, equipment, and manning.[103] Article 234 does not specifically forbid these types of standards. However, it does specify that a coastal State's laws must be for the prevention, reduction, and control of marine pollution. For Canada, the CDEM standards imposed pursuant to the AWPPA are arguably for that purpose. However, this issue is complicated by the fact that the United States and the European Union do not accept Canada's claim that waters of the Arctic archipelago are Canadian internal waters,[104] and the United States does not view Article 234 powers as overriding the Convention's rules for the territorial sea and international straits,[105] areas where coastal/bordering States cannot regulate foreign vessel CDEM standards. Hence, while the CDEM standards may comply with Article 234, the real challenge Canada may have is attempting to enforce them in the face of opposition.

Finally, the AWPPA clearly enables significant impacts on navigation in applicable waters. Denying a non-compliant ship access to an SSCZ, authorizing PPOs to board and inspect ships, requiring a ship under orders from a PPO to assist with pollution response, and empowering a PPO to seize a ship or cargo could seriously hamper navigation for an offending foreign vessel. Nonetheless, Article 234 does not forbid impacts on navigation but rather requires that navigation be given 'due regard' under the coastal State's laws. Safeguards written into the AWPPA may ensure this happens. Pollution prevention officers' powers affecting navigation are often made subject to the existence of "reasonable grounds" or other similar constraints.[106] And, in the case of ship seizure, a pollution prevention officer must first obtain consent of the GIC before making an arrest.[107]

Again, the biggest test here may be what Canada can affect in practice rather than what it can prescribe on paper. Given the EU and US rejection of Canada's internal waters claim for the Arctic archipelago and the US position that the Northwest Passage is an international strait through which foreign vessels

---

103 AWPPA, n. 1 above, s. 12(1)(a).
104 Roach and Smith, n. 4 above, p. 111; Kraska, n. 3 above, pp. 265, 272 (note: mistakenly states that Canada's Arctic baselines established in 1967 and 1968); European Commission, Maritime Affairs and Fisheries, "Legal and Socio-economic Studies in the Field of the Integrated Maritime Policy for the European Union," in *Legal Aspects of Arctic Shipping, Summary Report* (Luxembourg: Publications Office of the European Union, 2010), p. 7.
105 Roach and Smith, id., p. 318; Kraska, id., p. 275.
106 For example, AWPPA, n. 1 above, ss. 15(4)(b)(i), (iii), (c), 16, 23(1).
107 Id., s. 23(1).

enjoy a right of non-suspendable transit passage, will Canada be able to, for example, board and inspect a vessel traversing the NWP that appears to have discharged waste into Arctic waters? Does Canada even have the capacity to monitor, let alone enforce, compliance in its Arctic waters? These are the real tests when it comes to Canada's Arctic pollution prevention regime.

B.   *Regulations*

Though the AWPPA establishes the essential framework for Canada's pollution prevention activity in Arctic waters, several regulations lie at the heart of how Canada manages the region.

1a.   Summary of the Arctic Shipping Pollution Prevention Regulations
The Arctic Shipping Pollution Prevention Regulations (ASPPR) set out the specific CDEM standards authorized under Section 12 of the AWPPA. For the most part, these regulations apply to ships of 100 tons or more.[108]

The regulations provide different requirements for non-Canadian ships depending on whether a vessel is a "Safety Convention ship" or not. A Safety Convention ship is one "...that is of 500 tons or more and registered in a state that is a party to the Safety Convention" (International Convention for Safety of Life at Sea (SOLAS) 1960 or SOLAS 1974).[109] A non-Safety Convention ship, in order navigate in the SSCZs authorized under the AWPPA,[110] must comply with certain Canadian ship construction regulations (hull construction, hull inspection, marine machinery) as if it were a Canadian ship.[111] A Safety Convention ship, by contrast, need only comply with the requirements of the most recent Safety Convention to which its registering State is a party.[112]

The ASPPR works similarly with respect to load line requirements. In order to navigate in the SSCZs, non-Canadian, non-Arctic class ships registered in a State that is not a party to the International Convention on Load Lines, 1966, or the International Load Line Convention, 1930, must comply with Canadian Load Line Regulations like any Canadian ship.[113] Those registered in States that are parties to either international convention may navigate in an SSCZ as long as they comply with the applicable international convention.[114]

---

108   ASPPR, n. 87, s. 3(1).

109   Id., s. 2.

110   Established under the Shipping Safety Control Zones Order, CRC, c. 356 [SSCZO].

111   ASPPR, n. 87 above, s. 4(1).

112   Id.

113   Id., s. 5(1).

114   Id., s. 5(2).

The ASPPR have the greatest impact on ships "carrying oil in excess of 453 m^3." To receive permission to navigate in SSCZs, regular and Arctic class ships in this category must meet specific *construction standards* set out in schedules to the Regulations.[115] Ships that meet the construction standards must also follow the SSCZ entry parameters set out in Schedule VIII, which charts these allowances for 14 categories of ship ('Arctic class' and 'Type') and for each of 16 SSCZs with access ranging from 'No Entry', to entry within specified dates, to entry 'All Year'. The system established by Schedule VIII is known as the Zone-Date System (ZDS).

Subsections 6(3) and (3.1) of the Regulations introduce an alternative to the ZDS called the Arctic Ice Regime Shipping System (AIRSS). This system, detailed below, essentially substitutes for the Zone-Date chart, entry based on a combination of a vessel's class and the ice conditions/concentration present in a proposed navigation route.

In addition to the AIRSS, subsections 6(4) to (7) and (9) of the Regulations create a number of specific exceptions by which particular vessels at particular times and under certain conditions may navigate in shipping zones outside of the dates set out in Table VIII. The requirements laid out in these exceptions can be quite strict, including having an icebreaker available in the vicinity,[116] not carrying oil in direct contact with shell plating,[117] having on board a person in charge of the deck with specified ice navigating experience,[118] and the ship's being "equipped with a main hull girder stress monitoring and warning system."[119]

Subsection 6(8) creates an exception that further restricts rather than expands entry to SSCZs. Ships of Arctic class 3 or lower, when carrying oil or ore as cargo, may not navigate in Zone 6 after November 15 or in Zone 13 after December 15.[120]

Under Section 10 of the ASPPR, to navigate in SSCZs Arctic class ships must be fitted with bunkering stations on each side of the deck[121] and equipped with bunkering hoses[122] and facilities for safe bunkering hose link-up with other

---

115   Id., s. 6(1), Schedules V, VI and VII.
116   Id., ss. 6(4)(a), (5)(a).
117   Id., ss. 6(5)(b), (6)(c), (7)(a).
118   Id., ss. 6(6)(f), (7)(b).
119   Id., s. 6(7)(e).
120   Id., s. 6(8).
121   Id., s.10(a).
122   Id., s. 10(b).

ships.[123] The bunkering station flanges must match the dimensions detailed in Schedule IX of the Regulations.[124]

Section 26 sets out a requirement for ships to use an 'ice navigator' and specifies the qualifications for persons holding this title.[125] All tankers must use ice navigators when travelling in any SSCZ.[126] Other ships only have to use an ice navigator when operating in a zone outside of the times permitted under the ZDS.[127] There is an exception to the ice navigator requirement for both tankers and other ships during parts of their transit that are in "open water" as defined in the AIRSS.[128]

The ASPPR also mandate that ships carry minimum stores of fuel and fresh water to operate in SSCZs.[129] The requirements are higher for Arctic class ships which must have 30 days reserve fuel and water.[130] By contrast, other ships must have enough fuel and fresh water to either complete their intended voyage in and leave zones, or reach a place to obtain these stores in a zone inside their intended route.[131]

The Regulations' provisions end with sections that apply to all ships navigating in SSCZs regardless of their tonnage.[132] Section 28 permits the deposit into Arctic waters of sewage generated on board a ship (no minimum distance from shore is stipulated). Section 29 allows under certain conditions the deposit into Arctic waters of oil or an oily mixture from ships. The conditions are that (1) the oil deposit is made to save life or prevent the immediate loss of a ship;[133] (2) the deposit is made "through the exhaust of an engine or by leakage from an underwater machinery component where such deposit is minimal, unavoidable and essential to the operation of the engine or component";[134] and, (3) the deposit was accidental and the shipowner/master exercised due diligence to avoid the accident and mitigate damage from it.[135] More specifically, when a

---

123   Id., s.10(c).

124   Id., s.10(a).

125   Id., s. 26(3).

126   Id., s. 26(1).

127   Id., s. 26(2) (when using the AIRSS).

128   Id., ss. 26(4) and (5).

129   Id., s. 27.

130   Id., s. 27(3).

131   Id., s. 27(1).

132   Id., s. 3(2).

133   Id., s. 29(a).

134   Id., s. 29(c).

135   Id., s. 29(b).

deposit of oil or an oily mixture is "due to damage to or leakage from [a] ship as a result of stranding, collision or foundering," the deposit is allowed provided that "all reasonable precautions were taken" to avoid the accident "and to prevent or minimize the deposit."[136] Does this mean that Section 4(1) of the AWPPA does not set up a strict liability offence (in the civil sense) in every case? The definition of 'oil' in the Regulations is very broad: "oil of any kind or in any form"[137] and an 'oily mixture' is simply one with "any oil content."[138] The application of Section 29 of the ASPPR could significantly soften what is otherwise a 'zero discharge' regime under the AWPPA, at least for oil deposits. 'Waste' under the AWPPA, however, covers a much broader array of substances than just oil, and a due diligence requirement could be difficult to meet given the other standards and requirements imposed under the Regulations.

The Regulations' provisions are followed by nine schedules, the active ones being II, and V through IX. Schedule V sets out construction standards for ships of Types A to E by reference to the standards of ten international ship registries. A concise table lists the ship types on one axis and the registries on the other, with the names/abbreviations of specific standards filling the body of the table.

Schedules VI and VII apply specifically to Arctic class ships. Unlike the standards for 'Type' class ships, those found in these schedules are set out in great detail and not by reference to the standards of international ship registries. Schedule VI specifies the requirements of "Hull Design for Arctic Class Ships." It contains diagrams, dimensions, and tables and formulae for making calculations. Sections in Schedule 6 include those dealing with "Shell Plating and Framing," "Subdivision and Stability," and "Rudder and Steering Gear."

Schedule VII is equally detailed in addressing the "Machinery Requirements for Arctic Class Ships." With tables and formulae throughout, the Schedule's sections speak to, *inter alia*, "Power Requirements"; "Machinery Protection"; "Determination of Ice Torque"; "Propellers," "Shafting" and "Gearing"; and "Air Starting Systems."

As detailed earlier, Schedule VIII sets out the Zone-Date System for the 16 Shipping Safety Control Zones. The last schedule in the Regulations provides a diagram of Section 10's required bunkering flange for Arctic class ships.

Two features of the ASPPR not previously addressed provide for greater flexibility and potential efficiency in the regime's application. First, the Regulations permit certificates to be used in several instances as proof of compliance with

---

136 Id.
137 Id., s. 2.
138 Id.

requirements.[139] For example, pursuant to sections 12 and 13, the owner or master of a ship proposing to navigate in SSCZs may apply to designated persons for an Arctic Pollution Prevention Certificate (APPC). In the absence of evidence to the contrary, the certificate constitutes proof of the ship's compliance with the Regulations.[140] Safeguards to certificates being abused include a duty for owners/masters to report to a pollution prevention officer any change affecting the essential conditions under which the APPC was issued and the invalidation of the certificate if they fail to do so without reasonable cause;[141] a prohibition against issuing an APPC unless the vessel is actually in compliance;[142] and power for an inspector to invalidate an APPC where he believes a vessel does not comply with essential conditions or is in danger of depositing waste in a SSCZ contrary to Section 4(a) of the AWPPA.[143]

Second, the Regulations in Section 11 give pollution prevention officer's discretion to allow a ship to have different construction, machinery, fittings, appliances, apparatus, or materials, or to make different provisions than are called for under the Regulations if they are satisfied that these features and arrangements are at least equivalent to those required in the Regulations.[144] In 1995, Canada adopted regulations pursuant to this equivalency provision.[145] The Equivalent Standards for the Construction of Arctic Class Ships provide "...a complete and stand alone [sic] alternative for the hull construction provisions in Schedule VI of the Regulations."[146] They do not, however, provide alternatives for the machinery requirements of Schedule VII, which continue to apply.[147]

1b.   Compliance of the ASPPR with Article 234

The ASPPR potentially step outside Article 234's parameters in two areas. First, the ship standards imposed in the ASPPR touch on both maritime safety and mariner qualifications, areas normally reserved for international regulation

---

139   Id., ss. 4(3), 5(4), 12–18.

140   Id., s. 16.

141   Id., s. 18.

142   Id., s. 14.

143   Id., s. 17(2).

144   Id., s. 11.

145   Equivalent Standards, n. 65 above, (Under the heading, "Purpose," the government claims that the Standard "updates the requirements for the structure, subdivision and stability after damage .... [and] creates a more effective and safer structure with improved pollution protection of the waters of the Arctic").

146   Id., s. vii.

147   Id., s. viii.

with respect to foreign vessels. For example, the International Convention on Standards of Training, Certification and Watchkeeping for Seafarers (STCW) and its accompanying Code set out the international standards for "Special training requirements for personnel on certain types of ships" (Chapter V) and for "Watchkeeping" (Chapter VIII).[148] The Regulations' provisions concerning the deck watch on ships navigating SSCZs and prescribing qualifications for ice navigators tread in these same areas.[149] Similarly, many of the construction standards set out in the schedules could be said to relate at least as much to safety as to the prevention, reduction, and control of pollution.[150] Again, the main defense is that these impacts are incidental to the AWPPA's overall pollution prevention purpose. Also, international standards arguably do not deal with the unique conditions and hazards found in Arctic waters.[151] The level of CDEM standards imposed here certainly tests the limits of an 'incidental affects' argument. It is difficult to see, for example, how regulating a ship's supply of fresh water aims primarily at preventing pollution rather than at increasing maritime safety.

Second, the Regulations in some areas essentially forbid navigation. As noted, the Zone-Date system set out in Schedule VIII of the Regulations makes certain SSCZs 'No Entry' areas for ships of particular classes, while other areas may only be accessed during particular windows of the year. While from a common sense perspective restricting access to historically ice-covered and dangerous waters makes sense, without current and reliable information to support the dates and zones,[152] the system becomes arbitrary and potentially dangerous. Research performed in 2005 and 2006 to test the veracity of the ZDS revealed that it permitted vessels into ice areas where there was "a high potential" for damage while it often restricted vessels from entering areas

---

148 International Convention on Standards of Training, Certification, and Watchkeeping for Seafarers, 7 July 1978, see International Maritime Organization, available online: <http://www.imo.org/OurWork/HumanElement/TrainingCertification/Pages/Default.aspx> [STCW].

149 ASPPR, n. 87 above, ss. 6(6), (7); Id., s. 26(3).

150 Where maritime safety is dealt with under the Safety of Life at Sea Convention in its successive forms, 1 November 1974, see International Maritime Organization, available online: <http://www.imo.org/About/Conventions/ListOfConventions/Pages/International-Convention-for-the-Safety-of-Life-at-Sea-(SOLAS),-1974.aspx>.

151 At least not in mandatory instruments; note: IMO's Arctic Guidelines 2002 (amended 2009) and Guidelines on Voyage Planning for Passenger Ships in Remote Areas, 2007; also, "Recommendations" made in the Manila Amendments, 2010 for *STCW* "on measures to ensure the competency of masters and officers on ships operating in polar waters."

152 Timco and Kubat, see n. 75 above, p. 8.

where they could navigate safely.[153] Though the Regulations provide for an alternative system which accounts for ice conditions,[154] critics contend that this regime also needs tweaking to match available science.[155] Article 234 requires that "due regard" be taken of "the best available scientific evidence" and of "navigation." Given the questionable scientific basis of Canada's on-the-ground systems regulating access to ice-covered areas, it is unclear whether Canada can justify the impacts these Regulations create on navigation.

2a.   Summary of the Shipping Safety Control Zones Order
The Shipping Safety Control Zones Order establishes the safety control zones authorized under Section 11 of the AWPPA.[156] The Order creates 16 zones, described using geographic coordinates and place names in Schedule 1, and shown on the map in Figure 5.1. These zones form operational areas for many of the standards imposed under the Arctic Shipping Pollution Prevention Regulations. They are the 'zones' of the Zone-Date system.

2b.   Compliance of the Order with Article 234
Since the zones created under the Order completely enclose the waters of the Northwest Passage, the debate over the status of these waters arises once more. If the waters are an international strait, as the United States asserts, Canada's response is that Article 234 nonetheless permits impacts on navigation as needed to prevent pollution. If the waters are internal, either by virtue of an historic title or because enclosed by legitimate straight baselines, the regulations imposed in the zones are unquestionably lawful for whatever parts lie within the baselines, areas of complete Canadian sovereignty (Figure 5.1). For areas outside of Canadian internal waters, Canada would be limited to legislating within Article 234's scope, accepting existing international standards, or seeking other bilateral, regional, or international solutions.[157]

In addition, since three SSCZs follow the 141st meridian of longitude in the Beaufort Sea (Zones 1, 4 and 12), there is an issue concerning whether they

---

153   Id.
154   ASPPR, n. 87 above, s. 6(3)(a), (the AIRSS).
155   Timco and Kubat, n. 75 above, pp. 1, 8, 12, and 22.
156   SSCZO, n. 110 above.
157   For example, the bilateral arrangement with the United States for pollution prevention measures in the Beaufort Sea area, establishing other regional agreements like those reached on search and rescue (2011) and marine oil pollution and preparedness in the Arctic (May 2013), seeking to develop Arctic-specific standards in collaboration with other interested States through the IMO.

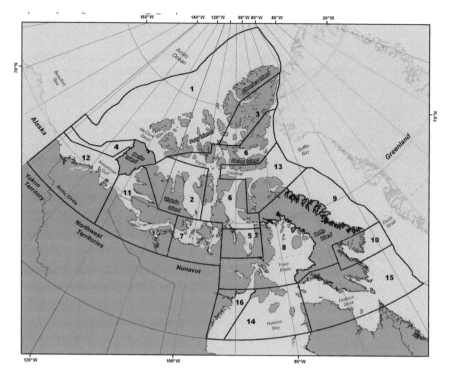

FIGURE 5.1 *Shipping safety control zones*
SOURCE: SCHEDULE 2 OF THE SHIPPING SAFETY CONTROL ZONES ORDER,
AVAILABLE ONLINE: <HTTP://LAWS.JUSTICE.GC.CA/PDF/C.R.C.,_C._356.PDF>.

apply along the contested boundary. Article 234 gives coastal States no powers outside of waters "within the limits of the exclusive economic zone."

Finally, as discussed above, the scientific basis of the zones may be challenged. Since the Order's zones form an integral part of Canada's legal regime for ice-covered waters, to conform with Article 234 they must reflect, at least to some extent, the best available scientific evidence. Insofar as the zones fail to do this, foreign States may fairly question their legitimacy under international law.

3a.   Summary of NORDREG SOR/2010-127
The Northern Canada Vessel Traffic Services Regulations (NORDREG) were initially introduced in 1977 and established a voluntary vessel reporting system in Canadian Arctic waters.[158] These regulations were made mandatory in 2010.[159]

---

158   Pharand, n. 2 above, p. 49.
159   Canadian Coast Guard, Vessel Traffic Reporting Arctic Canada Traffic Zone (NORDREG), Government of Canada, 24 June 2013, available online: <http://www.ccg-gcc.gc.ca/eng/MCTS/Vtr_Arctic_Canada> [CCG on NORDREG].

NORDREG applies in all Arctic Shipping Safety Control Zones, as well as in other specified northern waters of Canada.[160] The Regulations cover vessels of 300 gross tonnage or more; vessels engaged in towing or pushing another vessel if their combined gross tonnage is 500 gross tonnage or more, and vessels carrying a pollutant or dangerous goods as cargo or towing a vessel carrying such cargo.[161]

NORDREG functions in tandem with the foreign vessel pre-arrival information requirements imposed under the Maritime Transportation Security Regulations (MTSR).[162] Under the MTSR, a foreign vessel's master must report specified information to the Minister of Transport before entering Canadian waters at the following times: (1) if the voyage before entering Canadian waters is less than 24 hours, as soon as practicable before entering Canadian waters, but no later than when the vessel leaves its last port of call; (2) if the voyage before entering Canadian waters is between 24 and 96 hours, at least 24 hours before entering Canadian waters; and (3) in any other case, at least 96 hours before entering Canadian waters.[163]

NORDREG establishes four mandatory reports: a sailing plan report (SP), a position report (PR), a final report (FR), and a deviation report (DR).[164] A ship's master is responsible for ensuring that reports are completed properly and sent to a designated Marine Communications and Traffic Services Centre.[165] Under NORDREG, a sailing plan report must be provided at the following three times: (1) "when a vessel is about to enter the NORDREG Zone [Zone]"; (2) "more than one hour but not more than two hours" before a vessel leaves a berth within the Zone; and (3) "immediately before a vessel gets underway" within the Zone if it "has been stranded," stopped due to "breakdown in the main propulsion or steering system," or "involved in a collision."[166]

Position reports must also be made at specified times: (1) right after the ship enters the Zone; (2) daily at 4 PM Coordinated Universal Time, unless the ship is fitted with long-range identification and tracking equipment, and transmitting information as required under SOLAS V; and (3) if the ship is within or about to enter the Zone, as soon as possible after the ship's master becomes

---

160 *Northern Canada Vessel Traffic Services Zone Regulations*, SOR/2010-127, s. 2 [VTSZ Regulations].

161 Id., s. 3.

162 *Marine Transportation Security Regulations*, SOR/2004-144.

163 Id., s. 221(1).

164 VTSZ Regulations, n. 160 above, s. 5(1).

165 Id., ss. 4, 10.

166 Id., s. 6(1).

aware of certain situations, like "ice or weather conditions that are hazardous to safe navigation" or the presence of "a pollutant in the water."[167]

A deviation report is required when either a vessel's position "varies significantly" from what would be expected based on its sailing plan report, or its "intended voyage changes from the sailing plan report."[168] Not surprisingly, ships' masters must provide a final report immediately before leaving the NORDREG Zone, but they must also provide one upon arrival at a berth within the Zone.[169]

Each mandatory report is headed with 'NORDREG' followed by the two letters that correspond to the report type: SP, PR, DR, or FR.[170] The information required in each report varies according to its type and the circumstances requiring it to be made. Each type of information is given a letter 'designator' that must be used in the report, followed by the information set out next to that designator in the Schedule to the Regulations. So, for example, a ship about to enter the NORDREG Zone must send a sailing plan (SP) report including the designators A, B, C or D, E, F, G, H, I, L, O, P, Q, S, T, W and X and their associated information. Cross-referencing these designators with the Schedule, the required information for a hypothetical SP would be the following: information about the vessel (e.g., name, flag State, IMO number); the date and time corresponding to the vessel's position; the vessel's position indicated either by latitude and longitude or geographic name; the vessel's course; the vessel's speed; the vessel's last port of call; the estimated time and date the vessel will enter the Zone; the vessel's destination and ETA; the vessel's intended route; the vessel's maximum present static draught; the vessel's cargo; brief details about any defects, damage and deficiencies or any circumstances adversely affecting the vessel's normal navigation; a brief description of prevailing weather and ice conditions; the vessel's authorized representative, agent or owner; the number of persons on board the vessel; the amount of oil on board used as fuel or carried as cargo; if the vessel's master holds an Arctic Pollution Prevention Certificate, its expiry date and the name of its issuing authority; and finally, if applicable, the vessel's ice class.[171] As can be seen, the information required can be quite extensive.

---

167 Id., ss. 7(1), (2).
168 Id., s. 9.
169 Id., s. 8.
170 Id., s. 5(1).
171 Id., NORDREG Schedule, "NORDREG Information."

3b.   Compliance of NORDREG with Article 234

On 21 September 2010, following Canada's conversion of NORDREG from a voluntary to a mandatory regime, the United States and INTERTANKO sent a communication to the Maritime Safety Committee of the IMO expressing concerns over the amended regulations.[172] In their view, NORDREG does not comply with the IMO's requirements and guidance for mandatory ship reporting and vessel traffic services (VTS) systems. With respect to ship reporting, the parties claim that NORDREG was not properly submitted to the IMO for approval, following the process mandated under SOLAS V/11 and set out in Resolution A.851(20) and MSC/Circ. 1060.[173]

Similarly, the United States and INTERTANKO criticized the mandatory NORDREG Zone and the VTS system established within it on several fronts. First, they contend that under SOLAS V/12.3, a VTS system may only be mandatory in a coastal State's territorial sea.[174] They suggest that the geographic limits of the NORDREG Zone are unclear and its compliance with this requirement uncertain.[175] Second, they claim that a VTS system may be established outside a coastal State's territorial sea or in an international strait in only three ways: (1) gaining IMO approval under SOLAS V/12; (2) gaining IMO approval under SOLAS V/11; or (3) making the system voluntary.[176] Since Canada chose none of these methods to establish NORDREG, they allege it fails to comply with international requirements.[177] Third, the United States and INTERTANKO question whether Canada has the capacity to deliver the level of services suggested will be delivered under its mandatory VTS system.[178] For example, the parties question whether those delivering VTS under NORDREG have "suitable training for domain awareness, traffic clearances or providing advice on passage planning

---

172   INTERTANKO is the world's preeminent forum for independent owners and operators of oil and chemical tankers, available online: <http://www.intertanko.com/About-Us>; *Safety of Navigation: Northern Canada Vessel Traffic Services Zone Regulations*, submission by the United States and INTERTANKO to the Maritime Safety Committee of the International Maritime Organization, 21 September 2010, MSC 88/11/XX [US/INTERTANKO Submission].

173   "Guidelines for Vessel Traffic Services"; "Guidance Note on the Preparation of Proposals on Ships Routeing Systems and Ship Reporting Systems for Submission to the Sub-Committee on Safety of Navigation"; US/INTERTANKO Submission, id., paras. 2, 3.

174   Id. , para. 4.

175   Id.

176   Id., para. 5.

177   Id.

178   Id., paras. 6, 8, and 9.

and routeing," or whether "coherent and effective radar, AIS [automatic identification system] and radio coverage" is present in the NORDREG Zone.[179]

The submission concludes by recommending that the IMO's Maritime Safety Committee find NORDREG non-compliant with the requirements for mandatory ship reporting and VTS systems; that the IMO recommend that Member States encourage ships flying their flags to comply with Canada's regime only on a voluntary basis; and that the IMO request that Canada submit to it an appropriate proposal if it desires to make NORDREG mandatory.[180]

A close analysis of the US and INTERTANKO criticisms and claims is outside the scope of this article. However, a point highlighted in *Excessive Maritime Claims* concerning the interaction between SOLAS requirements and Article 234 provides an interesting insight.[181] The authors state that under international treaty law, an earlier treaty applies only to the extent that its provisions are compatible with a later treaty (assuming a State is a party to both).[182] In the case of the LOS Convention and SOLAS V/11 and V/12, the LOS Convention is the earlier treaty based on their date of adoption.[183] However, because the SOLAS regulations specifically state that nothing in them prejudices the rights of States under international law, the general rule is abridged, and these regulations become subordinate to the earlier treaty, the LOS Convention.[184] If this analysis is correct, it potentially weakens most if not all of the arguments adduced in the US/INTERTANKO Communication.

Aside from the Communication, NORDREG's compliance with Article 234 can be challenged for its "safety" focus, wide geographic scope and continuous application. The NORDREG regulations do not just apply during times when ice is present. They establish a continuous reporting requirement for vessels of a certain size or that carry particular cargo that enter or navigate within the NORDREG Zone. The Zone reaches from the undisputed internal waters of Hudson's Bay out to the limits of Canada's EEZ, from as low as 60° N in the East and beginning at the Arctic Circle in the West. While this is a massive and varied area, it must be remembered that Article 234 does not require continuous ice presence for the enactment and enforcement of measures, but only that ice

---

179   Id., paras. 8 and 9.

180   Id., para. 10.

181   Roach and Smith, n. 4 above.

182   Id. at 494; Vienna Convention on the Law of Treaties, 23 May 1969, 1155 *United Nations Treaty Series* 331, Art. 30(3).

183   Roach and Smith, n. 4 above, p. 494.

184   Id., pp. 494–495.

be present "for most of the year." In current climate conditions, the Zone may in fact meet this requirement despite its breadth.

Arguably, the reason NORDREG's coverage is so wide is because it was not crafted to only further Article 234 ends. While Canada asserts that the Regulations are "consistent with international law regarding ice-covered areas," it also states that they "...will enhance the safety of vessels, crew and passengers...."[185] Indeed, NORDREG was not enacted under the AWPPA, but pursuant to the *Canada Shipping Act*.[186] While Northern Canada Vessel Traffic Services undoubtedly supplies an important component of Canada's pollution prevention efforts in Arctic waters, it equally provides essential maritime safety services in the region.

Having made this concession, the validity of the US/INTERTANKO claims revive. If NORDREG is more than an Article 234 measure, the Regulations will need amendment to ensure compliance with SOLAS V/11 and 12, at least for application outside of Canada's internal waters and territorial sea. To achieve this, Canada could prepare an IMO submission to validate the regime as it exists, or potentially alter it so that the reporting requirements are only mandatory within the limits of its territorial sea and in Article 234 ice-covered areas.

4a.   Summary of the Arctic Ice Regime Shipping System Standards

The Arctic Ice Regime Shipping System (AIRSS) Standards flesh out the AIRSS established in subsections 6(3) and (3.1) of the ASPPR. The AIRSS is an alternative to the Zone-Date system. It is applied when a ship is navigating in a SSCZ outside the dates permitted under the ZDS.[187]

According to the Regulations, before deciding to enter a SSCZ under the AIRSS, a master must take account of key information, namely, (1) the manoeuvring characteristics of the ship and any escorting ship; (2) "the operating characteristics and condition of the ship and of any equipment on board designed for the purpose of detecting ice hazards"; (3) the probability that ice conditions will change during the intended transit and the probable effect of any such change; and (4) "weather conditions."[188] In the words of the Standards, what "the Regulations require [is] that the decision to enter an ice regime be based on the Master's assessment that the ship is capable to navigate safely through the ice regime."[189]

---

185   CCG on NORDREG, n. 159 above.

186   *Canada Shipping Act, 2001*, SC 2001, c. 26, s. 136(1)(a), (b), (i).

187   AIRSS Standards, n. 52 above, para. 1.

188   ASPPR, n. 87 above, s. 6(3)(b).

189   Id., para. 1.

The 'short guide' found at the beginning of the Standards provides a good overview of how the AIRSS works. It enumerates the following steps for the intended user of the system:

1. Obtain current ice information for the planned passage;
2. Select a desired route;
3. Determine the ice regime boundaries on the route;
4. Determine the Ice Numerals (IN) on the route for each separate ice regime;
5. If all the Ice Numerals are zero or greater, advise NORDREG, submit an Ice Regime Routing Message and proceed (Go to 8);
6. If the Ice Numeral for an ice regime is negative, consider the alternatives, such as selecting another route, waiting for improvement in ice conditions or requesting assistance of an icebreaker;
7. When an icebreaker or other vessel modifies a regime, or there is a change in the ice conditions, giving positive Ice Numerals, proceed after advising NORDREG; and
8. On completion of the voyage, send the After Action Report to Prairie and Northern Region – Marine (AMNS-OTT), Ottawa.[190]

Two aspects of the AIRSS require further explanation. First, though not mentioned in the short guide, the Regulations require that any ship using the AIRSS have an ice navigator on board.[191] The ice navigator can be anyone on board who has the qualifications set out in the Regulations.[192] Second, the term 'ice regime' means "a region covered with generally consistent ice conditions."[193] The size of an ice regime may vary drastically with its boundaries depending only on the existence of "...a relatively consistent distribution of any mix of ice types, including open water" in the area.[194] The path behind an icebreaker or another ship may constitute a separate ice regime; and a ship may potentially enter an ice regime even when the regime contains some ice "which is beyond the capabilities of [the] ship to pass through."[195] The decision to enter depends

---

190   Id., para. 4.
191   Id., s. 26(2).
192   Id., s 26(3). Note: There appears to be an inconsistency between the Regulations and the Standards. The latter state that the ice navigator need only meet the requirements of s. 26(3)(b), ASPPR – see para. 2, AIRSS Standards.
193   AIRSS Standards, n. 52 above, para. 8.1.
194   Id.
195   Id.

on the ability of the ship to pass through the regime safely, avoiding 'dangerous' ice.[196]

As indicated in the summary steps above, ships may only enter an ice regime when the Ice Numeral for the regime is 0 or higher.[197] To calculate the Ice Numeral, certain information is needed.

First, a master must determine the type of ice comprising the regime, of which there are nine varieties listed and described in the AIRSS' Standards.[198] Second, the master must estimate in tenths the concentration of each ice type found in the regime. Third, the master must assess whether any of the ice types in the regime are either "decayed" ("[have] thaw holes formed, or [are] rotten ice") or "ridged."[199] These characteristics lead to adjustment of the Ice Multipliers used in calculating the Ice Numeral. Fourth, the master must find the Ice Numeral for each ice type in the Ice Multiplier Table.[200] The table gives a number corresponding to each type of ice for each class of ship. If any ice type is decayed, the ice multiplier is increased by 1, and if any ice type is ridged, it is decreased by 1.[201] With this information, the master is able to calculate the Ice Numeral for the regime (region with more or less uniform ice conditions).

The Ice Numeral calculation is made by: (1) computing the product of the ice concentration and Ice Multiplier for each type of ice, and (2) adding these products together. The sum of the products is the Ice Numeral for that ice regime. If it is 0 or greater, that regime is considered 'safe' for navigation.[202] In reality, a proposed route through Arctic waters would likely cover several ice regimes, and an Ice Numeral must be calculated for each one. Assuming each Ice Numeral for a proposed route is 0 or greater, the master must send an Ice Regime Routing Message to NORDREG and receive acknowledgement of this message before proceeding into the zone(s) covered by the regime(s).[203] Within 30 days after completing a transit under the AIRSS, the master of the

---

196   Id.

197   Id., para 4; *ASPPR*, n. 87 above, s. 6(3)(a).

198   AIRSS Standards, n. 52 above, para. 6.2, 'Ice terminology', which establishes the following nine ice types in its 'Ice Multiplier Table': Open Water (OW); Grey Ice (G); Grey White Ice (GW); four stages of first year ice: Thin First Year 1st Stage (FY), Thin First Year 2nd Stage (FY), Medium First Year (MFY), and Thick First Year (TFY); Second Year (SY), and Multi Year (MY).

199   Id., paras. 3.2, 6.2, and 8.2.

200   Id., para. 5.

201   Id., para. 6.2 and 8.2.

202   Id., para. 8.2.

203   Id., para. 9.1; ASPPR, n. 87 above, s. 6(3)(c) and 6(3)(d).

ship must send an After Action Report, not to NORDREG, but to the Regional Director, Marine, Prairie & Northern Region.[204]

4b.   Compliance of the AIRSS with Article 234

In theory, the advantage of the AIRSS over the ZDS is that it provides greater flexibility. Rather than being confined to rigid times and set areas, the system relies on a vessel master's careful assessment of existing ice conditions and the capability of his vessel to navigate safely in and through them. The Foreword to the Standards states that the AIRSS is intended to eventually replace the ZDS scheme.[205] It also suggests that the AIRSS may require improvement before the ZDS is completely phased out.[206] This appears to be the case.

A 2007 study prepared for Transport Canada by researchers at the Canadian Hydraulics Centre concluded that neither the ZDS nor the AIRSS has a strong scientific basis.[207] In particular, when comparing the existing AIRSS to a modified approach, the researchers found the AIRSS was too restrictive, keeping vessels out of areas where they could have safely navigated.[208]

Article 234 requires a coastal State to have due regard for navigation and science. As was the case with other components of Canada's existing pollution prevention scheme, the AIRSS's weak scientific grounding means it may not only fail to meet Article 234's science criterion, but it may also unduly impact navigation as a consequence. Canada should take a careful look at both the ZDS and AIRSS to bring them up to date with current science.

IV.   Conclusion and Recommendations

A.   *Does Canada's Arctic Waters Regime Operate within Article 234's Scope?*

This article advanced the question whether Canada succeeded in legitimizing its Arctic waters pollution prevention measures by gaining insertion of Article 234 in the LOS Convention. If one interprets this question to include gaining general acceptance for some of Canada's more controversial claims, such as its position that the waters of the Arctic archipelago are Canadian internal waters, the answer is 'No'. However, if the question focusses instead on Canada's

---

204   AIRSS Standards, id., para. 9.2; ASPPR, id., s. 6(3.1).
205   AIRSS Standards, id., ii.
206   Id.
207   Timco and Kubat, n. 75 above, pp. 1, 8, 12, and 22.
208   Id., p. 12.

regulatory measures to protect the Arctic marine environment, the answer generally and largely is 'Yes'.

For the most part, Canada's measures operate within the geographic, climatic, and temporal limits of Article 234. Canada's regime applies uniformly to foreign vessels of all States. While Canada's regulations impact navigation, an effort has clearly been made to inject flexibility into the regime (e.g., the AIRSS) and, at least to some degree, to base it on available science and harmonize it with international standards (e.g., the Equivalent Standards). However, while Canada has achieved general compliance for its Arctic waters measures, there remain specific areas where its laws overstep Article 234's limits.

First, Canada's Arctic waters pollution prevention measures purport to apply to sovereign vessels.[209] While Canada may freely apply such measures to sovereign vessels traversing its internal waters, Article 236 of the LOS Convention clearly prohibits doing so under any of Part XII's provisions, including Article 234.

Second, Canada's Arctic pollution protection regime applies to disputed waters, not unequivocally within the limits of its EEZ, as required by Article 234. Specifically, the United States contests the Beaufort Sea boundary. Without resolution of this issue, Canada cannot effectively apply its regulations to that area.

Third, both the Zone-Date system and the alternative Arctic Ice Regime Shipping System lack correspondence with the best available scientific evidence, contrary to Article 234. While Schedule VIII's zones and dates may have at one time matched the ice concentrations occurring in Canadian Arctic waters, this is no longer the case.[210] And, though the AIRSS is more flexible and represents a closer match with current data, it too needs updating.[211] Because Canada's vessel traffic regulations lack sufficient scientific correspondence, they may either unnecessarily hinder or dangerously allow navigation. In the former case, infringing Article 234's navigation criterion, and in the latter, jeopardizing the very purpose of Canada's measures.

Finally, Canada's Arctic waters regulations in some instances go beyond laws and regulations for the prevention, reduction and control of marine

---

209   See, for example, in *Equivalent Standards*, n. 65 above, viii, where it is stated, "The possibility that large tankers would use the north-west passage as a regular route led to the enactment of the *Arctic Waters Pollution Prevention Act* in 1970. Civil Liability and Arctic Shipping regulations were promulgated in 1972, applicable to all vessels, sovereign or commercial in the Canadian Arctic. There has been no major amendment to the regulations since then."

210   Timco and Kubat, n. 75 above, p. 8.

211   Id., p. 12.

pollution. Specifically, stipulating the amount of fresh water a ship must carry, while unquestionably critical to crew safety in the vast expanses of the Arctic, is not primarily about pollution prevention. NORDREG may not be either. While it clearly enables pollution prevention, it equally serves maritime safety and security functions. It does not plainly fall within Article 234's scope.

B.   Recommendations

In light of the above conclusions, the following are suggestions for each of the highlighted compliance issues:

(1) *Stop applying Canada's pollution prevention regulations to sovereign vessels.*

Outside of Canada's internal Arctic waters, as established by straight baselines around the Arctic archipelago, Canada should accept that it cannot under international law apply pollution prevention regulations to sovereign vessels.[212] This should not be cause for alarm. First, Article 236 itself, while granting sovereign vessels immunity from the Convention's pollution prevention provisions, also requires that States operating such vessels "ensure, by the adoption of appropriate measures not impairing operations or operational capabilities...that such vessels...act in a manner consistent, so far as is reasonable and practicable, with [the] Convention."[213] In other words, States are not given a complete 'free ride' with respect to sovereign vessel pollution. Second, the cooperation of Arctic States on the Arctic Council and within the Council's working groups, such as Protection of the Arctic Marine Environment and Emergency Prevention, Preparedness and Response, demonstrates their collective commitment to protecting the Arctic's vulnerable marine environment. This is significant as these are the States most likely to be active in the region. Finally, the success of past arrangements, like the 1988 Canada-United States Arctic Cooperation Agreement managing the transit of US icebreakers through the Northwest Passage proves that non-binding political arrangements can sometimes be very effective at producing results.[214] Canada could potentially make similar arrangements with respect to sovereign vessel pollution prevention.

(2) *Establish the Beaufort Sea boundary with the United States.*

---

212   LOS Convention, n. 8 above, Art. 236.
213   LOS Convention, n. 8 above, Art. 236.
214   Kraska, n. 3 above, pp. 266–267; Pharand, n. 2 above, pp. 50–51.

Canada should seek to delimit the western boundary of its Arctic waters with the United States as soon as possible. It is in both Canada's and the United States' interest to reach an agreement over these waters for a number of reasons. One, the region is home to significant oil and gas reserves.[215] Delimiting the maritime boundary could open the door for sustainable and equitable development. Two, both nations are interested in making extended continental shelf claims in the Arctic. For the United States in particular, when combined with retreating sea ice, this would likely open access to significant additional hydrocarbon and mineral reserves.[216] Three, the area is ecologically fragile. Cooperation is needed to protect the region's living resources, wildlife, waters, and coastline.[217] Given the entrenchment of Canadian and US positions on this boundary, reaching an agreement would doubtless be very difficult. However, given the incentives listed above, the added impetus of climate change, and the two nations' record of past cooperation on matters like search and rescue, Canada and the United States just might find the political will to settle this matter to their mutual benefit.

(3)   *Modify or replace the current ZDS and AIRSS.*

Canada should modify or replace the current regime for regulating vessel traffic under its Arctic Shipping Pollution Prevention Regulations. The discussion paper for Transport Canada demonstrates that research has already begun to develop a better system. Given the United States' strength in scientific research, and the fact that it is with the United States that we have our biggest outstanding disputes in the Arctic (e.g., over the status of the NWP waters), cooperating with the Americans on the science to develop a new vessel regime for our Arctic waters could present a good opportunity for engagement. Canada could get more and better data while the United States would have little reason to claim the resulting system was not based on the best available science.

(4)   *Continue to push for better and Arctic waters-specific international standards, while simultaneously harmonizing Canadian standards with improved global ones as they come into force.*

---

215   AMSA Report, n. 47 above, p. 97.

216   R. Pedrozo, "Arctic Climate Change and U.S. Accession to the United Convention on the Law of the Sea," *International Law Studies* 89 (2013): 757–775 at 763.

217   See id., p. 773 on the US fishing moratorium in this area.

Canada's unilateral actions to protect Arctic waters beginning in the 1970s were arguably necessary to supply what was lacking under international law. Since the 1970s, however, much has changed. Arctic States have concluded binding agreements on search and rescue and oil pollution preparedness and response. Currently, the IMO is drafting a comprehensive International Code of Safety for Ships Operating in Polar Waters (the Polar Code), which will impose mandatory standards pertaining to the design, construction, equipment and operations of ships voyaging in waters surrounding the North and South Poles.[218] The Code's dual objectives relate to facilitating the safe operation of shipping while ensuring environmental protection measures are in place to safeguard the polar region's unique ecology. The IMO anticipates the approval and adoption of the Polar Code in November 2014 at the 94th meeting of its Maritime Safety Committee, in tandem with the approval the new draft Safety of Life at Sea Convention (SOLAS) Chapter XIV "Safety Measures for Ships Operating in Polar Waters."[219] Increased cooperation among Arctic States in fora such as the Arctic Council and the impending passage of comprehensive international standards regulating the safety of shipping and environmental protection in Polar Regions is evidence of a new international framework for Arctic regulation. Within this framework, it makes sense for Canada to seek, as much as possible, to harmonize its standards with a newly emerging international regime. Even if an international standard was marginally lower, it might be worth adopting for what Canada would likely gain in actual compliance.

As it stands now, Canada appears to lack the capacity to enforce much of its Arctic waters regulatory regime. Though cutting, the INTERTANKO/US criticisms of the mandatory NORDREG system may not be far off the mark with respect to Canada's ability to effectively manage such an immense vessel traffic services area. Canada should work to increase its capacity through careful investment in key infrastructure that responds to and meets actual needs.[220]

---

218   International Maritime Organization, Development of an International Code of Safety for Ships Operating in Polar Waters (Polar Code), available online: <http://www.imo.org/ MediaCentre/HotTopics/polar/Pages/default.aspx>.

219   International Maritime Organization, Maritime Safety Committee, Meeting Minutes of the 93rd Session of the Maritime Safety Committee, 14–23 May 2014, available online: <http://www.imo.org/MediaCentre/MeetingSummaries/MSC/Pages/MSC-93.aspx>. Editors' Note: The IMO adopted the Polar Code as expected in November 2014, see "Shipping in Polar Waters," available online: <http://www.imo.org/MediaCentre/ HotTopics/polar/Pages/default.aspx>.

220   See, for example, M. Byers and S. Webb, *Titanic Blunder: Arctic/Offshore Patrol Ships on Course for Disaster* (Ottawa: Rideau Institute and Canadian Centre for Policy Alternatives,

Canada played a key role in writing Article 234 into the LOS Convention. However, as conditions in the Arctic continue to change, Article 234 may diminish in significance, partly because it represents a 'snapshot' of ice-covered areas as they existed when it was drafted, but also because as Arctic States and those outside the region increasingly cooperate to protect ice-covered waters, both the need for and the legitimacy of unilateral coastal State action will decrease. Even so, Canada can continue to lead in this area. Canada should strive, through its seat on the Arctic Council and in other fora, to ensure that the unique challenges of the Arctic marine environment are never overlooked when global shipping standards are being developed. In this way, Canada's legacy of work to protect its ice-covered waters may not only continue, but also evolve and flourish.

April 2013), available online: <https://www.policyalternatives.ca/publications/reports/ titanic-blunder>.

Living Resources and Coastal Management

∴

Reforming European Union Participation in Fisheries Management and Conservation on the High Seas†

*Anna Antonova**
Department of Marine Affairs, University of Rhode Island, Kingston, Rhode Island, USA

Introduction

The European Union (EU) holds exclusive competence on matters of fishery conservation and management in European waters and in this role has participated actively in the international conventions and agreements that shape modern fishery management on the high seas. As the world's fifth largest fish producer in 2012[1] and a formidable political entity, the EU is well-positioned to influence further development in this regulatory network, as well as to address key weaknesses in the performance of regional fishery management organizations (RFMOs). The EU has shown its willingness to play a positive role within the external dimension of its Common Fisheries Policy (CFP), in which it proposes to 'strengthen and enhance' international compliance with RFMOs.[2] However, in the past the EU itself has been criticized heavily for its conduct in such organizations and has seemed to contribute to their overarching problems. To assess the potential legitimacy of the CFP claim to strengthen and enhance RFMO performance, this article explores the legal background for EU participation in international marine living resource management and the

---

† Editors' Note. – This article was the runner-up entry in the 2014 *Ocean Yearbook* Student Paper Competition.
* The author wishes to thank Professor Lawrence Juda in the Department of Marine Affairs at the University of Rhode Island for his teaching, guidance, and thoughtful comments.
1 European Commission, Facts and Figures of the Common Fisheries Policy (2012).
2 European Commission, Green Paper on Reform of the Common Fisheries Policy, COM(2009) 163, p. 5 [Green Paper].

Ocean Yearbook 29: 125–143
© KONINKLIJKE BRILL NV, LEIDEN, 2015 | DOI 10.1163/9789004297234_007

development of its role in the field, and evaluates two case studies of past EU conduct in two major RFMOs: the Northwest Atlantic Fisheries Organization (NAFO) and the International Commission for the Conservation of Atlantic Tunas (ICCAT).

Legal Overview

Legal Framework for EU Participation in International Fisheries Organizations

As the EU's CFP approached a new round of reform in 2012, its significance transcended EU waters by far.[3] The Union's power to affect the world's marine fisheries is enforced by sheer volume of production: collectively, the EU was the world's fifth largest harvester of fish in 2012 and it accounted for over five percent of world marine capture in 2011, while 20 percent of its landings were caught on the high seas.[4] The majority of this catch was extracted from the eastern Atlantic and Mediterranean, but EU fleets also operate globally and have been increasingly present on the high seas and in other countries' exclusive economic zones (EEZs) over the last few decades.[5] Additionally, the EU has the world's largest single market for fisheries products.[6] Given the breadth of its activity alone, therefore, the EU is an essential player in the realm of international fisheries management.

Within the context of international law, the role of the EU in fisheries is equally important, albeit more complex. Since the EU is a supranational organization, its degree of participation in any international institution (or treaty regime) is different from that of a sovereign state, and is determined both externally and internally.[7] Externally, the EU's involvement depends on whether the international institution in question allows for the participation of supranational organizations, and if it does, to what degree such participation is allowed, which is usually outlined in relevant provisions of the institution's constitutional treaty.

---

3   Id.

4   European Commission, n. 1 above; FAO for data on worldwide capture; Eurostat for capture by 27 Member States; European Commission, Directorate-General for Maritime Affairs and Fisheries, "Fishing Outside the EU," <http://ec.europa.eu/fisheries/cfp/international/index _en.htm> [DGMAF].

5   European Commission, n. 1 above; R. Watson, D. Zeller and D. Pauly, "Spatial Expansion of EU and Non-EU Fishing Fleets into the Global Ocean, 1950 to the Present," WWF Netherlands, 2012, available online: <http://www.wwf.org.uk/wwf_articles.cfm?unewsid=5623>.

6   DGMAF, n. 4 above.

7   R. Wessel, "The Legal Framework for the Participation of the European Union in International Institutions," Journal of European Integration 33, no. 6 (2011): 621–735.

For example, the 1982 United Nations Convention on the Law of the Sea (UNCLOS) includes in its final clauses the provision that "the Convention shall be open for signature by...international organizations,"[8] where the latter are defined as "intergovernmental organization[s] ...to which its member States have transferred competence over matters governed by this Convention."[9]

Accordingly, the second factor that defines the EU's capacity to participate in international institutions is determined internally, depending on how legal competences are divided between the EU and its Member States. As a supranational organization, the EU may hold legal competences that have been explicitly conferred unto it by its Member States, and these competences can be either exclusive or shared with the Member States.[10] Although the division of different competences is broadly outlined in the Treaty on the Functioning of the European Union (TFEU), their external implications are often implied or inferred from the external dimension of internal competences,[11] and from the general rights to cooperate with third countries granted to the EU in the TFEU.[12] Particular international competences of the EU are also often defined through agreements themselves, in which the EU often states its relative competences.

In the case of fisheries, the TFEU demarcates exclusive EU competence over "the conservation of marine biological resources under the common fisheries policy" and shared competence over other fisheries-related matters, such as research or technological development.[13] The exact scope of 'conservation' remains undefined in the TFEU, in large part because the extent of EU competence has expanded over the years along with the development of the CFP and with increased EU participation in relevant international institutions.

For the purposes of international law, current EU competence in fisheries relations is best defined by the EU declaration upon ratifying UNCLOS in 1998. The EU claims exclusive competence over "the conservation and management of sea resources" and the corresponding right "to adopt the relevant rules and regulations...and, within its competence, to enter into external undertakings

---

8   United Nations Convention on the Law of the Sea, 10 December 1982, *United Nations Treaty Series* 1833, Art. 305(1)(f) [UNCLOS].

9   Id., Annex IX (1).

10   Treaty of Lisbon Amending the Treaty on European Union and the Treaty Establishing the European Community, 13 December 2007, 2007 OJ (C 306) 1, Title I, Art. 5 [2007 Treaty on European Union].

11   Wessel, n. 7 above.

12   Consolidated Treaty on the Functioning of the European Union, OJ C 326, 26 October 2012, 47–390, Part V, especially Title V, Arts. 216–217.

13   Id., Part I, Title I, Art. 3(d); Id., Art. 4(d).

with third States or competent international organizations."[14] In short, when it comes to most fisheries matters – excluding flagging jurisdiction, which reverts to Member States, and research and technological development, which fall under the shared competences – the EU has exclusive competence to represent its Member States.[15]

On the basis of this competence, the EU has become a formidable force in international living marine resource management. It has taken on an active role in various multilateral fisheries organizations, often superseding previous participation by its Member States.[16] Where it comes to fisheries management and conservation, the EU represents its Member States' interests and negotiates and adopts measures within the framework of the international institutions. The EU is then also responsible for implementing measures from international treaties and agreements on an EU-level. This is accomplished through the Common Fisheries Policy.

International Significance of the Common Fisheries Policy

As the main legislation resulting from the EU's exclusive competence in living marine resource management and conservation, the CFP governs most aspects of fisheries policy in the EU. Its jurisdiction includes catch allocation, industry and market regulations, control and enforcement, and international relations.[17] Although it mainly sets regulations for fisheries within EU waters, the CFP has significant international implications. For one, it performs the important function of aligning internal law with international responsibility (the supranational equivalent of enabling legislation). Where this role of the CFP has previously been more implicit, it is now formally integrated into the legislation by the external policy provisions in the revised proposal of 2011.[18]

Needless to say, Member States' compliance with international agreements undertaken by the EU as a whole is crucial for maintaining the respectability of the EU as a competent international legal entity. The CFP governs the behavior of all EU vessels concerning living marine resources, whether they are

---

14   UNCLOS, n. 8 above. Declaration of the European Community upon signature (7 December 1998). Declaration made pursuant to Article 5(1) of Annex IX to the Convention and to Article 4(4) of the Agreement.

15   Id.

16   Lawrence Juda, Professor, University of Rhode Island, pers. comm. 2013.

17   Council of the European Union, Council Regulation (EC) No 2371/2002 of 20 December 2002 on the conservation and exploitation of fisheries resources under the Common Fisheries Policy. Official Journal of the European Communities, L 358/59, Art. 1(2).

18   European Commission, Proposal for a Regulation of the European Parliament and of the Council on the Common Fisheries Policy, COM(2011) 425 final [EC COM(2011)].

fishing in their flag state's territory, in wider EU waters, or on the high seas and in third countries' EEZs.[19] Breaches of compliance by individual Member States might therefore damage the international credibility of the EU as a whole, making third party States and multilateral organizations reluctant to trust it. Hence, the success of the CFP to integrate external policy into internal legislation and enforce it determines in part the extent of future EU participation in international fisheries institutions.

The significance of the CFP for the international community does not end there. As already observed, the EU holds a prominent role in the world's fisheries due to its considerable annual catch and its extensive consumer market for fish products. Consequently, the EU is an essential participant in successfully implementing international conservation measures and can exercise considerable political influence in the field. Because the CFP reflects the combined interests of all Member States, its regulations can be instrumental in ensuring that EU influence is used for the positive development and sustainable preservation of global living marine resources. This potential has understandably received international attention, including from academics, various institutions, and international non-governmental organizations (NGOs).[20] For instance, the World Wildlife Fund has actively called for responsible EU governance, asking the EU "to ensure that [its] fishing zeal is matched by the accountability to ensure its fleets fish sustainably, and to champion sustainable fisheries management on the international stage."[21]

The most recent reform of the CFP is therefore of interest. The CFP is based on multi-annual plans and is subject to review every ten years. As it approached the new review cycle in 2012, the European Commission called for fundamental reform of the CFP, "not...yet another piecemeal, incremental reform but a sea change cutting to the core."[22] While the main focus of the reform falls on addressing overarching issues with fisheries in EU waters, such as persistent overfishing, heavy industry subsidies, and fleet overcapacity, various documents of the reform process suggest that the new CFP intends to address its own international influence and responsibility. The 2009 Green Paper on Reform cites important worldwide resolutions with the clear

---

19   See n. 17 above.

20   Including a dedicated issue of *Ocean & Coastal Management* 70 (2012): 1–68.

21   WWF Global, "Wild West Fishing in Distant Waters," (2012) Press release report in response to R. Watson et al. 2012 study "Spatial Expansion of EU and Non-EU fishing Fleets into the Global Ocean, 1950 to the Present," requested by WWF Netherlands, 2013, available online: <http://wwf.panda.org/?203247/Wild-west-fishing-in-distant-waters>.

22   Green Paper, n. 2 above, p. 5.

intention of integrating them into the CFP: "The World Summit on Sustainable Development in 2002 spelled out specific targets for fisheries management... which must be taken on board by all fisheries managing authorities. Important steps have also been taken in the United Nations to limit the impact of fisheries in the high seas."[23] The 2011 reform proposal confirms this intention by including a section on external policy previously not present in the CFP. This new section aims, as explained in the proposal itself, to align the CFP more closely with international agreements and to ensure that EU participation in international multilateral organizations serves "to strengthen them and enhance their performance in the management and conservation of international fish stocks."[24] In short, the new CFP proposal shows awareness of its potential and actual role in the management of international living marine resources and purports to establish the EU as a positive leader in this field.

Modern International Fisheries Management and the EU

The external policy provisions in the revised CFP proposal represent only the latest step of EU participation in international fisheries management. As previously mentioned, the range of EU involvement expanded through the years in parallel with the development of modern international fisheries management. To properly understand the significance of the reformed CFP's claim, therefore, one must first comprehend how the current international fisheries regime developed, and what role the EU played in its progress.

Development of the Modern Fisheries Management Framework
The modern fisheries management framework emerged with the development of the EEZ in the 1970s and its codification in UNCLOS. Earlier, waters beyond coastal States' territorial seas were regarded as high seas subject to the 'freedom of the sea' and full freedom of fishing.[25] However, growing concern with distant water fishing fleets and dwindling stocks in the 20th century led many coastal States to extend their jurisdiction beyond three nautical miles, and eventually to integrate EEZs into international law under UNCLOS.[26]

---

23   Id.

24   EC COM(2011), n. 18 above, Explanatory Memorandum, p. 9.

25   H. Grotius, *Mare Liberum* (1609), as codified in Article 2 of the Convention on the High Seas, 29 April 1958, *United Nations Treaty Series* 450.

26   Lawrence Juda, Professor, Professor, of Rhode Island, pers. comm. (2013).

The EEZ was defined as an area up to 200 nautical miles (NM) from territorial sea baselines, in which coastal States have certain rights, jurisdiction, and duties over economic resources,[27] including determining total allowable catch (TAC), allocation, and necessary conservation measures.[28] EEZs were claimed by most coastal States globally, including ones that are not party to the Convention but view the EEZ as customary law.[29] At the time, it was estimated that over 95 percent of the world's fish came from areas over the continental shelf (due to the abundance of nutrients there), hence the EEZ's establishment ensured some form of authority over the majority of fishing resources worldwide.[30]

However, as ecological boundaries rarely coincide with human political borders, the migration patterns of fish resulted in issues with transboundary stocks (moving between two or more States' EEZs), straddling stocks (moving between the EEZs and the high seas), and highly migratory stocks (moving over extensive distances in the ocean).[31] The provisions addressing these issues in UNCLOS were only cursory as it was believed at the time that straddling and highly migratory stocks were of minor importance given the small share of catch extracted from them.[32]

Various incidents in the years after the conclusion of the Convention quickly proved this notion wrong. Distant water fishing fleets, increasingly excluded from their previous fishing grounds, began targeting straddling and highly migratory stocks instead. This often resulted in their overexploitation – as with pollock in the Bering Sea 'Doughnut Hole', groundfish on the Grand Banks of Newfoundland, and bluefin tuna in the Atlantic Ocean, among others.[33] Such incidents demonstrated the need for strengthened international cooperation on high seas fisheries and several agreements were adopted in the early 1990s. The Food and Agricultural Organization of the UN (FAO) drafted a 'soft law' Code of Conduct for Responsible Fisheries and the binding 1993 Compliance

---

27 UNCLOS, n. 8 above, Part V, Art. 55.

28 Id., Arts. 61 and 62.

29 The most prominent among these, of course, is the United States.

30 L. Juda, "The 1995 United Nations Agreement on Straddling Fish Stocks and Highly Migratory Fish Stocks: A Critique," *Ocean Development and International Law* 28 (1996): 147–166.

31 Id.

32 Id., as well as UNCLOS, n. 8 above, Part V, Arts. 63 and 64; Food and Agriculture Organization of the United Nations (FAO), *The State of World Fisheries and Aquaculture 2006* (Rome: FAO, 2007).

33 Id.

Agreement,[34] and in 1995, negotiations at the UN led to the Agreement on Straddling Fish Stocks and Highly Migratory Fish Stocks (Fish Stocks Agreement or UNFSA).[35]

The new regime changed the freedom of fishing on the high seas fundamentally. Previously unlimited,[36] fishing on the high seas was now subject to certain constraints, such as treaty obligations, the rights of coastal States, and cooperation for conservation measures.[37] Recognizing the inherent jurisdictional difficulty in cooperating to manage straddling species or highly migratory species (such as tuna), the Fish Stocks Agreement emphasized the importance of regional fisheries management organizations (RFMOs) as a mechanism for international cooperation.[38] UNFSA includes a binding obligation for its parties to enlist in such organizations and limits the access to stocks under any RFMO's jurisdiction to members of the particular RFMO and States complying with its measures.[39] Through such means, international ocean law seeks to limit unregulated fishing on the high seas.

However, despite subjecting most of the world's fisheries to some form of authority and conservation, the modern regime of fisheries management remains imperfect, particularly concerning high seas fishing. Straddling and highly migratory species are still the world's most heavily overexploited species.[40] Specific shortcomings of the management system have been emphasized. Generally, given the nature of international treaties, UNCLOS and UNFSA are only binding on States that are party to them, resulting in 'free riding' States that reap the benefits of the agreements without contributing to

---

34   FAO, Code of Conduct for Responsible Fisheries (CCRF), Report of the Conference of FAO, Twenty-Eighth Session, 20–31 October 1995, Annex 1 to the CCRF (Background to the Origin and Elaboration of the Code), available online: <http://www.fao.org/docrep/005/v9878e/v9878e00.htm>; FAO, Agreement to Promote Compliance with International Conservation and Management Measures by Fishing Vessels on the High Seas, 29 November 1993, FAO Conference Resolution 15/93, available online: <http://www.fao.org/docrep/MEETING/003/X3130m/X3130E00.HTM>.

35   Agreement for the Implementation of the Provisions of the United Nations Convention on the Law of the Sea of 10 December 1982 Relating to the Conservation and Management of Straddling Fish Stocks and Highly Migratory Fish Stocks, 4 December 1995, 2167 *United Nations Treaty Series* 88 [UNFSA].

36   See Article 2 of the Convention on the High Seas, n. 25 above.

37   UNCLOS, n. 8 above, Part VII, Arts. 116–119.

38   UNFSA, n. 35 above, Part III, Art. 8.

39   Id., Art. 8(4).

40   FAO, *The State of World Fisheries and Aquaculture 2011* (Rome: FAO, 2012).

conservation.[41] Moreover, RFMO efforts have been consistently limited by illegal, unreported, and unregulated (IUU) fishing. Interested States have attempted to address these issues through various means of international pressure, including blacklisting or banning fish product imports from non-complying States, a practice that the EU has adopted.[42] Such measures have proved only partially effective as banned States can often find other markets with relative ease.

Weaknesses have been observed with RFMO management itself. Many RFMOs predate the Fish Stocks Agreement and were originally established as international fora for quota allocation, making them ill-qualified to conserve the stocks.[43] In addition, the performance of many member States within RFMOs has been found lacking, while particular provisions in many RFMO constitutional treaties fail to limit bad faith actions.[44] In NAFO, for instance, provisions for opting out from the yearly catch quota agreements allowed members to disregard the conservation efforts of the organization on a continuous basis.[45] Recognizing the need to address these weaknesses, international attention has recently focused on strengthening the performance of RFMOs in order to better ensure successful conservation of global fisheries resources.

Developing EU Participation in the Modern Fisheries Management Regime

In the negotiations leading up to UNCLOS, the European Economic Community (EEC, the EU's predecessor) participated solely as an observer.[46] At the time the Convention was debated, the EEC did not yet hold exclusive competence over fisheries management. In fact, it was precisely the establishment of the EEZ system, especially in juxtaposition to the natural paths of fish and traditional fishing practices between Member States, that provided the original motivation for a common fisheries policy.[47] The first legislation establishing such a policy for

---

41 Lawrence Juda, Professor, University of Rhode Island, pers. comm. 2013.

42 Id.

43 K.M. Gjerde, D. Currie, K. Wowk and K. Sack, "Ocean in Peril: Reforming the Management of Global Ocean Living Resources in Areas beyond National Jurisdiction," *Marine Pollution Bulletin* 74, no. 2 (2013): 540–551.

44 Id.

45 A. Aneiros, "Spain, the European Union, and Canada: A New Phase in the Unstable Balance in the Northwest Atlantic Fisheries," *Ocean Development & International Law* 42 (2011): 155–172.

46 Id.

47 Green Paper, n. 2 above, p. 6.

the EEC was put into force in 1983,[48] shortly after the conclusion of the UNCLOS negotiations. In its first review in 1992, the EU Council claimed that the policy had "proved to be an effective instrument"[49] and thus the exclusive competence over fisheries was reinforced in the 1992 Maastricht Treaty on European Union.[50]

Once established as a competent legal entity in the field, the EEC sought to take part in subsequent developments of the modern fisheries management regime. It became increasingly active, participating in drafting the FAO Code of Conduct and the Compliance Agreement, as well in the negotiations for the 1995 Fish Stocks Agreement.[51] Upon signing UNCLOS in 1998, as noted above, the EEC attached an exhaustive declaration outlining its competence in fisheries conservation.[52] The declaration also included an important statement on fisheries jurisdiction: "The Community...wishes to declare [that it] does not consider the Convention to recognize the rights or jurisdiction of coastal States regarding the exploitation, conservation and management of fishery resources other than sedentary species outside their exclusive economic zone."[53] The statement was notable for two reasons. First, it stressed that the EEC was a legal entity with a uniform position on the development of international law in fisheries. Second, it declared this position very strongly: the EEC/EU's policy was to promote institutional cooperation on managing high seas fisheries rather than to promote extended coastal State jurisdiction.

The EEC/EU's ratification of the UNFSA in 2003 entailed a similar declaration of competence, which expanded upon the first with regard to shared competences and included port State measures and measures with respect to non-members of RFMOs and States not party to UNFSA.[54] This expansion is

---

48   Council of the European Communities, Council Regulation (EEC) No. 170/83 of 25 January 1983 establishing a Community system for the conservation and management of fishery resources.

49   Council of the European Communities, Council Regulation (EEC) No. 3760/92 of 20 December 1992 establishing a Community system for fisheries and aquaculture.

50   Treaty on European Union (Maastricht Treaty), 7 February 1992, 1992 OJ (C191) 1, Title II, Art. G(B)(3)(e).

51   See Aneiros, n. 45 above.

52   Declaration of the European Community upon signature (7 December 1998). Declaration made pursuant to Article 5(1) of Annex IX to the Convention and to Article 4(4) of the Agreement, available online: <http://www.un.org/depts/los/convention_agreements/convention_declarations.htm#EuropeanCommunityUpon signature> [EC UNCLOS Declaration].

53   Id.

54   Declaration concerning the competence of the European Community upon signature (27 June 1996) and upon ratification (19 December 2003), available online: <http://www.un.org/ depts/los/convention_agreements/fish_stocks_agreement_declarations.htm#EC> .

important because it marks the rising involvement pursued by the EU in international fisheries management. From a passive observer in the formation of UNCLOS, it had already become an active participant in negotiations and agreements with the establishment of its competences. Its expanded declaration of competences with the UNFSA declaration could be seen, especially in the context of subsequent claims and actions, as an overture to further strengthen its role, from an equal participant to a leader in developing future international fisheries management.

Certainly the expanded competence declared upon ratifying the Fish Stocks Agreement was justified by corresponding legal action. EU efforts to combat IUU fishing are outlined by a 2008 regulation citing the EU's international obligations to UNCLOS, UNFSA, and the Compliance Agreement.[55] Since the legislation's entry into force in 2010, the EU has been involved in placing import bans and other market limitations on seafood products from States that do not comply with RFMO measures or are otherwise seen as fishing unsustainably, and it has done so in reference to IUU vessels listed by the International Maritime Organization (IMO).[56] In the context of these actions, the EU's willingness to exert positive influence on global fisheries management, paying due regard to international law and competent international organizations, is indisputable. Understood in this light, the claim in the new CFP proposal – to "strengthen compliance in the international context"[57] – can be seen merely to express a continuing effort on the part of the EU.

At the same time, while aiming to enforce third States' compliance with RFMO measures, the EU has faced severe criticism in the past for its own conduct within RFMOs. Critics of the EU have pointed out its reluctance to use best practices within the management framework when those practices interfere with individual Member States' interests. In at least two instances – regarding Newfoundland turbot (Greenland halibut) resources managed by NAFO and bluefin tuna under ICCAT – the EU has been seen to exploit the weaknesses of the RFMO regime and undermine internal compliance with RFMO conservation measures rather than propagate best practices. As a result, the claim in the reformed CFP proposal appears to be subject to challenge;

---

55   Council of the European Union, Council Regulation (EC) No. 1005/2008 of 29 September 2008 establishing a Community system to prevent, deter and eliminate illegal, unreported and unregulated fishing, *Official Journal of the European Union*, L286/1.

56   European Commission, Directorate-General for Maritime Affairs and Fisheries, "Illegal fishing (IUU)," available online: <http://ec.europa.eu/fisheries/cfp/illegal_fishing/index_en.htm>.

57   EC COM(2011), n. 18 above, Explanatory Memorandum, p. 9.

however, more recent conduct in both RFMOs proves that the claim is instead an indication for changing policy.

Criticisms of EU Participation in RFMOs

EU Conduct in the Northwest Atlantic Fisheries Organization

The 1990s Newfoundland turbot (Greenland halibut) fisheries conflict between Canada and Spain has been studied in depth as an example of the clashing interests between coastal and distant water fishing States after the introduction of the new EEZ regime.[58] Indeed, the dispute was among the incidents that threw light on the UNCLOS regime's omissions and thereby inspired negotiations for the 1995 UNFSA. Following the 1977 establishment of Canada's 200-NM fisheries jurisdiction, Spain was excluded from its traditional operations on the Grand Banks fishing grounds and forced to retreat. However, as the 'nose' and 'tail' of the Grand Banks fell beyond the 200-NM limit, Spanish vessels continued to fish there for straddling species (mainly turbot, but also others) that have primary residence in Canadian waters.[59]

Straddling stocks in this area are subject to the jurisdiction of NAFO, which was established in 1979 with both Canada and the then EEC among its original founding members.[60] After the change in Canadian jurisdiction, Canadian representatives in NAFO reported intensified stock depletion due to overfishing on the nose and tail of the Grand Banks.[61] In response, TACs were set for many of these species, yet NAFO's conservation efforts stagnated when the EEC began making frequent use of an objection procedure under the NAFO Convention and opted out of the TACs systematically once Spain acceded to the EEC in 1986.[62] In the short period between 1986 and 1992, the EEC objected to various NAFO decisions 51 times.[63] Unsurprisingly, this conduct by the EEC/EU was severely criticized in the international community, not only by Canada,

---

58   See, for instance, Juda, n. 30 above; Y. Song, "The Canada-European Union Turbot Dispute in the Northwest Atlantic: An Application of the Incident Approach," *Ocean Development & International Law* 28 (1997): 269–311; Aneiros, n. 45 above; D. Day, "Tending the Achilles' Heel of NAFO: Canada Acts to Protect the Nose and Tail of the Grand Banks," *Marine Policy* 19, no. 4 (1995): 257–270.

59   Song, n. 58 above.

60   Id.

61   Day, n. 58 above.

62   Id.

63   Song, n. 58 above.

but also by other coastal States with a vested interest in preserving straddling stocks primarily residing within a coastal States' EEZs.[64]

The conflict escalated in March 1995 when the Canadian government extended the jurisdiction of its Coastal Fisheries Protection Regulations to encompass the nose and tail of the Grand Banks and proceeded to arrest the Spanish vessel *Estai*, which was fishing in that area.[65] Spain and the EU immediately protested the action, and Spain initiated proceedings at the International Court of Justice (ICJ) against Canada. As the ship was seized beyond Canada's 200-NM limit, Spain denounced the Canadian overreach in jurisdiction, which it perceived as a breach in "universally accepted norm of customary law codified in...the 1982 Convention on the Law of the Sea."[66] The EU's diplomatic note to Canada expressed a similar view, stating that "Canada is not only flagrantly violating international law, but is failing to observe normal behavior of responsible States."[67] It elaborated further, that the Canadian conduct "is particularly unacceptable since it undermines all the efforts of the international community...to achieve effective conservation through enhanced cooperation in the management of fisheries resources."[68]

Needless to say, the Canadian government regarded such language from the EU as markedly hypocritical. It had seen the Community's endless objections to NAFO quota measures in the previous years as illegal behavior hidden "under the mantle of legality"[69] and, therefore, as actions justifying due retaliation. For Canada, the issue of "enhanced cooperation in the management of fisheries resources" was indeed in question. Where Spain insisted before the ICJ that the case regards solely a matter of violated jurisdiction, Canada stressed the indivisibility of fisheries conservation from the subject of the dispute, and was joined in this opinion by the Court.[70] The conflict arose out of concern with preserving fisheries resources straddling the Canadian 200-NM limit, hence the matter of these stocks' conservation was to be addressed in resolving the conflict.

Thus the issue came down to alternate interpretations of the UNCLOS provisions on straddling stocks, with both sides trying to make a point about how international cooperation for the conservation and allocation of such resources

---

64   Lawrence Juda, Professor, University of Rhode Island, pers. comm. (November 2013).

65   Song, n. 58 above.

66   *Spain v. Canada*, [1998] I.C.J. Fisheries Jurisdiction, Jurisdiction of the Court, Judgment.

67   Id.

68   Id.

69   Day, n. 58 above.

70   *Spain v. Canada*, n. 66 above.

should develop. Canada stressed the UNCLOS provisions that subjected the freedom of fishing on the high seas to "the rights and duties of coastal States."[71] It preferred an interpretation of the obligation "to take, or to cooperate with other States in taking, such measures...as may be necessary for the conservation of the living resources of the high seas"[72] that would favor its interests in the stocks as a coastal State, and found its interests to be aligned with those of conservation.

The EU's position was founded in the opposing view. In particular, the EU acted in defense of Spain's interests in the Newfoundland fishing resources. But in more general terms, it also strove to protect the freedoms of the high seas against continuously extending coastal State jurisdiction. In the view of the EU Fisheries Commissioner at the time, Emma Bonino, Canada was an aggressor State using the case to impose its own interests: she stated that "Canada has not only taken an EU boat to satisfy its internal needs and to hide its inefficiency in fisheries management. Canada has taken the international community hostage."[73] Canada's extension of internal legislation to encompass waters beyond the 200-NM limit was regarded by the EU as a dangerous precedent for creeping jurisdiction. As the statement in the EU's declaration upon signing UNCLOS reveals,[74] the EU continued to oppose the codification of coastal States' interests in the international fisheries management framework.

The conflict abated when the EU and Canada agreed on an enhanced enforcement scheme for vessels fishing in the NAFO regulatory area, which was formally integrated into NAFO the same year.[75] While the EU discontinued its objection practice, its past abuse of the procedure renders some of its subsequent claims of strengthening international compliance with RFMO measures questionable. It bears noting, however, that the EU's conduct in NAFO was indicative both of the weaknesses in the developing regime and of the clashing views on managing high seas fisheries that largely caused these weaknesses.

---

71   UNCLOS, n. 8 above, Part VII, Art. 116.

72   Id., Art. 117.

73   "EU/Canada: EU Suspends Ties with Canada over Fisheries Dispute," *European Report*, 14 March 1995.

74   "The Community...wishes to declare [that it] does not consider the Convention to recognize the rights or jurisdiction of coastal States regarding the exploration, conservation and management of fishery resources other than sedentary species outside their exclusive economic zone." EC UNCLOS Declaration, n. 52 above.

75   Aneiros, n. 45 above.

EU Conduct in the International Commission for the Conservation of Atlantic Tunas

The 2008 Performance Review of ICCAT was harsh in assessing its failures in managing Atlantic tuna and tuna-like species under its international mandate; yet it was even harsher in evaluating the performance of its members. The review panel expressed the view that "rather than ICCAT failing in its mandate it is ICCAT that has been failed by its members" and that ICCAT's otherwise sound management approaches were "undermined by systematic failures by [members] to implement such rules and recommendations."[76]

Overall, the review addressed alarming declines in tuna populations in ICCAT's regulatory area during the 2000s. Atlantic bluefin tuna, in particular, was so severely overfished during that period that in 2009 it earned a nomination for protection under the Convention on International Trade in Endangered Species of Flora and Fauna (CITES).[77] ICCAT's estimate for catches in 2007 was between 39,000 and 54,000 tonnes – "substantially higher than the agreed TAC of 29,500 t and far in excess of the [scientific committee's] recommendation of 15,000 t."[78] ICCAT referred to this conservation failure by its contracting parties as "an international disgrace";[79] yet the organization's assessment that its members had largely failed its efforts by conducting IUU fishing and disrespecting quotas was echoed by others in the international community. A study by the WWF on the status of bluefin tuna in the eastern Atlantic and Mediterranean Sea in 2004–2005 found that EU fleets, especially French vessels, were responsible for much of the overexploitation of Mediterranean bluefin tuna stocks, fishing well beyond their quotas and underreporting their catch to ICCAT by thousands of tonnes.[80]

Rhetoric at the time suggested that the EU itself was displeased with the performance of individual Member States in the bluefin tuna fishery. Upon closing the fishery in 2008, Commissioner Joe Borg criticized Member States' conduct and pointed to specific failures of implementation and breaches in compliance, including "unreliable catch declarations, failure to respect

---

76   G.D. Hurry, M. Hayashi and J.J. Maguire, *Report of the Independent Review, ICCAT*, PLE-106/2008 (ICCAT, 2008), Executive Summary, p. 2 [2008 ICCAT Performance Review].

77   D.G. Webster, "The Irony and the Exclusivity of Atlantic Bluefin Tuna Management," *Marine Policy* 35, no. 2 (2011): 249–251.

78   2008 ICCAT Performance Review, n. 76 above, Executive Summary, Part III, p. 60.

79   Id.

80   World Wide Fund for Nature (WWF), *The Plunder of Bluefin Tuna in the Mediterranean and East Atlantic in 2004 and 2005: Uncovering the Real Story*, Report prepared by ATRT, S.L. for WWF (Rome and Madrid: WWF, 2006).

reporting deadlines, delays in submission of fishing plans, and failure to communicate satellite data on the movements of the vessels concerned."[81] Despite the Commissioner's motivation to "ensure a sustainable future for European fisheries,"[82] the EU's inability to control its fleets regardless of its best intentions suggested a degree of ineptitude and brought into question the EU's competence in international fisheries management.

This interpretation was especially pertinent on several occasions when Mediterranean States' interests were seen to sway important decisions for the fishery's international management. For instance, the EU was criticized by multiple NGOs (such as Greenpeace, WWF, and Oceana) for its role in negotiating 2009 ICCAT quotas for Mediterranean and eastern Atlantic bluefin tuna at levels significantly higher than the scientific recommendation.[83] The same year, the EU was also perceived as irresponsible when the proposed CITES trade ban of bluefin tuna received official support by the Fisheries Commission, but was nevertheless vetoed by the 'Club Med' of southern Member States that had commercial stakes in the fishery.[84]

The EU's conduct in the bluefin tuna fishery did not appear grounded in a consistent policy as it had been in the NAFO controversy. Instead, Commissioner Borg's rhetoric strongly suggested that the EU's policy had been compromised by Mediterranean Member States' lack of compliance,[85] whereas the quota and trade ban votes in 2009 suggested to the international community that those States' individual commercial interests were more likely to influence the behavior of the EU with regard to the bluefin tuna fishery than the reverse. Hence, the conservation failures here were in a way more dangerous to EU international authority. They raised the questions about its ability as a supranational organization to fully govern the actions of its members, even when granted exclusive competence. Therefore it is not surprising that subsequent actions by the EU – such as its ban on IUU fishing and an increased attention of RFMOs in general – began to address these weaknesses.

81   2008 ICCAT Performance Review, n. 76 above, Executive Summary, Part III, p. 59.

82   Id.

83   N. Williams, "Anger over Bluefin Tuna Decision," *Current Biology* 18, no. 24 (2008): R1110–R1111.

84   "Mediterranean EU Countries Block Bluefin Tuna Ban," *The Guardian*, 22 September 2009, available online: <http://www.theguardian.com/environment/2009/sep/22/eu-bluefin-tuna-ban-blocked>.

85   2008 ICCAT Performance Review, n. 76 above, Executive Summary, Part III, p. 59.

Reforming EU Participation in RFMOs

Given the criticisms leveled against the EU for its past participation in NAFO and ICCAT, the validity of its claim in the revised CFP proposal – to 'strengthen compliance' with RFMOs globally – could be questioned. However, when reviewed in the context of recent rhetoric from the Fisheries Commission and current Commissioner Maria Damanaki, the claim could also be seen as an indication of changing policy and a desire to shape a more positive leadership role for the EU through the CFP.

Commissioner Damanaki has shown particular sensitivity to the global significance of EU fisheries policy. Her speeches often emphasize the EU's responsibility for the sustainable management of international stocks. The Commissioner's rhetoric consistently reflects the external ambitions of the CFP reform. In response to a WWF study on the spatial expansion of EU fishing fleets, Commissioner Damanaki commented: "I can't agree more with those that see the reform of the Common Fisheries Policy as a unique opportunity to overcome once and for all the problem of overfishing, in EU waters as well as on a global scale."[86] Similarly, Damanaki's opening speech at a 2012 conference gathering leaders from fifteen RFMOs in Brussels conveyed her view that "taking care of European waters alone is not good enough. As a global player, the EU is also responsible for external waters and must prove that we assume our responsibility for sustainable ocean governance in RFMOs and other international fora."[87] The language of her speeches expresses both ambition for leadership and a sense of global responsibility, the latter of which may previously have been seen as lacking in EU fisheries policy.

The EU has shown a willingness to support its words with action. It is not coincidental that recent years mark the introduction of certification of all seafood products to ensure sustainable catches and regulations for banning IUU products,[88] nor that external policy is for the first time being integrated formally into the text of the CFP. Furthermore, the EU has taken steps recently

---

86   European Commission, "Commissioner Damanaki on New WWF Study on the External Dimension of the Common Fisheries Policy,": "Spatial Expansion of EU and Non-EU Fishing Fleets into the Global Ocean 1950 to Present," (25 January 2012) available online: <http://ec.europa.eu/commission_2010-2014/damanaki/headlines/press-releases/2012/01/20120125-3_en.htm>.

87   M. Damanaki, "Making Regional Fisheries Management Organisations Fit for the Future," Speech presented at Brussels, 1 June 2012, available online: <http://ec.europa.eu/commission_2010-2014/damanaki/headlines/speeches/2012/06/20120601_speech_en.htm>.

88   Id.; EC Reg. 1005/2008, n. 55 above.

toward positive leadership in the very same organizations where its participation had previously been criticized.

In NAFO, the EU helped drive reform in 2007 to enhance NAFO's overall performance.[89] It is a point of interest that the EU has done so by aligning its interests with Canadian ones, even while maintaining its principal opposition to the expansion of coastal States' jurisdiction.[90] A stronger NAFO proved to be in the interest of both sides because it would ensure better conservation of straddling stocks, thus alleviating Canadian concerns, but it retained the decision-making authority over high seas fishing measures for the organization, ensuring equitable control for all parties. As part of the exchange, the objection procedure was revised, allowing for objections only if measures are found to be inconsistent with the provisions of the NAFO Convention or discriminatory against the objecting member.[91] The amended NAFO Convention strengthened the authority of the organization through tougher compliance measures and included integrated approaches from UNFSA and the FAO Compliance Agreement.[92] While it remains imperative for the EU to continue to enforce NAFO regulations internally, its participation in the negotiations proved that the EU was capable of applying its policies internationally in a constructive manner.

Similarly in ICCAT, recent actions by the EU have been indicative of a more positive role. As its misconduct in this context was threatening to the international prestige of the EU in fisheries management, it is not surprising that in response the EU has stressed internal compliance heavily. In 2009, EU legislation addressed an ICCAT multi-annual recovery plan for bluefin tuna and included enforcement, monitoring, and control measures.[93] In addition to internal control, several contemporary ICCAT resolutions were integrated into EU law through this legislation, including the ICCAT regional observer program and its scheme of joint international inspection.[94] The legislation also prohibited all trade, import and export, or processing of bluefin tuna that does not comply with ICCAT measures.[95] In addition, as seen earlier, the EU

---

89   Aneiros, n. 45 above.

90   Id.

91   Id.

92   Id.

93   Council of the European Union, Council Regulation (EC) No 302/2009 of 6 April 2009 concerning a multiannual recovery plan for bluefin tuna in the eastern Atlantic and Mediterranean, *Official Journal of the European Union*, L96/1, Chapter V, Control Measures.

94   Id.

95   Id.

introduced a separate regulation battling against IUU fisheries catches by third States. Since then, the EU has also complied with a payback on quotas for 2012–2019 to compensate for the reported overfishing by the French fleet in 2007.[96] In short, recent actions by the EU suggest its strong intention to improve its standing with ICCAT, and assert a positive influence on the organization's performance.

In the context of these recent actions, EU rhetoric can therefore indeed be interpreted as an indication of changing policy. The CFP is after all in the process of reform, and it would seem that this includes in part reforming the EU's international role in global ocean governance. Significantly, this turn in conduct coincides with the EU's growing tendency to address environmental concerns with legislation, as exemplified by the recent Marine Strategy Framework Directive (MSFD). Indeed the reform of the CFP speaks to the need to integrate fisheries policy into the EU's increasingly comprehensive approach to marine policy as a whole.[97] Better science, ecosystem-based management, and the precautionary principle have been expressed as pillars of this new approach, which is reflected both in the internal regulations of the reformed CFP and in the international leadership role now sought by the EU.[98] Whether the reform succeeds in establishing the EU as a positive leader for the future of international fisheries and the role of RFMOs in managing them will depend on the continued compliance of its Member States. It is clear, however, that this is the role that the EU intends to take.

---

96   WWF, "Paving the Way for Recovery of Bluefin Tuna – an Example of EU Fisheries Reform," posted 21 November 2012, available online: <http://www.wwf.eu/?206799/ Paving-the-way-for-recovery-of-bluefin-tuna---an-example-for-EU-fisheries-reform>.

97   Green Paper, n. 2 above.

98   Damanaki, n. 87 above.

Tightening the Net: The Legal Link between Illegal, Unreported and Unregulated Fishing and Transnational Crime under International Law

Mary Ann Palma-Robles
Visiting Senior Fellow, Australian National Centre for Ocean Resources and
Security (ANCORS), University of Wollongong, Australia

Introduction

Fisheries crime is an increasingly significant threat not only to maritime
security but also to the sustainability of marine living resources. Although
increasingly recognized as a global challenge, its true scope remains difficult to quantify because of the elusive nature of these activities. To date,
only anecdotal evidence and a few studies document the existence of certain aspects of fisheries-related crime. More recently, international concerns have escalated with respect to fisheries crime in response to reports
on the opportunistic participation of transnational criminal groups in certain fisheries, and more importantly the increasing association with other
illicit activities such as narcotics trafficking, arms smuggling, trafficking in
people for forced labor, and the use of fishing vessels for acts of piracy at sea
and terrorism.

Illegal, unreported and unregulated (IUU) fishing and transnational crime
relating to the environment are equally important, but distinct issues. The relationship between IUU fishing and international environmental crime was raised
at the ninth meeting of the United Nations Open-Ended Informal Consultative
Process on Oceans and the Law of the Sea (UNICPOLOS) and at the meeting of
the Conference of Parties to the UN Convention against Transnational Organized
Crime (UNTOC) in 2008.[1] Divergent views emerged from these meetings on the
potential link between illegal fishing and organized crime. Participants decided
that further studies are required before such connection could be established.[2]

---

1   United Nations, Conference of Parties to the United Nations Convention against Transnational
    Organized Crime, Report of the Conference of Parties to the United Nations Convention
    against Transnational Organized Crime on its Fourth Session, Vienna, 8–17 October 2008,
    CTOC/COP/2008/19, 1 December 2008, para. 210.
2   United Nations General Assembly, Sixty-Third Session, Item 73(a) of the provisional agenda,
    Oceans and the Law of the Sea, Report on the Work of the United Nations and the Law of the
    Sea at its Ninth Meeting, A/63/174, 25 July 2008, paras. 71 and 73.

Ocean Yearbook 29: 144–165

On 19 March 2010, the UN General Assembly (UNGA) adopted Resolution 64/72 on sustainable fisheries where it

> (n)otes the concerns about possible connections between international organized crime and illegal fishing in certain regions of the world, and encourages States, including through the appropriate international forums and organizations, to study the causes and methods of and contributing factors to illegal fishing to increase knowledge and understanding of those possible connections, and to make the findings publicly available, bearing in mind the distinct legal regimes and remedies under international law applicable to illegal fishing and international organized crime.[3]

Succeeding meetings at UNGA and UNICPOLOS, as well as other UN forums, have also recognized concerns relating to transnational crime in fisheries.[4]

This article responds to the ongoing debate on the emergence of this new type of maritime security threat which is evolving to be an important global concern. It revisits the concept of IUU fishing within the context of international fisheries law and highlights the issues associated with categorizing activities that fall within the realm of fisheries management as crimes. It also explores the potential elements of fisheries crime based on concepts of transnational organized crime and environmental crime. The article argues that current practical measures undertaken by States to address the problem highlight potential synergies between distinct bodies of law that may be explored to develop an applicable international legal framework that will adequately address the problem. These areas of convergence are geared towards providing a clear definition and characterization of IUU fishing activities that fall within the ambit of transnational organized crime and environmental crime, strengthened regional cooperation, and amendments to domestic legislation that will enable enforcement authorities to combat fisheries crime.

---

3   United Nations, Sustainable Fisheries, including through the 1995 Agreement for the Implementation of the Provisions of the United Nations Convention on the Law of the Sea of 10 December 1982 relating to the Conservation and Management of Straddling Fish Stocks and Highly Migratory Fish Stocks and Related Instrument, *UNGA Resolution 63/112*, 5 December 2008, para. 59.

4   See UNGA and UNICPOLOS meeting reports to date. See also United Nations Economic and Social Council, Commission on Crime Prevention and Criminal Justice, Twenty-Second Session, Item 4 of the Provisional Agenda, Thematic discussion on the challenge posed by emerging forms of crime that have a significant impact on the environment and ways to deal with it effectively, Vienna, 22–26 April 2013.

IUU Fishing versus Fisheries Crime

Currently, there is no legal definition for fisheries crime, transnational crime in the fishing industry, or organized crime in fisheries although these expressions have been used interchangeably to describe illicit fisheries activities that resemble other types of transnational criminal activities. The concept that is most closely associated with fisheries crime is illegal fishing, or more broadly, IUU fishing. The conceptual link between IUU fishing and fisheries crime requires further understanding because of the legal and practical impact that criminalization of the former may have. For example, can fishing without a proper license by a domestic vessel in the exclusive economic zone be considered a wrongful behavior that the society may regard as harmful or potentially harmful within the context of criminal law and deserving of criminal sanction? Or can this conduct be better addressed through other forms of control? Is such an offence akin to other well-known types of crime such as murder, robbery, treason, or drug trafficking? Would the penalty be the same if a foreign fishing vessel were in breach of its licensing condition?

The concept of IUU fishing was established within the context of international fisheries law, primarily through the adoption of the Food and Agriculture Organization (FAO) International Plan of Action to Prevent, Deter and Eliminate Illegal, Unreported and Unregulated Fishing (IPOA-IUU) in 2001. The IPOA-IUU is a voluntary instrument supporting the implementation of the 1995 FAO Code of Conduct for Responsible Fisheries and based on relevant rules of international law, including the United Nations Convention on the Law of the Sea, the FAO Compliance Agreement, the UN Fish Stocks Agreement, the World Trade Organization (WTO) and the International Maritime Organization (IMO) agreements.[5] It describes the scope and quality of IUU fishing's

---

5 FAO, *International Plan of Action to Prevent, Deter and Eliminate Illegal, Unreported and Unregulated Fishing* (IPOA-IUU), adopted on 23 June 2001 at the 120th Session of the FAO Council, para. 5 [IPOA-IUU]. See also FAO, *Code of Conduct for Responsible Fisheries*, FAO Conference, 28th Session (31 October 1995), art. 1.1 [FAO Code of Conduct]; WTO, *Agreement on the Application of Sanitary and Phytosanitary Measures*, concluded on 15 December 1993, in force 1 January 1995, GATT Doc. MTN/FA Ii-A1A-4, 33 *International Legal Materials* XXX; WTO, *Agreement on Subsidies and Countervailing Measures*, concluded on 15 April 1994, 1867 *United Nations Treaty Series* 14, GATT Doc. MTN/FA Ii-A1A-4, 33 *International Legal Materials* XXX; International Maritime Organisation (IMO), *International Convention on Standards of Training, Certification and Watchkeeping for Fishing Vessel Personnel (STCW-F)*, concluded on 7 July 1995; IMO, *Torremolinos Protocol of 1993 relating to the Torremolinos International Convention for the Safety of Fishing Vessels 1977*, Torremolinos, Spain, concluded on 2 April 1993.

individual elements.[6] In summary, paragraph 3 of the IPOA-IUU characterizes IUU fishing as fishing in areas under national jurisdiction conducted by State or foreign vessels contrary to domestic regulations; fishing in waters managed by regional fisheries management organizations (RFMOs) in contravention of conservation and management adopted by that RFMO by vessels flying the flag of members and cooperating non-members, non-members, vessels without nationality, and fishing entities; mis-reporting, under-reporting and non-reporting of catch in national waters and in RFMO areas; and fishing in areas where and for fisheries in which there are no applicable regulations. These examples are mainly fisheries management and compliance concerns and ostensibly do not involve criminal acts.[7] Paragraph 3.4 of the IPOA also provides that "...certain unregulated fishing may take place in a manner which is not in violation of applicable international law, and may not require the application of measures envisaged under the International Plan of Action." This provision suggests that not all unregulated fishing activities are illegal, particularly fishing activities where no management measures are in place. It obscures establishing a conceptual link between IUU fishing and fisheries crime by suggesting that some IUU fishing activities may not be in breach of fisheries law.

Further examination of the IPOA-IUU also leads to the argument that the measures developed under this instrument are ill-equipped to address fisheries crime. The IPOA-IUU provides a wide range of measures that may be adopted by individual States and RMFOs to combat IUU fishing activities.[8] It provides flag, coastal, port, and market State, as well as RFMO measures to address various manifestations of IUU fishing in areas of national jurisdiction and on the high seas.

In summary, flag State measures include the exercise of effective jurisdiction and control over vessels flying the State's flag through fishing vessel registration, licensing, and records.[9] Flag States are required to enforce fisheries

---

6 IPOA-IUU, n. 5 above, para. 3.

7 For an in-depth analysis of IUU fishing terminology, see M.A. Palma, M. Tsamenyi and W. Edeson, *Promoting Responsible Fisheries: The International Legal and Policy Framework to Combat IUU Fishing* (Leiden, The Netherlands: Martinus Nijhoff, 2010), pp. 25–47.

8 IPOA-IUU, see n. 5 above, para. 8.

9 Id., paras. 34–41 and 44–47; United Nations Convention on the Law of the Sea, 10 December 1982, 1833 *United Nations Treaty Series* 3, 21 *International Legal Materials* 1261 (1982) (entered into force 16 November 1994), arts. 62, 91 and 94(1) and (2); United Nations Agreement for the Implementation of the Provisions of the United Nations Convention on the Law of the Sea of 10th December 1982 Relating to the Conservation and Management of Straddling Fish Stocks and Highly Migratory Fish Stocks, 4 August 1995, 34 *International Legal Materials* 1542 (1995);

laws and regulations by investigating alleged violations and cooperating with other States and institute proceedings against vessels that have violated global and domestic regulations and relevant RFMO measures.[10] Coastal State measures to combat IUU fishing center on the implementation of an effective monitoring, control and surveillance regime, which includes vessel monitoring systems, observer programs, boarding and inspection schemes, and application of sanctions of sufficient severity.[11] Port State measures apply to foreign vessels and include requirements for advanced notice of entry, port inspection, and port enforcement actions such as denial of port entry and refusal to land or transship fish.[12] Internationally agreed market measures include catch certification, trade documentation and trade restrictions such as fish import and export prohibitions.[13] The IPOA-IUU and WTO Agreements require port and market measures to apply in a fair, transparent and non-discriminatory way. The IPOA-IUU also provides for all State measures such as the implementation of international instruments, development of national plans of action, cooperation among States, application of sanctions, and adoption of measures against IUU fishing by vessels without nationality and vessels flying the flags of non-cooperating States to RFMOs.[14] States, acting under the auspices of a RMFO may also adopt measures to combat IUU fishing. These measures are similar to those that may be applied individually by States, and in addition, RFMOs may devise innovative ways to combat IUU fishing such as maintaining a record of vessels engaged in IUU fishing.[15] While these measures may present a comprehensive approach to addressing IUU fishing, and potentially certain aspects and causes of fisheries crime, none of them are specifically designed to address the diverse manifestations of fisheries crime discussed below.

The following sections identify the various dimensions of fisheries crime, compare and contrast the concept of fisheries crime as a transnational

---

2167 *United Nations Treaty Series* 88 (entered into force 11 December 2001), art. 18(3) [UN Fish Stocks Agreement]; Agreement to Promote Compliance with International Conservation and Management Measures by Fishing Vessels on the High Seas, 24 November 1993, 2221 *United Nations Treaty Series* 91 (entered into force 24 April 2003), art III(2), [FAO Compliance Agreement]; FAO Code of Conduct, n. 5 above, art. 8.2.2; IPOA-IUU, n. 5 above, paras. 34–41 and 44–47.

10   UN Fish Stocks Agreement, n. 9 above, Part VI; FAO Compliance Agreement, n. 9 above, art. III(8); FAO Code of Conduct, n. 9 above, art. 8.2.7.

11   IPOA-IUU, n. 5 above, para. 51.

12   Id., paras. 52–64.

13   Id., paras. 65–76.

14   Id., paras. 10–33.

15   Id., para. 81.4.

organized crime and an environmental crime, and as well examine certain issues in classifying illegal fishing and IUU fishing as such in legal regimes outside fisheries. They also identify some of the elements that may assist States in defining fisheries crime within the context of transnational crime and environmental crime.

Fisheries Crime as a Transnational Organized Crime

Transnational crime is governed by UNTOC and its three protocols addressing trafficking in persons, smuggling of migrants and trafficking in firearms.[16] UNTOC provides the framework for cooperation among States to prevent and combat organized crime by establishing criminal offences under domestic legislation for participating in an organized criminal group, money laundering, corruption, and obstruction of justice. It also provides a framework for extradition and mutual legal assistance among parties, as well as strengthening law enforcement.

UNTOC defines transnational organized crime with reference to three elements: (1) the transnational element, (2) involvement of an organized criminal group, and (3) conduct constituting a serious crime. With respect to the first element, UNTOC provides in Article 3(2) that an offence is transnational in nature if:

(a) It is committed in more than one State;

(b) It is committed in one State but a substantial part of its preparation, planning, direction, or control takes place in another State;

(c) It is committed in one State but involves an organized criminal group that engages in criminal activities in more than one State; or

(d) It is committed in one State but has substantial effects in another State.

The second element points to the involvement of an organized criminal group, which is defined as "a structured group of three or more persons, existing for a

---

16   United Nations Convention against Transnational Organized Crime, 15 November 2000, 40 *International Legal Materials* 335 (2001); UN Doc. A/55/383 at 25 (2000); UN Doc. A/RES/55/25 at 4 (2001), (entered into force 29 September 03), [UNTOC]. The three protocols to UNTOC are the Protocol to Prevent, Suppress and Punish Trafficking in Persons, Especially Women and Children, supplementing the United Nations Convention against Transnational Organized Crime; Protocol against the Smuggling of Migrants by Land, Sea and Air, supplementing the United Nations Convention against Transnational Organized Crime; and Protocol against the Illicit Manufacturing of and Trafficking in Firearms, Their Parts and Components and Ammunition, supplementing the United Nations Convention against Transnational Organized Crime.

period of time and acting in concert with the aim of committing one or more serious crimes established in accordance with this Convention, in order to obtain, directly or indirectly, a financial or other material benefit."[17] With respect to the third element, Article 2(b) of UNTOC defines a serious crime as "conduct constituting an offence punishable by a maximum deprivation of at least four years or a more serious penalty." Examples of transnational crime addressed under the auspices of UNTOC and the UN Office of Drugs and Crime (UNODC) include drug trafficking, trafficking in persons, including women and children, terrorism, internet-based criminal activities, money laundering, and corruption.

UNTOC does not provide an explicit definition or list of transnational organized crime; hence it can be argued that this can allow broader application to new types of crime that may emerge, including fisheries crime. However, the application of the UNTOC framework to fisheries crime comes with a number of challenges. One challenge stems from the evident disconnect between UNTOC's scope of application and domestic legal definitions of serious crime. Most fisheries offences under domestic legislation do not attract a level of punishment as required under UNTOC for an offence to constitute a serious transnational crime.

The second challenge relates to the complexity of issues associated with fisheries crime, which cannot be addressed exclusively by transnational criminal conventions. A UNODC study on the existence of transnational crime in the fishing industry highlighted the key linkages between organized crime and fisheries. The study focused primarily on trafficking in persons, migrant smuggling, and illicit drug trafficking. Its findings, listed below, reflect the complex interactions between fisheries and transnational criminal offences:

- Fishers suffer severe abuse when they are trafficked for the purpose of forced labor on board fishing vessels.
- There is frequent child trafficking in the fishing industry.
- Transnational organized criminal groups are engaged in marine living resource crimes in relation to high value, low volume species such as abalone, rock lobster, and some reef fishes, including protected species such as Napoleon wrasse.
- Laundering of illegally caught fish on the market is often conducted through the use of at-sea transshipments and fraudulent catch documentation.
- Fishing licensing and control systems are vulnerable to corruption.
- Fishing vessels are used for the purpose of migrant smuggling, illicit traffic in drugs (primarily cocaine), illicit traffic in weapons, and acts of terrorism.

---

17   UNTOC, n. 16 above, art. 2(a).

· Transnational fishing operators involved in marine living resource crimes are engaged in complex incorporation and vessel registration strategies and a high degree of logistical coordination of vessel support services at sea.[18]

A number of factors have also been highlighted as making the fishing industry susceptible to transnational organized crime. These include a fishing vessel's mobility and global reach, the lack of effective fishing vessel monitoring programs, the lack of transparency regarding the identity of fishing vessel's beneficial owners, the continuous depletion of global stocks, poor socio-economic conditions experienced by fishers and fishing communities, lack of effective flag and port State enforcement, corruption, and lack of international regulation on the safety of fishing vessels and working conditions of fishers.[19] The UNODC report also notes that fishers are often recruited by organized criminal groups due to their skills and knowledge of the sea and are seldom regarded as the masterminds behind organized criminal activities.[20] The bulk of these factors are fisheries management concerns that fall outside the scope of UNTOC instruments.

Specific examples of fisheries-related crime abound in many parts of the world. In Australia, criminal syndicates have been associated with IUU fishing for Patagonian toothfish.[21] There have also been reports on the involvement of international criminal networks in the illegal trade of Australian abalone, and other high value, low volume fisheries such as shark fin, seahorse, and trepang.[22] There are also similar incidents of the illegal capture and trade of abalone by organized criminal groups in South Africa.[23] There are accounts of drug trafficking employing fishing vessels in the Caribbean and Latin America.[24] There are equally incidents of persons engaged in piracy in the

---

18 See UN Office of Drugs and Crime (UNODC), *Transnational Organized Crime in the Fishing Industry: Focus on Trafficking in Persons, Smuggling of Migrants, Illicit Drug Trafficking* (Vienna: UNODC, 2010), pp. 1–3.

19 Id., p. 3.

20 Id.

21 G. Hayman and D. Brack, *International Environmental Crime: The Nature and Control of Environmental Black Markets* (London: Royal Institute of International Affairs, 2002), p. 7.

22 See for example, K.M Anderson and R. McCusker, "Crime in the Australian Fishing Industry: Key Issues," *Trends and Issues in Crime and Criminal Justice*, no. 227 (Canberra: Institute of Criminology, 2005).

23 UNODC, *Transnational Organized Crime in the Fishing Industry* (Vienna: United Nations, 2011), p. 92.

24 Id., p. 13.

western Indian Ocean employing fishing vessels of various sizes.[25] In 2008, an Indian fishing trawler, the MV *Kuber*, was hijacked for the purpose of transporting terrorists and arms to the Mumbai coast.[26] In 2013, the Environmental Justice Foundation detailed accounts of human trafficking for the purpose of forced labour in Thailand's fishing industry. The account alleged that the human trafficking occurred in a context characterized by bribery and corruption, preventing the apprehension of perpetrators.[27] These examples represent a limited sample of fisheries-related crime documented to exist in the fishing industry.

Among the examples of fisheries crime described above, only the laundering of illegally caught fish directly falls under the scope and nature of IUU fishing as provided in the IPOA-IUU. The rest display aspects of crime that fall outside the parameters of IUU fishing and cannot be addressed squarely under international fisheries law. In contrast, some of these types of fisheries crime may be addressed within the scope of UNTOC, such as the use of fishing vessels in the conduct of illicit activities such as smuggling of people, which may be subject to the measures available under Article 8 on the Protocol against Smuggling of Migrants. However, such an approach is limited in scope and may only address one or two aspects of fisheries crime while neglecting to address its root causes or consequences.

An example of a complex issue that requires consideration both within the context of international fisheries law and transnational criminal law is the impact of piracy off the coast of the Horn of Africa on fisheries in the Indian Ocean. The consequences of piracy in the region may be characterized as twofold. Due to incidents and fear of fishing vessels being hijacked, the Indian Ocean Tuna Commission (IOTC) noted a substantial relocation of effort in the western Indian Ocean. The IOTC reported the displacement of longline catch to other areas on the Indian Ocean, which subjected albacore tuna to overfishing.[28] Furthermore, vessels in the Indian Ocean of major fishing nations such as Iran, Japan, China, Taiwan, and the European Union have shifted fishing activities into other areas of the Indian, Atlantic and Pacific Oceans, increasing

---

25   UNODC, *The Globalization of Crime: A Transnational Organized Crime Threat Assessment* (Vienna: UNODC, 2010), p. 198.

26   *Mumbai Terrorist Attacks* (26–29 November 2008), p. 4, available online: <http://www.fas .org/irp/eprint/mumbai.pdf>.

27   Environmental Justice Foundation, *Sold to the Sea – Human Trafficking in Thailand's Fishing Industry* (London: Environmental Justice Foundation, 2013), (film).

28   Indian Ocean Tuna Commission (IOTC), *Report of the Sixteenth Session of the IOTC Scientific Committee*, Busan, Republic of Korea, 2–6 December 2013, para. 152.

pressure on certain species.[29] The second consequence is the decrease in compliance monitoring in the region. Piracy threats have resulted in a level of observer coverage below five percent – significantly less than the minimum requirement to monitor tuna fishing activities.[30] Although the combined efforts of navies to combat piracy in the region have also resulted in a gradual increase in fishing activities in the Indian Ocean since 2011, the link between fisheries and piracy largely remains unaddressed. Domestic fisheries legislation based on resource conservation objectives do not generally take into account criminal activities such as piracy at sea. Similarly, RMFOs have very limited enforcement jurisdiction with respect to these issues.

The third challenge in establishing fisheries crime as a transnational crime relates to the investigation and characterization of the organized element of the fisheries crime. Albanese defines organized crime as

> a continuing criminal enterprise that rationally works to profit from illicit activities that are often in great public demand. Its continuing existence is maintained through the use of force, threats, monopoly control, and/or corruption of public officials.[31]

Some of the illegal activities highlighted above may be the more obvious examples of organized crime in fisheries, such as human trafficking for purposes of forced labour in the fishing industry. Without adequate information, continuous investigation, and sufficient understanding of the modus operandi of persons involved in organized crime, the elements of the definition such as continuity of enterprise may prove to be difficult to establish. It may also be emphasized that within the context of organized crime, activities are not limited to those involved in criminal syndicates,[32] but clearly encompasses opportunistic activities of legitimate entities such as corrupt practices of government officials in fishing vessel licensing.

The unique nature of fisheries crime as a transnational organized criminal activity therefore requires further understanding of the synergies between international fisheries law and transnational criminal law, particularly in applying the UNTOC framework and its protocols within the context of fisheries. Based on the analysis above, the elements of transnational organized crime in fisheries may be summarized as follows. Transnational organized crime in

---

29   Id., para. 155–156.
30   Id., para. 157.
31   J.S. Albanese, *Organized Crime in our Times* (Newark: LexisNexis, 2007), p. 4.
32   Id., p. 5.

fisheries may refer to illegal activities within the realm of fisheries resource exploitation that are of a serious criminal nature, including the use of certain objects in fisheries such as fishing vessels as vehicles of crime. It is considered transnational in characteristic and may involve organized criminal groups as well as activities by non-criminal syndicates. Transnational organized crime in fisheries may also be associated with other types of transnational organized crime addressed within the UNTOC framework. While it is recognized that some of the illicit activities in question may have conservation implications, achievement of fisheries management objectives is not the main purpose of developing measures to address transnational organized crime in fisheries. Understanding these basic elements and characteristics may assist States in developing an appropriate legal framework that will address some of these problems.

Fisheries Crime as an Environmental Crime

Environmental crime, also known as eco-crime or crime against nature, refers to behaviors that contravene statutory provisions enacted to protect the ecological and physical environment.[33] Environmental crime is also characterized as certain behavior regarded as harmful or potentially harmful to the environment.[34] While an understanding of environmental harm is necessary in establishing control, precautionary and prevention measures, there are certain issues associated with this approach. One issue is that environmental crime presupposes that environmental harm is a crime. This raises questions not only on the legal definition of harm, but more importantly, on the set of criteria that will determine the elements of this type of crime.[35]

Although numerous studies have been conducted on criminal law's role in addressing resource and environment-related offences,[36] the classification of

---

33   N. Shover and A.S. Routhe, "Enironmental Crime," *Crime and Justice* 32 (2005): p. 321.

34   R. White, *Transnational Environmental Crime: Toward an Eco-global Criminology* (New York: Routledge, 2011), p. 4.

35   Id., p. 5.

36   A number of institutions have conducted studies on the protection of the environment by means of criminal law such as the United Nations Interregional Crime and Justice Research Institute (UNICRI), the United Nations Asia and Far East Institute of Crime Prevention and Treatment of Offenders (UNAFEI), the Max Planck Institute for Foreign and International Criminal Law, the Australian Institute of Criminology (AIC), and the International Centre for Criminal Law Reform and Criminal Justice Policy. See United Nations, Economic and Social Council, Report on the first session, Commission on Crime Prevention and Criminal Justice, 21–30 April 1992, Economic and Social Council Official Records 1992 Supplement No. 10, *E/1992/30, E/CN.15/1992/7*, para. IV(1)(a).

illegal and more broadly IUU fishing as an environmental crime has not been uniformly and clearly established in international law.[37] In his discussion of crimes against nature, Liddick highlighted illegal fishing as an example but the author more appropriately focused on the organized crime aspect of IUU fishing such as the trade of high value species, rather than more general examples of illegal fishing which can be addressed solely within a fisheries management context.[38] Based on his study and following the UNODC report on transnational crime in the fishing industry, the involvement of transnational organized criminal groups in the capture and trade of high value, low volume species such as abalone may be deemed as a clear example of an environmental crime. It may also include trade for certain species of fish or non-target species (e.g., tuna, Patagonian toothfish, southern bluefin tuna, and sharks), capture and trade against a threshold volume or value of fish, as well as specific trade of high value products (e.g., abalone, salmon roe, sturgeon caviar, and shark fin) contrary to legislation. However, White identifies the danger of conceptualizing harm based simply on the illegal nature of a fishing activity.[39] He correctly points out that such an issue is not as clear-cut in fisheries as both legal and illegal fishing activities have potential harmful impacts; hence, if we are to characterize fisheries crime based on harm, criminalization only of extant illegal fishing activities may not necessarily promote the ecological values we want to prevail in a fisheries crime prevention framework. This is particularly true in States where fisheries management is ineffective or where management or policy measures are not based on best scientific advice available.

A key concern for States regarding environmental crime is its transboundary or global impacts. Examples of these activities include the illegal movement of hazardous waste in breach of the 1989 Basel Convention, illegal trade in ozone depleting substances in breach of the 1987 Montreal Protocol on Substances that Deplete the Ozone Layer, and illegal trade of endangered species in contravention of 1972 Convention on International Trade in Endangered Species of Wild Fauna and Flora (CITES). Other examples have also been identified such as illegal whaling, biopiracy and the future possibility of illegal trade in genetically modified products in contravention of the Cartagena

---

37   Environmental Investigation Agency, *Environmental Crime: A Threat to Our Future* (London: Emmerson Press, 2008).

38   D.R. Liddick, *Crimes Against Nature: Illegal Industries and the Global Environment* (Santa Barbara: ABC-CLIO, 2011), pp. 72–93.

39   R. White, "Environmental Harm and Crime Prevention," *Australian Institute of Criminology: Trends and Issues in Crime and Criminal Justice*, no. 360 (June 2008), p. 3.

Protocol to the Convention on Biological Diversity.[40] One challenge in criminalizing acts with transboundary environmental effects is identifying the geographical range of impacts and potential victims. The victims of environmental crime vary depending on the transboundary reach of the offence, with some acts having more easily identified or localized casualties such as industrial discharge of toxic materials in a geographically defined area, while others have a more diffuse large-scale or global impact such as the release of persistent organic pollutants. Certain marine activities identified above are a relatively recent phenomenon. For this reason, it may take considerable time and capacity before a proper assessment of their potential and actual impacts is conducted. The biological diversity and scope of fisheries resources and their associated ecosystems, which do not respect manmade maritime boundaries, as well as the shared nature of the majority of commercially valuable species, make it difficult to limit potential impacts or affected stakeholders.

With respect to the infringement of international conventions, the capture and trade of a few commercially exploited aquatic species included in the CITES list may arguably be considered within the framework of fisheries crime. Examples of species of fish, molluscs, and echinoderms listed under CITES appendices include whale shark (*Rhincodon typus*), basking shark (*Cetorhinus maximus*), humphead (Napoleon) wrasse, Mediterranean date mussel, Caribbean queen conch (*Strombus gigas*), seahorses (*Hippocampus spp*), paddlefish and sturgeons (*Acipenseriformes* species), European eel, saw fishes (*Pristidae*), pipefishes, and sea cucumber.[41] It may also include a number of non-fish species which are either targeted in marine resource harvest or taken as bycatch in fisheries, including a number of whale species and marine turtle species listed in Appendix I.[42] These species' protection is also supported by the FAO in its technical guidelines and several RFMOs, including the Commission for the Conservation of Antarctic Marine Living Resources (CCAMLR) and the International Commission for the Conservation of Atlantic Tunas (ICCAT).[43]

---

40   D. Brack, "Combatting International Environmental Crime," *Global Environmental Change* 12 (2002), p. 144.

41   FAO, Convention on International Trade in Endangered Species of Wild Fauna and Flora (CITES) Implications to Fisheries, available online: <http://www.fao.org/fishery/cites -fisheries/en>.

42   Id.

43   CITES, Cooperation between CITES and the Commission for the Conservation of Antarctic Marine Living Resources Regarding Trade in Toothfish, Resolution Conf. 12.4, available online: <http://cites.org/sites/default/files/document/E12-04.pdf>; International Commission for the Conservation of Atlantic Tunas (ICCAT), Resolution by ICCAT on Cooperation with the Food and Agriculture Organization of the United Nations with

While this international agreement and supporting multilateral measures provide the basis for conserving these species, implementation is limited to the parties bound by these instruments and it will still be up to individual States to criminalize transport and trade in the listed species. Within this context, it is also emphasized that the descriptions of the terms 'illegal fishing', 'unreported fishing' and 'unregulated fishing' under paragraph 3 of the IPOA-IUU are too broad to form a solid basis of characterizing IUU fishing as an environmental crime.

One final issue associated with characterizing fisheries crime as an environmental crime is that the latter is not perceived to be of the same gravity as other forms of transnational crime. One reason for this is confusion surrounding the object of environmental crime when compared to arms smuggling, drug trafficking, or trafficking in people. Establishing criminal responsibility on the individual, society, and State is more straightforward in the latter categories of offences.[44] Hence, environmental threats are often considered "ambiguous crimes."[45] There is also limited knowledge on the extent of environmental crime, making it difficult for government authorities to readily recognize it as a threat.[46] Like illegal fishing, other forms of transnational environmental crime also often do not conform to the definition of serious crime under UNTOC, which requires a penalty of four or more years imprisonment to attach to an offence for it to be considered a serious crime. Other issues would also need to be dealt with if fisheries crime is to be addressed within the context of environmental crime prevention. These issues include identifying the drivers of trade in certain species such as the global demand for exotic species and the existence of black markets. Additionally, other issues requiring attention are those that permit the ongoing existence of fisheries crimes such as inadequate fisheries management regimes as well as ineffective environmental regulations and enforcement mechanisms.

In summary, a number of critical elements may be highlighted for the purpose of defining environmental crime in fisheries. Environmental crime in

Regard to Study on the Status of Stocks and By-catches of Shark Species, 21 December 1995; ICCAT, Resolution by ICCAT on Cooperation with the Convention on International Trade in Endangered Species of Wild Fauna and Flora, *93–08 MISC*; ICCAT, Resolution by ICCAT Concerning the Composition of the Delegations of ICCAT Contracting Parties to CITES 93–09 MISC.

44   L. Elliott, "Transnational Environmental Crime in the Asia Pacific: An Un(der)securitized Security Problem?" *The Pacific Review* 20, no. 4 (2007), p. 514.

45   R. Michalowski and K. Bitten, "Transnational Environmental Crime," in *Handbook of Transnational Crime and Justice*, ed. P. Reichel (Sage Publications, 2005), p. 139.

46   Elliott, n. 44 above, p. 514.

fisheries may be characterized as those activities that are harmful or potentially harmful to the health of marine living resources, the associated ecosystem, and the broader marine environment. The requisite level and quality of
harm is set within the ecological values identified by a State, authority, or community. Defining fisheries crime based on environmental harm may therefore
mean that some legal fishing activities fall within this category. Environmental
crime may involve the capture and/or trade of specific species or non-target
species that are of great commercial value and are highly vulnerable to certain
levels of exploitation. These species are generally protected under relevant
international agreements such as CITES, RFMO measures, and domestic legislation. Other illegal activities are associated with environmental crime in fisheries such as the use of fraudulent documentation and illegal transshipment.
Organized criminal groups may perpetrate some of these activities. Contrary
to transnational organized crime in fisheries, environmental crime in fisheries
does not often fall within the category of serious crime under UNTOC and
greater consideration is placed on relevant fisheries management concerns
such as the expected and quantified negative impact on a particular regional
area, marine ecosystem or resource, including overfishing on an overfished or
fully exploited stock.

Current State Practice in Addressing Fisheries Crime

While the international community continues to investigate and debate the
nature and legal characteristics of fisheries crime and the applicable legal
framework, States have developed practical and novel measures at the global,
regional, and domestic levels to combat the problem. These measures draw
upon existing legal mechanisms and channels to (1) address IUU fishing, and
(2) facilitate the collection and distribution of intelligence across institutions
and relevant multilateral organizations to address incidents of fisheries crime.
The most notable examples of these measures addressing aspects of fisheries
crime as both transnational organized crime and environmental crime include
the institutional listing of vessels found to have engaged in IUU fishing,
INTERPOL's Project Scale, the adoption of a regional code of conduct against
transnational crime by West and Central African countries, and domestic legislation adopted to address fisheries crime.

Identification and Listing of IUU Vessels
There have been several legal developments in combating IUU fishing in the
last decade. These developments include the implementation of binding

conservation and management measures by tuna and non-tuna organizations to list vessels engaged in IUU fishing. Various organizations share the IUU vessel lists to deter further activities of identified vessels in other regions. A significant trend in these developments is the adoption of measures which may be deemed more restrictive than the minimum requirements available under the IPOA-IUU. One example of these measures is listing vessels on the basis of their association with an identified IUU vessel of the same owner or company.[47] This measure, adopted by the Western and Central Pacific Fisheries Commission (WCPFC), the Inter-American Tropical Tuna Commission (IATTC), and the Southeast Atlantic Fisheries Organization (SEAFO) aims to increase the responsibility of vessel owners to ensure that all their vessels comply with regional conservation measures. A second example of a more stringent measure is the requirement by key fish importing nations such as the United States of America and the European Union to list States that are deemed non-cooperating in the global fight against IUU fishing.[48] Failure of listed non-cooperating States to take corrective actions against IUU fishing vessels may result in trade prohibitions or embargoes on fisheries products. These rigorous measures address a number of IUU activities, including fishing contrary to domestic and regional regulations and fishing activities with adverse impacts on vulnerable marine ecosystems.

Although the listing of vessels by RMFOs targets IUU fishing activities on the high seas conducted contrary to regional management measures, the use of this measure is now slowly being broadened to address vessels involved in fisheries crime to be investigated by INTERPOL. As an example, in 2013,

---

47 Western and Central Pacific Fisheries Commission, *Conservation and Management Measure 2010–03*, para. 3(j); Inter-American Tropic Tuna Commission, *Resolution to Establish a List of Vessels Presumed to Have Carried Out Illegal, Unreported and Unregulated Fishing Activities in the Eastern Pacific Ocean*, Resolution C-05-07, para. 1(i); Southeast Atlantic Fisheries Organization, *Establishing a List of Vessels Presumed to Have Carried Out Illegal, Unreported and Unregulated Fishing Activities*, Conservation Measure 08/06, para. 3(j). The same provision can be found in the *Agreement on the International Dolphin Conservation Program* (AIDCP), Resolution A-04-07, 20 October 2004.

48 *High Seas Driftnet Fishing Moratorium Protection Act*, 16 USC 1826k, s. 610(a) (2013); Council Regulation (EC) No. 1005/2008 of 29 September 2008 establishing a community system to prevent, deter and eliminate illegal, unreported and unregulated fishing, amending Regulations (EEC) No. 2847/93, (EC) No. 1936/2001 and (EC) No. 601/2004 and repealing Regulations (EC) No. 1093/94 and (EC) No. 1447/1999 OJ EU L 286 of 29 October 2008, art. 31(3); Council Regulation (EC) No. 1010/2009 laying down detailed rules for the implementation of Council Regulation (EC) No. 1005/2008 OJ EU L 280 of 27 October 2009, arts. 31, 35 and 51.

INTERPOL investigated FV *Snake* and FV *Thunder* for illegal activities upon the request of Norway and New Zealand, respectively. These vessels were first listed in CCAMLR's IUU fishing vessel list for non-cooperating parties in 2004 and 2006.[49] These vessels were suspected of changing flags and vessel names repeatedly to avoid detection and sanctions.[50]

INTERPOL's Project Scale

In recognition of the escalating severity of issues associated with fisheries crime, INTERPOL launched an initiative in 2013 dubbed Project Scale to detect, suppress, and combat fisheries crime. More particularly, the Project's objectives include generating awareness regarding fisheries crime and its consequences; establishing National Environment Security Task Forces to ensure cooperation between national and international agencies; assessing the needs of vulnerable member countries to effectively combat fisheries crimes; and conducting operations to suppress crime, disrupt trafficking routes, and ensure the enforcement of national legislation. INTERPOL established a Fisheries Crime Working Group under this initiative to develop the capacity, capability, and cooperation of member countries to effectively address fisheries crimes. The Fisheries Crime Working Group also aims to facilitate the exchange of information, intelligence, and technical expertise between countries for purposes of fisheries law enforcement.[51] To date, several countries have cooperated within the INTERPOL network and have called upon the international organization to issue 'Purple Notices' to illegal fishing vessels such as the FV *Snake* and FV *Thunder* discussed above. INTERPOL's Purple Notices are used to seek or provide information on the modus operandi, objects, devices, and methods used by criminals.

---

49   Commission on the Conservation of Antarctic Marine Living Resources (CCAMLR) website, Recent News, *INTERPOL and the IUU-Listed Vessel FV Snake*, 16 September 2013, available online: <http://www.ccamlr.org/en/news/2013/interpol-and-iuu-listed-vessel -fv-snake>; New Zealand Ministry for Primary Industries, New Zealand Requests Interpol Notice to Identify Illegal Fishing Vessel, 6 December 2013, available online: <http://www.mpi.govt.nz/news-resources/news/interpol-notice-to-identify-illegal-fishing -vessel>.

50   Information on the modus operandi of these vessels is available online at the INTERPOL website: <http://www.interpol.int>.

51   INTERPOL, Environmental Compliance and Enforcement Committee, Project Scale, available online: <http://www.interpol.int>.

Regional Code of Conduct in West and Central Africa

In 2013, 25 Western and Central African countries adopted the Code of Conduct Concerning the Repression of Piracy, Armed Robbery against Ships and Illicit Maritime Activity in West and Central Africa. The Code of Conduct recognizes IUU fishing as a "transnational organized crime in the maritime domain" together with other well-established transnational criminal activities.[52] Although the Code of Conduct does not provide specific characterization of IUU fishing activities that may constitute transnational criminal acts, it provides a strong framework for cooperation in the following areas:

(a)   sharing and reporting relevant information;
(b)   interdicting ships and/or aircraft suspected of engaging in transnational organized crime in the maritime domain, maritime terrorism, IUU fishing and other illegal activities at sea;
(c)   ensuring that persons committing or attempting to commit transnational organized crime in the maritime domain, maritime terrorism, IUU fishing and other illegal activities at sea are apprehended and prosecuted; and
(d)   facilitating proper care, treatment and repatriation of seafarers, fishermen and other shipboard personnel and passengers subjected to transnational organized crime in the maritime domain, maritime terrorism, IUU fishing and other illegal activities at sea, particularly those who have been subjected to violence.[53]

The repeated reference to IUU fishing emphasizes the importance the region attributes to the issue within a transnational criminal law and maritime security framework. The Code of Conduct also provides specific measures that may be undertaken cooperatively and individually by States to address transnational crime in the maritime domain. The regional code also incorporates elements of the Djibouti Code of Conduct in the Western Indian Ocean and the Gulf of Aden, as well as the Memorandum of Understanding on the Integrated Coastguard Function Network in West and Central Africa developed by the IMO and the Maritime Organization of West and Central Africa (MOWCA).[54]

---

52   The Code of Conduct Concerning the Repression of Piracy, Armed Robbery against Ships and Illicit Maritime Activity in West and Central Africa, Yaounde, 25 June 2013, art. 1(5)(i).
53   Id., art. 2(1).
54   IMO Sub-regional Meeting on Maritime Security, Piracy and Armed Robbery Against Ships for Western Indian Ocean, Gulf of Aden and Red Sea States, Code of Conduct Concerning the Repression of Piracy and Armed Robbery Against ships in the Western

Domestic Legislation Addressing Fisheries Crime

Fisheries-related crime is a distinctive maritime security concern that falls within the nexus of fisheries, environmental, and transnational criminal law. Correspondingly, creating a single legal instrument to address this problem may not only be impractical, it may also be impossible with respect to accounting for the regulatory and jurisdictional complexities that fisheries-related crime gives rise to. Nevertheless there is an impending need to support both global and regional initiatives to combat fisheries crime through more robust domestic legal frameworks.

A number of States have developed domestic legal mechanisms to address fisheries crime. One example of these mechanisms is legislation that integrates provisions against criminal acts within fisheries legislation. In 2009, Indonesia amended its *Fisheries Act Number 31* of 2004 and made reference to "theft of fish and other illegal fishing actions, not only inflicting losses to the State, but also threatening the interests of fishermen and fish cultivators, industrial climate, and the national fishery business."[55] Indonesian Law Number 45 of 2009 recognizes the limitations of Law Number 31 of 2004 in addressing these concerns and highlights key gaps in fisheries enforcement, application of sanctions, and jurisdiction or relative competence of district courts on criminal acts in the field of fisheries.[56] It institutes legal changes in the following key areas to address criminal aspects of fisheries: law enforcement and coordination mechanisms between agencies; investigations of criminal acts in fisheries; penal and administrative sanctions; judicial procedures on the determination of case investigation time limits; facilities of fisheries law enforcement, including the possibility of legal action in the form of sinking foreign vessels operating illegally in the Indonesian fisheries management zones; strengthening port measures; and extension of fisheries court jurisdiction, including the application of criminal penalties. These provisions may form the basis for developing specific regulations against transnational crime in fisheries. More specifically, the legislation provides for the investigation, prosecution, and punishment of criminal acts, which may be conducted by civil fisheries, naval, or police

---

Indian Ocean and the Gulf of Aden, Djibouti, Adopted 29 January 2009, IMO Council, 102nd Session, Agenda Item 14, C102/14, 3 April 2009; Maritime Organisation of West and Central Africa, Memorandum of Understanding on the Establishment of a Sub-regional Integrated Coast Guard Network in West and Central Africa, Dakar, 31 July 2008, 13th Session of the General Assembly, Item 6.2.1.1.c of the Agenda, MOWCA/XIII GA.08/8.

55   Republic of Indonesia, *Elucidation of Law of the Republic of Indonesia No. 45 Year 2009 Concerning Amendment to Law No. 31 of Year 2004 Concerning Fishery* (29 October 2009), Part I.

56   Id.

investigators.[57] Indonesia has provided for the establishment of fisheries courts in strategic areas to deal with criminal acts in fisheries. Fisheries courts, positioned within district courts, are special courts for the environment within the public court system.

In Australia, criminal syndicate involvement in illegal fishing and illicit trade in natural resources such as abalone and rock lobster have raised concerns that the penalties attached to fisheries offences are inadequate to address a problem that threatens the industry's viability. In response to these concerns, New South Wales has amended its relevant legislation – *Fisheries Management Act* (1994) – to incorporate provisions on 'trafficking in fish'. The state legislation provides for indictable species and quantities of fish, which are currently limited to 50 abalones (*Haliotis rubra*) and 20 eastern rock lobsters (*Jasus verreauxi*). Trafficking in fish under this provision is punishable with a minimum of ten years imprisonment. This legislation also provides that a court may also impose an additional pecuniary penalty for the offence equaling up to ten times the market value of the fish as determined by a number of factors including its market price and weight.[58] In Tasmania, under its *Living Marine Resources Management Act* (1995), a person is taken to traffic in fish without lawful excuse if he or she has taken fish, is in possession or control of fish, sells or purchases fish, delivers fish to or receives fish from another person, processes fish, transports fish, conceals fish, or engages with those who have dealt with trafficked fish.[59] A number of other states and territories in Australia have similar legislation prohibiting trafficking in fish for specific species, as well as businesses engaged in such illegal activity, including the control of, direction, supervision of the dealing, or provision of facilities or finance.[60] Legislative changes have resulted in increased monitoring over the sale and transport of abalone and eastern rock lobster as well as the successful prosecution of offenders in the country.

In the United States, the *Lacey Act* has been considered one of the most effective tools in preventing the possession of marine products illicitly obtained in foreign jurisdictions, effectively providing 'long arm national jurisdiction'. Under the *Lacey Act*, it is unlawful to import, export, transport, sell, receive, acquire, or purchase any fish or wildlife or plant taken, possessed, transported, or sold in violation of any law, treaty, or regulation of the United States or in

---

57   *Law No. 45*, Republic of Indonesia (29 October 2009), art. 73.

58   *Fisheries Management Act*, New South Wales, Australia (1994), sec. 21C.

59   *Living Marine Resources Act*, Tasmania, Australia (1995), sec. 264A.

60   *Fish Resources Management Act 1994*, Western Australia, Australia (1994), sec. 154; *Fisheries Management Act 2007*, South Australia (2007), sec. 74.

violation of any Indian tribal law.[61] It is also unlawful to commit the same when it occurs in interstate or foreign commerce and violates any law or regulation of any foreign law.[62] Depending on the degree of criminal intent, violations of these provisions may be considered as either serious offences or misdemeanors. Several cases have been prosecuted under the *Lacey Act*, the biggest of which is *United States v. Bengis* which concluded in June 2013.[63] In this case, a US court issued a restitution order in favor of South Africa in an amount over US$29 million for the illegal harvest of multiple tons of rock lobster.[64] This case not only demonstrated the effectiveness of carefully crafted domestic legislation in addressing fisheries crime in different jurisdictions, but also highlighted the possible application of various laws to fisheries crime such as fisheries and customs legislation.

The final example of domestic measures to address fisheries crime relates to anti-money laundering legislation adopted by the Philippines. A recent amendment to the Philippines' anti-money laundering legislation recognizes the relationship between illegal fishing and money laundering. Under the Philippine *Republic Act 10365*, which amended *Republic Act 9160*, an unlawful activity forming the predicate offence of money laundering now includes violations to sections 86 to 106 of the Philippine Fisheries Code,[65] which include a range of prohibited acts such as fishing during closed seasons, fishing using explosives, and other fishing activities that generally constitute fisheries management concerns. Although the implementation of this amendment to anti-money laundering legislation is yet to be tested, this amendment may be considered a milestone in addressing fisheries crime within the context of transnational crime. In most countries, offences of organized crime only include as predicate offences drug trafficking, trafficking in people, smuggling of firearms, smuggling of goods, kidnap for ransom, identity crime, computer crime, piracy, and armed robbery and terrorism, and sometimes environmental offences such as illegal logging. However, with the exception of the Philippines, no country has adopted fisheries infractions as predicate offences for transnational crimes. Anti-money laundering legislation includes

---

61   *Lacey Act*, 16 USC §3372 (1900), ss. (a)(2).

62   Id., ss. (a)(4).

63   J. Glazewski, "Current Developments: South Africa/United States, United States v. Bengis: A Victory for Wildlife Law and Lessons for International Fisheries Crime," *The International Journal of Marine and Coastal Law* 29 (2014): 173–183.

64   Id., p. 173.

65   *An Act Further Strengthening the Anti-Money Laundering Law of the Philippines*, Philippines Republic Act No. 10365 (2012), s. 2(21).

provisions for the freezing, seizure, and forfeiture recovery of money and property obtained from the proceeds of crime, provisions for international cooperation, provisions for the creation of financial intelligence units, requirements on customer identification, record keeping, and reporting of covered and suspicious transactions, which may now be possible in tracking the proceeds of fisheries crime in the Philippines.

Conclusion

Treating IUU fishing and fisheries crime as two separate concepts arises from distinct legal regimes that apply to these illicit activities. IUU fishing primarily relates to the depletion of fisheries resources and the need for conservation, which is in the realm of fisheries and environmental law. Other forms of criminal activities involving the fishing industry can be analysed within the context of transnational criminal law. Neither body of law is sufficient to adequately address IUU fishing and fisheries crime in itself. Accordingly, it is becoming increasingly apparent that the attempt to understand the intersection between these concepts unravels a range of complex issues that requires the development and adoption of a novel legal and policy framework at the global, regional, and domestic levels. A number of new approaches and collaborative efforts between States provide critical examples of responses to this burgeoning problem.

As States and multilateral organizations progress towards defining the extent of transnational crime in the fishing industry in particular regions and for particular fisheries, other issues will require rigorous discussion. Such issues include determining the appropriate criminal and administrative penalties, mutual legal assistance, and use of confiscated assets to develop and support programs designed to prevent and reduce fisheries crime. Another issue involves clarifying the jurisdiction exercised by a wide range of actors with functions relevant to addressing fisheries crime, including fisheries authorities, customs authorities, navies, coastguards, police, and multi-agency task forces such as anti-money laundering. The ongoing pursuit to establish stronger legal, policy, and administrative mechanisms to address transnational crime in the fishing industry will help tighten the net of fisheries concerns that not only contribute to the overexploitation of stocks, but also threaten the security of marine resources and peaceful use of the oceans.

Quality Counts: High Seas Marine Protected Areas in the Southern Ocean

Cheryle Hislop and Julia Jabour
Institute for Marine and Antarctic Studies
University of Tasmania, Hobart, Tasmania, Australia

Introduction

Designating vast marine protected areas (MPAs) of several million square kilometers in remote parts of the high seas beyond national jurisdiction may be favorable as well as inevitable. Yet, it is not unproblematic from conceptual, scientific, or political points of view. In 2001, the International Union for Conservation of Nature (IUCN), the World Wildlife Fund (WWF), and the World Commission on Protected Areas (WCPA) commissioned a report on the status of natural resources of the high seas. The research mandate was to assess threats to high seas biodiversity and review the existing political and legal framework so that avenues for the creation of MPAs in areas beyond national jurisdiction could be identified.[1] Later, environmental non-governmental organizations (ENGOs) met in Spain in 2003 at a workshop convened by IUCN, WWF, and WCPA. The aim of that workshop was to develop an action plan to promote a system of high seas MPAs to ensure long-term protection of ecosystem processes, biological diversity, and productivity beyond national jurisdictions.[2] Participants agreed that high seas MPAs were *an idea whose time had come* and that there appeared to be clear recognition of the need for new tools to manage risks to biodiversity on the high seas.[3] Contemporaneously, the 2002 World Summit on Sustainable Development (WSSD) placed a temporal target of 2012 on the establishment of a global representative network of MPAs and as a result, calls grew louder for the legitimization of high seas MPAs through a legally binding instrument. A 2010 assessment of the target concluded that despite a significant increase in the percentage of the world's ocean area under protection since 2003, only 1.3 percent of the ocean's surface area lay within

---

1   K. Gjerde and C. Briede, *Towards a Strategy for High Seas Marine Protected Areas,* Proceedings of the IUCN, WCPA and WWF Expert Workshop on High Seas Marine Protected Areas, 15–17 January 2003, Malaga, Spain (Gland, Switzerland: IUCN, 2003).

2   Id.

3   Id.

Ocean Yearbook 29: 166–191

marine protected areas.[4] Undeterred by the failure to meet temporal and spatial MPA targets, or to adopt a legally binding instrument, the 2010 Conference of Parties for the United Nations Convention on Biological Diversity (CBD) extended the ten percent target timeframe from 2012 to 2020.[5]

We contend that post-2002, oceans governance fora have become constrained by the terms of reference framing the concept of high seas MPAs, as well as by the magnitude of the task before them. While some ENGOs had proposed comparatively small-scale steps toward designation, such as pilot high seas MPAs, this approach has become largely peripheral in light of a growing preference for larger scale projects. This is significant because, given the contemporary preference for large-scale MPAs, international fora represent the primary venue through which these areas may be established. Constraints within those fora translate into a significant decrease in the uptake of MPAs and corresponding decrease in their ability to achieve ecological objectives.

Our objection is not with the concept of high seas MPAs *per se* but rather that they are seen as logical extensions of those MPAs in nation States' coastal zones. By neglecting to differentiate between the essential characteristics of distinct marine areas, the goal of enclosing ten percent of the 'marine environment' within a global representative system of MPAs becomes self-serving. In a study published in 2000, Agardy made useful distinctions concerning the differences between national marine and terrestrial protected areas.[6] In this article, to provide a structure for our analysis, we employ the comparative framework developed by Agardy and apply it to consider the differences between remote high seas and coastal marine protected areas. Relativity is the key to understanding our arguments.

The main variables within Table 8.1, which encapsulates part of our analysis are summarized as follows: (1) differences between jurisdictional boundaries, where responsibility goes from being multilateral for high seas 'commons' to unilateral for coastal marine areas; (2) relative ease of decision-making, implementation, and compliance in national waters; (3) size, where jurisdiction restricts unilateral designation of national MPAs; (4) differences in the level of

4 S. Butchart, M. Walpole, B. Collen et al., "Global Biodiversity: Indicators of Recent Declines," *Science* 328, no. 5982 (2010): 1164–1168.

5 Convention on Biological Diversity, Conference of the Parties 10 – Tenth Meeting of the Conference of the Parties to the Convention on Biological Diversity, Nagoya, Japan, 18–29 October 2010, Decision X/2, *Strategic Plan for Biodiversity 2011–2020* (United Nations Environment Programme, 2010).

6 T. Agardy, "Information Needs for Marine Protected Areas: Scientific and Societal," *Bulletin of Marine Science* 66, no. 3 (2000): 875–888.

TABLE 8.1   *Differences between high seas and coastal marine systems*

High Seas Marine Systems	Coastal Systems	Variable No.
Outside national jurisdiction	Designated jurisdictional boundaries	1
Require multilateral agreement	Permit unilateral action	2, 3
Significant barriers to implementation	Relative ease of implementation	2
Difficult to enforce compliance	Better capacity to enforce compliance	2
Large spatial scales	Potentially smaller spatial scales	3
Relatively poorly researched	Relatively well researched	4
Lack of resources to monitor and measure effectiveness against objectives	More resources available to monitor progress of objectives	5
Difficulty of reviewing objectives	Relative ease of review	5
Limited, if any, alternative conservation arrangements	Better availability of alternative conservation arrangements	6

SOURCE: ADAPTED FROM AGARDY, N. 6 ABOVE.

scientific knowledge about the marine environment and the conservation values derived from that knowledge; (5) relative differences in the ability to monitor and measure success and review objectives in light of effectiveness audits; and (6) the availability of alternative conservation arrangements including compliance monitoring through inspection systems.[7] To these factors we add political will – the *relative* ease of domestic decision-making to protect a State's interests, which stands in stark contrast to the lengthy and sometimes laborious negotiations to arrive at a multilateral decision at the international level.

In this article we argue that it is relatively easier to designate MPAs in coastal areas where all – or many – of the variables are the responsibility of one coastal State, or occasionally, the co-responsibility of a group of neighboring States. However, because coastal MPAs are likely to be small, the chance of achieving a ten percent globally representative MPA system by 2020 is improbable, particularly when it is considered that ten percent equals approximately

---

7   An exception to this is a feature of our case study – CCAMLR – wherein we argue that CCAMLR does have a whole suite of alternative conservation tools but decided to embrace MPAs in addition to these.

33 million square kilometers.[8] As of 2012, 1.6 percent or 5.3 million km² of the planet's oceans had been afforded some form of marine protection.[9] At the current rate of designation, the CBD's original target of "at least 10 percent of each of the world's ecological regions [including marine and coastal, which incidentally lags far behind the rate of terrestrial protected areas] effectively conserved [by 2010]" will not be achieved before, at the earliest, the middle of this century.[10] Knowing this, many developed States have embraced the concept of high seas MPAs as a means to boost domestic environmental credentials ('banking biodiversity'). Dulvy, commenting on domestic MPAs rightly asks: "In our rush for super-sized MPAs and other high-level conservation activities and values, are we missing the point?"[11] It is the authors' view that considering the size of MPAs proposed for international waters, Dulvy's query applies equally to areas beyond the reach of domestic management measures. In other words, do MPAs covering vast areas of the high seas achieve their original objectives with respect to environmental protection and biodiversity preservation? Or, do they miss the mark and represent a means of achieving ambitious conservation targets, without necessarily serving their underlying ecological objectives?

A number of international institutions have taken up the MPA challenge, including the Commission for the Conservation of Antarctic Marine Living Resources (CCAMLR).[12] In 2005, CCAMLR began its discussions on a representative system of MPAs following a workshop convened by its Scientific Committee and in accordance with WSSD targets.[13] By 2009, CCAMLR had established the first high seas marine protected area, around the South Orkney Islands southern

8   P.N. Trathan, E. Sala, A. Merkl et al., "The MPA Math: How to Reach the 10% Target for Global MPA Coverage," *MPA News* 13 (2012): 1–4.

9   Id.

10   L.J. Wood, L. Fish, J. Laughren et al., "Assessing Progress towards Global Marine Protection Targets: Shortfalls in Information and Action," *Oryx* 42 (2008): 340–351.

11   N.K. Dulvy, "Super-sized MPAs and the Marginalization of Species Conservation," *Aquatic Conservation, Marine and Freshwater Ecosystems* 23 (2013): 357–362 at 359.

12   Commission for the Conservation of Antarctic Marine Living Resources (CCAMLR), *General framework for the establishment of CCAMLR Marine Protected Areas*, CCAMLR Conservation Measure 91–04 (2011), available online: <http://www.ccamlr.org/en/measure-91-04-2011>. Note that all Commission and Scientific Committee meeting reports referred to hereafter are also available online: <http://www.ccamlr.org/publications> and all conservation measures at <http://www.ccamlr.org/en/conservation-and-management/browse-conservation-measures>.

13   *Report of the Twenty-fourth Meeting of the Scientific Committee for the Commission for the Conservation of Antarctic Marine Living Resources*, SC-CAMLR-XXIV, paras. 3.51 to 3.65.

continental shelf.[14] At 94,000 km^2 in size, this MPA went some way towards boosting total global representation, however subsequent proposals for Southern Ocean MPAs have failed to reach the consensus required for their adoption.

With respect to high seas MPAs, CCAMLR represents an important and interesting case study. Despite having the means to sustainably regulate access to marine living resources taking into account the whole of the Southern Ocean ecosystem and acting in a precautionary way when scientific information (or lack of it) demonstrates the requirement to do so, CCAMLR decided to embrace the challenges associated with a globally representative system of MPAs within the area of its application, the majority of which is beyond national jurisdiction.

CCAMLR Management

CCAMLR is a body whose members are bound by obligations contained within the multilateral Convention on the Conservation of Antarctic Marine Living Resources and the subsequent legally binding conservation measures adopted by consensus at its annual meetings.[15] The Convention is part of the legal regime known collectively as the Antarctic Treaty System.[16] While it constitutes a free-standing international legal instrument, historic ties connect it to the Antarctic Treaty and its Antarctic Treaty Consultative Meeting (ATCM), and the Protocol on Environment Protection and its Committee for Environmental Protection (CEP).[17] While the Treaty does not deal expressly with marine living resources protection through MPAs, it does give the parties a mandate to create laws relating to matters of interest in the Antarctic. Through the mechanism outlined in the Treaty's Article IX, the marine living resources convention and environmental protocol were both negotiated and adopted. CCAMLR is the subject of our case study. Yet, it is equally important to note that the CEP provides directions for designating Antarctic Specially Managed

---

14   CCAMLR, *Protection of the South Orkney Islands southern shelf*, CCAMLR Conservation Measure 91–03 (2009).

15   Convention on the Conservation of Antarctic Marine Living Resources (adopted 20 May 1980, in force 7 April 1982) 19 *International Legal Materials* 837.

16   The System includes the Antarctic Treaty (adopted in Washington, D.C., 1 December 1959, in force 23 June 1961, 402 *United Nations Treaty Series* 71) and the Protocol on Environmental Protection to the Antarctic Treaty (Madrid Protocol adopted in Madrid, 4 October 1991, in force 14 January 1998) 30 *International Legal Materials* 1416.

17   The CEP meets in the first five days of an ATCM, agrees and adopts a report, and presents this, along with recommendations, to the ATCM. The CEP is advisory only and cannot make legally binding rules.

and Antarctic Specially Protected Areas. Further, when a marine component is included, Article 6.2 of the CEP's Annex V requires prior approval from CCAMLR. This does not mean, however, that the ATCM, which receives CEP recommendations, plays a reciprocal role in the designation of CCAMLR MPAs. Rather, as we will show, the ATCM, while actively encouraging the CCAMLR MPA process, does not itself get involved.

CCAMLR is required to identify conservation needs and analyse the effectiveness of its conservation measures according to its functions outlined in Article IX. In fact, its principal objective is the conservation of Antarctic marine living resources, noting that 'conservation' includes rational use. In other words, its conservation efforts are to accommodate the rational use of marine living resources. This philosophy is defined in Article II, which specifies the temporal and ecological principles upon which harvesting and associated activities, in other words, 'rational uses', are judged. It is important to note that the majority of the 25 members of the Commission fish in the Southern Ocean and/or possess strong scientific research interests.[18] The Convention's Articles III, IV and V provide a formal nexus to the Antarctic Treaty: any State or regional economic integration organization interested in research or harvesting may accede to the Convention without first being an Antarctic Treaty contracting party. If they are not, they agree to do nothing contrary to the principles and purposes of the Treaty. In the case of regional economic integration organizations, the rules for accession involve having one or more States who have transferred their competence for fisheries matters to the organization and who are also members of CCAMLR (Article XXIX).

There are a number of well-formulated ways CCAMLR supports the sustained conservation of marine organisms in the Antarctic. First and foremost, members are obliged to take full account of the recommendations and advice of their Scientific Committee. Practically, in light of this advice CCAMLR members designate regions and sub-regions based on species population distribution; set catch limits for specific regions and sub-regions;[19] determine species requiring special protection; designate age, size, and sex of harvested species; open and close seasons; open and close areas, regions and sub-regions for study or conservation (approximately 42 percent of the CCAMLR area is currently closed to fishing); and regulate effort, gear, and methods of harvesting. In other words, CCAMLR takes whatever decisions the members feel are

---

18 24 States parties and the European Union; see CCAMLR, "Members," available online: <http://www.ccamlr.org/en/organisation/membership>.

19 CCAMLR fisheries are known as 'olympic', meaning that catch limits are allocated to the fishery as a whole rather than to individual members.

necessary to fulfil its mandate, based on the best scientific evidence currently available.

Furthermore, the Convention provides for a broad approach to determining conservation measures by taking into account dependent and associated species and their interactions in Antarctic ecosystems. As such, the results of scientific research on, for example, the foraging habits of penguins and other seabirds such as albatrosses and petrels, and marine mammals such as seals and whales are crucial in the decision-making process since they provide important information on ecosystem dynamics, ranging far beyond the mere knowledge of commercial fish stocks.

CCAMLR has identified a number of vulnerable marine ecosystems (VMEs) – areas such as the tops of seamounts, hydrothermal vents, cold water coral, and sponge beds – that can be seriously perturbed by bottom fishing.[20] Notifications about the location of VMEs from fishers are submitted to scientific working groups for discussion, review, assessment and updating of information on fishing impact. It is possible to establish exclusion zones to protect VMEs from the direct impacts of fishing. However, active monitoring of these particularly vulnerable areas does not occur. Rather, CCAMLR has adopted a number of alternative conservation measures that prohibit deep sea gillnetting, restrict the use of bottom trawling gear in the high seas, provide general regulations on bottom fishing and urge members to notify the Scientific Committee of so-called 'risk' (vulnerable) areas encountered during fishing.[21] The Commission then reaches decisions regarding their special protection by consensus.

CCAMLR MPAs

Given CCAMLR's broad-ranging powers to achieve conservation outcomes, we ask the question: Why have the members adopted the global call to designate

---

20   CCAMLR, *Protection of registered vulnerable marine ecosystems in subareas, divisions, small-scale research units, or management areas open to bottom fishing*, Conservation Measure 22–09 (2012); CCAMLR, *Interim measure for bottom fishing activities subject to Conservation Measure 22–06 encountering potential vulnerable marine ecosystems in the Convention Area*, Conservation Measure 22–07 (2013).

21   See, for example, CCAMLR, *Restrictions on the use of bottom trawling gear in high-seas areas of the Convention area*, Conservation Measure 22–05 (2008); CCAMLR, *Interim prohibition on deep-sea gillnetting*, Conservation Measure 22–04 (2010); and CCAMLR, *Protection of registered vulnerable marine ecosystems in subareas, divisions, small-scale research units, or management areas open to bottom fishing*, Conservation Measure 22–09 (2012).

MPAs in addition to exercising those other powers under their mandate? We see high seas MPAs as an unnecessary additional layer of regulation over the Southern Ocean and Antarctic waters and therefore also ask, what would define their success beyond what CCAMLR has already achieved (and is globally recognized for) in the sustainable management of activities in the high seas? As Dulvy and others note, fisheries management measures are, at a minimum, as effective as macro scale and highly restrictive marine protected areas. These measures have the advantage of being routinely used by fishers and are within the capability of fisheries institutions, whereas MPAs (especially those in the high seas) give rise to the challenges associated with multiple institutions and jurisdictions.[22] Nevertheless, CCAMLR has the honor of having designated the world's first high seas MPA.

South Orkney Islands Southern Shelf MPA

The South Orkney Islands MPA was the world's first high seas marine protected area, encompassing 94,000 km^2 of the southern shelf zone of the island of South Orkney. The Commission, at the recommendation of its Scientific Committee, adopted it in 2009.[23] Discussion at the table was mixed: while some States applauded the proposal by the United Kingdom (which proposed the MPA) to exclude fishing areas, others did not.[24] If there was agreement at all, it was – as expressed by the United States – that MPAs should be established on a case-by-case basis and that, as far as is practicable, the objectives of the Convention should be met.[25]

Two years later, CCAMLR adopted a general framework for the establishment of MPAs, based on a significant amount of work by the Scientific Committee and its recommendations to CCAMLR.[26] It is important to note that, as a conservation measure, the members agreed to this general framework by consensus (i.e., through the absence of formal objection).

The framework for the establishment of CCAMLR MPAs outlines the strategy for aiming to meet all of the six objectives:

---

22   Dulvy, see n. 11 above. See also J. Wiegand, E. Hunter and N.K. Dulvy, "Are Spatial Closures Better than Size Limits for Halting the Decline of the North Sea Thornback Ray *Raja clavata?*," *Marine and Freshwater Research* 62 (2011): 722–733.

23   This was achieved through a CCAMLR Conservation Measure, 91–03 (2009), n. 14 above.

24   CCAMLR, *Report of the Twenty-Eighth Meeting of the Commission*, CCAMLR-XXVIII 2009, paras. 7.1–7.19.

25   Id., para. 7.8.

26   CCAMLR Conservation Measure 91–04 (2011), n. 12 above.

- maintaining the viability and integrity of representative examples of marine ecosystems
- protecting key ecosystem processes, habitats, and species
- establishing scientific reference areas
- protecting vulnerable areas
- protecting features critical to local ecosystems
- protecting the resilience of areas to climate change

MPA proposals must also take full account of the CCAMLR mandate that conservation includes rational use. It could be argued that five of these six MPA objectives could reasonably be achieved using the collection of sustainability measures that CCAMLR has at its disposal now. Protecting and promoting the resilience of areas to climate change is possibly the outlier here, since information on the impact of the many variables within the changing climate remains sparse. In this case it is clear that precaution would be invoked where there is a lack of scientific evidence, and we feel that this approach underlies the broader philosophy of CCAMLR MPAs.

Subsequent MPA Proposals

At the 2012 CCAMLR meeting, members submitted four MPA proposals for consideration under the general framework – CM91-04. The framework prescribes – in addition to the six key objectives that potential MPAs should aim for – other rules, including the adoption of a management plan for achieving those objectives.

Proposals were received from (1) New Zealand for the Ross Sea Region; (2) the European Union (EU) for under collapsed ice shelves, glaciers, and ice tongues around the east and west of the Antarctic Peninsula; (3) France, Australia, and the EU for East Antarctica; and (4) the United States for the Ross Sea Region.[27] These proposals followed a number of MPA technical workshops convened by the Scientific Committee and organized according to the spatial delimitation of the CCAMLR area into nine so-called 'planning domains' that included the areas the four proposals referred to.[28]

The MPA proposals generated considerable discussion, consultation, and revision of language and approaches. Although progress was made, consensus eluded participating members. Concerns, as reflected in the meeting report,[29] rested partly on the scientific justification for the MPAs and partly on the

---

27   CCAMLR, *Report of the Thirty-First Meeting of the Commission* (2012), para. 7.60.
28   Id., para. 5.57.
29   Id., paras. 7.60–7.109.

erroneous perception that all MPAs would automatically become no-take fishing zones. These concerns resulted in all bids failing to achieve consensus. Nevertheless, as already conceded, CCAMLR had accepted the concept of MPAs *per se*, and had adopted the framework for assessing and approving them. The next steps were thought to involve building consensus on specific proposals emanating from the Scientific Committee, and subsequently recommending them to the Commission.

As a general rule, non-adopted proposals cannot be reconsidered until the next meeting of CCAMLR. However, in 2012, it used its discretion to convene extraordinary meetings, and in doing so scheduled only the second special meeting of the Scientific Committee and Commission in its history.

CCAMLR-SM-II, Bremerhaven, 2013

The first-ever special inter-sessional meeting of the Scientific Committee was convened immediately prior to CCAMLR-SM-II, and its advice was considered in the CCAMLR meeting. However, these Scientific Committee proceedings were not subject to the usual simultaneous interpretation into the four official languages of CCAMLR meetings (i.e., English, Spanish, French, and Russian). In light of a reported comment by the Russian Federation about this, it remains to be seen how influential the lack of interpretation was on discussions in the CCAMLR Special Meeting during which several members, including the Russian Federation, withheld their consensus on the MPA proposals.[30]

The Commission considered two resubmitted proposals: The first was a revised joint proposal by Australia, France, and the European Union for what they called the 'East Antarctic Representative System of Marine Protected Areas'. The second was a joint proposal by New Zealand and the United States for an MPA in the Ross Sea Region.[31] The latter contained a consolidated and revised version of the two individual proposals not accepted by the CCAMLR XXXI meeting in 2012.[32]

---

30   SC-CAMLR-IM-I *Report of the First Intersessional Meeting of the Scientific Committee,* Bremerhaven, Germany, 11–13 July 2013. A synthesis of this and the Commission discussion can be found in CCAMLR-SM-II *Report of the Second Special Meeting of the Commission, Bremerhaven, Germany, 15–16 July 2013.* The statement by the Russian Federation is at para. 3.17.

31   Full details of the proposals are not publicly available. As with all CCAMLR working documents, permission must be sought from the authors before the Secretariat can release a document. The reference for the East Antarctic proposal is SM-II/03 and information on how to apply for access is available online: <https://www.ccamlr.org/en/ccamlr-sm-ii/03>.

32   Id. The Ross Sea Region proposal is document SM-II/04.

The Ross Sea Region proposal sought to enclose approximately 1.3 million km², with roughly half of that ocean space designated as a no-commercial-take zone.[33] However, the proposal also offered three multi-use zones. The first was a General Protection Zone, in which commercial fishing would be prohibited. This zone – the most comprehensive of the three – was intended to achieve all ten of the MPA's specific conservation and scientific objectives. The proposal also outlined a Special Research Zone in which commercial fishing could continue, for purposes that included maintenance of an existing toothfish tagging program as a tool for assessing population status. The third zone was aimed at protecting spawning grounds. Here, there was to be a closed season, allowing only summer fishing between 1 December and 31 March.[34]

The two parties informed the meeting that the MPA would be reviewed every ten years (in accordance with CM91–04), and reaffirmed or modified, or a new MPA adopted, 50 years after its entry into force.[35]

Looking objectively at this proposal, the obvious conclusion – the time-frame for review and duration notwithstanding – is that the measures proposed align with CCAMLR's existing ability to open and close seasons and areas, direct scientific fishing and research efforts, and adopt any conservation measures thought necessary for the maintenance of ecosystems and biodiversity. The only difference is that the proposal had the label – and one might suggest, the burden – of 'marine protected area'.

The joint Australian/French/EU proposal fared no better than that of the Ross Sea. It too was a pared down iteration of the one not adopted at the previous Commission meeting. The new proposal was for only 1.6 million km². Had it, along with the Ross Sea proposal been accepted, together they would have encompassed almost 3 million km² of the Southern Ocean, a proportion roughly equal to the Southern Ocean's share of the world's total oceanic area.

Following their comment at SC-CAMLR about lack of simultaneous interpretation, the Russian Federation then questioned whether CCAMLR could, in fact, legally adopt MPAs. The meeting's final report noted that the Russian Federation concerns were based on

> the current lack of a definition for the concept of a CCAMLR marine protected area, upon which, in its opinion, the full legal foundation of the

---

33   Id., para. 3.8. The size was originally about 2.27 million km², prior to the resubmission in Bremerhaven.

34   See n. 30 above, paras. 3.8 and 3.9.

35   Id., para. 3.11.

Commission's activities in relation to the establishment of such areas should be based.[36]

Indeed this is correct; while the academic literature contains ample definitions of MPAs, the framework adopted by CCAMLR does not. Rather, it outlines a set of six objectives,[37] and lists five crucial substantive elements required for conservation measures established following advice from the Scientific Committee to bring an MPA into effect.[38]

CCAMLR members resubmitted the non-adopted MPA proposals at the October 2013 and 2014 meetings, where again they failed to achieve consensus. It is anticipated that the October 2014 CCAMLR meeting will be presented with the proposals in some form or another and perhaps pared down even further. Whatever the case, proponents of the MPAs will no doubt lobby vigorously for member support during the inter-sessional period with the objective of gaining consensus.

Summary

The high seas cover approximately 64 percent of the world's oceans. While the adoption of the MPA concept in coastal waters is impressive, it has been slower in areas outside national jurisdiction.[39] Universal acceptance of high seas MPAs has not been forthcoming because of the challenges outlined in Table 8.1, as well as the lack of both a demonstrated urgency and a convincing counterfactual of what would happen if large-scale MPAs were not established. Further, the success of MPAs is not guaranteed by virtue of their establishment alone, since the tensions between conservation and rational use are often very significant. In 2005, the CCAMLR Scientific Committee had sought indications from its working groups about "what percentage of the range of a known harvestable resource could be covered by protected areas within a statistical unit before CCAMLR would need to determine if a proposed protected area might impact on rational use."[40] Nevertheless by 2011, CCAMLR had adopted the conservation measure that became the framework for adopting and establishing future MPAs.

---

36   See n. 30 above, para. 3.18.

37   See n. 12 above, at para. 2(i)–(vi).

38   Id., para. 3(i)–(v).

39   R. Devillers, R.L. Pressey, A. Grech et al., "Reinventing Residual Reserves in the Sea: Are We Favouring Ease of Establishment Over Need for Protection?" *Aquatic Conservation, Marine and Freshwater Ecosystems* (2014) DOI: <10.1002/aqc.2445>.

40   See n. 13 above, extract from para. 3.63.

The very fact that CCAMLR has developed a planning framework is acknowledgement that it recognizes the need to adapt its thinking to changing circumstances. It will no doubt continue to use all the tools at its disposal to manage impacts on Southern Ocean ecosystems until such time as there is sufficient confidence in the MPA concept to achieve consensus on proposals. Some would argue that there is sufficient confidence now in the concept, but as our evidence shows, this is unsubstantiated in CCAMLR since that confidence did not translate into the consensus required to adopt conservation measures (the medium through which MPAs become legally binding).

Discussion

The previous sections have described the context in which CCAMLR adopted the first high seas MPA but failed to adopt subsequent proposals. We now turn to the Jacobson and Brown Weiss'[41] implementation and compliance model to frame our theoretical discussion exploring why this occurred. The fact that only a couple of members withheld agreement is important as one dissenting voice is all that is required to halt the adoption process and once this has occurred, no-one else need speak up.

Jacobson and Brown Weiss provide an intuitive and rational framework within which to explore and analyse international environmental agreements and general issues surrounding implementation and compliance. Their implementation and compliance model, based on extensive research into the efficacy of a number of existing multilateral environmental instruments, provides insight into the way in which key factors interact to impact implementation and compliance processes, in addition to providing insight into the relative importance of each. The factors (generalizations) are broadly grouped into the following four broad and inextricably linked categories:[42]

1. The characteristics of the activity involved.
2. The characteristics of the accord.[43]

---

41   H.K. Jacobson and E. Brown Weiss, "Assessing the Record and Designing Strategies to Engage Countries," in *Engaging Countries: Strengthening Compliance with International Environmental Accords*, eds. H.K. Jacobson and E. Brown Weiss (Cambridge, MA: MIT Press, 1998).

42   Id.

43   We use the terms *accord* and *agreement* interchangeably in this article to indicate informality. Both terms have the same meaning.

3.   The international environment.
4.   Factors involving the country.

Factors Influencing the Adoption, Implementation, and Enforcement of International Environmental Accords
The Characteristics of the Activity Involved

Jacobson and Brown Weiss' study of several international environmental accords confirms the conventional wisdom that the smaller the number of actors involved in an agreement, the easier and less resource intensive it is to reach consensus and guide the actions of the parties to that agreement. CCAMLR's 25 'voting' members and the diversity of members' agendas in the MPA context underscore the difficulties associated with corralling a relatively large number of parties toward consensus.[44] Indeed, the difficulties associated with reaching an agreement multiply when it takes only one dissenting voice to hobble the achievement of a goal.

The effect of economic incentives is also important. The likelihood of reaching agreement and inspiring compliance improve when there are complementary or non-competing economic interests among parties. Intuitively then, the likelihood of non-compliance increases when conflicting economic interests are present. In the CCAMLR case, the members with the largest fishing interests in the Southern Ocean (including China, Norway, Japan, Russia, and Korea) have thus far failed to support MPA proposals that included no-take fishing zones and thus avoided compliance issues for the time being. In fact, there has been a call to re-open areas currently closed to fishing:

> In the absence of an established mechanism of international cooperation in international researches and surveys, including the system of data exchange and accumulation, the establishment of large-scale MPAs may lead to the development of vast blank areas in the East Antarctic lacking scientific and fishery data.[45]

The decision to take up the call for a representative network of MPAs was a global approach to what was perceived as a global problem. Yet, in actual practice, the members encountered greater difficulty in fitting the mechanism to the high seas CCAMLR area than they did to their own domestic waters. The tag 'lowest common denominator' is traditionally applied to consensus-based

---

44   Relative in contrast to the number of parties (usually one) involved in establishing marine protected areas in coastal waters, as outlined in Table 8.1.

45   See n. 30 above, at para. 2.51.

decisions, as was the case with the designation of the South Orkney Islands southern shelf MPA. This area, while lauded as the world's first high seas protected area, excluded adjacent regions with the greatest ecological value. Without question, this exclusion was non-accidental given the commercial importance of adjacent regions as prime krill fishing grounds.[46]

Characteristics of the Accord

According to Jacobson and Brown Weiss, the characteristics of the accord matter implementation and compliance with the accord, will be enhanced if parties feel that the obligations are equitable, precise, simple, and clear.

Because of the often highly technical nature of environmental accords and the dynamic economic and scientific environment in which they exist, they require provisions for collecting and using scientific and technical advice. Environmental accords equally require broad consensus among parties regarding scientific and technical issues,[47] and a shared respect for the sources of information that are accessed. In the case of CCAMLR, there was important input from the Scientific Committee by way of recommendations supporting the MPA proposals and MPA designation architecture. The fact that one MPA (albeit with the fishing area excised) and the framework for the designation of future MPAs was recommended by the Scientific Committee and adopted by the Commission members by consensus underscores this point, even though the case for, and legitimacy of further MPAs in the CCAMLR region has been questioned by the Russian Federation, for example.

Requiring parties to report regularly on relevant domestic policies and regulations represents one of the few opportunities available for evaluating the extent of implementation and compliance.[48] However, domestic and international commitments might not gel into one consistent approach to MPAs, nor should they. As noted in Table 8.1, implementation and compliance are particularly challenging in the high seas, not least because of the prohibitive costs of policing such vast and isolated areas, and the corresponding lack of political appetite to invest resources in enforcement. In the remote CCAMLR area it is essential to have fishing and/or research projects in place to effectively monitor ecosystems. However, sometimes these measures are insufficient, as illustrated by their ostensible failure to address problems related to illegal, unreported, and unregulated (IUU) fishing. CCAMLR has a mandatory vessel

46   C.M. Brooks, "Competing Values on the Antarctic High Seas: CCAMLR and the Challenge
      of Marine Protected Areas," *Polar Journal* 3, no. 2 (2013): 277–300.

47   See Jacobson and Brown Weiss, n. 41 above.

48   Id.

monitoring system (VMS) that relies on licensed fishing vessels keeping their VMS active. Some members also have access to satellite monitoring, for example, by employing an automatic identification system (AIS). However, effective monitoring relies on the AIS being active, something that is not always the case. Additionally, effective CCAMLR compliance assessment would require the continuous monitoring of satellites and cooperation in sharing satellite-derived information irrespective of its commercial confidentiality or security status. It is fair to say that CCAMLR struggles with effective at-sea monitoring. This is underscored by its recent initiatives towards remedying this problem through collaboration with INTERPOL's Fisheries Crime Working Group.[49]

At the coastal marine environment level, a balanced mix of incentives and coercive mechanisms can enhance implementation and compliance. Financial and/or administrative assistance can help parties comply with their obligations under an accord.[50] In contrast to coastal marine environments, the very nature of high seas governance and the broad physical scope of the world's marine system make it much more difficult to use incentives and/or coercion to any meaningful advantage. CCAMLR's continued battle with IUU fishing, for example, and the fact that CCAMLR members themselves have in the past conducted illegal and unreported fishing, underscores this.

Further, the specter of compromise politics came into play at CCAMLR's 2013 meeting when only two MPAs were considered for discussion, both of which had been significantly reduced in size. As noted by Johnston,[51] in the broader arena of international legal regimes the primary danger in contemporary global diplomacy is the propensity to generate 'over-expectations' through grand and seemingly successful negotiations, with goals such as ecosystem-based or integrated oceans management setting a compelling but potentially unrealistic agenda. Indeed, selling "such an ambitious, and potentially sophisticated goal is a stirring challenge to the art of salesmanship."[52] The intrinsic limitations of large-scale structures at global or macro-regional levels – the structural, political, hierarchical, and financial restrictions inherent in all large-scale state government bureaucracies – cannot be overstated, which are further constrained by the inter-cultural, strategic, and ideological limitations

---

49   CCAMLR, Report of the Standing Committee on Implementation and Compliance, Annex VI to the *Report of the Thirty-second Meeting of the Commission*, 2013.

50   Id.

51   D.M. Johnston, "The Challenges of International Ocean Governance: Institutional, Ethical and Conceptual Dilemmas," Paper presented at the Second Australia Canada Ocean Research Network (ACORN II) Conference, Canberra, Australia, May 2002.

52   Id.

that operate at the international community level. Even in the best of circumstances where an international organization functions with minimal friction, the "politics of conference diplomacy at the global or macro-regional level is rarely simple."[53]

The characteristics of these MPA proposals in the Antarctic region have become increasingly specious given that consensus has, thus far, been unattainable. The massive size reduction in the Ross Sea MPA proposal was very probably a bid to achieve consensus through compromise, but in so doing, sent a poor message, warranted or otherwise, about the scientific and diplomatic merit of the original two proposals. After numerous failed attempts, those proposing MPAs in the CCAMLR region will need to refine their sales pitch even further in the hope of achieving consensus, but at what cost to the ecological objectives that underpinned the original proposals?

The International Environment

A multitude of factors shaped the international environment in which a global commitment to a representative network of MPAs emerged, including ENGO advocacy, public awareness campaigns, media mobilization, major international conferences, regional concerns, and – importantly – the state actors spearheading the issues.[54] In the CCAMLR context, however, it is often difficult to pinpoint unequivocally the position of each State actor, since the text of both the CCAMLR and Scientific Committee final meeting reports represents negotiated and agreed language that does not always record the full nuance of discussions or name individual countries (e.g., 'some Members supported...'). As mentioned earlier, failure to achieve consensus requires only one dissenting voice. However, it is certain that the Russian Federation questioned the legality of CCAMLR's MPA mandate, which not only surprises (since they participated in the consensus decision to adopt the framework) but concerns these authors.[55]

Without wishing to undermine the process that CCAMLR has set in motion, we feel that the success of proposals for additional MPAs in the Southern Ocean hinges on the increased recognition of the importance of the ecological issues MPAs respond to, as well as the increased recognition of their legitimacy and effectiveness as proposed solutions. Much depends on the distribution of individual CCAMLR member control over the activities impacting 'the

---

53   Id.

54   These factors receive further elaboration in H.R. Hall and M. Haward, "Enhancing Compliance with International Legislation and Agreements Mitigating Seabird Mortality on Longlines," *Marine Ornithology* 28, no. 2 (2000): 183–190.

55   See n. 30 above.

environment' in the relevant marine areas, and how this will influence the degree of acceptance and compliance for proposals. *Legitimacy* is critical. The challenge lies in the proposals for additional MPAs in the Southern Ocean maintaining their relevance and legitimacy in a constantly changing environment.

In international relations theory, legitimacy comprises two parts: (i) the "property of a rule or rule-making institution" which should "itself exert a pull toward compliance on those addressed normatively"; and (ii) the actors addressed by a rule or rule-making institution must perceive "that the rule or institution has come into being and operates in accordance with generally accepted principles of right process."[56] The rule-making institution in this case is CCAMLR and its 'consensus norm' which makes it difficult to draw all members (i.e., 'actors') toward acceptance of, and ultimately compliance with the proposed MPA regime[57] we are examining in this article.

The legitimacy of international regimes can be evaluated according to two sets of criteria: (1) the extent to which the rules are applicable (applicability), and (2) the level of acceptance of these rules by those to whom they apply (acceptability).[58] There are both internal and external aspects to these sets of criteria. Internal applicability covers the extent to which rules are considered by agents as supporting the solution to the problem, the internal consistency of those rules, and the clarity of the 'message', that is, the need for the text of a rule to spell out clearly and succinctly what is required.[59] External applicability refers to the structural and normative components of a regime or instrument and its consistency with significant developments in the international community,[60] in other words, its relevancy and legitimacy in a dynamic environment.

This discussion's key points are that a problem first needs to be identified (is it scientific uncertainty about the impact of changing climatic factors on the marine environment?); and second, are the proposed rules (i.e., MPAs)

---

56   T.M. Franck, *The Power of Legitimacy among Nations* (Oxford: Oxford University Press, 1990), cited in Hall and Haward, n. 54 above.

57   Regimes are: "Implicit or explicit principles, norms, rules and decision-making procedures around which actors' expectations converge in a given area of international relations." S.D. Krasner, "Structural Causes and Regime Consequences: Regimes as Intervening Variables," in *International Regimes*, ed. S.D. Krasner (Ithaca, NY: Cornell University Press, 1983).

58   O.S. Stokke and D. Vidas, *The Effectiveness and Legitimacy of the Antarctic Treaty System* (Ithaca, NY: Cornell University Press, 1996) cited in Hall and Haward, n. 54 above.

59   See Franck, n. 56 above.

60   Id.

internally consistent, clear and relevant? Because CCAMLR members failed to reach consensus on three occasions, it is fair to state that the rules are not acceptable in their current form, and that MPAs and other conservation tools currently at the CCAMLR's disposal require improvement. Consensus is the critical component – even if only one dissenting voice is heard, the members must rectify the proposal's perceived lack of legitimacy. Failing this, there will be no consensus.

Internal acceptability encompasses the extent to which the parties to a regime or accord acknowledge, implement, and adhere to its provisions, together with the level of support demonstrated by parties in international fora and in interactions with other parties.[61] External acceptance involves the level of acceptance by third parties and is usually revealed through their attitudes to the regime or accord on a scale encompassing opposition, criticism, indifference, acquiescence, acknowledgement, and/or accession.[62]

In the CCAMLR context, both internal and external acceptability have shown times of greater and lesser successes. Greater successes have consisted in overall compliance with conservation measures, undertaking important management decisions such as the *Dissostichus* catch documentation scheme, and pursuing excellence in conservation science. There are still significant shortcomings with respect to preventing IUU fishing (occasionally conducted by member-flagged vessels), as well as unacceptable by-catch levels (particularly, but not exclusively, of seabirds).[63] These examples raise questions about the levels of internal and external acceptability of CCAMLR's current suite of management tools. For example, do CCAMLR members themselves feel that they need more options, such as MPAs, to deal with the unknown but inevitable impacts from the changing climate? Would the addition of MPAs necessarily resolve issues of acceptability? This brings us to consider the perceived legitimacy of the CCAMLR MPA accord.

An accord with high levels of internal and external applicability and internal and external acceptability has a correspondingly high level of legitimacy, which in turn motivates compliance with the rules of the accord. This underlines the importance of building legitimacy in order to strengthen compliance.

---

61   Id.

62   Id.

63   Once the seabird by-catch problem was identified, mitigation measures were put in place, but not all members adopted the solutions uniformly or in a timely manner. J.P. Croxall, "The Role of Science and Advocacy in the Conservation of Southern Ocean Albatrosses at Sea," *Bird Conservation International* 18 (2008): S13–S29.

If we consider the global applicability and acceptability of MPAs in their current form, it is possible to see how their perceived legitimacy may be lacking. As noted earlier, the failures of the current generation of decision-makers to meet the spatial and temporal targets for MPA adoption gave rise to the trend of 'biodiversity banking', where super-sized zones for protection are identified in remote and difficult to reach locations and slated for protection as MPAs. Should they be implemented, those MPAs would represent the lowest hanging fruit of marine conservation.[64] In the case of those areas where human activities are managed by CCAMLR, the legitimacy (that is, the internal and external applicability and internal and external acceptability) of MPAs is questionable, and indeed has been questioned by some member states on several occasions. With this in mind, one could argue that the proposed CCAMLR MPAs are at best politically motivated veneers of environmental protection (albeit sanctioned by scientific investigation), essentially paper parks that offer 'little more than a false sense of security', where the ability to enforce compliance is illusory.[65]

Factors Involving the Country

At the heart of this discussion, however, are the factors important to the success or otherwise of the accord – the features of the countries involved. A country's history, culture, physical characteristics, political institutions, and economic conditions influence (directly and indirectly) its implementation of, and compliance with an international environmental regime or accord. Other important dynamics involve the country's behavioral history and attitudes during negotiations for previous environmental agreements, as well as its participation in discussions regarding the issues being addressed at the international level.[66]

While these factors are important, Jacobson and Brown Weiss identify four key proximate factors that impact on the performance of a country in the international environmental arena: (1) administrative capacity; (2) leadership; (3) ENGOs; and (4) knowledge and information.

Intuitively, countries that possess strong administrative capacity do better than those that do not. Access to knowledge and information, educated

---

64   Trathan et al., n. 8 above; Devillers et al., n. 39 above.

65   D. Cressy, "Uncertain Sanctuary," *Nature* 480 (2011): 166–167; see also A.N. Rife, B. Erisman, A. Sanchez and O. Aburto-Oropeza, "When Good Intentions are Not Enough. Insights on Networks of 'Paper Park' Marine Protected Areas," *Conservation Letters* (2012): DOI: <10.1111/j.1755-263X.2012.00303x>.

66   See Jacobson and Brown Weiss, n. 41 above.

personnel, financial support, and an appropriate legal framework create the preconditions for strong administrative capacity and competency to meet the demands placed upon it. These preconditions and the administrative capacity that they underpin will play an important role in determining a country's ability to meet the obligations inherent in its agreement to be a party to an international instrument.

CCAMLR membership is diverse, ranging broadly from developing to developed States, as well as supranational organizations such as the European Union.[67] Member State capacity to commercially exploit the marine environment through fishing for instance, and to conduct marine scientific research is not uniform resulting in differences in perceptions, interpretations, and sensitivities among them, which may inhibit consensus in manifold ways.

The role of ENGOs in the international arena can be bittersweet. On the one hand, they can mobilize public opinion through concerted media campaigns, exert pressure on governments to respond to environmental issues and correspondingly influence the political agenda at both the national and international level. In the three decades since the work of Jacobson and Brown Weiss, the role of industry and ENGOs has strengthened, particularly as they now have at their disposal the powerful tool of mass social media. ENGOs provide public access to a wealth of information on ecological issues, and many have become highly adept at lobbying governments and existing multilateral convention administrations to take up their concerns at regional, national, or international levels, thereby influencing the direction and tenor of the negotiating process.

On the other hand, some ENGOs can be selective with the knowledge and information they access and share with the wider community.[68] At issue is not

---

67   The EU relationship in CCAMLR is complicated because the European Union is not a
      State with national interests but rather represents a common fisheries policy for its mem-
      bers, some of which are also CCAMLR members. See, for example, M. Salomon and
      K. Holm-Müller, "Towards a Sustainable Fisheries Policy in Europe," *Fish and Fisheries* 14
      (2013): 625–638; A. Smith, "Fishery Management: Is Europe Turning the Corner?" *Current
      Biology* 23, no. 15 (2013): R661–R662.

68   For example, the Antarctic Ocean Alliance (AOA) conducted a measured campaign directed
      to an international audience in support of MPA proposals at CCAMLR in 2012 and the two
      meetings in 2013. Their multilingual website invited visitors to sign a petition, stating that
      "[t]his year [2012] the fate of Antarctica's ocean, 10 percent of the world's seas, will be
      decided by 25 countries behind closed doors. Let them know the world is watching." Their
      frame of reference was the 10,000 species that call Antarctica home. The Alliance is a coali-
      tion of ENGOs and other organizations interested in Antarctic conservation. In the CCAMLR
      meeting report for 2012, Antarctic Ocean Alliance had five members listed as being mem-
      bers of the Antarctic and Southern Ocean Coalition, a regular CCAMLR non-governmental

only the information itself, but also how it is used. For example, the use of powerful information and dramatic language at a campaign's outset may leave little space for growth, prematurely exhausting a campaign's long run impact. Similarly, the potential for creating 'environmental fatigue' exists where information depicted repeatedly in strong terms may cause the audience to 'switch off', which again limits campaign effectiveness. Further, countries involved in multilateral negotiations are often highly selective with the knowledge and information they share with ENGOs, providing only that which may paint the incumbent government in a favorable political light. There are also issues concerning diplomacy and commercial confidentiality which countries must account for during an accord's negotiation, agreement, implementation, and compliance phases.

Leadership is the final proximate factor involving a country's implementation of, and compliance with, an international environmental accord. According to Jacobson and Brown Weiss, agents (including states, individuals, and NGOs) do make a crucial difference, whether it is motivating action or encouraging implementation of and compliance with an accord. One need only recall Ambassador Arvid Pardo's stirring oration to the UN General Assembly in 1967 about the potential mineral wealth that lay on the seafloor and how it ultimately led to the inclusion of the concept of 'the common heritage of mankind' in the Law of the Sea Convention. There are no such statesmen or stateswomen in the CCAMLR context *per se* because of the unique legal and political nature of the Antarctic. The seven claimants to Antarctic territory, and the two which reserve their right to claim, have a significant amount of perceived, if not actual power. They are the original Antarctic Treaty Consultative Parties (i.e., decision-makers in the Antarctic Treaty Consultative Meetings) and also CCAMLR members. This means that while they might exercise significant influence over meetings because they have the power of veto, other States that are also Consultative Parties and members of CCAMLR have the same power of veto. This provides all members with important leverage in issues of national interest, particularly when those interests are at odds with conservation measures that exclude rational use of marine living resources. Despite potential displays of leadership in Antarctic fora, influence is diminished by the need to gain consensus.

Summary of the Implementation and Compliance Model
To conclude with respect to the implementation and compliance model, the first key point is that when fewer actors participate in an agreement, the less

---

observer, but AOA was not represented at the meeting in its own right and while it did gather tens of thousands of signatures through its online petition, its efforts were to no avail. See Antarctic Ocean Alliance, <http://www.antarcticocean.org>.

difficult and resource-intensive it will be to achieve consensus and guide parties' conduct.[69] While the number of CCAMLR members is comparatively small relative to other international fora, the challenge of achieving consensus among its 25 parties is evident in the failure thus far to establish large-scale MPAs in the CCAMLR area of responsibility. That CCAMLR has made significant progress in implementing its multitude of management measures for the seas surrounding the Antarctic without recourse to MPAs should be and is recognized and applauded globally.

The second key point addresses the *characteristics of the accord* itself. An effective accord needs to be built on equity, simplicity, clarity, and precision. It should comprise a competent secretariat, regular reporting mechanisms, and a regular reporting schedule, and implement a file sharing process to enhance knowledge and information pertaining to the accord.[70] Certainly, CCAMLR has the administrative expertise in place in providing a competent secretariat and has a sound reputation for reporting. Nonetheless the progress of establishing high seas MPAs elsewhere has been glacial, despite several decades of discussion, negotiation, and pressure. This indicates that there are issues concerning the equity, simplicity, clarity, and precision of high seas MPA proposals and those in the CCAMLR region are no exception.

The third key point, the *international environment*, concerns issue momentum in the multinational arena, both publicly and diplomatically. A significant point in this category is the legitimacy of the issue *and* the proposed solutions. In international relations theory, legitimacy relates to the properties of the rule or the rule-making institution and the perceptions of those who are the targets of the rule.[71] Internal and external applicability and acceptability of the solution, the rules imposed to reach the solution, and the normative and structural components of the regime or accord are also crucial factors in shaping the relevancy and legitimacy of the proposed solution in a dynamic international environment.[72] As has already been noted, legitimacy appears paramount in the context of CCAMLR MPA discussions. Whether legitimate or not, in a consensus-based environment, it takes only one dissenting voice to question the legitimacy of MPA proposals and halt their adoption.

The fourth key point concerns country-specific factors, including (1) the member country's culture, international and national behavioral history and patterns; (2) its administrative culture and capacity; (3) the influence of NGOs on its

---

69   See Hall and Haward, n. 54 above.

70   See Jacobson and Brown Weiss, n. 41 above.

71   See Franck, n. 56 above.

72   Id.

policy agenda settings; and (4) the strength of leadership, and the level of knowledge and information about the issue under negotiation which determines its involvement (or non-involvement) in relation to the accord or regime being proposed.[73] While we have not gone into any detail about any particular dissenting parties' national culture and administrative capacity, we chose to explore the factors involving the CCAMLR's decision to embrace the global MPA network concept against the backdrop of ENGO influence and recognition of the absence of a uniform administrative capacity among all 25 CCAMLR parties. There is a clear disjunction between the campaigns of well-resourced ENGOs and the capacity, economy, and political will (the latter sometimes influenced by lack of resources to improve the former) of countries involved in negotiations. The campaign to establish MPAs in the CCAMLR region appears to be no exception.

Summary and Conclusion

This article has examined proposals for super-sized MPAs in the Southern Ocean – areas managed by CCAMLR – against the backdrop of global MPA targets and within the framework of Jacobson and Brown Weiss' implementation and compliance framework. We have set out the architecture of CCAMLR and its procedures and processes for decision-making, as well as the suite of measures its members have at their disposal to protect and conserve the ecological integrity of the marine environment. We explored the constraints that post-2002 oceans governance fora have imposed, not least because of the spatial and temporal magnitude of the task that has been set, especially as including the high seas in global targets has become *de rigueur*. While some comparatively small-scale steps toward designation have been proposed over the intervening decades – for example, pilot high seas MPAs – the emerging theme of *big is best* has endured.[74] We are of the view that some members within CCAMLR have become captive to this mantra as a way of meeting their obligations through the banking of biodiversity.

Universal acceptance of high seas MPAs has not been achieved. Existing MPAs cover less than 2.5 percent of the marine environment – most of this in national waters.[75] The adoption of the MPA concept in CCAMLR has been achieved, insofar as a framework for MPA establishment is in place. However, the actual designation of MPAs has been slow (with one exception), reflecting

---

73   See Jacobson and Brown Weiss, n. 41 above.

74   See Devillers et al., n. 39 above.

75   Id.

a range of concerns about size, scientific justification, monitoring, enforcement, and legitimacy. Nevertheless, CCAMLR was the first international governance institution to declare a high seas MPA, that of the South Orkney Islands.

Jacobson and Brown Weiss' implementation and compliance framework has provided a useful lens for exploring the lack of consensus for MPA proposals within CCAMLR. Analysis of proposals for adopting MPAs in the Southern Ocean revealed that the likelihood of non-compliance increases when conflicting economic interests are at play. Members with the largest fishing interests in the Southern Ocean (including China, Norway, Japan, Russia, and Korea) have thus far failed to fully support MPA proposals that include no-take fishing zones.

Examination of the characteristics of the accord exposed the specter of compromise politics at CCAMLR's 2013 meeting in Bremerhaven when only two MPAs were considered for discussion, both of which had been significantly reduced in size. The move from four to two proposals implies that the motivation of proponents may be to conserve political opportunity rather than to advance any overriding ecological, ecosystem, or biological feature based on sound scientific evidence. As such, the characteristics of MPA accords in the Antarctic have become somewhat elastic.

International negotiations surrounding high seas MPA proposals indicate that their legitimacy can be challenged. The deficit of MPAs with reference to numerous spatial and temporal targets has given rise to calls for super-sized zones for protection in areas beyond national jurisdiction. If implemented, these MPAs would represent the lowest hanging fruit of marine conservation, particularly when they occur in remote areas where the conflict between ecological protection and rational use is less prevalent, than, for example, in more heavily fished areas.

Finally, we examined the members involved in the negotiations. Not only are they all members of CCAMLR, many are also Antarctic Treaty Consultative Parties, which means they have significant interest in the outcomes of discussions and, along with all other States, enjoy the privilege of veto, providing all with important leverage in issues of national interest. While the Antarctic Treaty Consultative Meeting (through the Committee for Environmental Protection) itself acknowledges the work of CCAMLR in establishing a representative system of MPAs and its legitimacy to do so, it eschews discussion of the details of MPAs in this forum, to the point recently of failing to adopt a resolution to support CCAMLR's efforts.[76]

---

76   *Final Report of Antarctic Treaty Consultative Meeting XXXV*, Brussels, 2013, available online: <http://www.ats.aq>, paras. 102–104.

High seas marine protected areas might well be an idea whose time came a decade or so ago. However, significant work remains to embed this philosophy in the minds of all CCAMLR members. Protecting marine biodiversity so that it can be studied, understood, and valued is already within the power of those members. Adding the burden of enclosing huge swathes of the Southern Ocean with extra layers of rules undermines CCAMLR's ability to fulfil its mandate, diverts attention from other serious matters (such as management of the expanding krill fisheries), and inadvertently raises questions about its view of its own management capacity given the suite of tools it already has in place. Demarcating areas of the marine environment should be premised on the integrity that the protective measure would bring to that area. It is about quality, not size.

Gender Approach in the Integrated Coastal Zone Management Program at Sevilla, Cuba

Ofelia Pérez Montero†
Director, Multidisciplinary Study Center of Coastal Zones (CEMZOC)
Universidad de Oriente, Santiago de Cuba, Cuba

Pedro Aníbal Beatón Soler
Ministry of Science, Technology and Environment (CITMA), Santiago de Cuba
Delegation, Cuba

José Abelardo Planas Fajardo
Center of Solar Energy Research, CITMA, Santiago de Cuba, Cuba

Isabel Poveda Santana
CEMZOC, Universidad de Oriente, Santiago de Cuba, Cuba

Mirka Morales Hierrezuelo
Municipal University Center, Guamá, Cuba

Introduction

Since 1999, actions have been taken in Cuba to introduce the integrated coastal zone management (ICZM) approach in post-graduate programs at Cuban universities. The development of capacity for ICZM in Cuba has its most significant antecedent in the Tier II Project: Education for the Integrated Management of Coastal Zones in Cuba, developed in 1994 and 2004 and financed by the Canadian International Development Agency (CIDA) in cooperation with Dalhousie University, Halifax, Canada. Today, over 100 graduates hold master's degrees in science that are busy progressing ICZM practice in Cuba. However, ICZM programs have failed to delve into the gender approach to narrow the gender gap in Cuba's coastal population, and there is no module that explicitly refers to gender issues in ICZM in the master's degree curriculum in Cuba.

† The authors acknowledge the support of the former Canadian International Development Agency for financing the development of the research project Local Integrated Coastal Zone Management in Southeast Cuba, with coordination by Dalhousie University, Halifax, Canada.

In 2007, the Cuban Ministry of Science, Technology and Environment (CITMA) established the declaration process for Zones under the Regime of Integrated Coastal Management (Sp. ZBRMIC). This is a national process the objective of which is the assessment and approval of integrated coastal management initiatives in different areas of the country.[1] Each area is vetted to guarantee the minimum organizational, functional, technical, and methodological requirements to start integrated coastal management, however, there is no explicit reference to gender issues in any variables or indicators.

The project Local Integrated Coastal Zone Management in Southeast Cuba (2010–2014) introduced gender-based research in an ICZM program. This research explored the following questions: How does one move from gender indicators to concrete actions within ICZM programs? What does a gender approach contribute and what difference does it make in ICZM programs? How can one promote participation by both men and women in decision-making to resolve coastal zone conflicts? What tasks should be developed to empower women and men in a patriarchal cultural environment to assume the added vulnerability inherent in their gender role? This research tests the idea that social gender roles assigned to men and women culturally influence the level of their relations with coastal resources, so the management of coastal resources would be more equitable and sustainable if it incorporates gender perspectives in its program.

Among the key issues ICZM programs have dealt with are coastal water quality, coastal resources and ecosystems, and coastal threats and development. The programs are mostly related to conservation and protection and sustainability of resources and the coastal zone in general. ICZM programs focusing on physical, natural, socio-economic, institutional, and legal problems of the coastal zone seem unable to define differences in gender roles and power relations among men and women in the management and sustainability of resources.

ICZM is a valid management tool in Cuba given the complexity of environmental problems. The most threatening environmental issues for the Cuban archipelago are climate change and sea level rise, soil degradation, changes to forest cover, pollution from liquid and solid wastes, atmospheric emissions, noise pollution, dangerous chemical products and wastes, loss of biodiversity,

---

1   D. Salabarría and L. Brito, *Declaración de zonas bajo régimen de manejo integrado en Cuba. Memorias de la V Conferencia Internacional de Manejo Integrado de Zonas Costeras* (Santiago de Cuba: CARICOSTAS, 2011, ISBN: 978959207409-5).

and water availability and quality. Cuba's National Environmental Strategy (2011–2015) also outlines concerns that these diverse aspects converge in the management of overlapping physical space.

There has been an increased intensity and frequency of extreme meteorological events affecting coastal settlements. Strong winds and rain, seawater inundation, flooding, landslides, acceleration of desertification processes and droughts, the salinization of soil and groundwater, forest fires, and loss of coastlines and settlements have affected Cuba. In 1990, Cuba passed the Program for the Cuban Society to Face Climate Change, the creation of which involved scientists in different specialties from several institutions in the country. Studies published on this topic in Cuba focus their attention on the impacts that climate change will generate for ecosystems and human settlements, except for social studies dealing with how gender approach might contribute to the adaptation program of Cuba.

Gender Approach and the Problems in Coastal Zones: Interaction of Variables

Gender approach is a social science analysis perspective that contributes tools to visualize and promote actions to narrow the differences between genders in aspects of political, social and economic life. In the present study, the variables associated with gender relate to the coastal zone, mainly the interaction of gender roles with environmental conflicts and problems that impact the quality of life of men and women who use coastal resources.

In this article, three main concepts are distinguished in relation to the gender approach. First, the concept of gender is understood as the social, historical and cultural construction that establishes the set of standards for women and men and the practices that women and men should carry out on the basis of gender. Such standards establish and determine the relations between genders. Secondly, the concept of gender roles refers to the activities, functions and spaces distributed for men and women according to what society regards as feminine or masculine. Thirdly, the concept of gender gap refers to the differences in terms of opportunities, access, use, control and enjoyment of the benefits of coastal resources that permit individual, family and community well-being.

The complex problems occurring in coastal zones are intertwined not only in the physical, geographical, and natural elements, but also in the social, economic, and gender aspects. Observing gender relations within the coastal environment permits the design and implementation of sustainable development programs that minimize differences in the use and control of coastal resources and enhances the quality of life of men and women. The principle of participation in decision-making in the coastal zone favors non-discrimination on a gender basis and takes into account the needs and interests that are occasionally different between men and women working toward the same objectives in coastal development.

What constitutes a gender approach in the coastal zone? Different authors have shown the need to understand the social and cultural factors limiting women's and men's participation in such processes.[2] Other studies use gender variables to study models of human behavior, as in the case of migration to coastal communities;[3] the consumption of seafood;[4] the role of women in managing fisheries;[5] or from the perspective of participation of the family group in fisher communities.[6] On the study of cultural contexts, other authors contribute understanding on the role of participation in programs and strategies for the management of fishing resources,[7] or about the perception of risks of consumption of invading species as related to gender and race.[8] To a lesser extent, problems with natural resource management are approached from a gender perspective. Di Ciommo and Schiavetti highlight women's participation in the management of marine protected areas in

---

2   L. Aguila and I. Castañeda, Sobre marinos, marinas, mares y mareas: perspectiva de género en zonas marino-costeras. UICN – Ed. Absoluto (S.A. San José, Costa Rica, 2000); R. Rodríguez, Villalobos. Compartiendo secretos: sistematizando desde la equidad, Cantera, Rednas Centroamericanas. 1a. ed., (San José, Costa Rica 1999: UICN: Absoluto, 42 p. (Serie Hacia la Equidad, Módulo no. 8) ISBN: 996874326–7; J. Tobey and E. Torell, "Coastal Poverty and MPA Management in Mainland Tanzania and Zanzibar," *Ocean & Coastal Management* 49 no. 11 (2006): 834–855.

3   M. Corbett, "All Kinds of Potential: Women and Out-migration in an Atlantic Canadian Coastal Community," *Journal of Rural Studies* 23, no. 4 (October 2007): 430–442.

4   C. Cardoso, H. Lourenço, S. Costa, S. Gonçalves and M.L. Nunes, "Survey into the Seafood Consumption Preferences and Patterns in the Portuguese Population. Gender and Regional Variability," *Appetite* 64, no. 1 (May 2013): 20–31.

5   E. Bennett, "Gender, Fisheries and Development," *Marine Policy* 29, no. 5 (September, 2007): 451–459.

6   A. Davis and J. Wagner, "A Right to Fish for a Living? The Case for Coastal Fishing People's Determination of Access and Participation," *Ocean & Coastal Management* 49, no. 7–8 (2006): 476–497.

7   Ma. E.T. Aldon, A.C. Fermin and R.F. Agbayani, "Socio-cultural Context of Fishers' Participation in Coastal Resources Management in Anini-y, Antique in West Central Philippines," *Fisheries Research* 107, no. 1–3 (January 2011): 112–121.

8   T.C. Haab, J.C. Whitehead, G.R. Parsons and J. Price, "Effects of Information about Invasive Species on Risk Perception and Seafood Demand by Gender and Race," *Resource and Energy Economics* 32, no. 4 (November 2010): 586–599.

Brazil,[9] and Wells et al. refer to women's participation in a management program in coastal Tanzania.[10]

Gender studies integrated with ICZM programs do not have any significant weight in the scientific literature. Gender approach, according to most researchers, means the quantification of actions on the basis of gender participation. Few understand the gender relations that underlie human interactions occurring in the coastal zone. The early studies referred to above only deal with the inclusion of gender-based actions within ICZM programs, while the gender mainstreaming of such programs undoubtedly is a complex task.

As current gender behaviors are a historical, social, and cultural construction achieved after centuries, the androcentric and patriarchal vision has marked the development of full generations. Added to this is a male chauvinist culture, rooted both in men and women, which reproduces task differentiation among men and women, and women subordination in many societies. Cuba has suffered this situation throughout its history, however, the country shows sustained progress in gender equity thanks to over 50-years of social policy that put Cuba in fifteenth place among 136 countries assessed for gender equity.[11]

Why is Gender Approach so Linked to Sustainable Development of Coastal Zones?

Sustainable development programs are more efficient when they observe the diversity of interests of the population at which they are aimed. These diverse interests are not only economic, but also political, social and gender-based. Regarding gender, "it means to recognize that the development actors are women as much as they are men, and that both sexes confront differentiated limitations, often unequal ones; that is why women and men may have different and even sometimes contrary needs and priorities."[12]

Coastal resource damage affects daily life quality in coastal settlements. The gender approach leads to understanding that the impact of environmental problems in coastal zones affects men and women differentially in relation to

---

9   R.C. Di Ciommo and A. Schiavetti, "Women Participation in the Management of a Marine Protected Area in Brazil," *Ocean & Coastal Management* 62 (2012): 15–23.

10   S. Wells, M. Samoilys, S. Makoloweka and H. Kalombo, "Lessons Learnt from a Collaborative Management Programme in Coastal Tanzania," *Ocean & Coastal Management* 53, no. 4 (April 2010): 161–168.

11   "Cubanas en primeros puestos de igualdad de género del mundo," GRANMA Newspaper, October 26, 2013.

12   E. Skinner. *Género y cambio climático. Informe general BRIDGE development gender*, (Institute of Development Studies, 2011, ISBN: 978-1-78118-011-2), p. 10. Translations were provided by a translator.

coastal resources. If men and women have different interests, then development programs should consider these differences in the implementation actions adopted.

Coastal problems associated with soil salinization, desertification, and droughts generate resource and food scarcity, limiting home income and affecting family nutrition, for which women are generally responsible. This increases household tensions when men, in their role as provider, cannot meet household needs. Under such conditions, an increase in gender violence, alcohol consumption, and gambling is usually observed, along with a distortion in men's and women's activities and use of time.

What does Gender Approach Contribute to ICZM Programs?

The gender approach visualizes the different tasks, spaces, and relations with coastal resources that men and women have, mediated by the power and subordination relations historically constructed by society. This social and cultural construction, learned by men and women in their socialization processes, assigns definite roles to each gender. One role consists of women as responsible for non-remunerated tasks of caring and tending the family's health, girls' and boys' education, and the transmission of family and community tradition. On the other hand, men are responsible for family safety and for providing household income and resources from their work. Both men and women struggle with the impacts of misuse of water and soil and the effects of climate change in the coastal zone; these struggles influence the execution of their gender role.

The Legal Framework in Gender-Environment Relations

The legal framework in gender-environment relations has advanced worldwide according to the Bridge Report.[13] Cuba has been party or signatory to every international convention on this topic. The country has advanced its legal framework and developed initiatives for the introduction of the gender approach in its legislation. This is no easy task in a population with deeply-rooted male chauvinist behavior. An important initiative consists of improving the Family Code, which is currently under discussion in Cuba, with the introduction of gender approach in its formal content. Cuba implements international agreements and conventions by means of national programs that develop initiatives to promote policies for conservation and protection of natural resources, community adaptation to climate change, and sustainable development. However, there are no initiatives to introduce the gender approach in

---

13   Id., p. 10.

environmental laws. In *Decree-Law 212* on coastal zone management,[14] for example, neither male–female relations with coastal resources are, nor men's or women's roles in decision-making processes are mentioned. Clearly there is a need to introduce gender approach in Cuba's environmental legislation.

Local Scale Integrated Coastal Management: The Case of the Sevilla River Basin at Guamá Municipality

Within the capacity development project for local coastal management in the southeastern part of Cuba, a research sub-project was developed to implement an integrated management program in the Sevilla River basin at Guamá municipality. In this project a research line was developed on the integration of the gender approach. The study was carried out with the participation of a multidisciplinary team of researchers from the social, natural and technical sciences. Contributions of gender approach theories to integrated coastal zone management and local development were considered in this research. The research objective emphasizes learning how gender could be an important analytical tool for decision-making within ICZM, and an element for social inclusion in group participation of natural resource users by a group that is usually forgotten.

To achieve these goals, a triangulated methodological strategy was carried out. The qualitative methodology used described the population's productive and reproductive activities and the influence of these profiles in gender relationships in the Popular Council of El Madrugón, in the coastal municipality of Guamá. Forty-five semi-structured interviews were carried out in rural homes at Guamá municipality to determine the lifestyle features and how coastal environmental problems affect family quality of life. Fifteen women who had been living in the community for over 20 years completed in-depth interviews in order to define the roles assigned to men and women and to determine the level of gender awareness in households and the community.

Three workshops were held with the participation of authorities, women community leaders, and community men and women, which facilitated identification of their main socio-economic problems, conflicts affecting their quality of life, and development priorities. Two gender workshops were also held with the secretariat of the Cuban Women's Federation (FMC) to learn about the organizational strategy and policy for raising gender awareness in the municipality.

---

14   *Gaceta Oficial de la República de Cuba. Decreto-Ley 212*, Gestión de la Zona Costera, 2000 (Centro de Investigaciones Tecnología de Medioambiente, Santiago de Cuba, Cuba), 18 pp.

A matrix technique was applied to determine interactions and use conflicts with household activities and those of public circles assigned to men and women in the community. Concurrently, the technique of content analysis was applied to contextualize the research from documents on municipal level research, statistics, and planning and program reports.

Integrating macro- and micro-social analyses to understand the complexity of gender issues in ICZM and of the dialectical relationship between both levels is important in ICZM programs, which confirms the necessary vertical and horizontal integration in coastal development policies. The tendency in variable behavior at the micro-level does not necessarily follow the pattern of statistics at the macro-level. The social micro-level is influenced by stochastic factors determined by socio-cultural features of the population and the specificities of social management at the local scale, which may be different among municipalities and should be observed in ICZM programs at such a scale.

Cuba has advanced in gender equity at the macro-level; however, such advances do not always manifest in the same way at the community scale, such as the coastal rural communities under study, where behaviors indicated backwardness compared to the national average. This is why integrating analyses at social macro- and micro-levels reveals the need to adjust ICZM programs to each community's development demands.

At the social macro-level, Cuba exhibits gender indicators that express women's integration in society in an active way and with wide social recognition. Cuban women have been able to insert themselves in the working world by increasing their educational capacity.[15] Even if social policies for education, health, and employment have been implemented, indicators show that there is less development in relation to the social macro-level average. This is due to the fact that conditioning or socio-cultural factors (e.g., customs, habits, and models of behavior that reproduce from generation to generation) play an important role at the social micro-level. Women's employment in Guamá is low and only 27 percent of the 2012 land plots distributed went to them. Studies carried out in Cuba reflect that

> this situation is given both because the process up to now does not show specific actions to favor women joining in the workforce, and because of the permanence of gender stereotypes that keep women in their reproductive role, as household care managers, and frequently put them in non-remunerated family help situations in the agricultural circles. The scarce

---

15   J.L. Centella Gómez, "En torno a Cuba y los derechos humanos," *Granma Newspaper* (5 December 2013); A.P. Vidal and O.E. Pérez. *Miradas a la economía cubana. El Proceso de actualización* (La Habana: Editorial Caminos, 2012), p. 127.

development of support services in rural areas for children, elderly and disabled people's care keeps women in the family circle in their caring role. In some rural areas electricity and water services either do not exist or are unstable. The little development of this infrastructure worsens the community population's lives, but it especially does so in the case of women, as they have the burden of the most demanding activities or services from which all the family benefits, such as cooking, cleaning, washing, pressing the clothes. On the other hand, the poor state of ways, the transportation shortages and the long distances from the land to usufruct limit the inhabitants' mobility, especially women's, thus making commercialization of the produce of the lands they exploit even more difficult.[16]

In the case of Guamá municipality, demographic statistics reflect a population inhabiting rural coastal environments, without the advantages of urbanization, with a birth rate above the national average. The structure of the population reflects higher male presence in nearly all age groups. Women migrate more than men, thus affecting sex ratios in the municipality. Women's participation in senior decision-making roles in Guamá municipality production or services institutions is still very low. At the municipal level, 65.8 percent of executive decision-makers are men. The Popular Council of El Madrugón has 85.7 percent of the electoral districts governed by men, and 83 percent of productive institutions and 100 percent of farmers' associations are also directed and managed by men.

The male presence in decision-making at the coastal community scale should not be ignored in ICZM programs as they are associated with decision-making on coastal resources. A different vision and relationship, taking into account gender relations, should be integrated programs that respond to men's and women's interests in the coastal zone. These actions should have a social macro- and micro-integration element, depending on their intervention scale (i.e., municipal, provincial, regional, and national).

Results and Discussion

Guamá is a municipality of Santiago de Cuba province in the Orient of Cuba that includes the Sevilla River basin (Figure 9.1). The baseline of the ICZM program was created on the characterization of the physical, natural, economic, social, and legal-institutional subsystems related to the coastal resources of Guamá municipality, as explained in the ICZM program of the Sevilla River basin.

---

16   See Vidal and Pérez, id.

FIGURE 9.1 *Geographical location of the Guamá municipality in the province of Santiago de Cuba*
SOURCE: PLANAS ET AL., 2013, N. 17 BELOW

The Sevilla River basin is an area of abundant natural resources that constitute the basis for economic and social development of Guamá municipality. The river is 18.6 kilometers long, with an average slope of 24 percent. The main tributaries of this river are El Jobo, La Magdalena and El Ají. However, water supply difficulties, deforestation, and mountain erosion create a complex site for economic and social development. Erosion processes occur in the littoral dunes, with sand loss and damage to coastal vegetation, leading to dynamic processes of beach degradation. There are also problems associated with poor soil management and unproductive activities. Communities suffer from an absence of basic services, which becomes more acute due to continuous periods of fluvial floods affecting transportation by land.[17]

Population

The population at Guamá is 35,442, of which 18,562 are male (52.4 percent) and 16,880 female (47.6 percent). In Figure 9.2 the increased presence of men in the last six years may be observed. The population's way of life at Guamá reproduces the rural culture of mountain and coastal environments. Men and women farmers and field workers conduct their daily lives mainly in agricultural work to satisfy their families and communities. Human settlements are concentrated on the coast as a result migration from the mountains. There is some disperse population in the Sierra Maestra mountains.

17   J.A. Planas et al., *Project Report: Local Integrated Coastal Zone Management in Southeast Cuba* (Santiago de Cuba: Multidisciplinary Center of Coastal Zone, Oriente University, 2012).

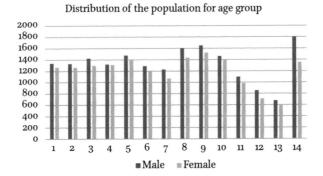

FIGURE 9.2 *Gender composition of the population in Guamá municipality*
SOURCE: 2012 EDITION OF GUAMÁ STATISTICAL
YEARBOOK, OFFICE OF NATIONAL STATISTICS OF CUBA

Guamá municipality has a population with a negative migration balance. The total population leaving the municipality is three times that of the population settling in it. Women participate more than men in the internal migration to other municipalities in the country. The most important outward migration trend is toward Santiago de Cuba municipality as migrants seek urbanization and the improved services generated by it. Of the interviewees, 54 percent were immigrants. The immigrants into Guamá municipality came from the province of Santiago de Cuba, from municipalities such as Contramaestre and Songo La Maya, and from other provinces such as Granma, Holguín, and La Habana.

The population of Guamá is young, with 29.5 percent under 20 years of age in contrast with the aged Cuban population. More than 57 percent of the population of Guamá is of working age and only 13 percent are over 60 years. Women between 20 and 50 years are always fewer than men of the same age group. This situation is reflected in the representation of age groups in the People's Council.

The Guamá population has a higher birth rate than the national average. Although the birth rate was 16.8 births per 1,000 people in 2010 and it dropped to 12.7 per 1,000 people in 2011, Guamá continues to have an average birth rate higher than the national rate shown in Figure 9.3, while mortality in Figure 9.4 suffered a slight increase at 6.8 deaths per year per 1,000 people.

The municipality of Guamá was the last site of the struggle for the independence of Cuba (1956–1959). Its mountain population were protagonists of the Rebel Army battles led by Fidel Castro Ruz in the Sierra Maestra heights. Currently, it contains numerous historical sites, among which over 14 places stand out in the memory of military and political events of that heroic age.

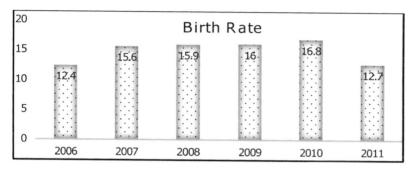

FIGURE 9.3 *Birth rate in Guamá municipality*
        SOURCE: 2012 EDITION OF GUAMÁ STATISTICAL YEARBOOK, OFFICE
        OF NATIONAL STATISTICS OF CUBA

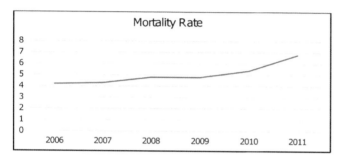

FIGURE 9.4 *Mortality rate per 1,000 inhabitants in Guamá municipality*
        SOURCE: 2012 EDITION OF GUAMÁ STATISTICAL YEARBOOK, OFFICE
        OF NATIONAL STATISTICS OF CUBA

Guamá counts on cultural development and the infrastructure supporting it, including four culture houses, four libraries, three bookstores, two cinemas, an art gallery, and two museums. The population develops diverse cultural activities, among which stand out literary workshops, musical ensembles, carnivals and the yearly culture celebration week. There are four archaeological sites in the area: two Indian-Cuban and two colonial sites.

Guamá has health and education infrastructure, guaranteeing the development and health of its inhabitants with free and universal access to such services, something almost non-existent in Guamá before 1959. Today, the municipality has more than 57 healthcare facilities, hospitals, polyclinics and quality medical assistance. The municipality has 119 education facilities at all teaching levels. With 1,383 students, the Municipal University Center of Guamá offers higher education programs in law, accountancy, agronomy, health technology, nursery, socio-cultural studies, physical culture, and social communication, as well as pedagogical professional programs aimed at local development of the municipality.

Guamá has a legal institutional order with municipal structures subordinate to Santiago de Cuba province. Municipal officials in education, health, culture, food, agriculture science and technology, environment, and the army, among others, are responsible for developing the municipal strategy to enhance the quality of life of the population. However, regarding the coastal zone, the following problems are identified in the legal institutional order:

· Insufficient knowledge of decision-makers about coastal zone features;
· Predominance of sectoral approaches in the municipal development programs;
· Violations of what has been legislated for the use of coastal resources and territorial organization;
· Short-term vision in the development strategy concerning the use of coastal resources;
· Lack of an integrated strategy for the management of coastal resources and their relation with gender equity; and
· No inclusion in the municipal political agenda of actions relating to gender awareness of its population with regard to coastal use conflicts.

First Cycle of Integrated Coastal Management with a Gender Approach

For the first integrated coastal management cycle, the Popular Council of El Madrugón was selected. The criterion for deciding upon the management area was defined by the development priorities of the municipal council administration. One hundred percent of the coastal population of the Sevilla River basin is rural. The human settlements with larger populations are the towns of El Madrugón and Sevilla. El Madrugón has the larger population and is the center for meetings and activities.

The Popular Council of El Madrugón has a population of 1,715 distributed across the following age ranges: 0–2 years: 87 people; 2–6 years: 115 people; 7–13 years: 186 people; 14–64 years: 1,188 people; and over 64 years: 139 people. Over 77 percent of Guamá's population is of working age. In the river basin there are 18.14 people per km^2, with the highest density between 1.5 and 4 km from the coastline. The majority of the population are males (56.3 percent), and 43.6 percent are females, so the approximate sex ratio is 0.8 women per man.[18] The Popular Council of El Madrugón comprises six districts. There are two mini-hydroelectric stations that presently experience operational difficulties during the drought season.

---

18   Id.

Key Issues for the ICZM Program and Interactions with Gender Relations in El Madrugón

A multidisciplinary group comprising local people and government staff held workshops to discuss 24 problems in the coastal zone management program.[19] Given the shortage of time and money, however, a consensus was reached that the first cycle of the Sevilla River basin ICZM program should focus on two key issues:

1. Conflicts related to water access and shortages and their affects on the population's quality of life.
2. Conflicts regarding the use of land that contribute to increased deforestation and erosion in steep slope areas.

Key Issues and Their Relation to Gender Equity

Both key issues are directly related to the decline of the population's quality of life in terms of reduction in the quantity and quality of food; personal, family and community hygiene; increased gender tensions; the population's level of overall discouragement and dissatisfaction; and loss of the basin's environmental quality and its natural ecosystem functions. Men and women are affected by these key issues, but their impact is differentiated according to their gender needs and interests. The solution to the conflicts and tensions generated by these problems in the daily work and household life of men and women involves untying the knots that hinder local sustainable development.

Gender Profile at Guamá Municipality

In some integrated management programs there is more information about the ecosystem under study than the population that depends on that ecosystem, or about the social and institutional system that manages such ecosystems. Gender information is difficult and complex to obtain. It is not usually revealed by the population in a clear and explicit way, as it has an intimate, private component that generates reservations in exposing it to others. In this study, analysis has centered on gender roles. Gender roles refers to the activities, functions, and spaces that are distributed for men and women according to what the society assigns in terms of gender roles. To understand how people of Guamá assign their gender roles reveals the gender profile in relation to strategies and routines followed by men and women regarding the use of coastal resources and the impacts of coastal environmental problems on people.

The composition and structure of homes as well as the socio-demographics of the people in the Guamá municipality contribute features that are the

---

19   Id.

subject and object of ICZM programs. Such features reveal differences in needs and interests to be observed while managing coastal resources. What types of homes characterize the population where the ICZM program is developed? On what population groups should the ICZM program efforts be focused regarding development and education for sustainability? Which population groups are most affected by coastal use conflicts? These and other questions find some of their answers in the present profile.

The last population and housing census reported a total of 11,012 homes in Guamá municipality. Of these, 23 percent include elderly people, 49.2 percent were childless, and 50.8 percent had children. Of the total homes with children, 57.4 percent have one child; 31.7 percent have two children, and only 10.9 percent have three or more children. This describes a rural home pattern that is not consistent with the traditional pattern of large numbers of children in rural areas. The number of people living in each home in Guamá municipality varies. Thus, 17.3 percent of Guamá homes consist of one person, 45.2 percent consist of two or three people, 30.3 percent of homes have four or five people, 6.3 percent are inhabited by six or seven people, while there are eight or more in 0.8 percent of homes. Kinship relationships in Guamá homes reveal that 11,024 individuals are heads of their homes, 19.5 percent have relationships with spouses, 30.9 percent have daughters and sons, and 3.9 have stepchildren; 1.4 percent have sons- and daughters-in-law, whereas grandchildren represent 5.9 percent, parents and in-laws at 0.9 percent, and 4 percent other relatives.

Regarding the marital status of males and females in Guamá, a predominance of consensual unions exist, i.e., not involving matrimonial contract. Guamá's males prefer consensual unions and 42 percent of them assume such relationships, whereas only 16.1 percent choose marriage. Thirty-seven percent of males were single during the census. Women's behavior is similar in preferring consensual unions, with 48.3 percent in this kind of relationship. Only 18.5 percent of had married their partner and 26 percent were single at the time of the census.

Gender Profile in Guamá's Daily Life

Regarding gender relations and roles in Guamá municipality, the results show that the population demonstrates traditional behaviors, although in the process of socialization in Cuban society men have progressed in housekeeping and women have made great strides in public service employment while keeping up with the burden of housekeeping. Such a profile generates information about the complexity of daily life in conflict conditions involving coastal resource use. The variables of gender role and the impacts of environmental problems intersect in Guamá's homes and communities, thus revealing individual, family and community tensions that should trigger action in ICZM programs aimed at minimizing or resolving such tensions.

In a sample of 28 homes in the coastal area of Guamá with 97 people, 46.3 percent of the females and 53.7 percent of the males reveal their perceptions and criteria about gender relations in their homes. Interviewees think that family care is the mother's responsibility (32.1 percent) and 7.1 percent consider it the father's responsibility. Fathers and mothers, according to 10.7 percent of interviewees, should equally share family care, while 18 percent concluded that the responsibility for family care is the mother's, and 10.7 percent said it was the father's. If those who regard both spouses as being responsible in the role of parents is included, this figure would increase to 82.2 percent for those who think it is the woman as mother or wife who is responsible for tending the home and family.

All interviewees regard the contribution of all family members to housekeeping as important and necessary. However, in practice, housework keeps falling to the women, a social and cultural role that is reproduced in Guamá. Forty-three percent of the interviewees consider that the inadequate contribution of men and women in the distribution of family chores generates conflicts in the home. Women continue to be responsible for cooking, laundry, housecleaning, ironing clothes, and tending to children and husbands. Some men declare that they "contribute" by giving money to buy food, by "buying the food at the grocery store" and in similar activities. Thus, 67.85 percent of women in the interviewees' homes have a double workload as they share housekeeping and out-of-the-house work.

The interviewees described the impact of coastal community environmental problems on their personal, family, and community life by mentioning the following:

1. Distress for family members suffering health issues (e.g., provoked by air pollution, smoke emissions due to improper burning, disagreeable smells from non-hygienic conditions of pigpens);
2. Physical and mental health effects and damage and loss of material goods belonging to family members (e.g., provoked by hurricanes, earthquakes, seawater penetration and flooding);
3. Family and household distress (e.g., provoked by intense rains and droughts); and
4. Distress in municipality management (e.g., generated by the lack of a management program integrating the interface of land-air-sea, and aimed at the sustainable development of the municipality).

Gender Profile at the Community Level in the Management Area

The communities belonging to the People's Council of El Madrugón have a profile of productive activities linked mainly to agriculture. Men's and women's lives revolve around planting and harvesting vegetables, legumes, coffee, and fruit, and sheep, pig, or goat raising. Productive activity takes place on the banks and the valley of the Sevilla River basin. The gender profile regarding productive activities shows the active participation of men, who are the main owners of the soil resource, in direct production. They represent 73 percent of the land tenants and mainly own their working tools.

In Guamá municipality, by the end of March 2013, among the 1,144 usufruct landowners under *Decree-Laws* 300,[20] of which 308 were women (27 percent). Few women at the People's Council of El Madrugón are usufruct landowners, but the majority of women help their husbands, brothers, and fathers in agricultural tasks during harvest and plantation time. The interviewees agreed by noting:

> Here most women dedicate themselves to agriculture because there is nothing else to do. (A female farmer).
> ... If any farmer needs help, we women go and help him. Women have stood out picking coffee, and to the fields we go mainly to work, but we are not landowners. There is no activity looking for women's income for women, there is nothing else other than agriculture. Each farmer in need of a labor force uses his family, although at the coffee harvest women go and do get paid. (A female inhabitant)[21]

Both men and women have access to bank loans, however, there is poor knowledge about the use and application process for loans, which results in few men and women farmers resorting to bank loans. "Farmers have access to loans, for example, my son-in-law has one to buy oxen and my daughter is a landowner and has another loan I think to buy oxen too, but the large majority do not know how to apply for it." (A female inhabitant)

Meanwhile, the gender relations profile regarding reproductive activities reflects patriarchal relationships. Women continue to be "responsible for the home"; they are the ones to tend the families' feeding, dressing and healthcare, even if men have "progressed" in "helping" with some of the family chores. "In my house, I prepare the meals, but the men also help and they are now taking

---

20   *Gaceta Oficial de la República de Cuba.* "*Decreto-Ley Sobre la entrega de tierras estatales ociosas en usufructo,*" 20 de septiembre 2012.

21   English translation provided by the authors.

more part in housekeeping" (A female inhabitant). Housekeeping tasks are mainly the women's responsibility. In this endeavor, women face the harshness of field labor, with a lack of some resources for clothing and food, which they have to obtain at the municipality administrative center.

The most pressing problem affecting family life quality is that of water resources. Recent studies indicate that the water pipeline originating at the Los Morones reservoir was destroyed by the flooding of Sevilla River 15 years ago,[22] so the supply has been guaranteed by means of extension of pipe sections from mountain springs. In general, drinking water supply and sanitary services in the area are deficient. Over 80 percent of the population have found solutions for their water supply with no treatment. The rest of the population has to carry the water directly from the river. Other water comes from artesian wells built privately by farmers and agricultural cooperatives.

The studies reveal that women are more collaborative in community activities. They participate in neighborhood organization activities and with women in their residence area. In the community socialization spaces, men and women do share in parties, sports activities, and entertainment.

Interaction between Household Tasks and Coastal Resources

The main household tasks carried out by women in this community have a significant interrelationship with coastal resources: soil, water, flora, mangrove swamps, fauna and the sea. These resources are the basis of products that support feeding and caring of the family, which reveals that the way of managing such resources will affect their daily lives. Ecosystem health directly affects the performance of community gender roles (Table 9.1).

In the study, feeding, entertainment, and hygiene activities were identified as the activities most associated families, whereas fishing, construction, and agriculture were the most significant activities that interviewees carry out for family support and quality of life. The interviews show that activities related to family feeding highly interact with the following coastal resources: soil, water, flora, and the sea. The state of health of community members depends on the quality of food products.

Providing coastal homes and communities with electricity might have a high interaction with water and ocean resources, as ocean energy and the river might be used for mini-hydroelectric plants. However, even if they have a high interaction theoretically, no in-depth analysis was made of the features and the potential of such resources for home energy generation. Additionally,

---

22   Planas et al., n. 17 above.

TABLE 9.1   *Matrix of the interaction of activities by men and women in their daily lives with the selected coastal resources*

Activities/Coastal resources	Soil	Water	Flora	Beaches	Mangrove swamps	Sea	Fauna
Food	H	H	H	L	A	H	H
Energy	NI	H	NI	NI	NI	H	NI
Entertainment	L	H	A	A	L	A	A
Hygiene keeping	NI	H	NI	L	NI	B	NI
Fishing	NI	H	L	H	H	H	H
Construction	H	H	L	H	NI	H	L
Agriculture	H	H	A	NI	NI	NI	H

Legend: H: High Interaction; A: Average Interaction; L: Low Interaction; NI: No Interaction
SOURCE: MONTERO, 2013, N. 24 BELOW

entertainment at rural coastal communities is largely associated with the use of resources such as water, beaches, sea, and fauna for swimming and enjoying nature. However, home and personal hygiene has a high interaction with water resources, as does keeping livestock pens and domestic animals clean.

Fishing is also carried out by farmer families. Although agricultural activity predominates in the study area, some people were dedicated to fishing. In this sense, fishing interacts highly with water resources, beaches, fauna, and mangrove swamps. Fishing is carried out either as a sports activity or as a source of family sustenance through the commercialization of marine products.

Construction is another activity carried out in the coastal zone and occasionally generates coastal erosion when houses are located on the coastline. Damage to coastal infrastructure can also be caused by seawater penetration or river floods when houses are located on river banks or near the coast. This is a highly vulnerable zone with regard to the impact of hydro-meteorological events. Meanwhile, agriculture interacts highly with soil, water, flora, and fauna. Access to soil and water can be difficult and the productive capacity of both of these resources has deteriorated in some areas due to misuse by humans and changes resulting from desertification and droughts. Table 9.2 sets out the level of compatibility of family activities with productive activities. Construction is the most incompatibile with other activities.

TABLE 9.2   *Matrix use compatibility*

	Feed	Energy	Entertainment	Hygiene keeping	Fishing	Construction	Agriculture
Feeding		C	C	PC	C	I	C
Energy	C		C	C	I	I	C
Entertainment	C	C		C	C	I	I
Hygiene keeping	C	C	C		I	I	I
Fishing	C	I	C	I		I	I
Construction	PC	PC	PC	PC	PC		I
Agriculture	C	C	C	PC	I	I	

Legend: C: Compatible, I: Incompatible; PC: Poorly Compatible
SOURCE: MONTERO, 2013, N. 24 BELOW

Gender Conflicts and Coastal Problems: Their Impact on Gender Relations

Men and women deal with conflicts associated with water and soil resources in coastal areas differently. Both genders are at high risk with regard to identified dangers in the coastal area. Women are responsible for household life and family matters according to their gender role and tensions are increasing for them as a result of these dangers. Men are vulnerable due to their home provider role and the difficultly of providing money or products for their homes, which is related to their gender role. Table 9.3 sets out five key dangers facing men and women in the coastal zone and outlines the impacts of a gender approach and Table 9.4 shows the probability of a danger occurring and the consequences for gender relations.

These environmental problems identified in Table 9.3 become dangers for the population inhabiting the coastal zone and significantly affect gender equality. These dangers demand management action to eliminate the environmental problem they created, as in the case of Peril 5, as water pollution may generate unhealthy human conditions. Perils 2, 3 and 4, water shortages, food shortages, and sea level rise respectively, demand mitigating actions that may generate new alternatives for exploiting soil resources, altering practices according to changes in soil characteristics, and conservation of aquifers and identification of areas to excavate new wells to obtain safe drinking water. Perils 1 and 2 require reduction and mitigation actions. Alternatives that integrate government action with local community entrepreneurial action are needed to reduce the gradual loss of productive soil capacity and to deal with water shortages.

TABLE 9.3   *Matrix of impact of identified dangers from a gender approach perspective*

Danger	Probability	Consequences for gender relations	Impact
Peril 1 desertification and drought	Almost Certain	Women, girls, and boys walk about 2–4 km to collect water for household tasks. Loss of employment options for men and women due to the decrease in production volume and the harvest times. Women have less time for education and income-generating activities. Decrease in the length of employment of women.	Very High
Peril 2 water shortage	Almost certain	Damage to the harvest produce and food security. Decreased personal, family, and home hygiene. Women are forced to walk longer distances to reach a water source. Women can be subject to sexual harassment and rape during these longer walks.	Very High
Peril 3 food shortage	Probable	Tensions in feeding the family. Tensions in home provisioning. Loss or reduction of family diet. Household stress.	Average

Peril 4 sea level rise	Probable	Salinization of drinking water sources. Reduction of the quantity and quality of household water. Loss of water sources. Material damage and loss of houses, affecting families living on the coastline. Loss of human lives.	Average
Peril 5 water pollution	Probable	Increase of water-transmitted diseases (e.g, cholera, diarrhea, malnutrition, malaria, and dengue). Loss of live or damage to health of men, women, boys and girls.	Extreme

SOURCE: MONTERO, 2013, N. 24 BELOW

TABLE 9.4   *Impact matrix of probability of danger occurrence/consequences for gender relations*

AP				P5	
P					P1, P2
M				P3, P4	
LP					
R					
	I	L	M	VH	E

Legend: *Probability*: R: Rare; LP: Low Probability; M: Moderately Probable; P: Probable; AP: Almost Probable

Consequences: I: Improbable; L: Low; M: Moderate; VH: Very High; E: Extreme

Perils: P1: Desertification and Drought; P2: Water Shortage; P3: Food Shortage; P4: Sea-level Rise; P5: Water Pollution

SOURCE: MONTERO, 2013, N. 24 BELOW

The ICZM Program with a Gender Approach

Mainstreaming of the gender approach in ICZM programs is a challenge, but it is necessary to add it to the principles of ICZM (see Table 9.5). The principles of sustainable development are consistent with gender and could direct the implementation of gender issues in ICZM programs. The results permit us to introduce the gender approach in the ICZM cycle as shown in Table 9.6. The larger the ICZM cycle loops, the greater the achievement of sustainable development goals and the narrower the gender gap among the coastal population.[23]

The integrated management program from a gender perspective in Sevilla has the following objective: To reduce the gender gap regarding coastal problems and conflicts related to water and soil use by means of integrated management, so that it improves men's and women's quality of life and sustainability in the Sevilla coastal zone. The specific objectives are

1.   to make the gender gap visible and reduce it in regard to coastal conflicts related to water and soil resources;

---

23   GESAMP (IMO/FAO/UNESCO-IOC/WMO/WHO/IAEA/UN/UNEP Joint Group of Experts on the Scientific Aspects of Marine Pollution), *The Contributions of Science to Integrated Coastal Management* (Rome: Food and Agriculture Organization of the United Nations, 1996, (rev. p. 6) 72 pp.

TABLE 9.5   *ICZM principles with gender approach assumption*

Principles	Definition in relation to the coastal environment and gender relations
Interrelation and integration	Understanding the different levels of relations and interrelations among coastal issues and the various sectors, between the environment and development, among men and women and coastal resources.
Inter- and Intra-generational equity	Guaranteeing, with present day's actions, that future generations are able to enjoy the natural resources that allow them to develop their lives in a healthy and conserved environment and considering men's and women's need and interests in the distribution of coastal development benefits through time.
Right to development	A basic right, offering equal opportunities to men and women regarding coastal resources use, control and benefits.
Environmental safeguard	To take preventive steps that permit environmental conservation against human impacts, with strong and effective regulatory frameworks that guarantee men's and women's quality of life and coastal ecosystem health.
Precaution	Lack of information and scientific uncertainty are not reasons to postpone environmental protection actions against potential and irreversible menaces and their incidence in gender relations, which could affect sustainable development and contribute to widening the gender gap in coastal communities.

SOURCE: MONTERO, 2013, N. 24 BELOW

2. to maximize the actions contributing to raise gender awareness in the presence of conflicts identified in the coastal community; and
3. to eliminate coastal pollution and to improve family life quality in communities and coastal ecosystem health.[24]

As a result of this research, the indicators in Table 9.7 were defined to show progress in gender gap reduction and coastal dimensions selected as key issues. These indicators permit evaluation of the levels of participation and advances in the use and control by men and women of coastal resources. Gender roles in the daily lives of the Sevilla River basin population are related to the use of coastal resources. The management of coastal resources is more equitable and

---

24   The authors arranged guidelines for the fulfillment of these objectives. See O.P. Montero, *Informe del Proyecto Formación de capacidades para el manejo costero local en el sureste de Cuba*, Universidad de Oriente, INEDITO, Santiago de Cuba 2013.

TABLE 9.6   *Essential steps to integrate a gender approach in the ICZM cycle*

Steps	Essential actions
Step 1. Identification and assessment of key issues related to gender	A. Identify and assess the main environmental, social, institutional, and gender issues and the implications of gender issues B. Identify the main actors and their interests and needs regarding their gender roles and their interrelation with coastal resources C. Verify the feasibility and governmental and non-governmental leadership, as well as the political agenda related to gender issues in the selected items D. Select the issues upon which the management initiative will focus and those issues which, for their impact on gender issues, are a priority for the program to succeed E. Define the goals of the ICZM initiative in relation to the gender approach
Step 2. Preparation of the program with enhancement of gender awareness	A. Document the conditions of the baseline including gender B. Carry out the research identified as a priority for the management of coastal resources in their relation with gender behaviors C. Prepare the management plan and the institutional structure under which the program will be implemented, considering men's and women's roles in decision-making D. Start the development of the local technical capacity in ICZM issues and those of gender E. Plan financial support F. Test implementation actions at a piloting scale G. Carry out a program of public education and gender awareness
Step 3. Formal adoption and funding provisions with equal opportunities for men and women within the program	A. Present the program to the Municipal Administration Council and obtain governmental approval of the proposal B. Implement the basic institutional framework of ICZM and obtain governmental support for the different institutional adjustments C. Include the ICZM program and the gender issues in social organizational agendas

Steps	Essential actions
	D. Provide equal funding opportunities to men and women for the implementation of the development actions approved in the program
	E. Provide the required funds to implement the program
Step 4. Implementation with gender inclusion	A. Modify the program strategies as needed
	B. Promote the fulfillment of the ICZM policies and strategies with gender equity
	C. Strengthen the institutional and the legal frameworks of the program, with emphasis on the relationship among gender, environment, and sustainable coastal development
	D. Strengthen the commitment of administration and personnel to the strategy and the results
	E. Strengthen the entrepreneurial, technical, gender, and financial management capacities of the program
	F. Ensure the construction and maintenance of the physical infrastructure
	G. Encourage open participation of those who support the program
	H. Implement conflict resolution with gender equity
	I. Encourage political support and the program presence in important national, provincial, and municipal discussions
	J. Monitor program development and ecosystem tendencies
Step 5. Assessment of program progress and gender gap reduction	A. Adapt the program to the present experience and to new and changing environmental, political, social, and gender conditions
	B. Determine assessment purposes and impacts
	C. Assess program progress and gender gap reduction in the coastal zone

SOURCE: OLSEN, 1999, MODIFIED BY MONTERO, 2013, N. 24 ABOVE

sustainable if it incorporates gender perspectives in its program. A greater human vision based on the cultural construction contributes to coastal management and highlights the significance that coastal resources have for the local population. The modification of implementation phases of the ICZM program guarantees gender mainstreaming in each cycle of the integrated management process in coastal zones.

TABLE 9.7   *Selected ICZM principles that allow integration of gender indicators in assessing ICZM programs*

Participation	Integration	Interaction	Prevention	Precaution	Governance
Level of women's participation in decision-making processes	Women's access to bank loans	New forms and organization of community services (care) that ease men's and women's participation in productive and service activities	Number of clean-up activities	Number of government agreements at the municipal scale and level of fulfillment regarding gender issues in the ICZM program	Initiatives and communal action for the management of water
Women in executive positions at the head of community organizations	Women land owners	Men-women relation regarding access, use, control, and benefits derived from soil use	Number and type of disease for women and men	Number of technologies introduced and transfer level	Initiatives and communal action for the management of soil
Women and men solving coastal problems and conflicts	Women's access to resources (e.g., animals, tools, seeds)	Men-women relation regarding access, use, control, and benefits derived from water use	Development activities on gender and resolving coastal conflicts	Water and soil quality parameters	Number of production and services entities that implement the system of integrated environmental management at the basin level

SOURCE: MONTERO, 2013, N. 24 ABOVE

Conclusion

From the results and discussion of this study, the following conclusions may be reached on gender issues in the integrated coastal zone management program at Sevilla, Guamá municipality, Cuba. The seashore of Sevilla is highly sensitive with high ecological, environmental, socioeconomic and cultural values. Coastal resources (e.g., soil, water, flora, fauna, beaches, and mangroves) are directly related to the quality of life of Guama's population. Gender relations with coastal resources are differential regarding gender roles. The ICZM program may contribute to higher gender equity levels as each program cycle increases the indicators of women's well-being, access, awareness, participation, and control of problems and conflicts generated in their life environment, which are limited at present. The ICZM program at Sevilla River basin added the gender approach for program efficacy and sustainability in a wider women's empowering framework. The profile of influences permitted the identification of factors affecting gender differences, determined in the profiles of productive, reproductive, and community activities. Among the influences are the following:

· Socio-cultural factors: Persistence of a male chauvinist and patriarchal culture that dominates and reproduces itself in men's and women's environments. Low levels of education among farmers and women's economic dependence on their husbands influences such persistence, as does the reproduction of gender roles in productive and reproductive activities related to use of water and land resources.
· Infrastructure-related factors: Difficulties in access to drinking water for household and agricultural use in communities and dwellings. Deterioration of community infrastructure for the provision of certain services to the population, including hair-dressers, barbershops, transportation, daycare centers, elder care centers, and other public services.
· Socioeconomic factors: Few employment sources for women and the issue of boys and girls not involved in either studies or work. Poor local entrepreneurial spirit for problem solving related to the well-being of a community affected by drought.
· Gender awareness-related factors: The community organization lacks goals associated with raising gender awareness that permit women to organize and participate consciously to overcome women's inequality with men in coastal resource decision-making.

It was shown that men and women face coastal conflicts associated with water and soil resources, with a significant impact due to desertification and droughts. Both genders are subject to high risks in the face of perils related to coastal problems, as women are responsible for household life and family care, the tensions of which increase in periods of conflict. Men face tensions in their home provider role when bringing home money or products, which can also be hampered by coastal problems.

Household activities, especially those carried out by women in the community, have high interrelations with coastal resources, e.g., soil, water, flora, mangrove swamps, fauna, and the sea. These resources are the base of products that provide family nutrition and care. Thus the way in which resources are managed will affect daily life. Ecosystem health directly affects the performance of the community gender roles. The interaction between household activities and the selected coastal resources is high, which justifies integrated management of resources with inclusion of the gender approach. This approach reveals the necessary information for decision-making for the use, control, and distribution of the benefits of coastal resources, which contribute to individual, family, and community well-being.

As for water resources that are not only vital to agricultural development in coastal and rural municipalities, but also for domestic utilities and hygiene, water management is related to family health risks. Management of soil resources is directly related to family food security, through the generation of personal and family revenues. Dysfunctional, poor families led by women are more vulnerable and more prone to flawed decision-making about water and soil use, decisions they do not generally participate in. Indeed, women-led families generally have low access to productive resources (e.g., land, cattle, agricultural tools and credit), which makes them still more vulnerable. The situation described above contributes to widening the gender gap in coastal communities.

The integration of macro- and micro-social analyses of the coastal reality indicates that although Cuba is internationally recognized in the development of gender equity, there are socio-cultural factors associated with gender that delay such development at the micro-community level. This is shown by socio-demographic indicators such as birth rate, migration rates above the national average, and low women's participation in local decision-making in relation to their potential given Cuba's social and educational policy over the last 50 years. At the local level, actions are proposed to empower the most vulnerable group in decision-making on coastal conflicts and programs that promote women empowerment in coastal zones.

Cuba has advanced its legal framework and developed initiatives for the introduction of the gender approach in its legislation. However, there no initiatives yet for the introduction of the gender approach in the legal framework related to the coastal zone. For example, *Decree-Law 212* on coastal zone management does not reflect gender relationships with coastal resources, or the role that each gender plays in decision-making processes.[25]

Gender mainstreaming within ICZM is a challenge. It is necessary to apply the precautionary principle so as to achieve the proposed goals and to incorporate the gender approach in the principles guiding the implementation of ICZM programs. Management authority staff should be trained to adequately implement the gender approach program. Failing to do so would reproduce subordinate gender relations found before ICZM program implementation.

Steps to implement the ICZM program were modified in this research by including those that visualize coastal problems from male and female viewpoints, and by searching for inclusive, participatory and empowering solutions for vulnerable groups, together with raising gender awareness in the coastal community of the People's Council of El Madrugón. Assessing the progress of ICZM in each cycle should be accompanied by a narrowing gender gap from the implementation of actions for women's and men's empowerment. The indicators to be assessed answer the needs identified in the gender diagnostic carried out in the Sevilla River basin, but they may be enhanced in other experiences and contexts.

---

25   See *Decreto-Ley 212*, n. 14 above.

Oil and Gas and Renewable Energy

∵

Re-conceptualizing Environmental Governance in Ghana's Offshore Oil and Gas Development

Godwin Eli Kwadzo Dzah*
Faculty of Law, Ghana Institute of Management and Public Administration, Ghana

Introduction

Offshore petroleum development in Ghana has been rapid. To date, there are at least seven offshore gas discoveries with estimated recoverable reserves of 4.845 trillion cubic feet,[1] and oil production from fields that are already at the exploratory and appraisal phase is expected to reach 600,000 barrels per day (bpd) in 2018. These figures will put Ghana in the top 50 global petroleum producers in the next few years.[2] The fast-paced nature of exploration and production has created challenges for sustainable resource development. However, offshore oil and gas development has eclipsed environmental concerns. To address this problem, the critical question is how does Ghana maximize the benefits of offshore drilling and at the same time manage the negative environmental impacts of oil and gas development.

Ghana's biggest challenge is how to establish both regulatory and institutional frameworks capable of addressing the emerging environmental consequences in the burgeoning petroleum industry. Ghana's present petroleum regulatory and institutional frameworks lack specific legislative prescrip-

---

* I sincerely wish to express my gratitude to Richard J. Lazarus, Howard J. and Katherine W. Aibel Professor of Law at Harvard Law School for supervising my research work during my LL.M. studies at Harvard Law School. I would also like to thank Sharon B. Jacobs, Lecturer on Law at Harvard Law School for her constructive suggestions. I also wish to thank Teresa Saint-Amour of the Harvard Law School Library for her research support. This article is a product of my LL.M. thesis at Harvard Law School.

1 Public Interest and Accountability Committee, *Report on Management of Petroleum Revenues for the Period 1st January 2012 to 30th June 2012* (Accra: 15 September, 2012), p. 5.

2 KPMG Africa, Ghana's Oil Prospects, available online: <http://www.blog.kpmgafrica.com/ghanas-oil-prospects/>.

Ocean Yearbook 29: 223–270

tions and the agency organization needed to deliver effective environmental management to ensure that the oil find does not become the nation's curse.[3] Therefore, the issues to consider include:

1. What should be the role of law in addressing the emerging environmental challenges that attend the oil and gas industry in Ghana?
2. Through law, can there be a balance between economic and environmental interests in Ghana?, and
3. More importantly, how does Ghana create a legal and regulatory regime capable of striking that balance?

These are questions with significant implications for the crafting of an appropriate institutional design for environmental law-making and legal enforcement over time in Ghana.

Ghana's existing petroleum environmental regulatory regime is inadequate. The regime does not provide the robust institutional design and legislative prescriptions needed to regulate the very powerful and important oil and gas industry. Consequently, poor environmental management of the extractive industry has persisted because the State relies heavily on revenue from the industry. Therefore, the State must develop a progressive environmental protection regime that provides adequately for the current challenges, and anticipates the emerging environmental consequences of offshore drilling. This requires an approach that utilizes constitutional provisions to provide broadly for environmental rights. Reliance on constitutional provisions has its limitations, but it is a significant step in elevating environmental protection from obscurity to prominence in national discourse. More specifically, and in addition to constitutionally guaranteed rights, Ghana will have to develop context-specific and appropriate legislative prescriptions targeted at environmental protection and remediation. The institutional design will have to be reformed as well. Regulatory agencies like the Ghana National Petroleum Corporation (GNPC) and the Petroleum Commission that are better suited for the promotion of resource development must be confined to this primary objective, and their environmental protection responsibilities placed under other agencies with the requisite environmental expertise like the Environmental Protection Agency (EPA).

This article asserts that Ghana's capacity to do this will lead to good political governance. Environmental protection and management is often seen

---

3   E. Duruigbo, "The World Bank, Multinational Oil Corporations, and the Resource Curse in Africa," *University of Pennsylvania Journal of International Economic Law* 26 (2005): 1, p. 31.

as sustainable development. However, environmental protection is more than just sustainable development. A reconceptualization of environmental protection and remediation as both sustainable development and good political governance will engender national consciousness as well as promote environmental protection within socio-economic rights adjudication. To this end, good political governance concerns must not be restricted to the traditional notions of corruption, lack of transparency, and gross human rights abuses, but also expanded to include poor environmental regulation of resource extraction.[4]

The dearth of academic publications relating to environmental protection in the petroleum industry in Ghana complicates the understanding it needs to provide for environmental protection in this area. Recent academic writings have been targeted at the transformation of the State's oil corporation into a national oil champion within the emerging petroleum industry.[5] In other writings, the focus has been a discussion of the strengths and weaknesses of the various industry regulators within the oil and gas industry and how they manage petroleum resources including environment, health and safety, among other concerns.[6] While these writings are important, they do not address the critical question of why environmental regulation has lagged behind resource development. This question is central to this article.

A de-prioritization of economic activity and a re-engagement with environmental protection is a necessary first step in analysing the present state of affairs and an antecedent in the protection, preservation and management of the environment. This is crucial to the sustainable use of natural resources and the delivery of good political governance on the part of the State through environmental protection preservation, and management. Therefore, this article analyses the State's willingness to develop legal rules and enforcement procedures necessary to ensure sound environmental management of the oil industry. The article argues that existing petroleum development statutes promote resource extraction at the expense of environmental protection. The article, also, critically examines government's ability and commitment to back enforcement measures with the requisite State power that can induce and impel compliance on the part of industry actors. This analysis shows the entire

---

4 F.N. Botchway, "Introduction," in *Natural Resource Investment and Africa's Development,* ed. F. Botchway (Cheltenham, Northampton: Edward Elgar, 2011), p. 7.

5 K.O. Acheampong, "Transnational Corporations in Ghana's Emerging Oil Industry: For a Sweet or Bitter Romance?" (LL.M. Thesis, Harvard Law School, 2013), p. 56.

6 H. Annie-Seini, "The BP Oil Spill and Its Implications for Ghana: Avoiding the Resource Curse through Adequate Regulation," (LL.M. Thesis, Harvard Law School, 2011), p. 14.

spectrum of possibilities available to a developing country with a burgeoning oil economy. In this regard, the analysis is premised on the study of statutes, government regulations, journal publications, reports, newspaper articles, and online features that relate to the study.

The article proceeds in five parts. The first part provides an account of oil and gas development in Ghana. It also offers a brief account of the environmental consequences of oil and gas development in Ghana. Additionally, it evaluates the consequences of these environmental impacts on Ghana's economy. The second part describes the existing legal and regulatory infrastructure for oil development in Ghana. The discussion focuses on constitutional provisions and the priorities reflected in the background environmental statute and supporting regulations. This Part also examines the major oil and gas-specific laws to identify the extent to which these laws inadequately provide for environmental compliance and enforcement. This Part concludes with a discussion of resource contracts, since contractual provisions in resource development agreements also provide alternative means to environmental protection.

The third part critically evaluates Ghana's existing legal and regulatory system and its preparedness to respond to the emerging environmental problems in Ghana's offshore drilling industry. A case study involving the uncontrolled discharge of toxic oil-based drilling mud that occurred in Ghana's offshore operations is used to highlight gaps in the existing regulatory system. Part four draws on the Nigerian and the United States' (US) experiences in petroleum development to show the extent of regulatory failure and its consequences. This analysis shows how regulatory functions were overshadowed by licensing and revenue generation. Consequently, the State failed to protect the environment, nor undertake remediation measures.

The final part summarizes the arguments and prescriptions in part four. It also foreshadows the potential international effects of a poorly crafted environmental regulatory system in Ghana. The relatively short coastlines of adjacent States in West Africa require a broader and concerted regional effort at containing offshore environmental challenges within national borders and developing cross-border responses in the event of major incidents. This will minimize transboundary pollution and related international disputes. Successful domestic management of the environmental consequences in Ghana's offshore drilling will inform measures adopted by other African States struggling with similar issues. The article concludes by asserting that environmental protection, management, and remediation in Ghana must be reconceptualized as serving a dual purpose, that is, sustainable development and good political governance.

Oil and Gas Development in Ghana

This part provides a brief account of the development of the oil and gas industry in Ghana. After discovering oil in commercial quantities in 2007, Ghana intensified exploratory activities offshore leading to significant discoveries and strong indication of potential for future oil finds. This is followed by a discussion of the environmental impacts of the offshore industry. It also critically examines the new environmental problems within Ghana's oil and gas industry and concludes with an evaluation of the environmental consequences on Ghana's economy.

Development Activities to Date and Future Potential

Oil and gas prospecting in Ghana began in the colonial era. The West Africa Oil and Fuel Company and Société Française de Petrole were the first companies to conduct exploratory activities between 1896 and 1909.[7] However, these efforts were mostly unsuccessful, and interest in exploration was only renewed after independence.

In the late 1970s and early 1980s there was an indication of commercial deposits of oil in Ghana.[8] From 1978 to 1985, Signal Amoco produced a total of 3.47 million barrels of oil from the Saltpond Fields and over 14 billion cubic feet of associated gas was flared.[9] This led the government to become much more aware of the economic potential of oil as a major catalyst for Ghana's development.[10]

This success and promise of better results set the tone for the development of a dedicated legal and regulatory framework in the 1980s. Ghana established a national oil company, the Ghana National Petroleum Corporation[11] (GNPC) to undertake exploratory activities.[12] During this period, Signal Amoco was

---

7   Ghana Oil Almanac, "History of Oil and Gas Industry in Ghana," available online: <http://booktype-demo.sourcefabric.org/ghana-oil-almanac/historical-overview/>.

8   A.J. Afful, "The Legal Regime of Ghana's Upstream Petroleum Industry and the Role of the GNPC as Player and Regulator," *Ghana Policy Journal* 4 (2010), p. 69. The drive to join the global oil production chain was fueled by economic crisis in the 1980s. As a result, the petroleum-related laws were economic in character.

9   Ghana Oil Almanac, n. 7 above.

10   Id.

11   Established under the *Ghana National Petroleum Corporation Act*, 1983 (P.N.D.C.L. 64) [GNPC Law or GNPC Act].

12   Other petroleum-related statutes including the *Petroleum (Exploration and Production) Act*, 1984 (P.N.D.C.L. 84) , and the *Petroleum Income Tax Act*, 1987 (P.N.D.C.L. 188) were adopted within the same period. Additionally, Ghana's sole oil refinery underwent rehabilitation in anticipation of crude oil from the oil fields. These statutes are described in detail in Part II of this article.

licensed to prospect in ten blocks in Ghana's eastern coastal waters. Diamond Shamrock was licensed to explore the Keta basin, and Petro-Canada International was licensed to explore the Tano basin area. Most of these exploratory activities yielded no results, or the amounts of oil drilled were negligible, however, the GNPC continued to license exploration.[13]

The GNPC and its partners in the Jubilee field operations, led by Tullow Oil and Kosmos Energy, announced the discovery of oil in commercial quantities in 2007.[14] With an initial estimated capacity of 1.5 billion barrels, this find was by far one of the largest in Africa in recent times.[15] Commercial production began in earnest in 2010, and currently, output averages 120,000 bpd.[16]

With new discoveries like the Tweneboa-Enyenra-Ntomme (TEN) oil field, production is expected to reach 180,000 bpd by 2016.[17] Current projections indicate output will reach 250,000 bpd by 2021.[18] While these figures may appear modest, current exploratory activities show that Ghana's future potential to produce even more oil looks promising since the current estimates are quite conservative.[19] In all, Ghana has entered into ten petroleum agreements with oil companies for oil exploitation in its coastal waters.[20] Therefore, Ghana's offshore

---

13   C. Ackah, E. Mochiah, O. Morrissey and R. Darko Osei, Managing the Macroeconomy in an Oil Rich Country: The Case of Ghana (London: International Growth Center Working Paper, 2013), available online: <http://www.theigc.org/sites/default/files/Final%20Report _June.pdf>.

14   Ghana National Petroleum Corporation, "Harnessing Petroleum Resources for Ghana's Sustainable Growth," available online: <http://www.gnpcghana.com/SitePages/Content Page.aspx?ItemID=17&ItemTitle=E%20And%20P%20Operations>.

15   D. Amanor, "Ghana oil begins pumping for first time," BBC News, 15 December 2010, available online: <http://www.bbc.co.uk/news/world-africa-11996983>.

16   "Ghana's Jubilee oil fields near output plateau," Reuters, 23 April 2013, available online: <http://www.reuters.com/article/2013/04/23/ghana-jubilee-idUSL6NoDA59S20130423>.

17   "Ghana oil output to hit 180,000 barrels per day by 2016," Oil & Gas Eurasia, 28 October 2013, available online: <http://www.oilandgaseurasia.com/en/news/ghana-oil-output-hit -180000-barrels-day-2016>.

18   E. Dontoh, "Ghana oil output to more than double with new fields," Bloomberg, 23 April 2013, available online: <http://www.bloomberg.com/news/2013-04-24/ghana-oil-output -to-more-than-double-by-2021-with-new-fields.html>.

19   "Tullow to develop new oil wells to increase Ghana's oil production," Global Times, 10 April 2013, available online: <http://www.globaltimes.cn/content/815617.shtml# .UwoFKvldWSo>.

20   Ghana has a coastline of 539 kilometers. This is relatively short compared with Nigeria's 853 kilometers. But, the rapid pace of offshore development demonstrates the intensity of offshore petroleum activity in Ghana's coastal waters.

waters hold significant deposits of oil and gas "waiting to be discovered and harnessed."[21]

Offshore development has been fast-paced, and projections are that Ghana will become a major producer and exporter of oil in West Africa.[22] Revised Jubilee field estimates indicate a reserve capacity of two billion barrels from an initial capacity of 1.5 billion barrels. In 2011, 14 new discoveries were made, with some going on-stream as early as 2016. Another discovery with an estimated reserve of 114 million barrels and 1.3 trillion cubic feet of gas is expected to come on-stream by the end of 2017. Ghana's oil output will increase with these new finds. Also, GNPC has invested heavily in seismic data collection in onshore areas as well.[23] The cumulative effect of these activities is that Ghana will soon become an active oil State. Additionally, Ghana's stable political climate in the West African sub-region makes the country an investor's choice for investment in the petroleum industry.

The benefits of oil revenue for Ghana are numerous, with economic transformation and energy security being prominent. In many respects, Ghana has managed this transformation well. For example, the *Petroleum Revenue Management Act* 2011[24] was passed to address the challenge of economic governance, transparency and accountability of oil revenue. In the first year of drilling, Ghana received US$1 billion in petroleum export revenue. This amount is expected to increase to US$1.8 billion annually for the next two decades.[25]

Also, Ghana's energy independence will receive a boost from the associated gas. Ghana's first gas processing plant is scheduled to be completed in 2015. The gas reserves from the offshore fields will play a critical role in Ghana's energy generation and security. Consequently, Ghana's manufacturing sector is expected to be revived with a steady supply of electric power.[26]

---

21   F. Kokutse, "Ghana looks to raise oil output with new fields," Africa Review, 24 April 2013, available online: <http://www.africareview.com/Business---Finance/Ghana-looks-to-raise-oil-output-with-new-fields/-/979184/1757064/-/xjitjfz/-/index.html>.

22   "Ghana: Economy," Global Edge, available online: <http://globaledge.msu.edu/countries/ghana/economy>.

23   "GNPC earmarks $40 million onshore oil exploration in Volta Basin," available online: <http://gbcghana.com/index.php?id=1.700515>.

24   *Petroleum Revenue Management Act*, 2011 (Act 815) [PRMA].

25   "Ghana: Transparency Snapshot," Natural Resource Governance Institute, available online: <http://www.revenuewatch.org/countries/africa/ghana/transparency-snapshot>.

26   Ecobank, "Ghana: The LNG Regasification Option and Domestic Gas Demand," 26 February 2014, available online: <http://www.ecobank.com/upload/2014022603240770 570QhVuNrxU5S.pdf>.

However, the environmental aspects of offshore drilling have not seen the transformation that the economy and energy sectors are currently undergoing. The environmental consequences are fairly new, and the existing statutes did not fully anticipate these new challenges before offshore development begun. The post-oil discovery statutes also do not provide adequately for these new challenges. The present situation is further complicated because petroleum export revenue is boosting government finances, thus overshadowing substantive discussions of environmental management and protection of petroleum operations. The emergence of these new problems and Ghana's response is ever more important as Ghana seeks to increase petroleum operations both offshore and more recently, onshore. Therefore the State must act decisively to address these emergent environmental consequences to ensure the nation and its citizens benefit from the oil industry.

Environmental Impacts

The impacts associated with petroleum exploitation are aquatic, atmospheric, and human. The associated aquatic pollutants include oily ballast discharge, introduction of invasive species, oil spills, and other drill fluid discharges including toxic oil-based drilling mud.[27] Atmospheric pollution includes the release of carbon dioxide, nitrogen oxide, and hydrogen oxide.[28] Also, human interference has considerable adverse effects. Vessel navigation in the offshore area and activities on the floating production, storage, and offloading (FPSO) units can adversely affect marine resources.

Major environmental consequences arising from Ghana's offshore operations are oil spills and the discharge of harmful effluents such as toxic oil-based drilling mud.[29] These substances can negatively affect the health of coastal ecosystems and marine resources, especially endangered marine species. The operation of oil support vessels within the catchment area also interferes with fishing.[30]

The uncontrolled toxic oil-based drilling mud discharge by Kosmos Energy in 2009 and 2010 adversely affected fishing activities in the catchment area.[31] The discharge was detected by coastal communities close to the offshore area.

---

27   G. Asamoah, "The Potential Impacts of Oil and Gas Exploration and Production on the Coastal Zone of Ghana: An Ecosystem Service Approach," (M.Sc. Thesis, Wageningen University, 2010), pp. 25–28.

28   "Airborne Oil Pollution," Global Marine Oil Pollution Information Gateway, available online: <http://oils.gpa.unep.org/facts/airpoll.htm>.

29   R. Amorin and E. Broni-Bediako, "Major Challenges in Ghana's Oil and Gas Discovery: Is Ghana Ready?" *ARPN Journal of Science and Technology* 3 (2013), p. 21.

30   Asamoah, n. 27 above, p. 28.

31   Amorin and Broni-Bediako, n. 29 above, p. 21.

The communities included Asemkow, Adjoa and Mpatato in the Ahanta West District of the Western Region.[32] It is estimated that the discharge covered about 80 kilometers of coastline.[33] The oil-based drilling mud discharge washed ashore, thus disrupting fishing activities and rendering fishing waters inaccessible. Also, dead fish were washed ashore.[34]

Additionally, oil spills may deprive the nation of the use of coastal tourism resources. Ghana's Western Region is a major heritage and ecotourism destination.[35] After the Kosmos Energy toxic oil-based drilling mud incident, the Ghana Tourist Authority indicated that tourism was badly affected. Beaches and other coastal tourist attractions were inaccessible and remained unusable well after the discharge had reached the shore.[36]

Gas flaring is another major problem. Presently, Ghana has a no-gas flaring policy. For every 1,000 barrels of oil produced from the Jubilee field, there is an associated gas production of 1.2 million standard cubic feet. Tullow Oil and its Jubilee field partners continue to re-inject gas into the underground reservoirs. Despite the government's no-gas flaring policy, there is some amount of ongoing flaring. There is no domestic capacity to use the gas, therefore, gas flaring is considered necessary in maintaining the integrity of the oil reservoirs.[37] Continuous flaring of gas is harmful to the environment and coastal communities. Carbon dioxide and methane released during gas flaring negatively affect the environment and contribute to disruptive climate change. Also, the atmospheric emissions can cause respiratory diseases among coastal communities close to the offshore area.[38]

Environmental impacts of the oil industry can adversely affect land and water resources as well. Ghana is constructing a gas processing plant onshore

---

32   G. Otoo, "Where there is oil, there is spillage," MC Modern Ghana, 18 December 2012, available online: <http://www.modernghana.com/news/436208/1/where-there-is-oil-there-is-spillage.html>.

33   Id.

34   The Kosmos Energy incident is discussed extensively in the fourth part of this article.

35   See Ghana Tourism, available online: <http://www.touringghana.com/regions/western_region.asp>.

36   M.D. Aklorbotu, "Oil spill on Ahanta West coast," MC Modern Ghana, 6 November 2011, available online: <http://www.modernghana.com/news/359569/1/oil-spill-on-ahanta-west-coast.html>.

37   Oxford Business Group, The Report: Ghana 2012, p. 128, available online: <http://www.oxfordbusinessgroup.com/country/Ghana>.

38   M. Iddrisu, "Ghana: The State of Oil and Gas Industry in Ghana – The Nagging Issues," AllAfrica, 26 February 2014, available online: <http://allafrica.com/stories/201402261325.html>.

to receive and process associated gas from the oil fields. This project involves laying undersea pipelines from the gas fields to bring gas onshore. Ghana's energy requirements are expected to receive a boost from the gas processing. The processed gas will be used in power generation to support Ghana's industrial drive. Farmlands situated in the area zoned for this project have been destroyed to make way for this project. Also, water and air quality are under threat. The Amanzuri River has been identified as the potential receiver of a heavy pollution load from the gas processing plant.[39] Proper management of hazardous waste is required to minimize or prevent this occurrence. The environmental impact statement (EIS) for the onshore processing plant indicates that in the event of failure of the treatment systems, there could be uncontrolled discharge of hazardous effluents that can adversely affect the environment.[40]

Consequences of Environmental Impacts on Ghana's Economy

The implications of the emerging environmental problems on the local economy cannot be discounted. The fishing industry is the worst affected. Artisanal fishing is the mainstay of the local communities in the catchment area. These communities and their local economies thrive on fishing. However, with increased offshore drilling and poor environmental protection, these communities will be rendered jobless and poverty levels will increase.[41]

Traditional fishing grounds are inaccessible.[42] There are two million people, ten percent of Ghana's population, involved in the fishing industry, especially coastal fishing. These include fisherfolk, fish processors and traders.[43] These fisher folk have lost access to traditional fishing grounds as a result of offshore drilling. The mandatory safety zones established around offshore oil installations require fishing boats to stay 500 meters away from the outer points of the offshore installations. A major function of the safety zones is that they reduce the incidence of fishing boats colliding with offshore installations. As a result, fishermen continue to record low catches, and in response they have resorted

---

39   Ghana National Gas Company, "Draft Environmental Impact Statement: Onshore Processing Plant Component of the Gas Infrastructure Project," (2012), p. 46.

40   Id.

41   Friends of the Nation, "Fisheries in Ghana – Danger looms: 5% of GDP at stake," *Greenlines Newsletter* 1 (April 2013), available online: <http://fonghana.org/wp-content/uploads/2013/04/130429_nl_amh.pdf>.

42   Ghana Maritime Authority, "Legislation," available online: <http://www.ghanamaritime.org/en/about-us/programmes/legislation.php>.

43   Ministry of Food and Agriculture, "Fisheries," available online: <http://mofa.gov.gh/site/?page_id=244>.

to the use of illegal, unregulated, and unlicensed methods of fishing like the use of banned substances and dynamite, with potentially harmful consequences for consumers of the fish and the marine environment.[44] A responsive environmental regime ready to anticipate and address these emerging challenges is plainly needed.

Also, as offshore oil drilling is ongoing, newer environmental problems have emerged. These problems threaten both marine and onshore resources. The problems also pose significant health risks for communities close to the catchment area. The adverse effects of these environmental impacts on fishery resources, coastal tourist attractions, and the contamination of coastal waters is a wake-up call for Ghana to respond in timely manner. A large oil spill could easily contaminate Ghana's relatively short coastline with devastating consequences for major economic activities such as coastal fishing. Notwithstanding the rapidly expanding industry and potential for environmental harm, the existing legal infrastructure is inadequate to ensure sustainable development. Also, the occurrence of new health challenges will require increased public health costs with consequences for the national expenditure.

Existing Legal and Regulatory Infrastructure

This part describes the existing legal and regulatory architecture for offshore oil and gas development in Ghana. The first section is focused on the constitutional structure and its prescriptions for natural resource management and environmental protection in Ghana. It is followed by a description of Ghana's framework statute for environmental protection. The next section discusses oil and gas-specific statutes and the extent to which they provide for environmental protection in the petroleum industry. An analysis of contractual provisions, which constitute an important alternative to environmental protection where statutory provisions are deficient, concludes this part.

Constitutional Provisions

Ghana's Constitution vests all minerals in their natural state in the President on behalf of, and in trust for, the citizens.[45] The citizens are the beneficiaries in this trust relationship. The Constitution also provides that any contract that involves the grant of a right to natural resource exploitation must be ratified by

---

44   Friends of the Nation, n. 41 above, p. 6.
45   The Constitution of the Republic of Ghana, 1992 [Ghana Constitution].

Parliament.[46] To ensure effective and efficient management of resources, the Constitution provides for the establishment of a commission that is responsible for the regulation and management of the utilization of the natural resource concerned and the coordination of related policies.[47] Consequently, after the discovery of oil, a commission was established to regulate and manage petroleum resources.

Ghana's Constitution also provides that the State shall take appropriate measures to protect and safeguard the environment for posterity.[48] The specific reference to 'posterity' underscores the intergenerational equity principle, which forms part of the broader scope of sustainable natural resources utilization.[49] Additionally, every citizen is under a duty to protect and safeguard the environment.[50] Articles 36(9) and 41(k) are part of the Directive Principles of State Policy (DPSPs).[51]

The DPSPs are policy directives. The Report of the Committee of Experts on Proposals for a Draft Constitution of Ghana[52] indicated that the DPSPs were the "core principles around which national political, social and economic life will revolve."[53] This Report recommended the adoption of the proposal for the inclusion of environmental protection in the Constitution, specifically under the DPSPs.[54] The proposal was subsequently adopted as Article 36(9) under Chapter 6 of the 1992 Constitution.

The justiciability of the DPSPs has been the subject of many debates in Ghana. In 2008, Ghana's Supreme Court stated that the Constitution as a whole is presumptively justiciable.[55] The Court also held that a presumption of justiciability would strengthen the legal status of the DPSPs;[56] however, the Court

---

46   Id., Art. 268(1).

47   Id., Art. 269(1).

48   Id., Art. 36(9).

49   E. Abotsi, "Ghana's environmental framework law and the balancing of interests," in *The Balancing of Interests in Environmental Law in Africa*, eds., M. Faure and W. du Plessis (Pretoria: Pretoria University Law Press, 2011), Chap. 7, p. 143. [*Balancing of Interests*].

50   Ghana Constitution, n. 45 above, Art. 41(k).

51   Id., Chap. 6.

52   Committee of Experts, *Report of the Committee of Experts (Constitution) on Proposals for a Draft Constitution of Ghana* (Accra: 1991) (A Special Committee for the drafting of Ghana's 1992 Constitution).

53   Id., p. 49.

54   Id., p. 55.

55   *Ghana Lotto Operators Association & Others v. National Lottery Authority*, S. Ct. Ghana. L. Rep. [2007–2008] 1088, pp. 1105–1107 [*Ghana Lotto Operators*].

56   Id., p. 1113.

indicated that there may be provisions in Chapter 6 which are unenforceable by the courts.[57] However, the Court did not elaborate on these provisions.

In addition, Ghana's Constitution Review Commission recommended the adoption of a constitutionally guaranteed right to a clean environment.[58] This recommendation was accepted by the government.[59] The reasons advanced in support of this proposed constitutional amendment include according prominence to environmental rights in line with international judicial and legal developments in India,[60] South Africa,[61] Kenya,[62] and most importantly, the African Charter on Human and People's Rights,[63] to which Ghana is a signatory.[64]

Background Environmental Statute

Beyond the broad provisions of the Constitution, Ghana's *Environmental Protection Agency Act*, 1994 (EPA Act) remains the most significant environmental protection statute.[65] The historical origins of the EPA as an executive agency can be traced to the period immediately following the United Nations Conference on the Human Environment (Stockholm Conference) in 1972. The Environmental Protection Council (EPC) was established in 1974 after the Conference,[66] as part of Ghana's commitment to environmental protection and

---

57   Id., p. 1106.

58   Constitution Review Commission, *Report of the Constitution Review Commission: From a Political to a Developmental Constitution* (Accra: 2011), at p. 737 [CRC Report]. This proposed constitutional amendment is yet to take effect. It will be incorporated into the Constitution depending on the outcome of a referendum on the amendments.

59   Republic of Ghana, *White Paper on the Report of the Constitution Review Commission of Inquiry* (WP. No. 1/2012), (June 2012), p. 43.

60   The Indian Supreme Court set the stage for this global evolution, especially in the developing world. The Court interpreted the right to life and liberty to include the right to a wholesome environment. See generally D. Chouhan and P. Dalei, *Right to live in a Healthy Environment – In framework of Indian Constitution*, 230, at p. 230, paper presented at the International Conference on Humanities, Economics and Geography, 17–18 March 2012, Bangkok, p. 230, available online: <http://psrcentre.org/images/extraimages/312150.pdf>.

61   The Constitution of the Republic of South Africa, 1996, s. 24.

62   The Constitution of Kenya, 2010, s. 42 and 70.

63   African Charter on Human and Peoples' Rights, 21 *International Legal Materials* 58 (1982), Art. 24.

64   CRC Report, n. 58 above, p. 737.

65   *Environmental Protection Agency Act*, 1994 (Act 490).

66   M. Anane, "Toward sustainable development in Ghana," Voices From Africa, no. 6 (UN Non-Governmental Liaison Service, undated), available online: <http://www.un-ngls.org/orf/documents/publications.en/voices.africa/number6/vfa6.03.htm>.

consciousness. The EPC was established under a military regime.[67] Its powers were confined in scope, and the constant change in administrative supervision of the EPC adversely affected its work; reflecting the difficult times in which the EPC operated.[68] In its 20 years of existence, the EPC adopted an *ad hoc* approach to environmental issues, attempting to address issues as and when they arose.[69] The EPC enjoyed limited success. However, this was a modest effort considering its rather difficult beginning, and at a time the EIS requirement did not exist.[70]

The EPA Act was passed in 1994 to consolidate the law relating to environmental protection, and the EPC was subsequently replaced by the EPA. The EPA's mission embraces a precautionary approach to environmental protection.[71] The EPA is required to liaise with other agencies in pollution control and protection of the environment in the performance of its functions.[72]

The EPA is also tasked to ensure that activities, especially industrial activities are undertaken in a manner that ensures protection and preservation of the environment. Where the EPA determines that an undertaking or activity will have or has had a significant adverse impact on the environment, the EPA may serve notice on the person responsible for the undertaking to submit an environmental impact assessment (EIA).[73] The EPA shall not issue an environmental permit for the undertaking unless the EIA requirement has been complied with.[74] The EPA is required to inform the executive branch agency that is responsible for issuing a license or approving that undertaking or activity causing the pollution not to grant the license or approval until the EPA's notice has been complied with and the EPA has issued its permit.[75] Therefore, the EPA shares regulatory authority with pro-development executive agencies. For example, in the petroleum industry, the EPA issues an environmental permit after an acceptable EIA has been submitted, and then the Minister for Energy and Petroleum

---

67   The government at the time was the National Redemption Council (NRC) led by Col. Ignatius Kutu Acheampong.

68   A.A. Tutuah Mensah and K. Yeboah, "40 Years of Environmental Protection Agency," 30 January 2014, available online: <http://www.ghana.gov.gh/index.php/2012-02-08-08-32 -47/features/4614-40-years-of-environmental-protection-agency>.

69   CRC Report, n. 58 above, p. 738.

70   An EIS is a statement that describes both positive and negative impacts of a proposed activity. The EIS also states contingent and remedial measures that will be adopted to mitigate the adverse effects of the proposed activity.

71   CRC Report, n. 58 above, p. 738.

72   Act 490, n. 65 above, s. 2(j).

73   Id., s. 12(1).

74   Id., s. 12(2).

75   Id., s. 12(2).

approves the petroleum development plans before the commencement of operations.[76]

The procedure for the conduct and compliance with the EIA is provided in the Environmental Assessment Regulations.[77] The Regulations implement the EPA Act's EIA requirement. The Regulations require an EIA for certain categories of undertakings or activities before the EPA issues an environmental permit.[78] Petroleum activities are included on this list.[79] These activities are oil and gas field development, construction of offshore and onshore pipelines, construction of oil and gas separation, processing, handling and storage facilities, and construction of oil refineries.[80]

EPA can suspend, cancel or revoke an environmental permit where the permit holder violates the terms of the permit.[81] The EPA may not issue an environmental permit until the proponent of an undertaking has complied with the EIA requirement under both the EPA Act and the Environmental Assessment Regulations. Therefore, oil companies must comply with this requirement before the Minister for Energy and Petroleum approves the petroleum development plans.

Public participation is provided for under the Environmental Assessment Regulations. The EPA is required to publish the EIS submitted by the proponent of the undertaking in the mass media and to display it in places it considers necessary.[82] The public can make comments and suggestions in respect of the EIS. In addition, the EPA is required to hold a public hearing where it appears there is adverse public reaction to the EIS.[83] The public can also make submissions at this hearing.[84] If the EPA determines that the EIS is unacceptable or insufficient, the applicant must be notified and asked to submit a revised EIS.[85] If the EPA determines the EIS is acceptable, it must notify the applicant and the environmental permit will be issued.[86]

EPA may also exercise control over an activity or undertaking by serving an enforcement notice on the person responsible for the undertaking if that

---

76   *Petroleum (Exploration and Production) Act*, n. 12 above, s. 10(2).
77   *Environmental Assessment Regulations*, 1999 (L.I. 1652).
78   Id., reg. 3.
79   Id., Schedule 2.
80   Id., Schedule 2(12).
81   Id., reg. 26.
82   Id., reg. 16(2).
83   Id., reg. 17(1).
84   Id., reg. 17(5).
85   Id., reg. 18.
86   Id., reg. 19.

activity is a source of serious threat to the environment.[87] The enforcement notice may include a direction for the cessation of the offending activity.[88] Failure to comply with the enforcement notice attracts a fine, a term of imprisonment, or both.

In addition to the EPA Act and the Environmental Assessment Regulations, the EPA has developed guidelines specific for the oil and gas industry.[89] These guidelines are non-binding and are "intended to help" managers in the oil and gas sector to mainstream environmental concerns into offshore operations.[90]

Oil and Gas-Specific Development Statutes

The initial, albeit limited, success of oil production in the late 1970s became a catalyst for the development of a legal regime to regulate the industry. This promise of better results set the tone for a dedicated legal and regulatory framework starting in the 1980s. Petroleum development-related statutes including the *Ghana National Petroleum Corporation Act*, 1983,[91] *Petroleum (Exploration and Production) Act*, 1984,[92] and the *Petroleum Income Tax Act*, 1987[93] were adopted within four years. These laws were adopted when Ghana was again under military rule.[94] There was a hiatus in legislative development until after the discovery of oil in commercial quantities in 2007, when another wave of petroleum development law-making took place. This led to the passage of the *Petroleum Revenue Management Act*, 2011 (PRMA)[95] and the *Petroleum Commission Act*, 2011[96] within a year, and after drilling had begun.

Ghana National Petroleum Corporation Act, 1983

The *Ghana National Petroleum Corporation Act*, 1983 is the preeminent legislation in Ghana's oil and gas industry.[97] The law primarily established the GNPC.

---

87   Act 490, n. 65 above, s. 13(1).

88   Id., s. 13(2)(d).

89   Environmental Protection Agency (Ghana), Guidelines for Environmental Assessment and Management in the Offshore Oil and Gas Development (2010).

90   Id., p. 13.

91   GNPC Act, n. 11 above.

92   *Petroleum (Exploration and Production) Act*, n. 12 above.

93   *Petroleum Income Tax Act*, n. 12 above.

94   Ghana returned to democracy on 7 January 1993. This brought to an end eleven years of uninterrupted military rule. Thus, statutes passed since 1993 are products of an elected legislature.

95   PRMA, n. 24 above.

96   *Petroleum Commission Act*, 2011 (Act 821) .

97   GNPC Act, n. 11 above.

The GNPC has a unique place in Ghana's petroleum industry and it is both an industry player and a regulator.[98] The GNPC is mandated "to undertake the exploration, development and disposal of petroleum."[99] The GNPC is also obligated to ensure that exploration and production of petroleum resources are carried out in a planned and orderly manner.[100]

The GNPC is also mandated to ensure the country derives the "greatest possible benefits" from the development of petroleum resources.[101] In this regard, the GNPC can engage in petroleum resource development by itself or in concert with others,[102] by entering into an agreement for the development of the resource.[103] After its establishment, the GNPC licensed exploration and also participated in joint activities. The GNPC invested heavily in data and research to support its participation in exploration activities.[104] Therefore, from the outset, the GNPC, in outlook and substance, has been oriented towards active participation in the oil economy.

The agency is also mandated to ensure petroleum operations are conducted in a manner that prevents adverse impacts on the environment, other resources and the citizens.[105] In this regard, the GNPC is empowered to ensure industry operators carry out their operations in an environmentally friendly, safe, and healthy manner. The GNPC, must therefore, regulate its own activities when it is involved in the development of petroleum resources. This is the dual-track duty responsibility of the GNPC.

Petroleum (Exploration and Production) Act, 1984

The *Petroleum (Exploration and Production) Act* complements the GNPC Act and reinforces the role of the GNPC as the lead agency in petroleum resource development.[106] Whereas the GNPC Act establishes the GNPC and sets out the functions of the corporation, the *Petroleum (Exploration and Production) Act* sets out in finer detail the exploration, production and development aspects of petroleum resources and related matters. Additionally, the GNPC is made a party to all petroleum agreements.[107] Oil drilling and revenue generation from petroleum development is the mainstay of this legislation.

---

98   Afful, n. 8 above, p. 69.
99   GNPC Act, n. 11 above, s. 2(1).
100   Id., s. 2(2)(a).
101   Id., s. 2(2)(b).
102   Id., s. 4.
103   Id., s. 3(b) and (c).
104   Id.
105   Id., s. 2(2)(e).
106   *Petroleum (Exploration and Production) Act*, n. 12 above, s. 2(1).
107   Id.

The law also provides for safety measures and some environmental protection in petroleum operations. The law states that a contractor, that is an oil company, is obliged to establish adequate mechanisms to address concerns such as fire and oil spills.[108] The law also requires a contractor to carry out its activities in accordance with best international practices.[109]

Petroleum Revenue Management Act, 2011

There was no law to regulate the utilization of petroleum revenue when offshore drilling began in 2010. The *Petroleum Income Tax Act*, which is still in force, only provides for tax assessments on petroleum income.[110] Consequently, Ghana passed the PRMA as a framework statute for the collection, allocation, and management of petroleum revenue in a responsible, transparent, and accountable manner. The first of two post-oil discovery statutes, this law was passed pursuant to Ghana's economic objectives as provided under its Constitution.[111]

Unlike Ghana's past history in the management of mining revenue, this statute introduced significant prudent financial measures for the management of petroleum revenue. All petroleum revenue is deposited in a Petroleum Holding Fund established under the Act, and disbursements are made out of this fund.[112] The law also established the Ghana Stabilization Fund. This fund "is to cushion the impact on or sustain public expenditure during periods of unanticipated petroleum revenue shortfalls."[113] Most importantly, the Act established the Ghana Heritage Fund. This fund provides development endowment support for future generations when petroleum reserves have been exhausted. These provisions are significant improvements in resource revenue management.

The Act also provides that a portion of petroleum revenue be used as budgetary support, namely the Annual Budget Funding Amount.[114] This support forms part of the national budget.[115] The use of this budgetary support includes maximization of economic development and promotion of economic opportunities.[116] The PRMA anticipates the use of this support within the broad

---

108   Id., s. 23(17).

109   Id., s. 3(1).

110   *Petroleum Income Tax Act*, n. 12 above, s. 1.

111   Ghana Constitution, n. 45 above, Art. 36.

112   PRMA, n. 24 above, s. 2.

113   Id., s. 9.

114   Id., s. 18.

115   Id., s. 21(1).

116   Id., s. 21(2).

framework of a long-term national development plan; however, in the absence of such a plan, the law provides that the budgetary support expenditure shall give priority to a list of programs and activities including environmental protection, and sustainable utilization and protection of natural resources.[117] The Minister for Finance, the supervising minister under the PRMA, shall specify four priority areas from the list of programs and activities for which this budgetary support may be used. This involves ministerial discretion, and the four priority areas are subject to ministerial review every three years.[118]

Petroleum Commission Act, 2011

The second post-oil discovery statute established the Petroleum Commission. The Petroleum Commission regulates and manages the utilization of petroleum resources and coordinates policies in relation to this objective.[119] According to the explanatory memorandum accompanying the introduction of the bill, the Commission was to absorb some of the regulatory functions of the GNPC and resolve GNPC's conflicting duties as industry player and regulator.[120] The Petroleum Commission is also authorized to promote efficient petroleum operations to "achieve optimal levels of resource exploitation."[121] The law tasks the Commission to "ensure compliance with health, safety and environmental standards in petroleum activities in accordance with applicable laws, regulations and agreements."[122] Under the Act, the Ministry of Energy and Petroleum is designated as the supervisory ministry. The Minister has residual powers to provide for effective implementation of the Act through a set of regulations.[123] The Minister may, therefore, provide for specific environmental standards in subsidiary legislation.

Contractual Provisions

Operational standards and practices are often set out in resource contracts.[124] Ghana's Model Petroleum Agreement provides for some environmental protection in the oil industry. Article 17 of the Agreement provides for inspection, safety and environmental protection. Article 17.2 tasks the contractor (an oil

---

117 Id., s. 21(3)(g).

118 Id., s. 21(5) and (6).

119 *Petroleum Commission Act*, n. 96 above, s. 2.

120 Explanatory Memorandum to the Petroleum Commission Bill, p. i (2013) [Memorandum].

121 *Petroleum Commission Act*, n. 96 above, s. 3(a).

122 Id., s. 3(d)(i).

123 Id., s. 22(c).

124 E. Laryea, "Contractual arrangements for resource investment," in *Natural Resource Investment and Africa's Development*, n. 4 above, Chap. 4, pp. 107–133 at 107.

company) to conduct its activities in accordance with applicable environmental laws. Article 17.3 provides that the contractor must provide an effective system for the disposal of waste water, oil-based drilling mud, and drill cuttings in accordance with accepted petroleum practice.

Problems with Existing System and Kosmos Energy Case Study

Ghana's Constitution, the general environmental statutory framework, and petroleum-related statutes provide for environmental protection in petroleum operations. However, the existing network of laws and rules does not provide the necessary environmental safeguards required in offshore oil and gas development. The first section of this part critically analyses the problems with the existing legal and regulatory structure. The second section is a case study premised on the fallout from Kosmos Energy's uncontrolled toxic oil-based drilling mud discharge. It examines how these regulatory shortfalls created a lax system that failed to respond to the adverse effects of the discharge.

Problems with Existing System

This section proceeds with a discussion of constitutional provisions relating to environmental protection. It is followed by a discussion of statutory provisions. First, Ghana's background environmental statute is considered. Second, environmental protection-related provisions in oil and gas development statutes are discussed. An evaluation of the shortfalls of Ghana's petroleum agreement concludes this section.

Constitutional Protections Non-Justiciable

Ghana's Constitution exhorts the State to safeguard the national environment, thus the enforceability of this provision is questionable.[125] The justiciability of the DPSPs is critical because the constitutional provision on environmental protection is part of the DPSPs, and the DPSPs are considered non-justiciable. Article 36(9) of Ghana's Constitution provides that the State shall take steps to protect and safeguard the national environment.

The enforceability of the DPSPs has been the subject of many debates in Ghana's constitutional history, lending itself to varied interpretations until 2008. In 2008, Ghana's Supreme Court held, in the landmark case of *Ghana Lotto Operators Association & Others v. National Lottery Authority*,[126] that all

---

125   Ghana Constitution, n. 45 above, Art. 36(9).
126   *Ghana Lotto Operators*, n. 55 above, p. 1106.

provisions in the 1992 Constitution including Chapter 6 are presumptively justiciable. However, the Supreme Court noted that if a particular provision in
Chapter 6 does not lend itself to enforcement, then the presumption of justiciability would be rebutted. On the basis of this decision, some scholars contend that the State is obligated to protect and provide a clean and healthy
environment.[127] This new thinking on the enforceability of the DPSPs remains
doubtful though.[128]

The proponents of the amendment of the Constitution to include an express
right to a clean and healthy environment to mediate the competing interests
between natural resource development and environmental protection and
sustainability do not proffer any standards for balancing these two contending
issues. An approach based entirely on constitutional guarantees obscures the
difficult policy questions that are central to the creation and application of
pollution control standards and environmental protection, preservation and
management requirements. At best, it promotes the power of the judiciary to
stultify legislative innovation through judicial decision-making and pronouncements in respect of matters that are best resolved through specific and
targeted legislative interventions.

Weak and Scattered Environmental Provisions in Petroleum-Related Statutes

Ghana's oil and gas statutes are characterized by weak, scattered and minimal
environmental provisions. The scattered nature of environmental protection
provisions leads to duplication of roles and inter-agency conflicts. Often EPA's
precautionary position clashes with the outlook of other executive agencies
that both lack environmental expertise and are governed by statutory provisions that make economic development their primary objective.[129] The cumulative effect of these regulations is that standards are low and non-compliance
is the norm.

---

127   Abotsi, n. 49 above, p. 143; Ghana Constitution, n. 45 above, Art. 33(5).

128   Ghana is in the process of amending its Constitution to include a right to a clean and
      healthy environment. Therefore, it cannot be true that there is an environmental right,
      because that would have been sufficient, and there would have been no need to review
      the Constitution in that regard.

129   Generally, functions are not well-coordinated. Therefore some institutions experience
      conflicts in the execution of their responsibilities leading to duplication of roles and
      efforts, gaps in regulation, institutional resistance and over-protection of institutional
      independence. Environmental Protection Agency, *National Implementation Plan of the
      Stockholm Convention on Persistent Organic Pollutants*, (2007), pp. 49–50.

In addition to weak and scattered environmental standards, institutional problems have rendered enforcement mechanisms ineffective. The GNPC's dual-track position as regulator and industry player weakens its enforcement capacity as industry regulator. The GNPC is required to ensure petroleum operations are conducted in a manner that prevents negative environmental consequences against its pro-resource development orientation.[130] The GNPC's regulatory function is not made any easier since the GNPC law does not specifically spell out what the agency must do to prevent these adverse impacts in the first place, nor does it outline any remedial steps that must be followed in the event that this provision is breached. The GNPC, therefore, does not prioritize these environmental obligations even though the statutory language could be read fairly to authorize the agency to do so.

The specific placement of environmental management of the oil industry under the supervision of an industry player like the GNPC suggests a deliberate intention to limit any future control by any other statutory body tasked with environmental protection. Ultimately, the inherent conflict a pro-resource development agency like the GNPC faces when assigned environmental protection responsibilities means the agency will focus on the more attractive option, *viz.*, petroleum operations. The *status quo* is reinforced in other laws and petroleum agreements signed by the GNPC and oil companies.

In similar fashion, as is the case with the GNPC law, the *Petroleum (Exploration and Production) Act* does very little to promote environmental protection objectives. While resource development provisions are detailed, the scant provisions on environmental regulation contained in the law are either vague or merely a reproduction of standard and general environmental provisions. The law does not outline the specific components of the environmental protection obligation. The law also states that petroleum operations must be carried out in accordance with best international practices, but there is no indication as to what is meant by these best international practices. Ultimately, this leaves such critical policy decisions to oil companies as they determine and adopt interventions based on widely permissible choices. These vague provisions portray the dearth of environmental safeguards regulating the petroleum industry.

The Petroleum Revenue Management statute, as its name suggests, is devoted entirely to revenue allocation and utilization. The statute is plainly not suited for environmental protection because of its focus on petroleum revenue allocation. One would have thought that the PRMA would have provided

---

130   GNPC Act, n. 11 above, s. 2(2)(e).

specific budgetary allocation for environmental remediation, but this is also absent.

Institutionally, there is uncertainty over the jurisdiction of the GNPC and the Petroleum Commission. The *Petroleum Commission Act* purportedly absorbs the regulatory functions of the GNPC.[131] The intended purpose was to provide the GNPC the freedom a national oil company requires to be an efficient market player. But, this is not exactly the case in the enacted law. Section 24(2) of the *Petroleum Commission Act* provides that

> ...the Ghana National Petroleum Corporation shall cease to exercise any *advisory* functions in relation to the regulation and management of the utilization of petroleum resources and the coordination of policy in relation to that function. [Emphasis added]

Thus, it is uncertain if the GNPC ceases to perform the actual regulatory functions relating to safety, health and environment, or it is just the GNPC's advisory role that has been annexed by the Petroleum Commission.[132]

The Petroleum Commission is also tasked to ensure compliance with environmental standards in petroleum operations.[133] But, once again, this is just a statement of general application, and follows similar statutory language used in the GNPC law and the *Petroleum (Exploration and Development) Act*. The *Petroleum Commission Act* suggests that apart from the Petroleum Commission, all other agencies are excluded from regulating and managing the utilization of petroleum resources and coordinating related polices. Section 24(3) provides that "subject to the other provisions of this Act, a Government agency or authority shall not exercise any function in relation to the *regulation* and *management* of the utilization of petroleum resources and the policies in relation to that function" [emphasis added].[134] The Act also provides that all government agencies shall cooperate with the Commission in the performance of its duties.[135] Again, it is uncertain if the law creates an inter-agency approach because it appears to subordinate the roles of other critical agencies like the EPA, or even the GNPC's environmental protection function, to that of the Petroleum Commission. The EPA is an agency under the supervision of the Minister for Environment. Therefore, the exclusive jurisdiction apparently

---

131 Memorandum, n. 120 above, p. i.
132 Acheampong, n. 5 above, p. 62; *Petroleum Commission Act*, n. 96 above, s. 24(3).
133 *Petroleum Commission Act*, n. 96 above, s. 3(d)(i).
134 Id., s. 24(3).
135 Id., s. 21(1).

created by section 24(3) of the *Petroleum Commission Act* raises issues of duplication, and further weakens an already poor regulatory system. Thus, it appears
once an EIS has been prepared and submitted to the EPA, and it issues an environmental permit to the company, the EPA ceases to exercise control over
environmental issues in the petroleum industry. This type of statutory ambiguity weakens any collaborative effort, and perpetuates inter-agency conflicts
and turf wars.

> Problems with Contractual Provisions in the Absence of a
> Comprehensive Statutory Regime

While contractual provisions could be an effective means to ensure environmental compliance, Ghana's Model Petroleum Agreement does not contain
specific standards. Article 17 of the Agreement provides for environmental protection, but this provision is insignificant. The obligations provided for under
Article 17 of the Agreement are replete with the expression "...in accordance
with accepted petroleum practice," however, the Agreement provides no reference to the 'practice' that should be followed. Article 17.2 requires contractors
to carry out their activities in accordance with environmental laws, however,
there are no specific environmental and pollution standards in either general
environmental- or petroleum-related statutes to which this provision refers to.

In developed countries, critical operational standards are provided in specific details under statutory provisions and not contracts. The United States
and the United Kingdom are two notable examples.[136] This complex legislative
network for pollution control and environmental protection is what Gao refers
to as the multi-statutory approach.[137]

Another approach has emerged beyond the contractual and multi-statutory
approaches. This is the comprehensive or integrated legislative approach
where all the environmental aspects of upstream activities are regulated under
one law. China introduced this approach in its offshore petroleum regulation
in 1982.[138] Thus, all the relevant components of the industry, including the conduct of an EIA, discharge standards, anti-pollution records, resource protection standards and requirements, liability for violations, compensation,
offshore decommissioning, and abandonment, are put together under a single

---

136   Z. Gao, "Environmental Regulation of Oil and Gas in the Twentieth Century: An
        Introduction and Overview," in *Environmental Regulation of Oil and Gas*, ed. Z. Gao
        (London, The Hague, Boston: Kluwer Law International, 1998), Chap. 1, pp. 32–33.
137   Id., p. 32.
138   Id., n. 136 above, p. 37.

statute.[139] This law is referenced in the petroleum agreement. In the absence of such a comprehensive legislative regime, contractual safeguards are of even greater importance.

The distinctive feature of the contractual approach is that it is favored by developing countries for the obvious reason; these countries prefer economic development to environmental sustenance.[140] This is still the practice in some jurisdictions, including Ghana. As Gao notes, in the absence of comprehensive legislation, the petroleum agreement becomes the most viable alternative despite its shortcomings, particularly with regard to environmental protection.[141]

Insufficient Enforcement of EPA Requirements

Statutory enforcement mechanisms are also inadequate. EPA's enforcement measures are not sufficient to deter offenders from repeating environmental violations.[142] The enforcement mechanisms include a fine, imprisonment or both. The threshold for the fine is quite low; therefore, these fines do not serve as effective deterrence.[143] First, the fine is general in character and applies equally to every offending activity. It is not calibrated with different thresholds for different activities. Second, the amount is woefully inadequate, thus is incapable of preventing recurrence of prohibited activity.

The EIA requirement is also not fully complied with. Although the EIA is considered necessary, and must be complied with before an environmental permit is issued, in practice this is not the case. An oil company is required to conduct an EIA and submit a report to that effect. Based on this report, an environmental permit will be issued and the Minister for Energy and Petroleum approves the petroleum development plan. However, the EIS submitted by the oil companies for Ghana's Jubilee field operations has been described as insufficient. The Bretton Woods Project, a project that scrutinizes the work of the World Bank and the International Monetary Fund (IMF), stated that all

---

139   Id., at 37.

140   Id., at 35.

141   Id., at 36.

142   W.K. Tamakloe, "State of Ghana's Environment – Challenges of Compliance and Enforcement," available online: <http://www.inece.org/indicators/SOE_CE_Ghana.pdf>, p. 5.

143   Act 490, n. 65 above, s. 13(3) provides that the fine shall not exceed 250 penalty units. In Ghana, a penalty unit is GHC12.00. 250 penalty units is GHC3000.00 (equivalent of US$1,083.03). Presently, US$1 is equivalent of GHC2.77. Bank of Ghana, "Daily Interbank FX Rates," (22 April 2014), available online: <http://www.bog.gov.gh/index.php?option =com_wrapper&view=wrapper&Itemid=89>.

interested parties admit "that the companies have not submitted a full environmental and social impact assessment (ESIA) to the government."[144]

There is also uncertainty regarding the effect of a suspension or revocation of an environmental permit on approvals made thereunder. The EPA can suspend or revoke an environmental permit it has already issued if there is a violation of the terms of the permit.[145] But, it is uncertain whether that operates to automatically revoke the approval given by the other executive agency that licensed the activity or development. In the petroleum subsector, it is unclear if such revocation operates to terminate the approval given by the Minister for Energy and Petroleum.

Executive control also hinders the Agency's effectiveness and efficiency. In the performance of its functions, the EPA is subject to supervision and ministerial direction of the Minister for Environment.[146] The President appoints ministers and can revoke their appointments at will.[147] Therefore, the supervisory minister can direct or influence the EPA not to sanction companies if the President has a pro-resource development view.

Critical components of Ghana's petroleum extraction were rushed, including compliance with environmental standards. As a developing country, it is apparent Ghana was more interested in tapping into the revenue from oil drilling, and the government was in a haste to see the first oil proceeds as opposed to putting in place the proper regulatory structures before drilling begun. Therefore, the statutes that were passed even after oil drilling begun did not provide specific environmental safeguards.

Kosmos Energy Example

The uncontrolled toxic oil-based drilling mud discharge by Kosmos Energy is illustrative of the legal and regulatory system's failure to respond to the emerging petroleum-based environmental problems and the inherent weaknesses in the existing legal and regulatory framework. Kosmos Energy, an oil producing company, discharged more than 600 barrels of toxic oil-based drilling mud into Ghana's marine environment during offshore operations between 2009 and 2010.[148] The toxic discharge adversely affected coastal and marine resources as

---

144   B. Akolgo, "Ghana's Off-shore Nightmare," Bretton Woods Project, 17 April 2009, available online: <http://www.brettonwoodsproject.org/2009/04/art-564175/>.

145   Act 490, n. 65 above, s. 26.

146   Id., s. 3.

147   Ghana Constitution, n. 45 above, arts. 58(3) and (4).

148   Amorin and Broni-Bediako, n. 29 above, p. 22.

well as socio-economic activities including fishing and tourism.[149] In response, the Minister for Environment set up a ministerial committee to investigate the cause of the discharge. The committee found there was inadequate supervision.[150] Consequently, it found Kosmos Energy negligent and recommended a fine. Acting upon the findings and recommendations, the Minister imposed a fine on Kosmos Energy in the amount of US$35 million. Kosmos Energy contested the fine. It argued that there was no law in Ghana that empowered a Minister to impose fines in respect of environmental damage. Therefore, the Minister for Environment had no power to levy a fine for the alleged violations.[151] In the end, Kosmos Energy did not pay.[152] Interestingly, Kosmos Energy and the Ministry of Environment later entered into a settlement agreement under which Kosmos Energy undertook to support the Ministry's capacity-building in environmental protection.[153]

Kosmos Energy's response to the findings of the ministerial committee, its subsequent refusal to pay the fine, and the government's willingness to settle with Kosmos Energy are demonstrative of a *lacuna* in Ghana's law regarding environmental damage arising from the petroleum industry. Kosmos Energy's internal investigation showed that the discharge was preventable.[154] Kosmos Energy's Incident Investigation Report stated that there was a failure to comply with procedures as well as low training compliance. The Report also stated that there was a complete breakdown of supervision and lack of management involvement.[155] This constituted enough grounds for a good case for the state, but the government did little to redress the problem.

The discharge adversely affected the use of coastal resources, but the full extent of these adverse effects on marine resources is difficult to ascertain. Under the *Fisheries Act*,[156] a person who plans to conduct or undertake an

---

149   Id.

150   "Kosmos Energy objects to $35 million fine for environmental accident," Joy Online, 22 August 2010, available online: <http://business.myjoyonline.com/pages/news/201009/52611.php>.

151   F.B. Npong, "Kosmos bullies Ghana over 400 Million fine," TH!NK Post, 11 November 2010, available online: <http://climatechange.thinkaboutit.eu/think4/post/kosmos_bullies_ghana_over_400_million_fine>.

152   Kosmos Energy objects, n. 150 above.

153   B.A. Gyampoh, "Setting precedence in managing future oil spillage disasters," Joy Online, 10 August 2011, available online: <http://opinion.myjoyonline.com/pages/feature/201101/58989.php>.

154   Kosmos Energy, *Incident Investigation Report* (2010), p. 7.

155   Id., p. 6.

156   *Fisheries Act*, 2002 (Act 625).

activity other than fishing is required to conduct a fisheries impact assessment (FIA) on fisheries and aquatic resources prior to the commencement of that activity. The FIA is necessary to determine conservation measures for fishery resources that will be significantly affected by the proposed activity.[157] The Fisheries Commission may require that person to adopt mitigation measures pursuant to the FIA.[158] The requirement for the conduct of an FIA is exclusive of an EIA.[159] Notably, the oil companies did not conduct an FIA before proceeding with the development of the oil fields. The EIA submitted under the Ghana Jubilee Field Phase 1 Development purportedly incorporates an assessment of fisheries.[160] This purported incorporation of a fisheries assessment under the EIA is contrary to provisions of section 93 of the *Fisheries Act*. Section 93(3) of the *Fisheries Act* requires the conduct of an FIA as exclusive of any other statutory assessments including an EIA. However, there has been no follow-up to ensure the Jubilee field operators comply with the provisions of the *Fisheries Act*. Consequently, the Fisheries Commission has been unable to ascertain the full extent of the impact of the offshore activities on marine fishery resources.[161]

While the EPA Act empowers the EPA to revoke or suspend an environmental permit that it has already issued if there is a violation of a term in that permit,[162] the EPA did not suspend Kosmos Energy's permit. The uncontrolled and avoidable discharge of toxic effluents into the marine environment is a violation of good corporate environmental practice, and the EPA could have suspended the permit and ensured mitigation measures were undertaken before restoring the permit. But, it is implausible to imagine the EPA calling for a cessation of oil drilling in Ghana where oil revenues are in excess of US$1 billion annually. The EPA would also have had to surmount the ambiguous effect of a suspension or revocation of an environmental permit on the Minister for Energy and Petroleum's approval for petroleum development. In all, a decision to cease operations requires political will, and the poor nature of the resolution of Kosmos Energy's uncontrolled oil-based drilling mud discharge and its aftermath suggest lack of such will.

---

157   Id., s. 93(1).

158   Id., s. 93(3).

159   Id., s. 93(1).

160   Tullow Ghana Limited, (5 August 2009), pp. L-LI, available online: <http://www.elaw.org/system/files/Jubilee+Field+Draft+EIA+Non+Technical+Executive+Summary_6+Aug+09.pdf>.

161   N. Kow, "Ghana's oil exploration affects fishing in Western (Province) Region," Global Times, 30 June 2012, available online: <http://www.globaltimes.cn/content/718046.shtml>.

162   Act 490, n. 65 above, s. 26.

When the processes and recommendations of the committee set up by the Minister for Environment to investigate Kosmos Energy's toxic oil-based mud drilling discharge are examined against this conflicting regulatory framework, it appears very little can be achieved in terms of environmental protection in offshore operations. Licensing agencies and regulators of petroleum resources will not aggressively pursue environmental standards when that power is given to them as part of their regulatory functions. The reason is that revenue generating agencies are looked upon favorably by the government because their activities ensure a steady stream of receipts to support the nation's economic development. Without clear rules and well-defined statutory implications of executive agency decisions, pro-environmental executive agencies like the EPA will remain ineffective in the discharge of their functions.

In the event of a large spill, like the 2010 BP Deepwater Horizon oil spill in the Gulf of Mexico, it is questionable whether Ghana could adequately respond. The absence of specific environmental standards and clearly delineated jurisdiction of respective State agencies emboldens oil companies like Kosmos Energy to challenge imposition of fines for uncontrolled discharges even while admitting the incidents were avoidable. Kosmos Energy's willingness to settle suggests an intention to maintain good relations with the government in respect of securing additional drilling leases in the future. On the other hand, the government's acquiescence indicates its readiness to promote oil drilling to the detriment of the environment.

Prescriptions

Environmental regulation has lagged behind offshore oil development in Ghana. This article argues that Ghana has been preoccupied with revenue generation, thus environmental protection is a secondary concern. This is the focus of the first section of this part. The second section discusses remedies for the current deficiencies in Ghana's legal and regulatory framework. This includes an analysis of both legal rules and institutional measures, drawing on lessons from regulatory failures in Nigeria and the United States. This part concludes with an analysis of how these changes can be made with emphasis on those that are likely to be adopted.

Why has Environmental Regulation been Left Behind?
In Africa, resource development is fraught with sub-standard practice and a lax regulatory regime.[163] These standards make general reference to applicable

---

163 Botchway, n. 4 above, p. 12.

environmental statutes, which may be non-existent or not detailed enough. Gao notes that early national petroleum statutes, especially laws made in the early part of the 20th century, made little reference to environmental protection and pollution control.[164] In situating this in an historical context, Gao states that it may have been overly ambitious to expect these countries to include rather stringent environmental provisions in domestic laws.[165] However, this article asserts that accidents, spills and the resultant damage, such as the recent BP oil spill, should induce a change in perspective and bring about reforms.

While it is acknowledged that environmental protection is a necessary component of sustainable natural resource development, in Ghana's oil and gas industry, environmental protection has failed to move in tandem with petroleum operations. Ghana's preoccupation with resource development means its environmental protection needs are outstripped by the expected petroleum revenue inflows and energy security requirements. The analysis of Ghana's regulatory and institutional design shows that both general environmental and petroleum-related statutes are insufficient in providing the sound regulatory and institutional regime required in Ghana's offshore operations.

Government preoccupation with revenue generation has been a major cause of regulatory failure. In the United States, the government's preoccupation with revenue generation overshadowed environmental protection concerns. At the height of offshore drilling, the EIS requirement under the *National Environmental Policy Act*[166] (NEPA) was scaled back.[167] Two significant characteristics of an EIS with respect to petroleum development are that it is undertaken before operations commence, and that it provides useful information for other governmental bodies, citizens, and even industry.[168] However, some aspects of US offshore operations were excluded from NEPA review, consequently watering down the environmental management aspects of offshore drilling.[169] Significantly, a category of leasing activities in the Gulf of Mexico was excluded.[170] Over time, exclusion became the established practice.

---

164   Gao, n. 136 above, p. 12.

165   Id.

166   *National Environmental Policy Act*, 1970, 42 U.S.C. 4321 [NEPA].

167   Id., s. 102(2)(c).

168   J.E. Hickey, Jr., "Environmental Regulation of Oil and Gas Industry in the U.S.A.," in *Environmental Regulation of Oil and Gas*, n. 136 above, Chap. 8, p. 219.

169   National Commission on the BP Deepwater Horizon Oil Spill and Offshore Drilling Report, *Deep Water: The Gulf Oil Disaster and the Future of Offshore Drilling: Report to the President*, (2011), p. 81 [BP Commission Report].

170   Id.

Relatedly, the Minerals Management Service (MMS) was overstretched by the performance of four discrete functions, that is, offshore leasing, revenue collection, permitting, and safety and environmental protection. It was just a matter of time before things got out of control.[171]

Nigeria presents one of the classic examples of statutory preoccupation with petroleum development as opposed to environmental protection. In Nigeria, the oil industry represents the biggest challenge in reconciling the struggle between environmental protection and resource extraction through sustainable development.[172] Although Nigeria is Africa's largest producer of oil, it has no specific oil pollution law.[173] Its legal system continues to be oriented toward resource extraction and revenue generation rather than environmental protection.

Nigeria's *Petroleum Act* is the main legislation governing the exploitation of petroleum resources.[174] The law directs the Minister for Petroleum Resources to suspend "operations which in his opinion are not being conducted in accordance with good oil field practice..."[175] However, this ministerial discretion has no well-defined parameters since the law does not specify the constituent elements of good oil practice.

The Petroleum (Drilling and Production) Regulations[176] complements Nigeria's *Petroleum Act*. The Regulations purport to provide for oil pollution prevention. The Act provides for the application of precautionary steps in the production process.[177] The Act also provides for the maintenance of drilling apparatus and environmentally safe operations. But, these provisions, like many other petroleum-related laws in other developing countries, are vague and do not set specific thresholds for operations nor do the regulations stipulate the environmental standards that are to be applied in the course of drilling.[178]

The *Associated Gas Re-Injection Act*[179] is another important law in Nigeria's regulatory framework, yet again it does very little to provide for effective

---

171   Id., p. 67.

172   E. Emeseh, "Limitations of Law in Promoting Synergy between Environment and Development Policies in Developing Countries: A Case Study of the Petroleum Industry in Nigeria," *Journal of Energy and Natural Resources Law* 24 (2006), p. 582.

173   Id., p. 587.

174   *Petroleum Act, 1969*, Cap 350, LFN, 1990.

175   Id., s. 8(1)(g).

176   *Petroleum (Drilling and Production) Regulations*, LN 69 of 1969.

177   Id., reg. 25.

178   R. Ako, "Resource exploitation and environmental justice: the Nigerian experience." in *Natural Resource Investment and Africa's Development*, n. 4 above, pp. 72–104.

179   *Associated Gas Re-Injection Act*, 1979 (Cap. A25) [AGR Act].

environmental protection. This statute regulates gas flaring in Nigeria. Originally, the law sought to ban gas flaring by the end of 1994. But, the end date has been postponed several times.[180] Communities exposed to the negative effects of atmospheric emissions took to the courts to seek redress, and the courts declared gas flaring illegal.[181] However, gas flaring persists because the Minister for Petroleum Resources may suspend the no-gas flaring policy where he/she considers reinjection or utilization of associated gas inappropriate, not feasible or a threat to the integrity of underground reservoirs.[182] Again, this discretion is exercised in favor of economic interests. Consequently, gas flaring is conducted under 'government supervision' while the host communities are exposed to harmful atmospheric emissions without any protection.[183] In short, petroleum-related statutes have failed to provide adequate environmental safeguards in Nigeria.

Procedural shortcomings also account for environmental regulation being left behind in Ghana. These shortcomings include lack of transparency and information deficit. In Ghana, early petroleum development statutes were adopted when the nation was under military rule.[184] During this period, the executive and legislative powers were fused and exercised by a military council, leaving no room for public scrutiny of proposed legislation. Thus the foundational statutes, the GNPC and Petroleum (Exploration and Production) laws, were adopted with little public input.

Second, the post-oil discovery statutes passed show that there is an information deficit. Admittedly, offshore oil development is fairly new in Ghana, and the understanding of the environmental implications is evidenced in the rudimentary nature of the environmental protection provisions in these statutes. For, example, the *Petroleum Commission Act* that was passed after drilling begun provides for environmental compliance in general terms without specific environmental and pollution standards.

The lack of transparency in the adoption of early petroleum statutes and the paucity of information reflected in the minimal environmental provisions in post-oil discovery laws suggest a disconnect between public aspirations and actual environmental protection measures the political elite have recognized

---

180   Ako, n. 179 above, p. 89.

181   *Gbemre v. Shell Petroleum Development Company and Others*, Suit. No. FHC/B/C153/05 (Federal High Court of Nigeria, Benin Division).

182   AGR Act, n. 180 above, s. 3.

183   Ako, n. 179 above, p. 88.

184   The government at the time was the Provisional National Defence Council (PNDC) led by Flt. Lt. Jerry John Rawlings.

or are willing to admit. While the public is more concerned with environmental protection, the political elite are more oriented towards revenue generation.

Nigeria's experience is illustrative of this disconnect between the public and political elite. Oil revenue is very important to Nigeria's economy, and the State's focus has been on revenue maximization as opposed to environmental remediation. As Africa's leading oil producer, Nigeria exported crude oil worth US$94.64 billion in 2013, which accounts for about 70 percent of total export revenue.[185] The ineffective nature of Nigeria's regulatory framework has led to the prevalence of environmental pollution from oil and gas activities in Nigeria. The physical environment in Nigeria's oil-producing areas, especially in the Niger Delta, is heavily polluted, with large swaths of land and water resources remaining polluted to date.[186]

In Nigeria, communities affected by oil pollution have had to seek redress in court due to the unwillingness of regulatory agencies to take action. These suits have been successful to some extent, but this success is anecdotal.[187] Public interest litigation, in this instance, cannot be considered as an alternative to State inaction. In Nigeria, just as in other African countries with a common law system, the rather strict standard on legal standing has proved to be a major barrier for mounting successful legal action.[188] In recent times, host communities have resorted to militant action since the State has failed to address environmental pollution in oil-bearing regions.[189] With increasing environmental challenges and pollution within a weak political governance context, a system that looks to short-term returns from oil revenue, Nigeria's minimal environmental regulatory system will remain ineffective in the foreseeable future. In Ghana's case, the possibility that communities within the catchment area will pursue court action even if the EIS is inadequate is quite low because these are indigent communities.

A recent report by the United Nations (UN) concluded that the present state of petroleum-induced pollution in Nigeria will take up to 30 years to clean up.

---

185   Organization of the Petroleum Exporting Countries, "Nigeria: Facts and figures," (from *Annual Statistical Bulletin, 2013*), available online: <http://www.opec.org/opec_web/en/about_us/167.htm>.

186   A.B.M. Marong, "The Role of Sustainable Development: A Case Study of the Petroleum Industry in Nigeria," (Ph.D. Thesis, McGill University, 2003), pp. 168–169.

187   Emeseh, n. 173 above, p. 598.

188   Id., p. 602.

189   F.A.E. Paki and K.I. Ebienfa, "Militant Oil Agitations in Nigeria's Niger Delta and the Economy," *International Journal of Humanities and Social Science* 1 (2011), p. 142.

The initial investment for this exercise will require a commitment of US$1 billion for the first five years, and sustained financial investment in environmental remediation will have to be increased for the subsequent years. The UN report indicates that the restoration of Nigeria's oil-producing enclave and host communities could end up becoming the world's most extensive and long-term oil clean-up program if the nation's ecosystems are to be restored to full health.[190] Remediation of the oil-polluted environment will require huge public expenditure, and budgetary allocations for pollution remediation will inevitably scale back short-term revenue gains and divert funds away from economic development. The Nigerian government is not committed to ecological restoration because this will come at great financial cost. Therefore, sustainable resource development does not look attainable in Nigeria. Ghana, as a new oil-producing country in the West African sub-region, must ensure that it does not repeat Nigeria's mistakes.

Institutional shortcomings constitute one of the major challenges for environmental regulation. Pro-resource development executive agencies are empowered to regulate the environmental aspects of oil drilling. This can lead to lax regulation and jurisdictional overlaps, often with disastrous consequences. In Ghana's case, the Minister for Energy and Petroleum is vested with residual powers under the *Petroleum Commission Act* to make regulations for the effective implementation of the Act.[191] But, it is plausible for the Minister to make regulations that do not focus on progressive environmental protection objectives while insisting that those regulations are required for optimal resource exploitation. Therefore, it is difficult to see how the Petroleum Commission, primarily tasked with ensuring optimal benefits of petroleum exploitation, will aggressively pursue environmental standard-setting and compliance given the nature of Ghana's political and regulatory history.

In the United States, a major institutional challenge was that agency reforms were met with stiff opposition from both industry and government.[192] In the face of these challenges, the viable option left for the MMS was to pursue a regime characterized by voluntary compliance by industry.[193] Also, technological changes outstripped regulation in terms of advances in drilling in deeper waters. As a result, safety regulations lagged behind the technological advances.[194]

---

190   "Cleaning up Nigerian oil pollution could take 30 years, cost billions," UN News Centre, 4 August 2011, available online: <http://www.un.org/apps/news/story.asp?NewsID=39232 &Cr=pollution&Cr1#.UzXjmfldWSo>.

191   *Petroleum Commission Act*, n. 96 above, s. 22(c).

192   BP Commission Report, n. 170 above, p. 71.

193   Id., p. 72.

194   Id., pp. 72–73.

In Ghana, the President appoints the governing body of the Petroleum Commission.[195] As a result, the President can revoke a member's appointment at any time.[196] The exercise of this presidential discretion may discourage a pro-environmental governing body, whose views could conflict with a President who has a pro-resource development outlook. In the absence of environmental protection-specific provisions detailing pollution standards and remediation measures, an agency such as the Petroleum Commission may be unable to successfully implement its rather general environmental protection obligation.

Once again, the Nigerian experience is instructive. The Federal Environmental Protection Agency (FEPA) was established by the *Federal Environment Protection Agency (FEPA) Act.*[197] FEPA was responsible for environment management in Nigeria. However, environmental regulation of the petroleum industry was excluded from FEPA's general environmental oversight responsibility. The Department of Petroleum Resources (DPR), the technical arm of the Ministry of Petroleum Resources, was responsible for environmental management of the petroleum industry. In this specific instance, DPR, which is a sectoral regulatory agency, was empowered to exercise supervisory jurisdiction over FEPA.[198] This legislative design was interesting in that it subordinated the role of FEPA, which originally had general jurisdiction over the environment, to that of DPR. Therefore, a federal agency suited to the technical aspects of the petroleum industry with limited environmental expertise was put in charge of environmental management of the industry.

The jurisdictional overlap between FEPA and the DPR in the area of petroleum-related environmental protection[199] rendered FEPA ineffective in the discharge of its functions.[200] The jurisdictional friction between FEPA and DPR exacerbated an already bad situation where non-compliance was the regular pattern.[201] Also, FEPA was hindered by constant struggle with other federal executive agencies.[202] These challenges contributed to the perception

---

195   *Petroleum Commission Act,* n. 96 above, s. 4(2).

196   Id., s. 5(5).

197   FEPA Act, 1988, No. 58. This statute was amended several times until 2004.

198   Emeseh, n. 173 above, p. 589.

199   Id.

200   FEPA Act, n. 198 above, s. 5.

201   Marong, n. 187 above, pp. 162–63.

202   O. Ajai, "Balancing of interests in environmental law in Nigeria," in *Balancing of Interests,* n. 49 above, Chap. 14, p. 384.

that FEPA, Africa's first national institutional mechanism for environmental protection,[203] exercised an "overbearing, over-ambitious jurisdiction."[204]

After almost two decades, FEPA was reorganized and joined with other departments to form a new ministry, presently the Federal Ministry of Environment (FME). This new arrangement did not have the legal structure to carry out its functions until the *National Environmental Standards and Regulations Enforcement Agency (NESREA) Act*[205] was passed in 2007. The NESREA Act established the necessary legal enabling framework that had been absent following the establishment of FME.

The NESREA Act is quite significant. First, it repealed the FEPA Act. Second, it brought together the fragmented parts of Nigeria's federal environmental regulation under a single piece of legislation. But, the NESREA Act continued most of the old provisions in the FEPA Act, including the exclusion of FEPA jurisdiction over the oil and gas industry.[206] NESREA, like its predecessor FEPA, has oversight jurisdiction over hazardous substances and waste, except in the oil and gas sector.[207] DPR continues to exercise jurisdiction over the oil and gas sector with little control over petroleum pollution. Oil spill incidents have increased from 92 in 1989 to 297 in 2001. Within this period, a total of 2,441 oil spills were recorded with a total volume of 598,468 barrels spilled.[208] These figures are not conclusive since the DPR relies on oil companies' records. Therefore, the incidence of under-reporting is probably high.[209] In the end, the Nigerian physical environment remains heavily polluted as a result of this ineffective institutional setup.

The exclusion of the oil and gas sector from NESREA's jurisdiction reinforces the notion that Nigeria continues to privilege oil revenue over the attendant environmental consequences. Oil companies are left to apply different standards of pollution control with little or no State control. In the absence of proactive regulatory and institutional design, Ghana may end up with a situation similar to that of Nigeria.

---

203   National Environmental Standards & Regulations Enforcement Agency, "About NESREA," available online: <http://www.nesrea.gov.ng/about/index.php>.

204   Ajai, n. 203 above, p. 384.

205   National Environmental Standards & Regulations Enforcement Agency (NESREA) Act, 2007, No. 25 [NESREA Act].

206   Id., s. 7(g) and (h).

207   M.T. Ladan, "Review of NESREA Act 2007 and Regulations 2009–2011: A New Dawn in Environmental Compliance and Enforcement in Nigeria," *Law, Environment and Development Journal* 8 (2012), p. 124.

208   Emeseh, n. 173 above, p. 594.

209   Id., p. 593.

The difficulty in striking a balance between revenue generation and environmental protection associated with oil drilling is not limited to developing countries. A major criticism of the US system was overlapping jurisdictions involving licensing, safety and environmental regulation.[210] The aggregation of competing responsibilities from licensing through revenue collection to environment and safety regulation in one agency will invariably lead to the subjugation of environmental protection and management, and in the context of offshore drilling, risk environmental catastrophe. The MMS, comparable to the GNPC in Ghana, was tasked with licensing and regulatory oversight for offshore drilling, including safety and environmental enforcement duties. Federal regulation of the industry had begun on an awkward footing with the combination of two priorities, namely, environmental protection on the one hand and energy independence and more importantly oil revenue on the other.[211] The economic benefits derived from offshore operations created a false sense of security for both industry and government.[212]

Complacency can also run down a relatively stable and efficient petroleum-based environmental regulatory system. While no major incident comparable to the BP oil spill has happened in Ghana's offshore, the possibility of such an occurrence is not remote. In the United States, the BP oil spill showed how political leadership tends to prioritize revenue generation from offshore operations to the disregard of environmental protection.[213]

The US experience with the BP oil spill is a powerful example of how a good system can deteriorate over time. In the United States, the federal government is both the owner of the offshore petroleum resources, as well as regulator of offshore drilling.[214] The US petroleum industry is primarily a private one[215] as opposed to that of Ghana. In Ghana, the State is made a necessary party to all petroleum agreements in addition to its power to license exploration and production as well as participate in the industry.

In the United States, offshore drilling is regulated under federal authority. The United States operates a highly developed and complex system of regulation of the petroleum industry. At the federal level, over 25 statutes are relevant to the petroleum industry, with some having a bearing on the environmental

---

210   See BP Commission Report, n. 170 above.
211   Id., p. 55.
212   Id., p. x.
213   Id.
214   Id., p. viii.
215   Id.

aspects of the industry.[216] The US regulatory regime, however, has had to respond over time and adopt new rules due to accidents, notably the *Exxon Valdez* in 1989, which led to the *Oil Pollution Act*[217] (OPA), and more recently the BP oil spill in 2010, which was described as avoidable.[218] OPA provides for, among other requirements, legal liability, pollution prevention, double-hull tanker construction, enhanced penalties for non-compliance, and criminal and civil liabilities for violations.[219] Nonetheless, the US has no national environmental policy to direct the adoption and application of a uniform set of environmental regulatory rules for the petroleum industry.[220] Complacency led to negligence.[221] Over the course of time, revenue maximization led to government weakness, inadequate federal regulation and oversight.

In the end, the MMS focused on revenue generation to the neglect of other responsibilities. Pockets of corruption among agency officials also had a negative effect on agency effectiveness.[222] Overall, the agency adopted a minimalist approach to environmental regulation of the industry.[223] Thus, a good system was allowed to deteriorate. This led to the biggest US environmental disaster with long-term adverse social and ecological effects.[224] About five million barrels of oil were spilled into the Gulf of Mexico continuously for 87 days before the well was successfully capped. Eleven rig workers were killed in the accident.[225] It is reported that the oil from the accident has entered the ocean food chain, and will remain in the marine ecosystem for a long time to come.[226]

After the BP oil spill, the MMS was split up and reorganized for reasons many referred to as its shortfalls over the years to regulate the industry that led to an accident.[227] The MMS was separated into three bodies with separate mandates: Bureau of Ocean Management, Bureau of Safety and Environmental Enforcement, and Office of Natural Resource Revenue. The names of these

---

216   Hickey, n. 169 above, p. 218.

217   *Oil Pollution Act*, 1990, 33 U.S.C., Ch. 40.

218   BP Commission Report, n. 170 above, p. vii.

219   Gao, n. 136 above, p. 33.

220   BP Commission Report, n. 170 above, p. 33.

221   J.L. Weaver, "Offshore Safety in the Wake of the Macondo Disaster: Business as Usual or Sea Change?" *Houston Journal of International Law* 36 (2014), pp. 165 and 205.

222   BP Commission Report, n. 170 above, p. 76.

223   Id., p. 84.

224   D.M. Uhlmann, "After the Spill is Gone: The Gulf of Mexico, Environmental Crime, and the Criminal Law," *Michigan Law Review* 109 (2011), p. 1414.

225   Weaver, n. 222 above, p. 157.

226   Id., p. 159.

227   BP Commission Report, n. 170 above, p. 55.

new offices even suggest the enormity of the tasks that the MMS had to perform in the 30 years of its existence, which included increasing revenue by licensing drilling at deeper depths offshore while ensuring environmental protection remained a cornerstone of operations.[228] Revenue generation, or the economic benefits from offshore activities, were more attractive and gradually pushed environmental concerns to the fringes of regulation. It must, however, be noted that though the benefits were economic in character, these were informed by political considerations including the drive for energy independence in the 1970s.[229] Going forward, Ghana's regulatory system must be informed by these experiences, and the government must guard against complacency.

Remedying the Deficiencies

Constitutional provisions, although limited in specificity, present a logical entry point for resource and environmental protection. For example, in Nigeria, the Constitution directs the "State to protect and improve the environment and safeguard the water, air and land, forest and wildlife of Nigeria."[230] Additionally, section 17(2)(d) provides that the exploitation of natural resources other than for the good of the community must be prevented. These provisions form part of the Fundamental Objectives and Principles and Directive Principles of State Policy. Thus, as Ajai notes, these provisions do not create substantive rights capable of enforcement, but "they are ideologically potent as objectives and principles that the Nigerian State is obliged to pursue."[231] However, as observed in Nigeria, the reality is that "environmental laws are largely unenforced, corruptly enforced, or often times enforced with a *revenue collection motive*, ignoring core issues of environment management as prescribed by law, standard or best practice..."[232] [emphasis added].

In Ghana's case, based on the Supreme Court's recent decision in *Ghana Lotto Operators*,[233] the initial understanding that the DPSPs were not justiciable appears to have been rejected by some Ghanaian scholars. Here, the view is that, the right to a clean environment is an inherent feature of a constitutional democracy. As Abotsi puts it, "...the Ghanaian Constitution provides a right to a clean environment."[234] Abotsi states further that, "[I]t is thus clear that the

---

228   Id., p. 56.

229   Id., p. 55.

230   The Constitution of the Federal Republic of Nigeria, s. 20.

231   Ajai, n. 203 above, p. 388.

232   Id., p. 381.

233   *Ghana Lotto Operators* , n. 55 above, p. 1088.

234   Abotsi, n. 49 above, p. 143.

Constitution intends to promote the dual concepts of sustainable use and intergenerational equity in the management and exploitation of Ghana's environmental resources."[235] Respectfully, however, this article asserts that this approach remains a doubtful resolution of the debate on the enforceability of the DPSPs because the meaning ascribed to the Supreme Court's decision appears to be rather wide.

Notable environmental law experts like Sarpong have urged a better approach, that is, the adoption of an express constitutional right to a clean and healthy environment to resolve any ambiguities with the current understanding of the DPSPs' enforceability.[236] In Sarpong's opinion, an express constitutional right should come under Chapter 5 of Ghana's Constitution.[237] Chapter 5 is considered the 'Bill of Rights', and the rights provided for under this chapter are directly enforceable at the courts.[238] Sarpong's argument follows the Indian Supreme Court's jurisprudence on the construction of Directive Principles to make them directly enforceable. However, recent studies into the implementation and enforcement of the Indian courts' decisions show that a greater part of these decisions are not enforced or poorly enforced. Therefore, express constitutional provisions are not the panacea they are made out to be.[239] However, in a developing world context, a constitutional environmental right provision is significant in the sense that it elevates environmental protection from obscurity to mainstream socio-economic rights adjudication. In Ghana, judicial activism in socio-economic rights is on the increase, and a constitutional environmental right will be a good starting point for further development in regard to environmental protection.

The understanding of constitutional rights and obligations within a resource development context is, especially from a developing country's perspective, necessary for the broader application and enforcement of environmental protection-related statutes. However, it is not to be assumed that constitutional guarantees like the right to a clean and healthy environment are conclusive

---

235   Id.

236   G.A. Sarpong, "Environmental Justice in Ghana," *Review of Ghana Law* XX (1996–2000), p. 95. This article was written four years after Ghana's Constitution came into force, however, it remains relevant even today.

237   Ghana Constitution, n. 45 above, Chapter 5 is titled "Fundamental Human Rights and Freedoms."

238   Id., Art. 12(1).

239   See generally, G. Sahu, "Implications of India's Supreme Court's Innovations for Environmental Jurisprudence," *Law, Environment and Development Journal* 4 (2008), p. 1.

solutions.[240] The right to a clean and healthy environment cast as a consti-tutional provision will end up as unenforceable rhetoric if specific comple-mentary legislative provisions are not designed to support the implementation of this right, and an efficient and robust institutional design is not put in place to balance the competing interests of petroleum development and environ-mental protection.

As part of the re-conceptualizing process, Ghana can amend its Constitution to include the proposal on a right to a clean and healthy environment as accepted by the government during the country's constitution revision proc-ess. Admittedly, this provision by itself is not enough to ensure environmental compliance, but it reinforces the public trust doctrine where the State's duty as trustee of natural resources will be taken more seriously. Therefore, every gov-ernment that is mindful of its constitutional mandate as a means to achieving good governance would have to give equal prominence to environmental pro-tection as well as the revenue generation component of resource development. Thus, this right complements specific legislative standards and engenders good political governance.

The Constitution is the basic law of the land, and it contains the most important rules on political governance. The inclusion of an environmental right in Ghana's Constitution will ensure the State's public trust duties are given constitutional prominence.[241] The procedural steps for the realization of this right should equally be spelled out in detail. The State's failure to perform the obligations of this trust, here environmental protection, will then amount to a breach of constitutionally guaranteed rights.[242] This right must be comple-mented by specific legislative provisions on environmental protection and management.[243] This is how to achieve good political governance through environmental protection.

Effective environmental protection requires an expanded regulatory net-work that transcends general constitutional guarantees and includes specific provisions on operational and pollution standards. Beyond the Constitution, Ghana must look to petroleum development statutes and amend these laws to reflect specific environmental and pollution standards. Ghana's *Petroleum (Exploration and Production) (Amendment) Bill* which was introduced in

---

240   P.D. Okonmah, "Right to a Clean Environment: The Case for the People of Oil-Producing Communities in the Nigerian Delta," *Journal of African Law* 41 (1997), p. 67.

241   B.S. Cohen, "The Constitution, the Public Trust Doctrine, and the Environment," *Utah Law Review* (1970), p. 392.

242   Id.

243   Okonmah, n. 241 above, p. 67.

Parliament in 2010 was withdrawn due to serious deficiencies. Civil society organizations rallied against the passage of the bill because it did not provide extensive environmental safeguards.[244] Subsequently, a new bill has been drafted. The purpose of this bill is to improve the existing legal and regulatory framework for petroleum operations in Ghana.[245] This new bill provides a more expanded view on environmental protection.[246] The draft law introduces strict liability for pollution damage caused by a licensee or a contractor. The licensee or the contractor is obligated to remedy the damage.[247] The draft law also includes compensation for pollution damage[248] and insurance in respect of pollution damage.[249]

The innovative measures introduced by the draft bill are commendable, but they are still not detailed enough. Also, the institutional shortcomings that attend the present regulatory system remain. The Ministry of Energy and Petroleum is the supervisory ministry, and the Petroleum Commission is the primary implementing agency under this draft law. If passed in its current state, it is difficult to envisage a pro-environmental protection Petroleum Commission functioning optimally within a Ministry with a pro-resource development orientation. The better approach is the distinct separation of environmental protection obligations from licensing and revenue generation as adopted by the United States after the BP oil spill.

Ghana's approach should be marked by a well-crafted and comprehensive petroleum environmental legislation informed by setting specific standards for pollution limits, liability, specific provisions for citizen law suits, a compensation scheme, corporate accountability, and practical enforcement mechanisms. Also, EPA's non-binding guidelines for oil and gas development should be made binding. This comprehensive petroleum legislation must redistribute responsibilities, carefully shifting environmental protection to the EPA. The law must provide for clear points of inter-agency cooperation between regulatory agencies thereby reducing duplication of roles and inter-agency conflicts. Consequently, this law should be referenced in all petroleum contracts entered into by Ghana.

---

244   "Petroleum Bill in limbo," GhanaWeb, 10 December 2012, available online: <http://www .ghanaweb.com/GhanaHomePage/business/artikel.php?ID=259020>.

245   Cover Memorandum of Draft Petroleum (Exploration and Production) (Amendment) Bill, 2013.

246   Id., clauses 76–86 titled 'Health, Safety, Security and Environment'.

247   Id., clause 81(1).

248   Id., clauses 83–86.

249   Id., clause 94.

In this regard, pro-resource development agencies must focus primarily on licensing and participation in the offshore oil industry. The environmental management functions of these pro-resource development agencies should be placed under the EPA's jurisdiction, the more competent agency for environmental management. Beyond legislation, the EPA must be well-resourced to prepare it for the expansion of the petroleum industry and the possibility of environmental incidents. The State can explore the possibility of industry paying fees to support regulatory oversight. However, the government must guard against this support scheme becoming a source of agency capture.[250]

All outstanding regulatory requirements like the conduct of the FIA as required under section 93 of the *Fisheries Act* should be carried out by the oil companies operating in the offshore area. One significant regulatory failure in the US case was that MMS paid little attention to the impact of offshore activities on marine fishery resources.[251] This situation echoes similar concerns in Ghana where, to date, no FIA has been carried out, although the *Fisheries Act* requires it.[252] Therefore, Ghana must insist on the satisfactory performance of outstanding regulatory requirements like the FIA.

Criminal liability should be adopted as part of environmental reforms, but it must be restricted to extremely serious breaches and used sparingly. The environmental and ecological damage as a result of the BP oil spill was unprecedented. Thus, there were calls for criminal prosecution to deter future occurrence. As Uhlmann notes, the BP oil spill "will become the classic environmental crime,"[253] and it will have a significant impact on shaping perceptions of environmental crime, especially of corporate actors.[254] Uhlmann asserts that egregious environmental violations are often committed by companies that do not attach significant attention to environmental observance;[255] in his opinion, the companies involved in the Deepwater operations were culpable.[256] Although criminal prosecution may be necessary at some point, Uhlmann

---

250   This was one of the recommendations made by the US National Commission on the BP Deepwater Horizon Oil Spill designed to enhance regulatory oversight capacity. However, the related risk of agency dependence on such revenues unwittingly promotes agency capture. Richard J. Lazarus (Professor of Law at Harvard Law School and Former Executive Director of the US National Commission on the BP Deepwater Horizon Oil Spill), pers. comm. (11 April 2014).

251   BP Commission Report, n. 170 above, p. 83.

252   *Fisheries Act*, n. 157 above, s. 93.

253   Uhlmann, n. 224 above, p. 1461.

254   Id., p. 1439.

255   Id.

256   Id.

notes that the key to preventing future accidents, or at least minimizing their reoccurrence, is vigilant regulation.[257]

Other eminent US environmental law experts advise against the frequent use of criminal prosecution in environmental cases. Lazarus notes that environmental standards are hardly based on the classical conception of criminal liability.[258] Criminal sanctions for environmental violations should, therefore, not simply be used as "another enforcement tool in the regulator's arsenal to promote public policy objectives."[259] Criminal liability must be a last resort and used sparingly for serious cases to deter recurrence and no more. This will ensure corporations are not discouraged from investing in resource development. This is particularly very important from a developing country perspective.

Contractual provisions are important pathways to environmental compliance, however, this approach also requires elaborate prescriptions or else little can be achieved. A foreign direct investor's primary motive is maximizing returns. The investor looks to reduce his or her production cost, including through contractual provisions.[260] For State parties, the main interest is economic development.[261] And while these interests can co-exist, they do not always work well together. The basic interests of each party are regularly in conflict.[262] In the absence of specific legislation, the closest source of environmental regulation is the petroleum contract.

Presently, Ghana's Model Petroleum Agreement falls short as a progressive resource contract that provides adequately for environmental standards. Ghana's Agreement is not any different from that of Nigeria. As the largest producer of oil in Africa, Nigeria's Model Production Contract (MPC), 1995 is "surprisingly silent on environmental protection."[263] This sums up the dearth of environmental consideration in the petroleum industry in Nigeria. Ghana's petroleum contracts must move away from those of Nigeria. Ghana's resource contracts must be revised to include specific environmental standards, and petroleum agreements must expressly refer to applicable environmental statutes.

---

257   Id., p. 1461.
258   R.J. Lazarus, "Assimilating Environmental Protection into Legal Rules and the Problem with Environmental Crime," *Loyola of Los Angeles Law Review* 27 (1994), p. 882.
259   Id., p. 883.
260   Laryea, n. 124 above, p. 107.
261   Id., p. 108.
262   Id.
263   Gao, n. 136 above, p. 36.

Pockets of success in respect of good corporate environmental observance in most developing countries are as a result of loan conditions set by international financial institutions (IFIs) like the World Bank and the IMF for transnational corporations, not enforcement of national laws.[264] While IFIs can play a significant role in ensuring compliance, their involvement can pose serious challenges to State sovereignty.

The World Bank Group, through its affiliate the International Finance Corporation (IFC), provided loans of US$100 million and US$115 million to Kosmos Energy and Tullow Oil respectively, two developers in Ghana's oil fields.[265] As a part of the loan package, the IFC supported the oil companies in preparing environmental and social management plans for the Jubilee field project.[266]

This approach is not the best since it portends a great deal of interference with the internal affairs of host countries. For example, the IFC was engaged in advising these oil companies on how to enhance the project's benefit through local communities and stakeholder engagement.[267] It is difficult to ascertain the kind of advice the IFC gave these oil companies in respect of community engagement. As a creditor, the IFC is inclined to protect the interests of its borrowers so it can recoup its investments, thus the possibility of meddling in domestic affairs is even greater. At best, the role of IFIs must be seen as complementary.

Agency reorganization must complement a revamped legal system. Institutional restructuring must be undertaken if environmental protection is to receive the prominence and enforcement it deserves. The current arrangement, which involves scattered implementation of scant environmental

---

264   I.F.I. Shihata, "The World Bank and the Environment: A Legal Perspective," *Maryland Journal of International Law and Trade* 16 (1992), pp. 13–20. Shihata notes that as part of the Morocco-Jerada Coal Mine Modernization and Expansion Project, the World Bank and Morocco agreed to the incorporation of a provision on health and safety standards in the loan agreement. Further, it was agreed by the parties that the borrower, i.e., Morocco, would implement these measures. This incorporation was effected by a supplementary letter to the loan agreement. Shihata, also, recounts a similar development with respect to the Uganda Forest Rehabilitation Project. Uganda was required to adopt a new forest development policy that was favorable to the World Bank. The credit agreement also contained certain provisions that required Uganda to fully give effect to the new policy by adopting legislative measures acceptable to the Bank.

265   International Finance Corporation, "Supporting best practices in Ghana's oil and gas sector," News, available online: <http://www.ifc.org/wps/wcm/connect/region_ext _content/regions/sub-saharan+africa/news/kosmos_ghana>.

266   Id.

267   Id.

protection under the GNPC, the Petroleum Commission, and the EPA, weakens any prospect of effective environmental protection and management. Ghana must dedicate an executive agency like the EPA to environmental regulation of the offshore petroleum industry. This agency must be endowed with the requisite technical capacity and training schemes to keep abreast of technological developments in oil drilling, especially in deeper waters.

Effecting Change

In looking to effect change, Ghana must examine the range of options available. This includes constitutionalizing environmental rights, detailed and specific statutory provisions on pollution and environmental standards, and agency reorganization according to institutional strengths.

The most likely first option to be implemented in Ghana is the amendment of the Constitution to provide for environmental rights.[268] Although this choice is not the strongest link in the chain of regulatory efforts, it will unlock the dilemma of environmental protection as public trust and engender a new outlook of environmental protection as part of the enforcement of rights that contribute to good political governance. Ghanaians are more likely to vote in favor of the inclusion of this right because during the constitution review process, many Ghanaians submitted proposals to that effect.[269]

The better approach is the adoption of a comprehensive petroleum environmental statute. This calls for an expansion of the Draft Petroleum (Exploration and Production) Bill before it is passed into law. In its current state, the bill does not reflect the discrete agency reorganization that progressive regimes like the United States have adopted following the BP oil spill in 2010. Attempts to reorganize the institutional design will require political will since it involves reducing rent seeking. Also, agency restructuring can reduce the incidence of regulatory capture.

Complementary contractual provisions can support both constitutional and detailed statutory provisions. It is important that Ghana looks toward a new and effective approach in achieving sound environmental regulation in the petroleum industry. This approach must be informed by progressive and specific standard-setting that address every aspect of petroleum operations. These standards, provided for in comprehensive legislation, must be expressly incorporated into petroleum agreements. Altogether, Ghana must reform its

---

268   F. Badu, "EC to hold referendum on constitutional amendments," Graphic Online, 30 January 2014, available online: <http://graphic.com.gh/news/politics/16625-ec-to-hold -referendum-on-constitutional-amendments.html>.

269   CRC Report, n. 58 above, p. 735.

current regime away from the approach that leans towards resource exploitation with vague general environmental protection obligations, coupled with inter-agency conflicts and duplication of roles.

Conclusion and Final Observations

This article focused on re-conceptualizing the economic development and environment debate within the offshore petroleum industry in Ghana. The analysis in this research shows that Ghana's petroleum environmental protection regime lacks the requisite general rules as well as specific standards and practices to allow for effective enforcement. The institutional architecture also allows political control that seems calculated to prevent the responsible institutions from developing and actually enforcing rules, standards and practices to ensure that resource development does not leave offshore areas polluted and un-remediated. Poor management of resource development can adversely affect Ghana's quest to achieve sustainable development. In this regard, the article asserts that effective environmental governance must be conceived as serving two ends, sustainable development and good political governance. The regulatory frameworks of Nigeria and the United States were studied, and the lessons drawn from these two countries illustrate the regulatory failures from both developing and developed oil-producing countries' perspectives.

The article focused on the extent to which Ghana's environmental protection and management regime provides adequate safeguards for the environment in respect of the country's burgeoning offshore oil and gas development. In this regard, this article makes a number of salient recommendations. These include a constitutionally guaranteed right to a clean and healthy environment, the development of comprehensive petroleum legislation that provides for specific environmental standards, reorientation of the institutional structure insulated from political interference, and good corporate environmental compliance.

In moving forward, the proximity of Ghana's offshore operations to Côte d'Ivoire's eastern border raises the likelihood of transboundary pollution and a potential source of cross-border dispute. Like Ghana, Côte d'Ivoire has a moderate upstream oil industry. Therefore, Ghana and Côte d'Ivoire must institute joint environmental protection efforts in the border region.

In addition, the Gulf of Guinea has become a choice destination for oil companies. From the shores of Mauritania to Nigeria, petroleum exploitation has increased. Consequently, it is imperative that coastal States in the West African sub-region develop regionally acceptable offshore petroleum environmental standards.[270] Notwithstanding the apparent advantages of standardization, the sub-region's legal pluralistic governance context and the marked imbalance in economic development pose tremendous challenges to the creation of robust and concrete efforts targeted at harmonizing standards. It is also uncertain if these States will back the development of common standards with the requisite political will.

Long-term unresolved oil pollution concerns may lead to potentially destabilizing political action like militancy, as witnessed in the oil-bearing areas of Nigeria. Political instability can expand into cross-border armed conflict and subsequently erode modest political and economic gains that have been made in the sub-region. However, the processes and standards in this regard must essentially reflect a development owned by these West African nations, and not foreign remedies foisted upon them.

---

270   West African coastal States have started processes to develop detailed standards suited to their offshore petroleum development effort and with an eye on what implementation and enforcement challenges they may face in putting these standards into effect. 11th Meeting of the Conference of the Parties to the Convention for Cooperation in the Protection, Management and Development of the Marine and Coastal Environment of the Atlantic Coast of West, Central and Southern Africa (Abidjan Convention), "Note on the Process of Developing a Protocol for the Prevention of Offshore Oil and Gas Exploration and Exploitation Pollution in West, Central and Southern Africa," UNEP(DEPI)/WACAF/COP.11/Inf.4; J. Rochette et al., *Seeing Beyond the Horizon for Deepwater Oil and Gas: Strengthening the International Regulation of Offshore Exploration and Exploitation* (Paris: Institut du développement durable et des relations internationals, IDDRI Study, No. 1, 14 February 2014), at p. 16, available online: <http://www.iddri.org/Publications/Collections/Analyses/ST0114_JR%20et%20al._offshore%20EN.pdf>.

Offshore Renewable Energy Governance in Nova Scotia: A Case Study of Tidal Energy in the Bay of Fundy

*Meinhard Doelle**

Professor of Law, Schulich School of Law, Dalhousie University, Halifax, Canada

Introduction

The Bay of Fundy is a large estuary that separates portions of Nova Scotia and New Brunswick on the Atlantic coast of Canada. The Bay is about 300 kilometers (km) long and 100 km wide at its mouth. Due to its shape and location it experiences extreme high tides of up to 16 meters in the upper Bay. In addition, the Bay of Fundy contains narrow passages that result in ocean currents of over six meters/second (m/sec) during each tidal cycle. These features combine to provide some of the highest potential for tidal energy development anywhere in the world.

This article considers the governance approach (including the legislative context, the regulatory system, and relevant policy context) to offshore renewable energy developments in Nova Scotia, with a focus on tidal energy in the Bay of Fundy. It explores applicable regulatory processes at the federal and provincial levels as well as the contribution of strategic environmental assessments (SEAs) carried out in 2008 and 2013. The article assesses the ability of the current governance approach to encourage integrated decision making that considers environmental, social, and economic factors, such as various environmental impacts and benefits, energy security, economic development opportunities, and interaction with other uses.

The potential for tidal power development in the Bay of Fundy region of the Atlantic coast of Canada has been recognized for decades (Figure 11.1). Not surprisingly, there have been previous attempts to develop offshore renewable energy. In the 1980s, barrage-based tidal power technology was piloted in Annapolis Royal, Nova Scotia. A combination of technical, economic, and environmental concerns identified as a result of this pilot project prevented any large-scale

* The research assistance of JD candidate Benjamin Ojoleck is gratefully acknowledged.

development of the resource at that time.[1] In recent years, offshore renewable energy has become of interest again.

There have been considerable changes in the technologies considered since previous efforts in the 1980s. Pilot projects underway around the world are using new, open turbine technology that is expected to significantly reduce costs and environmental impacts. This technology operates on principles similar to a wind turbine, except it is anchored or otherwise secured on the seabed in tidal waters. These turbines are able to take advantage of flows of water in both directions, and offer power in predictable intervals during most of the tidal cycle.[2]

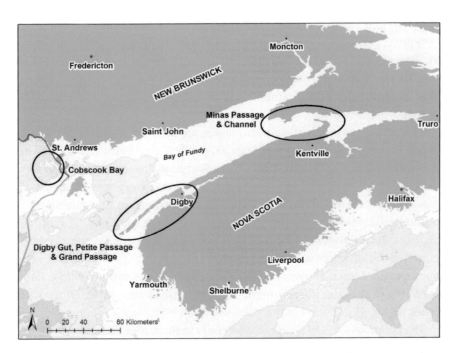

FIGURE 11.1   *Bay of Fundy area with circled areas indicating highest tidal energy potential*
SOURCE: THE AUTHOR.

1   See, for example, M. Conley and G. Daborn, eds., *Energy Options for Atlantic Canada* (Halifax: Formac Publishing, 1983).

2   For background information on tidal energy technologies, see AECOM, *Tidal Energy: Strategic Environmental Assessment (SEA) Update for the Bay of Fundy*, (January 2014) at 31–46, available online: <http://www.oera.ca/marine-renewable-energy/strategic-environmental -assessment>.

The economics of tidal power have also changed as a result of recent fluctuations in energy prices, and the projections for long-term energy supply and demand. Energy security is becoming a growing concern around the world. The environmental imperative for a switch from traditional non-renewable, fossil fuel-based energy sources to renewable, low greenhouse gas emitting energy sources has become a pre-occupation of governments in Canada and the United States. Finally, economic diversification has become critical for Maritime communities significantly dependent on the exploration of dwindling resources and on energy intensive manufacturing.[3]

All this adds up to considerable pressure to utilize all sources of renewable energy that are technically and economically within reach. Tidal energy is no exception. Numerous potential developers of tidal energy have been pushing governments in Canada to clarify the rules under which this industry will operate, and to allow pilots to be put into the water to demonstrate the viability of new technologies. Some developers are already pursuing commercial scale developments. At the same time, utilities are trying to understand how tidal energy will fit into the existing and future energy mix, the capacity of the grid to utilize the power generated, and the role of tidal in meeting increasing demand for greener power. The 2013 SEA estimates the realistic potential for power production in the Bay of Fundy to be in the range of 1.7 gigawatts (GW) of power, with the theoretical potential well in excess of 7 GW.[4]

Although there are no in-stream tidal turbines deployed in the Bay of Fundy at the time of writing, there have been deployments in the past, and there are several proposals for turbines to be deployed on a 2015/16 timescale. There are four major developers interested in placing turbines at one of the available berths at the Fundy Ocean Research Center for Energy (FORCE): OpenHydro, Minas Energy, Atlantis Resources Corporation, and Black Rock Tidal Power.

OpenHydro, a company based in Ireland and owned by DCNS, partnered with Nova Scotia Power in 2009 to deploy North America's first tidal turbine in the Bay of Fundy. This 1 megawatt (MW), open-center turbine was soon damaged and rendered out-of-commission because the tidal forces in the Bay of Fundy greatly exceeded previous estimates and pushed the blades of the six-meter turbine off the rotor. The base and entire turbine were recovered

---

3　One Nova Scotia, *Now or Never: An Urgent Call to Action for Nova Scotians – The Report of the Nova Scotia Commission on Building Our New Economy* (February 2014), available online: <http://onens.ca/report/>.

4　R. Karsten, "Measuring and Assessing the Tidal Resource," (2013) as cited in AECOM, n. 2 above, at 6.2.1.

from the water the following year.[5] OpenHydro has since developed plans for a 4 MW tidal array, consisting of two 16-meter 2 MW turbines. This array was awarded a berth at FORCE by the Nova Scotia Department of Energy, and is on schedule to be deployed in 2015. The turbines are 16 m tall and weigh approximately 275 tonnes.[6]

Black Rock Tidal Power, a Halifax company, was awarded a berth at FORCE in March 2014 and will be testing the Triton S36 tidal turbine array.[7] This array consists of 36 individual three-meter turbines arranged on a horizontal axis, with an energy production capacity of 2.5 MW. The array will initially start with 16 individual turbines in 2015, and is expected to increase to 36 turbines by 2016.[8]

Atlantis Resources Corporation is designing the AR1500 turbine for deployment at FORCE with the help of Irving Shipbuilding and Lockheed Martin. This turbine will have a 1.5 MW rated energy capacity and, at 18 meters in diameter, will be one of the largest single-rotor turbines ever developed.[9] This turbine is scheduled for deployment by 2016/17 after testing is completed in China.[10]

Minas Energy, partnered with Bluewater and Siemens, has proposed a design for a 2 MW SeaGen F floating tidal current turbine – the first of its kind in the Bay of Fundy. Minas Energy aims to have this turbine deployed by 2015/16.[11]

---

5   OpenHydro, "Bay of Fundy Tidal Energy Project: 2015–2020+" (2014), available online: <http://www.openhydro.com/download/OPENHYDRO-FUNDY-PROJECT-FACT-SHEET .pdf>.

6   Fundy Ocean Research Center for Energy, "OpenHydro" (2014), available online: <http:// fundyforce.ca/technology/openhydro-nova-scotia-power/>.

7   Nova Scotia Government, "Government Funds Tidal Industry, Welcomes New Players" (2014), available online: <http://novascotia.ca/news/release/?id=20140328006>.

8   TidalStream, "Triton S36 – Force" Black Rock Tidal Power, (2013), available online: <http:// www.blackrocktidalpower.com/wp-content/uploads/2013/11/TRITON-S36-FORCE-.pdf>.

9   Fundy Ocean Research Center for Energy, "Atlantis/Lockheed Martin/Irving Shipbuilding" (2014), available online: <http://fundyforce.ca/technology/atlantis/>.

10   B. Erskine, "Atlantis to Test Turbine in China before Fundy Project," The Chronicle Herald (7 April 2014), available online: <http://thechronicleherald.ca/business/1198657-atlantis -to-test-turbine-in-china-before-fundy-project>.

11   Marine Current Turbines Ltd., "Siemens, Bluewater and Minas to Install Floating Tidal Current Turbines in Canada's Bay of Fundy" (2014), available online: <http://www .marineturbines.com/News/2014/04/04/siemens-bluewater-and-minas-install-floating -tidal-current-turbines-canadas-bay>.

The Digby Neck area of the Bay of Fundy also holds significant potential for tidal energy in Nova Scotia. Fundy Tidal Inc. has already received community feed-in tariffs from the provincial government for three sites totaling almost 3 MW.[12] A project description was submitted to a variety of government agencies, as well as to the One-Window Committee for the Outer Bay of Fundy Tidal Energy Project in 2011, which mentions several developers as potential berth holders in the Fundy Tidal Inc. location. The four main companies that are being considered are NECI, Nautricity, Tocardo, and ORPC.[13]

This article assesses the overall governance approach currently in place for this emerging new industry in the Bay of Fundy. In considering the governance approach, the article first considers the existing constitutional and regulatory context. The constitutional context is briefly considered in Part 1. As we will see, the jurisdictional context has not been formally resolved, though there appears to be political acceptance of provincial territorial jurisdiction in the Bay of Fundy.

A number of existing federal and provincial regulatory processes will apply to tidal energy projects; however, there is currently no regulatory process in place specifically designed for tidal energy. The federal and provincial regulatory context are each considered below. It is this regulatory framework that government decision makers have had to work with since they were first approached to approve tidal pilot projects around 2005. It has been adapted somewhat in preparation for the industry, but it has not fundamentally changed.

Provincial officials initiated an SEA in 2007 to guide future decision-making on whether, where, and under what conditions tidal energy development should be approved. The tidal SEA was carried out without any legal foundation, and with limited federal engagement. It was updated in 2013. The fourth part of this article focuses on the role of this SEA in improving decision making for new industries in Nova Scotia. Lessons learned are discussed in the fifth part and the article concludes with an assessment of Nova Scotia's overall governance approach to tidal energy.

1   The Constitutional Context

The roles of the provincial and federal levels of government in Canada with respect to tidal energy projects will very much depend on whether the projects

---

12   Fundy Energy Research Network, "Digby Neck" (2014), available online: <http://fern.ac adiau.ca/briar-island.html>.

13   Fundy Tidal Inc., "Regulatory" (2014), available online: <http://www.fundytidal.com/ index.php?option=com_content&view=category&layout=blog&id=19&Itemid=47>.

are located within the territory of a province or outside. Unfortunately, while international maritime boundaries are relatively well-established as a result of the broad acceptance and adoption of the 1982 United Nations Convention on the Law of the Sea,[14] some provincial maritime boundaries within Canada are still unresolved. In the case of Nova Scotia, a strong legal claim can be made that a portion of the Bay of Fundy is part of the territory of Nova Scotia, but the issue has not been formally settled either through negotiations or litigation.[15]

Where tidal development takes place entirely within the territory of the province of Nova Scotia, both the provincial and federal levels of government will have jurisdiction to deal with aspects of tidal energy projects. Provincial laws would apply to the production of electricity and to certain aspects of its export. Section 92A(1)(c) of the *Constitution Act, 1982*[16] provides the basis for provincial jurisdiction over the production of tidal power within the province. It provides that:

> 92A (1) In each province, the legislature may exclusively make laws in relation to... (c) development, conservation and management of sites and facilities in the province for the generation and production of electrical energy.

The province also has jurisdiction over local works and undertakings under section 92(10), property and civil rights under section 92(13), and other matters of a local and private nature under section 92(16). Relevant areas of federal jurisdiction would include navigation and shipping under section 91(10), marine pollution,[17] and inland and seacoast fisheries under

---

14   United Nations Convention on the Law of the Sea, 10 December 1982, 21 *International Legal Materials* 1261 (1982).

15   For Supreme Court of Canada cases that have considered how to determine the territorial offshore boundaries of Canadian provinces, see *Reference re Offshore Mineral Rights of British Columbia* [1967] S.C.R. 792 (*B.C. Offshore Minerals Reference*), *Reference Re Bed of the Strait of Georgia and related Areas* (*Georgia Strait Reference*), [1984] 1 SCR 388, and *Hibernia Reference* [1984] 1 SCR 86. See also G.V. LaForest, "Canadian Inland Waters of the Atlantic Provinces and the Bay of Fundy Incident," *Canadian Yearbook of International Law* 1 (1963): 149, and E.C. Foley, "Nova Scotia's Case for Coastal and Offshore Resources," *Ottawa Law Review* 13 (1982): 281–308.

16   *Constitution Act, 1982*, being Schedule B to the *Canada Act 1982* (UK), 1982, c. 11. See also s. 92A(2), (3), and (4).

17   As established by the Supreme Court of Canada under 'peace, order, and good government' in *R v. Crown Zellerbach Ltd.*, [1988] SCJ No 23, [1988] 1 SCR 401.

section 91(12).[18] As a result, developers of tidal energy within the territory of the province of Nova Scotia have to comply with regulatory requirements at both levels of government. The current federal and provincial regulatory frameworks as they apply to tidal energy are briefly explored in the following sections.[19]

2 The Federal Regulatory Framework[20]

Regardless of any claims to provincial territorial jurisdiction in areas with high potential for tidal development, it is clear that the federal government does have jurisdiction over aspects of tidal power development. Federal jurisdiction over navigation, fisheries, and inter-provincial undertakings are obvious examples. As a result, a number of federal actors will be involved in Fundy tidal power development decision making, most notably the Canadian Environmental Assessment Agency, the National Energy Board, the Department of Fisheries and Oceans, Environment Canada, Transport Canada, and Natural Resources Canada. The following is a brief overview of federal regulatory regimes that are most relevant, although other federal legislation would apply depending on the circumstances.[21]

The Fisheries Act

Certain provisions of the *Fisheries Act*,[22] administered by the Department of Fisheries and Oceans, will be triggered in case of impact on fish or fish habitat, and in case of water pollution resulting from the construction, operation, and

---

18   For a more detailed discussion of jurisdictional considerations for tidal energy development in the Bay of Fundy, see M. Doelle, D. Russell, P. Saunders, D. VanderZwaag and D. Wright, "The Regulation of Tidal Energy Development off Nova Scotia: Navigating Foggy Waters," *UNB Law Journal* 55 (2006): 27–70 at 34.

19   The developer will have to be given some form of property right to develop tidal energy in a given area to the exclusion of others and to install its equipment. For a discussion of this issue, see Doelle et al., id., p. 42.

20   This section is an updated version of the author's contribution to a regulatory summary in Doelle et al., id., p. 49.

21   An example would be the disposal of waste produced during the construction phase of a tidal project, which would require a 'Disposal at Sea' permit under s. 127 of the *Canadian Environmental Protection Act*, SC 1999, c. 33, and the *Regulations Respecting Applications for Permits for Disposal at Sea*, SOR/2001-276 and *Disposal at Sea Regulations*, SOR/2001/275.

22   *Fisheries Act*, RSC 1985, c. F-14, as amended by *Jobs, Growth and Long-term Prosperity Act*, SC 2012, c. 19, ss. 132–156.

decommissioning of tidal projects. A tidal project may trigger section 35(1) which contains a general prohibition against "serious harm" to fish, defined in section 2(2) as death to any fish, or permanent alteration or destruction of any habitat. Although section 35(1) generally prohibits serious harm to fisheries, section 35(3) allows the minister to pass regulations exempting specified works, undertakings or activities from this prohibition. Furthermore, section 35 aims to prevent serious harm to fish only if they are part of a recreational, commercial or Aboriginal fishery, or are fish that support such a fishery. This version of section 35 only recently came into force, so there is no case law to date on its application. A tidal project could also trigger section 36(3) if in the course of constructing, operating or decommissioning the project a deleterious substance is deposited into water frequented by fish. The deposit of certain deleterious substances can be permitted by regulations under section 36(4). Finally, section 37 allows the minister to require the submission of certain information in case of serious harm to fish, or in case of a deposition of a deleterious substance in water frequented by fish.[23]

The Canadian Environmental Assessment Act

The *Canadian Environmental Assessment Act* (CEAA),[24] administered by the Canadian Environmental Assessment (CEA) Agency, has the potential to apply to some tidal energy projects in the Bay of Fundy. Its actual application will depend on the size and nature of the proposed project, the exercise of discretion by the CEA Agency and the federal minister, as well as the application of the provincial EA process to the project.[25]

The application of the CEAA is limited to projects. Projects are defined to include any project included in the designated project regulation. The threshold for in-stream tidal projects is 50 MW and for other tidal projects, such as tidal lagoons, it is 5 MW. Certain expansions of existing facilities, depending on the size of the original facility and the scale of the expansion, are also designated projects under the regulations. Not all designated projects require an assessment under CEAA. Rather, there is ultimately broad discretion to determine on a case-by-case basis whether an assessment of a project is required.[26]

---

23   Fisheries and Oceans Canada, *Fisheries Protection Policy Statement* (Ottawa: Fisheries and Oceans Canada, 2013), available online: <http://www.dfo-mpo.gc.ca/pnw-ppe/pol/PolicyStatement-EnoncePolitique-eng.pdf>.

24   *Canadian Environmental Assessment Act, 2012*, SC 2012, c. 19, s. 52 [CEAA].

25   *Regulations Designating Physical Activities*, SOR/ 2012–147.

26   The FORCE site in the Bay of Fundy, in addition to being federally reviewed under CEAA, underwent a provincial environmental assessment process in 2009, and was approved

There are two process options under CEAA: standard assessments and panel reviews. Legal requirements for standard assessments are limited; the process is designed to be flexible and efficient. There are opportunities for substitution and equivalency with provincial EAs, making it unlikely that there will be standard assessments of projects subject to a provincial EA. The standard assessment is the default process option; panel reviews are carried out at the discretion of the minister. Panels are independent and have to conduct public hearings. CEAA provides for joint panel reviews with other jurisdictions.

The Species at Risk Act

The *Species at Risk Act* (SARA),[27] under the shared responsibility of Environment Canada and the Department of Fisheries and Oceans, applies to all federal land as defined in the Act, including the territorial sea and internal waters of Canada.[28] SARA is designed primarily to protect listed species on federal lands. It does so through general prohibitions against activities harmful to species listed under section 15 as extinct, extirpated, endangered, threatened or of special concern, in combination with more proactive recovery strategies. The listing process and the general prohibitions associated with it work in combination with a permitting process that can override the general prohibition for certain activities.

Listed species that potentially could be affected include the blue whale (Atlantic population), North Atlantic right whale, fin whale, great white shark, harbour porpoise, leatherback sea turtle, piping plover (*Charadrius melodus*), Atlantic salmon, peregrine falcon (*anatum* subspecies), northern wolffish (*Anarhichas denticulatus*) and spotted wolffish (*Anarhichas minor*).[29] Depending on jurisdictional issues and the project's technology and implementation, sections 32(1), 33, and 58 all potentially apply. Section 32 generally prohibits harming or killing of listed species. Section 33 deals with harm to the residence of listed species, and section 58 seeks to protect critical habitat. SARA essentially requires consideration of any potential impact of a project on listed species, their residences and habitats, and requires projects to avoid negative impacts.

---

later that year by both authorities. Information about the EA process can be found on the FORCE website online: <http://fundyforce.ca/monitoring-and-research/enviromental-assesment/>.

27   *Species at Risk Act*, SC 2002, c. 29 [SARA].

28   See SARA, id., s. 2(1), definition of 'federal land'.

29   See SARA Registry online: <http://www.sararegistry.gc.ca>.

Section 32(1) applies if the construction or operation results in the death, harm, harassment, capture or taking of an individual of a species that is listed as an extirpated species, an endangered species or a threatened species. Section 33 comes into play if the project damages or destroys the residence of one or more individuals of a wildlife species that is listed as an endangered species or a threatened species. Section 58 applies in cases where critical habitat has been identified in a recovery strategy of a listed species. It provides for the protection of critical habitat through a general prohibition in combination with more specific provisions depending on whether the listed species is found in a national park, federal land, or provincial or private land.

It should be noted that the critical habitat and residences of all the marine species that could be affected by a Fundy tidal energy project have not yet been identified and some recovery plans do not yet exist. This means that as tidal projects proceed, attention will have to be paid to the ongoing development of recovery plans and the identification of residences and critical habitat.

Finally, depending on the circumstances, proponents may be able to enter into an agreement with the minister or obtain a permit pursuant to section 73 with respect to activities otherwise prohibited. Section 73 gives the minister limited discretion to allow activities otherwise prohibited due to their risk to listed species.

The Navigation Protection Act

The *Navigation Protection Act* (NPA),[30] currently administered by Transport Canada, will apply because the Bay of Fundy is a navigable water listed in the Schedule to the Act. Pursuant to section 5, a permit is required for a work that is built or placed in, on, over, under, through or across any listed navigable water. The permitting process under section 5 involves submitting a proposal to the minister, along with a fee, at which point the minister will determine if the project 'substantially interferes' with navigable waters, assessing a variety of factors under section 5(4). Factors the minister may take into account under the new section 5(4) include the characteristics of the navigable water in question, safety of navigation, current or anticipated navigation in the navigable water, impact of the work on navigation, and the cumulative impact of the work on navigation in that navigable water.

---

30   *Navigation Protection Act* RSC 1985, c. N-22 [NPA].

The National Energy Board Act[31]

The National Energy Board (NEB) is generally responsible for energy projects of an interprovincial or international nature. Specific to tidal power projects in the Bay of Fundy, if a project crosses provincial boundaries, extends beyond the territory of a province, or includes an interprovincial (section 58.4) or international (section 58.1) power line, a certificate (section 58.16) or permit (section 58.11) must be obtained from the National Energy Board pursuant to Part III.1 of the *National Energy Board Act* (NEBA).[32] It is unlikely that the NEBA will apply to the construction and operation of most tidal energy project projects. If infrastructure improvements are needed to export some of all of the electricity generated from the tides of the Bay of Fundy to New England, a certificate of public convenience and necessity would be required. These permits and certificates may be subject to "terms and conditions respecting the matters prescribed by the regulations as the Board considers necessary or desirable in the public interest" (section 58.35). In the issuance of permits the Board may consider "the impact of the construction or operation on the environment" as well as "the effect of the power line on provinces other than those through which the line is to pass" (section 58.14).

Complexities regarding overlapping authority or interests between provincial powers and the NEB have, in some cases, been dealt with through memoranda of understanding (MOUs). For example, provincial energy bodies in both Alberta and British Columbia have an MOU with the NEB.[33] Similarly, the NEB, the Canada-Newfoundland and Labrador Offshore Petroleum Board (C-NLOPB) and the Canada-Nova Scotia Offshore Petroleum Board (C-NSOPB), together with executives from the Newfoundland and Labrador and Nova Scotia Departments of Energy and Natural Resources Canada (NRCan), have formed the Oil and Gas Administrators Advisory Council (OGAAC)[34] to efficiently deal with issues in their sector. A cooperative approach in the tidal energy sector can help address some of the complexities in identifying the respective roles of federal and provincial energy agencies and departments, but there are constitutional limits to harmonization through cooperation.[35]

---

31   *National Energy Board Act*, RSC 1985, c. N-7 [NEBA].

32   The Supreme Court of Canada considered the limits of federal jurisdiction in *Westcoast Energy v. Canada (National Energy Board)*, [1998] 1 SCR 322, 156 DLR (4th) 456.

33   The NEB-BC MOU is available online: <http://www.neb-one.gc.ca/clf-nsi/rpblctn/ctsndrgltn/mmrndmndrstndng/lgscmmssn2007-eng.pdf>. The Alberta MOU is available online: <http://www.neb.gc.ca/clf-nsi/rpblctn/ctsndrgltn/mmrndmndrstndng/lbrtnrgtltbrd200601-eng.pdf>.

34   See *Canada Oil and Gas Operations Act*, RSC 1985, c. O-7, s. 5.4

35   See Doelle et al., n. 18 above, p. 42.

3   The Provincial Regulatory Framework[36]

As discussed, the geographic extent of provincial jurisdiction over the Bay of Fundy remains unresolved. It is not surprising therefore, that there are only limited signs that the province of Nova Scotia has applied its regulatory regime below the low-water mark in marine waters around Nova Scotia. The Nova Scotia *Environment Act*, for example, has until recently not been applied to activities in the Bay of Fundy. There is some indication that this is changing. Tidal energy developments, for example, have been added as undertakings requiring approval under the provincial environmental assessment process.[37]

Other provincial laws may apply, but no formal steps have been taken to date to clarify their role. Some of the key provincial regulatory provisions that may have relevance for tidal power are briefly summarized below, all with the understanding that their actual application depends on the constitutional issues briefly raised above (i.e., is the area within or outside the province) and decisions at the provincial level to extend their application to marine waters below the low-water mark.

The Nova Scotia Environment Act

Part IV of the *Nova Scotia Environment Act* (NSEA) requires an environmental assessment for certain tidal energy projects.[38] Tidal energy projects of at least 2 MW are listed as Class I undertakings in Schedule A of the Regulations. There are other energy undertakings in the list of Class II undertakings, but they would likely not apply to most tidal power projects. An example would be a hydroelectricity generating facility with a production capacity of over 25 MW.

Class I and II undertakings have to be registered with the minister in accordance with the *Environmental Assessment Regulations*. No work can be commenced on a project that falls within Class I or II until the minister has granted an approval following the conclusion of the EA process (section 32(1)). Section 47 of the NSEA comes into play if the undertaking is also subject to the environmental assessment or other review requirements of a municipality or the federal government (as discussed below, a likely scenario for this project). Section 47 allows the minister to enter into an agreement with the other government to carry out a joint assessment.

---

36   This section is an updated version of the author's contribution to Doelle et al., id., p. 45.

37   *Environmental Assessment Regulations*, OIC 95–220 (March 21, 1995), NS Reg. 26/95, as amended up to OIC 2013–19 (January 22, 2013), NS Reg. 18/2013, Schedule A, Section D(2) (a).

38   *Nova Scotia Environment Act*, SNS 1994–95, c. 5 [NSEA].

Part V and VI of the NSEA dealing with approvals and releases will also be applicable. Part V requires an approval for any activity so designated by regulations. It establishes the process for granting approvals, imposing terms and conditions and for changes to approvals. Part VI prohibits activities that may cause an adverse effect unless authorized by an approval under Part V. These provisions combine to require approvals of listed activities and other activities that may have adverse environmental effects. Most importantly an approval can be used effectively to ensure implementation of any conditions and mitigation measures identified during the EA of a particular project. While tidal power projects would most likely not meet the description of activities currently listed under Part 9 of Division V of the activities designation regulations for approval, the minister would have the discretion under Division VI, section 29(1), of the regulations to add tidal power projects to the list, likely based upon the size or magnitude of the project, the sensitivity of the site, or the use of new technology during the proposed activity.

The Fisheries and Coastal Resources Act

The *Fisheries and Coastal Resources Act* (FCRA),[39] which, *inter alia*, deals with the approval of aquaculture operations, provides a rare example of the application of provincial laws to marine waters below the low-water mark. Depending on the precise location of the tidal resource to be developed, there may be geographic and ensuing conflicts involving existing property interests. At present, licenses or leases to carry on aquaculture are issued by the minister pursuant to the FCRA (Part V). Under section 52(1)(a) a lease "shall be granted for a specific geographic area..." The initial term of the lease is ten years "with a right of renewal by the licensee, at the Minister's option, for further terms of five years each" [section 52(2)(a)]. Under section 51(3) or 52(2)(g) the lease can be terminated for various unmet conditions.

There is potential for conflicting uses involving aquaculture and tidal projects. Relevant to this are sections 52(3) and 44(3) which both acknowledge the aquaculture leaseholder's exclusive right to the water column and sub-aquatic land described in the license. There does not appear to be a provision considering a circumstance arising during a license term where a grantee would be asked to change the location of the operation. There are provisions allowing the minister to impose certain conditions and restrictions on a lease (section 56) and for the minister to terminate a lease in the event of a breach of terms or conditions of the lease (sections 52 and 58) and for the minister to

---

39   *Fisheries and Coastal Resources Act*, SNS 1996, c. 25 [FCRA].

decide between two competing aquaculture lease applications, but there is no explicit discussion of ministerial discretion to move an aquaculture lease in the event of competing interests between aquaculture and other marine activities.

Obviously, more specific data are required in terms of development-friendly tidal power areas and existing aquaculture leases, but this potential conflict may not materialize if tidal energy is developed in areas with high current velocities that are unsuitable for aquaculture projects. Similar potential conflicting uses will have to be explored for other existing and potential uses of the Bay of Fundy, such as fishing, tourism, recreation, biodiversity, and potential for other resource extraction activities.

The Endangered Species Act

The key obligations under the *Endangered Species Act* (ESA) apply to listed endangered or threatened species.[40] The Act essentially prohibits interference with such species unless specifically authorized in the ESA or through a permit or approval. Sections 13 and 14 of the Act include the key provisions on prohibitions and permits with respect to listed species.

Listed species that may be affected by the use of coastal lands for a tidal power project include the piping plover (*Charadrius melodus*) and two species of flora indigenous to southwestern Nova Scotia bogs and wetlands – the thread-leaved sundew (*Drosera filiformis*) and the eastern mountain avens (*Geum peckii*). Consistent with the application of the Act to the low-water mark, marine species such as leatherback turtles, right whales and other endangered species found in the Bay of Fundy are not listed.[41]

Other provincial statutes may also apply depending on the landfall of related infrastructure, such as transmission lines or service infrastructure. They include the *Provincial Parks Act*, the *Beaches Act*, and the *Wilderness Areas Protection Act*.[42]

The Energy Resources Conservation Act

The purposes of the *Energy Resources Conservation Act* (ERCA) suggest that it could be utilized to play a role in the strategic development of Nova Scotia's

---

40   *Endangered Species Act*, SNS 1998, c. 11 [ESA].

41   For the most up-to-date list of wildlife species protected under the ESA in Nova Scotia as established by the Species at Risk Working Group (pursuant to s. 9), see online: <http://novascotia.ca/natr/wildlife/biodiversity/species-list.asp>.

42   *Provincial Parks Act*, RSNS 1989, c. 367; *Beaches Act*, RSNS 1989, c. 32; *Wilderness Areas Protection Act*, SNS 1998, c. 27.

tidal power resources.[43] The Act aims to regulate and ensure efficient practices in the exploration for and development, production, transmission, and transportation of energy resources (section 3(b)); provide for the economic, orderly, and efficient development in the public interest of energy resources (section 3(d)); appraise the reserves and production capacities of energy resources (section 3(e)); and appraise the need for energy resources and appraise markets outside the province for the province's energy resources (section 3(f)).

It is important to note that Section 3 does claim jurisdiction beyond the low-water mark. It states that, "This Act applies to all Nova Scotia lands, which means the land mass of Nova Scotia including Sable Island, and includes the seabed and subsoil off the shore of the land mass of Nova Scotia, the seabed and subsoil of the continental shelf and slope and the seabed and subsoil seaward from the continental shelf and slope to the limit of exploitability." The ERCA authorizes the creation of regulations pertaining to development of energy resources in Nova Scotia, which could include tidal energy. To date this legislative authority has primarily been employed to create regulations for the offshore and onshore oil and gas sector.

The Electricity Act

The *Electricity Act* (EA) has changed the landscape of Nova Scotia's electricity sector.[44] First, it authorizes regulations regarding 'renewable energy standards' in the form of a Renewable Portfolio Standard (RPS) system. This system mandates electricity providers to supply a certain proportion of electricity generated from renewable energy sources. It includes a target of 25 percent by 2015 and 40 percent by 2020.[45] The *Renewable Energy Regulations* include provisions on community feed-in tariffs, and developmental tidal array tariffs as well as tariffs for single devices. Developmental tidal arrays, as defined in section 3 of the Regulations, refer to either a single device or multiple devices in a generating facility with a production capacity of over 0.5 MW. The tariffs associated with developmental tidal arrays require the generation facility to meet a number of requirements, as set out in section 22(2). These requirements include being located in Nova Scotia, interconnecting to the electrical grid, being approved for a feed-in tariff, and meeting the definition of 'developmental tidal array' as described in the Regulations. Community feed-in tariffs

---

43   *Energy Resources Conservation Act*, RSNS 1989, c. 147, s. 1 as amended by SNS 2000, c. 12, as amended by SNS 2001, c. 15 [ERCA].

44   *Electricity Act*, 2004, SNS c. 25 [EA].

45   *Renewable Electricity Regulations*, OIC 2010–381 (12 October 2010), NS Reg. 155/2010, as amended up to OIC 2014–26 (28 January 2014), NS Reg. 14/2014.

generally have more defined requirements, as set out in section 20 of the Regulations. Section 20(1) of the Regulations and section 4A(8)(a) to (e) of the Act list a variety of approved generators that have access to a community feed-in tariff, such as universities, municipalities, co-operatives, community economic development corporations and subsidiaries of municipalities. The Regulations also require the generator to own a generation facility as well as meet all the requirements set out in section 20(3), such as being located in Nova Scotia, and conveying electricity at distribution as opposed to transmission levels, meaning at voltages less than 69 kV. Sections 19 and 21 set out how the tariffs are to be set. Section 28 details the ability of the Minister to approve or reject an application for a feed-in tariff.[46]

Once a developer has been approved for a feed-in tariff in Nova Scotia, section 32(2) of the *Renewable Electricity Regulations* requires the developer and Nova Scotia Power Inc. (NSPI) to enter into a power purchase agreement. This agreement can either be crafted from a standard form agreement prepared by the minister and NSPI or from a unique form agreement, as elaborated on in section 32(1) and (1A). A draft of the standard form agreement is available online.[47]

A 2013 hearing by the Nova Scotia Utility and Review Board (NSUARB) resulted in the adoption of a proposal from a consulting firm (Synapse Energy Economics Inc.) to develop three separate tidal energy tariff rates in Nova Scotia.[48] A developer now has the choice between the Developmental Tariff path or the Test Tariff path, but not both. Under the Developmental Tariff, developers would have access to the tariff rates for 15 years for a given tidal array, with rates set at C$530 per megawatt hour (Mwh) for the first 16,560 Mwh produced in a year, decreasing to C$420 per Mwh produced above the 16,560 Mwh per year. The Test Tariff is implemented in two phases. The Phase 1 Test Tariff, available only to single-turbine projects located at FORCE, and lasting for a term of three years, has a rate of C$575 per Mwh for the first 3,300 Mwh produced in a year, decreasing to C$455 per Mwh afterwards. Once the three-year term on Phase 1 has expired, the developer will have access to Phase 2 test rate, which lasts for a 15-year term. Phase 2 rates apply to either a single unit or an array of turbines, and offer C$495 per Mwh for the first

---

46   Id., s. 24A(1).

47   Nova Scotia, "Power Purchase Agreement for Renewable Energy (DRAFT)" (Halifax: Department of Energy, 2012), available online: <http://0-fs01.cito.gov.ns.ca.legcat.gov.ns.ca/deposit/b10653478.pdf>.

48   Tidal Energy Feed-in Tariffs (Re), 2013 NSUARB 214 (CanLII).

16,560 Mwh per year, decreasing to C$375 per Mwh for anything produced after that in a year.

Second, the Act mandated NSPI to develop an Open Access Transmission Tariff (OATT). It was intended to open the Nova Scotia electricity market to more inter-provincial and international import and export, while also allowing 'any competitive supplier' to supply electricity to NSPI or one of the six municipal electricity suppliers. This means that a tidal project, whether privately or publicly owned and operated, will be able to sell electricity generated to NSPI or to any of the municipal suppliers, all of whom must comply with the RPS. The OATT was approved by the NSUARB, and came into effect in 2005, while the *Electricity Act* came into effect in 2007. The OATT is accessible to registered users through the online Open Access Same-time Information System (OASIS).[49]

In 2013, the government of Nova Scotia passed the *Electricity Reform (2013) Act*, a bill that amended the *Electricity Act*.[50] This Act focuses on the ability of retail suppliers of electricity to sell directly to retail customers. For the purposes of the Act, 'retail suppliers' are defined as a person other than NSPI or a municipal utility that is authorized to sell renewable, low-impact electricity. This amendment allows smaller producers of electricity to enter into the market, eliminating the monopoly that NSPI and municipal producers of electricity have in the province.

The *Wholesale Market Rules Regulations* under the *Electricity Act* may also affect the development of tidal energy in Nova Scotia.[51] These regulations require all generating facilities in the province to register with the Nova Scotia Power System Operator (NSPSO), and enter into a participation agreement with NSPSO. This participation agreement allows the facility to receive service under the open access transmission tariff. In this regard, any new tidal generating facilities would have to register under these regulations, provided they fit the requirements under the regulations.

The Public Utilities Act

The *Public Utilities Act* (*Utilities Act*) primarily deals with the procedural activities of the Utility and Review Board (UARB) and its regulatory powers over

---

49   Nova Scotia Power Inc., *Open Access Transmission Tariff* (Nova Scotia: NSPI, 2005), available online: <http://oasis.nspower.ca/site/media/oasis/ApprovedOATT052005.pdf>.

50   Bill 1, *An Act to Amend Chapter 25 of the Acts of 2004, the Electricity Act, Respecting the Sale of Renewable Energy*, 1st session, 62nd General Assembly, Nova Scotia, 2013 (Assented to 12 December 2013).

51   *Wholesale Market Rules Regulations*, NS Reg. 36/2007.

NSPI.[52] This Act may be implicated in a number of ways depending on the specifics of the construction process, as well as the parties involved. Currently, according to section 3B of the *Electricity Act*, the authority of the UARB does not extend to the market for tidal power produced by private producers independent of NSPI. In the context of the UARB rate hearings in 2004, the Board found that the *Utilities Act* did not authorize the Board to consider the appropriateness of rates offered by NSPI to independent energy producers.[53] For tidal power in Nova Scotia, this would suggest that the market, not the government, currently controls the price to be paid to producers (at least for provincial markets). Given that NSPI is still essentially a vertically integrated monopoly, it controls the price, subject only to UARB oversight as to whether NSPI has paid more than necessary for its power, although some measure of change has occurred in the way of the *Electricity Reform Act*. Increasing the percentage of renewable energy required under the existing RPS might be a way to influence the price NSPI would be willing to pay for tidal power. If the RPS is sufficiently high that NSPI cannot meet it using wind alone, it may be required to purchase tidal even if the price was higher than wind. One other factor that may influence the amount of tidal energy necessary to fulfill the RPS is the requirement of NSPI to purchase 20 percent of the electricity generated at the Muskrat Falls Generating Station under section 6A(2)(c) of the *Renewable Electricity Regulations*, provided the infrastructure is complete, in normal operation, and the UARB has approved the assessment under the *Maritime Link Act*. Other factors, such as the predictability of tidal energy would likely also influence NSPI's choice. An alternative would be to determine a fixed or minimum price for each form of renewable energy. This is generally referred to as the feed-in tariff approach. It would in effect allow the province to set the price to be paid by NSPI for tidal power produced.[54]

The Environmental Goals and Sustainable Prosperity Act

The *Environmental Goals and Sustainable Prosperity Act* (EGSPA) sets the overall goal of fully integrating environmental sustainability and economic

---

52   *Public Utilities Act*, RSNS 1989, c. 380 [Utilities Act].

53   Rather it is solely concerned with charges to be paid by customers. See *Nova Scotia Utility and Review Board, In the Matter of the Public Utilities Act, and, In the Matter of Nova Scotia Power Incorporated and complaints from seven individuals concerning the rates and conditions set out by NSPI in its solicitation for renewable energy under 2 MW* (2004). See online: <http://www.canlii.org/ns/cas/nsuarb/2004/2004nsuarb118.html>.

54   See J. Lipp, "Lessons for Effective Renewable Electricity Policy from Denmark, Germany and the United Kingdom," *Energy Policy* 35 (2007): 5481–5495.

prosperity through continuous improvement in measures of social, environmental, and economic indicators of prosperity.[55] The Act sets more specific targets that are relevant to the development of tidal energy, including goals with respect to greenhouse gas emissions and the use of renewable energy for the generation of electricity. The overall goals and specific targets do not directly translate into decisions on whether, where, when and under what conditions to encourage or permit tidal power development, because they treat renewable energy collectively, but they provide important context for future decisions on this emerging industry.

Pending Marine Renewable Energy (MRE) Legislation

A working draft of MRE legislation is scheduled to be released in 2014. It is expected to be consistent with the Marine Renewable Energy Strategy and the recommendations in the Fournier Report.[56] A key recommendation is the need for collaboration between federal and provincial authorities to engage in a dialogue to work toward harmonization of legislation, policies, and regulations. This recommendation seeks to reduce the complexity of the regulatory system. To date, an informal One-Window Standing Committee has been used, bringing together representatives from provincial and federal departments. Although the Fournier Report concluded that the One-Window Committee was an important first step, the Report suggests evolving this approach to keep pace with the increasing rate of development.

4   The SEA Process

In this section, we consider the role of a SEA carried out in 2007–08 and updated in 2013 in the governance of tidal energy in the Bay of Fundy. The SEA was initiated in 2007 to consider whether, where, and under what conditions offshore renewable energy developments should be encouraged and approved in the Bay of Fundy. The review of the SEA process will take place in three stages. The SEA process is first outlined. The outcomes of the SEA are then considered.

---

55   *Environmental Goals and Sustainable Prosperity Act*, SNS 2007, c. 7, as amended by 2012, c. 42 [EGSPA].

56   R.O. Fournier, *Marine Renewable Energy Legislation – A Consultative Process* (*'The Fournier Report'*), (Nova Scotia: 2011). available online: <http://www.oera.ca/wp-content/uploads/2013/05/Fournier-Final-Report.pdf>.

The tidal SEA process was initiated as a result of a request by the Nova Scotia Department of Energy to the Offshore Energy Environment Research Association (OERA).[57] OERA is a not-for-profit corporation established in 2006 with funding from the province of Nova Scotia. OERA is a collaboration between the provincial government and academic institutions in Nova Scotia interested in research on the environmental implications of ocean energy development around Nova Scotia. OERA was formally asked to carry out the SEA in April 2007.

The Minister asked OERA to complete its work on the SEA within 12 months, and with a C$250,000 budget. The SEA process was placed in the hands of a subcommittee of OERA made up of 15 individuals representing the governments of Nova Scotia, New Brunswick and Canada, fishing and environmental interests, academics with backgrounds ranging from engineering and biology to law, and a retired civil servant.[58] The SEA process designed by OERA consisted of the following key components:

·   An interactive website (www.bayoffundysea.ca)
·   A newsletter published regularly throughout the SEA process
·   Informal meetings with stakeholders on request
·   Regular meetings of the OERA subcommittee to guide the process
·   A consultant hired to serve as the 'process-lead' for the SEA process
·   Six community forums held in August, 2007 in affected communities
·   Two rounds of participant support funding for community-based research
·   A background report prepared by an environmental consulting firm
·   A round table of about 25 interested stakeholders[59]

Early efforts to engage Nova Scotians were intended primarily to help identify key issues to be addressed through the SEA process. The main vehicles for identifying issues of concern were the six community forums held in August 2007 and some informal meetings with key stakeholders. The forums in particular provided important guidance to the OERA subcommittee and the process-lead on the values, concerns, and priorities of affected communities, and potentially affected industry sectors such as fisheries and tourism. To this end, participants in the forums were asked two questions:

---

57   During the 2008 SEA process, the acronym OEER was also used for the Association. The change resulted from an internal re-organization.

58   OEER, *Fundy Tidal Energy Strategic Environmental Assessment: Final Report* (Nova Scotia: OEER, 2008), p. 5.

59   Id., p. 5.

· What information is needed before decisions can be made about whether, where, and under what conditions tidal energy should be permitted or encouraged in the Bay of Fundy?
· What information are you aware of that may be relevant to this process?

In parallel with the forums, OERA hired Jacques Whitford, an environmental consulting firm, to prepare a background report on the technologies, the receiving environment, and their potential interaction. The backgrounder was intended to serve as a starting point for the SEA process. As such, it sought to identify the state of knowledge and encourage participants to consider the implications of the state of knowledge for the SEA process.

Given the short time frame and the limited resources available to carry out the SEA, there clearly was no real opportunity to fill information gaps identified. Some effort was, nevertheless, made to fund efforts by community groups to supplement the information provided through the backgrounder. Topics covered included native fisheries in the Bay of Fundy, how to enable community benefits from tidal energy development, integrated resource management in the Bay of Fundy, research on submerged ice, and the gathering of local and traditional knowledge relevant to the SEA.[60]

The round table commenced its work after the conclusion of the community forums. Interests represented at the round table include municipalities, fisheries, aquaculture, community development, environmental organizations, tourism, marine transportation, the local power utility, and tidal developers. It met a total of seven times between October 2007 and April 2008. Given the time available and the diversity of interests and perspectives, a surprising level of consensus was reached. At the same time, it must be recognized that the limited time and resources, as well as the size of the round table, made a deeper level of agreement on the substance impossible. As a result, many of the SEA recommendations are general in nature. They will require ongoing engagement of stakeholders to become meaningful and clear, and to ensure that some of the unresolved issues underlying these general recommendations are not forgotten as time passes.

Following the conclusion of the round table process, the OERA subcommittee prepared the SEA report. The report was submitted to the provincial government on 1 May 2008. A final round of hearings in May 2008 sought further feedback on this report. OERA submitted a community comment report that summarized the final feedback received by way of follow-up to the SEA report.

---

60   For information on the funding program and the results of funded initiatives, see online: <http://www.oera.ca/>.

In July 2008, the provincial government released its response to the SEA report.[61]

The provincial government accepted most of the recommendations either explicitly or in principle. This is not surprising given the close connection between the Nova Scotia Department of Energy and OERA. The province proceeded to start the work of implementing the 29 recommendations of the report. Key next steps in the development of tidal energy in the Bay of Fundy included the approval of the research facility following an environmental assessment,[62] the first testing of an in-stream tidal turbine at the research facility,[63] and efforts to improve the legislative and regulatory basis for this new industry.[64]

In 2013, the province decided to update the 2008 SEA. It commissioned a private consulting firm, AECOM, to prepare an update to the SEA. AECOM, in coordination with OERA, followed a process similar to the 2008 SEA. It started by updating the backgrounder that had formed the information basis for the 2008 SEA. AECOM struck a round table and held community meetings. It submitted its report to OERA in January 2014.

SEA Outcomes
The 2008 SEA report included 29 recommendations to the province of Nova Scotia. The recommendations were supported by all members of the OERA subcommittee and were generally supported by the round table. The following are some of the key recommendations in the 2008 SEA:

- The province should adopt and apply ten sustainability principles as a framework for decision-making on renewable energy development in the Bay of Fundy.
- Pilot in-stream tidal projects should be permitted to proceed carefully and incrementally.
- There should be ongoing consultations and participation in decision-making, and a community participation and benefits strategy should be developed.

---

61   Nova Scotia, Department of Energy, *Bay of Fundy Tidal Energy: A Response to the Strategic Environmental Assessment, NS Department of Energy* (July 2008), available online: <http://energy.novascotia.ca/resources-and-publications/document-database/>.

62   AECOM, *Environmental Assessment Registration Document–Fundy Tidal Energy Demonstration Project. Volume 1: Environmental Assessment* (10 June 2009), available online: <http://www.novascotia.ca/nse/ea/minas.passage.tidal.demonstration.asp>.

63   OpenHydro, "OpenHydro Successfully Deploys 1 MW Commercial Tidal Turbine in the Bay of Fundy," News Release (17 November 2009), available online: <http://www.openhydro.com/news/OpenHydroPR-171109.pdf>.

64   See n. 51 above.

- The province should develop new legislation and amend existing legislation to improve the regulation of this industry.
- A research agenda should be developed to fill knowledge gaps.
- Efforts should be made to maximize local benefits from any development of renewable energy in the Bay of Fundy.
- The province should place a high priority on conservation, efficiency, and to ensuring that electricity from tidal developments replaces fossil fuel-based electricity.
- The capacity of the power grid in Nova Scotia to accept power from tidal power projects needs further study.
- The potential for impacts on other users needs to be considered. The report recommends an integrated approach to resource management in the Bay of Fundy.

The provincial response was generally positive. In addition to responding to the recommendations, the government highlighted the following measures:

- The government committed to providing funding and finding other ways of encouraging the research needed to fill the information gaps identified through the SEA process.
- The province decided to proceed with a demonstration facility for in-stream tidal (FORCE) and with a demonstration program for other forms of renewable energy.
- The government committed to remove devices in case of adverse environmental effects.
- The government confirmed the need to ensure compensation agreements are developed with other users of the Bay of Fundy.
- The government confirmed its desire to encourage collaboration with all affected jurisdictions and stakeholders.[65]

The 2013 SEA update included a review of the implementation of the recommendations of the 2008 SEA. It concluded that 26 of the 29 recommendations had been implemented or were in the process of being implemented. Two of the remaining recommendations were dependent on cooperation from other jurisdictions. The most notable recommendation not implemented is the integrated regional planning process. In addition, the commitment for compensation agreements for users affected by tidal developments appears to have been abandoned.

---

65   See Fournier, n. 56 above, p. 5.

The 2013 SEA update identifies some key developments since the 2008 SEA. It concludes that tidal in-stream technology has evolved significantly since 2008. Two distinct scales of development have emerged, a commercial scale intended for power production at the lowest possible cost, and a smaller scale technology designed to meet local power needs. These scales are reflected locally in the efforts of FORCE to encourage commercial scale developments, and the efforts of Fundy Tidal Inc. to deploy smaller units in the Digby Neck area.

Knowledge gaps in terms of the social and environmental impacts largely remain. The OpenHydro unit was not in the water long enough to provide an opportunity to fill knowledge gaps regarding the interaction of the turbines with marine species. The pilots planned for the next few years, both by FORCE and in the Digby Neck area, are expected to help fill some of these gaps. Uncertainty also remains with respect to social and economic benefits, risks, and uncertainties associated with tidal developments, and opportunities to maximize these benefits. In addition, the 2013 SEA update identifies the following technical challenges:

1. Sensors and instrumentation: assessing the resource, monitoring the devices, and monitoring environmental effects;
2. Deployment and recovery: installation and maintenance of devices and cables;
3. Subsea electrical grid: to transmit and condition the electricity generated by the devices;
4. Turbines/moorings: the devices and equipment that generate the electricity and maintain the position of that equipment and related infrastructure; and,
5. Cabling and connectors: between the land-based infrastructure and the subsea grid, both for electricity and communications.[66]

The impact of the SEAs on tidal energy governance in Nova Scotia is apparent. One of the most important elements of the 2008 SEA was the constructive engagement by stakeholders. Opportunities for mutual learning were evident during the process. Developers provided valuable insight into conditions for development for a variety of technologies. Members of the fishing industry provided valuable insight into local conditions, particularly some of the high current velocity passages. Other users were able to identify concerns over potential use conflicts. Exchanges on these issues at the round table allowed

---

66   AECOM, n. 2 above , p. 58.

everyone to develop a better understanding of the range of potentially suitable sites.

It seems clear that the Nova Scotia government has taken the recommendations of the SEA seriously. While much work is still to be done, the SEA has resulted in Nova Scotia being much more prepared for the industry than it was in 2008. More aggressive renewable energy targets, feed-in-tariffs for tidal energy, an operational research facility, a tidal research network, and the expected release of a Marine Renewable Energy Act are all significant steps forward.[67]

Lessons Learned from Tidal Governance in the Bay of Fundy

This section explores the lessons that can be drawn from the Nova Scotia experience with tidal energy in the Bay of Fundy. One category of observations deals with opportunities to improve tidal energy governance in Nova Scotia, and how other jurisdictions interested in tidal energy can benefit from the experience in Nova Scotia. A second category of observations deals with lessons more broadly on how jurisdictions such as Nova Scotia can develop effective governance approaches for newly emerging industry sectors.

Perhaps the most important general observation with respect to tidal energy governance in Nova Scotia is that the SEA process has provided important guidance for governments and key stakeholders involved in the development of the industry. The SEA process was an important step forward from past practice in Nova Scotia, as it initiated a proactive approach to developing an effective governance approach.

It is encouraging that the province of Nova Scotia took this more proactive approach to tidal energy. Early indications are that the benefits include constructive relationships with other users of the areas affected by tidal developments, some regulatory coordination and review early in the evolution of the industry, good coordination between development of the industry and research to better understand impacts and risks, and broad public support for the industry.

The tidal SEA process, of course, has had its limitations. It was limited by its *ad hoc* nature. This limitation is best addressed by providing a clear legislative foundation for SEAs carried out in Nova Scotia. Such legislation, perhaps under the *Nova Scotia Environment Act*, would establish rules on when an SEA is to be

---

67   Id., p. 59.

carried out, on the process to be followed, and on the role of the SEA in guiding future decision-making.

A key element of any legislative foundation for SEA is the connection of the SEA to higher and lower tier decision-making. Higher tiers in this regard refer to decision-making that goes beyond the tidal energy industry, such as regional planning, economic development at a provincial level, and energy planning. SEA legislation should set out clear expectations for how the results of the SEA feed into higher level decision-making, and how changes in high level policy feeds into the SEA. Lower tier decision-making refers to project-level decisions in the tidal sector. A legislative foundation for SEA would include clear direction on how the SEA will guide project EAs and regulatory decisions. Federal and municipal government involvement in the SEA would be required to maximize the opportunity for proper integration of the SEA into higher and lower tier decision-making. However, even integration at the provincial level would significantly enhance the governance approach.

The tidal SEA process was also limited in terms of the time and resources available. Knowledge gaps with respect to the environmental, social, and economic implications of this industry were identified but generally not filled. A number of issues, such as which approach to tidal energy is most likely to maximize long-term benefits to Nova Scotia (particularly rural development benefits) were identified but not resolved in the 2008 SEA. It is encouraging the see the effort to update the SEA in 2013, as periodic updates provide the opportunity to track knowledge gaps and ensure adjustments to the governance approach as we learn more about the benefits, impacts, risks, and uncertainties associated with tidal energy production. Based on the 2013 update, it appears that some progress has been made, but significant knowledge gaps remain.

For these reasons alone, further implementation and refinement of the SEA will continue to be critical. It has to continue to track knowledge gaps and continue the dialogue on values and priorities and how best to pursue them. For example, the interaction of turbines with marine life remains poorly understood. It remains unclear whether it would be in the best long-term interest of the province to focus on making the Bay of Fundy a testing, research and manufacturing site for tidal technology or on producing energy at a large scale? What are the key economic opportunities associated with the industry? Are they related to the production and use of the energy produced, or are they related to research and manufacturing?

As decisions continue to be made about individual pilot projects, as experience is gained about the technical, social, economic, and environmental feasibility of tidal energy, it will be critical that communities continue to feel as informed and as involved as they were at the start in decisions about whether, where, and under what conditions tidal energy projects ought to be permitted in the Bay of Fundy. The pilots will play an important role in the decision-making process for this new industry. It will be critical that the pilots are utilized to fill in some of the information gaps, particularly gaps in the understanding of the interaction between the various technologies and the receiving environment.

Continuity in terms of transparency of decision-making and public engagement is also critical. It is clear that the tidal SEA in Nova Scotia has developed a new level of trust and expectation in terms of transparency and public engagement in decision-making. The constructive relationships developed will be at risk if the expectations are not realized as the sustainability principles developed and other recommendations are applied to individual tidal projects.

The role of government decision-makers in the SEA process must be carefully considered. It needs to be designed to ensure independence and credibility of the process on the one hand, and active engagement of key decision-makers on the other hand. As with project EAs, early triggering of the tidal SEA was key. An effective way of addressing the challenges identified with the tidal SEA would be to provide a legislative foundation for SEAs at the provincial and federal levels. Initially, the legislation will have to retain considerable flexibility to be able to adjust to experience and unforeseen circumstances. As jurisdictions gain experience with SEAs, flexibility should gradually be replaced with legislative guidance.

The absence of integrated planning in the Bay of Fundy will limit the long-term effectiveness of tidal governance in Nova Scotia. It may be reasonable for purposes of deciding on whether to move ahead with pilot projects to assume the status quo of resource use and management will and should continue. It is more difficult to see how decisions about commercial-scale developments can be made in the absence of integrated planning, even with an incremental approach. This means that an integrated planning process for the Bay of Fundy will be critical to the success of tidal energy governance as it moves from pilots to commercial scale developments.

In the end, appropriate decisions about the role of this new industry, and how to maximize long-term sustainable benefits to Nova Scotians, cannot be made until an integrated management plan is in place for the Bay of Fundy. The main role of a SEA should be to update integrated management plans in light of the evolution of this new industry, not to eliminate the need for integrated planning and management.

Changes are also warranted on the regulatory side. To date, the focus has been on the coordination of existing regulatory requirements for tidal developments in combination with some new regulatory measures to encourage tidal developments, mainly in the form of feed-in tariffs and renewable energy targets. What remains is nevertheless a patchwork of federal and provincial regulatory requirements that seem unnecessarily complex, and that are not carefully designed to meet the goals and priorities set by the SEA. The marine renewable energy legislation that is currently being drafted provides an opportunity to set out the regulatory goals and objectives in legislation and to design an effective, efficient and fair regulatory system that furthers those goals and objectives, rather than the current patchwork that is based on a range of policy objectives that pre-date the emergence of the industry.

The 2008 SEA makes several recommendations in this regard. It proposes that the legislation should encourage the development of marine renewable energy resources in a safe and environmentally sound manner. It should require interested parties to obtain licenses for the rights to develop. Such licenses should be conditional on undertaking activity that will promote timely development. The legislation should provide for immediate disclosure of all environmental information and, after appropriate confidentiality periods, disclosure of technical information related to the resource. The legislation should provide for the province to receive revenues from the licensing and/or development of the resource and provide opportunities for affected communities to benefit from the development. Finally, the SEA proposes that the legislation provide incentives for the net reductions of greenhouse gases in the province.

These are all recommendations that should be considered carefully in the design of the pending marine renewable energy legislation. Furthermore, the legislation should set clear regulatory goals and objectives consistent with the conclusions of the SEA, be fully transparent to protect the social license the industry currently enjoys, ensure effective monitoring and research is conducted to learn from the experience, and continue to engage those interested and potentially affected by this industry in the evolution of the regulatory system.

Conclusion

Tidal energy governance in Nova Scotia is largely a good news story. Through proactive efforts over the past decade, the province seems reasonably well-prepared for this emerging new industry. Considerable work remains however. In particular, it is high time for an integrated planning process for the Bay of Fundy to ensure tidal plays an appropriate role in the sustainable use of the resources the Bay of Fundy has to offer. Furthermore, the current regulatory system is complex, and not designed to further the goals and priorities identified for the industry in the SEA. The pending marine renewable energy legislation in Nova Scotia provides an opportunity to reform the regulatory system at the provincial level.

Renewable Ocean Energy and the International Law and Policy Seascape: Global Currents, Regional Surges

*Sarah McDonald and David L. VanderZwaag**

Marine & Environmental Law Institute, Schulich School of Law
Dalhousie University, Halifax, Canada

Introduction

There is an urgent need to increase global renewable energy production as a method of lowering greenhouse gas (GHG) emissions in order to avoid the more devastating effects of climate change and ocean acidification. The latest figures, from the *Fifth Assessment Report of the Intergovernmental Panel on Climate Change* (IPCC), suggest that the international community must reduce anthropogenic GHG emissions by 40 to 70 percent from 2010 levels by 2050, and should aim for near zero emissions by 2100.[1] This would likely keep temperature change below 2°C relative to pre-industrial levels, and would therefore reduce the risk of predicted effects of climate change, such as inland flooding, extreme weather events, food insecurity, and the loss of marine and coastal ecosystems and biodiversity.[2]

The development of renewable energy plays an important role in the effort to mitigate climate change. The IPCC estimates that a tripling to nearly a quadrupling of the share of zero- and low-carbon energy from renewables in the

---

* The authors acknowledge the research support of the Social Sciences and Humanities Research Council of Canada and the Marine Environmental Observation Prediction and Response Network (MEOPAR). Based at Dalhousie University, MEOPAR is part of the Networks of Centres of Excellence (NCE) program.

1 IPCC, "Summary for Policymakers," in *Climate Change 2014: Mitigation of Climate Change: Contribution of Working Group III to the Fifth Assessment Report of the Intergovernmental Panel on Climate Change*, ed. O. Edenhofer, R. Pichs-Madruga, Y. Sokona, et al. (Cambridge: Cambridge University Press, 2014), p. 13.

2 IPCC, "Summary for Policymakers," in *Climate Change 2014: Impacts, Adaptation, and Vulnerability, Part A: Global and Sectoral Aspects, Contribution of Working Group II to the Fifth Assessment Report of the Intergovernmental Panel on Climate Change*, ed. C.B. Field, V.R. Barros, D.J. Dokken, et al., (Cambridge: Cambridge University Press, 2014), p. 13.

---

global energy supply is required by 2050.[3] In light of this need, renewable energy projects, including ocean renewable energy, are bound to increase in number in the coming years and decades. For instance, the *World Energy Outlook* predicts that electricity generation from both onshore and offshore wind will increase at an average annual rate of six percent between 2011 and 2035.[4] In 2013, 1630.9 megawatts (MW)[5] of offshore wind energy were added, making the total worldwide 7045.9 MW.[6] Tidal and wave energy remain mostly in the testing phases, with over 60 tidal energy sites undergoing testing or generating commercially, and approximately the same number of wave energy sites in development.[7] Other ocean energy technologies being explored include ocean currents, salinity gradients, and ocean thermal energy conversion. Though the nascent stage of development of most ocean renewable energy means it is unlikely to contribute significantly to GHG reductions in the short term, its effectiveness is expected to increase steadily with experience and the evolution of improved technologies.[8] The IPCC has estimated that ocean energy, excluding offshore wind, has the potential to generate 7,400 exajoules (EJ)[9] per year, which exceeds both current and future human energy needs.[10]

However, though marine renewable energy devices (MREDs) are an important part of the global effort to mitigate climate change and ocean acidification, various environmental concerns surround their implementation. These include noise during construction (such as pile driving) and operations (such as vibrations from windmills and shipping support activities), reduction of visual amenities, loss of access to space, collision of wildlife with

---

3   IPCC, "Summary for Policymakers," in *Climate Change 2014: Mitigation of Climate Change: Contribution of Working Group III to the Fifth Assessment Report of the Intergovernmental Panel on Climate Change*, ed. O. Edenhofer et al. (Cambridge: Cambridge University Press, 2014), p. 13.

4   International Energy Agency, *World Energy Outlook 2013* (Paris: International Energy Agency, 2013), p. 210.

5   A megawatt is equivalent to one million watts.

6   Global Wind Energy Council, *Global Wind Report: Annual Market Update 2013* (Brussels: Global Wind Energy Council, 2014), p. 55.

7   UNEP et al., *Green Economy in a Blue World* (Nairobi: United Nations Environment Programme, 2012), pp. 61–63.

8   O. Edenhofer, R.P. Madruga, Y. Sokona, K. Seyboth, P. Matschoss, S. Kadner, T. Zwickel, P. Eickemeier, G. Hansen, S. Schlömer and C. von Stechow, ed., *Renewable Energy Sources and Climate Change Mitigation: Special Report of the Intergovernmental Panel on Climate Change* (New York: Cambridge University Press, 2012), p. 501.

9   An exajoule is equivalent to one quintillion (10^{18}) joules.

10   Edenhofer et al., n. 8 above, p. 501.

structures and turbines, interference with migratory pathways, electromagnetic fields, and changes in water quality and currents.[11]

The evaluation of environmental impacts is complicated by a number of factors. To begin with, the effects of MREDs vary in duration. Those associated with construction and decommissioning, such as seismic explorations and drilling, may have short- or medium-term impacts, whereas electromagnetic fields and the presence of the structures themselves may have long-term impacts.[12] In addition, the technologies available are highly varied in nature. For example, close to 50 different wave energy devices have been proposed, and tidal energy harvesting can involve barrages, floating turbines, and structures placed on the seabed, each of which may have specific effects.[13] Furthermore, it has not yet been determined whether the impacts are proportional to the number of devices employed or more complex.[14]

Despite the complexity of the potential environmental impacts of renewable ocean energy projects, it may be possible to mitigate or prevent a number of the issues through marine spatial planning and specific efforts tailored to the different types of devices, installations, and sites.[15] To this end, the international community has developed a governance framework to address MREDs. This article will first examine 'global currents' – the international agreements, documents, and initiatives that have emerged to oversee ocean renewable energy activities. The central 'gyre' is the 1982 United Nations Convention on the Law of the Sea (UNCLOS), which establishes the overall jurisdictional framework for ocean energy developments, granting coastal States the right to exploit such energy resources within their exclusive economic zones while also setting out various responsibilities such as the obligation to protect and preserve the marine environment.[16] Key multilateral agreements such as the Convention on Biological Diversity,[17] the Convention on the Conservation of

---

11   D. Wilhelmsson, T. Malm, R. Thompson, J. Tchou, G. Sarantakos, N. McCormick, S. Luitjens, M. Gullström, J.K. Patterson Edwards, O. Amir and A. Dubi, *Greening Blue Energy: Identifying and Managing the Biodiversity Risks and Opportunities of Offshore Renewable Energy*, ed. D. Wilhelmsson et al. (Gland: International Union for Conservation of Nature and Natural Resources, 2010), pp. 16–25.

12   *Report of the Secretary-General*, UNGAOR, 67th Session, Supp. No. 76 (a), UN Doc. A/67/79, (2012), p. 22.

13   Id.

14   Id.

15   Id., pp. 22–23.

16   United Nations Convention on the Law of the Sea, 10 December 1982, 1833 *United Nations Treaty Series* 3 [UNCLOS].

17   Convention on Biological Diversity, 5 June 1992, 1760 *United Nations Treaty Series* 79 [CBD].

Migratory Species of Wild Animals,[18] the Convention on Wetlands of International Importance,[19] and the International Whaling Convention[20] form 'upwellings'. 'Ripples' encompass the International Maritime Organization's (IMO) routeing measures and Guidelines for Safety Zones and Safety of Navigation around Offshore Installations and Structures,[21] as well as measures adopted by the International Civil Aviation Organization to regulate wind farm developments. Finally, soft 'side currents' round out the global perspective with various relevant non-legally binding documents including UN General Assembly resolutions and outcome documents from global Earth Summits.

This article will continue with a selected survey of how ocean renewable energy has been addressed at the regional level. "Regional surges" include regional sub-agreements under the Convention on Migratory Species as well as regional sea initiatives and provisions, notably from the Northeast Atlantic (OSPAR)[22] and the Mediterranean (the Barcelona Convention[23] and the Protocol on Integrated Coastal Zone Management).[24]

Global Currents

'Central Gyre': United Nations Convention on the Law of the Sea
UNCLOS provides the overall governance framework for offshore renewable energy developments by establishing both State rights and responsibilities. In terms of rights, the Convention clearly grants coastal States exclusive rights to exploit and regulate renewable energy sources in their offshore waters.[25] It is

---

18   Convention on the Conservation of Migratory Species of Wild Animals, 23 June 1979, 1651 *United Nations Treaty Series* 333 [CMS].

19   Convention on Wetlands of International Importance especially as Waterfowl Habitat, 2 February 1971, 996 *United Nations Treaty Series* 245 [Ramsar Convention].

20   International Convention for the Regulation of Whaling, 2 December 1946, 161 *United Nations Treaty Series* 72 [IWC].

21   IMO, "Guidelines for Safety Zones and Safety of Navigation Around Offshore Installations and Structures," IMO Ref. T2-OSS/2.7.1, SN.1/Circ.295 (2010).

22   The Convention for the Protection of the Marine Environment of the North-East Atlantic, 22 September 1992, 2354 *United Nations Treaty Series* 67 [OSPAR Convention].

23   Convention for the Protection of the Marine Environment and the Coastal Region of the Mediterranean, 16 February 1976, 1102 *United Nations Treaty Series* 27 [Barcelona Convention].

24   Protocol on Integrated Coastal Zone Management in the Mediterranean, 21 January 2008, available online: <http://195.97.36.231/dbases/webdocs/BCP/ProtocolICZM08_eng.pdf> [ICZM Protocol].

25   D. Leary and M. Esteban, "Climate Change and Renewable Energy from the Ocean and Tides: Calming the Sea of Regulatory Uncertainty," *The International Journal of Marine and Coastal Law* 24 (2009): 617–651 at 631.

generally accepted that coastal States have complete sovereignty over their internal waters, and there are no explicit restrictions under international law on the development or regulation of ocean energy by coastal States in these areas.[26] The relevant UNCLOS provisions, however, relate to the control exercised by coastal States in the zones outside their internal waters. Article 2 provides that the sovereignty of a coastal State extends beyond its internal waters to its territorial sea.[27] Though States do not have complete sovereignty over their exclusive economic zone (EEZ), Article 56 stipulates that coastal States maintain the sovereign right to exploit and manage the production of energy from the water, currents, and winds in these areas.[28] This provision is not exhaustive, and may therefore extend to other types of marine energy, such as bioenergy, tidal barrages, and oceanic thermal energy conversion.[29] Furthermore, coastal States have limited sovereign rights over their continental shelves. Article 80 (in combination with Articles 56 and 60) establishes the exclusive right of coastal States to construct and regulate the use of installations and structures on the continental shelf for economic purposes, including for the production of offshore renewable energy.[30] Though offshore renewable energy facilities will generally be constructed in States' internal waters, territorial sea, or EEZ (which in certain cases encompasses the continental shelf),[31] all States have the additional right to develop renewable ocean energy sources in the high seas. This is illustrated by Article 87, which provides States with the freedom to construct installations permitted under international law[32] and to lay submarine cables.[33]

UNCLOS also sets out relevant State responsibilities with regard to three main areas: marine environmental protection, international navigation, and other marine uses on the high seas. Article 192 establishes States' general

---

26   Id.

27   UNCLOS, n. 16 above, Art. 2(1).

28   Id., Art. 56(1)(a).

29   M.A. Castelos, "Marine Renewable Energies: Opportunities, Law, and Management," *Ocean Development & International Law* 45 (2014): 221–237 at 226.

30   UNCLOS, n. 16 above, Art. 80. However, if an offshore renewable energy project with no connection to the seabed were to be proposed in the water column above an extended continental shelf, the issue of whether the proposal would be subject to the freedom of the high seas regime might arise. See J. Roderburg, "Marine Aquaculture: Impacts and International Regulation," *Australian & New Zealand Maritime Law Journal* 25 (2011): 161–179 at 170–171.

31   D. Leary and M. Esteban, "Recent Developments in Offshore Renewable Energy in the Asia-Pacific Region," *Ocean Development and International Law* 42 (2011): 94–119 at 108.

32   UNCLOS, n. 16 above, Art. 87(d).

33   Id., Art. 87(c).

obligation to protect and preserve the marine environment.[34] In addition, States have various pollution prevention and control responsibilities. The definition of pollution in Article 1(4)[35] is broad enough to encompass substances introduced into the marine environment during the construction, operation, and decommissioning of ocean energy facilities, and may arguably also include noise emitted by turbines. However, it is questionable whether this definition extends to the perceived negative aesthetic impact of wind turbines.[36] Among other things, Article 194 requires States to take all necessary measures to prevent, reduce, and control pollution from any source using best practicable means and in accordance with their capabilities.[37] In addition, States must ensure both that activities under their jurisdiction or control do not cause damage by pollution to other States or their environment and that pollution from activities under their jurisdiction or control does not spread beyond areas where they exercise sovereign rights.[38] Article 194 further compels States to take necessary measures to protect and preserve rare or fragile ecosystems and the habitat of depleted, threatened, or endangered species.[39] The responsibility to carry out environmental impact assessments is contained in Article 206, which requires States to do so where planned activities under their jurisdiction or control may cause substantial pollution or significant and harmful changes to the marine environment.[40]

With regard to international navigation, UNCLOS allows coastal States to regulate shipping in the vicinity of offshore renewable energy installations subject to some restrictions. Within the territorial sea, the coastal State's sovereignty is limited by the right of innocent passage of foreign-flagged vessels.[41] It is generally accepted, however, that coastal States may install ocean energy facilities in their territorial seas provided they do not preclude or unreasonably

---

34   Id., Art. 192.

35   "(4) 'pollution of the marine environment' means the introduction by man, directly or indirectly, of substances or energy into the marine environment, including estuaries, which results or likely to result in such deleterious effects as harm to living resources and marine life, hazards to human health, hindrance to marine activities, including fishing and other legitimate uses of the sea, impairment of quality for use of sea water and reduction of amenities." Id., Art. 1(4).

36   K.N. Scott, "Tilting at Offshore Windmills: Regulating Wind Farm Development within the Renewable Energy Zone," *Journal of Environmental Law* 18, no. 1 (2006): 89–118 at 104.

37   UNCLOS, n. 16 above, Art. 194(1).

38   Id., Art. 194(2).

39   Id., Art. 194(5).

40   Id., Art. 206.

41   Id., Art. 17.

interfere with the right of innocent passage.[42] Article 21 grants coastal States broad regulatory powers to protect their offshore facilities, installations, and cables.[43] In addition, Article 22(1) allows coastal States to require foreign ships exercising their right to innocent passage through the territorial sea to use such sea lanes and traffic separation schemes as may be prescribed to ensure the safety of navigation.[44] In taking such measures, coastal States must consider the recommendations of the competent international organization (i.e., IMO), any channels customarily used for international navigation, the special characteristics of particular ships and channels, and the density of traffic.[45] Furthermore, States are required to clearly indicate sea lanes and traffic separation schemes on navigational charts.[46]

In the EEZ and on the continental shelf, Articles 60 and 80 establish that coastal States must give due notice of the construction of offshore installations and structures, and maintain a permanent means for giving warning of their presence.[47] In addition, though coastal States may establish reasonable safety zones around offshore installations, these zones must not exceed a distance of 500 meters around each structure except as authorized by generally accepted international standards or recommended by the competent international organization.[48] The IMO has not yet adopted standards on this subject.[49] Finally, due notice must be given of the safety zones, and offshore installations and structures and safety zones around them may not be established where they might interfere with the use of recognized sea lanes essential to international navigation.[50]

Lastly, UNCLOS outlines States' responsibilities towards other marine uses on the high seas. When engaging in any ocean renewable energy activity on the high seas, Article 87(2) requires States to have due regard for both the interests of other States in the exercise of their freedoms and for the rights of other States to explore for or exploit minerals in the deep seabed.[51] In addition, Article 113 provides that every State has the obligation to make it an offence

---

42 Leary and Esteban, n. 25 above, p. 633.
43 UNCLOS, n. 16 above, Art. 21.
44 Id., Art. 22(1).
45 Id., Art. 22(3); Leary and Esteban, n. 31 above, p. 109.
46 Id., Art. 22(4).
47 Id., Arts. 60(3) and 80.
48 Id., Arts. 60(4), 60(5) and 80.
49 Castelos, n. 29 above, p. 226.
50 UNCLOS, n. 16 above, Arts. 60(5), 60(7) and 80.
51 Id., Art. 87(2).

under its national law for its flagged ships or persons under its jurisdiction to willfully or negligently break or injure a high seas submarine cable.[52]

'Upwellings': Key Multilateral Environmental Agreements

The international community has addressed renewable ocean energy both directly and indirectly through several multilateral agreements. The key environmental agreements that will be addressed in the following section are the Convention on Biological Diversity (CBD), the Convention on Migratory Species (CMS), the Convention on Wetlands of International Importance (Ramsar Convention), and the International Whaling Convention (IWC). The parties to each of these agreements have produced decisions and other documents which, while aiming to fulfill the objectives of the conventions themselves, also contribute to the establishment of a global governance framework for marine renewable energy. The following section reviews the relevant documents and discusses the significance of their overall contribution to the regulation of the adverse environmental impacts of renewable ocean energy.

Convention on Biological Diversity

The CBD does not specifically address marine renewable energy. However, the Convention and subsequent decisions and initiatives made pursuant to the Convention are relevant in three main areas. The first is with regard to environmental impact assessment (EIA) and strategic environmental assessment (SEA). In particular, Article 14(1)(a) of the CBD requires parties to introduce appropriate environmental impact procedures for proposed projects that are likely to have significant adverse impacts on biological diversity with a view to avoiding or minimizing such effects.[53] In addition, Article 14(1)(b) requires the implementation of appropriate arrangements to ensure that the environmental consequences of programmes and policies that are likely to have significant adverse effects on biological diversity are duly taken into account.[54]

In 2006, the CBD issued the Voluntary Guidelines on Biodiversity-Inclusive Impact Assessment, which outline methods for tailoring EIA and SEA processes to address biodiversity in marine and coastal areas, including areas beyond national jurisdiction.[55] These guidelines were updated in 2012 by the

---

52   Id., Art. 113.

53   Id., Art. 14(1)(a).

54   Id., Art. 14(1)(b).

55   CBD Conference of the Parties, UNEP/CBD/COP Decision VIII/28, "Voluntary Guidelines on Biodiversity-Inclusive Impact Assessment," 8th Ordinary Meeting of the COP, March 2006.

Revised Voluntary Guidelines for the Consideration of Biodiversity in Environmental Impact Assessments and Strategic Environmental Assessments in Marine and Coastal Areas.[56] Though the revised guidelines do not explicitly mention offshore renewable energy, certain provisions are especially relevant. For example, with regard to EIA, the guidelines urge the application of the precautionary approach in decision-making in cases of scientific uncertainty where there is a significant risk of harm to biodiversity. In addition, the guidelines recommend including noise emissions and activities in ecological corridors in screening criteria for determining the need for and required level of EIA. With regard to SEA, the guidelines suggest the need to both apply SEA where a proposed policy, plan, or programme substantially affects the occupation of water areas, and to ensure public participation and transparency in decision-making.

The second relevant CBD initiative area relates to ocean noise.[57] In 2010, the Conference of the Parties (COP) recognized ocean noise as an emerging issue requiring increased attention.[58] Subsequently, in 2012, a Scientific Synthesis Report on the Impacts of Underwater Noise on Marine and Coastal Biodiversity and Habitats was prepared under the auspices of the CBD Secretariat.[59] This report reviews both the numerous sources of ocean noise, including offshore wind farms, and the state of scientific knowledge on the impacts of ocean

---

56   CBD Conference of the Parties, UNEP/CBD/COP Decision XI/18, "Revised Voluntary Guidelines for the Consideration of Biodiversity in Environmental Impact Assessments and Strategic Environmental Assessments in Marine and Coastal Areas," 11th Ordinary Meeting of the COP, Oct. 2012.

57   The following are additional relevant CBD decisions on ocean noise: CBD Conference of the Parties, UNEP/CBD/COP Decision X/29, "Marine and Coastal Biodiversity," 10th Ordinary Meeting of the COP, October 2010; CBD Conference of the Parties, UNEP/CBD/ COP Decision XI/18, "Marine and Coastal Biodiversity: Sustainable Fisheries and Addressing Adverse Impacts of Human Activities, Voluntary Guidelines for Environmental Assessment, and Marine Spatial Planning," 11th Ordinary Meeting of the COP, October 2012. Decision X/29 asks the Executive Secretary to gather and synthesize the available scientific information on anthropogenic underwater noise and its effects on marine life. In Decision XI/18, the parties welcome the Secretary's report and encourage parties and other governments to take various actions, including promoting research and awareness of ocean noise as an issue.

58   CBD Conference of the Parties, UNEP/CBD/COP Decision X/13, "New and Emerging Issues," 10th Ordinary Meeting of the COP, October 2010.

59   CBD Subsidiary Body on Scientific, Technical and Technological Advice, UNEP/CBD/ SBSTTA/16/INF/12, "Scientific Synthesis on the Impacts of Underwater Noise on Marine and Coastal Biodiversity and Habitats," 16th Meeting of the SBSTTA, May 2012.

noise on marine biodiversity. In addition, it provides an overview of the complex array of global and regional efforts to understand the effect of ocean noise and summarizes possible mitigation measures. Also in 2012, the COP requested that the Executive Secretary organize an expert workshop on underwater noise.[60] This workshop took place in February 2014 at the IMO headquarters in London. The aim of the workshop was for participants to share knowledge on underwater noise and its impacts on marine and coastal biodiversity, and to develop practical guidance on how to best minimize and mitigate its significant adverse effects.[61]

Finally, the third relevant CBD initiative area is marine spatial planning (MSP). The parties addressed this issue in Decision X/29 on coastal and marine biodiversity.[62] This decision invited parties and other governments to increase efforts to apply marine spatial planning tools, and requested the Executive Secretary to synthesize information on national and international experiences with MSP. The Synthesis Document on the Experience and Use of Marine Spatial Planning was subsequently published in 2012.[63] Furthermore, at the COP in 2012, the parties passed Decision XI/18 which called for efforts such as the development of a web-based information sharing system on MSP, the convening of an expert workshop to provide consolidated practical guidance and a toolkit for MSP, and the organization of training workshops on MSP (especially for developing country parties).[64]

Convention on Migratory Species

The CMS addresses MREDs through Convention commitments, resolutions, and regional sub-agreements (though the latter will be discussed under "Regional Surges"). The Convention itself lists numerous marine species, including over a dozen cetaceans, on the endangered migratory species list in Appendix I, and over 40 cetaceans in Appendix II, which consists of species with an unfavorable conservation status or those that would significantly benefit from international cooperation.[65] There is evidence that cetaceans may be

---

60   CBD Conference of the Parties, UNEP/CBD/COP Decision XI/18, n. 57 above.

61   CBD Expert Meeting, UNEP/CBD/MCB/EM/2014/1/2, "Report of the Expert Workshop on Underwater Noise and Its Impacts on Marine and Coastal Biodiversity," February 2014.

62   CBD Conference of the Parties, UNEP/CBD/COP Decision X/29, n. 57 above.

63   Secretariat of the Convention on Biological Diversity, *Marine Spatial Planning in the Context of the Convention on Biological Diversity: A study carried out in response to CBD 10 decision X/29*, CBD Tech. Series No. 68 (2012).

64   CBD Conference of the Parties, UNEP/CBD/COP Decision XI/18, n. 57 above.

65   CMS, n. 18 above, appendix I–II.

especially sensitive to MREDs.[66] For endangered migratory species listed in Appendix I, Article III requires parties that are Range States to conserve and restore important habitats and to prevent, remove, compensate for, or minimize the adverse effects of activities or obstacles that seriously impede or prevent the migration of the species.[67] Article IV urges Range States to conclude further conservation and management agreements for species listed in Appendix II.[68]

The COP has adopted several resolutions that apply to offshore renewable energy developments, some of which explicitly address various marine renewable energy technologies. The first relevant resolution, Resolution 7.5 on Wind Turbines and Migratory Species, was adopted in 2002 and addresses the potential risks of marine wind farm installations.[69] Unique risks of offshore wind energy include large numbers of turbines per farm: a wind farm may number up to several hundred turbines with heights of up to 150 meters. Wind farms may have a number of adverse effects on migratory species and may even present obstacles to flyways. The resolution therefore calls on parties to identify areas where migratory species are vulnerable to wind turbines and to apply comprehensive strategic environmental protection procedures where major developments of wind turbines are proposed, in order to identify appropriate construction sites. Furthermore, it suggests that parties assess the cumulative environmental impacts of installed wind turbines on migratory species and use the precautionary principle when developing wind turbine plants.

A second key CMS resolution is Resolution 9.19 on Adverse Anthropogenic Marine/Ocean Noise Impacts on Cetaceans and Other Biota.[70] This resolution urges parties to control the impact of noise emissions in habitats of vulnerable species and in areas where marine mammals or other endangered species may be concentrated. In addition, it advises that parties both consult with marine renewable energy companies and scientific researchers and recommend best practices for noise pollution avoidance or mitigation.

---

66 S. Dolman and M. Simmonds, "Towards Best Environmental Practices for Cetacean Conservation in Developing Scotland's Marine Renewable Energy," *Marine Policy* 34 (2010): 1021–1027 at 1021.

67 CMS, n. 18 above, Art. 3.

68 Id., Art. 4.

69 CMS Conference of the Parties, UNEP/CMS Resolution 7.5, "Wind Turbines and Migratory Species," 7th Meeting of the COP, September 2002.

70 CMS Conference of the Parties, UNEP/CMS Resolution 9.19, "Adverse Anthropogenic Marine/Ocean Noise Impacts on Cetaceans and Other Biota," 9th Meeting of the COP, December 2008.

The parties passed a second resolution addressing underwater noise at the 2011 COP. Resolution 10.24 on Further Steps to Abate Underwater Noise Pollution for the Protection of Cetaceans and Other Migratory Species reaffirms the need for further internationally coordinated research on the impacts of underwater noise and urges parties to develop an appropriate regulatory framework or to implement relevant measures to ensure a reduction or mitigation of anthropogenic underwater noise.[71] It further recommends that parties use noise reduction techniques for offshore activities, including air-filled cofferdams, bubble curtains, pile drilling (as opposed to pile driving), and alternate foundation types such as floating platforms or gravity foundations.

Finally, Resolution 10.19 on Migratory Species Conservation in the Light of Climate Change urges parties to develop environmental sensitivity and zoning maps that include critical sites for migratory species as an essential tool for selecting sites for climate change mitigation projects.[72] It further calls on parties and the energy sector to undertake post-construction monitoring of the environmental impacts of climate change mitigation projects (especially wind power), and encourages the minimization of migratory species mortality due to renewable energy structures through, for example, short-term shutdowns of MREDs or the modification of wind turbine speeds.

An additional resolution on Renewable Energy and Migratory Species, which may endorse new guidelines, appears likely to be adopted at the 11th CMS COP in November 2014. The proposed guidelines, Renewable Energy Technologies and Migratory Species: Guidelines for Sustainable Deployment, would encourage the application of SEA and EIA to ocean energy projects.[73]

Convention on Wetlands of International Importance

Parties to the Ramsar Convention have emphasized the need to consider the protection of wetland ecosystems as the number of renewable energy projects continues to increase. For example, Resolution XI.10 on Wetlands and Energy Issues provides guidance for addressing the impacts of the energy sector,

---

71   CMS Conference of the Parties, UNEP/CMS Resolution 10.24, "Further Steps to Abate Underwater Noise Pollution for the Protection of Cetaceans and Other Migratory Species," 10th Meeting of the COP, November 2011.

72   CMS Conference of the Parties, UNEP/CMS Resolution 10.19, "Migratory Species Conservation in the Light of Climate Change," 10th Meeting of the COP, November 2011.

73   CMS Scientific Council, UNEP/CMS/ScC18/Doc.10.2.2, "Renewable Energy Technologies and Migratory Species: Guidelines for Sustainable Deployment," 18th Meeting of the Scientific Council, July 2014.

including tidal and wave energy projects, on wetlands.[74] Among other things, it recommends the rigorous application of SEA and EIA processes to proposed renewable energy projects that may alter the ecological character of wetlands, and urges the adoption of a precautionary approach when energy proposals may seriously or irreversibly impact wetlands of international importance.

International Convention for the Regulation of Whaling

Finally, the IWC has addressed the adverse environmental effects of marine renewable energy through the work of its Scientific Committee. In particular, the Scientific Committee has discussed and studied the issue of underwater anthropogenic noise associated with renewable ocean energy projects since 2003.[75] In 2010, the Committee strongly recommended that countries cooperate to limit the impacts of MREDs on marine wildlife.[76] The next year, the Committee emphasized the importance of properly assessing the effectiveness of measures aimed at mitigating the effects of pile driving sound on cetaceans.[77] More recently, in 2012, the Committee endorsed the conclusions and recommendations of a 2012 IWC Workshop on Interactions between Marine Renewable Energy Projects and Cetaceans Worldwide.[78] The Workshop

---

74   Ramsar Convention Conference of the Parties, Ramsar Resolution XI.10, "Wetlands and Energy Issues," 11th Meeting of the COP, July 2012.

75   The following Scientific Committee reports have examined the adverse effects of ocean noise on cetaceans: IWC Scientific Committee, SC/55, "Report of the Scientific Committee," 55th Meeting of the Scientific Committee, May–June 2003; IWC Scientific Committee, SC/56, "Report of the Scientific Committee," 56th Meeting of the Scientific Committee, June–July 2004; IWC Scientific Committee, SC/57, "Report of the Scientific Committee," 57th Meeting of the Scientific Committee, May–June 2005; IWC, SC/58, "Report of the Scientific Committee," 58th Meeting of the Scientific Committee, May–June 2006; IWC, SC/59, "Report of the Scientific Committee," 59th Meeting of the Scientific Committee, May 2007; IWC, SC/60, "Report of the Scientific Committee," 60th Meeting of the Scientific Committee, June 2008; IWC, SC/61, "Report of the Scientific Committee," 61st Meeting of the Scientific Committee, June 2009; IWC, SC/62, "Report of the Scientific Committee," 62nd Meeting of the Scientific Committee, June 2010; IWC, SC/63, "Report of the Scientific Committee," 63rd Meeting of the Scientific Committee, June 2011; IWC, SC/64, "Report of the Scientific Committee," 64th Meeting of the Scientific Committee, June 2012; IWC, SC/65, "Report of the Scientific Committee," 65th Meeting of the Scientific Committee, June 2013; IWC, SC/66, "Report of the Scientific Committee," 66th Meeting of the Scientific Committee, May 2014.

76   IWC Scientific Committee, SC/62, n. 75 above.

77   IWC Scientific Committee, SC/63, n. 75 above.

78   IWC Scientific Committee, SC/64, n. 75 above. In its 2013 report, the Scientific Committee evaluated the impacts of the workshop in question on policy-making: IWC Scientific Committee, SC/65, n. 75 above.

concluded, among other things, that Parties must take a strategic approach to planning MREDs, and in particular must consider the transboundary nature of cetacean behavior.[79] Furthermore, it highlighted the necessity of a staged approach to development in order to be adequately precautionary in light of the uncertainties surrounding the environmental impacts of MREDs. The Workshop also recommended that parties determine the overall noise tolerance for each region based on the best available cetacean science and refrain from exceeding that limit.

'Ripples' from the International Maritime Organization (IMO) and the International Civil Aviation Organization (ICAO)

Though they do not explicitly discuss the potential adverse environmental effects of renewable ocean energy, both the Convention on International Civil Aviation (Chicago Convention) and other relevant documents released by the IMO and the ICAO propose further restrictions on marine renewable energy developments. These relate primarily to minimizing any possible threats that ocean energy structures may pose to international shipping and civil aviation. The following section discusses the content of the pertinent IMO and ICAO documents and assesses their contribution to the broader MRED governance framework.

International Maritime Organization

The IMO is relevant to offshore renewable energy developments in two main ways. First, the International Convention for the Safety of Life at Sea (SOLAS Convention) recognizes the IMO as the only international body with the authority to establish traffic separation schemes and other ship routeing systems in major shipping areas.[80] Therefore, countries that wish to route international shipping away from ocean energy structures in the EEZ must work through the IMO for routeing measures. In addition, these countries must consider the IMO's Guidelines for Safety Zones and Safety of Navigation around Offshore Installations and Structures. Among other things, these Guidelines urge States to indicate all permanent offshore installations and structures on appropriate navigational charts, and request governments to depict designated

---

79   IWC Scientific Committee, SC/64/Rep6, "Report of the Workshop on Interactions between Marine Renewable Projects and Cetaceans Worldwide," 64th Meeting of the Scientific Committee, June 2012.

80   International Convention for the Safety of Life at Sea, 1 November 1974, 1184 *United Nations Treaty Series* 278, Chap. 5, reg. 10.

safety zones around offshore structures or installations on navigational charts using the legends, symbols, and notes recommended by the International Hydrographic Organization.[81]

The IMO has also minimally addressed the issue of noise from commercial ships, including those used to service renewable ocean energy developments. In April 2014, the Organization issued the Guidelines for the Reduction of Underwater Noise from Commercial Shipping to Address Adverse Impacts on Marine Life. This second relevant set of guidelines emphasizes the need to design the propellers, hulls, and onboard machinery of new ships to minimize noise, and urges proper maintenance such as propeller polishing and underwater hull surface cleaning to help reduce noise emanating from existing ships.[82] Furthermore, it suggests making speed reductions and precautionary routeing decisions to avoid sensitive marine areas, including well-known marine life habitats or migratory pathways.[83]

International Civil Aviation Organization

The Chicago Convention and related documents published by the ICAO establish specific requirements and recommendations for wind farm developments. Though the Chicago Convention does not specifically refer to offshore wind turbines, the rules it enacts with regard to wind turbines more generally are certainly applicable to marine wind farms given the heights these installations may reach in civil airspace.[84] The goal of these stipulations is to minimize the threat posed by wind turbines to civilian aircraft. For example, Section 6.2.4.1 of Annex 14 requires that wind turbines be marked and/or lighted if they are determined to constitute obstacles as defined in Section 1.1.[85] Sections 6.2.4.2, 6.2.4.3, and 6.2.4.4 elaborate on this requirement with recommendations for the types of markings and lighting to be used. Section 6.2.4.2 advises that the rotor blades, nacelle, and upper two-thirds of the supporting masts of all wind turbines be painted white.[86] With regard to lighting, Section 6.2.4.3 suggests

---

81   IMO, SN.1/Circ.295 (2010), n. 21 above, Arts. 2 and 4.3.

82   IMO Marine Environmental Protection Committee, MEPC.1/Circ.833, "Guidelines for the Reduction of Underwater Noise from Commercial Shipping to Address Adverse Impacts on Marine Life," 66th Session, September 2014, pp. 3–5.

83   Id., p. 6.

84   Castelos, n. 29 above, p. 227.

85   Convention on International Civil Aviation, 7 December 1944, 15 *United Nations Treaty Series* 295, Annex 14 Arts. 1.1 and 6.2.4.1.

86   Id., Annex 14 Art. 6.2.4.2.

among other things that when lighting is deemed necessary, medium-intensity obstacle lights should be used.[87] Finally, Section 6.2.4.4 recommends that obstacle lights be installed in such a manner as to provide an unobstructed view for aircraft approaching from any direction.[88]

In 2009, the ICAO released the second edition of the European Guidance Material on Building Restricted Areas.[89] This document provides direction for determining whether a structure's physical presence may have a negative impact on the availability or quality of communications, navigation and surveillance (CNS) signals of various ICAO-recognized facilities. It outlines a two-step process for the approval of buildings and other structures (such as wind turbines) that may adversely affect CNS facilities. Step one is to use the general input screening method to determine whether the application may be approved directly or should be passed to the appropriate engineering authorities.[90] Structures requiring further study then move on to step two, during which the engineering authorities in question carry out a detailed analysis of all aspects of the CNS facility to be protected and of the possible effects of the proposed structure on the CNS signal.[91]

Soft 'Side Currents': Non-legally Binding Documents

In addition to legally binding conventions and related documents, the international governance framework for marine renewable energy comprises various non-legally binding recommendations and commitments. These can be found in the outcome documents from the UN Earth Summits, UN General Assembly (UNGA) resolutions, and the International Renewable Energy Agency's (IRENA) ocean energy technology briefs. As discussed in the following section, through these documents parties to each of the three international bodies have addressed not only the importance of expanding the use of renewable ocean energy technologies, but have noted the potential adverse environmental impacts of MREDs and made recommendations for their prevention and mitigation.

Earth Summits

The UN has convened an Earth Summit every ten years since 1992. The outcome documents from each of these Summits, though they do not directly

---

87   Id., Annex 14 Art. 6.2.4.3.

88   Id., Annex 14 Art. 6.2.4.4.

89   ICAO, ICAO EUR DOC 15, "European Guidance Material on Managing Building Restricted Areas," September 2009, 2nd ed.

90   Id., p. 3.

91   Id.

address marine renewable energy, encourage the increased development and use of marine renewable energy technologies as a method of mitigating climate change. The 1992 UN Conference on Environment and Development (UNCED) resulted in the adoption of Agenda 21, which establishes a global partnership for sustainable development.[92] As part of this partnership, Agenda 21 contains numerous recommendations for action by States and multilateral organizations, including encouraging the environmentally sound use of renewable sources of energy.[93] Subsequent provisions require States to take various measures in accordance with UNCLOS to prevent, reduce, and control the degradation of the marine environment.[94] These measures include, for example, ensuring adequate prior assessment of activities that may have significant adverse environmental effects.[95] In combination with the provisions on the environmentally responsible use of renewable energy, these requirements establish the relevance of Agenda 21 to MREDs.

The 2002 World Summit on Sustainable Development resulted in the Johannesburg Plan of Implementation. This document does not address the potential adverse environmental impacts of renewable energy, but simply calls for the development and dissemination of renewable energy technologies with the aim of increasing their share of the global energy mix.[96] This appeal is further emphasized in the Rio+20 outcome document *The Future We Want*, which reaffirms the conference participants' support for increasing the use of renewable energy sources as a method of addressing climate change.[97]

United Nations General Assembly

The UNGA has not adopted any resolutions that directly address the potential adverse environmental effects of marine renewable energies. However, several recent resolutions have endorsed the conclusions of the three Earth Summits discussed above, including the need to expand the use of renewable energy.[98]

---

92   United Nations Conference on Environment and Development, UN Doc A/Conf.151/26, "Agenda 21," June 1992, para. 1.1.

93   Id., para. 4.18(e).

94   Id., para. 17.22.

95   Id., para. 17.22(b).

96   World Summit on Sustainable Development, UN Doc A/Conf.199/20, "Johannesburg Plan of Implementation," 2002, para. 20(c).

97   United Nations Conference on Sustainable Development, UN Doc A/Res/66/288, "The Future We Want," June 2012, paras. 127–128.

98   Earlier resolutions on this subject not mentioned above include: UN General Assembly, Resolution 61/195, "Implementation of Agenda 21, the Programme for the Further Implementation of Agenda 21 and the outcomes of the World Summit on Sustainable

Resolutions 63/212, 64/236, and 65/152 each call on governments and both international and regional organizations to ensure the effective implementation of the commitments adopted at the World Summit on Sustainable Development.[99] These resolutions also specifically demand the fulfillment of the provisions contained in the Johannesburg Plan of Implementation.[100] In addition, Resolutions 67/203 and 68/210 approve the outcome document of Rio+20 and urge it to be implemented promptly.[101]

The UN General Assembly has also adopted a series of resolutions on the promotion of new and renewable sources of energy.[102] For example, Resolution 64/206 stresses the need to increase the share of renewable energy sources in the global energy mix.[103] More recently, Resolution 67/215 emphasizes that increasing the use of renewable energy is essential for sustainable development, and encourages governments to ensure the promotion and use of renewable energy technologies.[104]

Development," 20 December 2006; UN General Assembly, Resolution 62/189, "Implementation of Agenda 21, the Programme for the Further Implementation of Agenda 21 and the outcomes of the World Summit on Sustainable Development," 19 December 2007.

99   UN General Assembly, Resolution 63/212, "Implementation of Agenda 21, the Programme for the Further Implementation of Agenda 21, and the outcomes of the World Summit on Sustainable Development," 19 December 2008, para. 3; UN General Assembly, Resolution 64/236, "Implementation of Agenda 21, the Programme for the Further Implementation of Agenda 21, and the outcomes of the World Summit on Sustainable Development," 24 December 2009, para. 3; UN General Assembly, Resolution 65/152, "Implementation of Agenda 21, the Programme for the Further Implementation of Agenda 21 and the outcomes of the World Summit on Sustainable Development," 20 December 2010, para. 4.

100 Id.

101 UN General Assembly, Resolution 67/203, "Implementation of Agenda 21, the Programme for the Further Implementation of Agenda 21 and the outcomes of the World Summit on Sustainable Development and of the United Nations Conference on Sustainable Development," 21 December 2012, para. 1; UN General Assembly, Resolution 68/210, "Implementation of Agenda 21, the Programme for the Further Implementation of Agenda 21 and the outcomes of the World Summit on Sustainable Development and the United Nations Conference on Sustainable Development," 20 December 2013, para. 1.

102 Another notable resolution not mentioned above is the following: UN General Assembly, Resolution 62/197, "Promotion of New and Renewable Sources of Energy," 19 December 2007. Among other things, this resolution emphasizes the need to expand research and development in support of renewable energy.

103 UN General Assembly, Resolution 64/206, "Promotion of New and Renewable Sources of Energy," 21 December 2009, para. 2.

104 UN General Assembly, Resolution 67/215, "Promotion of New and Renewable Sources of Energy," 21 December 2012, paras. 5 and 8.

Finally, the UNGA has referred specifically to marine renewable energy in several other resolutions. Through Resolution 65/37 the parties decided that the thirteenth meeting of the Informal Consultative Process on Oceans and the Law of the Sea would focus on renewable ocean energy.[105] The UNGA recalled this decision in Resolution 66/231.[106]

The thirteenth meeting of the Informal Consultative Process addressed a number of different issues relating to renewable ocean energy, including its impact on the marine environment.[107] Meeting participants called for States to bear in mind their rights and obligations under UNCLOS when planning marine renewable energy development.[108] In addition, several delegations emphasized the importance of assessing the adverse environmental impacts of offshore renewable energy.[109] More specifically, it was noted that further study of the effects of tidal barrages on the marine environment is required.[110]

Meeting participants also discussed important tools for mitigating the effects of MREDs, including marine spatial planning, SEAs, EIAs, and ecosystem-based management.[111] One panelist recommended that any assessment of the impacts of noise pollution should take all sources of such pollution into account when considering methods for its reduction.[112] Furthermore, participants suggested that baseline data should be gathered to facilitate future assessments of the cumulative environmental effects of renewable ocean energy technologies.[113]

International Renewable Energy Agency

The Statute of the International Renewable Energy Agency (IRENA) affirms that the Agency's objective is to promote the increased adoption and sustainable use of all forms of renewable energy.[114] It defines renewable energy as

105 UN General Assembly, Resolution 65/37, "Oceans and the Law of the Sea," 7 December 2010, para. 231.

106 UN General Assembly, Resolution 66/231, "Oceans and the Law of the Sea," 24 December 2011, para. 234.

107 United Nations Open-Ended Informal Consultative Process on Oceans and the Law of the Sea, UN Doc A/67/120, "Report on the Work of the United Nations Open-ended Informal Consultative Process on Oceans and the Law of the Sea at Its Thirteenth Meeting," 13th Meeting, May 2012.

108 Id., para. 9.

109 Id., para. 58.

110 Id., para. 39.

111 Id., para. 57.

112 Id., para. 59.

113 Id.

114 *Statute of the International Renewable Energy Agency*, 26 January 2009, 2700 *United Nations Treaty Series* 45, Art. 2.

including both ocean energy (such as wave and ocean thermal energy) and wind energy.[115] Though IRENA has not released any recommendations on methods for mitigating the adverse environmental effects of marine renewable energy, it has published ocean energy technology briefs on four technologies: ocean thermal energy conversion, salinity gradient energy, tidal energy, and wave energy.[116] Each of these briefs contains a section outlining the ecological implications of the specific technology in question. For example, the tidal energy technology brief discusses the environmental constraints of traditional tidal range technology, which requires streams or river arms to be closed with dams or impoundments.[117] In addition, the wave energy technology brief notes that the main environmental impact of wave energy is a reduction of the wave climate, and consequently of wave height. However, little is currently known about the long-term effects of either the underwater noise produced through construction and operation or the electromagnetic fields generated from sea cables.[118]

Selected 'Regional Surges'

In addition to global agreements, marine renewable energy developments, especially offshore wind farms, have been addressed under regional agreements including four CMS sub-agreements and two regional sea initiatives.[119]

---

115 Id., Art. 3.

116 R. Kempener and F. Neumann, *Ocean Thermal Energy Conversion Technology Brief* (Abu Dhabi: IRENA, 2014); R. Kempener and F. Neumann, *Salinity Gradient Energy Technology Brief* (Abu Dhabi: IRENA, 2014); R. Kempener and F. Neumann, *Tidal Energy Technology Brief* (Abu Dhabi: IRENA, 2014); R. Kempener and F. Neumann, *Wave Energy Technology Brief* (Abu Dhabi: IRENA, 2014).

117 Kempener and Neumann, *Tidal Energy Technology Brief*, id., p. 27.

118 Kempener and Neumann, *Wave Energy Technology Brief*, n. 116 above, pp. 20–21.

119 There are several other relevant regional agreements that could not be discussed in detail. Among the more significant initiatives are the European Landscape Convention (Florence Convention) and the Convention on the Conservation of European Wildlife and Natural Habitats (Bern Convention). Among other things, the Florence Convention commits each party to implement policies for landscape protection, management, and planning. Importantly, it includes marine areas within its defined scope. European Landscape Convention, 20 October 2000, C.E.T.S. no. 176, Arts. 2 and 5. The Bern Convention aims to protect endangered species and habitats. In 2004, its Standing Committee adopted Recommendation 109 on minimizing adverse effects of wind power generation on wildlife. This recommendation advises parties to take measures to minimize the adverse

The four relevant CMS sub-agreements are the Agreement on the Conservation of Cetaceans of the Black Sea, Mediterranean Sea, and Contiguous Atlantic Area (ACCOBAMS); the Agreement on the Conservation of Small Cetaceans of the Baltic, North East Atlantic, Irish and North Seas (ASCOBANS); the Agreement on the Conservation of African-Eurasian Migratory Waterbirds (AEWA); and the Agreement on the Conservation of Populations of European Bats (EUROBATS).[120] The two regional sea initiatives in question are the OSPAR Convention and the Barcelona Convention along with its Protocol on Integrated Coastal Zone Management (ICZM Protocol).[121] Each of these agreements addresses the adverse environmental impacts of marine renewable energy as they pertain to the region and species on which the agreement is based through resolutions and various other documents. In this way, they contribute to the establishment of a global regulatory framework for renewable ocean energy.

Regional Sub-agreements under the CMS
Agreement on the Conservation of Cetaceans of the Black Sea, Mediterranean Sea and Contiguous Atlantic Area
The first of the CMS sub-agreements is ACCOBAMS. ACCOBAMS has issued various resolutions on anthropogenic underwater noise.[122] Through Resolution

---

effects of wind turbines on wildlife, and to use monitoring and surveillance to improve their understanding of the environmental impacts of wind farms. Bern Convention Standing Committee, Recommendation No. 109 (2004), "Minimising Adverse Effects of Wind Power Generation on Wildlife," 3 December 2004.

120   Agreement on the Conservation of Cetaceans of the Black Sea, Mediterranean Sea and Contiguous Atlantic Area, 24 November 1996, 2183 *United Nations Treaty Series* 303; Agreement on the Conservation of Small Cetaceans of the Baltic and North Seas, 17 March 1992, 1772 *United Nations Treaty Series* 217; Agreement on the Conservation of African-Eurasian Migratory Waterbirds, 16 June 1995, available online: <http://www.unep-aewa .org/en/documents/agreements-text>; Agreement on the Conservation of Populations of European Bats, 4 December 1991, 1863 *United Nations Treaty Series* 101.

121   OSPAR Convention, n. 22 above; Barcelona Convention, n. 23 above; ICZM Protocol, n. 24 above.

122   Earlier ACCOBAMS resolutions on ocean noise are: ACCOBAMS Meeting of the Parties, Resolution 2.16, "Assessment and Impact Assessment of Man-Made Noise," Second Meeting of the Parties, November 2004; ACCOBAMS Meeting of the Parties, Resolution 3.10, "Guidelines to Address the Impact of Anthropogenic Noise on Marine Mammals in the ACCOBAMS Area," Third Meeting of the Parties, October 2007. Resolution 2.16 urges parties to take various actions to reduce the threat of anthropogenic noise, including avoiding the use of ocean noise in areas where marine mammals or endangered species may be concentrated. Resolution 3.10 does not explicitly refer to MREDs, but encourages

4.17, parties adopted the Guidelines to Address the Impact of Anthropogenic Noise on Cetaceans in the ACCOBAMS Area.[123] These Guidelines include provisions for coastal and offshore construction works. For example, they urge parties to schedule activities creating noise so as to avoid critical periods of cetacean concentrations and migrations, and to consider alternative construction technologies. In addition, the Guidelines recommend the use of noise reduction measures, such as bubble curtains, and the establishment of exclusion zones in which developers undertaking noise-producing activities would have to ensure the absence of cetaceans before beginning operations. Specifically with regard to MREDs, the Guidelines call for offshore wind farms to be designed and operated to produce the lowest possible noise in all phases.

Most recently, in 2013 the parties adopted Resolution 5.15.[124] Among other things, this resolution urges relevant national and international bodies to develop standards for methodologies to measure underwater noise and evaluate its impact on marine life, and to require the application of best practice to eliminate or reduce anthropogenic noise. It further calls on parties to consider the mitigation requirements outlined in Resolution 4.17 when developing national legislation.

Agreement on the Conservation of Small Cetaceans of the Baltic and North Seas

Parties to ASCOBANS have also adopted various resolutions on noise and other disturbances to cetaceans. Resolution 5.4, which supplanted Resolution 4.5, invites parties and Range States to conduct further research into the effects of industrial activities, including wind farms, on small cetaceans.[125] It also emphasizes the importance of developing appropriate mitigation measures and guidelines to minimize the adverse effects of the anthropogenic noise generated by the activities in question. In 2009, the parties adopted Resolution 6.2

---

parties to develop quieter and more environmentally friendly acoustic techniques and to implement mitigation and monitoring measures for noise producing activities in the ACCOBAMS area.

123   ACCOBAMS Meeting of the Parties, Resolution 4.17, "Guidelines to Address the Impact of Anthropogenic Noise on Cetaceans in the ACCOBAMS Area," Fourth Meeting of the Parties, November 2010.

124   ACCOBAMS Meeting of the Parties, Resolution 5.15, "Addressing the Impact of Anthropogenic Noise," Fifth Meeting of the Parties, November 2013.

125   ASCOBANS Meeting of the Parties, Resolution 4.5, "Effects of Noise and of Vessels," Fourth Meeting of the Parties, August 2003; ASCOBANS Meeting of the Parties, Resolution 5.4, "Adverse Effects of Sound, Vessels and Other Forms of Disturbance on Small Cetaceans," 5th Meeting of the Parties, September 2006.

on the Adverse Effects of Underwater Noise on Marine Mammals during Offshore Construction Activities for Renewable Energy Production.[126] This resolution recommends that parties and Range States undertake SEAs and EIAs prior to authorizing renewable ocean energy developments. In addition, it requests that both parties and Range States issue precautionary guidelines for renewable ocean energy developments. These could include avoiding construction during periods of high density of small cetacean populations, ceasing work that involves high levels of noise when cetaceans are in the vicinity, alerting small cetaceans to the onset of potentially harmful construction noise, and adopting noise reduction techniques.

Agreement on the Conservation of African-Eurasian Migratory Waterbirds

One key resolution has been adopted pursuant to AEWA. Resolution 5.16 on Renewable Energy and Migratory Waterbirds urges parties to undertake various measures to protect migratory waterbirds.[127] Suggested measures include subjecting new renewable energy installation proposals to SEA and EIA and avoiding sites located in the marine migration corridors of migratory waterbirds with high population densities, such as wetlands. In addition, the resolution invites parties to minimize bird mortalities at marine wind farms, for example, by introducing short-term shutdowns during peak migration periods and minimizing lighting in wind farms. Finally, it requests that parties encourage the dismantling of wind turbines in existing installations should high waterbird mortality have an effect on the population status of a species and mitigation measures prove to be insufficient.

AEWA's Guidelines on How to Avoid, Minimize, or Mitigate the Impact of Infrastructural Development and Related Disturbance Affecting Waterbirds set out detailed guidance on methods for addressing concerns relating to migratory waterbirds in SEA and EIA processes.[128] The Guidelines reference key publications on bird census techniques and monitoring approaches, and provide websites relating to waterbird flyways and important habitat sites.

---

126 ASCOBANS Meeting of the Parties, Resolution 6.2, "Adverse Effects of Underwater Noise on Marine Mammals during Offshore Construction Activities for Renewable Energy Production," 6th Meeting of the Parties, September 2009.

127 AEWA Meeting of the Parties, Resolution 5.16, "Renewable Energy and Migratory Waterbirds," 5th Meeting of the Parties, May 2012.

128 G. Tucker and J. Treweek, *Guidelines on How to Avoid, Minimize or Mitigate Impact of Infrastructural Developments and Related Disturbance Affecting Waterbirds*, Technical Series No. 26, *AEWA Conservation Guidelines No. 11* (Bonn: AEWA, 2008).

Agreement on the Conservation of Populations of European Bats
Finally, parties to EUROBATS have developed both resolutions and guidelines
on offshore wind farms.[129] The Guidelines for Consideration of Bats in Wind
Farm Projects, which were adopted in 2008, highlight the need to survey and
consider bat migration routes when siting offshore turbines.[130] In 2010, parties
adopted Resolution 6.11 on Wind Turbines and Bat Populations.[131] This resolution emphasizes the reality that several bat species forage offshore, and as a
result, that offshore wind farms may negatively affect bat populations. It therefore encourages the adoption of measures to mitigate bat mortality, such as the
use of blade feathering, the prevention of freewheeling, and the allowance of
spinning only at very low revolutions per minute (generally less than one rpm).
However, Resolution 6.11 was repealed by Resolution 7.5 on Wind Turbines and
Bat Populations, which was recently adopted at the 7th Meeting of the Parties
in September 2014. Resolution 7.5 broadens the mitigation measures aimed at
preventing bat mortalities to include higher turbine cut-in wind speeds and
shutting down turbines.[132] In addition, it urges parties to acknowledge that the
potential impact on bat populations will make certain locations altogether
unsuitable for wind farm construction.

Regional Sea Agreements and Provisions

OSPAR Convention
The OSPAR Commission has published both guidelines and impact assessments relevant to MREDs. The OSPAR Guidance on Environmental

---

129   The following resolutions on wind farms should also be noted: EUROBATS Meeting of the
      Parties, Resolution 4.7, "Wind Turbines and Bat Populations," 4th Session of the Meeting
      of the Parties, September 2003; EUROBATS Meeting of the Parties, Resolution 5.6, "Wind
      Turbines and Bat Populations," 5th Session of the Meeting of the Parties, September 2006.
      Through Resolution 4.7, parties request the Advisory Committee to evaluate the impacts
      of wind turbines on bat populations and develop guidelines for reducing these
      impacts. Resolution 5.6 addresses parties and Range States, encouraging them to raise
      awareness of both the potential adverse impacts of wind turbines on bat populations and
      the existence of unsuitable habitats for the construction of wind farms.
130   L. Rodrigues, L. Bach, M.J. Dubourg-Savage, J. Goodwin and C. Harbusch, *Guidelines
      for Consideration of Bats in Wind Farm Projects*, Publication Series No. 3 (Bonn: EUROBATS,
      2008).
131   EUROBATS Meeting of the Parties, Resolution 6.11, "Wind Turbines and Bat Populations,"
      6th Session of the Meeting of the Parties, September 2010.
132   EUROBATS Meeting of the Parties, Resolution 7.5, "Wind Turbines and Bat Populations,"
      7th Session of the Meeting of the Parties, September 2014.

Considerations for Offshore Wind Farm Development provides general directions for addressing environmental and conflict of use issues in the five main stages of offshore wind farms, namely, location, licensing, construction and operation, monitoring, and removal/decommissioning.[133] In addition, the Guidelines on Best Environmental Practice in Cable Laying and Operation highlight the risk posed by the electromagnetic fields generated by power cables to marine animals and, in particular, to elasmobranchs (a subclass of cartilaginous fish that includes sharks and rays).[134] They further recommend the application of the precautionary principle and the implementation of appropriate mitigation measures, such as burying cables to avoid the impairment of marine species by electromagnetic fields and routeing cables away from protected or sensitive marine areas.

Assessments have also been conducted pursuant to the OSPAR Convention on relevant issues. These include the environmental impact of offshore wind farms, the environmental effects of cables, and the impacts of underwater noise on marine life.[135]

Barcelona Convention

The Convention for the Protection of the Marine Environment and the Coastal Region of the Mediterranean (Barcelona Convention) and the Protocol on Integrated Coastal Zone Management set overarching legal frameworks for addressing renewable ocean energy in the Mediterranean. The Barcelona Convention outlines the various obligations of contracting parties. These

---

133 OSPAR Commission, Agreement 2008-3, "Guidance on Environmental Considerations for Offshore Wind Farm Development," 2008.

134 OSPAR Commission, Agreement 2012-2, "Guidelines on Best Environmental Practice in Cable Laying and Operation," January 2012.

135 OSPAR Commission, *Assessment of the Environmental Impact of Offshore Wind-farms*, Biodiversity Series 2008 (London: OSPAR Commission, 2008); OSPAR Commission, *Assessment of the Environmental Impacts of Cables*, Biodiversity Series 2009 (London: OSPAR Commission, 2009); OSPAR Commission, *Assessment of the Environmental Impact of Underwater Noise*, Biodiversity Series 2009 (London: OSPAR Commission, 2009). Additional relevant studies not mentioned above are the following: OSPAR Commission, *Review of the Current State of Knowledge on the Environmental Impacts of the Location, Operation and Removal/Disposal of Offshore Wind-Farms*, Biodiversity Series (London: OSPAR Commission, 2006); OSPAR Commission, *Review of the Environmental Impact of Non-Wind Renewable Energy Systems in the Marine Environment*, Biodiversity Series (London: OSPAR Commission, 2006); OSPAR Commission, *Overview of the Impacts of Anthropogenic Underwater Sound in the Marine Environment*, Biodiversity Series (London: OSPAR Commission, 2009).

obligations include applying the precautionary principle to prevent environmental degradation, undertaking EIAs for proposed activities that are likely to cause significant adverse impacts on the marine environment, and promoting cooperation between and among States in EIA procedures relating to activities that may have significant transboundary impacts.[136] Parties must also commit to promoting the integrated management of coastal zones and take all appropriate measures to protect and preserve marine biodiversity.[137] The ICZM Protocol calls on parties to both take an ecosystems approach to coastal planning and management, and to subject proposed infrastructure and energy facilities to authorizations in order to ensure that negative impacts are either minimized, or where appropriate, compensated by non-financial measures.[138]

Conclusion

A number of academics and public figures have called for further steps to be taken at the international level to support the widespread use of marine renewable energy technologies. For example, Bradbrook notes a lack of international action supporting renewable energy. In response, he calls for the establishment of a United Nations agency focused on sustainable development.[139] The 2012 *Report of the UN Secretary-General on Oceans and the Law of the Sea* identifies a number of potential opportunities for enhanced cooperation and coordination at the international level. Among other things, it suggests that IRENA could act as a focal point for intergovernmental cooperation and coordination, and points to the Sustainable Energy for All initiative as a method of mobilizing global action.[140]

Others have focused more specifically on improving international governance with regard to the environmental impacts of MREDs. These recommendations focus largely on incremental developments. For example, in its *Greening Blue Energy* report, the IUCN urges individual States to integrate wind farm development into integrated coastal zone management and spatial planning instruments.[141] More broadly, it recommends strengthening the

---

136   Barcelona Convention, n. 23 above, Arts. 4(3)(a), 4(3)(c) and 4(3)(d).

137   Id., Arts. 4(3)(e) and 10.

138   ICZM Protocol, n. 24 above, Arts. 6(c) and 9(2)(f).

139   A.J. Bradbrook, "Sustainable Energy Law: the Past and the Future," *Journal of Energy & Natural Resources Law* 30, no. 4 (2012): 511–522 at 517–518; *Report of the Secretary General*, n. 12 above, p. 26.

140   *Report of the Secretary-General*, id., pp. 24–25.

141   Wilhelmsson et al., n. 11 above, p. 27.

exchange of information between States to facilitate the coordination of conservation measures and wind farm development. The *Report of the UN Secretary-General on Oceans and the Law of the Sea* makes a similar recommendation, advocating close cooperation at the national level and between CMS focal points in order to develop coordinated solutions to the negative impacts of marine renewable energy on migratory species.[142] On a more global scale, Castelos emphasizes the importance of extending MSP to the high seas in order to address environmental impacts outside of national jurisdictions.[143] He suggests potential candidates for managing marine renewable energy in these areas, including the International Seabed Authority, the IMO, or the UNESCO Intergovernmental Oceanographic Commission.

In each of these reports, and many others like them, climate change is identified as the single most important issue requiring the switch from traditional energy sources such as oil and gas to renewable energy. The looming threat of climate change undoubtedly necessitates the exploration and development of many different types of sustainable energy, including marine renewable energy. Any efforts to regulate offshore renewable energy developments must be capable of doing so without significantly frustrating attempts to increase the development and deployment of marine renewable energy projects. However, the potential adverse environmental effects of renewable ocean energy projects cannot be ignored. It is essential that these projects be designed and implemented in such a way as to minimize their negative impact on marine ecosystems, many of which have already become vulnerable and strained as a result of pressures such as pollution, overfishing, and ocean acidification.

The overall international governance framework that has evolved to address the risks posed by offshore renewable energy projects to the marine environment stands out as being largely fragmented and recommendatory in nature, with the notable exception of certain binding obligations released by the IMO and ICAO. Multiple decisions, resolutions, and other documents have been adopted under international and regional conventions and organizations. These initiatives, agreements, and documents that have emerged together comprise the international governance framework for marine renewable energy. However, with no international organization with binding authority and a mandate covering renewable energy,[144] coastal States are left broad discretion to develop offshore renewable energy projects. This discretion is

---

142 *Report of the Secretary-General*, n. 12 above, p. 25.

143 Castelos, n. 29 above, p. 229.

144 Id., p. 232.

subject only to general law of the sea responsibilities and mostly procedural requirements, such as to subject project proposals to strategic environmental assessment and environmental assessment processes.

Evaluating the success of the numerous guidance efforts described in this article is difficult. The development and deployment of most marine renewable energy technologies is still in the early stages. As renewable ocean energy projects increase in number, however, the success or failure of these efforts will be an important factor in determining whether MREDs have an overall positive environmental effect, or constitute another source of pressure on our already vulnerable oceans. The international community should be prepared to adapt its efforts as this sector expands, in order to ensure that renewable ocean energy technologies contribute to climate change mitigation while allowing the world's oceans to be conserved for the generations to come.

Maritime Transport

∴

The Role of National Shipping Policy: A Scandinavian Perspective on Shipping Policies in a Global Economy

Martin Jes Iversen, René Taudal Poulsen and Henrik Sornn-Friese
Copenhagen Business School, Copenhagen, Denmark

Stig Tenold†
Norwegian School of Economics, Bergen, Norway

Introduction

Approximately one decade ago, Gunnar K. Sletmo published an article that asked whether globalization implied the end of national shipping policies.[1] A few years later, Selkou and Roe posed a similar question: "Is there a role for national shipping policy?"[2] The aim of this article is to discuss the extent to which shipping policies have affected the development of the shipping industry in the Scandinavian countries – Denmark, Norway and Sweden – in the period since the early 1970s. These countries provide us with two distinct development trajectories. In Denmark and Norway shipping continues to play an important role in society and the economy, while in Sweden the industry has been largely eradicated.

We analyse the role of nation states in shipping along the lines suggested by Selkou and Roe, distinguishing between international and supranational policies, on the one hand, and national policies – understood as the whole 'framework' or 'foundation' for maritime activities – on the other. The different fortunes of the shipping industry in the three Scandinavian countries can be understood as

† The authors would like to thank Siri Pettersen Strandenes and two anonymous referees for their comments. Corresponding author: Stig.Tenold@nhh.no.

1 G.K. Sletmo, "The End of National Shipping Policy? A Historical Perspective on Shipping Policy in a Global Economy," *International Journal of Maritime Economics* 3, no. 4 (2001): 330–350.
2 E. Selkou and M. Roe, *Globalisation, Policy and Shipping: Fordism, Post-Fordism and the European Union Maritime Sector* (Cheltenham: Edward Elgar, 2004).

the product of the combination of national shipping policies and shipping company strategies, utilizing the analytical framework developed in Tenold.[3]

Specifically, we discuss the roles played both by specific shipping policies, such as the access to foreign registry or establishment of open registries, and by more general policies that influence shipping, in particular tax policies. National level policies determined the extent to which shipping companies could respond to a changing market and evolve accordingly – their 'room to manoeuvre'. In Sweden, national level policies constrained the responsiveness of the shipping industry, stifling long-term growth. Conversely, in Norway and Denmark, the authorities successfully put in place national policies affording the shipping industry sufficient flexibility to develop in the long-term.

Thus, rather than spelling 'the end of national shipping policy', developments over the last 30 years suggest that policies are important and effective tools in determining the growth or decline of a country's shipping industry. Despite shipping's international character, the divergent Scandinavian trajectories suggest that national policies are more important than the policies of supranational bodies in determining the fate of a country's shipping industry.

The Theoretical Basis

Selkou and Roe present a spatial perspective for the analysis and evaluation of shipping policies by distinguishing between three levels of policies; international, supranational and national.[4] Within this framework comprising progressively smaller units, the constituent levels are interdependent. The national level on the one hand is affected by supranational and international policies. Yet, on the other, it may also influence these broader policies. Although the manner in which countries agitate in international fora presents an interesting question, it lies outside the scope of this article and will not be a subject of inquiry.

In evaluating the shipping policies of the three Scandinavian countries and their effects, we maintain the three-level framework of Selkou and Roe.[5] However, we nuance the national dimension and follow the analytical apparatus in

3   S. Tenold, "Boom, Crisis and Internationalised Revitalisation: Norwegian Shipping," in *Global Shipping in Small Nations: Nordic Experiences after 1960*, eds. S. Tenold, M.J. Iversen and E. Lange (Basingstoke: Palgrave MacMillan, 2012), pp. 26–60.

4   Selkou and Roe, n. 2 above.

5   As Selkou and Roe (n. 2 above) deal primarily with the policies of EU member countries, Norway is not subject to detailed discussion in their analysis of the cohesion of European shipping policies (Chapter 7).

TABLE 13.1   *Schematic overview of the playing field*

	Scheme A	**Scheme B**
Highest level	International policies – provide the overarching structure for the policies	International level – affected by international regulations, the demand for seaborne transport and competitors' policies
Intermediate level	Supranational policies – policies and laws superior to national legislation	National policies – directly shipping-related but also other policies affecting shipping companies
Bottom level	National policies	Shipping company strategies – aimed at profit-maximization, but restricted by the two levels above

SOURCE: SCHEME A: SELKOU AND ROE, N. 2 ABOVE AND SCHEME B: TENOLD, N. 3 ABOVE.

Tenold, where the growth or decline of a specific country's fleet is explained by a combination of developments at international, national and company levels.[6] Here, the bottom level is extended to include two dimensions, namely, the policies of the authorities and the strategies of the shipping companies. The two analytical schemes are presented in Table 13.1.

Although the international setting was identical for all three countries during the relevant period, the supranational level differed. Both Denmark and Sweden belong to the European Union (EU); Sweden since 1996 and Denmark since 1993, having been a member of the EU's precursor, the European Economic Community, since 1973. Norway, however, remains outside the EU. Despite these differences, most variation in shipping policy existed at the national level.

From the 1970s onwards, questions concerning a ship's flag have dominated shipping policy debates in many European countries. The growing use of flags of convenience, which brought about lost competitiveness or flagging out by their own shipping companies, meant that European authorities could either respond or accept the decline of their national merchant marines. The second question dominating shipping policy debates and forming a point of contention between shipowners and governments has been that of taxation. Both the flag and the tax questions reflect the inherently 'footloose' character of the shipping industry. The possibility of exiting the national context is far greater in shipping than in

---

6   Tenold, n. 3 above.

practically all other industries. This is in large part due to the low cost of such an exit in comparison with industries where capital equipment is immovable.[7]

The National Dimension

In 1970, Norway boasted a fleet of more than 31 million dead weight tons (dwt), positioning it as the world's fourth largest shipping nation, trailing only Liberia, Japan, and the United Kingdom. Sweden and Denmark were thirteenth and fourteenth on the same list, with fleets of approximately seven and five million dwt, respectively.[8] As of January 2013, Norway's fleet of 45 million dwt had slipped to ninth place on the list of countries and territories with the largest owned fleets. Denmark had climbed three places to eleventh, with a fleet of more than 40 million dwt, which had grown in size from its 1970 fleet by a factor of eight. Sweden, on the other hand, controlled a fleet that had shrunk in size relative to 1970, and had tumbled 20 places on the list. If, rather than control, we look at flag, Norway is fifteenth and Denmark is twenty-first. Sweden, with a Swedish-flagged fleet of around 1.9 million dwt, does not even make the Top 50.[9] Table 13.2 shows the shares of world tonnage represented by Scandinavian countries.[10]

We will attempt to explain in this article these three divergent trajectories in Scandinavian shipping: the Swedish decline, the Danish surge and the limited slippage of the Norwegian fleet. There are three intuitive explanations for these divergent trajectories. First, the disparity may be a result of different starting points, reflecting previous strategic choices. Second, it may have been caused

---

7   The only industry where the exit possibilities are similarly large is the airline industry, which is also characterized by extremely mobile equipment. This article deals solely with the *international* aspect of the countries' shipping industries, i.e., we do not discuss the role of coastal shipping.

8   United Nations Conference on Trade and Development (UNCTAD), *Maritime Transport* (Geneva: UNCTAD, 1971).

9   UNCTAD, *Review of Maritime Transport 2013* (Geneva: UNCTAD, 2013).

10   The table is based on data from Lloyd's and refers to registration for the period 1960–1990 and nationality of owner for subsequent years. The basis for the analysis is gross registered tonnage (grt); For details, see Tenold, Iversen and Lange, n. 3 above, p. 3; E. Ekberg, "Nordic Shipping: A Statistical Overview," in *Global Shipping in Small Nations*, n. 3 above, pp. 156–201. In the 1980s, in particular, there were large annual variations that are not picked up by these five-year data. There are a number of caveats in using simple data such as this, both problems of determining nationality and the fact that 'a ton is a ton' regardless of ship type, quality, and age.

TABLE 13.2 *Scandinavian shipping's share of world tonnage (grt), 1970–2008 (percent)*

	1970	1975	1980	1985	1990	1995	2000	2005	2008
Denmark	1.5	1.3	1.3	1.2	1.2	1.8	2.5	2.3	3.0
Norway	8.5	7.6	5.2	3.7	5.5	6.6	7.3	5.1	4.3
Sweden	2.2	2.2	1.0	0.8	0.7	2.0	1.5	0.9	0.9

by different strategies among the shipping companies in the three countries.[11] Third, the divergences may reflect the fact that across the three countries political conditions varied with respect to shipping policies and economic policies more broadly.

There is little doubt that both the first and the second explanation did have *some* effect on subsequent developments. We believe, however, that it is the third element, the policy dimension that has played the most important role, in particular via its effect on the economic opportunities available to shipping companies and, correspondingly, the long-term growth strategies which they would in turn develop.

With regard to the starting point, Denmark was 'the odd one out'. In the early 1970s, Norwegian and Swedish shipowners followed relatively similar strategies, investing primarily in large oil tankers and dry bulk carriers. The Danes, alternatively, had a more diversified fleet, with a higher proportion of liner vessels. These differences in fleet composition to some extent reflect shipping companies responding and adapting to each countries' respective policies during the 1950s and 1960s. However, because there were only minor variations in Scandinavian shipping policies during this period, the shipping companies' strategic decisions played an important role in determining the shape of the national shipping industry.

The picture becomes more complex when we evaluate the business strategies and management decisions followed by shipping companies in the three countries during the period in question. One reason for this is that these strategies are clearly affected by shipping policies. Thus, even if the starting points were identical, the varying effect of the political landscape clearly determined the shipping companies' room to manoeuvre. Consequently, what may have been a successful strategy in one country might have been unsuccessful or unfeasible in the other.

---

11 A related explanation, which we do not investigate here, is the existence of alternative business opportunities. If such opportunities are determined at the national level, the relative attractiveness of the alternatives becomes important.

While it is impossible to isolate the strategies developed by shipping companies from the political framework in which they operated, there is little doubt that the latter element varied greatly. A very brief introduction to the three political frameworks from the early 1970s until today may therefore be useful.

Denmark

Over the past two to three decades shipping has played a key role in Danish society, serving as a source of employment, a major contributor to the national balance of payments, and a driver for the internationalization of the Danish economy. After 2000, Danish shipping defined a successful growth pattern based on specialized functions such as operations of tanker and dry bulk fleets through pools and on charters, economies of scale in container shipping, close customer relations in liner businesses as well as specialized functions in offshore operations.

The background for this development was a combination of a specific political-institutional setting and individual, highly competitive corporate strategies, which together, in 2010 enabled Denmark to become the fourth largest ship-operating nation in the world. The interplay between the idiosyncratic strategic choices of the major Danish shipping companies and the development of an activist and highly shipping-friendly policy regime has thus made Denmark an important centre for international shipping.

Prior to the international shipping crisis of the 1970s and 1980s there was no explicit Danish maritime policy. However, during the second half of the 1970s, a strong coalition emerged between the major Danish shipping companies and their interest associations. They successfully collaborated with the government in drafting an ambitious and coherent set of maritime policy measures, including a Danish International Ship (DIS) register and a special tax exemption for seafarers under the DIS. The objective of these measures was to maintain a strong fleet under the Danish flag and thus preserve jobs and income in what was believed to be a national stronghold sector.[12] This was later augmented in 2002 by a tonnage tax scheme for ships registered in DIS.

This public-private coalition rested on three important pillars. First, there was the development of a shipping-friendly tax and ship registration regime

---

12   H. Sornn-Friese, R.T. Poulsen and M.J. Iversen, "Knowing the Ropes: Capability Reconfiguration and Restructuring of the Danish Shipping Industry," in *Global Shipping in Small Nations*, n. 3 above; H. Sornn-Friese and M.J. Iversen, "The Establishment of the Danish International Ship Register (DIS) and its Connections to the Maritime Cluster," *International Journal of Maritime History* 26, no. 1 (2014): 82–103.

founded on a 'level playing field approach' that, as a minimum, would match Danish framework conditions to those in other leading maritime nations such as Norway, Great Britain and The Netherlands. The second pillar was an active strategic maritime growth policy based on close public-private cooperation. This Michael Porter-inspired 'cluster policy' was introduced in the late 1980s and enhanced in the 2000s, when several maritime policy initiatives were developed in an intensive collaboration between the maritime authorities and maritime private actors, the latter often represented by the Danish Shipowners' Association.[13] The third important public-institutional pillar was Denmark's legal and political stability. As an industry marked by a combination of long-term investments, capital-intensive assets and unpredictable markets, shipping requires stability within the legal and political environment in which it operates. Since the mid-1990s, Denmark has enjoyed institutional stability, permitting shipowners to undertake large, long-term capital investments, trusting that taxation and legal conditions were not at risk of being dramatically altered in the wake of a changing political regime.

Norway

The shipping industry held a very special position in the Norwegian economy. In the century between the 1860s and the 1960s, shipping had been the country's most important export sector, accounting for between one-third and one-half of all export revenues. Shipowners also played an important role in society and politics – the closest thing to 'nobility' in a country where formal nobles did not exist.

Despite shipping's important role in the Norwegian economy, during this period the industry was largely left to its own devices. There had been periods of beneficial treatment (for instance in connection with access to foreign currency) and of adverse policy effects (when the authorities banned contracting at foreign yards during a booming market in the 1950s). However, Norwegian shipping companies generally operated with relative autonomy. Still, this freedom was subject to one caveat that required all Norwegian-owned ships to fly the Norwegian flag. This requirement had economic ramifications for Norwegian shipping companies. For example, it obligated shipping companies to employ Norwegian officers and crews, forcing companies to pay a higher wage bill relative to extra-nationally crewed vessels and effectively raising the costs of operating a shipping company in Norway.

The nationalist orientation of shipping policy was relatively irrelevant when the market was good during the 1960s and early 1970s and it was possible to

---

13   Sornn-Friese and Iversen, id.

neutralize the negative effects through strategic choices. By investing in ships that utilized economies of scale, or had a high capital-to-labor ratio, Norwegian shipping companies were able to remain competitive. A beneficial tax regime enhanced this strategy, with high depreciation rates favoring investment in shipping.

However, when the shipping crisis hit Norway in the 1970s and 1980s, previous strategies were no longer adequate. Banks forced indebted shipping companies to sell their tonnage. Other companies chose flagging out in an attempt to reduce costs. The latter practice had been explicitly illegal under the previous regime, but, the authorities reluctantly accepted "temporary" flagging out in the early 1980s. The end result was a marked decline in the size of Norway's shipping fleet, from approximately 50 million dwt in 1977 to less than ten million dwt a decade later.

In July 1987, Norwegian authorities established the Norwegian International Ship Register (NIS), which enabled the use of foreign low-cost crews on Norwegian ships, provided these vessels were not involved in domestic cabotage or on scheduled lines from Norway. A substantial reinvestment in the Norwegian fleet followed the introduction of the NIS, which became the prototype 'open register'. Improvements in the shipping market further increased industry investment. By the early 1990s, the tonnage losses of the pre-NIS decade had been regained. Parallel with this, the surviving Norwegian shipping companies revised their strategies, generally eschewing large tankers and bulk carriers and focusing instead on developing technologically advanced shipping for specialized markets and embracing possibilities related to offshore oil exploration.

Since the introduction of the NIS, policy debates in Norway have primarily concerned the question of taxation. In 1996, a tonnage tax regime replaced a tax regime enacted in 1992, which had drastically sharpened tax liabilities for shipping companies. The new regime, however, was based on tax deferral rather than tax exemption. This seemingly small distinction became problematic when a new tonnage tax regime – in line with the one by then introduced in most European Union countries – replaced the 'deferred tax' system in 2007.[14] Shipping companies were faced with substantial tax bills, and eventually, the case came before the Norwegian Supreme Court.

The Supreme Court case illustrated that there has been a schism between the manner in which the Norwegian authorities view the shipping industry

---

14   B.M. Høgberg, "Grunnloven § 97 etter plenumsdommen i Rt. 2010 s. 143 (rederiskatte-
      saken)," *Tidsskrift for Rettsvitenskap*, 04/05 (2010), 694–744.

and the industry's self-perception.[15] Despite the fact that the framework conditions for Norwegian shipping companies have been improved with legislation such as the NIS and the tonnage tax system, some shipping companies have left the country, threatened to leave or moved part of the value chain abroad. The basis for these actions has been dissatisfaction with regulation and legislation that shipowners see as being hostile to business and unpredictable.

Sweden

It is likely that national shipping policies reduced the international competitiveness of Swedish shipping companies from the early 1970s to the present. First, Swedish governments have imposed additional costs on Swedish companies relative to foreign competitors. Second, Swedish governments have responded more slowly to shipping industry requests than their counterparts in other countries, including Norway and Denmark. Swift implementation of new policy initiatives to support shipping companies is important in the global, mobile and volatile shipping industry. However, in Sweden's case such initiatives were implemented much later than in Norway and Denmark, if at all. Swedish governments have spent several years investigating new policy initiatives aimed at improving competitiveness, while the Danish and Norwegian governments have established these initiatives much faster.

The negative competitive effects of Swedish shipping policies are evident in three key areas. The first was the implementation of the 1977 *Flag Act,* which reduced Swedish companies' options for flagging out tonnage to low-cost ship registers. The second was the refusal of the government to establish an international shipping register similar to DIS or NIS in the late 1980s, which could have reduced crewing costs for shipowners. Finally, the government's refusal to introduce a tonnage-tax regime to replace ordinary corporate taxes in 2000, a measure which could have reduced the tax burden of the shipping companies, negatively impacted the competitiveness of Sweden's shipping industry. The end result was a decline in the size of the Swedish-flagged fleet and Swedish-controlled tonnage.

The bureaucratic organization responsible for Swedish shipping policy differs significantly from its Danish and Norwegian counterparts. In Denmark, the Ministry of Growth and Business is responsible for shipping, while in Norway responsibility lies with the Ministry of Business and Industry, which in 1988 assumed control of the sector from a previously dedicated Ministry of Trade

---

15   2010-02-12. Rt 2010 143. Utv 2010 s 511. Norges høyesterett – dom.

and Shipping. In contrast, Swedish shipping issues are handled by the Ministry of Communications and Infrastructure.

The bureaucratic set-up in Sweden indicates that the government and its officials view the shipping industry as a facilitator of national imports and exports, rather than a global business engaged in cross-trading. This perception is also clearly evident in the most recent government plan for Swedish shipping, launched in January 2013. To a large extent the plan focuses on the key role shipping has with regard to Swedish exports and national infrastructure. In other words the approach of the Swedish government remains more regional than global.[16] As stated by the Minister of Transportation, Catharina Elmsäter-Svärd in her opening remarks introducing the government plan:

> Shipping plays an important role in the Swedish transport system. Enormous trade flows across our oceans to end on our shop shelves, in our factories and homes. If one looks at our foreign trade with the outside world Sweden may almost be considered an island – around ninety percent of our foreign trade is transported by sea.[17]

This view of shipping solely as a support industry to the country's exports is mirrored in the government's ongoing evaluation of the pros and cons of introducing a tonnage tax regime. This measure, in place in Denmark more than ten years ago, is currently being discussed in a committee that has until November 2014 to present its recommendation. Furthermore, the committee's mandate reinforces shipping's role as a facilitator of Swedish trade rather than an independent commercial entity in itself, emphasizing that "Sweden is a country that is dependent upon efficient and competitive sea transport."[18]

While national shipping policies clearly hampered the competitiveness of shipping companies, Swedish shipowners have also contributed to the erosion of their own competitiveness. Poulsen, Sjögren and Lennerfors documented the effects of a series of unfortunate strategic choices made by Swedish

---

16 Swedish Government, Regeringskansliet, *Svensk Sjöfartsnäring – Handlingsplan för Förbättrad Konkurrenskraft* (2013), available online: <http://www.regeringen.se/content/1/c6/20/74/53/d8ca96c1.pdf>.

17 "Sjöfarten spelar en betydelsefull roll i det svenska transportsystemet. Enorma andelsströmmar korsar våra hav för att hamna i våra butikshyllor, fabriker och hem. Om man tittar på vår handel med omvärlden är Sverige i det närmaste att betrakta som en ö – runt 90 procent av vår utrikeshandel transporteras sjövägen." (Our translation).

18 Swedish Government, Regeringskansliet, Kommittédirektiv Dir 2013:6, "Tonnageskatt og andra stöd för sjöfartsnäringen" (24 January 2013), available online: <http://www.regeringen.se/sb/d/108/a/207832>.

shipowners between 1970 and 2010.[19] First, up until 1973, heavy overinvestment in new ships and shipbuilding proved a major burden for the shipping industry during the 1973–1987 shipping crisis.[20] Second, the unfortunate timing of asset sales during the late 1990s prevented the industry from reaping the full benefits of the 2002–2008 shipping boom. From 1970 to the present, only a few Swedish companies were able to demonstrate that they could consistently produce profits and generate employment in Sweden. The unfortunate corporate decisions by major Swedish shipping companies may have reduced the overall strength of shipping industry lobbyist arguments vis-à-vis the Swedish government.

This lack of corporate credibility, coupled with the relatively modest size of the Swedish shipping fleet, thwarted industry efforts to petition government for a beneficial shipping policy framework. This created a downward spiral where the lack of a beneficial framework reduced the number of companies, eroding political influence even more.

Shipping company performance and the national policy frameworks in which companies operate are clearly linked and co-constitutive. For this reason, it is impossible to attribute the Swedish shipping industry's losses in competitiveness solely to either unfavorable national policies or poor corporate strategies. However, it is possible to analyse shipping industry performance as a product of the dynamic between these influences.

Analysis

Based on the descriptions above, we can present two alternative and complementary schemes to illustrate the development in the Scandinavian countries. In Table 13.3 we use Scheme A, following Selkou and Roe.[21] In this scheme we see that Denmark and Sweden are identical at the top two levels, while the Norwegian position only corresponds at the highest level. At the national level, where all three countries differ, we have described the national shipping policies by the extent to which the authorities have advanced or worked against the interests of the shipping industry, according to the presentation above.

---

19   H. Sjögren, T.T. Lennerfors and R.T. Poulsen, "The Transformation of Swedish Shipping, 1970–2010," *Business History Review* 86, no. 3 (Autumn 2012): 417–445.
20   Swedish shipbuilding was more important, particularly to politicians, than the Swedish shipping sector, and it might be argued that Swedish politicians looked at shipping purely as a support industry.
21   Selkou and Roe, see n. 2 above.

TABLE 13.3   *The Scandinavian countries in Scheme A*

	Scheme A	Denmark	Sweden	Norway
Highest	*International policies*	Identical in all three countries*		
Intermediate	*Supranational policies*	Identical (EU)		Non-EU
Bottom	*National policies*	Strongly shipping positive	Shipping negative	Weakly shipping positive

SOURCE: SELKOU AND ROE (2004) AND PRECEDING ANALYSIS.
* The degree to which these policies will 'be heard' differs, however, as their participation and influence in, for instance, the International Maritime Organization varies.

Given the divergent trajectories, it is evident that according to Scheme A, the supranational level is relatively unimportant compared with the national level. The fact that the two extreme outcomes – Denmark's strong growth and the Swedish near-eradication – share the same superstructure at the international and supranational levels is a strong indication of this.

If we change the spatial distribution to Scheme B, as shown in Table 13.4, it becomes even more evident why the shipping sectors of the Scandinavian countries have developed so differently over the past decades. In the Swedish case, few shipping companies managed to find profitable strategies in a difficult working environment. Several of the large shipping companies shipped their oars, exiting the industry completely. Only two companies, Stena and Wallenius, can be said to maintain a large international presence today.

The Danish maritime cluster has not been characterized by the destruction seen in Sweden. Rather, the leading Danish shipping company, AP Möller-Maersk, has strengthened its international position during the relevant period and also provided a good learning environment for a large number of Danish shipping executives. Moreover, while there have been some newcomers in Denmark's shipping industry and certain older companies have failed, the industry's outstanding feature is its high level of stability. Additionally, existing firms have undertaken innovations, particularly those related to functional specialization and the operation of pools and chartered-in tonnage.

The Norwegian case is best described as 'creative destruction', as compared with creativity in Denmark and destruction in Sweden. The level of activity has

TABLE 13.4   *The Scandinavian countries in Scheme B*

	Scheme B	Denmark	Sweden	Norway
Highest	*International level*		Identical in all three countries	
Intermediate	*National policies*	Strongly shipping positive	Shipping negative	Weakly shipping positive
Bottom	*Shipping company strategies*	Functional specialization	Overinvestment and bad timing	Specialization and offshore oil support

SOURCE: TENOLD, IVERSEN AND LANGE, N. 3 ABOVE AND PRECEDING ANALYSIS.

remained relatively stable since the introduction of the NIS in 1987. However, before that time, a hemorrhaging of shipping companies occurred – between 1970 and 1987, the number of companies owning ships flying the Norwegian flag fell by two-thirds, while the number owning foreign-going ships (regardless of flag) fell by one-half.[22] Following this period, Norwegian shipping companies shifted towards specialized markets, such as those relating to servicing the offshore oil industry. Although Norway's individual shipping companies have experienced greater volatility than shipping companies in Denmark, its shipping industry as a whole has remained relatively stable. Explaining the stability and expansion of the Norwegian shipping industry is the fact that there has been "a steady influx of new risk-prone investors to replace those who had gambled and lost."[23]

The different strategies followed by Danish and Norwegian shipping companies are illustrated by examining their relative international position using alternative criteria. As previously mentioned, Norway is ninth and Denmark eleventh on UNCTAD's list of fleets by controlling nation. However, Denmark's position improves from eleventh to fourth if we look at operated, rather than controlled, tonnage. This reflects the large number of ships in Danish-operated pools or on charter to Danish operators. Similarly, the Norwegian strategy of investing in

---

22   S. Tenold, *Tankers in Trouble – Norwegian Shipping and the Crisis of the 1970s and 1980s* (St. John's, Newfoundland: International Maritime Economic History Association, 2006).

23   V.D. Norman, "A Future for Nordic Shipping?" in *Global Shipping in Small Nations* n. 3 above, pp. 202–214.

technologically advanced, specialized offshore ships takes the country from
ninth position, in terms of tonnage, to the fifth position on the list of the world's
leading fleets if we use the market value of the fleet as the criterion.[24]

Concluding Comments

The different developments in the shipping sectors of the Scandinavian countries over the last 30 years – and particularly after the shipping crisis of the
1970s and the 1980s – clearly shows that national shipping policies still play an
important role. Thus, even in the world's most globalized industry, the national
dimension remains significant. This implies that policy-makers at international, supranational, and, in particular, national levels, play an important role
in shaping the future of maritime industries.

Table 13.5 presents some of the major elements of the shipping policies of
the three Scandinavian countries. Denmark followed Norway in the establishment of an open register, but has since been leading the field when it comes to
a 'shipping friendly' attitude.

National shipping policies are, of course, related to the eternal struggle for
scarce resources and political patronage. It is therefore tempting to conclude
by reflecting on why this struggle produced different outcomes among the
Scandinavian countries.

The Danish pro-shipping policies can be partially attributed to effective
lobbying by strong business organizations. However, the self-perception of
Denmark as 'a nation of merchants and traders' must undoubtedly have
helped. Moreover, the strong position of the AP Möller-Maersk group, not only
within Danish shipping, but, in the Danish economy in general, has probably
been important.

TABLE 13.5   *Some important elements of Scandinavian national shipping policies*

	Denmark	Norway	Sweden
Open registry	1988	1987	No
Tonnage tax	2002	(1996)/2007	Currently under consideration
Cluster promotion policy	Strong	Limited	Non-existent

24   Menon, *Maritime Verdiskapningsbok* (Oslo: Menon, 2012).

Historically, Norway's shipping industry enjoyed greater importance within the national economy than that of Denmark. Additionally, the industry was traditionally perceived as being favored by the authorities. However, agitation for a level playing field *within* Norway – across various branches of industry – increased the burden on an industry that was challenged by developments in the international market. When the Norwegian shipping companies' tax obligations were equaled with those of other companies in the country, they faced a handicap relative to their international competitors. The Norwegian authorities gradually realized that it was impossible to neglect international liberalization without the country losing its status as an important maritime nation and reluctantly introduced both an open register and a tonnage tax regime.[25]

In Sweden, shipping is no longer considered an industry in its own right, but rather a vehicle for Swedish exports. In 2001, when the Swedish authorities half-heartedly introduced support for shipping companies in an attempt to create similar conditions as in competing countries, support was limited to "Swedish-flagged cargo ships and passenger ships that primarily are used in foreign-going traffic of importance to Swedish foreign trade or the Swedish services export."[26]

We can plug these facts into our two analytical schemes. In the Selkou and Roe scheme, Denmark and Sweden are identical at the top two levels, but differ greatly at the third – national shipping policy. Given that these two countries have the most extreme trajectories, with Denmark as the most successful and Sweden as the least, we illustrate that the national policy dimension plays a significant role in determining industry outcomes. Moreover, the middling fate of non-EU Norway, which does not share the supranational dimension with the two other countries, suggests that national policies are more important than supranational ones. If the EU policies were more important than what individual countries pursued at the national level, we would expect to see Sweden and Denmark developing similarly, with Norway being the odd one out. In summary, differential outcomes in the shipping industries surveyed in this analysis conform to predictions based on national rather than supranational policies, emphasizing the former's importance as determining factors.

We also extend the analysis to include two domestic levels – national policies and shipping company strategies – following the scheme in Tenold. Within

---

25   With regard to the Norwegian International Ship Register, the reluctance was not only confined to the authorities. The Norwegian Shipowners' Association was initially lukewarm to the idea; see A. Thowsen and S. Tenold, *Odfjell – The History of a Shipping Company* (Bergen: Odfjell ASA, 2006).

26   Swedish Government, Regeringskansliet, n. 18 above (our translation).

this framework, we see that both Danish and Norwegian shipping companies managed to utilize the benign political landscape and find feasible and sustainable strategies, leading to a vibrant and competitive shipping sector. The flight from the Swedish flag – partly caused by harmful policies, partly by strategic mistakes – reflected priorities in a country where shipping was treated as a support industry, rather than an industry in its own right.

China's Law and Practice as a Coastal State for the Prevention of Vessel-Source Pollution

Nengye Liu†
School of Law, University of Dundee, Dundee, Scotland, United Kingdom

Introduction

China is a major maritime nation with 18,000 km of mainland coastline.[1] The marine environment is of fundamental importance for China's economic development and environmental protection. According to the National Report on Social and Economic Development, in 2010, China imported 239.31 million tonnes of crude oil and 36.88 million tonnes of refined oil.[2] Approximately 95 percent of oil imports are carried by maritime transportation. This creates significant risk of marine pollution such as oil, oily wastes and invasive species from ballast water. Globally, maritime transport is responsible for 12 percent of total marine pollution.[3] The United Nations Convention on the Law of Sea (UNCLOS) deals with vessel-source pollution through Part XII on Protection and Preservation of the Marine Environment, Part II on the Territorial Sea and Contiguous Zone, and Part V on the Exclusive Economic Zone.[4] Under UNCLOS, the legislative or enforcement jurisdiction that a State may exercise in respect of a particular vessel varies according to whether it is a flag, coastal or port State.[5] UNCLOS creates a jurisdictional regime for the prevention of

---

† The author would like to thank two anonymous reviewers for their comments on an earlier draft.

1 As of 1 January 2013, Chinese ownership of vessels was ranked third in the world. Chinese shipowners control 11.78 percent of the total world deadweight tonnage. See United Nations Conference on Trade and Development (UNCTAD), *Review of Maritime Transport 2013* (Geneva: UNCTAD, 2013), p. 43.

2 See Table 9, *2010 National Report on Economic and Social Development Statistics*, National Bureau of Statistics of China, available online: <http://www.stats.gov.cn/tjgb/ndtjgb/qgndtjgb/t20110228_402705692.htm> (in Chinese).

3 International Shipping Facts and Figures – Information Resources on Trade, Safety, Security, Environment, Maritime Knowledge Center, International Maritime Organization, 2011, p. 24.

4 United Nations Convention on the Law of the Sea, *International Legal Materials* 21, no. 6 (1982): 1261–1354.

5 R. Churchill and A. Lowe, *The Law of the Sea*, 3rd ed. (Manchester: Manchester University Press, 1999), p. 344. Flag State is the State whose nationality a particular vessel has. The UNCLOS

vessel-source pollution. Furthermore, UNCLOS has designated the International Maritime Organization (IMO) as the competent international organization to deal with vessel-source pollution. Under the auspices of the IMO, a number of conventions have been adopted to tackle the aforementioned problems such as the International Convention for the Prevention of Pollution from Ships (MARPOL) and the International Convention for the Safety of Life at Sea (SOLAS).[6]

China signed UNCLOS in 1982 and ratified it in 1996. As early as 1983, China ratified MARPOL and its Annex I and II. China has also ratified MARPOL Annex III (in 1994), Annex IV and VI (in 2006), Annex V (in 1988), and SOLAS (in 1994). Most recently, China ratified the Anti-Fouling Convention in 2011, which came into force on 17 June 2011.[7]

However, in practice, how China implements and enforces UNCLOS and the IMO's conventions is to a large extent unknown. There is also limited public information that can be collected from desk-based research alone. In China, the prevention of vessel-source pollution has attracted little interest from academics to date. In addition, government decision-making processes are not widely available to the public. Although more may currently be known about China's policy deliberations and governmental administration than at any previous time, it remains difficult to find sufficient information for analysis. Without a comprehensive understanding of China's social system and culture, it can be challenging for outsiders to fully understand the complex structure of Chinese legislation and how it is implemented.[8]

---

does not define 'port' or 'coastal' State. According to Churchill and Lowe, coastal State is the state in one of whose maritime zones a particular vessel lies; port State is the state in one of whose ports a particular vessel lies. However, Molenaar suggests that account should not only be taken of the type of enforcement (in port or at sea), but also the locus of the violation and the type of standard subject to enforcement. What should nevertheless be clear is that port or coastal State jurisdiction always implies jurisdiction over foreign vessels. See E.J. Molenaar, *Coastal State Jurisdiction over Vessel-Source Pollution* (The Hague: Kluwer Law International, 1998), pp. 92–93.

6   International Convention for the Prevention of Pollution from Ships, *International Legal Materials* 12, no. 6 (1973): 1319–1444; International Convention for the Safety of Life at Sea, 1974, *International Legal Materials* 14, no. 4 (1975): 959–978.

7   International Convention on the Control of Harmful Anti-Fouling Systems on Ships, 2001, IMO Doc. AFS/CONF/26, 18 October 2001; Announcement of the Ministry of Transport, No. 22, 22 April 2011, the Entry into Force of the IMO Anti-Fouling Convention in P.R. China (in Chinese).

8   G. Xue, *China and International Fisheries Law and Policy* (Leiden: Martinus Nijhoff, 2005), p. 10.

In response to the limited literature on the prevention of vessel-source pollution under Chinese law, the author conducted semi-structured interviews in ten major port cities along China's coast between August 2011 and February 2012 (Dalian, Guangzhou, Haikou, Tianjin, Ningbo, Qinhuangdao, Qingdao, Shanghai, Shenzhen, and Yantai). Interviews were mainly conducted with representatives from China's Maritime Safety Administration (MSA), the competent authority for the prevention of vessel-source pollution in China. Additionally, unpublished (internally published) documents from China's MSA were collected and analysed.

Based on the literature and interview findings, this article focuses on the effectiveness of China's law and practice on the prevention of vessel-source pollution as a coastal State. The article first provides a brief overview of Chinese legislation on the prevention of vessel-source pollution. It then introduces the structure and function of the MSA and concludes by covering two major issues relating to China's role as a coastal State, namely, the identification of illegal discharge at sea and ship routeing/ship reporting systems. Flag State and port State measures are beyond the scope of the article and will not be considered.

Legislation

In order to implement UNCLOS and the IMO's conventions for the prevention of vessel-source pollution, China has promulgated the 1982 *Marine Environmental Protection Law* (MEPL), as amended in 1999.[9] The adoption of the MEPL in 1982 and amendments in 1999 can be seen as domestic responses to legal developments at the international level.[10] In 2010, the State Council of China enacted the Regulation on the Prevention and Control of Marine Pollution from Vessels (2010 Regulation),[11] which replaced the 1983 Regulation on Prevention of Pollution from Ships at Sea. The Ministry of Transport also

---

9   Decree of the President of the P.R. China (No. 26), Marine Environment Protection Law (revised), Standing Committee of National People's Congress Gazette, Issue No. 7, 1999.

10   For detailed discussions about MEPL and 2010 Regulation, see N. Liu and F. Maes, "Prevention of Vessel-Source Marine Pollution: A Note on the Challenges and Prospects for Chinese Practice under International Law," *Ocean Development and International Law* 42, no. 4 (2011): 356–367.

11   State Council of P.R. China, Order No. 561, 9 September 2009.

plays an important role for initiating and drafting the 2010 Regulation on the Prevention and Control of Marine Pollution from Vessels due to their superior institutional capacities. This is a common phenomenon in the Chinese system of law-making and is known as 'departmentalism' (*bumen lifa*).[12]

Under the framework set out by the 2010 Regulation, the Ministry of Transport adopted a set of supplementary rules of judicial practice between 2010 and 2012.[13] These include the Implementing Rules on the Insurance for Civil Liability of Damage by Vessel-Source Oil Pollution,[14] the Rules on the Prevention and Control of Marine Pollution from Ships and Relevant Operating Activities (Rule No. 7, 2010),[15] the Rules on the Contingency Plan and Contingency Response of Vessel-Source Marine Pollution,[16] and the Rules on the Investigation of Vessel-Source Pollution Accidents at Sea.[17]

Maritime Safety Administration

Both the 1999 MEPL and the 2010 Regulations designated the MSA as the responsible institution for marine pollution caused by non-military vessels:

> Art. 5 (3), 1999 MEPL: The State administrative department in charge of maritime affairs shall be responsible for the supervision and control over marine environment pollution caused by non-military vessels inside the port waters under its jurisdiction and non-fishery vessels and non-military vessels outside the said port waters, and be responsible for the investigation and treatment of the pollution accidents. In the event of a pollution accident caused by a foreign vessel navigating, berthing or operating in the sea under the jurisdiction of the People's Republic of

---

12 Y.N. Cho, "The Politics of Lawmaking in Chinese Local People's Congresses," *China Quarterly* 187, no. 3 (2006): 596–602.

13 For details about those supplementary rules, see B. Dong, L. Zhu and M. Luo, "Current Legal Developments: China: Combating Marine Pollution from Vessels: China's New Legislation," *International Journal of Marine and Coastal Law* 29, no. 1 (2014): 158–172. Rules play an important role in the Chinese legal system since they provide more details and guidelines for understanding and enforcement of laws and regulations. Until 30 November 2009, there are 596 valid implementing rules issued by MSA (Decree of the Ministry of Transport, No. 3, 2010 (in Chinese)).

14 Decree of the Ministry of Transport, No. 3, 2010 (in Chinese).

15 Decree of the Ministry of Transport, No. 7, 2010 (in Chinese).

16 Decree of the Ministry of Transport, No. 4, 2011 (in Chinese).

17 Decree of the Ministry of Transport, No. 10, 2011 (in Chinese).

China, inspection and treatment shall be conducted on board the vessel in question. Where the pollution accident caused by a vessel results in fishery damages, the competent fishery administrative department shall be invited to take part in the investigation and treatment.

Art. 4, 2010 Regulation: The State administrative department in charge of maritime affairs shall be responsible for the supervision and control over marine environment pollution caused by non-military vessels inside the port waters under its jurisdiction and non-fishery vessels and non-military vessels outside the said port waters. According to this Regulation, the maritime safety administration is responsible for specific supervision and administration of vessel-source pollution and relevant activities.

Although China established its new Coast Guard in 2013,[18] the MSA's capacity to enforce vessel-source pollution legislation was unaffected. The MSA is affiliated with the Ministry of Transport. The MSA's central authority is based in Beijing. There are 12 provincial MSAs along the coastline, under which approximately 90 local branches have been established. The MSA has a working team consisting of 25,000 officials, other working staff, and a patrol force of 1,300 vessels and crafts of various types.[19] Generally, each coastal province has its own provincial MSA, which is directly led by the MSA central authority based in Beijing.[20] These provincial MSAs are normally based in the capital city or the most important port city of that coastal province. Additionally, major port cities feature MSAs. City-level MSAs have several units (Maritime Safety Unit or *Haishichu*) responsible for enforcement and on-site inspections.

---

18   In 2013, the 12th National People's Congress adopted the Institutional Reform and Functional Change Plan for State Council. According to the Plan, a new China Coast Guard has been established, which incorporates the Sea Police, State Fisheries Administration, China Marine Surveillance (State Oceanic Administration), and Bureau of Anti-Smuggling at Sea. See Standing Committee of National People's Congress Gazette, Issue No. 2, 2013 (in Chinese).

19   Official website of the China MSA, available online: <http://en.msa.gov.cn>.

20   Along China's coastline, there are 12 provincial MSAs: Tianjin, Hebei Province MSA (based at Qinghuangdao), Shandong Province MSA (based at Qingdao), Liaoning Province MSA (based at Dalian), Jiangsu Province MSA (based at Nanjing), Shanghai MSA, Zhejiang Province MSA (based at Hangzhou however, the most important port in Zhejiang Province is Ningbo-Zhoushan port, which ranks as one of top ten busiest ports in the world), Fujian Province MSA (based at Fuzhou, however, the most important port in Fujian Province is the Xiamen Port), Shenzhen MSA, Guangdong Province MSA (based at Guangzhou), Guangxi Province MSA (based at Nanning), and Hainan Province MSA (based at Haikou).

The MSA has its own enforcement power at sea – the China Sea Patrol (*Zhongguo Haixun*).

Faure et al. refer to recent studies on the effects of decentralization on environmental management in developing countries that increasingly demonstrate the capture of decision-making processes by local elites. These studies suggest that in such cases local end-users are better off where there is direct intervention from the central government to enforce the law against local elites.[21] The MSA system is centralized (*chuizhi guanli*), and in the author's opinion, it generally functions effectively.

It has long been identified that local protectionism is a major problem for effective implementation of Chinese environmental legislation.[22] This does not appear to be the case with regards to the prevention of vessel-source pollution due to the fact that local governments have limited influence on the MSA. Local governments cannot directly control MSA personnel,[23] nor can they control budgetary or other related MSA arrangements at the provincial and city level. Individual offices within MSA bureaucracies are not responsible to superiors within local governments (*kuai*); rather, they are directly controlled by their functional administrative superiors (*tiao*) and have only consultative relationships with local government.[24] The provincial MSAs operate as relatively independent organizations under the control of the MSA central authority in Beijing.[25]

---

21   M. Faure, M. Goodwin and F. Weber, "Bucking the Kuznets Curve: Designing Effective Environmental Regulation in Developing Countries," *Virginia Journal of International Law* 51, no. 1 (2010): 121–122.

22   B. Van Rooij, "Implementing Chinese Environmental Law through Enforcement," in *Implementation of Law in the People's Republic of China*, eds. J. Chen, Y. Li and J.M. Otto (The Hague: Kluwer Law International, 2002), 162–163.

23   It is worth mentioning that the workforce of the MSA is made up of graduates from China's dedicated maritime universities (e.g., Dalian Maritime University and Shanghai Maritime University).

24   A.C. Mertha, "China's 'Soft' Centralization: Shifting Tiao/Kuai Authority Relations," *China Quarterly* 184 (December 2005): 791–810, 792.

25   Chinese administrative units generally distinguish between two types of political relationships: those governed by binding orders, and those based on non-binding instructions. Any political unit in China has the second type of relationship with any number of other units. But it has the first type of relationship with only one, its direct 'superior'. A relationship based upon such binding orders is referred to as 'leadership relations' or *lingdao guanxi*. The other type is based on 'professional relations' or *yewu guanxi*. Mertha, id., p. 797.

The MSA central authority is required to conduct an inspection of national legislation enforcement at least once every two years. Due to limits on the number of staff working in the central office, the inspection of legislation enforcement is carried out by a delegation consisting of staff from the central authority as well as one staff member from the provincial authority. The inspection requires overseeing the work of local MSA branches.[26] Provincial MSAs are required to inspect the work of local branches within their jurisdiction once annually.[27]

One successful case concerning the enforcement of legislation by the MSA is illustrated by their implementation of a zero discharge policy in the Bohai Sea. The Bohai Sea is a semi-enclosed body of water that borders China's coastline and is claimed as its internal waters.[28] It has a total area of 77,284 km², spans 3,784 km of coastline and has an average depth of 18 m. The Bohai Sea is the most polluted sea under China's jurisdiction. According to the Bulletin of China's Marine Environmental Status for 2010, 32,730 km² of the Bohai Sea is polluted during the summer months,[29] representing 40 percent of its total area. In 2001, to protect the marine environment of the Bohai Sea, the Chinese government adopted an Action Plan for Cleaning up the Bohai Sea.[30] The Ministry of Transport enacted the 2003 Procedural Rules on the Zero Discharge from Vessels (*Qianfeng*) in the Bohai Sea,[31] which provided that vessels (except for military and fishing vessels) docking, sailing or operating in the Bohai Sea for more than one month must seal their discharge facilities and discharge pollutants to reception facilities onshore.[32] The zero discharge measure has limited impact on vessels engaged in international voyages since these vessels rarely stay in the Bohai Sea for more than one month. The effectiveness of the zero discharge measure also depends on several factors such as sufficient

---

26 Interview with MSA staff (Qinghuangdao, Hebei Provincial MSA).

27 Rules on the Supervision of Maritime Administrative Law Enforcement, MSA, 1 May 2011 (in Chinese), Art. 40.

28 1958 Declaration on Territorial Sea by the Government of People's Republic of China (in Chinese).

29 Part 2, Marine Environmental Quality Status, Bulletin of China's Marine Environmental Status for the year 2010.

30 Circular on Adoption of Bohai Clean Sea Action Plan, No. 181, 2001, Ministry of Environmental Protection (in Chinese).

31 Circular on the Adoption of Procedural Rules on the Zero Discharge from Vessels (Qianfeng) in Bohai Sea, No. 32, 2003, Ministry of Transport (in Chinese). This was replaced by 2007 Rules on the Zero Discharge from Vessels (*Qianfeng*) in Coastal Sea Areas, No. 165, 2007, Ministry of Transport.

32 Procedural Rules on the Zero Discharge from Vessels (*Qianfeng*) in the Bohai Sea, Art. 3.

reception facilities onshore and effective inspection from the MSA. During interviews with MSA officers around the Bohai Sea (Dalian, Qinhuangdao and Tianjin), the MSA staff always referred to the 'Qianfeng' measures as a success.

Although in general the MSA system functions well, minor weaknesses exist that warrant mention. For example, unlike organizations in developed countries, such as the European Maritime Safety Agency (EMSA), which has hundreds of staff working on monitoring the work of EU Member States, the central authority of the MSA has fewer than ten personnel responsible for monitoring the work of the organization's provincial branches. Moreover, the effectiveness of internal monitoring is still unknown. According to Andrew Mertha, an associate professor of government specializing in Chinese politics, centrally managed administrative units are usually geographically distant from their functional and administrative superiors, and therefore difficult to supervise. It is easy for centrally managed units to establish a 'father-son relationship'; when the higher level unit discovers a problem, it might be reluctant to be overly strict with its subordinate unit.[33]

Practice

The Identification of Illegal Discharges at Sea
The identification of illegal discharges from vessels at sea is a difficult issue for practically all countries. The MSA's China Sea Patrol (*Zhongguo Haixun*) is responsible for this task. In 2000, the MSA adopted the Rules on the Administration of Patrols at Sea. The MSA replaced these rules in 2011 with a new set which provided that the MSA shall cruise in seas under China's jurisdiction to ensure compliance with maritime safety standards and prevent vessel-source pollution.[34] The Rules on the Administration of Patrols at Sea allocates MSA vessels over 80 meters in length to the control of the MSA's central authority, with MSA vessels less than 80 meters allocated to provincial MSAs.[35] To date, there are 207 MSA patrol vessels over 20 meters in length. Only three patrol vessels of 100 meters or longer (*Haixun 31, 21* and *11*) are responsible for patrol and emergency response operations outside the

33   See Mertha, n. 24 above, p. 804.
34   Rules on the Administration of Patrols at Sea, Art. 1.
35   Rules on the Administration of Patrols at Sea, Art. 3.

50-nautical mile offshore limit.[36] According to the Guiding Principles for the Development of Chinese Maritime Affairs (2005–2020) published by the Ministry of Transport, MSA vessels only expanded their patrol areas to 200 nautical miles from China's coastline since 2010.[37] The majority of MSA vessels cannot travel long distances. Consequently, MSA patrols have traditionally been confined to port or coastal areas. For example, the Wu Song Unit of the Shanghai MSA is responsible for patrolling the estuary of the Yangtze River. The unit has 11 vessels, the largest of which is 55 meters long.[38] Their main function is to maintain traffic order in the shipping routes of the Yangtze River estuary. The constraints faced by MSA vessels in terms of limited cruising range and competing functions demonstrate that the China Sea Patrol faces obstacles in enforcing vessel-source pollution regulations at sea.

The China Sea Patrol (*Zhongguo Haixun*) has, however, developed very rapidly over the past five years. Before the establishment of China's new Coast Guard, there was competition between the MSA and the State Oceanic Administration (SOA) for a dominant role in the Coast Guard. Therefore, both *Zhongguo Haixun* and China Marine Surveillance, the SOA's enforcement power at sea, were building more vessels to strengthen their capacity. These developments were therefore not strictly driven by the Chinese government's desire to enforce national and international legislation for the prevention of vessel-source pollution at sea. Rather, they have resulted from tensions in disputed sea areas between China and its neighbors, such as Japan (Diaoyu Islands, East China Sea), Vietnam, Malaysia and Philippines (South China Sea), as well as from the government's desire to strengthen its control and non-military presence in these disputed areas. The 2011 Rules on the Administration of Patrols at Sea also declare that one of the key reasons for MSA's patrol at sea is to protect China's sovereignty and national ocean interests,[39] which was not included in the 2000 Rules on the Administration of Patrols at Sea.

The MSA lacks its own satellites and as a consequence it lacks the internal capacity to indirectly monitor illegal discharges by vessels at sea. For indirect monitoring, the MSA relies on the SOA, which manages China's ocean satellites. This relationship requires the MSA to purchase satellite images in the

---

36   China MSA official website, "Maritime Equipment," available online: <http://www.msa .gov.cn/Static/zbjs> (in Chinese).

37   G. Liu, "Achievements of China Maritime Safety Administration in the 11th Five Years Plan Period," *China Water Transport* 2 (2006): 8–9 (in Chinese).

38   "Introduction to the Wusong Unit of Shanghai MSA," available online: <http://www .shwsmsa.cn/nr.aspx?id=1> (in Chinese).

39   Rules on the Administration of Patrols at Sea, Art. 1.

aftermath of oil spills to aid investigations. For example, in 2010, a pipeline explosion occurred at the northeast port of Dalian, causing oil to spread over an area of 430 km^2 and prompting a clean-up mission along the coast.[40] In order to facilitate the mission, the MSA purchased satellite images from the SOA.[41] This functions as an effective means for the MSA to perform indirect monitoring. However, one limitation stems from the fact that it is possible to do so only after serious oil spills have occurred rather than before due to the significant cost associated with SOA-provided satellite images. This was described as a constraint to the MSA discharging its duty of monitoring vessel-source pollution during the interviews.

Furthermore, the Rules on the Reward of Providing Information about Vessel-Source Pollution and Vessels Carrying Hazardous Goods provide that individuals who inform the MSA about illegal discharges from vessels will receive a financial reward. The effectiveness of this reward system is doubtful. The amount of the reward cannot exceed ten percent of the fine imposed on the vessel.[42] The maximum fine that can be imposed on illegal discharge from vessels is 100,000 Yuan (Chinese currency).[43]

> Art. 73, 1999 MEPL: In case of any of the following acts, in violation of the provisions of this Law, the department empowered by this Law to conduct marine environment supervision and control shall order a correction and impose a fine in accordance with the provisions of this Law: (1) discharging into the sea any pollutants or any other substances the discharge of which is prohibited by this Law; (2) discharging pollutants into the sea in a way inconsistent with the provisions of this Law, or discharging pollutants in excess of standards; (3) dumping wastes in the sea without obtaining a permit for dumping; and (4) failing to take prompt measures for a treatment in the event of an accident or any other contingency that has caused pollution to the marine environment. For any violation as mentioned in (1) and (3) of the preceding paragraph, a fine of

---

40   "China's worst-ever oil spill threatens wildlife as volunteers assist in clean-up," *Guardian*, 21 July 2010, available online: <http://www.guardian.co.uk/environment/2010/jul/21/china-oil-spill-disaster-wildlife>.

41   "High Technology Assists in Marine Cleaning," *China Maritime Safety* 8 (2010): 17 (in Chinese).

42   Rules on the Reward of Providing Information about Vessel-Source Pollution and Vessels Carrying Hazardous Goods, Circular on the Adoption of Rules on the Reward of Providing Information about Vessel-Source Pollution and Vessels Carrying Hazardous Goods, No. 63, 2011, Ministry of Transport (in Chinese), Art. 10.

43   Approximately US$16,000 under current exchange rates.

not less than RMB 30,000 yuan but not more than 200,000 yuan shall be imposed; for any violation as mentioned in (2) and (4) of the preceding paragraph, a fine not less than 20,000 yuan but not more than 100,000 yuan shall be imposed.

It is questioned to what extent seafarers, as employees, can refuse to obey their employer, or implicate them by reporting them to an authority that they know in the end may likely detain the ship, which is their instrument of contract and livelihood with that employer.[44]

Ship Routeing and Ship Reporting

The first shipping route in sea areas under China's jurisdiction was designated in 1984 (Da Sanshan, Dalian Port). Since that time, China has established 16 mandatory shipping routes along its coastal waters, of which 15 shipping routes are traffic separation schemes (TSS).[45] In 2011, the Ministry of Transport published the National Plan for Ship Routeing in Coastal Sea Areas. In the next decade, a total of 26 shipping routes will be designated. This includes six trunk lines (Laotieshan Shuidao, Cheng Shan Jiao, Estuary of Yangtze River, Taiwan Strait, Estuary of Pearl River and Qiongzhou Strait), five port areas (Dalian, Qingdao, Rizhao, Ningbo and Xiamen), and 15 other lines.[46] All these shipping routes are within China's territorial sea or in its internal waters or port areas. Considering the political situation between mainland China and Taiwan, the shipping routes designated in the Taiwan Strait by the People's Republic of China are within the sea areas under China's control.[47] To date, China has been modest in designating shipping routes and has not done so in sea areas disputed with its neighboring countries.

---

44 O.G. Anthony, "Criminalization of Seafarers for Accidental Discharge of Oil: Is there Justification in International Law for Criminal Sanction for Negligent or Accidental Pollution of the Sea?" *Journal of Maritime Law and Commerce* 37, no. 2 (2006): 219–232.

45 M. Wang, "The Urgent Need to Implement Ship Routeing System in the Coastal Waters of China," *China Maritime Safety* 11 (2011): 6 (in Chinese), 6–10.

46 "Ship Routeing will be Designated in Busy Traffic Sea Areas in the Coming 3–5 Years," available online: <http://www.moc.gov.cn/zhuzhan/jiaotongxinwen/xinwenredian/2011 2xinwen/201112/t20111223_1175907.html> (in Chinese).

47 "Taiwan Straits and coastal sea areas eastwards [to] Taiwan Island are both China's coastal waters. However, considering the current situation, the national plan only applied to sea areas of the Taiwan Straits bordering with the mainland China," Special Interpretation of the National Plan for Ship Routeing in Coastal Sea Areas, available online: <http://www .moc.gov.cn/zhuzhan/wangshangzhibo/11zhuantifbh/zhibozhaiyao/201112/t20111222 _1174902.html> (in Chinese).

SOLAS Chapter V (Safety of Navigation) states that governments may establish vessel traffic service (VTS) systems when, in their opinion, the volume of traffic or the degree of risk justifies such services.[48] The MSA is keen to establish a national VTS system. To date, there are 30 VTS systems operating along China's coastline. These VTS systems control 73,620 km² of sea area.[49] The MSA is responsible for vessel traffic while the VTS Centre affiliated with the MSA is responsible for the operation of the VTS system. In 1997, the MSA adopted the Rules for Vessel Traffic System Safety Management and the Rules for Vessel Traffic System Operation Management. Vessels in the VTS area must report to the MSA following the VTS User Guidelines published by the MSA.[50] Furthermore, when there is an accident, the vessel shall report to the VTS Centre as well.[51]

Regulation 19 of SOLAS Chapter V – Carriage Requirements for Shipborne Navigational Systems and Equipment – sets out navigational equipment to be carried onboard ships, according to ship type. In 2000, the IMO adopted a new requirement as part of a revised Chapter V for all ships to carry automatic identification systems (AIS) capable of automatically providing information about the ship to other ships and to coastal authorities.[52] The requirement came into force on 1 July 2002. The MSA issued a circular on 18 December 2001,[53] which requires three classes of Chinese ships to be fitted with AIS transponders: ships of 300 gross tonnage (gt) and upwards engaged in international voyages; cargo ships of 500 gt and upwards not engaged in international voyages; and all passenger ships. In 2010, the MSA adopted the Rules on AIS Equipment for Chinese Vessels engaged in domestic voyages.[54] This rule expanded the use of AIS to domestic shipping.

Conclusion

China has adopted a substantial amount of legislation to implement UNCLOS and the IMO's conventions for the prevention of vessel-source pollution. The MSA is the competent law-enforcement institution. On the whole, China's

---

48   IMO, "Vessel Traffic Services," available online: <http://www.imo.org/OurWork/Safety/Navigation/Pages/VesselTrafficServices.aspx>.

49   "The MSA's First National Conference on Ship Traffic Management held in Ningbo," *China Maritime Safety* 12 (2011): 16. (in Chinese).

50   Rules for Vessel Traffic System Safety Management, Art. 4.

51   Rules for Vessel Traffic System Safety Management, Art. 5.

52   IMO, "AIS Transponders," available online: <http://www.imo.org/ourwork/safety/navigation/pages/ais.aspx>.

53   Announcement on AIS Equipment, No. 2, 2001, MSA (in Chinese).

54   Circular on the Adoption of Rules on AIS Equipment for Chinese Vessels engaged in domestic voyages, No. 156, 2010, MSA (in Chinese).

centralized MSA system functions effectively. The highly educated workforce of the MSA, composed of graduates from China's dedicated maritime universities (e.g., Dalian Maritime University and Shanghai Maritime University), the international and technical nature of shipping issues, as well as the limited influence of and interaction with local government all contribute to the independence of the MSA. The relatively uncomplicated administrative structure enhances the efficiency and effectiveness of this system. As a coastal State, a current limitation of law enforcement by the MSA stems from the lack of infrastructure for patrol purposes. The MSA has not yet acquired sufficient capacity to identify illegal discharges in China's EEZ. China therefore needs to catch up and increase its procurement of ships and technology for this purpose.

Implementing the Maritime Labour Convention, 2006 in the Philippines: Rules, Organizations and Prospects

Joseph Anthony Loot
Interdisciplinary Studies Ph.D. Student, Dalhousie University, Halifax, Nova Scotia, Canada

Introduction

On 13 August 2012, the Senate of the Philippines approved a resolution on the ratification of the Maritime Labour Convention, 2006 (MLC) (Resolution 829).[1] Seven days later, upon depositing its instrument of ratification, which was registered by the Director General of the International Labour Organization (ILO), the Philippines became the thirtieth country with a registered ratification. In so doing, the MLC, 2006 entered into force 12 months later on 20 August 2013. ILO Director-General Juan Somavia commented on the Philippine ratification, together with the previous 29 States, as a "remarkable achievement" considering the 30 State ratifications totaled "nearly 60 percent...nearly double" the required shipping tonnage.[2] National government officials Senator Loren Legarda and Secretary Rosalinda Dimapilis-Baldoz of the Department of Labor and Employment (DOLE) also hailed the Philippine ratification and pointed out that the MLC, 2006 is vital to the country, particularly the numerous Filipino seafarers employed in domestic and international shipping.[3]

---

1   Philippine Senate, "Senate Concurrence in Ratification of Maritime Labour Convention, a Global Milestone – Legarda," available online: <http://www.senate.gov.ph/press_release/2012/0813_legarda1.asp>. The twenty-two Senators sitting in the Fifteenth Congress unanimously approved Resolution 829, which subsequently was adopted under Resolution 118. See Resolution No. 118, Resolution Concurring in the Ratification of Maritime Labour Convention, 2006, 13th Cong., 3rd Sess. (August 13, 2012) in <http://www.senate.gov.ph/15th_congress/resolutions/resno118.pdf>.

2   International Labour Organization (ILO), "Milestone ratifications of seafarers' labour rights charter," available online: <http://www.ilo.org/global/about-the-ilo/newsroom/news/WCMS_187660/lang--en/index.htm>.

3   Senator Loren Legarda was Chair of the Senate Committee on Foreign Relations and the sponsor of Resolution 829. See n. 1 above. Also, Department of Labor and Employment, "It's official: Philippines 30th ILO member-State to ratify MLC, 2006; Director General Somavia

© KONINKLIJKE BRILL NV, LEIDEN, 2015 | DOI 10.1163/9789004297234_016

This article discusses the Philippines' implementation of the MLC, 2006 one year after it entered into force. The discussion will (1) describe the Philippines' role as a maritime nation, (2) describe applicable primary and supporting national laws, (3) describe the structure, function and interconnection of government agencies tasked with implementation, and (4) analyse the opportunities and challenges associated with the Convention's implementation. With regard to the government agencies, this article does not cover any existing government and private sector (civil society and business) arrangements beyond mentioning the private sector organizations. On the implementation aspect, the article dwells mainly on the Philippines being a flag State and a seafarer labor-supplying country. This is in line with the compliance and enforcement provisions of MLC, 2006.

The Philippines as a Maritime Nation and the MLC, 2006

The Philippines is a maritime nation with flag State status and a seafarer supplying tradition. As a mid-ocean archipelago, vast bodies of water, notably the Pacific Ocean to the east and the South China Sea to the west, surround over 7,100 Philippine islands. Shipping is a vital national industry and ships are a major means of transporting goods and people to domestic and international destinations. As per the Maritime Industry Authority (MARINA) report in 2012, there are 8,112 vessels comprising the domestic merchant fleet.[4] As of 1 January 2013, according to the review of the United Nations Conference on Trade and Development (UNCTAD), there are 1,383 Philippine registered ships engaged in international seaborne trade with total deadweight tonnage of 6,417, which places the country as one of the 35 flag States with the largest registered fleet.[5] In the same review, the Philippines ranked nineteenth in number of vessels and thirty-second in deadweight tonnage out of the top 35 flags of registration with the largest registered fleets.

---

accepts ratification instrument," 19 October 2012, available online: <http://www.dole.gov.ph/good_news/view/132>.

4 Maritime Industry Authority, *The Philippine Maritime Industry: Prospects and Challenges in 2013 and Beyond*, available online: <http://www.marina.gov.ph/reports/report.htm>. Sixty percent (4,837) of the domestic fleet are passenger vessels, 28 percent (2,291) cargo ships, and 10 percent (795) tankers and tugboats.

5 United Nations Conference on Trade and Development (UNCTAD), *Review of Maritime Transport, 2013* (Geneva: UNCTAD, 2013), available online: <http://unctad.org/en/publicationslibrary/rmt2013_en.pdf>.

The Philippines is also the largest global supplier of officers, ratings, and service providers. In its 20 August 2012 news item, the ILO acknowledges the Philippines as "the largest source of the world's seafarers" and "home to nearly one third – 30 percent – of seafarers working on foreign flag ships."[6] As per government data, there were 366,865 overseas Filipino workers (OFWs) deployed in sea-based employment[7] in 2012 and 367,166 in 2013.[8] Filipino seafarers are hired to work overseas because they are (1) documented licensed professionals and certificated, thus, manifesting high training qualifications, (2) fluent in English – the lingua franca in international business including shipping, (3) in abundant supply due to the large Filipino population and high domestic unemployment rate and poverty incidence,[9] (4) widely branded and accepted as good, hard workers, and thus, increasing their brand recall,[10] and (5) graduates

---

6   ILO, "Philippines Ratification Marks Global Milestone for Decent Work for Seafarers," 20 August 2012, available online: <http://www.ilo.org/global/standards/maritime-labour -convention/WCMS_187712/lang--en/index.htm>.

7   The other classification of OFW is land-based, which, unlike sea-based seafarers, is comprised of various occupations deployed in numerous country destinations. Department of Labor and Employment, *Deployed Overseas Filipino Workers and Overseas Filipinos Remittances, Philippines: 2012 – April 2014*, available online: <http://www.bles.dole.gov.ph/ PUBLICATIONS/Current%20Labor%20Statistics/STATISTICAL%20TABLES/PDF/Tab43 .pdf>.

8   Id. There are no government data on the number of Filipinos employed in domestic merchant fleets. Generally, they are classified under the transport sector. Nonetheless, it can be surmised that the number would be large given the 8,112 vessels, as stated above, that sail within domestic waters. See n. 4 above.

9   A.M. Baylon and E.M.R. Santos, "The Challenges in Philippine Maritime Education and Training," *International Journal of Innovative and Interdisciplinary Research* (December 2011), p. 35. Per the National Statistics Coordination Board, population census as of 2010 is 92,337,852, with an annual growth rate of 1.90 percent; of the 63.8 percent labor force participation rate as of January 2014, the unemployment rate is 7.5 percent and underemployment is 19.5 percent; national poverty incidence in 2012 was 25.2 percent. National Statistics Coordination Board, *Statistics*, available online: <http://www.nscb.gov.ph/ stattables/>.

10   One possible explanation for the branding is the Filipino culture of resilience and hospitality. They have resisted centuries of foreign colonization, withstood natural (typhoons and volcanic eruptions) and human caused (oil spills) disasters, opposed dictatorship and rampant corruption in government, and lived in poverty for years. Amid all these trials, they remain patient, manage to smile, and struggle and live each day. On the other hand, Filipino hospitality presents a giving and forgiving attitude in a community spirit. With work and human relations, they practice service to others and submit to authority. Terry notes the following stereotype qualities of Filipinos that mark them as ideal workers in cruise lines: hardworking and flexible, subservient, family-oriented, happy, and nice.

of cadetship programs from maritime educational institutions receiving foreign funding support, which not only contributes to quality but provides assurance for employment.[11] In a more subtle way, as pointed out by Terry, government programs within the Philippines often conceive OFWs as 'unsung heroes' who sacrifice for their country and provide economic sustenance to the national economy. This places cultural pressure on workers to seek employment abroad.[12]

Historical, geographical, social, and economic factors drive Filipinos to work at sea despite occupational hazards and threats. Cabuang characterizes Filipinos as "island people" who dwell on islands and live by the seas (as opposed to "'inland people' who look at the waters as dividing lines that separate different islands").[13] He points out further that Filipino seafarers have been using the seas to bridge islands since the beginning of the Manila-Acapulco trade in 1565. The geographical attachment of Filipinos to the sea establishes seafaring as a common occupation despite the knowledge that work at sea involves hard labor and significant hazards. On the other hand, seafaring from a personal and family perspective, particularly overseas, is an opportunity for travel and a lucrative source of employment and income. Both personal and family interests are interconnected, with family interest being more prominent due to it being culturally regarded as a basic social unit. Thus, the family is a crucial influence in the decision by many Filipinos to engage in seafaring. Lamvik explains in his study that many Filipino seafarers endure the physical and psychological hardships on board ships because of their concern for family well-being and survival over and above personal struggles.[14] It is the family that invests resources for education and the recipient reciprocates by giving the family income from work in cash, in-kind or in enterprise investment (with the family as beneficiaries from investment income).[15]

W.C. Terry, "The Perfect Worker: Discursive Makings of Filipinos in the Workplace Hierarchy of the Globalized Cruise Industry," *Social and Cultural Geography* 15 (2014): 83–88.

11   Marine Café Blog, "The Filipino Seafarer Factory Revisited," 23 July 2012, available online: <http://www.marine-cafe.com/filipino-seafarer-factory-revisited/#.U8iz_JRdVgE>. Baylon and Santos, n. 9 above, p. 35.

12   Terry, n. 10 above, pp. 81–83.

13   F.S. Cabuang, "Filipino Seafarers Face Better Future!" *Tinig Ng Marino* (January–February 2014).

14   G.M. Lamvik, "The Filipino Seafarer – A Life between Sacrifice and Shopping," (Ph.D. diss. Norwegian University of Science and Technology, 2002), pp. 1–4.

15   Many of these investments are directly related to seafaring, such as marine educational and training institutions, which are lucrative given the numerous cadets and seafarers

The personal and family perspective is enhanced by government promotion of the seafaring profession. While government programs are intended to attract Filipinos into seafaring to address issues of population growth and domestic unemployment, these programs are at the same time aimed at expanding sources of national income. Seafarer remittance significantly contributes to national income. Total remittances of sea-based OFWs in 2013 amounted to US$5.2 billion, which is about 23 percent of overall total OFW remittances.[16] Furthermore, Amante points out that OFW remittances contribute to the balance of payments and foreign exchange stability and serve as a buffer against drastic Philippine peso devaluations that lead to inflation.[17] Apart from remittances, Filipino seafarers also contribute to the national finances indirectly through payments of required fees for education and training, and certifications. MARINA, in particular, collected PhP399.5 million (c. US$9.46 million) in 2012.[18] Filipino seafarers, moreover, also contribute to national social security.

The entry of new States providing seafarers – including those in Eastern Europe, Indonesia, Africa, and other developing economies – risks compromising the international shipping industry's ability to respond to the social, economic, and cultural factors that push Filipinos to seek employment as seafarers. This competition may result in Filipino seafarers becoming commodities that easily submit to exploitative and oppressive labor conditions,[19] especially in the absence of an international standard on decent employment. Such is the condition on board ships despite efforts of Philippine government agencies in securing fair and decent working conditions for Filipino seafarers.[20]

Enforceable international maritime labor standards are important for the Philippines as a flag State and a country from which many of the world's

---

      required by national regulatory bodies to undergo capacity building and documentation.

16   See Department of Labor and Employment, n. 7 above. The contributions of OFWs, particularly sea-based workers, are those officially reported and excludes money sent through unofficial means such as that sent through co-workers going home at the end of their contract.

17   M.S.V. Amante, *Philippine Global Seafarers: A Profile*, Research Report (Cardiff: Cardiff University, Seafarers' International Research Centre, 2003).

18   Maritime Industry Authority, n. 4 above.

19   E. Dela Cruz, "Turning the tide for seafarers," available online: <http://iboninternational .org/resources/pages/EDM/75/61>. This is unfair competition since Filipino seafarers compete for employment regardless of working conditions. This happens in the absence of a recruitment standard based on proficiency and competency.

20   ILO, "Preventing seafaring dreams from turning into nightmares," available online: <http:// ilo.org/global/about-the-ilo/newsroom/features/WCMS_219974/lang--en/index.htm>.

international seafaring workforce is drawn. In ratifying MLC, 2006, the Philippines is not only complying with the constitutional mandate for adherence to the general principles of international law, but also binds itself to protect the labor rights of all Filipino seafarers, including foreign nationals, on board Philippine-registered ships. The fundamental provisions for all seafarers in the MLC, 2006 are the stipulations of their fundamental rights,[21] their social and employment rights,[22] and State responsibilities for their protection through effective (and innovative) enforcement systems. The MLC, 2006 likewise establishes an important benefit for shipowners by establishing requirements aimed at helping to ensure fair competition. McConnell has noted the seafarers' right to a decent work-shipowners' level playing field equation established by the Convention, which the State should treat as inseparable and uniformly implemented.[23]

The MLC, 2006 is the fourth pillar of the international maritime regime complementing the three other pillar conventions of the International Maritime Organization (IMO), particularly the 1974 International Convention for the Safety of Life at Sea (SOLAS) and the 1978 International Convention on Standards for Training, Certification and Watchkeeping (STCW). The third IMO convention pillar is the International Convention for the Prevention of Pollution from Ships, 1973, as modified by the Protocol of 1978 relating thereto and by the Protocol of 1997 (MARPOL).[24]

Rules and Organizational Arrangements to Implement the MLC, 2006

When the Senate ratified the MLC, 2006, the Philippines already possessed national laws and organizational structures to establish and enforce adequate

---

21   The following are the fundamental rights under Article III:
    a)   freedom of association and the effective recognition of the right to collective bargaining;
    b)   the elimination of all forms of forced or compulsory labor;
    c)   the effective abolition of child labor; and
    d)   the elimination of discrimination in respect of employment and occupation.

22   Every seafarer has the right to a safe and secure workplace that complies with safety standards, to fair terms of employment, to decent working and living conditions on board ships, and to health protection, medical care, welfare measures, and other forms of social protection. See n. 3 above.

23   M. McConnell, "The Maritime Labour Convention 2006 – Reflections on Challenges for Flag State Implementation," *WMU Journal of Maritime Affairs* 10 (October 2011), p. 132.

24   The Philippines is a party to SOLAS, STCW, and MARPOL 73/78. As to the STCW, the Philippines has instituted domestic reforms in compliance with the requirements of the Convention, and included in the IMO 'White List' of countries.

labor standards in shipping (1987 Constitution, Republic Acts of Congress, presidential decrees and executive orders of the president, and administrative issuances of the designated department of the executive branch of government).[25] These laws defined the normative values of certain standards (specifically human or labor rights), mandated the implementation of international contractual obligations, and provided direction to achieve national goals. National laws also existed that established which government agency takes the lead and coordinates functions to implement the requirements of the Convention. After the Senate ratified the MLC, 2006 in 2012, DOLE, as the competent authority, issued department orders and labor advisories as measures to implement certain standards provided in MLC, 2006.

As already mentioned, this article describes only the organizational arrangements – structure and functions as provided in law – without delving into the hierarchy and system of administration. Moreover, although the focus of this article is on the implementation of MLC, 2006, this Convention, as noted above complements the IMO Conventions, particularly the STCW. This explains the inclusion of supporting agencies that form part of the total organization whose tasks may collectively and fully implement MLC, 2006.

National Laws
1987 Philippine Constitution: Relevant Provisions

The following provision in the Constitution embodies important principles relating to human rights' universality:

---

25   In the hierarchy of Philippine laws, the 1987 Constitution is the fundamental law followed by enactments of Congress, acts of the president, and administrative issuances of the departments of the executive branch. In Article VII of the same Constitution, executive power is vested in the president who heads the executive branch of government. However, during the rule of President Ferdinand E. Marcos prior to the 1986 'People Power' revolt that removed him from office, he issued presidential decrees that have the force of law given his legislative powers provided under the 1973 Constitution as amended in 1976 (Article XVII, Section 3, para. 2). Acts of the president and administrative issuances of executive departments other than the aforementioned presidential decrees also have the effect of law only as far as its consistency with the law it is sourced from. These issuances make possible the execution of laws by the executive branch of government and its instrumentality. For further explanation of this hierarchy, see also: A. Cruz-Trinidad, M.L. Maximo, J.L. Batongbacal, L.R. Pura and C.A. Courtney, "Hierarchy of Laws Governing Coastal Management in the Philippines," *OverSeas* 5, no. 9 (September 2002), available online: <http://oneocean.org/overseas/200209/the_hierarchy_of_laws_governing_coastal_mnmt_n_d_phil.html#source>. Treaties entered into by the President and ratified by the Senate, such as MLC, 2006, have the force and effect of a national law.

> The Philippines...adopts the generally accepted principles of interna-
> tional law as part of the law of the land and adheres to the policy of peace,
> equality, justice, freedom, cooperation, and amity with all nations.[26]

This directive provision of the Constitution contains two parts: the adoption of
incorporation doctrine in international law and the stipulation of adherence
to norms or principles accepted by nations. On the first part, the Supreme
Court held in a number of cases that by the incorporation method, accepted
principles of international law forms part of national law even if these principles are not derived from treaty obligations.[27] This provision articulates that
only "generally accepted principles of international law" are "accorded the status of national law." It therefore excludes principles which are not "generally
accepted."[28] The Supreme Court enunciates this in a human rights case of
Marcos v. Manglapus where a particular right that is a generally accepted principle of international law is part of national law (even though such right is not
stipulated in any domestic law).[29] On the second part, the Constitution indi-
vidualizes, though in rather vague concepts, the norms or principles adhered
to by the State as a matter of national policy. These principles are provided in
Article 2 of the Charter of the United Nations of which the Philippines is a
charter member.

The stipulation of the incorporation doctrine and the ratification of MLC,
2006 establishes the Philippine obligation to ensure promotion of the social
and economic rights of seafarers. In addition, the Philippines ratified the
International Covenant on Economic, Social and Cultural Rights (ICESCR) on
7 June 1974.[30] The rights provided in Article 7 of the Covenant are similar to the
social and employment rights in Article IV of MLC, 2006; the fundamental

---

26   1987 Philippine Constitution, Art. II, s. 2.

27   *Mijares v. Ranada*, 455 SCRA 397 (2005). SCRA refers to Supreme Court Reports Annotated.

28   M.M. Magallona, "An Essay on the Incorporation Clause of the Constitution as a Juridical
      Enigma," *The Integrated Bar of the Philippines Journal* 35 (August 2010), p. 19.

29   Id., p. 20. The Supreme Court ruled that "[t]he right to return to one's country is not
      among the rights specifically guaranteed in the Bill of Rights, which treats only of the
      liberty of abode and the right to travel, but it is our well-considered view that the right to
      return may be considered, as a generally accepted principle of international law and,
      under our Constitution, is part of the law of the land [Art. II, s. 2 of the Constitution]."
      The LAWPHiL Project, *Marcos v. Manglapus*, available online: <http://www.lawphil.net/
      judjuris/juri1989/sep1989/gr_88211_1989.html>.

30   iHumanRights Project, "Ratification of Human Rights Treaties," available online: <http://
      www.ihumanrights.ph/help-2/ratification-of-international-human-rights-treaties
      -philippines/>.

rights and principles in Article III of the MLC, 2006 are covered elsewhere in the Covenant. The ratification of these United Nations agreements effects the transformation of these rights and their protection under national law.[31] There are, however, specific provisions in MLC, 2006 on specific standards that are not provided in ICECSR that are adopted in particular national laws.

The protection of social and employment rights under MLC, 2006 is not only intended to prevent the abuses committed against seafarers. It also links human rights with social justice, both being key policies under the Constitution. Article II of the Constitution includes these key policies that directly relate to maritime labor:

> Section 10. The State shall promote social justice in all phases of national development;
> Section 11. The State values the dignity of every human person and guarantees full respect for human rights;
> Section 15. The State shall protect and promote the right to health...;
> Section 18. The State affirms labor as a primary social economic force. It shall protect the rights of workers and promote their welfare.

The value the Constitution places on labor strengthens the link between human rights and social justice. Article XIII, Section 3, on social justice and human rights mandates the protection of labor rights and recognizes the role of employers under the principle of shared responsibility, which can be understood in terms of both worker and employer standing on equal footing (such as both participating as key stakeholders in decision-making, particularly on issues relating to worker welfare)[32]:

---

31   The Supreme Court ruled in the case of *Pharmaceutical & Health Care Assn. of the Phil. v. Health Secretary Duque* that "[t]reaties become part of the law of the land through transformation pursuant to Article VII, Section 21 of the Constitution which provides that '[n]o treaty or international agreement shall be valid and effective unless concurred in by at least two-thirds of all the members of the Senate'." *Pharmaceutical & Health Care Assn. of the Phil. v. Health Secretary Duque*, G.R. No. 173034, 19 October 2007. G.R. refers to Government Reports.

32   In the case of *PAL, Inc v. NLRC* (1993), the Supreme Court noted the National Labor Relation Commission's observation: "In fact, our Constitution has recognized the principle of 'shared responsibility' between employers and workers and has likewise recognized the right of workers to participate in 'policy and decision-making process affecting their rights...'." The Court then held: "Indeed, industrial peace cannot be achieved if the employees are denied their just participation in the discussion of matters affecting their rights." *PAL, Inc v. NLRC*, G.R. No. 85985, (13 August 1993).

- The State shall afford full protection to labor, local and overseas, organized and unorganized, and promote full employment and equality of employment opportunities for all.
- It shall guarantee the rights of all workers to self-organization, collective bargaining, and negotiations, and peaceful concerted activities, including the right to strike in accordance with law. They shall be entitled to security of tenure, humane conditions of work, and a living wage. They shall also participate in policy- and decision-making processes affecting their rights and benefits as may be provided by law.
- The State shall promote the principle of shared responsibility between workers and employers and the preferential use of voluntary modes in settling disputes, including conciliation, and shall enforce their mutual compliance therewith to foster industrial peace.
- The State shall regulate the relations between workers and employers, recognizing the right of labor to its just share in the fruits of production and the right of enterprises to reasonable returns on investments, and to expansion and growth.

Presidential Decree 442 (as Amended): The Philippine Labor Code (1974)

The Philippine Labor Code is both social and labor legislation. As social legislation, it furthers the social justice objective of the Constitution.[33] As labor legislation, it draws the statutory standards of employment, labor rights, and labor relations. Article 3 lays down the basic policies that govern labor conditions in the country: protection of labor, promotion of full employment, ensuring equal work opportunities, and regulation of worker-employer relations.

The Code prescribes standards on employment conditions (Book III) and health and safety (Book IV). Included under Conditions of Employment are:

- hours of work (Articles 82–90)
- rest periods (Articles 91–93)

---

33   The 1973 Constitution was the fundamental law in force at the time the Labor Code took effect in 1974. In the Constitution, social justice is not linked to general human rights but to the social ends of dignity, welfare, and security of people. 1973 Constitution, Art. II, s. 6. With the continued effect of the Labor Code under the 1987 Constitution, the social justice context is broadened to establish its link with human rights. Further, the goals of dignity, welfare, and security can be achieved through the promotion of worker rights enumerated in Article XIII, Section 3.

- leaves (Articles 94–96)
- wages (Articles 97–129)
- employment conditions for women (Articles 130–138)
- employment conditions for minors (Articles 139–140)

Health and safety provisions of the Code include:

- medical and dental services (Articles 156–161)
- occupational health and safety (Articles 162–165)
- employees compensation and insurance fund (Articles 166–209)

Republic Act 8042: Migrant Workers and Overseas Filipinos Act (1995)

This law defines a Filipino 'migrant worker', institutes the rules on their recruitment, deployment, and employment, establishes the standards for promotion of families' rights and welfare in accordance with international enforcement mechanisms, and provides protection for overseas Filipinos in distress (such as their repatriation and needed legal assistance services while abroad).[34] Tasked with the enforcement of the law are the government foreign affairs and labor departments and designated attached agencies.

Republic Act 9295: Domestic Shipping Development Act of 2004

The relevant aim of this law is to establish a strong and competitive domestic merchant fleet manned by qualified Filipino officers and crew. The law applies to all Philippine registered ships engaged in trade and commerce in Philippine territorial waters. Under the law, all domestic ship operators are required to "comply with operational and safety standards for vessels set by applicable conventions and regulations, maintain its vessels in safe and serviceable condition, meet the standards of safety of life at sea and safe manning requirements, and furnish safe, adequate, reliable and proper service at all times."[35] This legal requirement is consistent with ship safety, human security, and quality ship management standards essential for implementation of MLC, 2006. MARINA is mandated to enforce this law.

---

34   *Migrant Workers and Overseas Filipinos Act, Republic Act 8042*, Secs. 24 and 25 (1995).

35   Maritime Industry Authority, *Mandates by virtue of Republic Act 9295*, available online: <http://marina.gov.ph/profile/mandates9295.htm>.

Republic Act 7471: Philippine Overseas Shipping Development Act (1992)

This law implements the national policy of developing and maintaining a Philippine Metropolitan Marine that is composed, among others, of well-equipped, safe, and modern Philippine registered vessels manned by qualified Filipino officers and crew. This earlier law complements R.A. 9295, particularly on maritime safety – an aspect vital to protecting Filipino seafarers' social and economic rights.

Administrative Issuances of the Department of Labor and Employment

Subsequent to the Philippine Senate ratification of MLC, 2006, DOLE issued the following department orders and labor advisories to implement the Convention and the national labor law:

- Department Order No. 129 – *Rules and Regulations Governing the Employment and Working Conditions of Seafarers Onboard Ships Engaged in Domestic Shipping* (7 June 2013). This order applies to 8,981 Philippine registered merchant or commercial ships engaged in shipping within Philippine territory.
- Department Order 130 – *Rules and Regulations Governing the Employment of Filipino Seafarers Onboard Philippine Registered Ships Engaged in International Voyage* (7 June 2013). This order applies to 125 Philippine registered merchant or commercial ships with 500 gross tonnage and above engaged in overseas voyage, excluding ships of traditional build, such as pump boats and fishing vessels.
- Department Order No. 130A-13 – *Guidelines on the Authorization of Recognized Organizations to Conduct Inspection and Certification of Philippine Registered Ships Engaged in International Voyages pursuant to the Maritime Labour Convention (MLC), 2006* (5 July 2013)
- Department Order No. 132-13 – *Guidelines on Maritime Occupational Safety and Health* (8 August 2013)
- Labor Advisory No. 02-2013 – *Requirements for Compliance with the Maritime Labour Convention, 2006* (8 July 2013)
- Labor Advisory No. 02-A-13 – *List of Additional Recognized Organizations Authorized to Conduct Inspection & Certification Pursuant to Maritime Labour Convention, 2006* (19 July 2013)
- Labor Advisory No. 04-2013 – *Requirements on Medical Certificates, Certificates on Catering Services, and Certificate of Inspection of Crew*

Accommodation Pursuant to the Maritime Labour Convention, 2006 and the Philippine Maritime Occupational Safety (8 August 2013)[36]

Administrative Issuances of the Philippine Overseas Employment Administration

There are numerous issuances by Philippine Overseas Employment Administration (POEA) prior to 2012 that set the rules and regulations on the recruitment and employment of seafarers. The following issuances reinforce the former in line with the implementation of MLC, 2006:

- Memorandum Circular No. 09 (Series of 2012) – *Clarification on the Implementation of the Double Wage and Compensation Benefits for Seafarers Transiting High Risk Zones/Areas.* This guideline, following the POEA Governing Resolutions 12 and 13 (2012), clarifies the implementation of benefits, particularly the inclusion of overtime and leave pay.
- Memorandum Circular No. 15 (Series of 2012) – *Continuing Agency Education Program.* Attendance of officers and staff of sea-based manning agencies in the Continuing Agency Education Program (CAEP) seminars of POEA is a mandatory requirement for issuance of a license.
- Memorandum Circular No. 06 (Series of 2013) – *Re-issuance of Manning Agency Licenses under the Provision of the 2006 Maritime Labour Convention (MLC 2006) of the International Labour Organization.* The re-issuance of a license is a procedure following the certification requirement under MLC, 2006.
- Memorandum Circular No. 02 (Series of 2014) – *Interim Implementation of the POEA-BI 'One-Stop OEC Validation System' for Departing Seafarers at NAIA Terminal 3.* The Overseas Employment Certificate (OEC) validation system is a procedure that secures the authenticity of working status and prompt departure of the seafarer working overseas.

Administrative Issuances of Maritime Industry Authority

MARINA issued numerous memorandum circulars concerning implementing and enforcing the STCW. The regulations and policies provided in these issuances regulate safety in domestic and overseas shipping and training and certifying maritime manpower.

---

36   These administrative issuances are published on the websites of the Department of Labor and Employment, available online: <http://www.dole.gov.ph/pages/view/37> and the ILO, available online: <http://www.ilo.org/dyn/normlex/en/f?p=1000:80024:0::NO::P80024_COUNTRY_ID:102970>.

Government Institutions: Structure and Functions

An executive department and two autonomous agencies attached to the government's Executive Branch comprise the three institutions designated as competent authorities in implementing the MLC, 2006.[37] Additional government agencies support these three competent authorities.

Department of Labor and Employment

DOLE is the lead organization tasked with enforcing rules on labor standards and relations. Created under Executive Order No. 292 of 1987,[38] otherwise known as the Administrative Code of the Philippines, the three-fold mandate of DOLE as the Executive Branch's primary policy-making, programing, coordinating, and administrative entity in the field of labor and employment is to

(1)   promote gainful employment opportunities and optimizing the development and utilization of the country's manpower resources;

(2)   advance workers' welfare by providing for just and humane working conditions and terms of employment; and

(3)   maintain industrial peace by promoting harmonious, equitable, and stable employment relations that assure equal protection for the rights of all concerned parties.[39]

DOLE performs the flag and labor-supplying State responsibility of the Philippines under Article V of MLC, 2006. The Department Secretary issues the Maritime Labour Certificate including the Declaration of Maritime Labour Compliance (DLMC) Part I and reviews and approves DMLC Part II, which covers shipowners and seafarers on board Philippine registered ships engaged in international voyages. DOLE also accepts applications from reputable international classification organizations (recognized organizations or ROs) and grants them authority to conduct inspections and certification of Philippine

---

37   ILO, "Philippines – MLC Country Profile," available online: <http://www.ilo.org/dyn/normlex/en/f?p=NORMLEXPUB:80021:0::NO::P80021_COUNTRY_ID:102970>.

38   In the hierarchy of Philippine laws, Executive Orders issued by President Corazon C. Aquino are laws arising from the grant of legislative powers to the President under the 1986 Provisional ("Freedom") Constitution (Article II, Section 1) and the 1987 Constitution (Article XVIII, Section 6). The legislative powers of the President ceased after the first Congress under the 1987 Constitution was convened.

39   Executive Order 292, Title VII, s. 2.

registered ships engaged in international voyages.[40] An attached agency of DOLE, hereunder described, performs regulatory functions over ship manning agencies and provides employment and deployment assistance (information, technical, and legal) to seafarers.

There are 12 autonomous agencies attached to DOLE for policy and program coordination and administrative supervision. The following five cater directly to seafarers:

(1) The Overseas Workers Welfare Administration (OWWA) is tasked with protecting and promoting the welfare of OFWs and their families. Being membership-based, OWWA sources its funds from members and utilizes the money to finance key social and economic programs. One example is the Seafarer's Upgrading Program that provides financial assistance for skills upgrading and expertise development training.

(2) The National Maritime Polytechnic (NMP) is the only government-owned maritime training center in the country that provides specialization and skills training required for employment acceptability of seafarers (officers and ratings). This training includes that required under the STCW.

(3) The Technical Education and Skills Development Authority (TESDA) is another government educational institution engaged in upgrading the employment qualifications of Filipinos. TESDA produces service-providing workers, such as those in the ship catering services (mess men and cooks) employed mostly on cruise ships.

(4) The Professional Regulation Commission (PRC) is the regulatory body that governs standards of professional occupations. It executes the regulatory policies of government, performs quasi-legislative functions by enacting rules with the effect of law, and exercises quasi-judicial functions on cases pertaining to erring examinees and professionals. (Note that in the succeeding discussion, the functions of PRC, along with TESDA, as regards seafarers' licensure and certification are assumed by MARINA under the policy of "single maritime administration").

(5) Finally, the National Labor Relations Commission (NLRC) is a quasi-judicial body that employs arbitration and alternative dispute

---

40   Labor Advisory No. 2, (2013). For the list of ROs, see ILO, "Philippines – Recognized Organizations," available online: <http://www.ilo.org/dyn/normlex/en/f?p=1000:80022:0 ::NO:80022:P80022_COUNTRY_ID:102970>.

resolution methods to resolve labor and management disputes. The aim of this function is the achievement of industrial peace through the establishment of healthy labor relations. The labor arbiters and commissioners comprising NLRC are granted with original and exclusive jurisdiction on the adjudication of labor cases.

Philippine Overseas Employment Administration

POEA is one of the six DOLE attached agencies (not included in the enumeration above) that is a competent authority to implement MLC, 2006. Created under Executive Order No. 797 (1 May 1982), it is governed by a Board (POEA Governing Board) headed by the Secretary of DOLE, with the POEA Administrator as vice-chairperson. POEA functions as labor recruitment industry regulator, employment and deployment facilitator, and worker's rights and welfare protector. As recruitment regulator, POEA accepts registration and grants licenses to labor-supplying agencies, specifically including ship manning companies. POEA has judicial functions, particularly to hear and arbitrate on cases (except money claims) involving violations of POEA rules filed by workers or employees against recruitment and manning agencies, foreign principals and employers, and overseas workers for reported violation of POEA rules and regulations.[41]

Maritime Industry Authority

An attached administrative and regulatory agency of the Department of Transportation and Communication, MARINA regulates shipping enterprises, registration of vessels, issuance of licenses, and safety concerns pertaining to vessel construction. In establishing MARINA as the 'Single Maritime Administration and Enforcement' of the STCW Convention, it assumes the functions of PRC, TESDA, the Commission on Higher Education (CHED), and the National Telecommunications Commission (NTC) "relative to issuance, validation, verification, correction, revocation or cancellation of certificates of competency, endorsement or cancellation of certificates of competency, endorsement, proficiency and documentary evidence required of all seafarers"

---

41   Philippine Overseas Employment Administration, "Core functions," available online: <http://www.poea.gov.ph/html/aboutus.html>. The functions of POEA are detailed in Executive Order No. 247 (1987 – Reorganizing The Philippine Overseas Employment Administration and for Other Purposes) and *Republic Act 9422* (2007) which reinforced the POEA functions by amending *Republic Act No. 8042* (the *Migrant Workers Act* described above).

and oversight of implementation matters.[42] Created under Presidential Decree
No. 474 in 1974, MARINA, as the Single Maritime Administration is governed by
the Maritime Industry Board and managed by the Maritime Administrator.

Other Supporting Government Organizations

The following executive departments provide additional administrative, legal,
social, and economic services in support of the national effort to protect seafarer labor rights: Department of Transportation and Communications
(DOTC),[43] Department of Health, Department of Justice, and Department of
Education. Constitutional bodies may also contribute by ensuring social justice and observance of universal human rights standards, e.g., the Commission
on Human Rights,[44] and accountability of public servants who cater to seafarers, e.g., the Civil Service Commission,[45] and the Office of the Ombudsman.[46]

Opportunities and Challenges for Implementation of the MLC, 2006

The Philippines' extensive regulatory and organizational framework indicates
its readiness to fully adopt and implement the MLC, 2006. However, pressing
legal, organizational, and political factors exist that may hinder government
from fully and promptly implementing the convention's maritime labour standards. These factors indicate two things: (1) the low level of importance the
government places on the maritime industry and seafarer well-being despite

---

42   *Republic Act 10635*, s. 4(c), (2013).

43   Apart from policy formulation, infrastructure development (such as ports), and interna-
      tional cooperation (such as implementation of internationally agreed maritime standards),
      DOTC regulates the shipping industry and its services. This is important particularly in the
      context of maritime safety and security, which directly link to the goal of protection of
      seafarer social and economic rights. Seafarer occupational health, for instance, is covered
      under safety and labor rights. On the other hand, an academic institution and two mari-
      time transport agencies are attached to DOTC: Philippine Merchant Marine Academy that
      trains and produces merchant marine officers (who also serve as auxiliary naval officers in
      times of conflict); Philippine Coast Guard (PCG), an armed and uniformed service that
      enforces national laws in territorial waters, conducts maritime security operations, safe-
      guards life and property at sea, and protects the marine environment and resource; and,
      Philippine Ports authority that is mandated to develop and maintain the country's ports.

44   1987 Philippine Constitution, Art. XII, s. 17.

45   Id., Art. IX(B).

46   Id., Art. XI, s. 12–13.

their contribution to the domestic economy,[47] and (2) the quality of human rights treatment as a developmental goal vis-à-vis the materialist contribution of industries, the shipping industry in particular, to economic growth.[48]

Rough Sailing: Challenges to Implementation

Barely a year after MLC, 2006 entered into force, the Philippines experiences rough sailing in implementing the Convention given the existing conditions of its maritime legal regime, the organizational framework, and social values.

Unresponsive Labor Laws

The Philippine Labor Code is the existing national law governing implementing MLC, 2006 provisions on the employment, health, and safety conditions of seafarers. It is doubtful, however, whether this law is responsive to seafarer's needs. The Labor Code provides for the generic rights and guarantees applicable to all types of labor. It does not distinguish sea-based labor from land-based labor, particularly on the qualification for employment and the hazardous work conditions. The Philippine Congress faces pending bills on the promotion of the rights of Filipino seafarers,[49] which manifest the need for specific

---

47   One way to illustrate how much sea-based OFWs are contributing to national income is by looking at what constitutes the country's surplus current account per the Philippine Central Bank statistics. During Q1 of 2014, the current account was US$1.961 billion, comprising OFW remittances of $22 million, trade of goods and services at minus $3.1 billion, and a net transfer of $4.997 billion. At 28 percent of total OFW remittances from sea-based sources (see n. 8 above), seafarers' contributions to the current account is $6.1 million. Simply put, the Philippine economy lives by remittances and gifts from Filipino workers and governments abroad! Bangko Sentral ng Pilipinas, *Selected Economic Indicators – Asian Countries 2010–2014*, available online: <http://www.bsp.gov.ph/statistics/spei_pub/Table%2060.pdf>.

48   "Strong rights, no remedy" characterizes the human rights situation in the Philippines according to the report of Asian Human Rights Commission (AHRC). Asian Human Rights Commission, *Philippines: The State of Human Rights in 2012*, available online: <http://www1.umn.edu/humanrts/research/Philippines/State%20of%20Human%20Rights%20in%20the%20Philippines%202012.pdf>. Although the report of AHRC dealt largely with violations of civil and political rights, its account on institutional remedies extends to treatment of social and economic rights. As common knowledge, the rights of seafarers are frequently violated.

49   There are three Bills pending in the Senate on the Magna Carta of Seafarers as of 27 August 2014: Senate Bill No. 21 filed by Senator Jinggoy Estrada on 1 July 2013; Senate Bill No. 673 filed by Senator Loren Legarda on 9 July 2013; and Senate Bill No. 1861 filed by Senator Joseph Victor Ejercito on 16 October 2013. The Senate Bills are available online: <https://www.senate.gov.ph/>. In the House of Representatives, there are two Bills on the

laws designed to recognize the unique nature of seafaring, acknowledge seafarers' contributions to national finances, and promote seafarers' social and
employment rights. Furthermore, these legislative initiatives identify seafarers
as part of a distinct group of workers with specific rights. Depending on the
importance that Congress gives to seafarers and their welfare through legislation in the near future,[50] the implementation of MLC, 2006 at the present time
will be difficult. The department orders of DOLE pertaining to seafarers are
inadequate as these are administrative issuances enforcing the existing labor
law. The department orders set the labor law enforcement guidelines and procedures without addressing the problems facing seafarers, which arise from
the lack of differentiation of labor rights and protection in the Labor Code.

Organizational Ambiguity

The confusion as to the relationships of the various government agencies
involved presents a difficulty in the implementation of MLC, 2006. As
McConnell points out:

> One of the main difficulties for implementation is that the MLC, 2006 is
> both a labour convention and a maritime convention. Interaction with
> the ILO including implementation of labour conventions is usually a
> matter dealt with by the labour departments or ministries in each coun-
> try. However, the compliance and enforcement approach in the MLC,
> 2006, including PSC [port State control] and the possible use of ROs and
> the express alignment with IMO instruments, is intended to "main-
> stream" it within the current flag State inspection and the PSC MOU
> approaches under the wider maritime regime. For some countries, the ques-
> tion of which department should handle the implementation of the
> MLC, 2006 has been difficult as this is a labour matter, usually involving

---

promotion of seafarer's welfare and their families: House Bill No. 3754 filed by Walden Belo
and Ibarra Gutierrez III on 27 January 2014; and House Bill No. 3895 filed by Joseph Gilbert
Violago and Juan Johnny Revilla on 11 February 2014. An earlier House Bill 122 on the Magna
Carta of Seafarers authored by Emmeline Aglipay was first read on 23 July 2013. The House
Bills are available online: <http://www.congress.gov.ph/download/?d=billstext_results#>.

50   The Bills filed in 2013 and 2014 and currently pending in both houses of Congress indicate the importance given to promoting seafarers' rights after the Philippine ratification of
MLC, 2006 in 2012. Incidentally, in 2007, former Senator Edgardo Angara filed Senate Bill
No. 214 for the enactment of the "Magna Carta of Filipino Seafarers." The Angara Bill was
in response to the inclusion of the Philippines on the "White List" of countries complying
with the STCW. A copy of this Bill is available online: <http://www.senate.gov.ph/lis/bill
_res.aspx?congress=14&q=SBN-214>.

labour inspectors; however, the Convention is obviously predicated, from a systemic perspective, on implementation by the competent authority or authorities that are already working with ship inspection and certification and with PSC. On the other hand, many of the topics such as social security or occupational safety and health and the possibility of implementation through collective bargaining agreements are not within the usual practice or jurisdiction of most maritime administrations.[51]

In the situation where multiple government departments or agencies regulate maritime labor, no standards exist to dictate whether the competent authority under MLC, 2006 is a coordinating collective or individual agencies operating independently of each other. McConnell suggests that a coordinating collective is a possibility, particularly in countries where State practice limits the jurisdiction of individual government agencies. Nonetheless, the purpose of a competent authority as defined in Article II paragraph 1(a) of MLC, 2006 is the implementation of the Convention by "the minister, government department or other authority having power to issue and enforce regulations, orders or other instructions having the force of law in respect of the subject matter of the (MLC, 2006) provision concerned." Thus, the organization of competent authority, whether a coordinating collective or an individual agency, is relevant when the involved government authority or authorities are able to issue rules and enforce laws that give effect to the provisions of the Convention. In the case when multiple government departments with different jurisdictions comprise the competent authority, MLC, 2006 can be implemented through a collective agreement that clearly defines both the powers and responsibilities of each department and the relationship between them. As McConnell points out above, there are topics in MLC, 2006 that are not within the jurisdiction of the maritime administration, which would require a collective bargaining agreement with other government agencies in order to implement the entire Convention.

In February 2014, DOLE and DOTC signed a memorandum of agreement (MOA) that created a 'coordinating mechanism' between the two executive departments by "spelling out the responsibilities of DOLE, DOTC, POEA, MARINA, and PCG [the Philippine Coast Guard]" in order to "harmonize government action towards effective compliance and implementation" of MLC, 2006.[52] Under the MOA, DOLE is "tasked to promote and protect workers' rights

---

51   McConnell, n. 23 above, p. 137.

52   Department of Labor and Employment, "DOLE and DOTC converge, sign agreement that creates coordinating mechanism to effectively implement Maritime Labour Convention, 2006," available online: <http://www.dole.gov.ph/news/view/2391>.

and welfare and to maintain industrial peace by promoting [a] harmonious relationship between workers and employers"; DOTC's "role is to promote, develop, and regulate a dependable and coordinated network of transportation and communications systems and fast, safe, efficient, and reliable transportation and communications services." More specifically, the MOA tasks DOLE with implementing the labor-supplying responsibilities under MLC, 2006, while the memorandum tasks DOTC with both flag State administration (through MARINA) and port State authority (through PCG). The Secretaries of DOLE and DOTC signed the agreement, and witnessed by the heads of the attached agencies (POEA, MARINA and PCG). DOLE, POEA, and MARINA comprise the competent authority in the Philippine compliance and implementation of MLC, 2006.[53]

The tasks of DOLE and DOTC in the MOA and the function of the competent authority in implementing MLC, 2006 creates a tricky situation, particularly considering that DOLE is an executive department with POEA as an attached agency, and MARINA is an attached agency of DOTC. The Philippine Administrative Code[54] established a hierarchy of executive organization with DOLE and DOTC directly under the control of the President and POEA and MARINA, as an attached regulatory agency, under the administrative supervision of DOLE and DOTC, respectively.[55] At this point, the relationship between the involved organizations is confusing: the coordination under the MOA is directly between DOLE and DOTC as parties, whereas no direct coordination exists between the identified competent authority, namely DOLE-POEA-MARINA. Furthermore, the relationship under the MOA creates a bureaucracy that may result in inefficiencies such as delays in responding to problems on seafarer working conditions onboard Philippine registered ships. For instance, under the MOA, DOLE "shall coordinate its enforcement and compliance-monitoring activities with the DOTC, through MARINA."[56] Presumably, since it is not clear whether MARINA can directly coordinate its activities with DOLE, MARINA shall also link the coordination through DOTC. This kind of bureaucracy complicates rather than simplifies, the process.

Lack of Political Will

Post et al. define political will as "the extent of committed support among key decision-makers for a particular policy solution to a particular problem."[57]

---

53   ILO, n. 37 above.

54   Executive Order No. 292 (1987).

55   Id., Chap. 9, s. 43. As attached agencies of departments in the executive branch, POEA and
       MARINA are also under the control of the president. 1987 Constitution, Art. VII, s. 17.

56   Department of Labor and Employment, n. 52 above.

57   L.A. Post, A.N.W. Raile and E.D. Raile, "Defining Political Will," *Politics & Policy* 38, no. 4
       (August 2010), p. 659.

Four components comprise this definition that can be used to analyse the absence or presence of political will: (1) a sufficient set of decision-makers; (2) a common understanding of a particular problem on the formal agenda; (3) a commitment to support; and (4) a commonly perceived, potentially effective policy solution.[58]

The author argues that lack of political will is a major stumbling block in the implementation of MLC, 2006, as evidenced by the lack of an ongoing commitment to support it by decision-makers. The lack of political will is manifest in the Convention's ratification process and in the legislative adoption of the Magna Carta of Filipino Seafarers.

In the case of the MLC, 2006 ratification, the 22 Senators sitting in the fifteenth Congress unanimously approved Resolution 829 (component 1), voted based on their common recognition of the social and employment conditions of seafarers, their contributions to national finances, and the need to protect their social and economic rights (component 2), and their decision to ratify is the result of their acceptance of MLC, 2006 as a guarantee for the promotion of seafarers' social and economic well-being. This satisfies political will's first two constituent components. However, the third component – commitment to support – is ostensibly absent in the ratification process. The main argument for this is the six-year period of public discussion and debate on the Convention's merits and demerits.[59] Six years is long enough for a flag State and major seafarer labor-supplying country to decide on ratification of an essential agreement. This slow decision-making process further manifests the lack of urgency and commitment on the part of legislators in protecting seafarer rights and providing them protection, indicating the lack of sufficient political will.[60]

---

58   Id.

59   It took the Senate 13 days to deliberate on and approve Resolution No. 829. As noted by a blogger Barista Uno, "[i]t was talking and squabbling between two state agencies that led to the failure of the Philippines to ratify ILO Convention No. 185 (revised Seafarers' Identity Documents Convention, 2003) before it came into force in February 2005. The same syndrome was behind the tardy action on MLC 2006. While so-called 'experts' prattled on the subject, some industry bigwigs insisted that domestic shipping be exempted from the Convention." Marine Café Blog, "MLC 2006 and Filipino Tardiness," 15 August 2012, available online: <http://www.marine-cafe.com/mlc-2006-and-filipino-tardiness/#.U9DgDuNdVgH>.

60   The lack of commitment is most likely the result of conflict of interest by decision-makers in government. According to Jeremy Cajiuat, project development officer of the non-governmental organization International Seafarer Action Center Philippines, a number of lawmakers and members of the executive branch of the government have interests in shipping and manning companies either as shipowners or shareholders. N.S. Barcelona, "Seafarer's groups fear non-ratification of maritime pact," *GMA News Online*, 2 March

The slow passage of the Magna Carta of Filipino Seafarers is another case where lack of commitment to support compromises political will (component 3). As indicated above, Congress has not passed into law any bill defining the seafarer and their rights and distinguishing them from land-based workers between 2007 and 2014 (component 4) despite the number of bills filed in Congress (component 1). This denotes the absence of commonly perceived, potentially effective policy solutions – compromising political will. The legislator's understanding of the urgent need to address the issues remains to be determined during the deliberations (component 2), and this aspect does not indicate presence or absence of political will. However, the common understanding of the particular problem is not present as indicated by the bills being filed by individual legislators. A common understanding of the concerned legislators expressed in a single unified bill would be even more strategic since more proponents pushing the initiative would most likely be given prompt attention.

Calm Waters Ahead: Opportunities for Smooth Sailing

Windows of opportunities exist that present solutions to the challenges described above. These opportunities are factors that can develop political will, particularly the core component of commitment to support a policy agenda that will lead to an effective policy solution to problems concerning seafarers' social and economic welfare. Such policy solutions are necessary for the full implementation of MLC, 2006.

Constitutional – MLC, 2006 Harmony

The Philippines approved and ratified the MLC, 2006. Except for some ambiguities, characteristic of general laws, the Convention is consistent with the principles embodied in the Constitution and provided in national laws. The principle of 'firm on rights, flexible on means of implementation' inherent in the Convention is not only a lure for ratification, but it recognizes the sovereignty of States in the implementation of its national laws. The promotion of human rights and protection of labor are key State policies.[61] The Convention and Constitution stipulate seafarers' social and economic rights.[62] Although there is need for a set of national laws protecting the rights of seafarers as a

---

2009, available online: <http://www.gmanetwork.com/news/story/151025/pinoyabroad/seafarers-groups-fear-non-ratification-of-maritime-pact>.

61   1987 Constitution, Art. II.

62   Maritime Labour Convention, 2006, 45 *International Legal Materials* 792 (2006), Arts. III and IV. 1987 Constitution, Art. XIII, s. 3.

separate occupational category, distinct from land-based workers, this is something that can be done through the active and vigilant action of civil society organizations such as seafarers' groups.[63] In as much as the State recognizes the contribution of civil society organizations (or people's organizations) in democratic nation building, these organizations are also guaranteed the right to participate in all levels of social, economic, and political decision-making.[64] This constitutional guarantee is consistent with the tripartite framework under MLC, 2006 wherein seafarer organizations are consulted as decision-making partners with governments (State) and shipowners (business).

Civil Society Initiatives

Private individuals with established experience in the shipping industry played a lead role in drafting the Philippine Maritime Code pending in Congress.[65] Indeed, civil society actors are key agents of change. They extend to public participation in policy-making, democratize social contracts, provide logistical and moral support for efficient delivery of public services, and grant legitimacy to government plans, policies, and programs. These are justifications for promoting the role and rights of people's organizations in national laws.[66]

Seafarer organizations form part of the tripartite institutional framework in formulating and implementing the MLC, 2006. The Convention emphasizes participation of these organizations under the principle of tripartism in dialogue to develop acceptable implementation and enforcement strategies.[67]

---

63 It is the policy of the State to encourage non-governmental, community-based, or sectoral organizations that promote the welfare of the nation. 1987 Constitution, Art. II, s. 23. The State policy is reiterated in the Philippine Labor Code: promotion of trade unionism to promote social justice and development, and fostering free and voluntary organizations to strengthen and unify the labor movement. The Philippine Labor Code, Art. 211, paras. 2 and 3.

64 1987 Constitution, Art. XIII, ss. 15–16.

65 Two House bills (HB 2382 and 1156) were filed in the House of Representatives but were not passed before the 2013 congressional elections. The measure was filed again under HB 00096 (*An Act Consolidating Admiralty and Maritime Laws, Updating Rules in Navigation, Safety Standards and Maritime Practices and for Other Purposes*) in the next Congress and passed the first reading in 23 July 2013. House of Representatives, House Bills/Resolutions referred to Committee on Transportation, available online: <http://www.congress.gov.ph/committees/search.php?id=E509&pg=bills#>.

66 Section 15, Article XIII of the 1987 Constitution states: People's organizations are *bona fide* associations of citizens with demonstrated capacity to promote the public interest and with identifiable leadership, membership, and structure.

67 McConnell, n. 23 above, pp. 131–132. Tripartism as an inherent approach is expressed in the Preamble of MLC, 2006 and stipulated in the governance framework under Article XIII.

Tripartism ensures the integration of seafarers' interests and their acceptance of the Convention and mechanisms for its implementation. There are 13 maritime manpower associations recognized by MARINA.[68] Beyond mere acknowledgement of its existence, these seafarer organizations are effective interest and pressure groups. As both proponent and recipient, they determine responsive approaches to promote seafarer rights. They engage in lobbying with legislators for passage of rights-based legislation. The United Filipino Seafarers (UFS), a MARINA-recognized maritime association, actively involves itself in advancing seafarer concerns through grassroots, government lobbying, private sector diplomacy, and mass media.[69]

Inter-agency Cooperation

Despite the organizational ambiguities identified above, cooperation between and among the involved departments and attached agencies is probable for two reasons: (1) although the labor and maritime aspects are distinguished in MLC, 2006 and the STCW, both conventions require their implementation following their natural complementary relationship,[70] and (2) the agencies are mandated by law to perform their independent functions in order to complete the work of the President as the government's chief executive.[71] The issue of ambiguity may be naturally resolved through time as the involved government agencies, in the performance of their functions, identify and address problems arising from the implementation of the MOA.

There is a growing demand for different government agencies to act on their mandates and collaborate with each other to implement MLC, 2006, particularly among seafarer organizations. The seafarers are visible workers and their presence is becoming even more widely known with the ratification of MLC, 2006. They have vigilant civil society organizations that keep a watchful eye on government policies and activities. They are represented in the House of Representatives by ANGKLA Party-list system, which authored the *Republic Act 10635*.[72]

---

68   MARINA, "Maritime Associations – Manpower Sector," available online: <http://www .marina.gov.ph/directory/dirmain.html>.

69   UFS publishes daily news online and a news magazine that comes out bimonthly. United Filipino Seafarers, available online: <http://unitedfilipinoseafarers.com.ph/>.

70   Inter-convention as contra-distinguished from the inter-agency complementary relationship discussed above as a threat to full implementation of MLC, 2006.

71   Administrative Code of the Philippines (1987), Book 4, Chap. 1, s. 1.

72   ANGKLA is Filipino term for anchor. ANGKLA is represented in Congress by Jesulito A. Manalo, a lawyer engaged in the transport business sector. Manalo, Jocson and Enriquez Law Offices, available online: <http://manalolaw.ph/lawyers/partners/>.

Conclusion

The Philippines is replete with legal, statutory, and institutional guarantees promoting labor rights. Yet, while these laws are commonly applicable to all types of labor, no specific laws exist to promote the rights of seafarers as a distinct group of workers and as contributors to national finances. Further, a lack of political will exists on the part of legislators to promptly act on a Magna Carta for seafarers despite the Philippine ratification of MLC, 2006. The Convention can only fill the gap through national enabling legislation. The lack of political will to legislate seafarer rights legislation is consistent with the lack of political will in the ratification of MLC, 2006, which may indicate difficulty in Philippine compliance with its treaty obligations. The ambiguous structure and interrelationship of government organizations involved in the implementation of MLC, 2006 may compound this difficulty.

Notwithstanding these issues, the rules and organizational arrangements do have positive aspects. There are legal, political, and even institutional factors that provide opportunities, and if steered in the right direction will contribute to securing the well-being of seafarers and the benefits they contribute. Perhaps, we can look beyond the horizon and perceive the future possibility of a unified set of rules, assigning one competent and proficient captain commanding a well-trained crew functioning independently as a concerted whole, and steering a soundly structured vessel along a well-defined route. In this case, both the crew and ship will sail safely into port.

The Indonesian Legal Framework on Navigational Aids, Shipping Telecommunications and Ocean Shipping Lanes for Navigational Safety in the Straits of Malacca and Singapore

Dikdik Mohamad Sodik
School of Law, Bandung Islamic University, Indonesia

Introduction

The geographic location of Indonesia between the Pacific and Indian Oceans makes some of its waters the most important sea lanes of communication in the world. The Straits of Malacca and Singapore ('the Straits') are a narrow 900-km stretch of water with its widest point at 350 kilometers and its narrowest point at less than three kilometers. The Straits comprise two of the world's chokepoints, with the daily transit of around 200 ships per day.[1] According to the International Maritime Organization (IMO), at least 50,000 ships transit the Straits each year, transporting oil to China and Japan (80 percent of Japan's and China's oil imports respectively) and about 30 percent of world shipping trade. In fact, the Straits are a route for the transport of one-third of the world's crude oil. Thus, the Straits constitute the second busiest shipping lane in the world and have significant strategic value.[2] However, the strategic importance of the Straits as a sea lane of communication brings with it a number of problems. These challenges are not only related to the problems of navigational safety and maritime security, but also to marine environmental protection.[3]

This article is particularly concerned with issues regarding navigational safety in the Straits that have led to increased cooperation among the three littoral States – Indonesia, Malaysia and Singapore – on measures to enhance

---

1   A.H. Oegroseno, "Threats to Maritime Security and Responses Thereto: A Focus on Armed Robbery against Ships at Sea at the Straits of Malacca and Singapore: Indonesian Experience," United Nations Open-ended Informal Consultative Process on Oceans and the Law of the Sea, Ninth Meeting, New York, 23–27 June 2008, p. 2.

2   N. Wisnumurti, "Maritime Security Issues in Southeast Asia: An Indonesian Perspective," *Indonesian Journal of International Law* 6, no. 3 (April 2009): 333–352.

3   Oegroseno, n. 1 above, p. 1.

Ocean Yearbook 29: 382–416
© KONINKLIJKE BRILL NV, LEIDEN, 2015 | DOI 10.1163/9789004297234_017

navigational safety through the IMO. The three littoral States have agreed to cooperate under Article 43 of the 1982 United Nations Convention on the Law of the Sea (UNCLOS)[4] to enhance navigational safety and to control ship-source pollution. The article highlights the IMO resolutions establishing the mandatory ship reporting system (STRAITREP), the vessel traffic management system (VTS), and sea lanes and traffic separation schemes (TSS) to enhance navigational safety in the Straits consistent with Article 41 of UNCLOS. The article assesses how international shipping safety regulations are implemented in Indonesian legislation in accordance with the relevant provisions of UNCLOS and other principal international legal regimes for maritime safety.

As a littoral State of the Straits, Indonesia has passed laws and regulations concerning navigational safety, namely the Regulation of the Minister of Transportation No. 25 of 2011 on Navigational Aids,[5] the Regulation of the Minister of Transportation No. 26 of 2011 on Shipping Telecommunications,[6] and the Regulation of the Minister of Transportation No. 68 of 2011 on Ocean Shipping Lanes.[7] It also has enacted the Decree of the Minister of Energy and Mining No. 300 of 1997 Regarding the Work Safety of Oil and Natural Gas Pipelines to complement the relevant provisions of Regulation No. 68. The Indonesian government has further enacted Law No. 32 of 2014 on Oceans, which came into force on 17 October 2014. This law provides authority to establish an effective institutional framework to deal with overlapping jurisdiction.

In recent years, navigational safety issues in Indonesian national waters of the Straits have become a major challenge. These issues include the effectiveness of legal and institutional frameworks, technological capability, and undelimited maritime boundaries with neighboring countries. Maritime navigation incidents have raised questions regarding the effectiveness of existing legal

---

4   United Nations Convention on the Law of the Sea, 1982, 1833 *United Nations Treaty Series* 397 [UNCLOS].

5   Peraturan Menteri Perhubungan Nomor: PM No. 25 Tahun 2011 tentang Sarana Bantu Navigasi Pelayaran (Regulation of the Minister of Transportation No. 25 of 2011 on Navigational Aids), available online: <http://atkonten/mm/uploadedpdf/34_Gabungan_Peraturan_Menteri _Perhubungan_Nomor_PM._25_Tahun_2011.pdf?p=pdf> [Regulation No. 25].

6   Peraturan Menteri Perhubungan Nomor: PM No. 26 Tahun 2011 tentang Telekomunikasi Pelayaran (Regulation of the Minister of Transportation No. 26 of 2011 on Shipping Telecommunications), available online: <http://kemhubri.dephub.go.id/perundangan/ images/stories/doc/permen/2011/pm._no._26_tahun_2011.pdf> [Regulation No. 26].

7   Peraturan Menteri Perhubungan Nomor: PM No. 68 Tahun 2011 tentang Alur Pelayaran di Laut (Regulation of the Minister of Transportation No. 68 of 2011 on Ocean Shipping Lanes), available online: <http://hukum.unsrat.ac.id/men/menhub2011_68.pdf> [Regulation No. 68].

and institutional frameworks, as well as the technological capability for navigational safety management.

This article will examine the adequacy of Indonesia's legislative and institutional frameworks that developed in accordance with relevant international instruments concerning maritime safety. It highlights the need for Indonesia to reform legal and institutional frameworks and to upgrade its technical capacity to cope with maritime navigational safety threats. At the same time, it is urgent to address technological constraints and to delimit unresolved maritime boundaries.

International Legal Frameworks for Maritime Safety in the Straits of Malacca and Singapore

Maritime safety is particularly focused on ensuring safety of life at sea, navigational safety, and the protection and preservation of the marine environment. The shipping industry has a significant role in that safety and many conditions on vessels must be properly constructed, regularly surveyed, adequately equipped (e.g., with nautical charts and publications), and appropriately manned. Crew must be well-trained, cargo must be properly stowed, and an efficient communication system must be on board.[8] However, shipping industry operators are mainly concerned with the maritime transportation system and the safe arrival of cargo at its destination without being interfered with or threatened by criminal activity.[9] *Maritime security* is defined by Hawkes as those measures used by owners, operators, and administrators of vessels, port facilities, offshore installations, and other marine organizations or establishments to protect against seizure, sabotage, piracy, pilferage, annoyance, or surprise.[10] The IMO has addressed matters of maritime security under the auspices

8   United Nations, *Oceans and the Law of the Sea Report of the Secretary-General*, 2008, UN Document A/63/63, available online: <http://www.un.org/Depts/los> [UN Secretary-General's Report].

9   C.Z. Raymond and A. Morrien, "Security in the Maritime Domain and its Evolution since 9/11," in *Lloyd's MIU Handbook of Maritime Security*, eds., R. Hebert-Burns, S. Bateman and P. Lehr (Boca Raton, LA: CRC, 2008): 3–11; K.N. Scott, "Maritime Security and Shipping Safety in the Southern Ocean," in *Maritime Security: International Law and Policy Perspectives from Australia and New Zealand*, eds., N. Klein, J. Mossop and D.R. Rothwell (London and New York: Routledge Taylor & Francis, 2010): 1–21.

10   M.Q. Mejia Jr., "Maritime Gerrymandering: Dilemmas in Defining Piracy, Terrorism and Other Acts of Maritime Violence," *Journal of International Commercial Law* 2, 2 (2003): 153–175.

of its Maritime Safety Committee since the 1980s.[11] It is important to be aware of the distinction drawn between maritime safety and maritime security. Maritime safety relates to preventive and responsive measures intended to protect the maritime domain against and limit the effect of accidental or natural danger, harm, and damage to the environment, risks or loss. Maritime security refers to preventive and responsive measures to protect the maritime domain against threats and intentional unlawful acts.[12]

Safe and efficient navigation depends on secure and crime-free navigational routes. Coastal States have an important role to play in this regard. In the case of a maritime casualty or incident, an adequate search and rescue regulation and response capability is essential to ensure safety of life at sea.[13] Hence, maritime safety and maritime security in straits used for international navigation must be seen in these two related perspectives. First, there is the benefit of the Straits for regional economic prosperity and development across the Straits, which need to be protected from maritime navigational safety threats. The second significant aspect is the protection of international navigation against threats and intentional unlawful acts. With the increasing occurence of incidents in straits used for international navigation, the tasks to ensure an appropriate balance between safety and security and marine environmental protection have become more important. Thus marine navigation policy in the Straits covers five aspects, namely navigational safety, shipping, technical navigation, the environment, and the economy.[14] National policy on marine navigation is designed to enhance safety and security, protect the marine environment, and support other marine activities in the Straits.

Article 41 of UNCLOS confers upon littoral States of straits used for international navigation the power to designate sea lanes and prescribe traffic separation schemes. Such sea lanes and traffic separation schemes must conform to generally accepted international regulations and be adopted by the IMO.[15] As the littoral States of the Straits, Indonesia, Malaysia, and Singapore have

---

11   Id., p. 153.

12   L. Feld, P. Roell and R.D. Thiele, "Maritime Security – Perspectives for a Comprehensive Approach," ISPSW Strategy Series: Focus on Defense and International Security, 222 (2013): 1–25.

13   UN Secretary-General's Report, n. 8 above.

14   I. Sutalaksana, *A Preliminary Report on the Guidance for Formulation on Navigational Safety in the Straits of Malacca and Singapore* (Bandung: Institute of Industrial Engineering and Management, Bandung Institute of Technology, 2012), p. 2.

15   R.C. Beckman, "PSSAs and Transit Passage: Australia's Pilotage System in the Torres Strait Challenge the IMO and UNCLOS," *Ocean Development and International Law* 38, no. 3 (2007): 325–357.

cooperated with each other and with the IMO in accordance with Article 41(5) to enhance safety in the Straits.[16] For example, upon the recommendation of the three littoral States, the TSS for the Straits was revised and extended in 1998 by the Maritime Safety Committee.[17]

In addition to the TSS and an Under Keel Clearance Scheme,[18] the three littoral States, with the assistance of members of the international community, have implemented other navigational safety measures in the Straits including the VTS in 1997[19] and STRAITREP in 1998.[20] STRAITREP came into force on 1 December 1998 through IMO Resolution MSC.73 (69) following the recommendation of the three littoral States.[21] In November 2004, the IMO as part of its Protection of Vital Shipping Lanes Initiative, convened a high-level conference to address the security of ships plying the Straits in collaboration with

---

16   UNCLOS, n. 4 above.

17   See International Maritime Organization (IMO), "New Amended Existing Traffic Separation Schemes," IMO Doc. COLREG.2/Cir.44 (May 26, 1998) cited in R. Beckman, "Singapore Strives to Enhance Safety, Security, and Environmental Protection in its Port and in the Straits of Malacca and Singapore," *Ocean and Coastal Law Journal* 14 (2009): 167–200.

18   The Joint Statement of the Tripartite Ministerial Meeting of 24 February 1977 stated, *inter alia*, "[v]essels shall maintain a Single Under Keel Clearance (UKC) of at least 3.5 metres at all times during the entire passage through the Straits of Malacca and Singapore. They also shall take all necessary precautions especially when navigating through the critical areas." M. Kusumatmadja and M. Danusaputro, "Elements of an Environmental Policy and Navigational Scheme for South-East Asia: With Special Reference to the Straits of Malacca," presented at the 11th Annual Conference of the Law of the Sea Institute, Honolulu, Hawaii, 14–17 November 1977, cited in M. Kusumatmadja, *Compilation on Law of the Sea* (Bandung, Indonesia: Binacipta Publisher, 1978), pp. 257–258. See also M.J. Valencia and A. Bakar Jaafar, "Environmental Management of Malacca/Singapore Straits: Legal and Institutional Issues," *Natural Resources Journal* 25 (1985): 195–232.

19   Vessel Traffic Service (VTS) is a service implemented by a Competent Authority, designed to improve the safety and efficiency of vessel traffic and to protect the environment. The service should have the capacity to interact with the traffic situations developing in the VTS area in Guidelines for Vessel Traffic Service, IMO Resolution A.857(20) adopted on 27 November 1997, 20th Assembly Session, Agenda item 9, A 20/Res.857, 3 December 1997, p. 3.

20   IMO, "Mandatory Ship Reporting Systems," SN/Circ.201, 26 May 1998, available online: <http://www.imo.org/blast/blastDataHelper.asp?data_id=8753&filename=201.pdf>. See also M.H. Bin Mohd Rusli, "Balancing shipping and the protection of the marine environment of straits used for international navigation: A study of the Straits of Malacca and Singapore," (Ph.D. Thesis, Australian National Centre for Ocean Resources and Security, University of Wollongong, 2012), p. 196.

21   IMO, *Report of the Maritime Safety Committee on its Sixty-ninth Session*, MSC 69/22/Add.1, 1 June 1998, Annex 10. See also Bin Mohd Rusli, id., p. 14.

Indonesia, Malaysia, and Singapore. Three meetings were held from 2005 to 2007. The outcome was the creation of a framework for cooperation in 2007 between users of the Straits and the littoral States, known as the Cooperative Mechanism. This was an historic breakthrough as Article 43 of UNCLOS was implemented for the first time.[22] The promotion of navigational safety and the protection of the marine environment dominate the work of the Cooperative Mechanism,[23] which comprises three components:

(1) Cooperation Forum: Main avenue for general dialogue and exchange of views on issues of common interest in the Straits between user States, industry, and other stakeholders with littoral States.

(2) Project Coordination Committee (PCC):[24] Implementation of projects through cooperation and burden sharing between littoral States and user States, industry, and other stakeholders.

(3) Aids to Navigation Fund (ANF): Provides means for users of the Straits to contribute financially towards the maintenance of aids to navigation (e.g., buoys, beacons in the Straits).[25]

22　Article 43 of UNCLOS, n. 4 above, prescribes that user States and States bordering a strait should by agreement cooperate in the establishment and maintenance in a strait of necessary navigational and safety aid and for the prevention, reduction and control of pollution of ships. J. Ho, "Enhancing Safety, Security, and Environmental Protection of the Straits of Malacca and Singapore: The Cooperative Mechanism," *Ocean Development and International Law* 40 (2009): 233–247.

23　In 2014 the Cooperative Mechanism published a pamphlet entitled, *Safe Passage: The Straits of Malacca and Singapore*, to provide navigational information for users of the Straits, available online: <https://www.bimco.org/~/media/Products/Manuals -Pamphlets/Safe_Passage_Straits_of_Malacca_and_Singapore/Safe_Passage_-_The _Straits_of_Singapore_and_Malacca_2014-05_Pamphlet.ashx>.

24　The PCC consists of six elements: (1) removal of wrecks in the TSS (India and Germany); (2) capability development to deal with spills (Australia, China, European Union, and United States); (3) development of automatic identification systems and prevention of collisions (Korea, Japan and Australia): (4) tide, current, and wind measurement system (China and India); (5) replacement and maintenance of existing aids to navigation in the TSS (Japan and Korea); and (6) replacement of aids to navigation destroyed by the 2004 tsunami (China). See L. Bernard, "Cooperation in the Straits of Malacca and Singapore," paper presented at the 37th Annual Conference of the Center for Oceans Law and Policy, "Global Challenges and Freedom of Navigation," Seoul, 1–3 May 2013, p. 26.

25　C. Li, Policy Analyst, IMO Public Affairs Office, "Updates on the Cooperative Mechanism on Safety of Navigation and Environmental Protection in the Straits of Malacca and Singapore (the 'Cooperative Mechanism')," Tripartite Technical Experts Group (TTEG) and the Marine Electronic Highway (MEH) (2012), p. 3.

The Cooperative Mechanism is based on the following principles:

(1) Recognition of the sovereignty, sovereign rights, jurisdiction, and territorial integrity of the littoral States over the Straits.

(2) The primary responsibility over navigational safety and environmental protection in the Straits lies with the littoral States.

(3) The sustained efforts and achievements of the Tripartite Technical Experts Group on Safety of Navigation to enhance navigational safety and protection of the marine environment in the Straits.

(4) Recognition of the role of the IMO, the user States, the shipping industry, and other stakeholders in cooperating with the littoral States to promote and enhance navigational safety and environmental protection, and to ensure the uninterrupted flow of traffic in the Straits.[26]

Several points should be noted about these principles. First, the three littoral States have primary responsibility to pass laws and regulations to govern navigational safety in the Straits. Secondly, these laws and regulations are to be interpreted and applied consistent with the rules of relevant international laws on maritime safety, namely UNCLOS, the International Convention for the Safety of Life at Sea (SOLAS) of 1974,[27] the Convention on the International Regulations for Preventing Collisions at Sea (COLREGS) of 1972,[28] and IMO resolutions and circulars. Thirdly, UNCLOS provides a role for the IMO as the competent international organization dealing with international shipping activities.[29] The IMO has adopted over 40 instruments addressing shipping safety,

---

26 "Kuala Lumpur Statement on Enhancement of Safety, Security and Environmental Protection in the Straits of Malacca and Singapore," (Kuala Lumpur, Malaysia, Meeting on the Straits of Malacca and Singapore: Enhancing Safety, Security and Environmental Protection, 18–20 September 2006), p. 3.

27 International Convention for the Safety of Life at Sea, 1974, 1 November 1974, 1184 *United Nations Treaty Series* 2, as amended, available online: <https://treaties.un.org/doc/Publication/UNTS/Volume%201184/volume-1184-I-18961-English.pdf> [SOLAS].

28 Convention on the International Regulations for Preventing Collisions at Sea, 20 October 1972, 1050 *United Nations Treaty Series* 16 [COLREGS].

29 IMO, "Implications of the United Nations Convention on the Law of the Sea for the International Maritime Organization," 26 January 2005, LEG/MISC/4, at 2, cited in Beckman, n. 15 above, p. 326.

maritime security, and marine environmental protection.[30] All rules of the IMO, including its conventions and other instruments, are to be consistent with UNCLOS.[31] These include, *inter alia*, the IMO resolutions on sea lanes and the TSS, STRAITREP, and the VTS governed by Article 41 of UNCLOS, which predates the Cooperative Mechanism. Significantly, Article 42(1)(a) of UNCLOS authorizes littoral States to adopt laws and regulations in respect of navigational safety and the regulation of maritime traffic as provided in Article 41, with which foreign ships exercising the right of transit passage must comply.[32] The advantage of implementing UNCLOS provisions in State legislation is that they become subject to enforcement by littoral State authorities under national law.[33]

Domestic regulations of littoral States are intended to strengthen the implementation and law enforcement of international rules governing navigational safety in straits used for international navigation. The following sections will assess the adequacy of the Indonesian legal and institutional frameworks and technological capability to address navigational safety in the Straits.

The Indonesian Laws and Regulations on Navigational Aids, Shipping Telecommunications, and Sea Lanes

As a littoral State of the Straits, Indonesia is a member of the IMO and has ratified UNCLOS (through Act No. 17 of 1985) and SOLAS (through Presidential Regulation No. 65 of 1980). It also accepted COLREGS (13 November 1979). Indonesia's international rights and obligations to facilitate the safe and

---

30   See IMO website for further information, including summaries of instruments and meetings: <http://www.imo.org>.

31   Beckman, n. 15 above.

32   D. Anderson, "The Legal Regime of the Channel/La Manche," in D. Anderson, *Modern Law of the Sea: Selected Essays* (The Hague: Martinus Nijhoff Publishers, 2008), p. 189. Article 34 of UNCLOS, n. 4 above, stipulates that (1) the regime of passage through straits used for international navigation shall not in other respects affect the legal status of the waters forming such straits or the exercise by States bordering the straits of their sovereignty or jurisdiction over such waters and their air space, seabed and subsoil and (2) the sovereignty or jurisdiction of the States bordering the straits is exercised subject provisions in this part of UNCLOS and other international law.

33   R.R. Churchill and A.V. Lowe, *The Law of the Sea*, 3rd ed. (Manchester: Manchester University Press, 1999), 108. Article 39(2)(a) of UNCLOS, n. 4 above, provides for ships in transit passage to comply with generally accepted international regulations, procedures, and practices for safety at sea, including COLREGS.

unimpeded transit of vessels engaged in maritime trade and commerce through coordinated management of the Straits arise from these key international instruments relating to maritime safety.[34]

Ministerial Regulation on Navigational Aids

An aid to navigation is defined as a device or system external to vessels that is designed and operated to enhance the safe and efficient navigation of vessels and/or a vessel.[35] Maritime navigational aids such as lighthouses, buoys, and beacons constitute a form of marine infrastructure. The function of navigational aids is not only to prevent marine accidents, but also to facilitate seaborne trade.[36] Regulation 13(1) Chapter 5 of the SOLAS Convention deals with establishment and operation of navigational aids.[37] This Regulation requires contracting governments to undertake to provide, as it deems practical and necessary, either individually or in cooperation with other contracting governments, such navigational aids as the volume of traffic justifies and the degree of risk requires.[38]

In the Straits, the high volume and value of cargo transiting the Straits means that any serious disruption to the flow of maritime traffic through these waters could have widespread and far-reaching detrimental effects.[39] The ANF, an important element of the Cooperative Mechanism, promotes navigational safety in the Straits. Contributions to the Fund come from States, shipping industries, oil industries, international organizations, or any non-governmental organizations that care for navigational safety and environmental protection in the Straits.[40] Several measures adopted under the ANF are important for enhancing maritime safety in Indonesian waters in the Straits.

---

34   M.H.E. Siang, "Implementation of Mandatory Ship Reporting in the Malacca and Singapore Straits," *Singapore Journal of International and Comparative Law* 3 (1999): 345–352.

35   *The IALA Aids to Navigation Guide (Navguide) Aid*, 4th ed. (St Germain en Laye: International Association of Marine Aids to Navigation and Lighthouse Authorities, IALA-AISM, 2001), p. 1.

36   M. Asteris, "The Funding of Marine Aids to Navigation in the European Union," Department of Economics, University of Portsmouth (2007), p. 1.

37   *Maritime Buoyage System and Other Aids to Navigations* (St Germain en Laye: International Association of Marine Aids to Navigation and Lighthouse Authorities, 2012), p. 7.

38   SOLAS, n. 27 above, Regulation 13, para. 2.

39   Ho, n. 22 above.

40   H. Djalal, "Regulation of International Straits," *Indonesian Journal of International Law* 6, no. 3 (April 2009): 315–332.

As a State party to SOLAS, Indonesia has implemented the provisions of Regulation 13(1) Chapter 5 through the Regulation of the Minister of Transportation No. 25 of 2011 on Navigational Aids. Under Article 2(2) of Regulation No. 25, navigational aids are to be put in place to determine vessel position, report existing danger and hampering in navigation, show the boundaries of navigation lanes, mark vessel traffic separation lanes, show zones and/or specific activity in water, and show the territorial boundaries of a State. The Regulation identifies three types of shipping navigation support facilities: visual, electronic, and audible.[41] The electronic navigational aids consist of the following measures: (a) a global positioning system (GPS)[42] at coastal radio stations, vessel traffic services, and local port services; (b) differential global position system (DGPS);[43] (c) radar beacons;[44] (d) a radio beacon, which is used in shipping navigation; (e) radar surveillance;[45] (f) medium wave radio beacon; (g) automatic identification system (AIS);[46] and (h) another electronic

---

41   Regulation No. 25, n. 5 above, Art. 2(1).

42   GPS is a positioning system based on a network of satellites that continuously transmit coded information. The information transmitted can be interpreted by receivers to precisely identify locations on Earth by measuring the distance from the satellite. Maryland NRCS, "Introduction to Global Positioning Systems (GPS)," prepared for USDA (2007), p. 3, available online: <http://www.nrcs.usda.gov/Internet/FSE_DOCUMENTS/nrcs144p2_024990.pdf>.

43   DGPS provides differential corrections to a GPS receiver in order to improve navigation accuracy and monitor the integrity of GPS satellite transmissions. Integrity monitoring of the reference stations is a vital feature of DGPS. Id., p. 8.

44   Radar navigation, especially radar beacons, provides an independent means of position fixing, situational awareness and collision avoidance. See N. Ward and M. Bransby, "Radar Aids to Navigation in the Age of GNSS," (General Lighthouse Authorities, Research & Radio Navigation Directorate, United Kingdom and Ireland, 2011), p. 1.

45   Careful selection of a VTS and coastal surveillance radar system is required to ensure the target types can be detected and tracked in the designated area. Visibility, precipitation rates, sea state, and propagation conditions for the individual radar site also require careful consideration by the radar supplier to enable the optimal system to be specified in VTS radar coastal systems. See Kelvin Hughes, "Coastal Surveillance Systems," available online: <http://www.kelvinhughes.com/surveillance/coastal/radar>.

46   The automatic identification system (AIS) is used by ships and VTS principally for identifying and locating vessels. AIS provides a means for ships to electronically exchange ship data including identification, position, course, and speed, with other nearby ships and VTS stations. AIS is intended to assist the vessel's watch standing officers and to allow maritime authorities to track and monitor vessel movements. It works by integrating a standardized VHF transceiver system with an electronic navigation system, such as a GPS receiver, and other navigational sensors on board ship. United States Coast Guard, "Projects," (2013), available online: <http://www.uscg.mil/hq/c3cen/projects.asp>.

shipping navigation support facility in line with technological development.[47] These electronic navigational aids are used to deliver information through radiowaves or another electromagnetic system for determining the direction and vessel position.[48] Through the ANF, Indonesia has installed 28 units of the principal navigational aids in the Straits, whereas Malaysia and Singapore have 18 units and 5 units respectively.[49]

With regard to the navigational aids under the authority of Indonesia, there are several challenges to implementing the Ministerial Regulation on Navigational Aids, in particular over hit-and-run incidents and theft and damage to navigational aids as well as damage caused by the 2004 tsunami in the Straits.[50] This damage makes it difficult for the Directorate General of Sea Transportation to have accurate data on vessel positions and to report potential navigational dangers in the Straits. The lack of such data could reduce the capability of Indonesia's navigational safety management authorities to exercise effective control and monitor vessels transiting the Straits. To address the problem of hit-and-run incidents, Indonesia has called for cooperation among littoral States, including sharing of related VTS data.[51] VTS data sharing should be established through trilateral cooperation within the framework of the Cooperative Mechanism.

Recognizing the serious consequences of problems to navigational safety, at the tenth ANF Committee Meeting, Indonesia submitted the 2012 Project 5 Report on Replacement and Maintenance of existing Aids to Navigation in the Traffic Separation Scheme. The Report noted that Indonesia carried out maintenance of 28 aids to navigation at a cost of US$1,315,657.[52] At the 11th ANF meeting, Indonesia affirmed that it would continue to maintain high standards in procuring equipment, and that it had taken the necessary measures to repair

---

47   Regulation No. 25, n. 5 above, Art. 6(2).

48   Id., Art. 6(1).

49   Directorate of Navigation, Directorate General of Sea Transportation, Ministry of Transportation of the Republic of Indonesia, "Traffic Separation Scheme in the Strait of Singapore: Aspect of Navigation Safety," (Jakarta: 14 November 2013), p. 10.

50   I. Sutalaksana, "Feedback for the Straits of Malacca and Singapore Study," Institute of Industrial Engineering and Management (2012): 1–2.

51   *Report of the 35th Tripartite Technical Experts Group (TTEG) Meeting on the Safety of Navigation in the Straits of Malacca and Singapore* (Yogyakarta, Indonesia, 4–5 October 2010), p. 2.

52   *Indonesian Report on Status Update of Project 5: Maintenance and Replacement of Aids to Navigation in the Straits of Malacca and Singapore*, 38th Tripartite Technical Experts Group (TTEG) Meeting on the Safety of Navigation in the Straits of Malacca and Singapore, Bali, Indonesia, 9–10 October 2013, p. 1.

faulty aids to navigation.[53] Nonetheless, Indonesia highlighted the urgency to repair aids to navigation to support navigational safety in the Straits, particularly at the northern approach where they have been out of service for nearly a decade. Indonesia emphasized its expectation that it would complete Project 6 in due course, and considered several options that could be decided to address obstacles to its completion.[54] Indonesia proposed a work program for 2014 that included maintenance of aids to navigation, procurement of spare parts, and replacement of light beacons totaling approximately US$1.1 million.[55]

The Directorate General of Sea Transportation has taken important steps within the framework of the Cooperative Mechanism on the ANF. While efforts have been made to achieve the main goal of the Ministerial Regulation on Navigational Aids, further efforts are needed to enhance capacity building and technical capability. To this end, the Directorate General of Sea Transportation requires technical assistance and human resource development to improve Indonesia's capacity to track and monitor vessels transiting the Straits to ensure compliance with international obligations.[56] Indonesia is encouraged to seek financial assistance from users of the Straits to support the implementation of the Regulation on Navigational Aids. Indonesia needs to enhance its capability to track and monitor vessel movements and collisions in the Straits.

Ministerial Regulation on Shipping Telecommunications

Despite the difficulty in measuring the effectiveness of VTS, there is considerable evidence to indicate that such measures reduce the risk of maritime collisions. In areas such as the Straits, it is essential to adopt mandatory coastal VTS because of the need for higher safety standards and increased concerns over environmental impacts caused by maritime incidents.[57]

---

53   *Official Meeting Report on 11th Meeting of the Aids to Navigation Fund Committee*, Singapore, 3–4 October 2013, p. 4 [11th ANF Meeting Report].

54   *Report of the 38th Tripartite Technical Experts Group (TTEG) Meeting on the Safety of Navigation in the Straits of Malacca and Singapore*, Bali, Indonesia, 9–10 October 2013, p. 4 [38th TTEG Meeting Report].

55   11th ANF Meeting Report, n. above 53, p. 5.

56   For further discussion, see UN Secretary-General's Report, n. 8 above, paras. 133–134.

57   J.F. Kemp and A.F.M. De Bievre, "A Regional Vessel Traffic Services for the North Sea: Perspective on Regional Environmental Cooperation," in *The North Sea: Perspectives on Regional Environmental Cooperation*, eds., D. Freestone and T. Ijlstra (London: Graham and Trotman, 1990), 173; D.R. Rothwell, "Coastal State Sovereignty and Navigational Freedoms: Current Issues in the Asia-Pacific Region," in *Rights and Responsibilities in the Maritime Environment: National and International Dilemmas*, eds., M. Tsamenyi and

It should be noted that the VTS has the purpose of improving vessel transit safety by providing vessel operators with advance information of other reported marine traffic and any additional information, advice and recommendations which will affect vessel traffic safety within the VTS area.[58] This is the reason why managing vessel traffic in ports, harbors, and coastal areas places significant demands on those responsible for safety, security, and protection of the environment. Higher traffic densities and greater vessel speeds mean that good outcomes increasingly depend on proven high-technology vessel monitoring solutions.[59]

The high volume of maritime activities and rapid vessel traffic in the Straits was anticipated by establishing the IMO-approved mandatory ship reporting system STRAITREP.[60] STRAITREP was adopted in accordance with SOLAS Regulation V/8-1, which obliges the contracting government to establish a ship reporting system. The government concerned is to take all measures necessary for the promulgation of any information needed for the efficient and effective use of the system.[61] The establishment of VTS centers in the Straits is consistent with Regulation 12(1) of SOLAS Chapter 5, which requires contracting governments to establish a VTS where, in their opinion, the volume of traffic or the degree of risk justifies such services. The use of a VTS, however, may only be made mandatory within the territorial seas of a coastal State.[62]

For a vessel transiting the Straits, there are three elements of STRAITREP to be considered: (a) reporting sectors, (b) participating in STRAITREP, and

M. Herriman, *Wollongong Papers on Maritime Policy*, no. 5 (Wollongong, Australia: Centre for Maritime Policy, Wollongong University, 1996), pp. 16–17.

58 Long Beach Vessel Traffic Service, *User Manual: Enhancing Safe, Environmentally Sound and Efficient Maritime Transportation for San Pedro Channel, Santa Monica Bay, Port of Los Angeles, and Port Long Beach, Los Angeles* (Marine Exchange of Southern California and United States Coast Guard, revised 1 June 2013), p. 1.

59 See for example, Transas, "Vessel Traffic Management System Solutions," available online: <http://www.transas.com/Port-and-Vessel-Traffic-Management-Solutions/Marine>.

60 The objectives of STRAITREP are to enhance safety of navigation, protect the marine environment, facilitate the movement of vessels, and support search and rescue and oil pollution response operations. "Paper on Information on the Development of Batam VTS Center for the Straits of Malacca and Singapore," Indonesia's paper presented at the 37th Meeting of the Tripartite Technical Experts Group on Safety of Navigation in the Straits of Malacca and Singapore, Directorate General of Sea Transportation of the Ministry of Transportation of the Republic of Indonesia, Singapore, 26–27 September 2012, p. 1.

61 SOLAS, n. 27 above, Regulation V/8-1(g).

62 See Regulation 12(3) of SOLAS, cited in Captain T. Hughes, "When is a VTS not a VTS," Fellow of the Nautical Institute and Royal Institute of Navigation (2006), p. 2.

(c) VTS.[63] In respect of reporting sectors, the Straits are divided into nine sectors. Sectors 1–5 and Sector 6 fall under the authority of Klang VTS and Johor VTS (Malaysia).[64] Sectors 7–9 are under the authority of the Singapore VTS Center and are also known as the Singapore Straits.[65] Malaysia and Singapore have recently installed fully operational VTS with six and three mandatory reporting sectors respectively.[66]

In the effort to establish a VTS center under the Cooperative Mechanism, Indonesia received Rp.177.6 billion (US$15 million) from the Japanese government in November 2008 to increase its ability to promote navigational safety in the Straits by establishing a VTS in Batu Ampar and as well as a number of sensor stations to collect information on vessel traffic.[67] The main reason for establishing this VTS Center is the increasing volume of vessel traffic as a result of trade development and shipping/dockyard industries in Batam.[68] Its main purpose remains the protection of navigation generally and protection of the right of freedom of passage through straits used for international navigation.[69]

At the 36th Tripartite Technical Experts Group (TTEG) Meeting on the Safety of Navigation in the Straits, Indonesia reported on the status of the Batam VTS and its planned involvement in STRAITREP. The project is being implemented in two phases. The first phase of the Batam VTS was completed in 2011. This phase comprises Batu Ampar, Batam (VTS Center as well as VTS sensors), Pulau Iyu Kecil (Small Iyu Island) (sensor station), and Tanjung Berakit (sensor station). The second stage of Dumai construction was expected

---

63 Safe Passage in the Straits of Malacca and Singapore, "Draft Content Text Ver. 24 September 2013," the 6th Cooperation Forum 7–8 October 2013, Bali, Indonesia, p. 2.

64 The primary function of a VTS is to provide information and assistance to commercial maritime traffic within channels, port approaches, or other areas that are difficult to navigate. G. Praetorius, F. van Westrenen, D.L. Mitchell and E. Hollnagel, "Learning Lessons in Resilient Traffic Management: A Cross-domain Study of Vessel Traffic Service and Air Traffic Control," in *Human Factors: A View from an Integrative Perspective. Proceedings of HFES Europe Chapter Conference*, Toulouse, eds., D. de Waard, K. Brookhuis, F. Dehais, C. Weikert, S. Röttger, D. Manzey, S. Biede, F. Reuzeau and P. Terrier (2012), p. 278.

65 X.Q. Meng and L. Suyi, *Ship Collision Risk Assessment for the Singapore Strait*, Department of Civil and Environmental Engineering, National University of Singapore and Centre for Maritime Studies, National University of Singapore (2012), p. 2.

66 Directorate of Navigation, n. 49 above, p. 5.

67 Djalal, n. 40 above.

68 "Paper on Information on the Development of Batam VTS Center," n. 60 above.

69 E.L. Miles and D.L. Fluharty, "U.S. Interests in the North Pacific," *Ocean Development and International Law* 22 (1991): 315–342.

to commence in 2013.[70] There will be three stations in the second phase, namely Dumai (VTS Sub-Center), Tanjung Parir (sensor station), and Tanjung Medan (sensor station).[71] More recently, the 37th TTEG Meeting noted that Indonesia agreed to provide the coordinates of the three working sectors of the Batam VTS sectors. It also noted that the Working Group's agreement that vessels engaged in support of authorized marine events and special operations, i.e., survey and salvage operations, should not be exempted from reporting to Batam VTS in order to ensure the safety of navigation.[72] Under SOLAS Regulation V/8-1(f),[73] however, the proposal for the Indonesian VTS Center is subject to agreement by Malaysia and Singapore,[74] and the proposal should be submitted to the IMO for its approval and adoption. The Republic of Indonesia has not yet submitted any proposal for the approval and adoption of the VTS Center through the IMO procedures.

Indonesia has enacted the Regulation of the Minister of Transportation No. 26 of 2011 on Shipping Telecommunications to support the establishment of the Batam VTS Center.[75] The purpose of the provisions of Regulation No. 26 is to ensure that vessels exercising transit passage through the Straits comply with UNCLOS and SOLAS. Under Article 2 of the Regulation, the shipping telecommunications facilities at Batam consist of a coastal radio station and VTS. Four types of shipping telecommunications are provided for, namely, Global Maritime Distress and Safety Systems (GMDSS), VTS, the Ship Reporting System (SRS), and the Long Range Identification and Tracking (LRIT) System (Article 3). Article 4 sets out the functions of the GMDSS, which are to alert concerning disasters (including location of the vessel in distress), search and research (SAR) coordination, facilitating location

---

70   *Report of the 36th Tripartite Technical Experts Group (TTEG) Meeting on the Safety of Navigation in the Straits of Malacca and Singapore*, Kuala Lumpur, Malaysia, 13–14 October 2011, pp. 4–5.

71   "Paper on Information of the Enhancement of Vessel Traffic Centre (VTS) System for the Straits of Malacca and Singapore," Indonesia's paper presented at the 36th Meeting of the Tripartite Technical Experts Group on Safety of Navigation in the Straits of Malacca and Singapore, Directorate General of Sea Transportation of the Ministry of Transportation of the Republic of Indonesia, Malaysia, 13–14 October 2011, p. 1.

72   *Report of the 37th Tripartite Technical Experts Group (TTEG) Meeting on the Safety of Navigation in the Straits of Malacca and Singapore*, Singapore, 26–27 September 2012, p. 6.

73   SOLAS Regulation V/8-1(f), n. 27 above, requires two or more governments having a common interest in a particular area such as the Straits to formulate proposals for a coordinated ship reporting system on the basis of agreement between them.

74   Directorate of Navigation, n. 49 above, p. 5.

75   "Paper on Information on the Development of Batam VTS Center," n. 60 above.

determination; communicating navigation safety information, and bridge-to-bridge communications.[76]

Article 5 of Regulation No. 26 sets out the functions of VTS, including monitoring shipping traffic and shipping sea lanes; enhancing shipping traffic security and navigation efficiency; protecting the marine environment; observing, detecting, and tracking vessels in the VTS coverage area; and assisting vessels as required.[77] VTS services are offered through service centers and sub-centers, sensor stations, and local port stations.[78] Standard equipment for VTS centers and sub-centers includes radar, closed circuit TV cameras, AIS, VHF radio, electronic navigation charts, and meteorological and hydrological receiving devices.[79] These provisions support the establishment of the Batam VTS Center, its VTS sub-center, and the VTS sensor station. Future VTS are expected to play a significant role in enhancing maritime safety and the efficiency of maritime transport as a key stakeholder of electronic navigation. To enhance VTS services, VTS operators need advanced functions to support VTS Services.[80]

VTS is particularly useful in areas of high traffic density or where there are narrow channels or other navigational difficulties such as the Straits. It is also appropriately used in environments that are either particularly sensitive or where dangerous cargoes are carried.[81] Eight critical areas have been identified along the Straits:

1.   One Fathom Bank: width: 1.4 nautical miles (NM), depth: 23.3 m (Choke Point 1);

---

76   The Global Maritime Distress and Safety System (GMDSS) is the technical, operational and administrative structure for maritime distress and safety communications worldwide. The GMDSS establishes the radio communications equipment that ships are required to carry, how this equipment shall be maintained and how it is used, and provides the context within which governments should establish the appropriate shore-based facilities to support GMDSS communications. "The Global Maritime Distress and Safety System (GMDSS)," International Mobile Satellite Organization (IMS), available online: <http://www.imso.org/GMDSS.asp>.

77   For a description of the functions of VTS, see "Vessel Traffic Services," Navigation Center, US Department of Homeland Security, United States Coast Guard (2013), available online: <http://www.navcen.uscg.gov/?pageName=vtsMain>.

78   Regulation No. 25, n. 5 above, Art. 14.

79   Id., Art. 17(3).

80   J.S. Jeong and G.K. Park, "Functional Requirements to Support Traffic Organization Service," *The International Journal of Marine Navigation and Safety of Sea Transportation* 7, no. 1 (March 2013): 115–118.

81   G. Plant, "International Legal Aspects of Vessel Traffic," *Marine Policy* 14 (1990): 71–81; Rothwell, n. 57 above, p. 16.

2. Northern Region of Medang Island: width: 3.7 NM, depth: 25 m (Choke Point 2);

3. North Tg. Balai Karmun: width: 2.9 NM, depth: 28.1 m (Choke Point 3);

4. Around RLB Takong: width: 0.5 NM, depth: 23 m (Choke Point 4);

5. Around the Strait of Durian: width: 0.75 NM, depth: 29 m (Choke Point 5);

6. Around Buffalo Rock (Kr. Banteng): width: 0.75 NM, depth: 24 m (Choke Point 6);

7. Around Batu Berhenti: width: 0.8 NM, depth: 23 m (Choke Point 7); and

8. Racon Delta around South Pelampung Suar Kardinal, where ship speed cannot reach 12 knots because ships must change course at a very sharp angle, so a ship has to turn off its engine and the ship's speed only reaches four knots.[82]

The Malacca Strait from One Fathom Bank (off Port Klang) south to the Singapore Strait is within the territorial sea of Indonesia and Malaysia.[83]

The third type of shipping telecommunications idenified in Regulation No. 26, SRS, serves the following functions: (a) to provide updated information on vessel movements; (b) to reduce contact time intervals with vessels; (c) to quickly determine locations of a vessel when it is in danger and its position is unknown; and (d) to enhance security and safety of persons and property at sea.[84] A SRS may be operated as part of a coastal radio station and VTS.[85] Standard equipment for a SRS includes a communication radio, AIS, a ship security alert system, and satellite communication.[86] SRS contribute to the safety of ships by providing information to vessels about navigational dangers, medical advice, directing the closest ship towards a vessel in distress, and defining the search area. The ship report is a precondition for providing such assistance. Ships submit their reports in pre-determined forms, at regular time

---

82 Directorate General of Sea Transportation, Ministry of Transportation of the Republic of Indonesia, "Workshop on Familiarization on the Result of the 36th Tripartite Technical Experts Group (TTEG) Meeting on Spatial Planning and Sea Lanes in the Straits of Malacca and Singapore," (Jakarta, Indonesia, 2011), p. 4.

83 R.C. Beckman, "The Significance to Asia of Cooperative Measures to Combat Piracy and Armed Robbery at Sea off the Coast of Somalia," The First Inter-Sessional Meeting on Maritime Security, Surabaya, 5–6 March 2009, ASEAN Regional Forum: *Promoting Peace and Security Through Dialogue and Cooperation in the Asia Pacific* (2009), p. 1.

84 Regulation No. 26, n. 6 above, Art. 6.

85 Id., Art. 20(1).

86 Id., Art. 20(2).

periods, or in some other agreed manner. Such systems can be voluntary or obligatory depending on national legislation.[87] Under Article 6 of Regulation No. 26, a SRS is mandatory in accordance with Regulation 12(3) of SOLAS.

The fourth type of shipping telecommunications, LRIT, detect vessels as early as possible, monitor vessel movement so that in case of disaster an action can be taken or anticipated, and assist in SAR operations.[88] Under Article 21(1), Indonesian vessels of a certain type and size that undertake international voyages are obliged to have an LRIT transponder on board. These vessels include high-speed passenger craft, high-speed craft of 300 gross tonnage (GT), and mobile offshore drilling units.[89] With regard to the mandatory reporting system, Article 52(1) of Regulation No. 26 obliges the operator or captain of a vessel to report the plan of ship arrival at the port to the harbourmaster via master cable to the port authority, or the harbourmaster through the coastal radio station no more than 48 hours prior to arrival.[90] The master cable contains information on the vessel name, call sign, Maritime Mobile Services Identity, date and time in reporting, real-time position reporting, and ports of departure and destination.[91] These provisions are in conformity with international maritime instruments that oblige the master of a ship to comply with requirements of the national ship reporting systems and to report to the appropriate authority all information required under relevant provisions of each system.[92] From a reporting perspective, Article 52 is of particular importance for obtaining information related to vessel arrivals and departures in the Port of Batam.

Challenges to Implementation

The effectiveness of Indonesia in controlling maritime incidents in the Straits is entirely dependent upon the existence of an adequate legal and institutional framework to tackle maritime concerns and the technical capabilities to implement such frameworks. Indonesia has a vital interest in providing safe and secure navigation through its archipelagic waters. International user States want Indonesia to maintain freedom of navigation and sea lanes passage through the Strait of Malacca and its archipelagic waters for their merchant shipping and naval vessels.[93] Indonesia has legitimate concerns over

---

87   K. Baljak and P. Vidan, *Global Ship Reporting System and Automatic Identification System*, p. 1, available online: <http://bib.irb.hr/datoteka/326010.326010.pdf>.

88   Regulation No. 26, n. 6 above, Art. 7.

89   Id., Art. 21(2).

90   Id., Art. 52(2).

91   Id., Art. 52(3).

92   SOLAS, n. 27 above, Regulation V/8-1(h).

93   Indonesian Navy Chief of Staff, "The Task of the Indonesian Navy in State Sovereignty and Law Enforcement in Maritime Zones under National Jurisdiction to Support the National

navigational safety, maritime security, and marine environmental protection of vessels exercising transit passage through the Straits. Therefore, ensuring maritime security and safety and marine environmental protection in the Straits constitutes an important element of Indonesian maritime policy.[94] From Indonesia's perspective, maritime safety and security as well as marine environmental protection in the Strait of Malacca are vital from an economic point of view, as the Strait is generally transited by merchant ships, oil and gas tankers, cargo vessels, and ships carrying nuclear and other dangerous goods.[95]

The implementation of Regulation No. 26 is not without problems as there have been maritime incidents in the Straits. For example, on 19 June 2011, a Marshall Island registered vessel, M/V *Al Rawdah* (175 GT) went aground in the Strait of Malacca. One person died and no marine pollution was reported due to the incident. On 19 August 2011, the Indonesian flagged *KLM Elvi Jaya* (286 GT) sank in the Strait of Malacca. No casualties or marine pollution was reported.[96] Such incidents and maritime collisions can be traced to a lack of interaction between vessels and VTS, and lack of coordination among wave guides,[97] tug boats, and port operators, as well as low levels of understanding and utilization of modern navigation systems such as electronic chart display and information systems, AIS, and radar.[98] In many cases, small vessels

---

Interest," paper presented at the Public Lecture of the Law of the Sea, Faculty of Law, Bandung Islamic University in Cooperation with the Indonesian Navy Headquarters of the Republic of Indonesia, Bandung Indonesia, November 4, 2008, pp. 3–4; D.M. Sodik, "The Indonesian Legal Framework on Baselines, Archipelagic Passage, and Innocent Passage," *Ocean Development and International Law* 43 (2012): 230–341.

94   Oegroseno, n. 1 above.

95   P. Susgiantoro (Minister of Defence), "Indonesian Waters are Vulnerable to Maritime Security Threats," 6 *Indonesian Maritime Magazine* (Indonesian Maritime Council of the Republic of Indonesia, 2011), p. 13.

96   "Status Report on Marine Casualty Affecting Traffic Movement Noted by Indonesia," 36th Meeting of the Tripartite Technical Expert Group on the Safety of Navigation in the Straits of Malacca and Singapore, 13–14 October 2011, Annex D, p. 1.

97   A wave guide is a structure that guides waves, such as electromagnetic waves or sound waves. There are different types of wave guides for each type of wave. The original and most common meaning is a hollow conductive metal pipe used to carry high frequency radiowaves, particularly microwaves. R.B. Marks and D.F. Williams, "A General Waveguide Circuit Theory," *Journal of Research of the National Institute of Standards and Technology* 97, no. 5 (September–October 1992): 533–562.

98   "Kerjasama 3 Negara Pantai dalam rangka Peningkatan Keselamatan Pelayaran dan Perlindungan Lingkungan Maritim," (Jakarta, Indonesia, Direktorat Jenderal Perhubungan Laut, Kementerian Perhubungan Republik Indonesia, November 2011), hlm. 14

navigating through or crossing the Straits may not be fully technologically equipped in terms of safety and environmental protection.[99] Accidents involving small boats colliding with large ships in the Strait of Malacca are often due to poor monitoring of navigation equipment by ships' crews.[100]

Indonesia faces several problems in implementing Regulation No. 26. First, despite the detail contained in the Regulation, the contents of the Regulation relating to VTS and SRS are not really centered on the key rules of STRAITREP. The failure of vessels to comply with the provisions concerning mandatory ship reporting is a further challenge and factor causing accidents and maritime collisions in Indonesian waters in the Straits.[101] Overall, the Regulation is inadequate to meet the standards set out in the IMO-approved STRAITREP.[102] According to the IMO-approved STRAITREP, information considered essential is not only vessel name and call sign as stipulated in Article 52(3) of Regulation No. 26, but also IMO identification number (if available), position, hazardous cargo and deficiencies of the vessel that may affect normal navigation. VTS authorities may request additional information considered necessary with regard to vessel course and speed.[103] Revision of Regulation No. 26 to incorporate these rules of STRAITREP would create an effective legal framework to strengthen Indonesia's call for stricter safety measures for ships entering Batam port and passing through its waters.

A second problem concerns damage to the Batam VTS, which was only operational for a few months in 2012, and a subsequent loss of valuable data.

"Cooperation Among Three Coastal States of the Straits of Malacca and Singapore in the Framework of Enhancing the Navigational Safety and Protection of the Marine Environment"), (Jakarta, Indonesia, Directorate General of Sea Transportation, Ministry of Transportation of the Republic of Indonesia, November 2011), p. 14 [Directorate General of Sea Transportation].

99   Djalal, n. 40 above.

100   R. Alsina, "New AIS System Reduces Rate of Maritime Accidents in Malaysia," *Cruise Ship Law Blog* (2013), available online: <http://blog.lipcon.com/2013/05/new_air_system_reduces_rate_of_maritime_accidents_in_malaysia.html#sthash.jlZMPdDt.dpuf>.

101   Report of the 37th (TTEG) Meeting, n. 72 above, p. 13.

102   Under IMO Resolution MSC.73(69), para. 1.1, on Mandatory Ship Reporting Systems in the Straits of Malacca and Singapore, the following categories of ships are required to participate in STRAITREP: (1) vessels of 300 gross tonnage and above; (2) vessels of 50 m or more in length; (3) vessels engaged in towing or pushing with a combined GT of 300 and above, or with a combined length of 50 m or more; (4) carrying hazardous cargo, as defined in paragraph 1.4 of Resolution MSC.43 (64); and (5) all passenger vessels which are fitted with VHF, regardless of length or GT; and (6) any category of vessels less than 50 m in length or less than 300 GT that are fitted with VHF and in an emergency uses the appropriate traffic lane or separation zone in order to avoid immediate danger.

103   Siang, n. 34 above.

Consequently, Indonesia does not have valid data on vessel traffic in the Straits to make predictions of what will happen in the future.[104] Indonesia has limited capabilities in identifying, directing, and controlling the vessel's voyage in the Straits due to acute technical constraints of the Indonesian VTS. The program offered by Indonesia through the Cooperative Mechanism Forum is directed more to navigational aids maintenance than VTS.[105] Meanwhile, Singapore is currently very active in encouraging international vessels to land at its port because of VTS capabilities, hardware, software, and human resources. Through professional management, Singapore's VTS has played an important role in boosting its economy from the maritime sector.[106]

To support the operation of the Batam VTS infrastructure, Indonesian technological capabilities have to be improved in order to ensure navigational safety of pilotage, traffic signals, among other things.[107] Indonesia needs enhanced human resource development in the field of VTS in order to cope with the tight implementation schedule of VTS in the Straits. For this purpose, Indonesia intends to seek cooperation through the TTEG to provide VTS training programs for personnel in accordance with Recommendation V-103 of the International Association of Marine Aids to Navigation and Lighthouse Authorities (IALA). This cooperation is expected to include the establishment of a VTS training center in Indonesia.[108] Such training programs are consistent with IMO Resolution No. A.857(20) of 1997, which provides guidance for planning and implementing a VTS as well as recruiting and training VTS operators.[109] These programs are expected to improve the technical capacity for implementing VTS and SRS rules and thus enable Indonesia to play a larger role in providing VTS or participating in STRAITREP. VTS and SRS personnel must be equipped with the technical know-how and skills in order to cope with the navigation safety concerns and safeguard the economy and the environment.

A further notable initiative is an integrated maritime safety system to support the Batam VTS Center, known as the Marine Electronic Highway (MEH),

---

104 "Laporan Draft Final Penyusunan Panduan Kebijakan Keselamatan Pelayaran di Selat Malakadan Singapura," (LETMI ITB, Kementerian Perhubungan Republik Indonesia, 2012), hlm. 35 ("Final Draft Report on Guidance Arrangements of Navigation Safety in the Straits of Malacca and Singapore," Bandung Institute of Technology, Ministry of Transportation of the Republic of Indonesia, 2012), p. 35 [Final Draft Report].

105 Id., p. 46.

106 Id., p. 78.

107 Id., p. 35.

108 "Paper on Information on Development of Batam VTS Center," n. 60 above, p. 2.

109 Hughes, n. 62 above.

which was agreed to at the 38th TTEG Meeting. At that meeting, Indonesia proposed a consolidated and integrated system including the MEH, electronic (E)-navigation, and the concept study of under keel clearance (UKC) and any other system that may arise in the future to avoid duplication and inefficiency.[110] The MEH Information Technology System for the Straits, which was managed by the IMO, was handed over to the Indonesian government in a formal ceremony in Batam in 2012. This marked the final stages of a demonstration project[111] and the potential move towards a full-scale MEH project in the Straits under the ownership of the littoral States.[112] The TTEG Meeting also noted Indonesia's request for funding support of US$70,000 for 2014 for the maintenance of the MEH Data Center.[113] However, Regulation No. 26 does not include provisions for the MEH system. It is recommended that the MEH provision be incorporated into the Ministerial Regulation for effectively supporting the MEH system in the Batam VTS Center.

A third problem is overlapping and competing jurisdiction between government agencies in handling shipping telecommunications technology. The Directorate General of Sea Transportation and the Ministry of Communications and Information Technology (MCIT) are the agencies claiming jurisdiction in marine telecommunications technology. These agencies reportedly do not share data and information, and often fail to communicate with each other.[114] This has hampered operations of the Batam VTS Center. The basic issue relates to the lack of a clear policy on the authority of the government agencies. Although the conflict between the Directorate General of Sea Transportation and the MCIT is basically domestic in nature, it affects the implementation and enforcement measures of the international maritime safety legal framework. Indonesia needs to pay more attention to international community concern over the safety of international navigation in the Straits as maritime incidents have serious negative effects on commercial maritime routes.

---

110   38th TTEG Meeting Report, n. 54 above, p. 6.

111   IMO, "Marine Electronic Highway (MEH) Demonstration Project in the Straits of Malacca and Singapore," <http://www.imo.org/OurWork/Safety/Navigation/Pages/MarineElectronicHighway.aspx>.

112   IMO, "Marine electronic highway IT systems handed over to Indonesia as Straits of Malacca and Singapore MEH comes closer to fruition," (2012), available online: <http://www.imo.org/MediaCentre/PressBriefings/Pages/29-MEH.aspx#.U5l8SEBQX74>.

113   38th TTEG Meeting Report, n. 54 above, p. 5.

114   Final Draft Report, n. 104 above; Sutalaksana, n. 14 above; See also B. Perciva, "Indonesia and the United States: Shared Interests in Maritime Security," USINDO, the United States Indonesia Society (June 2005), p. 28.

Law No. 32 of 2014 on Oceans provides a basis to establish an institutional framework for proper implementation of international maritime instruments. However, institutional reform is needed to establish a clear legislative mandate as well as a clear division of functions and responsibilities between the Directorate General of Sea Transportation and the MCIT. Coordination and cooperation between these government agencies are necessary to implement and enforce the international legal regime for maritime safety in the Straits.

Ministerial Regulation on Ocean Shipping Lanes

The IMO establishes sea lanes and traffic separation schemes as routeing measures under Regulation 10(1) Chapter 5 of SOLAS. Ships routeing systems are to contribute to safety of life at sea, safety and efficiency of navigation, and/or protection of the marine environment by separating opposing streams of traffic by appropriate means and by the establishment of traffic lanes.[115] Rule 10 of COLREGS regulates the behavior of vessels in or near traffic separation schemes adopted by the IMO.[116] Establishing traffic separation schemes in busy areas of difficult navigation[117] improves navigational safety in converging areas and in areas where the freedom of movement of shipping is inhibited by restricted space, the existence of obstructions to navigation, limited depths, or unfavorable meteorological conditions.[118]

These international instruments provide a legal framework for regulating maritime safety issues relating to vessel routeing systems, sea lanes, traffic separation schemes, archipelagic sea lanes passage, and innocent passage at the national level. The Indonesian government also considered the impact of disruptions of submarine telecommunications cables and the breaking of pipelines in its territorial sea and archipelagic waters on other marine activities in the Straits, including transit passage, in its maritime safety legislation as these issues are interlinked. Ministerial Regulation No. 68 on Ocean Shipping Lanes includes provisions to manage critical aspects of maritime safety in the Straits,

---

115   See also Beckman, n. 15 above.

116   Rule 10 of COLREGS, n. 28 above, applies to a vessel using a traffic separation scheme to proceed in the appropriate traffic lane in the general direction of traffic flow for that lane; so far as practicable keep clear of a traffic separation line or separation zone; and normally join or leave a traffic lane at the termination of the lane, but when joining or leaving from either side shall do so at as small an angle to the general direction of traffic flow as practicable. Further, so far as practicable a vessel is to avoid anchoring in a TSS or in areas near its terminations.

117   COLREGS, id., Rule 10: Traffic Separation Schemes.

118   A.M. Ibrahim, *Navigational Safety in the Straits of Malacca and Singapore: Current and Future Concern*, Marine Department Malaysia (2009), p. 18.

including vessel anchoring measures, vessel routeing systems and sea lanes, protection of submarine cables and pipelines, and charts and hydrographic surveys. Two further issues critical to implementation of these measures are also considered below, namely integrated oceans management and delineation of maritime boundaries with neighboring States in the Strait.

Anchoring

In conformity with Rule 10(g) of COLREGS, the IMO adopted Circular No. 282 of 27 November 2009 on Safety of Navigation Information Concerning Anchoring in the Traffic Separation Scheme in the Straits upon the recommendation of the three littoral States. The Circular reminds mariners not to anchor in all areas in the TSS of the Straits, as well as between the landward limits of the TSS and approaches to the ports. Vessels entering any port in the littoral States are to anchor only in the anchorages designated by the respective littoral States. Mariners are given notice that the maritime authorities of Indonesia, Malaysia, and Singapore closely monitor the identities and locations of vessels that anchor indiscriminately. The relevant authority will take appropriate action including reporting to the flag State of the vessel.[119]

Despite these measures, vessel anchorage outside the TSS without reporting to a local authority remains a problem in the Straits.[120] The 38th TTEG meeting noted Indonesia's concern with indiscriminate anchoring in the Straits, especially near or in the TSS area.[121] The TTEG noted the status reports by Indonesia and Singapore on contravention of Rule 10 of the COLREGS Convention.[122] Maritime accidents in the Straits are commonly due to the failure of vessel captains to comply with national and international rules on indiscriminate anchoring.[123] However, the Indonesian Ministerial Regulation No. 68 on Ocean Shipping Lanes contains no provisions on proscribed anchorage areas.[124] This absence is a significant factor contributing to such accidents. Regulation No. 68 needs to contain a prohibition on indiscriminate anchoring as set out under IMO Circular No. 282. This would assist Indonesian officials in exercising

---

119   IMO, Circular No. 282 of 27 November 2009 on Safety of Navigation Information Concerning Anchoring in the Traffic Separation Scheme in the Straits of Malacca and Singapore, Annex, "Prohibition of Anchoring in the Straits of Malacca and Singapore."

120   Directorate General of Sea Transportation, n. 82 above, p. 2.

121   38th TTEG Meeting Report, n. 54 above, p. 6.

122   Id., p. 2.

123   Directorate General of Sea Transportation, n. 98 above.

124   Id.

control and jurisdiction over indiscriminate anchoring of ships at non-designated anchorages.

Vessel Routeing Systems and Sea Lanes

Article 2 of Regulation No. 68 identifies two kinds of ocean shipping lanes: general and crossing, and port entry. Pursuant to Article 3, the Minister of Transportation is responsible for the designation of ocean shipping lanes, ship's routeing systems, traffic procedures, and port entry. The operation of ocean shipping lanes is conducted for vessel traffic order, vessel movement monitoring, and the application of innocent passage for foreign ships.[125] The Regulation also includes provisions for the development plan for ocean shipping lanes, including hydrographic surveys, technical design arrangements, working arrangements, and replacement of aids to navigation.[126] To ensure safe, smooth, and efficient navigation in specified waters, the designation of ship routeing systems includes traffic separation schemes, two-way routes, recommended tracks, deep water routes, areas to be avoided, inshore traffic zones, precautionary areas, and roundabouts.[127] Specified waters include TSS zones, Indonesian archipelagic sea lane waters, the territorial sea, and the designated water of a SRS. The designation of TSS zones,[128] two-way routes,[129] and roundabouts,[130] is to be determined by considering the width of shipping lanes, vessel dimension, shipping traffic congestion, the amount of dangerous goods shipped, specific characteristics of vessels, equipment, and lanes normally used for international navigation.

Article 20(3) of Regulation No. 68 stipulates that the recommended tracks are designated for guiding the master when entering ocean shipping lanesand clarifying a safe route for a ship. Article 20(4) sets out factors that are used to determine the designation of deep water routes including, *inter alia*, by the vessel's dimensions, under keel clearance, and draught, the condition of the seabed as listed on the charts, and dangers to navigation. Article 20(5) deals with the factors affecting the designation of areas to be avoided, which include the location of the designated anchorages, protected locations, the condition of the seabed as listed on charts, and identified dangers to navigation. Furthermore, inshore traffic zones are designated that consider vessels less

---

125   Regulation No. 68, n. 7 above, Art. 4.
126   Id., Art. 14.
127   Id., Art. 19(1).
128   Id., Art. 20(1).
129   Id., Art. 20(2).
130   Id., Art. 20(8).

than 20 meters in length, allocate routes for vessels transiting to and from port, allocate for fishing vessel operations around the TSS, and vessels that are not properly operating.[131] The designation of precautionary areas comprises temporary landing locations, joint areas for vessels entering the TSS, and areas identified for vessels taking a short-cut to a TSS.[132] Three precautionary areas have been identified in the Straits, namely Karimum Island, Batu Berhanti, and North Nongsa.[133]

Clearly, traffic separation schemes adopted by coastal states like Indonesia are designed to improve safety of life at sea and protect the marine environment while minimizing the inconvenience or cost to ship operators.[134] Existing maritime safety threats and challenges highlight the importance of designating a routeing system to improve maritime safety. In practical terms, the Straits are used for aquaculture and have highly diverse ecosystems, as well as an Indonesian fishing zone, submarine cables and pipelines. Indonesia is rich in diversity of marine habitats, protected marine plants,[135] mangroves, and coral reefs.[136] Although the deep water routes, critical lanes for deep draught vessels (DDVs) and very large crude carriers (VLCCs), are in Indonesian national waters, most of the traffic separation lanes in the Strait of Malacca are within Malaysian waters.[137] In 2011, the volume of traffic of all types and sizes passing through the Strait was approximately 28 percent Afframax (245 m) and Suezmax (285 m) respectively, 10 percent VLCC (350 m) and Malacca-Max (470 m) respectively, and 24 percent coastal tankers (205 m).[138] The 36th TTEG Meeting agreed to designate a routeing system in traffic separation schemes of the Straits from One Fathom Bank to Horshburg.[139] Article 19(3) of Regulation No. 68 provides that, *inter alia*, fishing areas; the existence or possibility of offshore exploration, development and exploitation of the seabed and sub-soil;

---

131   Id., Art. 20(6).

132   Id., Art. 20(7).

133   Directorate General of Sea Transportation, n. 98 above, p. 5.

134   G. Karandawala and B. Lewarn, "Implications for Shipping and Maritime Transport," in *The United Nations Convention on the Law of the Sea: What it Means to Australia and Australia's Maritime Industries*, eds., M. Tsamenyi, S. Bateman and J. Delaney, *Wollongong Papers on Maritime Policy*, No. 3 (Wollongong, Australia: Centre for Maritime Policy, University of Wollongong, 1996), p. 108.

135   Directorate of Navigation, n. 49 above, p. 7.

136   Bernard, n. 24 above, p. 12.

137   Directorate General of Sea Transporation, n. 98 above.

138   Directorate of Navigation, n. 49 above, p. 8.

139   Directorate General of Sea Transporation, n. 98 above, p. 20.

conservation areas; and the reliability of hydrographic surveys and charts must be considered in the designation of routeing systems.[140]

Submarine Cables and Pipelines

In territorial sea and archipelagic waters, there is significant incompatibility between the fast-growing, billion dollar submarine cable and fisheries industries, where fisheries cause damage, loss, huge repair costs, and lost revenues from cable disruptions.[141] Article 2(2) of UNCLOS allows coastal States to regulate the laying, maintenance, and repair of submarine cables and pipelines.[142] Under Article 21(1)(c) of UNCLOS, the coastal State has the right to pass laws and regulations concerning innocent passage through the territorial sea in respect of certain specified subjects, including the protection of submarine cables and pipelines provided that such laws and regulations are not discriminatory and are in conformity with the provisions of UNCLOS and other rules of international law.[143] This right also applies in straits used for international navigation between a part of the high seas or exclusive economic zone and the territorial sea of a foreign State.[144] Similarly, archipelagic States such as Indonesia and the Philippines have the right to regulate the laying, maintenance, and repair of submarine cables in their archipelagic waters. Article 51 of UNCLOS provides that archipelagic States must respect existing submarine cables laid by other States passing through their waters without making landfall.[145]

---

140   Regulation No. 68, n. 7 above, Art. 19(3).

141   S. Coffen-Smout and G. Herbert, "Submarine Cables: A Challenge for Ocean Management," *Marine Policy* 24 (2000): 441–448; F. Douvere and C. Ehler, "Ecosystem-Based Marine Spatial Management: An Evolving Paradigm for the Management of Coastal and Marine Places," in *Ocean Yearbook 23*, eds., A. Chircop, S. Coffen-Smout and M. McConnell (Leiden: Martinus Nijhoff Publishers, 2009): 1–26, p. 2.

142   Article 2(1) of UNCLOS, n. 4 above, states that the sovereignty of a coastal State extends to the air space over the territorial sea as well as to its bed and subsoil.

143   T. Davenport, "Submarine Communication Cables and Law of the Sea: Problems in Law and Practice," *Ocean Development and International Law* 43 (2012): 201–242.

144   Article 45(1)(b) of UNCLOS, n. 4 above, states that the regime of innocent passage, in accordance with Part 11, Section 3, shall apply in straits used for international navigation between a part of the high seas or exclusive economic zone and the territorial sea of a foreign State.

145   R. Beckman and T. Davenport, *Workshop Report, Workshop on Submarine Cables and Law of the Sea, Singapore, 14–15 December 2009* (Singapore, Centre for International Law, University of Singapore, 2009), p. 11.

The protection of submarine cables and pipelines in Indonesia is principally dealt with under Article 45(1) of the Regulation No. 68, which provides for
construction of submarine cables and pipelines using the burial method.
As stated in paragraph 1, burial is conducted subject to the following rules:
(a) their placement on the outer side of sea lanes; (b) in sea lanes with water
depths of less than 20 m, submarines cables and pipelines must be buried to
4 m under the natural seabed; (c) in sea lanes with water depths of 20 to 40 m,
submarines cables and pipelines must be buried to 2 m below the natural seabed; (d) in sea lanes with a water depth of more than 40 m, submarines cables
and pipelines must be buried to 1 m below natural seabed; and (e) in certain
locations to relieve anticipated shipping traffic congestion and harbor development and navigation congestion, a risk assessment is required, *inter alia*,
through an anchor drop test.[146] The legal framework pertaining to pipelines is
found in the Decree of the Minister of Energy and Mining No. 300 of 1997
Regarding the Work Safety of Oil and Natural Gas Pipelines. Specific protection
for international navigation is provided under Article 27(1), which obliges owners of pipelines to consider maritime safety when a pipeline is laid across the
seabed. Under paragraph 2, the owners of pipelines are required to post navigation signs in certain places, including shipping lanes, in accordance with relevant laws and regulations.[147] This legal framework for the protection of
submarine cables and pipelines is consistent with Articles 2(1), 21(2)(c), 45 and
51(2) of UNCLOS.

However, there remains a problem with improper laying of submarine
cables and pipelines in the Strait of Malacca's Indonesian Batam waters by
national and foreign stakeholders, which could interfere with navigation.[148]
Concerns have been raised about the consequences of inappropriate deployments as the Straits are criss-crossed by undersea cables and pipelines,[149]
including disruption of anchoring, fishing, and sand mining activities.[150]
Further, inadequately buried cables and pipelines can potentially damage
marine natural resources and marine protected areas. Improper deployments
are caused by the inadequate national legal and institutional frameworks to

---

146   UNCLOS, n. 4 above, Art. 45(2).

147   Article 44 of UNCLOS, n. 4 above., provides that States bordering straits shall not hamper
      and shall give appropriate publicity to any danger to navigation within a strait of which
      they have knowledge.

148   Sutalaksana, n. 14 above.

149   H. Djalal, "The Regime of Managing Safety and Security in the Straits of Malacca and
      Singapore," *Diplomacy Journal* 1, no. 2 (September, 2009): 8–26.

150   Final Draft Report, n. 104 above, pp. 71–72.

protect undersea cables and pipelines as provided for under Articles 21(1)(c), 45 and 51(2) of UNCLOS. Article 45(1) and (2) of Regulation No. 68 and Article 27 of Decree No. 300 do not specify liability of the owners of undersea cables and pipelines for improper laying of cables or pipelines that damage other marine activities. It is suggested that provisions holding an owner liabile for improper laying and failure to give accurate navigation information be included in the Regulation and the Decree. This would provide a basis for the Indonesian government's responsibility over navigational safety and protection of other legitimate uses of the sea in the Straits. Similarly, these provisions also do not confer liability on the owner and master of a vessel that damages a submarine cable or pipeline while exercising innocent passage and archipelagic sea lanes passage. It is further recommended that provisions holding the owner and master of a vessel liable for damage to a cable or pipeline in national waters be included in the Regulation and the Decree. Mariners must be made aware of protection arrangements regarding fisheries and resource management, discharge of harmful substances, as well as the protection of cables and pipelines. A single publication could provide information on all of these arrangements, along with detailed maps to indicate the visual extent of all protected areas.[151]

The improper laying of submarine cables and pipelines stems from institutional factors, *inter alia*, the absence of comprehensive and detailed maps on the deployment of cables and pipelines and whether they are active or decommissioned; inaction in designating corridors for the deployment of submarine cables and pipelines; the lack of clear policy and coordination among stakeholders relating to deployment guidance, including costs and economic benefits; and incomplete data on the number and location of submarine cables and pipelines.[152] The absence of clear policy and coordination is demonstrated by the fact that four working units under the Directorate General of Sea Transportation are directly involved in the deployment of submarine cables and pipelines, namely the Sub-Directorate of Salvage, Sub-Directorate of Traffic Signs, local navigation districts, and port authorities. Other government institutions might also be involved, including the Ministry of Energy and Mineral Resources, MCIT, the Ministry of Foreign Affairs, the Indonesian Navy,

---

151   V.A. Froude, "Area-based Restrictions in the New Zealand Marine Environment," Wellington: New Zealand Department of Conservation, 2004, available online: <http://www.doc.govt.nc/templates/MultiPageDocumentTOC.aspx/id=43055>; S. Kaye, "The Protection of Platforms, Pipelines and Submarine Cables under Australian and New Zealand Law," in Klein et al., n. 9 above, p. 200.

152   Final Draft Report, n. 104 above, pp. 71–72.

the Indonesian Naval Hydro-Oceanographic Office, the National Coordinating Agency for Surveys and Mapping, the Oil and Gas Upstream Business Executive Unit, and Stakeholders in Energy and Mineral Resources and Telecommunications.[153] Multiple institutions at the national level, lack of coordination, and jurisdictional conflicts make it difficult to build a comprehensive dataset of information on subsea deployments and the number and location of cables and pipelines.

To address these problems, all ocean-related ministries and agencies are required to follow the principles and rules contained in the Law No. 32 of 2014 on Oceans, though further details will be provided in a regulation. It is recommended that the division of functions and responsibilities for each ocean-related ministry and agency involved in the deployment of submarine cables and pipelines be included in this regulation. Specifically, the primary responsibility for deployments should be given to the Directorate General of Sea Transportation as it is in charge of the provision of services, infrastructure, communication facilities, and maintenance for sea transportation. Further, the regulation should contain provisions for policy collaboration between the Directorate General of Sea Transportation and other agencies. Improved coordination and cooperation are necessary to facilitate effective development and implementation of navigational safety measures.[154]

It is particularly important that industry should work with coastal States like Indonesia to develop a code of best practices for laying, repairing, and protecting submarine cables in the territorial sea and archipelagic waters.[155] The Indonesian government should consider developing guidance on deployment activities, both at the planning and implementation stages of a project and after project termination. Such guidance would set out the rights and duties of submarine cable and pipeline owners, relevant government agencies,[156] users, and operators. The main goal of such guidance would be to ensure that legitimate marine uses are not disrupted by laying submarine cables and pipelines.

Charts and Hydrographic Surveys

As noted in several places in the legislation, implementation of the regulatory framework must be done with due regard to hydrographic charts. Hydrographic

---

153   Sutalaksana, n. 14 above.

154   UN Secretary-General's Report, n. 8 above.

155   R. Beckman, "The Legal Framework on Permitting for Submarine Cables," paper presented at Submarine Networks World 2010, Permitting Workshop, 12 October 2010, Centre for International Law, National University of Singapore, p. 15.

156   Final Draft Report, n. 104 above, p. 72.

surveys are conducted to determine water depth for nautical chart production
and similar products for navigation safety. These surveys also determine the
configuration and nature of the seabed, obtain information on the heights and
times of tides, and identify hazards to navigation.[157] Safe and secure routes for
navigation and the reliability of accurate and appropriate hydrographic survey
coverage and up-to-date nautical information are crucial for navigational safety,
as well as the protection and preservation of the marine environment.[158]

The main functions of the Hydro-Oceanographic Office of the Indonesian
Navy are to conduct hydrographic surveys, scientific research, charting, produce relevant publications, protect the marine environment, and ensure navigational safety for the Indonesian National Navy and the general public. In this
context, the intense sea use in Indonesian waters requires consideration of not
only exploration and exploitation of oil and natural gas, marine tourism, international trade, port affairs, but also charting and maritime accidents.[159] The
duties of the Hydro-Oceanographic Office have become more important with
the recommendations of the 38th TTEG Meeting on the Concept Study on
Real-Time Monitoring of Under Keel Clearance to conduct multibeam hydrographic surveys in four areas and to carry out a test on real-time monitoring of
UKC in the Straits.[160]

Challenges to Implementation

The central issue considered in Regulation No. 68 is putting in place an effective and efficient regime to govern the navigational safety in the Straits. The
current approach to maritime safety is driven by the need to protect ocean
resources of the three littoral States. The conservation and management of
marine biodiversity and fisheries resources, the protection of submarine cables
and pipelines, and the promotion of navigational safety have a high profile
given the importance of marine natural resources to the coastal communities
of the three littoral States. Key aspects of Indonesian marine policy address the
need for compatibility between the desire to utilize fishing grounds, protect

157   B. Wilson and J. Kraska, "American Security and Law of the Sea," *Ocean Development and
       International Law* 40, no. 3 (2009): 268–290.
158   UN Secretary-General's Report, n. 8 above.
159   "Perspektif Hidro-Oseanografi dan Delimitasi Maritim di Perairan Selat Malakadan Singapora,"
       Jakarta, Indonesia, Dinas Hidro-Oseanografi Angkatan Laut Indonesia, (8 November 2011),
       hlm. 3–4. ("Hydrographic-Oceanography Perspective and Maritime Delimitation in the
       Straits of Malacca and Singapore,") (Jakarta, Indonesia, Hydro-Oceanographic Office of the
       Indonesian Navy, 8 November 2011), pp. 3–4 [Hydrographic-Oceanography Perspective].
160   38th TTEG Meeting Report, n. 54 above.

marine areas, and lay submarine cables and pipelines on the one hand, and promote navigational safety in the Straits on the other hand.

With the aim of promoting navigational safety in the Straits, appropriate and balanced legislative and institutional approaches need to be taken in conjunction with marine security and marine environmental protection measures. Five sub-issues can be identified in implementing such a regime in connection with Indonesia's interests in the Straits: (1) critical areas; (2) deep water routes; (3) rational utilization of fishing areas; (4) marine protected areas; and (5) protection of submarine cables and pipelines in the Indonesian territorial sea and archipelagic waters from shipping, fishing and other activities.[161] A holistic approach to deal with these competing marine activities is needed. Such an approach requires formulation and implementation of ocean policy and coordination among various national agencies. In order to achieve these objectives, it is also crucial to formulate an institutional framework to reduce conflicts among ocean uses and users. Further, ocean governance policy requires institutional capacity to deal with the maritime incidents in the Straits.

Several pieces of Indonesian legislation deal with the development of an integrated ocean governance policy. Article 42(1) of Law No. 32 of 2014 on Oceans provides that marine spatial management is to be conducted to (a) protect marine natural resources and the environment on the basis of environmental carrying capacity and local wisdom, (b) utilize potential futures of marine resources and/or activities in marine areas at both national and international levels, and (c) develop potential zones to become the focal points for production, distribution, and service activities. Article 42(2) provides further that marine spatial management covers planning, utilization, control, and surveillance. Marine spatial planning, according to Article 43(1), is to comprise national marine spatial planning, a zoning plan for coastal areas and small islands, and a zoning plan for marine areas. Article 69(1) and (2) further stipulates that the government should establish ocean governance policy and institutional frameworks, which include a legal system development plan, a planning system, and coordination, monitoring, and evaluation mechanisms for effective and efficient ocean development. Paragraph 4 provides that such an ocean governance policy and institutional framework will be regulated by government.

The absence of clear maritime boundaries between Indonesia and its neighbors has implications for ensuring navigational safety and marine environmental protection in this intensely used, narrow shipping lane.[162] Unclear

---

161 Beckman, n. 155 above, p. 19.
162 See J. Charney and L. Alexander, eds., *International Boundaries*, Vol. 1 (Leiden: Martinus Nijhoff Publishers, 1993).

territorial sea boundaries in the Straits create problems for law enforcement and jurisdiction that hinders navigational safety in the Straits.[163] Many vessels do not know the exact location of boundary lines, especially in the TSS. These uncertainties prevent Indonesia from being able to monitor and control the mandatory ship reporting system in overlapping zones and to determine ocean shipping lanes.

Indonesia has unsettled territorial sea boundaries with Malaysia and Singapore. Although Indonesia plans to determine its territorial boundaries with Malaysia on the western part of the Strait of Malacca (in the Karimun Sea), no agreement has been reached to date.[164] Indonesia also has not determined its territorial sea boundary with Malaysia in the eastern part of the Strait of Singapore between Bintan and Batam, which a few years ago became an issue after maritime enforcement agencies of the two states came face-to-face.[165]

The territorial sea boundary between Indonesia and Singapore in the Strait of Singapore in the area between Bintan and South Ledge, Middle Rock, and Pedra Branca/Batu Puteh has not been delimited and awaits further negotiation between Singapore and Malaysia following the International Court of Justice (ICJ) 2008 Judgement.[166] Indonesia must negotiate a boundary with Singapore and Malaysia in the eastern Strait of Malacca where the ICJ decision on sovereignty over Pedra Branca and Middle Rock paved the way for delimitation.[167] The delimitation of territorial seas between and among Southeast Asian countries is necessary.[168]

---

163   Djalal, n. 149 above.

164   H. Djalal, "Indonesian Maritime Boundaries," in *Negara Kepulauan Menuju Negara Maritim* (Archipelagic State Towards Maritime State), ed., C.M. Yusuf (Jakarta: Indonesian Maritime Institute, 2010), p. 114.

165   K. Akimoto, T. Imaizumi, M. Kunimi, A. Mori, W. Mukai, E. Sakai, T. Tomomori, H. Ueno, Y. Takada (Staff writers), "Singapore, Indonesia, Ratify Sea Boundary Treaty," *OPRF Marine Monthly*, August 2010 (Ocean Policy Research Foundation), p. 14. See also T. Hsien-Li, "Singapore, Indonesia Ratify Sea Boundary Treaty," (Bernama, 30 August 2010), *Asian Society of International Law Newsletter* 2010/9: 4.

166   *Case concerning Sovereignty over Pedra Branca/Pulau Batu Puteh, Middle Rocks and South Ledge (Malaysia/Singapore)*, [2008] *ICJ Reports*, pp. 1–84.

167   Id., cited in T. Davenport, "Southeast Asian Approaches to Maritime Boundaries," *Asian Journal of International Law* 4, no. 2 (2014): 309–357. See generally R. Beckman and C. Schofield, "Moving Beyond Disputes over Island Sovereignty: ICJ Sets Stage for Maritime Boundary Delimitation in the Singapore Strait," *Ocean Development and International Law* 40 (2009): 1–35; Charney and Alexander, n. 162 above.

168   Hydrographic-Oceanography Perspective, n. 159 above, p. 25.

The territorial sea boundary in the eastern part of the Strait of Singapore covering the maritime areas between Batam (Indonesia) and Changi (Singapore) has recently been agreed to by Indonesia and Singapore. The 2014 Territorial Sea Boundary Agreement[169] is the extension of the 1973 Territorial Sea Boundary Agreement in the central part of the Strait of Singapore and the 2009 Treaty on Maritime Boundaries.[170] The 2014 Agreement will give real benefits to Indonesia and Singapore in maintaining sovereignty and enforcing law in the territorial waters of both countries and in enhancing cooperation on navigational safety in the Strait of Singapore.

From a navigational safety perspective, the clear delimitation of the territorial sea boundary in the eastern part of the Strait of Singapore has two positive impacts. First, it provides the Indonesian government a definition of the area that is designated for port activities. Secondly, the delimitation is the basis for Indonesian participation in the IMO-approved mandatory STRAITREP in the Straits.[171] The delimitation of the territorial sea boundary has also been important to Indonesia in relation to the designation of a TSS within Indonesian territorial waters in the eastern part of the Strait of Singapore.[172] The designation of traffic separation schemes in the Indonesian territorial waters that are not immediately adjacent to a neighboring country will require, *inter alia*, coordination among ministries, hydrographic surveys, updated or new aids to navigation, and submission of a further proposal to the IMO Sub-Committee on Navigation, Communications, and SAR consistent with the provisions of

169   Treaty Between the Republic of Indonesia and the Republic of Singapore relating to the Delimitation of the Territorial Seas of the Two Countries in the Strait of Singapore in the Eastern Part of the Strait of Singapore, 3 September 2014, p. 4, available online: <http://treaty.kemlu.go.id/uploads-pub/5546_SGP-2014-0047.pdf>.

170   E.R. Agoes, "Indonesia: Problems Encountered in Some Unresolved Boundaries and the Outermost Islands," *Indonesian Journal of International Law* 9, no. 1 (October 2011): 1–18 states that Indonesia and Singapore succeeded in deliminating the border areas in the middle of the Strait of Singapore through the Treaty between the Republic of Indonesia and the Republic of Singapore relating to the Delimitation of the Territorial Seas of the Two Countries in the Strait of Singapore, 25 May 1973, ratified by Law No. 7 of 1973, State Gazette No. 59 of 1973. Following a series of negotiations, the two countries reached an agreement in the western extention of the existing boundary by signing the Treaty between the Republic of Indonesia and the Republic of Singapore relating to the Delimitation of the Territorial Sea of the Two Countries in the Western Part of the Strait of Singapore, 10 March 2009, available online: <http://treaty.kemlu.go.id/uploads-pub/4296_SGP-2009-0035.pdf>.

171   Directorate of Navigation, n. 49 above, p. 11.

172   Id.

UNCLOS.[173] The designation of a TSS that is immediately adjacent to a neighboring country requires a longer process and time than the first TSS in the Straits.[174] The designation of traffic separation schemes in Indonesian waters of the Straits can be completed if agreement can be reached on Indonesia's maritime boundary agreements with Malaysia and Singapore.

Conclusion

This article has demonstrated that gaps remain in the Indonesian legal and institutional frameworks relating to navigational safety and that technical capabilities are lacking. These problems contribute to maritime navigation incidents in the Straits. Actions need to be taken to address these problems. Legislative reform is required with regard to the regulation of VTS, SRS and the MEH, anchorage areas, and submarine cables and pipelines. Human resource development is required to improve the technical capability of Indonesian personnel in the operation of navigational aids, VTS, and SRS in order to tackle maritime navigation incidents in the Straits. An effective administrative structure needs to be set up to address problems of intergovernmental conflicts and the improper laying of submarine cables and pipelines. Indonesia, Malaysia, and Singapore have to reach maritime boundary agreements in the Straits in order to implement and enforce the mandatory IMO STRAITREP and to designate traffic separation schemes in the Straits.

---

173   See UNCLOS, n. 4 above, Art. 41(4).
174   Directorate of Navigation, n. 49 above, p. 5.

Corporate Social Responsibility and Quality Governance in Shipping

Johanna Yliskylä-Peuralahti, Daria Gritsenko and Jenna Viertola†
Brahea Center, Center for Maritime Studies, University of Turku, Finland

This article investigates the role of corporate social responsibility (CSR) in the governance of quality shipping. The specific emphasis is on the relationship between CSR as a form of private self-regulation and mandatory public regulation.[1] By governance of quality shipping we refer to a process by which rules, norms, and strategies that aim at improving safety, environmental protection, and economic sustainability in shipping are formed, applied, interpreted, and reformed. The concept of governance draws our attention to the fact that there is no single actor, institution, or source of authority that defines and steers quality in shipping, but there is instead a plurality of policy arrangements, understood here as "the substance and the organisation of policy domains in terms of policy discourses, coalitions, rules of the game and resources."[2] Our study seeks to identify how CSR fits within the broader maritime governance arrangements from the point of view of private actors, such as shipping companies and ports. The topic is approached empirically by studying the shipping industry in the Baltic Sea region (BSR).

In recent years the lack of capability to minimize negative social and environmental effects of shipping, sometimes referred to as a maritime governance failure, motivated the search for new forms of maritime governance.[3] Mandatory regulation in the form of international conventions administered by the International Maritime Organization (IMO) has been acknowledged as

---

† The authors thank the anonymous reviewer for constructive comments on an earlier version of the paper.

1 J-P. Gond, N. Kang and J. Moon, "The Government of Self-Regulation: On the Comparative Dynamics of Corporate Social Responsibility," *Economy and Society* 40, no. 4 (2011): 640–671.

2 B. Arts, P. Leroy and J. Van Tatenhove, "Political Modernisation and Policy Arrangements: A Framework for Understanding Environmental Policy Change," *Public Organization Review* 6 (2006): 93–106.

3 M. Roe, *Maritime Governance and Policy-Making* (London: Springer, 2013); M. Bloor, H. Sampson, S. Baker, D. Walters, E. Wadsworth and P. James, "Room for Manoeuvre? Regulatory Compliance in the Global Shipping Industry," *Social and Legal Studies* 22(1) (2013): 71–189.

Ocean Yearbook 29: 417–440

ineffective. Significant variation regarding how individual states implement and enforce IMO regulations made this command-and-control approach unable to eradicate low performing vessels and shipowners.[4] Attention has been paid to the potential of CSR as a form of self-regulation to contribute to quality shipping either directly by complementing mandatory regulation, or indirectly by serving as a precedent for renewal of public governance.[5] The direct effect emerges when companies engaged in CSR activities voluntarily aim to meet objectives that public policy failed to address (e.g., regarding the environment, welfare, employment, safety, or public health). Indirectly, shipping companies and their business partners engaged in CSR along the supply chains can change the prevailing attitude of "collective irresponsibility" in business practices and norms towards higher quality by acting in an environmentally, socially, and economically responsible manner. Furthermore, these higher standards put pressure on public regulators, and thus potentially contribute to policy renewal. While some actors are more optimistic towards the ability of CSR to change business norms, standards and practices, and thereby underpin future mandatory regulation,[6] others criticize the concept of CSR as being 'pure public relations' and lacking any practical content, thus, not bringing any real quality improvement.[7] Our aim is to investigate empirically these claims.

The theoretical goal of this study is to contribute to two voids in CSR research identified by Gond et al.: (1) the role of the public sector and government agency in influencing CSR, and (2) understanding how CSR has been altered when adopted in various industries with different regulatory settings in different parts of the globe.[8] Empirically this article focuses on how shipping companies and ports in the BSR see the relationship between CSR and mandatory regulations addressing quality shipping within maritime policy. We chose

4   T. Alderton and N. Winchester, "Globalisation and De-Regulation in the Maritime Industry," *Marine Policy* 26, no. 1 (2002): 35–43; Bloor et al., n. 3 above.

5   J. Yliskylä-Peuralahti and D. Gritsenko, "Binding Rules or Voluntary Action? A Conceptual Framework for CSR in Shipping," *WMU Journal of Maritime Affairs*, 13, no. 2 (2014): 251–268.

6   V. Haufler, *A Public Role for the Private Sector: Industry Self-Regulation in a Global Economy* (Washington, DC: Carnegie Endowment for International Peace, 2013).

7   M. Fougère and N. Solitander, "Against Corporate Responsibility: Critical Reflections on Thinking, Practice, Content and Consequences," *Corporate Social Responsibility and Environmental Management* 16, no. 4 (2009): 217–227; D. Kemp, J. Keenan and J. Gronow, "Strategic Resource or Ideal Source? Discourse, Organizational Change and CSR," *Journal of Organizational Change Management* 23, no. 5 (2010): 578–594.

8   Gond et al., n. 1 above.

to study this question within the specific geographical context as we seek to emphasize the spatial dimension of governance in globalized industries.[9] The data for the study was collected through a survey conducted in the BSR. The aim of the survey was to understand how CSR as a special form of self-regulation can develop in conditions where there already is a strict mandatory environmental and safety regulation in place, including standards for seafarers' working conditions onboard. Our main aim is to show how the context-specific features in a certain geographical area (the Baltic Sea), including natural conditions in the sea, regulatory architecture in place in the coastal countries, as well as their cultural and political traditions, influence the maritime actors' understanding of CSR. Thus, we address the variegated geography of responsibility.

The method of crisp-set qualitative comparative analysis (csQCA) is applied.[10] The QCA technique is based on the binary logic of Boolean algebra, and combines the strengths of case-oriented (qualitative) and variable-oriented (quantitative) approaches, allowing for analytically rigorous causal analysis of mid-range data. For this analysis a sample representative of the links between mandatory and self-regulation was selected. The results of QCA analysis are presented in the form of solution formulas: the combinations of causal conditions that jointly constitute paths to an explained outcome. Discussion of resulting explanatory models in the light of empirical evidence from the BSR as well as existing broader literature on CSR as a form of self-regulation allows the identification of mechanisms that link explanatory conditions to an outcome. The central findings of the article suggest that CSR as a form of self-regulation in shipping has the potential to become a driver for public policy-making in case actors involved in shipping operations realize there is room and need for private governance in shipping. Company engagement in CSR practices seems to add certainty, but does not determine CSR's success in the future maritime policy arrangements aimed at improvement of quality in shipping.

The article proceeds as follows. Section 2 discusses the concept of CSR and its relevance in shipping and introduces the theoretical framework of

---

9   A. Goldthau, "Rethinking the Governance of Energy Infrastructure: Scale, Decentralization and Polycentrism," *Energy Research and Social Science* 1 (2014): 134–140; K.R. Fabrizio and L.G. Thomas, "The Impact of Local Demand on Innovation in a Global Industry," *Strategic Management Journal* 33 (2012): 42–64; J. Neilson, "Institutions, the Governance of Quality and On-Farm Value Retention for Indonesian Specialty Coffee," *Singapore Journal of Tropical Geography* 28(2) (2007): 188–204.

10   C.C. Ragin, *The Comparative Method. Moving Beyond Qualitative and Quantitative Strategies* (Berkley and London: University of California Press, 1987).

regulation and governance. Section 3 presents data and elaborates on the QCA method and its main techniques. In Section 4, QCA analysis is reported step-by-step and its results are presented. Section 5 offers a discussion of results in light of theoretical propositions, putting the analysis in the empirical context of the BSR, and draws some conclusions and policy implications.

Preliminary Considerations

CSR and Shipping

Various definitions have been given to CSR. In this article we use the definition of CSR developed by the World Business Council on Sustainable Development: "CSR is the continuing commitment by business to behave ethically and con-tribute to economic development while improving the quality of life of the workforce and their families as well as community and society at large."[11] This concept of CSR has three dimensions: economic, environmental and social. When looking for an empirical proxy for these three dimensions, CSR in ship-ping can be linked with environmental protection, safety, labor issues, cus-tomer relations, impacts of shipping to coastal communities (at several geographical levels), and the increased transparency of operations.[12] In prac-tice, CSR is still unknown to the majority of maritime actors and its role is marginal in the shipping industry.[13] Shipping companies and ports link CSR activities most strongly with environmental and safety issues.[14] Framing CSR in terms of environmental sustainability is not unique for shipping, it is

---

11   World Business Council on Sustainable Development (WBCSD), "Corporate Social Responsibility (CSR)," available online: <http://www.wbcsd.org/work-program/business -role/previous-work/corporate-social-responsibility.aspx>.

12   Roe, n. 3 above; Bloor et al., n. 3 above.

13   Det Norske Veritas, *Corporate Social Responsibility and the Shipping Industry – Project Report*. Revision No. 1, 2004, available online: <http://www.he-alert.org/filemanager/root/ site_assets/standalone_pdfs_0355-/he00375.pdf>; J. Skovgaard, "Corporate Social Responsibility in the Danish Shipping Industry," (Paper Presented at Druid Academy Conference 2012, Cambridge, UK), available online: <http://druid8.sit.aau.dk/acc_papers/ 436055lixproo8mgnu655pfb6jhu.pdf>; L. Coady, J. Lister, C. Strandberg and Y. Ota, *The Role of Corporate Social Responsibility (CSR) in the International Shipping Sector. A Phase 2 Research Paper*, (2013), available online: <http://www.ligi.ubc.ca/sites/liu/files/ Publications/2013_Dec_CSR_UBC-Phase2_CSR-in-Shipping.pdf>.

14   L. Arat, *Corporate Social Responsibility in Shipping Companies in the Baltic Sea*, (University of Turku, Centre for Maritime Studies, 2011), available online: <http://www.merikotka.fi/ julkaisut/CafeCSRraportti_LauraArat.pdf>; V. Kunnaala, M. Rasi and J. Storgård, *Corporate*

characteristic of extractive industries as well.[15] The variation in CSR framing is usually associated with the company's specific position in the value chain.[16]

The social dimension of CSR in shipping is less developed than the environmental.[17] Several global socio-economic problems of shipping, such as difficult working and accommodation conditions of seafarers,[18] piracy threatening vessels and their crew,[19] corruption, and bribery in the form of "facilitation payments to authorities,"[20] and a widespread utilization of tax havens such as Panama, Liberia, Cyprus or Gibraltar to save labor costs and to avoid corporate taxes and regulation,[21] have received far less attention in companies' CSR portfolios. A tax haven[22] refers to a country or a jurisdiction that effectively imposes no or very low taxes on non-resident individuals or corporations, lacks transparency and effective exchange of information with foreign tax authorities regarding these assets, and requires no real operations regarding the foreign companies registered.[23] Among shipping companies, utilization of tax havens

---

Social Responsibility and Shipping, Report No. A70 (Centre for Maritime Studies, University of Turku, 2013).

15   H. Dashwood, "Sustainable Development and Industry Self-Regulation Developments in the Global Mining Sector," *Business Society* 53, no. 4 (July 2014): 551–582.

16   L. Fransen and B. Burgoon, "Privatizing or Socializing Corporate Responsibility Business Participation in Voluntary Programs," *Business Society* 53, no. 4 (July 2014): 583–619.

17   Coady et al., n. 13 above.

18   A.D. Couper, C.J. Walsh, B.A. Stanberry and G.L. Boerne, *Voyages of Abuse. Seafarers, Human Rights and International Shipping* (London: Pluto Press, 1999); N. Ellis and H. Sampson, "Corporate Social Responsibility and the Quality of Seafarers Accommodation and Recreational Facilities," in V. Kunnaala and J. Viertola, *IMISS2013. Proceedings of the International Scientific Meeting for Corporate Social Responsibility (CSR) in Shipping.* Report No. A71 (Centre for Maritime Studies, University of Turku, 2013).

19   X. Fu, A. Ng and Y.-Y. Lau, "The Impacts of Piracy on Global Economic Development: The Case of Somalia," *Maritime Policy and Management* 37, no. 7 (2010): 677–697; World Shipping Council, "Piracy," available online: <http://www.worldshipping.org/industry -issues/security/piracy>.

20   O. Andersen, "Maersk Line: Shipping Hit Hard by Widespread Corruption," *Shippingwatch*, 9 May 2012, available online: <http://shippingwatch.com/articles/article4644243.ece>.

21   R. Palan, R. Murphy and C. Chavagneux, *Tax Havens. How Globalisation Really Works* (New York: Cornell University Press, 2010); Roe, n. 3 above.

22   In addition to tax havens, secrecy jurisdictions and offshore financial centers are closely related terms and are often used as synonyms (see European Parliament 2013, n. 23 below).

23   European Parliament, Directorate-General for Internal Policies, *European Initiatives on Eliminating Tax Heavens and Offshore Financial Transactions and the Impact of These Constructions on the Union's own Resources and Budget* (Brussels: European Union, 2013), available online: <http://www.europarl.europa.eu/meetdocs/2009_2014/documents/cont/ dv/staes_study/staes_studyen.pdf>.

in the form of 'flagging out' vessels and registering them in open registers provided by the tax haven countries (in order to save labor and capital costs) has
been a widespread practice for a long time.[24] However, lax regulation together
with a lack of transparency in tax havens also enables widespread tax avoidance and money laundering. Several such malpractices have been discovered
among shipping companies.[25]

Likewise, voluntary programs to oversee and protect labor standards have
received far less attention in shipping compared to production industries such
as food production or clothing.[26] Discussion on the safety culture and the
human element in shipping has a limited reach in the discussion on CSR in
shipping. Whereas seafarer welfare has regained public attention around the
adoption of the Maritime Labour Convention (MLC) 2006 and speculation has
risen in regard to its potential to improve social responsibility in shipping,[27]
the weak representation of this dimension in companies' CSR profiles can be
seen as a substantial weakness of shipping CSR. Thus, shipping companies'
understanding of CSR is incremental, and some companies already engaged
with CSR do not act according to the normative principles of the concept.

CSR and the Baltic Context
Several studies show that CSR in particular is context specific and its application varies between industries and geographical areas.[28] Thus, it is vital to
study adoption of CSR in shipping tied with the specific geographical context.

---

24   "HS: Varustamot Rekisteröivät Veroparatiiseihin (Shipping Companies Register in Tax
      Havens)," *Kauppalehti*, 23 July 2013, available online: <http://www.kauppalehti.fi/etusivu/
      hs+varustamot+rekisteroivat+veroparatiiseihin/201307463615>; Palan et al., n. 21 above.

25   M. Dettmer and C. Reiermann, "Bailing Out Oligarchs. EU Aid for Cyprus a Political
      Minefield for Merkel," *Spiegel Online International*, 2012, available online: <http://www
      .spiegel.de/international/europe/german-intelligence-report-warns-cyprus-not
      -combating-money-laundering-a-865451.html>; "Tax Havens Face Tougher Scrutiny,"
      Lloyd's List, 18 July 2013.

26   T. Bartley, "Institutional Emergence in an Era of Globalization: The Rise of Transnational
      Private Regulation of Labor and Environmental Conditions," *American Journal of
      Sociology* 113, no. 2 (2007): 297–351; D. Vogel, "Private Global Business Regulation," *Annual
      Review of Political Science* 11 (2008): 261–282.

27   P. Milde, "The Maritime Labour Convention 2006: An Instrument to Improve Social
      Responsibility in the Cruise Industry," in P. Gibson, A. Papathanassis and P. Milde, eds.,
      Cruise Sector Challenges. Making Progress in an Uncertain World (Wiesbaden: Springer
      Gabler, 2011), 207–223.

28   J.P. Doh and T.R. Guay, "Corporate Social Responsibility, Public Policy, and NGO Activism
      in Europe and in the United States: An Institutional Stakeholder Perspective," *Journal of
      Management Studies* 43, no. 1 (2006): 47–73; S. Brammer, G. Jackson and D. Matten,

In this study, CSR is studied among shipping companies and ports in the context of the Baltic Sea. This sea area was chosen because of the urgent need to develop governance mechanisms to improve the state of the environment and to reduce safety risks of shipping in the heavily polluted, shallow Baltic Sea area with dense maritime traffic. The water in the sea is brackish with species adapted to living in low salinity. The natural conditions and need to protect the environment set limitations for shipping in the Baltic Sea: the sea is covered with ice in the winter, and the rocky and narrow fairways, especially in the northern part of the sea, pose a risk for vessel collisions and groundings. Thus, specific skills (e.g., winter navigation) are required by seafarers operating vessels in the Baltic Sea. Low salinity, cold climate, shallow depths, and long coastlines make the sea and coastal ecosystems very vulnerable to stress caused by pollution and make combatting oil pollution, for example, very difficult.[29] Due to these special characteristics the Baltic Sea was granted a particularly sensitive sea area (PSSA) status in 2005, enabling the introduction of additional regional measures to prevent environmental damages.[30] In 2008, the IMO designated the Baltic Sea as a sulphur emission control area (SECA) requiring a progressive reduction in sulphur oxide (SOx) emissions from ships by 2015.[31] Therefore, both the natural conditions and the regulations require additional investments by shipping companies in safety and environmental protection.

Whereas the overall regulatory framework for shipping is coherent in the BSR, the region is diverse in terms of corporate culture and state-business relations. In the Nordic countries the tradition to favor mandatory regulation is strong.[32] However, newly established businesses in post-communist countries, and in particular Russia, are often regarded as extremely neo-liberal in their

---

"Corporate Social Responsibility and Institutional Theory: New Perspectives on Private Governance," *Socio-Economic Review* 10 (2012): 3–28.

29   O. Lindén, A. Chircop, M. Pourzanjani, J.-U. Schröder and S. Raaymakers, *PSSA in the Baltic Sea: Present Situation and Future Possibilities* (World Maritime University Monograph/ Research Brief, 2006), available online: <http://www.balticmaster.org/media/files/ general_files_706.pdf>.

30   IMO, "Particularly Sensitive Sea Areas," available online: <http://www.imo.org/ourwork/ environment/pollutionprevention/pssas/pages/default.aspx>.

31   EMSA (European Maritime Safety Agency), *The 0.1% Sulphur in Fuel Requirement as from 1 January 2015 in SECAS: An Assessment of Available Impacts Studies and Alternative Means of Compliance*, Technical Report, 13 December 2010, available online: <http://ec.europa .eu/environment/air/transport/pdf/Report_Sulphur_Requirement.pdf>.

32   M. Gjølberg, "The Political Economy of Corporate Social Responsibility," Ph.D. Dissertation, University of Oslo, 2011, available online: <https://www.duo.uio.no/ bitstream/handle/10852/13346/dravhandling-gjolberg.pdf?sequence=3>.

corporate ideology. Denmark, Finland, Norway, and Sweden – where the so-called Nordic model marked with a high degree of private sector provision of public services developed multiple mechanisms for alignment of public and private interventions into public policy orchestrated by the welfare state – are increasingly recognized as leaders in CSR public policy.[33] The public systems emerging in the Baltic states, Poland and especially Russia were instead marked with a high degree of separation between state as a welfare provider and business as a profit-maker, the relationship between the two reduced to minimal interfaces. In terms of shipping CSR, the Baltic Sea region is interesting because these different cultures are connected by a mobile shipping network. As a result, the same ships calling at different ports are confronted with multiple attitudes regarding their role in society embedded in different incentive systems.

CSR in the Light of Regulation and Governance

CSR is a specific form of self-regulation that emerges together with the transformation of governance from a traditional command-and-control system to broader participatory governance. CSR first rose in the United States as a form of corporate strategy to address companies' impacts upon their social environment. Private actors, primarily US companies, took an active role in addressing public issues, thereby entering the governance domain traditionally occupied by the public sector.[34] Over time CSR has 'travelled' elsewhere on the globe. When adopted in a different (regulatory) environment and by actors in various industries, the meaning of CSR has changed from 'corporate-centered' to "corporate-oriented" phenomena where a wider set of actors take part.[35] Especially in Europe the public sector has increasingly started to promote CSR in its own policies.[36] In many countries, governments have set standards of socially responsible and sustainable behavior by encouraging companies to engage in

---

33   A. Midttun, M. Gjølberg, A. Kourula, S. Sweet and S. Vallentin, "Public Policies for Corporate Social Responsibility in Four Nordic Countries: Harmony of Goals and Conflict of Means," *Business and Society*, 18 July 2012.

34   A.B. Carroll, "Corporate Social Responsibility Evolution of a Definitional Construct," *Business and Society* 38, no. 3 (1999): 268–295; L. Albareda, "Corporate Responsibility, Governance and Accountability: From Self-Regulation to Co-Regulation," *Corporate Governance* 8, no. 4 (2008): 430–439.

35   A. Rasche, F.G.A. Bakker and J. Moon, "Complete and Partial Organizing for Corporate Social Responsibility," *Journal of Business Ethics* 115, no. 4 (2013): 651–663.

36   E.R.G. Pedersen, P. Neerdaard, J.T. Pedersen and W. Gwozdz, "Conformance and Deviance: Company Responses to Institutional Pressures for Corporate Social Responsibility Reporting," *Business Strategy and the Environment* 22, no. 6 (2013): 357–373.

CSR by providing information about the concept and by requiring mandatory CSR reporting.[37] Rasche et al. conclude that "CSR is now as much about the social, governmental and multi-actor regulation of business as about self-regulation of companies for community benefit."[38]

Can CSR improve the quality of shipping and contribute positively to solving problems facing the shipping industry? (Figure 17.1). We argue that the quality of shipping can be improved on the condition that maritime actors truly adopt the values of CSR and start acting accordingly, and that maritime regulatory structures support this aim. Safety, environmental protection, welfare of workers, human rights and ethical trading, business ethics, stakeholder involvement, local community impacts and benefits, and transparency and accountability should all be included in the operating principles of quality shipping companies.[39] Economically responsible shipping companies focus on long-term profits instead of short-term cost reductions that often undermine safety or environmental impacts. Economic responsibility and quality of the service provided is also tied to the reputation of the company: to protect their brand, shipowners need to prove to their clients and other stakeholders that their ships are safe and environmentally sound, and that their company's

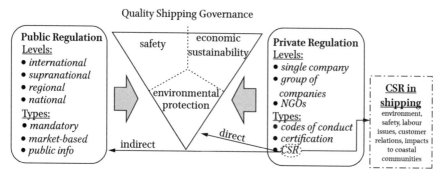

FIGURE 17.1   *Conceptual model for studying the place of CSR in quality shipping governance*
SOURCE: AUTHORS.

37   R. Steurer, A. Martinuzzi and S. Margula, "Public Policies on CSR in Europe: Themes, Instruments, and Regional Differences," *Corporate Social Responsibility Management* 19, no. 4 (2012): 206–227.

38   Rasche et al., n. 35 above.

39   S. Meidanis, "Sustainability of Shipping – Addressing Corporate Social Responsibility through Management Systems," Research Paper, 2013, available online: <http://www.maritimecsr.com/files/misc/SM_Sustainability_Paper.pdf>; Coady et al., n. 13 above.

activities do not cause negative societal effects.[40] Socially responsible shipping companies take into account human rights and create business practices that are beneficial to their labor force and to the region where the company operates. Socially responsible shipping companies fly a quality flag, recruit high quality crew, and invest in personnel well-being and training.[41]

Previous studies indicate that while there are many shipping companies that focus on high quality shipping and act according to the principles of CSR, there are also some who only focus on cost minimization and undermine safety.[42] Both types of companies occupy the shipping market, and the irresponsible shipping companies compete with the responsible ones.[43] The specific problem regarding economic, environmental and social sustainability and quality governance in shipping is how to lessen the gap between those companies that already do well and those that do not. Since the command-and-control regulation in the maritime domain has been ineffective towards sub-standard vessels, attention has turned to self-regulatory measures such as CSR[44] and practical enrollment of public, private, and third-party actors. CSR and other forms of self-regulation can complement 'hard law' regulations, but CSR does not develop in a 'vacuum'. Existing public regulation effects CSR and vice versa.[45]

With this study we investigate the relationship between CSR and mandatory public regulation (the 'Indirect' link in Figure 17.1) in a specific geographical context. Previous research indicates that the relationship between CSR and

40   D. Grewal and N.J. Darlow, "The Business Paradigm for Corporate Social Reporting in the Context of Australian Seaports," *Maritime Economics and Logistics* 9, no. 2 (2007): 172–192; D. Neef, "Corporate Social Responsibility Comes to Maritime Shipping," *Safety4sea News*, 26 September 2012, available online: <http://www.safety4sea.com/corporate -social-responsibility-comes-to-maritime-shipping/analysis-6-25>.

41   M. Progoulaki and M. Roe, "Dealing with Multicultural Human Resources in a Socially Responsible Manner: A Focus on the Maritime Industry," *WMU Journal of Maritime Affairs* 10, no. 1 (2011): 7–23.

42   H. Haralambides, "Quality Shipping: Market Mechanisms for Safer Shipping and Cleaner Oceans. Introduction of the Book," in *Quality Shipping: Market Mechanism for Safer Shipping and Cleaner Oceans*, H. Haralambides ed. (Rotterdam: Erasmus Publishing, 1998), available online: <http://www.maritimeeconomics.com/book/export/html/81>; M. Shinohara, "Quality Shipping and Incentive Schemes: From the Perspective of the Institutional Economics," *Maritime Economics and Logistics* 7, no. 3 (2005): 281–295.

43   R. Goss, "Social Responsibility in Shipping," *Marine Policy* 32, no. 1 (2008): 142–146.

44   J. Kuronen and U. Tapaninen, "Evaluation of Maritime Safety Policy Instruments," *WMU Journal of Maritime Affairs* 9, no. 1 (2010): 45–61.

45   Gjølberg, n. 32 above.

mandatory regulation can be twofold. Some authors hold the view that CSR can undermine regulation and act only as a smoke-screen for de-regulation.[46] Others claim that CSR can underpin future mandatory regulation directly, by complementing public governance and filling in gaps in existing legal arrangements, or indirectly by serving as a precedent for renewal of public governance.[47] The article aims at revealing which conditions contribute to consolidation of perception of CSR as a precedent for public policy-making among the shipping companies and ports in the BSR. We suppose that if CSR is to have some effect on quality in shipping, it shall become an organic part of shipping governance, and in particular be capable of driving public policies forward, which are often reluctant to change. A change in business practices towards quality shipping requires changes in attitudes and mindsets among all parties involved in maritime governance, stronger public pressure, credible sanctions towards both low-performing companies, as well as changes in the existing governance structures, especially the role of the IMO, so that it could directly enforce maritime conventions that ensure safety and sustainability by providing sanctions to non-complying companies and/or IMO member states.

Data and Methods

Data

Data were collected through an international survey during the autumn of 2013. The survey was developed with the aim of revealing CSR practices and attitudes among maritime stakeholders in the Baltic Sea Region. It consisted of over 30 questions organized in several blocks (e.g., background information, CSR in the company, motivations for CSR, CSR in the maritime sector, companies' CSR and public governance). The questionnaire was sent out via the web survey service Webropol to 2,122 respondents from shipping companies, ports, companies operating in forwarding, ship management, ship broking, chartering, pilotage, maritime authorities, research and education organizations, non-governmental organizations (NGOs), maritime industry associations in nine countries (Denmark, Estonia, Finland, Germany, Latvia, Lithuania, Poland, Russia, and Sweden), but the response rate was rather low (5.80 percent), constituting the main limitation of this method.[48] Nevertheless, the

---

46   Gond et al., n. 1 above.

47   Haufler, n. 6 above.

48   Th. Shih and X. Fan, "Comparing Response Rates from Web and Mail Surveys: A Meta-Analysis," *Field Methods* 20 (2008): 249–271.

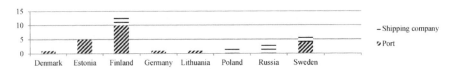

FIGURE 17.2   *Distribution of cases in the final sample (type and country). Total n = 32*
SOURCE: AUTHORS' COMPILATION

survey results provided a coherent sample for the purpose of mid-size data analysis using QCA. The final sample included only shipping companies (n = 10) and ports (n = 22) from eight Baltic region countries (n = 32; Figure 17.2). From the broad range of questions included in the survey, answers devoted to the relationship between CSR and regulation were selected.)

Methods

Qualitative comparative analysis (QCA) is a method based on analysis of necessary and sufficient conditions. Essentially, QCA is used for analysis of causal complexity, as it allows studying different combinations of causal conditions capable of generating the same outcome. Necessity and sufficiency in QCA are understood as implicational relationships between the outcome and conditions and the goal is to establish if any combination of conditions could possibly form a necessary and sufficient combination of conditions for the outcome to occur. Unlike statistical techniques based on estimation of regularity in large datasets, QCA is a configurational technique based on set theory reasoning that makes this method profoundly distinct from, e.g., correlational analysis. Set theory relations are not the same as correlational, since they are asymmetrical and make a distinction between necessity (outcome is a subset of the cause) and sufficiency (outcome is a superset of the cause). Among other features of QCA are its holistic approach to data (cases rather than variables), deterministic logic (invariant rather than probabilistic nature of the outcomes), configurational character (individual conditions are not over-interpreted, as the outcome is assumed to be a product of a combination of conditions), as well as assumption of causal heterogeneity (existence of alternative scenarios that may lead to the same outcome).[49] QCA is a case-oriented

---

49   Ragin, n. 10 above; J.E. Coverdill and W. Finlay, "Understanding Mills via Mill-Type Methods: An Application of Qualitative Comparative Analysis to a Study of Labor Management in Southern Textile Manufacturing," *Qualitative Sociology* 18, no. 4 (1995): 457–478; B. Grofman and C.Q. Schneider, "An Introduction to Crisp Set QCA, with a Comparison to Binary Logistic Regression," *Political Research Quarterly* 62, no. 4 (2009):

tool in that it allows one to establish similarities and differences between various configurations of conditions and relate the discovered causal paths to the initial cases used in the analysis, which enables one to systematically compare cases, not only the variables derived from the case material. The results of QCA – configurations of causal conditions leading to the explained outcome – shall be discussed in a dialogue between previous theory and case-related evidence.[50] Due to the need to keep relations with the initial case material, QCA is considered to be ideal for small and medium-size data (5–100 cases).[51] QCA has three main versions – crisp set, multi-value and fuzzy set.[52] Here crisp set analysis is used, the most basic and straightforward way to assess complex causality. In order to assist the analysis, fsQCA 2.0 software was used.[53]

QCA can be seen as consisting of six steps: (1) theoretical background (selecting outcome and conditions); (2) construct dichotomous dataset; (3) test for necessary conditions; (4) construct a truth table and resolve contradictions; (5) analyse the truth table (minimization, logical reminders); and (6) interpret the results.

In the first step, based on previous theoretical knowledge, the outcome of interest and relevant conditions that are expected to contribute to the outcome shall be identified. It is important to streamline, try to avoid duplication, and justify well why these conditions are expected to contribute to the outcome. In the second step, the dataset must be created and it is important to specify membership criteria: that is, when a case counts as a member of a certain set and which threshold is set for non-membership. The third step aims to look for necessary conditions, or conditions that always produce outcomes (although the dataset may not be sufficient for it!). Necessary conditions are often removed from further analysis, since they will be part of any solution formula. In the fourth step, a through table is created out of the available dataset, which means that all combinations of conditions are exhibited, even those without empirical instances. Often there are contradictory rows in truth tables – the same combination of conditions leads to the presence of the outcome in some cases, and to its absence in some others. There are good

662–672; C. Wagemann, "Qualitative Comparative Analysis (QCA) and Fuzzy-Sets: Agenda for a Research Approach and a Data Analysis Technique," *Comparative Sociology* 9, no. 3 (2010): 376–396.

50   B. Rihoux and C.C. Ragin, *Configurational Comparative Methods: Qualitative Comparative Analysis (QCA) and Related Techniques* (Thousand Oaks, CA: Sage, 2009).

51   Ragin, n. 10 above.

52   Rihoux and Ragin, n. 50 above.

53   See software site online: <http://www.u.arizona.edu/~cragin/fsQCA/software.shtml>.

practices for resolving the contradictory configurations[54] and knowledge of the cases is crucial, revealing the qualitative nature of QCA. The next step is analysis of the truth table, which includes minimization of the positive outcome (1) with and without counterfactuals, and the same procedure for the absence of the outcome (0). All the results are compared and explained in the last step of QCA analysis. The interpretation of the minimal formulas draws upon substantive knowledge and seeks to discover which causal paths are more important and why.

Analysis and Results

Selecting Outcome and Conditions

Theoretical considerations presented in Section 2 suggested that companies may see the potential of CSR as a governance instrument differently depending on their own experiences with CSR, as well as their understanding of the role and place of public and private regulation in the maritime sector. We selected the variable 'CSR can act as a precedent for policy-makers' as an outcome variable based on a positive answer to the survey question, "Can CSR and/or voluntary commitment to higher standards beyond mandatory regulation have an impact on policy-making?" Thus, the outcome is as follows:

> PRE = precedent; represents the maritime actors, who believe that CSR can serve as a precedent for public policy-making.

Even when rules come from a private body with no power to ensure their implementation, public regulations may require compliance with private standards.[55] Along with public rules that make private regulation compulsory, important roles can be played by economic incentives generated by the markets (reputation, power of exclusion, and market access) and governments (tax reductions, exemptions, and difference in monitoring).[56] The literature that deals with the relation between public and private regulation often raises a question if the two forms shall be seen as substitutes or as complements.

---

54   Rihoux and Ragin, n. 50 above, p. 48.

55   For example, the International Organization for Standardization (ISO), a voluntary organization established to set and maintain standards <http://www.iso.org>; Haufler, n. 6 above.

56   T. Büthe, "Special Issue: Private Regulation in the Global Economy: A (P)Review," *Business and Politics* 12, no. 3 (2010): 1–38 at 15–17.

Room for Private Regulation

Among the causal conditions, we were interested in questions that explicitly made a link between CSR/voluntary self-regulatory practices and public regulation. Whereas public politics can be understood as government-directed pressure on companies and society to follow certain rules of the game, private regulation emerges in the areas not covered at all or covered insufficiently by public regulation. Thus, an important factor is how actors perceive opportunity structure[57] for private regulation in the maritime industry. If room for private regulation (REG1 and REG2) is perceived by the actors as sufficient, they can be expected to be more positive about the effects of CSR. We have chosen two statements that shed light on actors' attitudes towards the prospects of CSR to be a complement and a driver for public policies: REG1 – the maritime industry is so strictly regulated that there is no room for voluntary actions, and REG2 – shipping has to be regulated by the public sector – voluntary initiatives cannot work in maritime industry. The first condition (REG1) uncovers how restrictive the perception of opportunity structure regarding CSR in shipping governance is. The second condition (REG2) deals with actors' belief in the effectiveness and success of voluntary initiatives. Disagreement with both statements was considered as an indicator of positive attitude towards CSR as a precedent for policy-making (coded as 1).

Regulatory Status Quo

Sometimes CSR is considered as a tool to preserve the regulatory status quo rather than as an opportunity for regulatory innovation.[58] In this case, actors interested and engaged in CSR may still be reluctant to see its potential in advancing current regulation and serve to make improvements at large. We introduce a condition, "CSR may help to uphold the regulatory status quo" (STQUO) as a control, as theoretically it has to be mutually exclusive with actors' optimism regarding the role of CSR as a precedent for public policy-making. We considered a positive answer to either of the following statements as a positive value on the STQUO variable: (1) if shipping companies or ports act responsibly there is no strong pressure for authorities to implement stricter

---

57   The concept of 'opportunity structure' was initially introduced in Robert Merton's *Theory of Deviance* (1959) and refers to the framework of rules people are encouraged to follow in order to reach something considered as a goal, achievement, or success in their environment.

58   B. Mark-Ungericht and R. Weiskopf, "Filling the Empty Shell. The Public Debate on CSR in Austria as a Paradigmatic Example of a Political Discourse," *Journal of Business Ethics* 70, no. 3 (2006): 285–297.

regulations; or (2) in a sense, implementation of stricter policies may be slowed down but probably the regulations are going to come into force regardless of the companies' CSR initiatives.

Engagement in CSR

Engagement of a company in CSR (ENG) cannot be considered as having a straightforward causal relation to how companies assess the potential of CSR to serve as a precedent for public policy-making. Nevertheless, we considered this condition to be important in the framework of our study as some studies showed that companies engaging in CSR are aware of its potential to influence regulatory arrangements.[59] By engaging in CSR, firms can, *inter alia*, attempt to raise their credibility in the role of self-regulating entities, thereby striving to delay, prevent or anticipate laws and regulations that may influence their competitiveness.[60] Moreover, ENG conditions allow follow up of the differences depending on the companies' CSR activities. The survey contained a question: Has your company implemented CSR measures in its operations?, with the alternatives yes (=1) and no (=0).

Business-to-business Industry

Shipping, as a transboundary and mobile business-to-business (B2B) industry, imposes severe limitations on the functioning of voluntary private regulation, including CSR. Whereas proximity to the end consumer increases companies' likelihood of community involvement and CSR initiatives,[61] in B2B industries the pressure from NGOs or directly from consumers is negligible.[62] If neither consumers nor NGOs are interested in how goods are transported,[63] so that their function of 'watchdogs' creating pressure on the industry is negligible,

---

59   Gjølberg, n. 32 above.

60   A. Kolk, R. Van Tulder and C. Welders, "International Codes of Conduct and Corporate Social Responsibility: Can Transnational Corporations Regulate Themselves," *Transnational Corporations* 8, no. 1 (1999): 143–180.

61   J. Haddock-Fraser and I. Fraser, "Assessing Corporate Environmental Reporting Motivations: Differences between 'Close-to-Market' and 'Business-to-Business' Companies," *Corporate Social Responsibility and Environmental Management* 15, no. 3 (2008): 140–155; S. Koos, "The Institutional Embeddedness of Social Responsibility: A Multilevel Analysis of Smaller Firms' Civic Engagement in Western Europe," *Socio-Economic Review* 10, no. 1 (2012): 135–162.

62   Skovgaard, n. 13 above.

63   C. Wolf and S. Seuring, "Environmental Impacts as Buying Criteria for Third Party Logistical Services," *International Journal of Physical Distribution and Logistics Management* 40 (2010): 84–102 at 95.

there will be little motivation for companies to engage in CSR or to believe in its regulatory effects. By including the statement "Shipping is a business-to-business (B2B) type of industry – the end consumer of transported goods has little influence upon the quality of transportation" (agreement coded as 1 and disagreement as 0), we introduce a B2B condition as potentially influencing an actors' attitude to CSR as a policy-making precedent.

Dichotomous Coding and Raw Data Matrix

Based on survey questions we coded all variables as absence or presence of quality in order to test their combinations in subsequent QCA analysis (Figure 17.3). Since variables were not interval, dichotomous coding did not require much compromising: value 1 was assigned for the presence and 0 for the absence of quality in question (Figure 17.3). The dichotomous dataset was created for all 32 cases, no missing data was detected (raw data matrix available on demand).

Analysis of Necessary Conditions

Analysis of necessary conditions revealed one necessary condition (STQUO, consistency score over 90 percent, see Table 17.1). Positive outcome on status quo is correlated with negative outcome on CSR as a precedent for policy-making. This condition (negated) will thus be part of any solution formula.

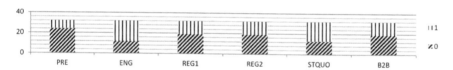

FIGURE 17.3   *Dichotomous coding of outcome and condition variables (frequencies)*
SOURCE: AUTHORS' COMPILATION

TABLE 17.1   *Analysis of necessary conditions (outcome variable: pre)*

Conditions Tested	Consistency	Coverage
ENG	0.750000	0.300000
STQUO	0.000000	0.000000
REG1	0.375000	0.230769
REG2	0.625000	0.384615
B2B	0.375000	0.230769

SOURCE: AUTHORS' COMPILATION

Truth Table Analysis: Resolving Contradictions

The truth table was created with the help of fsQCA 2.0 software. The first step in the truth table construction is a listing of all possible causal combinations, whereas the outcome value remains empty. In our analysis the initial truth table covered 32 (2 to the power of #conditions, i.e., 5) logically possible causal combinations, thereof 21 had instances, 19 had consistency of 0.00 or 1.00 (meaning that all cases that displayed this causal combination agreed with the outcome), and two were contradictory (meaning that cases that displayed those causal combinations displayed both positive and negative outcomes). In order to make the truth table ready for logical minimization, it is crucial to resolve such contradictory configurations. Rihoux and De Meur suggest eight practices to solve them,[64] including adding/removing conditions, re-examining cases (and excluding borderline cases), conditions, the outcome variable itself, recoding all contradictory configurations as 0 on outcome, and considering 'most frequent path' (if contradiction is produced by a few cases out of many). In both contradictory configurations there were only two cases that excluded the 'most frequent path' solution, and substantive knowledge of the cases did not allow making a clear distinction. One contradiction is for a case where engagement in CSR is present, whereas all other values are absent and the outcome both 1 and 0. According to theoretical knowledge, this case is more likely to be coded with 0 on outcome, since CSR engagement is not strictly connected to regulatory attitudes. In the second contradictory configuration we deal with two cases, with 1 on REG2 meaning that these cases do not believe in voluntary initiatives in the maritime sector. At the same time, one of them is still sure that CSR may act as a precedent for policy-making (German port), whereas another does not (Swedish shipping company). As this contradiction is also difficult to solve and knowledge is not enough to give grounds, we decided to code both of them as 0 on outcome to exclude them from the analysis (Table 17.2).

Truth Table Analysis: Logical Minimization

Minimization procedure in QCA can be performed in two ways: using the logical reminders (counterfactual cases) or not using them (Table 17.2). It is also crucial to test the opposite model, i.e., the one in which the outcome is negated. Since set theory analysis is not symmetrical, negation of conditions leading to the outcome must not be the causal path to absence of outcome.

---

64   B. Rihoux and G. De Meur, "Crisp-Set Qualitative Comparative Analysis (CSQCA)," in
      Rihoux and Ragin, n. 50 above, pp. 33–68.

TABLE 17.2 *Truth table ready for logical minimization*

ENG	STQUO	REG1	REG2	B2B	N	PRE	raw consist
0	0	1	1	1	1	1	1.000000
1	0	0	1	0	1	1	1.000000
1	0	0	1	1	2	1	1.000000
1	0	1	0	0	2	1	1.000000
0	0	0	1	0	2	0	0.500000
1	0	0	0	0	2	0	0.500000
0	0	0	0	0	1	0	0.000000
0	0	0	0	1	1	0	0.000000
0	1	0	0	1	1	0	0.000000
0	1	0	1	1	1	0	0.000000
0	1	1	0	0	1	0	0.000000
0	1	1	0	1	1	0	0.000000
0	1	1	1	0	1	0	0.000000
1	0	0	0	1	1	0	0.000000
1	1	0	0	1	1	0	0.000000
1	1	0	1	1	1	0	0.000000
1	1	1	1	0	1	0	0.000000
0	1	0	0	0	2	0	0.000000
1	1	0	0	0	3	0	0.000000
1	1	1	0	0	3	0	0.000000
1	1	1	1	1	3	0	0.000000

SOURCE: AUTHORS' COMPILATION

Table 17.3 presents solution formulas acquired for three models: (Model 1) pre = f(eng, stquo, reg1, reg2, b2b); (Model 2) pre = f(eng, stquo, reg1, reg2, b2b), where logical reminders are accepted and conditions REG1 and REG2 are (reg1 = present, reg2 = present); and (Model 3) ~ pre = f(eng, stquo, reg1, reg2, b2b). In accordance with good practice, we report all three solutions (complex – avoids using any counterfactuals, parsimonious – permits the use of any logical remainders, intermediate – uses counterfactuals input by hand based on theoretical and substantive knowledge).

Results of the CSQCA Analysis

Following the best practices and having reported all solutions acquired with the use of different analytical procedures, we shall stick to the intermediate

TABLE 17.3   *Simplification of outcomes: Solution formulas*

	Complex	Intermediate	Parsimonious
Model 1	eng* ~ stquo* ~ reg1*	reg2* ~ reg1* ~ stquo*eng	~ stquo*reg1
	eng* ~ stquo*reg1* ~ reg2* ~ b2b	~ b2b* ~ reg2*reg1* ~ stquo*	eng* ~ stquo*reg2
	~ eng* ~ stquo*reg1*reg2*b2b	b2b*reg2*reg1* ~ stquo* ~ eng	
Model 2	eng* ~ stquo* ~ reg1*reg2	reg2* ~ stquo*eng	~ stquo*reg1
	eng* ~ stquo*reg1* ~ reg2* ~ b2b	~ b2b *reg1* ~ stquo*eng	eng* ~ stquo*reg2
	~ eng* ~ stquo*reg1*reg2*b2b	b2b*reg2*reg1* ~ stquo	
Model 3	~ eng* ~ reg1* ~ reg2	~ reg1*stquo	stquo
	~ eng*stquo* ~ reg2	~ reg2*stquo	~ eng* ~ reg2
	~ reg1* ~ reg2*b2b	~ b2b*stquo	~ reg2*b2b
	stquo*reg1* ~ b2b	stquo*eng	
	stquo* ~ reg1*b2b	~ reg2* ~ reg1* ~ eng	
	stquo* ~ reg2* ~ b2b	b2b* ~ reg2* ~ reg1	
	stquo* ~ reg1* ~ reg2		
	eng*stquo*reg1*reg2		
	eng*stquo*reg2*b2b		

SOURCE: AUTHORS' COMPILATION. FOR MODELS 1 AND 2 SOLUTION COVERAGE: 0.750000; SOLUTION CONSISTENCY: 1.000000; FOR MODEL 3 SOLUTION COVERAGE: 0.916667, SOLUTION CONSISTENCY: 1.000000

solutions of Model 2, i.e., the model that permitted use of logical reminders selected by hand based on theoretical and substantive knowledge. Given a justified use of simplifying assumptions, the intermediate solution is recommended as the main point of reference for interpreting QCA results.[65] This solution is considered to be most accurate for interpretation since it bridges complexity and parsimony based on the substance of subject matter and allows overcoming the problem of limited diversity by emphasizing the qualitative element of QCA.

We selected the variable 'CSR can act as a precedent for policy-makers' as an outcome variable. The conditions to be tested included answers to two statements regarding regulation (REG1 and REG2), a status quo (STQUO) introduced as a control, respondent company's engagement in CSR (ENG), and a statement regarding the business-to-business nature and stakeholder pressure influencing CSR (B2B). Under the condition that counterfactual cases

---

65   C.C. Ragin, *Redesigning Social Inquiry. Fuzzy Sets and Beyond* (Chicago: Chicago University Press, 2008), pp. 160–175.

satisfying reg1 = present, reg2 = present are included, the QCA analysis showed three paths regarding how companies believe CSR can act as a precedent for maritime policy-making:

$$(1)\,reg2\!\sim\!stquo^*eng;(2)\!\sim\!b2b^*reg1^*\!\sim\!stquo^*eng;(3)\,b2b^*reg2^*reg1^*\!\sim\!stquo.$$

These formulas essentially mean that actors do recognize the potential of CSR to serve as a driver for public policy-making if one of the combinations of causal conditions is met. These three recipes shall be interpreted as combinations, and not reduced to weight of individual factors. As noted by Rihoux and De Meur, the solution formulas allow asking "more focused 'causal' questions about ingredients and mechanisms."[66] In respect to causal conditions that explicitly made a link between CSR/voluntary self-regulatory practices and public regulation (REG1 and REG2), the solution formulas reveal that the presence of at least one of them is necessary for the outcome. During the preliminary analysis, STQUO was indicated as a necessary condition and the final solution formulas are in agreement with this finding. Whereas absence of understanding CSR as a way to preserve the regulatory status quo ($\sim$STQUO) is a necessary condition, it is not a sufficient condition and cannot provide for the outcome outside the three combinations.

Ports and shipping companies already engaged in CSR activities (solution formulas 1 and 2) quite naturally believe in the effectiveness and success of voluntary initiatives, which in turn explains their optimistic views regarding CSR as a precedent. For the actors who engage in CSR practices it is important to see room for CSR in either form (REG1 or REG2). In addition, those ports and shipping companies who consider that the pressure from stakeholders or directly from consumers influences CSR in shipping are of the opinion that CSR appears to be a prominent tool to influence public regulation (formula 2). Thus, the actors' engagement in CSR, their views on the tightness of the mandatory regulations already in place, and their understanding on the stakeholder pressure are all connected with the outcome that CSR acts as a precedent for policy-making. Alternatively, independent from the actor's engagement in CSR, seeing need and room for CSR (REG1 and REG2) leads to an outcome, even when actors who are doubtful towards other stakeholders' ability to set pressure for maritime actors and to influence how maritime transport is carried out (formula 3). This view can be seen as a 'counter-reaction' towards forthcoming, tighter environmental regulation. This view also indicates that the existing regulatory framework has problems that self-regulation cannot fix.

---

66   Rihoux and De Meur, n. 64 above, p. 61.

Summing up, no assertion can be made in respect to the prevalence of any of the solutions over the others. Essentially this means that irrespective of actors' involvement in CSR in their own activities, their readiness to see the potential of CSR to influence public regulation is connected to their understanding of the role of regulation and the balance between public and private governance in the maritime industry at a more general level.

Concluding Remarks

This study investigated empirically how shipping companies and ports in the Baltic Sea region see the relationship between CSR and mandatory regulations within maritime policy. The findings of the QCA analysis suggest that maritime industry actors are aware of CSR's potential to influence regulatory arrangements, even when they are not engaged in CSR themselves. They also reckon that CSR can act as a precedent for policy-making. These findings are in line with previous studies that indicate that CSR activities of the companies can speed up adoption of new laws and also prompt development of new social norms among other actors within the industry,[67] and the governments, in turn, can use CSR initiatives as a basis for developing both soft and hard law.[68] The results of the analysis also support the argument that the adoption of CSR among some maritime actors may lead to changes that might strengthen both national and global governance with spill-over effects (e.g., along supply chains) beyond the companies that originally initiated CSR activities.[69]

Yet, the interpretation of the QCA results is only meaningful within the special circumstances of the BSR. Although international maritime regulation is uniform, enforcement of it varies significantly,[70] providing varying incentives for companies to engage or not to engage in self-regulatory measures. CSR is easier to implement by those companies that come from regions with strict regulation and high environmental standards because they most likely already comply with future regulatory requirements.[71] The survey respondents already engaged in CSR are very likely to be of this type, since there is strict regulation

---

67   A.G. Scherer and G. Palazzo, "The New Political Role of Business in a Globalized World: A Review of a New Perspective on CSR and its Implications for the Firm, Governance, and Democracy," *Journal of Management Studies* 48 (2011): 899–931.

68   Pedersen et al., n. 36 above.

69   Gjølberg, n. 32 above.

70   Alderton and Winchester, n. 4 above; Bloor et al., n. 3 above.

71   Gjølberg, n. 32 above, p. 65.

in place, especially in the Nordic countries, within the BSR. The 'shadow of hierarchy' in which most Baltic shipping companies and ports operate creates an environment favorable for private self-regulation, in which companies' CSR activities immediately complement mandatory rules thereby filling in the gaps in existing arrangements.

Social acceptance of voluntary commitments and societal expectation regarding firms' responsibilities vis-à-vis public sector and society vary in time and space.[72] The urgent need to develop governance mechanisms to improve the state of the Baltic environment and to reduce adverse effects of shipping is a commonly accepted discourse in the BSR. The existence of such an environmental imperative in the BSR may result in an opportunity structure raising perceived benefits from CSR; commitment to CSR allows companies to publicly express their care for the natural environment, as well as to show that they privately develop tools for managing quality in shipping. We suggest that the combination of the two factors specific to the BSR (shadow of hierarchy and public environmental awareness) create a context in which CSR initiatives can be seen as a reaction towards the pitfalls of existing maritime regulation and a renewed interest towards raising the quality of shipping. We thus argue that adoption of CSR should always be investigated in a particular time and space. Methodologically, this finding stresses that in the course of analysis, actors shall not be artificially separated from their operational environment, as the context supplies actors with unique territorially and substantially delaminated rationalities from which they derive their governance strategies.

Our main finding is that the success of CSR in the future Baltic maritime policy arrangements depends on both the private and public actors' capacity to accommodate private regulation within maritime governance. In a polycentric globalized shipping industry we cannot expect the public sector to 'take care' of quality matters and the private sector to 'blindly follow' the public regulation. Alignment of rules and incentives is much more an interactive/collaborative than hierarchical process that requires recognition of private rules within public governance schemes, as well as other forms of alignment that can improve perception of voluntary self-regulation as a precedent for public policy-making among private actors. This shall be a subject of further investigation. Put into a broader perspective, the results of the analysis highlight the difficulties likely to appear in any regulatory environment where a challenge of integrating private regulation into the overall public governance system needs

---

72   Carroll, n. 34 above; A. Dahlsrud, "How Corporate Social Responsibility is Defined: An Analysis of 37 Definitions," *Corporate Social Responsibility and Environmental Management* 15 (2008): 1–13.

to be addressed. At the same time they show how CSR can help to raise overall attention to the socio-economic and environmental problems shipping is causing. When finding policy solutions for these problems it is important to understand that the maritime industry is not uniform and both companies as well as policy-makers have differing premises to favor certain types of regulation depending on where they come from. The presence of strong (global) mandatory regulation helps to raise the standards and norms within the shipping industry as a whole. In the case of shipping, several gaps in global maritime policy, together with rather weak enforcement ensuring compliance, have led to the rise of private self-regulatory initiatives to complement public regulation. Future maritime policy should thus take into account the geographical differences regarding policy-making and preferences for regulatory instruments. In addition, future maritime policy should provide enough carrots for those companies that are motivated to do 'the right thing', and credible sticks for those who are irresponsible.

The IMO's Ballast Water Management Convention of 2004: A Decade of Evolution and Challenges

*Andreas Zink**
Institute for Environmental and Technology Law, Trier, Germany

Introduction

The International Convention on Management and Control of Ships' Ballast Water and Sediments (BWMC 2004)[1] was adopted in London on 13 February 2004. Ten years after its adoption, the BWMC 2004 has not yet entered into force.[2] The reasons for this delay are manifold,[3] and the most recent issues associated with its slow entry into force will be described and analysed in this article. In particular, it will be argued that the international community has developed legal approaches that, in effect, amend in advance of entry into force mandatory provisions that were understood as barriers to ratification. These approaches relate to the need for a more flexible time schedule that

---

* The author is member of the interdisciplinary graduate school, Cooperation of Science and Jurisprudence in Improving Development and Use of Standards for Environmental Protection – Strategies for Risk Assessment and Management, funded by the German Science Foundation (DFG, GRK 1319). The research for this article was done during a research visit at the Marine & Environmental Law Institute at Dalhousie University, Halifax, Nova Scotia, Canada, funded by the German Academic Exchange Service. The author would like to thank Amber Rose Maggio, LL.M. for her helpful comments.
1 International Convention for the Control and Management of Ships' Ballast Water and Sediments, IMO Doc. BWM/CONF/36, 16 February 2004 [BWMC 2004].
2 The BWMC 2004 enters into force 12 months after the date on which not less than 30 States that represent not less than 35 percent of the gross tonnage of the world's merchant shipping fleet have ratified, accepted or acceded the BWMC 2004 (Art. 18(1)). By the end of March 2015, 44 States had ratified the BWMC 2004. However, they represent only 32.86 percent of the gross tonnage of the world's merchant fleet. See IMO, "Status of Conventions," 10 March 2015, available online: <http://www.imo.org/About/Conventions/StatusOfConventions/Pages/Default.aspx>.
3 For actual reasons given by States for not becoming party to the BWMC 2004, see International Chamber of Shipping, "ICS Position on Ratification of IMO Ballast Water Management Convention, 2004," available online: <http://www.ics-shipping.org/docs/default-source/Submissions/IMO/ics-position-on-ratification-of-imo-ballast-water-management-convention575197D99DF7.pdf?sfvrsn=0>.

grants a longer transition period to shipowners in order to retrofit existing vessels with Ballast Water Management Systems (BWMS). In addition, the effort of the International Maritime Organization's (IMO) Marine Environmental Protection Committee (MEPC) and its sub-committees to adopt guidelines on port State control (PSC) under Article 9 of the BWMC 2004 will be discussed with regard to the need for uniformity and legal certainty for flag States and shipowners during vessel inspections in foreign ports.

The Ballast Water Problem

The purpose of the BWMC 2004 is to address and help to prevent the so-called 'ballast water problem' through uniform global rules and standards. The term 'ballast water problem' generally refers to the processes and patterns connected with the unintentional transfer of aquatic species in ships' ballast water between coastal regions. For millions of years, the transfer of aquatic species was influenced exclusively by natural phenomena such as ocean currents, winds, differences in water temperature and salinity, as well as the existence of land barriers in the form of continents.[4] The advent of shipping in the ancient world introduced ships as a vector for the transfer of aquatic species beyond natural biogeographic and ecological barriers.[5]

Following the invention of steel and advances in ship construction permitting watertight hulls, ballast water has been used to ensure ships' stability since the 1850s and completely replaced solid ballast in shipping by the end of the 19th century.[6] Ballast water can be defined as "water with its suspended matter taken on board of a ship to control trim, list, draught, stability or stresses of the ship."[7] Ballast water is an integral part of safe and efficient shipping because the position, stability, and maneuverability of a vessel are ensured at any given

---

4   S. Raaymakers, "The Ballast Water Problem: Global Ecological, Economic and Human Health Impacts," (Paper presented at the RECSO/IMO Joint Seminar on Tanker Ballast Water Management & Technologies, Dubai, 16–18 December 2002, available online: <http://www.imo.org/blast/blastDataHelper.asp?data_id=8595&filename=RaaymakersGlobRaaymakers Glob.pdf>.

5   J.T. Carlton, "The Scale and Ecological Consequences of Biological Invasions in the World's Oceans," in *Invasive Species and Biodiversity Management*, eds O.T. Sandlund, P.J. Schei and A. Viken (Dordrecht: Kluwer, 1999), pp. 195–212 at 195; G. Ruiz, J.T. Carlton, E.D. Grosholz and A.H. Hines, "Global Invasions of Marine and Estuarine Habitats by Non-Indigenous Species: Mechanisms, Extent, and Consequences," *American Zoologist* 37, no. 6 (1997): 621–632 at 621.

6   J.T. Carlton, "Trans-Oceanic and Interoceanic Dispersal of Coastal Marine Organisms – the Biology of Ballast Water," *Oceanography and Marine Biology* 23 (1985): 313–371 at 316.

7   BWMC 2004, n. 1 above, Art. 1(1).

moment through water in the ballast tanks.[8] Without ballast water, modern global shipping would not exist in its current form. Since more than 80 percent of commodities worldwide are transported using cargo ships, and due to the fact that ballast water is integral to shipping, it can be concluded that the transfer of aquatic organisms in ships' ballast water is both a by-product of, and directly connected to, the world economy and modern processes of globalization.[9] The use of ballast water in ships has had a direct effect on the spread of aquatic species. The first aquatic species recorded to have been transported through ballast water are the diatom (*Odontella sinensis*) into the North Sea in 1903 and the Chinese mitten crab (*Eriocheir sinensis*) into the estuary of the Elbe River in Germany during the 1930s.[10]

Ballasting, the operational process that can result in the transfer of aquatic species through ships' ballast water, is usually understood as involving three stages: uptake, transport, and discharge.[11] The first uptake stage occurs in ports or coastal waters and involves ships pumping seawater into their ballast tanks through intake hatches. These hatches are covered by mesh sieves, which prevent the uptake of larger organisms, but fail to prevent the intake of smaller aquatic organisms present in the water column near the ship.[12] A ship's ballast

---

8   T. Puthucherril, "Ballast Waters and Aquatic Invasive Species: A Model for India," *Colorado Journal of International Environmental Law and Policy* 19, no. 3 (2008): 381–425 at 385; M.L. McConnell, "Ballast and Biosecurity: The Legal, Economic and Safety Implications of the Developing International Regime to Prevent the Spread of Harmful Aquatic Organisms and Pathogens in Ships' Ballast Water," *Ocean Yearbook* 17 (2003): 213–255 at 217.

9   United Nations Conference on Transportation and Trade (UNCTAD), *Review of Maritime Transport 2011*, UNCTAD/RMT/2011, p. 26, available online: <http://unctad.org/en/Docs/rmt2011_en.pdf>; P. Hulme, "Trade, Transport and Trouble: Managing Invasive Species Pathways in an Era of Globalization," *Journal of Applied Ecology* 46, no. 1 (2009): 10–18 at 11.

10   C. Ostenfeld, "On the Immigration of *Biddulphia sinensis* Grev. and its Occurrence in the North Sea during 1903–1907 and on its Use for the Study of the Direction and Rate of Flow of the Currents," *Meddelelser fra Kommissionen for Havundersøgelser Serie: Plankton* (1908): 1–44 at pp. 9–10; L.-M. Herborg et al., "Spread of the Chinese Mitten Crab (*Eriocheir sinensis* H. Milne Edwards) in Continental Europe: Analysis of a Historical Data Set," *Hydrobiologia* 503 (2003): 21–28 at 23.

11   J.T. Carlton and J.B. Geller, "Ecological Roulette: The Global Transport of Nonindigenous Marine Organisms," *Science* 261 (1993): 78–82 at 79; McConnell, n. 8 above, p. 213; B. MacPhee, "Hitchhikers' Guide to the Ballast Water Management Convention: An Analysis of Legal Mechanisms to Address the Issue of Alien Invasive Species," *Journal of International Wildlife Law and Policy* 10 (2007): 29–54 at 29.

12   Carlton, n. 6 above, p. 315; J.T. Carlton, "Ballast," in *Encyclopedia of Biological Invasions*, eds D. Simberloff and M. Rejmánek (Berkeley: California University Press, 2011), pp. 43–49 at 46.

water capacity will vary according to the ship's type and size,[13] ranging from 100 cubic meters in the case of fishing vessels or passenger ferries, to more than 100,000 cubic meters in the case of crude oil tankers and ore carriers of the largest class.[14] The volume of ballast water carried in a ship is also influenced by weather conditions, the nature of the ship's cargo, and the voyage length.

The second transport stage of the ballasting process is composed of two distinct parts, the ballast leg and the cargo leg. During the ballast leg, a ship does not carry any cargo and its ballast tanks are filled with seawater. Conversely, during the cargo leg, a ship's holds are fully laden and its ballast tanks are nearly empty.[15] During the ballast leg, a ship carries, on average, a quantity of ballast water representing approximately 25 percent of the ship's gross tonnage, which may be less during short voyages under fair weather conditions and more during extended voyages under heavy weather conditions.[16] It is estimated that between 3 and 12 billion tons of ballast water are transported worldwide with cargo ships every year.[17] These estimates vary due to uncertainty regarding the exact vessel count in the world's merchant fleet, the volume and type of cargo transported, as well as the number and length of voyages. Despite these uncertainties, the volume of ballast water transported is high enough to cause an immense transfer of species, ranging from bacteria and other microbes to micro-algae, small invertebrates and the eggs, spores, seeds, cysts, and larvae of various aquatic plant and animal species.[18] Between 3,000 and 10,000 different species are transported each day at any given moment in the ballast tanks of cargo ships.[19]

---

13   McConnell, n. 8 above, p. 218.

14   IMO, "Alien Invaders – Putting a Stop to the Ballast Water Hitch-Hikers," available online: <http://www.imo.org/OurWork/Environment/BallastWaterManagement/Documents/LINK%2014.pdf>.

15   The number of species transported during the ballast leg is much higher than during the cargo leg, but since it is technically impossible to pump all ballast water out of the tanks and because the sediments at the bottom of the tanks cannot be pumped out either, a high number of species are transported in ballast tanks during cargo voyages as well.

16   D. Minchin and S. Gollasch, "Vectors – How Exotics Get Around," in *Invasive Aquatic Species of Europe*, eds E. Leppäkoski, S. Gollasch and S. Olenin (Dordrecht: Kluwer, 2002), pp. 183–192, at 187.

17   IMO, n. 14 above.

18   Raaymakers, n. 4 above; Carlton, n. 6 above, p. 314.

19   National Research Council, *Stemming the Tide: Controlling Introductions of Nonindigenous Species by Ships' Ballast Water* (Washington, D.C.: National Academy Press, 1996), p. 11; United Nations General Assembly, *Oceans and the Law of the Sea: Report of the Secretary-General*, UN Doc. A/64/66/Add.1, 25 November 2009, p. 64, para. 244; N. Bax, A. Williamson,

The third discharge stage refers to the process of discharging ballast water from the ship in port or coastal waters to allow the ship's cargo to be taken on board. The discharged ballast water necessarily includes any aquatic species that have been pumped into the ballast tanks during the uptake. These aquatic species are discharged into the port or coastal waters where the ship loads cargo. In many cases, species in ballast water do not survive these three stages or are unable to survive when discharged in foreign waters. However, the risk and potential impact of those that do survive is serious enough to count the transfer of aquatic organisms through the ballasting process as a major threat to global biodiversity.[20]

Those organisms that do survive, successful 'invaders', can have devastating ecological, economic, and social impacts. Generally, alien invasive species (AIS) are considered to be a threat to the biological diversity of species and ecosystems, because they are able to displace native species through predation, competition or hybridization and may alter food chains and other ecological processes.[21] The ecological impacts affect the levels of individual species, populations, communities, and ecosystems as well as the genetic diversity of organisms.[22] One of the best documented examples of an invasive species that affects ecosystems and subsequently causes high economic costs is the zebra mussel (*Dreissena polymorpha*), which was transported through ballast water from the region of the Black and Caspian Seas into the Great Lakes of the United States and Canada during the 1980s.[23] Zebra mussels are able to attach to all hard surfaces, including the metallic surfaces of ship hulls, navigation installations, and the piping of power stations and water works.

M. Aguero, E. Gonzalez and W. Geeves, "Marine Invasive Species: A Threat to Global Biodiversity," *Marine Policy* 27, no. 4 (2003): 313–323 at 313.

20　United Nations General Assembly, *Oceans and the Law of the Sea: Report of the Secretary-General*, UN Doc. A/65/69/Add.2, 31 August 2010, p. 63, para. 251.

21　P. Hulme, P. Pyšek, W. Nentwig and M. Vilà, "Will Threat of Biological Invasions Unite the European Union?" *Science* 324 (2009): 40–41 at 40; M. Vilà, J. Espinar, M. Hejda, P.E. Hulme, V. Jarošík, J.L. Maron, J. Pergl, U. Schaffner, Y. Sun and P. Pyšek, "Ecological Impacts of Invasive Alien Plants: A Meta-Analysis of their Effects on Species, Communities and Ecosystems," *Ecology Letters* 14 (2011): 702–708 at 707.

22　M. Kettunen, P. Genovesi, S. Gollasch, S. Pagad, U. Starfinger. P.U. ten Brink and C. Shine, *Technical Support to EU Strategy on Invasive Species (IAS) – Assessment of the Impacts of IAS in Europe and the EU* (Brussels: Institute for European Environmental Policy, 2009), available online: <http://www.ieep.eu/assets/448/ias_assessments.pdf>.

23　A.N. Cohen and B. Foster, "The Regulation of Biological Pollution: Preventing Exotic Species Invasions from Ballast Water Discharged into California Coastal Waters," *Golden Gate University Law Review* 30, no. 4 (2000): 787–883 at 795–796.

The costs for removal, as well as the costs for maintenance and repairs relating to damage caused by the zebra mussel in the United States have amounted to up to US$500 million annually.[24]

Furthermore, there are two hazards to human health specifically related to ballast water: cholera and paralytic shellfish poisoning (PSP).[25] PSP is caused through toxins produced by dinoflagellates which can accumulate in shellfish during algae blooms.[26] In cases when ships take up ballast water in regions where algae blooms occur, the uptake and transfer of toxic dinoflagellates is highly likely, meaning that the region receiving the discharged ballast water will face an elevated risk of PSP.[27] With regards to cholera, following an outbreak in Peru in 1991, the identical strain of cholera was detected in the ballast tanks of cargo chips in the port of Mobile, Alabama (USA). The examination and comparison of the strains of the cholera virus in Peru and the United States showed that ballast water is capable of transferring cholera between continents. The transfer of pathogens through ballast water poses significant risks to human health.[28]

Harmful Aquatic Organisms and Pathogens (HAOP): A New Legal Term

As explained above, the term 'ballast water problem' refers to the process through which aquatic species are transferred in the ballast water of ships and translocated beyond natural barriers, causing significant impacts on ecosystems, human health, and national economies. The BWMC 2004 defines those species as 'harmful aquatic organisms and pathogens' (HAOP): "aquatic organisms and pathogens which, if introduced into the sea including estuaries, or into fresh water courses, may create hazards to the environment, human

---

24   D. Pimentel, "Aquatic Nuisance Species in the New York State Canal and Hudson River Systems and the Great Lakes Basin: An Economic and Environmental Assessment," *Environmental Management* 35, no. 5 (2005): 692–702 at 699.

25   Ruiz et al., n. 5 above, p. 626.

26   G.M. Hallegraeff and C.J. Bolch, "Transport of Toxic Dinoflagellate Cysts via Ships' Ballast Water," *Marine Pollution Bulletin* 22, no. 1 (1991): 27–30 at 27.

27   C.J. Patrick, "Ballast Water Law: Invasive Species and Twenty-five Years of Ineffective Legislation," *Virginia Environmental Law Journal* 27, no. 1 (2009): 67–89 at 73.

28   S.A. McCarthy and F.M. Khambaty, "International Dissemination of Epidemic Vibrio Cholerae by Cargo Ship Ballast and other Nonpotable Waters," *Applied and Environmental Microbiology* 60 (1994): 2597–2601 at 2600; G.M. Ruiz, T.K. Rawlings, F.C. Dobbs, L.A. Drake, T. Mullady, A. Huq and R.R. Colwell, "Global Spread of Microorganisms by Ships," *Nature* 408, no. 2 (2000): 49–50 at 49; C.K. Takahashi, N. Lourenco, T.F. Lopes, V. Rall and C.A. Lopes, "Ballast Water: A Review of the Impact on the World Public Health," *Journal of Venomous Animals and Toxins including Tropical Diseases* 14, no. 3 (2008): 393–408 at 396.

health, property or resources, impair biological diversity or interfere with other uses of such areas."[29]

The term 'HAOP' is not another synonym for 'alien invasive species' (AIS), but rather, a discrete legal term that is narrower than the term 'AIS'.[30] Contrary to the widely accepted legal definition of AIS in the Guiding Principles for the Prevention, Introduction and Mitigation of Impacts of Alien Species that threaten Ecosystems, Habitats or Species[31] under the Convention on Biological Diversity (CBD),[32] HAOP refers only to aquatic organisms. By virtue of this definition, all terrestrial species are excluded from the scope of the BWMC 2004. In addition, the term HAOP explicitly encompasses pathogens. Since pathogens are able to survive under a wide range of environmental conditions, they are not tied to a specific habitat and may occur in terrestrial and aquatic habitats alike. To avoid an unnecessary restriction of the term HAOP and to apply the BWMC 2004 to all pathogens that may be transported in ballast water, the term 'aquatic' in the definition does not refer to pathogens.

As a specifically defined legal term, HAOP should be used in connection with the BWMC 2004 and the regulation of ballast water rather than the more general term AIS. Since Article 196 (1) of the United Nations Convention on the Law of the Sea (UNCLOS) relates to 'alien or new' species without providing a definition,[33] the term HAOP in the BWMC 2004 can be seen as a legal term that gives more precise meaning to Article 196 (1) of UNCLOS.

Regulation of Ballast Water on the International Level

The origin of the international regulation of the ballast water problem dates back to the 1973 IMO International Conference on Marine Pollution.[34] During

---

29 BWMC 2004, n. 1 above, Art. 8(1).

30 M.H. Fonseca de Souza Rolim, *The International Law on Ballast Water: Preventing Biopollution* (Boston: Martinus Nijhoff Publishers, 2008), p. 102.

31 Convention on Biological Diversity, "Guiding Principles for the Prevention, Introduction and Mitigation of Impacts of Alien Species that threaten Ecosystems, Habitats or Species," COP 6 Decision VI/23 (Annex), 2002, available online: <http://www.cbd.int/decision/cop/?id=7197>.

32 Convention on Biological Diversity, adopted on 5 June 1992, entry into force on 29 December 1993, 1760 *United Nations Treaty Series* 79; 31 *International Legal Materials* 818 (1992); available online: <http://www.cbd.int/doc/legal/cbd-en.pdf>.

33 United Nations Convention on the Law of the Sea, adopted on 10 December 1982, entry into force on 16 November 1994, 1833 *United Nations Treaty Series* 3; 21 *International Legal Materials* 1261 (1994), available online: <http://www.un.org/Depts/los/convention _agreements/convention_overview_convention.htm>.

34 Rolim, n. 30 above, p. 88.

this conference, not only was the well-known Convention for the Regulation of Vessel-source Pollution (MARPOL 73/78)[35] adopted, but also a non-binding resolution that gave both the World Health Organization (WHO) and the IMO (then the Inter-Governmental Maritime Consultative Organization) the mandate to conduct research on the connection between ballast water operations and the transmission of epidemic diseases such as cholera.[36] The resolution by the IMO underlined the importance of scientific research in the legal regulation of environmental problems and contained the prohibition of transboundary pollution in order to prevent the spread of disease into neighboring States through ballast water.[37]

On the initiative of Canada, New Zealand, and Australia, all having been affected by the impacts of HAOP since the 1980s, the MEPC adopted a resolution with Guidelines on Ballast Water Management in 1991.[38] The 1991 Guidelines contained several key elements addressing the ballast water problem, including ballast water management practices such as the Ballast Water Management Plan (BWMP), the Ballast Water Record Book (BWRB), and described the open-ocean exchange of ballast water (BWE) as one feasible option to reduce the risk of biological invasions in marine ecosystems.[39] In 1993, the IMO Assembly confirmed the 1991 Guidelines of the MEPC through

35   International Convention for the Prevention of Pollution from Ships as modified by the Protocol of 1978, adopted on 2 November 1973, entered into force on 2 October 1983, 1340 *United Nations Treaty Series* 184; 12 *International Legal Materials* 1319 (1973).

36   Inter-governmental Maritime Consultative Organization (IMCO), "Resolution 18: Research into the Effects of Discharge of Ballast Water containing Bacteria of Epidemic Diseases," IMCO Doc. MP/CONF/WP.29, 31 October 1973, p. 24.

37   Rolim, n. 30 above, p. 88; S.A. Lawal, "Ballast Water Management Convention, 2004: Towards Combating Unintentional Transfer of Harmful Aquatic Organisms and Pathogens" (LL.M. Thesis, Schulich School of Law, Dalhousie University, Halifax, Nova Scotia, Canada, August 2011) (unpublished), p. 66, available online: <http://dalspace .library.dal.ca/bitstream/handle/10222/14184/Lawal,%20Sabitiyu%20Abosede,%20 LLM,%20Law,%20August%202011.pdf?sequence=1>.

38   Marine Environmental Protection Committee (MEPC), "International Guidelines for preventing the Introduction of unwanted Aquatic Organisms and Pathogens from Ships' Ballast Water and Sediment Discharges," Resolution MEPC.50 (31), 4 July 1991; M.L. McConnell, *GloBallast Legislative Review – Final Report*, GloBallast Monograph Series No. 1 (London: IMO, 2002), p. 11, available online: <http://globallast.imo.org/ monograph1%20legislative%20review.pdf>.

39   MEPC, id., p. 7, para. 7.3.

an Assembly resolution.[40] This was done as a response to Agenda 21, which explicitly stated that the IMO should adopt mandatory rules for the regulation of the ballast water problem.[41] This in turn gave the Guidelines more international attention, because the IMO Assembly has more political weight than the MEPC, an IMO committee.[42] In 1997, the 1993 Guidelines were revised in order to develop further strategies and procedures for ballast water management and to adapt the Guidelines for scientific knowledge and technical progress. The 1997 IMO Guidelines contain elements such as the BWMP, the BWRB, and the BWE.[43] In addition, the requirements for the BWE are set out in greater detail, especially through new requirements on ship safety to ensure vessel stability and crew safety during ballasting operations on the high seas. The 1997 IMO Guidelines provided the foundation for a binding legal instrument for the international regulation of ballast water management and have been expressly adopted as an interim solution, until the final adoption of a binding instrument on ballast water management.[44] In the time period until the final entry into force of the BWMC 2004, the 1997 Ballast Water Guidelines remain the IMO's major instrument for regulating the ballast water problem. The BWMC 2004 will not replace the 1997 Guidelines after its entry into force. Consequently, these Guidelines remain important for States that will not become party to the BWMC 2004.

The Ballast Water Management Convention of 2004

After more than 14 years of discussion in the context of Guidelines, the International Conference on Ballast Water Management for Ships adopted a mandatory text, the BWMC 2004, with the consensus of the 74 States present.[45]

---

40   IMO, "Guidelines for Preventing the Introduction of Unwanted Aquatic Organisms and Pathogens from Ships' Ballast Water and Sediment Discharges," Assembly Resolution A.774(18), 4 November 1993.

41   United Nations Conference on Environment & Development, *Agenda 21*, June 1992, Chapter 17, para. 17.30 lit. a) vi), available online: <http://sustainabledevelopment.un.org/content/documents/Agenda21.pdf>.

42   J. Firestone and J.J. Corbett, "Coastal and Port Environments: International Legal and Policy Responses to Reduce Ballast Water Introductions of Potentially Invasive Species," *Ocean Development & International Law* 36, no. 3 (2005): 291–316 at 294.

43   IMO, "Guidelines for the Control and Management of Ships' Ballast Water to minimize the Transfer of Harmful Aquatic Organisms and Pathogens," Assembly Resolution A 20/Res.868, 1 December 1997.

44   S.A. Lawal, "Implementation of the 2004 Ballast Water Management Convention in the West African Region: Challenges and Prospects," *Ocean Yearbook* 27 (2013): 385–410 at 387.

45   GloBallast, Ballast Water News, Issue 16, January–March 2004, available online: <http://globallast.imo.org/BallastWaterNews16.pdf>.

The Secretary-General of the IMO described the Ballast Water Conference as the "culmination of many years of work."[46] The Conference adopted the text of the BWMC 2004 and developed consensus-based solutions to several major areas disputed between the State parties, i.e., the entry into force provision (Article 18), the right of State parties to adopt more stringent standards (Article 2(3)), and the standards for ballast water treatment (Regulation D-2).

The structure of the BWMC 2004 is similar to the structure of MARPOL 73/78 and follows the convention-annex approach.[47] The convention text of the BWMC 2004 consists of 22 articles on the general rights and obligations of the State parties and sets out the formal procedures to amend the text of the Convention or the Annex thereto. The Annex forms an integral part of the BWMC 2004, so any reference to the Convention constitutes at the same time a reference to the Annex.[48] The Annex to the Convention therefore has the same legal quality as the Convention text and is structured into five sections (A–E) that comprise material rules such as ballast water standards, a time schedule for implementation, and rules on survey and certification requirements:

- Section A – General Provisions
- Section B – Management and Control Requirements for Ships
- Section C – Special Requirements in Certain Areas
- Section D – Standards for Ballast Water Management
- Section E – Survey and Certification Requirements for Ballast Water Management

In addition, the MEPC adopted a set of 14 guidelines (G-1–G-14) on technical guidance and implementation of the BWMC after 2004. The Guidelines G-1–G-14 are not to be confused with the IMO Ballast Water Guidelines of 1991, 1993,

46   IMO, "Opening Statement by the Secretary-General," Doc. BWM/CONF/INF.8, 12 February 2004, p. 1.

47   M.L. McConnell, "Responsive Ocean Governance: The Problem of Invasive Species and Ships' Ballast Water – A Canadian Study," in *Understanding and Strengthening European Union-Canada Relations in Law of the Sea and Ocean Governance*, ed., T. Koivurova, A. Chircop, E. Franckx, E.J. Molenaar and D.L. VanderZwaag (Rovaniemi: University of Lapland Printing Centre, 2009), *Juridica Lapponica* 35, pp. 433–471 at 452; R. Balkin, "Ballast Water Management: Regulatory Challenges and Opportunities," in *Shipping, Law and the Marine Environment in the 21st Century: Emerging Challenges for the Law of the Sea – Legal Implications and Liabilities*, ed., R. Caddell and T. Rhidian (Oxford: Lawtext Publishing, 2013), pp. 137–149 at 143.

48   BWMC 2004, n. 1 above, Art. 2(2).

and 1997 mentioned above. The IMO Ballast Water Guidelines constituted guidance for States with respect to ballast water management. The Guidelines G-1–G-14 explicitly refer to the BWMC 2004, and must be understood as instruments to foster the uniform implementation of the BWMC 2004 through State parties. In general, the Guidelines G-1–G-14 are legally non-binding but nevertheless constitute an important manual for national administrations with regard to the application and enforcement of the BWMC 2004. The application of the Guidelines G-1–G-14 is not mandatory. National administrations of State parties may exercise discretion when deciding whether to apply the content of Guidelines G-1–G-14 in certain circumstances. However, this discretion might be restricted by State obligations arising from the law of the sea or international law.[49] The Guidelines G-1–G-14 deal with specific aspects of the implementation of the BWMC 2004 and contain more detailed rules and procedures for State parties:

- Guidelines for Sediment Reception Facilities (G1), MEPC.152(55), 13 October 2006
- Guidelines for Ballast Water Sampling (G2), MEPC.173(58), 10 October 2008
- Guidelines for Ballast Water Management Equivalent Compliance (G3), MEPC.123(53), 22 July 2005
- Guidelines for Ballast Water Management and Development of Ballast Water Management Plans (G4), MEPC.127(53), 22 July 2005
- Guidelines for Ballast Water Reception Facilities (G5), MEPC.153(55), 13 October 2006
- Guidelines for Ballast Water Exchange (G6), MEPC.124(53), 22 July 2005
- Guidelines for Risk Assessment under Regulation A-4 of the BWM Convention (G7), MEPC.162(56), 13 July 2007
- Guidelines for Approval of Ballast Water Management Systems (G8), MEPC.174(58), 10 October 2008
- Procedure for Approval of Ballast Water Management Systems that Make Use of Active Substances (G9), MEPC.169(57), 4 April 2008
- Guidelines for Approval and Oversight of Prototype Ballast Water Treatment Technology Programmes (G10), MEPC.140(54), 24 March 2006
- Guidelines for Ballast Water Exchange Design and Construction Standards (G11), MEPC.149(55), 13 October 2006

---

49   The discussion below deals with the question of circumstances under which the application of Guidelines G-1–G-14 through national administrations should be considered as mandatory.

- Guidelines on Design and Construction to Facilitate Sediment Control on Ships (G12), MEPC.150(55), 13 October 2006
- Guidelines for Additional Measures Regarding Ballast Water Management including Emergency Situations (G13), MEPC.161(56), 13 July 2007
- Guidelines on Designation of Areas for Ballast Water Exchange (G14), MEPC.151(55), 13 October 2006

Rights and Obligations of Flag States and Coastal/Port States under the BWMC 2004

The BWMC 2004 follows a two-tier approach for ballast water management and establishes uniform global standards (Tier 1) and allows coastal States to adopt more stringent special requirements in certain areas (Tier 2).[50] The exact extent of the rights and obligations of the State parties to the BWMC 2004 is complex due to the interaction of the Convention text and the regulations in the Annex to the BWMC 2004. Generally, the BWMC 2004 differentiates between State parties in their function as flag States and as coastal or port States. In short, all State parties have the obligation to "give full and complete effect to the provisions" of the BWMC 2004 and the Annex thereto "in order to prevent, minimize, and ultimately eliminate the transfer of HAOP through the control and management of ships' Ballast Water and Sediments."[51] However, as with most IMO conventions, the focus is on flag States. Flag States shall "require that ships to which the BWMC 2004 applies and which are entitled to fly its flag or operating under its authority comply with the requirements set forth in the BWMC 20,004, including the applicable standards and requirements in the Annex." Flag States "shall take effective measures to ensure that those ships comply with those requirements."[52] In their function as flag States, State parties must ensure that the ships flying their flag, *inter alia*, develop a BWMP, record all ballast operations in a BWRB, and perform the management of ballast water and sediments in line with quality standards and the time schedule for the application of standards.[53] Flag States are also competent to grant type approvals for ballast water management systems (BWMS), which have to be installed on ships in order to fulfill the requirements of the ballast water performance standard (Regulation D-2).

---

50   N. Liu, "Current Legal Developments: China: Prevention of Invasive Species from Ballast Water," *International Journal of Marine and Costal Law* 28, no. 1 (2013): 171–187 at 175.

51   BWMC 2004, n. 1 above, Art. 2(1).

52   BWMC 2004, n. 1 above, Art. 4(1).

53   Lawal, n. 44 above, at 396.

In their role as coastal and port States, State parties of the BWMC 2004 are obligated to ensure that ports and terminals under their jurisdiction provide adequate facilities for the reception of sediments removed from vessels during the dry-docking process.[54] Coastal States have the right to grant exemptions from the ballast water standards, to establish special areas for ballast water exchange, and to adopt more stringent standards in the waters under their jurisdiction and control.[55] Port States have the right and duty to control and inspect all vessels that are voluntarily in ports under their jurisdiction.[56] Port State control under the Convention is not restricted to the verification of the BWMP and BWRB documentation, but allows sampling and analysing the ballast water of a ship suspected to be non-compliant with the applicable ballast water standards. Port States have the right to sanction detected violations of the BWMC 2004 under their national law.[57]

As long as the BWMC 2004 has not entered into force,[58] and until the MEPC adopts guidelines on the extent and procedures of PSC with regard to sampling ballast water, it remains difficult to evaluate the rights and obligations of flag States and coastal/port States under the BWMC 2004 without practical evidence concerning the observance and enforcement of the instrument's provisions. Nevertheless, two issues can be identified as reasons for the reluctance of States to become party to the BWMC 2004: (1) the inflexible time schedule for the application of the Ballast Water Performance Standard (Regulation D-2) as laid down in Regulation B-3 of the Annex of the BWMC 2004, and (2) the unclear extent and procedures for sampling and analysis of ballast water for compliance purposes.

Evolution of the Ballast Water Management Convention since Adoption in 2004

International treaties are generally not subject to major changes in the rights and obligations of State parties during the period between the adoption and the entry into force. Nevertheless, more than ten years after its adoption through the Ballast Water Conference in London, the BWMC 2004 has undergone a process of 'evolution'. The significance of this process lies in the fact that

---

54   BWMC 2004, n. 1 above, Art. 5.
55   BWMC 2004, n. 1 above, regs. A-4 and C-1, Annex.
56   BWMC 2004, n. 1 above, Art. 9.
57   BWMC 2004, n. 1 above, Art. 8(2).
58   IMO, n. 2 above.

the BWMC 2004 has undergone changes without the application of the formal amendment procedure set out in Article 19 of the Convention, since this formal procedure is not applicable until the final entry into force of the BWMC 2004. In this context, the term evolution refers to (1) the adoption of the 14 Guidelines (G-1–G-14) necessary for the uniform application and interpretation of the BWMC 2004 by the MEPC, (2) the explanation of certain terms and concepts through circulars of the IMO, and (3) changes to the BWMC 2004 in form and content through IMO Assembly resolutions.

MEPC Guidelines G-1–G-14 on the Implementation of the BWMC 2004
The MEPC Guidelines G-1–G-14 on the implementation of the BWMC 2004 are not an integrated part of the Convention. Nevertheless, they constitute an essential instrument for the uniform application and interpretation of the provisions of the BWMC 2004 through State parties, national administrations, port authorities, and shipping companies. The function of the Guidelines G-1–G-14 is not restricted to ensuring the uniform application and interpretation of the BWMC 2004, but also to substantiating the general provisions of the BWMC 2004 with more detailed rules, standards, and procedures, as the Convention contains several cross-references to the Guidelines ("taking into account the Guidelines developed by the Organization").[59] The BWMC 2004 is dependent on the exact content of the Guidelines G-1–G-14, as these instruments may contain detailed rules, standards or processes for its core elements. The BWMC 2004 must therefore always be applied with the applicable Guidelines, leading to the question of the legal quality and binding character of the MEPC Guidelines G-1–G-14.[60]

In principle, neither the IMO nor the MEPC have legislative competence.[61] The Convention establishing the IMO does not empower any of the institutions,[62] i.e., the Assembly, the Council or one of the committees of the IMO, to adopt legally binding acts in relation to the Member States.[63] The Assembly of the IMO may only "recommend to Members for adoption regulations and

---

59   The function of the Guidelines is underlined by recital 8 of the preamble of the BWMC 2004 (n. 1 above): "[t]hat this issue, being of worldwide concern, demands action based on globally applicable regulations together with guidelines for their effective implementation and uniform interpretation."

60   Rolim, n. 30 above, p. 133.

61   J. Harrison, *Making the Law of the Sea* (Cambridge: Cambridge University Press, 2011), p. 24.

62   Convention on the International Maritime Organization, adopted on 6 March 1984, entry into force on 17 March 1958, 289 *United Nations Treaty Series* 3 (1958).

63   Rolim, n. 30 above, p. 83.

guidelines"[64] and the MEPC may only submit "proposals for regulations and for amendments" and "recommendations and guidelines."[65] These instruments have no binding force for the IMO Member States unless they agree otherwise, namely, in the form of ratification of an IMO convention or the transformation of IMO resolutions into national law. The Guidelines G-1–G-14, which have been adopted in the form of a resolution by the MEPC, are therefore legally non-binding on the State parties to the BWMC 2004.[66] Therefore, the binding character of the Guidelines G-1–G-14 must result from another legal basis, i.e., the Guidelines must either be already part of customary international law, or the BWMC 2004 as a legally binding international convention must contain a cross-reference to the Guidelines G-1–G-14, with the result that the Guidelines become mandatory after the BWMC 2004 enters into force.

The MEPC Guidelines G-1–G-14 are not part of customary international law because the two constitutive elements of customary law, state practice and *opinio juris*, are currently unfulfilled.[67] Since the majority of the Guidelines will not become relevant before the BWMC 2004 enters into force, most of the Guidelines are currently not applied by the State parties. Therefore, State practice cannot evolve at this time, which is a necessary constituent element of customary international law. With reference to Guidelines G-8 and G-9, which both relate to the process of granting type approvals for BWMS through national administrations, the application by State parties is based more on practical considerations than the *opinio juris* of States. These realities confirm that Guidelines G-1–G-14 are not yet part of customary international law.

The Guidelines G-1–G-14 might become legally binding once the BWMC 2004 enters into force if the BWMC 2004 contains cross-references to the Guidelines G-1–G-14.[68] It is a well-accepted IMO practice to insert references to instruments such as technical codes into existing international conventions in order to make the corresponding codes or guidelines legally binding. For

64   IMO Convention (n. 62 above), Art. 15(j).

65   Id., Art. 39(a) and (b).

66   The entry into force of the BWMC 2004 has no impact on the legally non-binding character of Guidelines G-1–G-14. The Guidelines' application is currently at the discretion of State parties and national administrations.

67   M.E. Villiger, *Commentary on the 1969 Vienna Convention on the Law of Treaties* (Leiden: Martinus Nijhoff, 2009), pp. 7–10; P.W. Birnie, A.E. Boyle and C. Redgwell, *International Law and the Environment*, 3rd ed. (Oxford: Oxford University Press, 2009), p. 22; Rolim, n. 30 above, p. 134.

68   Rolim, n. 30 above, p. 133.

instance, MARPOL 73/78 contains a reference to the IBC Code of 1983[69] in Article 11 (1) of Annex II,[70] meaning that the IBC Code of 1983, which has been adopted as a legally non-binding but recommendatory instrument, became legally binding for all MARPOL 73/78 State parties.[71] In this sense, non-binding IMO instruments can become legally binding for State parties of international conventions through cross-references in conventions, to the extent the convention requires that the guidance is followed. To ensure a uniform use of references and to avoid ambiguity, the IMO adopted a resolution with guidelines on the "Uniform Wording for Referencing IMO Instruments."[72] This guidance provides that where a cross-reference to a (non-binding) IMO instrument such as a technical code is intended, the reference to such instruments should be expressly stated in the text of the relevant convention regulations; it should be provided that future amendments to such instruments should follow the amendment procedures laid down in the relevant article of the parent convention (i.e., the tacit acceptance procedure) and that the use of terms in the cross-reference such as 'guidelines' or 'guidance', which might be misunderstood as implying recommendations, should be avoided as far as possible.[73] In the case of the BWMC 2004 and Guidelines G-2 and G-14, none of these requirements have been fulfilled. Firstly, the cross-references in the BWMC 2004 are very general and do not refer to a specific guideline but instead to "the Guidelines developed by the Organization."[74] Secondly, Guidelines G-1–G-14 do not constitute a uniform technical code in the same way as other instruments such as the IBC Code of 1983. The MEPC consciously decided to reject proposals to merge all guidelines into one 'Ballast Water Code'.[75] Thirdly, the designation of Guidelines G-1–G-14 as guidelines and guidance expresses the intention to create a recommendatory document rather than a legally

---

69   MEPC, "International Code for the Construction and Equipment of Ships carrying Dangerous Chemicals in Bulk (IBC Code)," IMO Doc. MEPC.119(52), 15 October 2004.

70   IMO, "Revised Annex II of MARPOL 73/78," Doc. MEPC.118(52), 15 October 2004, p. 15.

71   E. Anianova, "The International Maritime Organization (IMO) – Tanker or Speedboat?," in *International Maritime Organisations and their Contribution towards a Sustainable Marine Development,* eds P. Ehlers and R. Lagoni (Hamburg: LIT, 2006), pp.77–103 at 84.

72   IMO, "Uniform Wording for Referencing IMO Instruments," Assembly Doc. A 22/Res. 911, 22 January 2002.

73   Id., p. 2, para. 3.

74   See, for instance, Article 5 BWMC, Article 9(1)(c) BWMC, or Regulation A-4.1.4 of the Annex of the BWMC (n. 1 above).

75   IMO, "Proposal for Modification of Regulations A-4 and C-1, and Draft Guidelines on Assessment of Exemptions and Introduction of Additional Measures – Submitted by Norway," Doc. BWM/CONF/16, 19 January 2004, p. 4, para. 9.

binding act.[76] All guidelines contain the passage "[t]he MEPC *invites* Governments to apply these Guidelines as soon as possible, or when the Convention becomes applicable to them."[77] The IMO 'expects' all parties to UNCLOS to conform to resolutions of the Assembly or the MEPC.[78] It can thus be concluded that the IMO understands Guidelines G-1–G-14 as non-mandatory instruments. Finally, the cross-references in the BWMC 2004 to the Guidelines contain the expression 'shall take into account', which confirms the non-binding character of these instruments.[79] Strict compliance with the Guidelines is therefore not required, and discretion is available to the State parties when implementing the BWMC 2004 as well as the relevant Guidelines.[80]

In two circumstances, however, the discretion of national administrations of State parties to the BWMC 2004 to consider the applicable MEPC Guidelines appears to be restricted, because to do so and exercise the rights and obligations contained in the BWMC 2004 risks infringing certain rules of international law.[81] The clear wording of Regulation A-4 of the Annex to the BWMC 2004 expresses that the State parties may grant exemptions to any requirement but "only when they are...granted based on the Guidelines on risk assessment developed by the Organization." National administrations are therefore obliged to conduct risk assessments based on the procedure and requirements of the G-7 Guidelines before they can grant any exemption under Regulation A-4.[82] The legal background of this requirement can be found in Article 192 of UNCLOS and the obligation of States under international law to avoid transboundary environmental damage. This is reflected in Article 2 (6) of BWMC 2004, which provides that State parties "shall endeavor not to impair or damage their environment, human health, property or resources, or those of

---

76   IMO, n. 72 above, p. 5, para. 13.

77   See the resolution text in front of all of the Guidelines G-1–G14, for instance of the Guidelines for Ballast Water Sampling (G2), MEPC.173(58), 10 October 2008.

78   IMO, "Implications of the United Nations Convention on the Law of the Sea for the International Maritime Organization," IMO Doc. LEG/MISC/3/Rev.1, 6 January 2003, p. 5.

79   IMO, n. 72 above, p. 5, para. 14.

80   M. Tsimplis, "Alien Species Stay Home: The International Convention for the Control and Management of Ships' Ballast Water and Sediments 2004," *International Journal of Marine and Costal Law* 19, no. 4 (2005): 411–782 at 445.

81   "[I]t is proposed that the attached guidelines should be considered mandatory, i.e., if the provisions of Regulations A-4 and C-1 are to be used, the guidelines are to be applied," IMO, n. 75 above, p. 2, para. 4.

82   IMO, "Guidelines for Risk Assessment under Regulation A-4 of the BWM Convention (G7)," Resolution MEPC.162 (56), 13 July 2007.

other States." When State parties to the BWMC 2004 grant exemptions
without a prior assessment of the connected risk and danger, it might be
possible that damage occurs to the environment, human health, property or
resources of other States, a consequence that could have been avoided if the
exemptions had not been granted. Regulation A-4 and the procedure for
risk assessments under the G-7 Guidelines ensure that exemptions are only
granted in instances of low risk in order to prevent the spread of HAOP through
ships' ballast water. The purpose of the BWMC 2004 would otherwise be undermined, and the acting State would infringe its obligation to prevent transboundary harm to the environment of other States, the obligation under
Article 192 of UNCLOS to protect and preserve the marine environment and
the obligation under Article 196(1) of UNCLOS to prevent the introduction
of HAOP into the marine environment. The obligation of State parties under
Regulation A-4 of the Annex of the BWMC 2004 only to grant exemptions
based on the results of risk assessments conducted in line with the requirements of Guideline G-7 ensures that the State parties decide on a case-by-case
basis. State parties must identify the individual risks for each scenario under
which the grant of an exemption has been requested by a potential applicant
(shipowner or shipping company). Although the decision to grant or to deny
an exemption lies in the discretion of the State parties ('may grant'), the
content of Regulation A-4.3 indicates that exemptions may only be granted
if the impairment of or damage to other States can be excluded. The discretion
of State parties is therefore restricted with a view to the rights of other States
and the general principal in international environmental law to avoid transboundary harm for other States. In cases where State parties grant an exemption under Regulation A-4 although the results of a risk assessment indicated
high risks for the environment, human health, property or resources of other
States, the affected States may take legal action under international law for
damages suffered. This would comprise measures of dispute settlement under
Article 15 of BWMC 2004, as well as measures under the law of State responsibility. Under Regulation A-4, States that may be affected through the exemptions granted by other State parties have no right of direct intervention in
order to prevent the granting of an exemption but may refer to general diplomatic or judicial measures of dispute settlement and State responsibility under
international law.

Under Regulation C-1 of the Annex of the BWMC 2004, State parties have
the right to impose special requirements for ballast water management to
prevent, reduce, or eliminate the transfer of HAOP through ballast water and
sediments of ships. State parties that intend to impose such special requirements 'shall take into account' the applicable guidelines of the MEPC, namely

Guideline G-13.[83] The expression 'shall take into account' indicates the non-mandatory nature of the G-13 Guideline.[84] Nevertheless, there are circumstances under the law of the sea and international law which may transform the recommendatory Guideline G-13 into binding ones despite their non-binding character, with regards to the rights of other States in certain maritime zones. For example, in cases where State parties adopt special requirements in areas within their internal waters or ports, those measures are based on the territorial sovereignty of the acting State and do not infringe the rights of other States under UNCLOS or international law.[85] In circumstances where a State party adopts special requirements in its territorial waters or its exclusive economic zone, the rights of other States (i.e., innocent passage, approval by IMO) under UNCLOS and international law (i.e., prior notification) must be taken into account. The inclusion of a clear procedure of notification and assessment in Guideline G-13 ensures that State parties comply with their obligations under UNCLOS and international law, minimizing the risk of infringing other State's rights. Guideline G-13 is therefore mandatory for State parties of the BWMC 2004 in a limited way, as non-compliance may constitute an infringement of other State's rights under UNCLOS or international law.

The function of MEPC Guidelines G-1–G-14 is not restricted to providing guidance for State parties with regard to the uniform application and interpretation of the provisions of the BWMC 2004, but also ensures, through special procedures, that the rights of other States under UNCLOS and international law are respected. The Guidelines G-1–G-14 are not legally binding as such, but their application to State parties may be mandatory in certain circumstances due to legal obligations under UNCLOS and international law.

Circulars of IMO on Central Terms and Concepts of the BWMC 2004

Circulars and circular letters issued by the IMO and distributed between member States, stakeholders and the public have the function of providing information about actual developments with regard to particular IMO conventions. These circulars are communications only and indisputably non-binding in nature. However, they play an instrumental role in ensuring the uniform application and interpretation of the BWMC 2004, in tandem with the MEPC

---

83   IMO, "Guidelines for Additional Measures Regarding Ballast Water Management Including Emergency Situations (G13)," Resolution MEPC.161(56), 13 July 2007.

84   IMO, n. 72 above, p. 5 para. 14.

85   IMO, "Comments on the Draft Convention (as contained in BWM/CONF/2) – Submitted by the United Nations Division for Ocean Affairs and the Law of the Sea (UN-DOALOS)," Doc. BWM/CONF/9, 25 November 2003, p. 2, para. 2.4.

Guidelines G-1–G-14. All information submitted to the IMO by State parties of the BWMC 2004 is disseminated through circulars, such as granted type approvals of BWMS by national authorities, the intention to establish special areas for BWE, or the intention to grant specific exemptions for certain voyages or vessels. The IMO Secretariat uses circulars in order to clarify certain terms and concepts of the BWMC 2004 in answer to uncertainties expressed by State parties, national administrations or shipping companies. These clarifications include explaining the meaning of terms such as 'major conversion',[86] confirming the application of the BWMC 2004 to special vessels such as hopper dredgers or floating platforms,[87] the testing process for BWMS under Guidelines G-8 and G-9, and most importantly, developing the time schedule for the instrument's application under Regulation B-3.[88] In addition, IMO circulars inform all interested parties about the meetings of the Ballast Water Working Group (BWWG), a division of the Joint Group of Experts on the Scientific Aspects of Marine Pollution (GESAMP).[89] The BWWG evaluates active substances that are used in BWMS for the chemical/biocidal treatment of ballast water, and every statement by the BWWG is important for national authorities and manufacturers of BWMS during the process of type approval of BWMS that make use of active substances.

These considerations confirm that IMO circulars have no direct effect on the provisions of the BWMC 2004, as these instruments do not alter the content of the BWMC 2004. However, these circulars and clarifications are vital to enhancing the understanding of national authorities and stakeholders regarding the interpretation and application of the BWMC 2004. The function

---

86   IMO, "Clarification of 'major conversion' as defined in Regulation A-1.5 of the BWM Convention," Doc. BWM.2/Circ.45, 30 May 2013.

87   IMO, "Applicability of the Ballast Water Management Convention to Hopper Dredgers," Doc. BWM.2/Circ.32, 8 August 2011; IMO, "Application of the BWM Convention to Mobile Offshore Units," Doc. BWM.2/Circ.46, 31 May 2013.

88   IMO, "Guidance for Administrations on the Type Approval Process for Ballast Water Management Systems in Accordance with Guidelines (G8)," Doc. BWM.2/Circ.28, 5 October 2010; IMO, "Procedure for Approval of Ballast Water Management Systems That Make Use of Active Substances (G9)," Doc. MEPC.169(57), 4 April 2008; IMO, "Clarification Regarding the Application Dates Contained in Regulation B-3.1 of the BWM Convention," Doc. BWM.2/Circ.29, 7 October 2010; IMO, "Clarification Regarding the Application Dates Contained in Regulation B-3 of the BWM Convention," Doc. BWM.2/Circ.29/Rev.1, 26 September 2011.

89   IMO, "Establishment of the GESAMP – Ballast Water Working Group for the Review of Proposals for Approval of Active Substances Used for the Management of Ballast Water in Accordance with Resolution MEPC.126(53)," Doc. BWM.2/Circ.2, 7 November 2005.

of circulars is illustrated by the "Guidance on Ballast Water Sampling and Analysis for Trial Use in Accordance with the BWM Convention and Guidelines (G2)"[90] (in Circular 42), which "should be read in conjunction with the BWMC, the PSC Guidelines, the Guidelines for ballast water sampling (G-2), ..."[91] Without altering the legal character of the Convention and the Guidelines, Circular 42 provides the necessary information and guidance for competent authorities with regard to inspection procedures in ports and effective and uniform application of Article 9 by competent administrations. Circulars do not contribute directly to the 'evolution' of the BWMC 2004 but should be considered as important tools for enhancing the clarity and completeness of the BWMC 2004.

De facto Amendment of the BWMC 2004 through IMO Assembly Resolution A (28) 1088

In general, amendments to international conventions are subject to formal amendment procedures laid down in the provisions of that convention. For the BWMC 2004, the formal procedure for amendments of the Convention text or the Annex is described in Article 19. The BWMC 2004 may be amended within the IMO or by an international conference following a precise process; both amendment procedures have been included in previous IMO conventions.[92] Following the adoption of the BWMC 2004, it became apparent that the time schedule set out in Regulation B-1 of the Annex was inflexible and ineffective in ensuring adequate transition periods for existing ships. During the Ballast Water Conference, participating States agreed on a time schedule for the application of Ballast Water Performance Standard in Regulation B-3 with fixed dates of application (i.e., 2014 and 2016) rather than linking the time schedule for application to the date of entry into force of the BWMC 2004. The States argued that manufacturers of BWMS could only be motivated to intensify their efforts to develop and produce adequate BWMS when urged by an ambitious schedule of application with fixed dates.[93] States reasoned that only

---

90   IMO, "Guidance on Ballast Water Sampling and Analysis for Trial Use in Accordance with the BWM Convention and Guidelines (G2)," Doc. BWM.2/Circ.42, 24 May 2013.

91   Id. Annex I, p. 1.

92   Tsimplis, n. 86 above, pp. 424–426.

93   IMO, "Ballast Water Management for Ships – Regulation B-3 – Submitted by the United States," Doc. BWM/CONF/13, 5 January 2004, p. 1, para. 2; IMO, "Comments on the Draft International Convention for the Control and Management of Ships' Ballast Water and Sediments – Submitted by Norway," Doc. BWM/CONF/21, 22 January 2004, p. 4, para. 4.

a fixed schedule could provide the impetus necessary to develop solutions to outstanding problems within MEPC.[94]

More than ten years after the adoption of the BWMC 2004, the fixed time schedule in Regulation B-3 of the Annex is outdated. If the BWMC 2004 entered into force in 2014, the D-2 Standard would have been applicable to most of the existing and to all new vessels without an adequate transition period. Shipyards worldwide and manufacturers of BWMS currently do not have sufficient capacity for retrofitting the existing fleet of merchant vessels within one year. Accordingly, a high percentage of ships would be unable to comply with the D-2 Standard.[95] This problem led major flag States to consider not ratifying the BWMC 2004 under current circumstances.[96] For these reasons, the IMO decided to amend the time schedule in Regulation B-3 and insert new provisions that allow for flexible application in connection with the date of entry into force of the BWMC 2004.

From a legal perspective, the challenge for the MEPC was to adopt these amendments in a way that ensured their binding character for all State parties and also allowed these amendments to become effective in the shortest possible time period. Regulation B-3 was amended to accelerate the entry into force of the BWMC 2004. The MEPC discussed three options for amendments: (1) the adoption of an Assembly resolution which recommends that future State parties deposit a reservation concerning the new schedule, (2) the provisional application of the amendment procedure in Article 19 of BWMC 2004, and (3) the adoption of a resolution by the IMO Assembly which recommends the application of a new schedule.[97] After considering the legal consequences

---

94   IMO, "Comments on the Draft Convention – Submitted by the Netherlands," Doc. BWM/CONF/18, 20 January 2004, p. 4, para. 13; IMO, "Comments and Proposals on the Draft Convention – Submitted by Croatia," Doc. BWM/CONF/8, 25 November 2003, p. 2, para. 10.

95   It is estimated that 10,000 BWMS have to be installed per year in order to retrofit all existing vessels, IMO, "Preview of Global Ballast Water Treatment Markets – Submitted by the Institute of Marine Engineering, Science and Technology (IMarEST)," Doc. MEPC 63/INF.11, 23 December 2011, p. 5, para. 8; IMO, "Information for Examination and Analysis of the Applicable Requirements for Vessels Described in Regulation B-3.1 – Submitted by Japan," Doc. MEPC 61/2/17, 23 July 2010, p. 3.

96   IMO, "Challenges to Effective Implementation of the BWM Convention – Submitted by Liberia, the Marshall Islands, Panama, BIMCO, INTERTANKO, CLIA, INTERCARGO, InterManager, IPTA, NACE and WSC," Doc. MEPC 64/2/18, 27 July 2012, p. 2, para. 3.

97   IMO, "Report of the Correspondence Group on the Assembly Resolution on Application of the International Convention for the Control and Management of Ships' Ballast Water and Sediments, 2004 – Submitted by Japan," Doc. MEPC 65/2/11, 8 February 2013, p. 13.

of all three options, the MEPC agreed to finalize a draft resolution that contains the third option and to submit this draft resolution to the 28th session of the IMO Assembly.[98] In November 2013, the Assembly adopted Resolution A(28) 1088 with the new time schedule amending Regulation B-3 of the Annex of the BWMC 2004.[99]

As noted, the negotiating States agreed to follow the third option and to adopt a resolution in the IMO Assembly containing a recommendation for a relaxed enforcement schedule for compliance with the Ballast Water Standards in Regulation B-3.[100] The main advantage of this approach is that the State parties are not required to rely on the provisional application of a treaty provision under Article 25 of the Vienna Convention on the Law of Treaties (Vienna Convention)[101] or on the reservations of States, which leads to greater legal certainty for amending the BWMC 2004. The adopted Assembly Resolution A(28) 1088 contains a new schedule with relaxed transition periods for existing and new ships with regard to the application of the Ballast Water Standards in Regulations D-1 and D-2. The Resolution 'recommends' that State parties enforce the Ballast Water Standards in accordance with the new schedule, notwithstanding the existing schedule set forth in Regulation B-3. Legally, the Assembly Resolution neither amends the BWMC 2004 nor modifies the relations between the State parties, but simply recommends implementing the new schedule instead of the existing schedule that has been adopted as part of the BWMC 2004. This leads to the question, if and to what extent is the new schedule legally binding? With regard to resolutions adopted by the IMO Assembly, it can generally be said that these resolutions have no legal effect on IMO member States. The IMO has no legislative powers. Therefore, the member States are not obliged to comply with resolutions by the Assembly and/or the MEPC. Nevertheless, Resolution A(28) 1088 constitutes a kind of agreement between the States present and voting at the Assembly session. At the time the BWMC 2004 finally enters into force, the States parties are bound to this agreement under the general rule of Article 31(3)lit. (a) of the Vienna Convention, which states that "any subsequent agreement between the parties regarding the

---

98   IMO, "Report of the MEPC on its Sixty-Fifth Session," Doc. MEPC 65/22, 24 May 2013, p. 11, para. 2.30.

99   IMO, "Application of the International Convention for the Control and Management of Ships' Ballast Water and Sediments, 2004," Assembly Resolution A(28) 1088, adopted on 4 December 2013.

100   Id., p. 2, para. 2.

101   Vienna Convention on the Law of Treaties, adopted on 23 May 1969, entered into force 27 January 1980, 1155 *United Nations Treaty Series* 331 (1980).

interpretation of the treaty or the application of its provisions shall be taken into account when interpreting the treaty."[102] State parties may not enforce the BWMC 2004 in the wording of 2004 with the 'old schedule' in Regulation B-3 but are obliged, under Article 31(3)lit. a) of the Vienna Convention, to enforce the BWMC 2004 in line with the 'new schedule' contained in IMO Resolution A(28) 1088. Through Resolution A(28) 1088, the BWMC 2004 is modified prior to its entry into force without amending the Convention itself and the time schedule in Regulation B-3 in the legal sense and without applying the formal amendment procedure in Article 19 of BWMC 2004. This 'evolution' of the BWMC 2004 ensures legal certainty and confidence in the future application of the BWMC and assists the shipping industry in the timely planning of their operations. In addition, it encourages the early installation of BWMS.

Port State Control as a Barrier to the Entry into Force of the BWMC 2004

Although the modification of the time schedule in Regulation B-3 of the Annex was amended in 2013, the issue of enforcement through port States remains a major challenge that can be considered as a barrier to the early ratification and accession of BWMC 2004 by major flag States. In principle, the enforcement of BWMC 2004 is based on two pillars. The first pillar is the principle of primary flag State jurisdiction, one of the central principles of the law of the sea and laid down in Article 92 of UNCLOS. Regulation E of the Annex of the BWMC 2004 contains details about the enforcement of the provisions of BWMC 2004 through flag States by the means of issuance of the International Ballast Water Management Certificate (IBWMC). The system of survey and certification under BWMC 2004 is similar to the system of flag State jurisdiction under MARPOL 73/78, especially since the application dates in Regulation B-3 of the Annex are connected with the issuance of the International Oil Pollution Prevention Certificate (IOPPC) under Regulations 6–11, Annex I, MARPOL 73/78.[103] Generally, enforcement by flag States poses no new challenges, since this system of enforcement is well-accepted in conventions on marine environmental protection. The second pillar of enforcement of the BWMC 2004 constitutes port State control (Article 9 of BWMC 2004). The system of PSC is controversial due to the disputed balance between the jurisdiction of flag

---

102   IMO, "Legal Advice on the Draft Assembly Resolution on the Application of the BWM Convention – Note by the Secretariat," Doc. MEPC 65/2/18, 8 March 2013, p. 4, para. 16.

103   IMO, n. 99 above, p. 2, para. 2.6.

States and port States over ships in ports. Until the exact scope and extent of PSC under Article 9 is finalized, shipowners will continue to face legal uncertainties with regard to ship inspections in ports and the sampling procedures of ballast water by national administrations. The adoption of final guidelines on PSC through the MEPC during its next session is necessary to provide confidence for flag States and shipowners and to fulfill the interest of port States in comprehensive ship inspections.

MEPC Guidelines on Port State Control and Ballast Water Sampling

The MEPC and the competent sub-committees on Flag State Implementation (FSI, now: Implementation of IMO Instruments or III) and Bulk, Liquids and Gases (BLG, now: Pollution Prevention and Response or PPR) are currently working on Guidelines on Port State Control and Ballast Water Sampling under the BWMC 2004. The term 'PSC Guidelines' refers to two distinct areas of regulation. The first area relates to the general procedures of PSC through inspections in ports by port State control officers (PSCOs) under Article 9, while the second area comprises the sampling and analysis of ballast water in order to establish a vessel's non-compliance, especially with regard to Guideline G-2 for ballast water sampling. Sub-committee III is competent for the compilation of guidelines for PSC under the BWM Convention and must refrain "from discussing any ballast water sampling or analysis methodology until the appropriate methodology or protocols have been agreed by IMO."[104] The original plan was to adopt the PSC Guidelines by 2006,[105] but after the presentation of the first draft in 2010,[106] it became obvious that more time was needed to address all related issues. The finalization of consultations in Sub-committee III chaired by Canada is expected in 2015,[107] and the final PSC Guidelines might be adopted before the BWMC 2004 enters into force.[108] In 2013, the MEPC 65 adopted the "Guidance on Ballast Water Sampling and Analysis for Trial Use in Accordance

---

104 IMO, "Report to the MSC and the MEPC," Doc. FSI 21/18, 7 March 2013, p. 24, para. 8.8.2.

105 IMO, "Report of the Marine Environmental Protection Committee on its Fifty-Second Session," Doc. MEPC 52/24/Add.1, 1 November 2004, Annex 12: Work Programme for the Sub-Committee on Flag State Implementation (FSI).

106 IMO, "Harmonization of Port State Control Activities – Report of the Correspondence Group – Submitted by Australia," Doc. FSI 19/6, 19 November 2010, Annex 3.

107 IMO, n. 104 above, p. 24, para. 8.7–8.8.

108 IMO, "Report of the MEPC on its Sixty-First Session," Doc. MEPC 61/24, 6 October 2010, Annex 18: Biennial Agenda of the Sub-Committee on Flag State Implementation (FSI) and provisional Agenda for FSI 19; IMO, "Report of the MEPC on its Sixty-Fifth Session," Doc. MEPC 65/22/Add.1, 29 May 2013, Annex 44: Biennial Agenda of the Sub-Committee on Flag State Implementation (FSI) and Provisional Agenda for FSI 22 (deadline: 2015).

with the BWM Convention and Guidelines (G2)," developed by the competent Sub-committee BLG and disseminated as Circular 42 to all IMO member States.[109] In the following sections, the procedures under both the draft Guidelines on PSC and the circular on ballast water sampling are described and controversial issues with respect to the BWMC 2004 underlined.

Extent and Procedures of PSC under the Draft FSI Guidelines

The legal framework for the inspection of vessels in ports through PSCOs is laid down in Article 9 of BWMC 2004. The draft Guidelines on PSC contain specified procedures for inspection, define central terms such as 'initial' or 'detailed inspection', and describe the conditions under which the detention of a ship in port is allowed. These definitions supplement the text of the BWMC 2004, which does not specify these central terms and procedures. At the outset, PSCOs may only conduct an initial inspection of the ship in port. The initial inspection comprises the validation of all relevant certificates and documents onboard the ship. These include the IBWMC issued by the flag State of the ship, the BWMP, the Type Approval Certificate issued by the administration of the flag State or by a competent organization, and the BWRB.[110] The PSCO may also check the salinity of random ballast tanks in order to evaluate the effectiveness of the BWE or take indicative sampling and analysis of the ballast water discharge if the BWMS of the ship is not fitted with an onboard monitoring system indicating BWMS failure.[111] The initial inspection by the PSCO is confined to the above if the general impressions and visual observations on board confirm a good standard of maintenance with regard to the Convention. If, however, the initial inspection indicates that the ship presents a threat of harm to the environment, human health, property or resources, the PSCO should take steps to ensure the ship does not discharge ballast water until it can do so without further threat. The master of the ship may be directed to repair the BWMS, to retain part or all ballast water on board, exchange ballast water in a designated area, to discharge ballast water to a shore reception facility, or to treat the ballast water in accordance with an emergency ballast water treatment method approved by the port administration.[112]

---

109   IMO, "Report to the MSC and to the MEPC," Doc. BLG 17/18, 8 February 2013, Annex 5; IMO, n. 90 above; ClassNK, "Introduction to the Outcomes of MEPC 65," Technical Information TEC-0958, 18 July 2013, available online: <http://www.classnk.or.jp/hp/pdf/tech_info/tech_img/T958e.pdf>.

110   IMO, n. 106 above, Annex 3, pp. 1–2, para. 4.1.

111   Id.

112   Id., Annex 3, p. 4, para. 5.2.

A more detailed inspection may be warranted in cases where the ship presents a threat during the initial inspection. Grounds for finding that the ship presents a threat include, but are not restricted to, the identification of the ship as a potential risk to the environment or to the State; the absence of valid documents and certificates as described above; false entries in the BWRB; evidence or observation that the crew is not familiar with its duties; the condition of the ship or its equipment does not correspond substantially with the particulars of the certificate; the ballast water management performed is not in compliance with the application dates set out in Regulation B-3 of the Annex, or if information from third parties such as a report or complaint concerning violation of the Convention (Article 10(4)) has been received.[113] While conducting a more detailed inspection, the PSCO should verify that the BWMP is in accordance with the requirements in Guidelines G-4,[114] and that these requirements are understood by the master and crew. Depending on the indications from the initial and detailed inspections, the PSCO may require a representative sample and analysis of the ballast water discharge. Such sampling is to be conducted by a person recognized as being competent to sample a ship in accordance with the IMO Guidelines for Ballast Water Sampling (G2) and in accordance with the Protocols for Sampling and Analysis as developed by BLG and adopted through MEPC.[115] Without going into the technical and scientific details of sampling procedures, it can be said that the Protocols for Sampling and Analysis describe central terms, i.e., 'indicative', 'representative sample' or 'detailed analysis' and provide general recommendations on methodologies and approaches to sampling and analysis when testing for compliance with Regulations D-1 and D-2. The Protocols for Sampling and Analysis should therefore be read in conjunction with Guidelines G-2 on ballast water sampling, as only the interaction of both documents provides information on all requirements for sampling and analysis of ballast water and legal certainty for the detention of ships as a reaction to non-compliance.

The detention of a ship may be warranted as an enforcement measure by a competent PSCO in several cases, including the absence of a valid IBWMC, BWMP or BWRB, the indication that the vessel or its equipment does not correspond substantially with the particulars of the IBWMC, the designated officer of the vessel is not familiar with essential shipboard procedures relating to ballast water management, no ballast water management procedures have

---

113   Id., Annex 3, p. 2, para. 4.2.

114   IMO, "Guidelines for Ballast Water Management and Development of Ballast Water Management Plans (G4)," Doc. MEPC.127(53), 22 July 2005.

115   IMO, n. 90 above.

been implemented on board at all, the ship has not adhered to its BWMP, and finally, if sampling indicates a failure of the BWMS and the master has not taken action to prevent discharge of ballast water that may pose a threat to the environment, human health, property or resources.[116] Alternatively, the PSCO may permit a vessel to sail with deficiencies which do not pose an unreasonable threat of harm to the marine environment and the ship or crew.[117]

Controversial Issues of the Designated PSC System under the BWMC 2004

Before the MEPC can adopt final guidelines on PSC that cover both the procedures of PSC and the details on sampling and the analysis of ballast water for compliance purposes, several controversial issues remain which require resolution. These issues include the wording of Article 9 with regard to initial and detailed inspections, scientific uncertainties of sampling, and differences between methodologies of sampling for testing and for compliance purposes.

The wording of Article 9(1) describes measures that the PSCO can apply during the initial ship inspection. These compliance measures relate to the verification of documents and certificates (IBWMC, BWMP) as laid out above and provide the possibility for State parties to sample ballast water (Article 9(1) lit. c). Article 9 of BWMC 2004 implicitly recognizes the need for an efficient and practicable implementation of sampling procedures, since Article 9(1) lit. c) stipulates that the "time required for the analysis of ballast water samples shall not be used as a basis for unduly delaying the operation, movement or departure of the ship."[118] In addition, the wording of Article 9 (1) clearly expresses that the decision to sample and analyse a ship's ballast water during the initial inspection depends on the port State's discretion. Accordingly, port States may verify a ship's relevant documents and certificates during inspection procedures 'and/or' take a sample of the ship's ballast water.[119]

The inclusion of port States' right to take ballast water samples during the initial procedures appears imbalanced, as the procedures for 'detailed

---

116   IMO, n. 106 above, Annex 3, pp. 4–5, para. 6.

117   Id., Annex 3, p. 4, para. 6.1.

118   IMO, "Monitoring and Sampling of Certain Ballast Water Management Systems – Submitted by Germany," Doc. MEPC 64/2/15, 27 July 2012, p. 2, para. 5.

119   The expression 'and/or' has been introduced in the Convention text in order to indicate that sampling is not obligatory but an optional inspection method. See IMO, "Comments and Proposals on the Draft Convention – Submitted by Croatia," Doc. BWM/CONF/8, 25 November 2003, p. 2, para. 7; IMO, "Consideration of the Draft International Convention for the Control and Management of Ships' Ballast Water and Sediments – Submitted by Colombia," Doc. BWM/CONF/7, 17 November 2003, p. 2, para. 4.

inspections' under Article 9 (2) are not further specified. Article 9(2) contains only two circumstances that constitute 'clear grounds' for detailed inspections. Having regard to the fact that sampling and the analysis of a ship's ballast water is time-consuming and may take longer than the demurrage in port, including the right to sample and to analyse ballast water only under the procedures for 'detailed inspections' and not under 'initial inspections' would enhance the enforcement of the BWMC 2004. However, the wording of Article 9 is clear and without ambiguity with regard to 'initial and detailed inspections', and the Guidelines on PSC may only specify the extent and procedures of inspections, but cannot amend the wording of Article 9 without applying the formal amendment procedures in Article 19.[120] Until the final entry into force of the BWMC 2004, the formal amendment procedure of the BWMC is inapplicable. The MEPC must therefore find a reasonable interim solution to balance the extent of 'initial' and 'detailed inspections' under Article 9.

Moreover, State parties display concerns regarding the scientific uncertainties of sampling and the analysis of ballast water, which include the representativeness of samples, the lack of standardized procedures for conducting sampling and analysis and the limited level of confidence in the sampling process.[121] MEPC has already adopted the Guidelines for Ballast Water Sampling (G-2), which should provide "practical and technical guidance for the purpose of determining whether a ship is in compliance." However, the Guidelines only stipulate minimum requirements and lack a detailed sampling and analysis protocol. This protocol is yet to be developed through testing and analysis by laboratories, national administrations, and manufacturers of BWMS and requires standardization through MEPC to be valid under Article 9.

In addition, the concern was expressed that there is "the potential for properly used and maintained Type Approved [BWMS] being found non-compliant when assessed in accordance with the circular [Circular 42]."[122] During the testing procedures under Guidelines G-8 and G-9, all BWMS are tested to prove their ability and efficiency to comply with the requirements of the quality standard in Regulation D-2. For these purposes, treated ballast water is sampled during land-based and ship-based testing patterns and subsequently analysed. The results of this analysis constitute the basis for the decisions of

---

120   However, during the negotiations within MEPC it became clear that sampling should be a method of "detailed inspections" and not "initial inspections" of vessels. See IMO, "Outstanding Issues – Submitted by the United States," Doc. BWM/CONF/12, 5 January 2004, p. 2, para. 5.

121   IMO, n. 96 above, p. 2, para. 3.

122   Id., p. 6, para. 21.

national administrations or recognized organizations to grant or to deny a type approval for a BWMS. Therefore, it is crucial "that sampling and analysis procedures for port State control should be no more stringent than what is required for Type Approval of ballast water management systems."[123] Otherwise, it is probable that the BWMS aboard ships will be found to infringe the D-2 Standard, despite the fact that the potential for compliance has been previously certified.

The enforcement of the BWMC 2004 should be focused on "more rigorous Type Approval procedure and not in enforcement measures which go beyond the original testing parameters of the equipment."[124] However, the adjustment and harmonization of sampling and analysis procedures under Guideline G-8 and the Guidelines on PSC would require the amendment of Guideline G-8 and result in lengthy discussions and negotiations within MEPC and its sub-committees. For these reasons, MEPC 66 opposed current proposals from the shipping industry to amend Guideline G-8.[125]

In order to find a feasible solution for these concerns, State parties agreed during MEPC 64 to finalize the Guidelines on PSC under Article 9 as soon as possible and that "sampling for port State control should be no more stringent than the sampling used for type approval of a BWMS," enhancing legal certainty for manufacturers and shipowners.[126] In addition, certain delegations proposed that the results of sampling and analysis of ballast water for compliance purposes should not be used alone as a basis for enforcement measures such as criminal sanctions against officers or crew members.[127] Until final Guidelines on PSC and protocols for sampling and analysis are adopted, the principle of "no criminal sanctions solely on the basis of sampling" shall be applied, which means that "for ships that meet the requirements of the BWMC 2004, port States would refrain from initiating proceedings in accordance with their laws on the basis of sampling the ballast water discharge alone."[128]

---

123   IMO, "Report of the MEPC on its Sixty-Fourth Session," Doc. MEPC 64/23, 11 October 2012, p. 12, para. 2.36.

124   IMO, n. 96 above, p. 7, para. 23.

125   IMO, "The Continuing Compelling Need to Amend the Guidelines for Approval of Ballast Water Management Systems (G8) to ensure success of the BWM Convention – Submitted by ICS, BIMCO, INTERTANKO, INTERCARGO and WSC," Doc. MEPC 66/2/11, 24 January 2014, p. 3, para. 10.

126   IMO, n. 109 above, Annex 6, p. 1.

127   IMO, n. 98 above, p. 13, para. 2.43.

128   IMO, "Further Comments and Details on the Monitoring and Sampling of Certain Ballast Water Management Systems – Submitted by Germany," Doc. BLG 17/4/2, 30 November 2012, p. 2, para. 2.

Proceedings should still be taken if other violations of the BWMC 2004 occur, such as lack of an IBWMC or a BWMP or wrongful entries in the BWRB.

The BLG sub-committee considered these proposals and agreed in general that "the traditional port State control inspection practice and procedures should be maintained" and that "since the legal base of sampling is contained in Article 9, the legitimate right of a port State cannot be denied unless other alternative enforcement options are in place."[129] It was also agreed that criminal sanctions should not be based on the results of sampling and analysis of ballast water alone during a period of two to three years after the final entry into force of the BWMC 2004.[130]

In other words, emerging from MEPC 64, the right of port States to inspect ships under Article 9 remained intact. However, the BLG sub-committee proposed that sampling and analysis of ballast water should not be a central part of inspection procedures until uniform protocols are adopted through MEPC. During a 'trial period' of two or three years following the entry into force of the BWMC 2004, port States can apply the procedures for sampling and analysis as contained in Circular 42 in order to gather data and experience for future protocols and enforcement measures.[131] However, during the trial period, port States should "refrain from applying criminal sanctions or detaining the ship, based on sampling" alone. Port States would still have the right to take preventive measures to protect the environment, human health, property or resources, so proceedings could still be taken if other violations of the BWMC 2004 occur, such as lack of an IBWMC or a BWMP or wrongful entries in the BWRB.[132]

Concerning the controversial issues of PSC, the MEPC follows a two-tiered approach: the development and adoption of detailed final Guidelines on PSC in the near future and the application of sampling and testing protocols on an interim basis during a trial period of between two to three years without the application of enforcement measures such as detentions of ships or criminal proceedings. Following the trial period, the MEPC must nevertheless agree on final protocols for testing of BWMS and sampling and analysis of ballast water for compliance purposes. However, based on data and experience gathered during the trial period, such a protocol can be more robust and provide more

---

129   IMO, n. 109 above, p. 12, para 4.13.

130   Id., p. 14, para 4.22.

131   Id., Annex 6, p. 1.

132   MEPC, n. 118 above, p. 3, para. 9. The United States reserved its position on the suggested principle of "No criminal sanctions solely on the basis of sampling," refraining from applying criminal sanctions or detaining ships on the basis of sampling during the trial period. See IMO, n. 98, above, p. 13, para. 2.44.

scientific and legal certainty when adopted in the future. The intent of this approach is to encourage major flag States to ratify the BWMC 2004 so that its final entry into force can be attained in the foreseeable future, since the concept of PSC is still under review but aims at comprehensive procedures that give effect to the interests of both flag and port States.

Once the PSC Guidelines and the protocol on sampling and analysis are adopted, the comprehensive international system of PSC can be used in order to verify compliance with the BWMC 2004 through inspections in ports.[133] This PSC system has been established through various regional memorandums of understanding (MoU) on port State control between national port authorities.[134] Under these voluntary agreements,[135] national maritime authorities should maintain an effective system of PSC and ensure that vessels under foreign flags comply with the international standards laid down in the relevant international conventions.[136] For instance, the BWMC 2004 is included under the 1982 Paris MoU on Port State Control, so once the Convention enters into force, the national maritime authorities under the 1982 Paris MoU will give effect to the ballast water standards through inspections in port taking into account the PSC Guidelines and protocol on sampling and analysis of ballast water. The effective implementation of the BWMC 2004 is therefore not only dependent on flag State jurisdiction but will additionally be fostered through port State control with uniform inspection standards.

Conclusion

The entry into force of the BWMC 2004 more than ten years after its adoption through the International Ballast Water Conference will be a 'milestone' for the

---

133   Y. Tanaka, *The International Law of the Sea* (Cambridge, New York: Cambridge University Press, 2012), p. 286.

134   M. Gavouneli, *Functional Jurisdiction in the Law of the Sea* (Leiden: Martinus Nijhoff, 2007), p. 48. To date, nine regional MoUs on PSC have been established: the 1982 Paris MoU; the 1992 Viña del Mar Agreement (Latin America); the 1993 Tokyo MoU (Asia-Pacific); the 1996 Caribbean MoU; the 1997 Mediterranean MoU; the 1998 Indian Ocean MoU; the 1999 Abuja MoU (West and Central Africa); the 2000 Black Sea MoU; and the 2004 Riyadh MoU (Arab States of the Gulf).

135   Only the 1982 Paris MoU is mandatory and only for the Member States of the European Union, see Council Directive 95/21/EC of 19 June 1995, as amended through Directive 2001/106/EC of 19 December 2001.

136   R. Schiferli, "Regional Concepts of Port State Control: A Regional Effort with Global Effects," *Ocean Yearbook* 11 (1994): 202–217 at 204.

international regulation of HAOP and the protection of aquatic ecosystems. The ongoing process of 'evolution' of the BWMC 2004 is necessary, on the one hand, to articulate certain details of the Convention, i.e., the type approval of BWMS, the requirements to grant exemptions or to adopt more stringent measures in special areas. On the other hand, the evolution of the BWMC 2004 is necessary to remove barriers for its accelerated entry into force. An example of such a barrier and its removal is present in the replacement of the time schedule for application of the D-2 Standard in Regulation B-3 with a new, flexible time schedule based on the date of the entry into force of the BWMC 2004. When the BWMC 2004 comes into effect, the formal amendment procedure can be applied and amendments may be adopted more easily after consideration within MEPC through the tacit acceptance procedure. The entry into force of the Convention will lead to more legal certainty with respect to the application dates of the D-2 Standard, provide more confidence for investments in new BWMS and the retrofitting of existing ships, and allow the development of a global market for BWMS. One remaining challenge is the issue of PSC under Article 9. However, following the adoption of final Guidelines on PSC and protocols for sampling and analysis of ballast water in the future, no further reasonable grounds for the non-ratification of the BWMC 2004 may be put forward by State non-parties.

Book Reviews

∵

Tundi Agardy, *Ocean Zoning: Making Marine Management More Effective*
(London and Washington, D.C.: Earthscan 2010), xi, 220 pp.

Global and regional assessments of marine environmental status detail,
amongst other things, the continuing decline of marine biodiversity, the transformation of food webs, increasing marine pollution, and the acidification and
warming of the world's oceans. It is widely acknowledged that there needs
to be a radical reimagining of marine resource management if these problems are to be addressed. In *Ocean Zoning: Making Marine Management More
Effective,* Tundi Agardy argues that 'place' should play a central part in efforts
to develop innovative marine governance solutions to these problems. The
author argues that place matters, for various reasons, to marine planners,
managers, conservationists, and users, and that comprehensive ocean zoning
and marine spatial planning (MSP) allows us to be cognizant of the immense
value attached to coastal and marine places. The aim of this book is to provide
an overview of ocean zoning and marine spatial planning and to illustrate key
concepts and innovative practices through in-depth case studies.

The book can be divided in to three sections. Chapters 1–3 deal with the 'why'
and 'how' of ocean zoning. Section Two provides an account of ocean zoning
in practice. This section contains ten short chapters. Chapters 4–12 consist of
short case studies of ocean zoning from around the world, with Chapter 13
drawing together the key principles and concepts explored in each case study.
The final section contains two chapters that address issues relating to implementation and governance and summarizes the main points of the book.

The book begins with a synopsis of some of the most urgent marine
management issues facing coastal nations. Chapter 1 describes the physical,
biological, and chemical transformations wrought on marine and coastal
environments by human activity. Agardy postulates that addressing marine
governance fragmentation should be the top priority for those seeking to undo
or halt marine degradation. Ocean zoning is then advanced as a possible solution to this issue. Agardy argues that zoning has been repeatedly advanced as
an answer to these issues but that marine planners and conservationists often
circle around the topic without fully engaging with it. Therefore, until quite
recently, comprehensive ocean zoning has largely remained an idea rather

Ocean Yearbook 29: 475–527
© KONINKLIJKE BRILL NV, LEIDEN, 2015 | DOI 10.1163/9789004297234_020

than a practice. The rest of the chapter then traces the development of ocean zoning, from individual marine protected areas (MPAs), through networked MPAs to full scale ocean zoning. The chapter makes a convincing argument for the adoption of ocean zoning and is one of the strongest chapters in the book.

The second chapter provides an account of some of the challenges that may arise when adopting a zoning approach. Some of the challenges highlighted in the chapter include issues relating to scale; tackling property rights and the displacement of fishers; zoning in dynamic environments, particularly off-shore areas; and counteracting negative public perception. The chapter points the reader towards some interesting real world examples where these issues have occurred and other related studies.

In the third chapter, Agardy argues that ocean zoning is a process not a product. The zoning process consists of three distinct phases: visioning, planning, and implementation. The chapter then walks the reader through each phase and then discusses why MPAs are often the starting point in the ocean zoning process. This final section of the chapter seems a little out of place here and may have been better placed in Chapter 1.

The chapters in the second section of the book vary in quality. Chapter 4 provides an excellent account of the zoning process undertaken within the Great Barrier Reef Marine Park. This chapter details the operating principles adopted by the Great Barrier Reef Marine Park Authority (GBRMPA), as well as the legal framework within which zoning took place. The chapter also highlights how the GBRMPA team addressed some of the challenges outlined in Chapter 2. Chapter 5 provides a good account of various zoning initiatives in New Zealand and highlights some of the political and social realities of introducing marine and coastal zoning.

Chapters 6, 7, 10, 11, and 12, which outline marine management initiatives in the United Kingdom, Northeast Atlantic, Africa, Canada, the United States, respectively, are the weakest case studies in this section. Many of these chapters are highly descriptive and are lacking in detail. Part of the reason for this lack of detail and in-depth analysis is that some chapters describe processes that were at a very embryonic stage when this book was published. For example, Chapter 6 outlines the marine management framework that was emerging in the United Kingdom at the time the book was written. Other chapters, such as the chapters on Africa, Canada, and the United States, contain a number of mini case studies that provide only a brief description of each planning initiative. The chapter on zoning in Africa, for example, describes five different initiatives but only contains approximately nine pages of text. A more selective, in-depth approach in these chapters may have been more beneficial than describing the varying zoning initiatives underway within each country.

Chapter 8, which describes the zoning of the Asinara Marine Park of Italy, is the standout chapter of the book. This chapter is rich in detail and provides valuable insight into the comprehensive zoning process undertaken within the park. Agardy was part of the team which undertook this zoning process. This firsthand experience shines through in the chapter, as she leads the reader through the zoning process.

Section Two concludes with a chapter that describes the principles underscoring ocean zoning success. This chapter begins by drawing together some of the key lessons derived from the proceeding case studies. The chapter then outlines the European Commission's (EC) principles for MSP. These principles are not discussed in-depth nor are they related to the good practice lessons derived from the case studies. The addition of the EC's MSP principles seems a little unnecessary here and distracted a little from the core ideas advanced in the chapter. The chapter concludes with a brief discussion of 12 additional zoning principles derived from the case studies described in the book and from other MSP initiatives in various parts of the world. This makes it a little difficult for the reader to make the link between some of these lessons and the preceding case studies. It would have been useful to link particular lessons with particular case studies or to point the reader towards other relevant initiatives. Due to the absence of this information the reader is left wondering where these lessons were derived from.

Chapter 14 provides an excellent overview of the challenges of transition from planning to implementation within the zoning process and pays particular attention to governance issues. The final chapter reiterates some of the core arguments from section one and argues that ocean zoning makes sense. The chapter concludes with a call for States to show true leadership and to take on the challenge of ocean zoning – while it may be challenging, Agardy assures the reader that it will have been well worth the trouble.

Overall, this book provides a good introduction to ocean zoning. The book will be of most value to those new to this discipline. While those familiar with marine zoning and spatial planning may yearn for more detail in some of the case study chapters, they will undoubtedly appreciate the more comprehensive case studies.

Wesley Flannery, Ph.D.
Lecturer in Environmental Planning
Queen's University Belfast
Belfast, Northern Ireland

David Freestone, ed., *The 1982 Law of the Sea Convention at 30: Successes, Challenges and New Agendas* (Leiden/Boston: Martinus Nijhoff Publishers, 2013), 211 pp.

This book reproduces the contents of a special issue of *The International Journal of Marine and Coastal Law* (vol. 27, 2012, pp. 675–882) with the addition of an index and tables of cases and treaties. To make this material available in book form seems to me a very good idea, as it is one of the best collective reflections on UNCLOS thirty years after its opening to signature and almost twenty after its entry into force. It continues a discourse started in 1995 with the publication (edited by the same editor of the present book, David Freestone, and the late Gerard Mangone) of a special issue of the same journal entitled "The Law of the Sea Convention: Unfinished Agendas and Future Challenges" (10 IJMCL, 1995, pp. 157–334).

The book includes nineteen chapters authored by distinguished scholars of various generations and countries, preceded by an opening chapter by David Freestone and a closing chapter by Vaughn Lowe.

The opening chapter is entitled "Successes, Challenges and Open Agendas" of UNCLOS at 30. In David Freestone's view, the successes of the Convention concern especially its impact on customary law ("the main provisions of the Convention may now be regarded as customary law," p. 3); its contribution to the protection of the marine environment ("no discussion of marine environmental law can properly start without acknowledging the unparalleled and unequivocal obligation of Article 192 to 'preserve and protect the marine environment'," ibid.); and the consolidation of the institutions set up by the Convention. Although the work of the International Tribunal for the Law of the Sea is acknowledged in the introductory essay and in various essays in the book (see in particular the observations by Stephens and Rothwell, at p. 30f.), there is no insistence on the importance of the acceptance in the Convention of the principle of compulsory settlement of disputes. This seems to me one of the major contributions of UNCLOS to the progress of the law, and also a giant step forward as compared to previous codification conventions sponsored by the United Nations.

The concluding essay by Vaughn Lowe bears the challenging short title, "Was it worth the effort?" It is difficult to summarize this brilliant presentation. It is as short as full of thoughtful observations and of pertinent question marks. Vaughn Lowe is brief in evoking the massive effort that brought to the conclusion of the Convention and to what he calls with a remarkable neologism the "postparations" of UNCLOS, namely, the process followed to amend Part XI thus making it possible for most industrialized States to become parties. In answering the question put in the title, very sensibly Lowe observes that it depends on "what it was that one hoped that UNCLOS III would achieve" (p. 202). Such hopes range between a convention providing "reasonably clear answers to those questions that are most likely to arise," a convention setting out "the basic principles of the legal regime...and then letting it develop organically" and a convention based "upon the perception that there are certain key principles whose application must be secured in the face of the threat of erosion from a myriad of what may be apparently innocuous regulations and practices" (ibid.). The treaty-making style of the Convention, according to Lowe, is that of a chimera, in which "monumental, lapidary affirmations of basic principles...sit cheek by jowl with the *petit point* intricacies of article 76... and the still-born Annex III formula for the calculation of the production ceiling for seabed minerals" (p. 203). Lowe remarks that some issues have not been addressed because of their too controversial nature, while others find overabundant consideration. Answering the question whether the Convention has "the right mixture of general principle and detail," Lowe remarks that the need to adopt the 1994 Implementation Agreement "makes plain that the mixture was not optimal" (p. 207). Although uneven, "UNCLOS did succeed in building a comprehensive and remarkably resilient framework regime for the Law of the Sea" (p. 207). It was worth the effort "[i]f the appropriate lessons are learned from what UNCLOS III did well and from what it did badly" (ibid.).

The nineteen essays on specific topics range from the indication of defects or limitations of UNCLOS to its implementation, to subjects not left out of the conventional provisions.

Among essays addressing defects of the convention perhaps the most negative is Tullio Scovazzi's study on UNCLOS and the underwater cultural heritage. It is a radical (perhaps too radical) critique of the regime emerging from Article 303 and a presentation of the UNESCO-sponsored convention of 2001 as a defense against the looting of underwater cultural artifacts in the exclusive economic zone (EEZ) and continental shelf. Another defect of UNCLOS, signaled by Ellen Hey, is the persistence in the rules on fisheries of the notion of 'maximum sustainable yield'. The central role this notion plays in UNCLOS, and its confirmation in the UN Fish Stocks Agreement, point to factors "that are likely to increase pressures on fish stocks" (p. 92). Together with the ecosystem approach, the precautionary approach, adopted by the UN Fish Stocks Agreement, and examined in her essay by Rosemary Rayfuse, is seen also by Ellen Hey as the correct one in order to deal with fisheries.

Ambiguous, in fact intentionally ambiguous, provisions of the Convention have been interpreted differently by differently interested States. A clear example is Article 58(1) as regards military activities in the EEZ. Moritaka Hayashi illustrates this point with examples of incidents in the Asian seas. He also underlines the relevance in this context of the lack of definition of the term 'survey' and of its difference with 'marine scientific research', another undefined term in the UNCLOS. Philomene Verlaan informs about very interesting progress made as regards the definition of marine scientific research within the framework of the London 1972 Dumping Convention and of its 1996 Protocol. The Joint Scientific Groups established by the parties to these conventions have in fact agreed an Assessment Framework to determine whether a proposed activity demonstrate 'proper scientific attributes'. It is to be hoped that this document will be referred to in discussions on the interpretation of the notion of marine scientific research in UNCLOS.

A lacuna in UNCLOS is seen by Martin Tsamenyi and Quentin Hanish as regards rights and jurisdiction on fisheries in areas under the coastal State's sovereignty: internal waters, archipelagic waters, and territorial waters. The applicability of the UN Fish Stocks Agreement to these waters depends on the interpretation of the expression "waters under national jurisdiction" contained in that agreement. Contrary to Edeson's view, the authors hold that the correct interpretation is that these waters are not included in the scope of the Fish Stocks Agreement. They underline, however, that, in the present post-UNCLOS and post-Fish Stocks Agreement period, there is the "need to develop similar compatibility and cooperation provisions for waters under sovereignty for straddling stocks and highly migratory species" (p. 119). This is a remarkable statement that shows that the ecosystem approach, and multilateral treaty making, cannot stop at the borders of the coastal State's sovereignty. Further and more systematic development of this theme is in the essay by Richard Barnes on the prospects of an "Integrated Regulation of the Oceans."

Among the challenges for the future, Alan Boyle examines the implications for the law of the sea of climate change. Irini Papanicolopulu addresses the role of individuals in the law of the sea, a hitherto almost unexplored subject, and an indication that the law of the sea is not a 'self-contained' system and that bridges exist between it and other branches of international law, including human rights law. Kristina Gjerde and Karen N. Sen look at the protection of the marine environment beyond the limits of national jurisdiction respectively in general terms and from the point of view of marine protected areas. Gjerde touches upon the much debated question of a regime for genetic resources beyond the limits of national jurisdiction. While her remarks from the viewpoint of Part XII of UNCLOS are well taken, one regrets that the book does not include an essay dedicated to the last mentioned topic. Perhaps the editor thought that the literature concerning it is already abundant.

The implementation – or non-implementation – of UNCLOS is a theme envisaged in a number of essays. The role of the UN Secretariat is well illustrated in the essay by Tarassenko and Tani, as are those of the International Seabed Authority are in Michael Lodge's chapter, focused on the key notion of the common heritage of mankind. Stephens and Rothwell's assessment of the jurisdictional framework set out by UNCLOS is that it has well resisted pressures emerging especially in the aftermath of 9/11. They specify that there have been "few violations of flag State jurisdiction" and that "[i]nstead, States have sought through consensual arrangements to confer reciprocal rights of interdiction in relation to drug trafficking and fisheries" (p. 33).

Robin Churchill is less optimistic in his essay entitled "The Persisting Problem of Non-compliance with the Law of the Sea Convention: Disorder in the Oceans." Churchill gives, at p. 140f., examples of non-compliance. They include: (a) the drawing by some States of straight baselines which do not meet the requirement of Article 7 (a subject addressed also by Clive Schofield, who, however, sees the practice as due to the imprecision of the article which encourages maximum interpretation – see p. 53); (b) claims by four States of territorial seas exceeding 12 miles; (c) the inclusion by a number of States of security among the items on which they claim to exercise jurisdiction in their contiguous zone; (d) the delimitation of EEZs by some States taking into account inhabitable rocks; (e) non-conformity of a number of flag States with their obligations under Article 94 on the exercise of effective jurisdiction on their ships; (f) violation of the provisions on fisheries in the EEZ and on the high seas as evidenced by well documented data on overfishing; and (g) the failing to take necessary measures to protect and preserve rare or fragile ecosystems under Article 194(4), for instance by failing to prohibit the use of explosives in fishing near tropical reefs. Some of these examples of non-compliance are more important than others, some are more widespread than others; some are beyond discussion, and some are debatable. Still, we have to agree with Churchill's remark that "non-compliance matters," and that it "provokes disputes, denies States parties some of their LOSC rights, threatens good order at sea, and harms the marine environment" (p. 141). The remedies available through existing institutions – the Commission on the Limits of the Continental Shelf, the dispute-settlement bodies provided by the Convention, the UN Security Council – or through mechanisms provided by general international law such as protest, retortion, and countermeasures have some positive results. Churchill considers it useful, nonetheless, to raise the question of new mechanisms, such as a compliance committee to be established within the framework of the Meeting of States Parties. Reasonably, he is not very optimistic about such possibility. The conclusion Churchill reaches in his essay is that the Convention has failed to achieve its goals (p. 146). My view is that this is too harsh a conclusion. Compliance prevails over non-compliance although non-compliance must be fought. The other essays set out in this book, including the opening and concluding ones by Freestone and Lowe, confirm this view.

Tullio Treves
Professor of International Law, State University of Milano
Former Judge of the International Tribunal for the Law of the Sea

---

Duncan French, ed., *Global Justice and Sustainable Development* (Leiden/
Boston: Martinus Nijhoff Publishers, 2010), 416 pp.

Over thirty years after approving Agenda 21 (1992), the full application of the
essential principles for improving the conditions of human life in a situation of
fast growing needs and a world of finite resources remain a formidable challenge. The United Nations Environment Programme notes in its 2012 *Global
Environment Outlook* (GEO-5) report that adverse environmental impacts are
reaching the tipping point amidst the continuing global social and economic
development. Depletion of resources and widening socio-economic gaps
between people are the twin manifestations of the impact. One approach in
addressing this problem is to focus on legal standards that improve human
well-being, particularly on standards of human relationships in both domestic
and international settings. It is in this context that *Global Justice and Sustainable
Development* expounds the contribution of international law to the linkage
between justice and sustainable development. The linkage is indispensable in
the aim for the twofold objective of protecting and conserving natural resources
and improving human development. According to Professor Duncan French
(global) justice and sustainable development are truly mutually supportive
and normatively integrated in local, national, and international human societies. He strongly argues that the understanding of sustainable development
incorporates the innate belief for (global) justice. Further, since both goals are
indivisible, there is no dichotomy, precedence or hierarchy that sets global justice and sustainable development separate from each other.

The book generally explains the linkage between global justice and sustainable development. Professor French points out this linkage through the interplay of fairness, equity, and sustainability in the varied forms and extent of
human relationships. However, these standards are not limited only to human
cohesion but also to the solidarity of States and international organizations as
important actors in international relations. The book further looks at the connection between global justice and sustainable development from the lens of
mutuality, that is, their convergence rather than differences and separation.
This mutuality does not only give precision to the complex legal concept of

justice but also strengthens the argument in favour of the legal guarantees that promote the rights and welfare of vulnerable people and States.

There are nineteen papers comprising the collection in the book. Each paper discusses a different issue classified accordingly under three themes; the twentieth paper serves as a concluding discussion and synthesis. Each theme is part of a sequence of thought that clearly shows the progression of discussions. Starting with the foundational values that build sustainable development and global justice, the book then proceeds with the stipulation of these values in different areas of international law and the approaches to implementing the stipulations by the European Union and particular States. From a reader's perspective, the sequence of discussion can be viewed in the following logical progression: the conception of idea, the development of law, and the realization of the idea through the application of the law. Moreover, although there are cross-cutting discussions of the themes in a number of papers, all the papers tackle the main issues and clearly discuss each theme.

The multiple papers in the book present a multiplicity of perspectives that endeavor to prove the standards of equity, fairness, and sustainability as vital to the interaction between global justice and sustainable development. In Part One, discussions include the role of judicial bodies and stakeholder organizations, the contribution of law and religion, and an historical account on the normative development and practice of sustainability and justice. While it is ordinarily the case for judicial institutions to elucidate on concepts or ideas in its interpretation of existing fragmented domestic or international law, it is compelling to note how religious law ensures sustainable development amidst contesting values. Katja Samuel explains that sustainable development in Islamic law is founded on divine obligation, and the influence of Islamic concepts to the discourse at the United Nations poses a challenge to the development of the concept. The papers of Tim Stephens and Dire Tladi identify the authoritative role of courts in defining the concept of sustainable development in its interpretation of laws. These laws, explains Jaye Ellis using the autopoietic theory, are the products of consensus in a complex social system intended for desired outcomes – such as sustainable development. Stakeholder organizations form part of this social system and they, according to Karen Morrow, contribute to the elaboration of the sustainable development concept. Noteworthy in the above papers at this point is the continuing effort to improve human well-being through effective regulatory regimes, which as pointed out by Etienne Dunant, was desired even in ancient Greece.

Having defined the concept of sustainable development, Part Two discusses the integration of justice and sustainability in modern-day international environmental law. Though the papers discuss a limited number of aspects of international law – climate change, investment, trade, and human rights – particular significant developments in contemporary international law are explained. One of these developments is the transformation of the dominant State role to one where individuals, as emergent actors in international relations, are provided with personal rights. This is the case, as noted by David Ong, with the privatization of international law whereby the solely inter-state procedural obligation to notify, inform, and consult presently extends to include State-individual duty. The value of individual rights can be seen in the case of 'survival migration' or human mobility due to social, economic, and environmental causes as explained by Michèle Morel and Frank Maes. This phenomenon calls for the development of new legal protection and social order that can hurdle political obstacles. As gleaned from the paper of Joyeeta Gupta, a particular social order is needed that will establish an appropriate climate change paradigm to address its impacts and effect equity among countries and peoples. Investment and trade are two important sectors where environmental justice can be realized either as a matter of human rights or opportunity for development. In the adjudication of commercial disputes such as those related to international investment agreements, the apparent division between the prominent role of the State as regulator (suggested by Ximena Fuentes) and consideration for private (human) rights (noted by Owen McIntyre) are both, nonetheless, directed towards public good and sustainable development. According to Freya Baetens, these ends are also justified by the balanced application of non-discrimination rules in trade law to both developing and developed countries. Lastly, Elena Merino Blanco highlights the importance of ecological services and payments for them as economic mechanisms that ensure human environmental rights.

Further proof on global justice-sustainable development linkages continue in Part Three where regional and national experiences are presented. However, while the papers discuss varied approaches, these are limited in presenting a global view as regards the global dimension of justice and sustainable development the book purports to cover. Nonetheless, the case studies presented in the papers clearly explain the linkage of the key concepts. Silke Steiner notes the achievement and problems of the Renewed Sustainable Development Strategy of the European Union, the largest global donor and the only regional organization presented in the book, in addressing the challenges of the connection between global poverty and economic development. At the state level, three papers discuss European experiences, particularly in the United Kingdom: Peter Doran explains the role of individual freedom and the 'consumer citizen' in addressing consumerism and environmental constraints; Ole Pedersen, Aylwin Pillai, and Anne-Michelle Slater indicate that the Scottish government usage of environmental justice and sustainable development manifests the convergence of the two vague concepts; and Andrea Ross argues for legal recognition of sustainable development indicators as established in domestic policy. In Australia, the note of Jennifer McKay on the role of courts in interpreting "Ecologically Sustainable Development" in municipal law reiterates the importance of judicial decisions in establishing jurisprudence for law enforcement. Similarly, in discussing a Chilean experience, Dominique Herve highlights the necessity of incorporating the environmental justice concept in law and its enforcement.

As the book's conclusion, the paper of Suya P. Subedi is a timely review of international law as a measure to regulate State behaviour toward the natural environment. International law is still presently inadequate in regulating the State's exercise of its economic sovereignty particularly in the exploitation of certain high value natural resources. New ideas and experiences that extend the discussion on the value of international law provide needed insights for deeper understanding and valuation of the standards of justice and sustainable development. Professor Subedi's conclusion reiterates the eternal essence of (international environmental) law, that is, to protect the (global) environment and provide (economic) justice.

The book's collection of papers written by legal scientists and practitioners provides relevant insights and practical experience on the justice-sustainable development linkage. Apart from legal scientists and practitioners, the book is a useful reference for students studying international environmental law either as a sole subject or integrated with different disciplines. Moreover, the information in the book on the developments in international law as regards achieving the standards of justice and environmental protection is consistent with one of the main points in the GEO-5 report: that while international law is successful in addressing a broad range of environmental challenges, there is urgent need to strengthen it by aiming on targets that produce quantifiable results. This will mean the formulation and enforcement of regulations that, from the reflection of Professor French, are measurable and founded on the concept of justice and the overarching principles of sustainable development.

Joseph Anthony Loot
Interdisciplinary Studies Ph.D. Candidate
Dalhousie University
Halifax, Nova Scotia, Canada

Erik J. Molenaar, Alex G. Oude Elferink, and Donald R. Rothwell, eds., *The Law of the Sea and the Polar Regions: Interactions between Global and Regional*

Regimes (Leiden/Boston: Martinus Nijhoff Publishers, 2013), Publications on Ocean Development, Volume 76, 432 pp.

The Law of the Sea and the Polar Regions is a good book and is well worth reading. The authors and editors comprise an expert group with different backgrounds. This follow-up to the 2001 book project, *The Law of the Sea and Polar Maritime Delimitation and Jurisdiction*, is a pleasure to read from the beginning to the end. The book was developed by the authors in a seminar and seems coherent and systematically prepared. It does not pretend to say all that could be said about the theme, but what it says is generally interesting. This volume is not intended to be a handbook – the table of cases includes only ten cases – but it does present a number of interesting observations and an overview of a number of issues.

The first three chapters set the scene. The editors' introduction, "The Regional Implementation of the Law of the Sea and the Polar Regions" is followed by articles on the "Arctic Treaty System" by Shirley V. Scott and "The Developing Regional Regime for the Marine Arctic" by Betsy Baker. While the latter title seems to suggest that a regime akin to the Antarctic Treaty System is developing in the North, that situation neither seems to be true nor is it argued in the article.

"The Outer Limits of the Continental Shelf in the Polar Regions" is dealt with by Alex Oude Elferink in Chapter 4. The focus of this chapter, naturally, is the Arctic, as even territorial claims are disputed in the Antarctic, and exploitation seems more imminent in the North than in the South. This chapter gives an overview more concentrated on the process than on the principles. There are still many years until the Commission on the Limits of the Continental Shelf completes its work. Some wonder whether conflicts that might arise before the process has been finished should be addressed and, if so, how they should be resolved.

Marine protected areas in the Arctic and Antarctic are discussed by Suzanne Lalonde in Chapter 5 and Karen N. Scott in Chapter 6, respectively. It appears that the use of this regulatory technique is disproportionate to the alleged special vulnerability in these regions, perhaps especially in the Arctic. Robin Warner's chapter on environmental assessments as another approach to protecting the environment ties in well with this theme. While marine protected areas typically require command and control type rules, environmental assessments, by their nature, are procedural and are not meaningful unless the needed effort is put into conducting the assessment and considering the knowledge acquired. I note that observations along these lines are not the focus of the authors.

Laura Boone deals with "International Regulation of Polar Shipping" in Chapter 9, which is somewhat misplaced between chapters on migratory species and fisheries. I expected a more thorough discussion of Article 234 of the Law of the Sea Convention and the draft Polar Code, particularly the relation between them, but this was lacking, presumably due to space constraints.

Five chapters address different protective regimes. The overall impression of the law is of a badly organized and coordinated patchwork (p. 413). One chapter deals with migratory species, specifically birds and the warming of the polar oceans (Arie Trouwborst). Two chapters address fisheries management in the Antarctic and Arctic (Andrew Serdy and Erik J. Molenaar, respectively). Finally, two others focus on marine mammals (Joanna Mossop on the Antarctic and Nigel Bankes on the Arctic), telling the sad story of the dysfunctional International Whaling Commission (p. 411). Marine scientific research receives consideration in two full chapters by René Lefeber (Antarctic) and Yoshinobu Takei (Arctic). The last thematic chapter is on maritime security (Donald R. Rothwell). As rightly pointed out, there are few classical security issues in the Polar Regions for the simple reason that there are few significant commercial ports in the Arctic and none in the Antarctic (p. 382). The chapter defines the concept of security implicitly, very broadly and vaguely (p. 370–371).

The concluding chapter is the core of the book. The three editors attempt to identify trends and possibilities in interactions between global and regional regimes, including potential game changers. Game changers might not necessarily be as significant as analytical tools, such as the prospects of a major incident in the Antarctic or the Russian flag on the North Pole. However, the analysis of the interaction of systems, which was not the main focus earlier in the book, forms a very necessary part of it. After all, interaction between norms is a core focus, if not *the* core focus, of law.

For my part, I think that the Polar Code will prove to be the most important game changer, especially for better defining good shipping practices. Furthermore, implementation of the Code's norms will be mandatory, based on flag State jurisdiction, under the tacit amendment procedures of the maritime conventions. Finally, coastal State jurisdiction, including that over ice-covered areas, will be heavily influenced, if not eliminated, by these new rules.

This is a book by and for lawyers. Interdisciplinary work in the natural sciences is highly desired. The contributors to this volume seem well acquainted with examples of endangered species and other information from the life sciences, and in that sense, this book is interdisciplinary. For lawyers, interdisciplinary work can mean that they are well acquainted with other disciplines, work with other scientists, or take advantage of interaction with other scientists or disciplines to pose new problems and come up with new solutions. The interdisciplinary character of this book is not of the latter, more advanced kind. In many ways, the references to species serve only as illustrations (e.g., p. 166), with about the same relevance as photographs of sweet animals (usually omitted in legal science), carrying the implicit message that the authors are broad-minded and well-intentioned. True interdisciplinary research could contribute positively to discussions of the ecosystem approach to various sea management issues. The ecosystem approach is not unique to the Polar Regions but perhaps is especially relevant there because of the allegedly vulnerable and relatively untouched ecosystems.

Although the index is far from complete, the ecosystem approach is mentioned several times in the volume, but it is never defined. It is disappointing to see that the statement that there is not sufficient factual knowledge to establish an ecosystem approach in Arctic fisheries management is not accompanied by a footnote or a discussion of the interaction between facts and law (p. 249, 260). Such a discussion would have demonstrated the weakness of a concept such as the ecosystem approach and, thereby, shed light on the precautionary principle in this context.

Interdisciplinary potential lies not only in working with natural scientists. Collaboration with historians and social scientists would also have been relevant to this book, as its highlight is telling the story of how the current regimes recently developed to become what they are. However, I see no traces of the historical method in the book, and the few attempts to analyse the interplay of power are rather fragmentary and simplistic (p. 321), without a touch of social sciences methodologies. Had the volume made use of true interdisciplinary research wherever possible, it would have been rare and commendable. As is, the book still stands as a good, useful contribution. The authors, like most of us, presumably talk about real interdisciplinary research rather than actually taking advantage of it.

A final detail: There are many multi-letter acronyms in this book. A single, eight-line paragraph (p. 108) contains nine! Most are listed in a table, with notable exceptions such as SPLOS (State Parties to the Law of the Sea Convention) (p. 66). I think that, generally, if words are worth writing, they should be spelled out. Perhaps even bits of common jargon, such as "Banana Hole," "Donut Hole," and "Loophole" (p. 245), should be explained or footnoted.

Erik Røsæg
Scandinavian Institute of Maritime Law
University of Oslo, Norway

Myron H. Nordquist, John Norton Moore, Aldo Chircop and Ronán Long, eds., *The Regulation of Continental Shelf Development: Rethinking International Standards* (Leiden/Boston: Martinus Nijhoff Publishers, 2013), Center for Oceans Law and Policy, Volume 17, xviii, 374 pp.

The legal status of the submarine area beyond the limit of the territorial sea underwent significant upheaval in the 20th century, and many differing claims, before it became regulated internationally, first by the 1958 Convention on the Continental Shelf, and later by the United Nations Convention on the Law of the Sea (UNCLOS). Part VI of the UNCLOS governs the delineation of the outer limits of the continental shelf, as well as the right of the coastal State to carry out and regulate activities in this area. This is supplemented by other provisions in other parts of the Convention governing pollution, marine scientific research and protection of the marine environment. The framework provided in UNCLOS has been partially bolstered by subsequent, more specific treaties aiming to provide a more thorough regulatory structure for this part of ocean space.

Regulation of the continental shelf may be described as piecemeal, as although UNCLOS provides for the rights of the coastal State in relation to the exploration and exploitation of natural resources (Article 77 (1)), the laying of submarine cables (Article 79), artificial islands, installations and structures (Article 80), drilling (Article 81) and tunneling (Article 85), the framework set out in Part VI is couched in relatively general terms, as one would expect due to its being part of a much broader 'Constitution of the Oceans'. Moreover, the changes and technological developments that have occurred in the thirty plus years since the Convention has been concluded, many either not envisaged or unforeseeable, have irrevocably transformed the way in which we interact with the continental shelf and thus the way in which it requires to be regulated.

The Regulation of Continental Shelf Development: Rethinking International Standards is a collection of essays based on presentations given at the 39th Annual Conference of the Center for Oceans Law and Policy, University of Virginia School of Law, held on 21–22 June 2012, in Halifax, Nova Scotia, covering almost every imaginable area of modern continental shelf regulation, and the challenges faced therein. The collection fairly reflects a balance of focus on both law and policy in its assessment of the most important issues faced by regulators. Presumably reflecting the conference itself, some papers are long, detailed explorations of current issues, while others give brief synopses of areas affected by or affecting continental shelf regulation.

As is mentioned in the preface of the book, part of the rationale behind the conference was 'to glean lessons learned' from the 2010 Deepwater Horizon disaster in the Gulf of Mexico. In this vein, there is a particular focus in this book on environmental protection standards, risk, and liability for actions on the continental shelf. A recurring theme throughout the collection is the role of UNCLOS as the framework treaty for the regulation of activities carried out on the continental shelf, both within and beyond 200 nautical miles (NM). The appropriateness of the mere handful of provisions on the regulation of shelf activities, alongside the broader scope provisions on pollution and protection of the marine environment, is often brought into question, though the danger of fragmentation through the development of more specialized treaties is also highlighted repeatedly.

The collection of essays begins with context setting, in the shape of a paper by Shunmugam Jayakumar, Professor at the National University of Singapore, on reflections on the regime of the continental shelf under UNCLOS, thirty years after the treaty was concluded. The rest of the book is split into eight parts: Part 1, on contemporary uses of the continental shelf; Part 2, on emerging challenges to the development of the continental shelf regime; Part 3, on comparative best practices in environmental regulation of continental shelf activities; Part 4, on probabilistic risk assessment for continental shelf development; Part 5, on the decommissioning of offshore installations and structures; Part 6, on liability and compensation regimes; Part 7, on completing the unfinished business of UNCLOS III; and finally, Part 8 contains a special presentation given by Egdar Gold, Adjunct Professor at the Schulich School of Law and with the Marine Affairs Program, Dalhousie University, which briefly gives some reflections on his long career in the 'ocean business' and his thoughts on the current state of the world's oceans.

Part 1 gives readers the opportunity to better understand contemporary issues: offshore wind energy development and ecosystem-based marine management; submarine cables; and mining for marine minerals. What is notably absent from this section is any coverage of oil and gas issues, though greater attention is given to them in later parts. The decision not to include oil and gas issues in 'contemporary issues' may stem from the fact that such activities are long-standing continental shelf issues, though the same could be said for submarine cables. The paper by Ronán Long entitled "Offshore Wind Energy Development and Ecosystem-Based Marine Management in the EU: Are the Regulatory Answers Really Blowing in the Wind?" provides one of the most thorough pieces in the collection, with particular attention given to the current and potential future regimes for offshore wind energy production in the European Union. The second paper in this part entitled "Submarine Cables on the Continental Shelf" by Douglas R. Burnett may not be covering a contemporary issue in the broadest sense, but the case studies give an excellent overview of problematic state practice in relation to national regulatory structures which impede the right of States under Article 79 of UNCLOS to lay submarine cables on the continental shelf.

The final paper in Part 1 is aptly complemented by the first paper of Part 2, both covering aspects of deep seabed mining. While Georgy Cherkashov's paper on "Mining for Marine Minerals" presents factual data regarding the potential of shallow and deep-sea mineral deposits, Michael W. Lodge's paper on "International Seabed Authority Mining Standards" discusses ISA standards for mining in the Area, and their potential influence on the development of mining regulations by coastal States for mining carried out on the continental shelf.

Although Ted L. McDorman's paper assessing the International Tribunal for the Law of the Sea's judgment in the *Bay of Bengal Case* appears to fit with the subheading for Part 2 on Emerging Challenges to the Development of the Continental Shelf Regime, and certainly provides good, clear analysis of what is the most significant case concerning the continental shelf for many years, its coherence with the rest of the collection appears tenuous. While it is undisputed that the Tribunal's determination of entitlement and establishment of a boundary on the continental shelf between the two States *beyond* 200 NM raise complex issues, particularly in relation to the role of the Commission on the Limits of the Continental Shelf, the substance here seems slightly removed from that of the rest of the collection, relating as it does to more practical regulatory problems and standards. In a later paper (discussed below), there is discussion of these issues which highlights the relevance of these issues in the context of hydrocarbon resources in the Arctic, though explicit analysis of the importance of these issues in reference to regulation of continental shelf activities may also have been helpful at this stage.

The regulation of offshore drilling and other oil and gas industry regulatory issues are dealt with extensively in this volume, beginning with J. Ashley Roach's "International Standards for Offshore Drilling," which includes 28 pages reproducing relevant treaty provisions from international and regional treaties. Later papers, such as Preben H. Lindøc's and Ole A. Engen's "Offshore Safety Regimes – A Contested Terrain"; Bruce C. Glavovic's "Disasters and the Continental Shelf: Exploring New Frontiers of Risk"; and the entire Parts 5 and 6 on the decommissioning of offshore installations and structures and liability and compensation, explore other aspects. The amalgamation of different focal points relating to oil and gas and the continental shelf represents one of the greatest strengths of this volume, as it provides both a broad overview of the regulatory structures (or lack thereof) and detailed analysis of the more salient legal and technical problems. A particular highlight is the paper by Timothy J. Tyler et al. on "Developing Arctic Hydrocarbon Resources: Delineating and Delimiting Boundaries for Field Development in the Arctic," which assesses the importance of a regulatory framework for oil and gas exploration and exploitation and addresses the issues of delimitation and delineation, implicitly recognizing the importance and relevance of some of the issues in the *Bay of Bengal Case*.

The paper by Glavovic offers an in-depth analysis of the Deepwater Horizon disaster from a risk perspective. Glavovic here highlights the importance of placing the disaster in its historical, geographical and social context in order to understand its root causes, and demonstrates that in this case legal and technical uncertainties were compounded by an inconsistent and fragmented legal regime. The recommendation that "[p]revailing ocean and coastal management need to be reconceptualised as a transformative practice of deliberative governance" (p. 245) may offer little practical guidance for lawyers, but emphasizes the need for a new conceptual framework rooted in community-based political discourse in order to progress to the next stage of oceans governance and continental shelf regulation in which disasters like Deepwater Horizon can be better avoided.

In Part 7 on "Completing the Unfinished Business of UNCLOS III," Brian Flemming (perhaps somewhat prematurely) laments the end of the multilateral era, and in doing so seeks to highlight the fact that, as UNCLOS IV is most likely not around the corner, the next step ought to be an assessment of whether the framework of UNCLOS can effectively deal with modern problems in the law of the sea, with climate change identified as the biggest challenge. This ties in well with the theme referred to throughout the book on the appropriateness of the framework provided by UNCLOS. What does not appear to gel so well with the message transmitted in many of the other papers in the collection is his final caution against over-regulation, particularly in the wake of disasters such as Deepwater Horizon. A final comment is then offered by John Norton Moore which recalls the US experience with the UNCLOS and discusses his hopes for future ratification.

This volume is not tailored for those with no knowledge of the legal regime of the continental shelf, but rather aims to expand on the most important issues and problems faced by the regime today. Those that have read or made reference to an earlier volume in this series, *Legal and Scientific Aspects of Continental Shelf Limits* by M.H. Nordquist et al. (Leiden/Boston: Martinus Nijhoff Publishers, 2004), will find this collection particularly helpful in completing the picture of the legal regime of the continental shelf. The collection's variety can offer something for those generally interested in oceans governance from both a political and a legal perspective, whilst the particular focus on the framework of UNCLOS, pollution and risk aversion, and liability and compensation regimes provides interesting and helpful contributions for those interested in these more specific areas.

Amber Rose Maggio, LL.M.
Research Associate and Assistant Editor, UNCLOS Commentary Project
Institut für Umwelt- und Technikrecht der Universität Trier
Trier, Germany

Efthymios Papastavridis, *The Interception of Vessels on the High Seas Contemporary Challenges to the Legal Order of the Oceans* (Oxford and Portland, Oregon: Hart Publishing, 2013), Volume 43, Studies in International Law, 402 pp.

The 'peaceful use of the oceans' is a fundamental tenet of international law and has been the cornerstone of the evolution of the many principles of the law of the sea throughout the years. It has shaped and influenced the configuration of international uses of the oceans and even today in a world order that has changed so much, it continues to be the underlying principle that informs discussions on international relations and the oceans. One of the single biggest influences that have shaped world order in recent years have been the development of new technologies, the search for alternative energies and particularly the emergence of new threats that have changed the character of the traditional approaches to warfare. The transportation of radioactive material across the Atlantic and the Pacific Oceans, the threats of the use of weapons of mass destruction, terrorism, people smuggling, and increase in high seas piracy in the Indian Ocean have all challenged the legal order of the oceans and the principles of the law of the sea that have traditionally been applied to the use of force in the oceans. The factors that led the negotiators of the 1982 UN Convention on the Law of the Sea (UNCLOS) and the threats that faced the international community at that time are vastly different in nature and content to the threats that are faced today, and with it the questions of whether the legal principles of the law of the sea pertaining to high seas freedom and the right of visit are amenable to the forms of threats in the modern contemporary world. The emergence of non-State actors that pose threats to the traditional uses of the oceans like the Somali pirates, the increasing non-State to State

conflicts, and people smuggling have also raised issues about what legal principles should apply in terms of the appropriate responses to these threats.

Efthymios Papastavridis's book provides a welcome insight into the way in
which international law has morphed and continues to be the source of general powers for high seas interventions and enforcement. His book, *The
Interception of Vessels on the High Seas Contemporary Challenges to the Legal
Order of the Ocean,* provides an interesting insight into the questions pertaining to the "right to visit on the high seas" as a fundamental exception to the
freedom of the high seas, a principle that is *pacta sunt servanda.* In particular,
the book addresses the challenges posed by the changing nature of interceptions. These include interceptions to counter the threat of international terrorism, weapons of mass destruction, transnational crimes organized at sea like
people smuggling, and transport of narcotics. It might be said that heightened
terrorism and the availability of weapons of mass destruction poses a major
threat to world peace. The book starts with the premise that these challenges pose such a threat to global peace that it renders the principle of
non-interference on the high seas moot. This is probably an accurate assessment of the state of international law of the right of visit on the high seas given
what is happening in the world today.

The book's eight chapters cover the challenge to traditional international
order of the oceans, the freedom of the high seas, the right of visitation, and
the complexity arising from the emergence of threats perhaps not anticipated
when the principles on the right of visits on the high seas were discussed.

Chapter 1 provides an overall inquiry into the backdrop against which the
right of interception on the high seas was established, and discusses the contemporary challenges to the freedom of the high seas and maritime interception. These challenges include terrorism and weapons of mass destruction,
drug trafficking, illicit migration, piracy and armed robbery, and IUU fishing.
The author looks at these new threats and asks whether they provide a threat
to maritime security that would give rise to a right to visit on the high seas. This
is a pertinent question to ask especially in the circumstances of the current
geo-political and security environment.

Chapter 2 provides a historical overview and theoretical framework of right
to visit on the high seas, and offers a contemporary insight into the traditional
principles of *mare liberum* and *mare clausum.* the historical claim to the freedom of the high seas from the antiquity to the Middle Ages to the period of the
Battle of the Books is covered comprehensively in this chapter. The legal nature
of the high seas as it evolved from the medieval period to modern times is covered. The chapter also covers the contemporary right of visit on the high seas,
and the lessons that may be drawn from the theoretical framework of *mare*

liberum. Chapter 2 covers the traditional legal principles comprehensively including those pertaining to the claims for the maintenance of international peace and security, claims for the protection of the *bon usage* of the oceans, those relating to the maintenance of public order of States and the international community. The author is able to demonstrate that the theories of *mare liberum* and *mare clausum* were never mutually exclusive in so far as the freedom of navigation on the high seas is concerned. Importantly, the author argues that the freedom of the high seas was never an absolute principle and that it had always been qualified by *mare clausum* claims for jurisdiction an enforcement powers on the high seas for the purposes of maintaining peace and security, protection of the freedom of the high seas, and the maintenance of public order for the international community.

Chapter 3 provides an overview of the law of maritime interception on the high seas. In the first part of this chapter, the author discusses the right of visit in wartime. The author traces the legal development of the law of maritime interception by examining the law of naval warfare, the role of the UN Charter on contemporary law of naval warfare, and the application of UNCLOS to the law of naval warfare. The author highlights the belligerent right of visit and search and the rules and procedures underpinning these searches. Part 2 of the chapter examines the right of visit in peacetime. The modern contemporary treaties are examined, and the challenges to the customary right of approach are discussed including the contemporary practice of interception on the high seas. Of interest is the conclusion that the author draws. He argues that there is no self-contained regime that may be characterized as the law of interception or interdiction, but rather, the law of interception is made up of various rules of international law which collectively form the legal order of the oceans.

Chapter 4 addresses issues surrounding interception on the high seas in the context of peace and security and the right of visit in cases of armed conflict and the United Nations Security Council's actions. This is perhaps the more important discussion in so far as they relate to armed intervention and operations sanctioned by the Security Council. The author discusses the belligerent right of visit and search, and the contemporary application of those rights, if indeed they do exist, to the legal order of the oceans. The emergence of the United Nations and its sanctions on the use of force in certain armed conflict situations is discussed in this chapter. The author argues that the belligerent right of visit and search is still relevant in the contemporary law of armed conflict and indeed in many cases provide the more arguable justification for such interceptions on the high seas.

Chapter 5 encompasses the contemporary challenges to international peace and security through terrorism and the proliferation of weapons of mass destruction. The author discusses the responses and interdiction operations within the framework of the UN Security Council, NATO operations, the International Maritime Organization, and CARICOM. These institutions now play an influential role in dictating the responses to threats against navigation and the peaceful uses of the oceans. This is probably one of the biggest changes in that previously single States decided on whether they would exercise the right of intervention against vessels on the high seas. Increasingly, multilateral forums such as the Security Council are being used to frame responses to these new challenges. The author looks at these issues and discusses them in the context of responses by way of international institutional frameworks such as the Security Council, and responses beyond international organizations. These include bilateral boarding agreements and the Proliferation Security Initiative (PSI). The chapter covers the issue of legal justifications for unilateral interdiction measures under general international law. These are exceptions that may be found in the law of the sea, the principle of the right to self-defence, and in circumstances precluding the wrongfulness of interdiction under the law of State responsibility. This chapter shows the changes that have taken place in international law and the role that international institutions now play. The chapter concludes that only claims that can be justified by either the primary or secondary rules of international law relating to the right of visit can be accepted as legitimate *mare clausum* claims for the peaceful and orderly uses of the oceans.

Chapter 6 discusses two issues that have become problems in recent years. These are piracy and the threat that it poses to the freedom of navigation and commerce and illegal, unregulated and unlawful (IUU) fishing. The former relates to the problems that have happened in the Indian Ocean in recent years. The chapter highlights that in respect of interdiction operations to address piracy, the responses have generally kept within the parameters of international law. However, the author points out that there is some ambivalence on what constitutes 'reasonable grounds' and the practice has not always been consistent. The chapter highlights the threat that IUU fishing poses, and the evolution of the rules of high seas boarding and inspection incorporated in the 1995 UN Fish Stocks Agreement and its operationalization by regional fisheries management organizations (RMFOs). The author generally agrees with the conclusion that there is no agreed international law of boarding and inspection applicable to all high seas fisheries, and while Articles 21 and 22 of the UN Fish Stocks provide some guidance on the general principles, they do not, in and of themselves, generate any legal obligation of a general character.

Chapter 7 highlights the legal rights with regard to interception and interdiction for the purpose of drug enforcement, which is a major problem in many countries. The author discusses the international responses and highlights the fact that the international community has institutionalized claims that the high seas boarding and inspection of vessels suspected of trafficking drugs is necessary for the preservation of public order and therefore is an exemption to the freedom of the high seas. The legal rules in the 1988 Vienna Convention on Narcotic Drugs and the Caribbean bilateral agreements provide justification for the right of visit, which are also supported by Article 110 of UNCLOS Convention, which can be invoked by States to mount high seas inspection of vessels suspected of being involved in trafficking illicit drugs.

Chapter 8 considers the rules relating to trafficking human beings. The authors assess the interception activities on the high seas in relation to humans. This has become a problem in recent years. The author examined the treaty law justifications such as UNCLOS and the Smuggling Protocol. The contemporary practice of maritime interception of human beings serves two objectives, which are aimed at combating illicit migration by sea when it is associated with organized criminal organizations and also prevention of human trafficking and other forms of modern slavery. In this regard, the author argues in this chapter that the protection of human beings should be at the center of the interests of States when exercising the right of interception for humanitarian purposes on the high seas.

The right of visit on the high seas is a fundamental tenet of the construction development of the legal order of the oceans. This book is a valuable addition to the discussions that are now vogue in the international media. The threat of terrorism, the transportation of weapons of mass destruction, piracy, people smuggling are all issues that now occupy media headlines. This book is necessary reading in order to get a good understanding of the legal principles of what can be done to take preventative pre-emptive action. It makes a valuable contribution to a subject that has become important to international relations between States the continuing peaceful uses of the oceans for trade transportation.

Transform Aqorau
CEO, Parties to the Nauru Agreement Office
Senior Visiting Fellow, Australian National Centre for Oceans,
Resources and Security (ANCORS)
University of Wollongong, Australia

Rajendra Ramlogan, *Sustainable Development: Towards a Judicial Interpretation* (Leiden/Boston: Martinus Nijhoff Publishers, 2011), 292 pp.

Introduction

Even though the concept of sustainable development has ancient underpinnings, it was not until the publication of *Our Common Future* and the Rio Earth Summit of 1992 that sustainable development received a more substantive articulation. Since then, countless treaties and other international instruments, programs, national statutes, policies, etc., have been devoted to the development and realization of this concept, but sustainable development remains more or less a utopian ideal. While its practical and theoretical connotations are still in the process of evolution, it is generally accepted that 'sustainable development' cannot yet be precisely defined; nonetheless, attempts have been made to secure its practical implementation, despite not really knowing for certain what it is. Although this approach has achieved some progress, the lack of theoretical clarity has failed to encourage radical changes on the ground, prompting the need to revisit and strengthen the theoretical underpinnings of sustainable development. In this regard, an important source that affords a structure to this amorphous concept is the jurisprudence on sustainable development. International judicial bodies and national courts have expended considerable effort and resources to carry out this build-up.

Published as part of the Legal Aspects of Sustainable Development Series, whose objective is to add "flesh onto the bare bones" of this concept, the book under review is an interesting survey of sustainable development case law at national and international levels. Among the myriad of scholarly publications on this subject, this book stands apart as an excellent introduction that provides a basic overview of the judicial process in determining the evolving contours of sustainable development law and comparative jurisprudence on this subject. It unravels some of the theoretical complexities of the law on sustainable development and its treatment at judicial hands.

At the outset, it cannot be emphasized enough that the fundamental proposition this book expounds is that even though a "quiet revolution" is unfolding within the legal systems of several nations that favor judicial support for sustainable development, there is considerable divergence in terms of the legislative and judicial intervention in defining them. Therefore, "[t]he challenge is to determine the universal applicability of a value-system of development founded on the bedrock of sustainability, a system that seeks to strike a balance between development and the environment." Even though there is the need for a universal principle that can be applied across the spectrum in order to operationalize and encase sustainable development as a legal norm, the reality is that the North–South developmental dilemma works against this need. For the South, development is viewed as a tool for poverty alleviation, and therefore it is difficult for this group of countries to maintain a balance between the environment and development. In fact, in most of the South, sustainable development is pursued only within carefully set parameters so as to avoid the placing of unnecessary strictures on its drive for economic growth. As well, at the international level, it is argued that rather than expending efforts to foster a comprehensive and universal definition on sustainable development (given that sustainable development is more or less an umbrella concept that includes within its ambit different legal principles), it might be more beneficial to focus on the juridical development of the individual strands.

Correspondingly, the book identifies some of the major building blocks of sustainable development, such as the precautionary principle, the polluter pays principle, access to justice, the right to a healthy environment, inter- and intra-generational equity, and public participation, and organizes them into different chapters. Each chapter discusses and examines these individual pieces by referring to relevant international and regional instruments followed by relevant case law drawn from international and common law jurisdictions, thereby broadly covering the regions of Asia, North America, Africa, and the Caribbean. A succinct overview of the treatment that these concepts have received is provided below.

Themes

Given the worsening nature of environmental problems, there is growing demand to strengthen environmental human rights and to link these rights to the concept of sustainable development, since sustainable development cannot be realized without ensuring the basic rights to safe water, air, and land. Even though the link between the two is demonstrated in international and regional level instruments, it is at the national levels that this exposition has been most promising, particularly the development of the right to a clean and healthy environment. Here, the articulation has been at four main levels. First, in certain countries, the national constitutions impose a duty on citizens to protect the environment; second, the constitution can impose a responsibility on the state to protect the environment; third, a right to a safe and healthy environment can be vested in citizens; and fourth, courts in certain countries utilize constitutional standards, such as the right to life, privacy, health and family life, to recognize environmental human rights. It must also be noted that the right to a healthy environment is not always predicated on the presence of a constitutional norm and in certain cases can emerge even from statutory legislation.

The polluter pays principle is recognized as one of the more salient aspects of sustainable development. The underlying idea behind this concept is that the parties that generate pollution are to assume full responsibility and internalize the cost of its abatement. The population at large should not be made to subsidize the cost of the pollution. With its emphasis on cost allocation and cost internalization, a number of binding and non-binding instruments at the international level have facilitated the transformation of the polluter pays principle from an economic principle to a norm of environmental law. At the national levels, in certain jurisdictions, 'polluter pays' has even attained the force of law, either through legislative intervention or through the judicial process. Despite its importance and centrality in securing sustainable development, the principle remains largely idealistic, since it is seen as adding to production costs and thereby reducing competitiveness and economic opportunity. As pointed out, "[t]he complexity of deriving an appropriate formula for the implementation of the polluter pays principle ensures that it continues to hold a marginal role in the environmental legislation of most developing countries, primarily due to their adverse economic conditions."

Another important principle that can help control environmental pollution is that of precaution. Tracing its origin to the German *Vorsorgeprinzip*, the concept of precaution was popularized as Principle 15 of the Rio Declaration and incorporated into the United Nations Framework Convention on Climate Change and into the Convention on Biological Diversity, both of which are binding instruments. When it first appeared on the international horizon, the precautionary principle was directed mainly at addressing environmental and health issues. Subsequently, its ambit widened to include species protection, air pollution control, marine environmental protection, climate change, atmospheric emissions, fisheries, ocean dumping and mining, human rights protection, hazardous wastes control, and so on. The growing acceptance of the precautionary principle and its express reflection in many international treaties and documents has led many to hold that it is part of customary international law. Even international courts refer to it in their environmental decisions, reflecting a growing acceptance among judges that this principle is part of international customary law. As far as its incorporation into domestic legal systems is concerned, there is legislation in both developed and developing countries that recognize this principle. Even though it has acceptance in national jurisprudence, the approach has not been uniform, particularly when there is no legislative basis for applying the precautionary principle and reliance is placed on customary international law. Again, the formulation of the precautionary principle in itself raises several questions that add to the confusion, such as:

What is the threshold level that triggers the operation of the principle? Still, the precautionary principle is integral to sustainable development.

At the very heart of sustainable development, however, is a form of equity that manifests in two distinct ways. The first way – *inter-generational* equity – relates to the temporal dimension of equity, namely, equity between generations, while the second way describes equity within the existing generation, or *intra-generational* equity. Inter-generational equity is rooted in the idea of poverty eradication and the need to secure distributive justice. Intra-generational equity is concerned with equality within the present generation and the underlying idea that every human being has "an equal right to access the Earth's natural and cultural resources." Despite the realization that poverty removal can help protect the environment and ensure greater development, disparities in income distribution and the gulf between the rich and the poor continue to widen, thereby subverting sustainable development objectives. Furthermore, even though international legal instruments have dealt with the substantive content of intra-generational equity in much greater detail than with intergenerational equity, the treatment of intra-generational equity has been more in line with international equity among nations rather than with domestic equity. As far as the application of intra-generational equity at the national levels is concerned, national courts have relied on various juridical bases. For instance, courts in India treat this principle as an aspect of social justice, while in Kenya it is rooted in statutory requirements. Given the inequities in income at macro and micro scales, a major challenge before the international community in operationalizing sustainable development is to ensure linkages between equity and poverty eradication and inclusive economic growth.

With a nod to future generations' rights to Earth's resources and the inter-generational dimension of sustainable development, the Brundtland report defines sustainable development as "development that meets the needs of the present without compromising the ability of future generations to meet their own needs." Implicit in the concept of fairness or equity between generations is the idea that each is entitled to inherit a planet that is at least as good as that of the previous generation, and that the present generation is thus a custodian of Earth for future generations. As far as its recognition in international law is concerned, notwithstanding the absence of an express reference in several of the major international legal instruments, many of these do recognize the importance of considering the interests of future generations. Similarly, the International Court of Justice has also not endorsed the principle as being influential in its judicial deliberations. Despite this, national judiciaries have travelled considerable lengths and have relied on various legal bases to entrench this concept in their respective jurisprudence. For instance, Indian courts recognize this principle on the basis that inter-generational equity is part of customary international law; South African courts rely on "soft" international law as the legal basis; and courts in the Philippines rely on the right to a clean environment as including the right of future generations to a healthy environment. Even though the "moral imperative to act responsibly with regard to people not yet in existence has not been universally accepted," "much of the 21st century will be dedicated to safeguarding the legacy of future humanity while addressing the needs of those currently charged with stewardship of the earth."

The evolving nature of sustainable development has led to public participation being recognized as falling within its scope. Ever since the Rio Earth Summit, public participation in the environmental decision-making process has gained momentum. Nevertheless, very little attention has been devoted to its entrenchment at the international level in environmental matters. Despite this low profile, the importance of this principle has proliferated in several countries due mainly to the realization that public participation is a key part of the democratic process and that the public, which stands to be most severely affected by the consequences of environmental decisions, should be able to effectively influence its outcome. Generally, the basis of public participation in individual countries is based on legislation, whereas and in common law jurisdictions, reliance has been placed on common law principles. In this context, an important pathway to ensure public participation in environmental decision-making is through the critical tool of an environmental impact assessment (EIA). An EIA enables access to information, offers an opportunity to the affected to voice their opinions, ensures transparency in decision-making, and provides mechanisms for implementation and enforcement. In addition to the several international instruments that specifically make provisions for conducting an EIA, along with the recent judicial opinion by the International Court of Justice that emphasized the need to conduct EIAs in situations where there is an element of risk due to a proposed industrial activity involving a shared resource, there is growing jurisprudence at the national levels that links EIAs with public participation.

Closely related to the principle of public participation is the need both to access information and to create a justice dimension around sustainable development, since litigation is a form of public participation. In fact, public participation would have very little significance if citizens lacked the right to effective judicial review. Both governmental and non-governmental actors can affect environmental change through the judiciary. As pointed out, "[i]f protection of the environment is a necessary component of sustainable development, then there must be access to the judicial process." Access to justice has often been linked to the concept of public interest litigation, which is litigation for the protection and securing of public interests. Indeed, at the national level in various countries, the greatest thrust in securing access to justice is through public interest litigation. Even though the concept of public interest litigation is traceable to the decision of the United States Supreme Court in *Brown v. Board of Education*, it is the writ courts of India that "embraced the concept with almost evangelical fervor." While some national judiciaries root public interest litigation in constitutional principles, others base it on terms of common law and statute. Nevertheless, if sustainable development and its interrelated components have to be secured, it is crucial that ordinary citizens gain access to justice to realize sustainable development.

Discussion

Even though the unelected judges practically usurped to themselves the power to test the legality of laws enacted by the legislature, judicial review has become an integral component of democratic systems and has emerged as an effective bulwark against majoritarianism, ensuring constitutionalism and respect for the rule of law. Given the social engineering role of courts to vindicate public interest to secure a clean and healthy environment, it was only natural that judiciaries the world over would be called to balance the societal interests of economic development with environmental protection. As the author so eloquently argues, the judicial outpourings to entrench sustainable development values has ensured that the adjudication of environmental disputes is no longer an exercise to resolve claims of contending parties, but rather has become an effort to develop a legal order conducive to social justice, sound ecological management, and the promotion of sustainable development. Despite commitment on the part of the judiciary to strive to create links between development and environmental protection and the creation of a critical mass of rules to operationalize sustainable development, meaningful engagement between these interests is more difficult than ever to realize, given the complex nature of environmental, socio-economic, and scientific realties that confront the contemporary world. These are some of the recurring themes in the book under review.

Despite holding its ground as an impressive piece of work, *Sustainable Development: Towards a Judicial Interpretation* has certain limitations. In the editorial preface, Professor David Freestone points out that "the author lets the judges speak for themselves, often at length." And this is a major shortcoming. Given that this work is not intended to be a casebook, a more concise articulation of judicial opinions would have enhanced readability. While it is evident that the author has taken great pains to draw from a wide range of sources and judicial texts to trace out the judicial contribution, it is expected that scholarship that deals with the treatment of sustainable development at judicial hands should offer a discourse on certain issues germane to the discussion. For instance, why is the treatment of this concept so vastly different at the international and national levels, and how do these differences impact the juridical development of sustainable development? If confusion persists at the international level over its status, what then are the factors that impeded its crystallization into a rule of customary international law? What are the implications, given that some of the national judiciaries have entrenched sustainable development and its cognates into national law on the basis that these are part of customary international law, when its status as customary international law is still doubtful? Since sustainable development has more normative acceptance at the national level, what does this entail for the development of the concept at the international level? By being an activist in securing environmental human rights and securing its inter-relationship with sustainable development, is the judiciary overstepping its boundaries and thus guilty of violation of the separation of powers doctrine? And is this a legitimate exercise of judicial power?

Furthermore, why is it that, despite courts being over-enthusiastic in environmental matters, species are still disappearing and the air, bodies of water, and the ground continue to be polluted? Why do national judiciaries rely on different juridical standards to foster sustainable development and its building blocks? Even though the book under review examines the potential of environmental impact assessments as a means to secure public participation, it is consciously silent on the role of EIAs to implement the precautionary principle. Have the inconsistencies in treatment at judicial hands practically capped the evolution of sustainable development? Similarly, sustainable development and its cognates involve the application of multiple knowledge sources and specialized skills from a variety of sciences that a judge may not ordinarily know. How do judges wriggle out of such situations and still foster commitment to sustainable development values? Given the potential of climate change impacts to overturn development, what are the implications of climate change adaptation and mitigation for the future evolution of sustainable development? Are the components of sustainable development limited to what has been identified in this book or does it include other concepts like public trust, stewardship, and integration?

A dialogue on these aspects is conspicuous by its absence. Having light shed on these and similar issues would definitely have been helpful towards understanding why sustainable development and its components receive inconsistent treatment at judicial hands and continued recognition/non-recognition as part of international customary law. In fact, the lack of examination of such issues renders this contribution fairly tame and, in certain aspects, uncontroversial. Nevertheless, this book is still a valuable contribution to the emerging legal scholarship on sustainable development and its treatment at judicial hands. Perhaps the most important contribution of the book is identifying the various juridical bases that support sustainable development and its individual blocks and the comprehensive definition that the author affords to sustainable development, which reflects and interlinks the different strands. Without a doubt, *Sustainable Development: Towards a Judicial Interpretation* is a significant accomplishment that collates relevant international, regional and national instruments and judicial opinions and serves as an easy reference for the jurisprudence of sustainable development. It provides an essential useful starting point for those interested in exploring the role of the judicial process in securing and furthering sustainable development. Despite certain limitations, as noted above, the book is clearly an essential read for judges, judicial officers, all those involved in judicial education and training, practitioners, policy-makers, and researchers interested in the judicial dimensions of sustainable development and in comparative jurisprudence.

Tony George Puthucherril, JSD
Research Associate
Marine & Environmental Law Institute
Dalhousie University, Halifax, Nova Scotia, Canada

Harry N. Scheiber and Jin-Hyun Paik, eds., *Regions, Institutions, and Law of the Sea: Studies in Ocean Governance* (Leiden/Boston: Martinus Nijhoff Publishers, 2013), 554 pp.

The Law of the Sea Institute has organized and sponsored numerous international conferences and workshops on the law of the sea and ocean governance. This edited book is based on a collection of papers from a joint conference with the International Tribunal for the Law of the Sea (ITLOS) in Hamburg in 2010 (with the exception of Chapter 9). It is a book about international law specifically focusing on regulatory issues and institutional ocean governance arrangements since the inception of the Law of the Sea. While some edited books based on conference proceedings lack cohesiveness between chapters, this volume offers a thematic approach based on regions and institutions that clearly and logically links each chapter within each of the four parts. Significantly, its publication is timely, being released in 2013 just after the 30th anniversary of the UN Convention on the Law of the Sea (UNCLOS) in 2012.

This book is a long volume of 553 pages but it is sensibly structured, well-written and edited. The first part examines institutions with a specific focus on ITLOS as a system of courts and tribunals, the functions of the ad hoc Chamber, and ITLOS procedures. This part provides a detailed insight into ITLOS and law of the sea disputes that is expertly written and researched.

The second part focuses on non-judicial institutions and regimes in ocean governance including the FAO, the International Seabed Authority, the International Maritime Organization, and the Commission on the Limits of the Continental Shelf. It also investigates the areas where there is limited or laissez-faire regulatory provisions based on the pre-UNCLOS legal order (for example, iron fertilization of the oceans).

The third part of the book examines key issues in specific ocean regions and is divided into three sections. The first section studies oceans policies in the Asian region, including China, Korea, and Taiwan. This is followed by chapters on the European Union and Mediterranean ocean regimes. The last section of part three is an overview of additional regions – the Indian Ocean, Latin America, Africa, and the Arctic. Notably, the chapters in this part also reveal historical and political aspects of regional oceans policy-making. Other regional areas, such as the Antarctic or the Pacific, are noticeably missing as individual chapters, however, they are mentioned throughout the book with regard to disputes or institutional arrangements.

Part four, containing only of two chapters, addresses heightened current and future challenges. The first of the chapters reveals the difficulties with regulating piracy, and the second chapter deals with climate change and the oceans, an escalating issue of importance for the global community.

There is an absence of a concluding chapter to the book. Further analysis of ways forward in ocean governance in addition to an overview of the major conclusions of the book would have provided some closure to the salient issues raised. Nevertheless, this edited volume is a historically significant contribution to the understanding of international law, regime formulation, state and non-state actor behaviour, and the complexities of ocean governance on global and regional levels. The authors of each chapter are leading experts in international law and/or key representatives of the institutions they write about (for example, José Luis Jesus, Judge and former President of ITLOS). Consequently, this book offers an 'insider' perspective into the institutions it examines as well as an academic evaluation of these institutions, laws and policies. This book is unique and inspiring, and it will be utilized for many generations.

This book is heavily focused on the law and is most beneficial for law practitioners and students researching the intricacies of law making in global and regional ocean governance. However, its topics will also be of interest to a wider audience such as political scientists, geographers, and oceanographers.

Joanna Vince, Ph.D.
School of Social Sciences
University of Tasmania, Australia

Tim Stephens and David L. VanderZwaag, eds., *Polar Oceans Governance in an Era of Environmental Change* (Cheltenham, UK: Edward Elgar Publishing Limited, 2014), 384 pp.

Polar areas have received a lot of attention in recent years, and it is fairly obvious why this is happening, especially in the Arctic. Science tells us that climate change is melting the sea ice and opening new economic opportunities involving oil, gas, the movement of fish stocks, increased tourism, and shorter navigational routes. There are also many changes taking place in the Antarctic where human and economic presence is increasing, in addition to the consequences of climate change. As Tim Stephens and David VanderZwaag point out in their introduction to *Polar Oceans Governance in an Era of Environmental Change* [hereafter *Polar Oceans Governance*], climatic and other environmental changes are posing new types of challenges to the polar regions and their governance regimes.

Although the polar regions are connected in our heads, possibly for geographical and climatic reasons, they are not obvious places for comparison. After all, the Arctic consists of ocean surrounded by continents, whereas the Antarctic is a continent surrounded by ocean; the Antarctic also has no permanent human habitation, while the Arctic is inhabited. The two polar areas do however resemble each other in many respects: both have extreme climatic conditions, winters without daylight and summers without sunset, and ecosystems that have adapted to the cold environment. In such conditions, the ecosystems are simple, comprising of only a few key species. As such, they tend to be more vulnerable to human-induced disturbances or pollution than those of more temperate areas. Moreover, the polar regions tend to be topically and institutionally lumped together, in the approaches of many nation-States that are active in both polar regions.

More importantly, however, from the viewpoint of reviewing this book, the politico-legal bases of the polar regions are different and the importance of territorial sovereignty differs enormously. In the Antarctic, the sovereignty question has been "frozen" by way of the 1959 Antarctic Treaty and thus there are no active territorial sovereigns in the region. Seven States have claimed parts of the Antarctic as their sovereign area, but have agreed not to consolidate these claims into full sovereignty whilst the Treaty is in place. The situation in the Arctic contrasts sharply with this, because sovereignty and sovereign rights in the marine areas play a crucial role in the region.

There are an increasing number of research publications that address both polar regions. New journals and periodicals have emerged, such as the *Yearbook of Polar Law* and the *Polar Journal*. The Nordic Council of Ministers has also funded two textbooks on polar law, and in recent years, networks of legal scholars interested in polar and Arctic law issues have arisen, such as the symposia on polar law.

The pioneering research publication on polar governance is clearly Donald Rothwell's *International Law and the Polar Regions*, published in 1995 (Cambridge University Press). His contrast and comparison of the two polar regions sparked international interest and he has continued to follow this theme in his research career. This is to be seen in two notable books in this research genre. *The Law of the Sea and Polar Maritime Delimitation and Jurisdiction*, edited by Alex G. Oude Elferink and Donald R. Rothwell, was published in 2001 (Martinus Nijhoff Publishers). The 2013 book: *The Law of the Sea and the Polar Regions: Interactions Between Global and Regional Regimes*, edited by Erik J. Molenaar, Alex G. Oude Elferink and Donald R. Rothwell (Martinus Nijhoff Publishers) is the most recent and closest work to *Polar Oceans Governance*. Although there are some similarities between these books, they also have many differences. *Polar Oceans Governance* is produced by Australian and Canadian scholars, while *The Law of the Sea and the Polar Regions* has a more dispersed authorship. Moreover, *Polar Oceans Governance* is structured around themes which are addressed in the Arctic and Antarctica, whilst the 2013 volume has a more diverse thematic and structural orientation. However, these two books complement each other nicely, so anyone interested in oceans governance, the law of the sea, and the polar regions is well advised to familiarize themselves with both works. *Polar Oceans Governance* has its origins in a long-standing research co-operation between Canadian and Australian researchers on ocean policy and law – a co-operation that has already produced three monographs (p. xvi).

Content

The book is structured in five parts and contains chapters on: Environmental Change in the Polar Oceans; Geostrategic Dynamics in the Polar Oceans; Resources, Environment, Sovereignty and Jurisdiction – Bipolar Perspectives; Developing National and Foreign Policy Responses; and The Future of Polar Oceans Governance.

The introduction, written by the editors, nicely introduces the themes and topics of the book and acts as a brief summary of the overall work. Canadian scholarship on Arctic governance and Australian scholarship on Antarctic issues are to my mind at the forefront in the world, and this could have been perhaps more prominently flagged in the introduction. Also surprising is that neither the editors nor the forewords raise the interesting angles from which Australian and Canadian scholars look at polar governance issues: Canada is only a non-consultative party to the Antarctic Treaty Consultative Meetings, and Australia has not applied for observer status in the Arctic Council. I was surprised that this was not mentioned at all in the book, given that it must surely have an impact on how these countries orient themselves to the polar regions.

Part I considers environmental change in the polar oceans and is studied via two contributions. Marcus Haward and Julia Jabour go through the current environmental and resource governance arrangements, and in particular the challenges posed by climate change in the Antarctic. Their interesting and in-depth contribution focuses heavily on the Convention on the Conservation of Antarctic Marine Living Resources (CCAMLR) and how this regime regulates fisheries, and how it could be improved. In the second article in this section, Lorne Kriwoken addresses environmental change in the Arctic region in a wonderfully careful manner. Although he goes through all of the main environmental changes in the Arctic, he stops short of analyzing how these are or should be governed, and this seems to deviate from the book's focus on governance.

Part II addresses geostrategic dynamics in the polar oceans, and also follows the structure of two contributions. These each address the unique geopolitical developments taking place in each polar region, without any comparative aspect. Rob Huebert goes through the signs which point to an increase of militarization in the Arctic, e.g., more military investments and exercises conducted in the region. In his balanced overview, Huebert does not claim that there are immediate military conflicts on the horizon. However, he does point out that even if a degree of co-operative momentum has been created in the region, this does not isolate the Arctic from larger developments: "The security issues that cast the greatest shadow over the region's impressive advances in cooperation do not really originate as 'Arctic issues'. Rather, they are situated in the larger international security relationship between Russia and the United States" (p. 84). He continues that the decision-makers should not be complacent about the "threats that they will be facing both from within the Arctic region and from outside" (p. 85). Unfortunately, however, it seems that the Arctic cooperation is now facing exactly these threats as a result of the general worsening relations between Russia and the Western powers.

In her thoughtful piece "Power Politics in the Antarctic Treaty System" (ATS), Melissa Weber describes who are the current "hegemons" of the ATS, how they may be challenged, by which countries, and on which issues. She warns that "false confidence and stagnancy will upset the power within the organization" (p. 107), and that "diminished confidence will render stewardship in the larger forums impossible and the power of the ATS will diminish" (ibid.). Yet, she comes to the conclusion that currently, although there are many challenges, it is likely that the ATS will continue to be the main Antarctic organization.

Part III addresses bipolar perspectives on resources, environment, sovereignty, and jurisdiction. Rizal Abdul Kadir examines whether joint development zones could resolve some of the still unresolved maritime boundaries in the Arctic (e.g., the Beaufort Sea maritime boundary dispute between the United States and Canada), and those which may be forthcoming (such as the likely overlapping continental shelf entitlements around the North Pole between Canada, Denmark–Greenland, and the Russian Federation). As the author well demonstrates, joint development zones have been actively used in the Arctic, a practice that the International Court of Justice also favors.

The next two contributions by David Leary and Tim Stephens complement each other nicely. David Leary studies how media has paid a lot of undeserved attention to continental shelf "claims" in the Arctic and the Southern Ocean, and with this focus has missed something very important: how bioprospecting is being undertaken in both polar oceans, with gaps in its regulation. Tim Stephens provides a very clear, careful, and thought-provoking chapter of how the global process of delineating the outer limits of continental shelves has proceeded in both polar regions, and the orderly manner in which it has been conducted. He also raises an interesting question for both Canada and Australia: should they articulate the values underlying their polar shelf areas more clearly? In an era of environmental change, it might be apt for these two countries to ask whether these are areas to be reserved for resource extraction, or rather areas which require the highest levels of environmental protection.

The final contribution in this part is by Suzanne Lalonde. In a very engaging and solid manner, she steers the reader through a thought experiment to determine whether either the International Maritime Organizations (IMO) 'particularly sensitive sea areas' (PSSA) concept or the use of Article 234 of the UN Convention on the Law of the Sea could provide alternatives for Canada, should Canada change its policy and agree with the United States that the Northwest Passage straits are international straits from the viewpoint of the law of the sea, and considering the concomitant legal consequences. Using an example from Australia and Papua New Guinea of the way in which the PSSA proposal was used to protect the environment of the Torres Strait, Lalonde shows convincingly that there are severe problems with this approach, simply because PSSA designation does not give much additional power than States would have in using the law of the sea for protecting the environment. She also asks what if Canada just used Article 234 for environmental protection in this scenario? Her inquiry goes on to demonstrate that Article 234 has its limits in the polar context: as sea ice is diminishing with the intensifying climate change impacts, this hinders its use as the area of application would need to be ice-covered for most of the year. Another difficulty is that Canada could not apply the article to warships and government ships of other States as these ships enjoy sovereign immunity. She concludes that "Canada's sovereign control of the Northwest Passage remains the best guarantee of its effective protection" (p. 186).

Part IV addresses developing national and foreign policy responses, starting out with the contribution by Shelley Wright on Inuit perspectives on governance in the Canadian Arctic. An Inuit presence in the Arctic is one important part of why Canada can justify claiming waters inside its archipelago as historic internal waters, given that the Inuit have used these from time immemorial. Yet, as Wright points out, this does not manifest well in the federal policy of Canada, and the Inuit communities are therefore haunted by all kinds of social ills. The author examines more carefully the Nunavut territory resource developments – the Mary River iron ore mining project and the potential for oil and natural gas exploitation in Lancaster Sound – both of which pose difficult questions for the Inuit. The author emphasizes that for the Inuit, the discussions of sovereignty and decision-making power are perceived differently than by the federal government – they are human development questions of the highest order.

Meinhard Doelle examines climate policy at the federal and northern territories levels in view of the fact that climate change demonstrates its impacts most deeply in the Arctic regions. The author asks, "Are there signs that heightened awareness of impacts and vulnerability in the Arctic is translating into more progressive policies on adaptation, mitigation or development?" (p. 217). Doelle comes up with very interesting conclusions, especially as to the way that territories are approaching issues of climate change vis-à-vis the federal level. He contrasts their situation to that of developing nations versus developed ones in international negotiations over climate change, a situation in which nations that do not have the resources and know-how to counter the phenomenon need assistance from those industrialized States that have caused climate change in the first place. Even if the Canadian three northern territories now have more power than the federal level, they are less likely to criticize the federal level, given that they are significantly dependent on it, e.g., the facilitation of financial transfers. Yet, Doelle also points out that some advances have taken place in the territories, in the fields of adaptation and mitigation, despite the fact that the current negative attitude of the federal government towards climate change dominates his conclusions.

Rosemary Rayfuse examines whether the five coastal States of the Arctic Ocean have lived up to the promises they made in their Ilulissat Declaration in 2008 – to be stewards of the changing region, to strengthen and develop new measures to improve maritime safety, and to reduce the risk of ship-based pollution within the IMO. Rayfuse shows that this initial shared goal has not yet been fully realized in the context of negotiations concerning the mandatory Polar Code that is currently being negotiated under the auspices of the IMO. Rightly, Rayfuse argues that the Polar Code is a good governance test for the Arctic Five, indicating whether they can actually live up to their stewardship promise, given the future importance of shipping in the newly emerging ocean. However, I would have desired more coverage of the Arctic and Antarctic-specific aspects and also of issues relating to the negotiations over the Polar Code.

Ted McDorman provides an interesting update on where Canada and the United States are on those issues where they do not see eye to eye, such as the legal status of the Northwest Passage and the still unresolved Beaufort Sea boundary dispute. What makes his contribution very important is that he refers to actual sources of diplomatic communication, and the original document whereby Canada already in 1973 had outlined its historical internal waters argument (Note 9, p. 255). As McDorman points out, even if these remain disputed questions between the two neighbors, the evidence shows that relations will develop pragmatically and constructively, despite disagreements existing. Donald Rothwell offers an interesting insight into how Australian's multifaceted Antarctic policy has evolved, and the current questions and challenges it faces. Rothwell also provides very balanced conclusions, perceiving that as a middle power, Australia has so far succeeded in using a variety of international forums to advance its Antarctic goals.

Part V examines the development of the two polar regimes, the Antarctic Treaty System and the Arctic Council. Ruth Davis studies the durability of the Antarctic Treaty System via four criteria: responsiveness (the ability of the model to respond in a timely fashion to new issues as they arise); distinctiveness (the ability of the model to portray Antarctic issues as distinctive or exceptional, apart from global issues, and to present itself as a complete solution to those issues); cohesiveness (the provision of a united front based on cooperation and consensus decision-making, thereby maintaining the ability of the Antarctic Treaty Parties to control Antarctic issues); and authoritativeness (a strong moral foundation based on the concept of trusteeship and the primacy of science and peace) (pp. 292–293). I think this is a very engaging way to examine the durability of the ATS in the face of multiple challenges. Davis shows that on almost every front (perhaps most notably in terms of combating climate change), the ATS faces problems in responding to emergent issues. For this reason, I was slightly surprised by her positive evaluation of the ATS. On p. 306 she concludes that "it [ATS] is a durable model that is in a strong position to tackle the challenges of global climate change," and that overall it is likely to continue as a strong and durable organization (p. 307). Her analysis is intriguing in that she demonstrates the strong aspects of the ATS, while also highlighting inherent problems.

David VanderZwaag provides an interesting review of how the Arctic Council has been gradually beefing up its activities. He provides a very detailed view of what has been taking place in the Council, but is able to also convey the bigger picture of how the Council has become gradually stronger, thus placing the Council within the larger debates on the desirable direction of Arctic governance. VanderZwaag leaves the reader with lots to think about and points to various challenges (environmental and otherwise) that the Arctic Council is supposed to provide a solution to, but lacks the mandate or teeth for. His conclusion is probably the only one possible to draw: Yes, the Council is stronger, but the challenges that it faces seem to be ever-daunting. In the words of VanderZwaag, "One thing is certain however. Governance of human interests in and uses of the Arctic Ocean is certainly in the process of becoming messier" (p. 338).

General Evaluation

First of all, there is one minor issue in the book that I found myself struggling with. As Rizal Abdul Kadir states at the beginning of his contribution: "…five of these states border the Arctic Ocean, several with overlapping maritime *claims*, including to the continental shelf" (emphasis mine). What I found surprising with the use of the word "claim" is that we are talking of areas of continental shelf that need not be claimed. Kadir even refers in the accompanying footnote to Vladimir Golitzyn's article that specifically warns against using the word "claim" (Note 6, p. 111). Several other contributions to the volume also use the word "claim" when referring to extended continental shelf areas, which the Arctic States perceive as belonging to their continental shelf, yet only Tim Stephens dedicates a clarifying footnote to say that strictly speaking, the word "claim" should not be used (Note 5, p. 147). However, who should blame us if even States are using the term, for example, when they articulated the Ilulissat Declaration to read: "We remain committed to this legal framework [law of the sea] and to the orderly settlement of any possible overlapping claims." What I was left wondering is that if we international lawyers do not use the correct terminology, then who would do so?

A bigger substantive struggle I had was with the legal status of the Northwest Passage, and this is something that I have been thinking for some time. I am personally surprised how difficult it is for Canadian scholars to see anything problematic in their country's historic internal waters claim. It is as if the law of the sea community in Canada takes the historic internal waters as it is, and even tries to find further justifications for it, for example, as Michael Byers does in his otherwise impressive book *International Law and the Arctic*. In this regard, a more balanced approach, presenting a broader array of arguments would be of much importance from the Canadian legal academic community, given that the historical internal waters argument is questioned as being controversial.[1]

For instance, an excellent scholar as Suzanne Lalonde defends the historic waters argument with passion. She commences her contribution in an engaging manner: "At the end of a three hour impassioned lecture on the legal arguments supporting Canada's position on the Northwest Passage (NWP), an undergraduate student simply asked, would it really be so bad if Northwest Passage was an international strait?" (p. 166). If I had been in the audience, I would not have asked that question. In such a lecture, why would she only cover the supporting arguments for Canada's position, given the fact that serious concerns of the legal status of these waters do not center only on the arguments offered by the United States, but as a party to the Law of the Sea Convention, Canada has to comply with Article 8(2) and retain the rights of innocent passage (not transit passage). Lalonde erroneously comments on p. 167 that "only the United States has officially challenged Canada's sovereignty over the NWP," even though the EU/UK also protested against this

---

1   See generally C.R. Symmons, *Historic Waters in the Law of the Sea: A Modern Re-Appraisal* (Martinus Nijhoff Publishers, 2008).

historic claim in 1986. Since Lalonde also states that Canada can be taken to the International Court of Justice to defend its case (p. 168), it would seem important to enlighten us not only of whether the NWP could be designated as an international strait, but especially why Article 8(2) would not apply to those waters. It is evident that Suzanne Lalonde does not address this issue and in relation to her stated topic she does not have to: she only tries to demonstrate the problems that the IMO PSSA concept and Article 234 have for the protection of the NWP marine environment. Yet, my overall concern lies on why the Canadian law of the sea scholars do not critically examine this issue.

Another problem I struggled with was the editors' decision not to include a conclusion to the volume, given that we not only had perspectives on polar oceans governance from Australia and Canada, but that the work also examined oceans governance developments in both polar regions. A suitable conclusion could have summarized what can be gleaned from the developments in Arctic and Antarctic governance, both in relation to each other and also more generally to oceans governance. The structure of the book also promotes comparison, as each part addresses both polar regions and their governance evolution and challenges. Yet, as is apparent throughout the book, it is not very easy to compare these two so different regions from the perspective of oceans governance, as the editors tell in their introduction (p. 1; which is also manifested in the fact that there are two prefaces to the book, one devoted to each polar region). Even Part III (resources, environment, sovereignty and jurisdiction – bipolar perspectives) which specifically sets out to examine issues from a bi-polar perspective, does this only in two contributions (those of David Leary and Tim Stephens). The contributions of Kadir and Lalonde do not take a bipolar perspective, but rather study Arctic issues in the light of the development of international law. With such a varied approach, I was unsure as to whether some lessons learned could not perhaps have been teased out from the otherwise very interesting contributions of the book.

There is evidently some room for governance comparison and perhaps even for addressing the potential of learning between the region's governance arrangements. For instance, the ATS has been suggested as a possible model for regulating marine biodiversity in areas beyond national jurisdiction in the Arctic,[2] as well as on a more general level.[3] Comparable environmental changes

---

2   R. Rayfuse, "Protecting Marine Biodiversity in Polar Areas Beyond National Jurisdiction," *Review of European Community & International Environmental Law* 17, no. 1 (April 2008): 3–13.

3   E.J. Molenaar, "Current and Prospective Roles of the Arctic Council System within the Context of the Law of the Sea," *The International Journal of Marine and Coastal Law* 27, (2012): 553–595.

and their management schemes could be compared and contrasted, given that the Arctic is under the influence of global environmental protection regimes and the Antarctic is not. Such an examination might reveal whether they have adopted fairly similar approaches (e.g., in terms of biodiversity protection). If the editors of the volume had presented these questions from the outset of the project to the authors, then perhaps we would have received a more interesting work, from a position of polar oceans governance comparison. However, the approach taken by the editors is understandable, simply because the Poles are indeed so far apart in most governance issues. Thus, it seems sufficient that they canvassed the common challenges faced by the polar regimes in their respective oceans, especially given the politico-legal viewpoint. Moreover, they emphasize something that inspires us most in this field: both polar regions are extremely rich in terms of the types of governance arrangements that have emerged, and therefore require the scholar to know not only the results of natural and social sciences, but also the many branches and layers of the law. This is to me why I find both polar regions so interesting as a researcher.

When reading the book, I found myself wondering how quickly things really change. This volume was compiled really at the hype of Arctic governance. At the time, many were arguing that finally the Arctic Council was transforming to meet the vast challenges ahead, changing from a decision-shaping to a decision-making body. Concurrently, there were a lot of expectations that Arctic offshore hydrocarbons would be exploited, which would bring new wealth to the region, but also present more problems. Yet, what we have actually seen is that the whole energy landscape has been changed by the fracking revolution, and new technologies which have opened new sources of oil and gas have simultaneously taken demand away from conventional oil and gas resources, e.g., those located in Arctic offshore areas. Most dramatically, the Russian annexation of the Crimean Peninsula and the current conflict between Russia and the Western powers over Ukraine have created the very type of scenarios that Rob Huebert discusses in his contribution to this book. Such problems are not caused by Arctic-related factors, yet it has become increasingly difficult to keep the Arctic outside of the larger confrontation between East and West. This evidently manifests itself in the problems which are now influencing the processes of Arctic co-operation.

This book is excellent in many ways. It not only provides a much needed volume that focuses specifically on polar oceans governance, but its structure enables the reader to make a comparison between the regions. It achieves both of these objectives with a full degree of scientific rigor. The individual contributions are of the highest quality and contain almost no errors. For governance research communities, the Canadian and Australian contributors to this work have presented high-quality papers on key issues. As such, it fulfills its purpose as a high quality commentary on the current situation of polar oceans governance.

Timo Koivurova
Research Professor and Director of the Northern Institute for
Environmental and Minority Law, Arctic Centre
University of Lapland, Finland

Prue Taylor and Lucy Stroud, *Common Heritage of Mankind. A Bibliography of Legal Writing* (Malta: Fondation de Malte, 2013), 92 pp.

On November 1, 1967, Ambassador Arvid Pardo, Permanent Representative of Malta to the United Nations (UN), addressed the First Committee of the UN General Assembly for the first time. In a rather lengthy speech he called for "an effective international regime over the sea-bed and the ocean floor beyond a clearly defined national jurisdiction."[4] At the end, Pardo asked the General Assembly to adopt a resolution that declared the seabed and the ocean floor "a common heritage of mankind."[5] In the middle of the Cold War it was the representative of Malta – a small southern European country situated in the center of the Mediterranean that had just gained independence from Great Britain – who made an effort to establish a stable order on the world's oceans and to ensure a better management of ocean resources for the benefit of all.

In general terms, the common heritage of mankind is an ethical concept based on the ideas of non-proprietorship and participatory co-operation. Its main objective is the conservation of natural and cultural/intellectual resources for the benefit of all, including future generations. Although there is no universally accepted definition of the common heritage of mankind, it is of utmost importance to acknowledge that Pardo's proposal "was to be the basis for the concept of the common heritage of mankind being enshrined in international legal instruments and becoming a principle of international law."[6]

---

4 United Nations General Assembly, Twenty-Second Session. Official Records. A/6695; A/C. 1/952. First Committee, 1515th Meeting, Wednesday, 1 November 1967. Web. August 13, 2014.

5 Id.

6 H. Tuerk, *Reflections on the Contemporary Law of the Sea* (Leiden and Boston: Martinus Nijhoff Publishers, 2012), p. 33.

The concept was first spelled out as a legal regime to govern natural resources in Part XI of the United Nations Convention on the Law of the Sea.

Pardo could not anticipate what would come about in the aftermath of his proposal. Although the reaction of the world community had been rather positive at the beginning, the question of defining and implementing the concept of the common heritage of mankind was poised to cause huge controversies, especially in the political arena. From the moment Pardo had introduced the concept onto the stage of international law, a discussion about its very nature, legal content, and judicial status began. Over the last few decades, legal scholars have produced an almost unmanageable amount of literature discussing and analysing the common heritage of mankind within its various contexts.

Prue Taylor's and Lucy Stroud's book *Common Heritage of Mankind. A Bibliography of Legal Writing* reflects these different perspectives of scholarship over time and provides an overview of newly developed knowledge regarding the Common Heritage of Mankind in a remarkably comprehensive way. Taking the year 1967 as a starting point, the bibliography lists approximately 600 different titles in 14 different languages taken from 215 different journals. The bibliography contains a list of these journals as well. In addition, readers are invited to send updates to the editors in order to keep this project alive and up-to-date. To highlight the different contexts within which research on the common heritage of mankind (CHM) is being undertaken, the book is divided into ten different sections:

- CHM in the General Context
- CHM in Multi-Subject Areas
- CHM in the Outer Space Context
- CHM in Marine Context
- CHM in the Antarctic Context
- CHM in the Cultural and Natural Heritage Context
- CHM in the Climate Context
- CHM in the Biodiversity Context
- CHM in the Human Genome Context
- CHM in the Shared Water Resources Context

The chapters on the concept in both the general and marine contexts make up the most extensive sections of the book. The respective sections list the titles alphabetically by author. This particular way of structuring turns out to be highly effective and will be helpful to many researchers in different areas.

Prue Taylor, LL.B., LL.M. (Hons), LL.M. (Energy & Environment), is a senior lecturer at the School of Architecture and Planning at the University of

Auckland, New Zealand, and the deputy director of the New Zealand Centre for Environmental Law. Lucy Stroud, LL.B. (Hons), is a senior researcher at the New Zealand Centre for Environmental Law and a Ph.D. candidate in law at the University of Auckland.

Taylor is one of the leading scholars in the field of international environmental law. She has been published widely, especially on the topics of climate change, property rights, and environmental ethics. In her 1998 monograph *An Ecological Approach to International Law: Responding to Challenges of Climate Change*, Taylor enthusiastically argues for a fundamental change of consciousness in the human-nature relationship and suggests that "ecocentrism could be translated into a new principle of international environmental law which would operate as the guiding principle of a global environmental treaty."[7] Understood as an ethical concept and as a principle of environmental protection, the common heritage of mankind could be used as the basis for the formulation of such a new principle of international environmental law.[8] Taylor has been an outspoken advocate of the common heritage of mankind as a significant concept of environmental ethics. In general, her body of work offers a refreshingly comprehensible and straightforward account and analysis of this concept.[9]

According to Taylor, one way to achieve this change of consciousness and to keep the discussion about the common heritage alive is to flesh out and articulate the philosophical foundations of the common heritage of mankind.[10] Much more research needs to be done in this area. Taylor's and Stroud's introduction to their *Bibliography of Legal Writing* is especially interesting in this respect. Without contemplating too much on the history of the common heritage of mankind since Pardo's historic address to the United Nations, the authors go on to point out the significant contributions of Father Peter

---

7   P. Taylor, *An Ecological Approach to International Law. Responding to Challenges of Climate Change* (London and New York: Routledge, 1998), p. 43.

8   Id., p. 258.

9   See P. Taylor, "Common Heritage of Mankind Principle," in K. Bosselmann, D.S. Fogel and J.B. Ruhl, eds., *Berkshire Encyclopedia of Sustainability: Law and Politics of Sustainability* (Great Barrington: Berkshire Publishing Group, 2010), p. 64. Also P. Taylor, "The Common Heritage of Mankind: A Bold Doctrine Kept Within Strict Boundaries," in D. Bollier and S. Helfrich, eds., *The Wealth of the Commons: A World Beyond Market and State* (Amherst: Levellers, 2012), p. 353.

10 See P. Taylor, "The Future of the Common Heritage of Mankind. Intersections with the Public Trust Doctrine," in L. Westra, P. Taylor and A. Michelot, eds., *Confronting Ecological and Economic Collapse. Ecological Integrity for Law, Policy and Human Rights* (London and New York: Routledge, 2013), p. 32.

Serracino Inglott and Elisabeth Mann Borgese in the development of the concept. Serracino Inglott and Mann Borgese cooperated closely to illuminate the core essence of the common heritage of mankind. While Serracino Inglott came from the perspective of Christian theology, Mann Borgese followed a more holistic approach in developing a philosophical framework for the common heritage of mankind.

In general, Mann Borgese shared Arvid Pardo's notion of the common heritage of mankind, but she put more emphasis on environmental protection and conservation. She was able to expand and broaden the meaning of the concept profoundly. Mann Borgese supported a more holistic and universal view of the world. She tried to walk and cross the boundaries that for centuries have characterized the relationships between humankind and nature, the common and the private good, the individual and the community, myth and science, the outside and the inside of the individual (body and soul), and correspondingly the differentiations between the genders. In 1986, Mann Borgese briefly described her notion of the philosophy of the common heritage of mankind concept:

> It is based on a philosophy of transcendence of the individual, the blurring of his or her boundaries, and the continuity between 'inside' and 'outside' that the concept of the common heritage becomes 'natural', and therefore acceptable, because ownership and sovereignty become as open and permeable as the individual.[11]

Here, Mann Borgese does not talk about the concept itself, but about a "philosophical setting required for the application of that concept." Her approach to the philosophy of the common heritage of mankind is one step removed from the concept and acknowledges the fact that without major and universal changes in thought a new world order would not be possible. Mann Borgese's conception of the individual within the world at large is reflected in the boundlessness of the oceans: "When we deal with the oceans, everything flows, and boundaries are more fiction than reality as political boundaries, economic boundaries, and ecological boundaries no longer coincide."[12]

Mann Borgese's non-hierarchical and non-anthropocentric philosophy is based on the premise that human beings are part of a whole. Taylor's and

11   E. Mann Borgese, *The Future of the Oceans: A Report to the Club of Rome* (Montreal: Harvest House, 1986), pp. 125–134.

12   E. Mann Borgese, "Caird Medal Address," *Marine Policy* 25 (2001), p. 391.

Stroud's important contribution to the scholarship of the common heritage of mankind shows that they share Mann Borgese's philosophy.

Julia Poertner
Interdisciplinary Ph.D. Candidate
Dalhousie University
Halifax, Nova Scotia, Canada

Stefan Talmon and Bing Bing Jia, eds., *The South China Sea Arbitration: A Chinese Perspective* (Oxford: Hart Publishing, 2014), 274 pp.

The South China Sea is among the most intense spaces on the planet – critical for maritime traffic, for fisheries resources and hydrocarbons and has thus long been an object of State demands and claims. It is one of the world's large marine ecosystems, boasts more than half of the world's top 20 shipping ports,[13] is transited by 50 percent of global oil tanker traffic passing through some of the most heavily travelled international straits,[14] and as one of the world's most travelled shipping lanes accommodates $5.3 trillion of trade each year.[15] Recently, claims to access and control of this strategically critical marine space have intensified. The littorals of Brunei, China, Indonesia, Malaysia, the Philippines, and Vietnam have asserted claims to nearly 3.5 million square kilometers (1.4 million square miles) of marine space via diplomatic *notes verbale*, official media statements, positioning of national symbols and personnel, warship deployments, fishing vessels and positioning of drilling platforms. Yet, no claim invoked a formal tribunal constituted under widely accepted principles of international law until 22 January 2013, when the Philippines instituted arbitration proceedings against China "with respect to the dispute with China over the maritime jurisdiction of the Philippines in the West Philippine Sea."[16]

---

13 International Association of Ports and Harbors, Statistics: World Top 20 Ports, 2003–2012 (2013), available online: <http://www.iaphworldports.org/LinkClick.aspx?fileticket =PMewveDCUUg%3d&tabid=4879>.

14 US Energy Info. Admin., Independent Statistics & Analysis: South China Sea (last updated 7 February 2013), *available at* http://www.eia.gov/countries/regions-topics.cfm?fips=SCS.

15 B.S. Glaser, Council on Foreign Relations, Armed Clash in the South China Sea (2012), available online: <http://www.cfr.org/world/armed-clash-south-china-sea/p27883?cid =rss-asia-armed_clash_in_the_south_china-041112>.

16 See Philippines Notification and Statement of Claim reproduced in *The South China Sea Arbitration: A Chinese Perspective* (Stefan Talmon & Bing Bing Jia, eds., 2014), 206 Annex I.

The Philippines' claim requests relief on 13 points among which is a request that the tribunal declare that China's maritime claims in the South China Sea based on its "nine-dash line" are contrary to UNCLOS and invalid.[17] Philippine Foreign Secretary Albert del Rosario stated that the Philippines' case against China "is about defending what is legitimately ours...[and] guaranteeing freedom of navigation for all nations," thereby "preserv[ing] regional peace, security and stability."[18] This first South China Sea claim in a formal arena, a demand for dispute settlement via UNCLOS-authorized bilateral arbitration, is the subject of this most timely book.

The volume, *The South China Sea Arbitration: A Chinese Perspective*, is essential reading for anyone desiring thoughtful analyses of the case from the standpoint of China. The editors are Stefan Talmon, Professor of International Law and Director of the Institute for Public International Law in the University of Bonn and Bing Bing Jia, Professor of International Law in the Law School of Tsinghua University, Beijing. Each has also contributed substantive chapters to the volume. They are joined by contributing authors Michael Sheng-ti Gau, Professor of Public International Law at the Institute of the Law of the Sea, National Taiwan Ocean University in Keelung; Haiwen Zhang, a Vice-President and Senior Research Fellow of the China Institute for Marine Affairs and Secretary General of the Chinese Society of the Law of the Sea; and Chenxi Mi, Research Fellow of the China Institute for Marine Affairs and Ph.D. candidate at the Law School of Dalian Maritime University. Cumulatively, they bring great depth of scholarship and practical understanding of China law of the sea practice to this work.

By way of background, pursuant to UNCLOS Article 287 regarding choice of dispute settlement procedure, State parties are obliged to submit disputes concerning interpretation or application of the Convention to specified means of dispute settlement: (1) the International Tribunal for the Law of the Sea (ITLOS); (2) the International Court of Justice, (3) an arbitral tribunal constituted in accordance with UNCLOS Annex VII; or (4) a special arbitral tribunal constituted in accordance with UNCLOS Annex VIII. If States have not selected a means of dispute settlement, or, if States have not chosen identical means of dispute settlement, the dispute is to be submitted to an Annex VII Arbitral Tribunal. The Philippines Notification and Statement of Claim is a demand for arbitration pursuant to Annex VII.

---

17   Id.

18   *Philippines files case to UN in South China Sea dispute*, BBC News, Mar. 31, 2014, available online: <http://www.bbc.com/news/world-asia-26781682>.

The South China Sea Arbitration: A Chinese Perspective is divided into five chapters followed by annexes and accompanied by extensive footnotes to governmental and to independent scholarly sources. Chapter I, "The Disputes between the Philippines and China in the South China Sea," is co-authored by editors Professors Bing Bing Jia and Stefan Talmon. The authors describe the geography in context and present an overview of historical claims noting, "The proximity of the littoral States of the South China Sea means that disputes over regional control and influence are bound to arise almost automatically."

They review Chinese government cartographic exercises beginning in 1933 which led to the 1935 map describing South China Sea islands in both Chinese and English. By 1946, the map included the Xisha (Paracel) and Nansha (Spratly) recovered from Japan. In 1947, a government atlas described an eleven-dash line suggesting authority over greater South China Sea space. The authors explain that "In May 1949, the four island groups in the South China Sea and other attached islands were placed under the authority of the Hainan District of Guang Dong Province" (p. 4). They assert that "China has maintained its position since 1949 with only relatively minor changes over the years" (p. 4). Official government pronouncements ensued which the authors detail. Of critical import was the 7 May 2009 *Note Verbale* addressed to the United Nations Secretary-General stating that China "has indisputable sovereignty over the islands in the South China Sea and the adjacent waters and enjoys sovereign rights and jurisdiction over the relevant waters as well as the seabed and subsoil thereof" (p. 4). The note accompanied a map "illustrating the well-known Chinese position showing the islands and waters in the South China Sea enclosed by a nine-dash line, which has since been made the bone of contention by the Philippines" (p. 4).

The authors underscore that South China Sea claims have been manifested in a complex, and largely intractable, web of territorial and maritime jurisdictional disputes that became acute beginning the 1970s. The authors explain "[T]he issues that prompted the present arbitration have...a recent history and date back to the 1970s." They then proceed to highlight what in their view are "...the facts that gave rise, or are relevant to the Philippines' filing of the Notification and Statement of Claim against China in January 2013" (p. 3). They identify and describe those administrative acts accompanying the regulations that may have legal valence.

The authors then turn to the choice of arbitration, that is, recourse to the dispute settlement procedures of Part XV of UNCLOS. They note that there are regional mechanisms for the peaceful settlement of disputes within the Association of Southeast Asian Nations (ASEAN) framework, namely the ASEAN-China Declaration on the Conduct of Parties in the South China Sea

(DOC) and the Treaty of Amity and Cooperation in Southeast Asia, which provide for dispute settlement through "friendly consultations and negotiations" (p. 7). They underscore that neither is incompatible with UNCLOS, and in the authors' view, "consultations and negotiations continue to offer the best prospect for the peaceful settlement of the territorial and jurisdictional disputes in the South China Sea" (p. 7). They endeavor to place the Philippines' choice of arbitration in the context of "on-going efforts to resolve the disputes in the South China Sea in a spirit of friendship and cooperation..."

The authors describe the reasons China rejects arbitration: First, the dispute involves questions of territorial sovereignty over certain islands and reefs. Second, pursuant to ASEAN-China DOC 2002 the Philippines is bound by a commitment to resolve territorial and jurisdictional disputes with China through friendly negotiations. Third, China alleges the Philippines' *Note Verbale* and the Notification and Statement of Claims "contains serious errors in fact and law as well as false accusations against China" (p. 7). The authors explain the procedure by which the Tribunal has been constituted, the seat and registry of the arbitration, and explain that the rules of procedure have now been fixed.

Having set the stage, the ensuing chapters highlight critical issues of law and policy associated with the Philippines claim. In Chapter 2, Professor Stefan Talmon poses a critical question: "The South China Sea Arbitration: Is there a Case to Answer?" The chapter opens by articulating the position expressed by the Chinese Ministry of Foreign Affairs on 26 April 2013 that the arbitration would involve territorial sovereignty claims pertaining to islands and reefs which places the matter beyond the application or interpretation of UNCLOS. Thus China's default of appearance at this writing is likely. The author correctly emphasizes that "the absence of a State cannot be taken as an admission of the facts or the legal views of the applicant, or as showing that the absent party has no, or no convincing counter arguments to the applicant's case" and hence there is "a sovereign 'right' not to appear" (p. 16, 17). The chapter proceeds to place China's non-appearance in historical perspective, considers the consequences of default of appearance, and describes a range of preliminary objections to the Philippines claim including (subsets) of lack of jurisdiction of the arbitral tribunal, inadmissibility of the claims, and objections of a preliminary character such as indispensable third parties. The chapter concludes with Professor Talmon rebutting each of the thirteen points principally raised in the Philippines claim.

Chapter 3, "Issues in Jurisdiction in Cases of Default of Appearance," is by Michael Sheng-ti Gau. He squarely confronts the provision of UNCLOS Article 9: "Before making its award, the arbitral tribunal must satisfy itself not only that it has jurisdiction over the dispute, but also that the claim is well founded in fact and law" (p. 83, citing UNCLOS Annex VII, Article 9). Hence, the Tribunal is obliged to investigate whether it has jurisdiction. The writer explores how thoroughly and to what extent is the Tribunal is required to appraise the range of objections that China could conceivably raise and proceeds to the requirement that a dispute must exist between the parties. He examines five relevant groupings of claims – maritime areas, sovereignty of certain reefs, rock-status of certain reefs, claims to maritime zones and navigation claims. The author then characterizes and describes a threefold "real" Sino-Philippine dispute: (1) territorial dispute over the Spratly/Nansha Islands, (2) whether those islands generate maritime entitlements, and (3) a maritime delimitation dispute. He concludes by (tying) these to the jurisdiction of the Tribunal.

Chapter 4, "The Issues of Admissibility in Inter-State Arbitration," is by co-editor Bing Bing Jia. Professor Jia considers the Notification and Statement of Claim "on the hypothesis that it might actually be concerned with the interpretation or application of UNCLOS, which it is not..." He postulates that the Claim "may give rise to certain grounds of inadmissibility that may not easily be cured by the expected memorial" and proceeds to examine four plausible grounds of inadmissibility. The first is UNCLOS Article 281(1), specifically where no settlement has been reached by recourse to agreed means and where the agreement does not exclude any further procedure. The Article 281(1) provision is considered in light of the Declaration on the Conduct of Parties in the South China Sea of 4 November 2002 and the Treaty of Amity and Cooperation of 1976. Professor Jia effectively argues that there is no relevant and conclusive proof as to the failure of negation (p. 116). He concludes that two of the three Article 281(1) requirements have not been met.

The author then considers mootness and vagueness as indicative of the posits of two further defects in the Notification and Statement of Claim. He then raises the question of good faith and whether the filing itself rises to an abuse of rights and/or procedure and concludes that "[t]he act of filing clearly flows from and interpretation of the scheme of Part XV that should be firmly rejected by the Arbitral Tribunal for the sake of a stable and effective regime such as the one found in UNCLOS" (p. 130). Professor Jia also raises an interesting estoppel argument as a corollary to Article 281(1) and abuse of right. The argument is that the Government of the Philippines is estopped by a serious of official acts that by their nature are an engagement of the State and are binding under international law. On this point he cites relevant international jurisprudence in support of this argument – the *Nuclear Tests Case* (ICJ 1974), *Eastern Greenland* (PCIJ 1933), and *Temple of Preah Vihear* (ICJ 1962). The chapter concludes by citing the judgment of *Georgia v. Russia* where the ICJ found that Georgia had not availed itself of non-adjudicative mechanisms of dispute settlement provided in a precedent agreement entered into by the parties. The vector of Professor Jia's argument, founded on the non-fulfillment of Article 281(1) conditions, reaches the conclusion that the Government of the Philippines claims "should be declared inadmissible and rejected in their entirety by the Arbitral Tribunal" (p. 135).

Chapter 5 is co-authored by Haiwen Zhang and Chenxi Mi, "Jurisprudential Tenability of the Philippines v. China Arbitration on South China Sea Disputes?" After summarizing the Philippines claim as detailed in the Notification and Statement of Claim and reviewing the relief sought, the authors endeavor to answer the question as to why China has refused to accept the Philippines arbitration demand. These are, *inter alia*, a failure to fulfill good faith legal obligations under UNCLOS, legal flaws in the Notification and Statement of Claim, and breach of declarations and bilateral agreements. The authors explain Chinese policy on South China Sea disputes, discuss the attitudes of Vietnam and Taiwan toward the case, and conclude that China's position on resolving South China Sea disputes via bilateral negotiations is "in accordance with international law and has gained broad international support" (p. 158).

This reviewer found the documents contained as annexes in Chapter 6 especially useful. Annex I contains documents of the People's Republic of China and documents of the Republic of Philippines. These include ministry statements, *notes verbale*, position papers, declarations legislative acts, and municipal laws. It contains the Republic of the Philippines Notification and Statement of Claim. Annex II is comprised of a bibliography of the South China Sea disputes. The Annex III glossary of place names enumerates all islands, islets, and rocks referenced in the documents in both Chinese Pin-yin and English, which is extremely useful for readers limited in either language.

The process of State interactions that crystallize in claims can generate authoritative decisions that become accepted as international law. The calculus by according to which a State decides to assert a formal claim and the attendant choice of arena is strategic. The benefits and costs of that choice will have been carefully considered by one party, as will the cost and benefit of a default of appearance by the other party. This strategic dynamics is recognized by the authors of this book, particularly in a section entitled "The Politics of Arbitration" (p. 71). In the South China Sea, the opening strategic choices have been made and the arbitration has now been inserted into the regional constitutive process. The overwhelming question is whether this proceeding, and the behaviour of the parties, will advance the common interest of the oceans.

Those anticipating the answer and the range of potential outcomes will want to read *The South China Sea Arbitration: A Chinese Perspective*.

Charles H. Norchi
Professor of Law and Director
Center for Oceans and Coastal Law
University of Maine School of Law, Maine, USA

Annual Report of the International Ocean Institute

∵

Report of the International Ocean Institute, 2013[*]

Message from the President

More than 40 years ago, Elisabeth Mann Borgese founded the IOI with the aim of supporting the establishment of the international law of the sea. A year after its adoption, in 1983, I met Elisabeth and learnt from her about the work of the IOI. From that moment I became a supporter of her ambition to encourage enough states to ratify and implement the international law of the sea.

In many long conversations and discussions with Elisabeth, and during my work with her in reorganizing her library in the early 1980s – at the same time as I was graduating from the newly established training programmes in Halifax – I achieved a deep understanding of the foundations of her thinking about the sustainable use of the seas and of her untiring work towards a fairer world. On her advice I studied marine biology, and sought to contribute more substantially to her work in IOI through my support as a Board member of the Ocean Science and Research Foundation (OSRF) in the early 1990s.

After more than 30 years working with and in support of the IOI, I was elected President of the IOI in December 2013. This was an honour that I would never have imagined, but also a great challenge to which I commit myself wholeheartedly. Most of all, I feel that I have been given a responsibility, primarily towards the seas and oceans and the people who live near it and from it, but also towards keeping Elisabeth's heritage and her vision alive. From its humble yet ambitious beginnings, the international law of the sea has become a reality, but one that urgently needs to be amended based on new knowledge and new realities. An example that springs to mind is the requirement to establish large marine protected areas, where marine resources can recover from exploitation.

---

[*] Editors' Note.—This report is extracted from the *Report of the International Ocean Institute for 2013* (Malta: International Ocean Institute, September 2013), available online: <http://www.ioinst.org>. Due to space limitations it has been abridged and edited for publication in the *Ocean Yearbook*.

Ocean Yearbook 29: 529–567

Elisabeth Mann Borgese and the IOI contributed substantially to the development and the implementation of the law of the sea, the biggest legal settlement globally. Elisabeth would have been rightly proud of this achievement and so are we. Thus, the role of the IOI and the PIM conferences for the installation of the UN Convention on the Law of the Sea (UNCLOS) is not to be underestimated. At around the same time, Elisabeth became aware of the need to make this law more widely known and, above all, more accessible to people, since the law can only fulfill its function and be implemented in the correct spirit if people are aware of its implications and of what it means to interact with and govern the oceans. In this respect, IOI has established since the 1990s several operational centres to train people in the law of the sea and in how to apply this law to serve their needs. Most especially with the training courses held in Halifax, Canada, hundreds of students have been trained since 1981 and this success story continues today thanks to the IOI. Regular training courses are given in Malta and South Africa, and this programme of capacity building will continue since these training courses are considered to best serve IOI's core ambitions: to disseminate information and knowledge and to build capacity worldwide.

To continue to achieve these core ambitions, IOI basically focuses on two complementary approaches:

· The first is the publication of the *World Ocean Review*, which is reaching thousands of people and politicians worldwide and achieving success in increasing awareness of the needs of the oceans and seas. The *World Ocean Review* is published annually in many languages and disseminated free of charge by modern media such as the internet.[1]
· Another approach is the well-established regional and global ocean governance training programme series as well as a recently implemented Master in Arts degree programme in ocean governance at the University of Malta; the success of this capacity building and education series will be further continued, intensified and, above all, expanded to cover more regions and regional seas of the globe.

The implementation of the law of the sea and the dissemination of knowledge about the governance of the oceans should guide us in our future endeavours

---

1   The first three issues of the *World Ocean Review* may be downloaded as PDF files, free of charge, in English translation or in the original German, from <http://worldoceanreview.com/en/> and <http://worldoceanreview.com> respectively. The titles issued thus far are: *WOR 1: Living with the Oceans. A Report on the State of the World's Oceans; WOR 2: The Future of Fish – The Fisheries of the Future*, and *WOR 3: Marine Resources – Opportunities and Risks*.

and thus continue to complement and promote Elisabeth Mann Borgese's outstanding work.

Nikolaus Gelpke[2]

President of IOI

IOI Operational Centre Activities – 2013

In 2013, the IOI network worked through the actions of 22 active Operational Centres and 14 Focal Points worldwide, grouped according to five regions with each group being represented by one elected director. In this reporting year a new group of representative directors was elected following a re-organisation of the regional groupings. For clarity, reporting of network activities is structured along these new regions.

The IOI Operational Centres engage in a wide range of activities ranging from work at the community level to very specialised scientific research as part of large international programmes. The centres are embedded in the work programmes of their host institutes, which are mostly universities and independent research institutes. A few centres (e.g., South Africa, Canada and Ukraine) have reached an independent status of non-profit organisations. Extra funding is gained through the IOI network-wide development programme "Women, Youth and the Sea" that focuses on special training programmes for women and young people in coastal communities. These programmes are working especially on outreach, training and information dissemination and can reach several hundred people with their activities. Others concentrate on post-graduate students and are running small specialised courses. A total of more than 2,500 participants have been recorded in the different courses and events by the centres.

Flagship courses of IOI's training and capacity building programme remain the two-month training programme on Ocean Governance: Policy, Law and Management, organised by IOI-Canada at Dalhousie University, and the Training Programme on Regional Ocean Governance for the Mediterranean, Black, Baltic and Caspian Seas, organised by the IOI-Malta Operational Centre in Malta. However, an increasing number of regional governance courses for the western Pacific coast (IOI-China) in Tianjin, China, the dedicated Caspian Sea course in Turkmenistan and the newly developed course in South Africa to cover the African seas (IOI-Southern Africa), are bringing the issues of ocean governance closer to a greater audience. The Master of Arts degree in

---

2 Elected IOI President during the Governing Board Meeting in December 2013, succeeding Awni Behnam who was unanimously designated Honorary President of the IOI for life during the same meeting.

ocean governance offered in cooperation with the Faculty of Laws at the University of Malta is another institutionalized training programme of IOI in the field.

The network is represented at different global and regional meetings by the Chair of the IOI Directors or the regional representatives. The Executive Committee meeting held in Bangkok in September 2013 in conjunction with the International Forum on Sustainable Governance of the Oceans held in Bangkok, Thailand, was one of the major events to present IOI's expertise in various fields in the different sessions. Other meetings where the Chair of the network of IOI Operational Centre directors represented the work of the IOI were the ICES Working Group on Large Marine Ecosystem Programme Best Practices, which brings together since 2010 some 25 international experts on Large Marine Ecosystem Management; the IOC/UNESCO-IUCN-NOAA Consultative Meeting on Large Marine Ecosystems (LMEs) in Paris, France; and the Conference on China's Contribution on Security and Cooperation in the Indian Ocean Area in Shanghai.

The Buddenbrook-Haus, a museum in the old Hanseatic city of Lübeck dedicated to Thomas Mann, the father of Elisabeth Mann Borgese, created a specialised exhibition commemorating the work of IOI's founder, Elisabeth Mann Borgese. This exhibition was reported on extensively in earlier IOI publications, but 2013 saw the transfer of this exhibition to Bremen, the host city of IOI-Germany, in the autumn, before its eventual tour to Halifax for display at Dalhousie in connection with IOI-Canada in the future.

Regional Organisation and Representation within the IOI Network

The election of new representatives in 2013 led to a new grouping of the Operational Centres. While the regional groupings for Africa and the Americas remained the same, Europe, Asia and Oceania were re-organized to reflect new centre distributions. The new regional representative for Asia is the director of IOI-China, Mrs. Qin Li, while Oceania has become a region on its own merit and the director of IOI-Pacific Islands in Fiji, Dr. Joeli Veitayaki, is representing this region. The centres in Ukraine and Caspian Sea have been included in the region hosting the other European centres, and representatives for this group are the directors of IOI-Germany and IOI-Ukraine, Dr. Werner Ekau and Dr. Victoria Radchenko, respectively:

Africa	Adnan Awad, Vice-Chair (IOI-South Africa) with regional representation for the IOI Operational Centres in Egypt, Kenya, Nigeria and South Africa and the focal point in Egypt.
The Americas	Michael Butler (IOI-Canada) with regional representation for the IOI Operational Centres in Canada, Costa Rica, Cuba, Brazil and the United States and a focal point in the United States.
Asia	Qin Li (IOI-China) with regional representation for the IOI Operational Centres in PR China, Japan, Thailand, India, Indonesia as well as the focal points in Shanghai, PR China, Kazakhstan, Malaysia, Pakistan, Philippines, Republic of Korea and Singapore
Oceania	Joeli Veitayaki (IOI-Pacific Islands) with regional representation for the IOI Operational Centre of the Pacific Islands in Fiji and the focal point in Australia.
Europe	Werner Ekau, Chair (IOI-Germany) and Victoria Radchenko (IOI-Ukraine) with regional representation for the IOI Operational Centres in the Caspian Sea (Astrakhan, Russian Federation and in IR Iran), Germany, Malta, Romania, Slovenia and Ukraine, and the focal point in Cyprus, Finland, Lebanon and Turkey.

To better reflect the regional organisation of the IOI family, the reports of the centres' activities is presented by regional groupings.

Africa

The IOI-Southern Africa has restructured and registered itself in South Africa as a non-profit organization with tax exemption. It also moved its offices in February 2013 to the Kirstenbosch National Botanical Gardens, within the offices of the South African National Biodiversity Institute (SANBI). The year 2013 was dominated by preparations and running the first Ocean Governance Training Programme for Africa, reported on extensively in other parts of this annual report. Other projects have been running concurrently with continued and increased activity from the IOI-SA associates. IOI-SA continues to be supported through project work developed by the Director; however, a strategic approach has been initiated this year to seek and develop more sustainable mechanisms and partnerships for support. An intern from the United States was taken on board to work with the Director in the IOI-SA office for a period of six months to help develop an assessment of marine science and climate change initiatives in the region, as well as to assist with the running of the Ocean Governance Training Programme. 2013 also saw the launch of the new

IOI-SA website at www.ioisa.org and the launch of the IOI-SA Facebook Page with regular updates and photos on projects and activities: www.facebook .com/IOISouthernAfrica.

September 20th marked the last day of the IOI-SA four-week Ocean Governance Training Programme for Africa, but it also signified the official launch of AfriCOG (African Centre for Capacity Building in Ocean Governance). Although the Ocean Governance Training Programme was considered an AfriCOG imitative, this day marked the official beginning of AfriCOG as IOI-SA, along with 18 other partner organizations, signed AfriCOG's founding documents during an official signing ceremony; more information about AfriCOG is also available online: http://www.africog.net/news/11-new-partnership-supports-marine-resource-management-across-africa.html.

The IOI-West African Operational Centre (IOI-WAOC) in Nigeria has started an introductory course of basic oceanography for secondary school students. It also organized the World Ocean Day and activities related to the Women, Youth and the Sea Programme.

A group of about 50 students between 12 and 14 years old, from Basil International School, a privately owned Lagos-based secondary school, visited the host institution on an educational visit under the auspices of IOI-WAOC. The students were given lectures introducing them to the basics of marine science and emphasizing the importance of the ocean to life on this planet, a source of food and minerals, an avenue of world trade transport, and a moderator of the Earth's climate. The students were also shown a film on marine biodiversity and taken to the laboratory for some hands-on experience.

About two hundred people from the Nigerian Navy, Federal Department of Fisheries, Federal Ministry of Environment, Nigerian Shipper's Council, Fisheries Society of Nigeria (FISON), Department of Petroleum Resources (DPR), Etina Environmental Services, undergraduate and graduate students of marine science particularly from the University of Lagos, Lagos State University as well as research officers from the host institution participated in the celebration of World Ocean Day.

In its Women, Youth and the Sea Programme the centre worked on the introduction of fish farming to students of a coastal fishing community secondary school, A Catch Them Young initiative. This was the first in the series planned to be carried out in secondary schools in the Magbon-Orimedu Axis. For sustainability, the interest generated was encouraging as even some of the teachers expressed their intention to have their own fish farms in their backyards. The programme was also run in a participatory manner which gave the students the feeling of having a strong stake in the project.

The IOI Focal Point in Egypt, in collaboration with the Boy Scout Association, held a mini-seminar on ocean governance and protection, the aim of this event being to familiarize the group with the issues and to empower them to take action within their capabilities as an active NGO with wide social outreach. The group of 15 Boy Scouts attended the lectures held by Dr. Amer Dola (IOI Focal Point in Egypt) which centred around the role of oceans in our life, the challenges faced in ocean protection and how everyone can be involved in ocean governance even by small actions such as increasing awareness of the ocean's importance and also by acting to keep it clean. The group asked many questions about how they could start to implement what they had learnt such as by sharing information with the population in the Suez area and on the coast of the Red Sea. The seminar has empowered the group to work on these issues as well as to encourage them to influence positively more groups of young people and to share with them the ideas and activities of ocean governance.

The Americas

IOI-Canada's work particularly emphasised the 33rd annual course, attended by 12 participants from eight countries, and the ninth EMB Ocean Lecture which explored the important subject of Communicating the Oceans, held in conjunction with provincial celebrations of World Oceans Day. Both events are described in more detail in other chapters of this annual report. Information dissemination included the fourth Halifax Oceans Film Festival, as well as various outreach activities and presentations. Research activities included IOI-Canada's continued involvement in a multi-year, multi-million dollar project on small-scale fisheries. The senior research fellows contributed with a range of activities (e.g., training, information dissemination, research, and publications) and as ever, fundraising efforts continued to be an important focus. Accordingly, IOI-Canada has now established the Ocean Governance Training Foundation (OGTF) for which we are seeking charitable status.

IOI-Costa Rica was active in the Women, Youth and the Sea project continuing the successful work in local development by supporting a process of social support in the communities of Isla Venado, Isla Caballo, Cabuya and Lepanto. The implementation of an integrating methodological model is promoted because it takes into account the participation from the national Programmea de Desarrollo Integral Comunitario Costero (PDICC) assigned to the International Ocean Institute and as well as from other partners from the Universidad Nacional (host institute of the IOI Operational Centre in Costa Rica), such as the School of Planning and Social Promotion, the School of Sociology, the Institute of Woman Studies and Chorotega Regional Department. For 12 years this programme has been empowering communities and fostering good management by training over 300 individuals, most of them community representatives and leaders. Projects on the environment and productive project learning have been promoted, amongst others, and in each community research on different subjects is taking place: birds, potable water, mangroves, responsible fishing, natural hazard social risk, and youth empowerment.

Globe Florida-Costa Rica Programme: Together with the IOI-USA Operational Centre in Florida, the programme is being revised and new schools in Costa Rica are being supported by IOI-Costa Rica in the hope that funds for the purpose could be raised. In the context of the Globe program, a member of the Women, Youth and the Sea Programme team has introduced the Globe procedures in the community of Lepanto, Pacific side of Costa Rica, and currently is also helping the local IOI Globe coordinator develop the Globe routines in Puntarenas, Pacific side, and Sarapiquí inland community, in the north of the country. Lepanto and Sarapiquí celebrated this year's Oceans Day by organizing different marine science activities, including an exhibition of old oceanographic instruments.

Besides this IOI-funded project, the centre participates in other research projects such as "Determination of an index of risk due to rip currents in the Costa Rican beaches," where also a rip current meter measuring the current speed and direction was designed, constructed and tested in joint collaboration with the National Bureau of Tourism (ICT), the National Coast Guard (SNG) and the National Commission of Emergency (CNE) to extend the previous stage of the project from 100 beaches to over 200, to reduce the risk of fatalities and to support responsible tourism activities. Tsunami forecast models have also been implemented, as well as a proposal submitted to the CNE for determining the evacuation routes in the Costa Rican coastal zone.

The IOI-South Western Atlantic Ocean (IOI-SWAO, Brazil) together with its host institution opened the Brazilian section of the International Association for Promoting Geoethics (IAPG) as a multidisciplinary, scientific platform for widening the debate on problems of ethics applied to the geosciences. The backbone of one of the sessions at EGU 2014, co-organized by the Operational Centre's director, is a concept familiar to IOI: the Earth (Seas included) are a common heritage of humankind, and scientists have a great responsibility, particularly when dealing with natural (and human induced) hazards. IOI-SWAO is hosting the national section of IAPG.

IOI-SWAO continued organizing a network of researchers and practitioners in order to evaluate the coastal ecosystems and its relationship with human well-being (research and extension – national). This network was internationally recognized and invited to extend the experience working in an international network, under the Millennium Assessment Follow Up initiative umbrella (MAFU/UNEP), working with teams from Latin America and the Caribbean region (research and extension – international). Resources were obtained from local agencies, UNEP and UNU.

IOI-SWAO continues to "export" knowledge to primary and secondary schools in the coastal area, where there is a lack of resources, both human and material. Students and professors from the host university were encouraged to go into schools and create enthusiasm in primary and secondary school students and teachers regarding marine-related issues.

Ocean Day activities were performed together with the host institution, promoting an open get-together on the campus of the CEM, as well as a special presentation at the regular institute's event "Coffee with Science" session during Oceanographer Day on 8 June 2013.

In 2013, IOI-USA implemented initiatives with youth serving organizations and assessed the status of marine debris as a potential issue to develop programmes for 2014. The centre supported the Youth Ocean Conservation Summit in 2012 and 2013. The Summit is led by a university student with the goal to empower the next generation of ocean conservationists and help students learn skills necessary to implement conservation projects. Hosted by the renowned Mote Marine Laboratory, Sarasota, Florida, the YOC Summit provides opportunities for youth to share their experiences and learn from each other. Students that were funded in 2012 with mini-grants ranging from US$75 to US$200 presented their projects at the 2013 YOC Summit on Nov. 16, 2013. The projects addressed the following: mangrove cultivation and restoration, sea turtle support, shark awareness, oyster beds and water quality. All had extensive youth and community outreach efforts. To obtain the mini-grants, IOI-USA required that the students prepare and submit applications and prepare reports about their activities. Within this Summit, the IOI-USA executive director held a workshop on fundraising: "Hunting for Hidden Treasure." Approximately 35 high school students (ages 12–17) and 5 adult volunteers attended the two workshop sessions.

IOI-USA developed a new partnership with Girls Inc. (GI) of Pinellas County, which provides afterschool programmes to about 125 girls between 6 and 12 years old. The national network of Girls Inc. organizations serves 136,000 girls annually. The IOI-USA executive director was invited to serve on the newly created STEM Advisory Committee. To support development of a new marine science program, IOI-USA facilitated planning meetings with GI, the University of South Florida College of Marine Science and SRI St. Petersburg. The team tentatively agreed to develop a marine science education programme that will support science, math and reading objectives related to the Common Core, state requirements for grade schools but not afterschool programmes.

In another initiative, IOI-USA identified that non-governmental organizations and government agencies had been focused primarily on implementing and funding debris clean-up efforts. Exploratory conference calls were initiated with municipalities, NGOS and agencies to discuss their perceptions on programmes that would focus on prevention and reduction oriented initiatives. Universally, the organizations agreed that a more comprehensive approach was needed to address root causes, particularly land-based pollution. Together with the Ocean Conservancy and the environmental scientist and regional programme manager of the NOAA Marine Debris programme, future strategic priorities were discussed to develop contacts for regional partnerships and ideas for grants.

Asia

Through its host institute the State Oceanic Administration (SOA), IOI-China hosted the Training Programme on South East Asia Network Education and Training Project (SEA-NET) from August 20th to September 18th in Tianjin, China. This project was adopted during the 21st Workshop on Managing Potential Conflicts in the South China Sea held in 2011 in Indonesia. The SEA-NET Project consists of two phases in the second term of this project (the first term ran from 2010 to 2011). Phase I was implemented by Chinese Taipei in 2012. Phase II was implemented by China in 2013. Phase II was divided into two programmes, one being a training course and the other comprising a visiting scientist programme. The programme was implemented by the National Marine Data and Information Service, SOA, through the IOI-China Regional Centre for the West Pacific region.

As its major contribution to the IOI global programme for training, IOI-China organised the four-week second training course on Ocean Governance for Western Pacific Region from October 15th to November 8th 2013. Twenty seven participants attended the regional course; seven participants from outside China were supported by SOA, while the 20 participants from China were nominated and funded by their own agencies. More information is available in the section of the annual report specifically dedicated to training activities of the IOI.

Additionally, the IOI Operational Centre in PR China participated in the World Ocean Day and China Ocean Day activities on 8 June 2013 in Beijing, China and also regularly contributes to the editing and publication of the "China Polar Research and Strategy" in Chinese. Representatives from IOI-China attended the 23rd workshop on Managing Potential Conflicts in the

South China Sea in 2013 in Yogyakarta, Indonesia from the October 30th to November 2nd 2013.

IOI-India has been focusing on building its internal capacity for providing assistance to IOI's internet web-based GIS portal by evaluating other portals for their suitability for the purpose and performing training and working with geoportal technologies. In addition, an important activity has been to build connections with Indian governmental departments, specially the Planning Commission (http://planningcommission.nic.in/), and the National Knowledge Commission (http://knowledgecommission.gov.in/), and appraising them of the activities of IOI. The centre has assisted both of these organizations with their national GIS initiative (http://www.youtube.com/watch?v =iftoKMSa_b4). IOI-India is hoping to collaborate with these organizations in the creation of the India Coast Portal. IOI-India is currently working on creating a portal that presents all the Women, Youth and the Sea projects executed by the IOI in a geographic format.

The activities of IOI-Indonesia concentrated on training activities in environmental conservation education and community and human resources empowerment. Environmental conservation education and community empowerment training courses were held for awareness creation in different places in north Jakarta.

IOI-Japan forms an integral part of several councils and committees on ocean policy-making and research in Japan and the Director of IOI-Japan has been involved in the first and the second term of the three-year ICM (Integrated Coastal Management) model project organized by the Ocean Policy Research Foundation (OPRF, an affiliate of The Nippon Foundation), since April 2012 as a full-time Project Researcher of OPRF. In this respect she is in charge of five demonstration sites, Miyako (Tohoku where a tsunami hit), Shima City (Pacific coast), Bizen City (Seto Inland Sea coast), Obama City (Sea of Japan coast), and Sukumo Bay (Pacific coast of Shikoku Island), as a programme director/facilitator under the leadership of Mr. Hiroshi Terashima, Executive Director of OPRF. In this context various presentations were given on ICM and more than 170 ICM video/photo/essay clips have been uploaded on a website for outreach purposes (http://blog.canpan.info:oprficm/).

IOI-Thailand is very successfully engaged in fundraising for and organising workshops on Stakeholder Capacity Assessment on Critical Flooding/Flash Flood Events in Thailand (in cooperation with the Institute of Earth Systems, University of Malta; Pacific Disaster Centre, Hawaii, United States; and Thailand's National Disaster Warning Centre (NDWC)); a workshop on Small-Scale Fisheries Livelihoods, Well-being, Vulnerability and Governance; a fishery seminar in Phuket, Thailand; a workshop on oil spill risks; and a stakeholder consultation workshop on tsunamis. A major effort for the IOI centre was the organisation of the PIMXXXIV Forum on Sustainable Governance of the Ocean, 3–8 September 2013.

The Operational Centre continued in its active support of local capacity building by raising funds to support the travel of the IOI-Thailand coordinator, Mr. Wichayoot Boonkosol to attend the master degree programme in ocean governance at the University of Malta in October 2013; and the support of two participants from IOI-Thailand and the NDWC respectively, Ms. Usa Kerdsiri and Ms. Wasinee Sudpadrew and two participants, Ms. Natthawadee Bantiwiwatkul from the Department of Marine and Coastal Resources and Lt. Sutanee Sumanagkul from the Department of Fisheries (DOF), in collaboration with IOI-China, to attend the second IOI-China Training Course in Regional Ocean Governance for the Western Pacific Region, 16 October to 8 November 2013.

The IOI Focal Point in Malaysia organised, through its host institute (the Borneo Marine Research Institute of Universiti Malaysia, Sabah), the International Seminar on Marine Science and Aquaculture (ISOMSA), which was attended by about 150 delegates from several countries. This seminar comprised three keynote addresses and oral and poster presentations and was held 19–21 March in Kota Kinabalu, Sabah. The Marine Awareness Programme for Youth was organized at the request of the Ministry of Education with a programme for school students to provide them with guided exposure to the marine park. Activities included snorkelling, on-the-spot observations of intertidal habitats, video screening, a visit to the aquarium and a quiz contest (23–25 April 2013) website: http://www.ums.edu.my/ipmb.

The principal activity for the IOI Focal Point in Singapore was the organisation of the World Ocean Day outreach and information dissemination activities for seafarers on oceans and maritime environmental protection based on the UN's dedicated theme of "Oceans and People."

Oceania

The IOI Operational Centre for the Pacific Islands, based in Suva, Fiji was involved in the organisation of the 12th Pacific Science Inter-Congress at the host institute, the University of the South Pacific in Fiji in July 2013. The Inter-Congress was entitled Science for Human Security and Sustainable Development in the Pacific Region and the focus included physical, biological, and social sciences and encompassed terrestrial, marine, atmospheric, social/cultural subjects and approaches in the Pacific Islands and Rim region. According to IOI Operational Centre Director, Joeli Veitayaki, "This is a wonderful opportunity to share our vision, work and experiences on building a Pacific that is better suited for the future."

The principal activities of the IOI Focal Point in Australia involved issues pertaining to maritime boundaries through the Pacific Island Maritime Boundaries workshop in Sydney from February 20th to March 2nd, 2013. This workshop brought together 14 Pacific Island states to address issues surrounding the 22 unresolved maritime boundaries in the region. Other work was carried out on the problems facing artisanal fisheries, the acidification of coral reefs, and issues of climate interactions and the oceans. World Ocean Day was celebrated in 2013 by a lunchtime documentary screening at the University of Sydney. Ms Jill Storey, Research Affiliate, University of Sydney, was nominated as an IOI observer to the annual meeting of the International Maritime Organisation in London, United Kingdom.

Europe

In 2013, IOI-Germany continued its activities and projects in research and training and education. Contributions to the IOI network have been related to tasks as the Chair of the Regional Directors.

A new project started in February 2013 in cooperation with French and West African partners. The trilateral project on fisheries in West Africa, AWA – Ecosystem Approach to the management of fisheries and the marine environment in West African waters, investigates the scientific basis for a more sustainable management of the Bonga Shad, a clupeid species important for the artisanal coastal fisheries along the West African coast. The project is based in Dakar, Senegal and has a very strong capacity component.

The Buddenbrook-Haus, a museum in the old Hanseatic city of Lübeck dedicated to Thomas Mann, the father of Elisabeth Mann Borgese, developed and organized in 2012 an exhibition on the life of Elisabeth Mann Borgese. The IOI-Germany Operational Centre succeeded in collecting funds from various sponsors to present the exhibition in Bremen. The opening ceremony was on 31 August in the "Haus der Wissenschaft" in the city centre of Bremen. The exhibition in Bremen was officially opened on 31 August 2013 by Prof. Dr. Hildegard Westphal, director of the Leibniz Centre for Tropical Marine Ecology (ZMT) and Dr. Klaus Sondergeld, member of the board of the Haus der Wissenschaft (House of Science), Bremen. In his keynote address with the theme "Elisabeth Mann Borgese and the Drama of the Ocean," Dr. Werner Ekau, Director of the IOI-Germany Operational Centre, gave insight to the development of the law of the sea over the last centuries, the challenges arising during the first half of the 20th century, and the role and driving reasons of Elisabeth Mann Borgese and her companions in the development of the actual law of the sea.

The accompanying programme included several talks to the public, the presentation of a movie by Eberhard Görner about Elisabeth Mann Borgese, and a panel discussion on challenges in marine protected management governance. Some 2000 guests visited the exhibition and the different side events.

The GEF-funded Large Marine Ecosystem programmes strive for a strategic partnership with the International Council for the Exploration of the Sea (ICES). The idea is to probably establish a secretariat at ICES to guarantee a long-term perspective to the programmes and couple them closer to the scientific community. In this context an ICES Working Group on Large Marine Ecosystem Programme Best Practices was established in 2010 consisting of ca. 25 international experts, the German director of IOI Operational Centre being one of them. The fourth workshop was held in Paris, France, on 8–9 July 2013 back-to-back with the 15th IOC/UNESCO-IUCN-NOAA Consultative Meeting on Large Marine Ecosystems (LMEs). These events were used to advertise the regional and global courses on ocean governance of IOI.

The PIM XXXIV International Forum on Sustainable Governance of the Ocean was attended. A presentation on hypoxia as a growing threat to coastal waters was given in one of the sessions, and the closing plenary session included the acceptance of the Forum declaration co-chaired by the IOI-Germany director.

The IOI Operational Centre for the Caspian Sea in Astrakhan, Russian Federation regularly organises World Ocean Day activities in partnership with NGOs and the oil company Luk Oil MoreNeft involving 100 senior school students by realising displays, lectures, videos and cleaning of touristic sites in different districts of the Astrakhan Region. Many of these activities are performed in cooperation with IOI-Ukraine.

The Clean-Up Campaign for the Volga River channels was held on April 15th when the IOI-Caspian Sea Operational Centre conducted the annual regional cleaning campaign on the banks of the Volga River's main channels: Kutum, Buzan and Kigach. Taking part in the campaign were members of the Operational Centre, Astrakhan student environmental groups, students of secondary schools from Krasnoyarskiy region and students from the Krivobuzanskiy region of the Republic of Kazakhstan. All collected garbage was put in a special purpose container and carried out from the territory by employees of a waste recycling company. As a result of this campaign, some 100 km^2 of coastal areas and about 150 km^2 of water surface have been cleared; the total garbage volume removed was 3 tons of utility waste.

The centre continued its tradition to organize a summer ecological school in the Republic of Kazakhstan and work on distribution and migration of the Caspian seal. Within or connected to these works it also stimulates protection activity and conservation of biodiversity by encouraging several students of Astrakhan State Technical University (ASTU) to clean beaches and coasts of small rivers in Astrakhan Region. A partner in this initiative is the NGO Eco Mangistau; with the support of NCOC (North Caspian Operating Company) and together with these three organizations, IOI launched the educational programme "The Caspian Seal and Biodiversity of the Caspian Sea" with the aim to study the problems of conservation of flora and fauna of the Caspian Sea. The Forum was attended by experts from the competent public authorities, NGOs, academia and representatives of NCOC, as well as experts from ASTU, and the International Ocean Institute. Forum speakers provided information on the state of biodiversity of the Caspian Sea, as well as the steps that have been taken by all parties to save it, including new international practice.

The IOI-Islamic Republic Iran organised Ocean Day on 10th June 2013 at the conference hall of the Iranian National Institute for Oceanography in Tehran and used the opportunity to invite marine experts and oceanographers, university professors, as well as government officials from marine organizations to also hold a meeting of the Iranian National Committee for Oceanography. A number of official representatives were present, among others, Dr. Mahdi Iranmanesh, Deputy Minister and the Head of Marine Science and Technology Group of the Ministry of Science, Research and Technology. Attached to the meeting was an exhibition of marine handicraft artwork realised within the Women, Youth and the Sea programme.

The centre, in cooperation with other national institutions, also initiated another children's painting competition under the topic "Urbanization and the Sea" and several workshops with an outreach to Iranian experts as well as university and high school students. Such an activity was the Children's Workshop: An Introduction to Oceanography held from 27 to 29 October 2013; Tehran, I.R. of Iran. On the occasion of Science Week in Iran, IOI-IR Iran invited school students over three days to visit the oceanographic facilities and laboratories of the Iranian National Institute for Oceanography and Atmospheric Science (INIOAS) as a national oceanographic centre with the aim of introducing oceanography to students as a science and its related activities. The students from three secondary schools visited INIOAS laboratories and the equipment on 27–29 October 2013. Experts of different departments of INIOAS explained the applications and use of equipment and introduced different fields of oceanography for the students. During their visits, the students were acquainted oceanography, marine pollution, and what an oceanographer does. At the end of their visit, the students gathered at the conference hall of INIOAS and received brochures and small gifts from INIOAS and IOI-IR Iran and a presentation on oceanography and marine pollution by one of the INIOAS experts.

IOI-Malta Operational Centre (IOI-MOC) is a partner with the IOI-HQ in the organisation of the annual IOI Malta Training Programme on Ocean Governance for the Mediterranean, Black Sea, Caspian Sea and Baltic regions. Full information regarding this programme is given in the training section of this annual report. The centre also takes part in training and teaching activities through specialised courses, especially in relation to ocean governance and the law of the sea's managerial as well as scientific obligations on coastal states. This includes promoting awareness of the sea, on its naturalistic, scientific and cultural connotations, especially with the younger generation, and raising public awareness and, through an inter-sectoral approach, attempting to sustain at a national level the interaction between local institutions that are active in marine affairs.

The IOI Operational Centre in Malta successfully concluded the JERICO Summer School in Malta on 8–13 July 2013 with 35 participants. The young researchers came from all over Europe, including participants from the southern Mediterranean countries and the Black Sea, and hailed from a variety of disciplines. The intensive programme on operational oceanography in the 21st century with a focus on the coastal seas featured high-level lectures and practical sessions on all aspects of real-time acquisition and the continuous and sustainable delivery of high quality environmental data and information products related to the marine environment of European coastal seas. Experts discussed data acquisition technology, coastal observatories, data management, numerical modelling techniques, and the delivery of downstream services. The participants were able to work using software tools and applications. They also had a taste of putting things into practice with a visit to the CALYPSO HF radar installation in Malta.

The IOI Operational Centre in Slovenia concentrated on research related to operational oceanography (providing near real-time data on sea state including meteor-parameters, sea temperature, salinity, currents, waves, oxygen, and chlorophyll that can be viewed online); in cooperation with colleagues from Croatia and Italy.

Outreach activities culminated in organizing the World Ocean Day (7 June) and Researchers Night (27 September), attracting numerous visitors (about 400 youth and 50 adults) who enjoyed hands-on experience within interactive workshops (marine life under the microscope, diversity of marine organisms, preparation for diving, scientific work on a research boat, measurements at sea with small remotely operated vehicle, chemistry of the sea, microscopic life in sediments, a photographer's workshop and marine debris). Activities with youth have been organised with a contest for best essay and artwork under the theme "The ocean we want" and mentors and teachers discussed with children endangered seas, with the best essay being published in the daily journal *Dnevnik* (with the second highest circulation in Slovenia). The aim of the project Researchers for Nature Preservation and Technology use for the benefit of the society was to inform the public about the work-life of researchers, particularly in the field of natural and technology sciences.

Several exhibitions were organized entitled "Invisible Ties" (on the endangered species *Litophaga litophaga* in cooperation with the regional institute of nature protection) and the underwater photography exhibition on ecological investigations in the Port of Koper. The latter exhibition was presented also at Vienna, Austria, and at the Slovenian Research Institute.

A major area of activities in 2013 of IOI-Ukraine was related to environmental education, raising public awareness on environmental and sustainable development issues. It developed projects connected with environmental management in coastal communities and dissemination of maritime law knowledge by elaboration of an innovative set of lectures designed for students, crewing companies, staff and recruits. This was done in collaboration with the highly renowned Kyiv State Petro Konashevich-Sahaydachniy Maritime Academy to help meet the demand from shipping companies for highly qualified seafarers.

The centre was very successful in education and training. A training seminar on waste separation was conducted for community members in Ilyichevsk city jointly with city council and the municipal Department of Housing. The seminar was attended by municipal employees. Another example was the seminar on ecological management for hotel managers conducted upon a request from different hotel chains.

In the framework of the Women, Youth and the Sea Programme, a training course on Disaster Preparedness for Vulnerable Coastal Communities focused on children with disabilities, which was conducted on August 9th, 2013 in the interregional rehabilitation centre for people with disabilities in Yevpatoria. The course consisted of two modules on types of disasters, actions before, during and after different types of disasters, and personal preparation to deal with disasters for people with different types of disabilities. Twenty eight participants attended the training, including the three staff members expected to deliver such courses in the future.

Following his successful intervention as an invited keynote speaker at the AMER International Conference on Quality of Life in Malaysia, IOI-Cyprus Focal Point director Dr. Nicholas Kathijotes, was invited by LESTARI (the research Institute of the National University of Malaysia) for further discussions on future research collaborations between LESTARI and the International Ocean Institute. The meeting was chaired by Prof. Dr. Mazlin Bin Mokhtar, Director of LESTARI.

Dr Kathijotes also shared a presentation on the "Blue Economy: Environmental and Behavioural Aspects towards Sustainable Coastal Development," which was followed by an intensive discussion on the Blue Economy and issues on fisheries, aquaculture, maritime transportation, tourism, renewable energy and marine spatial planning. See http://www.ukm.my/lestari/en/ioi/.

The IOI Focal Point in Lebanon (Mr. Mohammed El Sarji) participated in the "Workshop ACR + MED Thematic Working Group Priority Waste Flows" on pollution through plastic bags, on March 25th in Brussels as part of the work of the EU's DG Environment. During this conference Mr. El Sarji spoke at length about the IOI and its mission, and the importance of working together as Mediterranean countries to protect and preserve the biodiversity of our sea to keep it healthy and pollution free and to encourage the sustainable use of its resources.

The IOI Focal Point in Turkey (Mr. Sezgin Tunca) in conjunction with its host institute carried out a study, which was conducted from December 2012 to March 2013, to find out the socio-economic characteristics of recreational fishing activities in Foça and Gökova Special Environmental Protection Areas (SEPAs). Data were collected via face-to-face interviews using specially designed questionnaire forms in Foça and Gökova (Karacasöğüt, Çamlı, Akyaka, Akçapınar, Akbük, Ören) SEPAs. In addition to the questionnaire surveys, authorities of charter and fishery cooperatives and local fishermen were also interviewed to support gathered information in both SEPAs. About 130 individuals in both SEPAs were queried. Recreational fishing in both SEPAs was also examined via SWOT (strengths, weaknesses, opportunities and threats) analysis. The current study was aimed at collecting more information for the site managers regarding recreational fishing in both Foça and Gökova SEPAs and to lead to management plans referring to the regulations for environmental protection and sustainability.

IOI Works towards Achieving the Millennium Development Goals

The eight Millennium Development Goals (MDGs) – which range from halving extreme poverty rates to halting the spread of HIV/AIDS and providing universal primary education, all by the target date of 2015 – form a blueprint agreed to by all the world's countries and the world's leading development institutions. They have galvanized unprecedented efforts to meet the needs of the world's poorest.

The MDG targets have been the principles guiding the development and progress of the IOI's Women, Youth and the Sea Programme since its inception in the millennium year. Focusing on the goals which fall within the IOI's core mission relating to the oceans and in keeping with IOI's work in favour of the holistic governance of the ocean, the projects funded through this programme have aimed to support in many ways the ocean community through offering training in sustainable activities and alternative employment to vulnerable communities that live on its borders, and governance and capacity-building courses for the global community of stakeholders that use its resources.

IOI's mission corresponds most closely to nine targets within four MDGs:

MDG	Target
Eradicate extreme poverty and hunger	2: Achieve full and productive employment and decent work for all, including women and young people
	3: Halve, between 1990 and 2015, the proportion of people who suffer from hunger
Promote gender equality and empower women	1: Eliminate gender disparity in primary and secondary education, preferably by 2005, and in all levels of education no later than 2015
Ensure environmental sustainability	1: Integrate the principles of sustainable development into country policies and programmes and reverse the loss of environmental resources
	2: Reduce biodiversity loss, achieving, by 2010, a significant reduction in the rate of loss
	3: Halve, by 2015, the proportion of the population without sustainable access to safe drinking water and basic sanitation
	4: By 2020, to have achieved a significant improvement in the lives of at least 100 million slum dwellers
Global partnership for development	1: Address the special needs of least developed countries, landlocked countries and small island developing states
	5: In cooperation with the private sector, make available benefits of new technologies, especially information and communications

In 2013, through the several programmes and projects financed under the IOI's Women, Youth and the Sea Programme work and carried out by the IOI's global network of Operational Centres, work continued on the eradication of poverty, the promotion of gender equality and the empowerment of women, the achievement of environmental sustainability through the promotion of holistic ocean governance, and the creation of synergies and partnerships between public and private entities, NGOs and communities of stakeholders worldwide.

The projects implemented through the actions of many Operational Centres and Focal Points in training, capacity-building, field projects, research and other actions have contributed in many significant ways to achieve the MDGs and specific targets. The cumulative effect of these efforts and the synergies created within the targeted communities should leave significant results with an impact on the sustainability of coastal communities and vulnerable populations and continue contribute strongly to achievement of the MDG targets, building on the work that the IOI network has achieved since the inception of the Women, Youth and the Sea Programme in 2000.

IOI's Women, Youth and the Sea Programme – 2013

IOI's Network-Wide Programme

The Women, Youth and the Sea Programme objective is to enhance the capacity and participation of women and youth from developing countries in ocean and coastal affairs and to help ensure environmental sustainability. Since 2000, it aims to provide both women and youth with an "opportunity space" to develop alternative knowledge and skills leading to a durable income earning environment. It seeks to address the needs of developing countries, particularly coastal communities and the role of women and youth, by increasing their abilities to develop and manage the ocean and coastal resources sustainably.

Eighteen projects were submitted for funding consideration in 2012 to the Women, Youth and the Sea Programme. Unfortunately funding limitations only allowed for 16 of these proposals to be implemented in 2013. The projects that were implemented continue the trends set in the first years with an emphasis on the sustainable development of coastal communities and capacity building; achieving these aims by diverse means and at several levels from grassroots community work in coastal villages and among vulnerable populations, alternative economic employment options using goods made from recycled materials, on to advanced training for ocean governance officials from developing coastal states. A commonality of values and aims guided the individual projects, and project work targets achieved by the various Operational Centres in different countries throughout this time are shown in Figure A.1.

A number of the proposals funded in 2013 continued to build on the achievements of prior Women, Youth and the Sea projects commenced over previous years, thus making them more effective and significant in further supporting the improved livelihood of women and youth in disadvantaged coastal communities. In these cases, synergies, partnerships, as well as communal trust achieved over the years were enhanced and the momentum of progress was maintained or increased. It is strongly felt that all these cumulative actions should leave significant positive impact on the sustainability of coastal communities and contribute to achieving the MDG targets.

Countries in which these projects have been carried out over the years are: Australia, Astrakhan – Russian Federation, Brazil, Canada, Costa Rica, Cuba, Egypt, Kenya, Indonesia, India, IR Iran, Japan, Malta, Nigeria, Pacific Islands, Senegal, Southern Africa, Thailand, Ukraine and the United States. Through the training programmes on ocean governance held annually in Canada and Malta, and now also in South Africa since 2013, dedicated scholarships make specialised training available to women from many developing countries worldwide increasing the effective outreach of this programme.

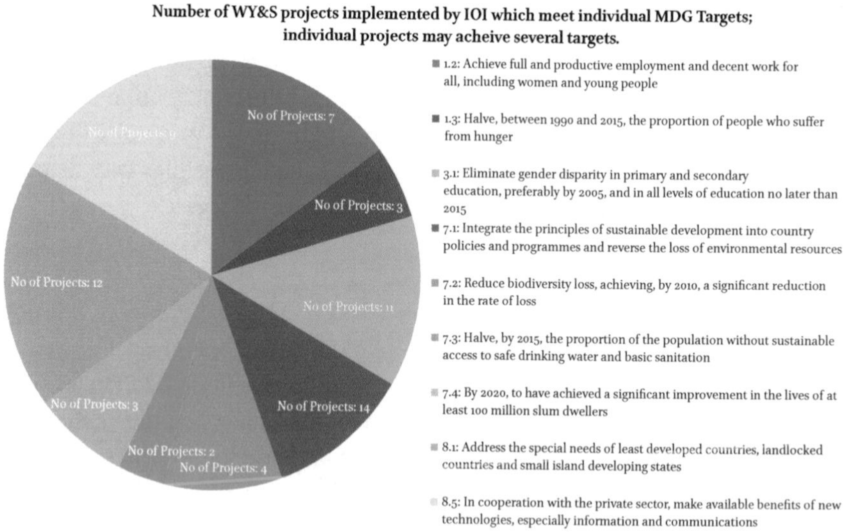
Number of WY&S projects implemented by IOI which meet individual MDG Targets;
individual projects may acheive several targets.
No of Projects: 7
No of Projects: 3
No of Projects: 11
No of Projects: 14
No of Projects: 4
No of Projects: 2
No of Projects: 3
No of Projects: 12
No of Projects: 9
1.2: Achieve full and productive employment and decent work for all, including women and young people
1.3: Halve, between 1990 and 2015, the proportion of people who suffer from hunger
3.1: Eliminate gender disparity in primary and secondary education, preferably by 2005, and in all levels of education no later than 2015
7.1: Integrate the principles of sustainable development into country policies and programmes and reverse the loss of environmental resources
7.2: Reduce biodiversity loss, achieving, by 2010, a significant reduction in the rate of loss
7.3: Halve, by 2015, the proportion of the population without sustainable access to safe drinking water and basic sanitation
7.4: By 2020, to have achieved a significant improvement in the lives of at least 100 million slum dwellers
8.1: Address the special needs of least developed countries, landlocked countries and small island developing states
8.5: In cooperation with the private sector, make available benefits of new technologies, especially information and communications

FIGURE A.1 *IOI women, Youth and the Sea Programme and MDG targets*

Special Section on IOI Activities in 2013

World Ocean Review (WOR) 2 the Future of Fish – The Fisheries of the Future

The WOR series is published by maribus gGmbH and is the fruit of cooperation between mare, the Kiel-based Cluster of Excellence "The Future Ocean," and the International Ocean Institute. The first review published in 2010, WOR 1, provided a panoptic overview of the state of the oceans with the intention of following this up with periodic updates and specialised reviews. The aim is to reveal the consequences of intense human intervention on the ocean realm, including the impacts of climate change.

The *World Ocean Review 2 – The Future of Fish: The Fisheries of the Future* is the first comprehensive analysis of the state of the world's fisheries, the consequences for the global food supply and the ocean ecosystem. On 21st February, WOR 2 was launched in the presence of the contributing partners. With the new report, published by the non-profit organization maribus gGmbH with support from the magazine mare, the International Ocean Institute and the Cluster of Excellence "The Future Ocean," scientists from Kiel together with other leading international fisheries experts have produced one of the most comprehensive investigations into the state of worldwide fisheries.

> This publication is a wakeup call for managing humanity's relations with the ocean. ...while promoting greater enforcement and compliance with international and regional agreements, is about future commitment to conservation, the creation of sustainable fisheries, the protection of high sea areas and sea mount biodiversity and the contribution to global food security that is underpinned by adherence to the principles of common heritage and the peaceful use of the ocean: principles very dear to the IOI and its founder, Professor Elisabeth Mann Borgese.
>
> AWNI BEHNAM, *President of IOI*

> This new report (WOR 2) focuses on fish and their exploitation... It is not our intention with this World Ocean Review 2 to press the panic button. But by pointing out the true facts surrounding fish stocks and fisheries we seek to come to grips with an extremely complex situation. Only sound knowledge – not alarmism or appeasement – will save these vitally important inhabitants of the world's oceans.
>
> NIKOLAUS GELPKE, *Managing Director of maribus gGmbH and publisher of mareverlag; Vice-President, IOI*

The second volume of the World Ocean Review is dedicated to fishery and throws light on the many different aspects of the topic... If we want to leave healthy, productive oceans for our grandchildren, we must take the long view and rethink fishery. The review gives good reasons – both ecological and economic – for modernizing today's fisheries! Any collapse of the stocks would put an end to the traditional trade of the fisherman. The prospect is real. Is that really what we want? What can we do to make sure this does not happen? What can be done at a regional level, and what must be negotiated in the national and international policy arenas? ...We give our best possible answers to all these questions, sharing our knowledge and assessing the situation, while at the same time identifying options for change. The future of the oceans is closely linked to the future of the fisheries and thus to the future of many – if not all – the world's peoples.

> PROF. DR. MARTIN VISBECK, *Spokesman for the Cluster of Excellence "The Future Ocean"*

The *World Ocean Review* is published in a print run of 60,000 copies (German/English). The publication is not for sale, but is available free of charge from http://www.worldoceanreview.com. An English version is available in addition to the German version and both versions in their entirety are available for download on the internet at http://www.worldoceanreview.com.

Unveiling of the Commemorative Bust of Professor Elisabeth Mann Borgese, Founder of IOI

On the morning of 12th December 2013 at the Msida Campus of the University of Malta, a memorial ceremony in honour of Professor Elisabeth Mann Borgese, founder of the International Ocean Institute, was held. The life size bronze bust of Professor Mann Borgese was donated by the IOI on the initiative of the IOI President, Dr. Awni Behnam, for display at the "Arvid Pardo and Pacem in Maribus Study Area" on campus in view of the strong links between Professor Mann Borgese and the IOI, and Arvid Pardo and Malta's work on the principle that the seabed constitutes part of the common heritage of mankind, a phrase that appears in Article 136 of the United Nations Convention on the Law of the Sea. This initiative was intended to honour Professor Mann Borgese and her contribution to the sustainable governance of the oceans and to recognise the strong link between the IOI and the University and the Government of Malta as host of the IOI-HQ.

The ceremony was presided by Dr. Behnam on behalf of the International Ocean Institute, and by Professor Alfred Vella, Pro Rector for Academic Affairs at the University of Malta and member of the Governing Board of the IOI, on behalf of the University of Malta. Invited guests to the ceremony included members of the IOI's Governing Board, representative Directors of the IOI network of Operational Centres, the staff of the IOI-HQ in Malta, faculty members and experts of the IOI Training Programme on Regional Ocean Governance for the Mediterranean, Black, Baltic and Caspian Seas, and other partners of IOI such as faculty members of the University of Malta-IOI joint Master of Arts degree in ocean governance.

Professor Mann Borgese's lifelong preoccupation was the search for peace and justice for all. She was known worldwide as "The Mother of the Oceans" and dedicated all of her later life to the understanding of ocean matters, to the development of a constitution for the oceans and to the consideration of the oceans as a "great laboratory for the making of a new international order based on new forms of international cooperation and organisation, on a new economic theory, on a new philosophy."

Pacem in Maribus (PIM) XXXIV International Forum on Sustainable Governance of the Ocean, Bangkok, Thailand

The International Ocean Institute successfully organized the 34th Pacem in Maribus (PIM) under the topic Sustainable Governance of the Ocean in Thailand during September 2013. The Forum was co-hosted by the IOI, the Office of National Water and Flood Management Policy (ONWF), the Office of the Prime Minister's Secretariat, the Department of Marine and Coastal Resources (DMCR), the Ministry of Natural Resources and Environment, DOF, the Ministry of Agriculture and Cooperatives, the NDWC, the Ministry of Information, Communication and Technology of Thailand, the Southeast Asian Fisheries Development Center (SEAFDEC), and the Association of Natural Disaster Prevention Industries (ANDPI).

More than 350 participants from 28 countries attended the Forum and the presentations of more than 70 speakers were moderated and supported by the 20 co-chairs and rapporteurs. PIM XXXIV addressed important and emerging global, regional and national issues on five themes namely:

Theme 1:   The Impacts of Climate Change and Ocean Related Hazards, Water and Flood Management Policy Implications

Theme 2:   Follow Up of the Outcome of Rio+20, Implementation of UNCLOS and Related Instruments in the Southeast Asian Region

Theme 3:   Integrated Ocean Web-Based Geographical Information System
Theme 4:   Leadership Seminar on Science on Tsunamis for Today's Society
             and its Input to Society Security and Sustainability
Theme 5:   Youth Online Dialogue 'The Ocean We Want' on the Rights of Youth
             in Sustainable Development

In addition, two national sessions were organized: "Thailand's Shoreline Change and Erosion Management" and "Expert Consultation on Thailand's Implementation of UNCLOS and Its Related Instruments."

The opening ceremony on September 4th was launched by a welcome from Dr. Cherdsak Virapat, Executive Director of IOI and Head of the Forum Secretariat. Official addresses were given by H.E. Dr. Plodprasop Suraswadi, Deputy Prime Minister of Thailand and the Forum Co-Chair; H.E. Dr. Phiraphan Phalusuk, Minister of Science and Technology of Thailand; Dr. Awni Behnam, President of IOI and also Forum Co-Chair; Dr. Wendy Watson-Wright, Executive Secretary of the Intergovernmental Oceanographic Commission (IOC) and Assistant Director General of UNESCO; Professor Salvino Busuttil, Representative of Malta to the IOI Governing Board and President of the Fondation de Malte; Mr. Chamnong Kaeochada, Deputy Permanent Secretary, Ministry of Information and Communication Technology; Mr. Suphot Tovichakchaikul, Secretary-General, ONWF, Office of the Prime Minister's Secretariat; Mr. Chirdsak Vongkamolchoon, Deputy Director-General, DOF, Ministry of Agriculture and Cooperatives; Dr. Chumnarn Pongsri, Secretary-General, SEAFDEC; and Mr. Pran Siamwalla, President, ANDPI.

The Forum received inspiring messages from the UN Secretary-General Mr. Ban Ki-moon; H.E. Sheikh Hamad bin Abdulaziz Al-Kawari, Minister of Culture, Arts and Heritage of Qatar and President of UNCTAD 13; Mr. Koji Sekimizu, Secretary-General of International Maritime Organization (IMO); Professor Dr. Martin Visbeck, spokesman for the Cluster of Excellence "The Future Ocean" in the University of Kiel, and Ms. Mary Shuttleworth, President of Youth for Human Rights International in the United States.

Following established tradition, the Elisabeth Mann Borgese Memorial Lecture was presented by a prominent person. During PIM XXXIV, Dr. Wendy Watson-Wright, Executive Secretary of IOC and Assistant Director-General of UNESCO, gave a lecture on the "Global Governance of the Changing Ocean: Risk Tolerance and the Science-Policy Gap."

Five keynote speakers presented in plenary: Dr. Behnam; Dr. Watson-Wright; Mr. K. Harald Drager, President, The International Emergency Management Society; Mr. Kit Miyamoto, President and CEO, Miyamoto International, Inc.; and Mr. Voradet Viravakin, Director-General, Department of Treaties and Legal Affairs, Ministry of Foreign Affairs of Thailand, followed by the thematic parallel sessions. The outcomes of the parallel session themes were presented in the final plenary session along with the Youth Online Dialogue.

Dr. Behnam, Professor Salvino Busuttil, Dr. Cherdsak Virapat, Mr. Kunjapong Anuratpanich and Mr. Wichayoot Boonkosol (Director and Coordinator of IOI-Thailand respectively) were granted an audience with HRH Princess Maha Chakri Sirindhorn on 6th September at Chaipatana Building, Chitralada Villa in Bangkok in connection with the award of the Elisabeth Mann Borgese Medal. The Princess was awarded the medal by the IOI in recognition of her contribution to issues of environmental protection and education in Thailand in support of Thailand's role in international fora through her outstanding leadership and initiatives aimed at using education as a means of community and social development and environmental protection.

The Forum Declaration was presented and accepted by the Conference which was brought to an end with a closing address. The Expert Consultation on Thailand's Implementation of UNCLOS and Its Related Instruments was convened 6th September and the IOI's 12th Executive Committee Meeting was held separately on 7th September. The PIM XXXIV Declaration and Thematic recommendations are summarized below.

Key Messages from the PIM XXXIV Declaration

Theme 1:   Regarding the impacts of climate change and ocean-related hazards: water and flood management policy implications, protection, mitigation and adaptation: We recognize the urgent need for well-planned and immediate action while being strategically vigilant of changing future needs. We maintain the necessity to retain vital sciences as a fundamental pillar in monitoring holistic processes and dynamics but crucially supported by policy frameworks and participatory approaches to ensure that community needs are well understood. Moreover, we acknowledge the necessity to address exigent issues of preparedness, adaptation and resilience, which are inherently so diverse on spatial and temporal scales, but are confident that the extant challenges can be overcome.

Theme 2:   Regarding the follow up of the outcome of Rio + 20: implementation of UNCLOS and related instruments in the Southeast Asian region: We firmly believe that, notwithstanding the existence of legal frameworks, more extensive regional cooperation is needed for sustainable management of marine resources at regional and sub-regional levels, especially enhanced regional cooperation to sustainably manage fisheries and coastal resources, notwithstanding the need to negotiate solutions to territorial disputes or maritime boundary agreements in areas of overlapping maritime claims. Moreover, it is felt that a better preparedness and cooperation in response to oil spills is needed as a result of the lack of preparation for major spills from tankers and platforms, which is exacerbated by a lack of international rules on prevention, liability and compensation in the event of pollution from oil platforms, especially transboundary spills. Thus, in order to protect resources within the marine environment, enhanced cooperation is further recommended. Additionally, and based upon a variety of national experiences, the adoption of a bottom-up approach in ICM is encouraged.

Theme 3:   Regarding the establishment of an integrated ocean web-based geographical information system: We recommend the establishment of such a system in order to capitalize on its potential benefits; these include the facilitation of scientific data exchange, the provision of support to policy-makers, and contributing towards the achievement of education/capacity building/ outreach targets, amongst others. Such systems may further enhance opportunities for collaboration and cooperation in matters of ocean governance.

Theme 4:   Regarding the science on tsunamis and other marine hazards for today's society and its input to society, security and sustainability: We emphasize the strong need for a new vision and the knowledge for further drastic improvement in various fields of marine hazards mitigation, such as hazard detection, warning, preparedness and response. The local preparedness and response to hazards and hazard warning were identified as very critical concerns since the warning time between marine hazard detection and transmission of information to the authorities and the public must be minimized. We emphasize further the key role of mass media in enhancing overall resiliency and post-disaster recovery when a tsunami or other marine disaster strikes. With its broad reach and power, the mass media can also help achieve long-term goals in enhancing, inter alia, tsunami and other marine disaster education. It was recommended that for students living in tsunami-prone coastal areas, the inclusion of education related to tsunami awareness is prioritized and made obligatory.

Theme 5:   Regarding the youth online dialogue: right of youth in sustainable development of the ocean, the ocean we want: We recognize the crucial role that younger generations play today and the unique position these hold in societal frameworks, in particular, the generational linkage with the present decision-making cohort of society, and, more importantly, their capacity to ensure continuity with respect to practices relating to governance and resource management. Education and awareness of the younger generation today has the capacity to determine future prospects for our planet and humankind.

The Forum recommended that IOI and all relevant agencies should continue to provide a forum for consensus building and leadership promotion by bringing together government representatives, civil society and the private sector to promote a common vision on coastal and ocean governance; to encourage governments, stakeholders and all those empowered in capacity development in ocean science and governance education to support the efforts in implementation, research and monitoring in marine science, engineering, technology and governance in all their facets, in particular to promote the concept of operational oceanography, and application of technologies for the mitigation of or adaptation to climate change and marine hazards, and ocean governance; and to foster the holistic, comprehensive and integrated management of coastal and marine systems in a framework firmly based on ecosystem and precautionary approaches. Such a framework should not only include regulatory measures and effective compliance, but also foster wider public awareness and appreciation of coastal and marine systems and enhanced public participation in decision-making processes; contribute to the informal consultative process (ICP) and further development in the implementation of initiatives relating to UNCLOS; and encourage the adoption of adaptive and evidence-based management practices, not only using insights from science as a basis for policy development and implementation, but also including ongoing monitoring and review of the effectiveness of implemented policies, plans and management measures. Such evidence and evaluation-based management cultures ensure the effective use of resources in the long term.

Capacity Development and Empowerment

IOI – Learning for Our Future Ocean

OceanLearn in Brief: IOI-*OceanLearn* is the system-wide programme for the coordination, delivery, quality assurance and development of global partnerships of the International Ocean Institute's capacity building activities. *OceanLearn* aims to develop an interdisciplinary and integrated culture of knowledge, inclusive and accessible to all, focusing on ocean affairs and ocean science, through which knowledge is distributed making use of modern techniques.

Report on IOI's Flagship Courses Delivered in Canada and Malta, 2013

The flagship courses in Canada and Malta were conceived as an integral component of IOI's *OceanLearn* capacity building and coordination mechanism and were designed in response to identified needs for capacity building by training mid-career professionals, particularly from developing and transition countries, in all related disciplines, functions and interests that may impact on the sustainable management of oceans, seas and coasts. The training courses respond to the mandate of the IOI as set out in Article 3:3, 4, 5, and 6 of its Statutes.

Through 2012 and 2013 work continued apace on the capacity building and training aspects of IOI's mission and the hard work by HQ and the Operational Centres yielded results in the form of a new regional ocean governance course in South Africa, a specialised course in the principles of sustainability and governance for the Caspian Sea, and the first Master of Arts degree in ocean governance offered at the Valletta campus of the University of Malta and the IOI. These training events are scheduled annually and in addition to the already existing courses offered in Malta, Canada and PR China.

33rd International Training Programme on Ocean Governance: Policy, Law and Management, Dalhousie University, Halifax, Canada

The 2013 IOI-Canada training programme on *Ocean Governance: Policy, Law and Management* was conducted at Dalhousie University in Halifax from 22nd May to 19th July. This was the 33rd annual course since Elisabeth Mann Borgese instituted the programme in 1981 and it was attended by 12 participants representing countries in Africa, Asia, the Caribbean, Eastern Europe and South America, and drawn from a wide range of disciplines and backgrounds. As usual, emphasis was placed on having strong female representation among the class, with women outnumbering the men this year. Approximately 90 speakers presented to the class, including local and international experts and practitioners, while over-all guidance was provided by Mike Butler as course director.

The syllabus included modules on Ocean Sciences, Integrated Coastal and Ocean Management, Law of the Sea and Principled Ocean Governance, Fisheries and Aquaculture, Communication and Negotiation, Maritime Security, Energy, and Marine Transportation. Woven through the course were "Toolbox" sessions providing an introduction to practical skills on topics such as GIS, information management, project cycle, negotiation, and performance management. There was also detailed coaching on how to make presentations and communicate to the media, with participants being filmed in one-on-one interviews which they could then review and learn from. Several exercises during the programme required active involvement by each member of the class, particularly the course-long simulation to prepare national and regional ocean policy documents for presentation to the final Round Table, as well as shorter exercises in negotiation and integrated maritime compliance and enforcement.

Outside the classroom, field trips enabled the participants to visit the Bedford Institute of Oceanography, Port of Halifax, *HMCS Sackville*, the Maritime Museum of the Atlantic, and the Eastern Canada Response Corporation. The group also went on a three-day trip to the Bay of Fundy, home of the world's highest tides, where they toured a tidal power station, seaweed research centre, and both land and sea-based aquaculture facilities. They experienced the lobster fishery first-hand while going to sea on a working lobster boat, explored the shoreline to collect edible seaweed and lunch on local periwinkles, and visited sites of historical and natural interest.

Other activities during the two months included the annual Oceans Film Festival, which IOI-Canada held over three evenings in partnership with various local organisations, as well as the annual Elisabeth Mann Borgese Ocean Lecture. The latter was delivered by Nikolaus Gelpke, President of OSRF and Vice-President of IOI, who gave a lively, beautifully illustrated presentation on Communicating the Oceans. Social events during the course included the opening and closing ceremonies, as well as the ever-popular international potluck, and participants also experienced local hospitality and sight-seeing trips though IOI's "hosting" scheme.

Elisabeth Mann Borgese Ocean Lecture, Canada 2013

The Elisabeth Mann Borgese Ocean Lecture Series was established by IOI-Canada in 2005 to commemorate and celebrate Elisabeth's life and work. It aims to create dialogue and stimulate discussion about global ocean issues and the implications for the future of the oceans. The ninth annual public lecture was held at Dalhousie University's Schulich School of Law on the 10th June and featured Nikolaus Gelpke, Vice-President of IOI and President of the Ocean Science Research Foundation. His illustrated presentation on Communicating the Oceans combined personal anecdotes about Elisabeth with discussion of oceans issues, from stories covered in his journal, mare, to key thematic issues featured in the *World Ocean Review* I and II. The lecture attracted a diverse audience of approximately 120 people and culminated in a lively reception. A video of the presentation is available upon request (e-mail: ioi@dal.ca).

9th Training Programme on Regional Ocean Governance for the Mediterranean, Black, Baltic and Caspian Seas 2013, Malta

Since 1972, issues of sound and sustainable practices contributing to ocean governance have been a major focus of IOI's work in all areas from policy direction to capacity building and it is in this spirit that the training courses provided by IOI through its main training and capacity building programmes in Canada, Malta, South Africa, Turkmenistan and China are organised and offered.

The five-week Training Programme held in Malta in 2013 was the ninth annual course organised in this region since 2005. This Programme focuses specifically on the governance of the Mediterranean, Black, Baltic and Caspian Seas through inter-regional comparisons and experiences, and the promotion of exchanges between participants from countries surrounding these seas with their diversity of experiences and realities.

The latest training programme was attended by 18 participants from ten countries around the regional seas – Egypt, Finland, IR Iran, Lithuania, Malta, Montenegro, Romania, Russia, Turkmenistan, and Ukraine, as well as observers from PR China – having different experiences and backgrounds in marine-related management, science, law, operational and policy undertakings. The faculty was composed of a diverse selection of experts in topical matters, coming from leading institutions and organisations working on regional seas issues from countries around the areas under study.

As well as traditional lectures, the course programme included field trips and a number of hands-on projects where the participants were expected to apply their knowledge to specific scenarios. Simulation sessions, role-playing games in maritime spatial planning and mock-ministerial meetings all allowed the class to use their new knowledge and experience the multidisciplinary approach to decision making in marine and maritime matters.

The essence of the course was the Regional Ocean Policy Frameworks Session for the Mediterranean, Black, Caspian and Baltic Sea groups where practical application of knowledge gained throughout the course was used in the theoretical solution of issues relevant to the Regional Seas for the creation of national, regional and inter-regional policy for an integrated and common approach to ocean management.

During the training course the specialised session on maritime spatial planning was supported by the Lighthouse Foundation. The programme was also supported by the Ocean Science and Research Foundation and the German Academic Exchange Service (DAAD) through the services of the Embassy of the Federal Republic of Germany in Malta.

First Training Programme on the Sustainable Development and Governance of the Caspian Sea, Turkmenbashi, Turkmenistan

The first training programme entirely dedicated to sustainable development and governance issues of the Caspian Sea was organised by the IOI through its *OceanLearn* programme at the express request of the State Enterprise on Caspian Sea Issues at the President of Turkmenistan in partnershipwith IOI. The training course provided by IOI in Turkmenistan offered dedicated training on Caspian Sea governance and sustainability issues. Participating candidates were nominated by the countries bordering the Caspian Sea on invitation of the official co-organisers in Turkmenistan.

The training programme was formally opened on the 11th March with welcome speeches by Mr. Murad Atajanov, Chairman, State Enterprise on Caspian Sea Issues at the President of Turkmenistan on behalf of the host country and commissioner of the course as well as by Dr. Awni Behnam, President of IOI and member of faculty with expertise on governance issues. The course was directed by Antonella Vassallo, IOI's *OceanLearn* Coordinator.

The training programme was attended by 20 participants from the five countries around the regional sea – Turkmenistan, Kazakhstan, IR Iran, Russia and Azerbaijan. Each hadhaving different backgrounds in issues of Caspian Sea management, research, operational and policy undertakings. This provided a rich source of experience for the project work undertaken during the course. The programme was structured in three main modules, namely:

Module 1:   Oceans and Seas, Governance Frameworks. This module covered issues of governance, legislation and also the issues specific to the Caspian Sea legal regime as well as the international principles on which good governance is based.

Module 2: Managing Our Relations With the Oceans nd Seas. In this module, tools for the management of sustainability and marine matters were introduced with topical examples of case studies relevant to the Caspian states. Thus, experts presented lectures on the principles of sustainable development, maritime spatial planning, and GIS and remote sensing as planning and decision support tools for the ocean and coastal manager amongst others. Each session was followed by a hands-on exercise by the class where the principles introduced were applied in themed exercises which fed into the final course work.

Module 3: Governance for the Caspian Sea. In this final part, the specific topics of Caspian regional governance framework were presented by experts from the region, with the Caspian Sea presented as a sea of challenges but also of immense opportunities for the surrounding countries.

The training programme reached its practical culmination in the work of the class groups on the "Caspian Sea: Vision 2025." The class was divided into four groups at the beginning of the programme and each group given a topic for which they were asked to formulate and present a series of possible scenarios/roadmaps for the management of issues pertaining to the Caspian Sea, to culminate in 2025, with the aim of achieving sustainable development and consolidated cooperation in the region. Each designated group had to apply the lessons, techniques and tools learnt during the training programme as well as their personal experiences on the Caspian Sea issues to give final presentations on the topics of eco-tourism, marine transportation, environmental monitoring and sustainable aquatic bio-resources management respectively. The group work during Module 2 also fed into this exercise.

The faculty commissioned by IOI was composed of a diverse selection of experts, many of which were already partners with IOI on other *OceanLearn* Courses. As well as traditional lectures, the course programme included a field trip to the coastal area of Turkmenbashy and the hands-on projects where the participants were expected to apply their knowledge to specific scenarios which allowed the class to use their new knowledge and experience the multidisciplinary approach to decision making in Caspian matters. The local media also actively covered the programme through various news articles and TV programmes.

First Ocean Governance Training Programme for Africa, Cape Town, South Africa

This inaugural course was successfully organized and hosted at the offices of the IOI-SA located within SANBI at the Kirstenbosch National Botanical Gardens in Cape Town, South Africa. The four-week course focusing on the vast array of pressing ocean governance issues in the African region was attended by 19 participants representing nine countries (including Côte d'Ivoire, Nigeria, Namibia, Mozambique, Kenya, Mauritius, Egypt, Maldives and South Africa). The participants were exposed to five modules each containing a series of core lectures, practical exercises, and field excursions and activities. The IOI-SA staff and associates, as well as subject matter experts involved in the course development, delivered the core programme, while guest speakers from various organizations and fields complemented the coursework with case studies and practical applications from their day-to-day experiences. The participants were also tasked with two projects conducted in working groups. A policy exercise ran the full duration of the course and the participants produced their oral reports for a panel discussion on the last two days. Also presented to the panel were the results of a marine spatial planning exercise that ran during the final week of the course. Extensive detail on the course is available on the website www.ioisa.org.

Much of the course delivery was made possible by in-kind contributions from a broad partnership network with common interests in capacity development in ocean governance. The IOI-SA has been playing a role to support the Agulhas and Somali Current Large Marine Ecosystem (ASCLME) programme in consolidating this network into the AfriCOG.

On the final day of the course the participants received certificates of completion and then attended the official launch of AfriCOG, which was organized by IOI-SA and held at a coastal venue in Cape Town. The launch served as the signing ceremony for the initial 18 members of AfriCOG, including academic, research, NGO and management institutions from all over Africa and beyond (e.g., World Maritime University). More information on this exciting new initiative is available at www.africog.net.

This course is the fruit of work by the IOI Operational Centre in Southern Africa over the past two years to develop a regional adaptation of the IOI *OceanLearn* ocean governance training approach customized for African countries. The funding for course development was provided by the IOI and the IMO. The course was completed, including extensive course notes, presentations and exercises, following a logical flow designed to provide participants with the knowledge and tools from a broad range of ocean and coastal management disciplines. The course was scheduled for delivery this year, with supporting funds for participants having been offered by the IOI's Women Youth and the Sea Programme, as well as other contributors including ASCLME programme, the Bay of Bengal Large Marine Ecosystem (BOBLME) Project, Nairobi Convention, and IW LEARN.

Second Training Course on Ocean Governance for the Western Pacific Region, Tianjin, PR China

IOI-China organised the four-week Training Course on Ocean Governance for Western Pacific Region, the second in this series of programmes for the western Pacific Ocean in Tianjin. The training programme was attended by 27 participants from five countries located in the Western Pacific Region of which seven regional participants (one each from Indonesia, Cambodia and Vietnam, and four from Thailand) and 20 local participants from coastal cities in mainland China. Support for the seven non-Chinese participants was provided by SOA while the 20 participants from China were nominated and funded by their own agencies. The training programme was directed by Margaret J. Wood (former Director of IOI-Canada) and Professor Qin Li (Director, IOI-China). The course lectures were structured within a framework of four modules:

· Global Ocean Governance Framework
· Managing Our Relationship with the Ocean
· Conflict Management and Consensus Building
· Ocean Governance for the Western Pacific Region

Each lecture provided participants with an understanding of the key principles and best practices required for effective ocean governance. The training programme ensured that all the participants from different backgrounds in research and application, managerial and other governmental posts, covering different disciplines and administrative areas, were exposed to the issues of the Western Pacific, and the programme encouraged the exchange of experiences and knowledge between the expert faculty and the class.

Dr. Cherdsak Virapat, Executive Director, IOI-HQ in Malta presented on the International Ocean Institute during the programme, and other technical lectures were given by experts, amongst which were long-standing friends of the IOI such as Professor Mao Bin.

The Master of Arts in Ocean Governance, University of Malta Valletta Campus, Malta

The Master's Degree Programme on Ocean Governance is being offered by the Faculty of Laws at the University of Malta in collaboration with the International Ocean Institute and, since commencement this October, is being held at the Valletta Campus of the University in Malta as part of the University's International Masters Programmes.

This degree programme is unique in its approach. It aims to forge a knowledge base that is essentially legal but which also serves to further enhance the development of learning and research in the field of marine resource management and maritime security from a multidisciplinary perspective. Emerging issues and threats, such as global maritime security, the sustainable use of the oceans and their resources, as well as linkages between natural sciences, socio-economic requirements and the law, necessitate a multidisciplinary approach for promoting learning and research on ocean governance. This programme adds an important dimension to the work of the IOI in capacity building in ocean governance issues by providing the first postgraduate level programme in this field.

The first cohort of international students from Canada, Germany, Malta, PR China, and Thailand started their lectures on October 1st at the Valletta Campus of the University of Malta in Malta. The course was launched with the first study unit given by Dr. Awni Behnam (President, IOI) on the contemporary definition of ocean governance. This unit traces human interaction with the ocean from its early history and the evolution of rules and laws that culminated in the adoption of UNCLOS, the constitution of the oceans. As a basic concept underpinning the degree and providing a leitmotif for the programme, the unit aims to give an understanding of its legal, economic, social and political implications; to develop an understanding of the role of international institutions in all dimensions of the governance architecture; and to identify the current governance deficit in the light of new and emerging challenges. The first nine months of this 13-month degree will provide the students with the tools for achieving sound governance through the application of a spectrum of disciplines and knowledge to truly reflect the complexities that must be considered to achieve holistic and sustainable ocean governance. The final months of the programme will be dedicated to the preparation and submission of a dissertation.

Award of a Scholarship for a Student of the Master of Arts in Ocean Governance

Phoenicia Energy Company Ltd., a subsidiary of Mediterranean Oil & Gas Plc and Genel Energy Plc, which is currently carrying out oil exploration offshore

Malta, offered a scholarship to cover tuition fees for a student attending the MA in Ocean Governance. In this era of globalization and sectoral integration, capacity building in the regulation of ocean governance plays a pivotal role and this MA degree programme continues to build the capacity that Malta, as a key maritime player in the region, needs to successfully manage its resources and obligations locally, regionally, and internationally. The support of this aspect of the programme by the Maltese government, academia and industry was amply highlighted during the scholarship award. The presentation of the scholarship to Maltese student, Mr. Liam Grech, was held on 21st October at the Valletta Campus of the University of Malta. Mr. Grech was selected by a specially set up board following a public call by the University of Malta inviting applications for the scholarship.

Award of IOI's Elisabeth Mann Borgese Bursary, 2013

The fourth IOI Elisabeth Mann Borgese Bursary (EMB Bursary) was awarded to Mr. Daniel Buhagiar from Malta to carry out research on ocean thermocline energy extraction using wind energy. This innovative research project aims to expand on the notion of renewable energy generation. By using offshore wind energy to simultaneously generate electricity and extract cooling energy from the deep sea we can move closer to obtaining renewable energy in the form in which it is actually required. Therefore, by directly using cold, deep seawater for cooling, substantial amounts of electricity are no longer required to operate air conditioning systems. This implies a very significant reduction in electricity use for cooling. The project consists of a detailed analysis of an offshore hydraulic-based wind turbine that will produce a combination of electrical and thermal energy. The wind turbine rotor is directly connected to a variable displacement pump that pressurises seawater and sends it to an onshore hydroelectric turbine. Electrical energy is therefore generated from the pressurized seawater. The aim of the current research is to assess alternative systems and address some shortcomings in the current preliminary design. The EMB Bursary funds will further extend the scope of this current work and enable the design of additional experiments and research to cover new issues and areas and extend the range of the simulations. Mr. Buhagiar has been awarded the sum of €3,500 to further his research studies over one year.

Conclusion of the Third EMB Bursary 2012–2013

The EMB bursary awarded to Dr. David Testa for his research related to the concept of State of disembarkation in the context of migration law and the examination of related concepts, was successfully concluded with the presentation of a specialized lecture on the topic during the Training Programme on Regional Ocean Governance for the Mediterranean, Black, Baltic and Caspian Seas; 10 November – 12 December 2013, Malta. The issues raised by Dr. Testa's work are of direct interest to the concept of governance of the regional seas since the work examines the current status of, as well as proposes improvements to, the regulatory framework, based also on the idea that cooperation is a vital element if the best solutions for all involved are to be found, especially when considering the trans-boundary nature of the issue in question. The two-hour lecture, held on 18 November 2013 and entitled "EMB Bursary Lecture: The concept of disembarkation of migrants and the examination of these principles under UNCLOS" was very well received by the class.

IOI's Danielle de Saint Jorre Scholarship Award, 2013

The scholarship has been established by IOI to honour the memory of the late Danielle de St. Jorre, Minister for Foreign Affairs, the Environment and Tourism of the Republic of the Seychelles and a member of the Governing Board of the International Ocean Institute, in consideration of all she did in her short life for the benefit of her country, the small island developing states and the world at large. Ms Silvia Patricia González Díaz from Cuba was awarded the Danielle de St. Jorre Scholarship and she chose to use this award to fund her attendance at the Ocean Governance: Policy, Law and Management Course held in 2013 in Dalhousie, organized by IOI-Canada.

IOI's Partnerships and International Cooperation

In 2013, IOI continued to implement its mission and objectives through fostering links of cooperation and establishing new partnerships, collaborative projects and programmes. IOI currently has 15 active MOUs. These include the Convention on Wetlands; IOC; IMO; the Global Invasive Species Programme; the Partnerships in Environmental Management for the Seas of East Asia; SOA of the People's Republic of China; the United Nations Human Settlements Programme (UN-HABITAT); the East China Normal University on establishment of the International Ocean Urbanology Institute; the Cluster of Excellence the Future Ocean, Christian-Albrechts Universitat zu Kiel, Germany; the European Centre for Information on Marine Science and Technology (EurOcean); the University of Malta concerning the establishment of the

Elisabeth Mann Borgese and Arvid Pardo Learning and Exhibition Centre; Pacific Disaster Center on Global Hazards Information Network; ZMT, Germany; and the High Sea Alliance.

Initiatives to establish collaboration and partnership with national and regional organisations in Thailand have been made through the organisation of *Pacem in Maribus* XXXIV in Bangkok, Thailand. These includes ONWF, Office of the Prime Minister; Ministry of Science and Technology, DMCR, Ministry of Natural Resources and Environment, NDWC, Ministry of Information and Communication Technology, DOF, Ministry of Agriculture and Cooperatives, SEAFDEC, BOBLME, and ANDPI.

Selected Documents and Proceedings

∵

Oceans and the Law of the Sea Report of the Secretary-General, 2014†

Summary

The present report has been prepared pursuant to paragraph 284 of General Assembly Resolution 68/70 of 9 December 2013, with a view to facilitating discussions on the topic of focus at the fifteenth meeting of the United Nations Open-ended Informal Consultative Process on Oceans and the Law of the Sea, on the theme entitled "The role of seafood in global food security." It constitutes the first part of the report of the Secretary-General on developments and issues relating to ocean affairs and the law of the sea for consideration by the Assembly at its sixty-ninth session. The report is also being submitted to the States Parties to the United Nations Convention on the Law of the Sea, pursuant to Article 319 of the Convention. In the light of the multifaceted nature of the topic being covered and the page limitations established by the General Assembly, the report does not purport to provide an exhaustive synthesis of available information.

---

† This document was provided by the United Nations Division for Ocean Affairs and the Law of the Sea (DOALOS) and is extracted from the United Nations General Assembly, Sixty-ninth session, UN Document A/69/71, 21 March 2014, available online: <http://www.un.org/Depts/los/>. The document has been edited for publication in the *Ocean Yearbook*.

© KONINKLIJKE BRILL NV, LEIDEN, 2015 | DOI 10.1163/9789004297234_022

I   Introduction

1.   In paragraph 274 of its Resolution 68/70 of 9 December 2013, the General Assembly decided that, in its deliberations on the report of the Secretary-General on oceans and the law of the sea, the United Nations Open-ended Informal Consultative Process on Oceans and the Law of the Sea (the Informal Consultative Process) would focus its discussions at its fifteenth meeting on the role of seafood in global food security. The present report addresses that topic.

2.   Food security and nutrition has become a pressing global challenge underscoring the need for sustainable food sources. Seafood already plays an important, albeit perhaps under-recognized, role in global food security as a key source of food and nutrition, as an input into the food production chain and as a source of revenue for individuals and States. The future role of seafood in global food security, however, faces considerable pressures, including overexploitation and other unsustainable practices in seafood exploitation, as well as other stressors on the marine environment, such as habitat loss, pollution, climate change, ocean acidification and invasive alien species, which affect the health, productivity and resilience of marine ecosystems.

3.   The present report highlights the current role of seafood in global food security as well as the pressures thereon. It also draws attention to activities and initiatives undertaken with a view to ensuring the continued role of seafood in global food security and highlights opportunities for, and challenges to, the future role of seafood in global food security.

4.   The Secretary-General wishes to express his appreciation to the organizations and bodies that contributed to the present report, namely, the European Union and the secretariats of the Convention on Biological Diversity and the Convention on the Conservation of Antarctic Marine Living Resources; the Council of Europe; the Department of Economic and Social Affairs of the Secretariat; the Food and Agriculture Organization of the United Nations (FAO); the Intergovernmental Oceanographic Commission of the United Nations Educational, Scientific and Cultural Organization (UNESCO); the International Atomic Energy Agency (IAEA); the International Commission for the Conservation of Atlantic Tunas; the International Council for the Exploration of the Sea; the International Coral Reef Initiative; the International Labour Organization (ILO); the North Atlantic Salmon Conservation Organization; the North East Atlantic Fisheries Commission; the North Pacific Anadromous Fish Commission; the Office for Disarmament Affairs of the Secretariat; the Parliamentary Assembly of the Mediterranean; the Partnerships in Environmental Management for the Seas of East Asia; the South Pacific Regional Fisheries Management Organization; the United Nations Industrial Development Organization (UNIDO); the United Nations University Fisheries Training Programme; and the World Meteorological Organization (WMO).[1] The report also draws on information from a number of other sources, but does not purport to provide an exhaustive synthesis of available information.

II   The Current Role of Seafood in Global Food Security

A   *Background*

5.   Despite the commitment of the international community in the United Nations Millennium Declaration (General Assembly Resolution 55/2) to reduce by half the proportion of people who suffer from hunger by 2015, persistent hunger and malnutrition remain the norm for close to 842 million people around the world suffering from hunger, approximately

---

1   Contributions authorized by the authors to be posted online are available at <www.un.org/Depts/los/general_assembly/general_assembly_reports.htm>.

2 billion suffering from micronutrient deficiencies[2] and more than 200 million children under five years of age suffering from malnutrition.[3] During the global food crisis of 2007–2008, a rapid rise in global staple food prices led to increased food insecurity and riots around the world.[4] The close connection between food security and economic growth and social progress as well as with political stability and peace has been underlined.[5]

6. According to the Declaration of the World Summit on Food Security, food security exists when all people, at all times, have physical, social and economic access to sufficient, safe and nutritious food to meet their dietary needs and food preferences for an active and healthy life. The four pillars of food security are availability, access, utilization and stability. The nutritional dimension is integral to the concept of food security.[6]

7 Food security is both a requirement for achieving sustainable development as well as one of the goals of sustainable development. Strong interdependencies exist between food security and nutrition and many other parts of the broader sustainable development agenda.[7] Food security also has a human rights dimension and the right to adequate food has been recognized in international human rights instruments.[8]

---

2 World Health Organization, World Food Programme and United Nations Children's Fund, "Preventing and controlling micronutrient deficiencies in populations affected by an emergency" (Geneva, World Health Organization, 2007), available online: <www.who.int/ nutrition/publications/WHO_WFP_UNICEFstatement.pdf>. According to the 2013 Fact Sheet on the Millennium Development Goals, "with concerted action by national Governments and international partners, the hunger target can be achieved" (see <www.un.org/millen niumgoals/pdf/Goal_1_fs.pdf>).

3 Food and Agriculture Organization of the United Nations (FAO), Committee on World Food Security, Global Strategic Framework for Food Security and Nutrition (CFS 2012/39/5Add.1/ Rev.1, para. 1); FAO, International Fund for Agricultural Development and World Food Programme, *The State of Food Insecurity in the World 2013: The Multiple Dimensions of Food Security* (Rome, FAO, 2013).

4 Edward H. Allison, "Aquaculture, Fisheries, Poverty and Food Security," Working Paper 2011– 65 (WorldFish Center, 2011), p. 13, available online: <http://aquaticcommons.org/7517/1/ WF_2971.pdf>.

5 Joint Statement on Global Food Security, adopted in L'Aquila, Italy, on 10 July 2009 <www .g8italia2009.it/static/G8_Allegato/LAquila_Joint_Statement_on_Global_Food_Security %5B1%5D,0.pdf>.

6 Declaration of the World Summit on Food Security (Food and Agriculture Organization of the United Nations, document WSFS 2009/2).

7 See "TST issues brief: food security and nutrition," available online: <http://sustainable development.un.org/content/documents/1804tstissuesfood.pdf>.

8 Interim report of the Special Rapporteur on the right to food (A/68/288, annex, paras. 1–3).

8.   As the role of seafood in global food security gains recognition, the issue is being addressed by a growing number of forums, including the Committee on World Food Security.[9] In the outcome document of the United Nations Conference on Sustainable Development, held in Rio de Janeiro, Brazil, from 20 to 22 June 2012, entitled "The future we want," world leaders reaffirmed their commitments regarding the right of everyone to have access to safe, sufficient and nutritious food, consistent with the right to adequate food and the fundamental right of everyone to be free from hunger. These leaders acknowledged that food security and nutrition had become a pressing global challenge and, in that regard, further reaffirmed their commitment to enhancing food security and access to adequate, safe and nutritious food for present and future generations. They also stressed the crucial role of healthy marine ecosystems, sustainable fisheries and sustainable aquaculture for food security and nutrition and in providing for the livelihoods of millions of people.[10]

9.   The present section highlights the current role of seafood in global food security both directly, as a source of food and nutrition (sect. B.1), and indirectly, as an input into food production (sect. B.2) or as a source of revenue (sect. B.3). It also underscores how pressures on the sustainable exploitation of seafood and on the marine environment affect that role. Inland fisheries are not addressed in the present report, but it is noted that their contribution to global food security is closely related to that of seafood.

B   *How Seafood Contributes to Global Food Security*
1   Seafood as Food

10.   For the purposes of the present report, seafood is considered to include all marine living resources used for food, including fish, shellfish, crustaceans, marine mammals, sea turtles and algae.[11] This definition promotes

---

9   For example, later in 2014, the Committee on World Food Security is expected to consider a report of its High-level Panel of Experts on Food Security and Nutrition on the topic "The role of sustainable fisheries and aquaculture for food security and nutrition" (www .fao.org/cfs/cfshlpe/en). The International Coalition of Fisheries Associations has also initiated work on this topic.

10   General Assembly Resolution 66/288, annex, paras. 108 and 113.

11   Popular definitions of seafood differ, e.g., "Food obtained from the sea; fish, crustacea, etc., used as food" (www.oed.com); "Fish and shellfish that live in the ocean and are used for food" (www.m-w.com); "Seafood is any sea animal or seaweed that is served as food or is suitable for eating, particularly seawater animals, such as fish and shellfish (including mollusks and crustaceans)" (http://seafood.askdefine.com); "animals from the sea that

a holistic view of the contribution of seafood to global food security. Due to space limitations, however, the present report will focus primarily on the contribution of marine living resources to global food security, in particular in the context of fisheries and aquaculture.

11. In order to meet the requirements of the four pillars of food security (see para. 6 above), it is important for seafood to have nutritional value (utilization) and for it to be available in sufficient quantities and on a consistent basis (availability). Individuals should be able to regularly acquire adequate quantities of seafood (access), and the supply of seafood should be resistant to spikes in price or temporary shortages (stability).[12]

12. *Utilization and nutritional value.* Seafood plays an important role in human nutrition, in particular as a key source of protein and essential micronutrients. Fish contributes about 17 percent to the world's animal protein intake, and is the main source of animal protein along with essential micronutrients and fatty acids for 3 billion people.[13] Populations in Africa and Asia rely even more on fish for their intake of animal proteins, and this contribution can reach up to 40 percent or more in some small island developing States.[14] According to one estimate, rural inhabitants of the Solomon Islands rely on fish and fish products for 94 percent of their animal protein.[15] Notably, seafood contributes almost a quarter of animal proteins consumed by people in low-income food-deficit countries.[16]

13. Although fish plays an extremely important role in the supply of protein worldwide, it has been considered more important as a source of micronutrients and lipids.[17] It is estimated that in excess of 2 billion people, especially in developing countries, are undernourished due to a lack of essential vitamins and minerals often contained in fish.[18] These deficiencies are believed to be "especially important at key stages of human life

---

can be eaten, especially fish or sea creatures with shells" (http://dictionary.cambridge.org/us/dictionary/british/seafood?q=seafood).

12   See <https://www.wfp.org/node/359289>.

13   FAO, Committee on Fisheries, Sub-Committee on Aquaculture, "Global Aquaculture Advancement Partnership (GAAP) Programme" (FAO document COFI:AQ/2013/SBD.2), and contribution of FAO.

14   Contribution of FAO.

15   Secretariat of the Pacific Community, "Fish and Food Security," Policy Brief 1/2008, available online: <www.spc.int/coastfish/en/publications/brochures/policy-briefs.html>.

16   For a definition of low-income food-deficit countries, see <www.fao.org/countryprofiles/lifdc/en/>.

17   See Allison, note 4 above, p. 7.

18   Ibid.

(pregnancy, breastfeeding, childhood)."[19] Seafood plays an important part in the diet of many indigenous peoples, for example, the diet of the Yup'ik Eskimos contains 20 times more omega-3 fats from fish than the diet of the people in the rest of the United States of America.[20]

14.   Important micronutrients provided by fish consumption include minerals, certain vitamins and omega-3 fatty acids,[21] as well as lysine, an essential amino acid.[22] Regular consumption (one to three times per week) of fish can reduce the risk of various diseases and disorders, particularly cardiovascular disease. It can also benefit brain health and development and relieve inflammatory conditions, and may help reduce the risk of premature birth.[23]

15.   Different types of seafood may have different nutritional value. For example, it has been suggested that "large farmed freshwater fish often possess micronutrient and lipid profiles inferior to those of small species derived from marine and inland capture fisheries."[24] In particular, levels of eicosapentaenoic acid and docosahexaenoic acid may be lower in certain types of farmed species.[25] However, many of the factors that affect the quality and nutritional value of fish can be monitored and controlled during farming.[26]

16.   Other types of seafood also serve as important sources of protein and micronutrients. For example, various types of seaweed contain protein, dietary fibre, vitamins, minerals and amino acids.[27] Seaweed is used for direct human consumption and hydrocolloids like agar, alginate and carrageenan have been extracted from seaweed and used as thickening and

---

19   Ibid.

20   See <www.sciencedaily.com/releases/2011/03/110324153712.htm>.

21   See for example, Charles R. Santerre, "The Risks and Benefits of Farmed Fish," *Journal of the World Aquaculture Society* 41, no. 2 (2010).

22   See Allison, "Aquaculture, Fisheries, Poverty and Food Security," p. 21.

23   Contribution of the European Union.

24   B. Belton and S.H. Thilsted, "Fisheries in Transition: Food and Nutrition Security Implications for the Global South," *Global Food Security* 3, no. 1 (2014): 59–66.

25   Albert G.J. Tacon and Marc Metian, "Fish Matters: Importance of Aquatic Foods in Human Nutrition and Global Food Supply," *Reviews in Fisheries Science* 21, no. 1 (2013): 28 and 35.

26   FAO, Committee on Fisheries, Sub-committee on Aquaculture, "The Role of Aquaculture in Improving Nutrition: Opportunities and Challenges" (FAO document COFI: AQ/VII/2013/7).

27   Dennis J. McHugh, *A Guide to the Seaweed Industry*, FAO Technical Fisheries Paper No. 441 (Rome, FAO, 2003), pp. 73–89, available online: <ftp://ftp.fao.org/docrep/fao/006/y4765e/y4765e00.pdf>.

gelling agents in food products. Seaweed meal is also used in animal and fish feed.

17. Crustaceans and shellfish similarly provide important nutritional bene-fits.[28] While not as widely consumed, for a variety of reasons, marine mammals can also provide an important source of nutrition, in particu-lar for certain groups of indigenous peoples.[29] Since 1990, people in at least 114 States have consumed one or more of at least 87 marine mammal species. These statistics include animals killed deliberately or uninten-tionally as by-catch or strandings.[30] A wide range of concerns have been expressed, however, over the consumption of marine mammals as food, arising from questions of sustainability and food safety[31] as well as cul-tural, religious and spiritual beliefs. Such concerns have, for example, led to support for an international moratorium on commercial whaling since 1986.[32] However, the food security needs of indigenous people are sup-ported through catch limits set for aboriginal subsistence whaling.

18. Food safety can affect the nutritional value of seafood. If not properly produced, transported, stored or prepared, some types of seafood are prone to spoilage. Environmental factors, such as pollution and poor eco-system health, may also affect the nutritional value of seafood, particu-larly through contamination. Food safety and environmental laws and regulations, effective quality control and consumer awareness can play an important role in minimizing the risks associated with the consump-tion of unsafe seafood.[33]

19. *Availability.* In 2012, global fish production amounted to approximately 157 million tons, with marine fisheries and aquaculture accounting for approximately 100 million tons.[34] With sustained growth in fish

---

28   See <www.fda.gov/downloads/Food/IngredientsPackagingLabeling/LabelingNutrition/ UCM169242.pdf>.

29   See <http://iwc.int/aboriginal>.

30   Martin D. Robards and Randall R. Reeves, "The Global Extent and Character of Marine Mammal Consumption by Humans: 1970–2009," *Biological Conservation* 144, no. 12 (2011): 2770–2786.

31   The cat parasite *Toxoplasma gondii*, which can cause blindness in people, has been identi-fied in a number of marine mammals, including beluga in the western Arctic and sea otters. See "Parasite in cats killing sea otters" (www.csgc.ucsd.edu/NEWSROOM/ NEWSRELEASES/2002/ParasitesKillingSeaOtters.html); "Cat parasite found in Arctic beluga" (www.bbc.com/news/science-environment-26197742).

32   See <http://iwc.int/commercial>.

33   FAO, *The State of World Fisheries and Aquaculture 2012* (Rome, 2012), pp. 158–164.

34   Contribution of FAO.

production and improved distribution channels, world fish food supply has grown substantially in the last five decades, with an average growth rate of 3.2 percent per year in the period 1961–2009, outpacing the increase of 1.7 percent per year in the world's population.[35]

20.   While fish production from marine capture fisheries has been fairly stable in recent years (around 80 million tons in 2007–2012; see the table below), the increasing demand for fish and fishery products has been steadily met by a robust increase in aquaculture production. This growth has been estimated at an average 8.1 percent yearly during the period 1970–2012.[36]

21.   In the past three decades, world food fish production of aquaculture has expanded by almost 12 times.[37] As a result, the average annual contribution of food fish from aquaculture for human consumption has increased sevenfold, from 6 percent in 1970 to 49 percent in 2012.[38] It continues to be the fastest growing food production sector in the world at nearly 6.5 percent a year.[39] Of this, 90 percent is produced in developing countries, primarily from small-scale aquaculture.[40] According to a recent study by the World Bank, fish production has the potential to increase by 23.6 percent between 2010 and 2030, principally through increases in aquaculture outputs.[41]

22.   It has been projected that future fish supplies will be dominated by aquaculture systems because, among other reasons, feed conversion rates for many farmed fish are more efficient than those of land-based animal production, and aquaculture is an efficient user of water.[42]

23.   Despite the relative stability of yields from capture fisheries and the increased yields from aquaculture in recent years, there are concerns regarding the future sustainability of current production levels. Overexploited stocks are less productive and prone to collapse. Rapid growth in aquaculture has been due in some regions to unsustainable practices that have negatively affected the marine environment upon which aquaculture yields depend. A wide variety of other anthropogenic pressures also continue to affect the marine environment and seafood yields (see sect. III below).

---

35   FAO, note 33 above, p. 84.

36   Contribution of FAO.

37   FAO, note 33 above, p. 8.

38   Contribution of FAO.

39   FAO, note 13 above, p. 3.

40   Contribution of the United Nations University.

41   World Bank, *Fish to 2030: Prospects for Fisheries and Aquaculture* (Washington, D.C., 2013), p. 44.

42   World Bank, *Strategic Vision for Fisheries and Aquaculture* (Washington, D.C., 2011).

Global Fish Production and Utilization, 2007–2012 (Millions of Tons)

	2007	2008	2009	2010	2011	2012 (estimated)
A. Production						
Capture fisheries						
Inland	10.1	10.2	10.4	11.2	11.1	11.5
Marine	80.7	79.9	79.6	77.7	82.4	79.5
Subtotal	90.7	90.1	90.0	89.0	93.5	91.0
Aquaculture						
Inland	33.4	36.0	38.1	40.9	43.9	46.4
Marine	16.6	16.9	17.6	18.1	18.8	20.1
Subtotal	49.9	52.9	55.7	59.0	62.7	66.5
Total	140.7	143.0	145.7	148.0	156.2	157.5
B. Utilization						
Human consumption	117.4	120.8	123.8	128.1	132.3	135.4
Non-food uses	23.3	22.3	21.9	19.9	23.9	22.1
Population (billions)	6.7	6.8	6.8	6.9	7.0	7.1
Per capita food fish consumption (kilograms)	17.6	17.9	18.1	18.5	18.9	19.1

SOURCE: FAO CONTRIBUTION.

24.   There is therefore concern that the availability of fish and fishery products may not be able to keep up with increased demand, as the world's population is expected to grow by 20.2 percent from 2010 to 2030.[43] For example, in approximately one half of Pacific island countries and territories, sustainable production is not expected to meet future needs based on predicted population growth and estimate sustainable catches.[44]

25.   *Access.* There are significant regional disparities in access to seafood. Of the 126 million tons available for human consumption in 2009, fish consumption was lowest in Africa (9.1 million tons, or 9.1 kg per capita), while Asia accounted for two thirds of total consumption. The corresponding per capita fish consumption figures for Oceania, North America, Europe and Latin America and the Caribbean were 24.6 kg, 24.1 kg, 22.0 kg and 9.9 kg, respectively.[45]

---

43   World Bank, *Fish to 2030: Prospects for Fisheries and Aquaculture.*
44   Secretariat of the Pacific Community, "Fish and Food Security."
45   FAO, note 33 above, pp. 3–4.

26. The supply of fish in Africa has been described as being "in crisis." Per capita consumption in sub-Saharan Africa is the lowest in all regions and it is the only part of the world where consumption is declining, principally owing to the levelling off in capture fish production and the increasing population. In order to simply maintain the current level of per capita supply of fish in sub-Saharan Africa (6.6 kg/year) up to 2015, fish production (capture fisheries and aquaculture) has to increase by 27.7 percent over this period.[46] Supply is also an issue in the least developed countries of South and South-East Asia and the small island developing States of the Pacific region.[47]

27. Some access gaps are alleviated by trade in seafood and seafood products. Fish and other types of seafood are among the most traded food commodities. A sizeable share of fish consumed in developed countries consists of imports and, owing to steady demand and declining domestic fishery production (down 10 percent in the period 2000–2010), their dependence on imports, in particular from developing countries, is projected to grow in coming years.[48] However, some concerns have also been expressed that, while it may bring economic benefits to exporting countries, trade in seafood can reduce access of the local populations in developing countries where the fish is caught, including by limiting the fish available to small-scale and artisanal fisheries.[49]

28. Transportability is also a key factor in access to seafood. Fish is very versatile as it can be processed into a wide array of products to increase its economic value and improve its transportability and durability. It is generally distributed in live, fresh, chilled, frozen, heat-treated, fermented, dried, smoked, salted, pickled, boiled, fried, freeze-dried, minced, powdered or canned form, or as a combination of two or more of these forms.[50] The available processing methods vary considerably, even within countries, and may affect access to fish.[51]

29. *Stability.* Although the global supply of fish from fisheries and aquaculture has been relatively stable, price fluctuations can occur in line with other food sources. During the global food crisis of 2007–2008, fisheries

---

46   C. Béné and S. Heck, "Fish and Food Security in Africa," *NAGA – the WorldFish Center Quarterly* 28, nos. 3 and 4 (2005): 10.

47   Allison, note 4 above, p. 6.

48   FAO, note 33 above, pp. 3 and 4.

49   Allison, note 4 above, pp. 34–38.

50   FAO, note 33 above, p. 63.

51   Ibid., pp. 63 and 64.

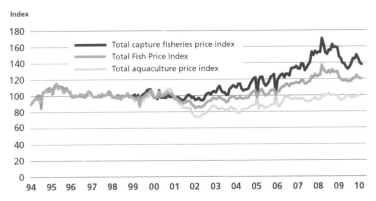

FIGURE B.1   *Trends in the FAO Fish Price Index and underlying indices*
                   SOURCE: FAO, THE STATE OF WORLD FISHERIES AND AQUACULTURE 2010
                   (ROME, 2010).
                   Note: 1998–2000 = 100.

products rose in value, according to the FAO Fish Price Index (see Figure B.1). The rise appeared to be more pronounced in the capture fisheries sector, where fuel costs for fishing vessels are a major input.[52]

30.   Local seafood stability may also be subject to fluctuations based on severe and recurring weather events (including El Niño), disease and pollution incidents. Stability in this regard, however, may counteract instability in land-based food sources caused by factors such as droughts and flooding. Disease outbreaks have cost the global aquaculture industry tens of billions of dollars over the last 20 years.[53]

31.   *Food safety and post-harvest losses.* Food safety more generally affects the stability of seafood availability and cost. Being highly perishable, fish needs timely harvesting and procurement, efficient transportation and advanced storage, processing and packaging facilities for its marketing. For example, in many parts of Africa, lack of infrastructure has led to post-harvest losses of greater than 30 percent of the catch.[54] Specific requirements and preservation techniques are therefore needed in order to preserve the nutritional quality of seafood, extend its shelf life, minimize the activity of spoilage bacteria and avoid losses caused by poor handling.[55]

---

52   Allison, "Aquaculture, Fisheries, Poverty and Food Security," p. 13.

53   Contribution of FAO.

54   Béné and Heck, note 46 above, p. 12.

55   FAO, note 33 above, p. 63.

32. For example, artisanal fisheries can suffer from high post-harvest losses because of low investment, low-level technology, variability in supply and contamination, especially during rainy periods. Spoilage and contamination of artisanal fisheries catch can create a significant source of food insecurity or even a public health hazard.[56]

2   Seafood and Seafood Products in Food Production

33. In addition to serving as food, seafood also contributes to food security as a key input in the production of food. In particular, fishmeal and algae can be used in feed for marine and freshwater aquaculture, livestock and poultry, as well as in fertilizers used to grow crops. Fish oils can also be used in the manufacture of edible oils and fats, such as margarine.[57]

34. Fishmeal, the crude flour obtained after milling and drying fish, is produced from whole fish, fish remains or other fish by-products resulting from processing. Many different species are used for fishmeal and fish-oil production, in particular anchoveta. The volume of fishmeal and fish oil produced worldwide annually fluctuates in line with catches of these species.

35. Another increasingly important source of raw material for the production of fishmeal is the processing waste from commercial fish species used for human consumption.[58] In 2010, 15 million tons of the 148 million tons of fish supplied by capture fisheries and aquaculture was reduced to fishmeal and fish oil.[59]

36. Aquaculture remains the largest user of fishmeal and fish oil. Aquafeeds are generally used for feeding omnivorous fishes, carnivorous fishes and crustacean species. According to FAO estimates, in 2008, about 31.7 million tons (46.1 percent of total global aquaculture production including aquatic plants) of farmed fish and crustaceans were feed-dependent, making up 81.2 percent of global farmed fish and crustacean production.[60] The fishmeal used for these diets varied between 2 and 10 percent, with the exception of those for tilapia and catfish in a few countries, where up to 25 percent fishmeal use has been reported.[61]

---

56   Contribution of the United Nations University Fisheries Training Programme.
57   See <www.fao.org/wairdocs/tan/x5926e/x5926e01.htm>.
58   FAO, note 33 above, p. 65.
59   Ibid., p. 13.
60   Ibid., p. 172.
61   Ibid., p. 13.

37.   While the total amounts of fishmeal and fish oil used in aquafeeds have
       grown, the use of fishmeal to feed land animals has decreased in recent
       years. However, the percentage of aquafeeds made up of fishmeal has also
       decreased as the costs of fishmeal have increased. Some alternative pro-
       tein sources have been identified.[62] For example, algal products can be
       used to enhance the nutritional value of food and animal feed owing to
       their chemical composition and thus play a crucial role in aquaculture.[63]

3   Seafood as a Source of Revenue

38.   Apart from being an important source of food, the seafood sector has also
       been an important provider of livelihoods and economic benefits to mil-
       lions of people engaged in harvesting, culturing, processing and trading
       seafood. This is especially true for coastal communities in developing
       countries, where large sections of the population have limited opportuni-
       ties for employment and fish trade is sometimes the only option open for
       earning a livelihood and improving the quality of lives.
39.   Worldwide, around 56 million people are directly employed in fisheries
       and aquaculture and some 200 million along the value chain from har-
       vesting to distribution. Thus the livelihoods of some 660 to 820 million
       people, representative of 9 to 12 percent of the global population, are
       dependent on the sector.[64]
40.   The value of the global fish trade exceeds the value of international trade
       in all other animal proteins combined.[65] Most trade is dependent on the
       labour of those who work on the world's merchant ships and commercial
       fishing vessels.[66] Trade in seafood, as well as the granting of fishing

---

62   Ibid., pp. 180–181.
63   Mohammad R. Hasan and Rina Chakrabarti, *Use of Algae and Aquatic Macrophytes as
      Feed in Small-Scale Aquaculture: A Review*, FAO Fisheries and Aquaculture Technical
      Paper, No. 531 (Rome, FAO, 2009).
64   Contribution of FAO. The 1995 Kyoto Declaration and Plan of Action on the Sustainable Con-
      tribution of Fisheries to Food Security (E/CN.17/1996/29, annex) recognizes and appreciates
      the significant role marine and inland fisheries as well as aquaculture play in providing
      global food security both through food supplies and economic and social well-being. See
      also the contribution of the Intergovernmental Oceanographic Commission of UNESCO.
65   World Bank, note 42 above.
66   Contribution of the International Labour Organization. Fishing continues to be one, if
      not the most hazardous occupation in the world, resulting in over 24,000 deaths annually,
      mainly on board small fishing vessels. The Maritime Labour Convention, 2006, of the
      International Labour Organization, sets out comprehensive rights and protection at work

licenses to foreign fishing vessels, can also be an important source of revenue for developing coastal States. However, some concerns have been expressed regarding the fair distribution of benefits from international fisheries between coastal States, particularly small island developing States, and distant-water fishing nations.[67]

41.   The value of the marine capture seafood production at the point of harvest is approximately 20 percent of the $400 billion global food fish market.[68] In 2012, the value of international trade in seafood was about $129 billion, while preliminary data for 2013 pointed to further growth to $136 billion. Over 53 percent of this trade originated in developing countries whose net trade income (exports minus imports), valued at $35 billion in 2012, is greater than the net trade income of the other agricultural commodities combined.[69]

42.   It is estimated that, overall, women accounted for at least 15 percent of all people directly engaged in the fisheries primary sector in 2010. As much as 60 percent of seafood is marketed by women in Asia and West Africa. In Africa, 59 percent of fishers (marine, inland and aquaculture) are women.[70] Commonly, in coastal artisanal fishing communities, women manage the smaller boats and canoes that go out fishing. Women are also involved in gathering shells, sea cucumbers and aquatic plants in the intertidal zone and contribute as entrepreneurs and provide labour before, during and after the catch in both artisanal and commercial fisheries.[71] By generating incomes for female workers, especially in fish processing and marketing, employment in aquaculture has enhanced the economic and social status of women in many places in developing countries, where more than 80 percent of aquaculture output occurs.

---

for the world's more than 1.5 million seafarers, who are indispensable to the carriage of 90 percent of international trade.

67   See, e.g., statements of Palau and Kiribati at the 63rd meeting of the General Assembly at its sixty-eighth session (A/68/PV.63), pp. 6 and 11–12.

68   The World Bank and FAO, *The Sunken Billions: The Economic Justification for Fisheries Reform* (Washington, D.C., World Bank, 2009), available online: <http://go.worldbank.org/MGUTHSY7Uo>.

69   Contribution of FAO.

70   African Union, concept note for the Second Conference of African Ministers of Fisheries and Aquaculture, Entebbe, Uganda, 14–18 March 2014, p. 3, available online: <www.africanfisheries.org/knowledge-output/second-conference-african-ministers-fisheries-and-aquaculture-camfa-iiconcept-note>.

71   FAO, note 33 above, pp. 46, 97 and 108–111.

43. However, pressures on the role of seafood in global food security are affecting the economic contribution of the seafood sector (see sect. III below). Recent studies have demonstrated that, as a result of overfishing, the difference between the potential and actual net economic benefits from marine fisheries is approximately $50 billion per year, equivalent to more than half the value of the global seafood trade. Thus, global marine capture fisheries are currently an underperforming global asset.[72]

44. Aquaculture has made important contributions to livelihoods, poverty alleviation, income generation, employment and trade, even though its potential has not yet been fully realized across all continents.[73] Mediterranean aquaculture, for example, which is a large and dynamic industry and plays an important social and economic role in the region, has grown substantially over recent years. Aquaculture can also provide opportunities to meet increased consumer demand for aquatic products, while reducing the dependence on often overexploited wild stocks.[74]

45. Global production of algae has been dominated by marine macroalgae, or seaweeds, grown in both marine and brackish waters. Aquatic algae production by volume increased at average annual rates of 9.5 percent in the 1990s and 7.4 percent in the 2000s – similar to the rates for farmed aquatic animals – with production increasing from 3.8 million tons in 1990 to 19 million tons in 2010. Cultivation has overshadowed production of algae collected from the wild, which accounted for only 4.5 percent of total algae production in 2010. The total value of farmed aquatic algae in 2010 is estimated at $5.7 billion, while that for 2008 is now re-estimated at $4.4 billion.[75]

46. In sharp contrast to fish aquaculture, the cultivation of aquatic algae is practised in far fewer countries. Only 31 countries and territories are recorded as having engaged in algae farming production in 2010, and 99.6 percent of global cultivated algae production comes from just eight countries in Asia and Africa.[76] China contributes 62.3 percent of global production.

47. The total value of seaweed production was estimated by FAO in 2003 at $6 billion, of which $5 billion was the value of seaweed for human consumption. Carrageenan seaweed farming is a profitable activity with great potential (see Figure B.2), especially for coastal communities with abundant

72   World Bank and FAO, note 68 above.

73   Ibid.

74   Contribution of the Parliamentary Assembly of the Mediterranean.

75   FAO, note 33 above, p. 40.

76   Ibid., pp. 40–41.

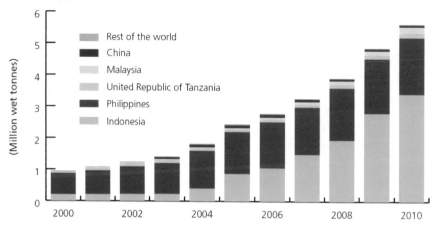

FIGURE B.2 *World carrageenan seaweed farming production (Millions of wet tons)*
SOURCE: FAO, *SOCIAL AND ECONOMIC DIMENSIONS OF CARRAGEENAN SEAWEED FARMING*, FAO FISHERIES AND AQUACULTURE TECHNICAL PAPER, NO. 580 (ROME, FAO, 2013), P. 9.

labour and few alternative activities. Among other advantages, it has a short production cycle, low capital requirement and relatively simple farming technology. The price of carrageenan in the international market was generally stable in the first half of the 2000s but has increased rapidly since the mid-2000s and become more volatile. Seasonality, disease, inclement weather and competition are the biggest risk factors for seaweed farming. The seaweed value chain involves four stages: cultivation, post-harvest treatment, trading and processing,[77] with women playing an important role in seaweed farming. In India, for example, women were the first and primary adopters of seaweed farming which offered them an income.[78]

III   Pressures on the Role of Seafood in Global Food Security

48.   The seafood industry faces numerous pressures that affect the current, as well as the future, availability, access, utilization and stability of seafood in global food security, including ecosystem degradation and unsustainable exploitation and production practices. The capacity of marine ecosystems to support the production of seafood to meet the food security

---

77   FAO, *Social and Economic Dimensions of Carrageenan Seaweed Farming*, FAO Fisheries and Aquaculture Technical Paper, No. 580 (Rome, FAO, 2013), pp. 6–20.

78   Ibid., pp. 42–43.

and nutritional needs of present and future generations is directly dependent on their health and resilience.

A   *Unsustainable Practices in the Exploitation of Seafood Resources*

49.   A wide range of unsustainable practices in marine capture fisheries,
       including overfishing, illegal, unreported and unregulated fishing and
       destructive fishing, as well as unsustainable aquaculture practices, can
       affect the health of marine ecosystems and, therefore, the sustainability
       of resource exploitation and food security.

50.   *Unsustainable exploitation of marine capture fisheries.* The share of
       marine fish stocks that are overexploited has increased during the last
       decades, from 10 percent in 1970 to nearly one third in 2009. A further
       52 percent of the fish stocks are fully exploited.[79] Overexploitation may
       also have other detrimental impacts on marine ecosystems, including by
       upsetting predator–prey relationships, particularly in relation to associ-
       ated and dependent species.[80]

51.   Harmful subsidies create overcapacity in the fishing industry and have
       resulted in marine capture fisheries underperforming as a global asset
       (see para. 42 above). These subsidies, such as support for vessel construc-
       tion and fuel tax waivers, reduce the real costs of fishing and enable
       unprofitable fishing to continue.[81] The cumulative economic loss to the
       global economy over the last three decades has been estimated to be in
       the order of 2 trillion dollars.[82]

52.   Technological advances have the potential to contribute to the role of
       seafood in food security (see sect. IV.B.3 below). However, they have also
       accelerated overfishing and contributed to by-catch, destructive fishing
       practices and ecosystem degradation. The effectiveness and efficiency of
       fishing fleets has increased through technological improvements, includ-
       ing advanced hydraulic power applications, stronger materials for fishing
       gear, electronic aids to navigation, seafloor mapping, fish finding, gear
       deployment and communication.[83] Many of these technologies are also

---

79   Contribution of FAO.

80   S.M. Garcia and others, *The Ecosystem Approach to Fisheries: Issues, Terminology,
      Principles, Institutional Foundations, Implementation and Outlook*, FAO Fisheries Technical
      Paper, No. 443 (Rome, FAO, 2003), pp. 9–11.

81   World Bank and FAO, *The Sunken Billions: The Economic Justification for Fisheries Reform.*

82   Contribution of the European Union.

83   P. Surronen and others, "Low Impact and Fuel Efficient Fishing – Looking beyond the
      Horizon," *Fisheries Research* 119–120 (2012): 135–146.

becoming more widely available, cheap and compact so they can be operated from smaller vessels.[84] The future modernization of small-scale and artisanal fisheries could increase their effectiveness and efficiency and further impact global fish catch.[85]

53. Discards are another contributor to overfishing. In its most recent global assessment of discards, FAO reports that 7.3 million tons of fish and other animals are captured and thrown away at sea annually. Much of the discarding is associated with the use of poorly selective fishing gears and often includes large quantities of juveniles of food fish species.[86]

54. Destructive fishing practices impair the ability of one or more key components of an ecosystem to provide essential ecosystem functions. While a few fishing practices are inherently destructive, such as the use of explosives and toxins, adverse impacts also occur from commonly used fishing gears, such as trawls, dredges, gillnets, pots, traps, hooks and lines.[87] The magnitude and extent of such impacts varies widely and depends to a large extent on the physical characteristics of the gear, the mechanics of its operation, where, when and how the gear is used and the extent of its use.[88] Synthetic pots, traps, gillnets and fish aggregating devices lost or discarded at sea can continue to catch and kill fish and other animals through a process known as ghost fishing.[89]

55. The practice of illegal, unreported and unregulated fishing, estimated globally at 11 to 26 million tons a year, further undermines efforts to manage fisheries sustainably and conserve marine biodiversity, often leading to the collapse of local fisheries.[90] This practice puts unsustainable pressure on fish stocks, marine wildlife and habitats, subverts labour standards and distorts markets.[91] Products derived from illegal, unreported and unregulated fishing enter local or overseas trade markets, thus undermining the local fisheries economy, depriving local communities of guaranteed food supplies and threatening the livelihoods of fishers and other fishery-sector stakeholders.[92]

---

84   Ibid.
85   See <www.fao.org/fishery/topic/14753/en>.
86   Contribution of FAO.
87   Ibid.
88   Ibid.
89   Ibid.
90   Ibid.
91   Contribution of the European Union.
92   Contribution of FAO.

56. Many factors contribute to illegal, unreported and unregulated fishing, including economic incentives that negate attempts to make fishing behaviour more responsible, as well as limited capacity or weak governance arrangements. Such fishing imposes significant economic costs on some of the poorest countries in the world, where dependency on fisheries for food, livelihoods and revenues is high, and undermines efforts by these countries to manage natural resources.[93]

57. *Unsustainable aquaculture practices.* Like any rapidly growing industry, aquaculture faces serious challenges. In many regions, ineffective governance and regulatory arrangements have failed to protect supporting ecosystems, with consequent impacts on marine resources and habitats. Aquaculture operations, for example, can negatively impact the local biophysical environment and thereby affect the food security of stakeholders competing with aquaculture for natural resources, such as capture fisheries.[94]

58. Capture fisheries and aquaculture may also compete with one another in relation to food security, with consequent trade-offs in relation to marine habitats, access to resources and fish utilization. Production from aquaculture may be economically profitable in the short term, but biologically wasteful processes may use more biomass to produce less.[95]

B   *Other Pressures on the Marine Environment*

59. *Habitat alteration and destruction.* Much of the world's marine production originates from coastal ecosystems, such as wetlands, mangroves, coral reefs and sea-grass beds. These ecosystems play a major role in the life cycle of many marine organisms by providing breeding, nursery and feeding grounds.[96] However, owing to a range of factors, including unsustainable coastal area development, unsustainable tourism, unsustainable aquaculture and destructive fishing practices (see sect. II.A above), major marine ecosystems and habitats have been degraded or lost,[97] with resultant threats to fisheries productivity. For example, destruction of mangroves removes the nursery grounds of many fish species and can result in reduced productivity of fish stocks.[98]

---

93   Contribution of the European Union.

94   Allison, note 4 above, pp. 43–44.

95   Belton and Thilsted, note 24 above.

96   FAO contribution.

97   See A/67/268.

98   Marine Resources Assessment Group, "Fisheries and Food Security," FMSP Policy Brief, No. 3 (United Kingdom, Department for International Development, Fisheries Management Science Programme, 2006).

60. *Pollution.* Pollution can have lasting effects on marine ecosystems. It originates from a number of marine and land-based sources, including riverine discharges, run-offs from industrial, agriculture and aquaculture operations, municipal wastewater, atmospheric deposition, dumping, accidents (e.g., oil spills), fishing operations, shipping and offshore installations. Marine pollution occurs in various forms, including heavy metals, persistent organic pollutants, pesticides, nutrients (nitrogen and phosphorus), plastics, abandoned, lost and otherwise discarded fishing gear, oil, hazardous substances, chemical munitions,[99] radioactive materials, and anthropogenic underwater noise.

61. The impacts of pollution include the formation of hypoxic zones in the oceans, where oxygen levels in surface water can no longer support life. Dead zones are linked with increasingly frequent outbreaks of harmful algal blooms, where mass mortality events of fish and marine mammals are caused by toxin build-ups owing to lower oxygen levels in their environment.[100] Seafood is also contaminated with toxins which may subsequently be transmitted to humans through consumption.[101] Through their bioaccumulation to levels that may adversely affect marine living resources and human health, marine pollutants can adversely affect productivity of stocks and international trade in seafood products.[102] Reproductive and developmental issues, behavioural problems, diseases and cancers have been linked to chemical and other pollutants in seafood.[103]

62. *Alien species.* There has also been a considerable increase in the accidental introduction of alien species, both from shipping through ballast water and from escaped farmed species. In favourable conditions, alien species may become invasive and out-compete local marine species and

---

99 Contribution of the Office for Disarmament Affairs of the Secretariat. Recent chemical weapons disarmament activities in the Syrian Arab Republic have drawn new attention to the safety and security of transport of chemical munitions and chemical agents by sea. Dumping of chemical and other munitions, lethal chemical agents, radioactive wastes are current issues of relevance being discussed in the disarmament context.

100 See A/67/268.

101 Contribution of the Intergovernmental Oceanographic Commission of UNESCO.

102 Contribution of IAEA.

103 T. Colborn, F.S. vom Saal and A.M. Soto, "Developmental Effects of Endocrine-Disrupting Chemicals in Wildlife and Humans," *Environmental Health Perspectives* 101, no. 5 (October 1993); L.S. Birnbaum, "Endocrine Effects of Prenatal Exposure to PCBs, Dioxins, and Other Xenobiotics: Implications for Policy and Future Research," *Environmental Health Perspectives* 102, no. 8 (August 1994); J.G. Vos and others, "Health Effects of Endocrine-Disrupting Chemicals on Wildlife, with Special Reference to the European Situation," *Critical Review in Toxicology* 30, no. 1 (2000): 71–133.

result in biodiversity loss, thereby impacting local marine ecology, complex food webs, food security and human health.[104] Genetic interactions between escaped farmed species, including possibly those that have been genetically modified, and wild fish populations may also affect the health and productivity of wild stocks.[105] Contamination of wild fish stocks, including from parasites and disease transmitted from farmed species to wild species,[106] can also create a significant source of food insecurity or even a public health hazard.[107]

63. *Climate change and ocean acidification.* The atmosphere and oceans have warmed, sea level is rising, and the concentrations of greenhouse gases have increased.[108] The ocean has absorbed about 30 percent of the emitted anthropogenic carbon dioxide, causing ocean acidification.[109] Although ocean acidification and climate change are separate phenomena, increased levels of CO_2 in the atmosphere contribute to both.[110]

64. Global climate change is expected to alter terrestrial inputs to the sea, the production of organic matter in the ocean, marine ecosystem composition and trophic interactions, the ice forming and melting dynamic, as well as the release of methane from permafrost areas in the Arctic, accelerating the green-house effect. As a result, the chemical composition of the organic matter may change accordingly with unknown consequences for global fish stocks.[111]

---

104   See A/67/268.

105   William M. Muir and Richard D. Howard, "Possible Ecological Risks of Transgenic Organism Release When Transgenes Affect Mating Success: Sexual Selection and the Trojan Gene Hypothesis," *Proceedings of the National Academy of Sciences* 96, no. 24 (23 November 1999): 13853–13856.

106   Albert G.J. Tacon, Marc Metian and Sena S. De Silva, "Climate Change, Food Security and Aquaculture: Policy Implications for Ensuring the Continued Green Growth and Sustainable Development of a Much Needed Food Sector," available online: <www.oecd.org/greengrowth/fisheries/45044794.pdf>.

107   Contribution of the United Nations University.

108   Intergovernmental Panel on Climate Change, "Summary for Policymakers," in *Climate Change 2013: The Physical Science Basis – Contribution of Working Group I to the Fifth Assessment Report of the Intergovernmental Panel on Climate Change*, eds. T.F. Stocker and others (Cambridge: Cambridge University Press, 2013), p. 4.

109   Ibid., p. 11. See also *Climate Change 2014: Impacts, Adaptation, and Vulnerability*, Summary for Policymakers, Working Group II Contribution to the Fifth Assessment Report of the Intergovernmental Panel on Climate Change, p. 16.

110   See A/68/159, para. 10. For information on the socioeconomic impacts of ocean acidification see A/68/71, paras. 33–39.

111   Contribution of IAEA.

65. Fisheries (both capture and aquaculture) and resulting food security are closely linked to weather and climate conditions. Extreme weather and long-term climate change pose important challenges to fisheries and food security. Owing to projected climate change by the mid-twenty-first century and beyond, global marine species redistribution and marine biodiversity reduction in regions sensitive to climate change will challenge the sustained provision of fisheries productivity and other ecosystem services.[112] Fishers, fish farmers and coastal inhabitants will bear the full force of these impacts through less stable livelihoods, changes in the availability and quality of fish for food, and rising risks to their health, safety and homes.[113]

66. The implications of climate change for food security and livelihood are of particular concern in developing countries, including small island developing States,[114] where undernourishment is already widespread and reliance on seafood as a source of food is high. Redistribution of marine fisheries catch potential towards higher latitudes poses risk of reduced supplies, income and employment in tropical countries, with potential implications for food security. Spatial shifts of marine species owing to projected warming will cause high-latitude invasions and high local extinction rates in the tropics and semi-enclosed seas. Species richness and fisheries catch potential are projected to increase, on average, at middle and high latitudes and decrease at tropical latitudes. This is shown by model projections for the years 2040 to 2060, based on evidence from the Global Ocean Observing System coordinated by the Intergovernmental Oceanographic Commission of UNESCO.[115] Moreover, effects of climate change on land-based food sources could also create increased reliance and pressure on seafood.[116]

67. In light of these pressures on fisheries and aquaculture, the question of how to meet increasing demand for fish in the face of climate change will increasingly pose a great challenge to fisheries and aquaculture management.[117]

112   Contribution of WMO. See also *Climate Change 2014*, note 109 above, p. 16.
113   Contribution of FAO.
114   Ibid.
115   Contribution of the Intergovernmental Oceanographic Commission of UNESCO.
116   Ibid.
117   C. De Young and others, "Building Resilience for Adaptation to Climate Change in the Fisheries and Aquaculture Sector," in *Building Resilience for Adaptation to Climate Change in the Agriculture Sector: Proceedings of a Joint FAO/OECD Workshop, 23–24 April 2012*, eds. A. Meybeck and others (Rome, FAO and Organization for Economic Cooperation and Development, 2012).

In fact, increasing climate variability will make fisheries management and the forecasts of fisheries production more difficult.[118]

IV   Opportunities for, and Challenges to, the Future Role of Seafood in Global Food Security

A   *Current Activities and Initiatives to Ensure the Continued Role of Seafood in Global Food Security*

68.   A wide range of ongoing activities and initiatives are being taken by the international community to address the pressures described in Section III above, including through strengthening implementation of the international legal and policy framework, protecting and restoring the health, productivity and resilience of marine ecosystems, enhancing the conservation and sustainable use of marine living resources and capacity-building and the transfer of technology.[119]

69.   The international legal and policy framework relevant to the role of seafood in global food security is drawn from a variety of binding and non-binding instruments. Of central importance among the binding instruments is the United Nations Convention on the Law of the Sea, which sets out the legal framework within which all activities in the oceans and seas must be carried out, including in relation to seafood and its role in global food security. The Convention contains detailed rights and obligations of States including regarding the equitable and efficient utilization of their resources, the conservation of living resources and the study, protection and preservation of the marine environment.

70.   The legal regime in the Convention is complemented by two implementing agreements, including the Agreement for the Implementation of the Provisions of the United Nations Convention on the Law of the Sea of 10 December 1982 relating to the Conservation and Management of Straddling Fish Stocks and Highly Migratory Fish Stocks, as well as a wide range of other instruments[120] relating to the conservation and management of marine living resources, the protection and preservation of the

---

118   Contribution of WMO.

119   Past reports of the Secretary-General on oceans and the law of the sea have provided information on past activities and initiatives (see www.un.org/Depts/los).

120   Ibid. Additional information on the legal framework for oceans and the law of the sea is set out in past reports of the Secretary-General.

marine environment, sustainable development, food security[121] and human rights.[122] Together they provide the international legal and policy framework for the role of seafood in global food security.

71.   National legal and policy frameworks are also vital to improving food security and ensuring the role of seafood in global food security. Given the wide variety of relevant international instruments, however, States are faced with challenges in incorporating their commitments in national legal frameworks.[123]

72.   The following sections, inter alia, provide information on initiatives and activities described in the contributions to the present report (see para. 4 above).

1   Protecting and Restoring the Health, Productivity and Resilience of Marine Ecosystems

73.   In the outcome document of the United Nations Conference on Sustainable Development, States committed themselves to protect and restore the health, productivity and resilience of oceans and marine eco-systems, to maintain their biodiversity, enabling their conservation and sustainable use for present and future generations, and to effectively apply an ecosystem approach and the precautionary approach in the management, in accordance with international law, of activities having an impact on the marine environment, to deliver on all three dimensions

---

121   For example, the 1995 Kyoto Declaration and Plan of Action on the Sustainable Contribution of Fisheries to Food Security (E/CN.17/1996/29, annex), 1996 Rome Declaration on World Food Security, 2004 Voluntary Guidelines to Support the Progressive Realization of the Right to Adequate Food in the Context of National Food Security (E/CN.4/2005/131, annex), and the 2012 Voluntary Guidelines on the Responsible Governance of Tenure of Land, Fisheries and Forests in the Context of National Food Security of the Committee on World Food Security of FAO (FAO document CL 144/9 (C 2013/20), Appendix D).

122   For example, Article 25 of the 1948 Universal Declaration of Human Rights (General Assembly Resolution 217 A(III)) and Article 11 of the International Covenant on Economic, Social and Cultural Rights (General Assembly Resolution 2200 A(XXI), annex). See also the interim report of the Special Rapporteur on the right to food (A/68/288).

123   The Division for Ocean Affairs and the Law of the Sea of the Office of Legal Affairs of the Secretariat assists States in the uniform and consistent application of the provisions of the United Nations Convention on the Law of the Sea and its implementing agreements. It also maintains a collection of national legislation on maritime space on its website (www.un.org/Depts/los). FAO reported that it maintains a number of legal databases (http://faolex.fao.org/, http://faolex.fao.org/fishery/ and www.fao.org/fishery/psm/collection/en).

of sustainable development.[124] Many other forums have also recognized the importance to food security of healthy and productive ecosystems, as indicated below.[125]

74. *Increasing scientific understanding.* Good supporting science and data, which increase understanding of the biology and ecology of species and the key linkages among species,[126] are an essential underpinning for managing the health and resilience of marine ecosystems and food security.

75. The first global integrated marine assessment of the state of the marine environment of the Regular Process for Global Reporting and Assessment of the State of the Marine Environment, including Socioeconomic Aspects, to be completed by 2014, will provide the international community with a sound, scientific basis for decision-making. It will include assessments on food security and food safety.

76. A number of recent initiatives have also focused on assessing the impacts of ocean acidification, climate change and weather events on marine ecosystems. For example, IAEA is using nuclear and isotopic techniques to assess the effects of ocean acidification, increasing water temperatures and co-contaminants on marine organisms.[127] It also expanded its support for collaborations among international researchers on the effects of rising acidity of ocean water.[128] IAEA recently initiated a four-year coordinated research project focused on key ocean ecosystems south of 30°N latitude to evaluate potential biological and socioeconomic impacts of ocean acidification and the implications for sustainable food security.

77. WMO, in partnership with the Secretariat of the Pacific Regional Environment Programme, is organizing a regional consultation on the Global Framework for Climate Services for small island developing States in the Pacific to address weather, climate and water events and climate change effects that have an impact on the socioeconomic development of those States, including fisheries.[129]

---

124   General Assembly Resolution 66/288, annex, para. 158.

125   See 1995 Kyoto Declaration and Plan of Action on the Sustainable Contribution of Fisheries to Food Security (E/CN.17/1996/29, annex); Committee on World Food Security, Global Strategic Framework for Food Security and Nutrition, CFS 2012/39/5 Add.1/Rev.1.

126   J. Travis and others, "Integrating the Invisible Fabric of Nature into Fisheries Management," *Proceedings of the National Academy of Sciences* 111, no. 2 (14 January 2014).

127   Contribution of IAEA.

128   Ibid.; see also <www.iaea.org/ocean-acidification/download/ebook-ECONOMICS%20 OF%20OCEAN%20ACIDIFICATION.pdf>.

129   See <http://gfcs-climate.org/content/regional-consultation-gfcs-small-island-developing -statespacific>.

78. The North Pacific Anadromous Fish Commission encourages international cooperative research to provide the best available scientific information on ecological mechanisms regulating production of anadromous populations, climate impact on salmon populations in the North Pacific and the extent to which salmon populations can be used as indicators of conditions in marine ecosystems.[130]

79. *Integrated management and ecosystems approaches.* Increased emphasis is being placed on adopting integrated management and ecosystem approaches. Many initiatives adopt a suite of management tools in an integrated, cross-sectoral manner, including environmental impact assessments, area-based management tools, including marine protected areas and marine spatial planning,[131] management of land-sea interactions, watershed and catchment planning and management,[132] gear restrictions[133] and promotion of cleaner production and environmentally sound technologies,[134] as well as pollution prevention and control.[135]

80. Ecosystem approaches are also increasingly being implemented and promoted within sectors, in particular, the fisheries sector. Cooperation is also currently taking place to improve policy integration in ecosystem approaches between the fisheries and biodiversity sectors. For example, the Conference of the Parties to the Convention on Biological Diversity at its eleventh meeting, held in Hyderabad, India, from 8 to 19 October 2012, adopted decision XI/18 (see UNEP/CBD/COP/11/35, annex I), in which it encouraged inter-agency collaboration between biodiversity and fisheries bodies and the participation by a range of experts on biodiversity, indigenous and local communities in fisheries management, and invited fisheries management bodies to integrate biodiversity considerations into their work.[136]

81. The Partnerships in Environmental Management for the Seas of East Asia developed and implemented a multi-faceted, comprehensive,

---

130 Contribution of the North Pacific Anadromous Fish Commission; the next International Symposium on Pacific Salmon and Steelhead Production in a Changing Climate is scheduled for May 2015.

131 Contributions of the European Union and the Parliamentary Assembly of the Mediterranean.

132 Contribution of the Partnerships in Environmental Management for the Seas of East Asia.

133 Ibid.

134 Contribution of UNIDO.

135 Contributions of the Partnerships in Environmental Management for the Seas of East Asia and FAO. With regard to adapting to, and mitigating, the impacts of ocean acidification, see A/68/71 and A/68/159.

136 Contribution of the secretariat of the Convention on Biological Diversity.

ecosystem-based approach. Its Sustainable Development of Coastal Areas Framework calls for the creation of food security and sustainable livelihood programmes to directly address fisheries concerns in the context of other programmes that also support fisheries management, including habitat protection and restoration, management of water use and supply, pollution reduction and waste management and natural and manmade hazard prevention.[137]

82.   The Intergovernmental Oceanographic Commission of UNESCO and partners are supporting the development, with coastal States, of strategies for assessing, managing, recovering, and sustaining marine living resources in large marine ecosystems.[138]

2   Promoting Sustainable Fisheries and Aquaculture

83.   A wide range of activities and initiatives is being undertaken to promote sustainability in the capture fisheries and aquaculture sectors. Increasing emphasis has been placed on incorporating integrated and ecosystems approaches in the management of fisheries and aquaculture operations.[139]

84.   Despite these efforts, however, the international community has thus far been largely unsuccessful in reversing the trend of overfishing and habitat degradation.[140] In many parts of the world, economic growth in fisheries and aquaculture has only been accomplished through unsustainable exploitation of marine resources.[141]

85.   At the United Nations Conference on Sustainable Development, States committed themselves to ensuring the exploitation of marine biological resources at rates which maintain or restore populations of harvested stocks at least to levels that can produce the maximum sustainable yield by 2015. States have also been called upon by the General Assembly to take a number of actions to achieve sustainable fisheries, including to urgently reduce the fishing capacity of the world's fishing fleets to levels commensurate with the sustainability of fish, to eliminate subsidies that contribute to overfishing and overcapacity and illegal, unreported and unregulated fishing and to strengthen fisheries management capacities

---

137   Contribution of the Partnerships in Environmental Management for the Seas of East Asia.
138   Contribution of the Intergovernmental Oceanographic Commission of UNESCO.
139   Contribution of the Parliamentary Assembly of the Mediterranean.
140   Contribution of FAO.
141   Ibid.

and institutions.[142] The Strategic Plan for Biodiversity 2011–2020 and especially Aichi Biodiversity Target 6, also aims to ensure that, by 2020, all fish and invertebrate stocks and aquatic plants are managed and harvested sustainably, legally and applying ecosystem-based approaches.[143]

86. IAEA underlined the relevance of its isotopic and nuclear data to management decisions in areas such as fisheries closures/reopenings, choice of aquaculture species and the geographical seating of aquaculture facilities, and also potentially to risk assessments of contaminants in seafood.[144] The International Coral Reef Initiative is working to improve awareness and understanding of the importance of fish aggregations for food security.[145]

87. The European Union reported that its Common Fisheries Policy aimed to ensure that fisheries were environmentally, economically and socially sustainable in accordance with principles of good governance, including decision-making based on best available scientific advice and the precautionary principle and broad stakeholder involvement. New rules that took effect on 1 January 2014 implement the commitment undertaken at the United Nations Conference on Sustainable Development and contain measures to reduce unwanted catches and gradually eliminate discards, including through an obligation to land catches. The policy also foresees designating areas that are biologically sensitive as protected areas. The new external dimension of the reformed Common Fisheries Policy also strengthens its commitment to addressing fishing overcapacity at a global level.[146]

88. FAO highlighted that low impact and fuel efficient technologies and practices were being developed to address the energy consumption and environmental impacts of existing fishing technologies and practices.[147]

89. Regional fisheries management organizations reported on measures to improve the conservation and management of fish stocks and to contribute, directly or indirectly, to global food security.[148] For example, the

---

142   General Assembly Resolution 68/71, paras. 86 and 91.

143   Contribution of the secretariat of the Convention on Biological Diversity.

144   Contribution of IAEA.

145   Contribution of the International Coral Reef Initiative.

146   Contribution of the European Union.

147   Contribution of FAO; P. Surronen and others, note 83 above, pp. 135–146.

148   Contribution of the secretariat of the Convention on the Conservation of Antarctic Marine Living Resources, the International Commission for the Conservation of Atlantic Tunas, the North Atlantic Salmon Conservation Organization, the North East Atlantic Fisheries Commission and the North Pacific Anadromous Fish Commission.

secretariat of the Convention on the Conservation of Antarctic Marine Living Resources has contributed to global food security through management responses based on precaution and an ecosystems approach, including catch limits, by-catch mitigation practices, temporal and spatial closures, prohibited fishing gears and sustained efforts over more than 15 years to combat illegal, unreported and unregulated fishing.[149]

90.   FAO has continued to develop its programme to support implementation of the 2009 Agreement on Port State Measures to Prevent, Deter and Eliminate Illegal, Unreported and Unregulated Fishing of FAO, including through its global series of regional capacity-development workshops.[150]

91.   With regard to small-scale fisheries, FAO is currently facilitating the development of voluntary guidelines for securing sustainable small-scale fisheries that extend beyond the traditional realm of fisheries management and address crucial socioeconomic issues. The guidelines seek to enhance the contribution of small-scale fisheries to poverty alleviation, food and nutrition security and economic growth.[151]

92.   The Sub-Committee on Aquaculture of the Committee on Fisheries of FAO is addressing a wide range of issues relating to the role of aquaculture in global food security and improving its sustainability.[152] FAO is developing the Global Aquaculture Advancement Programme aimed at assisting States and civil society in making future aquaculture growth sustainable.[153]

93.   The International Council for the Exploration of the Sea has made aquaculture an area of strategic importance; its newly established working group on aquaculture will develop science and advice for aquaculture sustainability, addressing issues such as sea lice, pest and predator management, climate change and impacts on wild species and fisheries.[154]

94.   Recent attention has also focused on the development of eco-labelling and certification programmes to strengthen sustainability measures for aquaculture through market-based incentives.[155] In this regard, FAO is

---

149   Contribution of the secretariat of the Convention on the Conservation of Antarctic Marine Living Resources.

150   Contribution of FAO.

151   Ibid.

152   See FAO document COFI:AQ/VII/2013/1.

153   See FAO document COFI:AQ/VII/2013/9 and FAO, note 13 above.

154   Contribution of the International Council for the Exploration of the Sea.

155   See, for example, the schemes proposed by the Aquaculture Stewardship Council (www .asc-aqua.org).

currently undertaking work to assess the conformity of aquaculture certification schemes with aquaculture certification guidelines.[156]

95. FAO has also recently published a new technical paper that summarizes some of the issues facing aquaculture employment governance in a number of countries, current best practices and suggestions for improvements.[157]

96. The Common Fisheries Policy of the European Union gives a prominent role to the development of environmentally, socially and economically sustainable aquaculture and aims to promote aquaculture through an open method of coordination.[158]

3   Capacity-Building and Technology Transfer

97. The importance of human, institutional and systemic capacity for the sustainable management of the marine environment and marine resources cannot be overemphasized and is essential to unlocking the benefits of seafood for global food security.[159]

98. In General Assembly resolutions on oceans and the law of the sea and sustainable fisheries[160] and in "The future we want,"[161] States have reiterated the importance of human resource development, exchange of experiences and expertise, knowledge transfer, technical assistance, and the need to strengthen technical and scientific cooperation. Regional meetings held in preparation for the Third International Conference on Small Island Developing States have also highlighted the importance of strengthening national statistical and information systems, analytical capabilities for decision-making, and monitoring and evaluation systems for sustainable development.[162]

99. Presented below are some initiatives and activities on capacity-building and transfer of technology that were highlighted in the contributions to the present report.

---

156 FAO document COFI:AQ/VII/2013/1.

157 N. Hishamunda and others, *Improving Governance of Aquaculture Employment: A Global Assessment*, FAO Fisheries and Aquaculture Technical Paper, No. 575 (Rome, FAO, 2014).

158 Contribution of the European Union.

159 See A/57/57, paras. 571–639; A/57/80, part B, paras. 52–59. On the role of fisheries in sustainable development, see A/60/63, paras. 168–231 and A/60/99.

160 Resolutions 68/70 and 68/71.

161 General Assembly Resolution 66/288, annex, paras. 160 and 277.

162 See <www.sids2014.org/content/documents/251inter-regional%20synthesis%20for%20 sids2014.pdf>.

100. The secretariat of the Convention on Biological Diversity highlighted the 2010 Sustainable Ocean Initiative, which builds partnerships and enhances capacity, including in global food security, through the achievement of the Aichi Biodiversity Targets.

101. IAEA supports capacity-building for addressing ocean acidification, harmful algal blooms, pollutants, such as heavy metals and persistent organic pollutants, and uncontrolled releases of radioactivity.[163]

102. The FAO SmartFish Programme is increasing capacities for the sustainable exploitation of fisheries resources with the goal of improving fisheries policies and legal and regulatory frameworks and the quality of information systems.[164]

103. The United Nations University Fisheries Training Programme aims to strengthen institutional capacity to support the sustainable use of living aquatic resources in developing countries, with a focus on Africa and small island developing States.[165] The Western and Central Pacific Fisheries Commission has developed a project on capacity-building in fisheries statistics, regulations and enforcement for small island developing States.[166] The need to build capacity in small island developing States for negotiating trade and partnership agreements and navigating the complex requirements for accessing certain funds has also been identified.[167]

104. The European Union provides financial and technical support for the sustainable development of the fisheries sector of partner countries through fisheries partnership agreements. Regional programmes of the European Union in Africa, the Indian Ocean and the Pacific Ocean have focused on strategic governance issues, including control, surveillance and the fight against illegal, unreported and unregulated fishing.[168]

105. The World Bank's tsunami livelihood recovery project has trained fishing families along the coast of Somalia in new fishing techniques and creating better storage and refrigeration systems.[169]

---

163   Contribution of IAEA.

164   See <www.fao.org/fishery/smartfish/en>.

165   Contribution of the United Nations University Fisheries Training Programme.

166   Contribution of the Western and Central Pacific Fisheries Commission.

167   See para. 15 of the synthesis report of the three regional meetings held in preparation for the Third International Conference on Small Island Developing States, available from <www.sids2014.org/content/documents/251inter-regional%20synthesis%20for%20 sids2014.pdf>.

168   Contribution of the European Union.

169   See <www.worldbank.org/en/news/feature/2013/10/09/a-fisheries-project-on-somalia-s -easterncoast-helps-fight-hunger-and-poverty>.

B   *The Future Role of Seafood in Global Food Security: Challenges and*
        Opportunities

106. If seafood is to continue to play a critical role in food security and nutri-
      tion and in providing for the livelihoods of millions of people, greater
      efforts are needed at all levels. On the broadest level, fisheries and aqua-
      culture need to be promoted in a way that improves food security and is
      economically viable, while at the same time conserves marine biodiver-
      sity and ecosystems and does not impair the natural ecological processes
      that support food production systems.[170]

107. The level of contribution of seafood to food security depends principally
      on maintaining healthy, productive and resilient ecosystems, on the sus-
      tainable management of capture fisheries and aquaculture, and on mini-
      mizing wasteful practices during harvesting, processing, transportation
      and, eventually, access for consumption. Each of these elements, how-
      ever, requires appropriate levels of human, institutional and systemic
      capacity. In this regard, food security is directly affected by lack of capac-
      ity in every aspect of the seafood supply chain. Ongoing transfer of tech-
      nologies with respect to equipment and practices used for monitoring,
      assessment, pollution control and clean-up, as well as for finding, har-
      vesting, handling, processing and distributing seafood are also critical.[171]
      The capacity of institutions forming the components of the seafood sec-
      tor would also need to be reinforced along the entire chain, from the
      management of the resource to its consumption. Harmonized sectoral
      approaches can lead to enhanced capacity at the systemic and individual
      levels and promote integrated management.

1   Management Approaches to Human Activities that Affect the
          Productivity of Marine Ecosystems and the Safety of Seafood

108. While there is a comprehensive international legislative and policy
      framework in place for sustainable fisheries and aquaculture (see paras.
      69–71 above), effective implementation remains a challenge. Incentives
      and adequate resources are needed to adapt and implement this frame-
      work to secure political commitment and governance reform, including
      by building effective institutions that lead to the adoption of integrated

---

170   170 General Assembly Resolution 66/288, annex, para. 111.
171   FAO Fisheries and Aquaculture Department, "Sustainable Technology Transfer" (www
      .fao.org/fishery/topic/13301/en).

and ecosystem approaches to fisheries and aquaculture with fair and responsible tenure systems.[172]

109. *Cross-sectoral cooperation and coordination in integrated and ecosystem approaches.* In light of the interaction between the impacts of various activities and phenomena in the oceans and their cumulative effect on the health, productivity and resilience of marine ecosystems, the development of cross-sectoral cooperation and coordination in policy development, management and science would be a necessary step in the further implementation of integrated and ecosystem approaches in support of the role of seafood in global food security.

110. The General Assembly has repeatedly emphasized the need to consider ocean space as a whole through an integrated, interdisciplinary and intersectoral approach and to improve cooperation and coordination at all levels to support and supplement the efforts of States in the implementation and observance of the United Nations Convention on the Law of the Sea, and the integrated management and sustainable development of the oceans and seas.[173] It has also recognized the need to further integrate ecosystem approaches into fisheries conservation and management and, more generally, the importance of applying ecosystem approaches to the management of human activities in the ocean.[174]

111. These approaches are particularly important as the impacts of increased CO_2 emissions compound the effects of other causes of ecosystem degradation. There is, however, no one-size-fits-all approach and such tools need to be tailored to the specific ecological, social and economic circumstances of a particular area.[175]

112. Integrated and ecosystem approaches can minimize the impacts of exploitation of marine living resources on associated ecosystems and habitats, thereby preserving their long-term viability, as well as minimizing the impact of other stressors on fisheries and aquaculture operations.[176] However, increased efforts are needed in the development of long-term management plans for fisheries and aquaculture that take into

---

172   Contribution of FAO.

173   See, for example, General Assembly Resolution 68/70, preamble.

174   See, for example, General Assembly Resolution 68/71, preamble.

175   Following the seventh meeting of the United Nations Open-ended Informal Consultative Process on Oceans and the Law of the Sea in 2006, the discussions of which focused on ecosystem approaches and oceans, the General Assembly has consistently reaffirmed paragraph 119 of Resolution 61/222 of 20 December 2006 regarding ecosystem approaches and oceans.

176   Contribution of the Parliamentary Assembly of the Mediterranean.

account the marine ecosystem, optimal fishing capacity and integrated frameworks of cooperation and governance.[177] FAO noted that most regional fisheries bodies are struggling to fulfil their mandates, and need greater recognition and support from the international community.[178] The North Pacific Anadromous Fish Commission suggested that a combined database on vessels engaged in illegal, unreported and unregulated fishing could supply information on a global scale, appropriate to the degree to which intelligence exchange is required to combat such activities. In that regard, capacity-building and enabling mechanisms to support cooperation and consultation on issues related to conservation and management of marine living resources are needed.[179]

113. Progress could also be made in the development of market instruments, such as eco-labelling certification schemes, to inform the purchasing decisions of consumers and the procurement policies of retailers, including the relatively new practice of issuing government-sponsored national eco-labels.[180]

114. Management approaches will also need to take into account the impact of climate change on the role of seafood in global food security. There needs to be strengthened linkages between science and policy. Greater efforts are also needed in the development of specific adaptation and mitigation measures for fisheries and aquaculture that improve the resilience of marine ecosystems, respond to opportunities for and threats to food and livelihood security due to climate change, and help the fisheries and aquaculture sector reduce greenhouse gas emissions and support the ocean's natural carbon sequestration and storage capabilities.[181] For example, in the Pacific, specific measures are being taken to support food security while also adapting to, and mitigating the impacts of, increased CO_2 emissions, including managing and restoring vegetation to reduce transfer of sediments and nutrients to coasts and prevent damage to coral reefs, mangroves and sea-grasses supporting coastal fisheries; protecting coral reefs supplying recruits to fish populations on "downstream" reefs to help stocks recover after coral bleaching or cyclones; and promoting

---

177   Ibid.
178   Contribution of FAO.
179   Contribution of the North Pacific Anadromous Fish Commission.
180   Contribution of FAO.
181   Ibid.

mangrove replanting programmes to enhance habitat for coastal fisheries and capture carbon.[182]

115. Cooperation among States in addressing other human activities that adversely affect the productivity of marine ecosystems and the safety of seafood is also very important. Many measures have been adopted to address various pressures (see sect. IV.A above), but implementation needs to be strengthened, including through capacity-building.

116. *Community-based management.* The involvement of coastal communities and resource users in planning and management[183] is also a critical element of successful ecosystem approaches, given the role that humans have within marine ecosystems. Indigenous and local communities often possess traditional knowledge, innovations and practices that have global importance for conservation and sustainable use of marine biodiversity and resources.[184]

117. Initiatives and activities in co-management and/or community-driven marine management that recognize community rights to resources and provide for sustainable uses that benefit community livelihoods and well-being are likely to increase community ownership of conservation and management initiatives, and thus their sustainability in the long term, and thereby contribute to future food security at the local level.[185] Capacity-building is required to support general awareness raising within fishing communities.[186]

2   Potential Roles of Small-Scale Fisheries and Aquaculture in Global Food Security

118. *Small-scale fisheries.* Despite their importance, many small-scale fishing communities continue to be marginalized and their contribution to food security and nutrition, poverty eradication, equitable development and sustainable resource utilization has not been fully realized.[187] Particular

---

182   Secretariat of the Pacific Community, "Coastal Fisheries and Climate Change," Policy Brief 16/2012, available online: <www.spc.int/coastfish/en/publications/brochures/policy -briefs.html>.

183   Contribution of the European Union, FAO and the Parliamentary Assembly of the Mediterranean.

184   United Nations Environment Programme, document UNEP/CBD/SBSTTA/14/INF/6.

185   Ibid.

186   Ibid.

187   See Voluntary Guidelines for Securing Sustainable Small-scale Fisheries in the Context of Food Security and Poverty Eradication (FAO document TC-SSF/2014/2).

attention must be paid to the capacity of small-scale fisheries and marginalized groups, including women fish workers and indigenous peoples, as seafood is a significant component of their food security.[188]

119. Adopting a community-based approach to development (see paras. 116 and 117 above) could be one way to create an enabling environment to reduce current vulnerabilities and allow the small-scale fisheries sector to unfold its full potential.

120. Given the importance of small-scale producers for national food security, greater efforts are needed to protect the tenure rights of small-scale producers. In this regard, the 2012 Voluntary Guidelines on the Responsible Governance of Tenure of Land, Fisheries and Forests in the Context of National Food Security of the Committee on World Food Security have the overarching goal of achieving food security for all and supporting the progressive realization of the right to adequate food in the context of national food security. They represent an unprecedented global consensus on responsible principles and practices for governing access to and tenure security of rights to land, fisheries and forests.[189]

121. Artisanal fisheries also suffer from high post-harvest losses because of low investment, low-level technology, variability in supply and contamination, especially during rainy periods. Coordinated international efforts to provide training and infrastructural investment for improved fish handling and processing may assist in addressing spoilage and contamination concerns.[190]

122. *Aquaculture*. The potential contribution of aquaculture to food security cannot be fully realized without consistent, responsible policies and goals, effective institutional arrangements and regulatory frameworks and improved cooperation among stakeholders at national, regional and interregional levels.[191] Despite having achieved good progress in terms of expansion, intensification and diversification, aquaculture has not grown evenly around the world (see para. 44 above).[192]

123. The aquaculture sector is relatively underdeveloped in terms of human and technical resources. Marked intraregional and interregional and country variations continue in a number of areas, such as production level, species composition, farming systems and producer profile, which

---

188   See <www.un.org/depts/los/consultative_process/documents/adv_uned_mat.pdf>, para. 118.
189   Contribution of FAO.
190   Contribution of the United Nations University Fisheries Training Programme.
191   Contribution of FAO.
192   See FAO, note 13 above.

have given rise to key issues and challenges that need to be proactively addressed in order to achieve the aquaculture sector's goal of sustainable and equitable development.[193]

124. In terms of increasing production, meeting the future demand for food from aquaculture will depend in part on the availability of quality feeds in requisite quantities. Considering the past trends and current predictions, the sustainability of the aquaculture sector will probably be closely linked with the sustained supply of terrestrial animal and plant proteins, oils and carbohydrates for aquafeeds, as opposed to fishmeal and fish-oil resources.[194]

125. Further efforts are also needed in strengthening international cooperation for sustainable aquaculture development. Major aquaculture development constraining factors currently include access to vital resources and technology, enhancement of capacities and institutional development, access to financial resources, especially to small farmers, climate change impacts, food safety and biosecurity risks.[195]

3   Potential Innovations in Seafood Production

126. Throughout human history, scientific discoveries and technological innovations have repeatedly revolutionized food production methods and yields. In the seafood context, recent advances in aquaculture have enabled a dramatic growth in yields from aquaculture farms. However, the rapid growth has, in some cases, resulted in environmental damage to the very ecosystems which support aquaculture and affected the sustainability of such growth. Potential innovations in seafood production, of which three examples are provided below, may provide opportunities for enhancing the role of seafood in global food security, but may involve considerable challenges. A precautionary approach is therefore needed.

127. *Algae.* In considering the future role of seafood in global food security, the role and potential profitability of algae cannot be overlooked. As noted in paragraph 47 above, carrageenan seaweed farming is a profitable activity with great potential especially for coastal communities with abundant labour.

128. An extrapolation from current brown kelp production in China estimated that less than 1 percent of ocean area would be required to produce

---

193   Ibid.
194   Contribution of the United Nations University.
195   See FAO, note 13 above.

6 billion tons of algal biomass, notably without land or freshwater, and in some locations without fertilizers.[196]

129. Biofuel production from algae,[197] which can indirectly benefit food security by freeing up land currently used for biofuel production, also continues to be of interest.[198]

130. *Biotechnology.* The development of genetically modified, or transgenic, fish has been heralded as a part of the solution to meeting global food security, particularly in the light of declining fish stocks.[199] The process involves modifications intended to increase growth rate, provide better resistance to bacterial diseases, improve nutrient use and increase tolerance to colder temperatures of fish, as well as the possibility of using transgenic fish in the biocontrol of invasive species.[200] The first transgenic animal for human consumption, a fast-growing salmon, is undergoing regulatory processes in a number of countries, with Canada approving the production of salmon eggs for commercial purposes.[201]

131. However, concerns have been raised with regard to ecological risks,[202] for example, the threat to wild fish populations that would result from the escape of transgenic fish into the environment. Even when tight controls

---

196 Six billion tons was the amount of plant matter consumed in 2013. See J. Forster, "A Review of Opportunities, Technical Constraints and Future Needs of Offshore Mariculture – Temperate Waters," in *Expanding Mariculture Farther Offshore: Technical, Environmental, Spatial and Governance Challenges – FAO Technical Workshop, 22–25 March 2010, Orbetello, Italy*, A. Lovatelli, J. Aguilar-Manjarrez and D. Soto, eds., FAO Fisheries and Aquaculture Proceedings, No. 24 (Rome, FAO, 2013), pp. 77–99.

197 Noted in A/67/79, para. 23; A/66/70/Add.2, paras. 119 and 166; A/66/70, para. 63; and A/64/66/Add.1, para. 159.

198 A. Lovatelli, J. Aguilar-Manjarrez and D. Soto, eds., *Expanding Mariculture Farther Offshore: Technical, Environmental, Spatial and Governance Challenges – FAO Technical Workshop, 22–25 March 2010, Orbetello, Italy*, FAO Fisheries and Aquaculture Proceedings, No. 24 (Rome, FAO, 2013), annex 1, sect. 4.1.

199 Views differ as to the estimated value of such species (see "TST issues brief: oceans and seas," available online: <http://sustainabledevelopment.un.org/content/documents/2311 TST%20Issues%20Brief%20Oceans%20and%20Seas_FINAL.pdf>).

200 W.M. Muir, "The Threats and Benefits of GM Fish," *European Molecular Biology Organization Reports* 5, no. 7 (2004): 654–659.

201 See <www.nature.com/news/transgenic-fish-wins-us-regulatory-backing-1.12130>. The transgenic fish and eggs are awaiting further regulatory approval in Canada to be available for sale (http://aquabounty.com/documents/press/2013/20131125.pdf).

202 See International Union of Nutritional Sciences (www.iuns.org/statement-on-benefits-and-risksof-genetically-modified-foods-for-human-health-and-nutrition); also see Muir, "The Threats and Benefits of GM Fish."

on fish stocks are maintained, the possibility of human error and the effects of natural disasters have been highlighted.[203] It has been postulated that transgenic fish with greater environmental tolerances and disease resistance could expand into new environments, occupy new ecological niches affecting existing predator–prey relationships and possibly mate with wild stock, thereby modifying genes and altering wild stock.[204] Separating wild stocks would be important to maintain genetic diversity for future breeding programmes in addition to conservation and amenity values.[205]

132. With regard to the ultimate use of transgenic fish, consumer acceptance in the light of health and environmental concerns is also an issue which would need to be overcome.[206]

133. *Offshore mariculture.* Offshore mariculture is seen as offering potential to increase world food production in an environmentally sustainable way and, through its expansion, could contribute to world food security.[207] Expansion of offshore mariculture, however, faces a number of technical challenges which need to be overcome, as deeper waters are generally exposed to a greater range of wind and wave activity.[208] Possible solutions include the development of more robust mariculture architecture or mariculture systems that can be submerged to avoid wind and wave exposure.[209]

134. Offshore mariculture development has also been impeded by the relatively high production costs and the need to develop culture methodologies for species for which near-shore mariculture has not been carried

---

203　See Muir, note 200 above.

204　Ibid.

205　B.O. Acosta and M.V. Gupta, "The Genetic Improvement of Farmed Tilapias Project: Impact and Lessons Learned," in *Success Stories in Asian Aquaculture*, eds. S.S. De Silva and F.B. Davy (Dordrecht, Springer, 2010), pp. 149–170; and contribution of the North Atlantic Salmon Conservation Organization.

206　See International Union of Nutritional Sciences (www.iuns.org/statement-on-benefits -and-risksof-genetically-modified-foods-for-human-health-and-nutrition).

207　Mariculture has been understood as offshore "when it is located >2 km or out of sight from the coast, in water depths >50 m, with waves heights of 5 m or more, ocean swells, variable winds and strong ocean currents, in locations that are exposed (open sea, e.g. ≥180° open) and where there is a requirement for remote operations, automated feeding, and where remote monitoring of operating system may be required" (Lovatelli et al., note 198 above, p. 4).

208　Lovatelli et al., note 198 above, annex 1, Sect. 4.

209　Ibid.

out.[210] In addition, offshore mariculture systems need to address a number of operational issues, including seeding and juvenile supply, feeding, harvesting, cleaning and monitoring, especially in the potentially difficult and dangerous conditions in which the offshore mariculture systems would be deployed.[211]

135. Although progress has been noted, further development of offshore mariculture systems for fin fish, shellfish and macroalgae is needed to make them commercially viable.[212] Policy and regulatory frameworks have been called for to achieve the expansion of offshore mariculture as well as policies to facilitate the necessary technological developments.[213]

4 Mainstreaming Seafood in Global, Regional and National Measures on Food Security

136. Fisheries and aquaculture sectors are often overlooked in the development of food security strategies at national and international levels. In considering the future role of seafood in global food security, greater awareness is needed of the importance of incorporating or mainstreaming the fisheries and aquaculture sectors in these policy discussions.[214] Currently, policy integration appears most prominent only at the interagency and intersectoral levels in oceans law and policy, for example in promoting integrated and ecosystem approaches, as described above. At a minimum, it would be beneficial to create synergies between traditional management tools in the fisheries and aquaculture sectors and socioeconomic strategies.[215] Consideration could also be given to fully

---

210 Ibid., annex 1, Sect. 3.3.

211 Ibid., annex 1, Sect. 4.2.

212 Ibid., annex 1, Sect. 4.2.

213 Ibid., p. 3.

214 Contribution of FAO. For example, the Second International Conference on Nutrition, an inclusive intergovernmental meeting on nutrition jointly organized by FAO and the World Health Organization, in cooperation with the High-level Task Force on the Global Food Security Crisis, the International Fund for Agricultural Development, the International Food Policy Research Institute, UNESCO, UNICEF, the World Bank, WFP and the World Trade Organization, will be held at FAO headquarters in Rome from 19 to 21 November 2014 and will propose a flexible policy framework to address today's major nutrition challenges and identify priorities for enhanced international cooperation on nutrition.

215 It has been estimated that the potential economic gain from restoring fish stocks and reducing fishing capacity to an optimal level is in the order of $50 billion per year (see World Bank and FAO, *The Sunken Billions: The Economic Justification for Fisheries Reform*).

integrating the fisheries and aquaculture sectors into national climate change adaptation and food security policies and programmes.[216]

137. At the United Nations Conference on Sustainable Development, States supported mainstreaming the consideration of the socioeconomic impacts and benefits of the conservation and sustainable use of biodiversity and its components, as well as ecosystems, into relevant programmes and policies at all levels, in accordance with national legislation, circumstances and priorities.[217] Particular attention was drawn to the need to identify and mainstream strategies that further assist small island developing States in developing capacity to conserve, sustainably manage and realize the benefits of fisheries.[218]

138. Mainstreaming seafood in global, regional and national measures on food security will contribute to policy coordination and discussions on trade-offs in the production of seafood and other foods. As described in Section II.B above, different types of seafood from different sources can contribute to food security in different ways with varied levels of effectiveness. Each type and source of seafood may also be in competition with other types and sources of seafood or other foods, thereby creating the need for policy trade-offs which should be considered in developing policy frameworks or measures for any particular sector involved in global food security. For example, capture fisheries, algae farms and aquaculture may compete for ocean space in coastal areas. Large-scale fishing operations, which are more efficient and produce greater revenue, may be in competition with small-scale and artisanal fisheries, which create greater levels of employment and are more likely to provide food for local communities. Distant water fishing fleets may provide greater revenue to developing States through fishing licences, but may also affect local communities who rely on local fishery resources.

139. The most appropriate course of action for resolving such trade-offs will need to be determined on a case-by-case basis, taking into account all relevant considerations. By integrating food security considerations into coastal and marine area management and planning, as well as by involving relevant stakeholders in decision-making, States could effectively explore policy options for maximizing the role of seafood and seafood industries in food security. For example, small fish discards or by-catch

---

216   FAO, *Report of the FAO Expert Workshop on Climate Change Implications for Fisheries and Aquaculture: Rome 7–9 April 2008*, FAO Fisheries report No. 870 (Rome, 2008), p. 5.

217   General Assembly Resolution 66/288, annex, para. 201.

218   Ibid., paras. 174 and 175.

from fisheries which could be for human consumption could also be used to produce fishmeal destined for aquaculture.

V   Conclusions

140. Population growth in the face of the ongoing challenge of eradicating extreme poverty and hunger, as well as malnutrition, coupled with the effects of climate change, environmental degradation and other factors have given rise to concerns about global food security. Seafood plays a significant, but not yet fully recognized, role in global food security as a source of food and nutrients and as an input to food production, as well as a source of revenue. In particular, safe seafood can be a key source of protein, as well as other essential nutrients and micronutrients. Certain parts of the world, including many coastal communities in developing countries and small island developing States, are particularly reliant on seafood for food security, including nutritional aspects, livelihoods and economic well-being.

141. In terms of the future of seafood in global food security, it will be important for the international community to mainstream the role of seafood in policy discussions relating to food security at the global, regional and national levels. It will be equally important for the various sectors involved in the management of human activities that impact on oceans and their resources to consider specific measures within the broader context of food security. This, in turn, will assist policymakers in making informed decisions on how to ensure the continued contribution of seafood to food security, particularly with regard to its availability, access, utilization and stability. In this regard, decision-making processes would benefit from the informed participation of all relevant stakeholders, including coastal communities, small-scale and artisanal fishers and consumers. Co-management and/or community-driven marine management that recognize community rights to resources can be very effective in supporting seafood sustainability. Given the crucial role of women in coastal fishing communities, their capacity to engage in a productive manner in the fisheries and aquaculture sectors requires strengthening.

142. It is noted that communities living below the poverty level, in particular in developing countries, including small island developing States, face critical challenges in their efforts to ensure the availability of, access to and sustainability of seafood for food security. International cooperation and coordination is needed to assist States in addressing these challenges, including through capacity-building and transfer of technology.

143. The continued contribution of seafood to global food security will also depend on the ability of States to address, in an effective, efficient and timely manner, current pressures and challenges to seafood sustainability, including overexploitation and unsustainable practices in seafood exploitation, marine pollution, habitat destruction, climate change and ocean acidification. It is critical to maintain healthy, productive and resilient ecosystems to support the continued contribution of seafood to food security. Integrated and ecosystems approaches that consider the oceans as a whole are important tools to that end and to sustaining the role of seafood in global food security.

144. Finally, it is important for States to take advantage of opportunities to optimize the role of seafood in global food security, including through sustainable aquaculture and small-scale fisheries, as well as responsible technological innovation.

United Nations Convention on the Law of the Sea Report of the Twenty-Fourth Meeting of States Parties, 9–13 June 2014*

---

* This document was provided by the United Nations Division for Ocean Affairs and the Law of the Sea (DOALOS) and is extracted from the Report of the Twenty-fourth Meeting of States Parties, New York, 9–13 June 2014, SPLOS/277, 14 July 2014, available online: <http://www.un.org/Depts/los/>. The document has been edited for publication in the *Ocean Yearbook*.

Ocean Yearbook 29: 613–639
© KONINKLIJKE BRILL NV, LEIDEN, 2015 | DOI 10.1163/9789004297234_023

I　Introduction

1.　The twenty-fourth Meeting of States Parties to the United Nations Convention on the Law of the Sea[1] was held at United Nations Headquarters from 9 to 13 June 2014, in accordance with Article 319, paragraph 2(e), of the Convention and paragraph 40 of General Assembly resolution 68/70.

2.　The Meeting was attended by the representatives of States Parties to the Convention[2] and observers, including the International Seabed Authority, the Commission on the Limits of the Continental Shelf[3] and the International Tribunal for the Law of the Sea.[4]

II　Organization of Work

A　*Opening of the Meeting and Election of Officers*

3.　Ferit Hoxha (Albania), President of the twenty-third Meeting of States Parties, opened the twenty-fourth Meeting.

4.　The Meeting observed a minute of silent prayer or meditation.

5.　The Meeting elected Jeremiah Nyamane Kingsley Mamabolo (South Africa) as President of the twenty-fourth Meeting of States Parties, by acclamation.

6.　The Meeting elected Melivia Demetriou (Cyprus), Patricio Troya (Ecuador), Aleksas Dambrauskas (Lithuania) and Anniken Enersen (Norway) as Vice-Presidents, by acclamation.

Statement by the President

7.　The President noted the continued steady progress towards the goal of universal participation in the Convention, recalling that since the previous Meeting one more State, the Niger, had ratified the Convention, bringing the total number of Parties to 166, including the European

---

1　United Nations, *Treaty Series*, vol. 1833, No. 31363.

2　See rule 5 of the Rules of Procedure for Meetings of States Parties (SPLOS/2/Rev.4).

3　See rule 18 of the Rules of Procedure.

4　See rule 37 of the Rules of Procedure; For a list of participants at the twenty-fourth Meeting of States Parties, see SPLOS/INF/28.

Union. Drawing attention to the twentieth anniversary of the entry into force of the Convention and to the sixth observance of World Oceans Day, he pointed out that a strong and universally accepted and implemented international legal regime applicable to the oceans was essential for the maintenance of international peace and security and for the sustainable use of ocean resources, navigation and protection of the marine environment.

B   *Adoption of the Agenda and Organization of Work*

8.   The President introduced the provisional agenda (SPLOS/L.73), proposing the inclusion of an additional agenda item entitled "Commemoration of the twentieth anniversary of the entry into force of the United Nations Convention on the Law of the Sea." The agenda was then adopted, as amended (SPLOS/273).

9.   Following consultations with the Bureau, the President made proposals regarding the organization of work. The Meeting approved the organization of work on the understanding that it could be adjusted, as necessary, in order to ensure the efficient conduct of the Meeting.

III   Credentials Committee

A   *Appointment of the Credentials Committee*

10. On 9 June 2014, pursuant to rule 14 of its rules of procedure (SPLOS/2/Rev.4), the Meeting appointed a Credentials Committee consisting of the following nine States Parties: Angola, Argentina, Australia, Czech Republic, Denmark, Kenya, Iraq, Paraguay and Viet Nam. The Credentials Committee held one meeting on 10 June 2014 and elected Bjørn Kunoy (Denmark) as its Chair.

B   *Report of the Credentials Committee*

11. The Chair of the Credentials Committee introduced the report of the Committee (SPLOS/274) on 11 June 2014. He stated that the Committee had examined and accepted the credentials of representatives to the twenty-fourth Meeting from 155 Parties, including the European Union. He also pointed out that, following the meeting of the Committee, additional information concerning the appointment of representatives had

been received from Belize, Liberia, Marshall Islands, Papua New Guinea and Saint Kitts and Nevis. Consequently, the total number of credentials received was 160, of which 94 were in due form and 66 were received on the understanding that formal credentials would be communicated to the Secretariat as soon as possible.[5]

12. The Meeting then approved the report of the Credentials Committee.

13. On 12 June 2014, the Chair of the Committee updated the Meeting on the receipt of information concerning the appointment of the representatives of Dominica. The Meeting took note of that information on the understanding that formal credentials would be communicated to the Secretariat as soon as possible. Consequently, 161 Parties participated in the Meeting.

IV   Commemoration of the Twentieth Anniversary of the Entry into Force of the United Nations Convention on the Law of the Sea

14. On 9 June 2014, the Secretary-General of the United Nations opened the commemoration of the twentieth anniversary of the entry into force of the Convention. Referring to the Convention as one of the most significant and visionary multilateral instruments of the twentieth century, the Secretary-General highlighted its critical importance for the peaceful uses of the oceans, equitable utilization of their resources, conservation of their living resources and the study, protection and preservation of the marine environment. He noted that most of the provisions of the Convention, traditionally referred to as the "Constitution for the oceans," were now widely recognized as reflecting customary international law and that the Convention had shown its dynamic character through its ability to address new challenges. The Secretary-General encouraged States to recommit to the task of implementing the Convention in order to protect and safeguard oceans for the benefit of all humanity, for generations to come. He expressed concern regarding the many pressures facing the oceans as a result of overfishing, ocean acidification, land-based activities and, above all, climate change. He also emphasized the critical role of oceans in the achievement of the Millennium Development Goals and in the post-2015 development agenda.

---

5 Following the approval of the report of the Credentials Committee, the Secretariat received formal credentials, which replaced the provisional ones, from Chile and Costa Rica.

15.   In commemorating the twentieth anniversary of the Convention, delegations underscored its achievements as the "Constitution for the oceans." In particular, they recalled that it set out the legal framework within which all activities in the oceans and seas must be carried out and its universal and unified character.

16.   Delegations highlighted the fact that the Convention represented one of the most successful international treaties ever negotiated and a milestone for international cooperation. The Convention contributed to the strengthening of international peace and security, the equality of rights in the use of ocean resources, the promotion of economic advancement and protection of the marine environment. Several delegations paid tribute to the work of the drafters of the Convention, in particular the contribution of Ambassador Arvid Pardo of Malta.

17.   Reference was made to the universality of the Convention, with many delegations emphasizing that its provisions had codified existing customary international law or had developed into customary international law. Delegations reaffirmed their commitment to its further implementation. Delegations welcomed the Niger as the newest party to the Convention and called upon States that had not yet done so to become parties to the Convention.

18.   Delegations emphasized that the problems of ocean space were closely interrelated and needed to be considered as a whole, as provided for in the Convention. In this regard, the delicate balance between the interests of ocean users achieved under the Convention was highlighted, with attention being drawn by several delegations to specific provisions in the Convention, including those regulating the establishment of the exclusive economic zone, freedom of navigation and the common heritage of mankind. The role of the Convention in sustainable development and in promoting the equitable sharing of ocean resources was emphasized. In this connection, it was noted by some delegations that equitable sharing not only implied disbursement of resources between countries, but also had an intergenerational dimension.

19.   Several delegations underlined the need for oceans to be at the centre of the post-2015 development agenda, including through a stand-alone goal under the sustainable development goals. A view was expressed that a new strategy was needed to provide a global vision as to how to make the best possible economic use of the oceans, while ensuring the sustainable use of living and non-living resources.

20.   Several delegations highlighted the importance of the oceans for the development of national economies and elaborated on the role of

the Convention in the development of their marine resources, the establishment of their maritime zones, the exploration and exploitation of the continental shelf and the establishment of control over and access to fishing areas. Several delegations emphasized the crucial role of the Convention in efforts to promote the peaceful resolution of disputes, the maintenance of maritime security and the delimitation of maritime boundaries.

21. Delegations underscored the continued relevance and importance of the Convention and reiterated the need to strengthen and maintain its integrity. In this connection, several delegations stated their firm belief that the legal framework established by the Convention contained no gaps, emphasizing that even though certain activities might lack specific regulation, such activities fell nevertheless under the overall framework of the Convention and could be further regulated through an implementing agreement. A view was expressed that matters not regulated by the Convention should continue to be governed by the rules and principles of general international law, as this was in line with the principles of the international rule of law.

22. Several delegations noted technical advances and progress in the knowledge and understanding of the oceans since the drafting of the Convention. In that regard, several delegations emphasized that the Convention was a living instrument, which was flexible enough to adapt to new challenges that had emerged after its adoption, including new uses.

23. Many delegations drew specific attention to issues and gaps concerning marine biodiversity in areas beyond national jurisdiction, including marine genetic resources, which could potentially be addressed by a new implementing agreement within the framework of the Convention.

24. Existing challenges in ocean issues, including in the implementation of the Convention were also highlighted by delegations. Several delegations raised concerns regarding illegal, unreported and unregulated fishing and the consequent threat that the depletion of fish stocks posed to global food security. Delegations also raised concerns about maritime crime, including piracy and illicit trafficking in narcotics and people, and emphasized the need to keep maritime zones safe and secure for international transport. Attention was drawn to the need for greater efforts in the protection of the marine environment. Delegations also noted their ongoing efforts to integrate the Convention into national laws or otherwise ensure its implementation at the national level.

25. Several delegations elaborated on their efforts to promote implementation of the Convention through capacity-building initiatives. Other delegations stressed the need for further efforts to promote capacity-building to combat poverty and assist developing countries in the implementation of the Convention and the development of their marine resources, including through the transfer of technology and training. Attention was drawn to the importance of the Convention for small island developing States and the fact that 2014 marked the International Year of Small Island Developing States. Some delegations noted the need to consider the interests of landlocked States and called for the elimination of cumbersome trade barriers.

26. Delegations recalled the important role of the three institutions established under the Convention, the International Tribunal for the Law of the Sea, the International Seabed Authority and the Commission on the Limits of the Continental Shelf, and commended the contribution of those institutions to the legal order established by the Convention.

27. It was noted in this regard that the increasing number of cases brought before the Tribunal was a testament to its success, although the Tribunal still had not reached its full potential.

28. Attention was also drawn to the twentieth anniversary of the entry into force of the Agreement relating to the Implementation of Part XI of the United Nations Convention on the Law of the Sea of 10 December 1982 and the establishment of the Authority.

29. The significant workload of the Commission was acknowledged by several delegations. A view was expressed that States Parties should take pragmatic actions to enable the Commission to continue to perform its functions expeditiously, efficiently and effectively. Some delegations expressed concern over the conditions of service for members of the Commission, including with regard to medical insurance, and called on States to improve their conditions of service. Gratitude was expressed to States who had contributed to the Trust Fund for defraying the cost of participation of the Commission members from developing States.

30. Appreciation was expressed to the Division for Ocean Affairs and the Law of the Sea for the high level of services provided to States Parties and the Commission.

31. Attention was also drawn to the trust funds administered by the Division and the need for States to ensure their viability and continued support. A call for contributions to the Hamilton Shirley Amerasinghe Fellowship was made, emphasizing the importance of the fellowship in the dissemination of knowledge and research on ocean issues.

V   Matters Related to the International Tribunal for the Law of the Sea

A   *Report of the Tribunal for 2013*

32. The President of the Tribunal, Judge Shunji Yanai, introduced the annual report of the Tribunal for 2013 (SPLOS/267) and provided an overview of its judicial activities and the work carried out during the two sessions devoted to legal and organizational and administrative matters held since the twenty-third Meeting, namely the thirty-fifth and thirty-sixth sessions.

33. The President noted the continued increase in the judicial activities of the Tribunal, drawing attention to the fact that in 2013 the Tribunal had handled four cases involving a wide range of substantive and procedural issues. These issues encompassed provisional measures for the release of a detained vessel and persons on board; the lawfulness of the arrest and confiscation of a vessel; the status of bunkering in support of foreign vessels fishing in the exclusive economic zone; reparation for damage and illegal, unreported and unregulated fishing. From the procedural point of view, the Tribunal had dealt with two cases on the merits, one urgent proceeding and one advisory opinion. The President recalled that two of those cases were completed in 2013 and one in 2014, noting that the hearing concerning the request for an advisory opinion submitted by the Subregional Fisheries Commission (case No. 21) would be held in September 2014.

34. The President outlined the capacity-building and training activities undertaken by the Tribunal in 2013. In particular, he informed the Meeting that the Tribunal continued to hold regional workshops to provide representatives of States with information on the jurisdiction of the Tribunal and the procedural rules applicable to cases before it. In this connection, he recalled that the latest regional workshop had been held in Mexico City in June 2013 and that the next two workshops would be held in Kenya and Ghana in 2014.

35. In the ensuing discussions, several delegations reaffirmed their support for the work of the Tribunal and expressed appreciation for its work and timely and efficient handling of cases. They acknowledged the increasingly important role of the Tribunal in the peaceful settlement of maritime disputes and the rule of law at sea, as well as in the interpretation and application of the Convention, reflected in the increasing number of cases dealing with a wider range of issues before the Tribunal. Some delegations also expressed the hope that the Tribunal would play an

even greater role in the future development of the law of the sea. In this connection, a suggestion was made that more States Parties should refer their disputes to the Tribunal, rather than to arbitral tribunals, under the Convention.

36. Several delegations observed that the acceptance by States Parties of compulsory dispute settlement procedures represented a major achievement of the Convention. The importance of participating in such procedures and complying with the binding decisions resulting therefrom was emphasized, as was the need to avoid abuse of the limitations and exceptions to the compulsory procedures entailing binding decisions provided for under the Convention.

37. With reference to the request for an advisory opinion from the Subregional Fisheries Commission (case No. 21), some delegations underlined the importance of advisory opinions in strengthening the rule of law. A view was expressed that the advisory opinion might play an important role in shaping international efforts to combat illegal, unreported and unregulated fishing. Some delegations noted that the Tribunal sought the views of States Parties and international organizations on this matter, while others observed that the advisory jurisdiction of the Tribunal as a whole remained disputed.

38. Concern was expressed over the delayed payment of financial contributions to the Tribunal and a call was made to States Parties for their continued support to the Tribunal, including through making their payments in full and on time.

39. Several delegations noted with appreciation the capacity-building efforts of the Tribunal, in particular its regional workshops, and expressed gratitude to those who had made contributions to such activities. Some delegations reaffirmed their support for the work of the Tribunal through financial contributions to both the capacity-building activities and the Trust Fund, as well as the nomination of members of the Tribunal.

40. The Meeting took note of the report of the Tribunal for 2013.

B   *Financial and Budgetary Matters*
1   Report on Budgetary Matters for the Financial Periods 2011–2012 and 2013–2014

41. The Registrar of the Tribunal introduced the report on budgetary matters for the financial periods 2011–2012 and 2013–2014 (SPLOS/268), covering the matters outlined below.

(a)   *Surrender of Cash Surplus for the Financial Period 2011–2012*

42. The Registrar recalled that the cash surplus for the 2011–2012 financial
     period as at 31 December 2013 amounted to €879,051. The Tribunal had
     proposed that the amount be surrendered to States Parties and deducted
     from their contributions for 2015 and for earlier financial periods, where
     applicable.

43. The Meeting decided that an amount of €529,051 would be surrendered
     and deducted from the contributions of States Parties for 2015, in accord-
     ance with financial regulation 4. It further decided that the remaining
     amount of €350,000 would be transferred, on an exceptional basis, to the
     Working Capital Fund to cover expenses related to cases, to the extent
     that such expenses could not be met from the budget lines concerning
     case-related costs (see SPLOS/275).

(b)   *Provisional Performance Report for 2013*

44. The Registrar recalled that the total expenditure for 2013 provisionally
     amounted to €9,696,296, which represented 90.26 per cent of the appro-
     priations in the amount of €10,742,633 approved for that year. It was
     noted that the underperformance was primarily due to savings under
     "case-related costs" of €663,281, part of which would be used to cover
     expenses relating to deliberations in case No. 21 in 2014. If case-related
     costs were excluded, expenses would amount to 95.12 per cent of the
     appropriations.

45. In the ensuing discussions, some delegations encouraged the Tribunal
     to continue its efforts to realize savings and ensure the optimal use
     of resources, especially in light of the financial constraints faced by
     Governments worldwide. A view was expressed that implementa-
     tion rates for certain items had improved and that past performance
     rates should be reflected in future reports on budgetary matters. The
     Registrar cautioned against assessing overall performance based
     solely on performance rates in 2013 and explained that lower per-
     formance rates on some budget lines were the result of unforeseen
     circumstances.

46. In relation to the pension scheme for judges, the possibility of estab-
     lishing a pension fund to reduce costs in future years was suggested. In
     response, the Registrar noted that the current pension scheme had been
     adopted by the Meeting and that there had been no proposals for alterna-
     tive arrangements.

(c)   *Report on Action taken Pursuant to the Financial Regulations of the Tribunal*

47.   The Registrar outlined the information contained in Section III of document SPLOS/268 concerning the investment of funds of the Tribunal and the status of the Trust Fund for the Law of the Sea, the Nippon Foundation Trust Fund and the China Institute of International Studies Trust Fund.

48.   In the ensuing discussions, several delegations expressed concerns over arrears in the payment of assessed contributions and reiterated their appeal to States Parties to honour their commitments and make outstanding contributions in full and on time. Delegations expressed appreciation for the action taken by the Registrar in that respect and urged him to continue efforts to collect outstanding contributions.

49.   The Meeting took note with satisfaction of the report on budgetary matters for the financial periods 2011–2012 and 2013–2014 (SPLOS/268).

2   Draft Budget Proposals for the Tribunal for 2015–2016

50.   The Registrar introduced the draft budget proposals for the Tribunal for the financial period 2015–2016 (SPLOS/2014/WP.1). The proposed budget in the amount of €20,045,300 (see SPLOS/2014/WP.1, Annex I), represented a decrease of €1,193,820 compared to the budget approved for the 2013–2014 period (SPLOS/250).

51.   The Registrar underlined that the part of the budget proposals concerning recurrent expenditures was based on the same level of expenditures as that included in the budget for the 2013–2014 biennium.

52.   He noted that the increases in the costs for judges due to higher travel costs for meetings and daily subsistence allowance had to be considered against the decreases resulting from exchange rate fluctuations, changes in the post adjustment factor and the circumstance that no election would be held for the position of President of the Tribunal in the 2015–2016 period. He drew attention also to the increase in pensions for up to seven retiring judges, noting that the exact amount could be calculated only after establishing the exact number of judges that would retire following the outcome of the election of seven members of the Tribunal by the twenty-fourth Meeting.

53.   With respect to case-related costs, the Registrar described the expected preparations related to case No. 21 in 2014 and other judicial work and the calculation of costs for three urgent proceedings. He proposed

that the Meeting consider funding one of the urgent cases through the Working Capital Fund by transferring a portion of the 2011–2012 cash surplus to the Fund and surrendering the remainder to States Parties.

54. Regarding staff costs, the Registrar noted an increase of approximately €400,000, resulting from appropriations based on the United Nations standard costs, over which the Tribunal had no control. An additional increase was due to the proposed creation of a new post at the G-6 level and the reclassification of one post from the G-7 level to the P-2 level. Those increases were partly offset by decreases across separate lines of the budget for recurrent expenditures.

55. Regarding operating expenditures, the Registrar noted that maintenance of the premises comprised approximately three quarters of the operating expenditures of the Tribunal. He described increases due, for example, to the renewal of contracts for the management and security of the premises and decreases in certain costs, such as utilities.

56. In the ensuing discussions, delegations posed a number of questions and made proposals with a view to further clarifying the proposed budget. Many delegations expressed their appreciation for the efforts of the Tribunal to reduce its budget as compared to previous years.

57. Several delegations supported the draft budget as proposed and noted, in this context, the increased workload of the Tribunal and the need to support and strengthen its activities. Other delegations proposed a reduction in the new budget proposal in light of the underperformance of approved budget lines in the past. Some delegations also opposed any increase in the Working Capital Fund.

58. Concerning the principles that should be applied in the preparation of the budget, several delegations emphasized that a zero-growth approach should not apply to the budget, noting the importance of safeguarding the independence of the Tribunal. Several delegations expressed the need to strike a balance between the principle of zero nominal growth and the evolutionary approach.

59. Further discussions on these matters were held in the context of the Open-ended Working Group on financial and budgetary matters. On the basis of the recommendation of the Working Group, the Meeting adopted, by consensus, a decision in which it approved the amount of €18,886,200 as the budget of the Tribunal for 2015–2016 (SPLOS/275). The decision resulted in a reduction of €1,159,100 from the budget amount proposed by the Tribunal (SPLOS/2014/WP.1) and a decrease of €2,352,920 from the budget for the financial period 2013–2014 (SPLOS/250).

3   Proposal by the United Kingdom of Great Britain and Northern
          Ireland for a Mechanism to Scrutinize Budgets of the International
          Tribunal for the Law of the Sea

60.   The President of the Meeting recalled that, at the twenty-third Meeting, the
      United Kingdom of Great Britain and Northern Ireland had introduced
      a proposal for a mechanism to scrutinize budgets of the International
      Tribunal for the Law of the Sea (SPLOS/260 and Corr.1). The President
      also recalled that the United Kingdom had presented a new proposal on
      the same matter, contained in document SPLOS/271, regarding the estab-
      lishment of a facilitation group aimed at improving the understanding
      of States Parties as to how the Tribunal arrived at a draft budget. The
      United Kingdom explained that such a facilitation group would not have
      any mandate to negotiate changes in the draft budget or make recom-
      mendations, but would provide an opportunity for delegations to ask
      questions of the Registrar of the Tribunal about the proposed budget.

61.   In the ensuing debate, delegations emphasized the need for transparency
      and accountability in the budget approval process and for efficiency in
      the consideration of draft budgets. Some delegations expressed concern
      with regard to the existing budget approval process and expressed their
      general support for the proposal. In this context, the need for vigilance
      in budgetary matters and the benefits of supplementary and informal
      means or mechanisms to consider the draft budget of the Tribunal were
      emphasized. It was also suggested that all options to improve the proc-
      ess should be considered, such as creating a subsidiary body to review
      the draft budgets or expanding the mandate of the Open-ended Working
      Group on financial and budgetary matters.

62.   Other delegations expressed their support for the existing procedures
      and raised specific concerns regarding the proposal, such as the pos-
      sibility of adding complexity, duplicating work or weakening the level
      of scrutiny in the budget approval process. Delegations indicated that
      the Open-ended Working Group on financial and budgetary matters
      had the necessary mandate for detailed deliberations on any budget
      proposal and that the process was already legitimate, transparent and
      inclusive.

63.   According to some delegations, the discussions on the draft budget pro-
      posals for the Tribunal for the financial period 2015–2016 had been very
      fruitful and demonstrated the value of the Open-ended Working Group
      on financial and budgetary matters. Other delegations suggested that this
      experience had confirmed the need for improvements in the process,

given the length of time taken during the discussions and the desire for greater understanding of the budget preparation process.

64. Some delegations suggested that any concerns over the budget approval process could be addressed through improvements to existing procedures. In this context, it was noted that the draft budget was published well in advance of the Meeting and that, in the interim, States Parties had an opportunity to ask the Registrar questions in writing. Delegations suggested that the process could be further improved if responses to those questions could be circulated to all States Parties. It was also suggested that there was a need to improve the process for proposing amendments to any draft budget. It was proposed that interested delegations should submit proposals or engage in informal discussions on how to improve the process.

65. Some delegations asked whether consideration could be given to adjusting the organization of work for the Meeting of States Parties so that discussions on the budget could begin earlier and more time could be devoted to the consideration of these matters. A suggestion was made that at the next Meeting a separate agenda item should be devoted specifically to the budget approval process.

66. The Meeting decided to remain seized of the matter and to include the item in the provisional agenda of the twenty-fifth Meeting of States Parties.

VI   Information on the Activities of the International Seabed Authority

67. The Secretary-General of the Authority, Nii Allotey Odunton, provided information on the activities carried out by the Authority since the twenty-third Meeting of States Parties.

68. The Secretary-General encouraged all States Parties to attend the upcoming twentieth session of the Authority, recalling that its agenda would include election of the members of the Council for the period 2015–2018; the consideration and approval of the 2015–2016 budget; the development of regulations for the exploitation of mineral resources; and a special session to commemorate the twentieth anniversary of the establishment of the Authority. He also appealed to States Parties that were in arrears to pay their contributions to the budget of the Authority, noting that, according to the rules of procedure of the General Assembly (A/520/Rev.17), a State Party in this position would have no voting rights.

A further appeal was made to States that were not yet party to the Part XI Agreement to become a party to it.

69. The Secretary-General recalled that, as at 19 May 2014, 16 exploration contracts were in force, covering about 900,000 square kilometres in the Atlantic, Indian and Pacific Oceans, with 12 contracts covering polymetallic nodules and two each for polymetallic sulphides and cobalt-rich ferromanganese crusts. In this connection, he added that seven pending contract applications were to be considered during the twentieth session. Their approval would bring the total number of contracts for exploration to 26. He observed that the growing number of exploration contracts in force would have a significant impact on the workload of the Secretariat and of the Legal and Technical Commission. In this regard, he recalled that, at its nineteenth session, the Assembly of the Authority had adopted a decision requiring all contractors to pay an overhead charge that would allow the Authority to ensure sufficient resources to administer and supervise those contracts. At the twentieth session of the Authority, the Secretary-General will report on the implementation of the decision concerning overhead charges, in particular with respect to contracts which were already in force at the time of the decision.

70. Commenting on the experience gained in connection with the work of contractors, the Secretary-General emphasized that it had become clear that contractors required standardized data and information. In this connection, referring to environmental protection and preservation as an example, he noted the need for standardized taxonomy for three classes of fauna: megafauna, macrofauna and meiofauna with respect to each of the three mineral resources for which the Authority was developing regulations. He informed the Meeting that the Authority was pursuing its efforts to standardize the taxonomy of these classes of fauna in collaboration with contractors and the scientific community, including through a number of standardization workshops. The need for standardization in the information which contractors would have to provide to the Secretary-General of the Authority upon the expiration of their contracts was also highlighted. In this regard the Secretary-General informed the Meeting that a workshop would be convened with contractors involved in the exploration for polymetallic nodules.

71. Delegations expressed appreciation for the work of the Authority and congratulated it on the occasion of the twentieth anniversary of its establishment, underscoring its contribution to the success of the Convention.

72. Some delegations reiterated their concern with regard to the low attendance at the sessions of the Authority and expressed appreciation for the

continuing efforts of the Authority to address this issue through adjustments in its programme of work.

73. Support was expressed for the work that the Authority had started on the development of an exploitation code for marine minerals in the Area. In this regard, some delegations noted with appreciation the efforts of the Authority to seek the opinions and views of all stakeholders in the processes leading to the elaboration of those regulations. The view was expressed that the regulations should be in line with industrial and technological developments, while reflecting a rational balance between sound commercial interests, sustainable exploitation and the protection and preservation of the marine environment.

74. Some delegations noted the high number of applications for approval of plans of work for exploration pending before the Authority, including one from a small island developing State. The increase in both activity and contractors in the Area was considered to represent an expression of confidence in the regime established for the Area. In this connection, it was acknowledged that the growing number of applications necessarily entailed an increase in the workload of the Legal and Technical Commission and the Council. In this regard, support was expressed for the efforts of the Authority regarding standardization of the data and information required for the consideration of applications. The view was expressed that the growing number of applications also reinforced the central role of the Authority in ensuring global cooperation in activities in the Area. Some delegations informed the meeting of upcoming national colloquiums to build interest in the economic opportunities related to the Area.

75. Some delegations noted that the early contracts for the exploration of polymetallic nodules were scheduled to expire in the coming years. In this connection, it was suggested that contractors should be granted the right to request the extension of their respective contracts if they had not yet reached the commercial exploitation stage.

76. Some delegations welcomed the work of the Authority concerning taxonomic standardization of species in the Area. The important role of the Authority in ensuring the environmental protection aspects of activities in the Area was noted, specifically with regard to the development of scientific knowledge of the unique ecosystems and biological communities occurring in potential sites for seabed mining activities. A view was expressed that the competence of the Authority should be extended in order to ensure sustainable use of biological resources in the Area.

77. It was stressed that further contributions to the Endowment Fund were needed, as it enhanced the capabilities of developing countries to participate in fellowships and training programmes.

VII   Matters Related to the Commission on the Limits of the Continental Shelf

A   *Information Reported by the Chair of the Commission*

78. The Chair of the Commission, Lawrence Folajimi Awosika, made a statement providing information on the activities carried out by the Commission since the twenty-third Meeting of States Parties, drawing particular attention to the issue of the conditions of service of the members of the Commission.[6]

79. In the ensuing discussion, delegations highly commended the work of the Commission, especially in the light of the ever-increasing workload, and its role in the implementation of the legal order of the oceans established by the Convention.

80. Delegations welcomed the decision of the Commission, during its thirty-second session, to hold 21 weeks of meetings during 2014 and they encouraged the Commission to maintain this level, as a minimum, for the remainder of the current term of the Commission. Delegations also welcomed the decision of the Commission, during its thirty-fourth session, to increase to nine the number of subcommissions actively considering submissions.

81. Concern was raised by some delegations with regard to the fact that some submissions were being deferred, seemingly indefinitely, as a result of objections made by third States under rule 46 and Annex I to the rules of procedure of the Commission (CLCS/40/Rev.1).[7] It was observed that none of the disputes that had led to the deferral of submissions had been resolved, leading to further deferrals. In this regard, a view was expressed that the Commission should continue to work in accordance with its rules of procedure and the Convention.

82. Concern was also raised by several delegations with regard to the non-attendance of some members of the Commission, noting that this exacerbated the workload issues faced by the Commission. A delegation expressed its support for the decision of the Commission to remove such members from holding any role of officer within the Commission and its subsidiary bodies.

83. Delegations noted with appreciation the high quality of the services rendered by the Division for Ocean Affairs and the Law of the Sea as

---

6 See SPLOS/270. For more information on the work of the Commission during its thirty-second, thirty-third and thirty-fourth sessions, see CLCS/80, CLCS/81 and CLCS/83.

7 See also para. 113 below.

secretariat of the Commission, in particular noting that its work had facilitated the increased work pace of the Commission.

84. The Meeting took note of the information reported by the Chair of the Commission.

B   *Conditions of Service of the Members of the Commission*

85. The co-coordinators of the Open-ended Working Group on the conditions of service of the Commission, established by the twenty-third Meeting, Tomas Heidar (Iceland) and James Waweru (Kenya), informed the Meeting about the work carried out by the Working Group since the last Meeting. In particular, they drew attention to a draft decision proposed by the Working Group, as contained in document SPLOS/L.74. The co-coordinators emphasized that the mandate of the Working Group encompassed a large number of issues pertaining to the conditions of service of the members of the Commission, the most urgent being medical insurance coverage while the members were carrying out their duties at United Nations Headquarters. The Working Group had therefore decided to focus its initial work on that issue, although it remained committed to addressing all other issues related to the conditions of service of the members of the Commission.

86. The Secretariat informed the Meeting of its findings concerning the options for providing medical insurance coverage to members of the Commission from developing States, whose participation might be facilitated through the voluntary trust fund for the participation of the members of the Commission from developing States in the meetings of the Commission, while carrying out their Commission duties at United Nations Headquarters (see para. 78 of General Assembly resolution 68/70).

87. In this connection, the Secretariat stated that under the existing terms of reference, the trust fund could not be used to defray the costs of medical and dental insurance. The broadening of the terms of reference to include such coverage would require a decision by the General Assembly. The Meeting was informed that the health insurance programme administered by the United Nations at Headquarters was currently limited to staff members and retirees. However, the Organization was in the process of examining ways in which it could facilitate access to health insurance for short-term periods for non-staff personnel, if no other insurance coverage was carried by such personnel, a development that might be of future relevance for the members of the Commission.

88. The Secretariat also provided the Meeting with an overview of the status of the trust fund, informing the Meeting that contributions had been

received from China, Iceland, Ireland, Japan, Mexico and the Republic of Korea since the last Meeting. The Secretariat stated that the funds currently available would enable the trust fund to ensure financial assistance through the end of 2015, provided that the number of requests for financial assistance did not increase. Additional contributions were therefore needed to ensure the ability of the Commission to fulfil its mandate beyond that time, especially if the terms of reference of the trust fund were to be broadened through including coverage of the costs related to medical insurance.

89. In the ensuing discussion, several delegations noted that, since the Commission had modified its working methods and extended the number and length of its sessions, in accordance with the request of the twenty-first Meeting (see para. 1 of SPLOS/229), the Parties had had to ensure adequate conditions of service for the members of the Commission.

90. Several delegations emphasized that, in accordance with Annex II to the Convention, it was the obligation of nominating States to defray the expenses of the members of the Commission while carrying out Commission duties. Several delegations also emphasized the important role of the trust fund in enabling the participation of members of the Commission nominated by developing States and called for further contributions.

91. Delegations drew attention to the issues related to the conditions of service of the Commission other than medical insurance coverage and welcomed the continued work of the Working Group to address those issues in this regard. Noting the importance of the work of the Commission, a suggestion was made that permanent financing of the Commission, including through the regular budget of the United Nations, was an option.

92. On the basis of the draft prepared by the Working Group, the Meeting adopted, by consensus, a decision on the conditions of service of the members of the Commission on the Limits of the Continental Shelf (SPLOS/276).

93. In accordance with the aforementioned decision, the Working Group will continue consideration of other conditions of service of the Commission, as stipulated in paragraph 77 of the report of the twenty-third Meeting (SPLOS/263).

94. The Meeting decided to appoint Alexandra Lennox-Marwick (New Zealand) as co-coordinator to replace Mr. Heidar who, following his election as a member of the Tribunal, would not be able to continue as co-coordinator.[8]

---

8 See para. 103 below.

VIII   Elections

95. Two elections were held during the Meeting, namely the election of seven members of the Tribunal and the election of one member of the Commission.

A   *Election of Seven Members of the International Tribunal for the Law of the Sea*

96. On 11 June 2014, the Meeting proceeded with the election of seven members of the Tribunal to fill the seats of those members whose terms of office would expire on 30 September 2014. The elections were held in accordance with Article 4, paragraph 4, of the Statute of the Tribunal (Annex VI to the Convention). Members of the delegations of France, Guatemala, Malawi, Lithuania and Thailand acted as tellers.

97. The President recalled that the Registrar of the Tribunal, in accordance with the Statute of the Tribunal, had addressed a note to the States Parties to the Convention on 16 December 2013, inviting them to submit the names of candidates between 12 January and 12 March 2014 for election to the Tribunal.

98. The President referred to documents SPLOS/264 (note by the Registrar of the Tribunal on election procedures), SPLOS/265 (list of candidates to the Tribunal nominated by States parties) and SPLOS/266 (curricula vitae of the candidates).

99. The President informed the Meeting of the election procedures, recalling the relevant provisions of the Convention and the rules of procedure for Meetings of States Parties.

100. Concerning the composition and membership of the Tribunal, the President recalled Articles 2 and 3 of the Statute of the Tribunal, noting in particular that in accordance with Article 3, paragraph 2, there should be no fewer than three members from each geographical group, as established by the General Assembly. He also noted that for the purpose of conducting the election of the seven members of the Tribunal at the twenty-fourth Meeting, the arrangement for the allocation of seats on the Tribunal and the Commission (see SPLOS/201) would apply.

101. He stated that, consequently, the regional allocation of the seven seats for the election would be as follows: two members from the Group of African States; two members from the Group of Asia-Pacific States; one member from the Group of Eastern European States; one member from the Group of Latin American and Caribbean States; and one member from the Group of Western European and other States.

102. The Meeting agreed that the election would be based on the confirmed regional allocation of seats and that the election would be conducted in one step. The Meeting also agreed that five separate ballot papers would be distributed, each containing the list of candidates from one of the five regional groups. The Meeting further agreed that balloting would continue until the requisite number of candidates for each regional Group obtained the highest number of votes and the required majority.

103. After the completion of the voting process, the President announced the election of the following seven members of the Tribunal for a nine-year term of office commencing on 1 October 2014: Alonso Gómez-Robledo Verduzco (Mexico); Tomas Heidar (Iceland); Albertus Jacobus Hoffmann (South Africa); James Luta Kateka (United Republic of Tanzania); Jin-Hyun Paik (Republic of Korea); Stanisław Michał Pawlak (Poland); and Shunji Yanai (Japan) were elected.[9] On behalf of the Meeting, the President congratulated the members on their election.

B   *Election of One Member of the Commission on the Limits of the Continental Shelf*

104. On 12 June 2014, the Meeting proceeded with the election of one member of the Commission to fill the vacancy which resulted from the resignation of Sivaramakrishnan Rajan (India) on 23 February 2014. The election was held in accordance with Article 2, paragraph 3, of Annex II to the

---

9   The Secretariat verified the quorum required for the election. The election required one round of balloting. For the Group of African States, out of 159 ballots cast, with 0 invalid ballots and 3 abstentions, a majority of 104 votes was required for election. Having obtained the required majority of votes, Albertus Jacobus Hoffmann (South Africa) (154 votes) and James Luta Kateka (United Republic of Tanzania) (152 votes) were elected. For the Group of Asia-Pacific States, out of 159 ballots cast, with 2 invalid ballots and 0 abstentions, a majority of 105 votes was required for election. Having obtained the required majority of votes, Shunji Yanai (Japan) (142 votes) and Jin-Hyun Paik (Republic of Korea) (130 votes) were elected. For the Group of Latin American and Caribbean States, out of 159 ballots cast, with 4 invalid ballots and 2 abstentions, a majority of 102 votes was required for election. Having obtained the required majority of votes, Alonso Gómez-Robledo Verduzco (Mexico) (118 votes) was elected. For the Group of Eastern European States, out of 159 ballots cast, with 0 invalid ballots and 14 abstentions, a majority of 97 votes was required for election. Having obtained the required majority of votes, Stanisław Michał Pawlak (Poland) (145 votes) was elected. For the Group of Western European and other States, out of 159 ballots cast, with 4 invalid ballots and 1 abstention, a majority of 103 votes was required for election. Having obtained the required majority of votes, Tomas Heidar (Iceland) (154 votes) was elected.

Convention. Members of the delegations of France, Guatemala and Lithuania acted as tellers.

105. The President recalled that the Secretary-General of the United Nations had addressed a note to the States Parties to the Convention on 27 February 2014, in accordance with Article 2, paragraph 2, of Annex II to the Convention, inviting them to submit between 3 March and 2 June 2014 the names of candidates for election to the Commission.

106. The President referred to documents SPLOS/269 (note by the Secretary-General on the election of one member of the Commission on the Limits of the Continental Shelf), SPLOS/272 (list of candidates to the Commission nominated by States parties) and the curriculum vitae of the candidate nominated for the election (circulated electronically in advance of the Meeting – see www.un.org/depts/los/meeting_states_parties/twentyfourthmeetingstatesparties.htm).

107. The President informed the Meeting of the election procedures, recalling the relevant provisions of the Convention and the rules of procedure for Meetings of States Parties.

108. After the completion of the voting process, the President announced the election of Rasik Ravindra (India) as a member of the Commission.[10] Mr. Ravindra will serve for the remainder of the term of Mr. Rajan, namely from the date of election until 15 June 2017.

109. On behalf of the Meeting, the President congratulated Mr. Ravindra on his election.

IX   Report of the Secretary-General under Article 319 of the United Nations Convention on the Law of the Sea

110. The Meeting considered the annual reports of the Secretary-General on oceans and the law of the sea (A/68/71/Add.1 and Corr.1 and A/69/71). Delegations expressed their appreciation to the Secretary-General and to the Division for the useful and comprehensive reports. A view was expressed that regrettably the only recent report available to the Meeting related to the topic of focus of the fourteenth meeting of the United Nations Open-ended Informal Consultative Process on Oceans and the Law of the Sea (A/69/71).

---

10   The Secretariat verified the quorum required for the election. The election required one round of balloting; 117 ballots were cast, with one invalid ballot and 5 abstentions. Rasik Ravindra (India) received 111 votes and was thus elected.

111.   Some delegations highlighted the central role of the Convention in set-
        ting out the legal framework within which all activities in the oceans and
        seas must be carried out, including by defining the areas of sovereignty
        and jurisdiction of coastal States, and in maintaining and strengthening
        peace, security, cooperation and friendly relations among Parties. The
        balance of rights and duties of States Parties under the Convention was
        underscored. Some delegations emphasized the importance of coastal
        States discharging their obligations of deposit and due publicity under
        the Convention.

112.   Some delegations highlighted the work of the Ad Hoc Open-ended
        Informal Working Group to study issues relating to the conservation and
        sustainable use of marine biological diversity beyond areas of national
        jurisdiction. Emphasis was placed upon its mandate to make recommen-
        dations to the General Assembly on the scope, parameters and feasibil-
        ity of an international instrument under the Convention. In this regard,
        a view was expressed that the Authority should be fully involved in the
        Ad Hoc Open-ended Informal Working Group. The active participation
        of States in meetings of the Ad Hoc Working Group of the Whole on the
        Regular Process for Global Reporting and Assessment of the State of
        the Marine Environment, including Socioeconomic Aspects, was wel-
        comed. States were urged to continue supporting the Regular Process for
        Global Reporting and Assessment of the State of the Marine Environment,
        including Socioeconomic Aspects, through financial contributions to the
        relevant trust fund.

113.   Some delegations welcomed the consideration of the role of seafood in
        global food security in the context of the fifteenth meeting of the Informal
        Consultative Process and the accompanying report of the Secretary-
        General, especially in light of the importance of the sustainability of
        marine resources. Delegations recalled a wide range of issues of signifi-
        cance for governance of oceans and seas, including the challenges of
        illegal, unreported and unregulated fishing; pollution and degradation
        of the marine environment; climate change; and the disappearance of
        marine species, which affect the ecosystem balance in the oceans and
        therefore food security. A view was expressed that there was a linkage
        between food security and the root causes of piracy and armed robbery
        at sea off the coast of Somalia and therefore the international commu-
        nity needed to combat criminal activities at sea. A delegation expressed
        concern over the seemingly indefinite delaying of the consideration of
        some submissions to the Commission on the basis of objections by other
        States under paragraph 5(a) of Annex I to the rules of procedure of the

Commission.[11] It was suggested that the twenty-fifth Meeting might wish to consider establishing parameters that might guide further application of this provision. In this regard, a view was expressed that territorial disputes should be addressed through bilateral negotiations.

114. Attention was drawn to the importance of flag State compliance with the treaties related to maritime safety. The recent entry into force of the Maritime Labour Convention was welcomed. Some delegations noted with appreciation the preparations for the fourth commemoration on 25 June 2014 of the Day of the Seafarer by the International Maritime Organization.

115. Some delegations addressed recent developments in the South China Sea/East Sea. Among them, some delegations elaborated in detail on their respective positions regarding these developments. Among other things, States Parties were urged to respect the rights and interests of other States Parties in their respective maritime zones and for maritime disputes to be resolved peacefully under the Convention. A reference was made in this regard to the Declaration on the Conduct of Parties in the South China Sea. The need for bilateral cooperation in resolving maritime disputes was emphasized. A view was also expressed that bilateral disputes fell outside the purview of the Meeting of States Parties. Calls were made to respect the integrity of the Convention and to apply it in good faith, and the need to ensure stability in the region was underscored. After the closing of the list of speakers, some delegations took the floor to further clarify their positions, exercising their right of reply.[12]

116. Some delegations expressed appreciation for the capacity-building activities and training programmes offered by the Division, including through the United Nations, the Nippon Foundation Fellowship Programme of Japan and the Hamilton Shirley Amerasinghe Memorial Fellowship on the Law of the Sea. Delegations encouraged contributions to ensure the continuation of the Hamilton Shirley Amerasinghe Fellowship programme. In this connection, a proposal to include the Amerasinghe Fellowship in the regular budget of the United Nations was made.

117. Recalling the concern expressed by many delegations at the twenty-third Meeting over the initiative of the Secretary-General entitled, "Oceans compact: healthy oceans for prosperity," the decision not to undertake any activities under this initiative was noted with satisfaction. Some

---

11   See also para. 81 above.
12   See para. 121 below.

delegations stressed that the Division was the unit of the Secretariat with the expertise and overarching mandate in ocean affairs and law of the sea matters and that duplication of efforts should be avoided for the sake of efficiency in the work of the Organization.

118. Divergent views concerning the mandate of the Meeting to discuss matters of a substantive nature relating to the implementation of the Convention continued to be expressed. It was indicated that the Meeting had the full mandate to consider all issues pertaining to the application and implementation of the Convention. Other delegations were of the view that the Meeting should limit itself to the consideration of financial and administrative matters relating to the bodies established by the Convention, namely the Tribunal, the Authority and the Commission. Some delegations stressed that the Meeting should not be regarded as a forum for discussion and resolution of bilateral disputes concerning the application and interpretation of the Convention.

119. In response to a query from one delegation, clarification was provided by the Secretariat with regard to the publication of information and communications concerning maritime spaces received by the Division from both States Parties and non-Parties to the Convention. Among other things, it was pointed out that the posting of information on the website or publication in the *Law of the Sea Bulletin* did not imply the expression of any opinion whatsoever on the part of the Secretariat concerning the legal status of any country, territory, city or area or of its authorities, or concerning the delimitation of its frontiers or boundaries. Publication of information concerning developments relating to the law of the sea emanating from actions and decisions taken by States did not imply recognition by the United Nations of the validity of the actions and decisions in question.

120. The importance of the website of the Division and the *Law of the Sea Bulletin* as an authoritative source of information on maritime spaces was highlighted by some delegations.

121. Once the list of speakers under the agenda item entitled "Report of the Secretary-General under Article 319 of the United Nations Convention on the Law of the Sea" was closed, some delegations requested the floor in order to reply to certain statements.[13] In response to such requests, the President noted that the procedure for Meetings of States Parties provided for a right of reply,[14] but did not regulate in detail the modalities in

---

13   See para. 115 above.

14   See rule 41 of the Rules of Procedure for Meetings of States Parties (SPLOS/2/Rev.4).

which the right of reply was to be exercised. The President proposed that in such cases, the Meeting should seek guidance from the procedures and practices of other bodies, in particular, the General Assembly. Following this proposal, the Meeting decided to establish a practice, according to which the number of interventions in the exercise of the right of reply would be limited to two per agenda item, the first no longer than 10 minutes and the second no longer than 5 minutes.

122. The Meeting took note of the report of the Secretary-General under Article 319 and decided that the same agenda item would be included in the provisional agenda of the twenty-fifth Meeting.

X   Other Matters

Event in Honour of the Late Hamilton Shirley Amerasinghe

123. A delegation informed the Meeting about a round table that was being planned in Sri Lanka for the third quarter of 2014 to commemorate the twentieth anniversary of the entry into force of the Convention and to honour the work of the late Hamilton Shirley Amerasinghe. Invitations would be sent in due course.

Information Provided by the Secretariat

124. The Secretariat provided information on the current status and projected funding requirements of the voluntary trust funds established by the General Assembly to assist the work of the Commission and the Tribunal.

125. It was reported that, since the previous Meeting, a contribution had been received from Costa Rica to the Voluntary Trust Fund for the purpose of facilitating the preparation of submissions to the Commission on the Limits of the Continental Shelf for developing States, in particular the least developed countries and small island developing States, in compliance with Article 76 of the United Nations Convention on the Law of the Sea.

126. With regard to the Voluntary Trust Fund to assist States in the settlement of disputes through the International Tribunal for the Law of the Sea, a contribution had been made by Finland.

127. The Secretariat provided a brief overview of the status of several other trust funds administered by the Division, which contributed, inter alia, to the dissemination and wider appreciation of international law

and provided financial assistance for the participation of representatives from developing countries to meetings held at United Nations Headquarters.[15] Regarding the Voluntary Trust Fund for the Regular Process for Global Reporting and Assessment of the State of the Marine Environment, including Socioeconomic Aspects, contributions had been received from China, Ireland, New Zealand, the Republic of Korea and the United Kingdom. Monaco and Slovenia had made contributions to the Hamilton Shirley Amerasinghe Memorial Fellowship on the Law of the Sea Trust Fund. A contribution had been received from New Zealand for the Voluntary Trust Fund for the purpose of assisting developing countries, in particular least developed countries, small island developing States and landlocked developing States, to attend meetings of the United Nations Open-ended Informal Consultative Process on Oceans and the Law of the Sea.

128. The Secretariat expressed its gratitude to all States that had made contributions to the trust funds and reiterated the appeal to States and others that were in a position to do so to contribute to the trust funds administered by it. The Secretariat also called upon States for assistance in identifying intergovernmental organizations and institutions and natural and juridical persons, which or who would be in a position to contribute to the trust funds.

---

15   Hamilton Shirley Amerasinghe Memorial Fellowship on the Law of the Sea Trust Fund; Voluntary Trust Fund for the Regular Process for Global Reporting and Assessment of the State of the Marine Environment, including Socioeconomic Aspects; Voluntary Trust Fund for the purpose of assisting developing countries, in particular least developed countries, small island developing States and landlocked developing States to attend meetings of the United Nations Open-ended Informal Consultative Process on Oceans and the Law of the Sea.

Report on the Work of the United Nations Open-Ended Informal Consultative Process on Oceans and the Law of the Sea at Its Fifteenth Meeting, 27–30 May 2014†

Letter Dated 6 June 2013 from the Co-chairs of the Consultative Process Addressed to the President of the General Assembly

Pursuant to General Assembly Resolution 68/70 of 9 December 2013, we were appointed as the Co-Chairs of the fifteenth meeting of the United Nations Open-ended Informal Consultative Process on Oceans and the Law of the Sea.

We have the honour to submit to you the attached report on the work of the Informal Consultative Process at its fifteenth meeting, which was held at United Nations Headquarters from 27 to 30 May 2014. The outcome of the meeting consists of our summary of issues and ideas raised during the meeting and in particular, with regard to the topic of focus: "The role of seafood in global food security."

In line with past practice, we kindly request that the present letter and the report of the Informal Consultative Process be circulated as a document of the sixty-ninth session of the General Assembly, under the agenda item entitled "Oceans and the law of the sea."

(*Signed*) Milan Jaya Meetarbhan
Don MacKay
Co-Chairs

Co-chairs Summary of Discussions[1]

1. The United Nations Open-ended Informal Consultative Process on Oceans and the Law of the Sea (the "Informal Consultative Process") held

---

† This document was provided by the United Nations Division for Ocean Affairs and the Law of the Sea (DOALOS) and is extracted from the United Nations General Assembly, Sixty-Ninth session, UN Document A/69/90, 6 June 2014, available online: <http://www.un.org/Depts/los/>. The document has been edited for publication in the *Ocean Yearbook*.

1 The summary is intended for reference purposes only and not as a record of the discussions.

its fifteenth meeting from 27 to 30 May 2014 and, pursuant to General Assembly Resolution 68/70, focused its discussions on the topic entitled "The role of seafood in global food security."

2. The meeting was attended by representatives of 80 States, 15 intergovernmental organizations and other bodies and entities and nine non-governmental organizations.[2]

3. The following supporting documentation was available to the meeting: (a) report of the Secretary-General on oceans and the law of the sea (A/69/71); and (b) format and annotated provisional agenda of the meeting (A/AC.259/L.15).

Agenda Items 1 and 2

Opening of the Meeting and Adoption of the Agenda

4. The two Co-Chairs, Don MacKay (New Zealand) and Milan Jaya Nyamrajsingh Meetarbhan (Mauritius), appointed by the President of the General Assembly, opened the meeting.

5. Opening remarks were made by Gyan Chandra Acharya, Under-Secretary-General and High Representative for the Least Developed Countries, Landlocked Developing Countries and Small Island Developing States; Nikhil Seth, Director, Division for Sustainable Development, Department of Economic and Social Affairs on behalf of the Under-Secretary-General for Economic and Social Affairs; and Stephen Mathias, Assistant Secretary-General for Legal Affairs on behalf of the Under-Secretary-General for Legal Affairs and United Nations Legal Counsel.

6. The meeting adopted the format and annotated provisional agenda and approved the proposed organization of work.

Agenda Item 3

General Exchange of Views

7. A general exchange of views on the role of seafood in global food security, as reflected below (paras. 7–33), took place at the plenary meeting on

---

2   A list of participants is available on the website of the Division for Ocean Affairs and the Law of the Sea at <http://www.un.org/Depts/los/index.htm>.

27 May. The discussions held on the topic of focus within the Panel segments are reflected in paragraphs 34 to 83 below.

8. Continued support for the Informal Consultative Process was expressed by several delegations. It was noted that the Informal Consultative Process had been a successful facilitator of the work of the General Assembly in reviewing developments in ocean affairs and the law of the sea not least owing to the informal character of the Informal Consultative Process and the participation of the various disciplines and stakeholders in its meetings.

9. Many delegations highlighted the timeliness and critical importance of the topic of focus, which was considered of paramount importance for developing States. In this regard, delegations expressed appreciation for the report of the Secretary-General on oceans and the law of the sea (A/69/71).

10. Several delegations underlined the importance of the discussions on the topic of focus in the context of ongoing processes, in particular, the Open Working Group on Sustainable Development Goals, the post-2015 development agenda and the third International Conference on Small Island Developing States (Independent State of Samoa, September 2014). Reference was also made to the outcome of the "Global Oceans Action Summit for Food Security and Blue Growth" (the Netherlands, April 2014), which called for urgent coordinated action to secure the long-term well-being and food security of a growing population through a stand-alone sustainable development goal on oceans and seas.

11. Delegations underscored the important contribution of seafood to global food security and its relevance to the three pillars of sustainable development. They underlined that seafood played a significant but not yet fully recognized role in food security. The need to better integrate seafood into wider policy discussions on global food security was emphasized.

12. The importance of seafood as a means to improve food security and nutrition, particularly in developing countries where it was often the sole source of critical proteins, was highlighted by delegations. They noted that fish provided approximately 3 billion people with almost 20 per cent of their average animal protein and that fish was an important source of minerals, vitamins and micronutrients and an excellent source of long-chain omega-3 fatty acids, which were required for numerous normal body functions. Regular consumption of fish could reduce the risk of

various diseases and disorders and benefit brain health and development and inflammatory conditions. The important contribution of seafood to food security as a key input in the production of food, such as fishmeal, was also noted. The need for education on the benefits of seafood as a healthy diet choice was underlined.

13. Many delegations recalled international commitments regarding the right to access sufficient, safe and nutritious food, consistent with the right to adequate food and the fundamental right to be free from hunger. Reference was made in particular to Millennium Development Goal 1, for the eradication of extreme poverty and hunger, and to the recognition in the outcome document of the 2012 United Nations Conference on Sustainable Development, "The future we want"(Resolution 6/28, annex), that poverty eradication was the greatest global challenge. In that regard, several delegations noted ongoing challenges as reflected by continued high rates of chronic hunger and infant deaths caused by malnutrition, particularly in developing countries.

14. Delegations drew attention to the role of the seafood sector as a critical source of livelihood and income, in particular for developing countries that export fish products. It was noted that without fishing, many coastal communities would suffer. It was pointed out that fish was the single most traded food product in small island developing States, valued at $25 billion a year and was integral to economies around the world. In this regard, it was noted that women represented the majority in secondary activities related to marine fishing and marine aquaculture, such as fish processing and marketing. Employment in aquaculture had enhanced the economic and social status of women in developing countries. The seafood sector also offered opportunities for young people to remainwithin local communities and contribute to their long-term sustainability.

15. The crucial role of healthy marine ecosystems, sustainable fisheries and sustainable aquaculture for food security, nutrition and livelihood was stressed by many delegations. It was emphasized that protecting the health, the productivity and the resilience of marine ecosystems was critical for global food security.

16. Attention was drawn by several delegations to the range of pressures that could affect marine biodiversity and the ability of marine ecosystems to contribute to global food security, including climate change; ocean acidification; invasive alien species; and pollution. Biodiversity loss threatened the capacity of marine ecosystems to fully deliver much-needed

services and there was thus a need to balance sustainable use and conservation. Several delegations pointed out that economic incentives that lead to the loss of biodiversity needed to be balanced with those encouraging biodiversity conservation, including alternative employment opportunities.

17. The detrimental impacts on the marine environment from man-made pollutants that commonly entered the marine environment from land-based sources, including nanoplastics, persistent organic contaminants, antibiotics, pesticides, herbicides, chemical fertilizers, detergents, oil, sewage, plastics, heavy metals such as mercury and other solids were underlined. Several delegations also highlighted threats due to pharmaceuticals in the marine environment that had not been fully processed by the human body. These pollutants were collecting at ocean depths and consumed by small marine organisms, which then entered the global food chain. One delegation highlighted the threat of underwater noise pollution to at least 55 marine species, including 20 commercially valuable species of fish, and encouraged further studies on these links. It was noted that noise from air guns reduced fish catch rates for certain species including cod, haddock and herring, by 40 to 80 percent.

18. Many delegations drew attention to the effects of unsustainable exploitation practices on seafood availability, illegal unreported and unregulated (IUU) fishing and destructive fishing practices. The need to address by-catch and discards and other adverse impacts on the ecosystem from fisheries was also emphasized. Delegations also noted concerns about harmful fishing subsidies and overcapacity, as well as unsustainable aquaculture practices. It was noted that the difference between the potential and actual net economic benefits from marine fisheries was approximately $50 billion annually, more than half the value of the global seafood trade.

19. Many delegations highlighted that almost 30 per cent of marine fish stocks remained overexploited or depleted. It was stressed that ocean systems were being pushed to the point of collapse, which threatened long-term food security. The invasion of lionfish in the Caribbean and the outbreak of jellyfish in the Black Sea and the Mediterranean Sea were highlighted as illustrations of the disruption being caused to marine ecosystems. A delegation also drew attention to the decline in marine mammals and further underlined that many species of cetaceans lacked a global regulatory instrument.

20. The need to combat IUU fishing was stressed by many delegations, in particular as such practices contributed to overfishing, undermined

conservation and management measures and resulted in losses in revenue and local employment. Current measures to combat IUU fishing were not considered sufficient and delegations were encouraged to ratify and implement the Port State Measures Agreement of the Food and Agriculture Organization of the United Nations (FAO) and to adopt integrated governance frameworks. Several delegations noted the link between illegal fishing and transnational organized crime.

21. Delegations recognized the important contribution of sustainable fisheries to global food security in small island developing States. In this context, several delegations expressed concern about the rate and scale of overexploitation of marine resources in the Pacific region, which threatened food security of the wider international community. A call was made for the international community to share the burden in ensuring the sustainable management of these resources.

22. Several delegations expressed concern over limited access to seafood in developing countries. Particular concerns were raised over exports that reduced the local supply of seafood and foreign fishing in the context of access agreements, which constrained the access of developing States to their own fish resources. They underlined the need to enhance developing countries' capacity to profit in a sustainable manner from their own resources by building capacity for exploitation of resources, improving marine science and enhancing monitoring, surveillance and control.

23. The importance of access to export markets was also highlighted. Several delegations expressed concern that unilateral trade barriers were being applied to the detriment of some exporting developing States. They called on the World Trade Organization to urgently address fisheries subsidies, which could exacerbate overcapacity, contribute to IUU fishing and affect trade in fish products by developing countries. It was emphasized that fisheries resources should not be seen as simply a source of foreign licence revenues.

24. It was stressed by many delegations that the future role of seafood in global food security depended on achieving sustainable fisheries and aquaculture. In this context, several delegations highlighted the role that aquaculture would need to play in meeting growing demands for seafood, given the limited additional production available from capture fisheries. It was recalled that aquaculture was the fastest growing animal-food-producing sector and was set to outpace population growth. The potential for other seafood types, including algae and sea cucumbers, to address growing seafood demand was also noted.

25. In terms of sustainable management measures, delegations emphasized the need for management objectives to obtain the maximum benefit from harvesting without reducing the value of the marine environment. Some delegations indicated that these objectives could be met through ecosystem information, stock assessments and improved fishing methods. In this context, it was noted that there was a need to take full advantage of existing international processes and legal frameworks to reduce overfishing, while implementing precautionary and ecosystem-based approaches.

26. It was emphasized that management measures needed to be based on credible, science-based, affordable and effective practices. Research was needed, for example, on the life histories of endemic species to learn the most effective protection patterns. Scientific studies were also needed to investigate the impacts and potential solutions to a range of challenges, including pollution, invasive species, coastal development and fragile ecosystems like coral reefs.

27. Some delegations drew attention to the key role of regional fisheries management organizations in achieving sustainable fisheries and reaching the goal of a sustainable exploitation of marine resources and, by extension, of food security. To that effect, the responsibility of coastal States within their maritime zones was also underscored.

28. Several delegations reported on current efforts to ensure sustainable fisheries management based on good governance, the best available science, the precautionary principle, broad stakeholder involvement and a long-term perspective. The new European Union Common Fisheries Policy, for example, aimed to maintain harvest stock populations at sustainable yield as soon as possible but not later than 2020, while also reducing by-catch, eliminating discards on a case-by-case basis and improving selectivity through adaptations to fishing gear.

29. In achieving sustainable fisheries and aquaculture, some delegations also noted the need to balance competing uses for a limited aquatic space, including through holistic approaches and integrated coastal management. In this context, delegations emphasized the need to maximize synergies through coordination and cooperation. It was noted that all sectors of the food industry, including harvesters, producers and transporters, needed to be involved in addressing global food security. It was suggested that scientific research could promote cross-cutting measures for regulating ocean resources. The importance of traditional knowledge was also highlighted, as was the role of consumers.

30. Many delegations highlighted the need for capacity-building and transfer of marine technology in order to improve food security in developing

countries. Delegations recognized in this context the lack of infrastructure and capacity for the science-based management of resources. It was noted, for example, that lack of infrastructure had led to post-harvest losses equivalent to 30 per cent of catch in some areas. Several delegations underscored that actions needed to restore fish stocks to sustainable levels depended on the capacity of developing countries to conduct marine science and implement technology-based controls. Capacity-building in marine science was particularly important in undertaking scientific studies to establish the maximum sustainable yield of fish stocks. There was also a need for capacity-building in the enforcement of conservation and management measures, including assistance in the monitoring, control and surveillance of fishing activities.

31. Transfer of technology was highlighted by several delegations as an essential basis for the development of capacity-building and for benefit-sharing. In this regard, disparities in technologies threatened the sustainable use of resources. Several delegations reiterated the need in this context for the implementation of Part XIV of the United Nations Convention on the Law of the Sea.

32. Some delegations described current capacity-building initiatives to improve the sustainable management of fisheries resources in developing countries. A delegate proposed an initiative to double every fifth year the capacity-building measures in developing States for the conservation and sustainable use of living marine resources and to increase the economic benefits from the sustainable use of living marine resources by 2030. Information was provided on the EAF-Nansen Project, which was administered by FAO, as an example of a successfully running programme of capacity-building for sustainable and ecosystem-based fisheries management.

33. Some delegations suggested that the development and enhancement of capacity-building would be more effective if cooperative links between regional institutions through, for example, the establishment of mentoring and partnership linkages between north and south regional organizations, were created. In this regard, several delegations suggested that food security could also be a key element in developing concrete partnerships for small island developing States.

Area of Focus: The Role of Seafood in Global Food Security

34. In accordance with the annotated agenda, discussions in the Panel segments were structured around: (a) understanding global food security

and the current role of seafood therein; (b) the role of seafood in global food security in the context of the three pillars of sustainable development; and (c) opportunities and challenges for the future role of seafood in global food security. The segments were launched by presentations from panellists, followed by interactive discussions.

1   Understanding Global Food Security and the Current Role of
        Seafood Therein
(a)   *Panel Presentations*

35. In segment 1, Gro-Ingunn Hemre, of the National Institute of Nutrition and Seafood Research (Norway), highlighted the nutritional benefits of fish in the human diet and the challenge of addressing micronutrient deficiencies in developing countries and in low-income food-deficit countries. She explained that, as a rich source of protein and nutrients, such as iodine, zinc, vitamins A and D, calcium anphosphorous, and fatty acids, the consumption of fish had numerous benefits, including protection against nutrition-related diseases. The importance of sardines, anchovies and other small pelagic fish as some of the richest nutrient sources was highlighted.

36. Moses Amos, of the Secretariat of the Pacific Community, Division of Fisheries, Aquaculture and Marine Ecosystems, addressed the importance of fisheries resources to food security, livelihoods, economic growth and development in the Pacific Island countries and territories. He described the status of coastal fisheries resources, which were unable to meet demands for food security from a growing population. He also mentioned unsustainable patterns of economic growth and the impacts of climate change. Mr. Amos highlighted the need for effective fisheries management and improved access to fisheries resources, including oceanic fisheries such as tuna, as well as national food security policies and conservation measures to protect coastal fisheries resources.

37. Christophe Béné, of the Institute of Development Studies, Vulnerability and Poverty Reduction Team (United Kingdom of Great Britain and Northern Ireland) referred to the work of the High-level Panel of Experts of the Committee on World Food Security. He emphasized the importance of fish as one of the most efficient converters of feed into high quality food, and in providing income and livelihoods. He noted challenges to the ecological sustainability of fisheries and aquaculture, while highlighting the socioeconomic benefits of small-scale fisheries. Mr. Béné drew attention to ongoing debates concerning international fish trade and food

security in terms of maintaining the right to food of fishing communities while ensuring the availability of fish for all. He stressed that increasing demand for fish needed to be met by expansion in aquaculture.

(b)   *Panel Discussions*

38. Delegations emphasized the high nutritional value of seafood and noted the contribution of fish to the world's consumption of animal protein, which, for example, was higher than 60 per cent in some small island developing countries. Attention was drawn to the protein and nutritional value of different types of seafood. It was noted by the panellists that the protein content of fish of the same species, whether farmed or wild, was the same as it was determined by its genetic code; however, the nutritional content and level of fatty acids depended on what was consumed by the fish.

39. One panellist noted that the way seafood was prepared and consumed also had a considerable impact on its nutritional value. In this regard, marine pelagic fish that was consumed whole was considered to be the richest source of nutrients. It was suggested that production of smaller farmed fish that could be eaten whole could increase food security and provide better nutrition, particularly in developing countries.

40. One panellist indicated that fish could generally be grouped into four different categories, which generally reflected their nutritional profiles: lean freshwater, oily freshwater, lean marine and oily marine fish. It was noted that the nutritional difference between freshwater and marine oily fish was generally small, although some marine oily fish produced some level of fatty acids regardless of the feed used.

41. Given the high nutritional value of small pelagic fish such as sardines and anchovies, particularly if they were eaten whole, it was noted by an observer delegation that such species should be reserved for human consumption rather than used as fishmeal in aquaculture. One panellist indicated that their use as fishmeal could be justified in the light of continued technological advances that would reduce reliance on fishmeal for aquafeed and the promise of aquaculture for nutrition and food security. Another observer delegation wondered whether the worlds of aquaculture and agriculture would converge and allow for the symbiotic use of all food resources, so that agricultural resources could be used in aquaculture and fisheries resources (fishmeal) could be used in agriculture.

42. One delegation noted that scientific knowledge on the nutritional value of seafood could inform the activities of the international community

and decision-makers. In this regard, the report of the High-level Panel of Experts on Food Security and Nutrition on Sustainable Fisheries and Aquaculture was mentioned by a panellist as a possible starting point for discussions on food security and fisheries. A delegation highlighted the need to facilitate the granting of consent for marine scientific research in areas within national jurisdiction.

43.   Delegations also considered the recommended intake of fish protein and how alternative sources of nutrients, other than seafood, compared to fish nutrients in terms of cost and availability. In this regard, one panellist observed that all animal protein was considered to be beneficial and there was no established comparative advantage of one form of animal protein, such as fish protein, over another. It was noted, however, that animal protein in general compared more favourably to vegetable sources such as soy, which lacked key nutrients.

44.   One panellist emphasized the importance of developing alternative sources of fish and alternative sources of income to relieve pressure on coastal fisheries, particularly in the light of the choice faced by many communities between food security today and environmental sustainability tomorrow. The importance of education and raising awareness at the local level to improve resource management was also underscored. In this regard, it was noted that helping to identify low-cost alternative sources of nutrition would relieve pressure on fish stocks and ensure their sustainable management. The importance of preserving sensitive marine ecosystems, such as mangroves, was emphasized. It was pointed out that mangrove forests serve as physical barriers to storms, act as nurseries for fish, offer habitats for birds and stop land erosion.

45.   It was noted by one panellist that in the Pacific, initiatives were taking place to utilize fish aggregating devices for subsistence and artisanal fisheries, to redirect fishing efforts away from coastal fisheries and towards small pelagics and to develop the small-scale freshwater and marine aquaculture sector, including sea cucumber farming. The Secretariat of the Pacific Community provided scientific advice on management of fisheries resources to member countries and further assisted small-scale fishers to develop their capacity to access oceanic fish resources for subsistence purposes, with any excess sold in markets. Several delegations raised concerns over the use of fish aggregating devices, given their potential to act as an ecological trap for by-catch and alter stock migration of certain species such as tuna. In response, it was noted that the use of fish aggregating devices supported by the Secretariat of the Pacific Community was confined to coastal pelagics up to 500m from the shore.

46. Some delegations noted the effectiveness of aquaculture in providing food security compared to farming or other land-based activities. One panellist noted that community-based aquaculture contributed to food security by yielding high production at a low cost and by compensating for the declining supply from coastal fisheries. Another panellist indicated that aquaculture was much more efficient in terms of protein conversion compared to all other livestock production systems. It was suggested that aquaculture should be prioritized by States for the purpose of providing food security and nutrition.

47. Some panellists highlighted the substantial contribution of small-scale aquaculture to food security particularly in terms of improving the livelihoods of fish producers. One panellist noted technological innovation and progress in aquaculture development that would allow producers to meet the increasing demand for fish in a more sustainable way.

48. It was noted in this context that, although offshore mariculture could reduce competition over ocean space, the industry remained highly intensive, in terms of technological and financial inputs, and was not considered, at this stage, to be a long-term solution for food security for many countries.

49. Delegations also considered the safety of fish consumption in the light of the range of pollutants in the marine environment and new types of contaminants in farmed species. In this regard, it was noted that the risks associated with the consumption of seafood were outweighed by the nutritional benefits. One panellist noted in this context that all food sources were contaminated to some extent by pollutants and chemicals. In addition, many countries had in place regulations to monitor the contaminant levels in seafood to ensure fish and fish products were considered safe for human consumption.

2   The Role of Seafood in Global Food Security in the Context of the Three Pillars of Sustainable Development

(a)   *Panel Presentations*

50. In segment 2, Brian Crawford, of the University of Rhode Island, Graduate School of Oceanography, Coastal Resources Center (United States of America), focused on the importance of small pelagic fish and their nutritional role in the supply of protein for coastal communities in developing countries. He noted threats from overfishing and overcapacity, subsidies, poor governance and IUU fishing, and stressed the need for improvements in ecosystem-based management, access and user

rights regimes, the fish value chain and distribution systems, as well as enforcement. It was also essential to ensure that resource control and foreign investment did not divert locally needed fish to export markets. Mr. Crawford also highlighted the important role of women throughout the fish value chain.

51. Geoffrey Shaw, of the International Atomic Energy Agency (IAEA), discussed the need to build capacity to better understand changes in the marine environment, including from ocean acidification and widespread pollution, as well as related impacts to food security. He described the work of IAEA in providing expert advice on protecting consumers from radioactive and non-radioactive contamination of fish and shellfish; knowledge of nuclear and isotopic techniques for measuring occurrence, levels and impacts of pollutants and toxins in biota, including edible organisms; and capacity-building for assessing the sustainable and safe use and development of seafood.

52. Paúl Phumpiu, Vice-Minister for Fisheries, of the Ministry of Production (Peru), described the important contribution of small pelagic fishes to food security as a resource high in protein that was readily available and affordable, and the role of Peru in providing approximately one fifth of the world's production of pelagic fish, a significant portion of which was exported to developing countries. He highlighted Peru's "blue capital" approach, based on ecosystem sustainability, adaptive institutions, market organization and social responsibility, and an initiative to increase the biomass of pelagic fish and the proportion of fish production used for direct human consumption.

53. Margaret Nakato, of the World Forum of Fish Harvesters and Fish Workers, described challenges faced by small-scale fishers, such as competition with industrial fishing, that deprive local communities of food supplies and threaten livelihoods. She stressed the value of small-scale fishing as a model of production and the need to ensure that fishers and fish workers had the necessary rights to fishery resources and land, as well as a say in governance. She also stressed the human rights dimension of food security and the importance of the right to adequate food, as well as the need to empower women in the fishing sector, coordinate policy in food security, implement existing instruments and harmonize sectoral approaches and capacity-building.

54. Wan Izatul Asma binti Wan Talaat, of Universiti Malaysia Terengganu, Institute of Oceanography and Environment, highlighted efforts to enhance the role of seafood in food security and address threats facing the coastal and marine resources, including in the context of the Coral

Triangle Initiative. She described initiatives in Malaysia to establish marine-protected areas and aquaculture intensive zones and innovative approaches to bridge the gap between scientific research and governance.

(b)   *Panel Discussions*

55. The important role of small pelagic species, for example, anchovies and sardines, in the context of food security was highlighted, in view of their high nutritional value and low cost. One panellist noted that both industrial and small-scale fisheries should be developed in order to enhance the food security and economic potential of these species, with priority given to meeting the nutritional needs of local communities. One panellist noted that these species were mostly used in the production of fishmeal, for indirect human consumption; however, further consideration should be given to their use for direct human consumption by local communities and for exports. It was also important to ensure the continued role of these species in the trophic food chain and to take into consideration the needs of dependent species when determining catch allocations.

56. A delegation queried how to introduce small pelagic species into communities that did not consider them to be part of their traditional diets. One panellist noted initiatives to promote consumption of anchovies in Peru through marketing and education campaigns on the nutritional value of these species. It was recalled that these species could be used as fishmeal or fish oils for other food production practices, where direct human consumption was not considered an option.

57. Delegations also considered the need to address current pressures on small-scale fisheries. In this regard, one delegation highlighted the need for governance and management policies to address the impacts of overfishing and IUU fishing, particularly in the light of the reliance of fishing communities in developing countries on small-scale fisheries for food security. One panellist noted that technological devices, such as satellite-connected tracking devices, combined with the assistance of local communities as observers, were an effective tool to enhance monitoring, control and surveillance. The management challenges associated with the effects of climate change were also noted.

58. A delegation suggested that fishing overcapacity could be reduced by creating alternative livelihoods for fishers. In this regard, one panellist noted the difficulties in considering this challenge at scale, given the

number of people involved in fisheries and aquaculture and the limited employment opportunities at local community level. In order to significantly reduce overcapacity, social safety nets needed to be developed to mitigate the exit of thousands of fishers and fish workers from the industry. One panellist highlighted the benefits of training in literacy, credit and financing. The importance of diverse income streams within households was also highlighted.

59. A delegation underscored the need to develop equitable and responsible governance and trade systems, in view of the role that sustainable fisheries and aquaculture played in enhancing food security and economic development. Emphasis was placed in this regard on unlocking the economic potential of safe aquaculture practices for food security. It was noted that the adoption of responsible policies and effective institutions could enhance food security, in particular when governance frameworks facilitated the participation of small-scale fishing communities in decision-making. One panellist noted the benefits of rights-based management systems, to encourage responsible use of marine resources and participation in governance and to generate tax revenues.

60. Some delegations noted the need to carefully consider investments in other sectors, such as real estate and tourism, which could displace small-scale fishing communities and limit access to fishing grounds, thus reducing food security and income. One panellist noted that investment in these sectors was often poorly coordinated due to the different interests of the stakeholders involved. The importance of integrated management at all levels, including multisectoral management and integration to enhance food security was highlighted.

61. Concerns were also expressed by some delegations over the impact of marine pollution on seafood. One panellist noted that toxins were not eliminated by the freezing and cooking of seafood and highlighted the need for water and sanitation programmes to address sanitary concerns. Another panellist underscored the importance of detecting toxins before they entered the human food chain, including through nuclear technologies. In that regard, a delegation cited concerns over the use of nuclear and isotopic techniques in relation to seafood contamination. In response, a panellist noted that such techniques were routinely used in common research applications.

62. Some delegations welcomed information on empowering women in local fisheries management in order to eradicate poverty. It was noted in this regard that an increased role for women could lead to increased food security. One panellist emphasized that half of the workforce in fisheries

in some developing countries was comprised by women in very diverse roles. Delegations discussed the need to develop best practices to engage women in the fisheries industry and, in particular, to ensure access to credit, improved working conditions and improved sanitation in processing factories. The importance of education was emphasized, including education in the value of fish as a source of nutrition. There was also a need to enable access to credit and training in financing to allow women to diversify their role in the fishing industry beyond subsistence fishing and post-harvest work.

63. In this regard, another panellist noted the low percentage of women in larger scale fishing activities, due to lack of access to medium-scale credit. It was suggested that through associations women could aggregate their products and obtain access to larger credit sources and markets. This panellist also suggested that women should be granted an enhanced role in resource management, since fishing practices at sea could have an impact on their post-harvest activities.

64. More generally, delegations noted the importance of capacity-building, training and access to credit for sustainable small-scale fisheries. Capacity-building and infrastructure development, in particular, could address differences in per capita consumption of fish in coastal and inland populations, including in landlocked States. One panellist highlighted the need for infrastructure related to refrigeration and safe storage of fish, which could allow fresh seafood to reach inland populations. The need for additional financial resources, access to credit and training opportunities was highlighted in this regard.

65. A delegation noted that the discussions during this panel segment reinforced the importance for oceans to be part of the post-2015 development agenda. In this context, support was expressed for a stand-alone goal on oceans with a view to maintaining healthy and productive oceans and seas and hence supporting food security, livelihoods and the empowerment of women.

3   Opportunities and Challenges for the Future Role of Seafood in Global Food Security

(a)   *Panel Presentations*

66. In panel 3, Rohan Subasinghe, of FAO, Aquaculture Branch, described challenges in supplying safe and nutritious seafood to a growing global population, including the need to improve the contribution of capture fisheries through better management, ensure sustainable and increasing

growth in aquaculture and reduce waste in the seafood value chain. He highlighted opportunities and challenges in sustaining aquaculture growth including technology and innovations (for example, reducing fishmeal and fish oil in feed), investment and finance, policy and governance and improved public-private partnerships.

67. Manuel Barange, of Plymouth Marine Laboratory (United Kingdom of Great Britain and Northern Ireland), described anthropogenic climate change and population growth as the two main challenges in producing enough seafood. He indicated that meeting current seafood consumption rates was only feasible under certain conditions, namely managing and using global fish resources efficiently and sustainably, reducing the reliance of the aquaculture industry on wild fish for feed through significant technological development, and ensuring the effective distribution of wild fish products based on food needs. He explained that the impacts from climate change would not be consistent across regions and countries and would be mitigated or exacerbated based on dependency on the resources, which demonstrated a need to improve management effectiveness and trade practices.

68. Susan Singh-Renton, of the Caribbean Regional Fisheries Mechanism, highlighted regional challenges for enhancing food security, including lack of policy coherence across sectors and marginalization of fisheries issues, as well as limited advancement in statistics and research, technological developments and marketing and trade. Ms. Singh-Renton noted initiatives at the regional level to address these challenges, including by improving policy coherence, establishing fisheries management objectives based on food security, strengthening fisherfolk capacity for participatory fisheries management, developing technical capacity for ecosystem approaches to fisheries and increasing capacity for managing seafood safety and quality standards.

69. Roland Wiefels, of Centro para los servicios de información y asesoramiento sobre la comercialización de los productos pesqueros de América Latina, described challenges and opportunities related to post-harvest issues and stressed the need to adapt seafood processing, distribution and marketing networks and the location of production sites to population growth and geographical distribution. He emphasized the importance of increased diversification of aquaculture species, reduction of production costs through economies of scale, improved transport facilities and enhanced regional trade.

70. James Movick, of the Forum Fisheries Agency, described opportunities and challenges in the co-management of tuna fisheries of the western

tropical Pacific, and the need to increase economic growth for Pacific small island developing States(in whose exclusive economic zones most of the tuna resources were found), including through harvest control rules and rights-based management. Particular challenges included decision-making processes in regional fisheries management organizations, a disproportionate burden on small island developing States of the costs of conservation and management, high utility and transport costs and remoteness from export markets, and combatting IUU fishing in large maritime spaces with limited financial resources.

71.   Nobuyuki Yagi, of the University of Tokyo, Graduate School of Agricultural and Life Sciences, outlined the role of consumers in supporting responsible fisheries and marine ecosystem conservation and productivity through eco-labelling schemes. He noted that, while current eco-labelling schemes had positive aspects, further consideration needed to be given as to how to support the livelihoods of small-scale fishers in developing countries and to help maintain marine and coastal ecosystems services.

72.   Janos Pasztor, of World Wide Fund for Nature International, emphasized that healthy ocean ecosystems were a prerequisite for food security and livelihoods based on seafood and highlighted the need for a new integrated approach to management, based on what an ecosystem could sustainably produce. He noted that opportunities for oceans in future global food security depended on political will and the involvement of all stakeholders to address cumulative impacts, which required rebuilding and sustainably managing fisheries, mitigating impacts from land-based and sea-based activities and managing ocean uses in an integrated holistic manner. He expressed his support for an implementing agreement to the United Nations Convention on the Law of the Sea.

(b)   *Panel Discussions*

73.   In the ensuing discussions, delegations highlighted a number of particular challenges and opportunities for the future role of seafood in global food security. With regard to increasing population and demand for seafood, it was stressed that international trade should reflect the need for food instead of profit. It was noted, in this regard, that fish should not only go where the money is, but should go where the need is. In this context, an observer delegation noted that, beyond a certain per capita gross domestic product (GDP) level, demand for meat and seafood depended on cultural

preferences instead of need. Another panellist expressed the view that GDP per capita was not an effective index to assess the buying power of populations because it was an average figure. Another panellist explained that demand from industrialized countries sometimes jeopardized the interests of poorer countries and indicated that this issue needed to be addressed through intergovernmental processes.

74. Concerning the impacts of climate change and pollution, clarification was sought on whether ocean acidification was taken into account in models assessing the countries that might lose or gain in terms of fisheries production. One panellist elaborated that there were difficulties in assessing the impacts of ocean acidification. It was explained that ocean acidification would not halt production in the oceans; however, food webs would need to restructure themselves owing to impacts on different species. With regard to queries on how to regulate climate change, another panellist highlighted eco-labelling, such as an anti-climate change label, as a potential useful tool.

75. Attention was drawn to the impacts on fisheries and food security owing to pollution from ocean noise, including from the oil and gas industry, and a request was made for FAO to carry out further studies on the topic, as encouraged by the General Assembly. Some delegations supported the need for such studies and suggested that the Caribbean Regional Fisheries Mechanism could participate in this research.

76. A question was raised about whether marine-protected areas had a positive effect on food security, since such areas often excluded fisheries communities. In that regard, a panellist indicated that there had been an evolution in the implementation of marine-protected areas, including through greater involvement of, and access for, local communities so as to enhance their food security.

77. With regard to fisheries governance, one panellist noted that the merging of fisheries and agriculture departments in States has in some cases resulted in the relative marginalization of fisheries interests. The panellist explained that developing countries had limited capital. She also mentioned that there was little infrastructure for monitoring industry performance to promote better returns and consequent investments in the sector so that more attention could be given to fisheries under agricultural portfolios. The panellist suggested that a determined effort should be made to estimate the value of fisheries.

78. Some delegations highlighted the monitoring, control and surveillance systems used by Pacific small island developing States to combat IUU fishing. The success in the region was attributed by one panellist to

regional cooperative efforts, including with patrol support from developed countries, and shared IUU vessel lists. The panellist explained that foreign fishing vessels were required to refrain from fishing in specified high seas areas as a precondition to being allowed to fish in any exclusive economic zone of the coastal States in the region.

79. A delegation emphasized the need to build the capacity of developing countries with regard to IUU fishing and for cooperation in developing effective management mechanisms. Complications that may arise in relation to the management of fish stocks in the event that maritime areas are subject to overlapping claims were mentioned by a delegation.

80. In terms of bridging the gap in food demand and supply through the intensification of aquaculture, one panellist emphasized the need for sustainable intensification, as well as the need to improve social and environmental performance by promoting more efficient energy and resource use. The continued importance of wild fisheries in providing the base load supply of edible fish was emphasized by an observer delegation in this context. Developments in programmes to support disease prevention and management in aquaculture were noted, including difficulties in developing vaccines for tropical fish compared to temperate fish.

81. Concerns were also expressed about the challenges for developing countries in moving aquaculture off shore, given the capital investment necessary for equipment, logistics and vessels. One panellist acknowledged that current trials for offshore mariculture were expensive and not necessarily well-suited to resource-poor countries.

82. With regard to concerns over rapid price fluctuations and income inequality in the value chain, one panellist suggested the use of certification or eco-labelling schemes. Some delegations observed that eco-labelling could also result in income gaps owing to differences in the capabilities of various fisheries, especially those in developing countries, to comply with eco-labelling criteria, for example, in estimating maximum sustainable yield.

83. Another panellist noted that eco-labelling schemes did not generally take into account small-scale fisheries, in particular in developing countries, which relied on different practices. One panellist expressed the view that most consumers around the world, especially those in developing countries, did not consider eco-labelling when buying fish and were more likely to pay attention to religious dietary labels, for example, halal and kosher. It was suggested that one useful aspect of eco-labelling was in combating IUU fishing.

Agenda Item 4

Inter-agency Cooperation and Coordination

84. The Director of the Division for Ocean Affairs and the Law of the Sea made a statement on behalf of the focal point for UN-Oceans, the United Nations Legal Counsel/Division for Ocean Affairs and the Law of the Sea,[3] providing information on the activities of UN-Oceans since the approval, by the General Assembly in Resolution 68/70, of revised terms of reference for UN-Oceans. She recalled that the revised terms of reference provided for reporting by UN-Oceans to ensure transparency and accountability.

85. She informed the meeting that, in order to respond to the revised terms of reference on participation in UN-Oceans, an invitation dated 20 December 2013 had been circulated to United Nations system organizations with competence in ocean and coastal areas. As a result, the current membership of UN-Oceans now consisted of 22 United Nations entities and the International Seabed Authority.

86. She stated that UN-Oceans had convened three teleconferences and had held two face-to-face meetings on 5 February and 27 May 2014, the latter of which was held on the margins of the present meeting of the Informal Consultative Process. She highlighted that UN-Oceans had adopted a biennial work programme at its February meeting. Among the activities foreseen in that work programme, she noted that the development of an inventory of mandates and activities of the members of UN-Oceans was under way, for the purpose of facilitating the identification of possible areas for collaboration and synergies as mandated under the revised terms of reference. Furthermore, two ad hoc coordination teams had been established; one focused on World Oceans Day 2014, and the other on the third United Nations Conference on Small Island Developing States, which would take place from 1 to 4 September 2014, in the Independent State of Samoa. She stated that, at its 27 May 2014 meeting, UN-Oceans had exchanged information on planned events and activities, which would be posted on the UN-Oceans website, and had discussed continued updates and improvements to the UN-Oceans website, as well as refinements to the inventory of mandates and activities prior to making it available on the UN-Oceans website.

---

3 The full text of the statement is available on the website of UN-Oceans at <www.unoceans.org>.

She emphasized the importance placed by UN-Oceans members at the meeting on using the UN-Oceans mechanism, including its website, as a means of information-sharing.

87. Delegations expressed appreciation for the update on the work of UN-Oceans, welcoming the increased transparency and effectiveness in the work of UN-Oceans. They also expressed satisfaction with the work programme.

88. Several delegations emphasized the importance for UN-Oceans of continuing to focus on ensuring coherence within the United Nations system on ocean issues, in order to prevent duplication of efforts among relevant United Nations entities. They further expressed confidence that, under its revised terms of reference, UN-Oceans would strengthen coordination and cooperation among competent organizations in conformity with the United Nations Convention on the Law of the Sea and their respective mandates, and facilitate inter-agency information exchange, including best practices and experiences, tools and methodologies.

89. Delegations expressed their appreciation to and reiterated their support for the United Nations Legal Counsel/Division for Ocean Affairs and the Law of the Sea as focal point for UN-Oceans.

Agenda Item 5

Process for the Selection of Topics and Panellists so as to Facilitate the Work of the General Assembly

90. The Co-Chairs introduced item 5, noting that it reflected paragraph 268 of General Assembly Resolution 68/70. Delegations were invited to provide their views and make proposals on ways to devise a transparent, objective and inclusive process for the selection of topics and panellists, so as to facilitate the work of the General Assembly. Several delegations were of the view that the concept notes elaborating on the proposed topics should be circulated in time for consideration during the first round of informal consultations on the annual draft General Assembly resolution on oceans and the law of the sea. This would enable an exchange on the proposed topics during the first round of informal consultations and also allow for continued discussion during the second round of informal consultations, when the topic of focus would be agreed upon. The meeting noted that this method for making proposals had been successfully used in the past and could also facilitate the timely identification of suitable experts.

91. The Director of the Division for Ocean Affairs and the Law of the Sea provided an update on the status of the Voluntary Trust Fund for the purpose of assisting developing countries, in particular small island developing States and landlocked developing States, to attend the meetings of the Informal Consultative Process. It was pointed out that the Voluntary Trust Fund played an important role in facilitating the participation of representatives and panellists from developing States in meetings of the Informal Consultative Process and delegations were invited to consider contributing to it. New Zealand noted that its contribution to the Fund signalled the importance it assigned to the Informal Consultative Process and to the participation of developing States and small island developing States therein.

Agenda Item 6

Issues that Could Benefit from Attention in the Future Work of the General Assembly on Oceans and the Law of the Sea

92. The Co-Chairs drew attention to the composite streamlined list of issues that could benefit from attention in the future work of the General Assembly on oceans and the law of the sea and invited comments from delegations. No delegation requested the floor under this agenda item. The Co-Chairs invited any delegation wishing to propose additional issues for inclusion in the list to submit them to the Co-Chair or the Secretariat in writing before 30 May 2014. Subsequently, the Secretariat has received a proposal to add to the list of issues, "An examination of the threats, including cumulative impacts, to marine species from indirect human actions and an exploration of practical, ecosystem-based approaches to mitigate those threats. Such threats could include chemical and noise pollution, coastal development and other indirect human threats."

Notification of Amendments to the 1996 Protocol to the Convention on the Prevention of Marine Pollution by Dumping of Wastes and Other Matter (London Protocol 1996)†

1. This is to notify, in accordance with Article 21.4 of the London Protocol 1996, all national focal points in administrations responsible for waste disposal at sea under the London Convention and Protocol that the 8th Meeting of Contracting Parties to the Protocol, convened from 14 to 18 October 2013, agreed to amend the Protocol by adopting Resolution LP.4(8), in order to regulate the placement of matter for ocean fertilization and other geoengineering activities. The text of Resolution LP.4(8) is attached in the annex hereto.

2. In accordance with Article 21.3 of the Protocol, the amendments concerned, having been adopted on Friday, 18 October 2013, shall enter into force for the Contracting Parties which have accepted it on the sixtieth day after two-thirds of the Contracting Parties shall have deposited an instrument of acceptance of the amendment with the Organization. Thereafter the amendment shall enter into force for any other Contracting Party on the sixtieth day after the date on which that Contracting Party has deposited its instrument of acceptance of the amendment.

3. The full record of the discussion on the amendments and their adoption can be found in the report of the 35th Consultative Meeting/8th Meeting of Contracting Parties which will be distributed as soon as possible through the usual channels and in all six United Nations languages under the symbol LC 35/15.

---

† This document was provided by the International Maritime Organization and is extracted from IMO Doc. LC-LP.1/Circ.61, 25 November 2013. The document has been edited for publication in the *Ocean Yearbook*.

Ocean Yearbook 29: 663–675

Annex

Resolution LP.4(8)
On the Amendment to the London Protocol to Regulate the
Placement of Matter for Ocean Fertilization and Other Marine
Geoengineering Activities (Adopted on 18 October 2013)

The Eighth Meeting of Contracting Parties to the 1996 Protocol
to the Convention on the Prevention of Marine Pollution by
Dumping of Wastes and Other Matter 1972,

RECALLING the objectives of the 1996 Protocol to the London Convention
("London Protocol") that include the protection and preservation of the marine
environment from all sources of pollution,

RECALLING that, in implementing the London Protocol, Contracting Parties
are obliged to apply a precautionary approach to environmental protection,

RECOGNIZING the importance of the conservation and sustainable use of
the oceans and seas and of their resources for sustainable development and
that oceans, seas and coastal areas form an integrated and essential component of the Earth's ecosystem and are critical to sustaining it,

NOTING the ongoing work on geoengineering within the context of the
Intergovernmental Panel on Climate Change (IPCC) and the relevant parts of
the IPCC Fifth Assessment Report as well as the outcomes of the IPCC expert
meeting on geoengineering (Lima, Peru, 2011),

NOTING United Nations General Assembly Resolution A/RES/67/78 on
"Oceans and the law of the sea" which recalled the importance of marine scientific research for understanding and conserving the world's marine environment and resources; and United Nations General Assembly Resolution 62/215,
concerning "Oceans and the law of the sea," adopted on 22 December 2007,
which in its paragraph 98 "encourages States to support the further study and
enhance understanding of ocean iron fertilization,"

RECALLING Resolution LC-LP.1(2008) that agreed that the scope of the London
Convention and the London Protocol includes ocean fertilization activities,

REITERATING ongoing concerns about the potential environmental
impacts of ocean fertilization and noting the concerns about ocean fertiliza-
tion expressed by, inter alia, the United Nations General Assembly, the United
Nations Conference on Sustainable Development, the Conference of the
Parties to the Convention on Biological Diversity and the Intergovernmental
Oceanographic Commission of UNESCO,

RECALLING Resolution LC-LP.2(2010) which affirmed that the London Convention and the London Protocol should continue to work towards providing a global, transparent and effective control and regulatory mechanism for ocean fertilization and other activities that fall within the scope of the London Convention and the London Protocol and have the potential to cause harm to the marine environment,

CONCERNED about the potential widespread, long-lasting or severe impacts on the marine environment of the placement of matter from unregulated ocean fertilization activities and other proposed marine geoengineering techniques, and determined to put in place a science-based, global, transparent and effective control and regulatory mechanism for such activities,

NOTING decisions X/33 and XI/20 of the Conference of the Parties to the Convention on Biological Diversity which invited Parties to ensure, in accordance with the precautionary approach, that no climate-related geoengineering activities take place "in the absence of science-based, global, transparent and effective control and regulatory mechanisms for geoengineering and that the Eleventh Conference of the Parties to the Convention on Biological Diversity concluded "that there is no single geoengineering approach that currently meets basic criteria for effectiveness, safety and affordability and that approaches may prove difficult to deploy or govern,"

EMPHASIZING that ocean fertilization and other types of marine geoengineering should not be considered as a substitute for mitigation measures to reduce carbon dioxide emissions,

1. ADOPTS the following amendments to the London Protocol, in accordance with Article 21 of the Protocol, as set out in the annex to this resolution;

2. REAFFIRMS that Resolutions LC-LP.1(2008) and LC-LP.2(2010) continue to apply for all Contracting Parties, pending the entry into force of the amendments to the London Protocol set out in the annex to this resolution for those Contracting Parties that accept them;

3. CONFIRMS that the Assessment Framework for Scientific Research involving Ocean Fertilization adopted by the Contracting Parties to the London Convention and the London Protocol in 2010 is the relevant specific assessment framework referred to in Annex 4 for ocean fertilization and should continue to be used to determine, with utmost caution, whether a proposed ocean fertilization activity constitutes legitimate scientific research that is not contrary to the aims of the London Protocol;

4. REAFFIRMS that new and relevant scientific information and knowledge on ocean fertilization and other marine geoengineering activities should continue to be reviewed by the Contracting Parties to the London Protocol in the context of the amendments;

5. DECIDES that the Contracting Parties to the London Protocol should continue to develop guidance for listing additional marine geoengineering[1] activities in Annex 4 that includes a multi-stakeholder approach consistent with Article 21; and

6. DECIDES ALSO that Contracting Parties to the London Protocol should undertake further work to develop the arrangements for seeking independent expert advice referred to in paragraph 12 of Annex 5.

Annex

Amendments to Article 1 and New Article 6bis and New Annexes 4 and 5
Article 1
Definitions
Add new paragraph, as follows:

"5bis "Marine geoengineering" means a deliberate intervention in the marine environment to manipulate natural processes, including to counteract anthropogenic climate change and/or its impacts, and that has the potential to result in deleterious effects, especially where those effects may be widespread, long lasting or severe."

Add new article, as follows:

"Article 6bis
Marine Geoengineering Activities

1. Contracting Parties shall not allow the placement of matter into the sea from vessels, aircraft, platforms or other man-made structures at sea for marine geoengineering activities listed in Annex 4, unless the listing provides that the activity or the subcategory of an activity may be authorized under a permit.

2. Contracting Parties shall adopt administrative or legislative measures to ensure that the issuance of permits and permit conditions comply with

---

1   See also explanatory text in the Report of the Meeting of Contracting Parties, paragraph 4.12.

provisions of Annex 5 and takes into account any Specific Assessment Framework developed for an activity and adopted by the Meeting of the Contracting Parties. A permit shall only be issued after the activity has undergone assessment which has determined that pollution of the marine environment from the proposed activity is, as far as practicable, prevented or reduced to a minimum. A permit shall only be issued if the outcome of the assessment is that the activity is not contrary to the aims of the Protocol.

3. Article 4 does not apply to activities listed in Annex 4."

Add new annex, as follows:

"Annex 4
Marine Geoengineering Activities

1. OCEAN FERTILIZATION

.1 Ocean fertilization is any activity undertaken by humans with the principal intention of stimulating primary productivity in the oceans. Ocean fertilization does not include conventional aquaculture or mariculture or the creation of artificial reefs.

.2 All ocean fertilization activities other than those referred to in paragraph .3 shall not be permitted.

.3 An ocean fertilization activity may only be considered for a permit if it is assessed as constituting legitimate scientific research taking into account any specific placement assessment framework."

Add new annex, as follows:

"Annex 5
*Assessment Framework for Matter that May be Considered for Placement Under Annex 4
General*

1. The purpose of this Framework is:
   .1 to assess placement activities listed in Annex 4; and
   .2 to be the basis for developing Specific Assessment Frameworks for placement activities listed in Annex 4.

2. Specific Assessment Frameworks developed for placement activities listed in Annex 4 shall meet the requirements of this annex and may provide further guidance for assessing and issuing permits.

3. Parties meeting the terms of any Specific Assessment Framework that has been adopted by the Parties shall be deemed to be in compliance with this annex.

Description of Activity

4. It first has to be determined whether the proposed activity is an activity covered by the listing in Annex 4 and may be permitted in accordance with that annex. The determination requires a full description of the proposed placement activity, including its purpose and covering all stages. It furthermore requires a description of both the working practices during the different stages and the wastes produced (if any) in the relevant stage.

5. The proposal shall demonstrate that:
    *   the proposed activity is for a purpose other than mere disposal;
    *   it is designed to fulfil its purpose;
    *   the rationale, goals, methods, scale, timings and locations as well as predicted benefits and risks are stated as a clear justification for the proposal;
    *   the proposed activity has the financial resources available to fulfil the programme of work before it commences.

6. A detailed description and characterization of the placement and all its constituents is an essential precondition for the assessment of the proposed activity and the basis for a decision as to whether a permit may be issued. If the proposed activity is so poorly characterized that proper assessment cannot be made a permit shall not be issued.

Marine Scientific Research related to Marine Geoengineering

7. Potential marine geoengineering techniques may require specific marine scientific research in order to, inter alia:
    *   better understand the natural processes which will be affected;
    *   understand their potential impacts on the marine environment;
    *   understand their potential efficacy for geoengineering purposes; and
    *   be able to effectively apply the assessment framework(s) to proposals for marine geoengineering.

8. In case of such a specific marine scientific research activity, the following considerations apply:
    *   the proposed activity is designed to answer questions that will add to scientific knowledge. Proposals should state their rationale, research goals, scientific hypotheses and methods, scale, timings, duration and

locations with clear justification for why the expected outcomes cannot reasonably be achieved by other methods.

· the research methodology to be applied should be appropriate
and based on best available scientific knowledge and technology.
The methodology should be described in sufficient detail to allow a
peer review.

· the proposed activity is subject to scientific peer review at appropriate
stages in the assessment process.

· economic interests do not influence the design, conduct and/or outcomes of the proposed activity. There should not be any financial
and/or economic gain arising directly from the experiment or its outcomes. This does not preclude payment for services rendered in support of the experiment or future financial impacts of patented
technology.

· the proponents of the proposed activity make a commitment to publish the results in peer reviewed scientific publications and include a
plan in the proposal to make the data and outcomes publicly available
in an appropriate and specified time frame.

· the proposed activity has the financial resources available before the
work commences to fulfil the program of work.

9. Paragraphs 4 and 6 above also apply to marine scientific research.

Consultation

10. Where the placement activity proposed for consideration by a Contracting
Party may have any effect in any area of the sea in which another State is
entitled to exercise jurisdiction in accordance with international law or
in any area of the sea beyond the jurisdiction of any State, potentially
affected countries and relevant regional intergovernmental agreements
and arrangements should be identified and notified and a plan should be
developed for ongoing consultations on the potential impacts, and to
encourage scientific cooperation.

11. Contracting Parties should encourage proponents of listed activities to
initiate early consultations with stakeholders so that they can address
any issues prior to submitting proposals. Contracting Parties shall
establish a consultation process with all relevant stakeholders nationally or internationally when a proposal is submitted. This consultation
process shall be carried out during the assessment process and before
a final permit decision is made. Consent should be sought from all
countries with jurisdiction or interests in the region of potential

impact without prejudice to international law. Where the placement activity has the potential to have any effects on an area subject to a regional intergovernmental agreement or arrangement, the process should include consultation with the relevant regional organization, with a view to ensuring consistency with applicable regional objectives and requirements.

12. Contracting Parties should consider any advice on proposals for activities listed in Annex 4 from independent international experts or an independent international advisory group of experts, especially in situations where paragraph 10 applies. The advice could address scientific, technical, social or economic aspects of the proposal. It shall, as appropriate, include a peer review of the information and data provided by the proponent with regard to its scientific and technical quality. In situations where paragraph 10 applies, potentially affected countries could seek such advice from independent international experts or an independent international advisory group of experts.

Information for Assessment

13. A common set of information is required for each of the assessment elements of the framework below, namely:
   · Placement site selection
   · Assessment of matter to be placed into the marine environment
   · Assessment of potential effects including the Impact Hypothesis
   · Risk management
   · Monitoring including the environmental baseline.

Placement Site Selection

14. In order to address placement site selection, Contracting Parties shall require the following information, as appropriate, to evaluate and to justify the selection of the site(s):
   · the physical, geological, chemical and biological conditions at the proposed site and the area of potential impact, and the uncertainties in these conditions in relation to the proposed activity;
   · the impact on amenities, values and other uses of the sea at the proposed site and in the area of potential impacts;
   · any constituent fluxes associated with the activity in relation to existing fluxes of substances in the marine environment; and
   · economic and operational feasibility.

Assessment of Matter to be Placed into the Marine Environment

15.   Characterization and assessment of matter proposed to be placed into the marine environment, including its constituents shall take into account as appropriate:

.1   origin, total amount, form and average composition and fate;
.2   properties: physical, chemical, biochemical and biological;
.3   toxicity;
.4   persistence: physical, chemical and biological; and
.5   accumulation and biotransformation in biological materials or sediments.

Assessment of Potential Effects

16.   Assessment of potential effects shall lead to the "Impact Hypothesis," a concise statement of the expected consequences of the placement activity within the area of the activity and within the area of potential impacts, including transboundary effects. It provides a basis for deciding whether to approve, reject or suggest revisions to the proposed placement activity and for defining risk management and mitigation measures and environmental monitoring requirements.

17.   The assessment of potential effects should integrate information on the characteristics of the proposed placement activity, conditions at the proposed site(s), any relevant fluxes, and any proposed construction techniques. The assessment shall specify the potential effects on human health, on marine ecosystem structure and dynamics including sensitivity of species, populations, communities, habitats and processes, amenities and other legitimate uses of the sea. It shall define the nature, temporal and spatial scales and duration of expected impacts based on reasonably conservative assumptions.

18.   An analysis of the proposed placement activity should be considered in the light of an assessment of the following concerns: human health risks, environmental costs, hazards, (including accidents), economics and exclusion of future uses. Cumulative impacts from repeated activities or from other activities may also be a relevant consideration. If this assessment reveals that adequate information is not available to determine the likely effects of the proposed placement activity then this activity shall not be considered further.

19.   Each assessment of potential effects shall conclude with a statement supporting a decision to approve, reject or suggest revisions to a proposed placement activity.

Risk Management

20. Risk Management procedures are necessary to ensure that, as far as practicable, environmental risks are minimized, inter alia, through mitigation and contingency planning, and the benefits maximized and that a precautionary approach is applied.

21. Strategies to manage or mitigate risks need to be appropriate for the risks under consideration. They may be imposed as additional conditions by a Contracting Party or included as an intrinsic part of the proposal. The strategies may include temporal, spatial or operational restrictions.

22. Contingency planning will also need to be considered for responding to monitoring in cases where the Impact Hypothesis is found to be incorrect. This may include the cessation of placement activities.

Monitoring

23. A well-designed monitoring regime is necessary and should consider both short and long-term impacts and, where possible, determine whether the activity has achieved its purpose.

24. The purpose of monitoring is to verify that permit conditions are met – compliance monitoring – and that the assumptions made during the permit review and site selection process were correct and sufficient to protect the environment and human health – field monitoring. It is essential that such monitoring programmes have clearly defined objectives. The type, frequency and extent of monitoring will depend on the Impact Hypothesis as well as on predicted local and regional consequences.

25. Monitoring is also used to determine the area of impact and to ascertain that changes are within the range of those predicted. The establishment of baseline conditions prior to a placement activity as well as monitoring of control sites is essential for ongoing monitoring and the detection of any impacts beyond those predicted.

Permit and Permit Conditions

26. A decision to issue a permit shall only be made if:

    .1   the assessment has been satisfactorily completed and has shown that the proposed activity is an activity covered by the listing in Annex 4 and may be permitted in accordance with that annex;

    .2   the activity is designed to fulfil its purpose. It has to be demonstrated that the proposed activity has the financial resources available before it commences to fulfil the programme of work including any permit conditions requiring e.g. mitigation, contingency planning and monitoring;

.3   all impact evaluations are satisfactorily completed;

.4   the risk management and monitoring requirements have been determined;

.5   conditions are in place to ensure that, as far as practicable, environmental disturbance and detriment would be minimized and the benefits maximized;

.6   the consultation requirements are fulfilled pursuant to paragraphs 10, 11 and 12;

.7   it is determined that pollution of the marine environment from the proposed activity is, as far as practicable, prevented or reduced to a minimum, therefore not contrary to the aims of the Protocol.

27.   In case that adequate information is not available to make the determinations in paragraph 26, the permitting authority shall request additional information before taking a decision or shall not issue a permit.

28.   The provisions of the permit shall ensure, as far as practicable, that risks for human health and the marine environment are avoided, environmental disturbance and detriment are minimized and the benefits maximized. Any permit issued shall contain conditions specifying among others:

.1   the types and sources of matter to be placed;

.2   the location of the placement site(s);

.3   the methods to be used in achieving the placement activity;

.4   risk management, monitoring and reporting requirements; and

.5   removal and/or disposal/reuse/recycling of items, as appropriate, at the end of placement activity.

29.   Permits should be reviewed at regular intervals, taking into account the results of monitoring, the objectives of monitoring programmes and relevant research. Review of monitoring results will indicate whether field programmes need to be continued, revised or terminated and will contribute to informed decisions regarding the continuance, modification or revocation of permits. Monitoring provides an important feedback mechanism into future permitting decisions for the protection of human health and the marine environment.

Reporting

30.   The outcomes of any assessment and documentation of any permit issued shall be reported to the Secretariat and shall be made publicly

available at or shortly after the time the decision is made. The Secretariat should then inform Contracting Parties."

Consequential Amendments

Consequential amendments are shown, as follows:

Article 1.9 of the Protocol is amended as follows: "Permit" means permission granted in advance and in accordance with relevant measures adopted pursuant to Article 4.1.2, 6bis or 8.2

Article 3.1 of the Protocol is amended as follows: "In implementing this Protocol, Contracting Parties shall apply a precautionary approach to environmental protection from dumping of wastes or other matter or from placement of matter for marine geoengineering activities which may be considered for permits according to Annex 4."

Article 9.1.2 of the Protocol is amended as follows: "keep records of the nature and quantities of waste or other matter for which ~~dumping~~ permits have been issued and where practicable the quantities actually dumped, or placed in accordance with Article 6bis, and the location, time and method of dumping or placement; and"

Article 9.2 of the Protocol is amended as follows: "The appropriate authority or authorities of a Contracting Party shall issue permits in accordance with this Protocol in respect of wastes or other matter intended for dumping or, as provided for in Article 6bis, placement or, as provided for in Article 8.2, incineration at sea":

Article 9.3 of the Protocol is amended as follows: "In issuing permits, the appropriate authority or authorities shall comply with the requirements of Article 4 and Article 6bis, together with such additional criteria, measures and requirements as they may consider relevant."

Article 10.1.2 of the Protocol is amended as follows: "vessels and aircraft loading in its territory the wastes or other matter which are to be dumped, or incinerated, or placed in accordance with Article 6bis, at sea; and"

Article 10.1.3 of the Protocol is amended as follows: "vessels, aircraft and platforms or other man-made structures believed to be engaged in dumping, or incineration, or placement in accordance with Article 6bis, at sea in areas within which it is entitled to exercise jurisdiction in accordance with international law."

Article 13.1 of the Protocol is amended as follows: "Contracting Parties shall, through collaboration within the Organization and in coordination with other competent international organizations, promote bilateral and multilateral support for the prevention, reduction and where practicable elimination of pollution caused by dumping <u>or placement of matter for marine geoengineering activities</u> as provided for in this Protocol to those Contracting Parties that request it..."

Article 18.1 of the Protocol is amended as follows: "Meetings of Contracting Parties or Special Meetings of Contracting Parties shall keep under continuing review the implementation of this Protocol and evaluate its effectiveness with a view to identifying means of strengthening action, where necessary, to prevent, reduce and where practicable eliminate pollution caused by dumping, and incineration, <u>or placement in accordance with Article 6bis</u>, at sea of wastes or other matter. To these ends, Meetings of Contracting Parties or Special Meetings of Contracting Parties may".

Decision of the Council of the International Seabed Authority Relating to Amendments to the Regulations on Prospecting and Exploration for Polymetallic Nodules in the Area and Related Matters†

The Council of the International Seabed Authority,

1. *Adopts* the amendments to the Regulations on Prospecting and Exploration for Polymetallic Nodules in the Area as contained in the annex to the present document;

2. *Decides* to apply the amended Regulations provisionally from the date of their adoption by the Council, pending their approval by the Assembly of the International Seabed Authority;

3. *Requests* the Secretary-General, in the case of a pending application for approval of a plan of work for polymetallic nodules submitted prior to the entry into force of the amendments to the Regulations, to consult the applicant prior to the signature of the contract for exploration, with a view to incorporating any necessary revisions into the standard terms of contract;

4. *Requests* the Legal and Technical Commission of the Authority to make a recommendation for consideration by the Council at its twentieth session to bring Regulation 21 of the Regulations on Prospecting and Exploration for Polymetallic Sulphides in the Area[1] into line with Regulation 21 of the Regulations on Prospecting and Exploration for Cobalt-rich Ferromanganese Crusts in the Area;[2]

5. *Decides that*, pending the receipt of the recommendation of the Legal and Technical Commission referred to in paragraph 4, Regulation 21(1)(b) of the Regulations on Prospecting and Exploration for Polymetallic Sulphides in the Area shall not apply;

---

† Editors' Note.—This document was provided by the International Seabed Authority and is extracted from the Decision of the Council of the International Seabed Authority, Nineteenth session, 15–26 July 2013, Kingston, Jamaica, ISBA/19/C/17, 22 July 2013, available online: <http://www.isa.org.jm/en/mcode>.

1   ISBA/16/A/12/Rev.1.
2   ISBA/18/A/11.

© KONINKLIJKE BRILL NV, LEIDEN, 2015 | DOI 10.1163/9789004297234_026

6. *Further requests* the Legal and Technical Commission to review the provisions of the Regulations on Prospecting and Exploration for Polymetallic Nodules in the Area, the Regulations on Prospecting and Exploration for Polymetallic Sulphides and the Regulations on Prospecting and Exploration for Cobalt-rich Ferromanganese Crusts in the Area relating to the monopolization of activities in the Area and the option of offering an equity interest in a joint venture arrangement with a view to possibly aligning all three sets of regulations in this respect and to make a recommendation thereon for consideration by the Council at its twentieth session.

190th meeting
22 July 2013

Annex

Regulations on Prospecting and Exploration for Polymetallic Nodules in the Area
Preamble

In accordance with the United Nations Convention on the Law of the Sea of 10 December 1982 ("the Convention"), the seabed and ocean floor and the subsoil thereof beyond the limits of national jurisdiction, as well as its resources, are the common heritage of mankind, the exploration and exploitation of which shall be carried out for the benefit of mankind as a whole, on whose behalf the International Seabed Authority acts. The objective of this set of Regulations is to provide for prospecting and exploration for polymetallic nodules.

Part I. Introduction

Regulation 1. Use of Terms and Scope

1. Terms used in the Convention shall have the same meaning in these Regulations.
2. In accordance with the Agreement relating to the Implementation of Part XI of the United Nations Convention on the Law of the Sea of 10 December 1982 ("the Agreement"), the provisions of the Agreement and Part XI of the Convention shall be interpreted and applied together as a

single instrument. These Regulations and references in these Regulations to the Convention are to be interpreted and applied accordingly.

3.   For the purposes of these Regulations:

(a)   "Exploitation" means the recovery for commercial purposes of polymetallic nodules in the Area and the extraction of minerals therefrom, including the construction and operation of mining, processing and transportation systems, for the production and marketing of metals;

(b)   "Exploration" means the searching for deposits of polymetallic nodules in the Area with exclusive rights, the analysis of such deposits, the use and testing of recovery systems and equipment, processing facilities and transportation systems and the carrying out of studies of the environmental, technical, economic, commercial and other appropriate factors that must be taken into account in exploitation;

(c)   "Marine environment" includes the physical, chemical, geological and biological components, conditions and factors which interact and determine the productivity, state, condition and quality of the marine ecosystem, the waters of the seas and oceans and the airspace above those waters, as well as the seabed and ocean floor and subsoil thereof;

(d)   "Polymetallic nodules" means one of the resources of the Area consisting of any deposit or accretion of nodules, on or just below the surface of the deep seabed, which contain manganese, nickel, cobalt and copper;

(e)   "Prospecting" means the search for deposits of polymetallic nodules in the Area, including estimation of the composition, sizes and distributions of deposits of polymetallic nodules and their economic values, without any exclusive rights;

(f)   "Serious harm to the marine environment" means any effect from activities in the Area on the marine environment which represents a significant adverse change in the marine environment determined according to the rules, regulations and procedures adopted by the Authority on the basis of internationally recognized standards and practices.

4.   These Regulations shall not in any way affect the freedom of scientific research, pursuant to Article 87 of the Convention, or the right to conduct marine scientific research in the Area pursuant to Articles 143 and 256 of the Convention. Nothing in these Regulations shall be construed in such a way as to restrict the exercise by States of the freedom of the high seas as reflected in Article 87 of the Convention.

5.   These Regulations may be supplemented by further rules, regulations and procedures, in particular on the protection and preservation of the

marine environment. These Regulations shall be subject to the provisions of the Convention and the Agreement and other rules of international law not incompatible with the Convention.

Part II. Prospecting

Regulation 2. Prospecting

1. Prospecting shall be conducted in accordance with the Convention and these Regulations and may commence only after the prospector has been informed by the Secretary-General that its notification has been recorded pursuant to Regulation 4(2).
2. Prospectors and the Authority shall apply a precautionary approach, as reflected in principle 15 of the Rio Declaration on Environment and Development.[3] Prospecting shall not be undertaken if substantial evidence indicates the risk of serious harm to the marine environment.
3. Prospecting shall not be undertaken in an area covered by an approved plan of work for exploration for polymetallic nodules or in a reserved area; nor may there be prospecting in an area which the Council has disapproved for exploitation because of the risk of serious harm to the marine environment.
4. Prospecting shall not confer on the prospector any rights with respect to resources. A prospector may, however, recover a reasonable quantity of minerals, being the quantity necessary for testing and not for commercial use.
5. There shall be no time limit on prospecting, except that prospecting in a particular area shall cease upon written notification to the prospector by the Secretary-General that a plan of work for exploration has been approved with regard to that area.
6. Prospecting may be conducted simultaneously by more than one prospector in the same area or areas.

Regulation 3. Notification of Prospecting

1. A proposed prospector shall notify the Authority of its intention to engage in prospecting.

---

3 *Report of the United Nations Conference on Environment and Development, Rio de Janeiro, 3–14 June 1992* (United Nations publication, Sales No. E.93.I.8 and corrigendum), vol. I, *Resolutions adopted by the Conference*, Resolution 1, Annex I.

2.   Each notification of prospecting shall be in the form prescribed in Annex I to these Regulations, shall be addressed to the Secretary-General and shall conform to the requirements of these Regulations.

3.   Each notification shall be submitted:
      (a) In the case of a State, by the authority designated for that purpose by it;
      (b) In the case of an entity, by its designated representative;
      (c) In the case of the Enterprise, by its competent authority.

4.   Each notification shall be in one of the languages of the Authority and shall contain:
      (a) The name, nationality and address of the proposed prospector and its designated representative;
      (b) The coordinates of the broad area or areas within which prospecting is to be conducted, in accordance with the most recent generally accepted international standard used by the Authority;
      (c) A general description of the prospecting programme, including the proposed date of commencement and its approximate duration;
      (d) A satisfactory written undertaking that the proposed prospector will:
           (i)   Comply with the Convention and the relevant rules, regulations and procedures of the Authority concerning:
                 a. Cooperation in the training programmes in connection with marine scientific research and transfer of technology referred to in Articles 143 and 144 of the Convention; and
                 b. Protection and preservation of the marine environment;
           (ii) Accept verification by the Authority of compliance therewith; and
           (iii) Make available to the Authority, as far as practicable, such data as may be relevant to the protection and preservation of the marine environment.

Regulation 4. Consideration of Notifications

1.   The Secretary-General shall acknowledge in writing receipt of each notification submitted under Regulation 3, specifying the date of receipt.

2.   The Secretary-General shall review and act on the notification within 45 days of its receipt. If the notification conforms with the requirements of the Convention and these Regulations, the Secretary-General shall record the particulars of the notification in a register maintained for that purpose and shall inform the prospector in writing that the notification has been so recorded.

3. The Secretary-General shall, within 45 days of receipt of the notification, inform the proposed prospector in writing if the notification includes any part of an area included in an approved plan of work for exploration or exploitation of any category of resources, or any part of a reserved area, or any part of an area which has been disapproved by the Council for exploitation because of the risk of serious harm to the marine environment, or if the written undertaking is not satisfactory, and shall provide the proposed prospector with a written statement of reasons. In such cases, the proposed prospector may, within 90 days, submit an amended notification. The Secretary-General shall, within 45 days, review and act upon such amended notification.

4. A prospector shall inform the Secretary-General in writing of any change in the information contained in the notification.

5. The Secretary-General shall not release any particulars contained in the notification except with the written consent of the prospector. The Secretary-General shall, however, from time to time inform all members of the Authority of the identity of prospectors and the general areas in which prospecting is being conducted.

Regulation 5. Protection and Preservation of the Marine Environment during Prospecting

1. Each prospector shall take necessary measures to prevent, reduce and control pollution and other hazards to the marine environment arising from prospecting, as far as reasonably possible, applying a precautionary approach and best environmental practices. In particular, each prospector shall minimize or eliminate:
   (a) Adverse environmental impacts from prospecting; and
   (b) Actual or potential conflicts or interference with existing or planned marine scientific research activities, in accordance with the relevant future guidelines in this regard.

2. Prospectors shall cooperate with the Authority in the establishment and implementation of programmes for monitoring and evaluating the potential impacts of the exploration for and exploitation of polymetallic nodules on the marine environment.

3. A prospector shall immediately notify the Secretary-General in writing, using the most effective means, of any incident arising from prospecting which has caused, is causing or poses a threat of serious harm to the marine environment. Upon receipt of such notification the Secretary-General shall act in a manner consistent with Regulation 33.

Regulation 6. Annual Report

1.   A prospector shall, within 90 days of the end of each calendar year, sub-
       mit a report to the Authority on the status of prospecting. Such reports
       shall be submitted by the Secretary-General to the Legal and Technical
       Commission. Each such report shall contain:
       (a) A general description of the status of prospecting and of the results
            obtained;
       (b) Information on compliance with the undertakings referred to in
            Regulation 3(4)(d); and
       (c) Information on adherence to the relevant guidelines in this regard.
2.   If the prospector intends to claim expenditures for prospecting as part of
       the development costs incurred prior to the commencement of commer-
       cial production, the prospector shall submit an annual statement, in con-
       formity with internationally accepted accounting principles and certified
       by a duly qualified firm of public accountants, of the actual and direct
       expenditures incurred by the prospector in carrying out prospecting.

Regulation 7. Confidentiality of Data and Information from Prospecting Contained in the Annual Report

1.   The Secretary-General shall ensure the confidentiality of all data and
       information contained in the reports submitted under Regulation 6
       applying mutatis mutandis the provisions of Regulations 36 and 37, pro-
       vided that data and information relating to the protection and preserva-
       tion of the marine environment, in particular those from environmental
       monitoring programmes, shall not be considered confidential. The pros-
       pector may request that such data not be disclosed for up to three years
       following the date of their submission.
2.   The Secretary-General may, at any time, with the consent of the prospec-
       tor concerned, release data and information relating to prospecting in an
       area in respect of which a notification has been submitted. If, after hav-
       ing made reasonable efforts for at least two years, the Secretary-General
       determines that the prospector no longer exists or cannot be located, the
       Secretary-General may release such data and information.

Regulation 8. Objects of an Archaeological or Historical Nature

A prospector shall immediately notify the Secretary-General in writing of
any finding in the Area of an object of actual or potential archaeological or

historical nature and its location. The Secretary-General shall transmit such information to the Director General of the United Nations Educational, Scientific and Cultural Organization.

Part III. Applications for Approval of Plans of Work for Exploration in the Form of Contracts

Section 1. General Provisions

Regulation 9. General

Subject to the provisions of the Convention, the following may apply to the Authority for approval of plans of work for exploration:

(a) The Enterprise, on its own behalf or in a joint arrangement;

(b) States parties, State enterprises or natural or juridical persons which possess the nationality of States or are effectively controlled by them or their nationals, when sponsored by such States, or any group of the foregoing which meets the requirements of these Regulations.

Section 2. Content of Applications

Regulation 10. Form of Applications

1. Each application for approval of a plan of work for exploration shall be in the form prescribed in Annex II to these Regulations, shall be addressed to the Secretary-General and shall conform to the requirements of these Regulations.
2. Each application shall be submitted:
    (a) In the case of a State, by the authority designated for that purpose by it;
    (b) In the case of an entity, by its designated representative or the authority designated for that purpose by the sponsoring State or States; and
    (c) In the case of the Enterprise, by its competent authority.
3. Each application by a State enterprise or one of the entities referred to in Regulation 9(b) shall also contain:
    (a) Sufficient information to determine the nationality of the applicant or the identity of the State or States by which, or by whose nationals, the applicant is effectively controlled; and
    (b) The principal place of business or domicile and, if applicable, place of registration of the applicant.

4. Each application submitted by a partnership or consortium of entities shall contain the required information in respect of each member of the partnership or consortium.

Regulation 11. Certificate of Sponsorship

1. Each application by a State enterprise or one of the entities referred to in Regulation 9(b) shall be accompanied by a certificate of sponsorship issued by the State of which it is a national or by which or by whose nationals it is effectively controlled. If the applicant has more than one nationality, as in the case of a partnership or consortium of entities from more than one State, each State involved shall issue a certificate of sponsorship.
2. Where the applicant has the nationality of one State but is effectively controlled by another State or its nationals, each State involved shall issue a certificate of sponsorship.
3. Each certificate of sponsorship shall be duly signed on behalf of the State by which it is submitted and shall contain:
    (a) The name of the applicant;
    (b) The name of the sponsoring State;
    (c) A statement that the applicant is:
         (i) A national of the sponsoring State; or
         (ii) Subject to the effective control of the sponsoring State or its nationals;
    (d) A statement by the sponsoring State that it sponsors the applicant;
    (e) The date of deposit by the sponsoring State of its instrument of ratification of, or accession or succession to, the Convention;
    (f) A declaration that the sponsoring State assumes responsibility in accordance with Articles 139 and 153(4) of the Convention and Article 4(4) of Annex III to the Convention.
4. States or entities in a joint arrangement with the Enterprise shall also comply with this regulation.

Regulation 12. Financial and Technical Capabilities

1. Each application for approval of a plan of work for exploration shall contain specific and sufficient information to enable the Council to determine whether the applicant is financially and technically capable of carrying out the proposed plan of work for exploration and of fulfilling its financial obligations to the Authority.

2.   An application for approval of a plan of work for exploration submitted on behalf of a State or entity, or any component of such entity, referred to in paragraph 1(a)(ii) or (iii) of resolution II, other than a registered pioneer investor, which has already undertaken substantial activities in the Area prior to the entry into force of the Convention, or its successor in interest, shall be considered to have met the financial and technical qualifications necessary for approval of a plan of work for exploration if the sponsoring State or States certify that the applicant has expended an amount equivalent to at least 30 million United States dollars in research and exploration activities and has expended no less than 10 per cent of that amount in the location, survey and evaluation of the area referred to in the plan of work for exploration.

3.   An application for approval of a plan of work for exploration by the Enterprise shall include a statement by its competent authority certifying that the Enterprise has the necessary financial resources to meet the estimated costs of the proposed plan of work for exploration.

4.   An application for approval of a plan of work for exploration by a State or a State enterprise, other than a registered pioneer investor or an entity referred to in paragraph 1(a)(ii) or (iii) of resolution II, shall include a statement by the State or the sponsoring State certifying that the applicant has the necessary financial resources to meet the estimated costs of the proposed plan of work for exploration.

5.   An application for approval of a plan of work for exploration by an entity, other than a registered pioneer investor or an entity referred to in paragraph 1(a)(ii) or (iii) of resolution II, shall include copies of its audited financial statements, including balance sheets and profit-and-loss statements, for the most recent three years, in conformity with internationally accepted accounting principles and certified by a duly qualified firm of public accountants.

6.   If the applicant is a newly organized entity and a certified balance sheet is not available, the application shall include a pro forma balance sheet certified by an appropriate official of the applicant.

7.   If the applicant is a subsidiary of another entity, the application shall include copies of such financial statements of that entity and a statement from that entity, in conformity with internationally accepted accounting principles and certified by a duly qualified firm of public accountants, that the applicant will have the financial resources to carry out the plan of work for exploration.

8.   If the applicant is controlled by a State or a State enterprise, the application shall include a statement from the State or State enterprise certifying that the applicant will have the financial resources to carry out the plan of work for exploration.

9.   Where an applicant seeking approval of a plan of work for exploration
      intends to finance the proposed plan of work for exploration by borrow-
      ings, its application shall include the amount of such borrowings, the
      repayment period and the interest rate.
10.   Except as provided for in paragraph 2, each application shall include:
      (a) A general description of the applicant's previous experience, knowl-
           edge, skills, technical qualifications and expertise relevant to the
           proposed plan of work for exploration;
      (b) A general description of the equipment and methods expected to
           be used in carrying out the proposed plan of work for exploration
           and other relevant non-proprietary information about the charac-
           teristics of such technology; and
      (c) A general description of the applicant's financial and technical
           capability to respond to any incident or activity which causes seri-
           ous harm to the marine environment.
11.   Where the applicant is a partnership or consortium of entities in a joint
      arrangement, each member of the partnership or consortium shall pro-
      vide the information required by this regulation.

Regulation 13. Previous Contracts with the Authority

Where the applicant or, in the case of an application by a partnership or consortium of entities in a joint arrangement, any member of the partnership or
consortium, has previously been awarded any contract with the Authority, the
application shall include:

(a) The date of the previous contract or contracts;
(b) The date, reference number and title of each report submitted to
     the Authority in connection with the contract or contracts; and
(c) The date of termination of the contract or contracts, if applicable.

Regulation 14. Undertakings

Each applicant, including the Enterprise, shall, as part of its application for
approval of a plan of work for exploration, provide a written undertaking to
the Authority that it will:

(a) Accept as enforceable and comply with the applicable obliga-
     tions created by the provisions of the Convention and the rules,
     regulations and procedures of the Authority, the decisions of the

organs of the Authority and the terms of its contracts with the Authority;

(b) Accept control by the Authority of activities in the Area, as authorized by the Convention; and

(c) Provide the Authority with a written assurance that its obligations under the contract will be fulfilled in good faith.

Regulation 15. Total Area Covered by the Application

Each application for approval of a plan of work for exploration shall define the boundaries of the area under application by a list of coordinates in accordance with the most recent generally accepted international standard used by the Authority. Applications other than those under Regulation 17 shall cover a total area, which need not be a single continuous area, sufficiently large and of sufficient estimated commercial value to allow two mining operations. The applicant shall indicate the coordinates dividing the area into two parts of equal estimated commercial value. The area to be allocated to the applicant shall be subject to the provisions of Regulation 25.

Regulation 16. Data and Information to be Submitted before the Designation of a Reserved Area

1. Each application shall contain sufficient data and information, as prescribed in Section II of Annex II to these Regulations, with respect to the area under application to enable the Council, on the recommendation of the Legal and Technical Commission, to designate a reserved area based on the estimated commercial value of each part. Such data and information shall consist of data available to the applicant with respect to both parts of the area under application, including the data used to determine their commercial value.

2. The Council, on the basis of the data and information submitted by the applicant pursuant to Section II of Annex II to these Regulations, if found satisfactory, and taking into account the recommendation of the Legal and Technical Commission, shall designate the part of the area under application which is to be a reserved area. The area so designated shall become a reserved area as soon as the plan of work for exploration for the non-reserved area is approved and the contract is signed. If the Council determines that additional information, consistent with these Regulations and Annex II, is needed to designate the reserved area, it shall refer the matter back to the Commission for further consideration, specifying the additional information required.

3. Once the plan of work for exploration is approved and a contract has been issued, the data and information transferred to the Authority by the applicant in respect of the reserved area may be disclosed by the Authority in accordance with Article 14(3) of Annex III to the Convention.

Regulation 17. Applications for Approval of Plans of Work with Respect to a Reserved Area

1. Any State which is a developing State or any natural or juridical person sponsored by it and effectively controlled by it or by any other developing State, or any group of the foregoing, may notify the Authority that it wishes to submit a plan of work for exploration with respect to a reserved area. The Secretary-General shall forward such notification to the Enterprise, which shall inform the Secretary-General in writing within six months whether or not it intends to carry out activities in that area. If the Enterprise intends to carry out activities in that area, it shall, pursuant to paragraph 4, also inform in writing the contractor whose application for approval of a plan of work for exploration originally included that area.

2. An application for approval of a plan of work for exploration in respect of a reserved area may be submitted at any time after such an area becomes available following a decision by the Enterprise that it does not intend to carry out activities in that area or where the Enterprise has not, within six months of the notification by the Secretary-General, either taken a decision on whether it intends to carry out activities in that area or notified the Secretary-General in writing that it is engaged in discussions regarding a potential joint venture. In the latter instance, the Enterprise shall have one year from the date of such notification in which to decide whether to conduct activities in that area.

3. If the Enterprise or a developing State or one of the entities referred to in paragraph 1 does not submit an application for approval of a plan of work for exploration for activities in a reserved area within 15 years of the commencement by the Enterprise of its functions independent of the Secretariat of the Authority or within 15 years of the date on which that area is reserved for the Authority, whichever is the later, the contractor whose application for approval of a plan of work for exploration originally included that area shall be entitled to apply for a plan of work for exploration for that area provided it offers in good faith to include the Enterprise as a joint-venture partner.

4. A contractor has the right of first refusal to enter into a joint venture arrangement with the Enterprise for exploration of the area which was

included in its application for approval of a plan of work for exploration and which was designated by the Council as a reserved area.

Regulation 18. Data and Information to be Submitted for Approval of the Plan of Work for Exploration

Each applicant shall submit, with a view to receiving approval of the plan of work for exploration in the form of a contract, the following information:

(a)   A general description and a schedule of the proposed exploration programme, including the programme of activities for the immediate five-year period, such as studies to be undertaken in respect of the environmental, technical, economic and other appropriate factors that must be taken into account in exploration;

(b)   A description of the programme for oceanographic and environmental baseline studies in accordance with these Regulations and any environmental rules, regulations and procedures established by the Authority that would enable an assessment of the potential environmental impact, including, but not restricted to, the impact on biodiversity, of the proposed exploration activities, taking into account any recommendations issued by the Legal and Technical Commission;

(c)   A preliminary assessment of the possible impact of the proposed exploration activities on the marine environment;

(d)   A description of proposed measures for the prevention, reduction and control of pollution and other hazards, as well as possible impacts, to the marine environment;

(e)   Data necessary for the Council to make the determination it is required to make in accordance with Regulation 12(1); and

(f)   A schedule of anticipated yearly expenditures in respect of the programme of activities for the immediate five-year period.

Section 3. Fees

Regulation 19. Fee for Applications

1.   The fee for processing an application for approval of a plan of work for exploration for polymetallic nodules shall be a fixed amount of 500,000 United States dollars or its equivalent in a freely convertible currency, to be paid in full at the time of the submission of an application.

2.   If the administrative costs incurred by the Authority in processing an application are less than the fixed amount indicated in paragraph 1 above, the Authority shall refund the difference to the applicant. If the administrative costs incurred by the Authority in processing an application are more than the fixed amount indicated in paragraph 1 above, the applicant shall pay the difference to the Authority, provided that any additional amount to be paid by the applicant shall not exceed 10 per cent of the fixed fee referred to in paragraph 1.

3.   Taking into account any criteria established for this purpose by the Finance Committee, the Secretary-General shall determine the amount of such differences as indicated in paragraph 2 above and notify the applicant of its amount. The notification shall include a statement of the expenditure incurred by the Authority. The amount due shall be paid by the applicant or reimbursed by the Authority within three months of the signing of the contract referred to in Regulation 23 below.

4.   The fixed amount referred to in paragraph 1 above shall be reviewed on a regular basis by the Council in order to ensure that it covers the expected administrative costs of processing applications and to avoid the need for applicants to pay additional amounts in accordance with paragraph 2 above.

Section 4. Processing of Applications

Regulation 20. Receipt, Acknowledgement and Safe Custody of Applications

1.   The Secretary-General shall:
   (a)   Acknowledge in writing within 30 days receipt of every application for approval of a plan of work for exploration submitted under this Part, specifying the date of receipt;
   (b)   Place the application together with the attachments and annexes thereto in safe custody and ensure the confidentiality of all confidential data and information contained in the application; and
   (c)   Notify the members of the Authority of the receipt of such application and circulate to them information of a general nature which is not confidential regarding the application.

Regulation 21. Consideration by the Legal and Technical Commission

1.   Upon receipt of an application for approval of a plan of work for exploration, the Secretary-General shall notify the members of the Legal and

Technical Commission and place consideration of the application as an item on the agenda for the next meeting of the Commission. The Commission shall consider only applications in respect of which notification and information has been circulated by the Secretary-General in accordance with Regulation 20(c) at least 30 days prior to the commencement of the meeting of the Commission at which they are to be considered.

2. The Commission shall examine applications in the order in which they are received.

3. The Commission shall determine if the applicant:
   (a) Has complied with the provisions of these Regulations;
   (b) Has given the undertakings and assurances specified in Regulation 14;
   (c) Possesses the financial and technical capability to carry out the proposed plan of work for exploration and has provided details as to its ability to comply promptly with emergency orders; and
   (d) Has satisfactorily discharged its obligations in relation to any previous contract with the Authority.

4. The Commission shall, in accordance with the requirements set forth in these Regulations and its procedures, determine whether the proposed plan of work for exploration will:
   (a) Provide for effective protection of human health and safety;
   (b) Provide for effective protection and preservation of the marine environment including, but not restricted to, the impact on biodiversity;
   (c) Ensure that installations are not established where interference may be caused to the use of recognized sea lanes essential to international navigation or in areas of intense fishing activity.

5. If the Commission makes the determinations specified in paragraph 3 and determines that the proposed plan of work for exploration meets the requirements of paragraph 4, the Commission shall recommend approval of the plan of work for exploration to the Council.

6. The Commission shall not recommend approval of the plan of work for exploration if part or all of the area covered by the proposed plan of work for exploration is included in:
   (a) A plan of work for exploration approved by the Council for polymetallic nodules; or
   (b) A plan of work approved by the Council for exploration for or exploitation of other resources if the proposed plan of work for exploration for polymetallic nodules might cause undue interference with activities under such approved plan of work for other resources; or
   (c) An area disapproved for exploitation by the Council in cases where substantial evidence indicates the risk of serious harm to the marine environment; or

(d)   If the proposed plan of work for exploration has been submitted or sponsored by a State that already holds:

    (i)   Plans of work for exploration and exploitation or exploitation only in non-reserved areas that, together with either part of the area covered by the application, exceed in size 30 per cent of a circular area of 400,000 square kilometres surrounding the centre of either part of the area covered by the proposed plan of work;

    (ii) Plans of work for exploration and exploitation or exploitation only in non-reserved areas which, taken together, constitute 2 per cent of that part of the Area which is not reserved or disapproved for exploitation pursuant to Article 162(2)(x) of the Convention.

7.   Except in the case of applications by the Enterprise, on its own behalf or in a joint venture, and applications under Regulation 17, the Commission shall not recommend approval of the plan of work for exploration if part or all of the area covered by the proposed plan of work for exploration is included in a reserved area or an area designated by the Council to be a reserved area.

8.   If the Commission finds that an application does not comply with these Regulations, it shall notify the applicant in writing, through the Secretary-General, indicating the reasons. The applicant may, within 45 days of such notification, amend its application. If the Commission after further consideration is of the view that it should not recommend approval of the plan of work for exploration, it shall so inform the applicant and provide the applicant with a further opportunity to make representations within 30 days of such information. The Commission shall consider any such representations made by the applicant in preparing its report and recommendation to the Council.

9.   In considering a proposed plan of work for exploration, the Commission shall have regard to the principles, policies and objectives relating to activities in the Area as provided for in Part XI and Annex III of the Convention and the Agreement.

10. The Commission shall consider applications expeditiously and shall submit its report and recommendations to the Council on the designation of the areas and on the plan of work for exploration at the first possible opportunity, taking into account the schedule of meetings of the Authority.

11. In discharging its duties, the Commission shall apply these Regulations and the rules, regulations and procedures of the Authority in a uniform and non-discriminatory manner.

Regulation 22. Consideration and Approval of Plans of Work for Exploration by the Council

The Council shall consider the reports and recommendations of the Commission relating to approval of plans of work for exploration in accordance with paragraphs 11 and 12 of Section 3 of the Annex to the Agreement.

Part IV. Contracts for Exploration

Regulation 23. The Contract

1.   After a plan of work for exploration has been approved by the Council, it shall be prepared in the form of a contract between the Authority and the applicant as prescribed in Annex III to these Regulations. Each contract shall incorporate the standard clauses set out in Annex IV in effect at the date of entry into force of the contract.

2.   The contract shall be signed by the Secretary-General on behalf of the Authority and by the applicant. The Secretary-General shall notify all members of the Authority in writing of the conclusion of each contract.

3.   In accordance with the principle of non-discrimination, a contract with a State or entity or any component of such entity referred to in paragraph 6(a)(i) of Section 1 of the annex to the Agreement shall include arrangements that shall be similar to and no less favourable than those agreed with any registered pioneer investor. If any of the States or entities or any components of such entities referred to in paragraph 6(a)(i) of Section 1 of the annex to the Agreement are granted more favourable arrangements, the Council shall make similar and no less favourable arrangements with regard to the rights and obligations assumed by the registered pioneer investors, provided that such arrangements do not affect or prejudice the interests of the Authority.

Regulation 24. Rights of the Contractor

1.   The contractor shall have the exclusive right to explore an area covered by a plan of work for exploration in respect of polymetallic nodules. The Authority shall ensure that no other entity operates in the same area for other resources in a manner that might interfere with the operations of the contractor.

2.   A contractor who has an approved plan of work for exploration only shall have a preference and a priority among applicants submitting plans of work for exploitation of the same area and resources. Such preference or priority may be withdrawn by the Council if the contractor has failed to comply with the requirements of its approved plan of work for exploration within the time period specified in a written notice or notices from the Council to the contractor indicating which requirements have not been complied with by the contractor. The time period specified in any such notice shall not be unreasonable. The contractor shall be accorded a reasonable opportunity to be heard before the withdrawal of such preference or priority becomes final. The Council shall provide the reasons for its proposed withdrawal of preference or priority and shall consider any contractor's response. The decision of the Council shall take account of that response and shall be based on substantial evidence.

3.   A withdrawal of preference or priority shall not become effective until the contractor has been accorded a reasonable opportunity to exhaust the judicial remedies available to it pursuant to Part XI, Section 5, of the Convention.

Regulation 25. Size of Area and Relinquishment

1.   The total area allocated to the contractor under the contract shall not exceed 150,000 square kilometres. The contractor shall relinquish portions of the area allocated to it to revert to the Area. By the end of the third year from the date of the contract, the contractor shall have relinquished 20 per cent of the area allocated to it; by the end of the fifth year from the date of the contract, the contractor shall have relinquished an additional 10 per cent of the area allocated to it; and, after eight years from the date of the contract, the contractor shall have relinquished an additional 20 per cent of the area allocated to it, or such larger amount as would exceed the exploitation area decided upon by the Authority, provided that a contractor shall not be required to relinquish any portion of such area when the total area allocated to it does not exceed 75,000 square kilometres.

2.   The Council may, at the request of the contractor, and on the recommendation of the Commission, in exceptional circumstances, defer the schedule of relinquishment. Such exceptional circumstances shall be determined by the Council and shall include, inter alia, consideration of prevailing economic circumstances or other unforeseen exceptional

circumstances arising in connection with the operational activities of the contractor.

Regulation 26. Duration of Contracts

1. A plan of work for exploration shall be approved for a period of 15 years. Upon expiration of a plan of work for exploration, the contractor shall apply for a plan of work for exploitation unless the contractor has already done so, has obtained an extension for the plan of work for exploration or decides to renounce its rights in the area covered by the plan of work for exploration.
2. Not later than six months before the expiration of a plan of work for exploration, a contractor may apply for extensions for the plan of work for exploration for periods of not more than five years each. Such extensions shall be approved by the Council, on the recommendation of the Commission, if the contractor has made efforts in good faith to comply with the requirements of the plan of work but for reasons beyond the contractor's control has been unable to complete the necessary preparatory work for proceeding to the exploitation stage or if the prevailing economic circumstances do not justify proceeding to the exploitation stage.

Regulation 27. Training

Pursuant to Article 15 of Annex III to the Convention, each contract shall include as a schedule a practical programme for the training of personnel of the Authority and developing States and drawn up by the contractor in cooperation with the Authority and the sponsoring State or States. Training programmes shall focus on training in the conduct of exploration, and shall provide for full participation by such personnel in all activities covered by the contract. Such training programmes may be revised and developed from time to time as necessary by mutual agreement.

Regulation 28. Periodic Review of the Implementation of the Plan of Work for Exploration

1. The contractor and the Secretary-General shall jointly undertake a periodic review of the implementation of the plan of work for exploration at intervals of five years. The Secretary-General may request the contractor

to submit such additional data and information as may be necessary for the purposes of the review.

2. In the light of the review, the contractor shall indicate its programme of activities for the following five-year period, making such adjustments to its previous programme of activities as are necessary.

3. The Secretary-General shall report on the review to the Commission and to the Council. The Secretary-General shall indicate in the report whether any observations transmitted to him by States parties to the Convention concerning the manner in which the contractor has discharged its obligations under these Regulations relating to the protection and preservation of the marine environment were taken into account in the review.

Regulation 29. Termination of Sponsorship

1. Each contractor shall have the required sponsorship throughout the period of the contract.

2. If a State terminates its sponsorship it shall promptly notify the Secretary-General in writing. The sponsoring State should also inform the Secretary-General of the reasons for terminating its sponsorship. Termination of sponsorship shall take effect six months after the date of receipt of the notification by the Secretary-General, unless the notification specifies a later date.

3. In the event of termination of sponsorship the contractor shall, within the period referred to in paragraph 2, obtain another sponsor. Such sponsor shall submit a certificate of sponsorship in accordance with Regulation 11. Failure to obtain a sponsor within the required period shall result in the termination of the contract.

4. A sponsoring State shall not be discharged by reason of the termination of its sponsorship from any obligations accrued while it was a sponsoring State, nor shall such termination affect any legal rights and obligations created during such sponsorship.

5. The Secretary-General shall notify the members of the Authority of the termination or change of sponsorship.

Regulation 30. Responsibility and Liability

Responsibility and liability of the contractor and of the Authority shall be in accordance with the Convention. The contractor shall continue to have responsibility for any damage arising out of wrongful acts in the conduct of its operations, in particular damage to the marine environment, after the completion of the exploration phase.

Part V. Protection and Preservation of the Marine Environment

Regulation 31. Protection and Preservation of the Marine Environment

1. The Authority shall, in accordance with the Convention and the Agreement, establish and keep under periodic review environmental rules, regulations and procedures to ensure effective protection for the marine environment from harmful effects which may arise from activities in the Area.

2. In order to ensure effective protection for the marine environment from harmful effects which may arise from activities in the Area, the Authority and sponsoring States shall apply a precautionary approach, as reflected in principle 15 of the Rio Declaration, and best environmental practices.

3. The Legal and Technical Commission shall make recommendations to the Council on the implementation of paragraphs 1 and 2 above.

4. The Commission shall develop and implement procedures for determining, on the basis of the best available scientific and technical information, including information provided pursuant to Regulation 18, whether proposed exploration activities in the Area would have serious harmful effects on vulnerable marine ecosystems and ensure that, if it is determined that certain proposed exploration activities would have serious harmful effects on vulnerable marine ecosystems, those activities are managed to prevent such effects or not authorized to proceed.

5. Pursuant to Article 145 of the Convention and paragraph 2 of this regulation, each contractor shall take necessary measures to prevent, reduce and control pollution and other hazards to the marine environment arising from its activities in the Area as far as reasonably possible, applying a precautionary approach and best environmental practices.

6. Contractors, sponsoring States and other interested States or entities shall cooperate with the Authority in the establishment and implementation of programmes for monitoring and evaluating the impacts of deep seabed mining on the marine environment. When required by the Council, such programmes shall include proposals for areas to be set aside and used exclusively as impact reference zones and preservation reference zones. "Impact reference zones" means areas to be used for assessing the effect

of activities in the Area on the marine environment and which are representative of the environmental characteristics of the Area. "Preservation reference zones" means areas in which no mining shall occur to ensure representative and stable biota of the seabed in order to assess any changes in the biodiversity of the marine environment.

Regulation 32. Environmental Baselines and Monitoring

1. Each contract shall require the contractor to gather environmental baseline data and to establish environmental baselines, taking into account any recommendations issued by the Legal and Technical Commission pursuant to Regulation 39, against which to assess the likely effects of its programme of activities under the plan of work for exploration on the marine environment and a programme to monitor and report on such effects. The recommendations issued by the Commission may, inter alia, list those exploration activities which may be considered to have no potential for causing harmful effects on the marine environment. The contractor shall cooperate with the Authority and the sponsoring State or States in the establishment and implementation of such monitoring programme.

2. The contractor shall report annually in writing to the Secretary-General on the implementation and results of the monitoring programme referred to in paragraph 1 and shall submit data and information, taking into account any recommendations issued by the Commission pursuant to Regulation 39. The Secretary-General shall transmit such reports to the Commission for its consideration pursuant to Article 165 of the Convention.

Regulation 33. Emergency Orders

1. A contractor shall promptly report to the Secretary-General in writing, using the most effective means, any incident arising from activities which have caused, are causing or pose a threat of serious harm to the marine environment.

2. When the Secretary-General has been notified by a contractor or otherwise becomes aware of an incident resulting from or caused by a contractor's activities in the Area that has caused, is causing or poses a threat of serious harm to the marine environment, the Secretary-General shall cause a general notification of the incident to be issued,

shall notify in writing the contractor and the sponsoring State or States, and shall report immediately to the Legal and Technical Commission, to the Council and to all other members of the Authority. A copy of the report shall be circulated to competent international organizations and to concerned subregional, regional and global organizations and bodies. The Secretary-General shall monitor developments with respect to all such incidents and shall report on them as appropriate to the Commission, the Council and all other members of the Authority.

3. Pending any action by the Council, the Secretary-General shall take such immediate measures of a temporary nature as are practical and reasonable in the circumstances to prevent, contain and minimize serious harm or the threat of serious harm to the marine environment. Such temporary measures shall remain in effect for no longer than 90 days, or until the Council decides at its next regular session or a special session, what measures, if any, to take pursuant to paragraph 6 of this regulation.

4. After having received the report of the Secretary-General, the Commission shall determine, based on the evidence provided to it and taking into account the measures already taken by the contractor, which measures are necessary to respond effectively to the incident in order to prevent, contain and minimize serious harm or the threat of serious harm to the marine environment, and shall make its recommendations to the Council.

5. The Council shall consider the recommendations of the Commission.

6. The Council, taking into account the recommendations of the Commission, the report of the Secretary-General, any information provided by the contractor and any other relevant information, may issue emergency orders, which may include orders for the suspension or adjustment of operations, as may be reasonably necessary to prevent, contain and minimize serious harm or the threat of serious harm to the marine environment arising out of activities in the Area.

7. If a contractor does not promptly comply with an emergency order to prevent, contain and minimize serious harm or the threat of serious harm to the marine environment arising out of its activities in the Area, the Council shall take by itself or through arrangements with others on its behalf, such practical measures as are necessary to prevent, contain and minimize any such serious harm or threat of serious harm to the marine environment.

8. In order to enable the Council, when necessary, to take immediately the practical measures to prevent, contain and minimize the serious

harm or threat of serious harm to the marine environment referred to in paragraph 7, the contractor, prior to the commencement of testing of collecting systems and processing operations, will provide the Council with a guarantee of its financial and technical capability to comply promptly with emergency orders or to assure that the Council can take such emergency measures. If the contractor does not provide the Council with such a guarantee, the sponsoring State or States shall, in response to a request by the Secretary-General and pursuant to Articles 139 and 235 of the Convention, take necessary measures to ensure that the contractor provides such a guarantee or shall take measures to ensure that assistance is provided to the Authority in the discharge of its responsibilities under paragraph 7.

Regulation 34. Rights of Coastal States

1. Nothing in these Regulations shall affect the rights of coastal States in accordance with Article 142 and other relevant provisions of the Convention.

2. Any coastal State which has grounds for believing that any activity in the Area by a contractor is likely to cause serious harm or a threat of serious harm to the marine environment under its jurisdiction or sovereignty may notify the Secretary-General in writing of the grounds upon which such belief is based. The Secretary-General shall provide the contractor and its sponsoring State or States with a reasonable opportunity to examine the evidence, if any, provided by the coastal State as the basis for its belief. The contractor and its sponsoring State or States may submit their observations thereon to the Secretary-General within a reasonable time.

3. If there are clear grounds for believing that serious harm to the marine environment is likely to occur, the Secretary-General shall act in accordance with Regulation 33 and, if necessary, shall take immediate measures of a temporary nature as provided for in Regulation 33(3).

4. Contractors shall take all measures necessary to ensure that their activities are conducted so as not to cause serious harm to the marine environment, including, but not restricted to, pollution, under the jurisdiction or sovereignty of coastal States, and that such serious harm or pollution arising from incidents or activities in its exploration area does not spread beyond such area.

Regulation 35. Human Remains and Objects and Sites of an Archaeological or Historical Nature

The contractor shall immediately notify the Secretary-General in writing of any finding in the exploration area of any human remains of an archaeological or historical nature, or any object or site of a similar nature and its location, including the preservation and protection measures taken. The Secretary-General shall transmit such information to the Director General of the United Nations Educational, Scientific and Cultural Organization and any other competent international organization. Following the finding of any such human remains, object or site in the exploration area, and in order to avoid disturbing such human remains, object or site, no further prospecting or exploration shall take place, within a reasonable radius, until such time as the Council decides otherwise after taking account of the views of the Director General of the United Nations Educational, Scientific and Cultural Organization or any other competent international organization.

Part VI. Confidentiality

Regulation 36. Confidentiality of Data and Information

1. Data and information submitted or transferred to the Authority or to any person participating in any activity or programme of the Authority pursuant to these Regulations or a contract issued under these Regulations, and designated by the contractor, in consultation with the Secretary-General, as being of a confidential nature, shall be considered confidential unless it is data and information which:
   (a) Is generally known or publicly available from other sources;
   (b) Has been previously made available by the owner to others without an obligation concerning its confidentiality; or
   (c) Is already in the possession of the Authority with no obligation concerning its confidentiality.
2. Data and information that is necessary for the formulation by the Authority of rules, regulations and procedures concerning protection and preservation of the marine environment and safety, other than proprietary equipment design data, shall not be deemed confidential.
3. Confidential data and information may only be used by the Secretary-General and staff of the Secretariat, as authorized by the Secretary-General,

and by the members of the Legal and Technical Commission as necessary for and relevant to the effective exercise of their powers and functions. The Secretary-General shall authorize access to such data and information only for limited use in connection with the functions and duties of the staff of the Secretariat and the functions and duties of the Legal and Technical Commission.

4. Ten years after the date of submission of confidential data and information to the Authority or the expiration of the contract for exploration, whichever is the later, and every five years thereafter, the Secretary-General and the contractor shall review such data and information to determine whether they should remain confidential. Such data and information shall remain confidential if the contractor establishes that there would be a substantial risk of serious and unfair economic prejudice if the data and information were to be released. No such data and information shall be released until the contractor has been accorded a reasonable opportunity to exhaust the judicial remedies available to it pursuant to Part XI, Section 5, of the Convention.

5. If, at any time following the expiration of the contract for exploration, the contractor enters into a contract for exploitation in respect of any part of the exploration area, confidential data and information relating to that part of the area shall remain confidential in accordance with the contract for exploitation.

6. The contractor may at any time waive confidentiality of data and information.

Regulation 37. Procedures to Ensure Confidentiality

1. The Secretary-General shall be responsible for maintaining the confidentiality of all confidential data and information and shall not, except with the prior written consent of the contractor, release such data and information to any person external to the Authority. To ensure the confidentiality of such data and information, the Secretary-General shall establish procedures, consistent with the provisions of the Convention, governing the handling of confidential information by members of the Secretariat, members of the Legal and Technical Commission and any other person participating in any activity or programme of the Authority. Such procedures shall include:

   (a) Maintenance of confidential data and information in secure facilities and development of security procedures to prevent unauthorized access to or removal of such data and information;

(b)   Development and maintenance of a classification, log and inventory system of all written data and information received, including its type and source and routing from the time of receipt until final disposition.

2.   A person who is authorized pursuant to these Regulations to have access to confidential data and information shall not disclose such data and information except as permitted under the Convention and these Regulations. The Secretary-General shall require any person who is authorized to have access to confidential data and information to make a written declaration witnessed by the Secretary-General or his or her authorized representative to the effect that the person so authorized:

(a)   Acknowledges his or her legal obligation under the Convention and these Regulations with respect to the non-disclosure of confidential data and information;

(b)   Agrees to comply with the applicable regulations and procedures established to ensure the confidentiality of such data and information.

3.   The Legal and Technical Commission shall protect the confidentiality of confidential data and information submitted to it pursuant to these Regulations or a contract issued under these Regulations. In accordance with the provisions of Article 163(8) of the Convention, members of the Commission shall not disclose, even after the termination of their functions, any industrial secret, proprietary data which are transferred to the Authority in accordance with Article 14 of Annex III to the Convention, or any other confidential information coming to their knowledge by reason of their duties for the Authority.

4.   The Secretary-General and staff of the Authority shall not disclose, even after the termination of their functions with the Authority, any industrial secret, proprietary data which are transferred to the Authority in accordance with Article 14 of Annex III to the Convention, or any other confidential information coming to their knowledge by reason of their employment with the Authority.

5.   Taking into account the responsibility and liability of the Authority pursuant to Article 22 of Annex III to the Convention, the Authority may take such action as may be appropriate against any person who, by reason of his or her duties for the Authority, has access to any confidential data and information and who is in breach of the obligations relating to confidentiality contained in the Convention and these Regulations.

Part VII. General Procedures

Regulation 38. Notice and General Procedures

1. Any application, request, notice, report, consent, approval, waiver, direction or instruction hereunder shall be made by the Secretary-General or by the designated representative of the prospector, applicant or contractor, as the case may be, in writing. Service shall be by hand, or by telex, fax, registered airmail or e-mail containing an authorized electronic signature to the Secretary-General at the headquarters of the Authority or to the designated representative.

2. Delivery by hand shall be effective when made. Delivery by telex shall be deemed to be effective on the business day following the day when the "answer back" appears on the sender's telex machine. Delivery by fax shall be effective when the "transmit confirmation report" confirming the transmission to the recipient's published fax number is received by the transmitter. Delivery by registered airmail shall be deemed to be effective 21 days after posting. An e-mail is presumed to be received by the addressee when it enters an information system designated or used by the addressee for the purpose of receiving documents of the type sent and is capable of being retrieved and processed by the addressee.

3. Notice to the designated representative of the prospector, applicant or contractor shall constitute effective notice to the prospector, applicant or contractor for all purposes under these Regulations, and the designated representative shall be the agent of the prospector, applicant or contractor for the service of process or notification in any proceeding of any court or tribunal having jurisdiction.

4. Notice to the Secretary-General shall constitute effective notice to the Authority for all purposes under these Regulations, and the Secretary-General shall be the Authority's agent for the service of process or notification in any proceeding of any court or tribunal having jurisdiction.

Regulation 39. Recommendations for the Guidance of Contractors

1. The Legal and Technical Commission may from time to time issue recommendations of a technical or administrative nature for the guidance of contractors to assist them in the implementation of the rules, regulations and procedures of the Authority.

2.   The full text of such recommendations shall be reported to the Council. Should the Council find that a recommendation is inconsistent with the intent and purpose of these Regulations, it may request that the recommendation be modified or withdrawn.

Part VIII. Settlement of Disputes

Regulation 40. Disputes

1.   Disputes concerning the interpretation or application of these Regulations shall be settled in accordance with Part XI, Section 5, of the Convention.
2.   Any final decision rendered by a court or tribunal having jurisdiction under the Convention relating to the rights and obligations of the Authority and of the contractor shall be enforceable in the territory of each State party to the Convention.

Part IX. Resources other than Polymetallic Nodules

Regulation 41. Resources other than Polymetallic Nodules

If a prospector or contractor finds resources in the Area other than polymetallic nodules, the prospecting and exploration for and exploitation of such resources shall be subject to the rules, regulations and procedures of the Authority relating to such resources in accordance with the Convention and the Agreement. The prospector or contractor shall notify the Authority of its find.

Part X. Review

Regulation 42. Review

1.   Five years following the approval of these revised Regulations by the Assembly, or at any time thereafter, the Council shall undertake a review of the manner in which the Regulations have operated in practice.
2.   If, in the light of improved knowledge or technology, it becomes apparent that the Regulations are not adequate, any State party, the Legal and Technical Commission or any contractor through its sponsoring State

may at any time request the Council to consider, at its next ordinary session, revisions to these Regulations.

3.   In the light of the review, the Council may adopt and apply provisionally, pending approval by the Assembly, amendments to the provisions of these Regulations, taking into account the recommendations of the Legal and Technical Commission or other subordinate organs concerned. Any such amendments shall be without prejudice to the rights conferred on any contractor with the Authority under the provisions of a contract entered into pursuant to these Regulations in force at the time of any such amendment.

4.   In the event that any provisions of these Regulations are amended, the contractor and the Authority may revise the contract in accordance with Section 24 of Annex IV.

Annex I. Notification of Intention to Engage in Prospecting

1.   Name of prospector:
2.   Street address of prospector:
3.   Postal address (if different from above):
4.   Telephone number:
5.   Fax number:
6.   E-mail address:
7.   Nationality of prospector:
8.   If prospector is a juridical person:
     (a)   Identify prospector's place of registration;
     (b)   Identify prospector's principal place of business/domicile;
     (c)   Attach a copy of prospector's certificate of registration.
9.   Name of prospector's designated representative:
10. Street address of prospector's designated representative (if different from above):
11. Postal address (if different from above):
12. Telephone number:
13. Fax number:
14. E-mail address:
15. Attach the coordinates of the broad area or areas in which prospecting is to be conducted (in accordance with the World Geodetic System WGS 84).
16. Attach a general description of the prospecting programme, including the date of commencement and the approximate duration of the programme.

17. Attach a written undertaking that the prospector will:
    (a) Comply with the Convention and the relevant rules, regulations and procedures of the Authority concerning:
        i. Cooperation in the training programmes in connection with marine scientific research and transfer of technology referred to in Articles 143 and 144 of the Convention; and
        ii. Protection and preservation of the marine environment; and
    (b) Accept verification by the Authority of compliance therewith.
18. List hereunder all the attachments and annexes to this notification (all data and information should be submitted in hard copy and in a digital format specified by the Authority).

Date: _____   _____
                                    Signature of prospector's designated
                                    representative

Attestation:

_____
Signature of person attesting

_____
Name of person attesting

_____
Title of person attesting

Annex II. Application for Approval of a Plan of Work for Exploration to Obtain a Contract

Section I. Information Concerning the Applicant

1. Name of applicant:
2. Street address of applicant:
3. Postal address (if different from above):
4. Telephone number:
5. Fax number:
6. E-mail address:
7. Name of applicant's designated representative:
8. Street address of applicant's designated representative (if different from above):
9. Postal address (if different from above):

10. Telephone number:
11. Fax number:
12. E-mail address:
13. If the applicant is a juridical person:
    (a) Identify applicant's place of registration;
    (b) Identify applicant's principal place of business/domicile;
    (c) Attach a copy of applicant's certificate of registration.
14. Identify the sponsoring State or States.
15. In respect of each sponsoring State, provide the date of deposit of its instrument of ratification of, or accession or succession to, the United Nations Convention on the Law of the Sea of 10 December 1982 and the date of its consent to be bound by the Agreement relating to the Implementation of Part XI of the Convention.
16. A certificate of sponsorship issued by the sponsoring State must be attached with this application. If the applicant has more than one nationality, as in the case of a partnership or consortium of entities from more than one State, certificates of sponsorship issued by each of the States involved must be attached.

Section II. Information Relating to the Area under Application

17. Define the boundaries of the area under application by attaching a list of geographical coordinates (in accordance with the World Geodetic System WGS 84).
18. Attach a chart (on a scale and projection specified by the Authority) and a list of the coordinates dividing the total area into two parts of equal estimated commercial value.
19. Include in an attachment sufficient information to enable the Council to designate a reserved area based on the estimated commercial value of each part of the area under application. Such attachment must include the data available to the applicant with respect to both parts of the area under application, including:
    (a) Data on the location, survey and evaluation of the polymetallic nodules in the areas, including:
        (i) A description of the technology related to the recovery and processing of polymetallic nodules that is necessary for making the designation of a reserved area;
        (ii) A map of the physical and geological characteristics, such as seabed topography, bathymetry and bottom currents and information on the reliability of such data;

    (iii) Data showing the average density (abundance) of polymetallic nodules in kg/m² and an associated abundance map showing the location of sampling sites;

    (iv) Data showing the average elemental content of metals of economic interest (grade) based on chemical assays in (dry) weight per cent and an associated grade map;

    (v) Combined maps of abundance and grade of polymetallic nodules;

    (vi) A calculation based on standard procedures, including statistical analysis, using the data submitted and assumptions made in the calculations that the two areas could be expected to contain polymetallic nodules of equal estimated commercial value expressed as recoverable metals in mineable areas;

    (vii) A description of the techniques used by the applicant.

  (b) Information concerning environmental parameters (seasonal and during test period) including, inter alia, wind speed and direction, water salinity, temperature and biological communities.

20.   If the area under application includes any part of a reserved area, attach a list of coordinates of the area which forms part of the reserved area and indicate the applicant's qualifications in accordance with Regulation 17 of the Regulations.

Section III. Financial and Technical Information[a]

21.   Attach sufficient information to enable the Council to determine whether the applicant is financially capable of carrying out the proposed plan of work for exploration and of fulfilling its financial obligations to the Authority:

---

a An application for approval of a plan of work for exploration submitted on behalf of a State or entity, or any component of such entity, referred to in paragraph 1 (a) (ii) or (iii) of resolution II, other than a registered pioneer investor, which has already undertaken substantial activities in the Area prior to the entry into force of the Convention, or its successor in interest, shall be considered to have met the financial and technical qualifications necessary for approval of a plan of work if the sponsoring State or States certify that the applicant has expended an amount equivalent to at least 30 million United States dollars in research and exploration activities and has expended no less than 10 per cent of that amount in the location, survey and evaluation of the area referred to in the plan of work.

(a) If the application is made by the Enterprise, attach certification by its competent authority that the Enterprise has the necessary financial resources to meet the estimated costs of the proposed plan of work for exploration;

(b) If the application is made by a State or a State enterprise, attach a statement by the State or the sponsoring State certifying that the applicant has the necessary financial resources to meet the estimated costs of the proposed plan of work for exploration;

(c) If the application is made by an entity, attach copies of the applicant's audited financial statements, including balance sheets and profit-and-loss statements, for the most recent three years in conformity with internationally accepted accounting principles and certified by a duly qualified firm of public accountants; and

   (i)   If the applicant is a newly organized entity and a certified balance sheet is not available, a pro forma balance sheet certified by an appropriate official of the applicant;

   (ii) If the applicant is a subsidiary of another entity, copies of such financial statements of that entity and a statement from that entity in conformity with internationally accepted accounting practices and certified by a duly qualified firm of public accountants that the applicant will have the financial resources to carry out the plan of work for exploration;

   (iii) If the applicant is controlled by a State or a State enterprise, a statement from the State or State enterprise certifying that the applicant will have the financial resources to carry out the plan of work for exploration.

22. If it is intended to finance the proposed plan of work for exploration by borrowings, attach a statement of the amount of such borrowings, the repayment period and the interest rate.

23. Attach sufficient information to enable the Council to determine whether the applicant is technically capable of carrying out the proposed plan of work for exploration, including:

(a) A general description of the applicant's previous experience, knowledge, skills, technical qualifications and expertise relevant to the proposed plan of work for exploration;

(b) A general description of the equipment and methods expected to be used in carrying out the proposed plan of work for exploration and other relevant non-proprietary information about the characteristics of such technology; and

(c) A general description of the applicant's financial and technical capability to respond to any incident or activity which causes serious harm to the marine environment.

Section IV. The Plan of Work for Exploration

24. Attach the following information relating to the plan of work for exploration:

(a) A general description and a schedule of the proposed exploration programme, including the programme of activities for the immediate five-year period, such as studies to be undertaken in respect of the environmental, technical, economic and other appropriate factors which must be taken into account in exploration;

(b) A description of a programme for oceanographic and environmental baseline studies in accordance with the Regulations and any environmental rules, regulations and procedures established by the Authority that would enable an assessment of the potential environmental impact including, but not restricted to, the impact on biodiversity, of the proposed exploration activities, taking into account any recommendations issued by the Legal and Technical Commission;

(c) A preliminary assessment of the possible impact of the proposed exploration activities on the marine environment;

(d) A description of proposed measures for the prevention, reduction and control of pollution and other hazards, as well as possible impacts, to the marine environment;

(e) A schedule of anticipated yearly expenditures in respect of the programme of activities for the immediate five-year period.

Section V. Undertakings

25. Attach a written undertaking that the applicant will:

(a) Accept as enforceable and comply with the applicable obligations created by the provisions of the Convention and the rules, regulations and procedures of the Authority, the decisions of the relevant organs of the Authority and the terms of its contracts with the Authority;

(b) Accept control by the Authority of activities in the Area as authorized by the Convention;

(c) Provide the Authority with a written assurance that its obligations under the contract will be fulfilled in good faith.

Section VI. Previous Contracts

26. If the applicant or, in the case of an application by a partnership or consortium of entities in a joint arrangement, any member of the partnership or consortium has previously been awarded any contract with the Authority, the application must include:
     (a)   The date of the previous contract or contracts;
     (b)   The date, reference number and title of each report submitted to the Authority in connection with the contract or contracts; and
     (c)   The date of termination of the contract or contracts, if applicable.

Section VII. Attachments

27. List all the attachments and annexes to this application (all data and information should be submitted in hard copy and in a digital format specified by the Authority).

Date: _____

_____
Signature of applicant's designated
representative

Attestation:

_____
Signature of person attesting

_____
Name of person attesting

_____
Title of person attesting

Annex III. Contract for Exploration

THIS CONTRACT made the ... day of ... between the **INTERNATIONAL SEABED AUTHORITY** represented by its **SECRETARY-GENERAL** (hereinafter referred to as "the Authority") and ... represented by ... (hereinafter referred to as "the Contractor") **WITNESSETH** as follows:

Incorporation of Clauses

1.   The standard clauses set out in Annex IV to the Regulations on Prospecting and Exploration for Polymetallic Nodules in the Area shall be incorporated herein and shall have effect as if herein set out at length.

Exploration Area

2. For the purposes of this contract, the "exploration area" means that part of the Area allocated to the Contractor for exploration, defined by the coordinates listed in schedule 1 hereto, as reduced from time to time in accordance with the standard clauses and the Regulations.

Grant of Rights

3. In consideration of (a) their mutual interest in the conduct of exploration activities in the exploration area pursuant to the United Nations Convention on the Law of the Sea of 10 December 1982 and the Agreement relating to the Implementation of Part XI of the Convention, (b) the responsibility of the Authority to organize and control activities in the Area, particularly with a view to administering the resources of the Area, in accordance with the legal regime established in Part XI of the Convention and the Agreement and Part XII of the Convention, respectively, and (c) the interest and financial commitment of the Contractor in conducting activities in the exploration area and the mutual covenants made herein, the Authority hereby grants to the Contractor the exclusive right to explore for polymetallic nodules in the exploration area in accordance with the terms and conditions of this contract.

Entry into Force and Contract Term

4. This contract shall enter into force on signature by both parties and, subject to the standard clauses, shall remain in force for a period of fifteen years thereafter unless:
   (a) The Contractor obtains a contract for exploitation in the exploration area which enters into force before the expiration of such period of fifteen years; or
   (b) The contract is sooner terminated, provided that the term of the contract may be extended in accordance with standard clauses 3.2 and 17.2.

Schedules

5. The schedules referred to in the standard clauses, namely Section 4 and Section 8, are for the purposes of this contract schedules 2 and 3 respectively.

Entire Agreement

6.   This contract expresses the entire agreement between the parties, and no
     oral understanding or prior writing shall modify the terms hereof.
         IN WITNESS WHEREOF the undersigned, being duly authorized thereto
     by the respective parties, have signed this contract at ..., this ... day of ... .

Schedule 1

[Coordinates and illustrative chart of the exploration area]

Schedule 2

[The current five-year programme of activities as revised from time to time]

Schedule 3

[The training programme shall become a schedule to the contract when
approved by the Authority in accordance with Section 8 of the standard
clauses]

Annex IV. Standard Clauses for Exploration Contract

Section 1. Definitions

1.1   In the following clauses:
      (a)   "Exploration area" means that part of the Area allocated to the
            Contractor for exploration, described in schedule 1 hereto, as the same
            may be reduced from time to time in accordance with this contract
            and the Regulations;
      (b)   "Programme of activities" means the programme of activities which
            is set out in schedule 2 hereto as the same may be adjusted from
            time to time in accordance with Sections 4.3 and 4.4 hereof;
      (c)   "Regulations" means the Regulations on Prospecting and
            Exploration for Polymetallic Nodules in the Area, adopted by the
            Authority.
1.2   Terms and phrases defined in the Regulations shall have the same mean-
      ing in these standard clauses.
1.3   In accordance with the Agreement relating to the Implementation of
      Part XI of the United Nations Convention on the Law of the Sea of 10
      December 1982, its provisions and Part XI of the Convention are to be
      interpreted and applied together as a single instrument; this contract and

references in this contract to the Convention are to be interpreted and applied accordingly.

1.4 This contract includes the schedules to this contract, which shall be an integral part hereof.

Section 2. Security of Tenure

2.1 The Contractor shall have security of tenure and this contract shall not be suspended, terminated or revised except in accordance with Sections 20, 21 and 24 hereof.

2.2 The Contractor shall have the exclusive right to explore for poly-metallic nodules in the exploration area in accordance with the terms and conditions of this contract. The Authority shall ensure that no other entity operates in the exploration area for a different category of resources in a manner that might unreasonably interfere with the operations of the Contractor.

2.3 The Contractor, by notice to the Authority, shall have the right at any time to renounce without penalty the whole or part of its rights in the exploration area, provided that the Contractor shall remain liable for all obligations accrued prior to the date of such renunciation in respect of the area renounced.

2.4 Nothing in this contract shall be deemed to confer any right on the Contractor other than those rights expressly granted herein. The Authority reserves the right to enter into contracts with respect to resources other than polymetallic nodules with third parties in the area covered by this contract.

Section 3. Contract Term

3.1 This contract shall enter into force on signature by both parties and shall remain in force for a period of fifteen years thereafter unless:

(a) The Contractor obtains a contract for exploitation in the explora-tion area which enters into force before the expiration of such period of fifteen years; or

(b) The contract is sooner terminated, provided that the term of the contract may be extended in accordance with Sections 3.2 and 17.2 hereof.

3.2 Upon application by the Contractor, not later than six months before the expiration of this contract, this contract may be extended for periods of not more than five years each on such terms and conditions as the Authority and the Contractor may then agree in accordance with the Regulations. Such extensions shall be approved if the Contractor has made efforts in good faith to comply with the requirements of this contract but for reasons beyond the Contractor's control has been unable to complete the necessary preparatory work for proceeding to the exploitation stage or if the prevailing economic circumstances do not justify proceeding to the exploitation stage.

3.3   Notwithstanding the expiration of this contract in accordance with Section 3.1 hereof, if the Contractor has, at least 90 days prior to the date of expiration, applied for a contract for exploitation, the Contractor's rights and obligations under this contract shall continue until such time as the application has been considered and a contract for exploitation has been issued or refused.

Section 4. Exploration

4.1   The Contractor shall commence exploration in accordance with the time schedule stipulated in the programme of activities set out in schedule 2 hereto and shall adhere to such time periods or any modification thereto as provided for by this contract.

4.2   The Contractor shall carry out the programme of activities set out in schedule 2 hereto. In carrying out such activities the Contractor shall spend in each contract year not less than the amount specified in such programme, or any agreed review thereof, in actual and direct exploration expenditures.

4.3   The Contractor, with the consent of the Authority, which consent shall not be unreasonably withheld, may from time to time make such changes in the programme of activities and the expenditures specified therein as may be necessary and prudent in accordance with good mining industry practice, and taking into account the market conditions for the metals contained in polymetallic nodules and other relevant global economic conditions.

4.4   Not later than 90 days prior to the expiration of each five-year period from the date on which this contract enters into force in accordance with Section 3 hereof, the Contractor and the Secretary-General shall jointly undertake a review of the implementation of the plan of work for exploration under this contract. The Secretary-General may require the Contractor to submit such additional data and information as may be necessary for the purposes of the review. In the light of the review, the Contractor shall make such adjustments to its plan of work as are necessary and shall indicate its programme of activities for the following five-year period, including a revised schedule of anticipated yearly expenditures. Schedule 2 hereto shall be adjusted accordingly.

Section 5. Environmental Monitoring

5.1 The Contractor shall take necessary measures to prevent, reduce and control pollution and other hazards to the marine environment arising from its activities in the Area as far as reasonably possible applying a precautionary approach and best environmental practices.

5.2 Prior to the commencement of exploration activities, the Contractor shall submit to the Authority:

(a) An impact assessment of the potential effects on the marine environment of the proposed activities;

(b) A proposal for a monitoring programme to determine the potential effect on the marine environment of the proposed activities; and

(c) Data that could be used to establish an environmental baseline against which to assess the effect of the proposed activities.

5.3 The Contractor shall, in accordance with the Regulations, gather environmental baseline data as exploration activities progress and develop and shall establish environmental baselines against which to assess the likely effects of the Contractor's activities on the marine environment.

5.4 The Contractor shall, in accordance with the Regulations, establish and carry out a programme to monitor and report on such effects on the marine environment. The Contractor shall cooperate with the Authority in the implementation of such monitoring.

5.5 The Contractor shall, within 90 days of the end of each calendar year, report to the Secretary-General on the implementation and results of the monitoring programme referred to in Section 5.4 hereof and shall submit data and information in accordance with the Regulations.

Section 6. Contingency Plans and Emergencies

6.1 The Contractor shall, prior to the commencement of its programme of activities under this contract, submit to the Secretary-General a contingency plan to respond effectively to incidents that are likely to cause serious harm or a threat of serious harm to the marine environment arising from the Contractor's activities at sea in the exploration area. Such contingency plan shall establish special procedures and provide for adequate and appropriate equipment to deal with such incidents and, in particular, shall include arrangements for:

(a) The immediate raising of a general alarm in the area of the exploration activities;

(b) Immediate notification to the Secretary-General;

(c) The warning of ships which might be about to enter the immediate vicinity;

(d) A continuing flow of full information to the Secretary-General relating to particulars of the contingency measures already taken and further actions required;

(e) The removal, as appropriate, of polluting substances;

(f) The reduction and, so far as reasonably possible, prevention of serious harm to the marine environment, as well as mitigation of such effects;

(g) As appropriate, cooperation with other contractors with the Authority to respond to an emergency; and

(h) Periodic emergency response exercises.

6.2 The Contractor shall promptly report to the Secretary-General any incident arising from its activities that has caused, is causing or poses a threat of serious harm to the marine environment. Each such report shall contain the details of such incident, including, inter alia:

(a) The coordinates of the area affected or which can reasonably be anticipated to be affected;

(b) The description of the action being taken by the Contractor to prevent, contain, minimize and repair the serious harm or threat of serious harm to the marine environment;

(c) A description of the action being taken by the Contractor to monitor the effects of the incident on the marine environment; and

(d) Such supplementary information as may reasonably be required by the Secretary-General.

6.3 The Contractor shall comply with emergency orders issued by the Council and immediate measures of a temporary nature issued by the Secretary-General in accordance with the Regulations, to prevent, contain, minimize or repair serious harm or the threat of serious harm to the marine environment, which may include orders to the Contractor to immediately suspend or adjust any activities in the exploration area.

6.4 If the Contractor does not promptly comply with such emergency orders or immediate measures of a temporary nature, the Council may take such reasonable measures as are necessary to prevent, contain, minimize or repair any such serious harm or the threat of serious harm to the marine environment at the Contractor's expense. The Contractor shall promptly reimburse the Authority the amount of such expenses. Such expenses shall be in addition to any monetary penalties which may be imposed on the Contractor pursuant to the terms of this contract or the Regulations.

Section 7. Human Remains and Objects and Sites of an Archaeological or Historical Nature

The Contractor shall immediately notify the Secretary-General in writing of any finding in the exploration area of any human remains of an archaeological or historical nature, or any object or site of a similar nature and its location, including the preservation and protection measures taken. The Secretary-General shall transmit such information to the Director General of the United Nations Educational, Scientific and Cultural Organization and any other competent international organization. Following the finding of any such human remains, object or site in the exploration area, and in order to avoid disturbing such human remains, object or site, no further prospecting or exploration shall take place, within a reasonable radius, until such time as the Council decides otherwise after taking account of the views of the Director General of the United Nations Educational, Scientific and Cultural Organization or any other competent international organization.

Section 8. Training

8.1 In accordance with the Regulations, the Contractor shall, prior to the commencement of exploration under this contract, submit to the Authority for approval proposed training programmes for the training of personnel of the Authority and developing States, including the participation of such personnel in all of the Contractor's activities under this contract.

8.2 The scope and financing of the training programme shall be subject to negotiation between the Contractor, the Authority and the sponsoring State or States.

8.3 The Contractor shall conduct training programmes in accordance with the specific programme for the training of personnel referred to in Section 8.1 hereof approved by the Authority in accordance with the Regulations, which programme, as revised and developed from time to time, shall become a part of this contract as schedule 3.

Section 9. Books and Records

The Contractor shall keep a complete and proper set of books, accounts and financial records, consistent with internationally accepted accounting principles. Such books, accounts and financial records shall include information which will fully disclose the actual and direct expenditures for exploration and such other information as will facilitate an effective audit of such expenditures.

Section 10. Annual Reports

10.1 The Contractor shall, within 90 days of the end of each calendar year, submit a report to the Secretary-General in such format as may be recommended from time to time by the Legal and Technical Commission covering its programme of activities in the exploration area and containing, as applicable, information in sufficient detail on:

(a) The exploration work carried out during the calendar year, including maps, charts and graphs illustrating the work that has been done and the results obtained;

(b) The equipment used to carry out the exploration work, including the results of tests conducted of proposed mining technologies, but not equipment design data; and

(c) The implementation of training programmes, including any proposed revisions to or developments of such programmes.

10.2 Such reports shall also contain:

(a) The results obtained from environmental monitoring programmes, including observations, measurements, evaluations and analyses of environmental parameters;

(b) A statement of the quantity of polymetallic nodules recovered as samples or for the purpose of testing;

(c) A statement, in conformity with internationally accepted accounting principles and certified by a duly qualified firm of public accountants, or, where the Contractor is a State or a State enterprise, by the sponsoring State, of the actual and direct exploration expenditures of the Contractor in carrying out the programme of activities during the Contractor's accounting year. Such expenditures may be claimed by the contractor as part of the contractor's development costs incurred prior to the commencement of commercial production; and

(d) Details of any proposed adjustments to the programme of activities and the reasons for such adjustments.

10.3 The Contractor shall also submit such additional information to supplement the reports referred to in Sections 10.1 and 10.2 hereof as the Secretary-General may from time to time reasonably require in order to carry out the Authority's functions under the Convention, the Regulations and this contract.

10.4   The Contractor shall keep, in good condition, a representative portion of samples of the polymetallic nodules obtained in the course of exploration until the expiration of this contract. The Authority may request the Contractor in writing to deliver to it for analysis a portion of any such sample obtained during the course of exploration.

Section 11. Data and Information to be Submitted on Expiration of the Contract

11.1   The Contractor shall transfer to the Authority all data and information that are both necessary for and relevant to the effective exercise of the powers and functions of the Authority in respect of the exploration area in accordance with the provisions of this section.

11.2   Upon expiration or termination of this contract the Contractor, if it has not already done so, shall submit the following data and information to the Secretary-General:

(a)   Copies of geological, environmental, geochemical and geophysical data acquired by the Contractor in the course of carrying out the programme of activities that are necessary for and relevant to the effective exercise of the powers and functions of the Authority in respect of the exploration area;

(b)   The estimation of mineable areas, when such areas have been identified, which shall include details of the grade and quantity of the proven, probable and possible polymetallic nodule reserves and the anticipated mining conditions;

(c)   Copies of geological, technical, financial and economic reports made by or for the Contractor that are necessary for and relevant to the effective exercise of the powers and functions of the Authority in respect of the exploration area;

(d)   Information in sufficient detail on the equipment used to carry out the exploration work, including the results of tests conducted of proposed mining technologies, but not equipment design data;

(e)   A statement of the quantity of polymetallic nodules recovered as samples or for the purpose of testing; and

(f)   A statement on how and where samples are archived and their availability to the Authority.

11.3   The data and information referred to in Section 11.2 hereof shall also be submitted to the Secretary-General if, prior to the expiration of this contract, the Contractor applies for approval of a plan of work for exploitation or if the Contractor renounces its rights in the exploration area to the extent that such data and information relates to the renounced area.

Section 12. Confidentiality

Data and information transferred to the Authority in accordance with this contract shall be treated as confidential in accordance with the provisions of the Regulations.

Section 13. Undertakings

13.1 The Contractor shall carry out exploration in accordance with the terms and conditions of this contract, the Regulations, Part XI of the Convention, the Agreement and other rules of international law not incompatible with the Convention.

13.2 The Contractor undertakes:
   (a) To accept as enforceable and comply with the terms of this contract;
   (b) To comply with the applicable obligations created by the provisions of the Convention, the rules, regulations and procedures of the Authority and the decisions of the relevant organs of the Authority;
   (c) To accept control by the Authority of activities in the Area as authorized by the Convention;
   (d) To fulfil its obligations under this contract in good faith; and
   (e) To observe, as far as reasonably practicable, any recommendations which may be issued from time to time by the Legal and Technical Commission.

13.3 The Contractor shall actively carry out the programme of activities:
   (a) With due diligence, efficiency and economy;
   (b) With due regard to the impact of its activities on the marine environment; and
   (c) With reasonable regard for other activities in the marine environment.

13.4 The Authority undertakes to fulfil in good faith its powers and functions under the Convention and the Agreement in accordance with Article 157 of the Convention.

Section 14. Inspection

14.1 The Contractor shall permit the Authority to send its inspectors on board vessels and installations used by the Contractor to carry out activities in the exploration area to:
   (a) Monitor the Contractor's compliance with the terms and conditions of this contract and the Regulations; and
   (b) Monitor the effects of such activities on the marine environment.

14.2 The Secretary-General shall give reasonable notice to the Contractor of the projected time and duration of inspections, the name of the inspectors and any activities the inspectors are to perform that are likely to require the availability of special equipment or special assistance from personnel of the Contractor.

14.3 Such inspectors shall have the authority to inspect any vessel or installation, including its log, equipment, records, facilities, all other recorded data and any relevant documents which are necessary to monitor the Contractor's compliance.

14.4 The Contractor, its agents and employees shall assist the inspectors in the performance of their duties and shall:

(a) Accept and facilitate prompt and safe boarding of vessels and installations by inspectors;

(b) Cooperate with and assist in the inspection of any vessel or installation conducted pursuant to these procedures;

(c) Provide access to all relevant equipment, facilities and personnel on vessels and installations at all reasonable times;

(d) Not obstruct, intimidate or interfere with inspectors in the performance of their duties;

(e) Provide reasonable facilities, including, where appropriate, food and accommodation, to inspectors; and

(f) Facilitate safe disembarkation by inspectors.

14.5 Inspectors shall avoid interference with the safe and normal operations on board vessels and installations used by the Contractor to carry out activities in the area visited and shall act in accordance with the Regulations and the measures adopted to protect confidentiality of data and information.

14.6 The Secretary-General and any duly authorized representatives of the Secretary-General, shall have access, for purposes of audit and examination, to any books, documents, papers and records of the Contractor which are necessary and directly pertinent to verify the expenditures referred to in Section 10.2(c).

14.7 The Secretary-General shall provide relevant information contained in the reports of inspectors to the Contractor and its sponsoring State or States where action is necessary.

14.8 If for any reason the Contractor does not pursue exploration and does not request a contract for exploitation, it shall, before withdrawing from the exploration area, notify the Secretary-General in writing in order to permit the Authority, if it so decides, to carry out an inspection pursuant to this section.

Section 15. Safety, Labour and Health Standards

15.1 The Contractor shall comply with the generally accepted international rules and standards established by competent international organizations or general diplomatic conferences concerning the safety of life at sea, and the prevention of collisions and such rules, regulations and procedures as may be adopted by the Authority relating to safety at sea. Each vessel used for carrying out activities in the Area shall possess current valid certificates required by and issued pursuant to such international rules and standards.

15.2 The Contractor shall, in carrying out exploration under this contract, observe and comply with such rules, regulations and procedures as may be adopted by the Authority relating to protection against discrimination in employment, occupational safety and health, labour relations, social security, employment security and living conditions at the work site. Such rules, regulations and procedures shall take into account conventions and recommendations of the International Labour Organization and other competent international organizations.

Section 16. Responsibility and Liability

16.1 The Contractor shall be liable for the actual amount of any damage, including damage to the marine environment, arising out of its wrongful acts or omissions, and those of its employees, subcontractors, agents and all persons engaged in working or acting for them in the conduct of its operations under this contract, including the costs of reasonable measures to prevent or limit damage to the marine environment, account being taken of any contributory acts or omissions by the Authority.

16.2 The Contractor shall indemnify the Authority, its employees, subcontractors and agents against all claims and liabilities of any third party arising out of any wrongful acts or omissions of the Contractor and its employees, agents and subcontractors, and all persons engaged in working or acting for them in the conduct of its operations under this contract.

16.3 The Authority shall be liable for the actual amount of any damage to the Contractor arising out of its wrongful acts in the exercise of its powers and functions, including violations under Article 168(2) of the Convention, account being taken of contributory acts or omissions by the Contractor, its employees, agents and subcontractors, and all persons engaged in working or acting for them in the conduct of its operations under this contract.

16.4   The Authority shall indemnify the Contractor, its employees, subcontractors, agents and all persons engaged in working or acting for them in the conduct of its operations under this contract, against all claims and liabilities of any third party arising out of any wrongful acts or omissions in the exercise of its powers and functions hereunder, including violations under Article 168(2) of the Convention.

16.5   The Contractor shall maintain appropriate insurance policies with internationally recognized carriers, in accordance with generally accepted international maritime practice.

Section 17. Force Majeure

17.1   The Contractor shall not be liable for an unavoidable delay or failure to perform any of its obligations under this contract due to force majeure. For the purposes of this contract, force majeure shall mean an event or condition that the Contractor could not reasonably be expected to prevent or control; provided that the event or condition was not caused by negligence or by a failure to observe good mining industry practice.

17.2   The Contractor shall, upon request, be granted a time extension equal to the period by which performance was delayed hereunder by force majeure and the term of this contract shall be extended accordingly.

17.3   In the event of force majeure, the Contractor shall take all reasonable measures to remove its inability to perform and comply with the terms and conditions of this contract with a minimum of delay.

17.4   The Contractor shall give notice to the Authority of the occurrence of an event of force majeure as soon as reasonably possible, and similarly give notice to the Authority of the restoration of normal conditions.

Section 18. Disclaimer

Neither the Contractor nor any affiliated company or subcontractor shall in any manner claim or suggest, whether expressly or by implication, that the Authority or any official thereof has, or has expressed, any opinion with respect to polymetallic nodules in the exploration area and a statement to that effect shall not be included in or endorsed on any prospectus, notice, circular, advertisement, press release or similar document issued by the Contractor, any affiliated company or any subcontractor that refers directly or indirectly to this contract. For the purposes of this

section, an "affiliated company" means any person, firm or company or
State-owned entity controlling, controlled by, or under common control
with, the Contractor.

Section 19. Renunciation of Rights

The Contractor, by notice to the Authority, shall have the right to renounce its
rights and terminate this contract without penalty, provided that the Contractor
shall remain liable for all obligations accrued prior to the date of such renunciation and those obligations required to be fulfilled after termination in accordance with the Regulations.

Section 20. Termination of Sponsorship

20.1 If the nationality or control of the Contractor changes or the Contractor's
     sponsoring State, as defined in the Regulations, terminates its sponsor-
     ship, the Contractor shall promptly notify the Authority forthwith.
20.2 In either such event, if the Contractor does not obtain another sponsor
     meeting the requirements prescribed in the Regulations which submits
     to the Authority a certificate of sponsorship for the Contractor in the pre-
     scribed form within the time specified in the Regulations, this contract
     shall terminate forthwith.

Section 21. Suspension and Termination of Contract and Penalties

21.1 The Council may suspend or terminate this contract, without prejudice
     to any other rights that the Authority may have, if any of the following
     events should occur:
     (a) If, in spite of written warnings by the Authority, the Contractor has
          conducted its activities in such a way as to result in serious persis-
          tent and wilful violations of the fundamental terms of this contract,
          Part XI of the Convention, the Agreement and the rules, regulations
          and procedures of the Authority; or
     (b) If the Contractor has failed to comply with a final binding decision
          of the dispute settlement body applicable to it; or
     (c) If the Contractor becomes insolvent or commits an act of bank-
          ruptcy or enters into any agreement for composition with its credi-
          tors or goes into liquidation or receivership, whether compulsory or
          voluntary, or petitions or applies to any tribunal for the appoint-
          ment of a receiver or a trustee or receiver for itself or commences
          any proceedings relating to itself under any bankruptcy, insolvency

or readjustment of debt law, whether now or hereafter in effect, other than for the purpose of reconstruction.

21.2 The Council may, without prejudice to Section 17, after consultation with the Contractor, suspend or terminate this contract, without prejudice to any other rights that the Authority may have, if the Contractor is prevented from performing its obligations under this contract by reason of an event or condition of force majeure, as described in Section 17.1, which has persisted for a continuous period exceeding two years, despite the Contractor having taken all reasonable measures to overcome its inability to perform and comply with the terms and conditions of this contract with minimum delay.

21.3 Any suspension or termination shall be by notice, through the Secretary-General, which shall include a statement of the reasons for taking such action. The suspension or termination shall be effective 60 days after such notice, unless the Contractor within such period disputes the Authority's right to suspend or terminate this contract in accordance with Part XI, Section 5, of the Convention.

21.4 If the Contractor takes such action, this contract shall only be suspended or terminated in accordance with a final binding decision in accordance with Part XI, Section 5, of the Convention.

21.5 If the Council has suspended this contract, the Council may by notice require the Contractor to resume its operations and comply with the terms and conditions of this contract, not later than 60 days after such notice.

21.6 In the case of any violation of this contract not covered by Section 21.1(a) hereof, or in lieu of suspension or termination under Section 21.1 hereof, the Council may impose upon the Contractor monetary penalties proportionate to the seriousness of the violation.

21.7 The Council may not execute a decision involving monetary penalties until the Contractor has been accorded a reasonable opportunity to exhaust the judicial remedies available to it pursuant to Part XI, Section 5, of the Convention.

21.8 In the event of termination or expiration of this contract, the Contractor shall comply with the Regulations and shall remove all installations, plant, equipment and materials in the exploration area and shall make the area safe so as not to constitute a danger to persons, shipping or to the marine environment.

Section 22. Transfer of Rights and Obligations

22.1 The rights and obligations of the Contractor under this contract may be transferred in whole or in part only with the consent of the Authority and in accordance with the Regulations.

22.2 The Authority shall not unreasonably withhold consent to the transfer if the proposed transferee is in all respects a qualified applicant in accordance with the Regulations and assumes all of the obligations of the Contractor and if the transfer does not confer to the transferee a plan of work, the approval of which would be forbidden by Article 6, paragraph 3(c), of Annex III to the Convention.

22.3 The terms, undertakings and conditions of this contract shall inure to the benefit of and be binding upon the parties hereto and their respective successors and assigns.

Section 23. No Waiver

No waiver by either party of any rights pursuant to a breach of the terms and conditions of this contract to be performed by the other party shall be construed as a waiver by the party of any succeeding breach of the same or any other term or condition to be performed by the other party.

Section 24. Revision

24.1 When circumstances have arisen or are likely to arise which, in the opinion of the Authority or the Contractor, would render this contract inequitable or make it impracticable or impossible to achieve the objectives set out in this contract or in Part XI of the Convention or the Agreement, the parties shall enter into negotiations to revise it accordingly.

24.2 This contract may also be revised by agreement between the Contractor and the Authority to facilitate the application of any rules, regulations and procedures adopted by the Authority subsequent to the entry into force of this contract.

24.3 This contract may be revised, amended or otherwise modified only with the consent of the Contractor and the Authority by an appropriate instrument signed by the authorized representatives of the parties.

Section 25. Disputes

25.1 Any dispute between the parties concerning the interpretation or application of this contract shall be settled in accordance with Part XI, Section 5, of the Convention.

25.2 In accordance with Article 21(2) of Annex III to the Convention, any final decision rendered by a court or tribunal having jurisdiction under the Convention relating to the rights and obligations of the Authority and of the Contractor shall be enforceable in the territory of any State party to the Convention affected thereby.

Section 26. Notice

26.1 Any application, request, notice, report, consent, approval, waiver, direction or instruction hereunder shall be made by the Secretary-General or by the designated representative of the Contractor, as the case may be, in writing. Service shall be by hand, or by telex, fax, registered airmail or e-mail containing an authorized signature to the Secretary-General at the headquarters of the Authority or to the designated representative. The requirement to provide any information in writing under these Regulations is satisfied by the provision of the information in an e-mail containing a digital signature.

26.2 Either party shall be entitled to change any such address to any other address by not less than ten days' notice to the other party.

26.3 Delivery by hand shall be effective when made. Delivery by telex shall be deemed to be effective on the business day following the day when the "answer back" appears on the sender's telex machine. Delivery by fax shall be effective when the "transmit confirmation report" confirming the transmission to the recipient's published fax number is received by the transmitter. Delivery by registered airmail shall be deemed to be effective 21 days after posting. An e-mail is presumed to have been received by the addressee when it enters an information system designated or used by the addressee for the purpose of receiving documents of the type sent and it is capable of being retrieved and processed by the addressee.

26.4 Notice to the designated representative of the Contractor shall constitute effective notice to the Contractor for all purposes under this contract, and the designated representative shall be the Contractor's agent for the service of process or notification in any proceeding of any court or tribunal having jurisdiction.

26.5 Notice to the Secretary-General shall constitute effective notice to the Authority for all purposes under this contract, and the Secretary-General shall be the Authority's agent for the service of process or notification in any proceeding of any court or tribunal having jurisdiction.

Section 27. Applicable Law

27.1 This contract shall be governed by the terms of this contract, the rules, regulations and procedures of the Authority, Part XI of the Convention,

the Agreement and other rules of international law not incompatible
with the Convention.

27.2 The Contractor, its employees, subcontractors, agents and all persons
engaged in working or acting for them in the conduct of its operations under this contract shall observe the applicable law referred to in
Section 27.1 hereof and shall not engage in any transaction, directly or
indirectly, prohibited by the applicable law.

27.3 Nothing contained in this contract shall be deemed an exemption from
the necessity of applying for and obtaining any permit or authority that
may be required for any activities under this contract.

Section 28. Interpretation

The division of this contract into sections and subsections and the insertion of
headings are for convenience of reference only and shall not affect the construction or interpretation hereof.

Section 29. Additional Documents

Each party hereto agrees to execute and deliver all such further instruments,
and to do and perform all such further acts and things as may be necessary or
expedient to give effect to the provisions of this contract.

Regulations on Prospecting and Exploration for Polymetallic Sulphides in the Area †

Preamble

In accordance with the United Nations Convention on the Law of the Sea ("the Convention"), the seabed and ocean floor and the subsoil thereof beyond the limits of national jurisdiction, as well as its resources, are the common heritage of mankind, the exploration and exploitation of which shall be carried out for the benefit of mankind as a whole, on whose behalf the International Seabed Authority acts. The objective of this set of Regulations is to provide for prospecting and exploration for polymetallic sulphides.

Part I. Introduction

Regulation 1. Use of Terms and Scope

1. Terms used in the Convention shall have the same meaning in these Regulations.
2. In accordance with the Agreement relating to the Implementation of Part XI of the United Nations Convention on the Law of the Sea of 10 December 1982 ("the Agreement"), the provisions of the Agreement and Part XI of the United Nations Convention on the Law of the Sea of 10 December 1982 shall be interpreted and applied together as a single instrument. These Regulations and references in these Regulations to the Convention are to be interpreted and applied accordingly.
3. For the purposes of these Regulations:
   (a) "exploitation" means the recovery for commercial purposes of polymetallic sulphides in the Area and the extraction of minerals therefrom, including the construction and operation of mining, processing and transportation systems, for the production and marketing of metals;
   (b) "exploration" means searching for deposits of polymetallic sulphides in the Area with exclusive rights, the analysis of such deposits, the

---

† Editors' Note.—This document is provided by the International Seabed Authority and is extracted from the Regulations on Prospecting and Exploration for Polymetallic Sulphides in the Area, ISBA/16/A/12/Rev.1, adopted 7 May 2010, available online: <http://www.isa.org.jm/mining-code>.

Ocean Yearbook 29: 731–785
© KONINKLIJKE BRILL NV, LEIDEN, 2015 | DOI 10.1163/10.1163/9789004297234_027

use and testing of recovery systems and equipment, processing facilities and transportation systems, and the carrying out of studies of the environmental, technical, economic, commercial and other appropriate factors that must be taken into account in exploitation;

(c)   "marine environment" includes the physical, chemical, geological and biological components, conditions and factors which interact and determine the productivity, state, condition and quality of the marine ecosystem, the waters of the seas and oceans and the airspace above those waters, as well as the seabed and ocean floor and subsoil thereof;

(d)   "polymetallic sulphides" means hydrothermally formed deposits of sulphides and accompanying mineral resources in the Area which contain concentrations of metals including, inter alia, copper, lead, zinc, gold and silver;

(e)   "prospecting" means the search for deposits of polymetallic sulphides in the Area, including estimation of the composition, size and distribution of deposits of polymetallic sulphides and their economic values, without any exclusive rights;

(f)   "serious harm to the marine environment" means any effect from activities in the Area on the marine environment which represents a significant adverse change in the marine environment determined according to the rules, regulations and procedures adopted by the Authority on the basis of internationally recognized standards and practices.

4.   These Regulations shall not in any way affect the freedom of scientific research, pursuant to Article 87 of the Convention, or the right to conduct marine scientific research in the Area pursuant to Articles 143 and 256 of the Convention. Nothing in these Regulations shall be construed in such a way as to restrict the exercise by States of the freedom of the high seas as reflected in Article 87 of the Convention.

5.   These Regulations may be supplemented by further rules, regulations and procedures, in particular on the protection and preservation of the marine environment. These Regulations shall be subject to the provisions of the Convention and the Agreement and other rules of international law not incompatible with the Convention.

Part II. Prospecting

Regulation 2. Prospecting

1.   Prospecting shall be conducted in accordance with the Convention and these Regulations and may commence only after the prospector has been

informed by the Secretary-General that its notification has been recorded pursuant to Regulation 4, paragraph 2.

2. Prospectors and the Secretary-General shall apply a precautionary approach, as reflected in principle 15 of the Rio Declaration.[1] Prospecting shall not be undertaken if substantial evidence indicates the risk of serious harm to the marine environment.

3. Prospecting shall not be undertaken in an area covered by an approved plan of work for exploration for polymetallic sulphides or in a reserved area; nor may there be prospecting in an area which the Council has disapproved for exploitation because of the risk of serious harm to the marine environment.

4. Prospecting shall not confer on the prospector any rights with respect to resources. A prospector may, however, recover a reasonable quantity of minerals, being the quantity necessary for testing and not for commercial use.

5. There shall be no time limit on prospecting, except that prospecting in a particular area shall cease upon written notification to the prospector by the Secretary-General that a plan of work for exploration has been approved with regard to that area.

6. Prospecting may be conducted simultaneously by more than one prospector in the same area or areas.

Regulation 3. Notification of Prospecting

1. A proposed prospector shall notify the Authority of its intention to engage in prospecting.

2. Each notification of prospecting shall be in the form prescribed in Annex 1 to these Regulations, addressed to the Secretary-General, and shall conform to the requirements of these Regulations.

3. Each notification shall be submitted:
   (a) In the case of a State, by the authority designated for that purpose by it;
   (b) In the case of an entity, by its designated representative;
   (c) In the case of the Enterprise, by its competent authority.

4. Each notification shall be in one of the languages of the Authority and shall contain:
   (a) The name, nationality and address of the proposed prospector and its designated representative;

---

1 *Report of the United Nations Conference on Environment and Development, Rio de Janeiro, 3–14 June 1991* (United Nations publication, Sales No. E.91.1.8 and corrigenda), vol. 1: *Resolutions adopted by the Conference*, resolution 1, annex 1.

(b) The coordinates of the broad area or areas within which prospecting is to be conducted, in accordance with the most recent generally
accepted international standard used by the Authority;

(c) A general description of the prospecting programme, including the
proposed date of commencement and its approximate duration;

(d) A satisfactory written undertaking that the proposed prospector will:

   (i) Comply with the Convention and the relevant rules, regulations and procedures of the Authority concerning:

      a. Cooperation in the training programmes in connection
with marine scientific research and transfer of technology
referred to in Articles 143 and 144 of the Convention; and

      b. Protection and preservation of the marine environment;

   (ii) Accept verification by the Authority of compliance therewith; and

   (iii) Make available to the Authority, as far as practicable, such data
as may be relevant to the protection and preservation of the
marine environment.

Regulation 4. Consideration of Notifications

1. The Secretary-General shall acknowledge in writing receipt of each notification submitted under Regulation 3, specifying the date of receipt.

2. The Secretary-General shall review and act on the notification within
45 days of its receipt. If the notification conforms with the requirements
of the Convention and these Regulations, the Secretary-General shall
record the particulars of the notification in a register maintained for that
purpose and shall inform the prospector in writing that the notification
has been so recorded.

3. The Secretary-General shall, within 45 days of receipt of the notification,
inform the proposed prospector in writing if the notification includes any
part of an area included in an approved plan of work for exploration or
exploitation of any category of resources, or any part of a reserved area,
or any part of an area which has been disapproved by the Council for
exploitation because of the risk of serious harm to the marine environment, or if the written undertaking is not satisfactory, and shall provide
the proposed prospector with a written statement of reasons. In such
cases, the proposed prospector may, within 90 days, submit an amended
notification. The Secretary-General shall, within 45 days, review and act
upon such amended notification.

4. A prospector shall inform the Secretary-General in writing of any change
in the information contained in the notification.

5. The Secretary-General shall not release any particulars contained in the notification except with the written consent of the prospector. The Secretary-General shall, however, from time to time inform all members of the Authority of the identity of prospectors and the general areas in which prospecting is being conducted.

Regulation 5. Protection and Preservation of the Marine Environment during Prospecting

1. Each prospector shall take necessary measures to prevent, reduce and control pollution and other hazards to the marine environment arising from prospecting, as far as reasonably possible, applying a precautionary approach and best environmental practices. In particular, each prospector shall minimize or eliminate:
    (a) Adverse environmental impacts from prospecting; and
    (b) Actual or potential conflicts or interference with existing or planned marine scientific research activities, in accordance with the relevant future guidelines in this regard.
2. Prospectors shall cooperate with the Authority in the establishment and implementation of programmes for monitoring and evaluating the potential impacts of the exploration for and exploitation of polymetallic sulphides on the marine environment.
3. A prospector shall immediately notify the Secretary-General in writing, using the most effective means, of any incident arising from prospecting which has caused, is causing or poses a threat of serious harm to the marine environment. Upon receipt of such notification the Secretary-General shall act in a manner consistent with Regulation 35.

Regulation 6. Annual Report

1. A prospector shall, within 90 days of the end of each calendar year, submit a report to the Authority on the status of prospecting. Such reports shall be submitted by the Secretary-General to the Legal and Technical Commission. Each such report shall contain:
    (a) A general description of the status of prospecting and of the results obtained;
    (b) Information on compliance with the undertakings referred to in Regulation 3, paragraph 4(d); and
    (c) Information on adherence to the relevant guidelines in this regard.
2. If the prospector intends to claim expenditures for prospecting as part of the development costs incurred prior to the commencement of

commercial production, the prospector shall submit an annual statement, in conformity with internationally accepted accounting principles and certified by a duly qualified firm of public accountants, of the actual and direct expenditures incurred by the prospector in carrying out prospecting.

Regulation 7. Confidentiality of Data and Information from Prospecting Contained in the Annual Report

1.   The Secretary-General shall ensure the confidentiality of all data and information contained in the reports submitted under Regulation 6 applying mutatis mutandis the provisions of Regulations 38 and 39, provided that data and information relating to the protection and preservation of the marine environment, in particular those from environmental monitoring programmes, shall not be considered confidential. The prospector may request that such data not be disclosed for up to three years following the date of their submission.

2.   The Secretary-General may, at any time, with the consent of the prospector concerned, release data and information relating to prospecting in an area in respect of which a notification has been submitted. If, after having made reasonable efforts for at least two years, the Secretary-General determines that the prospector no longer exists or cannot be located, the Secretary-General may release such data and information.

Regulation 8. Objects of an Archaeological or Historical Nature

A prospector shall immediately notify the Secretary-General in writing of any finding in the Area of an object of actual or potential archaeological or historical nature and its location. The Secretary-General shall transmit such information to the Director-General of the United Nations Educational, Scientific and Cultural Organization.

Part III. Applications for Approval of Plans of Work for Exploration in the Form of Contracts

Section 1. General Provisions

Regulation 9. General

Subject to the provisions of the Convention, the following may apply to the Authority for approval of plans of work for exploration:

(a) The Enterprise, on its own behalf or in a joint arrangement;

(b) States Parties, State enterprises or natural or juridical persons which possess the nationality of States or are effectively controlled by them or their nationals, when sponsored by such States, or any group of the foregoing which meets the requirements of these Regulations.

Section 2. Content of Applications

Regulation 10. Form of Applications

1. Each application for approval of a plan of work for exploration shall be in the form prescribed in Annex 2 to these Regulations, shall be addressed to the Secretary-General, and shall conform to the requirements of these Regulations.

2. Each application shall be submitted:

(a) In the case of a State, by the authority designated for that purpose by it;

(b) In the case of an entity, by its designated representative or the authority designated for that purpose by the sponsoring State or States; and

(c) In the case of the Enterprise, by its competent authority.

3. Each application by a State enterprise or one of the entities referred to in subparagraph (b) of Regulation 9 shall also contain:

(a) Sufficient information to determine the nationality of the applicant or the identity of the State or States by which, or by whose nationals, the applicant is effectively controlled; and

(b) The principal place of business or domicile and, if applicable, place of registration of the applicant.

4. Each application submitted by a partnership or consortium of entities shall contain the required information in respect of each member of the partnership or consortium.

Regulation 11. Certificate of Sponsorship

1. Each application by a State enterprise or one of the entities referred to in subparagraph (b) of Regulation 9 shall be accompanied by a certificate of sponsorship issued by the State of which it is a national or by which or by whose nationals it is effectively controlled. If the applicant has more than one nationality, as in the case of a partnership or consortium of entities from more than one State, each State involved shall issue a certificate of sponsorship.

2.   Where the applicant has the nationality of one State but is effectively controlled by another State or its nationals, each State involved shall issue a certificate of sponsorship.

3.   Each certificate of sponsorship shall be duly signed on behalf of the State by which it is submitted, and shall contain:

     (a)   The name of the applicant;

     (b)   The name of the sponsoring State;

     (c)   A statement that the applicant is:

         (i)   A national of the sponsoring State; or

         (ii)   Subject to the effective control of the sponsoring State or its nationals;

     (d)   A statement by the sponsoring State that it sponsors the applicant;

     (e)   The date of deposit by the sponsoring State of its instrument of ratification of, or accession or succession to, the Convention;

     (f)   A declaration that the sponsoring State assumes responsibility in accordance with Article 139, Article 153, paragraph 4, and Annex III, Article 4, paragraph 4, of the Convention.

4.   States or entities in a joint arrangement with the Enterprise shall also comply with this regulation.

Regulation 12. Total Area Covered by the Application

1.   For the purposes of these Regulations, a "polymetallic sulphide block" means a cell of a grid as provided by the Authority, which shall be approximately 10 kilometres by 10 kilometres and no greater than 100 square kilometres.

2.   The area covered by each application for approval of a plan of work for exploration for polymetallic sulphides shall be comprised of not more than 100 polymetallic sulphide blocks which shall be arranged by the applicant in at least five clusters, as set out in paragraph 3 below.

3.   Each cluster of polymetallic sulphide blocks shall contain at least five contiguous blocks. Two such blocks that touch at any point shall be considered to be contiguous. Clusters of polymetallic sulphide blocks need not be contiguous but shall be proximate and confined within a rectangular area not exceeding 300,000 square kilometres in size and where the longest side does not exceed 1,000 kilometres in length.

4.   Notwithstanding the provisions in paragraph 2 above, where an applicant has elected to contribute a reserved area to carry out activities pursuant to Article 9 of Annex III to the Convention, in accordance with Regulation 17, the total area covered by an application shall not exceed 200 polymetallic sulphide blocks. Such blocks shall be arranged in two groups of

equal estimated commercial value and each such group of polymetallic sulphide blocks shall be arranged by the applicant in clusters, as set out in paragraph 3 above.

Regulation 13. Financial and Technical Capabilities

1. Each application for approval of a plan of work for exploration shall contain specific and sufficient information to enable the Council to determine whether the applicant is financially and technically capable of carrying out the proposed plan of work for exploration and of fulfilling its financial obligations to the Authority.

2. An application for approval of a plan of work for exploration by the Enterprise shall include a statement by its competent authority certifying that the Enterprise has the necessary financial resources to meet the estimated costs of the proposed plan of work for exploration.

3. An application for approval of a plan of work for exploration by a State or a State enterprise shall include a statement by the State or the sponsoring State certifying that the applicant has the necessary financial resources to meet the estimated costs of the proposed plan of work for exploration.

4. An application for approval of a plan of work for exploration by an entity shall include copies of its audited financial statements, including balance sheets and profit-and-loss statements, for the most recent three years, in conformity with internationally accepted accounting principles and certified by a duly qualified firm of public accountants; and

    (a) If the applicant is a newly organized entity and a certified balance sheet is not available, a pro forma balance sheet certified by an appropriate official of the applicant;

    (b) If the applicant is a subsidiary of another entity, copies of such financial statements of that entity and a statement from that entity, in conformity with internationally accepted accounting principles and certified by a duly qualified firm of public accountants, that the applicant will have the financial resources to carry out the plan of work for exploration;

    (c) If the applicant is controlled by a State or a State enterprise, a statement from the State or State enterprise certifying that the applicant will have the financial resources to carry out the plan of work for exploration.

5. Where an applicant referred to in paragraph 4 intends to finance the proposed plan of work for exploration by borrowings, its application shall

include the amount of such borrowings, the repayment period and the interest rate.

6. Each application shall include:

    (a) A general description of the applicant's previous experience, knowledge, skills, technical qualifications and expertise relevant to the proposed plan of work for exploration;

    (b) A general description of the equipment and methods expected to be used in carrying out the proposed plan of work for exploration and other relevant non-proprietary information about the characteristics of such technology;

    (c) A general description of the applicant's financial and technical capability to respond to any incident or activity which causes serious harm to the marine environment.

7. Where the applicant is a partnership or consortium of entities in a joint arrangement, each member of the partnership or consortium shall provide the information required by this regulation.

Regulation 14. Previous Contracts with the Authority

Where the applicant or, in the case of an application by a partnership or consortium of entities in a joint arrangement, any member of the partnership or consortium, has previously been awarded any contract with the Authority, the application shall include:

    (a) The date of the previous contract or contracts;

    (b) The date, reference number and title of each report submitted to the Authority in connection with the contract or contracts; and

    (c) The date of termination of the contract or contracts, if applicable.

Regulation 15. Undertakings

Each applicant, including the Enterprise, shall, as part of its application for approval of a plan of work for exploration, provide a written undertaking to the Authority that it will:

    (a) Accept as enforceable and comply with the applicable obligations created by the provisions of the Convention and the rules, regulations and procedures of the Authority, the decisions of the organs of the Authority and the terms of its contracts with the Authority;

    (b) Accept control by the Authority of activities in the Area, as authorized by the Convention; and

    (c) Provide the Authority with a written assurance that its obligations under the contract will be fulfilled in good faith.

Regulation 16. Applicant's Election of a Reserved Area Contribution or Equity Interest in a Joint Venture Arrangement

Each applicant shall, in the application, elect either to:
  (a) Contribute a reserved area to carry out activities pursuant to Annex III, Article 9, of the Convention, in accordance with Regulation 17; or
  (b) Offer an equity interest in a joint venture arrangement in accordance with Regulation 19.

Regulation 17. Data and Information to be Submitted before the Designation of a Reserved Area

1. Where the applicant elects to contribute a reserved area to carry out activities pursuant to Article 9 of Annex III to the Convention, the area covered by the application shall be sufficiently large and of sufficient estimated commercial value to allow two mining operations and shall be configured by the applicant in accordance with Regulation 12, paragraph 4.
2. Each such application shall contain sufficient data and information, as prescribed in Section II of Annex 2 to these Regulations, with respect to the area under application to enable the Council, on the recommendation of the Legal and Technical Commission, to designate a reserved area based on the estimated commercial value of each part. Such data and information shall consist of data available to the applicant with respect to both parts of the area under application, including the data used to determine their commercial value.
3. The Council, on the basis of the data and information submitted by the applicant pursuant to Section II of Annex 2 to these Regulations, if found satisfactory, and taking into account the recommendation of the Legal and Technical Commission, shall designate the part of the area under application which is to be a reserved area. The area so designated shall become a reserved area as soon as the plan of work for exploration for the non-reserved area is approved and the contract is signed. If the Council determines that additional information, consistent with these Regulations and Annex 2, is needed to designate the reserved area, it shall refer the matter back to the Commission for further consideration, specifying the additional information required.
4. Once the plan of work for exploration is approved and a contract has been issued, the data and information transferred to the Authority by the applicant in respect of the reserved area may be disclosed by the

Authority in accordance with Article 14, paragraph 3, of Annex III to the Convention.

Regulation 18. Applications for Approval of Plans of Work with Respect to a Reserved Area

1. Any State which is a developing State or any natural or juridical person sponsored by it and effectively controlled by it or by any other developing State, or any group of the foregoing, may notify the Authority that it wishes to submit a plan of work for exploration with respect to a reserved area. The Secretary-General shall forward such notification to the Enterprise, which shall inform the Secretary-General in writing within six months whether or not it intends to carry out activities in that area. If the Enterprise intends to carry out activities in that area, it shall, pursuant to paragraph 4, also inform in writing the contractor whose application for approval of a plan of work for exploration originally included that area.

2. An application for approval of a plan of work for exploration in respect of a reserved area may be submitted at any time after such an area becomes available following a decision by the Enterprise that it does not intend to carry out activities in that area or where the Enterprise has not, within six months of the notification by the Secretary-General, either taken a decision on whether it intends to carry out activities in that area or notified the Secretary-General in writing that it is engaged in discussions regarding a potential joint venture. In the latter instance, the Enterprise shall have one year from the date of such notification in which to decide whether to conduct activities in that area.

3. If the Enterprise or a developing State or one of the entities referred to in paragraph 1 does not submit an application for approval of a plan of work for exploration for activities in a reserved area within 15 years of the commencement by the Enterprise of its functions independent of the Secretariat of the Authority or within 15 years of the date on which that area is reserved for the Authority, whichever is the later, the contractor whose application for approval of a plan of work for exploration originally included that area shall be entitled to apply for a plan of work for exploration for that area provided it offers in good faith to include the Enterprise as a joint-venture partner.

4. A contractor has the right of first refusal to enter into a joint venture arrangement with the Enterprise for exploration of the area which was

included in its application for approval of a plan of work for exploration and which was designated by the Council as a reserved area.

Regulation 19. Equity Interest in a Joint Venture Arrangement

1. Where the applicant elects to offer an equity interest in a joint venture arrangement, it shall submit data and information in accordance with Regulation 20. The area to be allocated to the applicant shall be subject to the provisions of Regulation 27.

2. The joint venture arrangement, which shall take effect at the time the applicant enters into a contract for exploitation, shall include the following:

    (a) The Enterprise shall obtain a minimum of 20 per cent of the equity participation in the joint venture arrangement on the following basis:

        (i) Half of such equity participation shall be obtained without payment, directly or indirectly, to the applicant and shall be treated *pari passu* for all purposes with the equity participation of the applicant;

        (ii) The remainder of such equity participation shall be treated *pari passu* for all purposes with the equity participation of the applicant except that the Enterprise shall not receive any profit distribution with respect to such participation until the applicant has recovered its total equity participation in the joint venture arrangement;

    (b) Notwithstanding subparagraph (a), the applicant shall nevertheless offer the Enterprise the opportunity to purchase a further thirty per cent of the equity in the joint venture arrangement, or such lesser percentage as the Enterprise may elect to purchase, on the basis of *pari passu* treatment with the applicant for all purposes;[2]

    (c) Except as specifically provided in the agreement between the applicant and the Enterprise, the Enterprise shall not by reason of its equity participation be otherwise obligated to provide funds or credits or issue guarantees or otherwise accept any financial liability whatsoever for or on behalf of the joint venture arrangement, nor shall the Enterprise be required to subscribe for additional

---

2 The terms and conditions upon which such equality participation may be obtained would need to be further elaborated.

equity participation so as to maintain its proportionate participation in the joint venture arrangement.

Regulation 20. Data and Information to be Submitted for Approval of the Plan of Work for Exploration

1. Each applicant shall submit, with a view to receiving approval of the plan of work for exploration in the form of a contract, the following information:

    (a) A general description and a schedule of the proposed exploration programme, including the programme of activities for the immediate five-year period, such as studies to be undertaken in respect of the environmental, technical, economic and other appropriate factors that must be taken into account in exploration;

    (b) A description of the programme for oceanographic and environmental baseline studies in accordance with these Regulations and any environmental rules, regulations and procedures established by the Authority that would enable an assessment of the potential environmental impact including, but not restricted to, the impact on biodiversity, of the proposed exploration activities, taking into account any recommendations issued by the Legal and Technical Commission;

    (c) A preliminary assessment of the possible impact of the proposed exploration activities on the marine environment;

    (d) A description of proposed measures for the prevention, reduction and control of pollution and other hazards, as well as possible impacts, to the marine environment;

    (e) Data necessary for the Council to make the determination it is required to make in accordance with Regulation 13, paragraph 1; and

    (f) A schedule of anticipated yearly expenditures in respect of the programme of activities for the immediate five-year period.

2. Where the applicant elects to contribute a reserved area, the data and information relating to such area shall be transferred to the Authority by the applicant after the Council has designated the reserved area in accordance with Regulation 17, paragraph 3.

3. Where the applicant elects to offer an equity interest in a joint venture arrangement, the data and information relating to such area shall be transferred to the Authority by the applicant at the time of the election.

Section 3. Fees

Regulation 21. Fee for Applications

1. The fee for processing a plan of work for exploration for polymetallic sulphides shall be:
    (a) A fixed fee of 500,000 United States dollars or its equivalent in a freely convertible currency, payable by the applicant at the time of submitting an application; or
    (b) At the election of the applicant, a fixed fee of 50,000 United States dollars or its equivalent in a freely convertible currency, payable by the applicant at the time of submitting an application, and an annual fee calculated as set out in paragraph 2.
2. The annual fee shall be calculated as follows:
    (a) 5 United States dollars multiplied by the area factor from the date of the first anniversary of the contract;
    (b) 10 United States dollars multiplied by the area factor from the date of the first relinquishment in accordance with Regulation 27(2); and
    (c) 20 United States dollars multiplied by the area factor from the date of the second relinquishment in accordance with Regulation 27(3).
3. The "Area Factor" means the number of square kilometres comprised in the exploration area at the date upon which the periodic payment in question becomes due.
4. Upon notification by the Secretary-General that the amount of the fee has been insufficient to cover the administrative costs incurred by the Authority in processing an application, the fee set out in paragraph 1(a) of this regulation shall be reviewed by the Council.
5. If the administrative costs incurred by the Authority in processing an application are less than the fixed amount, the Authority shall refund the difference to the applicant.

Section 4. Processing of Applications

Regulation 22. Receipt, Acknowledgement and Safe Custody of Applications

The Secretary-General shall:
    (a) Acknowledge in writing within 30 days receipt of every application for approval of a plan of work for exploration submitted under this Part, specifying the date of receipt;

(b)   Place the application together with the attachments and annexes thereto in safe custody and ensure the confidentiality of all confidential data and information contained in the application; and

(c)   Notify the members of the Authority of the receipt of such application and circulate to them information of a general nature which is not confidential regarding the application.

Regulation 23. Consideration by the Legal and Technical Commission

1.   Upon receipt of an application for approval of a plan of work for exploration, the Secretary-General shall notify the members of the Legal and Technical Commission and place consideration of the application as an item on the agenda for the next meeting of the Commission. The Commission shall only consider applications in respect of which notification and information has been circulated by the Secretary-General in accordance with Regulation 22(c) at least 30 days prior to the commencement of the meeting of the Commission at which they are to be considered.

2.   The Commission shall examine applications in the order in which they are received.

3.   The Commission shall determine if the applicant:
(a)   Has complied with the provisions of these Regulations;
(b)   Has given the undertakings and assurances specified in Regulation 15;
(c)   Possesses the financial and technical capability to carry out the proposed plan of work for exploration and has provided details as to its ability to comply promptly with emergency orders; and
(d)   Has satisfactorily discharged its obligations in relation to any previous contract with the Authority.

4.   The Commission shall, in accordance with the requirements set forth in these Regulations and its procedures, determine whether the proposed plan of work for exploration will:
(a)   Provide for effective protection of human health and safety;
(b)   Provide for effective protection and preservation of the marine environment including, but not restricted to, the impact on biodiversity;
(c)   Ensure that installations are not established where interference may be caused to the use of recognized sea lanes essential to international navigation or in areas of intense fishing activity.

5.   If the Commission makes the determinations specified in paragraph 3 and determines that the proposed plan of work for exploration meets

the requirements of paragraph 4, the Commission shall recommend approval of the plan of work for exploration to the Council.

6. The Commission shall not recommend approval of the plan of work for exploration if part or all of the area covered by the proposed plan of work for exploration is included in:

   (a) A plan of work for exploration approved by the Council for polymetallic sulphides; or

   (b) A plan of work approved by the Council for exploration for or exploitation of other resources if the proposed plan of work for exploration for polymetallic sulphides might cause undue interference with activities under such approved plan of work for other resources; or

   (c) An area disapproved for exploitation by the Council in cases where substantial evidence indicates the risk of serious harm to the marine environment.

7. The Legal and Technical Commission may recommend approval of a plan of work if it determines that such approval would not permit a State Party or entities sponsored by it to monopolize the conduct of activities in the Area with regard to polymetallic sulphides or to preclude other States Parties from activities in the Area with regard to polymetallic sulphides.

8. Except in the case of applications by the Enterprise, on its own behalf or in a joint venture, and applications under Regulation 18, the Commission shall not recommend approval of the plan of work for exploration if part or all of the area covered by the proposed plan of work for exploration is included in a reserved area or an area designated by the Council to be a reserved area.

9. If the Commission finds that an application does not comply with these Regulations, it shall notify the applicant in writing, through the Secretary-General, indicating the reasons. The applicant may, within 45 days of such notification, amend its application. If the Commission after further consideration is of the view that it should not recommend approval of the plan of work for exploration, it shall so inform the applicant and provide the applicant with a further opportunity to make representations within 30 days of such information. The Commission shall consider any such representations made by the applicant in preparing its report and recommendation to the Council.

10. In considering a proposed plan of work for exploration, the Commission shall have regard to the principles, policies and objectives relating to activities in the Area as provided for in Part XI and Annex III of the Convention and the Agreement.

11.   The Commission shall consider applications expeditiously and shall sub-
        mit its report and recommendations to the Council on the designation
        of the areas and on the plan of work for exploration at the first possible
        opportunity, taking into account the schedule of meetings of the Authority.
12.   In discharging its duties, the Commission shall apply these Regulations
        and the rules, regulations and procedures of the Authority in a uniform and
        non-discriminatory manner.

Regulation 24. Consideration and Approval of Plans of Work for Exploration by the Council

The Council shall consider the reports and recommendations of the
Commission relating to approval of plans of work for exploration in accordance with paragraphs 11 and 12 of Section 3 of the annex to the Agreement.

Part IV. Contracts for Exploration

Regulation 25. The Contract

1.   After a plan of work for exploration has been approved by the Council, it
        shall be prepared in the form of a contract between the Authority and the
        applicant as prescribed in Annex 3 to these Regulations. Each contract
        shall incorporate the standard clauses set out in Annex 4 in effect at the
        date of entry into force of the contract.
2.   The contract shall be signed by the Secretary-General on behalf of the
        Authority and by the applicant. The Secretary-General shall notify all
        members of the Authority in writing of the conclusion of each contract.

Regulation 26. Rights of the Contractor

1.   The contractor shall have the exclusive right to explore an area covered
        by a plan of work for exploration in respect of polymetallic sulphides.
        The Authority shall ensure that no other entity operates in the same area
        for other resources in a manner that might interfere with the operations
        of the contractor.
2.   A contractor who has an approved plan of work for exploration only
        shall have a preference and a priority among applicants submitting
        plans of work for exploitation of the same area and resources. Such
        preference or priority may be withdrawn by the Council if the contrac-
        tor has failed to comply with the requirements of its approved plan of

work for exploration within the time period specified in a written notice or notices from the Council to the contractor indicating which requirements have not been complied with by the contractor. The time period specified in any such notice shall not be unreasonable. The contractor shall be accorded a reasonable opportunity to be heard before the withdrawal of such preference or priority becomes final. The Council shall provide the reasons for its proposed withdrawal of preference or priority and shall consider any contractor's response. The decision of the Council shall take account of that response and shall be based on substantial evidence.

3. A withdrawal of preference or priority shall not become effective until the contractor has been accorded a reasonable opportunity to exhaust the judicial remedies available to it pursuant to Part XI, Section 5, of the Convention.

Regulation 27. Size of Area and Relinquishment

1. The contractor shall relinquish the area allocated to it in accordance with paragraph 2 of this regulation. Areas to be relinquished need not be contiguous and shall be defined by the contractor in the form of sub-blocks comprising one or more cells of a grid as provided by the Authority.
2. The total area allocated to the contractor under the contract shall not exceed 10,000 square kilometres. The contractor shall relinquish parts of the area allocated to it in accordance with the following schedule:
   (a) By the end of the eighth year from the date of the contract, the contractor shall have relinquished at least 50 per cent of the original area allocated to it;
   (b) By the end of the tenth year from the date of the contract, the contractor shall have relinquished at least 75 per cent of the original area allocated to it; or
3. The contractor may at any time relinquish parts of the area allocated to it in advance of the schedule set out in paragraph 2, provided that a contractor shall not be required to relinquish any additional part of such area when the remaining area allocated to it after relinquishment does not exceed 2,500 square kilometres.
4. Relinquished areas shall revert to the Area.
5. At the end of the fifteenth year from the date of the contract, or when the contractor applies for exploitation rights, whichever is the earlier, the contractor shall nominate an area from the remaining area allocated to it to be retained for exploitation.

6.   The Council may, at the request of the contractor, and on the recommendation of the Commission, in exceptional circumstances, defer the schedule
of relinquishment. Such exceptional circumstances shall be determined
by the Council and shall include, inter alia, consideration of prevailing
economic circumstances or other unforeseen exceptional circumstances
arising in connection with the operational activities of the contractor.

Regulation 28. Duration of Contracts

1.   A plan of work for exploration shall be approved for a period of 15 years.
Upon expiration of a plan of work for exploration, the contractor shall
apply for a plan of work for exploitation unless the contractor has already
done so, has obtained an extension for the plan of work for exploration or
decides to renounce its rights in the area covered by the plan of work for
exploration.
2.   Not later than six months before the expiration of a plan of work for
exploration, a contractor may apply for extensions for the plan of work
for exploration for periods of not more than five years each. Such extensions shall be approved by the Council, on the recommendation of the
Commission, if the contractor has made efforts in good faith to comply
with the requirements of the plan of work but for reasons beyond the
contractor's control has been unable to complete the necessary preparatory work for proceeding to the exploitation stage or if the prevailing economic circumstances do not justify proceeding to the exploitation stage.

Regulation 29. Training

Pursuant to Article 15 of Annex III to the Convention, each contract shall
include as a schedule a practical programme for the training of personnel
of the Authority and developing States and drawn up by the contractor in
cooperation with the Authority and the sponsoring State or States. Training
programmes shall focus on training in the conduct of exploration, and shall
provide for full participation by such personnel in all activities covered by the
contract. Such training programmes may be revised and developed from time
to time as necessary by mutual agreement.

Regulation 30. Periodic Review of the Implementation of the Plan of
Work for Exploration

1.   The contractor and the Secretary-General shall jointly undertake a periodic review of the implementation of the plan of work for exploration at

intervals of five years. The Secretary-General may request the contractor to submit such additional data and information as may be necessary for the purposes of the review.

2. In the light of the review, the contractor shall indicate its programme of activities for the following five-year period, making such adjustments to its previous programme of activities as are necessary.

3. The Secretary-General shall report on the review to the Commission and to the Council. The Secretary-General shall indicate in the report whether any observations transmitted to him by States Parties to the Convention concerning the manner in which the contractor has discharged its obligations under these Regulations relating to the protection and preservation of the marine environment were taken into account in the review.

Regulation 31. Termination of Sponsorship

1. Each contractor shall have the required sponsorship throughout the period of the contract.

2. If a State terminates its sponsorship it shall promptly notify the Secretary-General in writing. The sponsoring State should also inform the Secretary-General of the reasons for terminating its sponsorship. Termination of sponsorship shall take effect six months after the date of receipt of the notification by the Secretary-General, unless the notification specifies a later date.

3. In the event of termination of sponsorship the contractor shall, within the period referred to in paragraph 2, obtain another sponsor. Such sponsor shall submit a certificate of sponsorship in accordance with Regulation 11. Failure to obtain a sponsor within the required period shall result in the termination of the contract.

4. A sponsoring State shall not be discharged by reason of the termination of its sponsorship from any obligations accrued while it was a sponsoring State, nor shall such termination affect any legal rights and obligations created during such sponsorship.

5. The Secretary-General shall notify the members of the Authority of the termination or change of sponsorship.

Regulation 32. Responsibility and Liability

Responsibility and liability of the contractor and of the Authority shall be in accordance with the Convention. The contractor shall continue to have responsibility for any damage arising out of wrongful acts in the conduct of its operations, in particular damage to the marine environment, after the completion of the exploration phase.

Part V. Protection and Preservation of the Marine Environment

Regulation 33. Protection and Preservation of the Marine Environment

1. The Authority shall, in accordance with the Convention and the Agreement, establish and keep under periodic review environmental rules, regulations and procedures to ensure effective protection for the marine environment from harmful effects which may arise from activities in the Area.
2. In order to ensure effective protection for the marine environment from harmful effects which may arise from activities in the Area, the Authority and sponsoring States shall apply a precautionary approach, as reflected in principle 15 of the Rio Declaration, and best environmental practices.
3. The Legal and Technical Commission shall make recommendations to the Council on the implementation of paragraphs 1 and 2 above.
4. The Commission shall develop and implement procedures for determining, on the basis of the best available scientific and technical information, including information provided pursuant to Regulation 20, whether proposed exploration activities in the Area would have serious harmful effects on vulnerable marine ecosystems, in particular hydrothermal vents, and ensure that, if it is determined that certain proposed exploration activities would have serious harmful effects on vulnerable marine ecosystems, those activities are managed to prevent such effects or not authorized to proceed.
5. Pursuant to Article 145 of the Convention and paragraph 2 of this regulation, each contractor shall take necessary measures to prevent, reduce and control pollution and other hazards to the marine environment arising from its activities in the Area as far as reasonably possible, applying a precautionary approach and best environmental practices.
6. Contractors, sponsoring States and other interested States or entities shall cooperate with the Authority in the establishment and implementation of programmes for monitoring and evaluating the impacts of deep seabed mining on the marine environment. When required by the Council, such programmes shall include proposals for areas to be set aside and used exclusively as impact reference zones and preservation reference

zones. "Impact reference zones" means areas to be used for assessing the effect of activities in the Area on the marine environment and which are representative of the environmental characteristics of the Area. "Preservation reference zones" means areas in which no mining shall occur to ensure representative and stable biota of the seabed in order to assess any changes in the biodiversity of the marine environment.

Regulation 34. Environmental Baselines and Monitoring

1. Each contract shall require the contractor to gather environmental base-line data and to establish environmental baselines, taking into account any recommendations issued by the Legal and Technical Commission pursuant to Regulation 41, against which to assess the likely effects of its programme of activities under the plan of work for exploration on the marine environment and a programme to monitor and report on such effects. The recommendations issued by the Commission may, inter alia, list those exploration activities which may be considered to have no potential for causing harmful effects on the marine environment. The contractor shall cooperate with the Authority and the sponsoring State or States in the establishment and implementation of such monitoring programme.

2. The contractor shall report annually in writing to the Secretary-General on the implementation and results of the monitoring programme referred to in paragraph 1 and shall submit data and information, taking into account any recommendations issued by the Commission pursuant to Regulation 41. The Secretary-General shall transmit such reports to the Commission for its consideration pursuant to Article 165 of the Convention.

Regulation 35. Emergency Orders

1. A contractor shall promptly report to the Secretary-General in writing, using the most effective means, any incident arising from activities which have caused, are causing, or pose a threat of, serious harm to the marine environment.

2. When the Secretary-General has been notified by a contractor or other-wise becomes aware of an incident resulting from or caused by a contrac-tor's activities in the Area that has caused, is causing or poses a threat of, serious harm to the marine environment, the Secretary-General shall cause a general notification of the incident to be issued, shall notify in writing the contractor and the sponsoring State or States, and shall report

immediately to the Legal and Technical Commission, to the Council and to all other members of the Authority. A copy of the report shall be circulated to competent international organizations and to concerned subregional, regional and global organizations and bodies. The Secretary-General shall monitor developments with respect to all such incidents and shall report on them as appropriate to the Commission, the Council and all other members of the Authority.

3. Pending any action by the Council, the Secretary-General shall take such immediate measures of a temporary nature as are practical and reasonable in the circumstances to prevent, contain and minimize serious harm or the threat of serious harm to the marine environment. Such temporary measures shall remain in effect for no longer than 90 days, or until the Council decides at its next regular session or a special session, what measures, if any, to take pursuant to paragraph 6 of this regulation.

4. After having received the report of the Secretary-General, the Commission shall determine, based on the evidence provided to it and taking into account the measures already taken by the contractor, which measures are necessary to respond effectively to the incident in order to prevent, contain and minimize serious harm or the threat of serious harm to the marine environment, and shall make its recommendations to the Council.

5. The Council shall consider the recommendations of the Commission.

6. The Council, taking into account the recommendations of the Commission, the report of the Secretary-General, any information provided by the Contractor and any other relevant information, may issue emergency orders, which may include orders for the suspension or adjustment of operations, as may be reasonably necessary to prevent, contain and minimize serious harm or the threat of serious harm to the marine environment arising out of activities in the Area.

7. If a contractor does not promptly comply with an emergency order to prevent, contain and minimize serious harm or the threat of serious harm to the marine environment arising out of its activities in the Area, the Council shall take by itself or through arrangements with others on its behalf, such practical measures as are necessary to prevent, contain and minimize any such serious harm or threat of serious harm to the marine environment.

8. In order to enable the Council, when necessary, to take immediately the practical measures to prevent, contain and minimize the serious harm or threat of serious harm to the marine environment referred to in paragraph 7, the contractor, prior to the commencement of testing of collecting systems and processing operations, will provide the Council

with a guarantee of its financial and technical capability to comply promptly with emergency orders or to assure that the Council can take such emergency measures. If the contractor does not provide the Council with such a guarantee, the sponsoring State or States shall, in response to a request by the Secretary-General and pursuant to Articles 139 and 235 of the Convention, take necessary measures to ensure that the contractor provides such a guarantee or shall take measures to ensure that assistance is provided to the Authority in the discharge of its responsibilities under paragraph 7.

Regulation 36. Rights of Coastal States

1. Nothing in these Regulations shall affect the rights of coastal States in accordance with Article 142 and other relevant provisions of the Convention.
2. Any coastal State which has grounds for believing that any activity in the Area by a contractor is likely to cause serious harm or a threat of serious harm to the marine environment under its jurisdiction or sovereignty may notify the Secretary-General in writing of the grounds upon which such belief is based. The Secretary-General shall provide the Contractor and its sponsoring State or States with a reasonable opportunity to examine the evidence, if any, provided by the coastal State as the basis for its belief. The contractor and its sponsoring State or States may submit their observations thereon to the Secretary-General within a reasonable time.
3. If there are clear grounds for believing that serious harm to the marine environment is likely to occur, the Secretary-General shall act in accordance with Regulation 35 and, if necessary, shall take immediate measures of a temporary nature as provided for in paragraph 3 of Regulation 35.
4. Contractors shall take all measures necessary to ensure that their activities are conducted so as not to cause serious harm to the marine environment, including, but not restricted to, pollution, under the jurisdiction or sovereignty of coastal States, and that such serious harm or pollution arising from incidents or activities in its exploration area does not spread beyond such area.

Regulation 37. Human Remains and Objects and Sites of an Archaeological or Historical Nature

The contractor shall immediately notify the Secretary-General in writing of any finding in the exploration area of any human remains of an archaeological or historical nature, or any object or site of a similar nature and its location, including the preservation and protection measures taken. The Secretary-General shall transmit such information to the Director-General of the United Nations Educational, Scientific and Cultural Organization and any other competent international organization. Following the finding of any such human remains, object or site in the exploration area, and in order to avoid disturbing such human remains, object or site, no further prospecting or exploration shall take place, within a reasonable radius, until such time as the Council decides otherwise after taking account of the views of the Director-General of the United Nations Educational, Scientific and Cultural Organization or any other competent international organization.

Part VI. Confidentiality

Regulation 38. Confidentiality of Data and Information

1. Data and information submitted or transferred to the Authority or to any person participating in any activity or programme of the Authority pursuant to these Regulations or a contract issued under these Regulations, and designated by the contractor, in consultation with the Secretary-General, as being of a confidential nature, shall be considered confidential unless it is data and information which:

   (a) Is generally known or publicly available from other sources;

   (b) Has been previously made available by the owner to others without an obligation concerning its confidentiality; or

   (c) Is already in the possession of the Authority with no obligation concerning its confidentiality.

   Data and information that is necessary for the formulation by the Authority of rules, regulations and procedures concerning protection and preservation of the marine environment and safety, other than proprietary equipment design data, shall not be deemed confidential.

2. Confidential data and information may only be used by the Secretary-General and staff of the Secretariat, as authorized by the Secretary-General, and by the members of the Legal and Technical Commission as necessary for and relevant to the effective exercise of their powers and functions. The Secretary-General shall authorize access to such data and information only for limited use in connection with the functions and duties of the staff of the Secretariat and the functions and duties of the Legal and Technical Commission.

3. Ten years after the date of submission of confidential data and information to the Authority or the expiration of the contract for exploration, whichever is the later, and every five years thereafter, the Secretary-General and the contractor shall review such data and information to determine whether they should remain confidential. Such data and information shall remain confidential if the contractor establishes that there would be a substantial risk of serious and unfair economic prejudice if the data and information were to be released. No such data and information shall be released until the contractor has been accorded a reasonable opportunity to exhaust the judicial remedies available to it pursuant to Part XI, Section 5, of the Convention.

4. If, at any time following the expiration of the contract for exploration, the contractor enters into a contract for exploitation in respect of any part of the exploration area, confidential data and information relating to that part of the area shall remain confidential in accordance with the contract for exploitation.

5. The contractor may at any time waive confidentiality of data and information.

Regulation 39. Procedures to Ensure Confidentiality

1. The Secretary-General shall be responsible for maintaining the confidentiality of all confidential data and information and shall not, except with the prior written consent of the contractor, release such data and information to any person external to the Authority. To ensure the confidentiality of such data and information, the Secretary-General shall establish procedures, consistent with the provisions of the Convention, governing the handling of confidential information by members of the Secretariat, members of the Legal and Technical Commission and any other person participating in any activity or programme of the Authority. Such procedures shall include:

    (a) Maintenance of confidential data and information in secure facilities and development of security procedures to prevent unauthorized access to or removal of such data and information;

    (b) Development and maintenance of a classification, log and inventory system of all written data and information received, including its type and source and routing from the time of receipt until final disposition.

2. A person who is authorized pursuant to these Regulations to have access to confidential data and information shall not disclose such data and information except as permitted under the Convention and

these Regulations. The Secretary-General shall require any person who is authorized to have access to confidential data and information to make a written declaration witnessed by the Secretary-General or his or her authorized representative to the effect that the person so authorized:

(a)   Acknowledges his or her legal obligation under the Convention and these Regulations with respect to the non-disclosure of confidential data and information;

(b)   Agrees to comply with the applicable regulations and procedures established to ensure the confidentiality of such data and information.

3.   The Legal and Technical Commission shall protect the confidentiality of confidential data and information submitted to it pursuant to these Regulations or a contract issued under these Regulations. In accordance with the provisions of Article 163, paragraph 8, of the Convention, members of the Commission shall not disclose, even after the termination of their functions, any industrial secret, proprietary data which are transferred to the Authority in accordance with Annex III, Article 14, of the Convention, or any other confidential information coming to their knowledge by reason of their duties for the Authority.

4.   The Secretary-General and staff of the Authority shall not disclose, even after the termination of their functions with the Authority, any industrial secret, proprietary data which are transferred to the Authority in accordance with Annex III, Article 14, of the Convention, or any other confidential information coming to their knowledge by reason of their employment with the Authority.

5.   Taking into account the responsibility and liability of the Authority pursuant to Annex III, Article 22, of the Convention, the Authority may take such action as may be appropriate against any person who, by reason of his or her duties for the Authority, has access to any confidential data and information and who is in breach of the obligations relating to confidentiality contained in the Convention and these Regulations.

Part VII. General Procedures

Regulation 40. Notice and General Procedures

1.   Any application, request, notice, report, consent, approval, waiver, direction or instruction hereunder shall be made by the Secretary-General or by the designated representative of the prospector, applicant or contractor, as the case may be, in writing. Service shall be by hand, or by telex, facsimile, registered airmail or electronic mail containing an

authorized electronic signature to the Secretary-General at the head-quarters of the Authority or to the designated representative.

2. Delivery by hand shall be effective when made. Delivery by telex shall be deemed to be effective on the business day following the day when the "answer back" appears on the sender's telex machine. Delivery by facsimile shall be effective when the "transmit confirmation report" confirming the transmission to the recipient's published facsimile number is received by the transmitter. Delivery by registered airmail shall be deemed to be effective 21 days after posting. An electronic document is presumed to be received by the addressee when it enters an information system designated or used by the addressee for the purpose of receiving documents of the type sent and is capable of being retrieved and processed by the addressee.

3. Notice to the designated representative of the prospector, applicant or contractor shall constitute effective notice to the prospector, applicant or contractor for all purposes under these Regulations, and the designated representative shall be the agent of the prospector, applicant or contractor for the service of process or notification in any proceeding of any court or tribunal having jurisdiction.

4. Notice to the Secretary-General shall constitute effective notice to the Authority for all purposes under these Regulations, and the Secretary-General shall be the Authority's agent for the service of process or notification in any proceeding of any court or tribunal having jurisdiction.

Regulation 41. Recommendations for the Guidance of Contractors

1. The Legal and Technical Commission may from time to time issue recommendations of a technical or administrative nature for the guidance of contractors to assist them in the implementation of the rules, regulations and procedures of the Authority.

2. The full text of such recommendations shall be reported to the Council. Should the Council find that a recommendation is inconsistent with the intent and purpose of these Regulations, it may request that the recommendation be modified or withdrawn.

Part VIII. Settlement of Disputes

Regulation 42. Disputes

1. Disputes concerning the interpretation or application of these Regulations shall be settled in accordance with Part XI, Section 5, of the Convention.

2. Any final decision rendered by a court or tribunal having jurisdiction under the Convention relating to the rights and obligations of the Authority and of the Contractor shall be enforceable in the territory of each State Party to the Convention.

Part IX. Resources other than Polymetallic Sulphides

Regulation 43. Resources other than Polymetallic Sulphides

If a prospector or contractor finds resources in the Area other than polymetallic sulphides, the prospecting and exploration for and exploitation of such resources shall be subject to the rules, regulations and procedures of the Authority relating to such resources in accordance with the Convention and the Agreement. The prospector or contractor shall notify the Authority of its find.

Part X. Review

Regulation 44. Review

1. Five years following the approval of these Regulations by the Assembly, or at any time thereafter, the Council shall undertake a review of the manner in which the Regulations have operated in practice.
2. If, in the light of improved knowledge or technology, it becomes apparent that the Regulations are not adequate, any State Party, the Legal and Technical Commission, or any contractor through its sponsoring State may at any time request the Council to consider, at its next ordinary session, revisions to these Regulations.
3. In the light of the review, the Council may adopt and apply provisionally, pending approval by the Assembly, amendments to the provisions of these Regulations, taking into account the recommendations of the Legal and Technical Commission or other subordinate organs concerned. Any such amendments shall be without prejudice to the rights conferred on any Contractor with the Authority under the provisions of a contract entered into pursuant to these Regulations in force at the time of any such amendment.
4. In the event that any provisions of these Regulations are amended, the Contractor and the Authority may revise the contract in accordance with Section 24 of Annex 4.

Annex 1. Notification of Intention to Engage in Prospecting

1. Name of prospector:
2. Street address of prospector:
3. Postal address (if different from above):
4. Telephone number:
5. Facsimile number:
6. Electronic mail address:
7. Nationality of prospector:
8. If prospector is a juridical person, identify prospector's
    (a) Place of registration; and
    (b) Principal place of business/domicile and attach a copy of the prospector's certificate of registration.
9. Name of prospector's designated representative:
10. Street address of prospector's designated representative (if different from above):
11. Postal address (if different from above):
12. Telephone number:
13. Facsimile number:
14. Electronic mail address:
15. Attach the coordinates of the broad area or areas in which prospecting is to be conducted (in accordance with the World Geodetic System WGS 84).
16. Attach a general description of the prospecting programme, including the date of commencement and the approximate duration of the programme.
17. Attach a written undertaking that the prospector will:
    (a) Comply with the Convention and the relevant rules, regulations and procedures of the Authority concerning:
        (i) Cooperation in the training programmes in connection with marine scientific research and transfer of technology referred to in Articles 143 and 144 of the Convention; and
        (ii) Protection and preservation of the marine environment; and
    (b) Accept verification by the Authority of compliance therewith.
18. List hereunder all the attachments and annexes to this notification (all data and information should be submitted in hard copy and in a digital format specified by the Authority):

Date: _____   _____

                              Signature of prospector's designated representative

Attestation:

_____

Signature of person attesting

_____

Name of person attesting

_____

Title of person attesting

Annex 2. Application for Approval of a Plan of Work for Exploration to Obtain a Contract

Section I. Information Concerning the Applicant

1. Name of applicant:
2. Street address of applicant:
3. Postal address (if different from above):
4. Telephone number:
5. Facsimile number:
6. Electronic mail address:
7. Name of applicant's designated representative:
8. Street address of applicant's designated representative (if different from above):
9. Postal address (if different from above):
10. Telephone number:
11. Facsimile number:
12. Electronic mail address:
13. If the applicant is a juridical person, identify applicant's
    (a) Place of registration; and
    (b) Principal place of business/domicile and attach a copy of the applicant's certificate of registration.
14. Identify the sponsoring State or States.
15. In respect of each sponsoring State, provide the date of deposit of its instrument of ratification of, or accession or succession to, the 1982 United Nations Convention on the Law of the Sea and the date of its consent to be bound by the Agreement relating to the Implementation of Part XI of the United Nations Convention on the Law of the Sea of 10 December 1982.
16. A certificate of sponsorship issued by the sponsoring State must be attached with this application. If the applicant has more than one nationality, as in the case of a partnership or consortium of entities from more

than one State, certificates of sponsorship issued by each of the States involved must be attached.

Section II. Information Relating to the Area under Application

17. Define the boundaries of the blocks under application by attaching a chart (on a scale and projection specified by the Authority) and a list of geographical coordinates (in accordance with the World Geodetic System WGS 84).

18. Indicate whether the applicant elects to contribute a reserved area in accordance with Regulation 17 or offer an equity interest in a joint venture arrangement in accordance with Regulation 19.

19. If the applicant elects to contribute a reserved area:

(a) Attach a chart (on a scale and projection specified by the Authority) and a list of the coordinates dividing the total area into two parts of equal estimated commercial value; and

(b) Include in an attachment sufficient information to enable the Council to designate a reserved area based on the estimated commercial value of each part of the area under application. Such attachment must include the data available to the applicant with respect to both parts of the area under application, including:

   (i) Data on the location, survey and evaluation of the polymetallic sulphides in the areas, including:

      a. A description of the technology related to the recovery and processing of polymetallic sulphides that is necessary for making the designation of a reserved area;

      b. A map of the physical and geological characteristics, such as seabed topography, bathymetry and bottom currents and information on the reliability of such data;

      c. A map showing the remotely sensed data (such as electromagnetic surveys) and other survey data used to determine the lateral extent of each polymetallic sulphide bodies;

      d. Drill core and other data used to determine the third dimension of the deposits and therefore used to determine the grade and tonnage of the polymetallic sulphide bodies;

      e. Data showing the distribution of active and inactive polymetallic sulphide sites and the age that activity ceased in inactive sites and was initiated at active sites;

      f. Data showing the average tonnage (in metric tonnes) of each polymetallic sulphide body that will comprise the mine site and an associated tonnage map showing the location of sampling sites;

g. Data showing the average elemental content of metals of economic interest (grade) based on chemical assays in (dry) weight per cent and an associated grade map for data among and within the polymetallic sulphide bodies;

h. Combined maps of tonnage and grade of polymetallic sulphides;

i. A calculation based on standard procedures, including statistical analysis, using the data submitted and assumptions made in the calculations that the two areas could be expected to contain polymetallic sulphides of equal estimated commercial value expressed as recoverable metals in mineable areas;

j. A description of the techniques used by the applicant;

(ii) Information concerning environmental parameters (seasonal and during test period) including, inter alia, wind speed and direction, water salinity, temperature and biological communities.

20. If the area under application includes any part of a reserved area, attach a list of coordinates of the area which forms part of the reserved area and indicate the applicant's qualifications in accordance with Regulation 18 of the Regulations.

Section III. Financial and Technical Information

21. Attach sufficient information to enable the Council to determine whether the applicant is financially capable of carrying out the proposed plan of work for exploration and of fulfilling its financial obligations to the Authority:

(a) If the application is made by the Enterprise, attach certification by its competent authority that the Enterprise has the necessary financial resources to meet the estimated costs of the proposed plan of work for exploration;

(b) If the application is made by a State or a State enterprise, attach a statement by the State or the sponsoring State certifying that the applicant has the necessary financial resources to meet the estimated costs of the proposed plan of work for exploration;

(c) If the application is made by an entity, attach copies of the applicant's audited financial statements, including balance sheets and profit-and-loss statements, for the most recent three years in conformity with internationally accepted accounting principles and certified by a duly qualified firm of public accountants; and

(i) If the applicant is a newly organized entity and a certified balance sheet is not available, a pro forma balance sheet certified by an appropriate official of the applicant;

(ii) If the applicant is a subsidiary of another entity, copies of such financial statements of that entity and a statement from that entity in conformity with internationally accepted accounting practices and certified by a duly qualified firm of public accountants that the applicant will have the financial resources to carry out the plan of work for exploration;

(iii) If the applicant is controlled by a State or a State enterprise, a statement from the State or State enterprise certifying that the applicant will have the financial resources to carry out the plan of work for exploration.

22. If it is intended to finance the proposed plan of work for exploration by borrowings, attach a statement of the amount of such borrowings, the repayment period and the interest rate.

23. Attach sufficient information to enable the Council to determine whether the applicant is technically capable of carrying out the proposed plan of work for exploration, including:

(a) A general description of the applicant's previous experience, knowledge, skills, technical qualifications and expertise relevant to the proposed plan of work for exploration;

(b) A general description of the equipment and methods expected to be used in carrying out the proposed plan of work for exploration and other relevant non-proprietary information about the characteristics of such technology;

(c) A general description of the applicant's financial and technical capability to respond to any incident or activity which causes serious harm to the marine environment.

Section IV. The Plan of Work for Exploration

24. Attach the following information relating to the plan of work for exploration:

(a) A general description and a schedule of the proposed exploration programme, including the programme of activities for the immediate five-year period, such as studies to be undertaken in respect of the environmental, technical, economic and other appropriate factors which must be taken into account in exploration;

(b)   A description of a programme for oceanographic and environ-mental baseline studies in accordance with the Regulations and any environmental rules, regulations and procedures established by the Authority that would enable an assessment of the potential environmental impact including, but not restricted to, the impact on biodiversity, of the proposed exploration activities, taking into account any recommendations issued by the Legal and Technical Commission;

(c)   A preliminary assessment of the possible impact of the proposed exploration activities on the marine environment;

(d)   A description of proposed measures for the prevention, reduction and control of pollution and other hazards, as well as possible impacts, to the marine environment;

(e)   A schedule of anticipated yearly expenditures in respect of the programme of activities for the immediate five-year period.

Section V. Undertakings

25.   Attach a written undertaking that the applicant will:

(a)   Accept as enforceable and comply with the applicable obligations created by the provisions of the Convention and the rules, regula-tions and procedures of the Authority, the decisions of the relevant organs of the Authority and the terms of its contracts with the Authority;

(b)   Accept control by the Authority of activities in the Area as author-ized by the Convention;

(c)   Provide the Authority with a written assurance that its obligations under the contract will be fulfilled in good faith.

Section VI. Previous Contracts

26.   Has the applicant or, in the case of an application by a partnership or consortium of entities in a joint arrangement, any member of the part-nership or consortium previously been awarded any contract with the Authority?

27.   If the answer to 26 is "yes", the application must include:

(a)   The date of the previous contract or contracts;

(b)   The date, reference number and title of each report submitted to the Authority in connection with the contact or contracts; and

(c)   The date of termination of the contract or contracts, if applicable.

Section VII. Attachments

28. List all the attachments and annexes to this application (all data and information should be submitted in hard copy and in a digital format specified by the Authority):

Date: _____

_____
Signature of applicant's designated representative

Attestation:

_____
Signature of person attesting

_____
Name of person attesting

_____
Title of person attesting

Annex 3. Contract for Exploration

THIS CONTRACT made the day of between the **INTERNATIONAL SEABED AUTHORITY** represented by its **SECRETARY-GENERAL** (hereinafter referred to as "the Authority") and represented by (hereinafter referred to as "the Contractor") **WITNESSETH** as follows:

Incorporation of Clauses
A. The standard clauses set out in Annex 4 to the Regulations on Prospecting and Exploration for Polymetallic Sulphides in the Area shall be incorporated herein and shall have effect as if herein set out at length.

Exploration Area
B. For the purposes of this contract, the "exploration area" means that part of the Area allocated to the Contractor for exploration, defined by the coordinates listed in schedule 1 hereto, as reduced from time to time in accordance with the standard clauses and the Regulations.

Grant of Rights
C. In consideration of:
(1) Their mutual interest in the conduct of exploration activities in the exploration area pursuant to the Convention and the Agreement;

(2)   The responsibility of the Authority to organize and control activities in the Area, particularly with a view to administering the resources of the Area, in accordance with the legal regime established in Part XI of the Convention and the Agreement and Part XII of the Convention respectively; and

(3)   The interest and financial commitment of the Contractor in conducting activities in the exploration area and the mutual covenants made herein, the Authority hereby grants to the Contractor the exclusive right to explore for polymetallic sulphides in the exploration area in accordance with the terms and conditions of this contract.

Entry into Force and Contract Term

D.   This contract shall enter into force on signature by both parties and, subject to the standard clauses, shall remain in force for a period of fifteen years thereafter unless:

(1)   The Contractor obtains a contract for exploitation in the exploration area which enters into force before the expiration of such period of fifteen years; or

(2)   The contract is sooner terminated provided that the term of the contract may be extended in accordance with standard clauses 3.2 and 17.2.

Schedules

E. The schedules referred to in the standard clauses, namely Section 4 and Section 8, are for the purposes of this contract schedules 2 and 3 respectively.

Entire Agreement

F. This contract expresses the entire agreement between the parties, and no oral understanding or prior writing shall modify the terms hereof.

IN WITNESS WHEREOF the undersigned, being duly authorized thereto by the respective parties, have signed this contract at ..., this ... day of ...

Schedule 1
[Coordinates and illustrative chart of the exploration area]

Schedule 2
[The current five-year programme of activities as revised from time to time]

Schedule 3
[The training programme shall become a schedule to the contract when approved by the Authority in accordance with Section 8 of the standard clauses.]

Annex 4. Standard Clauses for Exploration Contract

Section 1. Definitions

1.1 In the following clauses:
  (a) "exploration area" means that part of the Area allocated to the Contractor for exploration, described in schedule 1 hereto, as the same may be reduced from time to time in accordance with this contract and the Regulations;
  (b) "programme of activities" means the programme of activities which is set out in schedule 2 hereto as the same may be adjusted from time to time in accordance with Sections 4.3 and 4.4 hereof;
  (c) "regulations" means the Regulations on Prospecting and Exploration for Polymetallic Sulphides in the Area, adopted by the Authority.
1.2 Terms and phrases defined in the Regulations shall have the same meaning in these standard clauses.
1.3 In accordance with the Agreement relating to the Implementation of Part XI of the United Nations Convention on the Law of the Sea of 10 December 1982, its provisions and Part XI of the Convention are to be interpreted and applied together as a single instrument; this contract and references in this contract to the Convention are to be interpreted and applied accordingly.
1.4 This contract includes the schedules to this contract, which shall be an integral part hereof.

Section 2. Security of Tenure

2.1 The Contractor shall have security of tenure and this contract shall not be suspended, terminated or revised except in accordance with Sections 20, 21 and 24 hereof.
2.2 The Contractor shall have the exclusive right to explore for polymetallic sulphides in the exploration area in accordance with the terms and conditions of this contract. The Authority shall ensure that no other entity operates in the exploration area for a different category of resources in a manner that might unreasonably interfere with the operations of the Contractor.
2.3 The Contractor, by notice to the Authority, shall have the right at any time to renounce without penalty the whole or part of its rights in the exploration area, provided that the Contractor shall remain liable for all obligations accrued prior to the date of such renunciation in respect of the area renounced.

2.4 Nothing in this contract shall be deemed to confer any right on the Contractor other than those rights expressly granted herein. The Authority reserves the right to enter into contracts with respect to resources other than polymetallic sulphides with third parties in the area covered by this contract.

Section 3. Contract Term

3.1 This contract shall enter into force on signature by both parties and shall remain in force for a period of fifteen years thereafter unless:
   (a) The Contractor obtains a contract for exploitation in the exploration area which enters into force before the expiration of such period of fifteen years; or
   (b) The contract is sooner terminated, provided that the term of the contract may be extended in accordance with Sections 3.2 and 17.2 hereof.

3.2 Upon application by the Contractor, not later than six months before the expiration of this contract, this contract may be extended for periods of not more than five years each on such terms and conditions as the Authority and the Contractor may then agree in accordance with the Regulations. Such extensions shall be approved if the Contractor has made efforts in good faith to comply with the requirements of this contract but for reasons beyond the Contractor's control has been unable to complete the necessary preparatory work for proceeding to the exploitation stage or if the prevailing economic circumstances do not justify proceeding to the exploitation stage.

3.3 Notwithstanding the expiration of this contract in accordance with Section 3.1 hereof, if the Contractor has, at least 90 days prior to the date of expiration, applied for a contract for exploitation, the Contractor's rights and obligations under this contract shall continue until such time as the application has been considered and a contract for exploitation has been issued or refused.

Section 4. Exploration

4.1 The Contractor shall commence exploration in accordance with the time schedule stipulated in the programme of activities set out in schedule 2 hereto and shall adhere to such time periods or any modification thereto as provided for by this contract.

4.2 The Contractor shall carry out the programme of activities set out in schedule 2 hereto. In carrying out such activities the Contractor shall spend in each contract year not less than the amount specified in such programme, or any agreed review thereof, in actual and direct exploration expenditures.

4.3 The Contractor, with the consent of the Authority, which consent shall not be unreasonably withheld, may from time to time make such changes in the programme of activities and the expenditures specified therein as may be necessary and prudent in accordance with good mining industry practice, and taking into account the market conditions for the metals contained in polymetallic sulphides and other relevant global economic conditions.

4.4 Not later than 90 days prior to the expiration of each five-year period from the date on which this contract enters into force in accordance with Section 3 hereof, the Contractor and the Secretary-General shall jointly undertake a review of the implementation of the plan of work for exploration under this contract. The Secretary-General may require the Contractor to submit such additional data and information as may be necessary for the purposes of the review. In the light of the review, the Contractor shall make such adjustments to its plan of work as are necessary and shall indicate its programme of activities for the following five-year period, including a revised schedule of anticipated yearly expenditures. Schedule 2 hereto shall be adjusted accordingly.

Section 5. Environmental Monitoring

5.1 The Contractor shall take necessary measures to prevent, reduce and control pollution and other hazards to the marine environment arising from its activities in the Area as far as reasonably possible applying a precautionary approach and best environmental practices.

5.2 Prior to the commencement of exploration activities, the Contractor shall submit to the Authority:

(a) An impact assessment of the potential effects on the marine environment of the proposed activities;

(b) A proposal for a monitoring programme to determine the potential effect on the marine environment of the proposed activities; and

(c) Data that could be used to establish an environmental baseline against which to assess the effect of the proposed activities.

5.3 The Contractor shall, in accordance with the Regulations, gather environmental baseline data as exploration activities progress and develop and shall establish environmental baselines against which to assess the likely effects of the Contractor's activities on the marine environment.

5.4 The Contractor shall, in accordance with the Regulations, establish and carry out a programme to monitor and report on such effects on the marine environment. The Contractor shall cooperate with the Authority in the implementation of such monitoring.

5.5 The Contractor shall, within 90 days of the end of each calendar year, report to the Secretary-General on the implementation and results of the monitoring programme referred to in Section 5.4 hereof and shall submit data and information in accordance with the Regulations.

Section 6. Contingency Plans and Emergencies

6.1 The Contractor shall, prior to the commencement of its programme of activities under this contract, submit to the Secretary-General a contingency plan to respond effectively to incidents that are likely to cause serious harm or a threat of serious harm to the marine environment arising from the Contractor's activities at sea in the exploration area. Such contingency plan shall establish special procedures and provide for adequate and appropriate equipment to deal with such incidents and, in particular, shall include arrangements for:

(a) The immediate raising of a general alarm in the area of the exploration activities;

(b) Immediate notification to the Secretary-General;

(c) The warning of ships which might be about to enter the immediate vicinity;

(d) A continuing flow of full information to the Secretary-General relating to particulars of the contingency measures already taken and further actions required;

(e) The removal, as appropriate, of polluting substances;

(f) The reduction and, so far as reasonably possible, prevention of serious harm to the marine environment, as well as mitigation of such effects;

(g) As appropriate, cooperation with other contractors with the Authority to respond to an emergency; and

(h) Periodic emergency response exercises.

6.2 The Contractor shall promptly report to the Secretary-General any incident arising from its activities that has caused, is causing or poses a threat of serious harm to the marine environment. Each such report shall contain the details of such incident, including, inter alia:

(a) The coordinates of the area affected or which can reasonably be anticipated to be affected;

(b)   The description of the action being taken by the Contractor to prevent, contain, minimize and repair the serious harm or threat of serious harm to the marine environment;

(c)   A description of the action being taken by the Contractor to monitor the effects of the incident on the marine environment; and

(d)   Such supplementary information as may reasonably be required by the Secretary-General.

6.3   The Contractor shall comply with emergency orders issued by the Council and immediate measures of a temporary nature issued by the Secretary-General in accordance with the Regulations, to prevent, contain, minimize or repair serious harm or the threat of serious harm to the marine environment, which may include orders to the Contractor to immediately suspend or adjust any activities in the exploration area.

6.4   If the Contractor does not promptly comply with such emergency orders or immediate measures of a temporary nature, the Council may take such reasonable measures as are necessary to prevent, contain, minimize or repair any such serious harm or the threat of serious harm to the marine environment at the Contractor's expense. The Contractor shall promptly reimburse the Authority the amount of such expenses. Such expenses shall be in addition to any monetary penalties which may be imposed on the Contractor pursuant to the terms of this contract or the Regulations.

Section 7. Human Remains and Objects and Sites of an Archaeological or Historical Nature

The Contractor shall immediately notify the Secretary-General in writing of any finding in the exploration area of any human remains of an archaeological or historical nature, or any object or site of a similar nature and its location, including the preservation and protection measures taken. The Secretary-General shall transmit such information to the Director-General of the United Nations Educational, Scientific and Cultural Organization and any other competent international organization. Following the finding of any such human remains, object or site in the exploration area, and in order to avoid disturbing such human remains, object or site, no further prospecting or exploration shall take place, within a reasonable radius, until such time as the Council decides otherwise after taking account of the views of the Director-General of the United Nations Educational, Scientific and Cultural Organization or any other competent international organization.

Section 8. Training

8.1   In accordance with the Regulations, the Contractor shall, prior to the commencement of exploration under this contract, submit to the Authority for approval proposed training programmes for the training of personnel of the Authority and developing States, including the participation of such personnel in all of the Contractor's activities under this contract.

8.2   The scope and financing of the training programme shall be subject to negotiation between the Contractor, the Authority and the sponsoring State or States.

8.3   The Contractor shall conduct training programmes in accordance with the specific programme for the training of personnel referred to in Section 8.1 hereof approved by the Authority in accordance with the Regulations, which programme, as revised and developed from time to time, shall become a part of this contract as schedule 3.

Section 9. Books and Records

The Contractor shall keep a complete and proper set of books, accounts and financial records, consistent with internationally accepted accounting principles. Such books, accounts and financial records shall include information which will fully disclose the actual and direct expenditures for exploration and such other information as will facilitate an effective audit of such expenditures.

Section 10. Annual Reports

10.1   The Contractor shall, within 90 days of the end of each calendar year, submit a report to the Secretary-General in such format as may be recommended from time to time by the Legal and Technical Commission covering its programme of activities in the exploration area and containing, as applicable, information in sufficient detail on:

(a)   The exploration work carried out during the calendar year, including maps, charts and graphs illustrating the work that has been done and the results obtained;

(b)   The equipment used to carry out the exploration work, including the results of tests conducted of proposed mining technologies, but not equipment design data; and

(c)   The implementation of training programmes, including any proposed revisions to or developments of such programmes.

10.2   Such reports shall also contain:

(a) The results obtained from environmental monitoring programmes, including observations, measurements, evaluations and analyses of environmental parameters;

(b) A statement of the quantity of polymetallic sulphides recovered as samples or for the purpose of testing;

(c) A statement, in conformity with internationally accepted accounting principles and certified by a duly qualified firm of public accountants, or, where the Contractor is a State or a State enterprise, by the sponsoring State, of the actual and direct exploration expenditures of the Contractor in carrying out the programme of activities during the Contractor's accounting year. Such expenditures may be claimed by the contractor as part of the contractor's development costs incurred prior to the commencement of commercial production; and

(d) Details of any proposed adjustments to the programme of activities and the reasons for such adjustments.

10.3 The Contractor shall also submit such additional information to supplement the reports referred to in Section 10.1 and 10.2 hereof as the Secretary-General may from time to time reasonably require in order to carry out the Authority's functions under the Convention, the Regulations and this contract.

10.4 The Contractor shall keep, in good condition, a representative portion of samples and cores of the polymetallic sulphides obtained in the course of exploration until the expiration of this contract. The Authority may request the Contractor in writing to deliver to it for analysis a portion of any such sample and cores obtained during the course of exploration.

Section 11. Data and Information to be Submitted on Expiration of the Contract

11.1 The Contractor shall transfer to the Authority all data and information that are both necessary for and relevant to the effective exercise of the powers and functions of the Authority in respect of the exploration area in accordance with the provisions of this section.

11.2 Upon expiration or termination of this contract the Contractor, if it has not already done so, shall submit the following data and information to the Secretary-General:

(a) Copies of geological, environmental, geochemical and geophysical data acquired by the Contractor in the course of carrying out the programme of activities that are necessary for and relevant to the effective exercise of the powers and functions of the Authority in respect of the exploration area;

(b) The estimation of mineable deposits, when such deposits have been identified, which shall include details of the grade and quantity of the proven, probable and possible polymetallic sulphide reserves and the anticipated mining conditions;

(c) Copies of geological, technical, financial and economic reports made by or for the Contractor that are necessary for and relevant to the effective exercise of the powers and functions of the Authority in respect of the exploration area;

(d) Information in sufficient detail on the equipment used to carry out the exploration work, including the results of tests conducted of proposed mining technologies, but not equipment design data;

(e) A statement of the quantity of polymetallic sulphides recovered as samples or for the purpose of testing; and

(f) A statement on how and where samples of cores are archived and their availability to the Authority.

11.3 The data and information referred to in Section 11.2 hereof shall also be submitted to the Secretary-General if, prior to the expiration of this contract, the Contractor applies for approval of a plan of work for exploitation or if the Contractor renounces its rights in the exploration area to the extent that such data and information relates to the renounced area.

Section 12. Confidentiality

Data and information transferred to the Authority in accordance with this contract shall be treated as confidential in accordance with the provisions of the Regulations.

Section 13. Undertakings

13.1 The Contractor shall carry out exploration in accordance with the terms and conditions of this contract, the Regulations, Part XI of the Convention, the Agreement and other rules of international law not incompatible with the Convention.

13.2 The Contractor undertakes:

(a) To accept as enforceable and comply with the terms of this contract;

(b) To comply with the applicable obligations created by the provisions of the Convention, the rules, regulations and procedures of the Authority and the decisions of the relevant organs of the Authority;

(c) To accept control by the Authority of activities in the Area as authorized by the Convention;

(d) To fulfil its obligations under this contract in good faith; and

(e) To observe, as far as reasonably practicable, any recommendations which may be issued from time to time by the Legal and Technical Commission.

13.3 The Contractor shall actively carry out the programme of activities:

(a) With due diligence, efficiency and economy;

(b) With due regard to the impact of its activities on the marine environment;
and

(c) With reasonable regard for other activities in the marine environment.

13.4 The Authority undertakes to fulfil in good faith its powers and functions under the Convention and the Agreement in accordance with Article 157 of the Convention.

Section 14. Inspection

14.1 The Contractor shall permit the Authority to send its inspectors on board vessels and installations used by the Contractor to carry out activities in the exploration area to:

(a) Monitor the Contractor's compliance with the terms and conditions of this contract and the Regulations; and

(b) Monitor the effects of such activities on the marine environment.

14.2 The Secretary-General shall give reasonable notice to the Contractor of the projected time and duration of inspections, the name of the inspectors and any activities the inspectors are to perform that are likely to require the availability of special equipment or special assistance from personnel of the Contractor.

14.3 Such inspectors shall have the authority to inspect any vessel or installation, including its log, equipment, records, facilities, all other recorded data and any relevant documents which are necessary to monitor the Contractor's compliance.

14.4 The Contractor, its agents and employees shall assist the inspectors in the performance of their duties and shall:

(a) Accept and facilitate prompt and safe boarding of vessels and installations by inspectors;

(b) Cooperate with and assist in the inspection of any vessel or installation conducted pursuant to these procedures;

(c) Provide access to all relevant equipment, facilities and personnel on vessels and installations at all reasonable times;

(d) Not obstruct, intimidate or interfere with inspectors in the performance of their duties;

(e) Provide reasonable facilities, including, where appropriate, food and accommodation, to inspectors; and

(f) Facilitate safe disembarkation by inspectors.

14.5 Inspectors shall avoid interference with the safe and normal operations on board vessels and installations used by the Contractor to carry out activities in the area visited and shall act in accordance with the Regulations and the measures adopted to protect confidentiality of data and information.

14.6 The Secretary-General and any duly authorized representatives of the Secretary-General, shall have access, for purposes of audit and examination, to any books, documents, papers and records of the Contractor which are necessary and directly pertinent to verify the expenditures referred to in Section 10.2(c).

14.7 The Secretary-General shall provide relevant information contained in the reports of inspectors to the Contractor and its sponsoring State or States where action is necessary.

14.8 If for any reason the Contractor does not pursue exploration and does not request a contract for exploitation, it shall, before withdrawing from the exploration area, notify the Secretary-General in writing in order to permit the Authority, if it so decides, to carry out an inspection pursuant to this section.

Section 15. Safety, Labour and Health Standards

15.1 The Contractor shall comply with the generally accepted international rules and standards established by competent international organizations or general diplomatic conferences concerning the safety of life at sea, and the prevention of collisions and such rules, regulations and procedures as may be adopted by the Authority relating to safety at sea. Each vessel used for carrying out activities in the Area shall possess current valid certificates required by and issued pursuant to such international rules and standards.

15.2 The Contractor shall, in carrying out exploration under this contract, observe and comply with such rules, regulations and procedures as may be adopted by the Authority relating to protection against discrimination in employment, occupational safety and health, labour relations, social security, employment security and living conditions at the work site. Such rules, regulations and procedures shall take into account conventions and recommendations of the International Labour Organization and other competent international organizations.

Section 16. Responsibility and Liability

16.1 The Contractor shall be liable for the actual amount of any damage, including damage to the marine environment, arising out of its wrongful acts or omissions, and those of its employees, subcontractors, agents and all persons engaged in working or acting for them in the conduct of its operations under this contract, including the costs of reasonable measures to prevent or limit damage to the marine environment, account being taken of any contributory acts or omissions by the Authority.

16.2 The Contractor shall indemnify the Authority, its employees, subcontractors and agents against all claims and liabilities of any third party arising out of any wrongful acts or omissions of the Contractor and its employees, agents and subcontractors, and all persons engaged in working or acting for them in the conduct of its operations under this contract.

16.3 The Authority shall be liable for the actual amount of any damage to the Contractor arising out of its wrongful acts in the exercise of its powers and functions, including violations under Article 168, paragraph 2, of the Convention, account being taken of contributory acts or omissions by the Contractor, its employees, agents and subcontractors, and all persons engaged in working or acting for them in the conduct of its operations under this contract.

16.4 The Authority shall indemnify the Contractor, its employees, subcontractors, agents and all persons engaged in working or acting for them in the conduct of its operations under this contract, against all claims and liabilities of any third party arising out of any wrongful acts or omissions in the exercise of its powers and functions hereunder, including violations under Article 168, paragraph 2, of the Convention.

16.5 The Contractor shall maintain appropriate insurance policies with internationally recognized carriers, in accordance with generally accepted international maritime practice.

Section 17. Force Majeure

17.1 The Contractor shall not be liable for an unavoidable delay or failure to perform any of its obligations under this contract due to force majeure.

For the purposes of this contract, force majeure shall mean an event or condition that the Contractor could not reasonably be expected to prevent or control; provided that the event or condition was not caused by negligence or by a failure to observe good mining industry practice.

17.2 The Contractor shall, upon request, be granted a time extension equal to the period by which performance was delayed hereunder by force majeure and the term of this contract shall be extended accordingly.

17.3 In the event of force majeure, the Contractor shall take all reasonable measures to remove its inability to perform and comply with the terms and conditions of this contract with a minimum of delay.

17.4 The Contractor shall give notice to the Authority of the occurrence of an event of force majeure as soon as reasonably possible, and similarly give notice to the Authority of the restoration of normal conditions.

Section 18. Disclaimer

Neither the Contractor nor any affiliated company or subcontractor shall in any manner claim or suggest, whether expressly or by implication, that the Authority or any official thereof has, or has expressed, any opinion with respect to polymetallic sulphides in the exploration area and a statement to that effect shall not be included in or endorsed on any prospectus, notice, circular, advertisement, press release or similar document issued by the Contractor, any affiliated company or any subcontractor that refers directly or indirectly to this contract. For the purposes of this section, an "affiliated company" means any person, firm or company or State-owned entity controlling, controlled by, or under common control with, the Contractor.

Section 19. Renunciation of Rights

The Contractor, by notice to the Authority, shall have the right to renounce its rights and terminate this contract without penalty, provided that the Contractor shall remain liable for all obligations accrued prior to the date of such renunciation and those obligations required to be fulfilled after termination in accordance with the Regulations.

Section 20. Termination of Sponsorship

20.1 If the nationality or control of the Contractor changes or the Contractor's sponsoring State, as defined in the Regulations, terminates its sponsorship, the Contractor shall promptly notify the Authority forthwith.

20.2 In either such event, if the Contractor does not obtain another sponsor meeting the requirements prescribed in the Regulations which submits to the Authority a certificate of sponsorship for the Contractor in the prescribed form within the time specified in the Regulations, this contract shall terminate forthwith.

Section 21. Suspension and Termination of Contract and Penalties

21.1 The Council may suspend or terminate this contract, without prejudice to any other rights that the Authority may have, if any of the following events should occur:

(a) If, in spite of written warnings by the Authority, the Contractor has conducted its activities in such a way as to result in serious persistent and wilful violations of the fundamental terms of this contract, Part XI of the Convention, the Agreement and the rules, regulations and procedures of the Authority; or

(b) If the Contractor has failed to comply with a final binding decision of the dispute settlement body applicable to it; or

(c) If the Contractor becomes insolvent or commits an act of bankruptcy or enters into any agreement for composition with its creditors or goes into liquidation or receivership, whether compulsory or voluntary, or petitions or applies to any tribunal for the appointment of a receiver or a trustee or receiver for itself or commences any proceedings relating to itself under any bankruptcy, insolvency or readjustment of debt law, whether now or hereafter in effect, other than for the purpose of reconstruction.

21.2 The Council may, without prejudice to Section 17, after consultation with the contractor, suspend or terminate this contract, without prejudice to any other rights that the Authority may have, if the Contractor is prevented from performing its obligations under this contract by reason of an event or condition of force majeure, as described in Section 17.1, which has persisted for a continuous period exceeding two years, despite the Contractor having taken all reasonable measures to remove its inability to perform and comply with the terms and conditions of this contract with a minimum of delay.

21.3 Any suspension or termination shall be by notice, through the Secretary-General, which shall include a statement of the reasons for taking such action. The suspension or termination shall be effective 60 days after such notice, unless the Contractor within such period disputes the Authority's right to suspend or terminate this contract in accordance with Part XI, Section 5, of the Convention.

21.4 If the Contractor takes such action, this contract shall only be suspended or terminated in accordance with a final binding decision in accordance with Part XI, Section 5, of the Convention.

21.5 If the Council has suspended this contract, the Council may by notice require the Contractor to resume its operations and comply with the terms and conditions of this contract, not later than 60 days after such notice.

21.6 In the case of any violation of this contract not covered by Section 21.1(a) hereof, or in lieu of suspension or termination under Section 21.1 hereof, the Council may impose upon the Contractor monetary penalties proportionate to the seriousness of the violation.

21.7 The Council may not execute a decision involving monetary penalties until the Contractor has been accorded a reasonable opportunity to exhaust the judicial remedies available to it pursuant to Part XI, Section 5, of the Convention.

21.8 In the event of termination or expiration of this contract, the Contractor shall comply with the Regulations and shall remove all installations, plant, equipment and materials in the exploration area and shall make the area safe so as not to constitute a danger to persons, shipping or to the marine environment.

Section 22. Transfer of Rights and Obligations

22.1 The rights and obligations of the Contractor under this contract may be transferred in whole or in part only with the consent of the Authority and in accordance with the Regulations.

22.2 The Authority shall not unreasonably withhold consent to the transfer if the proposed transferee is in all respects a qualified applicant in accordance with the Regulations and assumes all of the obligations of the Contractor and if the transfer does not confer to the transferee a plan of work, the approval of which would be forbidden by Annex III, Article 6, paragraph 3(c), of the Convention.

22.3 The terms, undertakings and conditions of this contract shall inure to the benefit of and be binding upon the parties hereto and their respective successors and assigns.

Section 23. No Waiver

No waiver by either party of any rights pursuant to a breach of the terms and conditions of this contract to be performed by the other party shall be construed as a waiver by the party of any succeeding breach of the same or any other term or condition to be performed by the other party.

Section 24. Revision

24.1 When circumstances have arisen or are likely to arise which, in the opinion of the Authority or the Contractor, would render this contract inequitable or make it impracticable or impossible to achieve the objectives set out in this contract or in Part XI of the Convention or the Agreement, the parties shall enter into negotiations to revise it accordingly.

24.2 This contract may also be revised by agreement between the Contractor and the Authority to facilitate the application of any rules, regulations and procedures adopted by the Authority subsequent to the entry into force of this contract.

24.3 This contract may be revised, amended or otherwise modified only with the consent of the Contractor and the Authority by an appropriate instrument signed by the authorized representatives of the parties.

Section 25. Disputes

25.1 Any dispute between the parties concerning the interpretation or application of this contract shall be settled in accordance with Part XI, Section 5, of the Convention.

25.2 In accordance with Article 21, paragraph 2, of Annex III to the Convention, any final decision rendered by a court or tribunal having jurisdiction under the Convention relating to the rights and obligations of the Authority and of the Contractor shall be enforceable in the territory of any State Party to the Convention affected thereby.

Section 26. Notice

26.1 Any application, request, notice, report, consent, approval, waiver, direction or instruction hereunder shall be made by the Secretary-General or by the designated representative of the Contractor, as the case may be, in writing. Service shall be by hand, or by telex, facsimile, registered airmail or electronic mail containing an authorized signature to the Secretary-General at the headquarters of the Authority or to the designated representative. The requirement to provide any information in writing under these Regulations is satisfied by the provision of the information in an electronic document containing a digital signature.

26.2 Either party shall be entitled to change any such address to any other address by not less than ten days' notice to the other party.

26.3 Delivery by hand shall be effective when made. Delivery by telex shall be deemed to be effective on the business day following the day when the "answer back" appears on the sender's telex machine. Delivery by facsimile shall be effective when the "transmit confirmation report" confirming the transmission to the recipient's published facsimile number is received by the transmitter. Delivery by registered airmail shall be deemed to be effective 21 days after posting. An electronic document is presumed to have been received by the addressee when it enters an information system designated or used by the addressee for the purpose of receiving documents of the type sent and it is capable of being retrieved and processed by the addressee.

26.4 Notice to the designated representative of the Contractor shall constitute effective notice to the Contractor for all purposes under this contract, and the designated representative shall be the Contractor's agent for the service of process or notification in any proceeding of any court or tribunal having jurisdiction.

26.5 Notice to the Secretary-General shall constitute effective notice to the Authority for all purposes under this contract, and the Secretary-General shall be the Authority's agent for the service of process or notification in any proceeding of any court or tribunal having jurisdiction.

Section 27. Applicable Law

27.1 This contract shall be governed by the terms of this contract, the rules, regulations and procedures of the Authority, Part XI of the Convention, the Agreement and other rules of international law not incompatible with the Convention.

27.2 The Contractor, its employees, subcontractors, agents and all persons engaged in working or acting for them in the conduct of its operations under this contract shall observe the applicable law referred to in Section 27.1 hereof and shall not engage in any transaction, directly or indirectly, prohibited by the applicable law.

27.3 Nothing contained in this contract shall be deemed an exemption from the necessity of applying for and obtaining any permit or authority that may be required for any activities under this contract.

Section 28. Interpretation

The division of this contract into sections and subsections and the insertion of headings are for convenience of reference only and shall not affect the construction or interpretation hereof.

Section 29. Additional Documents

Each party hereto agrees to execute and deliver all such further instruments, and to do and perform all such further acts and things as may be necessary or expedient to give effect to the provisions of this contract.

Decision of the Assembly of the International Seabed Authority Relating to the Regulations on Prospecting and Exploration for Cobalt-Rich Ferromanganese Crusts in the Area†

The Assembly of the International Seabed Authority,

Having considered the Regulations on Prospecting and Exploration for Cobalt-rich Ferromanganese Crusts in the Area, as provisionally adopted by the Council at its 181st meeting, on 26 July 2012,

Approves the Regulations on Prospecting and Exploration for Cobalt-rich Ferromanganese Crusts in the Area as contained in the annex to the present decision.

138th meeting
27 July 2012

Annex

Regulations on Prospecting and Exploration for Cobalt-Rich Ferromanganese Crusts in the Area
Preamble
In accordance with the United Nations Convention on the Law of the Sea of 10 December 1982 ("the Convention"), the seabed and ocean floor and the subsoil thereof beyond the limits of national jurisdiction, as well as its resources, are the common heritage of mankind, the exploration and exploitation of which shall be carried out for the benefit of mankind as a whole, on whose behalf the International Seabed Authority acts. The objective of this set of Regulations is to provide for prospecting and exploration for cobalt-rich ferromanganese crusts.

---

† Editors' Note.—This document was provided by the International Seabed Authority and is extracted from the Decision of the Assembly of the International Seabed Authority, Eighteenth session, 16–27 July 2012, Kingston, Jamaica, ISBA/18/A/11, 22 October 2012, available online: <http://www.isa.org.jm/mining-code>.

Ocean Yearbook 29: 786–840
© KONINKLIJKE BRILL NV, LEIDEN, 2015 | DOI 10.1163/9789004297234_028

Part I. Introduction

Regulation 1. Use of Terms and Scope

1. Terms used in the Convention shall have the same meaning in these Regulations.
2. In accordance with the Agreement relating to the Implementation of Part XI of the United Nations Convention on the Law of the Sea of 10 December 1982 ("the Agreement"), the provisions of the Agreement and Part XI of the Convention shall be interpreted and applied together as a single instrument. These Regulations and references in these Regulations to the Convention are to be interpreted and applied accordingly.
3. For the purposes of these Regulations:
    (a) "Cobalt crusts" means cobalt-rich iron/manganese (ferromanganese) hydroxide/oxide deposits formed from direct precipitation of minerals from seawater onto hard substrates containing minor but significant concentrations of cobalt, titanium, nickel, platinum, molybdenum, tellurium, cerium, other metallic and rare earth elements;
    (b) "Exploitation" means the recovery for commercial purposes of cobalt crusts in the Area and the extraction of minerals therefrom, including the construction and operation of mining, processing and transportation systems, for the production and marketing of metals;
    (c) "Exploration" means the searching for deposits of cobalt crusts in the Area with exclusive rights, the analysis of such deposits, the use and testing of recovery systems and equipment, processing facilities and transportation systems and the carrying out of studies of the environmental, technical, economic, commercial and other appropriate factors that must be taken into account in exploitation;
    (d) "Marine environment" includes the physical, chemical, geological and biological components, conditions and factors which interact and determine the productivity, state, condition and quality of the marine ecosystem, the waters of the seas and oceans and the airspace above those waters, as well as the seabed and ocean floor and subsoil thereof;
    (e) "Prospecting" means the search for deposits of cobalt crusts in the Area, including estimation of the composition, sizes and distributions of deposits of cobalt crusts and their economic values, without any exclusive rights;

(f)   "Serious harm to the marine environment" means any effect from activities in the Area on the marine environment which represents a significant adverse change in the marine environment determined according to the rules, regulations and procedures adopted by the Authority on the basis of internationally recognized standards and practices.

4.   These Regulations shall not in any way affect the freedom of scientific research, pursuant to Article 87 of the Convention, or the right to conduct marine scientific research in the Area pursuant to Articles 143 and 256 of the Convention. Nothing in these Regulations shall be construed in such a way as to restrict the exercise by States of the freedom of the high seas as reflected in Article 87 of the Convention.

5.   These Regulations may be supplemented by further rules, regulations and procedures, in particular on the protection and preservation of the marine environment. These Regulations shall be subject to the provisions of the Convention and the Agreement and other rules of international law not incompatible with the Convention.

Part II. Prospecting

Regulation 2. Prospecting

1.   Prospecting shall be conducted in accordance with the Convention and these Regulations and may commence only after the prospector has been informed by the Secretary-General that its notification has been recorded pursuant to regulation 4(2).

2.   Prospectors and the Authority shall apply a precautionary approach, as reflected in principle 15 of the Rio Declaration on Environment and Development.[1]

3.   Prospecting shall not be undertaken if substantial evidence indicates the risk of serious harm to the marine environment.

4.   Prospecting shall not be undertaken in an area covered by an approval plan of work for exploration for cobalt crusts or in a reserved area; nor may there be prospecting in an area which the International Seabed

---

1   *Report of the United Nations Conference on Environment and Development, Rio de Janeiro, 3–14 June 1992* (United Nations publication, Sales No. E.93.I.8 and corrigendum), vol. I, *Resolutions adopted by the Conference*, resolution 1, annex I.

Authority Council has disapproved for exploitation because of the risk of serious harm to the marine environment.

5. Prospecting shall not confer on the prospector any rights with respect to resources. A prospector may, however, recover a reasonable quantity of minerals, being the quantity necessary for testing and not for commercial use.

6. There shall be no time limit on prospecting except that prospecting in a particular area shall cease upon written notification to the prospector by the Secretary-General that a plan of work for exploration has been approved with regard to that area.

7. Prospecting may be conducted simultaneously by more than one prospector in the same area or areas.

Regulation 3. Notification of Prospecting

1. A proposed prospector shall notify the Authority of its intention to engage in prospecting.

2. Each notification of prospecting shall be in the form prescribed in Annex I to these Regulations, shall be addressed to the Secretary-General and shall conform to the requirements of these Regulations.

3. Each notification shall be submitted:
    (a) In the case of a State, by the authority designated for that purpose by it;
    (b) In the case of an entity, by its designated representative;
    (c) In the case of the Enterprise, by its competent authority.

4. Each notification shall be in one of the languages of the Authority and shall contain:
    (a) The name, nationality and address of the proposed prospector and its designated representative;
    (b) The coordinates of the broad area or areas within which prospecting is to be conducted, in accordance with the most recent generally accepted international standard used by the Authority;
    (c) A general description of the prospecting programme, including the proposed date of commencement and its approximate duration;
    (d) A satisfactory written undertaking that the proposed prospector will:
        (i) Comply with the Convention and the relevant rules, regulations and procedures of the Authority concerning:
            a. Cooperation in the training programmes in connection with marine scientific research and transfer of technology referred to in Articles 143 and 144 of the Convention; and
            b. Protection and preservation of the marine environment;
        (ii) Accept verification by the Authority of compliance therewith; and

(iii) Make available to the Authority, as far as practicable, such data as may be relevant to the protection and preservation of the marine environment.

Regulation 4. Consideration of Notifications

1. The Secretary-General shall acknowledge in writing receipt of each notification submitted under regulation 3, specifying the date of receipt.

2. The Secretary-General shall review and act on the notification within 45 days of its receipt. If the notification conforms with the requirements of the Convention and these Regulations, the Secretary-General shall record the particulars of the notification in a register maintained for that purpose and shall inform the prospector in writing that the notification has been so recorded.

3. The Secretary-General shall, within 45 days of receipt of the notification, inform the proposed prospector in writing if the notification includes any part of an area included in an approved plan of work for exploration or exploitation of any category of resources, or any part of a reserved area, or any part of an area which has been disapproved by the Council for exploitation because of the risk of serious harm to the marine environment, or if the written undertaking is not satisfactory, and shall provide the proposed prospector with a written statement of reasons. In such cases, the proposed prospector may, within 90 days, submit an amended notification. The Secretary-General shall, within 45 days, review and act upon such amended notification.

4. A prospector shall inform the Secretary-General in writing of any change in the information contained in the notification.

5. The Secretary-General shall not release any particulars contained in the notification except with the written consent of the prospector. The Secretary-General shall, however, from time to time inform all members of the Authority of the identity of prospectors and the general areas in which prospecting is being conducted.

Regulation 5. Protection and Preservation of the Marine Environment during Prospecting

1. Each prospector shall take necessary measures to prevent, reduce and control pollution and other hazards to the marine environment arising from prospecting as far as reasonably possible, applying a precautionary approach and best environmental practices. In particular, each prospector shall minimize or eliminate:

(a)   Adverse environmental impacts from prospecting; and

(b)   Actual or potential conflicts or interference with existing or planned marine scientific research activities, in accordance with the relevant future guidelines in this regard.

2.   Prospectors shall cooperate with the Authority in the establishment and implementation of programmes for monitoring and evaluating the potential impacts of the exploration for and exploitation of cobalt crusts on the marine environment.

3.   A prospector shall immediately notify the Secretary-General in writing, using the most effective means, of any incident arising from prospecting which has caused, is causing or poses a threat of serious harm to the marine environment. Upon receipt of such notification the Secretary-General shall act in a manner consistent with regulation 35.

Regulation 6. Annual Report

1.   A prospector shall, within 90 days of the end of each calendar year, submit a report to the Authority on the status of prospecting. Such reports shall be submitted by the Secretary-General to the Legal and Technical Commission. Each such report shall contain:

(a)   A general description of the status of prospecting and of the results obtained;

(b)   Information on compliance with the undertakings referred to in regulation 3(4)(d); and

(c)   Information on adherence to the relevant guidelines in this regard.

2.   If the prospector intends to claim expenditures for prospecting as part of the development costs incurred prior to the commencement of commercial production, the prospector shall submit an annual statement, in conformity with internationally accepted accounting principles and certified by a duly qualified firm of public accountants, of the actual and direct expenditures incurred by the prospector in carrying out prospecting.

Regulation 7. Confidentiality of Data and Information from Prospecting Contained in the Annual Report

1.   The Secretary-General shall ensure the confidentiality of all data and information contained in the reports submitted under regulation 6 applying mutatis mutandis the provisions of regulations 38 and 39, provided that data and information relating to the protection and preservation of the marine environment, in particular those from

environmental monitoring programmes, shall not be considered confidential. The prospector may request that such data not be disclosed for up to three years following the date of their submission.

2. The Secretary-General may, at any time, with the consent of the prospector concerned, release data and information relating to prospecting in an area in respect of which a notification has been submitted. If, after having made reasonable efforts for at least two years, the Secretary-General determines that the prospector no longer exists or cannot be located, the Secretary-General may release such data and information.

Regulation 8. Objects of an Archaeological or Historical Nature

A prospector shall immediately notify the Secretary-General in writing of any finding in the Area of an object of actual or potential archaeological or historical nature and its location. The Secretary-General shall transmit such information to the Director-General of the United Nations Educational, Scientific and Cultural Organization.

Part III. Applications for Approval of Plans of Work for Exploration in the Form of Contracts

Section 1. General Provisions

Regulation 9. General

Subject to the provisions of the Convention, the following may apply to the Authority for approval of plans of work for exploration:

    (a) The Enterprise, on its own behalf or in a joint arrangement;

    (b) States parties, State enterprises or natural or juridical persons which possess the nationality of States or are effectively controlled by them or their nationals, when sponsored by such States, or any group of the foregoing which meets the requirements of these Regulations.

Section 2. Content of Applications

Regulation 10. Form of Applications

1. Each application for approval of a plan of work for exploration shall be in the form prescribed in Annex II to these Regulations, shall be addressed to the Secretary-General and shall conform to the requirements of these Regulations.

2. Each application shall be submitted:
   (a) In the case of a State, by the authority designated for that purpose by it;
   (b) In the case of an entity, by its designated representative or the authority designated for that purpose by the sponsoring State or States; and
   (c) In the case of the Enterprise, by its competent authority.
3. Each application by a State enterprise or one of the entities referred to in regulation 9(b) shall also contain:
   (a) Sufficient information to determine the nationality of the applicant or the identity of the State or States by which, or by whose nationals, the applicant is effectively controlled; and
   (b) The principal place of business or domicile and, if applicable, place of registration of the applicant.
4. Each application submitted by a partnership or consortium of entities shall contain the required information in respect of each member of the partnership or consortium.

Regulation 11. Certificate of Sponsorship

1. Each application by a State enterprise or one of the entities referred to in regulation 9(b) shall be accompanied by a certificate of sponsorship issued by the State of which it is a national or by which or by whose nationals it is effectively controlled. If the applicant has more than one nationality, as in the case of a partnership or consortium of entities from more than one State, each State involved shall issue a certificate of sponsorship.
2. Where the applicant has the nationality of one State but is effectively controlled by another State or its nationals, each State involved shall issue a certificate of sponsorship.
3. Each certificate of sponsorship shall be duly signed on behalf of the State by which it is submitted, and shall contain:
   (a) The name of the applicant;
   (b) The name of the sponsoring State;
   (c) A statement that the applicant is:
      (i) A national of the sponsoring State; or
      (ii) Subject to the effective control of the sponsoring State or its nationals;
   (d) A statement by the sponsoring State that it sponsors the applicant;
   (e) The date of deposit by the sponsoring State of its instrument of ratification of, or accession or succession to, the Convention;

(f)   A declaration that the sponsoring State assumes responsibility in accordance with Articles 139 and 153(4) of the Convention and Article 4(4) of Annex III to the Convention.

4.   States or entities in a joint arrangement with the Enterprise shall also comply with this regulation.

Regulation 12. Total Area Covered by the Application

1.   For the purposes of these Regulations, a "cobalt crust block" is one or more cells of a grid as provided by the Authority, which may be square or rectangular in shape and no greater than 20 square kilometres in size.

2.   The area covered by each application for approval of a plan of work for exploration for cobalt crusts shall be comprised of not more than 150 cobalt crust blocks, which shall be arranged by the applicant in clusters, as set out in paragraph 3 below.

3.   Five contiguous cobalt crust blocks form a cluster of cobalt crust blocks. Two such blocks that touch at any point shall be considered to be contiguous. Clusters of cobalt crust blocks need not be contiguous but shall be proximate and located entirely within a geographical area measuring not more than 550 kilometres by 550 kilometres.

4.   Notwithstanding the provisions in paragraph 2 above, where an applicant has elected to contribute a reserved area to carry out activities pursuant to Article 9 of Annex III to the Convention, in accordance with regulation 17, the total area covered by an application shall not exceed 300 cobalt crust blocks. Such blocks shall be arranged in two groups of equal estimated commercial value and each such group of cobalt crust blocks shall be arranged by the applicant in clusters, as set out in paragraph 3 above.

Regulation 13. Financial and Technical Capabilities

1.   Each application for approval of a plan of work for exploration shall contain specific and sufficient information to enable the Council to determine whether the applicant is financially and technically capable of carrying out the proposed plan of work for exploration and of fulfilling its financial obligations to the Authority.

2.   An application for approval of a plan of work for exploration by the Enterprise shall include a statement by its competent authority certifying that the Enterprise has the necessary financial resources to meet the estimated costs of the proposed plan of work for exploration.

3. An application for approval of a plan of work for exploration by a State or a State enterprise shall include a statement by the State or the sponsoring State certifying that the applicant has the necessary financial resources to meet the estimated costs of the proposed plan of work for exploration.

4. An application for approval of a plan of work for exploration by an entity shall include copies of its audited financial statements, including balance sheets and profit-and-loss statements, for the most recent three years, in conformity with internationally accepted accounting principles and certified by a duly qualified firm of public accountants.

5. If the applicant is a newly organized entity and a certified balance sheet is not available, the application shall include a pro forma balance sheet certified by an appropriate official of the applicant.

6. If the applicant is a subsidiary of another entity, the application shall include copies of such financial statements of that entity and a statement from that entity, in conformity with internationally accepted accounting principles and certified by a duly qualified firm of public accountants, that the applicant will have the financial resources to carry out the plan of work for exploration.

7. If the applicant is controlled by a State or a State enterprise, the application shall include a statement from the State or State enterprise certifying that the applicant will have the financial resources to carry out the plan of work for exploration.

8. Where an applicant seeking approval of a plan of work for exploration intends to finance the proposed plan of work for exploration by borrowings, its application shall include the amount of such borrowings, the repayment period and the interest rate.

9. Each application shall include:
    (a) A general description of the applicant's previous experience, knowledge, skills, technical qualifications and expertise relevant to the proposed plan of work for exploration;
    (b) A general description of the equipment and methods expected to be used in carrying out the proposed plan of work for exploration and other relevant non-proprietary information about the characteristics of such technology;
    (c) A general description of the applicant's financial and technical capability to respond to any incident or activity which causes serious harm to the marine environment.

10. Where the applicant is a partnership or consortium of entities in a joint arrangement, each member of the partnership or consortium shall provide the information required by this regulation.

Regulation 14. Previous Contracts with the Authority

Where the applicant or, in the case of an application by a partnership or consortium of entities in a joint arrangement, any member of the partnership or
consortium, has previously been awarded any contract with the Authority, the
application shall include:

  (a)   The date of the previous contract or contracts;
  (b)   The dates, reference numbers and titles of each report submitted
        to the Authority in connection with the contract or contracts; and
  (c)   The date of termination of the contract or contracts, if applicable.

Regulation 15. Undertakings

Each applicant, including the Enterprise, shall, as part of its application for
approval of a plan of work for exploration, provide a written undertaking to
the Authority that it will:

  (a)   Accept as enforceable and comply with the applicable obligations
        created by the provisions of the Convention and the rules, regula-
        tions and procedures of the Authority, the decisions of the organs of
        the Authority and the terms of its contracts with the Authority;
  (b)   Accept control by the Authority of activities in the Area, as author-
        ized by the Convention; and
  (c)   Provide the Authority with a written assurance that its obligations
        under the contract will be fulfilled in good faith.

Regulation 16. Applicant's Election of a Reserved Area Contribution
or Equity Interest in a Joint Venture Arrangement

Each applicant shall, in the application, elect either to:

  (a)   Contribute a reserved area to carry out activities pursuant to
        Article 9 of Annex III to the Convention, in accordance with regu-
        lation 17; or
  (b)   Offer an equity interest in a joint venture arrangement in accord-
        ance with regulation 19.

Regulation 17. Data and Information to be Submitted before the
Designation of a Reserved Area

1.   Where the applicant elects to contribute a reserved area to carry out
      activities pursuant to Article 9 of Annex III to the Convention, the area
      covered by the application shall be sufficiently large and of sufficient

estimated commercial value to allow two mining operations and shall be configured by the applicant in accordance with regulation 12(4).

2. Each such application shall contain sufficient data and information, as prescribed in Section II of Annex II to these Regulations, with respect to the area under application to enable the Council, on the recommendation of the Legal and Technical Commission, to designate a reserved area based on the estimated commercial value of each part. Such data and information shall consist of data available to the applicant with respect to both parts of the area under application, including the data used to determine their commercial value.

3. The Council, on the basis of the data and information submitted by the applicant pursuant to Section II of Annex II to these Regulations, if found satisfactory and taking into account the recommendation of the Legal and Technical Commission, shall designate the part of the area under application which is to be a reserved area. The area so designated shall become a reserved area as soon as the plan of work for exploration for the non-reserved area is approved and the contract is signed. If the Council determines that additional information, consistent with these Regulations and Annex II, is needed to designate the reserved area, it shall refer the matter back to the Commission for further consideration, specifying the additional information required.

4. Once the plan of work for exploration is approved and a contract has been issued, the data and information transferred to the Authority by the applicant in respect of the reserved area may be disclosed by the Authority in accordance with Article 14(3) of Annex III to the Convention.

Regulation 18. Applications for Approval of Plans of Work with Respect to a Reserved Area

1. Any State which is a developing State or any natural or juridical person sponsored by it and effectively controlled by it or by any other developing State, or any group of the foregoing, may notify the Authority that it wishes to submit a plan of work for exploration with respect to a reserved area. The Secretary-General shall forward such notification to the Enterprise, which shall inform the Secretary-General in writing within six months whether or not it intends to carry out activities in that area. If the Enterprise intends to carry out activities in that area, it shall, pursuant to paragraph 4, also inform in writing the contractor whose application for approval of a plan of work for exploration originally included that area.

2. An application for approval of a plan of work for exploration in respect of a reserved area may be submitted at any time after such an area becomes

available following a decision by the Enterprise that it does not intend to carry out activities in that area or where the Enterprise has not, within six months of the notification by the Secretary-General, either taken a decision on whether it intends to carry out activities in that area or notified the Secretary-General in writing that it is engaged in discussions regarding a potential joint venture. In the latter instance, the Enterprise shall have one year from the date of such notification in which to decide whether to conduct activities in that area.

3. If the Enterprise or a developing State or one of the entities referred to in paragraph 1 does not submit an application for approval of a plan of work for exploration for activities in a reserved area within 15 years of the commencement by the Enterprise of its functions independent of the Secretariat of the Authority or within 15 years of the date on which that area is reserved for the Authority, whichever is the later, the contractor whose application for approval of a plan of work for exploration originally included that area shall be entitled to apply for a plan of work for exploration for that area provided it offers in good faith to include the Enterprise as a joint-venture partner.

4. A contractor has the right of first refusal to enter into a joint venture arrangement with the Enterprise for exploration of the area which was included in its application for approval of a plan of work for exploration and which was designated by the Council as a reserved area.

Regulation 19. Equity Interest in a Joint Venture Arrangement

1. Where the applicant elects to offer an equity interest in a joint venture arrangement, it shall submit data and information in accordance with regulation 20. The area to be allocated to the applicant shall be subject to the provisions of regulation 27.

2. The joint venture arrangement, which shall take effect at the time the applicant enters into a contract for exploitation, shall include the following:

    (a) The Enterprise shall obtain a minimum of 20 per cent of the equity participation in the joint venture arrangement on the following basis:

        (i)   Half of such equity participation shall be obtained without payment, directly or indirectly, to the applicant and shall be treated pari passu for all purposes with the equity participation of the applicant;

        (ii) The remainder of such equity participation shall be treated pari passu for all purposes with the equity participation of the applicant except that the Enterprise shall not receive any profit distribution with respect to such participation until the applicant has recovered its total equity participation in the joint venture arrangement;

(b) Notwithstanding subparagraph (a), the applicant shall nevertheless offer the Enterprise the opportunity to purchase a further 30 per cent of the equity participation in the joint venture arrangement, or such lesser percentage as the Enterprise may elect to purchase, on the basis of pari passu treatment with the applicant for all purposes[2];

(c) Except as specifically provided in the agreement between the applicant and the Enterprise, the Enterprise shall not by reason of its equity participation be otherwise obligated to provide funds or credits or issue guarantees or otherwise accept any financial liability whatsoever for or on behalf of the joint venture arrangement, nor shall the Enterprise be required to subscribe for additional equity participation so as to maintain its proportionate participation in the joint venture arrangement.

Regulation 20. Data and Information to be Submitted for Approval of the Plan of Work for Exploration

1. Each applicant shall submit, with a view to receiving approval of the plan of work for exploration in the form of a contract, the following information:

(a) A general description and a schedule of the proposed exploration programme, including the programme of activities for the immediate five-year period, such as studies to be undertaken in respect of the environmental, technical, economic and other appropriate factors that must be taken into account in exploration;

(b) A description of the programme for oceanographic and environmental baseline studies in accordance with these Regulations and any environmental rules, regulations and procedures established by the Authority that would enable an assessment of the potential environmental impact, including, but not restricted to, the impact on biodiversity, of the proposed exploration activities, taking into account any recommendations issued by the Legal and Technical Commission;

---

2 The terms and conditions upon which such equity participation may be obtained would need to be further elaborated.

    (c)   A preliminary assessment of the possible impact of the proposed exploration activities on the marine environment;

    (d)   A description of proposed measures for the prevention, reduction and control of pollution and other hazards, as well as possible impacts, to the marine environment;

    (e)   Data necessary for the Council to make the determination it is required to make in accordance with regulation 13(1); and

    (f)   A schedule of anticipated yearly expenditures in respect of the programme of activities for the immediate five-year period.

2.   Where the applicant elects to contribute a reserved area, the data and information relating to such area shall be transferred by the applicant to the Authority after the Council has designated the reserved area in accordance with regulation 17(3).

3.   Where the applicant elects to offer an equity interest in a joint venture arrangement, the data and information relating to such area shall be transferred by the applicant to the Authority at the time of the election.

Section 3. Fees

Regulation 21. Fee for Applications

1.   The fee for processing an application for approval of a plan for exploration of cobalt crusts shall be a fixed amount of 500,000 United States dollars or its equivalent in a freely convertible currency, to be paid in full at the time of the submission of an application.

2.   If the administrative costs incurred by the Authority in processing an application are less than the fixed amount indicated in paragraph 1 above, the Authority shall refund the difference to the applicant. If the administrative costs incurred by the Authority in processing an application are more than the fixed amount indicated in paragraph 1 above, the applicant shall pay the difference to the Authority, provided that any additional amount to be paid by applicant shall not exceed 10 per cent of the fixed fee referred to in paragraph 1.

3.   Taking into account any criteria established for this purpose by the Finance Committee, the Secretary-General shall determine the amount of such differences as indicated in paragraph 2 above, and notify the applicant of its amount. The notification shall include a statement of the expenditure incurred by the Authority. The amount due shall be paid by the applicant or reimbursed by the Authority within three months of the signing of the Contract referred to in Regulation 25 below.

4. The fixed amount referred to in paragraph 1 above shall be reviewed on a regular basis by the Council in order to ensure that it covers the expected administrative costs of processing applications and to avoid the need for applicants to pay additional amounts in accordance with paragraph 2 above.

Section 4. Processing of Applications

Regulation 22. Receipt, Acknowledgement and Safe Custody of Applications

The Secretary-General shall:

(a) Acknowledge in writing within 30 days receipt of every application for approval of a plan of work for exploration submitted under this Part, specifying the date of receipt;

(b) Place the application together with the attachments and annexes thereto in safe custody and ensure the confidentiality of all confidential data and information contained in the application; and

(c) Notify the members of the Authority of receipt of such application and circulate to them information of a general nature which is not confidential regarding the application.

Regulation 23. Consideration by the Legal and Technical Commission

1. Upon receipt of an application for approval of a plan of work for exploration, the Secretary-General shall notify the members of the Legal and Technical Commission and place consideration of the application as an item on the agenda for the next meeting of the Commission. The Commission shall only consider applications in respect of which notification and information has been circulated by the Secretary-General in accordance with regulation 22(c) at least 30 days prior to the commencement of the meeting of the Commission at which they are to be considered.

2. The Commission shall examine applications in the order in which they are received.

3. The Commission shall determine if the applicant:

(a) Has complied with the provisions of these Regulations;

(b) Has given the undertakings and assurances specified in regulation 15;

(c) Possesses the financial and technical capability to carry out the proposed plan of work for exploration and has provided details as to its ability to comply promptly with emergency orders; and

(d) Has satisfactorily discharged its obligations in relation to any previous contract with the Authority.

4. The Commission shall, in accordance with the requirements set forth in these Regulations and its procedures, determine whether the proposed plan of work for exploration will:
   (a) Provide for effective protection of human health and safety;
   (b) Provide for effective protection and preservation of the marine environment, including, but not restricted to, the impact on biodiversity;
   (c) Ensure that installations are not established where interference may be caused to the use of recognized sea lanes essential to international navigation or in areas of intense fishing activity.

5. If the Commission makes the determinations specified in paragraph 3 and determines that the proposed plan of work for exploration meets the requirements of paragraph 4, the Commission shall recommend approval of the plan of work for exploration to the Council.

6. The Commission shall not recommend approval of the plan of work for exploration if part or all of the area covered by the proposed plan of work for exploration is included in:
   (a) A plan of work for exploration approved by the Council for cobalt crusts; or
   (b) A plan of work approved by the Council for exploration for or exploitation of other resources if the proposed plan of work for exploration for cobalt crusts might cause undue interference with activities under such approved plan of work for other resources; or
   (c) An area disapproved for exploitation by the Council in cases where substantial evidence indicates the risk of serious harm to the marine environment.

7. The Commission may recommend the approval of a plan of work if it determines that such approval would not permit a State party or entities sponsored by it to monopolize the conduct of activities in the Area with regard to cobalt crusts or to preclude other States parties from activities in the Area with regard to cobalt crusts.

8. Except in the case of applications by the Enterprise, on its own behalf or in a joint venture, and applications under regulation 18, the Commission shall not recommend approval of the plan of work for exploration if part or all of the area covered by the proposed plan of work for exploration is included in a reserved area or an area designated by the Council to be a reserved area.

9. If the Commission finds that an application does not comply with these Regulations, it shall notify the applicant in writing, through the

Secretary-General, indicating the reasons. The applicant may, within 45 days of such notification, amend its application. If the Commission after further consideration is of the view that it should not recommend approval of the plan of work for exploration, it shall so inform the applicant and provide the applicant with a further opportunity to make representations within 30 days of such information. The Commission shall consider any such representations made by the applicant in preparing its report and recommendation to the Council.

10. In considering a proposed plan of work for exploration, the Commission shall have regard to the principles, policies and objectives relating to activities in the Area as provided for in Part XI and Annex III of the Convention and the Agreement.

11. The Commission shall consider applications expeditiously and shall submit its report and recommendations to the Council on the designation of the areas and on the plan of work for exploration at the first possible opportunity, taking into account the schedule of meetings of the Authority.

12. In discharging its duties, the Commission shall apply these Regulations and the rules, regulations and procedures of the Authority in a uniform and non-discriminatory manner.

Regulation 24. Consideration and Approval of Plans of Work for Exploration by the Council

The Council shall consider the reports and recommendations of the Legal and Technical Commission relating to approval of plans of work for exploration in accordance with paragraphs 11 and 12 of Section 3 of the annex to the Agreement.

Part IV. Contracts for Exploration

Regulation 25. The Contract

1. After a plan of work for exploration has been approved by the Council, it shall be prepared in the form of a contract between the Authority and the applicant as prescribed in Annex III to these Regulations. Each contract shall incorporate the standard clauses set out in Annex IV in effect at the date of entry into force of the contract.

2. The contract shall be signed by the Secretary-General on behalf of the Authority and by the applicant. The Secretary-General shall notify all members of the Authority in writing of the conclusion of each contract.

Regulation 26. Rights of the Contractor

1. The contractor shall have the exclusive right to explore an area covered by a plan of work for exploration in respect of cobalt crusts. The Authority shall ensure that no other entity operates in the same area for other resources in a manner that might interfere with the operations of the contractor.

2. A contractor who has an approved plan of work for exploration only shall have a preference and a priority among applicants submitting plans of work for exploitation of the same area and resources. Such preference or priority may be withdrawn by the Council if the contractor has failed to comply with the requirements of its approved plan of work for exploration within the time period specified in a written notice or notices from the Council to the contractor indicating which requirements have not been complied with by the contractor. The time period specified in any such notice shall not be unreasonable. The contractor shall be accorded a reasonable opportunity to be heard before the withdrawal of such preference or priority becomes final. The Council shall provide the reasons for its proposed withdrawal of preference or priority and shall consider any contractor's response. The decision of the Council shall take account of that response and shall be based on substantial evidence.

3. A withdrawal of preference or priority shall not become effective until the contractor has been accorded a reasonable opportunity to exhaust the judicial remedies available to it pursuant to Part XI, Section 5, of the Convention.

Regulation 27. Size of Area and Relinquishment

1. The contractor shall relinquish the area allocated to it in accordance with paragraph 1 of this regulation. Areas to be relinquished need not be contiguous and shall be defined by the contractor in the form of sub-blocks comprising one or more cells of a grid as provided by the Authority. By the end of the eighth year from the date of the contract, the contractor shall have relinquished at least one third of the original area allocated to it; by the end of the tenth year from the date of the contract, the contractor shall have relinquished at least two thirds of the original area allocated to it; or, at the end of the fifteenth year from the date of the contract, or when the contractor applies for exploitation rights, whichever is the earlier, the contractor shall nominate an area from the remaining area allocated to it to be retained for exploitation.

2. Notwithstanding the provisions in paragraph 1, a contractor shall not be required to relinquish any additional part of such area when the remaining area allocated to it after relinquishment does not exceed 1,000 square kilometres.
3. The contractor may at any time relinquish parts of the area allocated to it in advance of the schedule set out in paragraph 1.
4. Relinquished areas shall revert to the Area.
5. The Council may, at the request of the contractor, and on the recommendation of the Commission, in exceptional circumstances, defer the schedule of relinquishment. Such exceptional circumstances shall be determined by the Council and shall include, inter alia, consideration of prevailing economic circumstances or other unforeseen exceptional circumstances arising in connection with the operational activities of the contractor.

Regulation 28. Duration of Contracts

1. A plan of work for exploration shall be approved for a period of 15 years. Upon expiration of a plan of work for exploration, the contractor shall apply for a plan of work for exploitation unless the contractor has already done so, has obtained an extension for the plan of work for exploration or decides to renounce its rights in the area covered by the plan of work for exploration.
2. Not later than six months before the expiration of a plan of work for exploration, a contractor may apply for extensions for the plan of work for exploration for periods of not more than five years each. Such extensions shall be approved by the Council, on the recommendation of the Commission, if the contractor has made efforts in good faith to comply with the requirements of the plan of work but for reasons beyond the contractor's control has been unable to complete the necessary preparatory work for proceeding to the exploitation stage or if the prevailing economic circumstances do not justify proceeding to the exploitation stage.

Regulation 29. Training

Pursuant to Article 15 of Annex III to the Convention, each contract shall include as a schedule a practical programme for the training of personnel of the Authority and developing States and drawn up by the contractor in cooperation with the Authority and the sponsoring State or States. Training programmes shall focus on training in the conduct of exploration, and shall provide for full participation by such personnel in all activities covered by the contract. Such training programmes may be revised and developed from time to time as necessary by mutual agreement.

Regulation 30. Periodic Review of the Implementation of the Plan of Work for Exploration

1. The contractor and the Secretary-General shall jointly undertake a periodic review of the implementation of the plan of work for exploration at intervals of five years. The Secretary-General may request the contractor to submit such additional data and information as may be necessary for the purposes of the review.
2. In the light of the review, the contractor shall indicate its programme of activities for the following five-year period, making such adjustments to its previous programme of activities as are necessary.
3. The Secretary-General shall report on the review to the Commission and to the Council. The Secretary-General shall indicate in the report whether any observations transmitted to him by States parties to the Convention concerning the manner in which the contractor has discharged its obligations under these Regulations relating to the protection and preservation of the marine environment were taken into account in the review.

Regulation 31. Termination of Sponsorship

1. Each contractor shall have the required sponsorship throughout the period of the contract.
2. If a State terminates its sponsorship it shall promptly notify the Secretary-General in writing. The sponsoring State should also inform the Secretary-General of the reasons for terminating its sponsorship. Termination of sponsorship shall take effect six months after the date of receipt of the notification by the Secretary-General, unless the notification specifies a later date.
3. In the event of termination of sponsorship the contractor shall, within the period referred to in paragraph 2, obtain another sponsor. Such sponsor shall submit a certificate of sponsorship in accordance with regulation 11. Failure to obtain a sponsor within the required period shall result in the termination of the contract.
4. A sponsoring State shall not be discharged by reason of the termination of its sponsorship from any obligations accrued while it was a sponsoring State, nor shall such termination affect any legal rights and obligations created during such sponsorship.

5.   The Secretary-General shall notify the members of the Authority of the termination or change of sponsorship.

Regulation 32. Responsibility and Liability

Responsibility and liability of the contractor and of the Authority shall be in accordance with the Convention. The contractor shall continue to have responsibility for any damage arising out of wrongful acts in the conduct of its operations, in particular damage to the marine environment, after the completion of the exploration phase.

Part V. Protection and Preservation of the Marine Environment

Regulation 33. Protection and Preservation of the Marine Environment

1.   The Authority shall, in accordance with the Convention and the Agreement, establish and keep under periodic review environmental rules, regulations and procedures to ensure effective protection for the marine environment from harmful effects which may arise from activities in the Area.
2.   In order to ensure effective protection for the marine environment from harmful effects which may arise from activities in the Area, the Authority and sponsoring States shall apply a precautionary approach, as reflected in principle 15 of the Rio Declaration, and best environmental practices.
3.   The Legal and Technical Commission shall make recommendations to the Council on the implementation of paragraphs 1 and 2 above.
4.   The Commission shall develop and implement procedures for determining, on the basis of the best available scientific and technical information, including information provided pursuant to regulation 20, whether proposed exploration activities in the Area would have serious harmful effects on vulnerable marine ecosystems, in particular those associated with seamounts and cold water corals, and ensure that, if it is determined that certain proposed exploration activities would have serious harmful effects on vulnerable marine ecosystems, those activities are managed to prevent such effects or not authorized to proceed.
5.   Pursuant to Article 145 of the Convention and paragraph 2 of this regulation, each contractor shall take necessary measures to prevent, reduce and control pollution and other hazards to the marine environment arising from its activities in the Area as far as reasonably possible, applying a precautionary approach and best environmental practices.

6. Contractors, sponsoring States and other interested States or entities shall cooperate with the Authority in the establishment and implementation of programmes for monitoring and evaluating the impacts of deep sea-bed mining on the marine environment. When required by the Council, such programmes shall include proposals for areas to be set aside and used exclusively as impact reference zones and preservation reference zones. "Impact reference zones" means areas to be used for assessing the effect of activities in the Area on the marine environment and which are representative of the environmental characteristics of the Area. "Preservation reference zones" means areas in which no mining shall occur to ensure representative and stable biota of the seabed in order to assess any changes in the biodiversity of the marine environment.

Regulation 34. Environmental Baselines and Monitoring

1. Each contract shall require the contractor to gather environmental base-line data and to establish environmental baselines, taking into account any recommendations issued by the Legal and Technical Commission pursu-ant to regulation 41, against which to assess the likely effects of its programme of activities under the plan of work for exploration on the marine environment and a programme to monitor and report on such effects. The recommendations issued by the Commission may, inter alia, list those exploration activities which may be considered to have no poten-tial for causing harmful effects on the marine environment. The contractor shall cooperate with the Authority and the sponsoring State or States in the establishment and implementation of such monitoring programme.

2. The contractor shall report annually in writing to the Secretary-General on the implementation and results of the monitoring programme referred to in paragraph 1 and shall submit data and information, taking into account any recommendations issued by the Commission pursu-ant to regulation 41. The Secretary-General shall transmit such reports to the Commission for its consideration pursuant to Article 165 of the Convention.

Regulation 35. Emergency Orders

1. A contractor shall promptly report to the Secretary-General in writing, using the most effective means, any incident arising from activities which have caused, are causing or pose a threat of serious harm to the marine environment.

2. When the Secretary-General has been notified by a contractor or other-
    wise becomes aware of an incident resulting from or caused by a contrac-
    tor's activities in the Area that has caused, is causing or poses a threat
    of serious harm to the marine environment, the Secretary-General shall
    cause a general notification of the incident to be issued, shall notify in
    writing the contractor and the sponsoring State or States, and shall report
    immediately to the Legal and Technical Commission, to the Council
    and to all other members of the Authority. A copy of the report shall be
    circulated to competent international organizations and to concerned
    subregional, regional and global organizations and bodies. The Secretary-
    General shall monitor developments with respect to all such incidents
    and shall report on them as appropriate to the Commission, the Council and
    all other members of the Authority.

3. Pending any action by the Council, the Secretary-General shall take such
    immediate measures of a temporary nature as are practical and reason-
    able in the circumstances to prevent, contain and minimize serious harm
    or the threat of serious harm to the marine environment. Such tempo-
    rary measures shall remain in effect for no longer than 90 days, or until
    the Council decides at its next regular session or a special session, what
    measures, if any, to take pursuant to paragraph 6 of this regulation.

4. After having received the report of the Secretary-General, the Commission
    shall determine, based on the evidence provided to it and taking into
    account the measures already taken by the contractor, which measures
    are necessary to respond effectively to the incident in order to prevent,
    contain and minimize serious harm or the threat of serious harm to
    the marine environment, and shall make its recommendations to the
    Council.

5. The Council shall consider the recommendations of the Commission.

6. The Council, taking into account the recommendations of the
    Commission, the report of the Secretary-General, any information pro-
    vided by the contractor and any other relevant information, may issue
    emergency orders, which may include orders for the suspension or
    adjustment of operations, as may be reasonably necessary to prevent,
    contain and minimize serious harm or the threat of serious harm to the
    marine environment arising out of activities in the Area.

7. If a contractor does not promptly comply with an emergency order to
    prevent, contain and minimize serious harm or the threat of serious
    harm to the marine environment arising out of its activities in the Area,
    the Council shall take by itself or through arrangements with others on
    its behalf, such practical measures as are necessary to prevent, contain

and minimize any such serious harm or threat of serious harm to the marine environment.

8. In order to enable the Council, when necessary, to take immediately the practical measures to prevent, contain and minimize the serious harm or threat of serious harm to the marine environment referred to in paragraph 7, the contractor, prior to the commencement of testing of collecting systems and processing operations, will provide the Council with a guarantee of its financial and technical capability to comply promptly with emergency orders or to assure that the Council can take such emergency measures. If the contractor does not provide the Council with such a guarantee, the sponsoring State or States shall, in response to a request by the Secretary-General and pursuant to Articles 139 and 235 of the Convention, take necessary measures to ensure that the contractor provides such a guarantee or shall take measures to ensure that assistance is provided to the Authority in the discharge of its responsibilities under paragraph 7.

Regulation 36. Rights of Coastal States

1. Nothing in these Regulations shall affect the rights of coastal States in accordance with Article 142 and other relevant provisions of the Convention.

2. Any coastal State which has grounds for believing that any activity in the Area by a contractor is likely to cause serious harm or a threat of serious harm to the marine environment under its jurisdiction or sovereignty may notify the Secretary-General in writing of the grounds upon which such belief is based. The Secretary-General shall provide the Contractor and its sponsoring State or States with a reasonable opportunity to examine the evidence, if any, provided by the coastal State as the basis for its belief. The contractor and its sponsoring State or States may submit their observations thereon to the Secretary-General within a reasonable time.

3. If there are clear grounds for believing that serious harm to the marine environment is likely to occur, the Secretary-General shall act in accordance with regulation 35 and, if necessary, shall take immediate measures of a temporary nature as provided for in regulation 35(3).

4. Contractors shall take all measures necessary to ensure that their activities are conducted so as not to cause serious harm to the marine environment, including, but not restricted to, pollution, under the jurisdiction or sovereignty of coastal States, and that such serious harm or pollution arising from incidents or activities in its exploration area does not spread beyond such area.

Regulation 37. Human Remains and Objects and Sites of an Archaeological or Historical Nature

The contractor shall immediately notify the Secretary-General in writing of any finding in the exploration area of any human remains of an archaeological or historical nature, or any object or site of a similar nature and its location, including the preservation and protection measures taken. The Secretary-General shall immediately transmit such information to the Director-General of the United Nations Educational, Scientific and Cultural Organization and any other competent international organization. Following the finding of any such human remains, object or site in the exploration area, and in order to avoid disturbing such human remains, object or site, no further prospecting or exploration shall take place, within a reasonable radius, until such time as the Council decides otherwise after taking account of the views of the Director-General of the United Nations Educational, Scientific and Cultural Organization or any other competent international organization.

Part VI. Confidentiality

Regulation 38. Confidentiality of Data and Information

1. Data and information submitted or transferred to the Authority or to any person participating in any activity or programme of the Authority pursuant to these Regulations or a contract issued under these Regulations, and designated by the contractor, in consultation with the Secretary-General, as being of a confidential nature, shall be considered confidential unless it is data and information which:
   (a) Is generally known or publicly available from other sources;
   (b) Has been previously made available by the owner to others without an obligation concerning its confidentiality; or
   (c) Is already in the possession of the Authority with no obligation concerning its confidentiality.
2. Data and information that is necessary for the formulation by the Authority of rules, regulations and procedures concerning protection and preservation of the marine environment and safety, other than proprietary equipment design data, shall not be deemed confidential.
3. Confidential data and information may only be used by the Secretary-General and staff of the Secretariat, as authorized by the Secretary-General, and by the members of the Legal and Technical Commission as necessary

for and relevant to the effective exercise of their powers and functions. The Secretary-General shall authorize access to such data and information only for limited use in connection with the functions and duties of the staff of the Secretariat and the functions and duties of the Legal and Technical Commission.

4. Ten years after the date of submission of confidential data and information to the Authority or the expiration of the contract for exploration, whichever is the later, and every five years thereafter, the Secretary-General and the contractor shall review such data and information to determine whether they should remain confidential. Such data and information shall remain confidential if the contractor establishes that there would be a substantial risk of serious and unfair economic prejudice if the data and information were to be released. No such data and information shall be released until the contractor has been accorded a reasonable opportunity to exhaust the judicial remedies available to it pursuant to Part XI, Section 5, of the Convention.

5. If, at any time following the expiration of the contract for exploration, the contractor enters into a contract for exploitation in respect of any part of the exploration area, confidential data and information relating to that part of the area shall remain confidential in accordance with the contract for exploitation.

6. The contractor may at any time waive confidentiality of data and information.

Regulation 39. Procedures to Ensure Confidentiality

1. The Secretary-General shall be responsible for maintaining the confidentiality of all confidential data and information and shall not, except with the prior written consent of the contractor, release such data and information to any person external to the Authority. To ensure the confidentiality of such data and information, the Secretary-General shall establish procedures, consistent with the provisions of the Convention, governing the handling of confidential information by members of the Secretariat, members of the Legal and Technical Commission and any other person participating in any activity or programme of the Authority. Such procedures shall include:

    (a) Maintenance of confidential data and information in secure facilities and development of security procedures to prevent unauthorized access to or removal of such data and information;

(b) Development and maintenance of a classification, log and inventory system of all written data and information received, including its type and source and routing from the time of receipt until final disposition.

2. A person who is authorized pursuant to these Regulations to have access to confidential data and information shall not disclose such data and information except as permitted under the Convention and these Regulations. The Secretary-General shall require any person who is authorized to have access to confidential data and information to make a written declaration witnessed by the Secretary-General or his or her authorized representative to the effect that the person so authorized:

(a) Acknowledges his or her legal obligation under the Convention and these Regulations with respect to the non-disclosure of confidential data and information;

(b) Agrees to comply with the applicable regulations and procedures established to ensure the confidentiality of such data and information.

3. The Legal and Technical Commission shall protect the confidentiality of confidential data and information submitted to it pursuant to these Regulations or a contract issued under these Regulations. In accordance with the provisions of Article 163(8) of the Convention, members of the Commission shall not disclose, even after the termination of their functions, any industrial secret, proprietary data which are transferred to the Authority in accordance with Article 14 of Annex III to the Convention, or any other confidential information coming to their knowledge by reason of their duties for the Authority.

4. The Secretary-General and staff of the Authority shall not disclose, even after the termination of their functions with the Authority, any industrial secret, proprietary data which are transferred to the Authority in accordance with Article 14 of Annex III to the Convention, or any other confidential information coming to their knowledge by reason of their employment with the Authority.

5. Taking into account the responsibility and liability of the Authority pursuant to Article 22 of Annex III to the Convention, the Authority may take such action as may be appropriate against any person who, by reason of his or her duties for the Authority, has access to any confidential data and information and who is in breach of the obligations relating to confidentiality contained in the Convention and these Regulations.

Part VII. General Procedures

Regulation 40. Notice and General Procedures

1. Any application, request, notice, report, consent, approval, waiver, direction or instruction hereunder shall be made by the Secretary-General or by the designated representative of the prospector, applicant or contractor, as the case may be, in writing. Service shall be by hand, or by telex, fax, registered airmail or e-mail containing an authorized electronic signature to the Secretary-General at the headquarters of the Authority or to the designated representative.

2. Delivery by hand shall be effective when made. Delivery by telex shall be deemed to be effective on the business day following the day when the "answer back" appears on the sender's telex machine. Delivery by fax shall be effective when the "transmit confirmation report" confirming the transmission to the recipient's published fax number is received by the transmitter. Delivery by registered airmail shall be deemed to be effective 21 days after posting. An e-mail is presumed to be received by the addressee when it enters an information system designated or used by the addressee for the purpose of receiving documents of the type sent and is capable of being retrieved and processed by the addressee.

3. Notice to the designated representative of the prospector, applicant or contractor shall constitute effective notice to the prospector, applicant or contractor for all purposes under these Regulations, and the designated representative shall be the agent of the prospector, applicant or contractor for the service of process or notification in any proceeding of any court or tribunal having jurisdiction.

4. Notice to the Secretary-General shall constitute effective notice to the Authority for all purposes under these Regulations, and the Secretary-General shall be the Authority's agent for the service of process or notification in any proceeding of any court or tribunal having jurisdiction.

Regulation 41. Recommendations for the Guidance of Contractors

1. The Legal and Technical Commission may from time to time issue recommendations of a technical or administrative nature for the guidance of contractors to assist them in the implementation of the rules, regulations and procedures of the Authority.

2. The full text of such recommendations shall be reported to the Council. Should the Council find that a recommendation is inconsistent with the intent and purpose of these Regulations, it may request that the recommendation be modified or withdrawn.

Part VIII. Settlement of Disputes

Regulation 42. Disputes

1. Disputes concerning the interpretation or application of these Regulations shall be settled in accordance with Part XI, Section 5, of the Convention.
2. Any final decision rendered by a court or tribunal having jurisdiction under the Convention relating to the rights and obligations of the Authority and of the Contractor shall be enforceable in the territory of each State party to the Convention.

Part IX. Resources other than Cobalt Crusts

Regulation 43. Resources other than Cobalt Crusts

If a prospector or contractor finds resources in the Area other than cobalt crusts, the prospecting and exploration for and exploitation of such resources shall be subject to the rules, regulations and procedures of the Authority relating to such resources in accordance with the Convention and the Agreement. The prospector or contractor shall notify the Authority of its find.

Part X. Review

Regulation 44. Review

1. Five years following the approval of these Regulations by the Assembly, or at any time thereafter, the Council shall undertake a review of the manner in which the Regulations have operated in practice.
2. If, in the light of improved knowledge or technology, it becomes apparent that the Regulations are not adequate, any State party, the Legal and Technical Commission or any contractor through its sponsoring State

may at any time request the Council to consider, at its next ordinary session, revisions to these Regulations.

3. In the light of the review, the Council may adopt and apply provisionally, pending approval by the Assembly, amendments to the provisions of these Regulations, taking into account the recommendations of the Legal and Technical Commission or other subordinate organs concerned. Any such amendments shall be without prejudice to the rights conferred on any contractor with the Authority under the provisions of a contract entered into pursuant to these Regulations in force at the time of any such amendment.

4. In the event that any provisions of these Regulations are amended, the contractor and the Authority may revise the contract in accordance with Section 24 of Annex IV.

Annex I. Notification of Intention to Engage in Prospecting

1. Name of prospector:
2. Street address of prospector:
3. Postal address (if different from above):
4. Telephone number:
5. Fax number:
6. E-mail address:
7. Nationality of prospector:
8. If prospector is a juridical person:
   (a) Identify prospector's place of registration;
   (b) Identify prospector's principal place of business/domicile;
   (c) Attach a copy of prospector's certificate of registration.
9. Name of prospector's designated representative:
10. Street address of prospector's designated representative (if different from above):
11. Postal address (if different from above):
12. Telephone number:
13. Fax number:
14. E-mail address:
15. Attach the coordinates of the broad area or areas in which prospecting is to be conducted (in accordance with the World Geodetic System WGS 84).
16. Attach a general description of the prospecting programme, including the date of commencement and the approximate duration of the programme.

17. Attach a written undertaking that the prospector will:
    (a) Comply with the Convention and the relevant rules, regulations and procedures of the Authority concerning:
        (i) Cooperation in the training programmes in connection with marine scientific research and transfer of technology referred to in Articles 143 and 144 of the Convention; and
        (ii) Protection and preservation of the marine environment; and
    (b) Accept verification by the Authority of compliance therewith.
18. List hereunder all the attachments and annexes to this notification (all data and information should be submitted in hard copy and in a digital format specified by the Authority).

_____   _____
Date   Signature of prospector's designated representative

Attestation:

_____
Signature of person attesting

_____
Name of person attesting

_____
Title of person attesting

Annex II. Application for Approval of a Plan of Work for Exploration to Obtain a Contract

Section I. Information Concerning the Applicant

1. Name of applicant:
2. Street address of applicant:
3. Postal address (if different from above):
4. Telephone number:
5. Fax number:
6. E-mail address:
7. Name of applicant's designated representative:

8.   Street address of applicant's designated representative (if different from above):

9.   Postal address (if different from above):

10.   Telephone number:

11.   Fax number:

12.   E-mail address:

13.   If the applicant is a juridical person:
      (a)   Identify applicant's place of registration;
      (b)   Identify applicant's principal place of business/domicile;
      (c)   Attach a copy of applicant's certificate of registration.

14.   Identify the sponsoring State or States.

15.   In respect of each sponsoring State, provide the date of deposit of its instrument of ratification of, or accession or succession to, the United Nations Convention on the Law of the Sea of 10 December 1982 and the date of its consent to be bound by the Agreement relating to the Implementation of Part XI of the Convention.

16.   A certificate of sponsorship issued by the sponsoring State must be attached with this application. If the applicant has more than one nationality, as in the case of a partnership or consortium of entities from more than one State, certificates of sponsorship issued by each of the States involved must be attached.

Section II. Information Relating to the Area under Application

17.   Define the boundaries of the blocks under application by attaching a chart (on a scale and projection specified by the Authority) and a list of geographical coordinates (in accordance with the World Geodetic System WGS 84).

18.   Indicate whether the applicant elects to contribute a reserved area in accordance with regulation 17 or offer an equity interest in a joint venture arrangement in accordance with regulation 19.

19.   If the applicant elects to contribute a reserved area:
      (a)   Attach a list of the coordinates designating the two parts of the total area of equal estimated commercial value; and
      (b)   Include in an attachment sufficient information to enable the Council to designate a reserved area based on the estimated commercial value of each part of the area under application. Such attachment must include the data available to the applicant with respect to both parts of the area under application, including:

     (i)   Data on the location, survey and evaluation of the cobalt crusts in the areas, including:

         a.   A description of the technology related to the recovery and processing of cobalt crusts that is necessary for making the designation of a reserved area;

         b.   A map of the physical and geological characteristics, such as seabed topography, bathymetry and bottom currents and information on the reliability of such data;

         c.   A map showing the survey data used to determine the parameters of cobalt crusts (thickness etc.) necessary to determine its tonnage within the limits of each block, clusters of blocks of the exploration area and the reserved area;

         d.   Data showing the average tonnage (in metric tons) of each cluster of cobalt crust blocks that will comprise the mine site and an associated tonnage map showing the location of sampling sites;

         e.   Combined maps of tonnage and grade of cobalt crusts;

         f.   A calculation based on standard procedures, including statistical analysis, using the data submitted and assumptions made in the calculations that the two areas could be expected to contain cobalt crusts of equal estimated commercial value expressed as recoverable metals in mineable areas;

         g.   A description of the techniques used by the applicant;

     (ii) Information concerning environmental parameters (seasonal and during test period) including, inter alia, wind speed and direction, water salinity, temperature and biological communities.

20.   If the area under application includes any part of a reserved area, attach a list of coordinates of the area which forms part of the reserved area and indicate the applicant's qualifications in accordance with regulation 18 of the Regulations.

Section III. Financial and Technical Information

21.   Attach sufficient information to enable the Council to determine whether the applicant is financially capable of carrying out the proposed plan of work for exploration and of fulfilling its financial obligations to the Authority:

    (a)   If the application is made by the Enterprise, attach certification by its competent authority that the Enterprise has the necessary financial resources to meet the estimated costs of the proposed plan of work for exploration;

(b)   If the application is made by a State or a State enterprise, attach a statement by the State or the sponsoring State certifying that the applicant has the necessary financial resources to meet the estimated costs of the proposed plan of work for exploration;

(c)   If the application is made by an entity, attach copies of the applicant's audited financial statements, including balance sheets and profit-and-loss statements, for the most recent three years in conformity with internationally accepted accounting principles and certified by a duly qualified firm of public accountants; and

   (i)   If the applicant is a newly organized entity and a certified balance sheet is not available, a pro forma balance sheet certified by an appropriate official of the applicant;

   (ii)   If the applicant is a subsidiary of another entity, copies of such financial statements of that entity and a statement from that entity in conformity with internationally accepted accounting practices and certified by a duly qualified firm of public accountants that the applicant will have the financial resources to carry out the plan of work for exploration;

   (iii) If the applicant is controlled by a State or a State enterprise, a statement from the State or State enterprise certifying that the applicant will have the financial resources to carry out the plan of work for exploration.

22.   If it is intended to finance the proposed plan of work for exploration by borrowings, attach a statement of the amount of such borrowings, the repayment period and the interest rate.

23.   Attach sufficient information to enable the Council to determine whether the applicant is technically capable of carrying out the proposed plan of work for exploration, including:

(a)   A general description of the applicant's previous experience, knowledge, skills, technical qualifications and expertise relevant to the proposed plan of work for exploration;

(b)   A general description of the equipment and methods expected to be used in carrying out the proposed plan of work for exploration and other relevant non-proprietary information about the characteristics of such technology;

(c)   A general description of the applicant's financial and technical capability to respond to any incident or activity which causes serious harm to the marine environment.

Section IV. The Plan of Work for Exploration

24. Attach the following information relating to the plan of work for exploration:
   (a) A general description and a schedule of the proposed exploration programme, including the programme of activities for the immediate five-year period, such as studies to be undertaken in respect of the environmental, technical, economic and other appropriate factors which must be taken into account in exploration;
   (b) A description of a programme for oceanographic and environmental baseline studies in accordance with the Regulations and any environmental rules, regulations and procedures established by the Authority that would enable an assessment of the potential environmental impact including, but not restricted to, the impact on biodiversity, of the proposed exploration activities, taking into account any recommendations issued by the Legal and Technical Commission;
   (c) A preliminary assessment of the possible impact of the proposed exploration activities on the marine environment;
   (d) A description of proposed measures for the prevention, reduction and control of pollution of other hazards, as well as possible impacts, to the marine environment;
   (e) A schedule of anticipated yearly expenditures in respect of the programme of activities for the immediate five-year period.

Section V. Undertakings

25. Attach a written undertaking that the applicant will:
   (a) Accept as enforceable and comply with the applicable obligations created by the provisions of the Convention and the rules, regulations and procedures of the Authority, the decisions of the relevant organs of the Authority and the terms of its contracts with the Authority;
   (b) Accept control by the Authority of activities in the Area as authorized by the Convention;
   (c) Provide the Authority with a written assurance that its obligations under the contract will be fulfilled in good faith.

Section VI. Previous Contracts

26. If the applicant or, in the case of an application by a partnership or consortium of entities in a joint arrangement, any member of the partnership or consortium has previously been awarded any contract with the Authority, the application must include:

(a)   The date of the previous contract or contracts;

(b)   The dates, reference numbers and titles of each report submitted to the Authority in connection with the contract or contracts; and

(c)   The date of termination of the contract or contracts, if applicable.

Section VII. Attachments

27.   List all the attachments and annexes to this application (all data and information should be submitted in hard copy and in a digital format specified by the Authority).

_____   _____

Date   Signature of applicant's designated representative

Attestation:

_____

Signature of person attesting

_____

Name of person attesting

_____

Title of person attesting

Annex III. Contract for Exploration

THIS CONTRACT made the...day of...between the **INTERNATIONAL SEABED AUTHORITY** represented by its **SECRETARY-GENERAL** (hereinafter referred to as "the Authority") and...represented by...(hereinafter referred to as "the Contractor")

WITNESSETH as follows:

Incorporation of Clauses

1.   The standard clauses set out in Annex IV to the Regulations on Prospecting and Exploration for Cobalt-rich Ferromanganese Crusts in the Area shall be incorporated herein and shall have effect as if herein set out at length.

Exploration Area

2. For the purposes of this contract, the "exploration area" means that part of the Area allocated to the Contractor for exploration, defined by the coordinates listed in schedule 1 hereto, as reduced from time to time in accordance with the standard clauses and the Regulations.

Grant of Rights

3. In consideration of (a) their mutual interest in the conduct of exploration activities in the exploration area pursuant to the United Nations Convention on the Law of the Sea of 10 December 1982 and the Agreement relating to the Implementation of Part XI of the Convention, (b) the responsibility of the Authority to organize and control activities in the Area, particularly with a view to administering the resources of the Area, in accordance with the legal regime established in Part XI of the Convention and the Agreement and Part XII of the Convention, respectively, and (c) the interest and financial commitment of the Contractor in conducting activities in the exploration area and the mutual covenants made herein, the Authority hereby grants to the Contractor the exclusive right to explore for cobalt crusts in the exploration area in accordance with the terms and conditions of this contract.

Entry into Force and Contract Term

4. This contract shall enter into force on signature by both parties and, subject to the standard clauses, shall remain in force for a period of fifteen years thereafter unless:
    (a) The Contractor obtains a contract for exploitation in the exploration area which enters into force before the expiration of such period of fifteen years; or
    (b) The contract is sooner terminated provided that the term of the contract may be extended in accordance with standard clauses 3.2 and 17.2.

Schedules

5. The schedules referred to in the standard clauses, namely Section 4 and Section 8, are for the purposes of this contract schedules 2 and 3 respectively.

Entire Agreement

6.   This contract expresses the entire agreement between the parties, and no oral understanding or prior writing shall modify the terms hereof.

IN WITNESS WHEREOF the undersigned, being duly authorized thereto by the respective parties, have signed this contract at..., this...day of...

Schedule 1
[Coordinates and illustrative chart of the exploration area]

Schedule 2
[The current five-year programme of activities as revised from time to time]

Schedule 3
[The training programme shall become a schedule to the contract when approved by the Authority in accordance with Section 8 of the standard clauses.]

Annex IV. Standard Clauses for Exploration Contract

Section 1. Definitions

1.1   In the following clauses:
   (a)   "Exploration area" means that part of the Area allocated to the Contractor for exploration, described in schedule 1 hereto, as the same may be reduced from time to time in accordance with this contract and the Regulations;
   (b)   "Programme of activities" means the programme of activities which is set out in schedule 2 hereto as the same may be adjusted from time to time in accordance with Sections 4.3 and 4.4 hereof;
   (c)   "Regulations" means the Regulations on Prospecting and Exploration for Cobalt-rich Ferromanganese Crusts in the Area, adopted by the Authority.
1.2   Terms and phrases defined in the Regulations shall have the same meaning in these standard clauses.
1.3   In accordance with the Agreement relating to the Implementation of Part XI of the United Nations Convention on the Law of the Sea of 10 December 1982, its provisions and Part XI of the Convention are to be interpreted and applied together as a single instrument; this contract and

references in this contract to the Convention are to be interpreted and applied accordingly.

1.4   This contract includes the schedules to this contract, which shall be an integral part hereof.

Section 2. Security of Tenure

2.1   The Contractor shall have security of tenure and this contract shall not be suspended, terminated or revised except in accordance with Sections 20, 21 and 24 hereof.

2.2   The Contractor shall have the exclusive right to explore for cobalt crusts in the exploration area in accordance with the terms and conditions of this contract. The Authority shall ensure that no other entity operates in the exploration area for a different category of resources in a manner that might unreasonably interfere with the operations of the Contractor.

2.3   The Contractor, by notice to the Authority, shall have the right at any time to renounce without penalty the whole or part of its rights in the exploration area, provided that the Contractor shall remain liable for all obligations accrued prior to the date of such renunciation in respect of the area renounced.

2.4   Nothing in this contract shall be deemed to confer any right on the Contractor other than those rights expressly granted herein. The Authority reserves the right to enter into contracts with respect to resources other than cobalt crusts with third parties in the area covered by this contract.

Section 3. Contract Term

3.1   This contract shall enter into force on signature by both parties and shall remain in force for a period of fifteen years thereafter unless:

(a)   The Contractor obtains a contract for exploitation in the exploration area which enters into force before the expiration of such period of fifteen years; or

(b)   The contract is sooner terminated, provided that the term of the contract may be extended in accordance with Sections 3.2 and 17.2 hereof.

3.2   Upon application by the Contractor, not later than six months before the expiration of this contract, this contract may be extended for periods of not more than five years each on such terms and conditions as the Authority and the Contractor may then agree in accordance with the Regulations. Such extensions shall be approved if the Contractor has made efforts in good faith to comply with the requirements of this contract but for reasons beyond the Contractor's control has been unable to complete the necessary preparatory work for proceeding to the exploitation stage or if the prevailing economic circumstances do not justify proceeding to the exploitation stage.

3.3 Notwithstanding the expiration of this contract in accordance with Section 3.1 hereof, if the Contractor has, at least 90 days prior to the date of expiration, applied for a contract for exploitation, the Contractor's rights and obligations under this contract shall continue until such time as the application has been considered and a contract for exploitation has been issued or refused.

Section 4. Exploration

4.1 The Contractor shall commence exploration in accordance with the time schedule stipulated in the programme of activities set out in schedule 2 hereto and shall adhere to such time periods or any modification thereto as provided for by this contract.

4.2 The Contractor shall carry out the programme of activities set out in schedule 2 hereto. In carrying out such activities the Contractor shall spend in each contract year not less than the amount specified in such programme, or any agreed review thereof, in actual and direct exploration expenditures.

4.3 The Contractor, with the consent of the Authority, which consent shall not be unreasonably withheld, may from time to time make such changes in the programme of activities and the expenditures specified therein as may be necessary and prudent in accordance with good mining industry practice, and taking into account the market conditions for the metals contained in cobalt crusts and other relevant global economic conditions.

4.4 Not later than 90 days prior to the expiration of each five-year period from the date on which this contract enters into force in accordance with Section 3 hereof, the Contractor and the Secretary-General shall jointly undertake a review of the implementation of the plan of work for exploration under this contract. The Secretary-General may require the Contractor to submit such additional data and information as may be necessary for the purposes of the review. In the light of the review, the Contractor shall make such adjustments to its plan of work as are necessary and shall indicate its programme of activities for the following five-year period, including a revised schedule of anticipated yearly expenditures. Schedule 2 hereto shall be adjusted accordingly.

Section 5. Environmental Monitoring

5.1 The Contractor shall take necessary measures to prevent, reduce and control pollution and other hazards to the marine environment arising from its activities in the Area as far as reasonably possible applying a precautionary approach and best environmental practices.

5.2 Prior to the commencement of exploration activities, the Contractor shall submit to the Authority:

(a) An impact assessment of the potential effects on the marine environment of the proposed activities;

(b) A proposal for a monitoring programme to determine the potential effect on the marine environment of the proposed activities; and

(c) Data that could be used to establish an environmental baseline against which to assess the effect of the proposed activities.

5.3 The Contractor shall, in accordance with the Regulations, gather environmental baseline data as exploration activities progress and develop and shall establish environmental baselines against which to assess the likely effects of the Contractor's activities on the marine environment.

5.4 The Contractor shall, in accordance with the Regulations, establish and carry out a programme to monitor and report on such effects on the marine environment. The Contractor shall cooperate with the Authority in the implementation of such monitoring.

5.5 The Contractor shall, within 90 days of the end of each calendar year, report to the Secretary-General on the implementation and results of the monitoring programme referred to in Section 5.4 hereof and shall submit data and information in accordance with the Regulations.

Section 6. Contingency Plans and Emergencies

6.1 The Contractor shall, prior to the commencement of its programme of activities under this contract, submit to the Secretary-General a contingency plan to respond effectively to incidents that are likely to cause serious harm or a threat of serious harm to the marine environment arising from the Contractor's activities at sea in the exploration area. Such contingency plan shall establish special procedures and provide for adequate and appropriate equipment to deal with such incidents and, in particular, shall include arrangements for:

(a) The immediate raising of a general alarm in the area of the exploration activities;

(b) Immediate notification to the Secretary-General;

(c)   The warning of ships which might be about to enter the immediate vicinity;

(d)   A continuing flow of full information to the Secretary-General relating to particulars of the contingency measures already taken and further actions required;

(e)   The removal, as appropriate, of polluting substances;

(f)   The reduction and, so far as reasonably possible, prevention of serious harm to the marine environment, as well as mitigation of such effects;

(g)   As appropriate, cooperation with other contractors with the Authority to respond to an emergency; and

(h)   Periodic emergency response exercises.

6.2   The Contractor shall promptly report to the Secretary-General any incident arising from its activities that has caused, is causing or poses a threat of serious harm to the marine environment. Each such report shall contain the details of such incident, including, inter alia:

(a)   The coordinates of the area affected or which can reasonably be anticipated to be affected;

(b)   The description of the action being taken by the Contractor to prevent, contain, minimize and repair the serious harm or threat of serious harm to the marine environment;

(c)   A description of the action being taken by the Contractor to monitor the effects of the incident on the marine environment; and

(d)   Such supplementary information as may reasonably be required by the Secretary-General.

6.3   The Contractor shall comply with emergency orders issued by the Council and immediate measures of a temporary nature issued by the Secretary-General in accordance with the Regulations, to prevent, contain, minimize or repair serious harm or the threat of serious harm to the marine environment, which may include orders to the Contractor to immediately suspend or adjust any activities in the exploration area.

6.4   If the Contractor does not promptly comply with such emergency orders or immediate measures of a temporary nature, the Council may take such reasonable measures as are necessary to prevent, contain, minimize or repair any such serious harm or the threat of serious harm to the marine environment at the Contractor's expense. The Contractor shall promptly reimburse the Authority the amount of such expenses. Such expenses shall be in addition to any monetary penalties which may be imposed on the Contractor pursuant to the terms of this contract or the Regulations.

Section 7. Human Remains and Objects and Sites of an
Archaeological or Historical Nature

The Contractor shall immediately notify the Secretary-General in writing of any finding in the exploration area of any human remains of an archaeological or historical nature, or any object or site of a similar nature and its location, including the preservation and protection measures taken. The Secretary-General shall transmit such information to the Director-General of the United Nations Educational, Scientific and Cultural Organization and any other competent international organization. Following the finding of any such human remains, object or site in the exploration area, and in order to avoid disturbing such human remains, object or site, no further prospecting or exploration shall take place, within a reasonable radius, until such time as the Council decides otherwise after taking account of the views of the Director-General of the United Nations Educational, Scientific and Cultural Organization or any other competent international organization.

Section 8. Training

8.1 In accordance with the Regulations, the Contractor shall, prior to the commencement of exploration under this contract, submit to the Authority for approval proposed training programmes for the training of personnel of the Authority and developing States, including the participation of such personnel in all of the Contractor's activities under this contract.

8.2 The scope and financing of the training programme shall be subject to negotiation between the Contractor, the Authority and the sponsoring State or States.

8.3 The Contractor shall conduct training programmes in accordance with the specific programme for the training of personnel referred to in Section 8.1 hereof approved by the Authority in accordance with the Regulations, which programme, as revised and developed from time to time, shall become a part of this contract as schedule 3.

Section 9. Books and Records

The Contractor shall keep a complete and proper set of books, accounts and financial records, consistent with internationally accepted accounting principles. Such books, accounts and financial records shall include information which will fully disclose the actual and direct expenditures for exploration and such other information as will facilitate an effective audit of such expenditures.

Section 10. Annual Reports

10.1 The Contractor shall, within 90 days of the end of each calendar year, submit a report to the Secretary-General in such format as may be recommended from time to time by the Legal and Technical Commission covering its programme of activities in the exploration area and containing, as applicable, information in sufficient detail on:

(a) The exploration work carried out during the calendar year, including maps, charts and graphs illustrating the work that has been done and the results obtained;

(b) The equipment used to carry out the exploration work, including the results of tests conducted of proposed mining technologies, but not equipment design data; and

(c) The implementation of training programmes, including any proposed revisions to or developments of such programmes.

10.2 Such reports shall also contain:

(a) The results obtained from environmental monitoring programmes, including observations, measurements, evaluations and analyses of environmental parameters;

(b) A statement of the quantity of cobalt crusts recovered as samples or for the purpose of testing;

(c) A statement, in conformity with internationally accepted accounting principles and certified by a duly qualified firm of public accountants, or, where the Contractor is a State or a state enterprise, by the sponsoring State, of the actual and direct exploration expenditures of the Contractor in carrying out the programme of activities during the Contractor's accounting year. Such expenditures may be claimed by the contractor as part of the contractor's development costs incurred prior to the commencement of commercial production; and

(d) Details of any proposed adjustments to the programme of activities and the reasons for such adjustments.

10.3 The Contractor shall also submit such additional information to supplement the reports referred to in Sections 10.1 and 10.2 hereof as the Secretary-General may from time to time reasonably require in order to carry out the Authority's functions under the Convention, the Regulations and this contract.

10.4 The Contractor shall keep, in good condition, a representative portion of samples and cores of the cobalt crusts obtained in the course of exploration until the expiration of this contract. The Authority may request the Contractor in writing to deliver to it for analysis a portion of any such sample and cores obtained during the course of exploration.

Section 11. Data and Information to be Submitted on Expiration of the Contract

11.1 The Contractor shall transfer to the Authority all data and information that are both necessary for and relevant to the effective exercise of the powers and functions of the Authority in respect of the exploration area in accordance with the provisions of this section.

11.2 Upon expiration or termination of this contract the Contractor, if it has not already done so, shall submit the following data and information to the Secretary-General:

(a) Copies of geological, environmental, geochemical and geophysical data acquired by the Contractor in the course of carrying out the programme of activities that are necessary for and relevant to the effective exercise of the powers and functions of the Authority in respect of the exploration area;

(b) The estimation of mineable deposits, when such deposits have been identified, which shall include details of the grade and quantity of the proven, probable and possible cobalt crust reserves and the anticipated mining conditions;

(c) Copies of geological, technical, financial and economic reports made by or for the Contractor that are necessary for and relevant to the effective exercise of the powers and functions of the Authority in respect of the exploration area;

(d) Information in sufficient detail on the equipment used to carry out the exploration work, including the results of tests conducted of proposed mining technologies, but not equipment design data;

(e) A statement of the quantity of cobalt crusts recovered as samples or for the purpose of testing; and

(f) A statement on how and where samples of cores are archived and their availability to the Authority.

11.3 The data and information referred to in Section 11.2 hereof shall also be submitted to the Secretary-General if, prior to the expiration of this contract, the Contractor applies for approval of a plan of work for exploitation or if the Contractor renounces its rights in the exploration area to the extent that such data and information relates to the renounced area.

Section 12. Confidentiality

Data and information transferred to the Authority in accordance with this contract shall be treated as confidential in accordance with the provisions of the Regulations.

Section 13. Undertakings

13.1 The Contractor shall carry out exploration in accordance with the terms and conditions of this contract, the Regulations, Part XI of the Convention, the Agreement and other rules of international law not incompatible with the Convention.

13.2 The Contractor undertakes:
  (a) To accept as enforceable and comply with the terms of this contract;
  (b) To comply with the applicable obligations created by the provisions of the Convention, the rules, regulations and procedures of the Authority and the decisions of the relevant organs of the Authority;
  (c) To accept control by the Authority of activities in the Area as authorized by the Convention;
  (d) To fulfil its obligations under this contract in good faith; and
  (e) To observe, as far as reasonably practicable, any recommendations which may be issued from time to time by the Legal and Technical Commission.

13.3 The Contractor shall actively carry out the programme of activities:
  (a) With due diligence, efficiency and economy;
  (b) With due regard to the impact of its activities on the marine environment; and
  (c) With reasonable regard for other activities in the marine environment.

13.4 The Authority undertakes to fulfil in good faith its powers and functions under the Convention and the Agreement in accordance with Article 157 of the Convention.

Section 14. Inspection

14.1 The Contractor shall permit the Authority to send its inspectors on board vessels and installations used by the Contractor to carry out activities in the exploration area to:
  (a) Monitor the Contractor's compliance with the terms and conditions of this contract and the Regulations; and
  (b) Monitor the effects of such activities on the marine environment.

14.2 The Secretary-General shall give reasonable notice to the Contractor of the projected time and duration of inspections, the name of the inspectors and any activities the inspectors are to perform that are likely to require the availability of special equipment or special assistance from personnel of the Contractor.

14.3 Such inspectors shall have the authority to inspect any vessel or installation, including its log, equipment, records, facilities, all other recorded data and any relevant documents which are necessary to monitor the Contractor's compliance.

14.4 The Contractor, its agents and employees shall assist the inspectors in the performance of their duties and shall:

(a) Accept and facilitate prompt and safe boarding of vessels and installations by inspectors;

(b) Cooperate with and assist in the inspection of any vessel or installation conducted pursuant to these procedures;

(c) Provide access to all relevant equipment, facilities and personnel on vessels and installations at all reasonable times;

(d) Not obstruct, intimidate or interfere with inspectors in the performance of their duties;

(e) Provide reasonable facilities, including, where appropriate, food and accommodation, to inspectors; and

(f) Facilitate safe disembarkation by inspectors.

14.5 Inspectors shall avoid interference with the safe and normal operations on board vessels and installations used by the Contractor to carry out activities in the area visited and shall act in accordance with the Regulations and the measures adopted to protect confidentiality of data and information.

14.6 The Secretary-General and any duly authorized representatives of the Secretary-General, shall have access, for purposes of audit and examination, to any books, documents, papers and records of the Contractor which are necessary and directly pertinent to verify the expenditures referred to in Section 10.2(c).

14.7 The Secretary-General shall provide relevant information contained in the reports of inspectors to the Contractor and its sponsoring State or States where action is necessary.

14.8 If for any reason the Contractor does not pursue exploration and does not request a contract for exploitation, it shall, before withdrawing from the exploration area, notify the Secretary-General in writing in order to permit the Authority, if it so decides, to carry out an inspection pursuant to this section.

Section 15. Safety, Labour and Health Standards

15.1 The Contractor shall comply with the generally accepted international rules and standards established by competent international organizations or general diplomatic conferences concerning the safety of life at sea, and the prevention of collisions and such rules, regulations and procedures as may be adopted by the Authority relating to safety at sea. Each vessel used for carrying out activities in the Area shall possess current valid certificates required by and issued pursuant to such international rules and standards.

15.2 The Contractor shall, in carrying out exploration under this contract, observe and comply with such rules, regulations and procedures as may be adopted by the Authority relating to protection against discrimination in employment, occupational safety and health, labour relations, social security, employment security and living conditions at the work site. Such rules, regulations and procedures shall take into account conventions and recommendations of the International Labour Organization and other competent international organizations.

Section 16. Responsibility and Liability

16.1 The Contractor shall be liable for the actual amount of any damage, including damage to the marine environment, arising out of its wrongful acts or omissions, and those of its employees, subcontractors, agents and all persons engaged in working or acting for them in the conduct of its operations under this contract, including the costs of reasonable measures to prevent or limit damage to the marine environment, account being taken of any contributory acts or omissions by the Authority.

16.2 The Contractor shall indemnify the Authority, its employees, subcontractors and agents against all claims and liabilities of any third party arising out of any wrongful acts or omissions of the Contractor and its employees, agents and subcontractors, and all persons engaged in working or acting for them in the conduct of its operations under this contract.

16.3 The Authority shall be liable for the actual amount of any damage to the Contractor arising out of its wrongful acts in the exercise of its powers and functions, including violations under Article 168(2) of the Convention, account being taken of contributory acts or omissions by the Contractor, its employees, agents and subcontractors, and all persons engaged in working or acting for them in the conduct of its operations under this contract.

16.4 The Authority shall indemnify the Contractor, its employees, subcontractors, agents and all persons engaged in working or acting for them in the conduct of its operations under this contract, against all claims and liabilities of any third party arising out of any wrongful acts or omissions in the exercise of its powers and functions hereunder, including violations under Article 168(2) of the Convention.

16.5 The Contractor shall maintain appropriate insurance policies with internationally recognized carriers, in accordance with generally accepted international maritime practice.

Section 17. Force Majeure

17.1 The Contractor shall not be liable for an unavoidable delay or failure to perform any of its obligations under this contract due to force majeure. For the purposes of this contract, force majeure shall mean an event or condition that the Contractor could not reasonably be expected to prevent or control; provided that the event or condition was not caused by negligence or by a failure to observe good mining industry practice.

17.2 The Contractor shall, upon request, be granted a time extension equal to the period by which performance was delayed hereunder by force majeure and the term of this contract shall be extended accordingly.

17.3 In the event of force majeure, the Contractor shall take all reasonable measures to remove its inability to perform and comply with the terms and conditions of this contract with a minimum of delay.

17.4 The Contractor shall give notice to the Authority of the occurrence of an event of force majeure as soon as reasonably possible, and similarly give notice to the Authority of the restoration of normal conditions.

Section 18. Disclaimer

Neither the Contractor nor any affiliated company or subcontractor shall in any manner claim or suggest, whether expressly or by implication, that the Authority or any official thereof has, or has expressed, any opinion with respect to cobalt crusts in the exploration area and a statement to that effect shall not be included in or endorsed on any prospectus, notice, circular, advertisement, press release or similar document issued by the Contractor, any affiliated company or any subcontractor that refers directly or indirectly to this contract. For the purposes of this section, an "affiliated company" means any person, firm or company or State-owned entity controlling, controlled by, or under common control with, the Contractor.

Section 19. Renunciation of Rights

The Contractor, by notice to the Authority, shall have the right to renounce its rights and terminate this contract without penalty, provided that the Contractor shall remain liable for all obligations accrued prior to the date of such renunciation and those obligations required to be fulfilled after termination in accordance with the Regulations.

Section 20. Termination of Sponsorship

20.1 If the nationality or control of the Contractor changes or the Contractor's sponsoring State, as defined in the Regulations, terminates its sponsorship, the Contractor shall promptly notify the Authority forthwith.

20.2 In either such event, if the Contractor does not obtain another sponsor meeting the requirements prescribed in the Regulations which submits to the Authority a certificate of sponsorship for the Contractor in the prescribed form within the time specified in the Regulations, this contract shall terminate forthwith.

Section 21. Suspension and Termination of Contract and Penalties

21.1 The Council may suspend or terminate this contract, without prejudice to any other rights that the Authority may have, if any of the following events should occur:

(a) If, in spite of written warnings by the Authority, the Contractor has conducted its activities in such a way as to result in serious persistent and wilful violations of the fundamental terms of this contract, Part XI of the Convention, the Agreement and the rules, regulations and procedures of the Authority; or

(b) If the Contractor has failed to comply with a final binding decision of the dispute settlement body applicable to it; or

(c) If the Contractor becomes insolvent or commits an act of bankruptcy or enters into any agreement for composition with its creditors or goes into liquidation or receivership, whether compulsory or voluntary, or petitions or applies to any tribunal for the appointment of a receiver or a trustee or receiver for itself or commences any proceedings relating to itself under any bankruptcy, insolvency or readjustment of debt law, whether now or hereafter in effect, other than for the purpose of reconstruction.

21.2 The Council may, without prejudice to Section 17, after consultation with the Contractor, suspend or terminate this contract, without prejudice to any other rights that the Authority may have, if the Contractor is prevented from performing its obligations under this contract by reason of an event or condition of force majeure, as described in Section 17.1, which has persisted for a continuous period exceeding two years, despite the Contractor having taken all reasonable measures to overcome its inability to perform and comply with the terms and conditions of this contract with minimum delay.

21.3   Any suspension or termination shall be by notice, through the Secretary-General, which shall include a statement of the reasons for taking such action. The suspension or termination shall be effective 60 days after such notice, unless the Contractor within such period disputes the Authority's right to suspend or terminate this contract in accordance with Part XI, Section 5, of the Convention.

21.4   If the Contractor takes such action, this contract shall only be suspended or terminated in accordance with a final binding decision in accordance with Part XI, Section 5, of the Convention.

21.5   If the Council has suspended this contract, the Council may by notice require the Contractor to resume its operations and comply with the terms and conditions of this contract, not later than 60 days after such notice.

21.6   In the case of any violation of this contract not covered by Section 21.1(a) hereof, or in lieu of suspension or termination under Section 21.1 hereof, the Council may impose upon the Contractor monetary penalties proportionate to the seriousness of the violation.

21.7   The Council may not execute a decision involving monetary penalties until the Contractor has been accorded a reasonable opportunity to exhaust the judicial remedies available to it pursuant to Part XI, Section 5, of the Convention.

21.8   In the event of termination or expiration of this contract, the Contractor shall comply with the Regulations and shall remove all installations, plant, equipment and materials in the exploration area and shall make the area safe so as not to constitute a danger to persons, shipping or to the marine environment.

Section 22. Transfer of Rights and Obligations

22.1   The rights and obligations of the Contractor under this contract may be transferred in whole or in part only with the consent of the Authority and in accordance with the Regulations.

22.2   The Authority shall not unreasonably withhold consent to the transfer if the proposed transferee is in all respects a qualified applicant in accordance with the Regulations and assumes all of the obligations of the Contractor.

22.3	The terms, undertakings and conditions of this contract shall inure to the benefit of and be binding upon the parties hereto and their respective successors and assigns.

Section 23. No Waiver

No waiver by either party of any rights pursuant to a breach of the terms and conditions of this contract to be performed by the other party shall be construed as a waiver by the party of any succeeding breach of the same or any other term or condition to be performed by the other party.

Section 24. Revision

24.1	When circumstances have arisen or are likely to arise which, in the opinion of the Authority or the Contractor, would render this contract inequitable or make it impracticable or impossible to achieve the objectives set out in this contract or in Part XI of the Convention or the Agreement, the parties shall enter into negotiations to revise it accordingly.

24.2	This contract may also be revised by agreement between the Contractor and the Authority to facilitate the application of any rules, regulations and procedures adopted by the Authority subsequent to the entry into force of this contract.

24.3	This contract may be revised, amended or otherwise modified only with the consent of the Contractor and the Authority by an appropriate instrument signed by the authorized representatives of the parties.

Section 25. Disputes

25.1	Any dispute between the parties concerning the interpretation or application of this contract shall be settled in accordance with Part XI, Section 5, of the Convention.

25.2	In accordance with Article 21(2) of Annex III to the Convention, any final decision rendered by a court or tribunal having jurisdiction under the Convention relating to the rights and obligations of the Authority and of the Contractor shall be enforceable in the territory of any State party to the Convention affected thereby.

Section 26. Notice

26.1	Any application, request, notice, report, consent, approval, waiver, direction or instruction hereunder shall be made by the Secretary-General or by the designated representative of the Contractor, as the case may be, in writing. Service shall be by hand, or by telex, fax, registered airmail or e-mail containing an authorized signature to the Secretary-General at the head-quarters of the Authority or to the designated representative. The requirement to provide any information in writing under these Regulations is satisfied by the provision of the information in an electronic document containing a digital signature.

26.2 Either party shall be entitled to change any such address to any other address by not less than ten days' notice to the other party.

26.3 Delivery by hand shall be effective when made. Delivery by telex shall be deemed to be effective on the business day following the day when the "answer back" appears on the sender's telex machine. Delivery by fax shall be effective when the "transmit confirmation report" confirming the transmission to the recipient's published fax number is received by the transmitter. Delivery by registered airmail shall be deemed to be effective 21 days after posting. An e-mail is presumed to have been received by the addressee when it enters an information system designated or used by the addressee for the purpose of receiving documents of the type sent and it is capable of being retrieved and processed by the addressee.

26.4 Notice to the designated representative of the Contractor shall constitute effective notice to the Contractor for all purposes under this contract, and the designated representative shall be the Contractor's agent for the service of process or notification in any proceeding of any court or tribunal having jurisdiction.

26.5 Notice to the Secretary-General shall constitute effective notice to the Authority for all purposes under this contract, and the Secretary-General shall be the Authority's agent for the service of process or notification in any proceeding of any court or tribunal having jurisdiction.

Section 27. Applicable Law

27.1 This contract shall be governed by the terms of this contract, the rules, regulations and procedures of the Authority, Part XI of the Convention, the Agreement and other rules of international law not incompatible with the Convention.

27.2 The Contractor, its employees, subcontractors, agents and all persons engaged in working or acting for them in the conduct of its operations under this contract shall observe the applicable law referred to in Section 27.1 hereof and shall not engage in any transaction, directly or indirectly, prohibited by the applicable law.

27.3 Nothing contained in this contract shall be deemed an exemption from the necessity of applying for and obtaining any permit or authority that may be required for any activities under this contract.

Section 28. Interpretation

The division of this contract into sections and subsections and the insertion of headings are for convenience of reference only and shall not affect the construction or interpretation hereof.

Section 29. Additional Documents

Each party hereto agrees to execute and deliver all such further instruments, and to do and perform all such further acts and things as may be necessary or expedient to give effect to the provisions of this contract.

Index